The

International Critical Commentary

on the Holy Scriptures of the Old and

New Testaments

UNDER THE EDITORSHIP OF

The Rev. CHARLES AUGUSTUS BRIGGS, D.D., D.Litt.

Edward Robinson Professor of Biblical Theology,
Union Theological Seminary, New York;

The Rev. SAMUEL ROLLES DRIVER, D.D., D.Litt.

Regius Professor of Hebrew, Oxford;

The Rev. ALFRED PLUMMER, D.D.

Master of University College, Durham.

The International Critical Commentary

on the Holy Scriptures of the Old and

New Testaments.

EDITORS' PREFACE.

THERE are now before the public many Commentaries,
written by British and American divines, of a popular or
homiletical character. *The Cambridge Bible for Schools*,
the *Handbooks for Bible Classes and Private Students*, *The
Speaker's Commentary*, *The Popular Commentary* (Schaff),
The Expositor's Bible, and other similar series, have their
special place and importance. But they do not enter into
the field of Critical Biblical scholarship occupied by such
series of Commentaries as the *Kurzgefasstes exegetisches
Handbuch zum A. T.;* De Wette's *Kurzgefasstes exegetisches
Handbuch zum N. T.;* Meyer's *Kritisch-exegetischer Kommentar;* Keil and Delitzsch's *Biblischer Commentar über das
A. T.;* Lange's *Theologisch-homiletisches Bibelwerk;* Nowack's
Handkommentar zum A. T.; Holtzmann's *Handkommentar
zum N. T.* Several of these have been translated, edited,
and in some cases enlarged and adapted, for the English-
speaking public; others are in process of translation. But
no corresponding series by British or American divines
has hitherto been produced. The way has been prepared
by special Commentaries by Cheyne, Ellicott, Kalisch,
Lightfoot, Perowne, Westcott, and others; and the time has
come, in the judgment of the projectors of this enterprise,
when it is practicable to combine British and American
scholars in the production of a critical, comprehensive

Commentary that will be abreast of modern biblical scholarship, and in a measure lead its van.

Messrs. Charles Scribner's Sons of New York, and Messrs. T. & T. Clark of Edinburgh, propose to publish such a series of Commentaries on the Old and New Testaments, under the editorship of Prof. C. A. BRIGGS, D.D., in America, and of Prof. S. R. DRIVER, D.D., for the Old Testament, and the Rev. ALFRED PLUMMER, D.D., for the New Testament, in Great Britain.

The Commentaries will be international and inter-confessional, and will be free from polemical and ecclesiastical bias. They will be based upon a thorough critical study of the original texts of the Bible, and upon critical methods of interpretation. They are designed chiefly for students and clergymen, and will be written in a compact style. Each book will be preceded by an Introduction, stating the results of criticism upon it, and discussing impartially the questions still remaining open. The details of criticism will appear in their proper place in the body of the Commentary. Each section of the Text will be introduced with a paraphrase, or summary of contents. Technical details of textual and philological criticism will, as a rule, be kept distinct from matter of a more general character; and in the Old Testament the exegetical notes will be arranged, as far as possible, so as to be serviceable to students not acquainted with Hebrew. The History of Interpretation of the Books will be dealt with, when necessary, in the Introductions, with critical notices of the most important literature of the subject. Historical and Archæological questions, as well as questions of Biblical Theology, are included in the plan of the Commentaries, but not Practical or Homiletical Exegesis. The Volumes will constitute a uniform series.

THE INTERNATIONAL CRITICAL COMMENTARY.

THE following eminent Scholars are engaged upon the Volumes named below:

THE OLD TESTAMENT.

Genesis The Rev. JOHN SKINNER, D D., Professor of Old Testament Language and Literature, College of Presbyterian Church of England, Cambridge, England.

Exodus The Rev. A. R. S. KENNEDY, D.D., Professor of Hebrew, University of Edinburgh.

Leviticus J. F. STENNING, M.A., Fellow of Wadham College, Oxford.

Numbers G. BUCHANAN GRAY, D.D., Professor of Hebrew, Mansfield College, Oxford. [*Now Ready.*

Deuteronomy The Rev. S. R. DRIVER, D.D., D.Litt., Regius Professor of Hebrew, Oxford. [*Now Ready.*

Joshua The Rev. GEORGE ADAM SMITH, D.D., LL.D., Professor of Hebrew, Free Church College, Glasgow.

Judges The Rev. GEORGE MOORE, D.D., LL.D., Professor of Theology, Harvard University, Cambridge, Mass. [*Now Ready.*

Samuel The Rev. H. P. SMITH, D.D., Professor of Biblical History, Amherst College, Mass. [*Now Ready.*

Kings The Rev. FRANCIS BROWN, D.D., D.Litt., LL.D., Professor of Hebrew and Cognate Languages, Union Theological Seminary, New York City.

Chronicles The Rev. EDWARD L. CURTIS, D.D., Professor of Hebrew, Yale University, New Haven, Conn.

Ezra and Nehemiah The Rev. L. W. BATTEN, Ph.D., D.D., Rector of St. Marks Church, New York City, sometime Professor of Hebrew, P. E. Divinity School, Philadelphia.

Psalms The Rev. CHAS. A. BRIGGS, D.D., D.Litt., Professor of Biblical Theology, Union Theological Seminary, New York.

Proverbs The Rev. C. H. TOY, D.D., LL D., Professor of Hebrew, Harvard University, Cambridge, Mass. [*Now Ready.*

Job The Rev. S. R. DRIVER, D.D., D.Litt., Regius Professor of Hebrew, Oxford.

Isaiah Chaps. I-XXXIX. The Rev. S. R. DRIVER, D.D., D.Litt., Regius Professor of Hebrew, Oxford.

Isaiah Chaps. XL-LXVI. The late Rev. Prof. A. B. DAVIDSON, D.D., LL.D.

Jeremiah The Rev. A. F. KIRKPATRICK, D.D., Master of Selwyn College, Regius Professor of Hebrew, Cambridge, England.

Ezekiel By the Rev. G. A. COOKE, M.A., Fellow Magdalen College, and the Rev. CHARLES F. BURNEY, M.A., Fellow and Lecturer in Hebrew, St. Johns College, Oxford.

Daniel The Rev. JOHN P. PETERS, Ph.D., D.D., sometime Professor of Hebrew, P. E. Divinity School, Philadelphia, now Rector of St. Michael's Church, New York City.

Amos and Hosea W. R. HARPER, Ph.D., LL.D., President of the University of Chicago, Illinois. [*Now Ready.*

Micah to Malachi W. R. HARPER, Ph.D., LL D., President of the University of Chicago.

Esther The Rev. L. B. PATON, Ph.D., Professor of Hebrew, Hartford Theological Seminary.

Ecclesiastes	Prof. GEORGE A. BARTON, Ph.D., Professor of Biblical Literature, Bryn Mawr College, Pa.
Ruth	Rev. CHARLES P. FAGNANI, D.D., Associate Professor of Hebrew, Union Theological Seminary, New York.
Song of Songs and Lamentations	Rev. CHARLES A. BRIGGS, D.D., D.Litt., Professor of Biblical Theology, Union Theological Seminary, New York.

THE NEW TESTAMENT.

St. Matthew	The Rev. WILLOUGHBY C. ALLEN, M.A., Fellow of Exeter College, Oxford.
St. Mark	The late Rev. E. P. GOULD, D.D., sometime Professor of New Testament Literature, P. E. Divinity School, Philadelphia. [Now Ready.
St. Luke	The Rev. ALFRED PLUMMER, D.D., sometime Master of University College, Durham. [Now Ready.
St. John	The Very Rev. JOHN HENRY BERNARD, D.D., Dean of St. Patrick's and Lecturer in Divinity, University of Dublin.
Harmony of the Gospels	The Rev. WILLIAM SANDAY, D.D., LL.D., Lady Margaret Professor of Divinity, Oxford, and the Rev. WILLOUGHBY C. ALLEN, M.A., Fellow of Exeter College, Oxford.
Acts	The Rev. FREDERICK H. CHASE, Norissonian Professor of Divinity, President of Queens College and Vice-Chancellor, Cambridge, England.
Romans	The Rev. WILLIAM SANDAY, D.D., LL.D., Lady Margaret Professor of Divinity and Canon of Christ Church, Oxford, and the Rev. A. C. HEADLAM, M.A., D.D., Principal of Kings College, London. [Now Ready.
Corinthians	The Right Rev. ARCH. ROBERTSON, D.D., LL D., Lord Bishop of Exeter, and the Rev. RICHARD J. KNOWLING, D.D., Professor of New Testament Exegesis, Kings College, London.
Galatians	The Rev. ERNEST D. BURTON, D.D., Professor of New Testament Literature, University of Chicago.
Ephesians and Colossians	The Rev. T. K. ABBOTT, B.D., D.Litt., sometime Professor of Biblical Greek, Trinity College, Dublin, now Librarian of the same. [Now Ready.
Philippians and Philemon	The Rev. MARVIN R. VINCENT, D.D., Professor of Biblical Literature, Union Theological Seminary, New York City. [Now Ready.
Thessalonians	The Rev. JAMES E. FRAME, M.A., Associate Professor in the New Testament, Union Theological Seminary, New York.
The Pastoral Epistles	The Rev. WALTER LOCK, D.D., Warden of Keble College and Professor of Exegesis, Oxford.
Hebrews	The Rev. A. NAIRNE, M.A., Professor of Hebrew in Kings College, London.
St. James	The Rev. JAMES H. ROPES, D.D., Bussey Professor of New Testament Criticism in Harvard University.
Peter and Jude	The Rev. CHARLES BIGG, D.D., Regius Professor of Ecclesiastical History and Canon of Christ Church, Oxford. [Now Ready.
The Epistles of St. John	The Rev. S. D. F. SALMOND, D.D., Principal of the United Free Church College, Aberdeen.
Revelation	The Rev. ROBERT H. CHARLES, M.A., D.D., Professor of Biblical Greek in the University of Dublin.

AMOS AND HOSEA

WILLIAM RAINEY HARPER

THE INTERNATIONAL CRITICAL COMMENTARY

A

CRITICAL AND EXEGETICAL COMMENTARY

ON

AMOS AND HOSEA

BY

WILLIAM RAINEY HARPER

PROFESSOR OF SEMITIC LANGUAGES AND LITERATURES
IN THE UNIVERSITY OF CHICAGO

NEW YORK
CHARLES SCRIBNER'S SONS
1905

Norwood Press
J. S. Cushing & Co. — Berwick & Smith Co.
Norwood, Mass., U.S.A.

To

ELLA DAVIDA HARPER

WHOSE DEVOTION TO HER HUSBAND AND TO HIS WORK
HAS BEEN HIS GREATEST SOURCE OF HELP AND STRENGTH
DURING THIRTY YEARS

PREFACE

THE agreement to prepare the volumes on the Minor Prophets for this series was entered into in 1890, — fourteen years ago. I did not then anticipate the serious obligations which were shortly to be assumed in other directions. But in all these years of administrative concern I have had recourse for change, comfort, and courage to my work on the Twelve Prophets. A large portion of the work had been finished as early as 1897, when the essential results on the structure of Amos appeared in *The Biblical World*. It is a significant fact that during these fourteen years there have been given to the world the noteworthy contributions of Oort (1890), Mitchell (1893, 1900), Müller (1896), Cheyne (in W. R. Smith, *Prophets*[2], 1895), Nowack (1897, 1903), George Adam Smith (1896), Volz (1897), Driver (1897), Wellhausen (3d ed., 1898), Budde (1899), Löhr (1901), Sievers (1901), Baumann (1903), Meinhold (1903), and Marti (1903).

The plan originally included two volumes for the Minor Prophets; this has been enlarged to three, of which the present volume, containing Amos and Hosea, is the first. Vol. II. will include Micah, Nahum, Habakkuk, Zephaniah, Obadiah; Vol. III., Haggai, Zechariah, Malachi, Joel, Jonah. It is hoped that the second and third volumes will appear within the next two years.

It cannot be said that the Twelve Prophets lack, either in the comprehensive relation which they sustain to the entire history of Hebrew life and thought, in the interest of the problems which they suggest, or in the almost infinite variety of these problems. In every field of study, the textual, the literary, the historical, the archaeological, and the theological, they furnish facts and suggest questions than which few others, perhaps, possess greater significance. One need only mention, by way

of illustration, the questions involved in determining the place
of Amos in the development of Hebrew thought, the problems of
criticism and interpretation which are suggested by the early
chapters of Hosea, the text and historical distribution of the
chapters now joined together under the name of Micah, the
complexity of the data included in the several portions of
Zechariah, not to speak of the fragmentary character of Obadiah, the peculiar phenomena presented in Jonah, and many
other equally puzzling but significant aspects of literary and
theological inquiry.   These facts and problems connect themselves with every important phase of the Old Testament activity
between 900 B.C. and 300 B.C., in other words, with the entire
creative period.

The books which occupy our attention in this first volume go
well together, not only because one follows the other chrono-
logically, but also because one supplements the other logically,
the two presenting a totality of expression in the light of which
each receives a clearer interpretation.   It seemed necessary to
take up, in connection with these first two of the immortal
Twelve, many questions that concern just as closely the others.
Especially was the force of this point felt in the Introduction ;
for an introduction to Amos and Hosea is really an introduction
to Prophecy.

Nowhere is it more necessary to distinguish sharply between
the actual words of an author and those that have been added
by later writers than in the case of Amos and Hosea.   The history of the Messianic idea, in whatever sense we employ that
term, is fundamentally involved in this distinction.   Care has
been taken, therefore, to keep separate the quite considerable
proportion of material (ascribed by tradition to these authors)
which may confidently be treated as of later origin.   This in
the case of Amos is about one-fifth of the whole, and in the case
of Hosea about one-fourth.

It is unquestionably the first duty of a commentator to reconstruct the text as best he may.   The contributions to the text-
criticism of Amos and Hosea, made within two decades, are
striking; but not more so than the unanimity with which the
more important emendations have received acceptance.   More-

over, many of the changes originally suggested, perhaps on
one or another basis (*e.g.* grammar, history, the versions, or the
strophic structure), have later received corroboration on other
grounds than those on which they rested primarily. This has
frequently occurred in my own experience; and when I recall
how often a twofold or even threefold substantiation of a conjecture has thus taken place, I am compelled to defend myself,
and others like myself, against Professor Driver's suggestion
that "it is precarious to base textual and critical inferences"
upon the "strophe."* I venture to suggest that in the near
future this comparatively new phase of critical study will be
"brought forth into a large place."† It is worthy of notice
surely that nearly every important piece of work on the Twelve
Prophets in fifteen years has taken into consideration the question of the measure and strophic arrangement (pp. clxv f.).
My own interest in this subject was aroused in 1887 by the
articles of Professor Briggs in *Hebraica*. No one can doubt
the good results in general which have followed the turning of
attention in this direction. It is unnecessary, and in a commentary impossible, to take up this phase of treatment in all
the detail worked out by Sievers; but it is equally impossible
now to study the thought of these prophetic sermons without
recognizing fully this fundamental factor in their form of composition. As a matter of fact, "strophic structure" is only
another name for "logical structure."

The textual notes preceding the general treatment and the
grammatical and philological notes following it have been intended to furnish the student of ordinary advancement the
more important data with which to reach his own conclusions.
I fear that in some cases these suggestions are too elementary
in their character; but I have had in mind that student of
Sacred Scripture who, with such help, might enter into a fairly
critical appreciation of the points raised; and I have felt that I
might advantageously omit a portion of this kind of material in
the succeeding volumes. The presentation of different readings which are not accepted, as well as of all the principal

* *Joel and Amos*, p. 116.   † *V.* p. clxix.

interpretations in every case, seemed to me to be required by
the emphasis which the editors of the series have placed upon
the importance of providing the history of the interpretation.
I am perfectly aware that the history of interpretation does not
consist in placing one after another a series of differing interpretations; but it is quite clear that space would not permit a fuller
discussion in every place, nor was such discussion necessary.
At the same time, upon the basis of the interpretations as thus
given, even when no comment is added, it is not difficult for
one to construct the history.   I have endeavored to note all
opinions really worthy of consideration; and I trust that the
fulness of citation in some passages may not prove too weari-
some to the reader who is not a student.

It is a source of great satisfaction to make acknowledgment
of the indebtedness which I owe to those who have preceded me;
and especially to Baur, Wünsche, Cheyne, Wellhausen, W. Robertson Smith, Nowack, Driver, George Adam Smith, Budde,
and Kautzsch (*v.* his article, "Religion of Israel," in Hastings's *Dictionary of the Bible*).   I have tried in each important
instance to indicate the position taken by those who have discussed that particular case; and likewise to recognize the
author who first suggested a reading or interpretation afterward adopted by others.   I regret that my manuscript was
already almost wholly in type before the appearance of Nowack's second edition and of Marti's commentary.   Use has
been made of these volumes in the revision of the sheets.   I
ought perhaps to mention that a considerable portion of my
manuscript has been thrown out because I had transgressed the
limits set for the volume.

A word more concerning the Introduction seems to be necessary.   It appeared to me that a brief summary of pre-prophetism
was required as the basis on which to place the work of Amos
and Hosea.   This would have been unnecessary if it were certain that all Hebrew thought really began with Amos.   But this
view I cannot accept, and so I have enlarged the Introduction
to include a résumé of the pre-prophetic activity.   In the presentation of this I have found myself greatly embarrassed for
lack of space.

The list of literature will be found fairly exhaustive as far as half a century back. Lists of the literature before that time are accessible in Gunning's *De Godspraken van Amos*, Driver's article on Amos in Smith's *Dictionary of the Bible* (2d ed.), Wünsche's *Hosea*, and in Lange's *Commentary*, Vol. XVI. The reader is requested to note the Addenda and Corrigenda on pp. xv, xvi, as well as the abbreviations on pp. xvii ff.

In conclusion, I wish particularly to acknowledge the help which has been given me in the preparation of the volume by my former pupil, now my colleague, Dr. John M. P. Smith. The assistance which he has rendered in gathering material, in verifying references, and in revising the manuscript and the printer's sheets, and the suggestions which he has made from time to time upon the subject-matter itself, have been of the greatest value. Without this help I doubt whether I should have been able to bring the work to a completion. My thanks are due also to my former pupil, Professor George R. Berry of Colgate University, for aid furnished, and to my colleague, Professor George S. Goodspeed, for important suggestions in connection with the historical material in Amos.

The publishers have coöperated most generously in securing a typographical excellence which, I am confident, will be greatly appreciated.

I think that I realize most keenly some of the defects of this commentary. Doubtless many that I do not perceive will be pointed out to me. I shall hope to make good use of all such criticisms and suggestions in connection with the two remaining volumes.

CHICAGO, NOVEMBER TWENTY-FOUR,
 THANKSGIVING DAY, 1904.

CONTENTS.

xiii

E. AMOS AND HOSEA.

ADDENDA AND CORRIGENDA.

———◆———

p. lv, line 1. The first mention of Phoenician prophets is found in the report of Wenamon, an Egyptian envoy to Byblos, in the reign of Ramses XII., probably about 1100 B.C. See J. H. Breasted, "The Report of Wenamon," *AJSL*. XXI. (Jan. 1905), pp. 101 f., 105.

p. lxxxix, line 14. For "Ju. 5^{46}," read "Ju. $5^{4f.}$."

p. cx. On the teachings of Amos, Hosea, and preceding prophets of the eighth century, see Köberle, *Sünde und Gnade im religiösen Leben des Volkes Israel bis auf Christum* (1905), pp. 96–153.

p. 4, line 12. For الحلاري, read الحازي.

pp. 15 ff. On the nations dealt with in Am. 1^3–2^4, see the article "Semites," in *DB*. V., by J. F. McCurdy.

p. 42, line 6 (from bottom). For ܪܡܚܣܡ, read ܪܡܚܣܡ.

p. 257, line 4. Omit *against me*, with 𝔖, as a gloss; see p. 256.

p. 277, note ‡. For *G VI.*, read *GI.*

p. 280, lines 27–29. The text of strophe 1, lines 7 and 8, is better arranged as in the translation on p. 283, viz.:

יחינו מימים ביום השלישי
יקמנו ונחיה לפניו :

p. 281, lines 1, 2. Transpose "6^{11a} is, of course, a gloss," to follow "In strophe 4 (6^{11}–7^2)." Dele "(1) v.^{11b} is suspected, but *v.i.*" For "v.^{11c}," read "v.^{11b}."

p. 287, line 2 (from bottom). For أَقْرَب, read أَقْرَب.

p. 291, line 15. For "also rejects," read "rejects all of."

p. 313, line 20. Orelli reads לְחֵמָא; see p. 320.

p. 329, line 1. Insert *it* after *eat*.

PRINCIPAL ABBREVIATIONS

I. GENERAL.

abs.	absolute.
acc.	accusative.
adv.	adverb, or adverbial.
apod.	apodosis.
art.	article.
Ass., or Assyr.,	Assyrian.
ca., or *cir.*	*circa*, about.
cf.	*confer*, compare.
circ.	circumstantial.
cl.	clause.
cod., codd.	codex, codices.
cog., or cogn.	cognate.
com.	commentators, or commentaries.
cons.	consecutive.
cont.	continue, continuing, etc.
cstr.	construct.
dat.	dative.
d.f., or dag. f.	dagesh forte.
f. or fem.	feminine.
fol.	following, follows, etc.
freq.	frequentative.
gen.	genitive.
Hiph.	Hiph'îl.
impf.	imperfect.
imv.	imperative.
indef.	indefinite.
inf.	infinitive.
intrans.	intransitive.

lit.	literal, or literally.
m., or masc.	masculine.
Ni.	Niph'al.
om.	omits, omit, etc.
p.	person.
pass.	passive.
pf.	perfect.
Pi.	Pi'el.
pl.	plural.
prec.	preceding.
pred.	predicate.
prep.	preposition.
pron.	pronoun, or pronominal.
ptcp.	participle.
rel.	relative.
rm.	remark.
sg.	singular.
stat.	stative.
str.	strophe.
subj.	subject.
suf.	suffix.
sugg.	suggest, suggestion, etc.
s.v.	*sub voce.*
trans.	transitive.
v.	verse.
v.	*vide*, see.
vb.	verb, verbal.
v.i.	*vide infra*, see below.
v.s.	*vide supra*, see above.

2. TEXT AND VERSIONS.

A.V.   Authorized Version (1611).

'A.   Aquila's translation, cited from Field's *Hexapla*.

Bab.Cod. *Prophetarum posteriorum codex Babylonicus Petropolitanus auspiciis augustissimi Imperatoris Alexandri II.* Edidit H. Strack (1876).

Complut. The Complutensian Polyglot.

𝕲   The Septuagint, cited from *The Old Testament in Greek according to the Septuagint;* edited by H. B. Swete; Vol. III (1894).

𝕲ᴺ   Codex Sinaiticus.

𝕲ᴬ   Codex Alexandrinus.

𝕲ᴮ   Codex Vaticanus.

𝕲ᵠ   Codex Marchalianus.

𝕲ᴸ   Lucian's Recension.

Kt.   Kᵉthîbh.

𝕷   The Old Latin Version, cited from Oesterley's *Studies in the Greek and Latin Versions of the Book of Amos* (1902) and "The Old Latin Texts of the Minor Prophets," *Journal of Theological Studies,* V. 76–88.

𝔐𝕿   The Massoretic Text.

O. T.   Old Testament.

Qr.   Qᵉri.

RV.   Revised Version (1885).

RV. m. Revised Version, margin.

𝔖   The Syriac translation, cited from the Paris Polyglot.

Σ.   Symmachus's translation, cited from Field's *Hexapla.*

Syr.-Hex. Syro-Hexaplar.

𝕿   The Targum, cited from the Paris Polyglot.

Θ.   Theodotion's translation, cited from Field's *Hexapla.*

𝖁   The Vulgate, cited from the Paris Polyglot.

3. AUTHORS AND BOOKS.

Abar. or Abarb. Abarbanel († 1508).

ABL.   *Assyrian and Babylonian Literature. Selected Translations.* Edited by Robert Francis Harper (1901).

AE.   Aben Ezra († 1167).

AJSL.   *American Journal of Semitic Languages and Literatures,* edited by William R. Harper.

AJT(h).   *American Journal of Theology,* edited by the Divinity Faculty of the University of Chicago.

Ba.	Baur, *Der Prophet Amos erklärt* (1847).
Bach.	Bachmann, *Alttestamentliche Untersuchungen* (1894)
Bach. *Pr.*	*Praeparationen zu den kleinen Propheten* (1890).
Bäd.	Bädecker's *Handbuch z. Palästina und Syrien* (5th ed. 1900; English, 1894).
Baethgen, *Sem. Rel.*	Baethgen, *Beiträge zur semitischen Religionsgeschichte* (1888).
Barth, *NB.*	J. Barth, *Die Nominalbildung in den semitischen Sprachen* (1889-91).
Barth, *ES.*	*Etymologische Studien* (1893).
BAS.	*Beiträge zur Assyriologie und semitischen Sprachwissenschaft*, herausgegeben von Friedrich Delitzsch und Paul Haupt (1890 ff.).
Baud. *Einl.*	Baudissin, *Einleitung in die Bücher des Alten Testamentes* (1901).
Baud. *Rel.*	*Studien zur semitischen Religionsgeschichte*, I. (1876), II. (1878).
Bauer,	G. L. Bauer, *Die kleinen Propheten übersetzt und mit Commentarien erläutert*, I., *Hoseas bis Micha* (1786).
Baumann,	*Der Aufbau der Amosreden* (Beihefte zur *ZAW*. VII. 1903).
BDB.	*A Hebrew and English Lexicon of the Old Testament, with an Appendix containing the Biblical Aramaic, based on the Lexicon of William Gesenius as translated by Edward Robinson*, edited by Francis Brown, with the coöperation of S. R. Driver and Charles A. Briggs (1891 ff.). Eleven parts have appeared thus far, extending as far as שָׁכַר.
Benz.	I. Benzinger.
Benz. *Arch.*	*Hebräische Archäologie* (1894).
BL.	Schenkel's *Bibel-Lexikon. Realwörterbuch zum Handgebrauch für geistliche und Gemeindeglieder*, 5 vols. (1869-75).
Bl. *Einl.*	F. Bleek, *Einleitung in das Alte Testament* (5th ed. by Julius Wellhausen, 1886).
Böckel,	*Hoseas* (1807).
Böttcher,	*Ausführliches Lehrbuch der Hebräischen Sprache*, I. (1866), II. (1868).
Briggs, *Hex.*	Chas. A. Briggs, *Higher Criticism of the Hexateuch* (1897).
Brugsch, *Hist.*	Heinrich Brugsch-Bey, *A History of Egypt under the Pharaohs* (1881).
Brüll,	"Beiträge zur Erklärung des Buches Hosea," *Jahrb. f. jüdischen Geschichte und Litteratur*, 1883, pp. 1-62.
BSZ.	Wilhelm Gesenius' *Hebräisches una Aramäisches Handwörterbuch über das Alte Testament* in verbindung mit Prof. Albert Socin und Prof. H. Zimmern bearbeitet von Dr. Frants Buhl. 13th ed. (1899),

Bu.   Karl Budde.
Bu. *Rel.*   *Religion of Israel to the Exile* (1899).
Buhl, *Pal.*   *Geographie des alten Palaestina* (1896).
Burkius,   *Gnomon in* 12 *Prophetas Minores* (1753).
Burney,   *Notes on the Hebrew Text of the Books of Kings* (1903).
BW.   *The Biblical World,* edited by William R. Harper.

Cal.   Calvin, *Commentaries on the Twelve Minor Prophets;*
                    transl. by J. Owen. Vols. I., II. (1846).
Cap(pellus),   *Critica sacra, sive de variis quae in sacris Veteris Testa-*
                    menti libris occurrunt lectionibus libri sex. Recensuit
                    multisque animadversionibus auxit Geo. Io. Lud. Vogel.
                    Tomus I. (1775), II. (1778).
Che.   T. K. Cheyne, *Hosea with Notes and Introduction* (The
                    Cambridge Bible for Schools and Colleges, 1884). In
                    the commentary on Hosea, "Che." always means this
                    work, unless otherwise indicated.
Co.   C. H. Cornill.
Co. *Einl.*   *Einleitung in das Alte Testament* (1891; 4th ed., 1897).
Cornelius a Lapide († 1637), *Commentarii* (1664).
COT.   *The Cuneiform Inscriptions and the Old Testament* (1885;
                    English transl. of *KAT.*[2]).
Crit. Bib. or *CB.* *Critica Biblica* or *Critical Notes on the Text of the Old*
                    Testament Writings, by T. K. Cheyne. Part II., *Ezekiel*
                    and the Minor Prophets (1903).
Crocius,   *Johannis Crocii . . . hypotyposes concionum in Prophetas*
                    Minores, etc. (1673).
Cyril,   Cyril of Alexandria († 444 A.D.).

Da.   A. B. Davidson.
Da. §,   *Hebrew Syntax* (2d ed., 1896).
Da. *Theol.*   *The Theology of the Old Testament* (1904).
Dahl,   J. C. Dahl, *Amos neu übersetzt und erläutert* (1795).
Dathe or Dat.   *Prophetae minores ex recensione textus Hebraei et versionum*
                    antiquarum latine versi notisque philologicis et criticis
                    illustrati a J. A. Dathio (1773).
DB.   *A Dictionary of the Bible,* edited by James Hastings. 4 vols.
                    (1898–1902) and an "Extra Volume" (1904), cited here
                    as Vol. V.
DB.[2]   *A Dictionary of the Bible,* edited by Sir William Smith and
                    J. M. Fuller. 3 vols. (2d ed., 1893).
De.   Franz Delitzsch.
de R.   de Rossi, *Variae Lectiones Veteris Testamenti,* etc., Vol. III.
                    (1786), and *Scholia Critica in Veteris Testamenti libros*
                    (1798).

DHM. *Proph.*   D. H. Müller, *Die Propheten in ihrer ursprünglichen Form*, 2 vols. (1896).

Di.   August Dillmann.

Di. *Theol.*   *Handbuch der Alttestamentlichen Theologie* (1895; edited by Kittel).

Dl.   Friedrich Delitzsch.

Dl. *Pr.* or *Prol.*   *Prolegomena eines neuen Hebräisch-Aramäischen Wörterbuchs zum Alten Testament* (1886).

Dl. *HWB.*   *Assyrisches Handwörterbuch* (1896).

Dl. *Pa.* or *Par.*   *Wo lag das Paradies* (1881).

Dl. *Hebr. Lang.*   *The Hebrew Language* (1883).

Dr.   S. R. Driver, *Joel and Amos* (The Cambridge Bible for Schools and Colleges; 1897).

Dr. §,   *A Treatise on the Use of the Tenses in Hebrew* (1874; 3d ed., 1892).

Dr. *LOT.*   *An Introduction to the Literature of the O. T.* (6th ed., 1897).

Dr. *Dt.*   *A Critical and Exegetical Commentary on Deuteronomy* (International Critical Commentary, 1895).

Dr. *Sam.*   *Notes on the Hebrew Text of the Books of Samuel* (1890).

Dru. or Drus.   Drusius, Commentary on Minor Prophets, in *Critici Sacri: s. doctissimorum virorum ad Sacra Biblia annott. et tractatus* (London, 1660).

Duhm, *Theol.*   Bernhard Duhm, *Die Theologie der Propheten* (1875).

Düsterdieck,   "Beiträge zur Erklärung des Propheten Amos, mit besonderer Rücksicht auf G. Baur, *Der Prophet Amos*," *Theologische Studien und Kritiken*, 1849, pp. 869–914.

EB.   *Encyclopaedia Biblica*, edited by T. K. Cheyne and J. Sutherland Black. 4 vols. (1899–1903).

Ed. Meyer, *GA.*   *Geschichte d. Alterthums*, Vol. I. (1884).

Eich.   Eichhorn, *Die Hebräischen Propheten* (1816 ff.).

Elh.   H. J. Elhorst, *De Profetie van Amos* (1901).

Enc. Br.   *Encyclopaedia Britannica*.

Eph. Syr.   Ephraem Syrus († 373).

Ew.   Heinrich Ewald, *Die Propheten des Alten Bundes* (1840; 2d ed., 1867; transl. as *Commentary on the Prophets of the Old Testament*, 5 vols., 1875–81).

Ew.[8]   *Ausführliches Lehrbuch der Hebräischen Sprache des Alten Bundes* (8th ed., 1870).

Ew. *Hist.*   *Geschichte des Volkes Israel* (3d ed., 1866), Engl. transl. *History of Israel* (1871).

Exp.   *The Expositor*, edited by W. Robertson Nicoll. (Superior figures indicate the series cited.)

Exp. T.   *The Expository Times*, edited by James Hastings.

Fürst, *Lex.*   *Hebräisches und Chaldäisches Handwörterbuch über das Alte Testament* (3d ed., 1876).

GAS.   George Adam Smith, *The Book of the Twelve Prophets* (The Expositor's Bible, Vol. I., 1896).
GAS. *HG.*   *Historical Geography of the Holy Land* (1895).
Geb.   Gebhard, *Gründliche Einleitung in die zwölf kleinen Propheten* (1737).
Geiger,   Abraham Geiger, *Urschrift und Uebersetzungen der Bibel in ihrer Abhängigkeit von der innern Entwickelung des Judenthums* (1857).
Ges.   Wilhelm Gesenius.
Ges. *Thes.*   Wilhelm Gesenius, *Thesaurus philologicus criticus linguae Hebraeae et Chaldaeae Veteris Testamenti* (1829).
GFM.   George Foote Moore.
GFM. *Ju.*   *Judges* (International Critical Commentary, 1895).
Giesebrecht,   *Beiträge zur Jesaiakritik, nebst einer Studie über prophetische Schriftstellerei* (1890).
GK.   Wilhelm Gesenius, *Hebräische Grammatik völlig umgearbeitet*, von E. Kautzsch (27th ed., 1902).
Gr.   H. Grätz, *Emendationes in plerosque Sacrae Scripturae Veteris Testamenti libros, secundum veterum versiones nec non auxiliis criticis caeteris adhibitis. Fasciculus secundus Ezechielis et Duodecim Prophetarum libros, etc., continens* (1893).
Gr. *Gesch.*   *Geschichte der Juden* (1853–76).
Grimm, *Lit. App.* *Euphemistic Liturgical Appendixes in the Old Testament* (1901).
Grot(ius),   *Annotata ad Vetus Testamentum*, Vol. II. (1644).
GSG. *Hist.*   George S. Goodspeed, *History of the Babylonians and Assyrians* (1902).
Gu.   H. Guthe; when no specific reference is added, the translation of the Minor Prophets in Kautzsch's *Die Heilige Schrift* (1896) is to be understood.
Gu. *Gesch.* or *G VI.*, *Geschichte des Volkes Israel* (1899).
Gun.   J. H. Gunning, *De Godspraken van Amos* (1885).

H.   W. R. Harper, *Elements of Hebrew Syntax* (1888; 5th ed., 1899).
Hal.   J. Halévy: (1) "Le livre d'Osée," *Revue Sémitique*, X. (1902), 1–12, 97–133, 193–212, 289–304.
                    (2) "Le livre d'Amos," *ibid.* XI. (1903), 1–31, 97–121, 193–209, 289–300; XII. (1904), 1–18.
Har.   J. C. Harenberg, *Amos Propheta expositus interpretatione nova latina, etc.* (1763).

Häv.	Hävernick, *Handbuch der historisch-kritischen Einleitung in das Alte Testament* (1837; transl. 1852).
Hd.	Henderson, *The Book of the Twelve Minor Prophets translated from the original Hebrew, with a Commentary, critical, philological, and exegetical* (1868).
Hebr.	*Hebraica*, Vols. I.–XI. (1884–95); continued as *American Journal of Semitic Languages and Literatures*.
Hes.	Heinrich Hesselberg, *Die zwölf kleinen Propheten ausgelegt* (1838).
Hi.	Hitzig, *Die zwölf kleinen Propheten* (1838; 4th ed. by Steiner, 1881).
Hirscht,	"Textkritische Untersuchungen über das Buch Amos," *Zeitschrift für wissenschaftliche Theologie*, Vol. XLIV. (1903), pp. 11–73.
Hng.	Hengstenberg, *Die Christologie des Alten Testaments* (2d ed., 1854–8; transl. 1863).
Hoffm.	Hoffmann, "Versuche zu Amos," *Zeitschrift für die Alttestamentliche Wissenschaft*, III. 87–126.
Holzinger, *Einl.*	*Einleitung in den Hexateuch* (1893).
Hom.	F. Hommel, *The Ancient Hebrew Tradition as Illustrated by the Monuments* (1897).
Hom. *GBA.*	*Geschichte Babyloniens und Assyriens* (1885).
Houtsma,	"Bijdrage tot de kritiek en verklaring van Hozea," *Theologisch Tijdschrift*, IX. (1875), 55–75.
Hux(table),	*Commentary on Hosea* (Bible Commentary, VI., 1892).
Jarchi =	Rashi = Rabbi Solomon ben Isaak († 1105).
Jastrow, *Rel.*	*The Religion of Babylonia and Assyria* (1898).
JBL.	*Journal of Biblical Literature.*
Jer.	Jerome († 420).
Jew. Enc.	*The Jewish Encyclopaedia* (of which 8 vols. are now published).
Jos. *Ant.*	Flavius Josephus, *The Antiquities of the Jews.*
JPTh.	*Jahrbücher für Prot. Theologie.*
JQR.	*The Jewish Quarterly Review.*
Jus.	C. W. Justi, *Amos neu übersetzt und erläutert* (1799).
K.	E. Kautzsch.
K. *DB. V.*	Art. "Religion of Israel," by Kautzsch, in Hastings's *Dictionary of the Bible*, extra volume (1904).
KAT.[2]	*Die Keilinschriften und das Alte Testament*, von Eb. Schrader (2d ed. 1883).
KAT.[3]	*Die Keilinschriften und das Alte Testament*, von E. Schrader. Dritte Auflage . . . neu bearbeitet von Dr. H. Zimmern und Dr. H. Winckler (1902).

KB.	*Keilinschriftliche Bibliothek*, herausgegeben von Eb. Schrader (1889 ff.).
Ke.	C. F. Keil, Commentary on the Twelve Minor Prophets in Keil and Delitzsch's *Biblische Commentar*, Vol. IV. (1866 ; transl. 1880).
Kenn.	B. Kennicott, *Vetus Testamentum Hebr. cum variis lectionibus* (1776–80).
Kent, *Hist.*	*A History of the Hebrew People*, I. (1896); II. (1897).
KGF.	*Keilinschriften und Geschichtsforschung*, von Eb. Schrader (1878).
Ki.	David Kimchi († 1230).
Kirk. *Doct.* or *Proph.*	A. F. Kirkpatrick, *Doctrine of the Prophets* (1892; 3d ed. 1901).
Kit.	Rudolph Kittel.
Kit. *Hist.*	*History of the Hebrews*, 2 vols. (1888–92 ; English transl. by John Taylor, 1895–96).
Klo.	Klostermann.
Kno.	Knobel, *Prophetismus der Hebräer* (1837).
Kö.	König, *Historisch-kritische Lehrgebäude der Hebräischen Sprache*, Vols. I.–III. (1881–97). Where there is no indication of the volume, the reference is to Part III., *Historisch-comparative Syntax der Hebr. Sprache* (1897).
Kö. *Einl.*	*Einleitung in das Alte Testament* (1893).
Kö. *Hauptprobleme, Die Hauptprobleme der altisr. Religionsgeschichte* (1884).	
Kö. *Stil.*	*Stilistik, Rhetorik, Poetik* (1900).
Kue.	Abraham Kuenen.
Kue. *Einl.*	*Historisch-kritische Einleitung in die Bücher des Alten Testaments* (2d ed. of Dutch, 1885 f.; German, 1887–93).
Kue. *Hibb. Lect.*	*National Religions and Universal Religions* (Hibbert Lectures, 1882).
Kue. *Proph.*	*De profeten en de profetie onder Israel. Historisch-dogmatische Studie* (2d ed., 1875 ; English, *The Prophets and Prophecy in Israel: an Historical and Critical Enquiry*, 1877).
Kue. *Rel.*	*The Religion of Israel* (Dutch, 1869 f.; English, 1874 f.).
Kurtz,	*Die Ehe des Propheten Hosea, chaps. 1–3* (1859).
Kusznitzki,	*Joel, Amos, Obadja qua aetate quibus de rebus sint locuti* (Inaugural dissertation, 1872).
Lag.	Paul de Lagarde.
Lag. *BN.*	*Uebersicht über die im Aramäischen, Arabischen und Hebräischen übliche Bildung der Nomina* (1889).
Lag. *Mit.*	*Mittheilungen*, Vols. I.–IV. (1884–91).
Levy, *NHWB.*	*Neuhebräisches und Chaldäisches Wörterbuch über die Talmudim und Midraschim*, von Jacob Levy (1876–89).

Linder,   "Bemerkungen über einige Stellen im Propheten Hosea," *Theol. Studien und Kritiken*, 1860, pp. 739 ff.

Loftm. or Loft.   Loftman, *Kritisk undersökning af den Masoretiska texten till prof. Hoseas bok* (1894).

Löhr,   *Untersuchungen zum Buch Amos* (Beiheft zur *Zeitschrift für die Alttestament. Wissenschaft*, IV., 1901).

Lu. or Luth.   Martin Luther.

Ma.   Manger, *Comm. in Hoseam* (1782).

Marck,   *Commentarius in Duodecim Prophetas Minores* (1784).

Marti,   *Dodekapropheton* (1903).

Marti, *Rel.* or *Gesch.*   *Geschichte der israelitischen Religion* (3d ed., 1897; 4th ed., 1903).

Mau.   Maurer, *Commentarius grammaticus historicus criticus in Prophetas minores* (1840).

Maybaum, *Proph.*   *Die Entwickelung des israelitischen Prophetenthums* (1883).

McC. *HPM.*   J. F. McCurdy, *History, Prophecy, and the Monuments.* 3 vols. (1895–1901).

Meinhold,   *Studien zur israelitischen Religionsgeschichte.* I., *Der heilige Rest.* Teil I., "Elias, Amos, Hosea, Jesaja" (1903).

Merc(erus),   *Commentarii locupletissimi in vates quinque priores, inter eos qui minores vocantur* (2d ed., 1695).

Mich.   J. D. Michaelis, *Deutsche Uebersetzung des Alten Testament mit Anmerkungen für Ungelehrte. Der erste Theil welcher die zwölf kleinen Propheten enthält* (1872).

Mit.   H. G. Mitchell, *Amos, an Essay in Exegesis* (1893; 2d ed., 1900).

Müller, *SK.*   "Textkritische Studien zum Buche Hosea," *Theologische Studien und Kritiken*, 1904, pp. 124–6.

Munster,   Commentary on Minor Prophets, in *Critici Sacri* (1660).

Muss-Arnolt, *Dict.*   Wm. Muss-Arnolt, *A Concise Dictionary of the Assyrian Language* (of which 16 parts, extending to *šaṭru*, are now published).

MV.   Gesenius's *Hebr. u. Aram. Handwörterbuch*, 11th ed. (1890) by Mühlau and Volck.

New. or Newc.   Newcome, *An Attempt towards an Improved Version, Metrical Arrangement, and an Explanation of the Twelve Minor Prophets* (1836).

Nö.   Theodor Nöldeke.

Now.   W. Nowack, *Die kleinen Propheten übersetzt und erklärt* (Handkommentar zum Alten Testament, 1897; 2d ed., 1903 = Now.[3]).

Now. *Arch.*   *Lehrbuch d. hebr. Archäologie* (1894).

Now.[H.]   *Der Prophet Hosea* (1880).

Oet. Oettli, *Amos und Hosea. Zwei Zeugen gegen die Anwendung der Evolutionstheorie auf die Religion Israels* (Beiträge zur Förderung christlicher Theologie, Fünfter Jahrgang, Heft 4, 1901).

Ols. J. Olshausen, *Lehrbuch der Hebr. Sprache* (1861).

OLZ. *Orientalistische Litteratur-Zeitung*, herausgegeben von F. E. Peiser.

Oort, H. Oort, (1) "De profeet Amos," *Theologisch Tijdschrift*, XIV. (1880), 114–58.
(2) "Hozea," *ibid.* XXIV. (1890) 345–64; 480–505.

Oort (*Em.*), *Textus Hebraici Emendationes quibus in Vetere Testamento Neerlandice vertendo usi sunt A. Kuenen, I. Hooykaas, W. H. Kosters, H. Oort.* Edidit H. Oort (1900).

Or. Orelli, *The Twelve Minor Prophets* (1888; transl. by J. S. Banks, 1893).

Os. Osiander, *Ezechiel, Daniel, Osee, Joel, Amos, Abdias, Jonas, etc. juxta veterem seu vulgatam translationem ad Hebraeam veritatem emendati, etc.* (1579).

PAOS. *Proceedings of the American Oriental Society.*

Pareus, *Hoseas proph. comm. illustr. cum transl. trip. ex Hebr. et Chald.* (1605–09).

Paton, *Hist.* L. B. Paton, *The Early History of Syria and Palestine* (1901).

PEF. Quarterly Statements of the Palestine Exploration Fund.

Perles, *Analekten zur Textkritik des Alten Testaments* (1895).

Po. Edward Pococke, *A Commentary on the Prophecy of Hosea* (1685).

PRE.[3] *Realencyklopädie für protestantische Theologie und Kirche*, begründet von J. J. Herzog; in dritter verbesserter und vermehrter Auflage . . . von A. Hauck (1896 ff.; 14 vols. are now issued).

Preiswerk, *Explication des douze derniers livres prophétiques de l'Ancien Testament* (1841).

PSBA. *Proceedings of the Society of Biblical Archaeology.*

Pu. E. B. Pusey, *The Minor Prophets with a Commentary, explanatory and practical, and Introductions to the several Books.* Vol. I. (1865).

I R., II R., III R., IV R., V R. Rawlinson's *Cuneiform Inscriptions of Western Asia*, 5 vols.

Ra. or Ras. Rashi, *i.e.* Rabbi Solomon ben Izaak († 1105).

Redslob, *Die Integrität der Stelle Ho. 7,4–10 im Frage gestellt* (1842).

Reu. Ed. Reuss, *Das Alte Testament übersetzt eingeleitet und erläutert*, Band II, *Die Propheten* (1892).

RFH.   Robert Francis Harper (see *ABL.*).
Riedel,   *Alttestamentliche Untersuchungen*, Part I. (1902), 1–36.
Ri(ehm), *HBA.* Riehm's *Handwörterbuch d. Biblischen Alterthums.*
Riehm, *Einl.*   *Einleitung in das Alte Testament*, Vol. II. (1890).
Rob. *BR.*² or *Pal.* Robinson, *Biblical Researches in Palestine*, 3 vols. (2d ed.,
                1874).
Ros.   Rosenmülleri, *Scholia in Vetus Testamentum in compen-*
                dium redacta ; post auctoris obitum edidit J. C. S. Lechner.
                Vol. VI. *scholia in prophetas minores continens* (1886).
*RP.*²   *Records of the Past* (new series), Vols. I–IV. (1889–92).
Ru.   Paul Ruben, *Critical Remarks upon Some Passages of the*
                Old Testament (1896).
Rückert,   *Hebräische Propheten, übersetzt und erläutert*, Vol. I. (1831).

Sanctius,   *Comm. in Proph. Min.* (1621).
Sayce, *Bab. Rel.* A. H. Sayce, *Lectures on the Origin and Growth of Reli-*
                gion as Illustrated by the Religion of the Ancient Baby-
                lonians (Hibbert Lectures, 1887).
Sayce, *HCM.*   *Higher Criticism and the Verdict of the Monuments* (3d
                ed., 1894).
Sayce, *Pat. Pal.* *Patriarchal Palestine* (1895).
SBONT.   *The Sacred Books of the Old and New Testaments. A New*
                English Translation with Explanatory Notes and Pic-
                torial Illustrations, prepared by . . . and edited, with the
                assistance of H. H. Furness, by Paul Haupt.
SBOT.   *The Sacred Books of the Old Testament. A Critical edi-*
                tion of the Hebrew Text, printed in Colors with Notes,
                prepared by . . ., under the editorial direction of Paul
                Haupt.
Schegg,   *Die kleinen Propheten übersetzt und erklärt*, Theil I. (1854).
Schleus.   J. F. Schleusneri, *Opuscula critica ad versiones Graecas*
                Veteris Testamenti pertinentia (1812).
Schlier, J.   *Die zwölf kleinen Propheten. Ein Wegweiser zum Verständ-*
                niss des Prophetenwortes für die Gemeinde (2d ed., 1876).
Schmo.   Schmoller, Exposition of the Books of Hosea and Amos in
                Lange's *Bibelwerk* (1872; transl. by J. F. McCurdy
                [Hosea] and T. W. Chambers [Amos], 1874).
Schmidt,   Sebastian Schmidt, *In Prophetam Hoseam commentarius*
                (1687).
Scholz,   *Commentar zum Buche des Propheten Hosea* (1882).
Schra.   Eberhard Schrader (see *KAT.* and *KB.* and *KGF.*).
Schrö.   J. F. Schröder, *Die kleineren Propheten übersetzt und*
                erläutert (1829).
Schultz, *Theol.* *Old Testament Theology* (1869 ; 5th ed., 1896 ; English,
                1892).

Seb.   Mark Sebök, *Die syrische Uebersetzung d. zwölf kleinen Propheten und ihr Verhältniss zu dem massoretischen Text und zu den älteren Uebersetzungen, namentlich den LXX. und dem Targum* (1887).

Seesemann,   *Israel und Juda bei Amos und Hosea nebst einem Exkurs über Ho. 1–3* (1898).

Sellin,   *Beiträge zur israelitischen und jüdischen Religionsgeschichte* (1896 f.).

Sharpe,   *Notes and Dissertations upon the Prophecy of Hosea* (1884).

Sim.   August Simson, *Der Prophet Hosea erklärt und übersetzt* (1851).

SK.   *Theologische Studien und Kritiken*, herausgegeben von E. Kautzsch und E. Haupt.

Skinner,   *Kings* (New-Century Bible, 1904).

Sm.   R. Smend.

Sm. *Rel.*   *Lehrbuch der alttestamentlichen Religionsgeschichte* (1893 ; 2d ed., 1899).

HPS. *O. T. Hist.*, H. P. Smith, *Old Testament History* (1903).

SS.   Siegfried und Stade, *Hebräisches Wörterbuch zum Alten Testamente* (1903).

St.   H. Steiner (see under Hi.).

Sta.   Bernhard Stade.

Sta. *GVI.*   *Geschichte des Volkes Israel* (1887–89).

Sta. §.   *Lehrbuch der Hebräischen Grammatik* (1879).

Sta. *SBOT.*   *The Books of Kings — Critical Edition of the Hebrew Text printed in Colors* (1904).

Sta. *Akad. Reden,* *Ausgewählte Akademische Reden und Abhandlungen* (1899).

Stäudlin,   *Neue Beiträge zur Erläuterung der biblischen Propheten* (1791).

Stek.   Schuurmans Stekhoven, *De Alexandrijnsche Vertaling van het Dodekapropheton* (1887).

Stru.   Struensee, *Neue Uebersetzung der Weissagungen Jesaias, Joels, Amos, Obadja und Micha nach dem Ebräischen Text mit Zuziehung der griechischen Version* (1773).

Stuck,   *Hoseas Propheta. Introductionem praemisit, vertit, commentatus est* (1828).

SV.   *Skizzen und Vorarbeiten*, von J. Wellhausen, Vols. I.–VI. (1884–89).

Tay.   J. Taylor, art. "Amos," Hastings's *Dictionary of the Bible.*

Theiner,   *Die zwölf kleinen Propheten* (1828).

Theod.   Theodoret, Bishop of Cyrus († 457).

T(h)LZ.   *Theologische Literaturzeitung.*

Thomson, *LB.*   *The Land and the Book; or Biblical Illustrations drawn from the Manners and Customs, the Scenes and Scenery, of the Holy Land,* by W. M. Thomson, 2 vols. (1859).

ThSt.   *Theologische Studiën.* Tijdschrift onder redactie van F. E. Daubanton en C. H. Van Rhijn.

ThT.   *Theologisch Tijdschrift.*

Torrey,   (1) " On the Text of Am. 5^{26} 6^{1-2} 7^2," *Journal of Biblical Literature,* XIII. (1894), 61–3.

       (2) " Notes on Am. 2^7 6^{10} 8^{13} 9^{8-10}," *ibid.* XV. (1896), 151–4.

Tött.   Töttermann, *Die Weissagungen Hosea's bis zur ersten assyrischen Deportation ($1-6^3$) erläutert* (1879).

Tristram, *NHB.*   *Natural History of the Bible* (1889).

TSBA.   *Transactions of the Society of Biblical Archaeology.*

Umb.   Umbreit, *Praktischer Commentar über die kleinen Propheten,* I. (1844).

Va.   Vater, *Amos übersetzt und erläutert mit Beifügung des Hebräischen Textes und des Griechischen der Septuaginta nebst Anmerkungen zu letzterem* (1810).

Val.   Valeton, *Amos en Hosea* (1894 ; German, 1898).

Vatablus,   Commentary on Minor Prophets, contained in *Critici Sacri* (1660).

Volz,   *Die vorexilische Jahweprophetie und der Messias* (1897).

Vol.   K. Vollers, " Das Dodekapropheton der Alexandriner," *Zeitschrift für die alttestamentliche Wissenschaft,* III. (1883), 219–72 ; IV. (1884), 1–20.

We.   J. Wellhausen, *Die kleinen Propheten übersetzt und erklärt* (1892 ; 3d ed. 1898 = We.[3]).

We. *Prol.*   *Prolegomena to the History of Israel.*

We. *SV.*   *Skizzen und Vorarbeiten,* Vols. I.–VI. (1884–89).

We. *Hex.*   *Die Composition des Hexateuchs und der historischen Bücher des Alten Testaments* (1889).

Wkl.   H. Winckler.

Wkl. *Untersuch.*   *Alttestamentliche Untersuchungen* (1892).

Wkl. *AOF.*   *Altorientalische Forschungen* (1893 ff.).

Wkl. *GI.*   *Geschichte Israels in Einzeldarstellungen,* 2 vols. (1895–1900).

W. Max Müller, *AE., Asien u. Europa nach Altägyptischen Denkmälern* (1893).

WRS. *Proph.*   W. R. Smith, *Prophets of Israel* (1882 ; new ed., 1895).

WRS. *Sem.*   *Lectures on the Religion of the Semites* (1889 ; 2d ed., 1894).

WRS. *OTJC.*[2]   *The Old Testament in the Jewish Church* (1881 ; 2d ed., 1892).

Wü.	Wünsche, *Der Prophet Hosea übersetzt und erklärt, mit Benutzung der Targumin der jüdischen Ausleger Raschi, Aben Ezra und David Kimchi* (1868).
ZA.	*Zeitschrift für Assyriologie,* herausgegeben von C. Bezold.
ZAW.	*Zeitschrift für die alttestamentliche Wissenschaft,* herausgegeben von Dr. Bernhard Stade.
ZDMG.	*Zeitschrift der deutschen morgenländischen Gesellschaft.*
ZDPV.	*Zeitschrift d. deutsch. Palaestina-Vereins.*
ZKW.	*Zeitschrift für kirchliche Wissenschaft und kirchliches Leben.*
ZLTh.	*Zeitschrift für Lutherische Theologie.*
ZWTh.	*Zeitschrift für wissenschaftliche Theologie.*

Biblical passages are cited according to the English enumeration of chapters and verses, except in the textual, strophical, and grammatical portions where the Hebrew enumeration is followed.

INTRODUCTION.

A. FACTORS IN THE PRE-PROPHETIC MOVEMENT.

§ 1. THE PRE-PROPHETIC MOVEMENT IN GENERAL.

FOR a proper understanding of the place of Amos and Hosea in connection with Hebrew prophecy it is necessary to consider briefly the principal manifestations, during the two preceding centuries, of what may be called " pre-prophetism " ; * the basis of this movement and its chief characteristics ; likewise its fundamental thought (concerning God, man, worship, life, and the future),† as wrought out in this period. In the same connection some attention must be given to Assyria, which in these times touches Israel so closely and exercises so marked an influence upon the development of Israelitish thought. ‡ With some of the data relating to these subjects in our possession, we shall be better prepared to take up the subjects connected with Amos and Hosea, viz. in each case the personal life, the message, the public ministry ; likewise the literary form of the prophetic work,

---

* The distinction between prophetism proper (*i.e.* written prophecy) and that out of which it sprang is important, and may be maintained by using for the latter the word " pre-prophetism." For the same reason, we may use *nabhi'* (pl. *nebhi'im*) in speaking of those (not *seers*) who preceded Amos. Cf. the use of the terms *Nebiïsmus* and *Prophetismus* by R. Kraetzschmar in *Prophet und Seher im Alten Israel* (1901).

† In other words, the theology of these times, as it has been preserved in contemporaneous writings and in tradition.

‡ A striking characteristic of Israel, in comparison with its sister nations, was a readiness to receive, from the outside, contributions in the form of new institutions and new thought. Much of this was bad and in time was lost; but much of it, being good, was retained. The gradual accumulation and assimilation of this outside material, under the guidance of an all-wise Providence, ultimately lifted Israel to a position of influence in world-history.

the versions in which it has come down to us, and the more important literature.*

The spirit of pre-prophetism was always alert and aggressive. Its manifestations were frequent, strong, and of a unique character. These manifestations were factors in preparing the way for that "point in the history of prophecy at which this great religious phenomenon rises — apparently, but surely not really — on a sudden to a higher level" (Che. *EB*. 3855); in other words, the point at which Amos and Hosea appear upon the scene of action. Unless a better explanation of the forward step taken at this time by the so-called *writing* prophets can be furnished than that which Budde (*Rel.* 131) proposes (viz. their utter failure to impress the people by oral speech), the question is to be regarded as a problem still unsolved.

§ 2. Pre-prophetic Participation in the Revolt of Jeroboam I.

The participation of the *nebhi'im* in the revolt which resulted in the disruption of the united kingdom may be assumed,† notwithstanding the late date of those portions of the narrative ‡ in which this participation is especially described.

---

* Much is gained in thinking of Amos and Hosea as together presenting a single unit of thought; for, while each is in sharp contrast with the other in temperament and in message, neither, by himself, is complete. They must both be taken to secure the whole idea.

† Kue. (*Rel.* I. 198 f.) says, "The revolt of the ten tribes from the royal house of David was undoubtedly countenanced by the prophets, especially by those of Ephraim " ; We. (*Prol.* 458), declares that they " actually suggested and promoted it " ; Kit. (*Hist.* II. 188) says, " Jeroboam was supported in his enterprise by a prophet, Ahijah of Shiloh " ; Kent (*Hist.* II. 20) maintains that it was supported by prophets who selected the leader. So also Gu. (*GVI*. 130–132), Wade (*O.T. Hist.* 313), Paton (*Hist.* 191). Cf. Che. (*EB*. 2406), who, though treating the narratives as unhistorical, regards it as possible that Jeroboam had friendly relations with Ahijah who lived at Shiloh, and certain that the northern prophets were on Jeroboam's side; and *contra* Winckler (*GI*. I. 159 f., II. 273) and H. P. Smith (*O.T. Hist.* 1903, pp. 177–80), who make no reference to prophetic influence; Sta. (*GVI.* I. 306 f.), who declares the narratives concerning the prophets to be without historical basis.

‡ There are four stories: (1) Ahijah, 1 K. 11²⁹⁻⁴⁰, of which vs.²⁹⁻³¹ may be early (so Kit. and Skinner) ; but all is considered late by Wkl. (*Untersuch.* 8 f.), Kamphausen, Benz., and Sta. (*SBOT.*) ; (2) Shemaiah, 1 K. 12²²⁻²⁴, clearly late; (3) "the man of God out of Judah" and "the old prophet at Bethel," 1 K. 13¹⁻³², all of which is late; (4) the visit of Jeroboam's wife to Ahijah, 1 K. 14¹⁻¹⁸, which, if early, has been thoroughly worked over by a later editor, the Hebrew text seeming to be a late recension of 𝔊.

This assumption is based upon (1) the fact that the early prophets in their intense conservatism stand opposed to every advance of civilization; cf. the general policy of Elijah (p. xxxvi), the attitude of the Judean narrative toward the beginnings of civilization in Gn. 4[16-24], and the opposition of Isaiah (2[6f.] 3[16-26]) to everything that seemed to favor luxury in life; not to speak of the representation of this same idea by the Nazirites and Rechabites who were closely associated with *nebhi'ism* and prophetism (p. xxxi); (2) the probability that the spirit which later actuated Elijah (as well as Amos and especially Hosea) in reference to the acknowledgment of other gods existed, at least in germ, in the minds of these earlier *nebhi'im* (so *e.g.* WRS. *Proph.* 48 ff.; Bu. *Rel.* 102); (3) the consistency of this pre-prophetic action with that of Elijah and Elisha in the conspiracy against the dynasty of Omri, as well as with the alleged conspiracy of Amos himself (Am. 7[10-13]) against Jeroboam II., at which time the prophetic temper was at all events regarded as revolutionary; and (4) the extreme likelihood that the prophetic stories, while late, represent in the main a true tradition, since they, at least, indicate one school of later opinion, the other school, led by Hosea (cf. Ho. 8[4] 13[11]) regarding the revolt or schism as a great blunder.

The effect of the disruption, in so far as the pre-prophetic movement is concerned, appears (1) in the fact that this movement takes place in the North, rather than under the Davidic dynasty in the South,* for until the last twenty years or so before the end of the Northern kingdom (721 B.C.) Judah produced little or nothing except the Judean narrative (p. lxix). This was true in part, because (2) a much greater liberty existed in the North, as a consequence of the failure of the Solomonic régime to maintain in Israel the obligations which it succeeded in imposing upon Judah; and with this liberty, there was possible also (3) a far greater simplicity of life than in the South; there existed, in fact, a more democratic atmosphere, the extreme class distinctions being less emphasized;† while (4) there was less interference from outside influence than would have been felt under a continuation of the Solomonic policy; likewise, (5) the disruption,

---

* Che. (*EB.* 3863), after making the words "Gilgal," "Carmel," "Ephraim," "Jordan," "Ramoth-gilead," etc. (as they occur in the narrative), corruptions of the all-pervading *Jerahmeel* of North Arabia, and after assigning the homes of Elijah and Elisha, as well as of Amos, to this region, says, "We cannot therefore be certain that there were any settlements of prophets in Northern Israel."

† Meinhold (p. 25) suggests that Yahweh was the champion of every Israelite against the despotism of Solomon, and that the *nabhi'*, therefore, as in later times the prophet, took the side of the deity against the despot.

in spite of the calves of Jeroboam, contributed very largely toward preparing the way for that ultimate separation of Yahweh from a place among the gods of the nations, and his elevation into the god of the heavens.* The revolt, in a word, was in some slight sense an anticipation of the later and more radical steps taken by Elijah and Elisha.

§ 3. The Pre-prophetic Manifestation under Elijah's Leadership.

1. Prophetic interference in the affairs of state took place under Elijah's leadership in the days of Ahab (*ca.* 875–850 B.C.). In estimating the importance of this very notable and unique manifestation of the pre-prophetic spirit, account must first be taken of the different strata of material preserved. On this point students are practically agreed.

Certain stories come from about 800 B.C., *i.e.* from within fifty years or so of Elijah's own times, *viz.* (*a*) the early trouble with Ahab and the drought; the contest on Carmel; and the visit to Horeb (1 K. 17¹–18³ᵃ·⁵⁻³⁰ 18³²ᵇ–19⁹ᵃ·¹¹ᵇ⁻²¹); (*b*) the story of Naboth's vineyard (1 K. 21¹⁻²⁰ᵃ·²⁷); (*c*) Elijah's encounter with Ahaziah's messengers (2 K. 1¹⁻⁴·⁵⁻⁸). From a period twenty-five to fifty years later comes the account of Elijah's last days with Elisha and his translation (2 K. 2¹⁻²⁵). To a much later time belong the story of Elijah's treatment of the companies sent out by Ahaziah (2 K. 1⁹⁻¹⁸) and certain additions to the early stories (*e.g.* 1 K. 18³ᵇ·⁴·³¹·³²ᵃ 19⁹ᵇ⁻¹¹ᵃ 21⁹ᵇ·²⁶·²⁸ᶠ·; Benzinger makes 2 K. 1⁵⁻⁸ also late, and Kamphausen the entire account, 2 K. 1¹⁻¹⁸). So substantially Kit., Benz., Kamphausen, Burney, and Skinner; but Sta. (*SBOT.*) calls all the Elijah and Elisha material late except 1 K. 18³¹⁻³²ᵃ 19⁹ᵇ·¹⁰·¹¹ᵃ·ᶜ· 21²⁰ᵇ·²¹ᶠ·²⁴ 2 K. 2¹ᵃ·²⁵ᵇ (cf. *GVI.* I 522, note); Meinhold (pp. 17–21) places the stories about 750 B.C. on the ground that such legends could not have developed in fifty years; and Todd (*Politics and Religion in Ancient Isr.* (1904), 195 ff.) minimizes Elijah's significance and makes the entire Baal-story an allegory coming from Manasseh's times.

2. In the interpretation of these stories, the earlier, as well as the later, must be acknowledged to show two tendencies of a decided character. The narrator's point of view is one strongly biassed by the attitude toward Baalism which prevailed in the times succeeding

---

* Cf. K. *DB.* V. 646 f.

Jehu. The picture of Ahab and his relation to Baalism is greatly overdrawn, a very large legendary element having entered into it.* Besides this, Elijah, called *nabhi'*, or prophet, only once in the entire narrative (viz. 1 K. 18²² where no other designation could have been employed), is everywhere (especially in 1 K. 17⁸⁻²⁴ 2 K. 1⁹⁻¹² 2⁸) represented as possessed of magical powers.†

3. But after making full allowance for these elements, we may feel confident that Elijah represents a true historical character of a remarkable type, and that a proof of his greatness is this very "stupendous and superhuman" image of him here sketched. ‡ We are not compelled to choose between the two extreme views, according to one of which, the prophet Elijah, while above the level of the *nebhi'im* of his time, is presented in greatly magnified form, the prophets of this period having had no such prominence as the narratives assign to them; § while the other treats him as a Titanic character creating a new epoch in Israel's history, to be placed side by side with Moses himself. ‖ His proper place may be determined by observing certain secondary points in connection with his contest with Ahab regarding Baalism, and with Ahab's relations to Naboth, and all of this must be studied in the light of the issue of the whole matter as it appears in the case of Jehu under Elisha's ministry.

Among other points, outside of the two main stories, the following should not be overlooked: (1) Elijah (*v.s.*) is not called *nabhi'*, because even at this time he is recognized as something different. He may not, however, be placed in the class of the writing prophets, because, unlike them, he has left

---

* This is the unanimous voice of critical opinion; cf. *e.g.* Kue. *Einl.* § 25; Kit. *Hist.* II. 267; Addis, art. "Elijah," *EB.*; We. *Prol.* 292 f.; Co. *Proph.* 29; Che. *EB.* 3859 f.; Meinhold; Sm. *Rel.*² 175 ff.; H. P. Smith, *O. T. Hist.* 188; K. *DB.* V. 655.

† This is in accordance with the earlier conceptions of *nebhi'ism* which Israel held in common with other nations; cf. the power of Moses with his magician's staff (Ex. 4²ᶠᶠ· 7²⁰ 9²³, etc.), that of Joshua and his spear (Jos. 18. 20), and the use of the arrow in divining referred to in 2 K. 13¹⁵ᶠᶠ· See K. *DB.* V. 650 f.; Sm. *Rel.*² 154; Kit. *Hist.* II. 266 f.; Che. *EB.* 3856 f.

‡ Cf. Co. *Proph.* 29.

§ We. *Prol.* 291; Sta. *GVI.* I. 526 f.; Todd, *op. cit.* 195 ff.; H. P. Smith, *O. T. Hist.* 191 ff.; Meinhold, 1–32.

‖ Co. *Proph.* 29; Kit. *Hist.* II. 266 f.; Addis, art. "Elijah," *EB.*; Strachan, art. "Elijah," *DB.*

nothing in written form ; and unlike them, he is closely associated with manticism and magic. On the other hand, the facts seem to make him both *seer*
and *nabhi'*. Witness the point already suggested in reference to manticism and
magic, and, in addition, the fact of his close relationship with the societies of
nebhi'im, and his apparent leadership among them, his farewell visit to the various headquarters of these societies, their strong interest in the occasion and the
manner of his final departure ; and, still further, those great characteristics
of sturdiness, strength, and courage which bespeak for him a place side by
side with the *seers* of the past, viz. Moses, Joshua, Samuel. (2) The suddenness of his appearances and disappearances, so frequently a subject of
comment (1 K. 17¹ 18⁷ ff. 2 K. 2¹⁶), is to be attributed to the *lacunae* of the
narrative, rather than to any effort upon the part of the writer to cultivate an
atmosphere of mystery.

(3) The impression of a magical personality (cf. the story of Samuel and
the witch of Endor) is conveyed, not only in the miraculous power ascribed
to him in general, but also in his special power over dew and rain (1 K.
17² 18¹· ⁴¹⁻⁴⁵), the deference paid to him by Obadiah (1 K. 18⁷ ff.), the use of an
extra quantity of water to prevent suspicion (18³³ ff.), the physical performance
in connection with his premonition of rain (18⁴²⁻⁴⁵), the ecstatic condition
in which he ran five hours from Carmel to Jezreel (18⁴⁶), the magical power
ascribed to his mantle (19¹⁹, cf. 2 K. 2⁸· ¹³ ff.), which Elisha may not resist,
and with which the waters are divided ; and especially in the account of
his marvellous translation by means of a chariot and horses of fire (2 K. 2¹¹ f.),
a later expression of the feeling that his activity was enduring, and that his
fellowship with God was "so close that its interruption seemed inconceivable" (K. *DB.* V. 655). In close connection with all this is (4) the strongly
pronounced nomadic spirit, which, naturally, stands opposed to everything
that indicates progress in civilization. This spirit appears in the simplicity
of his food and dress (1 K. 19⁶· ¹⁸ 2 K. 1⁸), in his isolation from his fellows,
and in his opposition to the religious policy of Ahab (*v.i.*). Perhaps this
furnishes the explanation, also, of the sudden character of his appearances
and disappearances (*v.s.*) : it is surely in accord with this that he is represented as living by the brook Cherith, which flows into the Jordan (1 K.
17²⁻⁷) ; sojourning outside of his own country at Zarephath in Phoenicia
(1 K. 17⁸ ff.) ; paying a visit to Horeb, after a journey of forty days and forty
nights (1 K. 19⁵⁻⁸) ; and moving about from place to place (2 K. 1, 2) ;
cf. the nomadic character of the Rechabites (p. lii), who arose about this
time (*v.i.*). (5) Not a little light is thrown upon the story of pre-prophetism
by the two incidents in Elijah's life, in connection with which he left his
native land and visited foreign countries. The earlier sojourn in Phoenicia,
at Zarephath, together with the nature of the work performed, indicates, on his
part, not only the nomadic tendency (in this case encouraged, doubtless, by
fear of Ahab), but also an attitude toward non-Israelites which is broad and
liberal, in spite of the narrow and intense zeal ordinarily attributed to him ;
and besides, a leniency which meant that the hatred shown in connection

with Baalism was not against that religion in itself, but only against its encroachment upon the realm of Yahweh (Sm. *Rel.*[2] 178; Co. *Proph.* 31), who had now become recognized as, indeed, the god of the land of Israel, although not god also of Phoenicia. The visit to Horeb (1 K. 19[8 ff.]), while illustrative of many elements in the prophet's character (*e.g.* the longing for solitude characteristic of the nomad, and a deep spiritual nature, as well as a tendency to deep despondency), also calls attention to the prophet's idea of Yahweh's original home and dwelling-place, *i.e.* the place in which one can most easily secure his oracle ; and is better understood in the light of Ju. 5[5] (cf. also Dt. 33[2] Hb. 3[8] Ps. 68[8]). This journey, although undertaken in a fit of discouragement, and because of Jezebel's inimical attitude, cannot be easily explained on any other supposition than that the *nabhi'*, in accordance with the general conviction, makes this pilgrimage, in the fashion of all ages, to a place regarded as sacred from the oldest times, because there Yahweh had dwelt in the beginning (Bu. *Rel.* 18 ; K. *DB.* V. 626 f. ; Barton, *Semitic Origins*, 277 ; Sta. *GVI.* I. 130 ff.).

(6) The chief elements in certain situations described in the Elijah-stories had already been anticipated in earlier history, *e.g.* Solomon had erected sanctuaries for his foreign wives (1 K. 11[7 f.]) just as Ahab does for Jezebel (*v.i.*), and probably this constituted one of the charges in the prophetic indictment of that monarch. Even earlier, Nathan had taken precisely the same stand against the abuse of royal power (2 S. 12[1-15]) as that taken by Elijah in the case of Ahab. Still further, the thought of Yahweh's using Syria (1 K. 19[15-17]) in order to punish Israel for wrong-doing, does not, of itself, imply that Yahweh is other than a national god, as is clear from the presence of this same conception not only in earlier Israelitish times (Nu. 14[40 ff.] [J, E] Jos. 7 [J]), but also among other nations (cf. the part played by the gods in the fall of Babylon in the Cyrus Cylinder,* and the representations concerning Yahweh's power at the time of the Exodus [J, E], and in the confusion of tongues at Babel [in J]; cf. Meinhold, 30 f.). On the further bearing of this, *v.i.* (7) Much turns upon the exact meaning assigned to the utterances concerning Yahweh and the Baalim in 1 K. 18[24. 27. 37. 3*] (Sm. *Rel.*[2] 178), *v.i.*

4. The uncertainty of the facts in the story of Elijah's struggle with Ahab and the priests of Baal explains, if it does not justify, the varying interpretations which have been founded upon them. We may consider here those points which relate to the form of

---

* The words of Sennacherib's general (2 K. 18[25] = Is. 36[10]) might also be cited, were it not probable that they represent a later Israelitish view rather than the thought of the Assyrian (cf. Sta., Benz., Marti, Duhm, *in loc.*). It is hardly likely that the haughty Assyrian would represent himself as acting in obedience to the command of the god of a small, despised people.

the story, the actual facts as nearly as they can be determined, and the problems raised by these facts. But since Elijah's contest is only part (or perhaps the beginning) of the great struggle which was closed, under the direction of Elisha, by Jehu, we shall state the problems and reserve a decision upon them until the additional help has been gained which is furnished by the events of Elisha's career and a consideration of the actual denouement (pp. xlviii f.).

(1) Reference has been made to the date of the material (*v.s.*), as well as to its prejudiced character. We cannot fail to note also its fragmentary form, *e.g.* its failure to furnish any introduction to the story of the challenge, from which an adequate knowledge of the events leading up to it may be obtained; the lack, also, of the end of the story, in which one might have expected to find out how Elijah executed the commission given him at Horeb, for surely I K. 19$^{19. 20}$ cannot be accepted as a fitting conclusion; and, still further, the absence of anything that will throw light on the fulfilment of the prediction in I K. 19^{17}. Perhaps the story of Naboth was intended, as Wellhausen suggests, to be the beginning of the judgment which overtook the worshippers of Baal. (2) The facts in the story itself are not always mutually consistent, and the statement throughout bears evidence of being too strongly colored against Ahab. The formal charge in I K. 16$^{30-33}$ represents him as being actually the greatest sinner that has yet occupied Israel's throne. But every accusation made, except that of building an altar in the house of Baal (v.^{32}), comes from the Deuteronomic period, nearly two and a half centuries later, when the official spirit had altogether changed. Was the extension of this courtesy to his wife worse than the similar act of Solomon ? And then, we may not think that Ahab had altogether forsaken Yahweh, or that Yahwism was in so bad a state, when we learn that of Ahab's children, three (I K. 22^{40} 2 K. 3^1 8$^{18. 26}$) were given names containing the word Yahweh as one element; that Ahab is able to find four hundred Yahweh prophets in one place, when there is occasion for their service (I K. 22^6); and that the number of those who had not bowed the knee to Baal was seven thousand, while, on the other hand, all of the Baal adherents are able a little later to be accommodated in one house (2 K. 10$^{21. 23}$). If, now, we add to this the statement of Jehu that Ahab served Baal only a little (2 K. 10^{18}), and the evidence that Jezebel was, indeed, a malicious and vindictive woman, we may well suppose not only that the situation was less serious than it is represented, but also that Jezebel, rather than Ahab, was the chief sinner. Ahab, following the policy of David and Solomon, sought to strengthen his throne and benefit the nation by alliance with outside powers, and did not appreciate the full meaning of the struggle as it presented itself to Elijah. He regarded the question as one in which the royal authority was involved, and, encouraged doubtless by the Tyrian influence, acted accordingly (WRS. *Proph.* 76 ff.). But, on the other hand, Jezebel was zealous and persistent in her efforts to

build up the Baal-party, for political as well as for religious purposes. The Tyrian Baal-worship threatened to a greater or less degree the Israelitish Yahweh-worship. (3) But these facts, even in this simpler and less sensational form, represent a contest. What was the point at issue ?

The question, in general, is this : Does Elijah here draw the line between the spiritual Israel (*i.e.* the seven thousand), and Israel of the flesh, who, though of the nation, are not members of the elect, known later as "the remnant"?* Are the spiritual and the worldly here for the first time brought into conflict ?† Does Elijah, then, give evidence of a conception of God higher than any that has yet been held? Or, on the other hand, shall we throw out this entire narrative of the Baal-struggle as absolutely unhistorical ; ‡ and understanding that it had its origin a century or a century and a half later than was indicated above, regard it as consequently the expression of a time not earlier than that of Amos and Hosea ? In either case may we suppose that, after all, Elijah's position is nothing more than Ahijah might have taken against Solomon, the fact being that the struggle is on behalf of the old idea, viz. an undefiled cultus, through a correct performance of which Yahweh's demands are satisfied, § and not in behalf of the new idea, emphasized by the writing prophets, that Yahweh's religion was something other than a cult ? Does Elijah represent Yahweh as about to bring great punishment on Israel, through Syria, because of failure to observe a pure cult, or because of ethical shortcomings ? This is the question at issue. The answer to it is of great concern in determining the value of the contribution of Amos and Hosea.

5. The Naboth story is perhaps more significant than anything else connected with the life of Elijah, for here there is spoken the condemnation of governmental unrighteousness which receives so large a notice from later prophets.

Some difficulties exist, likewise, in the form, as it is given us, of this story (1 K. 21). It is easy to see that it interrupts the connection of chaps. 20 and 22. If to this we add that in 𝔊 it immediately follows chap. 19, and that it has many points of affinity with the narrative in chaps. 17, 19 (*e.g.* the

---

* We. *Isr. u. jüd. Gesch.*[1] 54, note.　　　　† Sm. *Rel.*[2] 177 ff.
‡ Sta. *GVI.* I. 526 ff.; Todd, *op. cit.* 195 ff.　§ Meinhold, 24 ff.

representation of Ahab as a weak man controlled by Jezebel; also the apparent dependence of 21^{20a} upon 18^{17}), sustaining no relation to chaps. 20, 22, we have a fairly strong case for the order given in 𝕲 (*v.s.*). But now, if we put together the fact that Elijah is being introduced again by the same writer after his successor has been appointed (1 K. 19^{15-21}); the fact that the murder of Naboth contributed more largely to the ruin of Ahab's house than did his religious policy (Ew. *Hist.* IV. 71, 107; Co. *Proph.* 31 ff.; Skinner, 255); and the better understanding gained of the Carmel episode if we suppose the murder of Naboth to have preceded it, and to have excited the feeling of the people against Ahab (Skinner, 255; WRS. *EB.* 2670), — we are compelled to assume either that chap. 21 originally stood between vs.[18 and 19] of chap. 19, or that it is an independent document (cf. its resemblance to 14^{1-16}, and the view of Burney that it belongs to the same source as 2 K. 9^1-10^{28}).*

Keeping in mind the difficulties which the form of the story presents, we may note in reference to its content : (*a*) that the main point, rebuke of the king for an outrageous act, is the same as that found in the Nathan-David story (*v.s.*), and forms one of the principal topics in the discourses of Amos and Hosea ; (*b*) that, after all, Ahab's act was not an unusual thing for an oriental monarch (*v.s.*) ; but, in this case, the ancient spirit of freedom is again aroused (as in the days of the disruption) against a personal despotism ; (*c*) that it was this crime (*v.s.*), rather than Ahab's defence of Baalism, that cost him his throne, a significant fact in the history of national ethics and of a true conception of religion. In this same connection we may observe further : (*a*) the thing which Yahweh is here represented as doing is something quite unusual ; the threat that Ahab's house is to be destroyed by a foreign power, viz. Syria, plainly makes Yahweh something other than a merely national god (*v.i.*) ; (*b*) the Naboth-story is to receive practically the same interpretation, whether we suppose it

---

* To this may still be added the lack of harmony between chap. 21 and 2 K. 9; cf. the position of Naboth's "field" in 2 K. $9^{16ff.}$, a little way from Jezreel, and Naboth's "vineyard" close to Ahab's palace (in Samaria?), 1 K. 21^{18}, and the variants of 𝕲 in v.[1]; the visit of Ahab to his ill-gotten prize on the day after the murder in 2 K. 9^{26}, but apparently on the same day in 1 K. 21; also, the words of Jehu in 2 K. 9^{26} tell us a fact not in 1 K. 21^{11-16}, viz. that Naboth's sons were killed. On the basis of these and other facts chap. 21 is assigned to an independent source, as an appendix to chaps. $17-19^{21}$, by Kue. *Einl.* I[II.] 78 ; Meinhold, 12 ff.; Gunkel, *Preussische Jahrb.* XXVII. (1897), 18 ff.; Skinner; but cf. We. *Hex.* 283 ff.; WRS., art. "Kings," *EB.* 2670; Kit, 159–162; Benz. *in loc.*

to have preceded the Carmel event, and to be closely connected therewith (furnishing, in fact, the basis of that popular uprising), or to have followed it and been entirely independent of it. In either case it is a cry for justice to those oppressed. Upon the whole, something tangible is gained if the two stories are joined together; (*c*) with both stories there may be connected logically the opening message of Elijah to Ahab (1 K. 17¹) containing the threat of drought; for, after all, this is the question at issue; Who grants rain? Who is God? Yahweh or Baal? The chief purpose of this threat was " to demonstrate that the God, whose servant is Elijah, is the sole ruler of nature, against whose will no power in heaven or earth can prevail" (Skinner). This, in brief, was Elijah's great message (*v.s.*).

§ 4. Pre-prophetic Influences in the Time of Elisha.

1. Close coöperation of the prophet with the government, a conspiracy against the government and its overthrow by the instigation of the prophet, — all this took place in the days of Elisha (*ca.* 850–800 B.C.). In this we have the completion of the work initiated by Elijah.

The portions of 2 K. concerned with the life of Elisha may be classified: (1) 2¹⁻²⁵ 4¹⁻6²³ 8¹⁻¹⁵ 13¹⁴⁻²¹, a series of early prophetic narratives of a personal or biographical character, loosely strung together and laying special emphasis on Elisha's activity as a wonder-worker (to be designated by the symbol Eᵇ); (2) 3⁴⁻²⁷ 6²⁴⁻7⁷ 9¹⁻⁶· ¹¹⁻²⁸· ³⁰⁻10²⁷, a different collection of early prophetic narratives giving special attention to Elisha's influence in affairs of state and in the campaigns against Syria and other nations (Eᵖ); (3) 3¹⁻³ 7¹⁸⁻²⁰ 8¹⁶⁻²⁴· ²⁵⁻²⁹ 9⁷⁻¹⁰ 10²⁸⁻³¹· ³²⁻³⁶, a series of later additions chiefly from the pen of the Deuteronomic compiler of Kings. Cf. the comm. of Kit., Benz., Burney, Skinner; and Kue. *Einl.* Iᴵᴵ· 80 ff.; We. *Hex.* 286–90; Addis, art. "Elisha," *EB.*; Dr. *LOT.* 196 f.; WRS. and K., art. "Kings," *EB.*

This material presents some of the characteristics named above, notably, *e.g.* (*a*) the magical element (strikingly similar, and even stronger), but there is little or no basis for the opinion (H. P. Smith, *O. T. Hist.*, p. 194, and others; cf. *contra*, Addis, *EB.* 1276; Strachan, art. " Elijah," *DB.*; and the comm. of Kit., Benz., and Skinner) that the Elisha-memoirs are in large part a duplication of those of Elijah, and consequently unhistorical. (*b*) The lack of chronological order, as well as of chronological indication; and the result of this is to create a wrong impression of Elisha's career (cf. Addis, *EB.* 1276;

Strachan, *DB*. I. 694; Benz. 129; Kit. 185); for who really gathers from the narrative that Elisha lived forty-five years after the revolt of Jehu? A true conception of the case is prevented by the placing of this story at the end, with all the anecdotes but one preceding.

2. The following points, although of secondary interest, may not be ignored : —

(1) The first meeting, at which the call was extended (by Elijah, it would seem, rather than by Yahweh himself),* took place at the home of Elisha's family (which must have possessed substance ; and consequently Elisha, like Amos, was not an ordinary *nabhi'*), some time after Elijah's visit to Horeb,† perhaps six or seven years before Elijah's final disappearance,‡ in all a dozen years or so before the great revolution which unseated the dynasty of Omri. Elisha differed greatly from Elijah in appearance (cf. the phrase *hairy man*, 2 K. 18 [unless with Kittel, Benzinger, and Skinner, we refer this to the hairy mantle], with the epithet *bald-head*, 2 K. 2^{23}) and in dress (cf. the mantle, 1 K. 19^{19}, which Elisha does not seem to have worn in later life; note בגדים, 2 K. 4^{29}). He used a staff, which, with the mantle, served him in his work as a magician. In a true sense he was a *successor*, since he it was who gave political effect to Elijah's teaching,§ or, in other words, faithfully and resolutely carried out the policy of annihilating Baal and all that belonged to Baal, which was Elijah's great legacy to the nation.‖ In this case there is no exegetical nor historical sense in calling Elisha a " demagogue, conspirator, revolutionist, and agitator " (Co. *Proph.* 33); the phrase " father and guide of the Northern kingdom " (Addis, *EB*. 1276) seems more appropriate (p. xliv). (2) The story of *the separation* is late, and exhibits some peculiarities, two or three of which deserve mention ; *e.g.* how comes it that Elijah, who has always lived a solitary life, now sustains close personal relations with the prophetic societies? Perhaps he sees fit to change his habits now that the end is coming (Ew. *Hist.* IV. 80); or does this document present a different conception of Elijah (Skinner)? It is, rather, Elijah's emphatic way of introducing his successor, to whom he intrusts a task so terrible in its seriousness. The passage, therefore, has closer connection with the " Elisha-stories " than with the " Elijah-stories." The "double portion" (2^9) is not the portion of the first-born, Dt. 21^{17} (Thenius, Benz., Kit., Skinner, *in loc.*; and Addis, *EB*. 1277); nor may we follow the literalizing view of Sirach (that Elisha performed twice as many miracles as did Elijah); ¶ but rather it expresses Elisha's desire that, having an even larger enduement of the divine spirit than his master, he may be able to carry the struggle of Yahweh begun by

---

* Cf. cases of second-hand inspiration noted by Sm. *Rel.*[2] 80, note.

† Addis, *EB*. 1276 ; cf. Skinner, 242 ; Benz. 113 ; Kit. 153 f.

‡ Strachan, *DB*. I. 693.   § WRS. *Proph.* 85.   ‖ Kit. *Hist.* II. 279.

¶ Ecclus. 48^{12}, פי שנים אחות הרבה ומופתים כל מוצא פיהו.

Elijah to a successful issue (Maybaum, *Proph.* 76). On the purpose of the picture, as a whole, *v.s.*, p. xxxvi. (3) The fact that Elisha's habits were those of an agriculturalist at first, and later of a city dweller (in Jericho, 2 K. 2^{18}, Samaria, 6^{32}, Dothan, 6^{13}, Shunem, 4^{10}, Damascus, 8^{7}), plays an important part in contrast with Elijah's nomadic manner of life (p. xxxvi). It is not enough to observe simply that here, as frequently, those are associated who differ greatly from each other (*e.g.* Amos and Hosea, Isaiah and Micah); or that one kind of mind is needed for initiation, another for final execution. The case is incomplete, unless we realize the full significance, in this long ministry of, perhaps, fifty years, of Elisha's "easy familiarity" and gentle manners, not only when he is sought out by kings (2 K. 6^{21} 13^{14}), but also when he is visited on new moon or Sabbath (2 K. 4^{22} ff.) by the people who trust him implicitly. Was this demagoguery? Then Jesus also must have been a demagogue. Elijah's whole career was a protest against civilization. Not so Elisha's ; but rather an example of wise and effective adjustment, in spite of his strict religious views, to the new environment created by Ahab. This suggests (4) other points of character which come out in connection with some of the smaller events, such as the remarkable spirit of toleration (cf. Elijah during his residence in Zarephath) in the advice given Naaman the Syrian (Strachan, *DB.* I. 694); of humaneness, in his attitude toward the Syrian captives (6^{22}); of intense love for Israel, in his reply to Hazael's question, Why does my lord weep? (8$^{11-13}$) ; * of widely recognized sympathy, as shown by the coming to him of widows and orphans (4^{1}); of the tremendous energy and fruitfulness of his work, if we may accept the estimate placed in the mouth of king Joash (13^{14}), for had he not been more to Israel than its chariots and horsemen ? † It will be noted that the data suggestive of these elements in Elisha's character lie, for the most part, outside of the field of his political activity, and the circumstances connected with the revolution, on which *v.i.*

3. Nothing in prophecy, or indeed in the entire Old Testament scripture, is more suggestive of wonderland than the stories which recount Elisha's miracles. This idealization finds explanation in more than a single way ; *e.g.* the writer thus makes expression of the profound feeling of love and esteem entertained by the people for Elisha, as well as of an equally profound belief in the love of Yahweh for his people, a love exhibited in the beneficent activity of the great representative, Elisha. Whether emphasis is to be placed upon the first or the second of these ideas will be determined by one's final estimate of Elisha's work as a whole.

---

* With the reading, פני, *his face took on a fixed look of unutterable horror* (Skinner, X.; cf. Klo., Kit.).   † Addis, *EB.* 1278 ; Skinner *in loc.*

We cannot fail to make three comparisons: (1) Of these miracles with those of Elijah (*v.s.* p. xxxvi); but here we should regard Elisha's miracles neither, on the one hand, as grotesque and vulgar in so far as they are not pure imitation, and as altogether lacking in sanctification and grandeur,* nor, on the other, as something altogether ideal and above criticism of any sort.† (2) Of Elisha's relation to Samaria during the Syrian wars, with Isaiah's relation to Jerusalem in 701 B.C. during Sennacherib's invasion; but in making this comparison, we must remember that a century and a half full of good teaching for Israel has elapsed, and that while Elisha, as a matter of course, appears to less advantage than does Isaiah, it may well be questioned whether, upon the whole, the latter event was more critical than the former, and whether, likewise, the doctrine of Zion's inviolability established in connection with Isaiah's preaching in 701 B.C. was not far more injurious to the Israel of the future, both ethically and politically, than the severe and, indeed, terrible measures apparently sanctioned by Elisha in the uprooting of Baalism. (3) Of Elisha's miracles with those of Jesus Christ; were they not of the same general character ? Omitting the treatment of the children slain by bears, do they not represent the single idea of beneficence, that is, love ? From no other source does prophecy receive a contribution which so definitely represents or anticipates the Christlike element (Addis, *EB*. 1277). Surely this thought of love is a new idea in Israel's religion. But is it just to attribute it to Elisha ? His life and work furnished the conception. Even if the stories are very late, and even if little historical fact may be found in them, they, at all events, reproduced Elisha's character as it appeared to the people of his own times and of those that followed.

Much in these miracles relates to the pre-prophetic societies (§ 5). Elisha was strengthening and developing these societies for purposes of propaganda (Che. *EB*. 3863). These societies were capable of exercising great influence on Israel. This method of warfare was more diplomatic than that of Elijah. It does not mean, however, that Elisha lacked courage (2 K. 3^{13f.}). It is probable that in view of his feeling toward Joram, he did not use his house in Samaria to any great extent until after Jehu's accession, but lived much of the time with the societies. This work was to have great significance in the further development of prophecy.

4. The political activity of Elisha is full of interesting problems. (1) Pre-prophetism, acting through him, now controlled the state. He was not merely an adviser like Isaiah. He was himself an active participant in the affairs of administration, "a decisive power in court and camp " (Addis, *EB*. 1277). In this he followed the example of *all* his predecessors. The time had not yet quite

---

* So Co. *Proph.* 33; cf. Addis, *EB*. 1277.
† So most of the older commentators.

come for the introduction of a new policy, viz. that of non-inter-
ference except in so far as moral suasion might exert an influence.
(2) His relations with foreign kings and potentates are of a remarkable nature. They seek him out. His reputation must have
been widespread. Meinhold is right in pointing out that Wellhausen underestimates the influence of the prophets in these
times. It is quite inconceivable how certain writers * count Elisha
as of so small a value to Israelitish thought. Greater justice is
shown him by others.†

(3) The account of the Moabite campaign of the king of Israel (2 K. 3[4-27])
with his vassal kings of Judah and Edom possesses for us a larger interest
even than that which its relation to the well-known Mesha inscription (a
voucher for the historicity of this story) occasions, ‡ because, being evidently
from the series of political stories (p. xli), it assigns to Elisha an important rôle
as political adviser, and, besides, refers to certain facts in connection with the
prophet which aid us in formulating our estimate of him. We observe (a) the
custom of making inquiry of the *nebhi'im* concerning war (cf. 1 K. 22[6 ff.]), and
when we recall the times of Saul and the beginning of the work of the
nebhi'im, we find ground for the supposition that the primary aim of these
dervishes was to awaken the spirit of the nation for purposes of war (Schwally,
Semitische Kriegsaltertümer, I. (1901), 103 ff.; K. *DB.* V. 653); but (b) Elisha being discovered in the camp, the mere mention of his relation to Elijah
(as the pourer of water on the hands = servitor) gives him standing in the
eyes of the king of Judah, who in 1 K. 22 seems not to have known the
Northern prophets. There is to be noted next (c) the statement of the king
of Israel (v.[18]) which implies that the kings, in this case as in 1 K. 22,
have undertaken this expedition by prophetic advice for which Yahweh
was responsible; but (d) Elisha, following Elijah's policy, will have no
dealings with the king of Israel (whichever king it was) § ; for the sake,
however, of Judah's king he will speak. But he cannot speak except in trance,
and so (e) as was his custom (ויהי, *and it used to be*, is frequentative), he asks
for a musician (v.[15]) in order by the influence of music to excite himself into
the ecstatic condition. This act, attested by 1 S. 10[5], alluded to frequently
in Arabian literature (WRS. *Proph.* 392), and recognized to-day as a powerful
incentive to religious emotion (cf. the influence of music on Saul's evil spirit,
1 S. 16[16]), seems to bear witness to three things : that Elisha (*contra* Elijah)

---

* Co., Sta., H. P. Smith, Marti.

† Ew., WRS., Addis, Gu., Meinhold, Sm., Kit.; K. *DB.* V. 655 f.

‡ Mesha's inscription relates to the revolt in which he secured independence
from Israel. The campaign of Jehoram seems to have been an unsuccessful
attempt to reduce Moab to submission again.

§ Cf. comm. on 2 K. 3[7], and 𝕲L's substitution of Ahaziah for Jehoshaphat.

is in close companionship with the *nebhi'im;* that, while the spirit of Yahweh takes hold of Elijah spontaneously, artificial means are resorted to in Elisha's case ; and that consequently he belongs rather with those that preceded him in the prophetic work (*i.e.* a lower order) than with those who followed (*i.e.* Amos and Hosea). The first of these all will accept; but are the other inferences strictly legitimate ? May not this act in his case have been merely the conventional way of announcing the oracle ? Is it really any more derogatory to his standing as a prophet than the ecstatic visions of Amos or Isaiah or Jeremiah or Ezekiel (*v.i.*)? (*f*) The method adopted to secure water (vs.[16-19]) was adapted to the possibilities of the locality (known for its sand-pits); cf. the plagues of Egypt. (*g*) The evident recognition (3[26. 27]) of the efficacy of the sacrifice of the king's own son to Chemosh is of interest in fixing the theological point of view of the writer.

(4) Evidence of Elisha's political activity is seen, still further, in the stories of the healing of Naaman (5[1-19]), of the entrapping of the Syrians in Samaria (6[8-23]), of the siege of Samaria by Ben-hadad (6[24]-7[20]), with each of which important difficulties are connected; * but, in general, they show the high esteem in which Elisha was held by all classes of men, his international as well as national reputation, his almost unlimited influence at home and abroad, and, at the same time, the great breadth of his mind, and his entire devotion to the nation's God, Yahweh. We may not go so far as to infer that Elisha's international greatness and his international relations furnished the basis for the idea of an international god, which, in turn, prepared the way for Amos's position taken in chaps. 1 and 2; yet the high character of his work must be recognized.

5. The great revolution instigated by Elisha and executed by Jehu, described in 2 K. 9, 10, is one of the most important events in Israel's history ; this importance relates to the political situation, but also, and especially, to the history of the pre-prophetic movement, the relation, in that movement, of both Elijah and Elisha to the history of Israel's religion. This revolution placed on the throne the dynasty under which Amos and Hosea (in part) did their work. That Omri's dynasty had greatly strengthened Israel at home and abroad is universally acknowledged.† That seed was sown in this revolution, which in the end proved Israel's ruin, has not been denied since Hosea (1[4]) first announced it. We may call Jehu ambitious and bloodthirsty, and, since he undoubtedly believed

---

* *E.g.* the latter event is assigned to the reigns of Ahab (Benz.), Jehoram (We.; H. P. Smith, *O. T. Hist.* 196), Jehoahaz (Kue. *Einl.* I[II.] 81 f.).

† Kit. *Hist.* II. 262; We. *Prol.* 458 f.; Sta. *GVI.* I. 518, 522.

himself to be acting for and in the name of Yahweh, a fanatic.*
Sacred history fails to furnish a more ghastly series of official murders, beginning with the shooting of Jehoram in his chariot, and
closing with the horrible blood-bath of the Baal-worshippers in the
temple. But there was prophetic precedent for the revolution,
and the total destruction of the royal house, when dethroned,
has been the regular routine in all Oriental revolutions.† Although by the revolution there was gained a destruction of the
Baal cult, and although it was strictly in accord with Oriental
policy, from the political point of view it was a blunder. ‡

It is more difficult to reach a decision as to the meaning of this
event in connection with the pre-prophetic movement, and of the
rôle played by the individual prophets. Apparently no great fault
has ever been found with Elijah because of his share in it, and
yet it was he who conceived and initiated the movement, indicated the exact lines of its execution, and selected specifically
the agents who were to complete its execution. On whom, then,
rests the responsibility ? If one may judge Elijah's character by
the impression which it produced upon his contemporaries and
upon those immediately following him, he himself would have
done, in detail, just what Jehu did; for did he not (1 K. 18⁴⁰)
actually slay the prophets of Baal (four hundred and fifty)? Did
he not foretell the awful events which were to rid Israel of Baalism
(19¹⁶⁻¹⁸) ? §

On the other hand, severe criticism has been meted out to

---

* Cornill's characterization is too strong, viz. "one of the most contemptible
characters known in the history of Israel" (*Proph.* 33).

† Cf. Ju. 9⁵ 1 K. 15²⁹ 16¹¹; the Panammu Inscription from Zinjirli, line 3, mentions a slaughter of seventy kinsmen of the king in a conspiracy against the throne.
Che. *EB.* 2355.

‡ Sta. *GVI.* I. 545; Gu. *GVI.* 178; Co. *Proph.* 33.

§ Bu. (*Rel.* 122), concerning the reason for the prophets' support of Jehu, says:
"There can be no doubt that the reason why Jehu was made the candidate of the
prophets for succession to the throne was that he was known as a zealot for the
pure worship of Yahweh. For this reason alone we might be sure that he and his
successors were unremitting in their zealous endeavor to maintain the worship of
Yahweh in Israel pure and uncontaminated. This inference is fully confirmed —
if we may trust the popular tales of the Second Book of Kings — by the fact that
for full two generations the prophet is found firmly established alongside the king,
as the bulwark of the throne." Cf. also K. *DB.* V. 653.

Elisha, who, it is maintained, is scarcely to be justified for his participation in the deeds of Jehu, even from the point of view of his own times.* It is suggested that he was entirely deceived as to Jehu's character; † or, in any event, though meaning well, lived on that lower plane of religious life which, as in the case of the patriarchs, did not forbid intrigue and bloodshed. ‡ Now, in making our estimate of Elisha, let us recall (a) the lack of any word of disapproval from the pen of the narrators; (b) the wonderfully beautiful character portrayed by these writers, in which the features especially emphasized are humaneness, tenderness, compassion, and love, — the very opposite of those ascribed to Elijah (who can imagine Elisha as suggesting or favoring the policy of Jehu, except under the constraint of a controlling religious conviction?); (c) the strangely solemn circumstances of his appointment to office, and of his reception of Elijah's legacy; (d) the opinion of Joash, when Elisha's life is just closing, a strong testimony in favor of its magnificent value, while the estimate of Hosea is to be treated as we treat the anachronistic utterances of other prophets whose judgments concerning earlier events are determined by the sympathies and antipathies of a later age.

With these points in mind, the question briefly stated is this: Was the religious crisis one of sufficient magnitude to justify the revolution? We do not wish, in any sense, to justify the intrigue and bloodshed connected with the revolution.

6. It remains to present, in the form of propositions, the answers to the questions that have thus far been raised (cf. pp. xxxviii ff. and xliv f.), all of which pertain to the significance of the revolution in connection with the progress of Israel's religion.

(1) The contest, initiated by Elijah and completed by Jehu under Elisha's direction, was one for which the higher prophetism of the period (860 to 800 B.C.) was responsible. It signified for pre-prophetism a great victory, and lifted it higher than it had before reached.

(2) The contest was a struggle, not so much with the old Canaanitish Baalism, which had largely disappeared, but with

---

* Co. *Proph.* 33; Addis, *EB.* 1278.
† Cf. Kent, *Hist.* II. 68.   ‡ Kent, *loc. cit.*

Phoenician Baalism, a new form of syncretism which, in view of all the circumstances, involved far greater danger to the interests of the Yahweh-religion (*v.s.*).*

(3) The point at issue was nothing more nor less than that of Yahweh's existence; it was not simply that of giving him a lower place, but rather of his complete rejection; † for if Baalism had conquered, Yahwism would sooner or later have disappeared, just as Baalism disappeared after the victory of Yahwism.

(4) The conception of Yahweh which the prophets represent is higher than that of the past. For them he is, to be sure, a national God, but he sustains relations also to other nations, and exercises over them a large controlling influence. This is moving in the direction of an international God, although it has not reached that point.

(5) The religion for which they contend is something other than a cult such as had existed in the past, but with its corruption eliminated. ‡ It may be elected or rejected. It is one which makes ethical demands. Its ideal life for men is that of sympathy and love.

(6) The distinction is now for the first time drawn (though very vaguely) between the spiritual and the worldly, in other words between a true spiritual religion and nature-worship. §

The content of these propositions prepares the way for an examination of other pre-prophetic influences which antedated the work of Amos and Hosea; but before it receives a final formulation it requires a consideration of the other influences.

§ 5. The Pre-prophetic Societies.

1. The pre-prophetic societies constitute a phase in the development of pre-prophetism which bears closely on later prophecy. Omitting many points which do not stand in close relationship with the later development, the following may be regarded as the essential features for our immediate purpose, viz. (1) the numbers of the *nebhi'im*, including the closely related sects of the Nazirites and Rechabites; (2) the general purpose, character, and

---

* K. *DB*. V. 647.   † *Contra* Sm. *Rel.*[2] 155; but cf. Meinhold, 28.
‡ *Contra* Meinhold.   § *Contra* Meinhold; but cf. Sm. *Rel.*[2] 177 ff.; We.

habits of these associations; and (3) the question of their origin, their external and internal relations, and their place in history and prophecy.*

2. That these societies represented a large movement (whether patriotic, or religious, or both) is clear from the great numbers of *nebhi'im* referred to (viz. the one hundred hidden by Obadiah, 1 K. 18³; the four hundred in conference with Ahab, 1 K. 22⁶; the fifty or more residing at Jericho, 2 K. 2⁷·¹⁶), as well as the citation of some by name,† among whom we must select Micaiah ben Imlah for special mention, since a true estimate will place him side by side with Elijah and Elisha, and, in some respects, above both. These numbers signify not only deep interest in Yahweh-worship, but also an intense excitement because this worship was in danger from the Baalism of Tyre.

The failure of Eᵖ, which describes the public activity of the *nebhi'im*, to make any definite reference to the societies (but cf. 2 K. 9¹ = Eᵖ, and 1 K. 20³⁵, probably late), as well as the silence of Eᵇ concerning any public activity on their part, is not to be interpreted either as destroying the value of the representations made in each (for the narratives need not be taken as mutually exclusive ‡), nor as giving special weight to the opinion that the life of the societies was exclusively retired and devoted to worship and meditation, or, on the other hand, that it was largely public. As a matter of fact, it was both, the two narratives presenting different phases of the life of the *nebhi'im*.

From the lack of any mention of the societies between the days of Samuel and those of Elijah and Elisha, a period of more than one hundred and fifty years, we may not assume that with the passing of the Philistine struggle they had died out and were later revived by Elijah. Against this may be urged, not only the numbers just mentioned, but also the standing which they had in Ahab's time as an order that must be consulted (1 K. 22⁶ᶠ·).

---

* The most satisfactory treatments of this subject will be found in Kue. *Prophets and Prophecy*, 46 ff., and *Rel.* I. 193–202, 316 ff.; WRS. *Proph.* 85 f., 389–392; GAS. I. 20–30; Maybaum, *Die Entwickelung d. isr. Prophetenthums* (1883), 30–59; Da., art. "Prophecy," *DB.* IV. 109 f.; Bu. *Rel.*, 93–103; K. *DB.* V. 652 ff.

† Viz. Micaiah and Zedekiah, 1 K. 22¹¹ᶠᶠ·; Jehu, 1 K. 16¹.

‡ Cf. K. *DB.* V. 656 f.; note also the failure of the Elijah stories to mention the societies.

This silence may be accidental, or it may be due to the fragmentary and incomplete character of the narratives as they have come down. So few are the names of preëxilic writing prophets preserved in the historical narratives (Isaiah alone, and in Je. 26[18f.], Micah) * that, but for the preservation of their utterances, one might deny their very existence.

In addition to the many *nebhi'im*, named and unnamed, and the societies which are so marked a feature of the times, cognizance must be taken of two sects, perhaps orders, *viz.* the Nazirites and Rechabites, the members of which, while not reckoned as *nebhi'im*, share to some extent their ideas and their work as servants of Yahweh.

The Nazirites (pp. 56 f.), rarely mentioned, were individuals especially consecrated to Yahweh, the consecration taking the form of a vow or dedication in which some restriction was assumed (*e.g.* in the case of Samson, his unshorn hair, the possession of which secured to him Yahweh's spirit; note also the obligation placed upon his mother, during pregnancy, in reference to wine and unclean food). We are not here interested in the later codification (Nu. 6[2-8. 13. 21]), but two things seem very suggestive : (*a*) the fact that Samson's Nazirate involved exhibitions of great strength against Israel's enemies, and was, in fact, a vow of abstinence solely for *warlike* purposes.[†] Was this perhaps the motive that led also to the organization of the bands of *nebhi'im* (*v.i.*)? (*b*) The reference of Amos (2[11 f.]) to Nazirites, in parallelism with prophets, who had been caused to drink wine, a sin as great as that which was committed in forbidding the prophets to prophesy. From this we must infer that the prohibition of wine (which was regarded by all nomadic tribes as a luxury belonging to agricultural life,[‡] and was, like sensuality, a part of the routine of Baal-worship §), as well as that of cutting the hair was, at one time or another, the restriction assumed in the consecration; but further, that this service was one which, like the prophetic service, received Yahweh's approbation and was worthy of being cited along with it. Whether, now, this abstinence represented merely a service in war, uninterrupted by periods in which one yields himself to pleasure, that is, an absolutely unbroken service, ‖ or rather (as with the Rechabites, *v.i.*) a sworn protest against Baalism (wine being a special product of Baal's land),

---

* Bu. *Rel.* 103.

† Now. *Arch.* II. 134; Schwally, *Semit. Kriegsaltertümer*, I. 101 ff.; K. *DB.* V. 657 f.

‡ WRS., *Proph.* 84, 389; Schultz, *Theol.* I. 163; Kue. *Rel.* I. 316 f.

§ Cf. also the attitude of the ancient Greeks, and of Mohammedans to-day.

‖ Schwally, *loc. cit.*; K. *loc. cit.*

the general meaning is the same; for in both cases the purpose is protest, that is, consecration to war.

Another society or sect which seems to have been prominent in these times was that of the Rechabites, who appear and disappear in Israelitish history almost mysteriously. Assuming * that the Jehonadab whom Jehu took up into his chariot and thus joined with himself in his bloody work for Yahweh (2 K. 10¹⁵ᶠ·) was the Jonadab cited in Jeremiah, chap. 35, as the ancestor of the Rechabites, who prohibited to his descendants the drinking of wine, we may make three assertions : (a) in Elisha's times a sect or family or perhaps order existed, pledged not to drink wine (the symbol of a corrupted civilization), not to engage in agriculture or in the building of homes (that is, pledged to the primitive nomadic life); (b) this pledge was made in the service of Yahweh (cf. the names of those whom Jeremiah brought into a chamber of the temple, all of which end with *Yah*, and also Jeremiah's closing words, *viz.* that for Yahweh's service there shall always be sons of Jonadab); (c) the life of this society was a protest against luxury, intemperance, and idolatry, and against the Canaanitish civilization of the times; and was a reaction toward the primitive simplicity of Israel. We may leave unsettled the question whether this order was founded on the model of the Kenites † (cf. 1 Ch. 2⁵⁵, Ju. 1¹⁶, 1 S. 15⁶), or was really a family descended from them. "They represented in either case a type of anchoritism " (Kautzsch) which was closely related in form, and especially in spirit, to that of the *nebhi'im* and the Nazirites, the three together constituting a comparatively new and extraordinary propaganda for the old-fashioned idea of Yahweh as the god of the desert, and of storm and battle, — an idea which carried with it simplicity both of life and of cult.

3. A few points relating to the general character and the habits of these prophetic associations deserve consideration.

(1) While in Samuel's time these societies were bands of men roving from place to place (probably in order to draw others into their association by the contagion of their enthusiasm), in Elisha's time, they had adopted, more or less fully, a settled mode of life, their residences being at great sanctuaries like Gilgal (2 K. 4³⁸), Bethel (2 K. 2³), or at political centres like Samaria, bands of fifty or more living together (2 K. 2¹), and sometimes at a common table (2 K. 4³⁸), while some among them were married (2 K. 4¹).

(2) Samuel, although a prominent adviser, was probably never really a head (notwithstanding 1 S. 19²⁰), and surely never lived

* So Bu. *Rel.* 120; Sm. *Rel.*² 152 f.; K. *DB.* V. 659.

† Bu. *Rel.* 20, 30, and *New World*, 1895, p. 729; cf. Ew. *Hist.* IV. 79; Schra. *BL.* V. 46; Sm. *Rel.*² 93 f.; K. *DB.* V. 659.

with them (1 S. 19^{18}), unless Naioth means "dwellings"; * while it was a common custom for them to *sit before* (2 K. 4^{38}, cf. 6^1) Elisha, as disciples before a master.

(3) These associations have been improperly termed "schools"† since the members are already engaged in public work, and some of them are married, while no phrase occurs which would justify the use of the word. Moreover, the idiom of the title, *sons of the nebhi'im*, together with Semitic usage, requires the conception of guilds or corporations. Nevertheless, we are warranted in supposing that instruction was imparted (cf. 2 K. 4^{38} 6^1); and probably the prophetic technique and nomenclature which Amos found in existence had its origin among them. ‡

(4) The members of the association did not prophesy as individuals, but jointly in a body, and in their processions (1 S. 10^5) they were, in fact, conducting a kind of public worship at the various high places or sanctuaries (cf. Is. 30^{29}).

(5) The ecstasy (1 S. 19$^{18-24}$) was the physical and psychological condition § in which they performed their service, "the hand of Yahweh" (1 K. 18^{46} 2 K. 3^{15}) being upon them; and this "holy frenzy," which was frequently induced by music (cf. especially the case of Elisha), passed, according to E (Nu. 11$^{17.\,25\,ff.}$), in part, from Moses to the seventy elders, and lifted them into the condition of ecstasy. Still further, it may be inferred from 1 K. 20^{41} that the *nebhi'im* bore a peculiar mark, which distinguished their service. ‖

(6) In Samuel's time this uprising had its occasion in the Philistine crisis, when Israel's existence was threatened, and the result

---

* So Schultz, *Theol.* I. 241; WRS. *Proph.* 392; and most of the older commentators; but נָוֶה denotes a *pastoral abode*, and is hardly appropriate as a designation for a prophetic residence. Moreover, the absence of the article here counts against any appellative signification. It is now generally taken as the name of some locality in Ramah, the precise meaning being unknown. See especially, Dr. *Sam.* 124 f., and art. " Naioth," *DB*; H. P. Smith and Bu. on 1 S. 19^{18}; Che., art. " Naioth," *EB*; BSZ., and BDB.

† By Ew. *Hist.* III. 49 f.; Da. *DB.* IV. 109; Kue. *Rel.* I. 195; but *v.* WRS. *Proph.* 85.

‡ So Da. *DB.* IV. 109; cf. K. *DB.* V. 656.

§ Bu. *Rel.* 100 f.; Che. *EB.* 3872 f.; Giesebrecht, *Die Berufsbegabung d. alttest. Propheten*, 38–72.

‖ Kraetzschmar, *Prophet u. Seher im alt. Israel*, 9; K. *DB.* V. 656.

was "a national religious enthusiasm," which again came forward, perhaps more strongly, in the crisis of the Tyrian Baalism in the times of Elijah and Elisha. These national disasters are the expression of Yahweh's anger; hence the reaction in the form of patriotic spirit, in other words, the spirit of battle.

(7) That Saul is thought to be insane, Elisha's messenger "mad" (2 K. 9[11]); that the word הִתְנַבֵּא, to prophesy, means literally to drop (sc. foam), i.e. to foam at the mouth; and that the insane were looked upon in all Semitic antiquity with respect and awe as being controlled by demons (cf., e.g., David at the court of Achish, 1 S. 21[12 ff.]), — all point to the presence of a large element of superstition upon the subject of prophecy, and also show its emotional and ecstatic character. With these facts before us, we may conclude in general that the spirit of these associations, while intense and upon the whole correct, was nevertheless as narrow as it was intense, as crude as it was correct; and that it partook largely of the spirit of the four hundred and fifty Baal-prophets, an association of very similar nature (v.i.).

4. The questions of their origin, their external and internal relations, are of great interest. (1) Concerning the origin we actually know little, but certain points may be grouped for consideration: The character of ancient Semitic life (v. e.g. WRS. Sem.; We. SV. III.; Barton, Sketch of Semitic Origins; Lagrange, Études sur les religions sémitiques), especially as seen in its purest form in Arabia,* was but slightly changed in these early days of Israel; and Palestine, like Arabia, with its desert life, its compulsory fasts ("in which the soul easily detaches itself and hunger lends the mind a curious passion, mixed of resignation and hot anger" [GAS. HG. 29; cf. Schultz, Theol. I. 102 ff.]), its habit of continuous war, its uniformity of religious life (growing out of the exclusive attention to a tribal god), was well fitted to produce and develop fanaticism, as is shown by every century of past history, and by the presence to-day in the Mohammedan world of the dancing and howling dervishes, who, by a peculiar life and in strange ecstatic cries, seek to secure and to express their religious exaltation. Amid such surroundings the religious feeling, if at all awakened, becomes intense, and tends to an "entire self-surrender," which finds concrete expression in a frenzied state, that sometimes involves self-mutilation, human sacrifice, and the tribute of maidens (Schultz, Theol. I. 104).

---

* Every year since the work of WRS. brings Israel into closer relationship with Arabia; cf. the recent opinions of Barton, op. cit. 287 ff.; S. I. Curtiss, Primitive Semitic Religion To-day; and Che.'s Jerahmeelite hypothesis in EB., CB., and elsewhere.

(2) The presence of Baal-prophets among the Tyrians, together with the facts that most of the growth in Israel's ritual (and especially that of mantic and sorcery) came from the Canaanites, and that the idea of prophets or *nebhi'im* first appeared at this time, leads us to suppose that the pre-prophetic societies also were originally Canaanitish.* The occurrence of the word *nabhi'* in Phoenician, as well as in the Assyrian Nebo (= Hermes), points in the same direction. The Israelites, observing the prophesying (that is, the transport and frenzy) of the Canaanitish worshippers, adopted it, as they adopted many other rites (cf. the view that Yahweh himself was a Canaanitish god adopted by Israel; so Land, *ThT.* II. 160 ff.; Wkl. *Babel-Bibel und Bibel-Babel;* but *v.* Kue. *Rel.* I. 398 ff.; Kö. *Neue kirchl. Zeitschrift,* XIII. 828–883). This, of course, implies merely that the external form, as in the case of circumcision, was taken by the Israelites, for within a short time it was spiritualized. The connection of all this with the spirit of war developed by the Philistine oppression has already been noted. Cf. **1 S.** 10⁵, in which Saul is represented as entering into the state of frenzy at the very place in which the garrison (so AV., RV.), or pillar (so 𝕲, Thenius, Dr., Kit.; K. *DB.* V. 653), or administration (so H. P. Smith, BDB.) of the Philistines was placed.

(3) While in the earliest times, priest, seer, and *nabhi'* were one, they now begin to differentiate. But, until later, the relation of priest and prophet was very close, as, in these early days, was that of priest and seer (cf. Samuel, and the Arabic *kâhin,* denoting *seer,* or *soothsayer,* probably, in early times, one in charge of a shrine). In later days, when there seems to have been antagonism between priest and prophet, this difference existed, not so much between the two orders, as between the priestly order and individual prophets who had risen above their fellows, and represented the prophetic order in general as being on the same low level with the priests (cf. WRS. *Proph.* 85, 105 ff.). In Isaiah's time a priest (8²) was selected to witness concerning a prophecy, while Jeremiah, Ezekiel, and other prophets of later times were themselves priests. It is probable, therefore, that in the early times the *nebhi'im* were closely associated with the priests (McCurdy, *HPM.* § 488, note), as was true of the priests and prophets of Baal, and in Judah; cf. Je. 20¹˙² with 29²⁶ Lam. 2²⁰ (*v.i.*). The bearing of this upon the attitude of Amos and Hosea is significant; cf. Am. 7¹⁰⁻¹⁷ Ho. 4⁴⁻⁹ 5¹ 6⁹.

(4) The unity, or joint action, of the *nebhi'im* has been mentioned (*v.s.*). This was an essential element in their strength. Elijah and especially Elisha seem to have worked harmoniously with the various societies, although they stood far above them. In Elisha's own days, however, there lived a man who stood above and against his fellow-*nebhi'im,* and to whom the word prophet in its later and higher usage might well be given. This was Micaiah ben Imlah, whose story is told in 1 K. 22⁸ ᶠᶠ. (Eᵖ).† The essential point for us in

---

* K. *DB.* V. 653; Co. *Proph.* 13 f.; Kue. *Rel.* I. 216 f., 317 ; Toy, *New World,* V. 139; *contra* Schultz, *Theol.* I. 240 f.; Kö. *Offenbarungsbegriff d. A. T.* I. 63 ff.

† This is not from the narrative which furnishes the Elijah-stories, but from the

this story is neither (*a*) the large number of prophets living at the time,* nor (*b*) the fact that the word of Yahweh is called for through the body of prophets as if it were a matter of regular routine; nor (*c*) the fact that their advice is asked in reference to a matter of war, and that they return a unanimous answer. These things are interesting, but they do not constitute the essential element, which is (*d*) that Micaiah (who not infrequently prophesied in opposition to the king's wishes, and was for that reason obnoxious to him), when sent for, delivers a message which is remarkable in the history of pre-prophetism. The position taken by Micaiah in opposition to the others deserves notice, since he is the first to break the unity which had thus far existed, — "a cleavage in the ranks of the prophetic body, which runs through the whole subsequent history of the movement" (Skinner, *in loc.*). The significance of this cleavage is enhanced by certain features in the narrative, viz. the attitude of the king (already mentioned) (v.[8]); the earnest effort made by the messenger to bring Micaiah into harmony with those who have already spoken (v.[13]); the symbolical action of Zedekiah to corroborate and support the prediction of the four hundred (v.[11]); the statement of Micaiah that he will speak what Yahweh has sent to him (v.[14]); and his first utterance, which, after all, is identical with that already given, and promises success (v.[15]). This was probably a piece of irony, and was so recognized by Ahab. When adjured to speak the whole truth, and with the background thus indicated, he announces two visions, the first, a prediction of Ahab's death, and without special interest; the second, a vision in which (*a*) he distinguishes between Yahweh on the one hand, and on the other a spirit, evidently recognized as a superhuman power, which produces the prophetic ecstasy; (*β*) he clearly recognizes the independence of this agent, but this spirit, we are told, becomes a lying spirit in the mouths of the *nebhi'im*, and thus deceives them; (*γ*) he thus makes two strange representations, viz. that he, Micaiah, rather than the spirit, knows the will of Yahweh; and further, that the falsehood which the four hundred have just spoken is to be charged, not "to the imperfection of its human medium," but to the superhuman agent acting with Yahweh's approval (K. *DB.* V. 656; Che. *EB.* 3859). In all this, however, it is to be understood that (*δ*) he takes a position far above the ordinary *nebhi'im*, that knowledge comes to him which they do not share; in other words, that there are grades, or ranks, in the order, some higher and others lower. These "lower" or "narrow" or "false" prophets are thus pointed out even at this early time, although they are still understood to be made use of by Yahweh (Volz, *EB.* 3874 f.). They have been called "prophets of a narrow range of vision" (Volz), "the belated representatives of an earlier stage of

Ephraimite national narrative; it contains no reference to Elijah, and, in view of the four hundred prophets of v.[6], contradicts the impression (18[22]) that Elijah was the only Yahweh-prophet left (cf. also 18[13] 19[14]).

* Che.'s assumption that four hundred here and in the case of the Baal-prophets is a corruption of Arab-Jerahmeel is altogether groundless.

prophetic development," who "had closed their minds against the deepening of the idea of God to an unconditionally ethical conception, and were thus no longer able to penetrate into the depths of his counsel" (Bu. *Rel.* 131). We are immediately concerned with the bearing of this on the actual condition of the *nebhi'im* in the days of Elisha, and on Elisha himself (for if he occupies a high place, one, for example, side by side with Micaiah, how can he, neverthe-less, work harmoniously with the rest ?), and on the *nebhi'im* of Amos's day. It is not quite fair to say that "under the protection of Jehu's dynasty proph-ecy so-called sank to depths of hypocrisy and formalism " (WRS.). A better statement would be that at this time pre-prophetism continued to occupy the low place which it had always occupied, save when some great personality like Elijah, or Elisha, or Micaiah was raised up ; or, better still, let us dis-tinguish between *prophecy*, for which these great souls stood, and manticism (*i.e.* the *nebhi'ismus*), which is all that the others yet knew or cared for (Davidson, *O. T. Proph.* 111 ff.; Kue. *Rel.* I. 196-7). Amos plainly shows his estimate of this crowd of *nebhi'im*, when he maintains very forcibly that he is not one of them, and his words perhaps imply that it is no great honor to be regarded as one of their number (but *v.i.*).

5. It remains only to note the stages of this development and to indicate its place in the history of the pre-Amos time. Starting on the Israelitish side with *seers* (who are closely akin to priests), and on the Canaanitish side with *nebhi'im* (or *dervishes*), we see the two classes gradually growing together. From among them, or in close association with them, there arise from time to time certain great characters who share their peculiarities and adopt their methods, but at the same time reach far above them in their knowledge of the divine will. These men, not yet prophets in the technical sense, are the forerunners of the prophets, the connecting link between the old and the new, which begins with the *writing* prophets. This is their place in the development. What did these societies of *nebhi'im* do for the people among whom they lived? What influence did they exercise upon them?

It is certainly unjust to characterize them as "hotbeds of sedition " and to limit their activity almost entirely to the sphere of politics (HPS. *O. T. Hist.* 193), or to consider them "a species of begging friars," with but little influence among the people (Co. *Proph.* 13). It is with a truer appreciation of their services that Cheyne (*EB.* 3857 f.) declares them to have been "a recognized sacred element in society, the tendency of which was to bind classes together by a regard for the highest moral and religious traditions." Compare also the view of Kittel (*Hist.* II. 266), that their chief interest was the "fostering of religious thought," and that, as compared with the priests, they were "the soul, the latter the hand and arm, of religion"; the opinion of Marti (*Rel.* 81 f.), that in times of peace they had little influence, but in national crises were invaluable in kindling a spirit of patriotism and devotion to Yahweh; the estimate of Wellhausen (*Prol.* 461; similarly, WRS. *Proph.* 85 ff.), that they were not of "first-rate importance," historical influence having been exercised only by exceptional individuals among them, who rose above their level and sometimes opposed them, though always using them as a base of operations.

They constituted one of Israel's greatest institutions, which, like many others, came by adoption from the outside. But in its coming it was purified and spiritualized, and itself gave rise directly to an influence perhaps the most distinctive and the most elevating ever exerted on Israelitish life and thought.

§ 6. The Older and Younger Decalogues.

Two important documents known as decalogues were formulated, and probably promulgated, in the pre-prophetic period. These decalogues now form a part of the Judaean and Ephraimitic narratives, and might be considered in connection with those documents; but they were originally independent of them, and their especial importance warrants a separate treatment. It is essential to ask: What was their origin? What was their message to the times in which they were published? What prophetic element do they contain? What is their relation to prophecy in general? We may not suppose that these, with the Book of the Covenant (§ 7), are the only laws of this early period that have been handed down; others are probably to be found in Deuteronomy and in the Holiness Code; but these will be sufficient for the purpose we have in mind.

1. *The older decalogue,*[*] found in Ex. 34$^{12-26}$, consists, as reconstructed,[†] of ten regulations. These deal with the worship of

---

[*] Cf. We. *Hex.* 331 ff.; Bu. *ZAW.* XI. 216 ff.; Bacon, *Triple Tradition of the Exodus,* 139–158; Sta. *GVI.* I. 510; Holzinger, *Exodus,* 119 f.; Stärk, *Deuteronomium,* 30 f.; GFM. *EB.* 1446 f.; G. B. Gray, *EB.* 2733 f.; Bäntsch, *Exod.-Lev.-Num.* xlvi. f.

[†] We. (*Hex.* 331); cf. Holzinger, Bäntsch, Briggs (*Hex.* 189–210); *contra* K. *DB.* V. 633, who characterizes the so-called decalogue as "only an appearance," being "ceremonial prescriptions [inserted by the Redactor] which can be recognized at the first glance as parallels to the laws of the Book of the Covenant."

other gods, the making of molten images, the observance of three feasts and the sabbath, the offering of firstlings and first-fruits, and the avoidance of certain rites commonly practised in non-Israelitish religions.

This code, as well as the chapter of which it is a part, belongs to the Judaean narrative, but fits in badly with what precedes and follows it. It would seem to follow logically J's introduction to the Sinaitic Covenant (Ex. 19$^{20-22\cdot\ 25}$), for one would scarcely expect new legislation to be given after orders had been received (cf. Ex. 32^{34} 33$^{1-3}$) to leave Horeb. In Ex. 34^{28} it is called the *ten words*, and so naturally constitutes J's decalogue, corresponding to that of E in Ex. 20 and Dt. 5. (The discovery of this decalogue was made by Goethe in *Zwei wichtige bisher unerörterte Fragen*, 1773 A.D.) While there may be some doubt whether this decalogue was a part of J from the beginning or found its present place in J at the hand of the editor who much later joined J and E, no one disputes its very primitive character, and, consequently, its early age. Arising in connection with some Judaean sanctuary (GFM. *EB.* 1446), it represents a ritual of worship which is not only of an early age, but also indicative of a national religion. The very fact that it is so strongly ritualistic shows the pre-prophetic age ; and this is further attested by the pains taken to forbid certain rites (*e.g.* seething of a kid in its mother's milk) which were common in non-Israelitish religions. It is, as Moore (*EB.* 1446) says, "the earliest attempt with which we are acquainted to embody in a series of brief injunctions, formulated as divine commands, the essential observances of the religion of Yahweh." But, on the other hand, it had its origin after the conquest of Palestine, because the background is agricultural throughout.

The message of the Judaean decalogue might thus be expressed : "Worship Yahweh, and Yahweh alone, without images (such as Northern Israel uses) ; let the worship be simple and in accord with the old usage ; forbear to introduce the practices of your Canaanitish neighbors."

This message, notwithstanding its extremely ritualistic content, shows a perfect consistency with the pre-prophetic thought of 775–50 B.C. ; for in three of the ten injunctions (viz. "Thou shalt worship no other gods," "Thou shalt make thee no molten gods," "Thou shalt not seethe a kid," etc.) we have representations exactly in accord with the prevailing thought of the pre-prophetic reformers, while the other injunctions emphasize the simplicity of Yahweh's requirements in contrast with the elaborate and sensuous ritual of Baalism.

The earlier decalogue thus connects itself with the pre-prophetic movement as it has thus far found expression, and prepares the way for a higher expression later on. At the same time it was not instituted as a measure of reform, but rather as the codification of existing practice. The publication, however, was not simply for the sake of providing a law-book ; it was rather an expression of the general prophetic (sometimes called historical) spirit illustrated by J (cf. Gray, *EB.* 2732).

2. *The younger decalogue*, found in two forms, viz., Ex. 20 (E²) and Dt. 5 (D), presents a much larger field for conjecture and consideration.* This code consisted originally of ten injunctions, positive and negative, covering the relation of man to God and to his fellow-men.

In Ex. 19³ᵃ·⁹⁻¹⁹ we find, in a passage ascribed to E, the preparations leading up to the giving of the laws, and in 24³⁻⁸ occurs the ratification of the same. The intervening chapters contain two important pieces of legislation, the decalogue (chap. 20) and the Book of the Covenant (chaps. 21–23).† In spite of the appropriateness of the present order (*i.e.* a body of general and fundamental principles, followed by a series of detailed laws dealing with the life of Israel in all its aspects), we are compelled to believe that the two codes have no direct relationship to each other, because (1) no such relationship is recognized in the historical part of the material ; (2) chap. 20¹⁸⁻²⁶ contains no reference to CC; (3) chap. 24 shows no evidence for connecting the two ; (4) chaps. 32–34 make no mention of CC; (5) Dt., while it adopts the decalogue as the basis of its code, shows no acquaintance with any other law given at Horeb ; (6) Jos. 24 makes no reference to any other law. In view of these facts, it may be concluded that E's original Horeb legislation was not CC, but the (later) decalogue.

But we are confronted with two or three important questions : (1) Is there other E material which could possibly have been connected with the Horeb legislation? (2) Is the decalogue in its present form (either Ex. 20 or Dt. 5) the original? (3) How

---

* That this decalogue was not an original constituent of the E narrative is held by Sta., Co., Carpenter and Battersby, who assign it to a Judaean recension of E; by Stärk (*Deuteronomium*), who finds the original decalogue of E scattered through the Book of the Covenant; by Kue., We. (*SV.* I. 68), Meissner (*Der Dekalog*), Bäntsch, Sm. (*Rel.*² 273), Marti (*Rel.* 174), Addis (*EB.* 1050), and Matthes (*ZAW.* XXIV. 17–41), who assign it to the seventh century. Holzinger (*Exod., in loc.*) places it in the latter half of the eighth century.

† This may be called the Covenant Code, and represented by the symbol CC.

early in the history of E did the original decalogue occupy its present position?

(1) It is probably true * that there was an earlier legislation (E¹) of which only fragments now exist, viz. the account of the tent of meeting (33⁷⁻¹¹), with, perhaps, an account of the construction of the tent (for which P's elaborate description was substituted), and of the ark for which the tent was made, together with the ritual found in 20²⁴⁻²⁶. It will be noted that this earlier legislation of E, according to this hypothesis, was supplanted, partly by P's material concerning the ark and the tent, partly by the decalogue (and the story of the golden calf, Ex. 32, which may be called E²), leaving certain fragments only (v.s.).

(2) The present form of the decalogue gives evidence of considerable expansion from the original ten words, e.g. the very striking differences in the two versions as given in Ex. and Dt., the great difference in the length of the injunctions, and the internal character of the material itself. The original ten words, stripped of all these later additions, were probably as follows: —

1. Thou shalt have no other gods beside me.
2. Thou shalt not make for thyself any graven image.
3. Thou shalt not utter the name of thy God for an evil purpose.
4. Remember the sabbath day to sanctify it.
5. Honor thy father and thy mother.
6. Thou shalt do no murder.
7. Thou shalt not commit adultery.
8. Thou shalt not steal.
9. Thou shalt not bear false witness against thy neighbor.
10. Thou shalt not covet thy neighbor's house.

(3) How early, then, is the younger decalogue? (a) It cannot † come from the times of Moses, for tradition regards Ex. 34 as "the ten words"; it is unknown to CC; it is in a measure inconsistent with the ritualistic religion of the pre-prophetic time. (b) Is it then as late as the days of Manasseh (cf. Mi. 6⁶⁻⁸), ‡ and if so, is it the product of the ripest prophetic thought? The answer turns upon the fulness of interpretation given to the several commandments, the turning-point in the whole matter being the specific *prohibition of the use of images* in the second commandment, and the alleged highly developed ethical system underlying the whole. The former, it is claimed, cannot be earlier than the eighth century, for until this time there seems to have been no knowledge of such a prohibition. The latter must, it is thought, represent the

---

* GFM. *EB.* 1445; Stärk, *Deuteronomium*, 40 ff.; Meissner, *Dekalog*, 33.

† So We. *Hex.* 331 ff.; Bäntsch, *Bundesbuch*, 92 ff.; Sm. *Rel.* 273 f.; Marti, *Rel.* 68; Addis, *EB.* 1050.

‡ So Kue., Meissner (*Der Dekalog*), Bäntsch, Addis (*EB.* 1050).

result of the prophetic teaching at least down to and including Isaiah. The question, therefore, of the prophetic character of the decalogue and of its relation to prophecy depends wholly on the date, and this on the degree of ethical development which it is found to contain.

(c) We may not accept Eerdmans's suggestion (*ThT*. XXXVII. 18 ff., made with a view to placing the original as early as Moses) that some other commandment originally stood in the place of what is now the second (the present second belonging to the seventh century), or that in the original form there were seven instead of ten; but the principle underlying this suggestion, which has been accepted by Kautzsch (*DB*. V. 633ᵇ), is sound and is to be allowed a controlling place in our decision; viz. that the commands and prohibitions of the decalogue "have not an absolute, but a relative scope" (K.). This means that the ethical conceptions which are connected with the decalogue in our modern times have been read into it, and were not originally so understood. The earlier thought was one not of morals but of rights. Eerdmans goes still further and limits the application of the commandments, *e.g.* the killing to one's countrymen, and the coveting to the appropriation of property that was ownerless. Nor is Wildeboer's criticism (*ThSt.*, 1903, 109–118) of this valid when he says that thus the deeper moral sense of the decalogue is degraded.

(d) Concerning the second commandment in particular, it may be said in passing : Its close association with the chapter on the Northern calves (Ex. 32) has some significance. The fact that the central sanctuary in the times of Eli, David, and Solomon seems to have had no image indicates the presence of a strong sentiment opposed to image-worship, if not an actual prohibition. The non-observance of such a prohibition in Northern Israel is no evidence of the non-existence of the law. Account must also be taken of the sentiment in the South (as represented by Isaiah in his early ministry), which must have existed some time before Isaiah. The presence of a similar law in the older decalogue of J supports the early origin of the prohibition.

Upon the whole we shall be justified in assigning the formulation of the younger decalogue in its original form, even with the second commandment, to a period not much later than 750 B.C., the arguments for a still later date * not being convincing.†

The message of this younger decalogue to its times was three-fold : (1) Acknowledge (cf. in the older, *worship*) no other god, and follow not other religions in making images, or in using

---

* Addis, art. "Decalogue," *EB.;* GFM. *EB.* 1447; Marti, *Rel.* 174; We.; Kue.; Sm. *Rel.* 273 ; *et al.*

† So Gray, *EB.* 2733 f.; Paterson, art. "Decalogue," *DB.;* K. *DB.* V. 634; Wildeboer, *loc. cit.;* Kit., *Hist.* I. 248 f.; Montefiore, *Rel. of Anc. Hebrews*, 553–7 ; *et al.*

the divine name for purposes of sorcery; but observe the sabbath (as representing Yahweh's ordinances), and pay respect to Yahweh's representatives. These are Yahweh's *rights;* do not do violence to them. (2) Do not do violence to the rights of your neighbor, as they relate to his person, his wife, his property, or his reputation. Still further, (3) do not even *think* of doing violence to any of your neighbor's rights.

The younger decalogue thus harmonizes completely with the growth of the prophetic thought as thus far (760 B.C.) developed. With the higher conception of God (*v.i.*) a more rigid adherence to him is demanded, and a more concrete separation from the ritual customs which had been in vogue. Still further, sorcery must be banished. While as a corollary it follows that the institutions of Yahweh in their simplicity must be observed; and respect will be shown Yahweh by honoring those who, in his place, have power of life and death.* The prophetic element, in the first table, is clearly seen in the first, second, and third commandments; but did the prophets really advocate the observance of institutions? Yes; for (1) they could not do away with *all* institutions, and in the very act of rooting out the Baal ritual, they must fall back on *something;* and besides (2) their connection with ritual is seen in J's including the earlier decalogue, in E's including another decalogue, in D's including an enlarged code of ritual. As to the fifth commandment, while we are unable to distinguish the extent to which the spirit of ancestor-worship still influences opinion, it can hardly be supposed that all trace of it has yet disappeared.

The original obligation in the fourth commandment was (not that which P or D later inserted) to treat the Sabbath as Yahweh's property, and therefore not put it to the profane uses which had formerly been customary in connection with the heathen cult † (cf. Am. 8⁵ Ho. 2¹¹).

---

* *V.* references on ancestor-worship, pp. 40 f., note.

† The need of such a law and the prophetic character of it at once become apparent, if the supposition be correct that the sabbath was taken over from the Canaanites, who had themselves gotten it from Babylonia (so Reu. *Gesch. d. Alt. Test.* § 71, Anm.; Sm. *Rel.*² 160; Now. *Arch.* I. 144; Benz. *Arch.* 202, 465; Holzinger, *Exodus*, 73). The task of prophecy was to purify it from its Canaanitish associa-

In the commandments of the second table the case is even clearer. With the examples of David and Solomon and Ahab, in connection with whom the prophets have actually said the same things that are found in the sixth, seventh, eighth, and ninth commandments, it is easy to see that a prophetic redaction after Elijah must contain just these points (*v.s.* as to meaning of each). The important step forward which the tenth commandment contains, viz. not to *think* of violating one's neighbor's rights, is noticeable, but, after all, in harmony with the active intellectual effort of the times which produced the philosophical work of J and E (*v.i.*).

(6) With this understanding of the message, and of the prophetic element in it, we can discover its close connection with the pre-prophetic movement. Its formulation can be ascribed to the intense religious feeling which is just beginning to recognize the *rights* of Yahweh and of men; it is in a sense the product of prophetic thought, but, more strictly, that of pre-prophetic thought.

§ 7. The Book of the Covenant.

The Book of the Covenant (= CC), to which reference has already been made, was promulgated, substantially in its present form, with prophetic sanction, as early as 800 B.C., or half a century before Amos and Hosea. We may ask, as before, as to its origin and marks of date, its message, the prophetic element in the message, and its relation to the pre-prophetic movement.

1. This book (Ex. 21–23) contains two kinds of material. The first part (21^2–22^{17}) is a series of "hypothetical instructions, based presumably on precedent" (Gray, *EB.* 2734); in a single word, *judgments* (cf. Ex. 21^1, 24^3, Nu. 35^{24}), or judicial *decisions;* regulations, seemingly intended for the use of judges, and dealing with questions of civil and criminal law.* The second part (22^{18}–23^{19}) is a series (with some interruptions, *e.g.* 22^{22-27} $23^{4\,f.\,9\,b.\,13.\,15\,b.\,17.\,19\,a}$)

---

tions and to transform it into an institution thoroughly consonant with the spirit of Yahwism.

* The following subjects are treated in this portion : (1) Regulations regarding slaves, 21^{2-11}; (2) personal injuries, 21^{12-27}; (3) injuries and damages in connection with cattle, 21^{28-36}; (4) theft, 22^{1-4}; (5) damages to crops, 22^{5-6}; (6) breaches of trust, 22^{7-15}; (7) seduction, 22^{16} f.

of precepts relating to life and worship,* evidently other than legal in character; regulations of a moral and religious character, having especially to do with the deity and worship.†

2. An examination of the material soon discloses that (a) the original form of this material has suffered both in the way of mutilation and in actual loss, ‡ for all of which full allowance must be made; while (b) a considerable amount of new material, joined with the original text, must be set aside (*v.s.*) if we are to reconstruct the original document or documents; still further, (c) the laws on ritual (23^{14-19}) are practically identical, even verbally, with 34^{18-26} (the earlier decalogue), and belonged originally in chap. 34, whence they have been transferred by an editor; § (d) the second part ($22^{18}-23^{19}$) is more diverse in character than the first, and is itself plainly a compilation of different elements, ‖ some of which betoken a Deuteronomic origin; (e) the narrative (23^{20-33}), which in its present form is late, contains old material that originally stood in close connection with CC, viz. vs.$^{20-22.\ 25.\ 26}$, and especially vs.$^{28-31}$; ¶ (f) the regulations in 20^{23-26} have no connection with the preceding decalogue (vs.$^{1-17}$), and should be taken ** with the "words" (cf. 22^{28-31}).

3. CC, with such modifications as are involved in the preceding (cf. 2), now suggests two series of questions: (1) Did the author of the *judgments* also collect the *precepts?* or is CC, as we have it, a growth? Various schemes of reconstruction have been proposed,†† of which G. F. Moore's is,

---

* The chief subjects of this portion are: (1) three precepts on sorcery, bestiality, and worship of foreign gods, 22^{18-20}; (2) humanitarian laws, 22^{21}; (3) reverence and offerings, 22^{28-31}; (4) testimony, 23^{1-3}; (5) impartial administration of justice, 23^{6-9}; (6) Sabbath and sabbatical year, 23^{10-13}; (7) feasts and offerings, 23^{14-19}.

† Kent, *Student's O. T., in loc.*, describes 20^{23-26} $22^{29.\ 31}$ 23^{10-19} as duties to Yahweh in connection with the ritual which constitute E's terms of the covenant with Yahweh.

‡ *E.g.* $22^{2.\ 3a}$ seems to be a fragment now misplaced; so also $23^{4\,f.\ 13}$.

§ GFM. *EB.* 1448; cf. Jülicher, *JPTh.* VIII. 300 f.; Briggs, *Hex.* 190 ff., 229 f. According to Bu. (*ZAW.* XI. 217 ff.), the presence of these laws in Ex. 34 after this transfer is due to another still later editor; cf. also GFM.

‖ GFM. *EB.* 1448; Gray, *EB.* 2734.

¶ GFM. *EB.* 1448.

** *Contra* GFM. *EB.* 1444; cf. Kent, *Student's O. T.* 184.

†† Sta. (*GVI.* I. 636) recognizes two divisions, viz. "words" and "judgments," questions whether they originally had any connection with each other, and suggests that the words originally all stood together under their own superscription; and that when the latter was dropped the present confusion arose. Rothstein (*Bundesbuch*, 1888) regards CC as an expansion of the decalogue and attempts by a series of violent transpositions, resulting in worse confusion than that which now exists, to rearrange its contents in an order corresponding to that of the subject-matter in the decalogue. Stärk (*Deuteronomium*, 1894, 32 ff.) finds three strata of laws: (1) six laws, somewhat later than the J decalogue, viz. $21^{12.\ 15-19}$; (2) the "judgments" of

perhaps, the simplest, viz. there existed originally (*a*) a book of judgments; to this was added (*b*) the "main stock" of 22^{18}–23^{13}, *i.e.* the Horeb legislation of E; then (*c*) the ritual 23^{14-19} (taken from J, $34^{14\,\text{ff.}}$) was attached, probably by the editor who (*d*) wrote the closing story (23^{20-33}). In this case the substance of CC is as early as E (*v.s.*).

(2) Some suppose that CC formed a part of the original E; * in this case CC would be: (*a*) the law given at Horeb as the basis of the Sinaitic Covenant (but we have both what may fairly be regarded as the original basis (E^1), as well as the decalogue substituted (*v.s.*) for the original); or (*b*) a continuation of the decalogue (Ex. 20^{1-17}) and so a *part* of the Sinaitic Covenant (*v.s.*); or (*c*) the document which led up to the renewal of the covenant and so was connected with Moses' parting words in the plains of Moab † ; or (*d*) the "statute and ordinance" of Jos. 24^{25-27}, thus representing the law given as the basis of the covenant made at that time, whence it was removed by R^D to its present position. ‡   But no one of these suggestions is free from difficulties, although the consideration in favor of the proposition is important, viz. the general similarity of CC to E.

It seems upon the whole easier to believe that CC was a separate book from E, § inserted in E by the editor who was himself the compiler of CC.

21^2–22^{16}, from a later date than the preceding; and (3) a group of ethical and religious laws, a sort of programme of the prophetic activity, viz. 20^{24} ff. $22^{17.\ 20.\ 24\,\text{f.}\ 27\,\text{f.}}$ $23^{1-3.\ 6\,\text{f.}\ 10-12.\ 14}$. Bertheau (*Sieben Gruppen Mosaischer Gesetze*, 1840) first arranged CC in decades, viz. (1) 20^{3-17}; (2) 21^{2-11}, (3) 21^{12-27}, (4) 21^{28}–22^{16}, (5) 22^{17-30}, (6) 23^{1-8}, (7) 23^{14-19}; this involved the treatment of 20^{22-26} as four introductory commands, 23^{9-13} as an interpolation, and 23^{26-33} as a closing decalogue of promises. Briggs (*Hex*. 211–232) includes in the original CC only four pentades and one decalogue of "words," viz. 20^{23-26} 22^{27-29} 23^{1-3} 23^{6-9} 23^{10-19}. This was enlarged by the addition of two pentades, three decalogues, and a triplet of "judgments," viz. 21^{2-11} 21^{18-25} 21^{26-36} 21^{37}–22^3 $22^{4\,\text{f.}}$ 22^{6-16}. The remaining laws are later insertions showing traces of Deuteronomic redaction. Paton (*JBL*. XII. 79–93), by supposing Ex. 34 to contain another recension of CC, from which he supplements defective decalogues in CC, by considering 21^{22-25} $22^{1\,\text{f.}\ 11}$ $23^{4\,\text{f.}\ 9.\ 13.\ 14.\ 15\,c}$ as later additions, and by restoring two pentades from Dt. 22, obtains an original CC consisting of ten decalogues, each being symmetrically divided into two pentades.

* So Di. *Exod*. 219 f.; Jülicher, *JPTh*. VIII. 305 ; Kue. *Hex*. 152 f.; Co. *Einl*. 73 ff.; Carpenter and Battersby, *The Hexateuch*, II. 113, *et al.; contra* Bäntsch, *Bundesbuch*, chap. II.

† So Kue., Co., Carpenter and Battersby, *et al.;* in this case either (1) R^D (the editor who joined J and E with D) put D in the place formerly occupied by CC, at the same time removing CC to the earlier place which it now occupies; or (2) R^{JE} (the editor who joined J and E) took Ex. 34 (which was the basis of the Sinaitic covenant according to J) and used it as the basis of the renewal, at the same time pushing back CC to the decalogue and making the two (*i.e.* the decalogue and CC) the basis of the covenant.

‡ Holzinger, *Einl*. 179.

§ So Rothstein, *Das Bundesbuch*; Bäntsch, *Bundesbuch*, 77 ff.; We. *Prol. zur Gesch. Isr.*³ 420; GFM. *EB*. 1449.

The material in this case may have had its origin as follows (*v.s.*) * : (*a*) Ex. $23^{14\,ff.} = 34$ (J); (*b*) the *judgments* may have been a part of E standing after chap. 18, which itself originally stood later in the narrative; (*c*) the *precepts*, now somewhat obscured in $22^{18\,ff.}$ 23, were probably that part of the Horeb legislation (E¹) for which the decalogue (*v.s.*) was substituted.

It is to be observed that all of these various hypotheses agree in assigning to the substance of CC and in large measure to the form which we now have, an age contemporaneous with or preceding that of E (*v.i.*). CC embodies "the consuetudinary law of the early monarchy." †

4. The presence of CC in E (or JE) is due to a religious purpose on the part of the author or editor; this purpose, however, partakes of the historical spirit rather than of the legal or reformatory spirit. In other words, no effort was being made, as later in the case of the Deuteronomic code or the Levitical code, to gain recognition from the people for a new legislation. ‡ This appears, not only from the small proportion of the whole of E which CC constitutes, but also from the fact that its laws are based on long-established usage, or codify moral precepts which had already been taught; the presence of CC indicates also, from the point of view of E (or the editor), a complete harmony of thought between the content of CC and the material of E; the message of CC, therefore, becomes a part of the larger message of E, and receives interpretation from the latter.

The regulations ("judgments" and "precepts") are entirely consistent (1) in treating the deity as the direct and exclusive source of judgment and authority; (2) in recognizing that a time has now come in the affairs of the nation when the rights of the community are to be considered, with a view to restricting the action of individuals in so far as they are injurious to the community (cf. the decalogue); (3) in continuing to accept certain principles which have long prevailed in Semitic life, *e.g.* (*a*) that of retaliation, which included the *lex talionis*, (*b*) that of blood revenge, and money compensation for injuries committed, there

---

* As suggested by GFM. *EB.* 1449; cf. Bu. *ZAW.* XI. 218 f.

† Co. *Einl.* 75; cf. Dr. *DB.* III. 68; WRS. *OTJC.*² 340 ff.

‡ Cf. G. B. Gray, *EB.* 2731 f,

being no punishment by way of degradation ; (4) in having as a basis on which everything rests the agricultural form of life.

The regulations, as already indicated, (*a*) when studied from the point of view of worship, represent the customs of the past * in their comparative purity and simplicity, but at the same time emphasize the restriction of such worship to Yahweh (monolatry) ; nothing new is here presented ; (*b*) when considered from the point of view of ethics, emphasize two or three important points, viz. the setting apart of the sabbath as a day of rest, the giving to the poor of the produce of the land during one year in seven,† the distinction between murder and manslaughter, the securing of justice to the foreigner, the restoration of ox or ass to one's enemy, the urgency against oppression and maladministration of office.

In general, then, the message was one of an elevating character in its moral attitude, advocating, as it does, absolute "rectitude and impartiality" in methods of administration ; mildness, protection and relief from severe life for the poor, the foreigner, and the slave ; a generous attitude even toward one's enemy (23[4b]). ‡

5. The prophetic element is manifest ; so manifest, indeed, that many have regarded CC as the result of the later prophetic work. It is more correct, however, after making proper allowances for the Deuteronomic additions, to regard this as the expression of that religious and ethical development which had its source and strength in the movement of the times of Elijah and Elisha, and of J and E, and, therefore, as preparatory to the period of prophecy beginning with Amos and Hosea. § This view is to be accepted because of (1) the marked linguistic and phraseological affinity of CC to E ; (2) the large proportion of the code given to the treatment of secular matters (cf. the similar nature of the Code

---

* Viz. rude and simple altars, firstlings and first-fruits, three pilgrimages, no leaven, destruction of fat, burnt-offerings and peace-offerings, etc.

† *V.* my *Constructive Studies in the Priestly Element in the O. T.* (1902), 108–118.

‡ K. *DB.* V. 664 *b*, 665.

§ So K. *DB.* V. 664 f.; Carpenter and Battersby, *The Hexateuch*, I. 119; Dr. *DB.* III. 68; Co. *Einl.* 75; WRS. *OTJC.*[2] 340 ff.; Bacon, *Triple Tradition*, 110 ff.; Gray, *EB.* 2733; We. *Hex.* 89 f.; Addis, *Doc. of Hex.* I. 142 f.; *contra* Sta. *GVI.* I. 634; Steuernagel, *Deuteronomium u. Josua*, 278; Bäntsch, *Bundesbuch*, 122; *et al.*

of Hammurabi), a sign of a comparatively early date ; * (3) the primitive character of many of the regulations and ideas, *e.g.* "the conception of God as the immediate source of judgment" (Driver) ; the principle of retaliation and the law of blood revenge, ideas still dominant among the Bedouin; the more primitive tone of 22^{21} as compared with 34^{20} ; and the conception of woman which appears in the provision for the estimate of a daughter's dishonor, as so much damage to property, to be made good in cash (cf. the higher ideal of Hosea).

§ 8. THE JUDAEAN NARRATIVE (J).

This narrative of world- and nation-history had its origin within the century 850–750 B.C., and, with the closely related Ephraimitic narrative, is at once an expression of the pre-prophetic thought and the basis for a still higher development of that thought. What may be gathered from this most wonderful narrative, throughout prophetic in its character, for a better understanding of the pre-Amos period ?

1. Four propositions relating to the Hexateuch are now all but universally acknowledged and may be stated without discussion : —

(1) The Hexateuch is made up in general of three distinct elements, viz. the prophetic (JE), the prophetico-priestly, found mostly in Deuteronomy (D), and the priestly (P), these elements being joined together, first JE with D, and later JED with P.†

---

* It is still a question whether the relationship of CC to the Code of Hammurabi is (*a*) one of direct dependence (as close, indeed, as the relation of the early stories in Genesis to the Babylonian legends), since, in a number of cases, the laws are practically identical (so Johnston, *Johns Hopkins University Circular*, June, 1903) ; or (2) one of racial affinity, *i.e.* of common tradition, without any direct influence, much less, borrowing (so Cook, D. H. Müller, Kohler) ; or, perhaps, (3) one of entire independence, with CC, however, greatly influenced by a Babylonian environment (so Johns, *DB*. V. 610 ff.). While the existence of such a code as that of Hammurabi, at the early date of 2250 B.C., strengthens the arguments for an early date of CC, it does not furnish any proof that CC could have existed in its present form earlier than the stage of civilization (viz. the agricultural) in which it is plainly imbedded.

† The details do not concern us in this connection; for the most recent discussion of these details, *v.* Carpenter and Battersby, *The Hexateuch*, Vol. I.; Holzinger, *Einleitung in den Hexateuch;* Dr. *LOT.;* and the introductions to the various commentaries on the Hexateuch by Gunkel, Steuernagel, Bäntsch, G. F. Moore, Gray, Bertholet, Holzinger, and Driver.

(2) The prophetic element, with which alone we are now concerned, is itself the result of a union of two distinct documents; and while these two documents may not be clearly distinguished from each other in certain phases, they nevertheless stand apart, in the greater portion of the material, to an extent which is no longer seriously questioned.*

(3) J is a Judaean narrative, having its origin in the kingdom of Judah, while E (*v.i.*) arose in Northern Israel. The evidence of J's Southern origin is not so clear as is that of E's Northern origin, but with the practical certainty of the latter, the probability of the former follows. This, moreover, is strengthened when we observe (*a*) the prominence attached to certain distinctively Southern sanctuaries in the patriarchal narratives; (*b*) the conspicuous place assigned to Judah among Jacob's sons (Gn. 37^{26} 43^8 $44^{16, 18}$ 49^{10}), cf. the corresponding place assigned to Reuben and Joseph in E, and the absence in J of any very sure allusion to Joshua; (*c*) the improbability that two such similar narratives as J and E circulated side by side in the Northern kingdom, and (*d*) the presence in Gn. 38 of traditions concerning families of Judah, which would have little interest for a non-Judahite.†

(4) J, although for the sake of convenience spoken of as a narrative, or indeed as a narrator, represents a school of writers covering a period of perhaps a century or more. It is necessary, therefore, in the use of J to distinguish with care the different strata. For practical purposes, however, we may speak of J¹ as the original J, and of the material assigned to J² or J³ as additions. ‡

---

* Cf. the practical agreement existing among recent analysts, *e.g.* Carpenter and Battersby, Addis, Bacon, Driver, Kautzsch.

† Cf. Holzinger, *Einl.* 160–5; Kit. *Hist.* I. 83–5; E. Meyer, *ZAW.* I. 138; Sta. *GVI.* I. 547; Co. *Einl.* 51; Carpenter and Battersby, *The Hexateuch*, I. 104 ff.

‡ Cf. Carpenter and Battersby, *op. cit.* I. 108 f.; Holzinger, *Einl.* 138–60. This material is of more than a single kind, including, as it does, (1) additions to the *Urgeschichte*, having a different point of view or background, *e.g.* the narrative of the Deluge, which is unknown to J¹; (2) parallels in the patriarchal narratives, *e.g.* the story of Abraham and Sarah at the court of Pharaoh is a later form of the tradition as it appears in connection with Isaac and Rebekah at the Philistine court; (3) insertions pervaded by a loftier ethical and spiritual tone than the context, *e.g.* Gn. 18¹⁷ ff. 22 ᵇ⁻²³ᵃ Ex. 34⁶⁻⁹ Nu. 14¹⁷; (4) editorial additions made in connection

The time relations of J[1] seem to be those of 850 to 750 B.C., or possibly a little later. Only a few would assign a later date.* This unanimity of opinion rests upon (*a*) the fact that the prophetic character of J is less definite than that of Amos and Hosea, seeming, therefore, to belong to a more primitive stage in the development of the spirit of prophecy; (*b*) the probability that Am. 2⁹ Ho. 9¹⁰ 12³ᶠ· ¹²ᶠ· are based upon the written narrative of J; (*c*) the literary style and the religious development found in Amos and his immediate successors imply the existence of religious writings with which they and their listeners were familiar; (*d*) the fact that the narrative of J continues into the days of Joshua implies its post-Mosaic origin; (*e*) the national spirit everywhere characteristic of it did not exist until the age of the monarchy, when Israel for the first time realized its unity; (*f*) the probability that the same school of writers has contributed to the Books of Samuel and Kings; (*g*) the friendly attitude toward the Philistines appearing in the narratives concerning the dealings of Abraham and Isaac with them could not have arisen until a long time after the hostilities of the reign of David; (*h*) the reign of Solomon is evidently looked back upon as a sort of golden age (cf. Gn. 15¹⁸ and 1 K. 4²¹; Gn. 9²⁵ and 1 K. 9²⁰); (*i*) such names as Zaphenath-paneah and Poti-phera are unknown in Egyptian writings until the post-Solomonic period; (*j*) Jos. 6²⁶ points back to the reign of Ahab; cf. 1 K. 16³⁴.

2. The scope of J includes the history of the world from the creation of Adam down to Abraham, the history of Israel's patriarchal ancestors from the selection of Abraham down to the residence in Egypt, the history of the nation under the leadership of Moses and Joshua(?) down to the conquest of Canaan. It is altogether probable that the same school (*v.s.*) of writers continued the work down through the times of the monarchy, giving us the earlier portions of Samuel and Kings.†

The general framework of the narrative from the story of Eden

---

with the union of J and E, *e.g.* Gn. 22¹⁵⁻¹⁸ Ex. 32⁹⁻¹⁴; (5) Deuteronomic additions to the legislation of J, *e.g.* Ex. 19³ᵇ⁻⁶.

* Schra. (in De Wette's *Einl.*⁸) places J between 825 and 800; Kit. (*Hist.* I. 86), between 830 and 800; Kue. puts J[1] in the latter part of the ninth or the first years of the eighth century, and J[2] in the latter half of the seventh century; Bu. (*Urgesch.*) assigns J[1] to the ninth century or the latter years of the tenth, and J[2] to the reign of Ahaz; Di. dates J somewhat after 750 B.C., but prior to Hezekiah's reform; Carpenter and Battersby say, "J may, perhaps, be the issue of two centuries of literary growth, 850–650 B.C."; Steuernagel, *Deuteronomium u. Josua*, 280, names 900–700 B.C. as the period within which J arose (so Holzinger, *Genesis*).

† So Schra. in De Wette's *Einl.*⁸ 327–32; Bu. *Richter u. Samuel;* GFM. *Judges;* Now. *Richter-Ruth;* Sta. *ZAW.* I. 339; Co. *ZAW.* X. 96 ff.; *et al.*

to the settlement in Canaan discloses a definite purpose in the
mind of the author of this literary creation.*   The purpose is
twofold, relating on the one hand to the origin of Israel as a
nation and Israel's relation to the neighboring nations, and, on
the other, to the close connection of Yahweh with this origin and
development.   Nearly every story in the long series finds its true
interpretation from this point of view.†   This is in perfect harmony with the national motive which underlies the work of Elijah,
Elisha, and other *nebhi'im* (§§ 3–5), with the higher place which
Israel is just at this period taking among the nations, and, likewise, with the new ideas of Yahweh which were appealing with
such force to those who breathed the prophetic inspiration
(p. xlix).   This religio-political motive includes also the desire
to give expression to new and larger conceptions of God and man
and life (*v.i.*).   This historical interest does not concern itself
with matters of an institutional character (this was P's great
responsibility).   It is the heroes of ancient history and the scenes
of the olden times that the Judaean narrative delights in.   For this
reason practically no care is given to providing chronological
indications, and hardly more to the chronological arrangement
of the material. ‡   It is the spirit that controls throughout, nowhere
the letter.   It is not difficult to connect this expression of a true
religious spirit with the reformation in Judah, almost contemporaneous (six years later) with that of Elisha and Jehu in Israel,
which was, after all, only the conclusion of the former, resulting,
as it did, in the overthrow of Athaliah, the daughter of Ahab and
Jezebel.

3. One of the principal problems of the Judaean narrative
requires at least a passing glance, viz. that of the world-stories
with which the narrative of J opens. §   What was their origin?
What was their place in the narrative as a whole?   We cannot

---

* Reuss (*Gesch. d. heil. Schrift d. A. T.* § 214) not inappropriately characterizes
J as a "national epic."   Dr. (*The Book of Genesis*, p. xiv) declares J to be "the
most gifted and the most brilliant" of all the Hebrew historians.

† This is true (*contra* Dr.) even of stories like that of the mission of Abraham's
steward (Gn. 24).

‡ *V.* the author's articles in *Hebr.* V.–VI.

§ Viz. the stories of the Garden of Eden, Cain and Abel, the Deluge, and the
Tower of Babel.

longer deny the close formal connection of these traditions with the similar traditions of other peoples.* Nor can we suppose that the various forms which these same stories take on among other nations are derived from an original Israelitish form. Israel received this material from the same sources as those from which other nations received their stories. It is a heritage common to many nations. At the same time it is quite certain that Israel came into peculiar relations with the older Babylonian tradition, not so much in a direct way through the earliest ancestor Abraham,† as in a more indirect manner, viz. through the Canaanitish element, which itself contained much that was Babylonian. ‡ The transformation which these stories have undergone is strictly in accordance with the spirit of the narrative as a whole, and might well be taken to represent the whole, since it shows the prophetic motive, not only in general, but in detail, and illustrates practically every phase of that spirit. Moreover, these stories (found in Gn. 2–11) furnish not only the starting-point, but the basis, for the Judaean narrative, establishing at the very beginning the essential view-point of the narrative. This is seen especially (1) in the place assigned Yahweh in reference to the outside nations; (2) in the importance attached to the conception of sin, and likewise that of deliverance; (3) in the attitude shown toward the progress of civilization; (4) in the preparation already made for giving Israel her place among the nations; and (5) in the details of prophetic method and procedure.

4. This prophetic factor appears in several of the most important characteristics of the narrative. § Only a few of these may be mentioned : —

(1) The purpose and spirit (*v.i.*) are distinctly prophetic, since the writer assumes to be acquainted with the plans of the deity, and in fact to speak for that deity under all circumstances; *e.g.* he declares the divine purpose in the creation of woman (Gn. 2^{18-24});

---

* *V.* Lenormant, *Beginnings of History ;* Davis, *Genesis and Semitic Tradition ;* Gunkel, *The Legends of Genesis ;* and the enormous *Babel u. Bibel* literature resultant upon Friedrich Delitzsch's famous lectures.

† Jastrow, *JQR.*, 1901, p. 653.

‡ So Gunkel, *Genesis*, p. xli ; Dr. *Genesis*, 31 ; Sayce, Wkl., Zimmern, *et al.*

§ Dr. *Genesis*, pp. xxi ff.; Holzinger, *Einl.* 129 ff.; Carpenter and Battersby, *Hex.* I. 99.

he assigns the cause and motive of Yahweh's act in sending the Deluge (Gn. 6^{1-7}) ; he knows the exact effect of Noah's sacrifice upon the divine mind (Gn. $8^{21\,f.}$) ; he sees the divine purpose in the confusion of tongues (Gn. $11^{6\,f.}$) and in the selection of Abram (Gn. 12^{1-3}) ; he also describes the scene between Moses and Yahweh on the top of Pisgah (Dt. $34^{1\,d.\,4}$).

(2) The national element, so prophetic in its character, displays itself (*a*) in the great prominence given to stories in which the principal heroes are reputed national ancestors, such as those concerning Abraham, Isaac, Jacob, Judah, Joseph, Moses ; (*b*) in the recital of events which had to do with the national progress, such as the journey into Egypt, the Exodus, the covenant at Sinai, the conquest, the settlement, — these being the very foundations of the national history ; (*c*) in the evident desire to represent Israel as unique among the nations, since she, a direct descendant (through Noah, Abraham, and others) of the first man Adam, had been definitely chosen by Yahweh as his own peculiar people ; and to represent the affairs of the world as arranged in such a way as to secure the best interest of a single people, Israel ; * (*d*) in the naïve and primitive method adopted to show Israel's superiority to their more closely related neighbors, viz. by connecting some form of reproach with the origin of the nation concerned, *e.g.* Canaan in the story of Noah (Gn. $9^{25\,ff.}$) as a slave to other peoples ; Moab and Ammon (Gn. 19^{30-38}) as the offspring of Lot by incest ; † Ishmael (Gn. $16^{11\,ff.}$) as the son of a handmaid ; Edom as inferior in ability and character from the beginning ; various Arabian tribes as being descended from Keturah, Abraham's second wife, and as not receiving a share in Abraham's property (Gn. 25^{1-5}).

(3) The *predictive* element is, of course, prophetic ; " the patriarchal history is, in his (J's) hands, instinct with the consciousness of a great future " (Driver). (*a*) The history of sin is pictured (Gn. 3^{14}) with unerring accuracy, as a long and painful struggle

---

* This conception is clearly found in J (cf. 13^7 22^{18} 26^4), although the word " choose " is used first of Israel in Dt. 4^{37}.

† Cf., however, Gunkel's conjecture that this story is of Moab-Ammonite origin, and in early times bore no tinge of reproach ; but on the contrary was a eulogy of the daughters of Lot, who took such heroic measures to secure children, and also preserved thereby the purity of the tribal blood.

between humanity and the influences which tempt man to evil, a struggle which in the very nature of the case must mean victory for humanity; * (*b*) Israel's relations to other peoples are prophetically interpreted in Gn. 9^{25-29}; † (*c*) glimpses of Israel's future numbers and power are given to the patriarchs, Isaac (Gn. $27^{27\,\text{ff.}}$), Jacob (Gn. 48^{15-19} 49^{1-27}); while (*d*) a forecast of Israel's future relations to the world at large is placed in the mouth of a foreign prophet (Nu. 24^{17-19}).

These predictions represent the very thought of the prophet concerning the Israel of his own day, the position already gained, or that which, with the encouragement thus given (*i.e.* by the rhetorical and homiletical use of prediction), may be expected. They are, in other words, "prophetical interpretations of history" (Driver).

(4) The prophetic element is seen also in the *idealism* which permeates the narrative throughout. The writer makes word-pictures of events and characters in life, in order that his contemporaries, observing the ideal life thus represented (whether it is an ideal of good or an ideal of bad), may lift their life from the lower plane to a higher.

The story of Abraham is a pen-portrait presenting the ideal of intimate acquaintance and communion with Yahweh, and consequent faithfulness and obedience (cf. Che. *EB*. 24). In the story of Joseph, he pictures the final victory of purity and integrity in spite of evil machinations on the part of those who are rich and powerful (cf. Dr. *DB*. II. 770). In the picture given us of Israel's oppression in Egypt, and deliverance from the same by the outstretched hand of Yahweh, we see Israel as a nation brought face to face with the mightiest power on earth, and triumphing over that power with all its gods. ‡

---

* This passage implies, if it does not promise, victory; cf. Dr. *Genesis*, 48, 57, and *contra* Holzinger, *in loc.*, who denies to it ethical content and limits its meaning to an explanation of the well-known antipathy of man to the serpent family; also Gunkel, who interprets it as explaining the perpetual hostility of man and the serpent family, as a punishment for their league against Yahweh.

† Whether we understand (1) as formerly (also recently by Dr. *op. cit.* p. 111) the three great powers of civilization, the Semitic, the Japhetic, and the Hamitic, or (2) with We., Sta., Bu., Meyer, Holzinger, merely Israel, Canaan, and Philistia or Phoenicia; or (3) with Gunkel (Shem =) the Aramaean-Hebrew peoples, and (Japhet =) the northern peoples (*i.e.* the Hittites).

‡ On the Muṣri hypothesis of the Exodus this exalted conception of Yahweh's power disappears from the story in its original form, but, even if the hypothesis be accepted, the transformation into an Egyptian Exodus must have taken place prior to the times of J.

Stories of this kind, and there were many such, were intended to lead men into a higher life, and to give the nation a confidence in its destiny.*

(5) A true prophetic conception expresses itself in the attitude of the Judaean narrative toward the progress of civilization. Here J follows in the footsteps of those who preceded him, and joins hands with the Nazirite and the Rechabite (*v.s.*).

This antagonism, a corollary of the views entertained concerning sin (*v.i.*), shows itself in connection with (*a*) the story of the murder which accompanied the building of the first city (Gn. 4^{3-16}); (*b*) the beginnings of the arts, all of which led to the further spread of sin (Gn. 4^{20-24} 11^{1-9}); (*c*) the evident reproach joined to the beginning of the culture of the vine (Gn. $9^{20\,\text{ff.}}$); and (*d*) the beautiful representation everywhere made of the charm and simplicity of the pastoral life.

(6) The Judaean narrative clearly presents the prophetic idea of the covenant relation entered into between Yahweh and the people of Israel, with the circumstances leading up to the making of the covenant, the basis on which it was to rest, and its formal ratification (Ex. 19^{20-25} 24^{1-9} 34^{1-28}). We do not see the proof of the non-existence of this idea at this time in the assertion that the narratives (including that of E, cf. Ex. 20 and Dt. 5, and Ex. 24^{20-24}) are legendary and self-contradictory, that the early writing prophets make no use of the conception, and that, consequently, we are to understand the entire covenant idea to be the result of prophetic teaching,† rather than one of its fundamental positions from the very beginning.

This question will come up again, but it is well at this point to observe with Giesebrecht (*Die Geschichtlichkeit d. Sinaibundes*): (*a*) that while references to the fact of a Sinaitic covenant outside of JE are few and doubtful (*e.g.* 1 K. $19^{10,\,14}$, in which ברית is probably a later insertion, cf. 𝔊; on Ho. 6^7 and 8^1 *v.* commentary *in loc.*) until Jeremiah's time, this is not conclusive that such a covenant was unknown; since (*a*) Hosea in chap. 1–3

---

* This work of *transforming* appears all the more clearly, if we understand with Paton (*AJT.* VIII., Oct. 1904) that the real basis of these patriarchal stories is found in traditions concerning the relation and movements of the early tribes.

† We. *Isr. u. jüd. Gesch.* 12 f.; Sm. *Rel.*[2] 117; Schwally, *Semitische Kriegsaltertümer*, I. 2; Schmidt, art. "Covenant," *EB.*; *contra* Giesebrecht, *Geschichtlichkeit d. Sinaibundes* (1900); and K. *DB.* V. 630 ff.

plainly presents the fact of a covenant, although no name is used; (β) the primary meaning of בְּרִית (cf. Val. *ZAW*. XII. 1 ff., 224 ff., XIII. 245 ff.; Krätzschmar, *Die Bundesvorstellung im A. T.*; K. *DB*. V. 630; *contra* Schmidt, *EB*. 928 ff.) is covenant, agreement, the only way of putting a law into force being that of mutual agreement; (γ) the lack of more frequent reference to the existence of the covenant is explained in part on the ground that no writings from the older prophets have come down to us; in part, because few particular occasions called for such mention, and, besides, after the expiration of so long a period it was unnecessary to make allusion to the initial act, especially when, as history shows, every great change in the national situation was accompanied by a new pledge of Yahweh's loyalty and love. Furthermore, (*b*) the leaders, in their continuous effort to use the cultus as an example of the demands growing out of the covenant-relation, and at the same time to adapt the instruction to the changing needs of the people, emphasized the new relations, rather than the old covenant made by Moses. And if it is asked why should such emphasis have been placed on it in the days of Jeremiah, the answer is close at hand : Israel's religion is preëminently an historical religion ; the time had come when the covenant was to be broken; this fact necessarily brings the old covenant into great prominence. Concerning the relation of Amos and Hosea to this covenant-idea *v.i.*

(7) The prophetic element is seen still more strongly in the controlling place occupied in the narrative by the characteristic prophetic conception of *sin and deliverance*.* This factor seems to underlie everything else, beginning, as it does, with the story of the origin of sin in Eden and the forecast of its struggle with humanity (p. lxxv), and continuing with each forward step in the progress of civilization, until because of its terrible growth the race itself (except a single family) must perish. Starting again in the new world, it reappears in the account of Noah's vine-culture and in the scattering of the nations ; while the stories of the patriarchs, one after another, illustrate, for the most part, their deliverance by God's grace from evil situations consequent upon sin ; and the national stories seem to be chronicles only of sin and deliverance from sin,— in other words, of disgraceful acts of rebellion and backsliding, and rescue from enemies who, because of such sin on Israel's part, had temporarily become Israel's masters.

5. *The message* of the Judaean narrative was a rich and varied one, lifting the minds of the Israelites (of pre-Amos times) to the contemplation of : —

---

* *Contra*, Tennant in *The Fall and Original Sin* (1903).

(1) Yahweh, as a God who had controlled the affairs of humanity, since he first brought humanity into existence ; a God also who is celebrated for mercifulness and long-suffering, and for faithfulness (cf. Gn. 6^8 $8^{21f.}$ $18^{23ff.}$ 32^{12} etc.) ; a God, not only all-powerful, but ever-present with his people (Gn. 26^{3a} 28^{15} 39^2 Nu. 14^{9b}).

(2) The origin of sin, and with it of human suffering ; the power of temptation and the terrible results which follow its victory over man ; the awful picture of the growth of evil in civilization ; and, likewise, the possibility of deliverance from evil and distress through the kindness and love of Yahweh.

(3) Great characters, who, while not without fault, " on the whole maintained a lofty standard of faith, constancy, and uprightness of life, both among the heathen in whose land they dwelt, and also amid examples of worldly self-indulgence, duplicity, and jealousy, afforded sometimes by members of their own family " (Driver, *op. cit.*). This life is intended to bring about the establishment of a holy people in the world (Gn. $18^{18f.}$).

(4) A future mission *in* the world (perhaps not yet *to* the world), where Israel is to be conspicuous by reason of the special privileges accorded. These blessings will take the form of material prosperity (cf. the spiritual gifts so great as to attract the envy of all nations, suggested later in Gn. 22^{18} 26^4 [R.]).

6. The place of the Judaean narrative in prophecy and its relation to the later prophets may receive only a brief statement. (1) The ideas of Yahweh as just and hating sin, as merciful, and as faithful, are the very ideas afterward emphasized, respectively by Amos, Hosea, and Isaiah ; the representation of him as all-powerful, and ever-present with his people, precedes Amos's representation in chaps. 1, 2, and that of Isaiah's Immanuel. (2) The conception of sin, and the statement of its evil effects, contain the very substance of all subsequent prophetic utterance. (3) The germ of the Messianic hope, here appearing, in later years is to occupy a large place in religious thought. (4) The conception of Israel's mission in the world ultimately develops into the doctrine of the servant of Yahweh.

Besides this, the more specific allusions to J which are found in Amos and Hosea may be noted, *e.g.:* Am. 3^2, cf. Gn. 18^{19} ;

Ho. $4^{6.\ 10}$ 9^1, cf. Nu. 11^{20}; Am. 4^{11} Ho. 11^8, cf. Gn. 18^{20}–19^{27}; and the relation of the two conflicting estimates of Jacob in Ho. chap. 12 to J's attitude toward the patriarch.

§ 9. THE EPHRAIMITE NARRATIVE (E).

This narrative of Israel's early history took form as early as 800 B.C., and, with the Judaean narrative already discussed, furnishes us a remarkable picture of the life and thought of the period.

1. Certain preliminary points concerning E require brief consideration : (1) The evidence of E's Northern origin is found[*] in its interest in the sanctuaries of Northern Israel ; its assignment of the leadership in the Joseph story to Reuben (cf. J's assignment of it to Judah); its giving of a conspicuous place to Joseph in Dt. 33, the account of his covenant with the tribes at Shechem, and the interment of his bones at Shechem ; the mention of the tombs of many prominent persons, especially those located in the North ; some points of contact with Aramaic in its language ; the prophetic spirit which breathes through it and is characteristic of the North, the home of prophecy.[†]

(2) The date of E is 800 B.C. to 750 B.C.[‡] The general historical situation of the writers seems to be the same as in the case of J, namely, the period of the monarchy. But the general theological standpoint of E is unanimously conceded to be more advanced than that of J ; *e.g.* the conception of the deity is less anthropomorphic (cf. especially, Ex. 3^{14}); the idea of progress in revelation appears ; the whole representation of the method

---

[*] *V.* Carpenter and Battersby, *Hex.* I. 116 f.; Dr. *LOT.* 122; Holzinger, *Einl.* 212 ff.

[†] The oldest form of J has been assigned to the North by some scholars, *e.g.* Schra. in De Wette's *Einl.*[8] 321; Reuss, *Gesch. d. heil. Schriften d. A.T.*, § 213; Kue. *Hex.* 248 ff.; but this view does not commend itself.

[‡] That E was prior to J was the prevailing opinion until the appearance of We.'s *Gesch. Isr.* (I. 370 ff.) in which the opposite view was adopted, which is now generally accepted. For the old view, *v.* Di. *Num.-Dt.-Jos.* 620 ff., 630 ff.; Kit. *Hist.* I. 76 ff. Kue. (*Hex.* 248–52) dates E[1] about 750 and E[2] about 650 B.C.; so Co. *Einl.* 51. Sta. (*GVI.* I. 58 f.) places E about 750 B.C., and maintains the possibility of additions to it after 722 B.C. (p. 582, note 1). Holzinger (*Einl.* 225 f.) puts E[1] in the latter half of the eighth century and E[2] early in the seventh century. Carpenter and Battersby assign E[1] to the first half of the eighth century, and " affirm that E, like J, contains elements of various date, some of which may have been contributed to it after it had been adopted into the record of history and law preserved in Judah "; similarly Steuernagel, *Deuteronomium*, etc., 282 f. Wildeboer puts E[1] about 750 B.C. and E[2] somewhere before 621.

of the divine activity in the world is in the realm of the supernatural and superrational; the transcendent God makes known his will to men in dreams and visions and through angels, not by direct, personal speech as in J. Furthermore, in the case of stories common to J and E, not infrequently, the earlier form of the tradition is evidently that in J; *e g.* in Gn. 26$^{26-33}$ (J) and 21$^{22-31}$ (E), according to E the covenant is binding upon posterity, the oath becomes one of exculpation, and seven lambs are introduced in an attempt to explain the origin of the name Beer-sheba (cf. also Gn. 30$^{14-16}$ [J] with 30$^{17 f.}$ [E], and 30^{24} [J] with 30^{23} [E]). For a *terminus ad quem* 722 B.C. is the lowest possible date, since nowhere in E is there any allusion to the overthrow of the state, which a Northern writer must have mentioned had he been through that experience. The same may safely be said of the events of 734 B.C. The whole character of E's narrative reflects a period of prosperity such as the reign of Jeroboam II.; the tone is one of confidence and hope, with no consciousness of recent disasters nor premonitions of approaching misfortunes. The points of contact between Hosea and E (*v.i.*) also seem to point to the priority of the latter, and so confirm the assignment of E to the date 800–750 B.C.

(3) In comparing the scope of E with that of J, we observe (*a*) that in E the relation of Israel's tradition to the outside world is altogether ignored, the barest allusion (*e.g.* Gn. 20^{13} Jos. 24^{2}) being made to the Mesopotamian antecedents of Abraham's family; but (*b*) the history of the family, and later of the nation, proceeds on lines quite parallel to those of J. The more interesting variations are (*c*) the story of the intended sacrifice of Isaac (Gn. 22), the fuller statement of Jacob's intercourse with Laban, the special attention given to the Joseph-episode, the very independent account of Moses and his times, as well as of the ceremony at Horeb where the "ten words" are proclaimed and the covenant instituted, after which (Ex. 24$^{3-8}$) follow the reception of the tables of stone in the mountain and the apostasy of the golden calf. Out of this came the establishment of the tent of meeting (Ex. 33$^{7-11}$),* in connection with which certain events of important prophetic significance occur (the prophetic inspiration of the seventy elders, Nu. 11^{24b-30}, the vindication of Moses' peculiar prophetic office, 12$^{1-13}$). Thence the narrative passes on to the conquest and the distribution of the land and Joshua's final

* E's description of the tent of meeting has been omitted to make place for the more elaborate account of P.

leave-taking at Shechem (Jos. 24). The narrative unquestionably continues through Judges and Samuel,* thus reaching down at least into the early history of the monarchy, perhaps even to the Elisha stories in 2 Kings.†

(4) *The purpose* of this narrative is evidently to magnify the office of the leaders, and these leaders are prophets, *e.g.* Abraham (Gn. 20^7), Isaac (Gn. 27$^{39\,f.}$), Jacob (48$^{20\,f.}$), Joseph (50^{25}), and Moses (Nu. 12$^{1-15}$), to all of whom visions are granted of the future prosperity of the nation. Israel's government is a theocracy, in which the prophets speak *for God*. When Israel has obeyed the theocratic representatives, she has always been the recipient of divine favor, which signified peace and plenty. When Israel disobeyed, the divine anger was visited upon her in the form of disaster. It is not the secular rulers upon whom her success depends, but the theocratic guides. This teaching, which the narrative throughout was intended to convey, is admirably summed up in Joshua's farewell address (chap. 24).

2. The prophetic element in E, as has been said, is most conspicuous ; ‡ and the narrative, for this reason, is of especial interest to us. We may recall the representation of Abraham as a prophet (Gn. 20^7), the ascription to Joseph of the spirit of Elohim (Gn. 41^{38}), the unique place in pre-prophetism assigned to Moses (Nu. 12$^{1-14}$; cf. Dt. 34$^{10-12}$), the treatment of Miriam as a prophetess (Ex. 15^{20}), the recognition of the non-Israelitish Balaam as a prophet (Nu. 23$^{5-24}$), the prophetic inspiration and authority accorded to the seventy elders (Nu. 11$^{16\,f.\;24\,b-30}$), the characterization of Joshua as the minister of Moses and the servant of Yahweh, the forecasts of Israel's greatness made in the visions ascribed

---

* GFM. *Judges*, XXV. ff. ; Bu. *Richter* (*Kurzer Hand-Comm. z. A.T.*), XII.–XV, and *Samuel* (*SBOT.*).

† It is important to separate E^2, so far as possible, from E^1, for it is only the latter that preceded Hosea. Concerning the limits of E^2, however, there is as yet little agreement, the exceedingly fragmentary character of E as a whole rendering it peculiarly difficult to determine definitely the different strata within the document. The more important passages assigned to E^2 are : Gn. 34 35$^{1-4}$ Ex. 32^1–33^6 Nu. 11$^{14.\;16\,f.\;24\,b-30}$ 12$^{2-8}$ 21$^{32-35}$, and, by some, the Decalogue of Ex. 20 (but *v.s.*). Cf. Kue. *Hex.* 251 f. ; Co. *Einl.* 48 ff. ; Wildeboer, *Litteratur d. A. T.* 140 ; Carpenter and Battersby, *Hex.* I. 119 f.

‡ *V.* Holzinger, *Einl.* 209–11 ; Carpenter and Battersby, *Hex.* I. 113.

to dying patriarchs (Gn. $27^{30\,f.}$ 46^3 48^{20}), the hero-stories which were pictures intended to serve as the ideals of the times in which the narratives were written, and, in fact, as anticipations or predictions of Israel's future glory, and the general representation of theocratic guidance and control which is always present. In all this the prophetic element is pronounced. Furthermore, the emphasis of E upon ethical matters and everything pertaining to the impartial administration of justice is in keeping with its prophetic character; cf. the large amount of legislation concerning the rights of individuals and their mutual responsibilities incorporated in E, and especially the ethical character of E's decalogue (p. lxi ff.) as compared with that of J, and the evident effort to remove from the old traditions everything detrimental to the reputation of the prophetic heroes. This ethical interest is in the direct line of the development of thought which culminates in Amos and the writing prophets. E possesses also a larger interest in priestly matters than J, but this is wholly subordinate in comparison with his prophetic tendency.

3. The message of E * is after all quite distinct from that of J, although it contains very much, indeed, that is the same : —

(1) The teaching concerning God is characterized by (a) a recognition of three different stages of growth through which the conception has passed, viz. that of Israel's early ancestors, polytheism (Jos. 24^2), that of Abraham and Jacob, cf. the reformation instituted by the latter after seeing Elohim's angels at Bethel (Gn. 35^{2-4}), and that connected with the revelation of Yahweh (Ex. 3^{15}); (b) the important place assigned to representatives (viz. prophetic spokesmen or angelic messengers Ex. 14^{19}), as agents of the deity in his intercourse with the people, and to dreams as a method of communication, and the consequent absence of the crude, though picturesque, anthropomorphisms found in J; (c) the treatment of important events as the result, not of human effort in a natural way, but of the direct action of the deity (Ex. 17^{8-11} Jos. 6^{20}), and in this same connection, the employment by the deity of men to accomplish his plans in spite of their ignorance or hostility (Gn. 50^{29} 45^{58}); (d) the use in connection with

---

* V. especially Holzinger, *Einl.* 201–12.

the deity of certain peculiar forms and phrases, *e.g.* the plural of the verbal form (Gn. 20¹³ 31⁵³ 35⁷ Ex. 22⁹ Jos. 24¹⁹), the phrase "fear of Isaac" (Gn. 31⁴². ⁵³), the reference to the sacred stone (Gn. 28²²), the pillar at the door of the tent speaking (Ex. 33⁹), the stone of witness (Jos. 24²⁷), the "trying" of the people by the deity (Gn. 22¹).

The whole idea of God is more theological and abstract (cf. the new interpretation given the word יהוה, viz. אהיה אשר אהיה) than is the case in J. E's God is an exalted personality far removed from his people, and working almost entirely in the realm of the supernatural. He is a God of transcendent power and majesty and of unchanging purpose.

(2) Other characteristic elements in E's message, already mentioned, may be briefly summarized as follows: (*a*) A keener ethical sense than J's, as seen particularly in the evident desire to shield the reputation of the patriarchs by relieving them of the responsibility for certain transactions (*e.g.* Abraham expels Hagar only when commanded so to do (Gn. 21¹²), Jacob in his shrewd dealing with Laban is acting under the direct guidance of God (Gn. 31²⁴. ²⁹. ⁴²). (*b*) A very definite recognition of the patriarchal cultus, with its tent of meeting (Ex. 33⁷⁻¹¹), placed under the charge of Joshua, rather than of Aaron and his sons (Nu. 11¹⁶⁻³⁰), together with altars and pillars (Gn. 28¹⁸. ²² Ex. 24⁴), but no priests. (*c*) An utter lack of interest in the outside world, or in the connection of Israel's history with the outside world.

(3) E's message, briefly stated, was this : Israel's God is a being of wonderful majesty and exalted personality, with unlimited power. His purpose concerning the nation is unchanging. He is not close at hand to communicate with you in person, but makes known to you his will through definite agents, prophets, and messengers; there is no occasion to be ignorant of his wishes, which have been declared so clearly by these agents raised up to represent him. History has shown conclusively that when the voice of these agents has been heeded, the nation has had peace and prosperity; but when there has been rebellion against their injunctions, there have come ruin and disaster. In every important crisis of national history, Israel's God has shown his interest by direct action on Israel's behalf; but he has never hesitated to send punishment when Israel deserved the same. Israel may learn how Yahweh would have the nation act, if attention is given to the lives

of the old patriarchal ancestors and to the great events of early national history. These experiences of honor and glory will again be enjoyed, if only Israel will give heed to the lessons of the past, improve the standards of conduct, and worship Yahweh as did their ancestors.

4. The relation of E to other prophets is quite clear. It is more advanced and higher than J. In many points it is on a level with Amos and Hosea. It is like Hosea, rather than J and Amos, in showing little or no interest in the larger world-view. It is interesting to note that the broader conception is confined to the two documents of Judaean origin. E sees no such danger in the cult as is evidenced by Amos and Hosea. E's thought of sin is that of J. While E's ethical standards (cf. p. lxxxiii) are higher than those of J, they do not reach the level on which those of Amos and Hosea rest.

In E we have the close of the pre-prophetic movement, for with Amos, as all agree, real prophecy has begun. We may now ask, what was the basis and character of this movement, taken as a whole?

B. THE BASIS AND CHARACTER OF THE PRE-PROPHETIC MOVEMENT.

§ 10. THE RELATION OF PRE-PROPHETISM TO MOSAISM.

The question of the connection of pre-prophetism with Mosaism is as interesting as it is difficult. Such connection is taken for granted in J and E (likewise in D).* But does this assumption stand the historical test?† The answer to this question bears most directly

---

* Both J and E narrate the circumstances of Moses' work with great minuteness, and on all the main points there is a fair agreement. They unite in ascribing to him (1) leadership in the deliverance from Egypt and in the journey to Canaan; (2) the position as the representative of Yahweh to Israel; (3) the place as mediator in the making of a covenant between Yahweh and Israel; (4) the honor of founding Israel's legislation.

† Che. (*EB.* art. "Moses") makes the name Moses that of a clan; Wkl. (*Gl.* II. 86–95) makes the entire Moses story a transformation of an original Tammuz myth; but the historicity of the narratives, in a greater or less degree, is maintained by Sta. *GVI.* I. 130; We. *Prol.* 429–40; Sm. *Rel.*2 15 ff.; Kit. *Hist.* I. 227–39; WRS. *OTJC.*2 303 ff.; Giesebrecht, *Geschichtl. d. Sinaibundes;* Bennett, art. "Moses," *DB.*; H. P. Smith, *O. T. Hist.* 56 ff.; and many others.

upon the estimate which we shall finally place upon the work of Amos; for, in the fewest words, the case may thus be stated : Did the ethical idea which formed the essence of prophetic teaching have its origin in Amos? or is there clear trace of its existence before the days of Amos? Is it seen in the transforming work of J and E in their stories dealing with world-history and nation-history (*v.s.*)? Is evidence of its presence to be seen farther back, in the legal formulations found incorporated in J and E (*v.s.*)? Is it seen still earlier, in the motives and methods of Elijah, Elisha, and the *nebhi'im*, whose work began in the days of the seer Samuel? And is the germ of it all to be discovered in Mosaism?

If we are to reach a safe conclusion concerning Moses and his relation to the subsequent history of Israel and Israel's religion, more, perhaps, is to be stated in the form of negation than in the form of affirmation. This is true, partly because so much that is unfounded has been affirmed, partly also because it is practically impossible to draw a sharp line between Mosaism and the pre-prophetic religion, or to trace with perfect satisfaction the relations between the two.

1. It may safely be said that the pre-prophetic religion, even if this includes Mosaism as its basis, has little to do with Egypt or Egyptism ; * while, on the other hand, its relation to the desert of Sinai (or Horeb), and to the tribe of which Jethro was priest is very close. This locality, according to all tradition, was the scene and source not only of Moses' education, but also of the call from the deity, as well as of the work of Jethro, who became the guide (religious and secular) of Moses (and likewise his father-in-law);† and this, also, was the place, according to all tradition, in which Israel later entered into covenant with Yahweh (*v.s.*).

2. We must relinquish the conception (old and widely accepted as it may be) that Mosaism and the developments from it are identical, ‡ an idea which has been the occasion of much error

---

* This is granted by those who hold to the Egyptian bondage, *e.g.* Sm. *Rel.*[2] 37 ; Marti, *Rel.* 55 f.; Schultz, *Theol.* I. 127 ff.; Kue. *Rel.* I. 275 ff.; and follows as a matter of course upon the adoption of the Muṣri hypothesis.

† For explanations of the two names Jethro and Hobab, see the commentaries *in loc.*, and the articles "Hobab" and "Jethro" in *DB.*, *EB.*, and *PRE.*[3]

‡ Bennett (*DB.* III. 446) rightly recognizes the necessity and the difficulty of making this distinction.

and confusion; but we may regard it as established that Moses represents historically (*a*) the deliverance of Israel from Egypt,* (*b*) the union of several clans into one community (perhaps not yet a nation),† and (*c*) a new conception of deity expressed in, or in connection with, the word "Yahweh." ‡

3. We are no longer to argue, *a priori*, that the Moses of tradition must have been just what the tradition represented him as being, for, on this basis, we cannot explain "the ethical impulse and tendency, which, at any rate from the time of the prophet Amos (and Amos, be it remembered, presupposes that this impulse is no novelty), is conspicuous in the history of the Israelitish religion" (Cheyne); but we are entirely justified in believing that Moses was the founder of a religion, and "brought to his people a new creative idea (viz. the worship of Yahweh as a national God), which moulded their national life" (Stade, *G VI.* I. 130; cf. *Akad. Reden.*, 105 ff.). §

4. We may safely deny the ascription to Moses of literary work of any kind, even the songs with which his name is connected (*e.g.* Ex. $15^{1\text{-}18}$ Dt. $32^{1\text{-}45}$ $33^{2\text{-}29}$), or the "judgments and precepts" of CC (§ 7), and the decalogues of E (Ex. 20), and of J (Ex. 34); ‖ but, without much question, we may hold him responsible for the institution of the tent of meeting as the dwelling-place of the deity, together with the ark, and the beginning of a priesthood, and this

---

* Ew. *Hist.* II, 75; We. *Prol.* 429 ff.; Sm. *Rel.*[2] 15 ff.; Kit. *Hist.* I. 227 f.

† See especially Eerdmans, *ThT.* XXXVII. 19 ff.; Bu. *Rel.* 35 ff.

‡ Bu. *Rel.* 35 f.; K. *DB.* V. 624 ff.

§ Cf. We. (*Prol.*), "Moses was not the first discoverer of this faith (viz. that Yahweh is the God of Israel, and Israel the people of Yahweh), but it was through him that it came to be the fundamental basis of the national existence and history"; WRS. (*OTJC.*[2] 305), "He founded in Israel the great principles of the moral religion of the righteous Yahweh." Co. (*Hist. of the People of Isr.*) says of Moses' work at Sinai, "It is one of the most remarkable moments in the history of mankind, the birth hour of the religion of the spirit. In the thunderstorms of Sinai the God of revelation himself comes down upon the earth; here we have the dawn of the day which was to break upon the whole human race, and among the greatest mortals who ever walked this earth Moses will always remain one of the greatest."

‖ Moses was preëminently a man of affairs; the strenuous nature of his activities as leader and organizer of the tribes of Israel left no opportunity for literary pursuits. His work was "rather practical than didactic, the influence of an inspired life rather than the inculcation of abstract dogmas" (Bennett, *DB.* III. 446).

is the germ of much of the institutional element that follows in later years.

5. We may find greater or less difficulty in discovering the basis of an ethical development in Mosaism, either (*a*) in the essentially ethical character of the claim upon Israel, which grew out of the great act of mercy performed by Yahweh at the crossing of the Red Sea, Israel's religion taking on gradually thereafter a moral character, because she is constantly impelled to pay due regard to the claim ; * or (*b*) in the new conception of God, viz. that he controls nature and history, involving the truth that Yahweh was not the God of a country but of a people, the relation of a deity to a people being more spiritual than that of a deity to a country ; † or (*c*) in the mutual loyalty of the tribes to one another and their common loyalty to one God, in contrast with the individual henotheism of Moab, Ammon, etc.

It is probable, on the other hand, that a more reasonable hypothesis will be found in the view ‡ that this development has its roots in the fact that Israel's relation to Yahweh was not that of blood-kindred, as in the case of nature religions, nor that simply of long observance which had become something inevitable ; but, rather, a relation entered into by choice, one which, unlike that of a nature religion, could be broken, but also one which Israel was led to preserve, because Yahweh had wrought great works in her behalf. Budde's summary (p. 38) expresses this thought most exactly : " Israel's religion became ethical because it was a religion of choice and not of nature, because it rested on a voluntary decision, which established an ethical relation between the people and its God for all time."

6. We may acknowledge quite freely the insufficiency and uncertainty of the materials at our command, and, as well, the difficulty of giving proper credit to the various agents and movements concerned with the development of the great ethical ideas concerning righteousness, which had before been unknown ; but, at the same time, we cannot fail to recognize that certain facts

---

* Che. *EB*. 3214. † Bennett, *DB*. III. 446.

‡ So Tiele, *Manuel de l'histoire des religions* (1880), 84, and *Histoire comparée des anciennes religions* (1882), chap. IX.; Sta. *GVI*. I. 130 ff.; Bu. *Rel.* 1–38; Barton, *Sketch of Semitic Origins*, 275 ff.

have been established which fit into hypotheses more or less satis-factory, the fundamental factor in which is the close logical and historical connection between pre-prophetism and Mosaism. In-deed, it may be asserted that Mosaism is as fundamental to pre-prophetism as is pre-prophetism to prophetism itself.

§ 11. The Essential Thought of Pre-prophetism.

Is it possible now to think of this movement in its unity, and, in spite of the many difficulties which exist, to separate and dis-tinguish its thought from that which precedes and follows it? In making the effort to draw historical lines, we may observe : (1) That the case before us is, in some sense, a definite one, since we are concerned with Israel's religious thought during the period in which *Yahwism is in contact with Baalism as a rival religion.* This contact began when Israel entered Canaan ; it ended in the century in which Jehu, under the influence of the *nebhi'im*, up-rooted it.* We might go farther and say that we are dealing with Yahwism itself ; for, pure Yahwism, at the end of this period, passes into prophetism, which, still later, becomes Judaism. (2) Consequently, our question is a threefold one : What was Yahwism at the time of the entrance into Canaan? With what did Yahwism have to contend in the centuries from 1100 to 800 B.C. ? What had Yahwism become at the close of the con-test? Two or three subsidiary questions will arise, viz.: How was it that, in the end, Yahwism became supreme? Is the differ-ence between the Yahwism of 1100 B.C. and that of 800 B.C. the sum contributed by the *nebhi'im ?* or did Yahwism draw from Baalism itself much that was of vital significance? And further, were the institutions of Baalism made use of by Yahwism in securing this position of superiority?

1. It is natural to consider first the idea of God.

(1) When Yahwism, whatever may have been its origin,† came

---

* The effects of Baalism continue down to Hosea and later; some of them are, indeed, incorporated in Yahwism (*v.i.*).

† Whether, *e.g.* (1) in an original direct revelation (so most old interpreters) ; (2) in the old Arabian tribal religion (Schultz, *et al.*) ; (3) in the religion of the Kenites (Stade, Budde, *et al.*) ; or (4) in the esoteric monotheism of the Egyptian priesthood.

into Canaan, it was, so far as the conception of God was concerned, simple and primitive, very crude and naïve, monotonous and severe.

This appears in (*a*) the conception of Yahweh as the god of the mountain (Sinai), a conception which continued in one form or another until late in Israel's history (Dt. $33^{2\,f.}$ 1 K. 19^8 Ps. 68^8 Hb. 3^3). (*b*) The more widely prevailing conception of Yahweh as the god of war, an idea which found strong justification in the issue of the contest with Egypt (cf. also, the war-song with which camp was broken, Nu. 10^{35}), as well as that with the Canaanites (cf. the fear of the Philistines, 1 S. $4^{7\,f.}$, on account of Yahweh's presence in the ark). This is seen also in the allusion to Israel's armies as Yahweh's armies (1 S. 17^{26} 25^{28}), and in the very name, Yahweh Sabaoth (cf. 2 S. 5^{10}).* (*c*) The conception of him also *as the God of the desert* (*i.e.* of the nomad), and especially in connection with storms, *e.g.* at the giving of the law (Ex. 19), in the battle of Deborah (Ju. 5^{46}), in the storm exhibited to Elijah at Horeb (1 K. $19^{11\,ff.}$), and in later times, *v.s.* It is here that the nomadic temperament of pre-prophetism (*v.s.*) finds its basis.† (*d*) The conception of the *ark*, a materialistic symbol of Yahweh's presence, which plays a great rôle in this early period,‡ actually representing Yahweh, and not merely containing some image or symbolic stone. The history of its presence or absence in Israel's armies, its transportation hither and thither until at last it is deposited in the Temple (1 K. $8^{4.\,6\,ff.}$), is full of significance in showing the crude and crass conceptions of deity entertained, not only by the people, but also by the leaders.

(*e*) The use of *images*, involving family and clan conceptions of deity, distinct from that of Yahweh. § Some of these images, unquestionably, were employed to represent Yahweh, *e.g.* the פֶסֶל, originally of wood or stone, and probably of human form (Ju. $17^{3\,f.}$), ‖ likewise, the אֵפוֹד (p. 221), perhaps originally the garment used to clothe the image, and later, the image itself, and used in obtaining oracles. But the *teraphim* (p. 222), used very frequently of Yahweh, are also images of ancestors, of the tribal or family gods, as in the case of Rachel (Gn. $31^{19.\,34\,f.}$ cf. $^{30.32}$), and of the king of Babylon (Ez. 21^{26}).¶ It is understood that all of these usages existed in the earliest times of the pre-prophetic period.

---

* Cf. especially Schwally, *Sem. Kriegsaltertümer*, I. 4 ff.

† Cf. Bu. *Rel.* 27, who adds, also, the representation of the burning bush, the pillar of fire and smoke, the lightning as Yahweh's " fire " or " arrow," the thunder as his " voice," the rainbow as his " bow."

‡ K. *DB*. V. 628; cf. his foot-note for a careful survey of recent literature.

§ K. *DB*. V. 641 f.

‖ Not referred to in Ex. 34^{17}, and probably not in Ex. 20^{4-6}.

¶ So Schwally, *Das Leben nach d. Tode ;* Matthes, *ThT.*, 1900, pp. 97 ff., 193 ff.; 1901, pp. 320 ff.; but cf. K. *DB*. V. 614 f., 642, who wrongly denies the existence of even survivals of ancestor-worship in Israel.

(2) What, now, did Israel find in Canaan that required to be either assimilated or destroyed? To what extent, and through what means, in the course of the struggle was Yahwism itself modified?

(*a*) The distribution of the clans among the Canaanites involved a serious risk, for they now acted more or less independently of each other, and much that had been gained by their union was lost. With Canaanites on every side of them, they were compelled to give a certain recognition to the gods of the people, who were, likewise, the gods of the land; and especially was this true in view of the fact that they were unable to drive out the Canaanites, but lived with them side by side (Ju. 1^5 $18^{1\,ff.}$). How could they do other than express gratitude to the Baalim, *i.e.* the gods of the land, for the fruits which they gave?

(*b*) The new life, moreover, was an agricultural rather than a nomadic life, and demanded many modifications. The Israelites were the pupils of the Canaanites in all "the finer arts of field and vine culture," and the association needed for this could not fail to exert a great influence on Israel's life and thought.*

(*c*) The nation for the first time came into touch with real civilization, and civilization was for them identical with Baalism. This explains why the *nebhi'im* tended toward an isolated life, and seem in most cases to have opposed all progress toward civilization. The emblems of civilization, corn and oil, silver and gold, Israel believed, came from the Baalim (Ho. 2^8).

(*d*) The nature of Baalism itself† was something peculiarly attractive to people of a sensuous type. The great emphasis placed on reproduction and everything connected with it, whether in the realm of vegetable or animal or human life, gave it a pervasive influence, for all life in the narrower, if not in the broader, sense was involved. The strength of the ideas thus included is evident from the hold they took upon many nations of ancient times. There was a stimulus in all this, a warmth which, although greatly abused, produced also some good results.

(3) What actually occurred in the process of this long struggle was as follows: (*a*) Yahweh's residence is changed; he gradually

---

* Gu. *GVI.* 155 ff.; Sta. *Akad. Reden*, 109 ff., 116 ff.; K. *DB.* V. 645.

† Cf. A. S. Peake, art. "Baal," *DB;* WRS. *Sem.*² 93–113; WRS. and GFM., art. "Baal," *EB.;* Movers, *Die Phönizier*, I. 672–90.

takes up his dwelling in the new territory.   This means that the
Baalim whom men worshipped at many different points, under various names, Baal-Peor, Baal-Hermon, etc. (cf. also Baal-Berith,
Baal-Zebub), were displaced by Yahweh, who was worshipped at
all the sacred places and bore different names according to the
place (*e.g.* אל עולם, the eternal God, Gn. 21³³; אל בית־אל, the God
of Bethel, 31¹³ 35⁷; " שלום, Yahweh Shalom, Ju. 6²⁴, etc.).   All
this change has taken place before the times of J and E, for, as
Kautzsch points out (*DB*. V. 646), the patriarchal narratives do
not know of any Baal-worship in the land.   Yahweh has taken
Baal's place, but in so doing the Yahweh ritual has absorbed so
much of Baalism as to become, practically, a Baal ritual.   (*b*) The
idea grows that Yahweh "is enthroned as God in heaven."   This
means much, for it implies that he is superior to all other gods.
It is from heaven that he performs all those acts which indicate
his power over the elements (*e.g.* rain, dew, fire, Gn. 19²⁴) and
over the fruits of the soil.   He is called the God of heaven (Gn.
24⁷).   Messengers must now be employed to represent him, and
these angels call from heaven (21¹⁷ 22¹¹), and, indeed, go up and
down on ladders which unite heaven and earth (28¹²), the "house
of God" being identical with the "gate of heaven."   (*c*) His
nature as the God of the desert is changed; he is no longer hostile to civilization.   Yahwism could never have become without
change the religion of a civilized people, still less of humanity.
"He takes under his protection every new advance in civilization."*
(*d*) His nature as destroyer (war-god) is changed, for he is no
longer the deity of desolation and silence.   He is in continual
touch with man's activity, and everything is subordinated to secure
his influence and blessing.   The idea of beneficence and love has
come.   Warmth and color now exist, where all before was cold and
stern.   (*e*) Baalism, acting as a "decomposing reagent," brings
unity, solidarity, in so far as like conditions exist, and thereby all
cult and family images must disappear.   Hence arises the opposition to image-worship which forms so large an element in
prophetism beginning with Hosea.   (*f*) Attempts are made to
spiritualize the old physical conception of Yahweh.   Among these

---

* Cf. on this general subject, Bu. *Rel*. 72 ff.

are to be counted (a) the expression, "angel of Yahweh" (J), which was at first used when Yahweh was represented as coming into contact with man (Gn. 16[7 ff.] cf. [11]); in other words, a method of Yahweh's manifestation; * (β) *the face of Yahweh* (J), *i.e.* the person (Ex. 33[20-23]), but not the full being,† and (γ) *the name of Yahweh* (Ex. 20[24] 23[21]), in which "name" is a "personified power, placed side by side with the proper person of Yahweh." ‡ The use of these phrases § is an attempt to substitute something more spiritual for the thought of the human form, and marks great progress in the conception of God.

(4) The agencies which bring about this change are in part: (a) Those of the old Yahwism, the strength of which continues to be felt in spite of the additions that have been taken on ; (b) those also of Baalism, among the chief of which was prophetism, adopted and adapted by Israel (*v.s.*); but (c) the immediate occasion of the acute attack which enabled Yahwism to throw off the gradually increasing burden that had almost proved its ruin, was the attempt to force upon Israel a new form of this same Baalism, that of Tyre. The situation was now essentially different from that which existed in the early days of the conquest ; for at this time Yahweh had actually taken possession of the land, and the question was : Shall a foreign god, the deity of Tyre, who has already shown great power, come in and overpower the god of the land, who is now Yahweh ? ‖ On the nature of this struggle in detail, *v.i.* The old Baalism had become so intimate a part of Yahwism that at this time it is lost sight of in the new Baalism which threatens Israel. This distinction makes clear what at first seems contradictory, viz. the idea that Baalism was actually uprooted by Jehu, and the idea, which also existed, that Baalism was still a corrupting element in Israel's religion.

(5) At the close of the struggle, Yahwism is victorious ; ¶ the conception of God which has now developed being as follows :

---

* K. *DB*. V. 638 f.; Kosters, *Th T.*, 1875, pp. 367 ff.   † Cf. comm. *in loc.*

‡ Giesebrecht, *Die alttest. Schätzung des Gottesnamens u. ihre religionsgeschichtliche Grundlage*, 66; K. *DB*. V. 640 f.; F. J. Coffin, *JBL*. XIX. (1900), 166–188.

§ The phrase "glory of Yahweh" probably arose in this period, but there is no certain evidence of its existence until a slightly later date; cf. 1 S. 4[22] Ex. 33[18] (late J) Nu. 14[22] (JE).   ‖ K. *DB*. V. 647.   ¶ Bu. *Rel.* 106.

(*a*) Yahweh is a god irresistible in nature and among nations, the idea of a *merely* national god having been outgrown. This is seen in the power attributed to Yahweh over other nations, *e.g.* Egypt, and Canaan, as well as in the extra-national existence involved in his residence at Sinai, and likewise in the later conception of a heavenly residence (*v.s.*). The narrower idea of Yahweh as the god of a land has never existed. He has been and is a national god, *i.e.* Israel's God; but he is also something more than this, a god who controls nations and nature in Israel's favor. It is not in this same sense that we may speak of Chemosh or Ashur.

(*b*) He is, moreover, a god who is the moral ruler of his people; this has not gone so far as to affect individuals, being still limited to families and nations. The interests of the individual are indeed conceived of as under the protection of Yahweh, but they are wholly subordinate to those of the nation, being in themselves of too slight importance to merit the especial and continuous consideration of the deity, except in so far as they contribute to the national life and progress.* Yahweh's rule is characterized by justice, and his power to judge extends to heaven and to Sheol. Here we must estimate the true character of judgment in ancient times, for, although it came from Yahweh, it signified, not a "moral investigation and instruction," but "an oracular response obtained by means of a sacred lot" (Ex. 22[6 ff.] Jos. 7[16 ff. 38 ff.] 1 S. 14).† This, as Budde says, is not moral, but intellectual knowledge. But this primitive judgment has nevertheless given place to the verdict against kings pronounced by Nathan and Elijah (*v.s.*).

He is known for his personal interest and love, since he has shown himself to be, not only a helper and a friend, but, indeed, a father. ‡ This signifies something very great, for he is no longer simply a natural or even national god, and therefore compelled to render such service. If deliverances have been wrought, they have come through his affection. There is a sense, likewise, in which he is a *holy* god, and disobedience of his regulations is *sin*. This is implied in the claim of Elijah, who treats allegiance to any other god as sin; in representations of J and E, that disregard of Yahweh's will (cf. especially the story of the origin and progress of

---

* Cf. Sm. *Rel.*[2] 102 ff.   † Bu. *Rel.* 33 f.   ‡ Cf. Sm. *Rel.*[2] 96-101.

sin given by J in Gn. 3–11) is deserving of severe punishment and inevitably followed by judgment; in the decalogues, which present the ethical and the ritualistic demands of a god, himself holy, and therefore demanding an elevated character in those who serve him; and in CC, the regulations of which are everywhere regarded as the expression of the divine will.

(c) Yahweh alone is the God of Israel, and he only may be worshipped, — this was the truth for which Elijah had contended, and his contest had been won. The significance of this victory can scarcely be overestimated. The fact that Yahweh had made and enforced such a demand in itself challenged attention. It emphasized the fundamental and far-reaching difference between Yahweh and the nature gods of Canaan and the surrounding peoples.* This difference consisted chiefly in the essentially ethical and spiritual nature of Yahweh, which must of necessity find expression in demands upon his people for a worship arising from the heart and a life devoted to ideals of justice and purity.

2. In what has already been said, there is much that refers to the conceptions concerning man's duty to God, as expressed in *worship*. We may add the following brief statement: —

(1) The priest, hardly known before the entrance into Canaan, has attained an important place. The story of the priest-work of Micah (Ju. 17, 18), and that of Eli and his sons (1 S. 1^1–4^{22}), shed much light upon the early history of the priesthood. He was at first occupied with the care of the Ark (1 S. 4^4 2 S. $15^{24. 29}$), and with carrying or consulting the ephod (for no positive evidence exists that the priests participated in sacrifice†). Out of this function grew later the giving of *directions*, i.e. *tôrôth*, in matters relating to law or ritual. But with the erection of the Temple, the priests took on larger service and rose to a higher place in society and in governmental affairs. Strong societies were organized, at first in Jerusalem, and later in Northern Israel (cf. Dt. $33^{8 ff.}$ [E], in which the priesthood is recognized as organized and as possessing high dignity and power). At the same time CC contains no reference to a priest; the whole matter is custom, not law.

(2) The high places taken over from Baalism are still employed

---

* Cf. Kue. *Rel.* I. 367 f.   † 1 S. $2^{12 ff.}$ does not prove this.

without objection as the seats of popular worship. These represent the ancient holy places, and have now become thoroughly identified with Yahweh-worship, as distinguished from Baal-worship. The thought has not yet been suggested that worship shall be restricted to one place, Jerusalem. The impossibility of securing a pure worship at these high places has not yet been realized.

(3) Sacrifice is, after all, the chief feature of worship. It appears in the meal of communion (1 S. 14[4 ff.] 9[12 ff.]); the offerer may kill the victim, the fat is reserved for Yahweh, and a portion is given to the priest (1 S. 2[13 f.]); the flesh may not be eaten with the blood (1 S. 14[32 f.]). All sacrifices are *gifts* to the deity; the offerings of Gideon (Ju. 6[18 ff.]) and Manoah (Ju. 13[19]) represent the usage of the times.*

(4) The passover, Israel's only festival in pre-Canaanitish times, has now grown into several, among which are (*a*) the *Sabbath* (Ex. 34[21] 23[12] Dt. 5[12]), observed, however, with a humanitarian rather than a religious motive (*v.s.*); this same thing holds good also of (*b*) the *seventh year*, which is beginning to be observed. There are also (*c*) the new moon (1 S. 20[5 ff. 24 ff.]), with festivities lasting for two days, and (*d*) the three festivals at which all males were to appear with gifts (Ex. 23[14 ff.] 34[18 ff.]); these were occasions of great joy and feasting, reaching even to excess, for sacred women at the high places prostituted themselves as a part of the religious ritual. Cf. Amos and Hosea *passim*.†

(5) Custom has now in many cases been codified into law, for CC is clearly in existence (*v.s.*). These precedents are now recognized as having divine sanction ; and while their scope is not broad, the essential content includes reference to many of the more important of the religious institutions.

(6) The use of images continues, and oracles are consulted in order to ascertain the divine will. This was the use made of *Urim and Thummim*, which, in some way not quite clear, represented the sacred lot. Cf. 1 S. 14[41] (𝕲), and 14[3. 18. 36].‡ This usage, hardly consistent with a later and higher prophetism, was still a part of the system in vogue, and entirely consistent with that system.

3. It is not easy to formulate, as the expression of this Canaanitish-Israelitish age, the opinion which prevailed concerning the relation of man to his fellow-man, his obligations, or, in other

---

* For further details *v.* Schultz, "Significance of Sacrifice in O. T.," *AJT.* IV. 257–313; Now. *Arch.* II. 203 ff.; Dr., art. "Offering," *DB.;* GFM., art. "Sacrifice," *EB.;* and my *Priestly Element in O. T.*, 83–93.

† On early Israelitish festivals, see my *Priestly Element in O. T.*, 94–7; Benz., art. "Feasts," *EB.;* Now. *Arch.* II. 138 ff.

‡ GFM., art. "Urim and Thummim," *EB.*

words, the ethical standards which were in vogue. But certain things may be said, partly in the way of explanation, partly, also, in the way of interpretation : —

(1) It is unfair to the age, and to the subject, to base one's conclusions on the extreme cases of immorality. Such cases occur in our own day. The record of such cases (*e.g.* that of Judah and Tamar (Gn. 38), and that of David and Bathsheba (1 Sam. 11, 12)) is evidence, not of their common occurrence, but of their heinousness in the sight of the prophet who makes the record.

(2) While we may still hesitate concerning the actual basis of this ethical movement in Israel's history, and its origin, it is comparatively easy to point out, not only the elements in the remarkable growth which has taken place in this period, but also the occasion of the growth, viz. the advance in a true conception of Yahweh (pp. xc ff.).

(3) The conception of higher ideals is still restricted to the community (*i.e.* the family or clan), and has not received application to the individual.

(4) This higher conception has influenced the attitude of Israel neither toward outside nations, nor, indeed, toward the stranger inside Israel's gates. This is not to be regarded as strange in view of the definitely hostile relations which existed for the most part between every ancient nation and its neighboring nations. International comity and law must follow national law at a long distance.

(5) Custom is still, in great measure, the standard of action, but this is more and more influenced by religious thought. And, as already suggested, custom has now been formulated into law. Crime is regarded as affecting Yahweh himself (2 S. 12^{14}, following the reading of Lucian), and the enactments of CC, aside from its ritual content, take cognizance of the most common and important of the human relationships.

(6) The later decalogue, properly interpreted (*v.s.*), marks the stage of advancement now reached. This is splendidly supported and, indeed, developed in CC (pp. lxiv ff.).

(7) But, after all, the stories of the patriarchs give us the truest idea of the morals of the period.* They represent the highest ideals

---

* K. *DB.* V. 663 f.

of the teachers of Israel at the time they assumed literary form (cf. pp. lxxi, lxxix f.). Abraham is the type of the truly pious Israelite, exhibiting the qualities of faith and obedience under the most trying circumstances ; while Jacob is the successful man of affairs, whose prosperity is due, not alone to his own shrewdness, but also to his faithful adherence to his God. The moral delinquencies of the patriarchs must be estimated in view of (*a*) the fact that in large part the questionable transactions are in relations with foreigners, toward whom ethical requirements did not hold to such a high degree (*v.s.*) ; (*b*) the effort of E to minimize the faults of the patriarchs (*v.s.*), which shows an ethical advance toward the close of the pre-prophetic period ; (*c*) the indirect condemnation sometimes found within the stories themselves (cf. Gn. $20^{9\,f.}\,26^{9\,f.}\,27^{12}$).

(8) The stories of the kings enforce similar truths upon the attention. The special position of the king as " the anointed of Yahweh " and the most powerful personage in the nation added emphasis to the use of his life-story for purposes of moral and religious instruction. If David and his successors could achieve success only in so far as they obeyed Yahweh and refrained from evil, how much less could the nation at large disregard Yahweh's will and prosper? The direct teaching of these stories is evident.

4. Aside from the conceptions already considered, viz. those of God, of man in relation to God, and of man in relation to man, there are certain others with which the religious and ethical ideas are closely associated. These possess more of the speculative character and deal with the origins of things and the future.*

(1) *Ideas concerning the origin and nature of man* had taken on quite definite form, *e.g.* (*a*) the *body* of man (Gn. 2^7) is of earth and at death returns to the earth (Gn. 3^{19}) ; while the *breath* (*v.i.*) is re-absorbed in the great Spirit of the universe ; this *body* or *flesh* is transitory in its nature (cf. Is. 31^3) and always subject to decay and destruction ; it is, moreover, the occasion of moral weakness ; but it is never represented as in itself sinful (*i.e.* as equivalent to σάρξ) and unclean.

(*b*) The *blood* is the life only in the sense that it is the source,

---

* Di. *Theol.* 355 ff.; the recent statement of Kautzsch (*DB.* V. 665 ff.) furnishes an admirable survey of this entire field.

or vehicle, or seat, of life; consequently it must not be eaten (1 S. 14$^{32\,ff.}$; cf. Dt. 12^{23} Lv. 17^{11}), for in so doing another life might be absorbed. The desire to bring about just such an identification of different lives was the basis of the earlier sacrificial meals, of which, however, no instance occurs in O. T. literature. The significance of this conception of *blood* upon the later development of sacrifice is very evident.

(*c*) The *breath* or *spirit* (רוּחַ) occupied a still larger place in the older thought. This *breath* represented life, and had its origin in the breath of Yahweh himself, which he breathed into the first man (Gn. 2^{7}). When this divine breath (the spirit of life) is called back by Yahweh to himself (*i.e.* re-absorbed), death ensues. Nor was this spirit restricted to human beings, for animal life (Gn. 2^{17}) had the same origin (Nu. 16^{22} 27^{16}; cf. Ps. 104$^{29\,f.}$ Jb. 34$^{14\,f.}$), although it was reckoned inferior, as is shown by the fact that man was treated more directly and individually in the act of creation, animals being animated, so to speak, as a species; and further, although animals are represented as created for man's use, none of them is fit to be his "help." But now, this spirit, breathed into humanity once for all in the case of the first man (= traducianism, rather than creationism), and including life of every kind, viz. thought, will, and action, is everywhere a manifestation of the divine spirit (cf. Acts 17^{28}). *

(2) The origin and purpose of the universe does not occupy a large place in Hebrew pre-prophetic thought, and yet certain definite ideas are contained in J's statement in Gn. 2$^{4\,ff.}$ Perhaps something also is to be learned from what this passage does *not* contain (*e.g.* the lack of any mythical element). (*a*) This narrative, of which a portion (dealing with the creation of heaven and earth) doubtless has been lost, clearly points to Yahweh as the former of man and of man's home (but this is only what other religious cosmogonies have done, each in its own way, and does not contradict the position that the doctrine of Yahweh as Creator is exilic or post-exilic, *i.e.* subsequent to the acceptance of monotheism).†

---

* Cf. Di. *Theol.* 359 ff.; Da. *O. T. Theol.* 117–29; Briggs, *JBL.* XIX. (1900), 132 ff.; Shoemaker, *JBL.* XXIV. (1904), 13 ff., who finds no case of רוּחַ = *breath* until exilic times (*v.* p. 24).

† Sta. *ZAW.* XXIII. 178; Gunkel, *Schöpfung und Chaos,* 159; K. *DB.* V. 669.

(*b*) The interest is centred in man, for whose benefit alone the animals are formed ; and when no suitable companion is found for him among them, woman is created by another and different process ; while (*c*) the climax is found in the representation concerning marriage.*

(3) The origin and nature of sin is pictured in the story of the *fall,* for no other interpretation than that of a *fall* † will satisfy the demands.   Concerning all this, it was believed (*a*) that man, at one time, lived in close association and communion with the deity ; but (*b*) pride led him to overstep certain bounds that had been set ; (*c*) this act of disobedience was followed by trouble, misery, and suffering. ‡

(4) *The state after death* is a subject concerning which neither pre-prophecy nor prophecy had much to say, partly because the saying of anything would give encouragement to the superstitious survivals of animism, and partly, also, because no adequate teaching had as yet been worked out.   That the ideas which prevailed in early Israel concerning Sheol came from the Canaanites (and perhaps farther back from Babylon) is probable ; in any case, the popular belief was closely associated with necromancy, and consequently opposed to Yahwism.   This belief (Gn. 37^{35} 42^{38} $44^{29.\ 31}$ Nu. $16^{30.\ 33}$, for which we are indebted to J) included, at least, the following points : (*a*) Sheol is a space to which one goes *down;* (*b*) no one ever returns ; yet (*c*) by the influence of necromancers a " form " may be brought up, as in the case of Samuel (1 S. $28^{11\ ff.}$) ; while (*d*) only thick darkness prevails.   (*e*) It is a place of assembly for the departed ; but (*f*) there is no such thing as fellowship (Gn. 37^{35}).   (*g*) That which goes *down* is not the body (which decays in the grave), nor the spirit (which is absorbed by the spirit of God) ; but " an indefinable something of the personality " which (= *shade,* or *manes*) is invisible and does not live, but merely

---

* On the question of Babylonian influence upon this and the other early stories of Genesis, cf. the recent voluminous literature on Babel and Bible.

† Cf. the opinions that we have here : (1) an illustration of how sin arises in the case of *every* individual (cf. Di. *Theol.* 371) ; (2) the story of how humanity passed from rudeness to culture, or from unconsciousness to freedom (cf. Holzinger and Gunkel, *in loc.*) ; or (3) a culture-myth without moral content (Tennant).

‡ On the relation of this to the Babylonian, and especially the Zend, cf. Sta. *ZAW.* XXIII. 172 ff. ; Zimmern, *KAT.*[3] 527 f. ; K. *DB.* V. 667.

exists. How far this popular belief was a survival of animism, and the extent to which it was really antagonized by Yahwism, cannot here be discussed.*

5. The general character of the pre-prophetic movement may now be briefly summarized in view of its history up to this point, and, likewise, in view of the real prophetic activity which is to grow out of it and, at the same time, to follow close upon its heels :

(1) This movement is not exclusively or essentially Israelitish, but is of Canaanitish origin,† although itself at a later time hostile to Canaanitism and directly responsible for its destruction ; and in the long process of its growth it incorporates many Canaanitish ideas.

(2) The struggle between pre-prophetism and Baalism is between the later idea of a relation with the deity, based upon a pact or covenant, and the earlier idea of a relation based upon the natural tie. In this case, the covenant idea lives and works several centuries with the nature idea, and, in the end, shakes it off, but only after absorbing all that was good in it.

(3) The result of the movement, in so far as it concerns worship, is the endurance, if not the acceptance, of an elaborated cult, through which the religious sentiment has been enlarged and enriched, but in which Israel is soon to find that which will prove her ruin (cf. Judah and the doctrine of the inviolable Jerusalem).

(4) The influence of the movement on conduct has been to raise the standard in a marked degree, and to define more closely the relations of man to man, without, however, going outside of Israel, or developing anything higher than that which pertains to the tribe or family.

(5) The movement, in so far as it concerns the idea of God, is still henotheistic, not monotheistic.

C. AMOS.

§ 12. THE PERSONAL LIFE OF AMOS.

The facts of the life of Amos present many points of peculiar interest. 1. His home was in Judah (cf. p. 3).

---

* For the most important literature on this subject, see pp. 40 f.
† So Kue. *Proph.* 554 ff. ; K. *DB.* V. 653 ; Gu. *GVI.* 71 ; *et al.*

This may be accepted, notwithstanding (*a*) his seeming absorption in Northern Israel (cf. p. cxxi for the view that he always had Judah in mind as the home of Yahweh's religion in the future); * (*b*) the elevation of Tekoa, which is alleged to be too great for sycamore culture (p. 3); † (*c*) the lack of allusion to Judah in his writings; ‡ (*d*) the effort of Grätz § to identify Tekoa with Eltekeh of Jos. 19⁴⁴, making him a Danite; (*e*) the suggestion of Oort that he really lived in the North, and went to Judah only after his expulsion from Bethel (p. 3); (*f*) the desire of Che. || to transfer Tekoa to the Negeb, and transform many of the proper names in such a way as to place the entire activity of Amos in this region, which Che. supposes to have belonged to Northern Israel.

The location of Tekoa in the desert of Judah furnishes the possibility of just such a sense of natural grandeur ¶ as we are compelled to believe must have been the privilege through many years of one who was later able to express himself as did Amos. Nor may we deny the very great importance of the not far distant Arab influences, including the stimulating effect of the caravan routes close at hand (cf. the Dedanites, Is. 21¹³), although we may hesitate to see ** an actual Arabic idiom in עם שבי סוסיכם (4¹⁰), or to regard Tekoa †† as a great Arab-Israelitish literary centre, the Book of Job likewise having been written here, or to believe that the inhabitants of this general region, under the lead of the Jerahmeelites, were the occasion of all ancient Israelitish life and activity. ‡‡

There is nothing in 3⁷·⁸ to show, as Cheyne thinks, that Amos must have left Tekoa before receiving his call. Here, almost within sight of Jerusalem, in or near a village fortified at one time by Rehoboam (2 Ch. 11⁶), and celebrated for the visit paid to David (2 S. 14²ᶠᶠ·) by one of its wise women, which looked out upon a desolate, dreary, and savage world, in fact "an unmitigated wilderness," in an environment abounding in emptiness and stillness, was very naturally developed the being who was to possess, in fullest measure, the power of observation and reflection, the austere habits of the recluse, and the unpitying sharpness of the censor of his country's faults and vices. §§   No mention is made of a father, or of family.   Did he have no family record ?

---

* Meinhold, 63; cf. Marti, 150.

† Tekoa is about 2700 feet above sea level, while sycamores are never found in Palestine at a greater height than 1000 feet; cf. 1 K. 10²⁷ 1 Ch. 27²⁸; *v.* GAS. I. 77; Maspero, *Dawn of Civilization*, 26, 121; Post, *DB.* IV. 634 f.; M'Lean, *EB.* 4831 f.

‡ Cf. Marti, 146.   § *Gesch.* I. 403. || *EB.* 3888 f., and *CB.* II. 133 f.

¶ Che. *EB.* 148.   ** With We., and Che. *EB.* 148.

†† Stickel, *Hiob,* 269–77.   ‡‡ Che. *EB.* and *CB. passim.*   §§ GAS. I. 79–81.

2. But if this was the home of Amos, when and under what circumstances did he occupy it and do his work ? We may not accept (1) the view recently suggested * that the book is subsequent to the exile, later even than Joel; nor (2) its assignment to the date 744 or 745 B.C.,† on the ground that Assyria was inactive for twenty-five years previous to the accession of Tiglathpileser III. (745 B.C.); nor (3) the date indicated by Elhorst, viz. in the days of Josiah, 638–621.

Students of Amos are all but unanimous in agreeing that Amos delivered these sermons between 765 and 750 B.C. (p. 5). ‡ This view assumes the general accuracy of the statements made in chap. 7, and is in strict accord with the circumstances of this period as they are elsewhere found to exist. §

(a) The freedom of the people from anxiety on account of Assyria, and the vagueness of Amos in referring to Assyria ‖ (5^{27} 6^{14}) are both clear, when we note that during the reigns of Shalmaneser III. (783–773 B.C.), who was all the time engaged with the people of Urartu (i.e. Ararat), and Ašur-dan (772–755 B.C.), whose time was occupied principally in dealing with conspiracy and revolt at home, ample opportunity was afforded for the growth of Israel,¶ and the political situation was one which gave the people great confidence.

---

* Edward Day and Walter H. Chapin, AJSL. XVIII. 66–93. This argument is based on (1) the presence of many insertions generally acknowledged to be from a later hand, but these in nearly every case plainly interrupt the thought and fail to harmonize with the main portion, and this difficulty is not relieved by making the main portion also late; (2) the presence in the genuine Amos portions of many words and phrases which are "late," and yet words are called "late" by these authors which are found in the Song of Deborah (Ju. 5), or the Blessing of Jacob (Gn. 49); (3) the general post-exilic tone of these supposedly original parts, but since this same post-exilic tone is said to characterize all of Isaiah as well as Hosea, the whole question is begged. The vagueness of the utterances of Amos, here used as evidence against the early date, is precisely the strongest possible evidence for that date.

† Zeydner, ThSt., 1894, 59; Valeton, Amos und Hosea, 10; concerning this, Che. (EB. 150) is correct in saying that to any one not blinded by a fanatical religious belief this inactivity must have appeared temporary; and, moreover, if written after the events of 745 B.C., the predictions of destruction would have been fuller and more specific. Cf. Now., p. 121.

‡ So e.g. We., GAS., Now., Dr., Marti.

§ Dr. (p. 101), Che., Now., Marti.

‖ The word "Assyria" is not mentioned unless we read with ⑤BAQ אשור instead of אשרד (3^9).

¶ Within this period Assyria troubled Syria as follows: In 775, they came to (*b*) The religious situation is most intense. The keenest possible interest is taken in the cultus. The zeal of the worshippers attracts attention. The service is full and rich (4⁴ ᵇ· 5²¹⁻²³ 8¹⁴ 9¹). This is due, on the one hand, to the satisfaction with which the people regard the peace and prosperity they now enjoy since the wars with Syria have closed, and to the joy and gladness with which they hail the enlargement of the nation's territory; and on the other, to the anxiety aroused by earthquakes and pestilences (*v.i.*), the melancholy recollection of the treatment recently accorded them by the Syrians and Ammonites (1³· ¹³ 4⁶⁻¹¹), as well as the fear that, unless worshipped in this gorgeous fashion, Yahweh will bring back the troubles through which they have recently passed.

(*c*) The social situation is one in which the wealthy (and in these days of economic changes the number of the wealthy was large) are luxurious and given to debauchery (3¹² 5¹¹), cruel and oppressive (2⁶ ᶠ· 3¹⁰), the women taking their full share (4¹, cf. Is. 3¹⁶). Ivory houses (3¹⁵) and continual feasting (6⁴ ᶠᶠ·) furnish one picture; robbery, adultery, and murder (Ho. 4¹¹· ¹³ ᶠ· 7¹· ⁴ ᶠ·), another; while the lack of brotherliness and the prevalence of injustice (5⁷· ¹⁰· ¹² 6¹² 8⁴ ᶠ·) give still a third.

We cannot urge in favor of this date the interpretation of 6¹³ suggested by We. and adopted by Che. (*EB.* 149), that the people are rejoicing because of the capture of two cities in Gilead, Lo-debar and Karnaim (p. 156); but, at the same time, we do not find evidence against this date in 1⁵, because in 2 K. 16⁹ the fulfilment is represented as literally taking place; Kir here is probably an interpolation,* while Kir of 1⁵ was perhaps suggested by the tradition regarding Aram's origin (9⁷), no stress being placed upon the locality of the captivity.† Nor is a correct interpretation of 6² (p. 144) opposed to this date. The conquest of Gath by Uzziah (2 Ch. 26⁶; cf. 6² and the absence of any mention of Gath in 1⁶⁻⁸), the overthrow of Moab by Jehoshaphat (2 K. 3; cf. use of שפט rather than מלך in Am. 2³), as well as that of Aram (2 K. 14²⁸), seem to be presupposed.

Still further, notice may be taken of (*d*) the pestilences which prevailed in Assyria in 765 and 759 B.C., to which allusion, possibly, is made in 4¹⁰, although it is there styled "after the manner of Egypt"; (*e*) the solar eclipse referred to in 8⁹, assigned by the Assyrian eponym list to 763 B.C.; ‡ (*f*) the earthquake (1¹); this was the earthquake spoken of much later in Zc. 14⁴ (where the mention of it is possibly due to this superscription; cf. the statement of

---

Erini (*i.e.* Mt. Amanus, near the Gulf of Antioch); in 773, to Damascus; in 772, to Hadrach; in 765, again to Hadrach; in 755, a third time to Hadrach; in 754, to Arpad; and not again till 745. Syria, thus, was engaged with Assyria. Israel was let alone, and in consequence Jeroboam II. and Uzziah were enabled to build up their kingdoms to a higher point than ever before.

* So Benz., Kit., Oort, Che. (*EB.* 150); Kir is lacking in 𝔊.

† Che. *EB.* 150.

‡ Schra. *COT.* II. 193; Sayce, *TSBA.* III. 149; Marti, *EB.* 790.

Josephus, *Ant.* IX. 10, 4), and seemingly referred to in 4[11] as well as in 8[8] (not an interpolation, as We., Now., Elh., Che., maintain).* We cannot deny the occurrence of this earthquake, even though no other evidence for it is to be discovered. With the tradition thus substantiated, and with the recognition of the earthquake as a method of divine punishment found in 4[11] Is. 29[6], we may well accept the truth of the assertion, although, it is to be conceded, no help is gained from it for the more definite determination of Amos's date.

3. In the case of no other prophet is the question of occupation more interesting, since with this there stands closely connected the problem of Amos's preparation for his life-work. Four items require to be considered: (1) The prophet's own statement (7[14]) that he was not a prophet by profession, nor a member of one of the pre-prophetic societies. This implies that he does not wish to be reckoned as one of the *nebhi'im*, "the ecstatic enthusiasts," the crowd of diviners, who in recent years had come to have a definitely recognized professional position; and, besides that, since he is not one of them nominally, his work is characterized by a purpose and spirit different from theirs. What was this? I answer, that spirit of observation and recognition of general law, of philosophical insight and reasoning, which became the so-called wisdom-spirit when nationalism had passed away and the doctrine of individualism was beginning to assert itself. Amos, as it will be seen, is almost as much a sage as he is a prophet. He differs from the later sages in still being, like the *nebhi'im*, limited to a point of view which is largely national; but inside of his circle he exhibits the mood, the method, and the motive of the sage (*v.i.*). With this point in mind, it is easier to understand the other facts mentioned in the same passage (7[14]). (2) The prophet's real occupation was that of a "dresser of sycamores." This was a humble employment, and proves that Amos, like Micah, was one of the people. The evidence at hand does not clearly indicate whether he was really poor, or, perhaps, fairly well-to-do. Did he own a plantation of sycamores?† In any case he was independent

---

* Nothing could be more fanciful than G. Hoffmann's suggestion (*ZAW.* III. 123, approved by Che. *EB.* 149; Marti), that the remark in 1[1] is an inference of the editor, based upon the understanding that, according to 7[3.6] (cf. 7[8] 8[2]), Israel's punishment had been delayed twice, for a year each time.

† So Che. *EB.* 148.

enough to leave home. Or was he a dresser of sycamores in Northern Israel? and did he give up that occupation when driven out by Amaziah? This bears upon the place of his home as well as the character of his occupation (*v.i.*). It is immaterial whether Amos was a dresser or tender of the tree (p. 172), a collector and seller of the fruit,* or a pincher or scraper of the fruit, to insure a more rapid ripening.† We do not find in this occupation anything inconsistent ‡ with his Southern origin.

(3) The further statement that he was a shepherd, and had been taken by Yahweh from following the flock (cf. Elijah's call of Elisha), is entirely consistent with the preceding, inasmuch as a shepherd might in those days, as at the present time, cultivate fruit trees (the sycamore, although the poorest, was the most easily grown), for the purpose of varying the monotony of his milk diet.§ Since the word נקד (1¹) is not the ordinary word for shepherd (the word used in 𝔐𝕿 of 7¹⁴, בקר, being inconsistent with the following צאן, and so easily corrupted from נקד, is generally read נקד ‖), there is some doubt as to the exact idea meant to be conveyed; but, upon the whole, we may understand (*v.i.* on 1¹) that Amos was a wool-grower, that is, something more than a mere shepherd. As such, he would naturally make journeys from time to time, and meet men coming and going from all parts of the world as it was known in his day.¶

(4) While the language of Amos is rich in figurative speech drawn from many sides of life, nothing is more apparent than the influence exerted on his utterance by the life and occupation which he followed. This is seen, for example, in 2^{13} $3^{4\,f.\,12}$ $4^{1\,f.}$ $5^{11.\,17.\,19}$ 6^{12} $7^{1.\,4}$ 8^{1} 9^{3}. But the influence of his rustic life and humble occupation was not limited to the symbols and figures in which we find this thought expressed. The thought itself had birth in this same environment. The separation of the man from human companionship, and his consequent lack of human sym-

---

* G. E. Post, *DB*. IV. 634 f.   † GAS.

‡ So Oort and Grätz, on the ground that sycamores could not be cultivated so far above the sea as Tekoa is located (2700 feet) ; but it is easy to suppose that Amos, a nomadic shepherd, might have had opportunity at a place lower down, but within the general district of Tekoa, this name being applied to the whole territory down to the pasture-land on the shore of the Dead Sea.

§ GAS. I. 78.   ‖ *Contra*, GAS. I. 76.

¶ To such journeys "were probably due his opportunities of familiarity with Northern Israel, the originals of his vivid pictures of her town life, her commerce, and the worship at her great sanctuaries" (GAS. I. 79).

pathy, may account, at least in part, for the absence from his message (*v.i.*), as from that of Elijah, of anything that savors of tenderness or love. It is in the solitude of shepherd life that one gains most certainly the ability to concentrate attention even on the smallest details. Moreover, here it is that one most easily is "trained in that simple power of appreciating facts and causes which, applied to the great phenomena of the spirit and of history," constitutes the highest form of intellectual life.

4. The shepherd was taken by Yahweh from following the flocks, as Elisha was taken from following the oxen with the plough. But was there no call, definite and comprehensive, like those of Isaiah (chap. 6), Jeremiah (chap. 1), and Ezekiel (chap. 1)? And, in any case, where did this shepherd really obtain the intellectual preparation that justified the divine selection and is evidenced in his writings?

(1) We shall see that Amos is not an unlettered rustic, although many attempts, beginning with Jerome, have been made to prove him such. (*a*) There is nowhere to be found in the Old Testament an example of stronger or purer literary style. He is absolute master of the language which he uses. Where did he gain this mastery? (*b*) His knowledge of history and society is as marked as his literary style. He has seen things with his own eyes; his perception is as delicate as his human interest is broad. He knows of nations, but also, in each case, of the national character. He is an ethnologist, informing his auditors of the origin of nations, as well as an historian; a geographer, cognizant of the rise of the Nile, of the far distant Cush, and the equally distant Babylonia, as well as a sociologist. *V*. the Map of Amos and Hosea. (*c*) His conception of God and man and right (*v.i.*) is something that is thought to be marvellous. He is not credited with the ability to work miracles, as were his predecessors; but is he so detached from his environment, so abnormal in his attainments, so irregular in every way as to constitute in himself a real miracle? *

---

* We. (*Prol.* 472) says, "Amos was the founder of the purest type of a new phase of prophecy." Co. (*Proph.* 46) says, "Amos is one of the most marvellous and incomprehensible figures in the history of the human mind, the pioneer of a process of evolution from which a new epoch of humanity dates." WRS. (*Proph.* 120)

(2) He maintains for himself (7^{14}) that he was not called to his work by the usual technical methods, viz. through the prophetic societies. We do not understand, as many do,* that this statement indicates on the part of Amos an utter contempt for the order of *nebhi'im ;* because (*a*) elsewhere he speaks (2^{11} 3^7) of the *nabhi'* with great respect,† and in 7^{15} he is ordered to go as a prophet. (*b*) While he might feel as did Elijah and Elisha* toward the great mass of the *nebhi'im*, he was, after all, too much like Elijah and Micaiah ben Imlah in natural disposition, training, and theological position to do other than respect them and others like them. (*c*) He himself uses the technique of pre-prophetism, which had long years been taking form (p. cviii). (*d*) He stood by no means alone, preceded as he was by J and E, having Hosea as his contemporary, besides others whose names have not come down to us. Amos here ‡ merely emphasizes the fact that prophetism or ecstasy has not been *his* profession, and that, consequently, he is not to be identified with those who for so many generations have shown hostility to the government ; and further, that he should not be understood as uttering words such as he has spoken for the sake of reward or remuneration. He was, after all, in the line of the prophets, spiritually, if not literally.

(3) Reference has already been made to the superior discipline that gave him "desert-eyes," which, in a "desert-atmosphere," furnished the best possible training for an observer of human affairs, a student of cause and effect ; likewise, to the unsurpassed opportunities afforded him in the progress of travels, which were undertaken in connection with his occupation. (4) But, back of this, is the fact that in Eastern society superior culture is not uncommon in connection with the poverty of shepherd life. "At the courts of the Caliphs and their Emirs the rude Arabs of the desert were wont to appear without any feeling of awkwardness, and to surprise the courtiers by the finish of their impromptu verses, the fluent eloquence of their oratory, and the range of subjects on which they could speak with knowledge and discrimination. Among the Hebrews, as in the Arabian desert, knowledge and oratory were not affairs of professional education, or dependent for their cultivation on wealth and social status. The sum of book-learning was small; men of all ranks mingled with that Oriental freedom which is so foreign to our habits ; shrewd observation, a memory retentive of traditional lore, and the faculty of original reflection took the place of laborious study as the ground of acknowledged intellectual preëminence." §

---

calls Amos "the founder of a new type of prophecy." Marti says, "Amos is one of the most prominent landmarks in the history of religion." Che. (*EB.* 155) says, "The book of Amos forms a literary as well as a prophetic phenomenon."

* So *e.g.* Now. ; cf. Matthes, *Modern Review*, V, 421.

† Riedel, *SK.* 1903, p. 163 f., following 𝔊𝔖 and others (p. 171), uses the past tense, *I was no prophet*, etc., but, contrary to K. *DB.* V. 672, this does not make the case clearer.

‡ So Marti.   § WRS. *Proph.* 126.

(5) But are we quite certain that the more usual method of vision was not employed in the case of Amos? It is worthy of notice that in Amos, as well as in the latest prophets, the vision plays an important part. Is it not probable that the first visions, viz. those of the fire, locusts, and plummet, constituted, not only the beginning of Amos's work, but also, in large measure, his actual awakening and incitement to the task which he endeavored so faithfully to perform? * We cannot urge against this, that these initiatory visions are not recorded in the first chapter, for in Isaiah's case the call is found in chap. 6; and, further, we have no reason for expecting the sermons, in their written form, to be put in chronological order (*v.i.*).

(6) The antecedents of Amos's thought will be considered when we take up the substance of his message (*v.i.*); but we must, at this point, again touch upon the external facts connected with Amos's position in so far as they relate to the problem of his preparation; Amos must have had models. What were they? We may cite: (*a*) the prophets referred to by himself in $2^{11\,f.}$, and represented as of high repute; (*b*) Elijah and Elisha (*v.s.*); (*c*) the Judaean narrative and the Ephraimite narrative, in which, although mainly narratives, are contained many disconnected fragments of prophetic utterance; (*d*) the personal acquaintance with prophets or prophetic experience implied in 3^7; (*e*) the priestly literature which (Ho. 8^{12}) had already taken written form, a striking precedent for the prophet, cf. the decalogues and Book of the Covenant; (*f*) the prophetic formulas which, as employed by Amos, show long and technical usage, either written or handed down from mouth to mouth; † (*g*) the great poetical pieces which had come down from times that would have seemed ancient even to Amos, *e.g.* Ju. 5 Gn. 49 Dt. 33. This material, which Amos must have known, furnished the background or basis from which a literary style as perfect even as that exhibited by him might have been developed.

5. The character of Amos is quite plainly indicated in the facts already noted: (*a*) He was bold; but this boldness was that of indifference and reserve, rather than of passion. His courage had

---

* So Meinhold, 39; H. P. Smith, *O. T. Hist.* 211.   † Che. *EB.* 155 f.

its origin, not in enthusiasm, but in a certain kind of fatalism.
(*b*) He was accurate in his observations and scientific in his habits
of mind. He was able, not only to see the facts, but also to
describe them as they actually were. It was this that made it
possible for him to *write out* his utterances. This element in his
character contributed greatly to the new impulse given through
him to prophecy. This was the sage element. He recognizes
law. His sermons are the proclamation of divine law, not the
oracles of a soothsayer. He was more of a realist than an idealist.
He does not permit his fancy to picture the future. His utterance is a continuous, deadly monotone of ruin and destruction.
(*c*) He was nomadic in his instincts; like Elijah, hostile to the
softer influences of civilization; without the ties which bind
a man to country, and so without patriotism; without family
bonds, so far as we can ascertain, and so without much human
sympathy. To be sure, Northern Israel was to him a foreign
country; but we can imagine that his disposition toward Judah
would have been the same. (*d*) He was austere; but could such
a message as he was sent to deliver be other than austere? Hosea
announced the same doom in terms more terrible, but less severe.
His conception of God was that of the Puritan; his temperament,
stern and uncompromising. "Amos's nature was not a sensitive
or emotional one; it was not one in which the currents of feeling
ran deep : it was one which was instinct simply with a severe sense
of right."* He sat as judge, unmoved by the awful character of
the doom he was obliged to pronounce. In him justice does not
contend with love.† (*e*) In what sense was he spiritual? He
was not a devout man like Isaiah, nor was he, like Hosea, emotional. His spirituality, which was intense, consisted in loyalty to
truth and in antagonism to error, in recognizing the character of
Yahweh as spiritual, and as wholly inconsistent with that character
the round of ritualistic routine which, in his day, constituted
worship. The preacher who said, "Seek me and live," was a
preacher, not only of righteousness, but also of the truest
spirituality.

---

* Dr. III.   † *GAS.* I. 87 f.

§ 13. The Message of Amos.

Amos's message is in some respects the most important of any conveyed by an Old Testament writer. Great interest centres in and about this message, because (*a*) it is the first of a series of writings which stand alone in the world-literatures; (*b*) it places a stress upon the ethical side of religion greater than had before existed; (*c*) it marks a new epoch in the history of Israel's relations with the nations of the world — the Assyrian period.

1. The most general analysis of Amos's message discovers in it only two or three factors: (*a*) a profound conviction on certain subjects relating to God and human life; (*b*) a knowledge of certain facts in national and international history; (*c*) a conclusion, which follows the putting together of the conviction and the knowledge of the situation.*

The message of Amos must be obtained from words actually uttered or written by Amos himself. This involves the separation of insertions and additions coming from the pen of later prophets. Nearly one-fifth of the book which bears the name of Amos is thus to be set aside. It is to be conceded at once that the omission of these passages modifies very considerably the nature and content of the message. It is most important, however, in the interest of a true historical development of Israelitish thought, to restrict ourselves to those portions of the book the authenticity of which is incontrovertible. The other portions have just as important a place to occupy in the later literature.

2. The general circumstances under which the message of Amos was delivered have already been considered. It is necessary, however, to formulate more definitely the exact state of feeling and opinion against which the prophet felt compelled to array himself. We may call this the popular opinion; but it was more than this, for it represented, not only the mass of the people, but also the royal family and the court, the priests, and the vast majority of the prophets themselves.† What, precisely, was the consensus of thought to which the prophet made oppo-

* This has been well presented by GAS. I. 89.

† Just as pre-prophetism is not to be confounded with the true prophetism, so this latter must be kept distinct from what may be called popular prophetism. This is sometimes wrongly called false prophetism.

sition?* Or, in another form, What was the popular prophecy (or theology) from which true prophecy now separates itself as never before?

(1) The people held fast to the conception that Yahweh was *one* among other gods, invincible within the boundaries of his own land, and able to extend those boundaries against the power of other gods. He was no longer a deity whose residence lay outside of Canaan (*i.e.* at Sinai); for he had, with Israel, taken possession of the old sanctuaries in Canaan, and was now (especially since the rooting out of Baalism) in very truth the deity of the land. To be sure, he had, in idealistic fashion, been transferred to a residence in the heavens; and this had influenced somewhat the popular mind. Yet what was essentially *naturalism* controlled the life and thought of the masses.

(2) This involved the thought of Yahweh as exclusively interested in Israel, as satisfied, therefore, with a devotion which restricted itself to his worship. Service in the forms prescribed would secure the continued strength and existence of the nation. When "the day of Yahweh," thought to be not far distant, actually came, there would be relief from all difficulties, victory over all remaining foes. To think of Yahweh without Israel was absurd; for what could he do, how would he conduct himself, without his people? What would become of Yahweh if Israel were to perish? Whether this was on the basis of naturalism,† or on the ground of a voluntary act in the form of a covenant, ‡ it was none the less *nationalism*, and was accepted by the great body of prophets who had risen above what may have been the earlier and still more common belief in naturalism. But naturalism was itself a form of nationalism; the latter, consequently, included the former. The people, led by nearly all the leaders, interpreted the present period of peace and prosperity, growing out of the victories gained

---

* One might ask, Was Amos opposing an old order of things, or was he advocating something new? The answer is, He did both. The new idea, or the old idea which he emphasized, was definitely opposed to the existing current opinion. The presentation of it by Amos made it, for practical purposes, a new idea, although he clearly represented it as something not unknown even to the people.

† So *e.g.* We. *Prol.* 469; Sm. *Rel.* 116f., 119; Schwally, *Sem. Kriegsaltertümer*, I. 2.

‡ So *e.g.* Giesebrecht, *Die Geschichtlichkeit d. Sinaibundes;* K. *DB.* V. 631.

in the Syrian wars, as definite indication of Yahweh's pleasure and satisfaction. What more could he ask? Did he not himself share in this prosperity? Everything, as they viewed it, was in right condition.

(3) A corollary of nationalism (as well as of naturalism) was the belief that Yahweh was not only pleased to favor Israel, but also actually bound to protect their political interests, without reference to their moral conduct. He might show his anger for a time; but sooner or later, without reference to right or wrong, he must identify himself with those who were thus bound to him by the closest bond, whether that of nature or of covenant. To him was accorded no option in the matter. In other words, he could not act toward Israel on the basis of ethical consideration. The henotheism was non-moral, *i.e.* natural. The Israel of these times "neglected entirely his (Yahweh's) ethical character."

(4) A second corollary of nationalism was the feeling entertained concerning Yahweh's relation to other nations. It was his duty, in fact his highest function, to fight the battles of his people against their enemies; and his strength, compared with that of other deities, was measured by the success or failure of such battles. But, aside from this, Yahweh had nothing to do with outside nations, who, in each case, had their own gods. He is concerned with them *only* when they seek to injure Israel. For such injury he will use his best endeavor, in turn, to inflict injury upon them. He had thus shown his power against Egypt, in Canaan, and recently against Syria; but his relationship to these nations ceased when peace was declared. In any dealings, therefore, with other nations, Yahweh acts directly and exclusively for Israel. Israel is wholly his; he is wholly Israel's.

(5) It was, still further, the conviction of the people that Yahweh's favor was secured and his anger averted by following out, in its various forms, the ceremonial or cultus which prevailed at this period. The holding of festivals, the presentation of sacrifices, was something, on the one hand, indispensable to religion; and, on the other, altogether satisfying to the deity. What did he desire? Gifts, pilgrimages, and praises; since other things than these could hardly be expected. Yahweh demands these; nothing

more. The increasing costliness of these requirements promoted injustice and inhumanity.*

(6) The corollary of the preceding is contained in the words just used, "nothing more." The people understood that moral delinquencies (in so far, indeed, as they recognized the existence of any such) were entirely overlooked by Yahweh; provided, of course, they performed faithfully the routine of sacrifice. That they were not entirely ignorant of moral duties is clear, not only because certain moral distinctions were already known to all the world, but also because a code, largely moral in its character, had recently been formulated (p. lxiv). But notwithstanding their actual knowledge of right and wrong, at least in certain particulars, they did not believe that morality was a necessary factor in religion. It was, in fact, unnecessary, if the routine of worship was strictly observed. This conception was fundamental in the early Semitic religions,† and signified that moral defects were, upon the whole, comparatively unimportant. Perhaps the decalogue was not so clearly a moral code as we now regard it, or, if such, had not yet been taken as authoritative (p. lx ff.).

(7) Assyria was, of course, in the thought of the people; but they did not fear her. Why should they? Had not Yahweh given sufficient exhibition of his strength to warrant their supreme confidence in his ability? Egypt and Syria were equally interested with Israel and Judah in standing out against Assyria's claims. And Assyria, surely, could not overpower four nations thus closely interested in each other's protection. Besides, Assyria was often seriously engaged with revolts in other sections of " her huge and disorganized empire." ‡ In any case, Assyria did not uniformly sweep all before her. There was always a good chance of successful opposition. Were the prophets themselves so confident of Assyria's place and future success as to make unambiguous mention of her name in their predictions?

3. The convictions of Amos on the subjects mentioned above, whatever may have been their source, were radically different from those of the people at large. His training in the desert, his travels

---

* Che. *EB*. 156.

† GAS. I. 103. It is too much to say that it had never been challenged.

‡ Cf. GAS. I., chap. IV, " The Influence of Assyria on Prophecy."

to other countries, his acquaintance with the ideals of former generations, together with his appreciation of their ideals, his study of
Israelitish life, — these, combined with the qualities of mind and
heart bestowed upon him by an all-wise Providence, produced,
under the direction of that same Providence, certain convictions
which he was enabled to express in a form destined to influence
most vitally the whole trend of religious thought.

The thought of Amos is of two kinds : (1) Much is simply in direct antagonism with the prevailing thought. Knowledge of the popular feeling on this
or that subject means knowledge also of the position taken by Amos, since
the latter is the very opposite of the former. This, however, may not be
called negative, for there is always to be seen the larger, fuller teaching which
underlies. (2) Much, on the other hand, may be described as strongly
positive, *i.e.* as the statement or restatement of everlasting truth. Was this
the first statement, or only a restatement ? There were also some popular
beliefs, afterwards condemned, concerning which he does not speak (*v.i.*).

(1) The god of Amos was Yahweh of Hosts ($5^{13.14.27}$ $6^{8\,b.\,14\,b.}$) ; *
this included the hosts of heaven as well as of earth, nature, and
nations. One of his favorite expressions is " Lord Yahweh," †
which occurs fifteen times. To Amos, then, Yahweh was *all-
sovereign, omnipotent.*

(*a*) His power over nature is seen in his control of rain, mildew, locusts, and pestilence (4^{6-11}), as well as in the melting or
quaking of the earth, ‡ and in the rising and falling of the Nile
($8^8\,9^5$) ; and in history it is manifested, not only in bringing Israel
out of Egypt (9^7), but in bringing the Syrians from Kir, and the
Philistines from Caphtor (1^5), and in the direction of the destiny
which he assumes in the case of Philistia (1^{6-8}), Ammon (1^{13-15}),
and Moab (2^{1-3}) ; and further, it reaches even to heaven and Sheol,
along with Carmel and the bottom of the sea ($9^{2.\,3}$), — all this, in
addition to the management of Israel's own affairs, both spiritual
and material. We may not forget, however, that the nations
referred to in these statements are those near at hand (this power
is not *said* to be universal) ; that to the gods of other nations
their worshippers attributed the same powers ; that both J and E

---

* On interpretation of the phrase, *v.* p. lxxxix.
† Cf. Che. *EB*. 156 f.
‡ Other passages quoted (*e.g.* by Dr.) in illustration of this idea are late (*v.i.*).

had localized Yahweh in heaven before Amos spoke ; that criticism
has pronounced as late the passages of clearest import (*v.i.*) ; and
finally, that in Amos, so far as we can discover, Yahweh has personal intercourse only with Israel, and that, too, with Israel as a
nation.*

(*b*) This suggests the question whether we have here real
monotheism.† If Amos anywhere denied the existence of all
other gods, the case would be clear. But where is there such a
denial ? The intermediate step between the conception entertained by Israel and the later conception of monotheism was that
of unlimited power. This in itself did not entirely shut out the
idea that there were other gods. It is better, therefore, to understand that it is "a belief in the unqualified superiority of Yahweh
so absolute as to be practically a belief in his omnipotence," ‡ or
in other words, ethical monotheism not strictly, but " to all intents
and purposes." §

(*c*) But what relation would these other gods sustain to Yahweh,
now that he possessed this unlimited power ? If Yahweh brought
the Philistines from Caphtor and the Syrians from Kir (as, indeed,
he did bring Israel from Egypt), he must have acted in a way
contrary to the will of the gods of those countries, for no god
would willingly permit his people to be broken away from him.
These and other like heathen gods are, therefore, inferior and
subject to Yahweh. "They may for a time presumptuously
imagine themselves to have independent power, but in reality
they only carry out the will and commands of Yahweh " ‖ (cf.
Is. $10^{5\,\text{ff.}}$). Yahweh, then, is a God who in earlier times defeated
the gods of Egypt, Philistia, Canaan ; in more recent times, he
has overthrown the Phoenician Baal and the Syrians. It is easy
to see how the history of the past and the work of Elijah and
Elisha helped Amos to this point of view.

(*d*) What is to be said of the anthropomorphisms employed
in Amos, *e.g.* Yahweh as an armed warrior against Jeroboam's
house (7^9) ; the change of purpose due to pity for his people

---

* Duhm, *Theol.* 121 f.

† So Taylor, *DB.* I. 86; Dr. 106 ff.; Da. *O. T. Theol.* 65; Kö. *Hauptprobleme*,
chap. VI.

‡ Bu. *Rel.* 123.   § Che. *EB.* 157.   ‖ Bu. *Rel.* 124.

(7^3) ; the phrases " turn my hand " (1^8), " will not smell " (5^{21}), " eyes of the Lord Yahweh " (9^{8a}) ; the representation of Yahweh as taking an oath (4^2 6^{8a} 8^7) ; and the appearance of Yahweh in the visions ($7^{1.4.7}$ 8^1 9^1) ? These are not evidences of crude religious thought, but, like similar expressions in our own religious language,* arise from the difficulty which is inherent in any effort to represent the personality of deity. There is in this language no survival of the former naïve belief that Yahweh had the form of a human body. " A clear formula for the notion of bare spirituality such as we find in John 4^{24} was beyond the reach of the Old Testament." †

(*e*) But did Amos pass by the image-worship, so large a factor in his day, without remonstrance ? We know that no objection was made to the use of images in early times (even Ex. 34^{17}, the older decalogue, objecting only to molten images of metal),‡ and testimony to their use is found in the ephod, the presence in connection with the ark (Nu. 10^{35b}), and the teraphim (*v.i.*). It is in the later decalogue that we have the first prohibition (*v.s.*). Hosea (8^{4-6} 10^5 13^2) enters protest against image-worship. But does Amos ? Not in 2^4 (*their lies = their idols*), for this is unquestionably late ; nor in 8^{14}, since the text is wholly unsatisfactory (pp. 181, 184). § Elsewhere there is nothing to indicate his feeling on this point ; but we are by no means certain that he approved them.

(*f*) It remains to notice Marti's interesting statement on the relation of Amos's monotheism to that of other nations. He says : " No one can fail to observe how, in this belief of Amos, monotheism is present in essence, even if not in name, and what an altogether different kind of monotheism it is from that to which the priests in Babylon and Egypt are said to have attained ! There in Babylon and Egypt a monotheistic speculation, which possesses no force and is wholly indifferent toward the polytheism of the mass, whose gods this theory allegorizes and dissolves in a general conception ; here among the prophets in Israel a vigorous and vital faith in Yahweh, who suffers no gods alongside of himself, who watches jealously over

---

* Cf. Duhm's remark (*Theol.* 120 f.) to the effect that this does not indicate the nature religion, since nature religions do not *anthropo*-morphize ; they rather *physio*-morphize, since the physical is the common ground upon which deity and humanity meet and become like each other. Our metaphysical abstractions concerning the nature of God and the relations of God and Christ, their personality, etc., are much nearer physiomorphism than Amos's anthropomorphism.

† K. *DB.* V. 679.

‡ K. *DB.* V. 627; *contra* Kö. *ZKW.*, 1886, Heft 5, 6.

§ Cf. also Che. *EB.* 157; WRS. *Proph.* 175 f.; *contra* Da. *Biblical and Literary Essays*, 120 f. (reprinted from *Exp.*, 1887).

his own exclusive worship, and directs the destinies of men as the only God. A relationship and dependence between the monotheism in Babylon and that in the Bible does not exist ; their radically different origin is the basis of the difference. In Egypt and Babylon monotheism is theory ; in Israel, strength and life ; there it is the product of a speculating abstraction, won through a fusion of the gods ; here the experience of a higher Being, the inner realization of his moral and spiritual might, grown from a moral and religious deepening, from an intimate union with a special God who, moreover, does not disappear and dissolve, but remains the living one, and proves himself the only living one. There the empty concept of monotheism ; here, indeed, though the word (viz., monotheism) is not yet coined, the fulness of power and life which must indwell this faith, where it is a true faith. How vividly, however, Yahweh was experienced as power by Amos is shown by 3^{4-8}, perhaps, notwithstanding its simplicity, the most magnificent portion of his prophecy : not merely is God an hypothesis of the intellect, but the perception of him is a result of the announcement of God himself."

(2) Yahweh is never called " God of Israel " (*v.i.*) in Amos. He is, rather, the God of the world ; and yet he represents him (in common with all that precede) as sustaining a peculiar relation to Israel, and puts in his mouth the phrase, " my people " (7^{15}). This relation is not indissoluble ; it is, on the contrary, plainly conditioned, and will surely be annulled if the conditions are not complied with. (*a*) Amos does not grapple with the question, why Israel, rather than some other nation, was selected by Yahweh for this special relationship. It is evident that a deity so powerful among the nations as was Yahweh could have taken any other nation, *e.g.* the Philistines, whom he actually did bring from Caphtor, or the Syrians, who were removed from Kir. But (*b*) accepting this as a fact, he tells his contemporaries (3^2) that on this very account (viz. that Yahweh knew Israel out of all the nations of the earth) he would judge them all the more strictly for the sins which they had committed. " Obligation is the complement of privilege ; punishment, of sin." * Moreover (*c*), his interest is not in the world for Israel's sake, but rather in Israel for the world's sake. Israel, after all, is no more to him than are the Cushites (9^7). (*d*) If Israel will only seek him, the future will be safe (4^{14}) ; but the prophet has given up all hope that Israel, devoted as she now is to the sweet religion of the crowd, will ever do what he suggests (*v.i.*).

(3) The conception of Yahweh which Amos entertains is that

---

* Bu. *Rel.* 134.

of a god of justice. This thought Elijah (1 K. 21¹⁸ ᶠᶠ·) had already expressed, but Amos goes farther and makes the idea the very centre of his conception of God.* He is all the better able to reach this high point, because he has also conceived of Yahweh as standing in close relation to all nations. Yahweh's power being universal, it is necessarily impartial and consequently ethical. On the other hand, if Yahweh is ethical, he cannot be a national god, that is, show favor to Israel; he must be a world-god. Righteousness being a vital element in Yahweh's character, he not only will demand it in those who profess to be his followers, but also will enforce the demand. He cannot, however, have one standard for the nations and a lower standard for Israel. If, for any reason, Israel has enjoyed special privileges, the standard by which she shall be judged is to be placed all the higher. Two points, however, require notice, both pointed out by Duhm,† viz. (*a*) Amos has no adequate conception of sin; to him the life of man and God should naturally express itself in *good*. This good is an objective matter, something regarded as present, while all departures from it arouse the anger of Yahweh. Everything is regarded concretely, and at the same time negatively (*v.i.*). (*b*) There is no glimmer of a purpose on the part of Yahweh in the working out of this idea of righteousness, and " the ethical, apart from the teleological, remains unfruitful."

(4) Yahweh's relation to the outside nations follows closely upon the idea, already indicated, of Israel's relation to Yahweh. In fact, it precedes. To have unlimited power is to control the world. This includes Assyria, as well as the nations living in closer proximity to Israel. Egypt had already felt the power of Yahweh's hand. So had Canaan in days past, and Syria more recently. Does Yahweh's righteousness make demands of all these nations? Is it for lack of proper treatment of his nation Israel

---

* Cf. Gn. 18²⁵; but this lofty utterance can hardly have preceded Amos. We. (*Hex.* 27 f.) treats 18²²ᵇ⁻³³ᵃ as a late addition to JE; Kue. assigns it to J²; Di. argues for its retention in J (so Dr.); Co. declares it to be "theologically about a century later than J"; Bacon, Holzinger, and Gunkel also consider it a late expansion; while Carpenter and Battersby (*The Hexateuch*, II. 26) say that it "seems to belong to the group of probable additions in which the universal grandeur and sole sovereignty of Yahweh are again and again asserted in the most emphatic terms," *e.g.* Ex. 8¹⁰. ²²ᵇ 9¹⁴⁻¹⁶. ²⁹ᵇ.   † *Theol.* 120 ff.

that he will punish them? or because of their idolatry? No; but
in each case is cited, as the direct occasion of the doom, the violation of some dictate of universal morality, some principle of
the natural laws of humanity and mercy.* This is no narrow
point of view.

(5) It follows, still further, that Yahweh, in the opinion of
Amos, cannot be affected even by the strictest observance of
the ceremonial. In Yahweh's eyes, such observance is itself
transgression (פשע, 4^4). Israel's pilgrimages he hates; he despises
their feasts, their offerings he will not accept; their songs of
praise he will not hear (5^{21-25}). But this is not all. He stands
ready to destroy the nation's places of worship (3^{14} 5^5 7^9), and
to pursue to the bitter end those who worship at these places
(9^{1-4}). What does Amos (pp. 129–136) really mean? Does
he, perhaps, say more than he means? We must guard against
attributing to him what he never said. This is done by those
(p. 136) who wrongly interpret 5^{25} as suggesting that in the
days of the wilderness no sacrifices were offered.† What is it,
now, that Amos denounces? To have opposed sacrifice in itself
would have meant opposition to the only method yet known
to humanity of entering into communion with deity, in a word,
the abolition of all tangible worship. If the Old Testament,
even when its day was finished, had no true formulation for the
conception of God as a spirit, how shall we look for practically
this same thing in the days of Amos? It was, therefore, not sacrifice in general that Amos opposed; ‡ nor was it the belief that
sacrifice when duly performed can change the mind of Yahweh.
It was, rather, the belief that had become fixed, "a strange delu-
sion deeply rooted in Israel's heart," that the ritual *of itself* does
or can satisfy an ethical deity. Shall one observe the ritual?
Yes; but one may not stop there.

(6) Yahweh, then, has something to demand besides worship,

---

* WRS. *Proph.* 134.

† A prophet who has nothing to say against the use of images will surely not go
so far as to object altogether to sacrifice. Moreover, neither Amos nor any other
Israelite, preceding the exile, could have dreamed of a period in Israel's history
when no sacrifices were to be offered. This would actually have involved a purely
vegetarian diet.

‡ *Contra* Ew., Hi., We., Mit., Dr., Now., GAS.; Che. *EB.* 158; Marti, *et al.*

which has hitherto been understood to constitute the whole of religion. This grows out of Yahweh's ethical character, and is, in fact, an ethical demand (2^{6-8} 3^{10} 4^1 $5^{7.\ 10-15.\ 24}$ $6^{1-6.\ 12}$ $8^{4\,f.}$). It is a demand for justice, which, in its simplest and most natural form, includes honesty, integrity, purity, and humanity.* (*a*) This, it will be noted, is concrete, and includes the elementary duties of life, such as are recognized by all nations who have risen to the point of governmental organization.† (*b*) It is only this which Yahweh demands of other nations. (*c*) The demand does not necessarily depend upon a code of legislation; in other words, it is not legal justice. (*d*) It demands the utmost consideration of the poor and weak,—*moral* justice. (*e*) The prophet promises life and prosperity (5^4) to those who meet this demand, while all disaster is due to the wrath of Yahweh against those who fall short of this requirement (3^6). ‡

(7) This brings us to the prophet's position, touching the nation's future, including his conception of the "Day of Yahweh." Israel, in very truth, must suffer punishment; and the punishment, since everything else has been tried, will now be utter demolition. This is really the great thought of the message. Everything else is connected with this sentence. It is important (cf. Duhm), because no one had ever even dreamed of such a thing for the nation, and also because the overthrow contemplated was in no sense the plan of a party, nor had it anything of a political character. It is expressed many times and in many forms, always terrible and always irrevocable. § It is the unmistakable expression of the condemnation of wicked Israel by the absolutely righteous Yahweh. The sentence of destruction, however, is not wholly unconditional. That Amos pointed out a way of escape, viz. repentance, open perhaps only to a few, is clear from $4^{4.\ 6}$ $5^{14\,f.}$; that he should not have contemplated such a possibility of conversion is psychologically unintelligible, since it would leave his entire prophetic activity without a sufficient *raison d'être*. But whatever expectation he may have had at the opening of his ministry, it is practically certain that in the progress of his ministry all hope deserted him as he saw the utter lack of response to his message.

---

* Dr., p. 109.   † Duhm, *Theol.* 116.   ‡ Cf. Dr., p. 112.
§ Cf. K. *DB.* V. 691 f.; WRS. *Proph.* 129 ff.; Dr., pp. 108 ff.

We cannot prove that Amos saw in the future a brighter picture in case of repentance (9^{8-15} being surely of a later date) ; nor are we even reasonably certain that, being from Judah, he had it in his mind that Yahweh's true religion would be continued and developed by Judah after the destruction of Israel. The motto (1^2) would express this idea, if only it were from Amos's hand, but cf. pp. 9 f. On Amos's conception of the Day of Yahweh, *v.* pp. 131 f.

4. Did Amos and those who immediately followed him *create* Israelitish ethical monotheism ? Or can it be shown that, so far as essential content is concerned, Amos's teachings are rooted in the past ?

(1) The answer determines, not only the place of prophecy in the progress of the Old Testament development, but also the whole course of that development. If Amos had little or nothing before him in the way of antecedents, he is to be assigned the place ordinarily given to Moses as the founder of the religion. No one, certainly, in these days is disposed to minimize the high place which he has come to occupy, but we may fairly ask ourselves whether the emphasis has always been placed upon just the right point.

It is now clear that the Old Testament history, like other histories, was an evolution. Every period of great activity *grew out of* something that preceded. Was the wonderful movement which found expression through Amos, Hosea, and Isaiah entirely exceptional, in that it came forth without antecedents ? So some would have us believe.* This, at all events, is the real position of those who use the phrase " creators of ethical monotheism." It has been observed that Amos himself makes no direct appeal to something earlier than his own work. For example, he does not openly refer to a preëxisting code of laws as the basis of his system, any more than to miracles or institutions. But does this prove that his ideas are not rooted in the past, and that his work and that of his times are not merely the fruitage of seed sown long before ? †

(2) We cannot deny that the morality which forms the essence

---

* Cf. We. *Prol.* 472 ff.; Co. *Proph.* 45 f.; Sm. *Rel.* 184 ff.; GAS. I. 96.
† Cf. GAS. I. 92.

of his thought is, when closely analyzed, fundamental; but it is also simple and of long standing. The demands made for justice, including honesty, humanity, etc., go back to the earliest days of history. He surely did not discover or invent them. These are ideas that have appealed to men of all nations for all centuries. Are they not the basis on which rests the prophet's condemnation of the neighboring nations? Yet nothing more is asked of Israel than of them. But this is not all. Amos represents Israel as knowing these things, failing to do them, and, therefore, as deserving of punishment. Neither Israel nor the other nations would have merited destruction for failing to observe conditions or commands of which they were totally ignorant. "To neither man nor people can the righteousness which Amos preached appear as a discovery, but always as a recollection and a remorse." * Is this representation of Amos, then, an anachronism, or, perhaps, a piece of beautiful rhetoric, or, in plain words, a misrepresentation? But those who call it an anachronism give it the highest place of value. This does not seem consistent. Moreover, if we recall that Amos resided within sight of Jerusalem and, being the kind of man he was, must, therefore, have been in intimate relationship with much of the spirit as well as of the material of the nation's past experiences, it is fair to suppose on *a priori* grounds that Amos drew largely upon the accumulations of this already celebrated past. But we need not rest the case on an argument of this character.

(3) Amos actually shows a knowledge of the past history of Israel, and expresses this knowledge in a manner which indicates a supposition of knowledge on the part of the people; cf. his references to the exodus and the conquest ($2^{9\,f.}\,3^1\,5^{25}\,9^7$), to the religious history of his people ($2^{11f.}$), to the series of past chastisements inflicted by Yahweh (4^{6-11}), and his allusion to David (6^5).† Israel's ethics, in so far as they had yet developed, rested on the choice made of Yahweh, and the character of Yahweh (*v.i.*) as shown in history. Knowledge of history meant also acquaintance and familiarity, on the part of those who were at all intelligent, with this basis (*v.s.*).

---

* GAS. I. 98.   † Cf. Dr., pp. 113 f.

Moreover, the terminology of prophecy employed by Amos is the product of generations of prophetic activity.* Cf. his frequent use of the established formulas כה אמר יהוה ($1^{3.\ 6.\ 13}$ $2^{1.\ 6}$ $3^{11.\ 12}$ $5^{3.\ 4.\ 16.\ 17.\ 27}$ 7^{17}) and נאם יהוה (2^{11} 3^{10} $4^{5.\ 6.\ 8b.\ 9.\ 10.\ 11}$ $6^{8.\ 14}$ 8^{3} 9^{7}), and of the strongly prophetic title יהוה צבאות ; his employment of the vision as an impressive method of communicating Yahweh's message to Israel; and his recognition of the dirge as a most appropriate vehicle for his message of doom ($5^{1\ \mathrm{ff.}}$).

(4) We may be still more specific and note that in 2^{9-11} reference is made to "consecrated personalities," for whom a keen appreciation was manifested. Who were they? Not only Elijah and Elisha, but also J and E; and how many more of whom we now have no record! These make up the great pre-prophetic movement which we have already tried briefly to describe (§§ 1–11).

(5) That Amos knew written documents, such as the decalogues and the Book of the Covenant, is certain. But this is not all; for (*a*) national songs had already come into existence, which prepared the way, technically as well as spiritually, for his work, — among them may reasonably be included Ju. 5,† Deborah's song; Ex. 15 ‡ (in its earliest form), the song of the Red Sea; Gn. 49, § the tribal blessing, as well as Dt. 32 (?) ‖ and 33 ¶; and besides these (*b*) there were ancient proverbs and folk-lore. Some of these were already incorporated in J and E, *e.g.* Gn. 26^{23} $27^{27\ b.\ 28.\ 29.\ 39.\ 40}$;

---

* Cf. Kue. *Rel.* I. 207; Che. *EB.* 155.

† G. F. Moore calls this "the oldest extant monument of Hebrew literature"; so practically all recent interpreters.

‡ Carpenter and Battersby incline to a post-exilic date; so Holzinger; Baentsch declares it later than J and E, and perhaps later than JE. A genuine Mosaic kernel is discovered in it by Ew., De., Di., Strack, Dr.

§ Kö., Wildeboer, and Dr. (*Genesis*, 380), assign this to "the age of the Judges, or a little later"; Di., Carpenter and Battersby, and Gunkel place it in the Davidic period; Sta. (*GVI.* I. 150) locates it in Ahab's reign; Holzinger decides upon some time during the Syrian wars prior to the age of Jeroboam II.

‖ Placed about 780 B.C., by Knobel, Schra. (*Einl.* § 205^h), Di., Oettli, *et al.*; assigned by Ew., Kamphausen, and Reuss, to the period just before 722 B.C.; by Dr., to the age of Jeremiah and Ezekiel; by Co., Steuernagel, Bertholet, and Carpenter and Battersby, to the end of the exile.

¶ Dr., Schra. (*Einl.* § 204), Di., place this in the reign of Jeroboam I.; Graf, Bleek, Kue. (*Hex.* § 13, note 16), Sta. (*GVI.* I. 150 ff.), Co., Baudissin (*Priesterthum*, 74 f., 266), Steuernagel, Wildeboer, Bertholet, and Carpenter and Battersby put it about 780 B.C.

some, likewise, have probably been preserved in the collections of
Proverbs, although it is, of course, impossible at this date to distinguish them ; some, indeed, Amos himself preserves, for not a
little of the literary strength of his writings is due to his familiarity,
not only with history and sociology, but as well with folk-lore and
the speech and thought of the common people.

§ 14. THE MINISTRY OF AMOS.

With this summary of the work before us, we may consider the
external form of Amos's work, his ministry. If his teaching
forms an important part in the history of prophecy, his ministry
should be expected to contribute largely to the history of
prophetism. If Amos himself is responsible for the book which
bears his name (either in the present form or in an earlier form
of which the present is an edition enlarged and modified by
a later prophet), the literary work is a part of his ministry. This,
however, deserves separate and special consideration (p. cxxx ff.).
The historical background of the work, as well as the prophet's
personal life and the preparation for his ministry, have been
considered in § 12.

1. It is unfair to Amos either to regard the story of the man
of Judah (1 K. 13) as a distorted account of his ministry,[*] or
to accept the suggestion that the story of his ministry, like the
story of Jonah (in the book of Jonah), is a later invention or
fiction.[†] When we recall (a) that no miracle or wonder-story
is connected with his work, either directly or indirectly ; (b) that
no ecstatic frenzy is in any way suggested ; and (c) that, on the
other hand, all connection with that kind of thing is strongly
denied (7^{14}), we may at once concede that one has entered upon
his ministry who is a prophet in a new sense, at least in so far
as the external work is concerned. He receives visions, to be
sure ; but these are no ecstatic trances, for which music was
needed, as in Elisha's case. They are rather like the visions
of Isaiah and Jeremiah, manifestations of a lofty and sublime

---

[*] So We. in Bleek's *Einl.*[4] 244; Klostermann, *Samuel und Könige*, 349; Che.
EB. 148; Benz. *Könige*, 91.

[†] Cf. Day and Chapin, *AJSL.* XVIII. 66–93; Che. *EB.* 3864 f. ; Elh.

character, made not in dream, nor in trance, but through spiritual
enlightenment; dealing not with this battle or that promotion
to the throne, but with the fundamental truth of God. However,
we are surely able to see in these visions, not only the lineal
successors of the trance, but also an indication, if we note their
number and character, of the practical adoption by the new
order of the machinery of the old. If, however, Amos follows
closely the old style in receiving his message by vision (although
of a more elevated character),* he exhibits a more striking difference in the method of presentation. It is true that in many
cases we still have what seem to be only brief *oracles* or *texts*,
that is, fragmentary utterances. Even these differ from those
of older prophets, "which offered a hard and fast decision of the
moment for the moment"; † since in many cases they have now
taken on the form of sermons, and in all cases they present teaching concerning Yahweh's nature and his purposes for Israel. On
the public preaching of the prophet, as distinguished from the
writing of his sermons, *v.i.*

2. A most significant factor in the ministry of Amos is the
writing down of his sermons. In this service he is, perhaps, the
leader. ‡ The adoption of the new method, viz. that of writing,
was the outcome of certain factors in the situation, and itself the
occasion of certain others.

(1) It is to be remembered that in this century Israel was, for
the first time, enjoying the privileges of civilization. Many forces
are set in motion in a nation when it rises into this stage of life,
among others that of literature. § There was not only an incentive
to writing, but the opportunity for it, as provided in the long peace
of Jeroboam's reign. ‖ Torah-literature had already taken form
(Ho. 8¹²) in the laws that had been codified. Prophetic literature
also had come into existence in the form of the great epics of old

---

* We cannot suppose that these visions were used only as a method of presenting
the prophetic thought to the people. Here, as in Isaiah and Jeremiah, we have
survivals of the old trance, as the state in which the prophet received the message.
Cf. K. *DB.* V. 676.   † Bu. *Rel.* 133.

‡ The only rival for the honor is the author of Is. 15 and 16; but these chapters
are probably later; so Schwally, *ZAW.* VIII. 207 ff.; Duhm; Che. *Introduction,
etc., in loc.;* Marti. For an early date *v.* WRS. *Proph.* 91 f., 392; Di., GAS.; and
Dr. *LOT.* 215 f.   § Sta. *GVI.* I. 556; Kit. *Hist.* II. 315 f.   ‖ GAS. I. 35.

Israel, which J and E had taken pains to put together. Amos, after all, is not showing much originality in taking up the pen, for he is only following those who have already shown him the way.

(2) Then, too, certain changes had come about which led inevitably to this step. Israel's religion had passed upward to an entirely new position. It was no longer a matter of *worship*, *i.e.* ritual. It stood for certain new ideas, which could not be expressed in an institution, but must find for themselves a written record.* The prophetic utterance was no longer a temporary matter, uttered for a special time or set of circumstances; it had become something of eternal value, having to do with truth concerning vital subjects. Moreover, the prophet himself has taken on new functions and new responsibilities. He sees more clearly his position as it bears upon human affairs in general, and not merely the affairs of a single nation, nor of a certain time.

(3) The earlier prophets were men who sought to exert "an instantaneous influence." It was their business to act, as did Elijah, rather than to speak. And, then, it was a matter of supreme moment that now the prophet is expected to give a message with which the people will be displeased. He will no longer be the leader of the masses. His work will be outwardly a failure. His very ill success in reaching the hearts of the people actually forces him to put his words in writing.†

(4) In order that there may be secured permanent influence, the prophets' words must be read and studied. This, and this only, will bring a continuous development of Israel's religion, and a deepening of it in the hearts of the people. But to obtain this the prophet need not write out his words just as he had spoken them. He may give only the text of his address, or, possibly, a synopsis of it. The written form may omit much that had only local application. Nor did the writer himself always put his prophetic speeches into written form. This may have been left to a band of disciples such as history tells us Isaiah had (Is. 8^{16}), men who desired to see the words of the master justified as only time could justify them (cf. Dt. 18^{20-22} Je. $28^{8.9}$).

Amos was first among the prophets to appreciate all this.

---

* Kue. *Rel.* I. 209.   † WRS. *OTJC.*[1] 295 f.; Bu. *Rel.* 131.

Although he probably expected the end of Israel to come within his own generation, he saw the advantage of giving his thought a definite place. He may also have had in mind the possibility of transmitting it thus through disciples.

3. In his political activity, likewise, Amos exhibits variation from the older type of prophet. (1) The difference, however, is one, not in fact, but in method. He is as greatly interested in the national life as was Elijah or Elisha, but he makes no use of political influence. He himself is not an official of the government (as were Samuel and Elisha), just as he was not an official prophet. He sustained no special relation to the king, as did Nathan or Micaiah. He was only a private citizen. His interest in affairs was intense, but he established no organization to execute his mission. He does only one thing, *preach*.

(2) His political views (*v.s.*) concerning the nations near at hand he announces with consummate skill (p. 12), the method chosen being one which brings him into sympathetic touch with the Israelites themselves.*

(3) But his political sagacity is displayed most keenly in his interpretation of Assyria's relation to the world of that day, including Israel, and the use made of this interpretation. His mind was not at first clear in reference to the fall of Samaria, but certainly grows more definite with the progress of the visions.

4. The chronological order of the various stages in the ministry of Amos is uncertain, and its determination will rest upon our final decision as to the structure of the book itself (p. cxxx ff.). The following is suggested as a possible hypothesis : —

(1) In connection with his early shepherd life in Tekoa, he visits many points of interest at home and abroad ; and in the course of these visits learns, as an outsider might learn, the methods and work of the *nebhi'im* (3^7).† This was only a part of that information concerning the world at large which he obtained in these earlier years.

---

* Such is the interpretation placed by many scholars upon the arrangement of the first two chapters, *e.g.* We. on Am. 2^{14} ff.; Mit., Dr., Now., Marti.

† Che. (*EB.* 157) says, "Which (*i.e.* 3^7) Amos could hardly have written, unless he had had the most vivid and ocular evidence of the effects of a true prophetic impulse even before his own turn came to receive one."

(2) A time came when in visions given him, like those which he had seen others have (*v.s.*), a definite call to preach was received.* This call grew out of the message contained in the vision of the plumb-line, viz., the irrevocable destruction of Israel. In the two visions which precede, although he saw the doom threatened, he believed it might be averted; but gradually he becomes convinced that Assyria is the source of the danger (6^{14} 7^{17}), and that ruin is inevitable unless something extraordinary shall avert the catastrophe. He goes to Northern Israel, amazed that every one does not, like himself, foresee the coming disaster.†

(3) Having reached his destination, the work is opened by the proclamation, with diplomatic skill, of one oracle after another concerning Israel's neighbors. ‡ These may have been uttered on successive days, but, in all probability, were spread over weeks and months. When the proper time has arrived, to Israel (2^{6-16}) itself is announced the dreadful future with the reasons therefor. In the course of his wanderings he arrives at Bethel. The climax is reached in the sermon of chap. 6, in which captivity is threatened.

(4) This is probably followed by a popular interruption of his work. In any case, demand is made for his authority to utter such pessimistic denunciations, and to announce what really amounts to treason. § In justification of his words, he tells the story of his call, as it came in the visions of locusts, fire, and plumb-line. This closes with a specific threat against Jeroboam the king. ‖

---

* These (ecstatic) visions (1) connect Amos closely with the work of the *nebhi'im* ; (2) are not satisfactorily explained as being merely the vehicle of the prophet's publication of his message (cf. p. cxxv, and K. *DB.* V. 676 *a*) ; (3) are presented *after* the oracles and sermons (1–6), as the justification of the prophet's mission (cf. Is. 6), and form the continuation of his work after Amaziah's interruption.   † This (p. 74) is the proper interpretation of 3^7.

‡ The resemblance of these utterances to the short oracles of the *nebhi'im* cannot be overlooked. Their pleasing character would surely commend the prophet to his auditors. One cannot imagine Cheyne's reasons (*EB.* 154) for suggesting that these oracles could not have been spoken.

§ This seems to be a reasonable inference in view of the necessity of explaining the present position of the visions, for only in some such way as this can one account for hope contained in the first and second, when the most absolute statement of destruction has just been uttered in 6^{14}.

‖ The third vision indicates the position which Amos had held since coming to Northern Israel.

(5) Then follows the official attack by Amaziah, and the prophet's explanation of his work, with a scathing rebuke of the priest for his interference.* Whatever the plans for the future may be, he continues for a while the work which he had come North to perform.†

(6) Another vision (the fourth) is received revealing *Israel as ripe for destruction,* with an arraignment of the accused, a threat of earthquake and slaughter, followed by universal mourning, Yahweh's abandonment of his people, despair and destruction. A little later comes the fifth and last vision, *the downfall of the sanctuary,* with a picture of ruin which none may escape, and an assurance that the destruction will be complete.

(7) The prophet goes back to Judah, perhaps to Jerusalem, ‡ where he puts his addresses into literary form and intrusts them to the disciples of Yahweh, for the use of those who are to follow him (*v.i.,* on his literary work, p. cxxx ff.).

5. The turning-point in Amos's ministry, and, indeed, the only significant event that has been handed down to us, is the scene at Bethel. We cannot fail to appreciate : (1) The element of tragedy which it includes, for the throne of a king is at stake, the life of the priest is forfeited, and the fate of the nation is sealed. (2) The naturalness of it all, for is not Amos seeking to do just what his predecessors back to Samuel had done before him, viz. to unseat the king? How could his words be otherwise interpreted? How could king or priest fail to take cognizance of them? (3) The strange character of Amos's reply to this point. Is the prophet's language, in which he foretells Amaziah's doom, general or special? We answer, the former. The catastrophe which is soon to befall the whole nation will include the priest with the rest.

---

* This arrangement is, on the whole, better than (1) that which introduces the attack before the visions immediately after 6¹⁴ (so Baumann); or (2) that which places the attack after *all* the visions have been announced, and understands that Amos said nothing after his rebuke of Amaziah (so Löhr, Marti).

† It is hardly possible to regard this interference as in any sense a friendly one (Or.). Nor can we easily suppose that Amos was strong enough to disobey what was evidently the king's command, and not go away at all. At the same time one can scarcely imagine so bold a prophet not doing what this hypothesis takes for granted, viz. continuing to preach until he had finished his message.

‡ Was this a second visit (cf. 6¹), as Che. (*EB.* 154) suggests ?

6. In forming an estimate of the efficiency of Amos's ministry, we must note one or two facts : —

(1) There was in Amos a noticeable lack of the religious element, in the ordinary sense of that word ; and certainly the ministry was not one that could reach very many minds. There were probably not fifty people in Northern Israel who could understand him. It is quite certain that he did not himself have in mind a clear conception of the issue involved in his preaching. He was indifferent to everything that had to do with purpose or motive. As Duhm has said, the teleological element was lacking. The fact is, the new element in Amos was that which is represented by the sage. The union of a *nabhi'* and a sage in one person produced a prophet in the new sense, the sense in which Amos is entitled to that title.

(2) Amos's ministry, then, signifies a breaking away from the old ; or, better, an infusion into the old of a new spirit, that of observation, philosophical inquiry, acceptance of law. His work furnishes for future prophecy a new basis for development, one which will include thought, adjustment to environment, and growth of thought. Still further, although he was a moralist of an extreme type, requiring for the proper balancing of his ideas those of his contemporary Hosea, which were in striking contrast with his own, he nevertheless bequeathed to all mankind certain truths which time has shown to be unchangeable : —

"The truths that justice between man and man is one of the divine foundations of society ; that privilege implies responsibility, and that failure to recognize responsibility will surely bring punishment ; that nations, and, by analogy, individuals, are bound to live up to that measure of light and knowledge which has been granted to them ; that the most elaborate worship is but an insult to God when offered by those who have no mind to conform their wills and conduct to his requirements, — these are elementary but eternal truths." *

§ 15. The Literary Form of Amos's Writings.

The present form of the book of Amos suggests several problems. How much of the book did Amos himself leave ? What

---

* Kirk. *Doct.* 106.

portions are of later origin, and what motive suggested their insertion ? * Through what stages has the book gone ? What contact has it had with other literature ? And still further, what is the form of composition employed, and what special features of that form deserve attention ?

1. The table on p. cxxxii presents the contents of the book, showing (1) the larger divisions, viz. oracles, sermons, etc., (2) the smaller sections, and (3) the original and secondary elements within each section.

2. The secondary material indicated in the table on p. cxxxii includes the passages (with the exception of a few words or phrases, *v.i.*) which have been treated as interpolations in the commentary. An examination of these passages shows that they fall into five groups : —

(1) The Judaistic insertion, made after the promulgation of Deuteronomy, and referring to the approaching destruction of Jerusalem, viz. the judgment on Judah, $2^{4\,f.}$.†

(2) Historical insertions, from a post-exilic date, (*a*) adding judgments upon Tyre ($1^{9\,f.}$) and Edom ($1^{11\,f.}$), thus bringing the whole number (with Judah) to seven ; ‡ (*b*) adding reference to the fall of Calneh, Hamath, and Gath, 6^2 (cf. Is. 10^{9-11}).

(3) Theological insertions, from a post-exilic time, similar in tone and spirit to certain passages in Job § and Deutero-Isaiah. ‖

---

* Men in later days of prophecy seem to have regarded it as a pious duty to illustrate older utterances by making application to their own times. If the older form of utterance appeared too harsh for the later age, it was modified; if too obscure, it was explained. The intention was not to preserve and transmit what the prophet had actually said, but rather to indicate what, in the opinion of the later editor, he would have had to say in order "to fulfil the religious purpose which he once meant to serve" (cf. K. *DB.* V. 671; Carpenter and Battersby, *Hex.* I. 110).

† There is no basis for adding to this, with Marti, either $3^{1\,b}$, for surely Amos, himself a Judahite, could speak of the "whole family"; or $6^{1\,a}$, for was not Amos concerned also for Zion ? Even with these passages treated as insertions, there is no ground for supposing a special edition of Amos to have been issued for the Judahites.

‡ No good reason (*v. in loc.*) exists for regarding, with Marti, 2^{10} as such an historical addition (to 2^9, the difficulty involved in its position is entirely relieved by transposition), or 2^{12} (to 2^{11}), or 5^{26} (p. 130).

§ *E.g.* $3^{8\,ff.\ 25\ ff.\ 31\ ff.\ 34-38}$.

‖ *E.g.* $4^{0\,21\ ff.}$ $4^{5\,12.\ 18}$ $4^{8\,12\ f.}$.

ANALYSIS OF AMOS.

Original	Secondary	Subject *	§§
	1^1	*The Superscription.*	1
	1^2	*The Text or Motto.*	2
$1^{3\text{-}5. 6\text{-}8. 13\text{-}15}\ 2^{1\text{-}3}$	$1^{9\text{-}10.\ 11\text{-}12.}\ 2^{4\text{-}5}$	Judgments upon Neighboring Nations, viz. Syria, Philistia, *Tyre*, *Edom*, Ammon, Moab, *Judah*.	3
$2^{6\text{-}11.\ 13\text{-}16}$	2^{12}	Judgment upon the Nation Israel.	4
$3^{1\text{-}8}$		The Roar of the Lion: Destruction is coming.	5
$3^9\text{-}4^8$		The Doom of Samaria.	6
$4^{4\text{-}7a.\ 8b\text{-}12.\ 13e}$	$4^{7b.\ 8a.\ 13a\text{-}d}$	Israel's Failure to understand the Divine Judgment.	7
$5^{1\text{-}6}$	$5^{8\text{-}9}$	A Dirge, Israel's Coming Destruction.	8
$5^{7.\ 10\text{-}17}$		Transgressors shall come to Grief.	9
$5^{18a.\ c.\ 19\text{-}22a.\ 23\text{-}}6^{1.\ 3\text{-}8.\ 11b\text{-}14}$	$5^{18b.\ 22b.}\ 6^{2.\ 9\text{-}11a}$	The Doom of Captivity.	10
$7^{1a\text{-}c.\ 2\text{-}7.\ 8b.\ 9}$	$7^{1d.\ 8a}$	Three Visions of Destruction.	11
$7^{10\text{-}17}$		An Accusation and a Reply.	12
$8^{1.\ 2b\text{-}5.\ 7\text{-}10.\ 11b\text{-}14}$	$8^{2a.\ 6.\ 11a}$	A Fourth Vision, with Explanatory Discourse.	13
$9^{1\text{-}4.\ 7\text{-}8b}$	$9^{5\text{-}6}$	A Fifth Vision, with a Passionate Description of the Ruin.	14
	$9^{8c.\ 9\text{-}15}$	*A Later Voice of Promise.*	15

Row groups:
- The Oracles: $1^8\text{-}2^{16}$.
- The Sermons: $3^1\text{-}6^{14}$.
- The Visions: $7^1\text{-}9^{8b}$.

* Titles in *Italics* belong to late sections.

Here belong (*a*) the heading of the book, 1^2 (pp. 9 f.) ; (*b*) the well-known doxologies, 4^{13} * $5^{8\,b}$ $9^{5\,f.}$·†

(4) Technical or archaeological insertions, which take the form of expansion, thus adding details to the more simple statement of the original. Here belong, (*a*) "each woman straight before her," in 4^3; (*b*) "while yet there remained three months to the harvest," in $4^{7\,a}$ (p. 97), also, "together with the captivity of your horses," in 4^{10} (p. 100); (*c*) "one field being rained upon," etc., . . . "two or three cities staggering," etc., in $4^{7\,b.\,8\,a}$ (pp. 97 f.) ; (*d*) "and unto wailing those skilled in lamentation," in 5^{16} (p. 127); "and the peace-offerings of your fatlings I will not regard," in 5^{22} (p. 135); (*e*) the detail of the inner part of the house, in $6^{9\text{-}11\,a.}$ (p. 151) ; (*f*) "and lo ! there were full-grown locusts after the king's mowings," in $7^{1\,d}$; (*g*) the extra technique, involving the question of Yahweh to Amos, in $7^{8\,a}$ $8^{2\,a}$; (*h*) "buying the poor for silver," etc., in 8^6; (*i*) "your images, the star of," in 5^{26}, "and it devour," in 5^6, "and the oppressions within her," in 3^9, "O children of Israel," in 3^1, "with a storm in the day of tempest," in 2^{14}, "plumb-," in 7^7, "for thirst," in 8^{13}.

(5) The Messianic additions found in "Behold the days are coming," in $8^{11\,a}$, and the long closing passage $9^{9\text{-}15}$ connected with what precedes by $9^{8\,e}$, in which the interpolator announces that the original message of destruction was intended only for Northern Israel.

(6) Certain phrases, "The Lord," "God of Hosts," "It is the oracle of Yahweh," "Has Yahweh said," which have been inserted arbitrarily to emphasize some favorite thought of a reader, *e.g.* $1^{5.\,8}$ 2^{16} $3^{13.\,15}$ 4^3 5^{16} 7^6 8^9. Cf. also, "in that day," 8^3.

3. The internal history of the book (*i.e.* the various steps in the process of its growth) was probably as follows : —

(1) Amos himself left, not a book, but certain addresses or groups of addresses in writing.

(2) These became a book, in all probability through the work of his disciples, before the times of Isaiah (*v.i.*), who, says Cheyne, "steeped himself in the originality of Amos before displaying his

---

* Che. (*EB*. 153) includes also $4^{12\,b}$.

† We cannot include here, with Marti, 3^3 (p. 67), or 3^7 (also Duhm; Che. *EB*. 154; *v.* p. 71), or 5^{13} (p. 121), or 8^8 (p. 176), or $8^{11\text{-}14}$ (pp. 183 f.).

own truly original genius." *   Since Amos probably issued his addresses in Judah, it is questionable whether Hosea ever saw them (*v.i.*). †

(3) A Deuteronomic insertion consisting of $2^{4 \text{f.}}$ was probably made in Jeremiah's time. This address would fit in just before the fall of Jerusalem, almost as appropriately as before the fall of Samaria. It is perhaps too much to call this a Deuteronomic redaction.

(4) During the exilic experience (or a little after) important changes were introduced, viz. (*a*) those of an historical character (*v.s.*) in accord with the same spirit which gave rise to Obadiah$^{10-14}$ (cf. Is. 34 Ez. 25^{12} 35^{5} Ps. 137^{7}) Jo. $3^{2-6.\ 19}$; and (*b*) those of a theological character (*v.s.*) in accord with the same spirit which found expression in the descriptions of the deity that occur in Job and Deutero-Isaiah (*v.s.*).

(5) In a later post-exilic period there was added the large number of technical and archaeological explanations and expansions indicated above. At this time the superscription (1^{1}) probably had its origin. Many of these are glosses which found their way into the text without motive of any kind. Some, however, are the work of an editor who delighted to repeat in minute detail some point or description which had been passed over quite summarily. No definite line perhaps can be drawn between these two classes of additions.

(6) Finally, in the spirit of the days of Zechariah and Zerubbabel, when men were thinking of the restoration of the throne of David, or perhaps still later, there was added the Messianic promise of 9^{8c-15} (*v.s.*). This closed the internal history of the book.

4. The general structure of the book as understood by the present writer is indicated in the table (*v.s.*). Its character is extremely simple : A series of judgment oracles ; a series of judgment sermons ; a series of judgment visions. These various series have each its own unity of thought and its own unity of purpose. These have already been fully discussed.

It remains, however, to notice some of the more important hypotheses put forward in recent times which offer different explanations of Amos's structure.

---

* *EB.* 154.   † So We., Che.; but cf. Ba.

(1) Elhorst (1900) on the supposition that the text was originally written in parallel columns, the strophes being arranged so that 1, 3, 5, etc., fell in Column I. and 2, 4, 6, etc., in Column II. and that some copyist transferred the columns consecutively instead of alternating between the two, proposes the following order: $1^{1.\ 2.\ 11.\ 12.\ 3.\ 5.\ 13\text{-}15.\ 6\text{-}8}$ $2^{1\text{-}3}$ $1^{9.\ 10}$ $2^{4.\ 5.\ 6}$ $5^{6\,b.\ 7}$ $2^{7.\ 8}$ $5^{8.\ 9}$ $2^{9\text{-}12}$ $5^{10\text{-}12}$ $2^{13\text{-}16}$ $5^{13\text{-}15}$ $3^{1.\ 2}$ $5^{16.\ 17}$ $3^{3\text{-}8}$ $5^{18\text{-}20}$ $3^{9\text{-}14}$ $5^{21\text{-}25}$ $4^{1\text{-}3}$ $5^{26.\ 27}$ $4^{4\text{-}11}$ $6^{1\text{-}6}$ 4^{12} 6^{7} 4^{13} 6^{8} $5^{1\text{-}3}$ $6^{9\text{-}11}$ $5^{4.\ 5}$ $6^{12.\ 13}$ 5^{6} 6^{14} $7^{1\text{-}9.\ 10\text{-}17}$ $8^{1\text{-}6}$ $9^{1\text{-}6}$ $8^{7\text{-}14}$ $9^{7\text{-}15}$. With this rearrangement, the prophecy falls into four divisions: (a) $1^{1}\text{-}2^{5}$; (b) $2^{6}\text{-}6^{14}$; (c) $7^{1\text{-}17}$; (d) $8^{1}\text{-}9^{15}$.

(2) Löhr (1901) finds five main divisions; the first one consists of the introductory address, threatening Israel and her neighbors with punishment, and includes $1^{1\text{-}8.\ 13\text{-}15}$ $2^{1\text{-}3.\ 6\text{-}14.\ 16}$. The second one contains two addresses, announcing destruction because of the exploitation of the poor by the rich and powerful; the first address consists of $3^{1\,b.\ 2\text{-}4\,a.\ 5\,a.\ 6.\ 8\text{-}15}$ $4^{1\text{-}3}$ $8^{4\text{-}14}$ $9^{1\,b\text{-}4\,a}$, the second address comprises $5^{1\text{-}6\,a.\ 7.\ 10\text{-}12.\ 16\text{-}18\,b.\ 20\text{-}27}$ $6^{1.\ 3\text{-}8.\ 11\text{-}14}$. The third division contains the mere fragment of a sermon against the sanctuaries and the ritual, viz. $4^{4\text{-}12\,a.}$ $3^{14\,b.}$ $9^{1\,a.\ 7}$. The fourth division includes the four visions in $7^{1\text{-}9}$ $8^{1\text{-}3}$; and the fifth division consists of the historical episode in $7^{10\text{-}17}$.

(3) Riedel (1902), regarding the book as an anthology of the most significant utterances of Amos, collected and arranged by a later editor, and treating $7^{10\text{-}17}$ as a later addition, makes the following analysis: I. A poem announcing Yahweh's judgment on the nations in general, and Israel in particular, chaps. 1 and 2. II. The central division ($3^{1}\text{-}8^{3}$), falling into three sections: (a) three addresses beginning with "Hear this word," $3^{1\text{-}5}$ $4^{1\text{-}13}$ $5^{1\text{-}17}$; (b) two addresses beginning with "Alas," $5^{18\text{-}27}$ $6^{1\text{-}14}$; (c) the four visions, $7^{1\text{-}9}$ $8^{1\text{-}3}$. III. The closing address ($8^{4}\text{-}9^{15}$), likewise consisting of three sections: (a) $8^{4\text{-}14}$, which again begins with "Hear"; (b) $9^{1\text{-}10}$, again narrating a vision; (c) $9^{11\text{-}15}$, a word of promise, in part looking back to the first address (cf. 9^{12} with $1^{11\,ff.}$).

(4) Baumann* (1903) finds five addresses, all of similar structure. Each of the last four addresses has three main divisions, the last division in each case summing up the entire speech, and the second division, with one exception, consisting of four sections. First address: $1^{2\text{-}8.\ 13\text{-}15}$ $2^{1\text{-}3.\ 6\text{-}11\,a.\ 12.\ 11\,b.\ 13.\ 14\,a.}$ $^{16\,a.\ 14\,b.\ 15\,a^{a}\ 15\,b.\ 16\,b}$ (with an appendix, $3^{9\text{-}15}$). Second address: I. $3^{1\text{-}6\,b.\ 6\,a.\ 8}$; II. (a) $4^{1\text{-}3}$, (b) $8^{4.\ 5.\ 7.\ 8.\ 9.\ 10.\ 13.\ 14.\ 11\,a^{\beta}}$. Third address: I. $4^{4.\ 5}$; II. (a) $4^{6.\ 9\text{-}11}$, (b) $4^{12\,a}$ $5^{21\text{-}27}$; III. $5^{4\text{-}6}$. Fourth address: I. $5^{1.\ 2.\ 3.\ 16.\ 17\,b}$; II. (a) $5^{18\text{-}20}$, (b) 6^{1}, (c) $6^{3\text{-}7}$, (d) $6^{13.\ 12\,a.\ 8}$; III. $6^{14.\ 11.\ 12\,b.\ 9.\ 10}$. Fifth address: I. $7^{10\text{-}17}$; II. (a) $7^{1\text{-}3}$, (b) $7^{4\text{-}6}$, (c) $7^{7\text{-}9}$, (d) $8^{1\text{-}3}$; III. $9^{1\,a.}$ $3^{14\,b.}$ $9^{1\,b\text{-}4.\ 7}$. Baumann summarizes the thought in the form of a dialogue as follows: First division (Amos): Yahweh will bring destruction upon Israel's foes and also upon Israel; for every crime demands punishment. (Israel): How unheard of, to maintain that Yahweh would destroy his own people! Who would listen to such folly? Second division (Amos): What I speak is not folly, but the decree of God. Hear, therefore, especially you leaders in iniquity, of impending disaster.

---

* With whom Now.[2] is in essential accord.

(Israel) Our cultus at the sanctuaries will turn aside every sort of disaster. Third division (Amos) : Vain labor of love ! Have not past calamities taught you that Yahweh demands a better service? Seek him through the practice of morality and justice ! But no, all warning is useless. Because you will not listen, you cannot be helped. Fourth division (Amos) : It remains only to raise the funeral dirge and to wail over the blind. Destruction is inevitable. Fifth division (Amos's justification of his message in response to the protests of Amaziah and the people) : God, whom I have seen, has revealed to me what must come, and in spite of my earnest entreaties, has held fast to his decision.

(5) Marti (1903) finds in the original book (*a*) an announcement of judgment upon Damascus, Ammon, Moab, and Israel herself: $1^{3-5.\ 13-15}$ $2^{1-3.\ 6-9.\ 11.\ 13-16}$; (*b*) a series of fragments of fourteen sermons: $3^{1\,a.\,2}$ $3^{4-6.\,8}$ 3^{9-11} 3^{12} $3^{14\,b.\,15}$ 4^{1-3} $4^{4-7\,a^{a}\,8-12\,a}$ 5^{1-3} $5^{4.\,5\,a.\,6.\,14.\,15}$ $5^{7.\,10-12.\,16.\,17}$ $5^{18.\,20\,b.\,19.\,21-25.\,27}$ $6^{1.\,3-6\,a.\,7}$ 6^{8-10} $6^{11.\,12.\,13\,a.\,6\,b.\,13\,b.\,14}$; (*c*) the five visions and the historical episode: 7^{1-9} 8^{1-3} $9^{1-4.\,7}$ 9^{10-17}, and some fragments within 8^{4-14}, viz. $8^{4.\,5.\,7.\,11\,a.\,12.\,13\,b.\,14}$.

5. The external history of the book of Amos may be traced briefly through four periods : —

(1) Direct evidence of an external acquaintance with it by other prophets is perhaps slight. The similarity of expression found in certain passages in Hosea,* as compared with Amos, proves nothing ; the two were dealing with the same historical traditions and were working in the same environment. The same thing may be said of the two or three passages in which Isaiah and Amos use similar expressions.† In Jeremiah, on the other hand, because the situation is a similar (although not the same) one, more definite trace is found of Amos's influence. ‡ In Ezekiel, likewise, some points of external resemblance may be noted, espe-

---

* *E.g.* between Am. 2^5 etc. (sending fire upon the palace) and Ho. 8^{14} (which is late), Am. 2^{10} (the rescue from Egypt) and Ho. $12^{10\,f.}$, Am. 7^{17} (threat of captivity in an unclean land) and Ho. 9^3, Am. 8^5 (corruption of Ephraim, unjust scales) and Ho. 12^8, Am. 8^8 9^5 and Ho. 4^3, Am. 4^6 and Ho. 7^{10}.

† Cf. Is. 30^{10} with Am. 2^{12}; Is. $32^{9.\ 11.\ 17}$ (שאנן) with Am. 6^1; $3^{16\,ff.}$ with Am. $4^{1\,ff.}$; and $9^7-10^4 + 5^{25-39}$ with Am. 4^{4-13}.

‡ This is seen, perhaps, in the formulas employed at the beginning (כה אמר י׳) and at the end of the utterances against foreign nations; cf. 47^2 48^1 $49^{1.\ 7.\ 28.\ 34}$ and Am. $1^{3.\ 6}$ etc.; also $48^{25.\ 44}$ $49^{2.\ 6.\ 26.\ 39}$ with Am. $1^{5.\ 8.\ 15}$ 2^3; and in the similarities to be noticed in a comparison of Je. 17^{27} with Am. 2^5, 21^{10} with 9^4, 25^{30} with 1^2, 49^{27} with 1^4, 49^3 with 1^{15}, 46^6 with 2^{14}, 46^7 with 8^8, 48^{24} with 1^{12} 2^2, $49^{13.\ 20-22}$ with 1^{12}, 48^7 49^3 with 1^{15}. The phrase " virgin Israel " is found only in Am. and Je.; " days are coming " occurs in no other prophetic books.

cially in the passages directed against foreign nations.* In the other prophets, few cases of direct external influence may be discovered.†

But it is not in such external manifestations that we should expect to find traces of Amos's influence upon later prophets. That his ministry and message were known to them appears from several points in which they follow closely in his steps, *e.g.* in standing aloof from the great body of so-called prophets in their respective periods; in adopting the method of writing down their utterances; in the continued development of the sermonic discourse introduced by him; in following the fashion of directing a certain portion of their attention to the foreign nations; ‡ in basing their work on the fundamental doctrine of *national judgment* as presented by Amos; in holding up and completing the new ideas propounded by Amos concerning God and his ethical demands upon humanity.

(2) The external relation of the book of Amos to the wisdom literature is not indicated by anything that has come down to us. That its influence was felt can scarcely be doubted, since in it we have the first definite formulation of Yahweh's relation to the outside world, the idea which lay at the basis of all Hebrew wisdom; the assignment of Israel to a place upon a level with other nations (cf. the absence of any reference to Israel in the book of Proverbs); an example of Oriental learning in history, geography, social customs; the very essence of wisdom, in the emphasis placed upon honesty, purity, etc.; together with an almost total absence of the religious sentiment (*v.s.*).

(3) In later times reference is made to the Amos-book in Ecclus. 49[10], where "the twelve prophets" are mentioned, showing that at

---

* Cf. the introductory formula in Ez. 25[6. 8. 11. 15] 26[3. 7], etc., and the closing words in 25[7. 11. 14] 26[6. 14. 21]; also Ez. 27[2] 28[12] 32[2] with Am. 5[1], 28[26] with 9[14], 35[5. 6] with 1[11], 6[8] with 9[9], 7[2. 6] with 8[2], 28[18] with 1[10].

† Cf. Zp. 2[4 ff.], in which the same cities of Philistia are mentioned as in Am. 1[6-8] (Gath being omitted), and in the same connection a call issued for repentance in language almost like that of Am. 5[14]; also Zc. 9[1-7], in which Damascus, Phoenicia, and Philistia are threatened (Gath being again omitted in the list of cities); also Zc. 3[2] with Am. 4[11], Zc. 13[5] with 7[14], Hag. 2[17] with Am. 4[9]. On the resemblance of Is. 42[5] 45[7. 12] to Am. 4[13] 5[8 ff.], *v.* p. cxxxiv.

‡ *E.g.* Is. 10[5 ff.] 13[1 ff.] 14[28 ff.] 15[1]–19[25] 21 23 Je. 46 ff. Ez. 25 ff. Ob., Na. 2[8]–3[19] Zp. 2[4-15] Zc. 9[1-7].

that time there was a book of Amos ; in Tobit 2^6, where the book of Amos is first mentioned by name and a citation is made from 8^{10} ; in Acts $7^{42\,f.}$, where Am. $5^{25\,f.}$ is quoted and assigned to " the book of the prophets " ; and in Acts $15^{16\,f.}$, a quotation of 9^{11} in connection with other " words of the prophets."

(4) The place of the book in the Canon is naturally with " the twelve." Its position in the Hebrew Canon, viz., third (following Joel), is different from that in ⅏, where it is second (Joel being placed after Micah).

6. Partly on *a priori* grounds (it being thought impossible to conceive of a herdsman as a man of letters),* and partly on the ground of certain words which were wrongly spelled (these have more recently been discovered to be textual errors),† many explanations of the uncultivated and, indeed, rude speech of Amos have been deemed necessary. The fact has long been recognized, however, that these estimates were wrong. Recent writers, especially since W. Robertson Smith in 1882, have vied with each other in appreciation of the simplicity and refinement, as well as of the vigor of Amos's literary style. ‡ The latest critics go even so far as to deny that the figures which he employs are prevailingly those of the shepherd-life. §

(1) The regular and simple structure of the book (p. cxxxii) exhibits at once Amos's style of thought. What could be more natural and easy than the series of oracles, the series of sermons, and the series of visions? It is unfortunate that some recent critics seem as blind to the simplicity of Amos's style of expression as were the older critics to its refined nature.

(2) This regularity, or orderliness, exhibits itself in detail in the repetition of the same formulas *for three transgressions, yea for four*, etc., in the opening chapters (or, to put it otherwise, in the orderly arrangement of the nations) ; in the use of the refrain, *but ye did not return*, etc., in the poem describing Israel's past chastisements (4^{4-13} ‖) ; in the entire form of the first three visions

---

* Jerome, in his introduction to Amos, characterizes Amos as *imperitus sermone sed non scientia.*

† For these words, viz. מעיק 2^{13}, בושסכם 5^{10}, מחאב 6^8, מסרפו 6^{10}, ישחק 7^{16}, *v. in loc.* ‡ *V.* especially Mit.; Che. *EB.* 155. § Che. *EB.* 155.

‖ Isaiah followed closely this model in his celebrated poem 9^8-10^4 5^{26-30}, although a portion of this is probably later than Isaiah himself.

(7^{1-9}); in the almost artificial symmetry of form seen in the accusation (7^{10-14}) and the reply (7^{14-17}); in the series of illustrations employed with such effect in $3^{3\,\text{ff.}}$; in the structure, in general, of the several pieces (*v.i.*). Moreover, these various series, "while not so long as to become tiresome, are long enough to impress upon the mind of the reader the truths that they are intended to illustrate and justify the use of them by the prophet." There is here the skill, not only of the poet and the speaker, but also of the teacher. Every poem in the book is a notable example of this same direct, straightforward orderliness of thought.

(3) The imagery of Amos, like that of Isaiah, is worthy of special study. Tradition has probably been wrong in emphasizing too strongly the prevailingly shepherd-characteristics (*v.s.*) which mark the figures employed by Amos. But no one will deny that he is especially fond of drawing his language from *nature;* and what, after all, is this but the field of rural life? He not only cites certain facts of agricultural significance, *e.g.* the recent drought, blasting and mildew ($4^{7\,\text{ff.}}$), the oppressive taxation of crops (5^{11}), and the cheating of the grain merchants (8^{5}), but he finds picturesque illustrations and comparisons in "threshing instruments" (1^{3}), the loaded wagon on the threshing-floor (2^{13}), the height of the cedars and the strength of the oaks (2^{9}), the roar of the lion in the forest ($3^{4\,8}$), the shepherd rescuing remnants from the lion (3^{12}), the snaring of birds (3^{5}), the "kine of Bashan" (4^{1}), wormwood ($5^{7}\ 6^{12}$), the lion, bear, and serpent (5^{19}), the perennial stream (5^{24}), horses stumbling upon rocks and ploughing the sea with oxen (6^{12}), swarms of locusts devouring the aftermath ($7^{1\,\text{f.}}$), and the "basket of summer fruit" (8^{1}).

(4) Other features of Amos's style, which may only be mentioned, are (*a*) its originality (sometimes called unconventionality or individuality),* as seen in a certain kind of independence, probably due to the fact that he was a pioneer in the application of writing to prophetic discourse; (*b*) its maturity, for nothing is more clear than that he had predecessors in this work who had developed, in no small degree, a technical nomenclature of prophecy (*v.s.*); (*c*) its artistic character, which is seen not only

---

* Cf. Mit. 8.

in strophes with refrains, but in the entire strophic structure of the various pieces, together with the measure and parallelism, *v.i.* It is probable that Amos's style, as well as the substance of his message, is to be explained largely by the circumstances of his environment (*v.s.*).

D. HOSEA.

§ 16. The Personal Life of Hosea.

The facts of Hosea's life, while altogether different from those relating to Amos, are equally interesting and instructive.

1. There is no evidence to prove that the man Hosea was of the tribe of Reuben (a view based on the resemblance of his father's name, Beeri, to Beerah, 1 Ch. 5^6) ; * or of the tribe of Issachar (p. 202) ; or of the tribe of Judah, for the passages in which Judah is mentioned are for the most part doubtful, since they seem to be part of a plan (p. clix), and even if authentic would prove neither the prophet's Judaean birth,† nor the suggestion that the book was written out in Judah, when the prophet (like Amos) had been sent away. ‡ On the name Hosea, *v.* p. 205 ; on the bearing of the superscription 1^1, *v.* pp. 203 f. It is hardly to be questioned that he was a citizen of the Northern kingdom ; *v.* p. 202, to which may be added, § as matter of detail, that (*a*) the interest in Northern Israel is seen in his intimate acquaintance with the historical conditions and foreign interests of the North, as well as with the policies of intrigue of the two political parties ; (*b*) the particular places with which familiarity is shown, all of which lie in North Israel, are Mizpah in the east and Tabor in the west (5^1), Samaria (frequently mentioned, 7^1 $8^{5\,f.}$ $10^{5.\,7}$ 13^{16}), Gilead (6^8 12^{11}), Shechem (6^9), Gilgal and Bethel (4^{15} 9^{15} $10^{5.\,15}$ 12^{11}), Gibeah and Ramah (5^8 10^9) ; (*c*) the difference between Amos's point of view and that of Hosea illustrates

---

* So, many Rabbis ; cf. Jer. *Quaestiones in Paralipomena.*

† Jahn and Mau. ; *v.* p. 202.

‡ Umb., Ew.

§ Certain Aramaicisms, *e.g.* תרגיל (11^3), נחה (5^{13}), קאם (10^{14}), and the frequent use of the long form אנכי, are commonly cited in support of Hosea's northern origin ; but too great stress may not be laid upon these ; cf. Kautzsch's *Aramaismen in A. T.*, which recognizes no Aramaic words in Hosea.

well the difference between a visitor and a resident; (*d*) the great historical significance of the book of Hosea is largely affected by the question of his citizenship in the Northern kingdom.

2. The date and circumstances of Hosea's life and work are, upon the whole, quite definitely settled. While the superscription 1^1 (pp. 203 f.) is from a later date, it is in part consistent with the facts. Hosea sustains to the fall of the Northern kingdom the same relation which Jeremiah sustained a century and a half later to that of the Southern kingdom.

(1) Can we, however, determine how early he began his work? or how late he continued to prophesy?

The following indications of date may be considered: (*a*) That he was preaching in 743 B.C. is certain in view of the threat concerning Jezreel (1^4), which must have been uttered before the fall of Jehu's house, that is, before the death of Jeroboam II.; for Zechariah's reign was very short, and immediately thereupon came the period of anarchy. If 1^4 was uttered in 743, the prophet's marriage and the birth of his oldest son must be understood to have preceded. (On the date of the writing of chaps. 1–3, *v.* § 19.) (*b*) That he lived in the midst of the period of anarchy which followed the death of Jeroboam II. (*i.e.* 743–736 B.C.) seems to be shown by the utterance found in 7^7 (perhaps also $7^{3 \text{ ff.}} 8^4$), which reflects the condition of things in this period.* (*c*) The lack of allusion of any kind to the Syro-Ephraimitish war of Pekah and Rezin against Judah (Is. 7, 2 K. $15^{37. \, 38}$) would indicate that Hosea was not in active service at that time (734–733 B.C.), for one cannot imagine silence on his part with reference to events of such importance.† (*d*) Still further, Gilead in Hosea's day was still a part of Northern Israel ($5^1 6^8$ 12^{11}); but in 734–733 B.C. Gilead and Naphtali passed under the yoke of Tiglathpileser. ‡

The certain dates, then, are 743 B.C. and 734 B.C. How much earlier than 743 Hosea may have preached cannot be determined.

(2) The historical events of the period just indicated (cf. 2 K. 15) fit in admirably with the descriptions of Hosea's times found in his addresses. (*a*) In the earlier part, the times are

---

* Zechariah, son of Jeroboam II., is assassinated within six months by Shallum, son of Jabesh, who, in turn, is killed after a month by Menahem, son of Gadi. He reigns about six years, paying tribute to Assyria for his protection. His son Pekahiah, after a reign of about two years, is assassinated by Pekah, son of Remaliah (736 B.C.).   † So Now., Marti, *et al.*

‡ On the impossibility of treating 10^{14} as an indication of date, thus bringing Hosea's work down as late perhaps as 725 B.C., *v.* discussion *in loc.*

represented as prosperous, just as in the days of Amos ; evidences of wealth and ease are seen on every hand, and punishment is still in the future ($2^{5 \text{ f. } 9 \text{ ff.}}$) ; (*b*) a little later the situation is greatly changed ; lawlessness is prevalent (4^2 5^1 7^1), the panic-stricken rulers are vacillating between Assyria and Egypt (5^{13} 7^{11} 12^1), political dissolution has already begun (7^9 8^8), the powerlessness of the kings is generally recognized (10^3 13^9), the religious and political leaders are the worst violators of the laws ($4^{8 \text{ f.}}$ 5^1 9^{15}), conspiracies and revolution are rife (5^{13} 7^{11} 10^6 12^1), and anarchy prevails.

(*c*) While the situations described by Amos and Hosea have much in common, there is also much that is different. Hosea actually sees the chaos and confusion, the decay, of which he preaches. Nor are the evils of the times, as seen by him, limited to those of the ruling classes (cf. $4^{1 \text{ f. } 8 \text{ f. } 11\text{-}14}$ 9^{15}), as for the most part in Amos. Moreover, Hosea seems to be himself a part of the situation, in a sense in which Amos, not being a resident of Israel, could not have been. He did not see so widely, but he saw more deeply.

3. Concerning Hosea's occupation and social standing, we are able only to draw inferences of a more or less uncertain character. (*a*) Was he a member of the prophetic society? Nothing is to be found which would point in this direction.* (*b*) Was he a priest, and for this reason was he enabled to speak against the evil practices of his class as no one else could have done?† This is an interesting conjecture, with perhaps as little evidence in its favor as against it. His intimacy with life of every kind, in nature and among men, those of the country as well as those of the city, does not oppose this view. (*c*) His acquaintance with life in general, and especially with that of the priests, taken in connection with his familiarity with the plans of both political parties, and his intimate knowledge of his country's history (pp. cliii, cliv), may reasonably warrant us in the opinion that he occupied a "distinguished position" as a citizen in his native land.

4. Hosea's call and preparation constitute a tragedy in domestic

---

* WRS. *Proph.* 156.

† So Duhm, *Theol.* 130 f.; cf. Sta. *GVI.* I. 577 f.; Marti, p. 2.

life, and give us even a deeper insight into his career and prophetic work than we could obtain concerning Amos from the data in his book.* It is important, however, not to make use of later material in forming this estimate. We are to put aside, without hesitation, 1^7 1^{10}–2^1 $2^{2b.\ 4.\ 6.\ 7.\ 10.\ 14-16.\ 18-23}$ 3^5. This leaves us (v. pp. 205 ff.) the story of Gomer's harlotry ($1^{2-6.\ 8f.}$), the story, continued, of her purchase as a slave, and her retention "many days," 3^{1-4}. While $2^{2a.\ c.\ d.\ 3.\ 5.\ 8f.\ 11f.\ 13.\ 17}$ are from the prophet's own hand, they furnish us light upon his life only as this may be reflected in his own interpretation of that life in connection with Yahweh and Israel.

(1) The story is this: He marries a woman who, afterward, proves unfaithful to him. At the birth of the first son (whose father is another than Hosea, although the latter is as yet ignorant of his wife's infidelity), Hosea calls him Jezreel (p. 211), a name of symbolical character (cf. the names of Isaiah's children). When the next child, a daughter, comes (also in sin), Hosea, now cognizant of his wife's unfaithfulness, names the child *No-love*. Still another son is born, who is called by Hosea *Not-my-Kin*. The woman, it would seem, now leaves home and falls into the hands of some man whose slave-concubine she becomes. But Hosea, who has loved her from the beginning and in spite of all her shame, purchases her at the price of a slave. The relationship of wife, however, is not reëstablished; how could it be? She is placed where she will, in discipline, be shut off from intercourse with men, even from the legitimate intercourse with her husband. This period of seclusion will last "many days." How long? No indication is given.

(2) It is to be especially noticed that (*a*) the conclusion of the story is not given us. We do not know whether in the end she was finally restored to full companionship. (*b*) While according to Israelitish law and custom the wife was a part of the possessions or property of the husband, and the marriage relation was based upon this idea, in Hosea's case the relationship was one of love, so strong that it forced him to do unheard-of things. (*c*) The period required for these transactions must have covered six or seven years. (*d*) The "tragic isolation" of Hosea through all these years is clearly evi-

---

* On the various views entertained of the transaction in the first chapter and the literature of the same, *v.* pp. 204 ff.

dent. (*e*) The feeling which suggests the naming of the first child is widely different from that connected with the naming of the second and third children.

(3) The truth of these representations concerning the domestic life of Hosea rests partly upon the general interpretation of the narrative which is adopted, and partly upon our acceptance of 3^{1-4} as belonging to the original narrative. (*a*) Concerning the general interpretation and the objections to it, *v.* pp. 208–210. But these objections are largely imaginary; for it is pure assumption that a call to prophesy may come *only* in a vision, and that consequently this must be a vision. The years required for all these events need not have exceeded six or seven (*v.s.*), leaving abundant time for prophetic activity. The fundamental point to be noted is that the principal contribution of the domestic experience was not the message concerning the destruction of Israel, but that concerning the great love of Yahweh in spite of faithlessness. It is just as easy to suppose that the prophet kept Gomer in his house after becoming cognizant of her infidelity, as to suppose that he imagined himself so doing. The fact that Gomer's infidelity did not develop until after the marriage is not ignored in the text, but plainly indicated in the use of the phrase *wife of whoredoms* (1^{2a}) rather than זנה (p. 207). The usage of speech, as well as the psychological conception involved in the command of Yahweh to marry a woman, who, as Yahweh knows, will break her marriage vows, is to be compared with representations concerning the hardening of Pharaoh's heart (Ex. 10^1 11^{10} 14^4), and the commission to Isaiah ($6^{9f.}$), these being really *not* commands, but events which in the light of later history are so interpreted. Still further, it was not the purpose of the marriage to teach that Yahweh was Israel's husband, nor is it so to be understood; it was rather to teach the wonderful *love* on the part of one who was released from all obligations of nature or contract. Moreover, we may well understand that this experience, which was primarily a revelation to Hosea, also served in the prophet's work as a means of communicating to the people the thought which it first conveyed to the prophet himself. (*b*) In opposition to the view that 3^{1-4} is from a later hand and to be treated wholly as allegory, I would urge (in addition to what has been said, p. 217) that the change in conception from the *land* as Yahweh's bride (1^2 and chap. 2) to the *sons of Israel* is only a rhetorical effort toward personification and individualization, common enough and thoroughly Hebraic. The phrase *other Gods* (3^1) refers to the Baalim (p. 218), whose existence Hosea, as well as Amos, certainly recognized (p. cxlviii f.), whatever may have been his feeling toward the images of Yahweh. It is unquestionable that the later utterances of Hosea are permeated through and through with the idea of Yahweh's love (p. cxlix), notwithstanding the large place occupied also by the opposite conception, viz. Yahweh's righteous indignation. There is really nothing tangible that has been offered by any one to prove the later date of chap. 3.

(4) The consideration of this domestic experience as the basis of the prophet's call or of his preparation for his message belongs properly under

the topic of his message (*v.i.*); but in this connection two things may be mentioned: (*a*) The narrative of this experience, written some time afterward, shows, as do the similar cases of Isaiah (chap. 6) and Jeremiah (chap. 1), that the prophet has interpreted into the narrative much of his later experience. In other words, the logical order was the experience, the great truth which it suggested, the narration of the experience in the light of this truth. (*b*) This is exactly analogous to the case of Amos; for while the one heard the voice of God in the rising Assyrian situation, which itself was the occasion of both the form and the content of his visions, the other heard it in the ruin of his home. It was in neither case merely a vision, but rather a psychological experience extending over a considerable period.

(5) The basis of the prophet's own interpretation of his experience was found in that most common Semitic conception that the national deity was the husband of the land; but he puts an entirely new thought into the old form of the conception (*v.i.*). Love, as such, was not a necessary accompaniment of marriage in the olden times. Here the entire emphasis is placed upon this phase of the marriage experience.

5. If one can imagine a character almost the opposite of that of Amos, he will have pictured Hosea to himself. (1) This picture, however, would be misleading if Hosea were thought of as weak. In this particular, as in all others, he was not inferior to Amos; but his strength was of another kind. It was that of endurance under incalculable agony; and also of persistence against the combined forces of the leaders of his times. (2) His character was as complex as that of Amos was simple. There is manifestation everywhere of contending and conflicting feelings; of tenderness side by side with indignation, of love and hate commingled; of leniency passing swiftly into severity and the reverse, and of hope for the future actually turning before the gaze into an almost absolute despair. "The swift transition, the fragmentary, unbalanced utterance, the half-developed allusions, that make his prophecy so difficult to the commentator, express the agony of this inward conflict." * (3) This means a nature strongly emotional. So true is this of Hosea (cf. the strikingly parallel case of Jeremiah) that not infrequently he seems to lose his self-control, and to become subject to these same emotions. (4) One side of this emotional nature is seen in his affectionate character, of which the entire family story is an expression. The depth of his affec-

---

* WRS. *Proph.* 157.

tion, the gentleness which characterized it, and, likewise, the passion, of which a glimpse is now and then obtained, all point to a personality unique in Old Testament history. (5) Still another phase, closely associated with the emotional, is his strongly marked religious temperament, in contrast with the ethical, as it is seen in Amos. "Amos is the stern moralist; Hosea is the man of religious affection. Amos sees the righteous will of Yahweh pronouncing and executing judgment upon Israel; Hosea has a vision of the loving heart of Yahweh grieving over his erring children." * (6) But Hosea was not illogical, as he has so frequently been represented. His ability, notwithstanding conflicting feelings, to give expression to a system of theology which was to serve henceforth as the basis of all Israelitish thought, is a factor worthy of consideration in any estimate of his character. He was, in a strange and true sense, a typical Israelite, and his thought, as time shows, was the thought which Israel would accept. This must have come about, at least in part, because his character was fundamentally the Israelitish character, viz. strong, complex, emotional, religious.

§ 17. THE MESSAGE OF HOSEA.

Hosea's message is hardly less important than that of Amos. The special interest lies in three facts, viz.: (1) the personal element which pervades it throughout, for one feels that, after all, the message is not so much a part of the political situation, nor, indeed, of the religious, as the man himself; (2) the supplementary relation which it sustains to that of Amos, both together giving the two sides of one great conception; (3) the fact that in connection with the delivery of this message the end of Northern Israel is rapidly approaching, for within a dozen years all will be over.

1. The general thought of Hosea's message is summed up briefly in connection with a very few propositions: (a) Israel is wicked through and through, and her condition morally is that of rottenness. (b) Israel is politically doomed, the last stages of decay having now been reached. (c) Yahweh is Israel's father,

---

* H. P. Smith, *O. T. Hist.* 221.

with all a father's love and interest; he is Israel's husband, with
all a husband's love and devotion. (*d*) Israel fails to comprehend
Yahweh; has a totally wrong conception of him; in short, Israel
does not know Yahweh. (*e*) Israel deceives herself in her acts
of repentance; but there is a repentance which consists in turning
back to Yahweh.* (*f*) Israel's present attitude toward Yahweh's
love means, in the end, her total destruction.

2. The question of insertions sustains even a closer relation to the message
of Hosea than in the case of Amos. (For the passages which a scientific
criticism denies to the original utterance, *v.i.* p. clx, and for the considerations
which have led to the opinion thus expressed, *v.* each passage *in loc.*, as
well as p. clix.) There is involved in this, especially, the question whether to
Hosea or to later writers we shall ascribe the strongly expressed teaching of
Israel's restoration, which is found in the book as it is now constituted. The
most careful consideration seems to show that this thought is non-Hoseanic
(p. clix).

3. Again it may be said : Hosea followed Amos. But what did
that signify? What did Amos do that Hosea need not do again?
What did Amos leave undone, which Hosea must now do? † Amos
aroused the conscience of Israel to a perception of the real state
of affairs; but, aside from the most general injunction, *Seek Yahweh
and ye shall live* (Am. 5⁴), he refers neither to a restoration (9¹²⁻¹⁵
being late) nor to any plan for securing such a restoration. That
Yahweh loved his people, and had manifested this love on many
occasions of great national importance, was evident. This love
was indeed the basis in some measure of the ethical development thus far wrought out. But although this love was already
recognized, there remained, in view of the emphasis which Amos
lays on universal law, another problem to be solved, viz., "to
prove in God so great and new a mercy as was capable of
matching that law," ‡ in other words, it is necessary for a prophet
" to arise with as keen a conscience of law as Amos himself, and
yet affirm that love was greater still; to admit that Israel was
doomed, and yet " (not " promise their redemption," but) show
that redemption, *i.e.* repentance, is possible; and that the basis

---

* A later writer (12⁷) includes also the maintaining of true love and justice, and
the waiting continually on God.   † GAS. I. 227 ff.   ‡ GAS. I. 229.

of this redemption is as fundamental as is the basis of law itself. This was what Hosea had to do ; and in doing it he is marking out the lines (*v.s.*) of all subsequent prophecy. 3^{1-4} (v.⁵ being late) clearly involves (*a*) Israel's continued relationship with Yahweh, (*b*) her days of punishment for the sake of discipline, (*c*) her acquisition of a new spirit and her return or redemption ; but, while (*a*) and (*b*) are definitely expressed, (*c*) is only implied. This was left so, because the means and method were outside of Hosea's vision ; not so, however, the fact and its philosophy.

4. The circumstances of Hosea's earlier life were practically the same as those under which Amos worked. But in the later period of his ministry everything had changed (*v.s.*). We are not to suppose, however, that the popular feeling (pp. cx ff.) on fundamental questions had been greatly altered. Hosea takes cognizance of certain phases of this opinion which Amos seems not to have noticed, *e.g.* image-worship, the platforms of the two great political parties, the national feeling as to the past history of the nation. These and other subjects constituting the popular usage or opinion which Hosea opposed will be taken up briefly in connection with the statement of his convictions (*v.i.*).

5. Hosea, when compared with Amos, is found to deal very differently with the same question. While Amos was broader, Hosea goes deeper ; Amos is controlled solely by the ethical spirit, Hosea by the religious spirit. The more important details are the following : —

(1) The god of Hosea was omnipotent as truly as was that of Amos ; but this idea of power occupies no such place in Hosea's thought as in that of Amos.

(*a*) Yahweh's power over nature is seen in the fact that not Baal, but Yahweh, had been the giver of Israel's gifts (2^8), in the affliction which the land and the beasts thereof are soon to suffer (4^3 9^2), as well as in the control of Sheol itself (13^{14}). In history his hand has wrought many wonderful things which have occurred in Israel's own life as a nation (*e.g.* the deliverance from Egypt, 11^1 12^9 $13^{4, 5}$; tender guidance in their early history, $11^{3, 4}$; the sending of prophets, 12^{10}); but Hosea exhibits no interest in the work of Yahweh outside of Israel.

(*b*) Was Hosea more truly a monotheist than was Amos ? It cannot be said that Hosea has a narrower conception of the deity; but for him, as for his predecessor, Yahweh is a national god (3^4 9^3 13^4), especially concerned with a single nation. His representation of this god, now as the light (6^5), again as a lion (5^{14} 13^7), or a gnawing worm (5^{12}), vividly expresses the writer's conception of the divine attitude and power. The anthropomorphism is strong and startling. Yahweh is always represented as speaking, there being only a single case in chaps. 4–14 of an introductory formula (4^1). The representations of love on Yahweh's part (especially those of the father and the husband), and those also of indignation and threatened destruction ($5^{10.\ 14\,f.}$ 12^{14} $13^{7\,f.}$) bespeak a poetic nature, but at the same time present ideas of the deity of a peculiarly fundamental character (*v.s.*).

(*c*) The image-worship of these times, passed over in silence by Elijah, Elisha, and Amos (p. cxvi), is the subject of "incessant polemic" on the part of Hosea ($8^{5.\ 6}$; cf. 1 K. 12^{28} Ex. $32^{4.\ 5}$). This idea, not altogether new (cf. the decalogues, pp. lviii ff.), plays a large part in Hosea's conception. Hosea, looking deeper than those who preceded, sees in the traditional Yahweh-worship of his times what he believes to be the worship of other gods (3^1; *v.s.*). Yahweh regards it as sinful to make idols or to worship them (13^2), and all this applies to the calf-worship of Hosea's times. Why was it Hosea rather than Amos who took this position? Because, as W. Robertson Smith has suggested,* while Amos looked at the national practices from the ethical point of view and that of the administration of justice, Hosea thought of them rather as they affected the personal relation of the nation to Yahweh himself. Israel, in idol-worship, shows no true conception of the love due Yahweh. She is, in fact, an adulteress. The worship given the calves is morally false, and therefore inadequate and injurious (*v.i.*).

(2) The fundamental idea of Hosea is his conception of Yahweh as a *god of love* (3^1 11^{1-4}). The word חסד *love, kindness*, "leal love" (never found in Amos), represents an act or feeling of dutiful or loyal affection ($6^{4.\ 6}$ 10^{12}). There is a relationship (6^7) between Yahweh and Israel which calls upon both to exercise this feeling toward each other. The obligation is not merely a legal one; it is likewise moral. We may not overlook the fact that, although

---

* *Proph.* 176 f.

this relationship is in one sense multiform (viz. *grace* on the part of Yahweh to Israel, *piety* on the part of Israel to Yahweh, and *love* [equivalent to *humanity*] on the part of one Israelite to another), this multiformity was lost in the unity of the conception. Yahweh is not only the head of a state demanding justice, he is the head (*i.e.* the father) of a family, for which he has a deep and never ending love. This love is the basis and the principal factor of religion. Because Yahweh loves Israel, Israel should be true to him, *i.e.* moral.*

(3) His most bitter complaint against his people is that *they do not know Yahweh* (2^8 $4^{1.6.}$ 5^4 6^6 8^2; cf. *in loc.*).† In brief, we are to take *know* as meaning not only *knowledge, but also the practical application which knowledge calls for*. It is understanding, or comprehension, but more; for *to know God* is to feel the force of the deity and to act accordingly, *i.e.* to have the feeling (of love, or duty, or whatever else) which a knowledge of God implies. *To come to know God*, then, means to come into a new state of mind. Now, (*a*) Hosea is not asking Israel to accept knowledge which the nation once possessed, but has lost; it is something really *new* in religion which he is holding out to them, although in 13^6 this ignorance is rhetorically styled *forgetfulness;* moreover, (*b*) he clearly indicates the obstacles in the way of their reaching up to this new knowledge, viz. their evil life ($4^{1\,ff.}$) and the failure of the religious leaders, priests and prophets, to do their duty ($4^{6\,ff.}$ $5^{1\,ff.}$); but (*c*) if these difficulties should be removed, how might Israel gain this true knowledge of Yahweh? ‡ Through the many deeds in which Yahweh has made manifestations of himself in history (*v.s.*); through the prosperity and abundance with which she has been blessed (2^8); and, still further, through the laws or teachings which have already taken formal shape (4^6); but, so hardened and insensible has Israel become to these and all similar influences, that Yahweh will be compelled to come upon them in violence and with disaster, in order to make impression on their minds. This is the doom of the immediate future (13^{16}).

---

* Cf. WRS. *Proph.* 160 ff.; GAS. I. 346 ff.; Now. 9 f.; Marti, 5 f.

† An admirable discussion of the full meaning of *know*, as it is here used, will be found in GAS. I. 320 ff.   ‡ Cf. GAS. I. 326 f.

(4) While the exact relation of Yahweh to Israel,* represented under the various figures described above, is that of a covenant (6^7), or a marriage ($2^{2\text{ff.}}$ $3^{1\text{ff.}}$), or that of father and son ($11^{1\text{ff.}}$), what does Hosea understand his relation to be to the outside nations? To this question no definite answer can be given. As has been noted, Hosea concerns himself little with the world outside. He realizes that there is such a world; he teaches that Egypt and Assyria will be used in the chastisement of Israel; he gives, therefore, a place of superiority to Yahweh over the nations and over their gods. Further than this he does not go. This is in accord with the general fact that Hosea, unlike Amos, is not interested in state or nation history. He thinks of Israel, not as a state, but as a family; not so much as a government, but as an individual, either child or wife. It is everywhere the personal attitude that is made most of.

(5) The substance of Hosea's message on the cultus ($4^{13\text{f.}}$ 6^6 8^{11-13}, 10 throughout, $13^{1\text{f.}}$) is the same as that of Amos (p. cxix), and need not be dwelt upon.† It is only to be noted, as above, that because so much emphasis is placed upon the personal element, the faithlessness of Israel in the matter of acts of worship appears all the greater. The physical and sensual character of the cultus, taken over from the Canaanitish worship of the Baalim, was wholly foreign and repugnant to Hosea's conception of the truly spiritual relation of Yahweh to his people. His opposition to the calf-worship in particular was in large part due to its carnal tendencies. These things were fundamentally antagonistic to the new conception of Yahweh for which Hosea stood; hence it is that the denunciation of the cultus occupies a much larger place in the utterances of Hosea than in those of Amos.

(6) The immorality of Israel is pictured even more vividly by Hosea than by Amos. The situation was the darkest possible (*v.s.*); for the land is full of " harlotry " and " adultery." The fact that this general immorality is in part due to the Canaanitish influence makes the prophet's case all the stronger from his point of view. His lamentation is frequently and strongly expressed

---

* Cf. WRS. *Proph.* 161, 162.

† Cf. GAS. I. 286 ff.; WRS. *Proph.* 175 f.; HPS. *O. T. Hist.* 222; Sm. *Rel.* 207 f.; Duhm, *Theol.* 128 f.

(4^8 $5^{1.\ 10\text{-}13}$ 6^4 11^{12}). A heinous thing is the fact that the leaders, particularly the priests, encourage this immorality for the gain which they derive from it (cf. 4^6). The sanctuaries, he declares, are dens of thieves; while the priests are the actual leaders in crime (6^9). Against all this Hosea (a) utters scathing rebuke, (b) makes earnest effort to stir the public conscience, and (c) preaches חסד, which means just as truly *love to man*, as *love of God* or *love to God*. The strange thing is that he finds in religion itself the responsibility for the situation.

(7) The political situation * at home and abroad is treated in much detail. Hosea is convinced (a) that Israel's *home policy* from the beginning has been wrong. Israel's kings, as distinguished from those of Judah (8^4), are not of divine appointment. In other words, the schism is condemned, and while he does not " yearn for the healing of the schism by a Davidic king " (Cheyne),† he sees no future for a kingdom whose religion is represented by calves ($8^{5.\ 6}$). Moreover, while 8^4 may refer to the original schism, it is general enough to include the kings who come one after another in his own day. His attack upon the anarchy and confusion of his day (cf. $8^{4\text{-}13}$) is most violent ($10^{3\ \text{ff.}}$ $7^{1\text{-}7}$ $8^{7\ \text{ff.}}$). He declares that society is a " cake not turned " (7^8), *i.e.* half raw, half baked to a cinder; ‡ that Israel has no leaders worthy of the name; that the strength of the people is worn out; that they are actually held in contempt by the outside nations. This was the natural outcome of (b) their *foreign policy*, which was one of vacillation between Egypt and Assyria, one of half-hearted substitution of other gods for Yahweh, the result of which is seen in the actual deposition of their kings and the appointment of Assyrian vicegerents on the Israelitish throne. § But another political party will not accept Assyrian supremacy and turns to Egypt. Thus they are divided among themselves; and, whatever unity might have gained, all is lost in this conflict of interests.

---

* GAS. I. 269–289; Che. 25 f.; WRS. *Proph.* 183 f.; HPS. *O. T. Hist.* 224 f.; We. *Prol.* 417.

† 3^5 is not from Hosea. ‡ GAS.

§ Menahem held his throne as a vassal of Assyria (2 K. $15^{17\text{-}20}$; Tiglathpileser's Annals, l. 150), while Hoshea seems to have been an Assyrian appointee (Tiglathpileser's small Inscription, col. I., ls. 15 ff.; cf. *KAT.*[3] 264 f.).

(8) Hosea's mind dwells minutely on Israel's past history, which he interprets in the light of the situation of his own days.* This interpretation was carried forward, and became the basis of all later treatment of the past. This fact is one of the most significant in connection with Hosea's career; and in the influence thus exerted he proved himself, perhaps, the greatest of Israel's prophets. We have four great interpretations of Israel's early history, that of JE, which, after all, is hardly an interpretation in the sense in which we now use that term; that of Hosea; and, after him, that of the Deuteronomist and that of the priestly guild. Just as Israel is about to die, "Hosea sees the tenderness and the romance of the early history." † Did Yahweh select Egypt or Assyria or Phoenicia, all great nations? No; but Israel (11^1). Yet her whole career from the "days of Gibeah" has been one of conspiracy and bloodshed (1^4 5^{13} 7^{3-7} 10^9) and rebellion against Yahweh ($7^{13 ff.}$). The purity of the early days has been lost (9^{10}). Yea, from the very beginning the tendency to evil manifested itself (12^{3a}); while Yahweh has never ceased sending his messengers with the call to repentance ($12^{9 f.}$). The prophet's point of view is clear; how can Israel, after the great favors shown her, exhibit to Yahweh such ingratitude?

(9) Israel's immediate future is one of doom. Hosea has no bright message, for 14^{1-8} is surely late. ‡ If we could assure ourselves that such passages as $1^{10}-2^{1.\ 14-16.\ 18-23}$ 3^5 $11^{10 f.}$ were genuine, the case would be entirely different. Hosea saw more clearly than did Amos; and his hope for the future of Israel, based upon the divine love, was more tangible and definite; but he promised nothing. He contributed a conception of Yahweh which made such a future not only possible, but, indeed, probable; whether he supposed Northern Israel might still enjoy the divine favor is a question, yet it is just as questionable whether he transferred the hope to Judah. He taught the possibility of repentance and the true nature of repentance if it would be availing (2^2 5^4 6^6 10^{12}); but would Israel, accustomed to a fitful repentance, ever enjoy the true experience? Hosea scarcely expected Israel's deliver-

---

* WRS. *Proph.* 183 ff.   † GAS. I. 290.

‡ Cf. Meinhold's attempt to separate the work of Hosea into two periods, in the latter of which predictions of exile and return may be found, *e.g.* 11^{8-11} 14^{1-8}.

ance from Assyria's hand. It was too late. There was a possibility, but it was only a possibility. Israel would not lift herself from the depths of degradation into which she had fallen. The future is altogether dark.* While Yahweh's heart was filled with love, it nevertheless burns now with indignation; so let the worst come ! " Shall I deliver them from the hand of Sheol ? Shall I redeem them from death ? Where are (*i.e.* come with) thy plagues, O death ? Where (*i.e.* come with) thy destruction, O Sheol ? Repentance is hid from my eyes " (13^{14}).

6. Hosea was more intimately acquainted with the nation's past than was Amos. At all events he makes larger use of it. On what authority did he depend ? The documents J and E were already in existence (§§ 8, 9), and Hosea must be supposed to have known them. 8^{12} presupposes his acquaintance with written laws such as the Decalogue and the Book of the Covenant, while the allusions in $9^{10\,b}$ $12^{3\,a}$ might well be based upon the narratives of J and E, though the possibility of oral tradition as the source is not excluded here,† and is probably to be accepted in the case of 8^{13} $9^{3.\,10\,a}$ 10^9 $11^{1.\,5}$ $13^{4f.}$. That he was in possession of information not contained in any documents now existing is clear from 11^8, and his independence of judgment concerning the past appears in 1^4 10^5.

7. The character of Hosea's message has already been indicated in the character of the man himself. Whatever one was, that, also, was the other. Was the man a typical Israelite ? The message, as we have seen, was likewise a truly national expression, since its content is the basis of all succeeding Israelitish thought. If Amos's message was universal, Hosea's was more narrowly national; if Amos's was ethical, Hosea's was religious. There is no lack of the tender and the spiritual element. " The two men are types of a contrast which runs through the whole history of religious thought and life down to our own days. The religious world has always been divided into men who look at the questions of faith from the standpoint of universal ethics, and men by whom moral truths are habitually approached from a personal

---

* Cf. WRS. and Marti, *EB*. 2125 f.

† Cf. Dr. *LOT*.⁶ 123; Carpenter and Battersby, *Hex*. I. 107.

sense of the grace of God. Too frequently this diversity of stand-point has led to an antagonism of parties in the church. Men of the type of Amos are condemned as rationalists and cold moderates; or, on the other hand, the school of Hosea are looked upon as enthusiasts and impractical mystics. But Yahweh chose his prophets from men of both types, and preached the same lesson to Israel through both." *

§ 18. The Ministry of Hosea.

In an examination of Hosea's ministry let us prepare ourselves for something as different as possible from that of Amos. It will be the ministry of a poet, not a philosopher; of a man dealing with his own home and country, not a foreigner; of a man living and working largely in privacy, rather than in connection with rulers; of a mystic, not a moralist.

1. His call, together with the message which he was to preach, came not in a vision, but in an experience, one of the saddest known in life.† As in most cases, long years were occupied in the communication of the truth which he was ultimately to preach. The experience was historical and psychological: historical in the sense that it had to do with external facts; psychological in that it was more largely an operation of mind or soul, since both call and message were in reality a spiritualizing of an ordinary event, and an old tradition. We cannot be certain that Hosea did not have a vision of the ecstatic order; but there is no testimony which favors this, and all the facts are explicable without it.

---

* WRS. *Proph.* 163 f.

† To the suggestion (cf. A. B. Davidson in *DB.*) that Hosea was already a prophet when the first child was born (as indicated by the name *Jezreel*), and that at this time he had no knowledge of his wife's infidelity, and that consequently the experience had nothing to do with the call, it may be replied: (1) Unquestionably the prophet's knowledge of Israel's faithlessness and of Yahweh's goodness was a matter of historical observation; likewise, the relationship of Yahweh as husband was an old Semitic idea; but (2) Hosea's prophetic mission (including his call) was not merely to foretell a coming disaster (Amos had done this); it was much more than this, viz. to picture Israel's wicked ingratitude over against the love of Yahweh, which had been manifested through centuries in spite of this ingratitude; (3) the call to preach this message was one which only years of experience and reflection made certain and definite.

As the crushing force of the home tragedy begins to touch this man, possessed of a deeply emotional and religious nature, he feels, in the very touch, a voice saying, "This experience of your married life is a reflection of Yahweh's experience with Israel"; and the voice that speaks is Yahweh's voice. It did not come in a single day, nor in a year; but extended itself over many years, becoming more and more distinct until he no longer doubted its tone or its truth.

2. He seems to have presented his message in the ordinary way. Three or four details in the method employed may be noted: (1) He gives his children symbolical names, each of which conveys (to all who hear it) a significant teaching. In this method, as in many other points, Isaiah followed closely in his track.

(2) He makes public recital of his disgrace and sorrow, not for the sake of sympathy nor with sensational motive, but because in no other way could he present his message. He thus employs a story (personal to be sure) through which to teach his fellow-countrymen. The unique thing is not the event itself, which is too usual, nor the story of the event, which in another's mouth would have been ordinary scandal; but the telling of it by him who was the victim of the situation described. That this produced a profound impression is beyond any question, and this, we may well suppose, was the motive of the prophet in narrating it. Perhaps he wishes to explain just how he came into possession of the message (*v.s.*); but this, after all, was only to make the message itself more definite and more authoritative.

(3) He preaches, as did Amos, discourses (in all thirteen) which were intended to persuade the people to accept the new point of view which he, at bitter cost, had attained. These discourses (*v.i.*), though modified by later insertions, yet more greatly by corruption of the text, still show the evidence of passion in their delivery.

(4) Still another method of presentation was adopted after the example of Amos, when the prophet committed his addresses to writing, and thus secured their preservation for all time (*v.i.*). The suggestion of Marti that these prophecies were never spoken in public, but were originally written and intended for private

reading among the people, lays too much emphasis upon their present form, and, in any case, finds insufficient basis in the mere fact that they consist of "poems which do not give the impression of having been popular addresses." Poetry was the most popular form of address before an Oriental audience.

3. Hosea falls in with Amos in the new policy of political action. He holds no office, exercises no direct control. But more than this, he, like Micah, lives in an atmosphere more retired than that of Amos or Isaiah. The latter came into direct contact with the royal power, while the relations of the former were, at least, indirect. It was, in other words, a private rather than a public ministry. (1) His political views (p. clii) were more definite, perhaps, than those of Amos, and they had to do more distinctly with home affairs. This fact, together with the unpleasant prominence given him by his domestic relations, and especially the political character of the period (pp. cxli f.), made his work one of peculiar difficulty. The prophet must still have been accorded large freedom to have been permitted to speak so freely in times of such political confusion. (2) Hosea's readiness to differ from the prophets of earlier days, in reference to political matters, is noteworthy. To differ from Elijah and Elisha in connection with the Jehu episode was a daring thing to do, but it was even more remarkable that he should go back and pass an opposing judgment as to the division of the kingdom (v.i.). His political ministry thus passes in review the national history of two centuries. Time has shown the wisdom of his position. (3) His attitude toward the prophetic policy of the past is no more severe than that which he holds toward the priests and prophets of his own times (9^7). (4) With his political attitude toward Judah is involved the question of the Judaistic references now generally assigned to a later date (p. clix).

4. The chronological order of the various stages in the ministry of Hosea is not even as clear as in the case of Amos, since neither the structure of the book nor the external events make contributions of a very definite nature.

(1) At the time of his marriage (750 B.C.?) he was presumably a young man, and, if his occupation was that of a priest (p. cxlii), his mind had been dwelling on sacred things for many years. At

first hand he gained his knowledge of the evil practices of his fellow-priests, and their close associates, the prophets.

(2) Within two or three years (747 B.C.) he has satisfied himself as to the doom of Jehu's dynasty; this is announced in connection with the birth of his son (Jezreel). He, doubtless, expected Israel's collapse to be contemporaneous.

(3) Within six or seven years the tragedy of his life has been enacted; the real call to preach has come; the great message has been received; Jeroboam has died, and anarchy has set in; important announcements concerning the future have been made (in the symbolic names given to the three children of his wife).

(4) During the next six or seven years (742–735 B.C.), with his wife put away (for he cannot now live with her, however much he loves her), he preaches his impassioned sermons, breathing into them all the warmth and all the pain of an agonizing heart. These are the years of revolution and vacillation, of decay approaching close to death, — years without any hope, yet with a faith in Yahweh that is strong and steadfast.

(5) What next? We do not know. It is improbable that, like Amos, he left home and went to Judah, there to put his writings into form, and to include the Judaistic references which are in the present book.* It is probable that he was spared the worst agony of all, that of seeing Samaria in ruins and Israel carried captive. We have nothing from his lips or pen later than 735 B.C. (v.s.).

5. The efficiency of Hosea's ministry is even more clearly perceived than was that of Amos. The fact stated above (p. cliv) that Hosea's teaching forms the basis of subsequent Hebrew prophecy, the fact that these utterances produced so great an impression as to find preservation, the additional fact that they were so strongly felt as to require for their elucidation and interpretation the comments and amendments of later generations, prove an efficiency of service and a permanency of character of the highest order.

§ 19. The Literary Form of Hosea.

The corrupt state of the text of Hosea makes the study of its literary problems both difficult and unsatisfactory.

---

* Umb., Ew.

1. The table on p. clx exhibits a view of the book as we now have it, with (*a*) the larger divisions,* and (*b*) a separation of the original and secondary elements.

2. The secondary passages † in the following table fall into four groups : (1) References in Hosea to Judah are for the most part the work of a *Judaistic* editor. The basis for this decision is found ‡ in the fact that in the great majority of cases no sufficient motive can be discovered to explain their Hoseanic origin, while the motive of the later editor is clearly evident ; besides, these passages in nearly every case contain phrases which are late, or interfere with the rhythmic structure. The principal cases are the following : 1^7, exempting Judah from the coming destruction (p. 213), the change of "Israel" to Judah in $5^{10.\ 12.\ 13.\ 14}$ 6^4 10^{11b} $12^{3\ (2)}$; 6^{11a}, threatening Judah with judgment (p. 291) ; 8^{14}, coupling Judah with Israel in transgression (p. 324) ; 12^{1b} (11^{12b}), contrasting Judah's faithfulness with Israel's treachery (pp. 376 f.). While Kuenen is certainly too conservative in his treatment of the Judaistic passages, we cannot agree with Marti (p. 8) that Hosea never in a single case referred to Judah ; one can scarcely conceive the possibility of such a thing. In 4^{15} and 5^5 there is nothing which demands a later origin.

(2) It is impossible to reconcile with Hosea's situation and declarations certain passages referring to Israel's future, the so-called Messianic allusions. The prophet plainly represents Israel's ruin as close at hand (*v.i.*). Moreover, it is apparently an irretrievable disaster (13^9) which is threatened. In any case death and Sheol are first to do their work (13^{14}), nor is Yahweh a man to repent (11^9 13^{14}). These passages, therefore, are entirely inconsistent with Hosea's point of view, and directly contra-

---

* There is no ground for the suggestion of Grätz (*Gesch.* II. 93 ff., 214 ff., 439 ff.) that there are two Hoseas (chs. 1–3 and 4–14) with an interval of fifty years, for the great changes between the times of Jeroboam II. and those which immediately followed are entirely sufficient to explain the differences. Cf. Kue. *Einl.* II. 324, who gives a brief list of expressions common to both divisions.

† The integrity of the Book of Hosea was first impeached by Stuck (1828), who regarded 9^{7-9} as displaced. Redslob (1842) rejected 4^{6-7} 7^{4-10}; Grätz (1853) made chaps. 4–14 late; while Sta. *GVI.* I. 577, prepared the way for Co., We., Che., Now., and others.

‡ Cf. We. *Prol.* 417 ; Sta. *GVI.* I. 577; GAS. I. 224–226; Co. *ZAW.* VII. 285–289; on the contrary Kue. *Einl.* II. 322 f.

ANALYSIS OF HOSEA.

ORIGINAL	SECONDARY*	SUBJECT†	§
	1^1	*The Superscription.*	1
$1^{2, 6, 8f}$	1^7	Harlotry of Hosea's Wife.	2
3^{1-4}	3^5	Purchase of Gomer as a Slave, and her Retention "many days."	3
$2^{4-7, 10-14, 15, 19}$	$2^{4b, 6, 12, 18}$	Israel's Harlotry and her Punishment therefor.	4
	$2^{8-9, 16-17, 20-25}, 1^{1-3}$	*Later Voices describing Israel's Return to Yahweh.*	5
4^{1-19}		Yahweh's Contention with Israel on Account of Sins encouraged by the Priests.	6
5^{1-14}		Guilt of Priests and Princes.	7
$5^{15}-7^7$	$6^{11a, b}\ 7^4$	Fitful Repentance Insufficient to remove Guilt.	8
7^8-8^3	8^{1b}	Confusion of the Nations.	9
$8^{4-8a, 9, 11-13}$	$8^{8b, 10, 14}$	Israel's Kings and Idols Displeasing and Destructive.	10
9^{1-8}	9^9	Israel's Exile.	11
9^{10-17}		Israel's Corruption.	12
$10^{1, 2, 5-8}$	$10^{3, 4}$	Israel's Wickedness as Great as her Prosperity.	13
$10^{9, 11-14a, 15}$	$10^{10, 14b}$	Israel's Past History one of Sin.	14
$11^{1-8a, 9b, 10a}$	$11^{8b, 9a, 10b, 11}$	Israel loved by Yahweh as his Son.	15
$12^{1a, 2-4a, 8-11}$	$12^{1b, 4b-7, 13, 14}$	Israel's Falsity and Faithlessness from the Beginning.	16
13^{1-11}		Israel's Destruction Absolute.	17
$13^{12}-14^1$		Ephraim condemned to Sheol.	18
	14^{2-9}	*Later Words of Hope.*	19
	14^{10}	*The Lesson to be learned.*	20

* This list includes only the more important of the additions and glosses. † Titles of later sections are in *italics.*

dict the representations which are fundamental in his preaching; nor can it be shown that they are spoken, either, to a different audience (viz. the faithful for their encouragement), or at a later time in Hosea's ministry.* Besides, they interrupt the logical development of the thought in particular passages (*v. in loc.*), and show a definite connection with the thought of later prophecy. This material is unquestionably from exilic times.

The more important pieces are the following: 2^{1-3} ($1^{10}-2^1$), promising restoration to Yahweh's favor, great increase of population, and the reunion of Israel and Judah under one king (pp. 245 f.); $2^{8.9}$ $^{(6.7.)}$ describing the disciplinary measures adopted by Yahweh to restore Israel to her senses (p. 236); 2^{16-18} $^{(14-16)}$, setting forth Yahweh's purpose to restore Israel to the purity and joy of her first love (p. 238); 2^{20-25} $^{(18-23)}$, picturing the universal harmony and prosperity that will prevail when Yahweh again betroths Israel to himself (pp. 241, 244); 3^5, announcing Israel's return to Yahweh and the Messianic King in the days to come (pp. 216, 223); $11^{8b.9a.10b.11}$, giving the assurance that Yahweh's anger is appeased and that he will recall the exiles from Egypt and Assyria (p. 372); 14^{2-9} $^{(1-8)}$, containing a call to repentance followed by a description of the great prosperity and peace consequent upon the restoration to Yahweh's favor (pp. 408 f.).

(3) A third group includes, as in the case of Amos (p. cxxxiv), phrases and sentences of a technical, archaeological, or historical character, inserted by way of expansion and explanation.

Here belong, *e.g.* 4^{13d}, "for good is its shade"; 5^6, "with their flocks and their herds"; 7^4, the comparison of the princes to an oven and a baker kindling the fire; 7^{16c}, "this their scorn"; 8^{8b}, "as a vessel wherein none delighteth"; 9^{1b}, "corn"; 9^{9a}, "as in the days of Gibeah"; 9^{10}, "in its first season"; 10^5, "on account of his glory because it has gone into exile from him"; 10^{14b}, "as Shalman spoiled Betharbel in the day of battle"; 12^{14} $^{(13)}$, magnifying the prophetic phase of Moses's work; 13^{4b-7}, presenting Jacob in a favorable light.

(4) The fourth group will include miscellaneous glosses and interpolations for which, perhaps, no special motive may be discovered. As examples of the kind may be cited: 8^4, "that they may be cut off"; 8^5, "how long will they be incapable of

---

* Meinhold.

punishment "; $8^{10.14}$ 9^{1a}; 9^{8a}, " with my God "; 9^{8b}, " enmity." (5) Ch. 14^{10} stands by itself, and is a product of the later wisdom period (pp. 416 f.).*

3. The internal history of the Book of Hosea was perhaps as follows : —

(1) Hosea himself prepared the collection of sermons (v.s.), together with the introduction explaining his call to preach. In this case the explanation of the call comes at the beginning (rather than, as in Amos, after the sermons of chaps. 3–6, or in Isaiah, after the sermons of chaps. 2–5) either because it was only a part of the book and had never been preached or made public, or because it was thought necessary to a proper understanding of what followed. (2) The fulfilment of Hosea's threats in the fall of Samaria (721 B.C.) must have given great prominence to the book in Judah ; in any case it was known to Isaiah, who follows Hosea † in using the words ואין מציל (Ho. 5^{11} = Is. 5^{29}), the thought of Ho. 10^8 in the refrain of his terrible prophecy on the day of judgment (Is. $2^{10.21}$), and the phrase שריהם סררים (Ho. 9^{15}, Is. 1^{23}). (3) At some time, the book was worked over in a kind of Judaistic revision. This was not preëxilic, occurring in the days of Josiah, ‡ but post-exilic ; § because (a) 1^7 is apparently inserted with reference to the deliverance from Sennacherib, and its point of view presupposes the lapse of considerable time since that event, (b) the inclusion of Judah in 8^{14} reflects the disaster of the exile. (4) At a later time, following Ezekiel and Deutero-Isaiah, the Messianic insertions (v.s.) were made which entirely changed the character and function of the book. (5) From time to time during all these periods modifications of a less important character were incorporated ; and the book did not take its present form until the Greek period, since 14^{10} was probably not a part of it until that time.

4. The general structure ‖ of the book as understood by the

---

* Cf. 𝕲's addition to 13^4 (p. 392).   † Marti, p. 10.

‡ Oort, Th T., 1890, pp. 345 ff.

§ Marti.

‖ Cf. Marti, who denies the usual division between 1–3 and 4–14 on the ground that (a) 1–3 are not from an earlier period than 4–14, (b) chap. 3 was not a part of the original book, (c) chap. 2 has more in common with 4–14 than with 1 and 3.

present writer has been presented essentially above. It includes three or four propositions : —

(1) 1^{2-9} 3^{1-4} is a story, briefly and simply told, of the prophet's own family experience, narrated in part to make known how he came to *see* the message which he was to deliver to his people.

(2) $2^{4-7.\ 10-14.\ 18.\ 19}$ is the prophet's suggestion of the *meaning*, obtained in the light of his own experience, in its explanation of Israel's situation.

(3) Discourses uttered from time to time, put together without chronological or logical relationship,* — a group of thirteen, presenting, under varying circumstances, the double thought of *guilt and inevitable punishment* (4^1-14^1).

5. The external history of the Book of Hosea may be briefly traced. (1) On its connection with other prophetic books, *v.* pp. cxlvii f. ; and on its more direct influence on prophetic thought, *v.* p. cxlvi. (2) In the apocryphal literature, Ecclus. 49^{10} mentions the "twelve prophets," and it is quite certain that Hosea constituted one of the twelve. (3) Philo quotes Ho. 14^8 and 14^{10}, while Josephus † speaks of Isaiah and "the others which were twelve in number," undoubtedly referring to the existing book of the twelve prophets. (4) In the New Testament : Ho. 2^{25} is quoted in Rom. $9^{25\ f.}$ (where the prophet is mentioned by name) ; 6^6 in Mat. 9^{13} 12^7 ; 10^8 in Luke 23^{30}, Rev. 6^{16} ; 11^1 in Mat. 2^{15} ; and 13^{14} in 1 Cor. 15^{55}. (5) Its place in the Canon at the head of the Book of the Twelve is probably due to its comparatively large volume. ‡ Its right to a place in the Canon has never been questioned.

---

* GAS. I. 222 (following Hi. and Kue. *Einl.* II. 319) exaggerates this characteristic when he says, "It is impossible to separate the section, long as it is, into subsections, or into oracles, strophes, or periods." Cf. Ew.'s division (for detailed refutation *v.* Sim. 30 ff.) into three parts, (*a*) 4-$6^{11\ a}$, God's arraignment of Israel; (*b*) $6^{11\ b}$-9^9, Israel's punishment; (*c*) 9^{10}-14^{10}, review of early history, with words of warning and comfort. Also Dr.'s arrangement, (*a*) 4-8, dealing with Israel's guilt; (*b*) 9-11^{11}, threatening punishment; (*c*) 11^{12}-14^{10}, a fusion of the two preceding thoughts with a promise of hope. † *Ant.* X. 2, § 2.

‡ Cf. the Babylonian Gemara, *Baba Bathra*, fol. 14 *b*-15 *a* : "The order of the prophetical books is Jos., Ju., Sa., Ki., Je., Ez., Is., the Twelve. Inasmuch as Hosea was the first, as it is written, 'the beginning of the word of the Lord by Hosea' (Ho. 1^2), we should expect the book of Hosea to occupy the first place, at least of the four contemporary prophets, Ho., Is., Am., Mi. But because his prophecy is written together with those of the latest prophets, Hg., Zc., and Mal., he is counted with them" (Wildeboer's translation in *Origin of the Canon of the O.T.*, p. 13).

E. AMOS AND HOSEA.

§ 20. THE POETICAL FORM OF AMOS AND HOSEA.

1. The analogy of other ancient literature should have suggested long ago the probability that Israel's early prophetic literature was poetry, and that its particular form was one adapted to its peculiar purpose and function. Its efficiency was determined in no small measure by its capability of transmission. If we keep in mind not only the character of early literary effort among other nations,* but also the wonderful series of poetical pieces in the O. T., beginning with Deborah's song (Ju. 5), we may not doubt that the old oracle-form would be followed by something of the same kind, but higher in art, as well as in thought. One will expect a much larger freedom in form in pieces which were spoken rather than sung, and likewise a greater variety. This it is that occasions the chief difference between prophetic poetry and psalm poetry.†

2. As far back as 1813 a beginning was made by Kösters ‡ in pointing out the indications of strophic formation. In 1840 Ewald § used the word "strophe" in describing the divisions of a chapter or piece of prophetic diction. In 1847 Baur recognized the presence of strophes in Amos, chaps. 1–4. Schlottmann, in 1884, presented a treatise on the strophic structure in Hebrew poetry ; and in 1887, Charles A. Briggs, in a series of articles, ‖ opened up the subject more widely to the English-speaking world. The publication of Müller's *Die Propheten in ihrer ursprünglichen Form* (1895) ¶ aroused a new interest in the subject. He recognized the existence of strophes as divisions according to

---

* The poetic character of ancient literature is illustrated by the Gilgamesh epic of the Babylonians and the Homeric poems of Greece.

† Sievers, *Metrische Studien*, I. 93.

‡ *Das Buch Hiob und der Prediger Salomos nach ihrer strophischen Anordnung übersetzt* (1813).

§ In *Die Propheten des Alten Bundes* (1st ed. 1840).

‖ *Hebraica*, IV. 161 ff., 201 ff., being a development of the chapter on Hebrew Poetry in his *Biblical Study* (1883).

¶ Followed in 1898 by his *Strophenbau und Responsion*, in the preface of which Zenner (*Chorgesänge im Buche der Psalmen*, 1896) is charged with appropriating the idea and the terminology first used by Müller.

the thought, but maintained further that a new element existed which bound the strophes together in a discourse, just as parallelism bound together lines in a verse. This he called *Responsion.*

Before seeing Müller's work, and Zenner's (1896) somewhat similar arrangement of Am. 1^2–2^{16}, the present writer had prepared and given to his classes the scheme of strophic structure (for Amos) presented in this commentary. The first chapters were published in January, 1897, and later the entire book in August, September, October, 1898.† The structure of Hosea as here presented, although finished in 1898, was first published in part in October, 1900.‡

Contributions to the structure of Amos came very frequently in and after 1900. (1) Elhorst (1900), supposing the book to have originated between 638 and 621 B.C., advanced the view that it was written in two parallel columns, the strophes alternating between the columns. Since both of his premises are wrong, the results do not prove satisfactory. The theory as to the date presupposes the essential unity of the book, and no additions are recognized. The column theory involves many transpositions, few of which improve the present connection, while some are distinctly inferior. In addition, irregularity in the length of lines is a marked feature of the arrange-

---

* " In a case of responsion completely carried out every line of one strophe corresponds to its fellow in the next strophe either with verbal exactness or in thought, as a parallel or an antithesis " (Müller, *Die Propheten*, I. 191). " Along two lines the thought endeavored to modify the form; on the one hand in that responsion appears only partly made evident, though always in the same position, *i.e.* in corresponding lines; on the other, in that it exhibits itself not in parallel fashion and in like words, but through antithesis and through like-sounding or similar words, which re-emphasize in a greater or less degree the same or similar thoughts " (*ibid.* I. 192). While this theory, which has failed to gain general recognition, contains much that is interesting, and, in some cases, may really cover the facts, two serious difficulties oppose the acceptance of it as a widely prevailing feature of the early poetry, viz. (1) the arbitrary measure assumed for lines, the line in each case being made as long or as short as the theory demands, *e.g.* in one strophe (Am. 3^{9-12}) are found heptameters, hexameters, and trimeters; in another (Am. 7^{7-9}) are found hexameters, pentameters, trimeters, and dimeters; (2) the utter indifference of the author to the universally acknowledged results of lower and especially higher criticism.

† See *AJT.* I. (January, 1897), *The Biblical World*, XII. (1898), and the entire text with a parallel translation in my *Structure of the Text of the Book of Amos* (Decennial Publications of the University of Chicago, 1904).

‡ *AJSL.* XVII. 1–15; the remainder of the text (chaps. 4–14) may be found in *AJSL.* XX. 85–94, XXI. 1–21; and the corresponding translation in *Biblical World*, December, 1904.

ment. (2) Löhr (1901) presents a scheme which has much in common with that of this commentary (cf. *e.g.* the two treatments of 1^3–2^3 and 7^{10-17}). But his fundamental premise that the original order of the book has been much broken into and disturbed seems unwarranted. The transpositions suggested do not justify themselves (cf. *e.g.* his third address 3^{1-15} 4^{1-3} 8^{4-14} $9^{1-4\,a}$). (3) Sievers (1901)* gives a treatment of Hosea 1–2 and Amos 1–3, which brings out the possibilities of the poetic form in so far as this concerns the metre, *i.e.* the tone-phrase, the line, and the period. He practically ignores the strophic structure, although recognizing its existence (pp. 123 ff.). This treatment is peculiarly defective in its failure to take into account even the most commonly accepted modifications of the text. (4) Condamin (July, 1901) adopts Zenner's choral system, and arranges the text of Amos (with the exception of 2^6–4^{11} 6^8–7^{17}) in a series of strophes occurring constantly in the order: strophe, antistrophe, alternate strophe, supposed to have been chanted by two choirs alternately. In addition to the self-evident defects of the theory *per se*, Condamin gives no attention to the results of historical criticism, and shows an indifference to keen logical analysis; *e.g.* 5^{1-6} cannot be brought into close relation with $5^{7.\ 10-15}$. (5) Baumann (1903) proceeds, upon Löhr's theory of the present disorder of the Amos text, to reorganize it into five addresses (*v.s.*). Aside from the unnecessary transpositions involved in the arrangement, this work is characterized by its careful application to the entire text of Amos of the metrical principles worked out by Sievers. (6) Marti (1903) bases his commentary on the strophic structure of the book, but has such frequent recourse to glosses and interpolations as to render his poetical structure very uncertain. The shattering of 3^1–6^{14} into fourteen fragments of addresses, and the treatment of the visions and the historical episode as mere prose, can certainly not be justified. (7) Nowack (August, 1903), in the second edition of the *Hand-Kommentar* adopts Baumann's presentation, but makes no practical use of the structure in his commentary.

Contributions to the structure of Hosea have not been so numerous. On Müller (DH.),† Sievers (1901),‡ Condamin (July, 1902),§ and Marti (1903), the same general statement may be made as that already presented concerning their respective treatments of Amos (*v.s.*). As a matter of fact, only Müller and Marti have really given any adequate consideration to this question.

3. The standard unit in the system of Hebrew Poetry, as it is now most generally understood, may be called the *foot*, or *tone-phrase, i.e.* a word or combination of words having a single beat

---

* See his *Studien zur Hebräischen Metrik*, pp. 467–71, 473–9.

† Cf. *Die Propheten* (1896), chaps. 5, 6, 10; *Strophenbau* (1898), chaps. 2, 4, 7.

‡ *Op. cit.*, pp. 466–70, where chaps. 1 and 2 are treated.

§ *Revue Biblique*, XI. 386–91, a rearrangement of chap. 2.

or accent. The possible varieties of the tone-phrase are four,
viz.: a word (accented) of *one* syllable, thus, $\angle$, אֵשׁ (1^4) ; * one
or two words making *two* syllables with the second accented, thus,
$\_ \angle$, אָמַר (1^3) or עַם־אָרָם (1^5) ; one or more words making *three*
syllables, with the second or third accented, thus, $\_ \angle \_$ or
$\_ \_ \angle$, הַבַּרְזֶל (1^3), בֶּן־הֲדַד (1^4) ; one or more words making
four (or more) syllables, with the third or fourth accented,
thus, $\_ \_ \angle \_$ or $\_ \_ \_ \angle$, בְּחֻומֹת־רַבָּה, לִקְרַאת־אֱלֹהֶיךָ (1^{14}).

It is to be noted that (1) the essential thing is the *tone*, the
number of syllables being a matter of no consequence. (2) The
Măqqēph plays an important part in combining two or even three
words into one. (3) In any effort to express the rhythmic movement of a line, much care must be given to a consideration of the
details connected, *e.g.* with Segholate forms (in which the helping
vowel does not count in forming a syllable) ; the use of Šᵉwâ,
which may or may not count as a vowel and thus form a syllable ;
the treatment of particles (prepositions, conjunctions, adverbs,
negatives, pronouns, etc.) as proclitics and enclitics ; the recession
of the accent for various reasons ; the pausal forms.

4. The *line*, in Hebrew poetry, is usually a combination of
two or more tone-phrases. The possibilities of line-structure are
numerous. Those most frequently found in Amos and Hosea are
(*a*) the dimeter, made up of two tone-phrases, *e.g.* $1^{6e.\,7b}$ 6^{14c}.
The dimeter is found, for the most part, either as a shortened
(*i.e.* brachycatalectic) trimeter (1^{14b} 2^{8d}), or in a combination of
two dimeters, thus making a tetrameter ($2^{7c.\,d}$ $4^{1c.\,d}$), or in the
Qînah-measure ($5^{2b.\,d.\,3c.\,e.\,4b.\,c}$). (*b*) By far the most common
movement is that of the trimeter, consisting of three tone-phrases,
e.g. דִּרְשׁוּ טוֹב וְאַל־רָע (4^{4a}), בָּאוּ בֵית־אֵל וּפִשְׁעוּ (1^{5d}), וְגֹלוּ עַם־אֲרָם קִירָה
(5^{14a}). (*c*) Rarer combinations of tone-phrases are of *four*, *i.e.*
tetrameter, with a caesural pause after the second (3^{12d} 5^{25a}) ;
five, *i.e.* pentameter (2^{9c}), in most cases to be taken rather as a
combination of $3 + 2$ or $2 + 3$; *six*, *i.e.* hexameter (*v.i.*), which
is either $4 + 2$, $2 + 4$, or $2 + 2 + 2$ (5^{19b}).

5. The poetical *period* (ordinarily called parallelism) consists
of two or more closely connected lines. We find a variety of com-

---

* The examples cited are from Amos, unless otherwise indicated.

binations; *e.g.* (*a*) The most common period is the *bi-trimeter*, *i.e.* double trimeter ($1^2\ 4^4$), which, in some cases, may easily be reckoned an hexameter ($3^{4.\ 5}$). (*b*) Much rarer is the bi-tetrameter, *i.e.* double tetrameter ($4^{1\,c.\ d}\ 7^{14\,b.\ c}$). (*c*) Quite frequently there is used the combination of $3 + 2$, rarely $2 + 3$. This is the so-called Qînah-measure (pp. 108 f.). (*d*) Other combinations are that of $4 + 3$ ($5^{15\,a.\ b}$), rarely $3 + 4$ (6^{13}), $4 + 2$ ($6^{8\,c.\ d}$), as well as 3×2 (*i.e.* triple dimeter) ($6^{14\,c}$).

6. The *strophe* is a combination of periods, or of periods and lines, which, in every case, constitutes a logical unit.* A variety of combinations occurs : (*a*) Groups, consisting only of periods, of which there may be two ($3^{4.\ 5}\ 5^5$), three ($5^{18-20.\ 21-24.\ 25-27}$), four (Ho. $2^{4\,f.}$), five ($5^{7.\ 10\,f.\ 12-14.\ 15-17}$), or six (Ho. $4^{1-3}\ 5^{1-3}$). (*b*) Groups, consisting of periods and independent lines, in various combinations, *e.g.* bi-trimeter and trimeter, *i.e.* $3 + 3$ and 3 ($1^{4.\ 5\,a}$) or bi-trimeter and dimeter, *i.e.* $3 + 3$ and 2 (1^{15}), or three bi-trimeters and a trimeter (Ho. 11^{5-7}, etc.). (*c*) Groups, consisting of lines and periods, in combinations like those given above, *e.g.* a trimeter and five bi-trimeters (Ho. 9^{1-4}), a trimeter and a bi-trimeter (Am. 7^{16}).

It is to be noted further concerning strophes, (1) that in Amos the six-line strophe occurs most frequently, while the four-line strophe is next in order of frequency, and no strophe exceeds ten lines. In Hosea, on the other hand, the strophes are, as a rule, longer than in Amos, twelve lines being not an uncommon length, while eight-, nine-, and ten-line strophes are of frequent occurrence. (2) In a few cases the strophes are indicated by external signs, *e.g.* Am. 1 and 2 by the recurrence of certain introductory and closing formulas; in Am. 4^{4-13} by the recurrence of the refrain; but in the remaining cases the thought is usually so distinct and separate as to render the strophic division comparatively certain.

7. The many introductory and concluding expressions must be considered, each on its own merits. — (*a*) It is frequently a question whether the introductory words relating to the *utterance* †

---

* Cf. Sievers, pp. 134 f., who, however, lays greater emphasis upon the necessity of formal resemblance.

† *E.g.* ויאמר (Ho. 1^4 3^1), כה אמר י׳ (Am. 1^8 $5^{3\,a}$).

should be treated as a part of the poetical form, and consequently as one of the lines, or tone-phrases. It does not seem possible to lay down an absolute rule, as is done by Baumann.* In Am. $1^{3.\ 6.\ 9.\ 11.\ 13}\ 2^{1.\ 4.\ 6}$ it matters little whether these words are counted or not. In Ho. $1^{2.\ 4.\ 6.\ 8}$ they stand outside of the strophe. In Am. $3^{11.\ 12}\ 7^{10.\ 11.\ 12.\ 14.\ 17}$ they can scarcely be omitted. (*b*) There is the same question in the case of such introductory phrases as " Behold, the days are coming " ($8^{11\ a}\ 9^{13}$), " hear this word, etc. " ($3^1\ 4^1\ 5^1\ 8^4$). (*c*) The same question arises concerning similar phrases at the end. Some omit them entirely,† as in $1^{5.\ 8}\ 2^{16}$ $3^{13.\ 15}\ 4^3\ 8^9$. Others retain them. ‡

8. A splendid example of the refrain occurs in Am. 4^{4-13}, in which five strophes close with the words, " But ye did not return unto me — it is the oracle of Yahweh." Cf. Is. 9^8–10^4 (which was probably modelled after Amos) ; also Ps. $39^{6.\ 12}\ 42^{6.\ 12}\ 43^5\ 46^{(4)\ 8.\ 12}$ $49^{13.\ 21}\ 57^{6.\ 12}\ 59^{6.\ 12.\ 18}$. Something approaching to a refrain is seen in Ho. $5^3\ 6^{10}$, " Thou, O Ephraim, hast committed harlotry, and Israel is defiled."

9. Textual criticism has found a great ally in this new work of metrical and strophic structure. § Evidence of this appears in every recently published commentary. A new criticism has arisen, distinct from the textual (or lower) and from the historical (or higher). We may call this the *strophic* (including metrical) criticism. By the application of this criticism, (*a*) introductory and concluding formulas will be thrown out, *e.g.* $1^{5.\ 8}\ 2^{16}\ 3^{15.\ 13}$; (*b*) glosses and variants are detected, while repetitious phrases and unnecessary adjectives are given their proper place, *e.g.* $5^{23}\ 7^{8\ a}\ 8^{2\ a.\ 13}$; (*c*) lacunae are recognized, *e.g.* $2^{10.\ 13}\ 3^2\ 4^{1.\ 11}\ 5^6\ 7^7\ 8^1$; (*d*) additions made merely for explanation or by way of expansion are separated from the original text, *e.g.* $1^{14\ d}\ 2^{12\ c}\ 3^{1.\ 9\ e}$ $4^{3.\ 7\ a.\ 7\ b.\ 8\ a.\ 10\ b}\ 5^{16\ e}$; while (*e*), as the most important service of all, the great divisions of thought are clearly marked (*v.s.*). This criticism, while " lower " (having to do with the form) is also " higher," since it is largely a logical criticism.

---

* Following Sievers, §§ 240–246.   † Sievers, Baumann.

‡ Müller, Condamin, Löhr.

§ Cf. Sievers, §§ 240–246 ; Da. *O. T. Proph.* 242 f.

§ 21. The Language and Style of Amos and Hosea.

Reference has already been made to the character of the language of these earliest prophets, as also to certain alleged Aramaicisms in Amos (p. cxxxviii), and in Hosea (p. cxl). The general characteristics of the style of Amos have been noted (pp. cxxxix f.). It is entirely in accord with the sentiment of modern scholarship to designate the language of both Amos and Hosea as classic Hebrew. This becomes much more clear in Hosea's case, when one separates from the original Hosea the secondary material that belongs to a later age; and especially when the original text of the separate pieces appears in its clearness and logical unity, after excluding the elements which, by their interpolation, have given an entirely wrong conception, as against the straightforwardness and lucidity of Hosea's method of expression.*

1. Concerning Amos, in particular, certain facts of a linguistic character deserve consideration. Among these are : —

(1) Those elements which point to a fully developed, and, indeed, thoroughly artistic style, viz.: (*a*) the rhythmical flow of the language, which moves on easily and smoothly in stately periods; this rhythmic factor is very marked and furnishes one of the strongest arguments for the poetic character of the book; (*b*) the use of chiasm, *e.g.* 2⁶· ¹⁴ 4⁷ 5⁵· ¹⁰· ²⁴ 6⁸· ¹² 7⁹· ¹¹ 8¹² 9¹; (*c*) the occurrence of paronomasia, *e.g.* 5⁵ 8² 7¹⁰; (*d*) the employment of assonance, *e.g.* 2¹⁶ᵇ 4¹ 6⁷ 9¹.

(2) Those instances of phraseology or syntax which are either rare or very frequent, viz.: (*a*) rare phrases and constructions are seen in the use of the accusatives שרע (3¹²) and פרצים (4³); the construction of the numerals in 5³; the sequence of tenses in והמטרתי and אמטיר (4⁷ᵃ), יאכל (4⁹), and ואכלה (7⁴); the various usages of ל in הרבו לפשע (4⁴), לשלשת . . . לבקר (4⁴), ולשבית (8⁴), and להקטין וגי (8⁵); the adverbial use of מִי in מי יקום (7²· ⁵); the use of ל with the direct object as in Aramaic (6³ 8⁹); the use of ב with אריח in 5²¹ (only here and Ex. 30³⁸ Lv. 26³¹; in Is. 11³ probably a dittograph); and the phrase מהלאה ל in 5²⁷ (only here and Je. 22¹⁹ Gn. 35²¹).

(*b*) Among the favorite phrases and constructions are the following: The use of the participle is frequent, especially in descriptions, where it furnishes

---

* Cf. on the one side, the clearness and smoothness of 13¹⁻¹¹, which has preserved its original form with only slight corruption ; and on the other, the confusion of chap. 12, as found in 𝔐𝔗, and the obscurity of chap. 11, due to its corrupt text.

a convenient substitute for a relative clause, *e.g.* 2^7 $3^{10.\ 12}$ $4^{1.\ 11}$ $5^{3.\ 7.\ 10.\ 12.\ 18}$ $6^{1.\ 3.\ 4.\ 5.\ 6.\ 7.\ 13}$ $8^{4.\ 14}$ 9^1; elsewhere it is used as a vivid substitute for a perfect or imperfect, *e.g.* 2^{13} 5^1 $6^{8.\ 14}$ $7^{7.\ 8.\ 16}$. The idiom לא אוסיף עוד occurs in $7^{8.\ 13}$ 8^2 (cf. 5^2 8^{14}). The rhetorical question is made use of in $3^{3-6.\ 8}$ $5^{20.\ 25}$ $6^{12.\ 13}$ 8^8 9^7; and conciseness is attained by the use of the circumstantial clause with אין in $3^{4.\ 5}$ $5^{2.\ 6}$.

(*c*) Examples of words, or usages of words, which are rare or frequent, *e.g.*:
(*a*) words found only in Amos*: נעלים, 2^6 8^6 (in dual); תעיק and מעיק, 2^{13}; בדל and דמשׁק, 3^{12}; פרות (used of women), 4^1; הרצות (in this form), 4^1; רוגה and צנות, 4^2; סירות (fem. pl.), 4^2; הי, 5^{16}; אפל, 5^{20}; עצרות (in pl.), 5^{21}; הפרטים, 6^5; מזרקי (used of wine), 6^6; רסיסים, 6^{11}; הלקשׁ, 7^1; אנך, 7^7; בולס, 7^{14}; נשׁקעה (in Niph.), 8^8; כְּשָׁיִם, 9^7 (pl. of this form only here). To these may be added words found in Amos, and only once elsewhere: נקדים, 7^{14} (1^1) 2 K. 3^4; חסון, 2^9 Is. 1^{31}; עקב כי, 4^{12} 2 S. 12^{10}; בַּר, 5^{11} (8^6) Ps. 72^{16} (elsewhere בָּר); המנדים, 6^3 Is. 66^5; מרוח, 6^7 Je. 16^5; בקעים, 6^{11} Is. 22^9; נבי, 7^1 Na. 3^{17}; כלוב, $8^{1.\ 2}$ Je. 5^{27}; בצעם, 9^1 Jo. 2^8 (in similar sense); and also words found in Amos, and only two or three times elsewhere: חרצות, 1^3 Is. 28^{27} 41^{15} Jb. 41^{22}; עמיר, 2^{13} Mi. 4^{12} Je. 9^{21} Zc. 12^6; נכחה, 3^{10} (in fem. sg. only here and Is. 59^{14}; in fem. pl. Is. 26^{10} 30^{10}); ברעים, 3^{12} (only occurrence outside of P); באש, 4^{10} Is. 34^3 Jo. 2^{20}; אור, 4^{11} Is. 7^4 Zc. 3^2; מבליג, 5^9 (ptcp. only here; cf. Jb. 9^{27} 10^{20} Ps. 39^{14}); מתאוים, 5^{18} (ptcp. only here and Pr. 13^4 Nu. 11^{34}); סרחים, $6^{4.\ 7}$ Ez. 17^6 23^{15} Ex. 26^{13}; מרבק, 6^4 1 S. 28^{24} Je. 46^{21} Mal. 3^{20}; גוי, 7^1 Dt. 18^4 Jb. 31^{20} Ps. 72^6; ישחק for יצחק, $7^{9.\ 16}$ Je. 33^{26} Ps. 105^9; תתעלפנה, 8^{13} (in Hithp. only here and Jon. 4^8 Gn. 38^{14}); נחש, 9^3 (in mythological sense, also Is. 27^1 Jb. 26^{13}); שקעה, 9^5 (in Qal only here and Je. 51^{64} Nu. 11^2); פְלִשְׁתִּיִם, 9^7 (this form of pl. only here and Gn. 10^{14} 1 Ch. 14^{10}).

(*β*) Favorite words and ideas are the following: Expressions for *the poor and needy*, viz. אביון, 2^6 5^{12} $8^{4.\ 6}$; דלים, 2^6 4^1 5^{11} 8^6; ענוים, 2^7 4^1 8^4. Words for *justice, righteousness*, viz. משׁפט, $5^{7.\ 15.\ 24}$ 6^{12}; צדקה, $5^{7.\ 24}$ 6^{12}. Expressions for *destruction*, viz. "send fire upon," 1^4, etc.; "kindle a fire," 1^{14}; "cast fire on," 5^6; "break the bar," 1^5; "cut off inhabitants, etc.," $1^{5.\ 8}$ 2^3; "go into exile," $1^{5.\ 15}$ $5^{5.\ 27}$ 6^7 $7^{11.\ 17}$; "turn my hand against," 1^8; "slay," 2^3 4^{10}; "visit upon," $3^{2.\ 14}$; "the sword," 4^{10} $7^{9.\ 11.\ 17}$ 9^1; "famine," 8^{11}; "end is come," 8^2; "groan," 2^{13}; "smite," 3^{15} 4^9 6^{11} 9^1; "taken with hooks," 4^2; "send pestilence," 4^{10}; "overthrow," 4^{11}; "hurl down," 5^2; "pass through the midst of," 5^{17}; "day of calamity," 6^3; "deliver up," 6^8; "crush," 6^{14}; "lay waste," 7^9; "darken the earth," 8^9; "put mine eye on them for evil," 9^4; "destroy," 9^8. Titles of the Deity, viz. Yahweh (33 times), Lord Yahweh (15 times), Yahweh God of hosts (4^{13} $5^{14.\ 15.\ 27}$ $6^{8b.\ 14b}$), the Lord ($7^{7.\ 8b}$ 9^1), thy God (4^{12}), God (4^{11}).

2. Concerning Hosea, in particular, notice may be taken of the following phenomena: (1) Certain characteristics of linguistic

---

* Cf. Carrier, *Hebraica*, V. 135 f.

usage that indicate his possession of a mature and well-formed literary style : (*a*) While the rhythm of Hosea is on the whole inferior to that of Amos, there being many passages in which the movement is halting and broken, yet there are portions of which the rhythm is as marked and fine as that of Amos, *e.g.* 9^{1-8} 13^{1-9}.

(*b*) Chiasm is of comparatively rare occurrence, but is definitely recognized and employed, *e.g.* $4^{4.\ 9.\ 13\ d.\ e}$ $5^{3\ a.\ b}$ $7^{7\ b.\ c}$ $10^{14\ a.\ b}$.

(*c*) A number of cases of paronomasia occur, *e.g.* יזרעאל (1^4), בית און (4^{15} 10^5), יפריא and אפרים and פרי (9^{16}), אפרים and פרא (8^9), ואל תשבעו בבאר שבע (4^{15}), אפרים (13^{15}), שב and ישבו (9^8), שוב in two senses (11^5), גלים and גלגל (12^{12}), מצא in two senses (12^9).

(*d*) Assonance appears in 2^7 (repetition of suffix י), 3^4 4^1 (repetition of מצרים תקצרם), $4^{16\ a}$ 5^1 . . . מצפה, רשת פרושה פח, also שחת השטים ($8^{7\ b}$ $9^{6\ b}$), שריהם סררים (9^{15}), מזבחות and מצבות ($10^{1.\ 2}$), מף תקברם ($10^{1.\ 2}$).

(2) Syntactical usage, phraseology, and vocabulary : (*a*) Rare and irregular constructions are common in the Massoretic text of Hosea, but many of them disappear when the text is properly corrected (pp. clxxvi f.).

Among those still remaining are : the ellipses before לכסות (2^{11}) and ונגלה (7^2), the omission of the object of יתנו (5^4), the force of מן in עקבה מדם (6^8), the construction of גרודים (6^9), the force of ל in להוציא (9^{13}), use of ל with direct object (10^{12} 11^3), the force of ב in בעזרך (13^9), the construct followed by relative clause with relative omitted (1^2), the gender of אותה (4^{19}), בלי with a participle (7^8), use of ל expressing *time at which* (9^5), and the use of the jussive אוסף (9^{15}).

(*b*) Among the favorite constructions of Hosea are his use of asyndeton (more frequent than in any other O. T. book), *e.g.* $2^{13.\ 14}$ $4^{6\ e.\ 7.\ 10.\ 11.\ 18}$ $5^{6.\ 8.\ 10.\ 11.\ 15}$ $6^{3.\ 10}$ $7^{12.\ 16}$ $9^{6.\ 7.\ 9.\ 15}$ $10^{1.\ 2\ b.\ 6.\ 11\ b.\ 13}$ 11^4; the frequent introduction of clauses by עתה, *e.g.* 4^{16} 5^7 7^2 $8^{3.\ 13\ b}$ $10^{2\ a}$ 13^2; verbal apposition, 1^6 $5^{11.\ 15}$ 6^4, and the frequent use of אין (especially with the meaning *without*), $3^{3.\ 4}$ 4^1 $5^{2.\ 14}$ $7^{7.\ 11}$ 8^7 13^4.

(*c*) Hosea's vocabulary is extensive and varied ; though speaking almost continually upon the same subject, he is ever finding new words in which to express his thought. Hence the number of "favorite" words is comparatively small.

Among those most frequently occurring are : זונים (1^2 2^4 4^{12} 5^4), זנה (1^2 2^7 3^3 $4^{10.\ 11.\ 12.\ 13.\ 14.\ 18}$ 5^8 6^{10} 9^1), פקר (1^4 2^{15} $4^{9.\ 14}$ 8^{13} $9^{7.\ 9}$ 12^3), ירע (2^{10} $5^{3.\ 4.\ 9}$ 6^3 7^9 $8^{2.\ 4}$ $9^{2.\ 7}$ 11^3 $12^{4.\ 5}$), רעת (4^1 $6^{3.\ 6}$), נאף (3^1 $4^{2.\ 13.\ 14}$), שכח (2^{15} 4^6 8^{14} 13^6), חטא (4^7 8^{11} 12^9 13^2), חטאה (4^8 $9^{7.\ 9}$ 10^9 13^{12}), עון (4^8 5^5 7^1 8^{13} $9^{7.\ 9}$ 10^{10} 12^9 13^{12}), אשם (4^{15} 5^{15} 10^2 13^1 14^1), טמא (5^3 6^{10} $9^{3.\ 4}$), חסר (4^1 $6^{5.\ 6}$ 10^{12}).

Among the rarer words and forms in Hosea may be noticed those that occur nowhere else, viz.: לחך (3^2), נאפפיה (2^4), אתנה (2^{14}), חליתה (2^{15}), נבלתה (2^{12}), יגהה (5^{13}), עקבה (6^8, in this sense), יתבולל (7^8, in this form), זרקה (7^9, intransitive), שׂד (7^{13}, as particle of denunciation), שבבים (8^6), הכבי (8^{13}), משטמה (9^8), בקק (10^1, intransitive), לחם אונים (9^2), יערף (10^2, in this sense), תרגלתי (11^3, in this form), עבתות (11^4, in this form), רתח (13^1), תלאבות (13^5), סגור (13^8), נחם (13^{14}), יפריא (13^{15}), לצצים (7^5, in this form), ישדד (10^2, in Po.), אוכיל (11^4, in Hiph.), זו (7^{16}), התנו and יתנו (8^9), יקוש (9^8), צמקים (9^{14}), הריותיו (14^1).

Of words that occur not more than three times outside of Hosea there are: אשישי (3^1 Ct. $2^{5\,f.}$ 2 S. 6^{19} 1 Ch. 16^3 Is. 16^7), אכרה (3^2 Jb. 6^{27} 40^{30} Dt. 2^6), שקווי (2^7 Ps. 102^{10} Pr. 3^8), זנונים (1^2 $2^{4.\,6}$ 4^{12} 5^4 Ez. $23^{11.\,29}$ 2 K. 9^{22} Na. 3^4), רקב (5^{12}, in this sense, Jb. 13^{28}), מזור (5^{13} Je. 30^{13}), ילבט (4^{14} Pr. $10^{8.\,10}$), שערורׂיה (6^{10} Je. 18^{13}), פותה (7^{11} Jb. 5^2), כמריו (4^4 10^5 Zp. 1^4 2 K. 23^5), מגן (11^8 Gn. 14^{20} Pr. 4^9), עקב ($12^{4\,a.\,8}$ Je. 9^8 Gn. 27^{36}), תמרורים (12^{15} Je. 6^{26} 31^{15}), לרה (9^{11} 2 K. 19^3 Is. 37^3 Je. 13^{21}), משבר (13^{13} Is. 37^3 2 K. 19^3), קטב (13^{13} Is. 28^2 Dt. 32^{24} Ps. 91^6), אחו (13^{15} Gn. $41^{2.\,18}$ Jb. 8^{11}), נירו (10^{12} Je. 4^3), ניר (10^{12} Je. 4^2 Pr. 13^{23}), יושר (10^{14} Is. 33^1, in Hoph.).

Of other uncommon or poetical forms may be cited: the archaic ending ון (10^{11}), אהבתי (4^3), אמלל (4^3), ירדפו (8^3), סופתה (8^7), ישׁרׂנׂי (5^{15} 6^3), ישׁרׂני (9^{16} 11^2 13^2), אלות (10^4), כמו (7^4 8^{12} 13^7), קאם (10^{14}).

It cannot be maintained that the peculiarities of Hosea furnish any considerable data toward the hypothesis of a Northern dialect as distinguished from the Southern.

§ 22. TEXT AND VERSIONS OF AMOS AND HOSEA.

1. The text of Amos is as well preserved as perhaps any text in the Hebrew Bible, the number of unintelligible passages being remarkably small (cf. 3^{10} 4^9 5^6 $6^{1.\,2}$ 7^2).

The text of Hosea, however, is one of the most corrupt in the O. T., the number of passages which almost defy interpretation being extremely large. Among these are 4^{18} $5^{2.\,8.\,11.\,15}$ $6^{3.\,5.\,9}$ $7^{2.\,6.\,12\,c.\,16}$ $8^{5\,a.\,10\,b}$ $9^{8.\,13}$ $10^{5.\,9.\,10}$ $11^{2.\,3.\,7.\,9\,b.\,10}$ $12^{9.\,12}$ $13^{1.\,9.\,10.\,15}$ $14^{3\,b}$. Hosea's reputation for obscurity is due in large measure to the corrupt form in which the text of his message has reached us. That this corruption began at a comparatively early date is evident from the fact that some of the errors of 𝕸 appear already in 𝕲, e.g. $7^{12\,c}$, בְּשֵׁמַע, ἐν τῇ ἀκοῇ ; 7^{16}, עַל לֹא, εἰς οὐθέν ; 11^9, אָבוֹא בְעִיר, εἰσελεύσομαι εἰς πόλιν. For the restoration of the original text much help may be derived from the versions, but in many cases resort must be had to critical conjecture.

(1) In the correction of 𝕸𝕿, 𝔊 is most helpful. That the textual basis of 𝔊 is different from 𝕸𝕿 appears from the large number of cases in which the reading of 𝔊 cannot have come from 𝕸𝕿, e.g. Am. 1¹⁵, הוא, οἱ ἱερεῖς αὐτῶν=כהניו; 2¹¹, אקים, ἔλαβον=אֶקַּח; Ho. 2¹⁷, תקוה, σύνεσιν αὐτῆς = תְּבוּנָה(?); 8¹⁰, ממשא, τοῦ χρίειν = ממשח; 4¹⁸, סר סבאם, ἥρέτισεν Χαναναίους. 𝔊's rendering was evidently made before 𝕸𝕿 had become the standard text. The character of 𝔊's rendering is in general the same in Amos and Hosea as elsewhere.* The translation of Hosea seems to be inferior to that of Amos, but this is probably due, in large measure, to the greater difficulty of the text. Sometimes 𝔊 is very free, e.g. Am. 3⁹. ¹⁰. ¹¹, ארמנות, χῶραι; 5²¹, לא אריח בעצ', οὐ μὴ ὀσφρανθῶ θυσίας ἐν ταῖς πανηγύρεσιν ὑμῶν; Ho. 2⁷, שקויי, πάντα ὅσα μοι καθήκει; 5¹³, וישלח, καὶ ἀπέστειλεν πρέσβεις; in other cases excessive literalness is aimed at, e.g. in Am. 7². ⁵ the synonyms סלח and חדל are differentiated; 5¹⁸, למה זה, ἵνα τί αὕτη; Ho. 2¹, במקום אשר, ἐν τῷ τόπῳ οὗ; the idiom לא אוסיף וגו' is regularly rendered, οὐ μὴ προσθήσω, κ.τ.λ., e.g. Ho. 1⁶ 9¹⁵ 13², etc. Inaccurate renderings are of common occurrence, e.g. Am. 6¹, שאננים, ἐξουθενοῦσι; 3¹², בפאת מטה, κατέναντι τῆς φυλῆς; Ho. 9¹⁰, כבכורה, ὡς σκοπόν; 7¹³, שר, δείλαιοι; 5¹¹, הואיל, ἤρξατο; 7⁶, ישן, ὕπνου ἐνεπλήσθη.

Occasionally ignorance of the meaning is shown by resort to transliteration, e.g. Am. 1¹, בנקרים, ἐν 'Ακκαρείμ; and, perhaps, 3¹², ערש, ἱερεῖς.

When due allowance is made for the errors of 𝔊, there still remain many passages in which its text is preferable to 𝕸𝕿. In this commentary 𝔊 has suggested corrections of 𝕸𝕿 in Am. 2⁷. ¹⁵ᵇ 3⁵. ⁹ 4³. ¹⁰ 5⁹. ²⁶ 8¹¹ᵇ Ho. 2⁸ 4⁴. ¹⁰. ¹⁹ 5⁸. ¹¹. ¹⁵ 6¹. ³. ⁵. ⁹ 7¹. ⁶. ¹² ᶜ. ¹⁴ 8¹² 9². ⁹. ¹³. ¹⁴ 10⁵. ¹². ¹³ᵇ. ¹⁵ 11². ³. ⁷ 12². ³. ⁹ 13². ⁴. ⁵. ⁶. ⁷. ⁹. ¹⁰. ¹⁴ 14³. ⁹.

(2) The remaining Greek versions present the same characteristics in Amos and Hosea as elsewhere.† (a) Aquila's pedantic literalness is illustrated by Am. 1², βρυχήσεται, שאג; cf. 𝔊 ἐφθέγξατο; 2¹⁶, καὶ ὁ καρτερὸς καρδίαν αὐτοῦ ἐν δυνατοῖς γυμνὸς φεύξεται; Ho. 2¹⁸, ἔχων με = בעלי; 5¹³, δικασόμενον = ירב; 8¹³, θυσίας φέρε φέρε = זבחי הבהבי. His fondness for transliteration is frequently indulged, e.g. Am. 5²³, ναβλῶν σου, נבליך; 7¹, τῆς γάζης τοῦ βασιλέως, גזי המ'; 2¹², Ναζαραίους, נזירים; cf. 𝔊 ἡγιασμένους; 6¹⁰, ἡσυχώθητι, הס כי לא; Ho. 9⁹ and 10¹⁰, where הגבעה is transliterated, though 𝔊 translates it in both cases. 'A. also translates many proper names, cf. e.g. Ho. 4¹⁵ 5⁸. ¹³ 9¹³ 10⁶. ¹⁴. His etymological tendency crops out often, e.g. Am. 3¹⁰, ὀρθότητα, נכחה; 7¹, ὄψιμος, לקש. The rendering of Aquila presup-

---

* See especially Swete, Introduction to the O. T. in Greek, 315-41.

† See Swete, Introduction, 29-58.

poses a text different from 𝕸𝕿 in very few cases, e.g. Am. 1³, כהניו for הוא;
4¹⁰, באפ׳ for ובאפ׳; 8³, αἱ στρόφιγγες = צירות, 𝕸𝕿 שירות; 8⁸, σκεπασθήσεται
for עלתה; Ho. 11⁷ 12⁵·⁹ 13¹. The version of Aquila is thus of little value for
the correction of 𝕸𝕿. Readings of Aquila have been adopted only in two
cases, Am. 4¹⁰ (omission of ו in ובאפכם) and Ho. 11⁷ (עֹל for עַל of 𝕸𝕿), both
of which have the support of other versions.

(b) The version of Symmachus is the very opposite of Aquila's in that
it strives after an expression of the idea in pure and graceful language rather
than an exact and literal reproduction of the Hebrew. Examples of this
freedom may be found in Am. 1³ 4¹ 5¹². While using 𝕸𝕿 as a basis, Σ.
shows familiarity with 𝕲, ᾽A., and especially Θ. He exhibits, however, a
certain amount of independence. His rendering involves a different textual
basis from 𝕸𝕿 in Am. 1¹⁴ 4¹⁰ 8⁸ (all agreeing with ᾽A., v.s.); 5⁹, יביא for
יבוא; 5²⁶, סַכַּת for סכות; 6¹, הַנִּקָּבִים for נקבי; and Ho. 3¹ 7¹⁵ 8⁹ 11⁴·⁷ 12⁵·¹² 13²·⁶.
Readings of Σ. have been adopted in Am. 4¹⁰ 5²⁶ 6¹ Ho. 11⁷ (two), in only
one of which, viz. Ho. 11⁷, וַיְקָרִיאֵהוּ, is any independence of other versions
exhibited.

(c) Theodotion's version is a revision of 𝕲, and of practically no independent value for the correction of 𝕸𝕿. That he had the Hebrew text
before him is evident from his frequent transliterations, e.g. Am. 1¹, ἐν νωκεδειμ,
בנקדים; 7⁷, ἀδωναι, ארני. In no case does he furnish a text independent
of both 𝕲 and 𝕸𝕿. He supports the readings adopted in Ho. 9¹³, דְּוָיו;
10⁵, לְעֵגֶל; 11⁷, עֹל.

(3) The fragments of the Old Latin version are of much value for the
correction of 𝕲. The version is on the whole a literal translation of 𝕲, but
presents many variations in agreement with the recension of Lucian. Its most
significant departure from 𝕸𝕿 and 𝕲 is in Am. 1¹ (q.v.). Little use of it
has been made in this commentary, since it was not accessible till the textual
work was practically finished and much of it in type.

(4) The Syriac furnishes a fairly careful and accurate rendering. In
general it follows 𝕲, but shows frequent independence, e.g. Am. 1¹¹ follows
𝕸𝕿; 1¹⁵ takes מלכם as proper name; Ho. 3⁴ 2¹⁰·²⁰ 4⁴ 5¹³ 6¹⁰. It presupposes
a different text * from 𝕸𝕿 and 𝕲, e.g. in Am. 1¹¹·¹⁴ 2⁸·¹⁰·¹⁶ 3²·⁵·¹¹·¹³ 4⁵·⁹ 5¹⁶
6¹·³·⁷ 7⁵ 8¹·³·⁴ Ho. 1⁶ 3² 4⁵·⁷·¹²·¹⁸ 5⁴·⁷ 6⁹·¹⁰ 7⁶·⁸·¹¹ 8⁶ 9¹ 10⁷·¹⁰ 11⁴·⁸ 12¹·²·⁵·¹⁰·¹²
13¹·¹⁰·¹³. Its readings have been adopted in preference to 𝕸𝕿 or 𝕲 in
Am. 1¹¹ 3¹¹ 5¹⁶ 6¹ Ho. 4⁷·¹²ᶜ·¹⁹ 6¹ 7⁶ 8⁶ 9¹ 11⁴ 12²·³·¹⁹.

(5) The Targum of Jonathan is a paraphrase rather than a translation,
and is characterized by its adherence to the letter of the text, and by its
theological point of view, e.g. all anthropomorphisms are carefully removed.
Consonantal departures from 𝕸𝕿 are of rare occurrence, variations from the
vocalization of 𝕸𝕿 being more frequent. No emendation has been adopted
on the basis of 𝕿 independently of 𝕲 and other versions.

(6) The Vulgate follows 𝕸𝕿 very closely, but sometimes borrows Greek

---

* For details see textual treatment in commentary.

renderings. The literalness of 'A. is sought after at times, but, as a rule, the translation is made with considerable freedom, and this, together with Jerome's imperfect knowledge of Hebrew, which not infrequently caused him to err (*e.g.* Am. 5²⁴, *revelabitur*, וְיִגַּל; 6⁷, *factio*, מרוח), and the uncertain state of 𝔙's own text, renders 𝔙 an unsafe guide to the original text. No readings have been adopted here on 𝔙's authority uncorroborated by that of other versions.

2. The following transpositions have been made: (1) In Amos: 2², המת בשאון מואב, follows לשדר (2¹); 2⁷ follows 2⁸, and 2⁹ follows 2¹⁰; 2¹¹ᵇ follows 2¹²; 2¹⁵, רכב הסום, exchanges places with ערום in 2¹⁶; 2¹⁶ᵃ follows לא ימלט in 2¹⁵ᵇ; 3¹⁵ follows 3¹¹; 5³ᵃ follows 5¹; 5³ᶜ, לבית ישראל, follows והיוצאת מאה; 5⁵ᶜ follows 5⁴; 5⁷ precedes 5¹⁰; 5⁸, יהוה שמו is placed at beginning of verse; 6⁸ᵇ follows 6⁷; 6¹⁴ᵇ follows ¹⁴ᶜ; 8³ follows 8⁹.

(2) In Hosea: 2¹⁰·¹¹ are connected with 2⁷; 2¹⁴ follows 2¹¹; 2¹³ precedes 2¹⁵; 2¹⁹ is joined to 2¹⁵; 4¹⁴ᵈ follows 4⁴; 4¹²ᵃ·ᵇ precedes 4¹¹; 7¹²ᶜ precedes 7¹¹; 8⁵ᵇ precedes 8⁵ᵃ; 9³ comes between 9⁴ ᵃⁿᵈ ⁵; 9¹⁶ follows 9¹¹; 9¹²ᶜ follows 9¹⁵; 10⁷ comes between 10⁸ ᵃ ᵃⁿᵈ ⁸ᵇ; 12¹³ is connected with 12¹ᵇ; 12¹⁵ comes between 12¹¹ ᵃⁿᵈ ¹²; 14⁴ᶜ follows 14³.

3. The errors of 𝔐𝔗 may be classified as follows: (1) Changes in vocalization: Am. 2⁷ 8⁴, הַשֹּׁאֲפִים for הֹשֲׁאֲפִים; 2¹⁵ᵃ, יְמַלֵּט for יִמַלֵט; 5²⁶, סִכּוּת for סְכּוּת; 6¹, נְקֻבֵי for נַקְּבִים; 8³, שִׁירוֹת for שָׁרוֹת, and הָשְׁלִיךְ for הִשְׁלִיךְ; 9¹⁰, סָכַת for סֻכַּת; תָּחֻדֵם for תַּקְרִים; Ho. 5¹¹, עָשׁוּק for עָשֻׁק, and רצוץ for רוֹצֵץ; חָגִישׁ for תָּגִשׁ, and הַקְּרִים for תַּקְרִים; אֶנְחָרֵם for אֲנִסֵרֵם; 6⁸, יוֹרֶה for יָרֹוֶה; 7¹²ᶜ, אִפְּהֵם for אַפְּהֶם; יַנְהֶה for יְנַהֵּה; 5¹³, תוֹרְתִי for תּוֹרֹתִי; 8¹¹, כִּי שְׁבָבִים for כְּשֹׁבְבִים; 8⁴, עָשׁוּ for עֲשֹׁו; יָסוֹרוּ for יָסוּרוּ; 7¹⁴, חָלָק for חֵלֶק; 10², שָׂחַתוּ for שֻׁחֲתוּ; 10⁵, לֶעֱגְלוֹת for לְעֶגְלֹות; 9⁸, צָפֶּה for צָפֶה; תּוֹרָתִי; 11², קָרָאִי for קֹרְאִי; עָלַי for עַל; 10⁹, חָטָאת for חַטַּאת, and שְׁכֵנִי for שֻׁכְנֵי, and לְעָגֵל for שְׁכֵן; 11⁴, יַקְרִיאֵהוּ for יְקָרְאֵהוּ; וְאַט for וָאַט; 11⁷, עַל for עֹל, and כְּמָרִים for כְּמָרִים; 12², חָטָא for חֵטְא; יָנְעִיו for יִגְעִיו, and יוּבָל for יוּבַל; 12⁹, יִבְלוּ for יִוֹבְלוּ; יָרֻבוּ for יַרֻּבֻּה; 13¹, אָשׁוּר for אַשֹּׁר; נָשָׂא for נָשָׂא; 13², זֹבְחֵי for זֹבְחֵי; 13⁶, שָׂבְעוּ for שָׂבֵעַ; 13⁷, שָׁבֻּעַ for שָׁבַע; 13⁹, שְׁחָתֶךָ for שִׁחֲתָךְ; 13¹⁵, אָחוּ for אֲחִים, and וַיֵּבֹשׁ for וַיּוֹבִישׁ; אוֹצֵר for אוֹצָר; 14³, פְּרִי for פָּרִים.

(2) The consonantal corrections may be grouped under: (*a*) Incorrect division of words: Am. 6¹², ובקרים for בבקר ים; 7², בבקר יֹם for וכלה אם והיה; Ho. 4⁴, ועמי ככמריו for ועמך כמריבי; ושחת הששים for ושחטה שטים; 5², מכלה; 8¹, כנשר for כשר; משפטי כאור for משפטיך אור; 6⁵, כשחרנו כן נמצאהו for כשחר נבון מצאו; 8⁶, מפני הם for מפניהם; 11², כשבבים for כי שבבים; 12²·³, יובל וריב for כי נשר for יובלו ריב.

(*b*) Dittography and haplography: Am. 5⁶, כאש for אש, and בית for בבית; 5⁸, מגבולם גבלכם for מגבולכם; 6², בוסכם for בושסכם; 5¹¹, ללילה for לילה; 7⁷, דבר for דבר; Ho. 3³, חומה חומת אנך for אני; 8¹¹, השלך for השליך הס; 8³, אהבו for אהבו הבו; 4¹⁸, ויומם for יומם; 4¹⁹, מזבחותם for מבחותם; 5⁸, בית for מסו; 9¹, לחטא added; dittog. of דגן; 9⁴, לחמם for לחם להם; 9¹³, אל הרע for בבית; 8¹¹ᵃ, גרן; שורים, 12¹², מעל for על; 11⁴, זרועתי for זרועתיו; 11³, להרגה for להרגה; 12⁹, עון for לעון; 13², אנכי for כי; 13⁹, עם זבחים לשדים for זבחי; 14⁸, ישבי for וישבו, and יחיו for ויחיו.

(c) Confusion of ד and ר: Am. 2⁷, הגערה for הנערה; 5¹⁶, אדני for ארנין;
Ho. 4¹⁸, סר סבאם for סבאם; 7², יערמו for יעמרו; 7¹²ᶜ, לערתם for לצרתם; 7¹⁴,
יתגוררו for יתנוררו; 9², ירעם for ידעם; 9¹³, לצור for לציד; 10¹³, בדרכך for ברכבך;
12¹², שורים for לשרים; 13⁵, ידעתיך for רעיתיך.

(d) Confusion of א and ע: Am. 6⁸, מתאב for מתעב; Ho. 5³, עתה for אתה;
7², יאמרו for יעמרו.

(e) Confusion of צ and שׂ: Am. 5⁶, יצלח for ישלח; Ho. 5¹¹, צו for שׁוא.

(f) Confusion of שׁ and שׂ: Am. 2¹, לשׂיד for לשׂדד; Ho. 5², שׂטים for שׂטים;
9¹²ᶜ, בשׂורי for בשׂורי.

(g) Confusion of ו and י: Am. 5⁹, יבוא for יביא; Ho. 9¹³, לצור for לציד;
13¹⁰, ושׁפטוך for ושׁפטיך; 12⁹ and 14⁹, לי for לו.

(h) Transposition: Am. 3¹², ברל for לבר; Ho. 5², ואני for ואין; 7³, ישׂמחו
for ימשׂחו; 10⁹, עלוה for עולה; 13¹⁰·¹⁴, אהי for איה.

(i) Confusion of ב and כ: Ho. 7¹, כרפאי for ברפאי; 7¹²ᶜ, כשמע for בשבע;
9⁴, יערבו for יערכו.

(j) Omission or insertion of א: Ho. 4⁶, ואמאסאך for ואמאסך; 5¹⁵, יאשׁמו for
ישׁמו; 8⁵, זנח for אזנח; 10¹⁵, עשׂה for אעשׂה; 11³, קחם for אקחם.

(k) Confusion of suffixes: Ho. 2⁸, דרכך for דרכה; 4¹²ᶜ, התעה for התעם; 8⁷,
לו for לה; 9², בה for בם; 12⁵, עמנו for עמו.

(l) Omission or insertion of copula: Ho. 4⁵, דמיתי for 'ור; 6¹, יך for וויך;
8⁶, והוא for 'ה; 8¹⁰, שׂרים for 'וש; 12², וברית for בר; 12³, ולפקד for 'לפ; 12⁴ᵇ,
ובאנו for 'בא.

(m) Theological change: Ho. 7¹⁶, לא על for לבעל; 9¹⁰, בשׁת for בעל.

(n) Miscellaneous corruptions: Am. 2², ומת for המת; 3⁵, פח for פני; 4⁹,
ההרבות for החרבתי; 5⁹, שׁד for שׁבר; 5¹², חטאיכם for חטאתיכם; 9¹⁰, בערינו for עדינו;
Ho. 1⁹, לכם for אלהיכם; 4⁷, המורו for אמיר; 4¹⁰, ירצו for יררצו; 5⁸, אחריך for
החרידו; 6⁹, חבר for חבאו; 6¹⁰, זנות לא' for זנית א'; 7², ללבבם for בל'; 7⁶, קרבו
for בערו; 7¹⁴, משׁכנותם for מזבחותם; 8¹⁰, ויחלו for וחלו, and ממשׂא for ממשׂח; 9⁶,
הלכו for ילכו, and משׁד for אשׁור, and מחמד לכ' for מחמדי כ'; 9⁷, החטאה omitted;
9¹³, שׁתולה for שׁתו; 10¹, ישׁה for ישׁגיא; 10⁵, יגילו for יחילו; 10⁶, בשׁנה for בשׁת;
10¹², לפי for לפרי, and וורה for פרי; 11², לבני for כדי; 11⁵, לא for לו; 11⁶,
יחד לא and ממעצותיהם for במבצריהם; 11⁷, תלואים למשׁובתי for הלאני במשׁובתיו; 11⁹,
ירומם for הוא חרל לרחמו; 11¹⁰, אבוא for אדם; 12², יגער כאריו for בעיר אחריו; 12²,
היו and בגל for אם גלעד; 12¹², ללעקב for לעקב; 12⁸, את for אל; 12⁵, וישׁוא for ושׁד
for עשׂו; 13², כתבונם for כתמונתם; 13⁹, בי for מי; 13¹⁰, בכל עריך for וכל שׂריך
13¹⁵, ורוו for דגן; 14⁸, כבין מים אחו for בין אחים.

4. The more important special studies on the text of Amos and Hosea are:
Vollers, "Das Dodekapropheton der Alexandriner," *ZAW.* III. (1883),
219–72; Zeydner, "Bijdragen tot de textkritiek op het O. T.," *ThSt.* IV.
(1886), 196–207; Sebök, *Die syrische Uebersetzung d. zwölf kleinen Propheten
und ihr Verhältniss zu dem massoretischen Text und zu den älteren Uebersetzungen, namentlich den LXX. und dem Targum* (1887); Treitel, *Die
Alexandrinische Uebersetzung des Buches Hosea* (1887; only chaps. 1–3);
Idem, "Die Septuaginta zu Hosea," *Monatsschrift für Geschichte und Wissenschaft des Judenthums,* 1898; Schuurmans Stekhoven, *De Alex. Vertaling van*

het Dodekapropheton (1887); Patterson, "The Septuagint Text of Hosea Compared with the Massoretic Text," *Hebraica*, VII. (1891), 190–221; H. Graetz, *Emendationes in plerosque sacrae Scripturae Veteris Testamenti libros, secundum veterum versiones nec non auxiliis criticis caeteris adhibitis. Fasciculus secundus Ezechielis et duodecim prophetarum libros etc. continens* (1893); Bachmann, "Zur Textkritik des Propheten Hosea I.-VII.," *Alttestamentliche Untersuchungen* (1894), 1–37; Loftman, *Kritisk undersökning af den Masoretiska texten till prof. Hoseas bok* (1894); Torrey, "On the text of Am. 5^{26} 6$^{1.\,2}$ 7^{2}," *JBL*. XIII. (1894), 61–63; *Idem*, "Notes on Am. 2^{7} 6^{10} 8^{3} 9$^{8-10}$," *ibid.*, XV. (1896), 151–154; Ruben, *Critical Remarks upon Some Passages of the Old Testament* (1896); Oort, *Textus Hebraici Emendationes quibus in Vetere Testamento Neerlandice vertendo usi sunt A. Kuenen, J. Hooykaas, W. H. Kosters, H. Oort; edidit H. Oort* (1900); W. R. W. Gardner, "Notes on Certain Passages in Hosea," *AJSL*. XVIII. (1902), 178–83; Bewer, "Text-critical Suggestions" (Ho. 12^{1} 4$^{4.\,8}$, etc.), *JBL*. XXI. (1902), 108–14; *Idem*, "Critical Notes on Am. 2^{7} 8^{4}," *AJSL*. XIX. (1903), 116 f.; Hirscht, "Textkritische Untersuchungen über das Buch Amos," *ZwTh*. XLIV. (1903), 11–73; Müller, "Textkritische Studien zum Buche Hosea," *SK*. 1904, pp. 124–26; and W. O. E. Oesterley, *Studies in the Greek and Latin Versions of the Book of Amos* (1902); *Idem*, "The Old Latin Texts of the Minor Prophets, I." (Hosea), *Journal of Theological Studies*, V. (Oct. 1903), 76–88. These last two studies are of especial value in the effort to determine the original text of 𝕲, but were not received in time to .be of material assistance in the preparation of this volume.

§ 23. Literature on Amos and Hosea.

Of the older commentaries the more important are those of Jerome († 420 A.D.), Aben Ezra († 1167), Kimchi († 1230), Luther, Calvin, Pococke (on Hosea, 1685), Mercerus (1698), Gebhard (1737), Harenberg (Amos, 1763), Manger (on Hosea, 1782), Vater (Amos, 1810); Stuck, *Hoseas Propheta* (1828); Maurer (1836); Hitzig (1838; 3d ed. 1863); Ewald (1840); and Umbreit (1844).

From 1845 to 1880 may be mentioned: Baur, *Der Prophet Amos erklärt* (1847); Düsterdieck, "Beiträge zur Erklärung des Propheten Amos," *SK.*, 1849, pp. 869–914; Simson, *Der Prophet Hosea erklärt u. übersetzt* (1851); Kurtz, *Die Ehe d. Propheten Hosea* (1859); Linder, "Bemerkungen über einige Stellen im Propheten Hosea," *SK.*, 1860, pp. 739–49; Pusey, *Minor Prophets*, I. (1861); Löwe, *Beiträge zum Verständniss des Propheten Hoseas* (1863); Ewald, *Propheten d. Alten Bundes* (2d ed. 1867; English, 1875); Wünsche, *Der Prophet Hosea übersetzt und erklärt mit*

Benutzung der Targumim u. der jüdischen Ausleger (1868); Henderson, *The Book of the Twelve Minor Prophets* (1868); Schmoller, Exposition of Hosea and Amos in Lange's *Bibelwerk* (1872; English translation of Hosea by J. F. McCurdy, of Amos by T. W. Chambers, 1874); Duhm, *Die Theologie der Propheten* (1875), 109–41; Houtsma, "Bijdrage tot de kritiek en verklaring van Hozea," *ThT.* IX. (1875), 55–75; Hermann, "Exegetisch-kritische Bemerkungen zu einigen Stellen aus Hosea," *SK.* III. (1879), 515–7; A. B. Davidson, "The Prophet Hosea," *Exp.*[1] IX. (1879), 241–64; Töttermann, *Die Weissagungen Hoseas bis zur ersten assyrischen Deportation erläutert* (1879).

During the last twenty-five years much attention has been given to the Minor Prophets in general, and more to Amos and Hosea in particular. The list of works includes: Oort, "De profeet Amos," *ThT.* XIV. (1880), 114–59; Nowack, *Der Prophet Hosea erklärt* (1880); Buhl, "Beiträge zur Erklärung des Propheten Hosea," *ZKW.* 1881, pp. 227–35; W. R. Smith, art. "Hosea," *Enc. Br.* XII. (1881); Keil, *Minor Prophets*, in Keil and Delitzsch's *Biblische Commentar*, I. (1866; 2d ed. 1873; transl. 1880, 2d ed. 1888); Hitzig-Steiner, *Die zwölf kleinen Propheten erklärt* (4th ed. of Hitzig's Commentary, by Steiner, 1881); W. R. Smith, *Prophets of Israel* (1882; new edition, with Introduction by Cheyne, 1895); Scholz, *Commentar zum Buche des Propheten Hosea* (1882); Hoffmann, "Versuche zu Amos," *ZAW.* III. (1883) 87–126; Brüll, "Beiträge zur Erklärung des Buches Hosea," *Jahrb. f. jüd. Geschichte u. Litteratur*, 1883, pp. 1–62; Cheyne, *Hosea, with Notes and Introduction* (Cambridge Bible, 1884); Sharpe, *Notes and Dissertations upon the Prophecy of Hosea* (1884); Gunning, *De Godspraken van Amos* (1885); Zeydner, "Het Vaderland van Amos," *Stemmen voor Waarheid en Vrede*, 1886, pp. 548–53; de Visser, *Hosea de Man des Geestes* (1886); Cornill, "Hosea 12¹," *ZAW.* VII. (1887), 285–9; A. B. Davidson, "The Prophet Amos," *Exp.*[2] V. (1887), 161–79; VI. 161–73; Mitchell, "The Idea of God in Amos," *JBL.*, Dec. 1887, pp. 33–42; Orelli, *Die zwölf kleinen Propheten* (1888; transl. by J. S. Banks, 1893); Schuurmans Stekhoven, "Het Vaderland van Amos," *ThSt.* VII. (1889), 222–8; Sayce, "The Book of Hosea in the Light of Assyrian Research," *JQR.*

1889, pp. 162–72 ; Bachmann, *Praeparationen zu den kleinen Propheten* (1890) ; Zeydner, " Nog iets over den profeet Amos," *Stemmen voor Waarheid en Vrede*, 1890, pp. 613–34; Oort, "Hozea," *ThT.* XXIV. (1890), 345–64, 480–505 ; *Idem*, "Het Vaderland van Amos," *ThT.* XXV. (1891), 121–6 ; Kirkpatrick, *Doctrine of the Prophets* (1892 ; 3d ed. 1901), 83–142 ; Wellhausen, *Die kleinen Propheten übersetzt und erklärt* (1892 ; 3d ed. 1898) ; Lagrange, " La nouvelle histoire d'Israel et le prophète Osée," *Revue biblique*, I. (1892), 203–38 ; Smend, *Lehrbuch der alttestamentlichen Religionsgeschichte* (1893 ; 2d ed. 1899), 179–86, 204–18 ; Michelet, *Amos oversat* (1893) ; Mitchell, *Amos, an Essay in Exegesis* (1893 ; 2d ed. 1900) ; Billeb, *Die wichtigsten Satze d. alttestamentlichen Kritik vom Standpunkt der Propheten Amos und Hosea aus betrachtet* (1893) ; Driver, art. "Amos," Smith's *Dictionary of the Bible* (2d ed. 1893); Kirkpatrick, art. "Hosea," *ibid.;* Beer, "Zu Hosea XII.," *ZAW.* XIII. (1893), 281–93 ; Boehmer, " Die Eigenart des Heilspredigt des Amos," *SK.*, 1893, pp. 35 ff.; Guthe, Translation and notes in Kautzsch's *Heilige Schrift d. A. T.* (1894 ; 2d ed. 1896); Valeton, *Amos en Hosea. Een hoofdstuk uit de geschiedenis van Israels godsdienst* (1894 ; German, 1898) ; N. Schmidt, " On the Text and Interpretation of Am. 5^{25-27}," *JBL.* XIII. (1894), 1–15 ; Paton, " Did Amos Approve the Calf-Worship at Bethel ? " *ibid.*, 80–91 ; Cornill, *Isr. Prophetismus* (1894 ; English, 1898), 37–55 ; Skipwith, " Note on the Order of the Text in Hosea 1–3," *JQR.* VII. (1895), 480 ff.; Oettli, " Der Kultus bei Amos und Hosea," *Greifswalder Studien* (1895), pp. 1–34 ; Tesch, *Setzt der Prophet Amos autoritatives Gesetz voraus ?* (1895) ; Paton, " Notes on Hosea's Marriage," *JBL.* XV. (1896), 9–18 ; George Adam Smith, *The Book of the Twelve Prophets*, I. (1896) ; Loftman, *Kommentar till prof. Hoseas bok* (1896) ; Nowack, *Die kleinen Propheten übersetzt und erklärt* (1897; 2d ed. 1903) ; Cheyne, " Notes on Obscure Passages of the Prophets," *Exp.*[5] V. (1897), 41–51 ; *Idem*, "A New German Commentary on the Minor Prophets," *ibid.*, VI. (1897), 361–71 ; Volz, *Die vorexilische Jahweprophetie und der Messias* (1897) ; Budde, " Die Überschrift des Buches Amos und des Propheten Heimat," in *Semitic Studies in Memory of Rev. Dr. Alexander Kohut* (1897), 106–10 ; Driver,

Joel and Amos (Cambridge Bible, 1897) ; Seesemann, *Israel und Juda bei Amos und Hosea, nebst einem Exkurs über Ho. 1–3* (1898) ; Hartung, *Der Prophet Amos nach dem Grundtexte erklärt* (1898) ; Volz, "Die Ehegeschichte Hosea's," *ZwTh*. 1898, pp. 321–35 ; Taylor, art. "Amos," *DB*. I. (1898) ; Cheyne, art. "Amos," *EB*. I. (1899) ; A. B. Davidson, art. "Hosea," *DB*. II. (1899) ; Vetter, "Die Zeugnisse der vorexilischen Propheten über den Pentateuch ; I. Amos," *Theologische Quartalschrift*, 1899, pp. 512–52 ; Vienney, *Amos de Tekoa, son époque et son livre* (Dissertation, 1899) ; Elhorst, *De Prophetie van Amos* (1900) ; Giesebrecht, *Die Geschichtlichkeit des Sinaibundes untersucht* (1900) ; Muss-Arnolt, "Amos $5^{26 (21-27)}$," *Exp.*[6] II. (1900), 414–28 ; Houtsma, *ThT*. XXXIV. (1900), 429 ff. (review of Elhorst) ; W. R. Smith and K. Marti, art. "Hosea," *EB*. II. (1901) ; Procksch, *Die Geschichtsbetrachtung bei Amos, Hosea und Jesaia* (1901) ; Budde, art. "Amos," *Jew. Enc.* (1901) ; Oettli, *Amos und Hosea, zwei Zeugen gegen die Anwendung der Evolutionstheorie auf die Religion Israels* (Beiträge zur Förderung christlicher Theologie, Jahrgang 5, Heft 4, 1901) ; Grimm, *Liturgical Appendixes in the Old Testament* (1901), 60–78, 88–93 ; Day and Chapin, "Is the Book of Amos Post-Exilic?" *AJSL*. XVIII. (1902), 65–93 ; Nowack, "Die Zukunftshoffnungen Israels in der Assyrischen Zeit," in *Theologische Abhandlungen* (Festgabe für H. J. Holtzmann, 1902), 33–59 ; Riedel, *Alttestamentliche Untersuchungen*, Heft I. (1902), 1–36 ; Boehmer, "Die Grundgedanken der Predigt Hosea's," *ZwTh*. XLV. (1902), 1–24 ; Halévy, "Le livre d'Osée," *Revue Sémitique*, X. (1902), 1–12, 97–133, 193–212, 289–304 ; *Idem*, "Le livre d'Amos," *ibid.*, XI. (1903), 1–31, 97–121, 193–209, 289–300 ; XII. (1904), 1–18 ; Meinhold, *Studien zur israelitischen Religionsgeschichte*, I. *Der heilige Rest* (1903), 33–88 ; Cheyne, *Critica Biblica*, II. (1903) ; Marti, *Dodekapropheton* (Kurzer Hand-Commentar z. A.T., 1903) ; J. A. Montgomery, "Notes on Amos," *JBL*. XXIII. (1904), 94–96 ; R. F. Horton, *The Minor Prophets, Hosea–Micah* (The New-Century Bible, 1904) ; von Ryssel, art. "Hosea," *Jew. Enc.* (1904).

Literature on the poetical form and the text is given in connection with §§ 20 and 22, pp. clxv f., clxxvii f.

CHRONOLOGICAL TABLE OF ISRAELITISH LIFE AND THOUGHT DURING THE DIVIDED KINGDOM

ISRAEL'S HERITAGE FROM CENTURIES PRECEDING 933 B.C.

Pre-Prophetic Religious Activity	Extra Pre-Prophetic Religious Activity
The Song of Deborah (Ju. 5).	The Book of Jasher (Jos. 10¹³; 2 S. 1¹⁸).
Nathan's Parable (2 S. 12¹⁻⁴).	The Book of the Wars of Yahweh (Nu. 21¹⁴ ᶠ·).
The Blessing of Jacob (Gn. 49).	Jotham's Fable (Ju. 9⁷ ᶠ·).
The Oracles of Balaam (Nu. 23, 24).	David's Lament over Saul and Jonathan (2 S. 1¹⁷ ᶠᶠ·).
The Stories of Creation, the Deluge, etc.	
The Song of the Exodus (Ex. 15, earliest form).	David's Lament over Abner (2 S. 3³³ ᶠ·).
The Patriarchal Traditions.	Early Proverbs (1 S. 10¹¹ ᶠ·; 24¹³).
Traditions of the Conquest.	Popular Riddles (Ju. 14¹⁴⁻¹⁸; 15¹⁶).
State Annals.	Ancient Folk-lore.
Traditional Customs.	Ancient Legends and Songs—*e.g.:*
The Order of Seers.	Lamech's Song (Gn. 4²³ ᶠ·).
The *Nebhi'im*.	Song of the Well (Nu. 21¹⁷ ᶠ·).
The Nazirites.	Ancient Laws (*e.g.* 1 S. 30²⁴ ᶠ·).
The Institution of the Kingdom.	Religious Institutions—*e.g.:*
The National, or Patriotic, Spirit.	Sacrifice.
The Life and Work of Samuel.	Feasts.
The Prophet Nathan.	The Sabbath.
Gad, the Seer.	Clean and Unclean.
The Oracle, Ephod, Teraphim.	Circumcision.
	The Ark.
	The Priesthood.
	Local Sanctuaries.
	The Temple.

CHRONOLOGICAL TABLE OF ISRAELITISH LIFE AND THOUGHT (933–721 B.C.).

DATE	POLITICAL EVENTS		RELIGIOUS ACTIVITY		CONTEMPORANEOUS HISTORY		DATE
	JUDAH	ISRAEL	PROPHETIC	EXTRA-PROPHETIC	SYRIA, MOAB, ETC.	ASSYRIA AND EGYPT	
933	Disruption of Rehoboam	the Kingdom Jeroboam I and Israel	Ahijah (1 K. 11:29); Shemaiah (1 K. 12:22 f.)	Golden Calves			
929	Wars between Judah	dah and Israel				Shishak I of Egypt	929
916	Shishak invades Judah	and Israel					
	Abijam			Development of temple-ritual; Gradual differentia-tion of priest-hood			912
912	Wars between Judah	Nadab; War against Philistia; Baasha			Philistia invaded by Israel		
911	Asa	and Israel	Hero-stories in Judges; Nazirites	Contact with Ca-naanitish Life and Thought			900
	Wars between Judah		NEBHI'IM		Rise of Damascus; Ben-hadad of Da-mascus invades Is-rael	Northern campaigns of Tukulti-Ninib II	890–885
c. 890	Asa appeals to Damas-cus for aid against Is-rael	Baasha loses territory to Syria; Elah; Omri; Civil war; factions led by Omri and Tibni; Tibni slain; Omri builds Samaria	Pre-prophetic soci-eties		Philistia attacked by Elah of Israel	Ashurnasirpal III; north-ern campaigns, 885, 884, 883, 880, 867; eastern campaigns, 882, 881; campaigns in West Mesopotamia, 884, 879, 878–875 (?); reaches Mediterranean, 876 (?)	885–860
885		Judah and Israel; Ahab; Alliance with Phoeni-cia	Elijah (875–850); Early world-stories		Phoenicia and Israel allied		
875	Long peace between	Wars with Syria	Judaean Decalogue		Wars with Israel; Mesha's revolt; Mo-abite stone		
872	Jehoshaphat	First contact with As-syria: Battle of Kar-kar	Micaiah ben Imlah		Central and South Syria invaded by Shalmaneser II (in 854–832); battle of Karkar	Shalmaneser II; constant war; campaigns in Bab-ylonia, 852, 851; in West Mesopotamia, 859–856; in South Syr-ia, 854, 849, 846, 842, 839; in Central Syria, 850, 843, 841, 832; in North Syria and North-west, 840, 838, 837, 835, 834; in North, 860, 855, 853, 845, 833, 831–828; in East, 844, 836.	c. 860
854		Ahab against Syria; Ahaziah; Joram			War between Syria and Israel		860–825
853	Jehoshaphat aids	Joram against Moab	Elisha (850–800); Early Saul and Da-vid stories; J[1] (850–750)	Gradual develop-ment of Hebrew civil and religious law, later codified in Deuteronomy and in the Holi-ness Code; Priests under Jehoi-ada overthrow	Moab attacked by Israel, Judah, and Edom; Edom and Libnah rebel against Judah; War between Syria and Israel		
850	Jehoshaphat aids Jehoram; Revolt of Edom and Libnah						
843	Ahaziah; Ahaziah aids Joram	War against Syria against Syria; Joram slain by Jehu; Jehu tributary to Shalmaneser II	Prophets support Jehu's revolution; Rise of Rechabites				843
842	Ahaziah slain by Jehu						
836	Athaliah; Joash						

Date	Judah	Israel	Literature	Temple	Hazael or Damascus smites Gilead, Gath, etc.	Assyria	Date
c. 830	Joash gives tribute to Hazael of Syria	Hazael smites Gilead, Gad, etc.		Joash repairs temple		Insurrection in Assyria; Shamshi-Adad IV; quells insurrection, 822; three campaigns in North, six in Babylonia. Adadnirari III; campaigns against Syria, 806–803, 797; eight campaigns against Medes; six campaigns in Northeast. Ethiopians subdue Upper Egypt	c. 830 / 827–822 / 825–812
814		Jehoahaz; Syria's long oppression of Israel			Syria humiliates Israel		812–783
800		Jehoash; Victories over Syria	Book of the Covenant		Damascus subdued by Assyria		c. 800
797	Amaziah		Elijah-stories E¹ (800–750)		Syria defeated by Israel in days of Jehoash		797
795	War against Edom; Jehoash smites Jerusalem; Uzziah	War with Amaziah	Early narratives in Samuel and Kings; Elisha-stories; Prophet Jonah (II K. 14:25) J²	Parable of Jehoash (II K. 14:9)	War between Edom and Judah		
c. 785 / 783		Jeroboam II; Syria expelled from Israel	Blessing of Moses (Deut. 33); Ephraimite Decalogue	Blessing of Moses (Deut. 33)	Syria repulsed by Israel	Shalmaneser III; decline of Assyria and growth of kingdom of Urartu; campaigns against Aramaeans in North Babylonia, and against Damascus (773)	783–773
765 / 763	Total Eclipse of Sun	on June 15, visible in Syria	Amos (765–750)		Damascus attacked by Shalmaneser III; Hadrach attacked by Assyria, 772, 765	Ashurdan III; Assyria's decline continued; campaigns in Central Syria, 772, 765; insurrection in Assyria, 763	773 / 773–755
745 / 742		Zechariah (6 months); Shallum (1 month); Menahem	Hosea (745–735)		Arpad attacked by Assyria, 754	Ashurnirari II; campaign against Arpad, 754; downfall of dynasty	755–745
739 / 738		Menahem sends tribute to Tiglath-pileser; Pekahiah; Pekah	E²; Isaiah	Jotham repairs the Temple	Arpad besieged and captured by Assyria (743–740); Hamath attacked by Assyria	Tiglath-pileser III; revival of Assyria. Campaigns against Aramaeans in Babylonia, 745; in East, 744, 737; in Syria, against Arpad, 743–740; against Hamath, 738; against Damascus, Israel, and Philistia, 734–732; against Kaldi, 731, 729, 728	745–727
736 / 735	Jotham; Ahaz; Judah invaded by	Pekah and Rezin of Syria			Damascus and Israel invade Judah		735
734	Ahaz sends tribute to Tiglath-pileser	Tiglath-pileser deports inhabitants of Gilead, Galilee, and Naphtali; Hoshea, an Assyrian vassal		Ahaz introduces Assyrian elements into temple-ritual	Kingdom of Damascus destroyed		733
730 / c. 725 / 724–721 / 721		Hoshea rebels against Assyria; Siege of Samaria; Fall of Samaria	Micah			Shalmaneser IV; campaign against Syria and Palestine, 725; siege of Samaria, 724–722. Sargon; acme of Assyrian power; expedition to the West, 722	727–722 / 722–705

A COMMENTARY ON THE BOOK OF AMOS.

———◆———

§ 1. The superscription: *Occupation and residence of Amos; date of his work.* 1^1.

The superscription contains the title, the author's name, his occupation, his home, the subject treated, and the date; the last in two forms.* This is the most exact and complete of all the superscriptions to prophetic utterances.† Although it may well be supposed that Amos prepared, perhaps in Jerusalem, the edition of his sermons, which, with some modifications has been handed down to us, it is improbable that so early an author would have prepared such an elaborate superscription; it is better to understand that it comes from a post-exilic period. ‡ The editor evidently makes Amos precede Hosea, since only Uzziah is mentioned among the kings of Judah. It is important to note that, whatever may be the age of the superscription, it is entirely con-

---

* Uhland, *Annotationes*, 3–30; Juynboll, *Disputatio de Amos*, 1–8, 11–18, 27–32; Ba. 38–110; Oort, "De Profeet Amos," *ThT.* XIV. 122–7; Matheson, "Studies in the Minor Prophs.," *Exp.* III. (1882), 342–4; WRS., *Prophs.* 120 ff., 395; Sta. *GVI.* I. 562–75; Da. *Exp.* V. (1887), 161–79; Stekhoven, "Het vaderland van Amos," *ThSt.* 1889, 222–8; Mit. 1–22; Gun. 13 ff.; Now. 121 ff.; GAS. I. 67 f.; Che. *EB.* I. 147 ff.; Dr. 93 ff., 125 ff.

† Ho. gives title, author, parentage, date; Mi., title, author, country, date, subject; Na., title, subject, author, country; Zp., title, author, parentage (fully), date; Hb., title, author, occupation (prophet); Hg., no proper superscription, the first verse contains date (to the day), title, author, occupation (prophet), those to whom his message was addressed; Zc., date, title, parentage, occupation (prophet); Mal., title, subject (to Israel), author; Ob., title, author; Jo. and Jon., title, author, parentage.

‡ So Che. *EB.;* Tay. *DB.;* Bu. *Jew. Enc.;* Now.; Houtsma, *ThT.* 1900, p. 432.

sistent with the contents of the book and is to be accepted as historical.

1. אשר היה בנקדים] a gloss; orig. text, *words of Amos of Tekoa*, cf. Ju. 12[8] [Bu. in Kohut's *Semitic Studies* (1897), 106–10; id. *Jew. Enc.* I. 530; Now.; Löhr, 3]; present structure very awkward; but cf. Or. (fol. De.) who makes אשר ... תקוע a later addition; and Oet. (p. 65) who suggests that in this case הַתְּקוֹעִי (2 S. 23[26]) would have been used. בנקדים] Ⓖ ἐν ᾽Ακκαρείμ, probably for ἐν Νακκαρείμ, initial ν having been lost after ἐν [so Drusius, Grotius, Vol. Cf. the suggestion of Hirscht (*ZwTh.* XLIV. 45) that Ⓖ is based on a marginal gloss אכָּרִים, added in explanation of נקדים]; cf. Νωκῆθ, 2 K. 3[4]; some codd. of Ⓖ καριαθιαρείμ; ᾽Α. ποιμνιοτρόφοις; Σ. τοῖς ποιμέσιν (= *herdsmen*); Θ. νωκεδείμ. Ⓣ מָרֵי גִתֵּי. Ⓢ ‎ܒܢ‎, merely transliterating the Heb. ישראל] Ⓖ ᾽Ιερουσαλήμ, probably confusing similar abbreviations. Ⓢ *sons of Israel*. Cf. the form of the superscription in 𝕷: — *sermones Amos quos vidit super Hierusalem.*

1 a. *The words of Amos*] The titles of the prophetic books [*] generally contain some reference to Yahweh, as the author of the words spoken, or some technical expression which implies such authorship (Na. 1[1] Hb. 1[1]). This phrase (Je. 1[1] Hg. 1[12]) contains no allusion to a specifically active human element,[†] since the words are recognized as Yahweh's words. Nor does the plural designate the writing as composed of distinct prophecies, [‡] since every book is similarly made up of distinct prophecies. There is likewise no reason to suppose that the original superscription was limited to these words.[§] The Amos of this book has sometimes been confounded with the father of Isaiah,[‖] but for the most part tradition has rightly distinguished between the two. Concerning Amos see Introduction (§ 12). *Who had been among the shepherds*] *v.s.* That is, he was one of the shepherds in Tekoa; not with the distinctive use of the preposition, *viz.* he was great among them.[¶] Here one must compare 7[14]

---

[*] Cf. (1) the similar introduction of Je.; (2) "the word of ᾽" of Ho., Mi., Zp., and Jo.; (3) "the burden" of Na. and Hb.; (4) "the burden of the word of ᾽," of Mal.; (5) "the vision" of Is. and Ob.; (6) the introductory formula "and it came to pass" of Ez.; (7) "was the word of ᾽ by Hg. the prophet"; (8) "was the word of ᾽ unto Z."   † Cf. Ba.   ‡ Geb.   § Implied by Val. 79 ff.

‖ Clem. of Alex. and Pseudepiph (see Ba.).

¶ Ki., Ephraem; cf. Bu. (in Kohut, *Semitic Studies*, 20, 106 ff.), who translates: who had been among the sheep breeders, (a man) of Tekoa; so Che. in *EB.* I. 147; but in *Crit. Bib.* he treats נקדים as a proper name.

in which Amos calls himself a herdsman (but see p. 8). Was
Amos an *owner* of sheep, and wealthy? So most Jewish interpreters, who urge that this is implied in the use of the same word
of the King of Moab (2 K. 3⁴) ; and that if a slave or servant, he
could not have left his work for an excursion of this kind ; but the
fuller description in 7¹⁴, in which reference is made to his indigent
circumstances, the etymology of the word, and the answer made
to Amaziah (7¹⁵), "Yahweh took me, etc." point to a simple
shepherd. There is no reason to suppose that he was a slave.*
— *From Tekoa*] This was certainly in Judah, although it has been
placed in Zebulon,† in Asher, ‡ in the south of Palestine, but
belonging to Ephraim, § (*i.e.* the ten tribes). ‖ In favor of
Judah are (1) the evidences elsewhere found that Amos was
of Judah, *e.g.*, the command of the priest (7¹²) to Amos to flee to
Judah; likewise "the exact scenery of his visions" which is seen
from Tekoa ; ¶ (2) the references in 2 S. 14² 23²⁶ Je. 6¹ 2 Ch. 20²⁰
1 Macc. 9³³. The place lies six miles south of Bethlehem (twelve
miles south of Jerusalem).** The hill, four or five acres, is broad
at the top and not steep. The surrounding country is sterile and
rocky, but rich in pasturage. The wilderness of Tekoa (2 Ch. 20²⁰)
is part of the wilderness of Judah.†† The preposition "from"
indicates that, like other shepherds, Amos came from Tekoa, but
remained in the wilderness or vicinity. ‡‡ While the Jewish fancy
that Amos was wealthy has no basis, it is just as unfounded to
say §§ that Tekoa is mentioned as especially poor to show God's
ability to confound the rich with the poor. Was Tekoa too high for
the cultivation of sycamores? It is reasonable to suppose that the
reference is to some low lying district in the Shephelah owned by
Amos ‖‖ at some distance perhaps from Tekoa. — *Which he saw*]
This word originally marked the method of reception of the

---

* *V.* Ba.   † Pseudepiph. *de vitis prophetarum*, 245.   ‡ Ki.   § Cyril.

‖ Cf. Har. 45–9, who locates it on Carmel; Graetz, *Gesch.* I. 403, who identifies
it with Eltekeh of Jos. 19⁴⁴, making Amos a Danite; Oort, *ThT.* XXV. 121–6, who
makes him belong to the ten tribes.   ¶ GAS. *HG.* 315.

** Its ruins, "extensive, but uninteresting," still remain, bearing the name of
Teḳu'a (تَقُوع). *PEF.* 1874, p. 27.

†† See also Ba.; Rob. *BR.*² I. 486 f.; Stickel, *Das Buch Hiob*, 269–77; Kue.
*HCO.*² II. 355 f.   ‡‡ Hi.   §§ Cal., Os.   ‖‖ Che. *EB.*

divine communication as by vision. The vision may have been merely a dream, a vision of the night, or a half-sleeping, half-waking condition, as with the Syrian monks of the present day; or the ecstasy or trance. It is impossible, in the majority of cases, to distinguish between these forms. Such visions came to non-prophets (1 K. 3⁵ 1 S. 28⁸ᶠᶠ·) as well as to prophets (1 K. 19⁶ 1 S. 3¹⁻¹⁴).

An earlier and a later usage may be noticed: (1) In the earlier period חזה (as well as ראה of which it is often the poetic equiv.) marks the *reception* of the message, which is seen as well as heard (cf. ראיתי Am. 9¹ Is. 6¹; הראני Am. 7¹·⁴·⁷ 8¹ 2 Ki. 8¹⁰·¹³; this is in accordance with the Arab. الحلاري used of clairvoyants, soothsayers, those who can foretell the future (cf. Hoffm. *ZAW*. III. 92 f.). At this time נָבִיא had reference to the speaking or impartation of the communication to others. נביא is not (*a*) a passive formation from a root נבא = נבע to bubble forth; Arab. نَبَع to well forth (Redslob, *Der Begriff des Nabi* (1839); and Ho. 7⁴⁻¹⁰, p. 30; Ke. on Gn. 20⁷; Kue. *Proph.* 42; Maybaum, *Die Entwickelung des isr. Prophetenthums*, 113; Baud. *Einl.* 314); nor (*b*) a noun, designating an ordinary *speaker* from נבא, cf. Arab. نَبَأَ *utter a low sound*, Assyr. נבא *nabû, name, call* (*Or. Proph.* 11 f.; Kö. II. 1, pp. 133, 407; BDB.; cf. WRS. *Proph.* 390 f.); but (*c*) as is seen from the use of the Niph'al *to prophesy*, an involuntary speaker, one who speaks under compulsion that which has been communicated to him (Hoffm.; Arab. نبا *raise up, speak softly*, hence نباة *soft wine*). Perhaps it is an active transitive (cf. רכיל; אפיק; פליל; פקיד; פקורה; יהיל) its object being נאם, which he apprehends quietly but imparts vehemently with deep breaths, cf. Bewer, *AJSL*. XVIII. 120. (2) In the later period, the distinction between חזה (also ראה) and נביא is broken down, the former, as well as the latter, meaning to utter or announce prophecy (Is. 2¹ Mi. 1¹ (חזות), Is. 29¹¹ 21²). In this verse, חזה has its later usage; and since the distinction between revelations "heard" and "seen" is made by the compiler of the book (cf. chaps. 1-6 with 7-9), the date of the expression would seem to be still later than the compilation. (Ba., Hoffm. *ZAW*. III. 95.)

1 *b*. *Concerning Israel*] The words of Amos were intended for the North, *viz.* Israel, not the South. The Northern Kingdom, therefore, seems to have been regarded by him as Israel proper, of which Judah was a fragment (1 K. 11²⁹⁻³⁹ 2 K. 17¹⁸).* His utterances

---

* See Seesemann, *Israel und Juda bei Amos und Hosea* (1898), pp. 1-17, in which it is shown that Amos always means *Ephraim* when he uses the name *Israel*, thus following the usage of the old sources of the historical books, *e.g. K* in

concerning foreign nations, Syria, Moab, etc., like the similar
utterances of Isaiah, Jeremiah, and Ezekiel, were intended for the
ear of Israel.   There is no reason to suppose that the outside
nations ever heard them.   In a true sense, however, even these
utterances were *concerning Israel,* since the attitude of God
therein depicted was the same as that assumed by him toward
Israel and Judah ; and the affairs of Israel were so closely woven
with those of the nations named as to make everything concerning
them related in some way also to Israel.   The fact that so much
of the prophetic material has to do with the outside nations,
coupled with the probability that no part of this material was
given to them, points indisputably to the opinion here expressed,
and justifies and explains the use of the phrase — *concerning Israel.*
In the days of Uzziah . . . and . . . Jeroboam] In corroboration of this statement may be cited (1) the plain historical narrative ($7^{9\,\mathrm{ff.}}$) in which Jeroboam plays an important part ; (2) the
consistency between the representation made in 2 K. 14^{25} as to
the extent of Israel's kingdom and the allusions in Am. 6^{14} (the
borders of Ephraim) and 6^2 (the destruction of Hamath) ; (3) the
consistency between the situation which forms the background of
the discourses of Amos and that which, as gathered from other
sources, existed in the days of Jeroboam.   The work of Amos
would fall between 765 and 750 B.C.* (see Introduction, § 12, 2).
Uzziah] The long reign of Uzziah,† during which there was
co-regency with Amaziah at the beginning and with Jotham at the
end, was, in general, a period of comparative peace, and of great
political prosperity.   Judah was probably in a certain kind of subordination to Israel ; ‡ the Philistines were severely defeated and

---

1 K. $12^{18\,\mathrm{ff.}}$.   Though certainly familiar with the broader significance of the name
Israel, he probably refrained from thus using it because of Ephraim's unwillingness
to allow Judah to share it, and because after the division of the kingdom, ordinary
usage limited the use of the name Israel to the North, the South being called
Judah.

* For a presentation of the view that the Book of Amos is really post-exilic, see
AJSL. Jan. 1902, an article by Edward Day and Walter H. Chapin.

† According to the old chronology B.C. 810–758 ; but 791–740, Schra. ; 783(?)–
737, Kit. *Hist.* II. 239 f. ; 767–716, Sta. *GVI.* I. 559 ; 790(?)–740, Marti, *EB.* I. 795 ;
790–739, *KAT³.* I. 320 ; 783–738, *HPM.* III. 435.

‡ Kit. *Hist.* II. 331 ; Gu. *EB.* II. 2242 ; Paton, *Hist.* 205, 225 ff. ; cf. *KAT³.* I.
262 f.

their fortifications at Gath, Jabneh, and Ashdod destroyed ; in the
south the Arabs and Maonites were defeated ; the walls of Jerusalem were strengthened.   Uzziah probably accompanied Jeroboam
in his campaigns against Syria and after Jeroboam's death made
an independent expedition there.*   He appears about 738 B.C.
as head of a coalition of Syrian states against Tiglathpileser III.†
His name in the Book of Kings and in the Tiglathpileser inscriptions is Azariah.   *Religiously* Judah, while zealous for the temple
ceremonial, was to a large extent under the influence of Israel
and the outside nations.   The power of the priests was increasing, and it is probable that Uzziah was brought into conflict with
them and that the mysterious incident (2 Ch. 26^{16-25}) really means
that Uzziah was deposed and isolated by the priestly faction. ‡
Jeroboam] The reign of Jeroboam § lasted about forty years and
was marked by great political prosperity.   While many wars were
waged, peace existed during a large part of his reign.   In the
wars with Syria much northern territory (the district east of the
Jordan) was recovered.   This was accomplished the more easily
because the Syrians were weakened by wars with Assyria.   The
limits of the kingdom assumed the widest extent (2 K. $14^{25\,ff.}$),
though the statement that his dominion extended to Hamath is
thought to be an exaggeration. ‖   The calf-worship was zealously
observed at Bethel and Dan ¶ and a similar worship at other
places.   While this worship was conducted in the name of Yahweh,
it was largely corrupt, including Teraphim, Maṣṣeboth, the Ephod,
and the Asherah.**   The prophets of the period tell us †† that this

---

* Kit. *Hist.* II. 335 f.

† III R. pl. 9, II, ls. 3, 4, and III, ls. 23, 31. But this identification of Azriya'u of
Ya'udi with Uzziah of Judah is called in question by an increasing number of schol-
ars who maintain that the Ya'udi of Tiglathpileser's narrative is a district in Northern
Syria mentioned in the inscriptions recently discovered at Sinjirli. So, *e.g.* Wkl.
Forsch. I. 1–23 ; *Id. KAT³.* I. 262 ; W. E. Barnes, *DB.* II. 512 ; Paton, *Hist.* 233 f. ;
Gu. *Gesch.* 188 f. ; Hom. *Trad.* 319 ; Kit. *Könige*, 263 ; Benz. *Könige*, 166 ; G. S.
Goodspeed, *History of Babylonians and Assyrians* (1902), 230 f. ; Smith, *O. T. Hist.*
(1903), 226 f. ; but *v.* McCurdy, *HPM.* I. 413 f.   ‡ Kit. *Hist.* II. 331.

§ According to the old chronology 825–784 ; but 790–749, Schra. ; 781–741, Sta.
GVI. I. 559 ; 781–740, Kit. *Hist.* II. 240 ; 783–743, *HPM.* § 262 ; 785–745, *KAT³.*
I. 262 ; 784–744, Paton, *Hist.* 223, 231.   ‖ Sta. *GVI.* I. 570.

¶ Ho. $8^{5.\,6}$ 10^5 Am. 8^{14}.   ** Kit. *Hist.* II. 305 f. ; Ho. $2^{13.\,17}$ 3^4 10^2.
†† Am. $2^{6\,ff.}$ 3^{15} 4^1 $5^{7.\,10\,ff.}$ $6^3\,ff$ $8^4\,ff.$ Ho. $4^{1\,f.\,11\,ff.}$ $6^{8\,f.}$ $12^7\,f.$

reign was characterized by gross immorality, inordinate luxury of the rich, and by oppression and injustice toward the poor. *Two years before the earthquake*] This phrase, contrary to Keil, is intended to mark a date. Since earthquakes (the view which makes it a civil commotion is untenable) are not infrequent in Palestine,* as may be gathered from their frequent mention in poetic descriptions, this must have been an especially severe one. Reference is made to it certainly in Zc. 14⁵, possibly also in Am. 8⁸·⁹ (an interpolation) and Mi. 1²⁻⁴.† Tradition, according to Josephus, ‡ connects it with Uzziah's attempt to act as priest (2 Ch. 26¹⁶) and with a shattering of the temple in the year of Uzziah's death (Is. 6⁴). On closer examination, however, we may ask, Does the editor mean to imply that this earthquake was a beginning of the fulfilment of the prediction of Amos? § Had there, in other words, been an interval of two years, a period of repentance, between the last words of warning and this the first flash of the lightning which consumed them? ‖ Does this chronological statement carry with it the implication that his work was of short duration, limited, perhaps, to the one year, "two years before the earthquake,"¶ or may it be inferred with Pusey from 7¹⁰ 2¹¹·¹² that he had a long ministry, and that the discourses were written out only after a period of at least two years? The answers to these questions depend partly on one's conception of prophecy, but more largely upon data which are not at hand. Jerusalem itself seems seldom to have been affected by earthquakes, and this may account for the lack of reference to specific earthquakes by O. T. writers, this being the only case mentioned in O. T. literature.**

עָמוֹס] Only in this book, 1¹ 7⁸·¹⁰·¹⁴ 8². 𝕲 'Aμώs which stands also for אָמוֹץ; proper names of the same form are עָמוֹק, Ne. 12⁷·²⁰; אָמוֹן, 2 K. 21¹⁸ ff.; אָמוֹץ, Is. 1¹; צָדוֹק, 2 K. 15³³; זָנוֹחַ, Jos. 15³⁴; עָכוֹר, Jos. 7²⁴; the original vowels are not ă — ŭ (Lag. *BN*. 28 f.), but ă — â (Barth. *NB*. 41, cf. 59; Lag. *BN*. 69 f.). This form is found in adjectives (cf. גָּדוֹל, *great*), abstract substantives (cf. שָׁלוֹם, *peace*); with active significance (cf. עָשׁוֹק, *oppressor*; רָזוֹן = רָזַן); perhaps never as passive. The etymologies suggested may be classified: (1) עָם and

* *V.* Pu. I. 286; Dr. 172; Che. *EB.* II. 1150 f.; E. Hull, *DB.* I. 634 f.
† Cf. also Jo. 2¹⁰.   ‡ *Ant.* IX. 10⁴.   § Cal.   ‖ Pu.   ¶ Bl. *Einl.* 363.
** Hoffm. (*ZAW.* III. 123) regards this case as an exegetical inference from 7³·⁶ (cf. 7⁸ 8²), the thought being that Israel's punishment is twice postponed, for a year each time; so Che. *EB.* I. 149; and Marti, *EB.* I. 776.

מוּשׁ *a people put away, populus avulsus* (Jer.; cf. Ba.), (2) connection with
the Egyptian Amasis or Amosis (Ges. *Thes.* 1044), (3) for עָמוּס, *carried (in
the bosom)* or for עָמֵס, *carrying, burden-bearer,* related to עָמָל (MV.; cf.
Jer. in introd. to Jo.), (4) *a hard or heavy people* (Jer. in introd. to Is.), or
heavy-tongued, lisping (Jer. on Am.), used of Am., who according to the
Rabbins used בּוּלֵס (7¹⁴) for בּוּלֵשׁ, cf. Ju. 12⁶.   Of these (1) and (2) are
absurd, (3) and (4) uncertain.   The root (cf. عَمَسَ, *to be oppressed;* Phoen.
עמס, *to burden, v.* Levy, *Phön. Wört.* 38), means (*a*) to lift and carry, Is. 46⁸,
(*b*) to load an animal, Gn. 44¹³. It is probable, therefore, that the word is a
simple adjective meaning *heavy* (Ba.). — הָיָה נֹקֵר, cf. הגם שאול = [היה בנקרים,
בנביאים, *Is Saul also among* (one of) *the prophets ?* (1 S. 10¹¹), also 2 S. 15³¹
Ps. 118⁷; cf. the ἐν of 'A. and Σ. *v.s.* The word נקרים is of interest from
every point of view: (1) בוקר of 7¹⁴ is probably a corruption of it; (2) the
Hebrew forms from the same stem, viz. נָקוּר, *punctured,* נְקֻדָה, *point,* נְקֻרִים,
bread-crumbs, indicate a root (not occurring as such in Hebrew) meaning
puncture; (3) the cognate forms, Ass. nâkidu (Dl. *Pr.* 47 and *HWB.* 479;
Muss-Arnolt, *Dict.* 719; Evans, *Essay on Assyriology,* 74) and Arab. نَقّاد
mean *shepherd,* the latter (Lane, 2837) being used of a particular kind of
sheep, viz., نَقَل, a kind having short legs and ugly faces, but furnishing
the best kind of wool; (4) Syr. ‎نَصَم‎, *shepherd,* and Moabitish נקר (Mesha
stone, l. 30 [reading doubtful]; *v.* Dr. *Heb. Text of Sam.* LXXXV. ff. and in
Authority and Archaeology, 90; Smend and Socin, *Die Inschrift des Königs
Mesa von Moab;* Lidzbarski, *Handbuch zur Nord-Semitischen Epigraphik,*
I. 415 ff.; W. H. Bennett, *DB.* III. 404 ff.), cf. 2 K. 3⁴; (5) suggestions have
been made: (*a*) from a root meaning *pierce* (cf. نَقَب, used of a bird's boring,
and of the bite of a serpent) from which is developed the idea *distinguish,*
used particularly of separating good money from bad; hence نَقَل, applied
to a kind of sheep distinguished for choice wool (*v.s.*); hence نَقّاد
= נִקֵּר (*v.s.*); (*b*) from a root meaning *to puncture* explained by "stimulo
hastae utuntur, pungentes calcem et pedes bovum posteriores" (Har.);
(*c*) *shepherd,* so called because many of his sheep are נָקוּר (Ki.). — The
idea of רעשׁ], as of its cognates رَعَسَ (also رَعَشَ), Aram. רעשׁ, is *to
shake, tremble.* It is used, therefore, only of noises which are connected with
a trembling or shaking movement, *e.g.* of the quivering spear, Jb. 41²¹; of
the thundering rattle of horses' hoofs, Jb. 39²⁴; of the roll of wagon wheels,
Na. 3² Je. 47³. Very appropriately, therefore, is it used of an earthquake,
1 K. 19¹¹ᶠ· Is. 29⁶ Zc. 14⁵. Interestingly enough the root is not used of
earthquakes in the other Semitic dialects, which, however, employ words of
similar significance (Aram. זִיעָא, Syr. ‎أَوَم‎ (from זוע, *move one's self*), Arab.
زَلْزَلَة from زَلْزَلَ, *move, shake).*

§ **2. The text or motto of the book.** 1². When Yahweh manifests his power and majesty, all nature feels the terrible influence
of the manifestation. The essence of the teaching of Amos seems
to be presented in this verse, which serves as an introduction, prepared either by himself or the editor. In any case it is a separate
section and not to be immediately connected with what follows.*
The verse is a stanza of four lines, in trimeter movement.† The
parallelism is exact, lines 1 and 2 being synonymous, 3 and 4
synonymous; lines 1 and 2 synthetic with 3 and 4. The rhythm
of the verse is inimitable : —

[ויאמר] יהוה מציון ישאג
ומירושלם יתן קולו
ואבלו נאות הרעים
ויבש ראש הכרמל

For an interesting theory as to its relation to the following
stanzas, in which it is suggested that Amos went to the headquarters of the Northern King, accompanied by a chorus, and
that the entire passage (Chs. 1, 2) was presented in strophe and
antistrophe, *v.* Müller. ‡ Against the authenticity of the verse may
be urged : (1) the phraseology is similar to that found in Joel and
later authors (*v.* p. 12) ; § (2) the words suit the context better in
Joel than here ; (3) the tone of lamentation seems inconsistent with
the severe announcements which follow ; (4) the extremely finished and artistic character of the verse (*v.i.*), in contrast with the
spoken addresses which follow ; ‖ (5) the lack of point in making
Jerusalem so prominent in an address delivered to the citizens of
Northern Israel ; ¶ (6) the hostility, implied toward the high-
places of the North, did not exist until after Amos's time. It is

---

* So Dat., Ba., Reu., Gun., We., Now., GAS., Dr., *et al.*

† See my articles in *AJT.* I. (1897), 140–5, and *BW.* XII. (1898), 86–9, 179–82,
251–6, 333–8.

‡ *Die Propheten in ihrer ursprünglichen Form* (1896) ; cf. Löhr, *Untersuchungen
zum Buch Amos* (1901), p. 3 ; Kö. *Stilistik, Rhetorik, Poetik* (1900), 348 ff. ; Zenner,
Die Chorgesänge im Buche der Psalmen, I. (1896), 5–8 ; Sievers, *Metrische Studien,*
I. (1901), 134–41, 472–9 ; Baumann, *Der Aufbau der Amosreden* (1903) ; and on
Hebrew Poetry in general, Briggs, *General Introduction to the Study of Holy Scrip-
ture* (1899), 355–426.

§ Che. in Introd. to WRS. *Proph.* XV. f., and art. "Amos," *EB.*

‖ Seesemann, p. 5.   ¶ Volz, 19 f. ; Bu. art. "Amos," *Jew. Enc.*

not enough to claim that Amos uses this utterance earlier, because
in Joel the effect of Yahweh's indignation is very much exaggerated
as compared with the effect described by Amos; * or that the
passage is not hostile to the high-places but implies merely that
Jerusalem is the most prominent of the places at which Yahweh is
worshipped.† The verse introduces the entire book and not the
first chapters.

2. ישאג] Greek versions variously: 𝕲 ἐφθέγξατο; Ἀ. Σ. βρυχήσεται;
Θ. ἐρεύξεται; while 𝕮𝕵𝕾 translate as future. נאות הרעים] 𝕮 *habitations of
Kings;* 𝕵 *speciosa pastorum;* 𝕾 *oasis inhabited by shepherds.* ראש הכרמל]
𝕮 *fortification of their strongholds.*

2. *And he said*] This phrase is used after "words" of 1¹ instead of the more common "saying," because of the number of
subordinate sentences intervening; cf. Ho. 1². *Yahweh roars
from Zion, and utters his voice from Jerusalem*] This is found
in Jo. 3¹⁶, but in a different connection. The verse is neither
original with Amos and, with what follows, a reflection of his shepherd-life; borrowed therefore by Joel who, in this case, lived later; ‡
nor is it original with Joel and repeated, somewhat later, by Amos,
because though still unfulfilled he wishes to give assurance of
fulfilment; § but by the hand of a post-exilic editor who inserts
it here from Joel‖ (*v.s.*). The "roaring" is that of the lion,¶ not
that of thunder (as perhaps in Joel and Je. 25³⁰) nor of waves,
though this is found elsewhere, cf. Is. 5³⁰; the phrase "utters his
voice" is the Hebraistic expression for "thundering" (Ps. 46⁶
Jb. 37⁴); the idea of both phrases is the manifestation of majesty
and power. *Zion*] originally applied (*a*) to the hill Ophel,
(*b*) to the ridge on which the temple stood, and later (*c*) to the
entire city ** (so here and in 6¹ and Is. 2³), and *Jerusalem*] of the

* Mit.   † Now.

‡ Cocceius, quoted by Ba.; We.; Mit.; Dr. 75; *Id.* art "Joel," *EB.*; Now.;
GAS.; Elh. 137.

§ Ba.; Reu.; Kirk. *Doct.* 63 ff.; G. G. Cameron, *DB.* II. 675.

‖ Volz, 19 f.; Taylor, *DB.* I. 86; Che. *EB.* I. 151; Day and Chapin, *AJSL.*
XVIII. 72 f.; Houtsma, *ThT.* 1900, p. 432; cf. Bu. *Jew. Enc.* I. 532.

¶ Ju. 14⁵ Am. 3⁴·⁸ Ps. 104²¹; so Dr.; *et al.*

** Klaiber, *ZDPV.* III. 189 ff., IV. 18 ff.; Riehm, *HBA.* II. 1839 ff.; Starck, *Pal.
u. Syrien,* 86 f.; Smith's *DB²*. II. 1650 f.; Mühlau, art. "Zion" in Riehm's *HBA.*;
BSZ. *s.v.* ציון.

synonymous parallelism, are too local to be understood as meaning the mass of the faithful children of God.* To the pure and devout worshippers of Yahweh, at the time of this utterance (*i.e.* after the exile), the place represented by these names was the centre of the national life, as well as of the theocracy. *The pastures of the shepherds mourn*] The shepherd life of the author (whoever he was) shows itself in these words, which stand in relation of consequence to the first half. The Targumic " habitations " instead of " pastures " has no basis ; nor is the translation " perish " instead of " mourn " on the ground of the parallel " wither " † well taken. The present tense‡ presents the descriptive idea better than the future " shall " or " will." *The top of Carmel*] § does not refer to the Carmel of 1 S. 25⁵ in Southern Palestine, ‖ the home of Nabal which, according to Eusebius and Theodoret, was a village south of Jerusalem, not a mountain ; nor may it be taken in a general way, " the best of cornfields," * but designates the mountain ordinarily so called (cf. 9³) on the coast of Palestine, west of the plain of Esdraelon. The word, being originally an appellative meaning *the garden*, like certain other geographical terms,¶ has the article. No part of Palestine was more beautiful or fertile than the ridge of Carmel (S.E. to N.E. 12 miles, 1800 ft. high at the S.E., 500 ft. high at the N.W.).** The greatest calamity imaginable would be the withering of Carmel, Is. 33⁹ Na. 1⁴. The prophet speaks of a general characteristic of Yahweh with special reference to an impending judgment. In semi-proverbial form we have the essence of the prophetic thought ; the verse serves also, from the point of view of the editor, as a motto or text. The chapters which follow are merely the expansion of this thought, and the explanation of it. There will be locusts and drought (7¹·⁶) ; but the end will come about through Assyria (5²⁷ 7¹⁷).

---

* Geb.   † Calv.

‡ So We.; Or.; Gun.; GAS.; Now.; Elh.; but cf. Dr.

§ Ba. 191–5; WRS. *Sem.* 156; Bädeker, *Pal.*⁴ 259; *ZDPV.* VIII. 110; Mit. 55 f.; Starck, *Pal. u. Syrien*, 103; GAS. *HG.* 150, 152–note, 337–41; Buhl, *Geog.* 23, 163; Jastrow, *JBL.* XI. 115. For the city Carmel in Judah, cf. BSZ. 387; Rob. *BR.*² I. 495–8.

‖ Jer.; Mich.; Justi; BSZ. 387.   ¶ *E.g.* הגלער, v.²; הבשן, 4¹.

** F. R. Conder and C. R. Conder, *Handbook*, 209.

2. יהוה] the position of this word makes the first half of the v. subordinate to the second, the force being, "When Yahweh out of Zion roars, and from Jerusalem utters his voice, the pastures of the shepherds mourn," etc.; GK. 142 *c*; Dr. § 165; H. 45, 3, *b*. The other alternative, to treat יהוה as emphatic, is scarcely possible. The emphasis rests on ציון and ירושלם which stand out of the usual order. A rhetorical climax is seen in both members, the roar of the lion passing into that of thunder; the waste of Carmel's top following the desolation of the pasture-land. If we omit ויאמר the first word, and pronounce אדני for יהוה and לֶם for לֶם, we find that 21 of the 28 vowels in the verse are long (ô (7), â (6), ê (3), û (3), î (2)), in other words the very vowel sounds with the frequently recurring sibilants (5) and liquids (13) suggest the thunder in its rollings. יתן, ישאג] ᴳ uses aorist or pf. (*v.s.*), ᴛᴴ𝕾, the impf., the former adopting the gnomic, the latter the prophetic interpretation; for variation in other Grk. versions *v.s.* Likewise in the case of ואבלו and ויבש the same variation occurs. The use of the present expresses the thought as generic. H. 21, 3; Dr. § 35; GK. 107 *g*. ואבלו, נאות, ישאג, ויבש] The usage of these words is of a late character; אבל is used figuratively as in Jo. 1¹⁰ Is. 24⁴·⁷ 33⁹; but cf. Ho. 4³; נאות as in Jo. 1¹⁹ᶠ· 2²²; יבש as in Jo. 1¹²; שאג is used of ʼ only in Jb. 37⁴ Je. 25³⁰ Ho. 11¹⁰ Jo. 4¹⁶, all post-exilic passages. Note further the similarity of v.²ᵇ to Je. 9⁹ 23¹⁰ 25³⁷ Is. 33⁹ Na. 1⁴, all post-exilic except the first (*v.* Che. *EB.* I. 151, n. 2).

§ 3. Approaching judgments upon the surrounding nations.*

1³–2⁵. The real work of Amos is to preach to Israel; he begins his work, however, by announcing the judgment which is to fall upon the neighboring nations. In this he has a threefold purpose : —

1) To gain the good-will of those in whose welfare he is interested, and to whom his words are addressed. In this is seen the art of the prophetic method. 2) To show that a judgment is coming, which is to include all nations; shall Israel be omitted? 3) To raise the question, whether, if these nations, without the truth as given by Yahweh's prophets, must suffer, Israel shall not suffer most of all. The literary work of Amos (though belonging to the earliest period of written prophecy) exhibits evidence of the highest poetical skill. A study of the utterances of Amos, with reference to their original form, discloses some interesting facts. Since the connection of thought and, in many cases, the very wording of the text, are largely dependent upon the results of such study, it will be necessary in each section, or closely allied group

---

* Ba. 65–110; Ew. I. 151–5; WRS. *Proph.* 127 ff.; We. 67–71; Or. 109–12; Mit. 56–84; DHM. *Die Propheten*, I. 62–66; McC. *HPM.* I. 337–46; GAS. I. 121 ff,

of sections, to present a reconstruction of the text, including divisions into strophes, arrangement in lines, transposition, at times, of clauses or lines, and changes in the reading of words.

Chaps. 1^3–2^5 constitute a literary unit and present the characteristics of Amos as clearly as any other portion of the book.*

Its divisions are :

$1^{3-5.\ 6-8}$ against Damascus and Gaza, Strophes of 5, 3, and 4 lines.
$1^{9-10.\ 11-12}$ against Tyre and Edom,   Strophes of 5 and 2 lines.
$1^{12-15}\ 2^{1-3}$ against Ammon and Moab,   Strophes of 5, 3, and 3 lines.
2^{4-5} against Judah,   Strophes of 5 and 2 lines.

The symmetry of the arrangement is not only striking, but significant. The significance of the variation in form in divisions II. and IV. will be considered in their detailed treatment. The arrangement of Müller † does not bring out all the facts, and his theory of the poetical form of Amos requires an adjustment of the material so artificial as to throw the greatest doubt upon the whole scheme.

I. 3–5. *Judgment upon Syria.* — In his forecast of impending national catastrophes, the prophet begins with Syria, and charges the nation with sins, as a punishment for which Yahweh will send desolation and captivity.

The strophic arrangement, if the opening and closing words, "thus has Yahweh said" and "said Yahweh" are included, is 5, 3, and 4; the clause "and I will break," etc. goes with strophe 2, because it completes the thought of the strophe, forming its culmination; while the structure of the following sentence excludes it from strophe 3, including reference as it does to "common people," "ruler," "whole people." It will be noted that the arrangement of 1^{6-8} is precisely that of 1^{3-5}. Müller's arrangement, 5, 2, and 5, ignores the logical connection of the members, and the parallelism of 1^{3-5}. Line 5 of strophe 1, and line 4 of strophe 3 are shorter than the rule; and it is possible to treat them as parts of the preceding lines. Cf. Löhr, 3.

3. אשיבנו] 𝕷 here and in v.^{13} has fem. suf. *eam;* so also 𝕲^L. Hoffm. אַשִּׁיבֶנּוּ(?) (*ZAW*. III. 97, *v.i.*); Elh. אָשְׁבֶנּוּ. — וגו׳ [דושם 𝕲 ἔπριζον (= שורם(?))

---

* For the view that this entire section is exilic, see Houtsma, *Th T.* 1900, p. 432.
† *Die Propheten* I. 63, 64; II. נה, נר,

πρίοσιν σιδηροῖς τὰς ἐν γαστρὶ ἐχούσας τῶν ἐν Γαλαάδ (1 Ch. 20³, וישר, 𝔊 διέπρισεν); the additional words here (and in 𝔏) are perhaps an insertion from 1¹³ (Vol.), unsupported by the other versions. — **4.** ארמנות] 𝔊 τὰ θεμέλια; 'Α., Σ., βάρεις; Θ., τὰς αὐλάς; 𝔙 domos. — בן־הדד] 𝔊 υἱοῦ Ἀδέρ, reading ר for final ד. — **5.** וישברתי] goes with strophe 2 (v.s.). — און] 𝔊, Θ., Ὤν; 𝔖 ܒܠ, so 𝔙 idoli; but 'Α. ἀνωφελοῦς; Σ., Ε., ἀδικίας. — ותומך] 𝔊 om. — בית עדן] 𝔊 ἀνδρῶν (cf. Ho. 1⁷) Χαρράν (= חרן); 𝔙 domo voluptatis. — קירה] 𝔊 ἐπίκλητος = קריא (cf. Nu. 1¹⁶ 16²); 'Α., Κυρήνην; 𝔙 Cyrenen.

3 a. *Thus has Yahweh said*] Usual formula for the introduction of each utterance, cf. 1⁶·⁹·¹¹·¹³ 2¹·⁴·⁶. The tense (pf. not impf.) implies no particular time in the past at which the revelation has been given. The imperfect would have suggested a repeated statement on the part of Yahweh. Amos, like the other prophets, is represented as Yahweh's spokesman. — *For three transgressions, yea for four*] Compare similar expressions in Je. 36²³ Pr. 30¹⁵·¹⁸·²¹·²⁹ Ecclus. 26⁵. The numbers were taken literally by the Rabbins, who understood that three transgressions had actually been committed which were to be forgiven, while the fourth was of such a nature as to make forgiveness impossible.* A symbolical interpretation, however, has been generally adopted : (1) Four and three added together = *seven*, a complete number ;† (2) three, the complete number, four, more than enough ;‡ (3) three, representing many, four the thing which calls for punishment ;§ or, as seems most probable, the two numbers together representing the idea of indefiniteness or lack of limitation.‖ The word rendered *transgression* really means *rebellion* against authority (cf. 1 K. 12¹⁹ 2 K. 1¹). — *Damascus*] The country (cf. v.⁵, in which the city is thus designated) of Syria, or that portion of it of which Damascus was capital. From the days of Baasha and Ben-hadad I. (1 K. 15¹⁸ ᶠᶠ·) there had been constant struggle between Israel and Syria, in which Israel had suffered grievously (2 K. 10³² 13²²). At this time, however, the southern territory of Syria must have been in Israel's hands (2 K. 13²⁵ 14²⁵).

---

* So essentially Ew.
† Cal., Os.
‡ Pu., Dr.
§ Dat.
‖ Gun., We., Mit., Val., Now., Marti.

The country of Aram (אֲרָם, Homer and Hesiod, Ἄριμοι; later Συρία and
Σύρος, shortened from ᾿Ασσουρία; Ar. الشَّأْم, i.e. North-land, as Yemen
meant South-land; the root سمو, be unlucky, 3d form go to the left, hence,
north) included the territory between the Taurus Mountains and the Arabian
desert, the Tigris and the Mediterranean, except the coast land occupied by
the Phoenicians and Philistines, and the possessions of Israel, Edom, Moab,
and Ammon. The Aramaeans, or Syrians, were closely related to the Hebrews,
and in the earliest times they seem to have lived in close relationship with each
other. The early traditions, as presented in the Old Testament, connect the
two families in the migration from Ur of the Chaldees (Gn. 11³¹ 24¹⁰. ²⁹ 27⁴³);
represent the Hebrews as coming to Canaan, while the Aramaeans remained
in Mesopotamia; describe the residence of Nahor in Mesopotamia; introduce Balaam of Pethor on the Euphrates (Nu. 22⁵ 23⁷; Pethor is identified
by Schr., KAT^2. pp. 155 ff.; KB. I. 133, with the Assyrian *Pitru* located on
the river Sagur, near Hierapolis; this, if correct, involves a slight inaccuracy
in the Biblical statement that Pethor is on the Euphrates; cf. Che. on Pethor
in EB.); and mention Cushan-rishathaim, King of Aram (Ju. 3⁸ ¹⁰). The
Priest-writer of the Hexateuch uses the geographical term פדן ארם (BSZ. 655;
cf. Nö. EB. I. 278), the field of Aram. Other references of interest are
Gn. 22²⁰ ff. 25¹⁰ 28² (cf. 10²² ff.) 31⁴⁷ Is. 36¹¹ Ezra 4⁷ ff. ¹⁷ f. 6² ff. In the time of
Saul, Zobah had become the centre of Aramaean power (1 S. 14⁴⁷ cf. 2 S. 10⁶);
and in David's time the King of Zobah, Hadadezer, was Israel's most dangerous enemy (2 S. 8³ ff. 10¹⁶ ff.). The different branches of Aram, viz.
(1) ארם דמשק (2 S. 8⁵ ff.), (2) ארם בית רחוב (2 S. 10⁶ cf. Nu. 13²¹), (3) ארם
מעכה (1 Ch. 19⁶ cf. 2 S. 10⁶ Jos. 13¹¹), (4) טוב (2 S. 10⁶ cf. Ju. 11³), (5)גְּשׁוּר
occurring chiefly in connection with מעכה (Dt. 3¹⁴ Jos. 12⁵ 13¹³ 2 S. 15⁸), were
united under Hadadezer, and with the exception of גְּשׁוּר, all took part in the
war against David. At this time the dominion of the King of Zobah extended
to Damascus and Hamath (2 S. 8⁵. ⁹. ¹⁰) and beyond the Euphrates (2 S. 10¹⁶).
The capital of Zobah was between the Euphrates and the Orontes (the Saba
mentioned by Ptolemaus; Ew., cf. Ba.; also BSZ. 696). David defeated
Hadadezer twice (2 S. 10¹³. ¹⁸) and gained control of the country. A little
later, a kingdom was established in Damascus under Rezon, one of Hadadezer's captains (1 K. 11²³⁻²⁵). In Solomon's reign this new kingdom was continually at war with Israel (1 K. 11²⁵). Henceforward Damascus was the
capital city and seat of the kingdom of Aram, the word Aram itself, when not
otherwise defined, being used for this kingdom (1 K. 15¹⁸ 2 K. 5¹ 6⁸. ²⁴ Am. 1⁵).
Only during the reign of Hezion, Rezon's successor, was there peace (1 K. 22¹).
For the view that Hezion and Rezon are identical, v. Ew. *Hist.* IV. 24, n. 5;
GAS. *EB.* I. 990; Thenius and Klo. on 1 K. 11²³ 15¹⁸; and KAT^3. 134; but
cf. Che. art. "Hezion," EB. I.; Kit. on 1 K. 15¹⁸. Wkl. *Untersuch.* 60 ff. reads
Hazael on basis of 𝔊ᴬᴸ. Tabrimmon, son of Hezion, seems to have made a
covenant with Judah against Israel (1 K. 15¹⁸. ¹⁹). With Ben-hadad I., the son

of Tabrimmon, the relations became still more delicate. A treaty was made
with Baasha, King of Israel, but afterwards at the request of Asa, King of Judah,
it was broken, and certain cities in the north of Israel were captured (1 K.
15²⁰ ᶠᶠ·). Ben-hadad II. was frequently repulsed by Ahab, King of Israel, with
whom Jehoshaphat of Judah was allied (1 K. 20¹ ᶠᶠ· 22³ ᶠᶠ· 2 K. 6⁸· ²⁴; for the
view that the opponent of Ahab was Ben-hadad I. *v.* Wkl. *Untersuch.* 60 ff.;
Che. art. "Ben-hadad," *EB.*; but cf. Gu. *GVI.* 154). Ahab, fearing Shalmaneser II. (860–825) of Assyria, dealt very leniently with Ben-hadad, though
victorious over him, because it was deemed expedient to keep Syria as a
power between Assyria and Israel (F. Brown, *Assyriology*, 60 f.; Kit. *Hist.*
II. 272). When Shalmaneser attacked Ben-hadad, Ahab and other neighboring princes came to the assistance of Syria, but all were defeated in the
battle of Karkar (854 B.C.; see Shalmaneser-Monolith, col. II. 91 f.; Schr.
KGF. 359–64; *KB.* I. 172; *COT.* I. 182–90; We. *SV.* I. 31 ff.; Sta. *GVI.* I.
528 f.; McC. *HPM.* I. 272–80; R. F. Harper, *ABL.* 43). In the year following (853 B.C.) Ahab took advantage of a respite from Assyria to make his
fatal campaign against Ben-hadad (1 K. 22¹⁻⁴⁰). Hazael, the usurper, successor
of Ben-hadad II., captured the land east of the Jordan (2 K. 10³²ᶠ· 13³· ⁵· ⁷· ²²)
from Jehu and Jehoahaz, and made a campaign against the Philistines (2 K.
12¹⁷ᶠ·), in which Jehoash of Judah secured the safety of Jerusalem by giving
him presents. But Hazael's son, Ben-hadad III., was defeated by Joash of
Israel three times, and Jeroboam II. took away from him Hamath and
Damascus, or, at least, part of the territory belonging to Damascus (2 K. 13²⁵
14²⁵· ²⁸). Moreover, Adad-nirari III. (812–783 B.C.) of Assyria besieged Damascus and compelled its king, Mari, to pay heavy tribute. In the time of
Amos, therefore, Syria was greatly weakened, but was probably giving signs
of renewed hostility.

3 *b, c. I will not revoke it*] Cf. Is. 55¹¹. The pronoun "it" is
ambiguous here as in Nu. 23²⁰ Is. 43¹³ 48¹⁶; it probably refers to
the anger of Yahweh, *i.e.* the threatening which is involved in the
preceding verse, and in this case the idea is that Yahweh will not
avert the punishment which he has already threatened.* Others
refer it to the specific threatening which is to be uttered in verses
⁴ ᵃⁿᵈ ⁵.† A different turn is given to the verb by translating it
"repay," "pay back," ‡ and making the sentence interrogative,
although without the sign of interrogation. Hesselberg, however,
giving the verb the same force but taking the connection differently,
arrives at this interpretation, " I will not repay Syria for the inde-

---

* Jus., Hi., Ew., Pu., Or., We., Now., Dr.   † Marck, Mau.

‡ The other meaning of השיב, *revoke, turn*, regularly requiring חָרוֹן or אַף.
So Va.

finable number of lesser crimes of which she has been guilty, but on account of her threshing Gilead," etc. Some refer the pronoun to Syria, the verb being translated "convert." * Others refer "it" to some earlier prophecy, the fulfilment of which has been delayed, but according to Amos will not be revoked.† The translation "I will not bring them back," ‡ requires a late date for the prophecy. By a change of pointing (v.s.) Hoffmann translates, "I will not let them dwell in peace." — *Because they have threshed Gilead* §] The country, not the mountain, of Gilead is intended. The word is derived, according to Gn. 31⁴⁷ ᶠᶠ·, from the Aramaic words meaning hill (גַּל) and witness (עֵד), ‖ and accordingly was used at first as the name of the mountainous region forming the boundary between Israel and her Aramaean neighbors. For a good example of this narrower usage, see Ct. 4¹. At an early period, however, it took on a larger meaning and designated, in contrast with Canaan, west of the Jordan, all the territory east of the Jordan except Bashan (cf. Dt. 3¹³ Jos. 13¹⁰· ¹¹· ³¹ ᶠ·). In Dt. 34¹ Bashan seems to be included.¶ It stands specifically for the territory of the two and a half tribes (*e.g.* Nu. 32²⁶· ²⁹· ³⁹ Jos. 12²· ⁵). In 1 S. 13⁷ Gad and Gilead are joined. That Amos used the word in the latter sense appears from 2 K. 10³² ᶠ·, although even here it is used in two senses in the same passage. ** — *With threshing instruments of iron*] The reading of 𝔊 (v.s.) is without basis. References in the O. T. to threshing machines or instruments are easily classified according as they speak (1) of the ordinary work of such machines (2 S. 24²² 1 Ch. 21²³ Is. 28²⁷· ²⁸) ; (2) of their use as instruments of torture (here, and 2 S. 12³¹ 1 Ch. 20³), or (3) in a figurative sense (Jb. 41³⁰ of the crocodile ; Is. 41¹⁵ of Israel). To understand their use as instruments of torture we must note the three forms which are described as still found in Oriental countries,

---

* Jer.   † Mit.   ‡ Day and Chapin, *AJSL.* XVIII. 73 f.

§ Cf. the similar phraseology used by Tiglathpileser III.: "the land Bît-Amuk-kâni I threshed as with a threshing instrument; all its people, and its possessions I brought to Assyria" (*KB.* II. 4 f.; cf. *ABL.* 54).

‖ Cf. suggestion of Ba. גַּל עַד *hill of eternity*, Hb. 3⁶ (הַרְרֵי עַד) and Gn. 49²⁶ (גִּבְעוֹת עוֹלָם).

¶ Cf. GAS. *HG.* 548 f., 575–90; S. Merrill, art. "Gilead," *DB.*; Che. art. "Gilead," *EB.*   ** Ba.

C

viz. (1) that seen by Niebuhr at Yemen,* *a great stone*, in
the shape of a wooden drag, drawn over the grain by two oxen;
(2) that seen by Niebuhr in Syria,† *a sledge*, made of planks
underneath which are fixed sharp flints, or pieces of sharp iron;
(3) that described by Girard, ‡ *a threshing wagon*, consisting of
a square frame of wood across which, parallel with two of the
sides, run two axletrees, on one of which are three, and on
the other four flat iron wheels. § Only prisoners of war were
thus tortured; the custom was not uncommon of placing them
on the ground like grain, and driving the machine over them.
Other cruelties (cf. 2 S. 12^{31}) were practised at the same time.
The cruelties here represented, whether literally or figuratively,
were probably those practised by Hazael (842–802 B.C), in the
incursions during the reigns of Jehu and Jehoahaz (cf. 2 K. 8^{12}
10$^{32\,f.}$ 13^7).— **4.** *Send a fire*] For fire as a symbol of war, see
Ju. 9^{20}; of divine wrath, which frequently finds expression in war,
Dt. 4^{24} 32^{22}. The same words are used in Ho. 8^{14} and Je. 17^{27}
21^{14} 49^{27} 50^{32}. It is hardly.to be taken either as literal fire, or as
lightning; ‖ cf. Ju. 20^{48} and 2 K. 8^{12}.— *In the house of Hazael*]
Hazael,¶ the founder of the dynasty which sat upon the throne
of Syria in the times of Amos, was a contemporary of Joram
(2 K. 8^{29}), Jehu (2 K. 10^{32}), and Jehoahaz (2 K. 13^{22}). His occupation of the throne was foretold by Elisha (2 K. 8$^{7-13}$). The
allusion here may be to Damascus, or to a royal palace in
Damascus, as favored by the parallelism, or to the dynasty of
Hazael. In any case the thought is essentially the same.—
The palaces of Ben-hadad] A phrase practically parallel with
"house of Hazael." The name scarcely refers to Ben-hadad I.
(about 900), or Ben-hadad II. (about 874), both of whom preceded Hazael, but rather to Ben-hadad III. (2 K. 10^3 13^{25}),**
the son and successor of Hazael. The suggestion †† that this

---

* *Reisebeschreibung von Arabien*, 158.   † *Ibid.* 158. Post, *PEF.*, 1891, p. 114.

‡ *Mémoire sur l'agriculture, l'industrie et le commerce de l'Égypte*, II. 504 f.
(cf. Ba.).

§ Cf. Dr. 227 f.; Now. *Arch.* I. 232 ff.; Benz. *Arch.* 209 f.   ‖ Schrö.; GFM. *Ju.* 21.

¶ Ri. *HBA.* I. 572; *COT.* I. 196 ff., 202 ff.; Sta. *GVI.* I. 540–6, 562–6; Che.
art. "Hazael," *EB.*; C. F. Burney, art. "Hazael," *DB.*

** Or., Dr.; *v.* GAS. art. "Damascus," *EB.*; and *KAT*^{3}. 134, on the question
of two or three Ben-hadads.   †† Cf. Mit.; *KAT*^{3}. 134.

may be the same as Mari whom Adad-nirari III. (803 B.C.)
conquered is hardly tenable. By some the name is thought
to be a title of Syrian kings as Pharaoh was of the Egyptian
kings ; * others think Hazael and Ben-hadad are used as typical,
representative names of the kings of Damascus.† — **5.** *The
bars of Damascus*] The bars employed in ancient cities to
fasten the gates are frequently used by synecdoche for the defences of a city (Ju. 16³ 1 K. 4¹³ Je. 51³⁰ Lam. 2⁹). The power
of Yahweh will break in pieces the defences of the city. — *An
inhabitant*] *i.e.* the common people ; either so, or with equal
appropriateness, *the one sitting on a throne ;* the former is favored
by the context which has another term for ruler (*v.i.*) ; for
the latter, cf. Ps. 2⁴ 22³. — *The valley of Aven*] If the Hebrew text be read with ⑤ ןוא, ‡ instead of ןוא, and it be remembered that On was the Egyptian name for Heliopolis, a name
given also to Baalbek, because it was a centre of the sun-worship,
the prophet must have had in mind " the valley of the Lebanon "
(Jos. 11¹⁷ 12⁷), the Coele-Syria of the Greeks, the modern El-
buka'a. With this may be compared Ezekiel's similar treatment of
the Egyptian On (30¹⁷). If the Hebrew text is retained, the pun
is introduced to bring out more distinctly the idolatry. § The interpretation, valley of idolatry, ‖ presents no satisfactory explanation.
— *The sceptre holder*] This phrase in Ju. 5¹⁴ means *governor*, in
Am. 2³ *judge*.¶ It evidently denotes the supreme officer, whether
king or judge, and is either synonymous with *inhabitant* of the
preceding member, or in contrast with it. — *From Beth-Eden*] The
localities suggested for this designation are (1) old Jûsieh, near
Riblah, thirty miles N.E. from Baalbek ;** (2) the modern Jubb-
'Adin, twenty-five miles N.E. from Damascus, perhaps a country
seat of the Syrian kings ;†† (3) 'Ehden or Bêt Jenn, near the foot
of Hermon, eastward ;‡‡ (4) 'Ehden, on the N.W. slope of Lebanon, near the great cedars ; §§ (5) the Eden of Ez. 27²³, ‖‖ (cf.

---

* Jer., Bauer, Schrö.; cf. Je. 49²⁷.   † We., Now., Marti.
‡ See against this view *EB.* I. 390.
§ So Dahl, Hi., Ba., GAS.; but *v.* We., Now., Dr.   ‖ ƻ. Os., Gun., Or.
¶ So Hi.   ** Hi., Ke.   †† St.; Hoffm. *ZAW.* III. 97.
‡‡ Ros., cf. Ba.   §§ Bauer.
‖‖ Ri. *HBA.* I. 176; *COT.* II. 11 f.; Wkl. *Forsch.* I. 104; Now.; but *v.* Che.
EB. I. 551 f.; Dr. 228 f.

2 K. 19^{12} Is. 37^{12}), which is the Bît-Adini of the Assyrian inscriptions (often mentioned by Ashurnaçirpal and Shalmaneser II.), an Aramaic kingdom, on both banks of the Middle Euphrates. — *The people of Aram*] *v.s.* under Damascus. — *Shall go into captivity*] The word גָּלָה meaning *to be* or *make naked* is here for the first time used in the sense of *go into captivity*. The earlier word שׁבה *to carry captive* is used of captives as individuals, although individuals are, of course, included in a general captivity (cf. 7^{17}). גלה, on the other hand, stands for a national captivity or exile, when a whole nation is deported. Since the Assyrians (under Tiglathpileser III.) were the first to introduce this policy, the idea had not existed among the Hebrews before the time of Amos.* The policy, as history shows, was one which contributed to the fall of the Assyrian empire. — *To Kir*] The following suggestions have been made : (1) The original home of the Aramaeans (cf. 9^7) ; † (2) the place to which they were afterwards carried (2 K. 16^9) ; ‡ (3) to be pointed קוּר and taken as the name of the river which rises in the Caucasus and empties into the Caspian Sea ; § (4) Cyropolis ; ‖ (5) the Syrian province, Cyrrhestica ; ¶ (6) Cyrene ; ** (7) Kurenia in Media, cf. Is. 21^2 22^6 ; †† (8) Kuris, north of Aleppo ; ‡‡ but nothing certain has yet been discovered. The latest suggestions are to emend קיר to קוֹע, the name of a nation mentioned in Ez. 23^{23}, corresponding to the Ḳutû or Ḳuê of the Assyrian inscriptions ; §§ to emend to קוֹר and identify it with the Karians whom Arrian (III. 8^5) mentions in connection with the Sittakenians. ‖‖ In the mind of the prophet the world power by which this judgment was to be executed was Assyria. This is evident from the historical situation of the times, in which Assyria, of all the nations, was the only one capable of accomplishing such a thing ; from the

---

* McC. *HPM.* I. 327 f. But cf. GSG. *History*, 170, 239, who claims that this was introduced as early as Tig. Pil. I. (1100 B.C.), and developed by Tig. Pil. III.

† Ḳi., Ba. ‡ Jus.

§ Mich.; Bauer, cf. Jus.; but the name of this river begins with *K* not *Q*, and the river lies outside of the territory that was dominated by Assyria.

‖ Struensee, 214. ¶ Har.; Furrer, *BL.* III. 534. ** 𝔗, 'A, 𝔙.

†† Bochart, *Reise.*, cf. Ba. ‡‡ Socin.

§§ W. Max Müller, art. "Kir," *DB.;* Wkl. *Untersuch.* 177; cf. Klo., Co., and Bredenkamp on Is. $22^{5\,f.}$ ‖‖ So. Wkl. *Forsch.* II. 254 ff.; cf. *EB.* art. "Kir."

"deportation" policy referred to in נלה (v.⁵), a policy peculiar to
Assyria; and from the direct naming of Assyria by Hosea (10⁶)
the younger contemporary of Amos. The historical statement of
the overthrow of Syria by the Assyrians is given in the Annals
of Tiglathpileser III.*

3. אמר] Indefinite pf. *v.* H. 17, 3; Dr. §9; cf. Kö. *Stil.* 112 f.— על שלשה
וגו׳] So also vs.⁶. ⁹. ¹¹. ¹³ 2¹. ⁴. ⁶; for this use of numbers to express the idea of
indefiniteness *v.* GK. 134*s*; Kö. *Stil.* 163 f.; for a similar use of *one* and *two*,
Dt. 32³⁰ Je. 3¹⁴ Jb. 33¹⁴ 40⁵ Ps. 62¹² Ecclus. 38¹⁷; *two* and *three*, Jb. 33²⁹
Is. 17⁶ 2 K. 9³² Ho. 6² Am. 4⁸ Ecclus. 13⁷ 23¹⁶ 26²⁸ 32⁷ 50²⁵; *four* and *five*,
Is. 17⁶; *five* and *six*, 2 K. 13¹⁹; *six* and *seven*, Jb. 5¹⁹ Pr. 6¹⁶; *seven* and *eight*,
Mi. 5⁴ Ec. 11²; *nine* and *ten*, Ecclus. 25⁷; the same usage exists in Arab.
(cf. Spitta, § 132*b*), in Syriac (cf. Nö. *Syr. Gram.* § 240 *B*), in the Tel-
el-Amarna Letters (87, l. 44; 120, l. 32), in Greek (*Odys.* V. 306) and
Latin (Horace, *Carm.* I. 21, 13; Virgil, *Aen.* I. 94).— פשעי] a stronger
word than עבר, always containing the idea of wilful opposition, whereas the
latter is the etymological equivalent of *transgress*, *i.e.* overstep the limit;
cf. חטא *to miss* (the mark).— אשיבנו] It has been urged against the usual
interpretation of this (1) that the suffix cannot refer to יד, since this has
not been mentioned and is not readily supplied from the preceding context, (2) that it cannot refer to the threat in v.², since v.² contains nothing
touching foreign nations and, moreover, to represent ׳ as uttering a threat
and at once declaring his purpose not to withdraw it is to compromise him,
(3) that the suffix is not sufficient to designate an unspoken oracle, (4) that
punishments are always revoked on account of *repentance*, not "on account of
three or four transgressions" as here (so Hoffm. *ZAW.* III. 97; Elh. 139).
But the emendations proposed (*v.s.*) are certainly no less objectionable, *e.g.*
if it referred to the people the pl. suffix would be more natural, especially in
view of the immediately following דושם; furthermore לא אשיבנו is a very weak
expression of the thought of exile.— בחרצות] The more ordinary word is מורג
with which חרוץ is used as a descriptive term in Is. 41¹⁵; the primary meaning
of חרץ = *cut*, cf. Assy. ḫarâṣu = *dig;* the חרוץ is mentioned again in Is. 28²⁷
Jb. 41³⁰; and possibly in 2 S. 12³¹ where it is vocalized חָרִיץ. The modern
name for the מורג in Palestine is *nauraj*, and among the common people
mauraj; it is still called *môrâg* in the Ḳalamûn mountains around Ma'lûlâ

---

* The passage relating to the conquest of Damascus is badly mutilated; in part
it reads as follows: "In order to save his life, he fled alone . . . I entered the
chief gate of his city; his chief officer I captured alive . . . impaled him and subdued his land . . . I captured his city and shut him up like a bird in a cage . . .
his groves which were innumerable I cut down and left not a tree standing . . . the
house of the father of Rezin of Damascus, impassable mountains. . . ." See
Layard, *Inscriptions in the Cuneiform Character*, pl. 72, ls. 3–16; *COT.* I. 252–7;
Rost, *Die Keilschrifttexte Tiglat-Pilesers III.*, I. 34–7.

(*PEF.*, 1891, p. 114; Dr. 227 f.). The אוֹפַן עֲגָלָה and גִּלְגַּל עֶגְלָתוֹ of Is. 28²⁷ f. point to the third form of threshing instrument mentioned above (*v.* p. 18). —**4.** ארמנות] A poetic word which does not occur in the Hexateuch, Ju., or S., and is used chiefly in the prophets. It is sometimes considered a formation from ארם (BSZ.; BDB.; Kö. II. 1, pp. 154, 203). It is probably a loan word of uncertain origin (Ew.⁸, 496). Its usual meaning is clearly *palace*, but it has also the meaning *fortress, citadel.* Cf. Assyr. ulmânu, *palace*, and almattu, *castle* (Muss-Arnolt, *Dict.*). — בן־הדד] In view of 𝔊 υἱοῦ 'Αδέρ, Assy. *Dad-'idri*, or better *Bir-'idri* (= (*ilu*)IM-'idri; Shalmaneser-Obelisk, 59, 88; *KB.* I. 134; Wkl. *Untersuch.* 68 ff.; Hilprecht, *Assyriaca*, 76 ff.; Sayce, art. "Ben-hadad," *DB.*; Che. art. "Ben-hadad," *EB.*), and the reading הדר עזר, (1 Ch. 18³, for הדר עזר) the proper form is בן הדר or better בר הדר. The divine name *Bir* seems to have been confused by the Hebrew scribes with the Aramaic *bar = son*, and was thus rendered *ben*. The meaning of the name is "Bir is my glory." The name *Adores* used by Justin (36, 2) is identified by Nöldeke (*BL.* I. 392) with our Ben-hadad. On the use of the name of this god in Syrian proper names *v.* Sayce, *Hibbert Lectures* (1887), 55 f.—**5.** און] Macrobius (*Sat.* I. 23) and Lucian (*de Dea Syria*, § 5) state that the worship of the sun at Heliopolis in Syria was derived from Heliopolis in Egypt (quoted by Rob. *BR²*. III. 518). On the supposition that this is correct, the name *On* is explained as having been carried over from Egypt also; cf. Egyptian *Aûnû*. But the statements of Macrobius and Lucian are without further support and, as Dr. suggests, may be "nothing more than inferences from the fact of two celebrated temples being dedicated to a similar cult "; if so, the name *On* together with the Egyptian theory of its origin, must go. In any case On was the secular, not the religious, name of the Egyptian Heliopolis. We. suggests the possibility that און is a corruption of the name of some god, and doubts whether Heliopolis was an Aramaic city in the time of Amos (so also *EB.* I. 390; cf. Wkl. *Untersuch.* 183 n.; Hirscht, *ZwTh.* XLIV. 46 f.; Kö. *Stil.* 297).—ותומך שבט] The Hadad inscription of Zinjirli, ll. 15, 20, and 25, contains the Aramaic equivalent of this phrase, *viz.* אחז חטר (DHM. *Die altsemit. Inschriften von Sendschirli* (1893), 20 f.; quoted by Dr.). Cf. the σκεπτοῦχος βασιλεύς of Homer (*Il.* II. 26; *Od.* II. 231). —מבית עדן] The Assyrian *Bît-Adini* was the occasion of more than one campaign on the part of Ashurnaçirpal and Shalmaneser II. The latter gives a full account (Monolith Inscription, col. I. 12–29, II. 1–35) of the capture of Aḫuni, the son of Adini, the ruler of Bît-Adini; the inhabitants of Bît-Adini seem to have been called בני עדן; the Assyrian inscriptions likewise speak of *Bît-Am-mân, e.g.* Bu-du-il šar Bît-Am-ma-na (*KB.* II. 149, *ABL.* 86.) while the O. T. mentions the בני עמון. The objection that Bît-Adini had long been subject to Assyria, hence cannot be the place referred to here, seems fatal (Che. *EB.* I. 552; cf. Wkl. *Untersuch.* 183; Rogers, *History of Babylonia and Assyria*, II. 74; GSG. *Hist.* 191, 198, 213); Χαρράν in 𝔊 is due to confusion of ר and ר. —וגלו] Cf. Arab. جَلاَ *uncover, emigrate*, and جلو *make bare, go into* *exile;* so Aram. and Syriac. It is applied but rarely to the exiling of individuals, *e.g.* 2 S. 15^{19}, and is sometimes used figuratively of lifeless things, *e.g.* Pr. 27^{25} I S. 4$^{21 f.}$ Is. 24^{11} Ho. 10^5. שבה seems to have been the earlier word (cf. Arab. سَبَى, *be captured;* Syr. ܫܒܐ, *take;* Assyr. šabû, *to overpower, attack*). גלה does not appear in this sense prior to the coming of the Assyrian forces westward. — ארם] cf. Assyr. *Aramu,* which is never applied to people west of the Euphrates, who are always called *Ḥatti.* — קירה] W. Max Müller, art. "Kir," *DB.,* suggests that וגלו עם ארם קירה is an interpolation based upon 9^7; urging that if Kir was the original home of the Aramaeans (9^7) the Assyrians would certainly never have deported them thither, but rather to some strange region.

6–8. *Judgment upon Philistia.* — Next in order Philistia is upbraided for the sins of which her cities have been guilty, in punishment for which the entire country shall perish.

The strophic arrangement of vs.$^{6-8}$ is like that of vs.$^{3-5}$, viz. $5 + 3 + 4$. The parallelism is exact, if the line, "and I will turn my hand against Ekron," be transposed from the middle of v.^{8} to be the last line of v.^{7}. Even a hasty comparison of the two pieces shows that by this change, the lines of each piece beginning with "and I will cut off" are brought into the same position; likewise, in the case of the lines beginning with "and the one holding, etc.," while the climactic arrangement of strophe 3 is thus preserved.

6. [אשיבנו] 𝔊 renders suf. αὐτούς. — [על] 𝔊 ἕνεκεν; cf. ἀνθ' ὧν in v.^{3}. — שלמה] 𝔊 τοῦ Σαλωμών (= שְׁלֹמֹה, or an error of a copyist for the transcribed σαλημα). — [להסגיר] Wkl. treats as a gloss based on v.^{9} (*Untersuch.* 183; so Löhr.); but לאדום cannot well follow הגלותם (Now., Oet.) — **7.** [חומת] 𝔊𝔖𝔗 pl.; but cf. חומך ,יושב ,בריח. — **8.** [יושב] 𝔊 pl. — [חומך] 𝔊 ἐξαρθήσεται. — [פלשתים] 𝔊 τῶν ἀλλοφύλων, the regular rendering outside of the Hex. — [והשיבותי] to be transposed (*v.s.*). — [אדני יהוה] 𝔊 Κύριος.

6 a. *Gaza*] As Damascus (v.^{3}) represented Syria, so Gaza, as the largest city of the Philistines, and perhaps as the centre of the slave traffic here rebuked, is used for Philistia (*v.i.*). On this city *v.* George Adam Smith.*

The name of the Philistines is similar in all the languages of their neighbors. In Egyptian it is *Purasati,* and in Assyrian *Palastu, Pilistu,* and *Pilištu.* The Philistines were immigrants into Palestine from Caphtor (Am. 9^7 Dt. 2^{23}), an island (Je. 47^1), doubtless in the Mediterranean. This place has been variously identified, *e.g.* with Cyprus, Κάρπαθος, and Crete. The last

---

* *HG.* 181 ff.

seems most probable both from its size and from notices in which the Philistines are called פְּרֵתִים (𝕲 Κρητῶν) and similar expressions (1 S. 30[14, 16] Ez. 25[15.16] Zp. 2[6]; Ba., GAS. *HG.* 171). The view which places Caphtor in Egypt (Ebers, *Aegypten u. Bücher Mose's,* 127 ff.) is untenable, although possibly the Philistines dwelt there for a time before their final location (Gn. 10[14]). A Semitic origin has been claimed for them by many (Ew., Sta. *GVI.* I. 142; cf. W. J. Beecher, art. "Philistines," *DB.*), chiefly on the ground of the proper names. But from part of the names and from their general un-Semitic characteristics, a non-Semitic origin is more probable (Ba., Wkl. *GI.* I. 216; McC. *HPM.* § 192). The available evidence indicates that they were probably Aryan pirates whose first settlement in Palestine was made about the age of Ramses III. (Ew., GFM. *Ju.* 80; Brugsch, *Egypt under the Pharaohs,* 329 ff.; Ed. Meyer, *GA.* I. 319 f.). Probably in the patriarchal time they occupied a small territory between Egypt and Gaza (Ba., Beecher, Wkl., *et al.*), since the early references to them are too numerous to be explained as later additions. They were so formidable at the time of the Exodus that the Hebrews were not willing to take the direct road to Palestine (Ex. 13[17]). They were either partially conquered under Joshua and some of their cities taken (Ju. 1[18]), the view of many; or else they had not yet occupied those cities, but toward the close of the period of the Judges were greatly strengthened by numerous immigrants directly from their original home, summoned because of their fear of the growing power of the Hebrews (Ba.). Near the close of the period of the Judges they became so strong that they invaded the territory of the Hebrews and subdued them (Ju. 14[4] 15[11]). We have records of their defeating Israel (1 S. 4 ff.), and only in the time of Samuel were they defeated (1 S. 7[3 ff.] especially v.[14]). Saul had frequent contests with them (1 S. 17[1 ff.] 18[6] 19[8] 23[1 ff.] 29[1] 31[4]). After this time, they appear to have been so far conquered that they are seldom mentioned. Cf. the view of W. Max Müller, *AuE.* 389 f., that the last Egyptian king of the 21st dynasty conquered them. This explains why David and Solomon had little trouble with them (2 S. 8[1]).

6 b. *Because they carried into complete captivity*] Cf. Je. 24[5] 28[4] Ob.[20]. This has been taken to mean: (1) a peaceful captivity, *i.e.* "captivity of those who lived peacefully with them, and had not injured them," * (2) a holy or pious captivity,† (3) captivity of Solomon as in 𝕲, which (although a copyist's error) is defended by Theodoret,‡ while (4) Jerome understands it to mean a perfect captivity, *i.e.* the hardest service ; § but the phrase here and in v.[9] refers rather to a complete captivity, *i.e.* one of the whole people, neither age nor sex being spared (cf. Je. 13[19]).‖ Cf.

---

* Geb., Grotius. † Jus. ‡ Cf. Ba. § Va. ‖ Cal., We., Now., *et al.*

the translations of Driver, *they carried into exile entire popula-*
tions; Ewald, *whole villages,* and Winckler (*v.s.*). — *To deliver*
them up to Edom] Either *to deliver up* as a fugitive slave to his
master * (cf. Dt. 23¹⁵), or *to deliver over* to Edom to be resold.
From this reference, and from v.⁹, Edom, in these early days, must
have been engaged in the slave trade between different nations.†
There seems to be allusion to an historical incident, for the
definite recovery of which the data are insufficient. According
to Hitzig, the Phoenicians (see v.⁹) sold the slaves to the Philistines, who again sold them to the Edomites, the greater activity
of the Philistines being reflected in the use of הגלות rather than
הסגיר, and in the order of the names in vs.⁶⁻¹⁰, Philistines, Phoenicians, since Jo. 3⁴ gives them in the reverse order. According to
Baur ‡ the Philistines sold them to the Phoenicians, and they again
to the Edomites, Tyre being the chief slave market. For this it is
urged that הגלות, used of the Philistines, means their actual removal
from the land, while הסגיר of the Phoenicians refers only to their
dealing in them. Slavery was an essential element in ancient
civilization, and the supply of slaves was in large part recruited
from captives taken in war. The large demand for them under
the ancient régime is evidenced by the gigantic pyramids of
Egypt, by representations on Assyrian bas-reliefs, and by the
legislation concerning them in the Hammurabi code; cf. *e.g.*
§§ 15–20, 118, 119, 175, 176, 226, 227. Does Jo. 3³⁻⁶ refer to
the same event? and is the event that which is described as
occurring under Jehoram (2 Ch. 21¹⁶) § or Ahaz (2 Ch. 28¹⁸) ‖ ?
It seems best either to understand that reference is made to
both of them and to any other similar event,¶ or that there
is no specific reference intended.** Indeed, it is not certain
that גלות refers at all to the Israelites.†† The sons of Javan (Jo. 3⁶)
may refer to an Arabian tribe (cf. Ez. 27¹⁹, *v.s.*) rather than to the
Greeks. ‡‡ — **7.** *Gaza*] Gaza was the most southern (2 K. 18⁸)
and important of the five Philistine cities (1 S. 6¹⁷). Being the

---

* Kusznitzki.

† Cf. also Ez. 27¹⁶ (reading אדם (Edom) for ארם (Aram), as do 𝔊, 𝔖, 'A., Da.
Toy, Co., Hi., Kraetzschmar, *et al.*).   ‡ p. 96; so also Ew.

§ Mit.   ‖ Ros., Schrö.   ¶ Jus.   ** Os.   †† We.

‡‡ Ba.; cf. Che. art. " Javan," *EB.;* Sta. *Das Volk Javan* (1880).

last town on the road to Egypt, it was always closely connected
with Egypt.*

Its situation on the edge of the desert made it important to caravans. It
was located on a hill about a hundred feet high, three miles from the Mediterranean, and fifty miles S.W. of Jerusalem. In ancient times it was the centre
of great caravan routes north to Jerusalem, Damascus, Tyre, etc., and south
to Egypt, South Arabia, Petra, and Palmyra. In the Tel-el-Amarna period it
was held by Egypt. Early Israel probably never captured Gaza (Ju. 1¹⁹ 3³
Jos. 13³). To the contrary effect are Jos. 15⁴⁷ Ju. 1¹⁸ (cf. 𝔊), which are probably later additions. Gaza (= Assyr. *Ḥa-az-za-tu* or *Ḥa-zi-ti*) suffered severely
at the hands of the Assyrians in the times of Tiglathpileser III. (734 B.C.).
In the Nimrud Inscription, l. 62, Hanno of Gaza is mentioned as paying
tribute; see *ABL.* 57; *KB.* II. 21. In the annals of Tiglathpileser (III.
R 10, 2, ls. 19 ff.) in connection with the attack upon Israel, we read, "As for
Hanno of Gaza [who] had fled [before] my [weapons] and escaped to
Mutsri — Gaza [I captured], its possessions, [its] gods [I carried away]
... and my royal image [I set up]." See *KB.* II. 32 f.; *COT.* I. 247.

8 c. *And I will turn my hand*] Strike with repeated blows,†
rather than extend in a new movement. ‡ Cf. also Ju. 6⁹ Is. 1²⁵
Zc. 13⁷ Ps. 81¹⁴. This has been transposed (*v.s.*). — *Ekron*] The
northernmost of the four cities named, was of importance because
it possessed an oracle of Baalzebub (2 K. 1²), and was on a
good trade route, being on the northern frontier of Philistia, nine
miles from the sea, in the vale of Sorek, where a pass breaks
through the low hills to Ramleh. It was on a branch of the line
of traffic. Hence, possibly, it is mentioned only once in the
Egyptian lists, viz. by Thutmosis III. It was thus the nearest
of the Philistine cities to Judah. — **8 a, b.** *Ashdod*] Was a well-
fortified city, south of Ekron, 21 miles N.E. of Gaza and three
miles from the seacoast; cf. Jos. 13³ 1 S. 6¹⁷ᶠ·. It was anciently
of importance as the halfway station on the road from Gaza to
Joppa. It was well watered, and situated at the mouth of the
most broad and fertile valley of Palestine. The cult of Dagon
was especially associated with Ashdod (cf. 1 S. 5 f. 1 Macc. 10⁸³
11⁴). From 3⁹ it may be supposed to have been in the times of
Amos a place of some repute. — *Askelon*] mentioned as early as

---

* Cf. the lists of Ramses II. and III. which are treated in *RP²*. VI. 24 ff., 31 ff.;
W. M. Müller, *A. und E.*, 159, 164 ff., 227 ff., 393; Sayce, *Patriarchal Palestine*, 235-
40; cf. Paton, *Hist.* 78 (map).   † Ros., Ba.   ‡ Mit.

on Meneptah's Israel-stele, was situated in a rocky amphitheatre immediately on the coast. It was isolated from the other Philistine cities by its location.

Letters from its governor form a part of the Amarna correspondence (Am. Tab. 207, 211 f.; see transl. of No. 207 in Paton, *Hist.* 101; Wkl. *Amarna Letters*). It is mentioned as a part of the Philistine territory in the days of Samson (Ju. 14[19]), Samuel (1 S. 6[17]), David (2 S. 1[20]), Zephaniah (2[4.7]), Jeremiah (25[20] 47[5.7]), and the later Zechariah (9[5]). Metinti of Askelon is mentioned among the tributaries of Tiglathpileser III. (Nimrud Inscription, l. 61, *v. ABL.* 57).

8 d. *The remnant of the Philistines shall perish*] Not the inhabitants of the cities and villages (including Gath) unmentioned before * (cf. Je. 39[3] Ne. 7[72]), nor the last man of the Philistines † (cf. אחרית, 4[2] 9[1]), but the remnant of the Philistines wherever they may be, *i.e. all the Philistines.* Cf. Ez. 36[3.4]. Other predictions against Philistia will be found in Is. 11[14] 14[29-32] Je. 25[20] 47 Zp. 2[4-7] Ez. 25[15-17] Zc. 9[5-7]. — *The Lord Yahweh*] The most common designation for the deity in Amos, occurring fifteen times.

6. על הגלותם גלות שלמה] The pron. suf. used as subj. GK. 115 *h*; Kö. 229 *d*; H. 29, 2 *b*(1); the cogn. acc. GK. 117 *p, q*; H. 32, 2 ; prep. and inf. expressing causal clause, GK. 158 *c*; Kö. 403 f; lit. because they carried into exile an entire exile, *i.e.* exiled company; cf. Is. 45[13], the fem. being used collectively, GK. 122 *s*; Kö. 255 *d*; so also the other deriv. גילה (cf. Je. 29[1]). — [להסגיר לאדם הסגיר is followed by אל (Dt. 23[16]), ביד (1 S. 23[11.12.20]), and as here ל (Ps. 78[48.50.62]); this would seem to be a poetic usage. The Hiph. like the Pi. = *shut one up to, deliver over to;* the acc. of the person is omitted here as in 1 S. 23[12]. The inf. with ל = purpose ; GK. 114 *f, g*; H. 29, 3 *a* ; Kö. 407 *a*.

9, 10. *Judgment upon Tyre.* — The world-catastrophe which the prophet sees includes also Phoenicia. The relationship between Phoenicia and Israel had been very close (*v.i.*) ; but the threats of destruction here uttered continued to be made to the very end (cf. Is. 23 Je. 25[22] Ez. 26–28 Zc. 9[2b]).

The structure of this oracle (and of the following one), viz. 5 and 2, is very different from that of the preceding. Strophe 1 is the same including (1) line 1, the divine authority; (2) lines 2, 3, the use of the symbolical numbers, marking the transgression in a general way, as one often repeated; (3) lines 3, 4, 5, the more specific charge; while strophe 2 is a reproduction of the first

---

* Jer.   † Ew., Now.

two lines of strophe 2 of the preceding oracles.   There is nothing to correspond to strophe 2, line 3, and all of strophe 3, including the closing אמר יהוה.
This striking variation of form in the utterances against Tyre (vs.⁹·¹⁰), Edom
(vs.¹¹·¹²), and Judah (2⁴·⁵) is to be explained, not upon the ground of a
desire to condense, in order to avoid too much monotony and repetition,
for it would be impossible in that case to understand why the condensation
is made in one case rather than in another; but upon the supposition, for
which there is other support, that these particular utterances, viz. concerning
Tyre, Edom, and Judah, are not from Amos, but are interpolations from a later
time.   The considerations to be noted here are: (1) If the geographical
order   prevailed   as   elsewhere,   from   N.   to   S.,   vs.⁹⁻¹¹ would   have   preceded
vs.⁶⁻⁸;   (2) the charge made here is the same as that made against the
Philistines;   (3) the אמר י is lacking here as in the section on Edom (vs.¹¹·¹²).
Cf. We., Now., Löhr; Che. *EB.* I. 151; Baumann. — **9.** צר] Wkl. (*KAT.*³ I.
147; so Che. *Crit. Bib.*) מצר referring to the N. Arabian Muçri. — שלמה] ⑮
(as in v.⁶) שְׁלֹמֹה. — אחים] ᚨ أَسْمَهُ.‸. — לאדם] not לאדם, for Amos would have
said Damascus; Wkl. (*GI.* I. 199 note) omits, since it really comes from v.⁶;
but this is not certain.

9 a. *Tyre*] *i.e.* Phoenicia.   According to the usual view, the
Phoenicians were a Semitic people, who, like the Aramaeans and
Hebrews, formed a part of the great Semitic westward immi-
grations.

That they were originally related to the Hebrews may be concluded from
their Semitic speech, which can hardly have been borrowed by either nation.
They are named with the Hamites in Gn. 10⁶ for good reasons, as that table
does not contemplate actual relationship but geographical distribution.   The
oldest settlement of the Phoenicians was Sidon.   The Assyrian inscriptions
mention a great and a small Sidon (Sennacherib, Taylor Cyl. II. 38; *COT.* I.
87; RFH. *ABL.* 71).   From that point they spread, first to the north on
the coast (cf. Gn. 10¹⁵), and later to the south, where Tyre was founded as a
colony of Sidon (cf. Is. 23¹², where it is called בַּת־צִידוֹן).   Tyre, the prominence
of which dates from about 1197 B.C., was first built on the mainland, thirty
furlongs south of the later island-city, called by the old writers Παλαίτυρος (Jos.
Ant. 9, 14, 2; Strabo, 16, 2, 24; Diodorus, 17,4; Curtius, 4, 2, 18; Ba. 239).
Old Tyre is probably meant by מִבְצַר צֹר (Jos. 19²⁹ 2 S. 24⁷).   It existed at the
time of the Exodus, but seems to have been of little importance, in view of
the above passage in Joshua, which contains the only mention before David's
time, and represents it to have been conquered by the tribe of Asher, although
other Phoenician cities, as Acco, Sidon, were not so treated (Ju. 1³¹).   Homer
often mentions Sidon, but never Tyre (*Il.* VI. 289; XXIII. 743; *Odys.* XIV.
84; XIII. 285; XV. 425), but both are mentioned in the Tel-el-Amarna letters
(*e.g.* Nos. 17 and 18).   By reason of their increase, the Tyrians founded the
new city on an island four furlongs from the mainland, and being thus pro-

tected from enemies they soon rose to importance. In David's time they had their own powerful king (2 S. 5¹¹), and from that time on are frequently mentioned. By the year 900 B.C. they had taken the supremacy of the Phoenicians away from Sidon, as shown by the fact that in 1 K. 16³¹ Ethbaal is King of the Sidonians, while according to Josephus (*Ant.* VIII. 13, 2) he was King of Tyre. On Tyrian coins of Antiochus Epiphanes, we read "metropolis of the Sidonians," the Phoenicians generally being called Sidonians. Tyre is often mentioned in the Assyrian inscriptions (*v.i.*). Both Sidon and Tyre are written with the determinatives for city or for country, but with Tyre the latter is more common. At the time of Amos, Tyre, the chief city, naturally represented the whole country. By its geographical position it was more intimately connected with Israel than was any of the other cities. The settlement of the Hebrews in Canaan did not bring them into much trouble with Phoenicia. In the times of David and Solomon Phoenician influence was great (2 S. 5¹¹ 1 K. 5¹ ᶠᶠ·), being seen especially in everything that relates to art, architecture, and, indeed, the common affairs of life (Perrot and Chipiez, *Phénicie-Cypre*). After the division, the intimacy became even greater, Jezebel, the daughter of Ethbaal, king of Phoenicia (1 K. 16³¹), being queen of Israel, and her daughter Athaliah, the wife and successor of Ahaziah, being queen of Judah (2 K. 11¹). In the times of the prophets, perhaps as early as those of Amos, there came a reaction against Phoenicia, due, in part, perhaps, to the character of the two women just mentioned, and in part to the work of Elijah and Elisha.

9 b. *The brotherly covenant*] From 1 K. 9¹³, in which Hiram calls Solomon brother, and from 2 S. 5¹¹ 1 K. 5¹ ᶠᶠ· 16³¹ we may conclude that friendly relations existed between Israel and Tyre before, during, and after the time of Solomon. A covenant is mentioned between Solomon and Hiram (1 K. 5¹²), which possibly contained a provision against selling the Hebrews as slaves.*
This was a spiritual covenant as well as a worldly one, 1 K. 5⁷.†
It may be an objection to this that the covenant was one of individuals (Solomon and Hiram) and not of the two nations; ‡ since it seems quite clear that vs.⁹· ¹⁰ are a late interpolation (*v.s.*). The reference is not to a supposed covenant between Edom and Israel which Phoenicia had forgotten, although Israel and Edom are called brothers in v.¹¹, because (1) the relationship with Edom was that of blood, not of covenant; § (2) this relationship had long ago been changed to one of deadly enmity; ‖ (3) Phoenicia would not be responsible, but Edom;

---

* Pu.   † Geb.   ‡ Düsterdieck.   § Cal., Ew., Düsterdieck.   ‖ Ba.

at all events Philistia would be equally responsible. It has been suggested * that the slaves turned over to Edom were taken by Tyre, not from Israel, but from various cities of the Phoenicians or of the Canaanites. This would constitute the breach of the covenant. Cf. Winckler's view (*v.s.*). — **10**. *And it shall devour her (Tyre's) palaces*] Cf. Is. 23 Je. 25^{22} Ez. 26$^{15\,ff.}$ Zc. 9$^{2f.}$. This prediction was fulfilled in the relationship which Tyre sustained to Assyria and the empires that followed.

Up to the time of Amos the city had paid tribute to Ashurnaçirpal (*Annals*, col. III. 86) and Adadnirari III. who says, ". . . from above the Euphrates, Ḥatti, Aḥarri, to its whole extent, Tyre, Sidon, the country of Omri, Edom, Palastu as far as the great sea of the setting of the sun, I brought to submission, and taxes and tribute I placed on them" (1 R. 35, 12; *v.* RFH. *ABL.* 52), and a little later to Tiglathpileser III. *v.* Nimrud Inscription: "I sent my military governor, the chief officer, to Tyre; from Mitenna, of Tyre, (I received) one hundred and fifty talents of gold . . ." (*ABL.* 57; cf. *COT.* I. 242).

9. על הסגירם . . . ולא זכרו] Inf. continued by pf., GK. 114 *r*, 158 *c*; Kö. 413 *d*. — ברית אחים] an attributive gen., *v.* Kö. 335 *c*; GK. 128 *p*. Primary meaning of ברית appears in Assyr. *birîtu* (*barû* = bind), *fetter*, also *treaty*, *covenant* (Zimmern, *Busspsalmen*, 59, 82; Dl. *Die Sprache der Kossäer*, 7, and *HWB.*, *s.v.*). ברית might be made either (*a*) between men, or (*b*) between God and man. Of the former there were at least two kinds, those between individuals, *e.g.* 1 S. 18^3 20^8 23^{18} 2 S. 3$^{12\,ff.}$; and those between tribes or nations, *e.g.* 1 K. 5^{26} 15^{19} Ho. 12^2 Gn. 26$^{26\,ff.}$ 31$^{44\,ff.}$. A divine covenant is said to be at the basis of the great institutions of the O. T., viz. Israel's claim to the land of Canaan (Gn. 15), the perpetual monarchy of the Davidic house (2 S. 7 23^5 Ps. 89^3), and the perpetual priesthood of the Levites (Ex. 32^{29} Dt. 33^9 Je. 33^{21} Ma. 2$^{4\,ff.}$). The usual expression for making a covenant is כרת ברית, the significance of which is illustrated by Gn. 15. The idea of communion of life secured by eating together seems to have been the original conception lying at the root of the custom of covenant-making (cf. Jos. 9$^{14\,f.}$); this fellowship might be established by drinking each other's blood, or by partaking together of the blood of a sacrificial animal, or by eating salt together, or by eating any food in common. It is probable that the covenant was usually ratified by some distinctly religious rite. The full ceremony of making a covenant was as follows: (*a*) a statement of the terms agreed to; (*b*) an oath on the part of each party to the agreement to observe the terms agreed to; (*c*) a curse invoked upon himself by each one in case of failure to keep his agreement; (*d*) a solemn ratification of the curse made by pass-

---

* We., Dr.

ing between the parts of a sacrificed animal (probably a later development of the custom of eating the sacrifice together). The expression ברית אחים occurs only here, and the covenant alluded to is wholly unknown. On covenants *v.* Kraetzschmar, *Die Bundesvorstellung im A.T.* (1896); N. Schmidt, art. "Covenant," *EB.;* Da. art. "Covenant," *DB.;* WRS. *Sem.* 312 ff., 479 ff.; Val. *ZAW.* XII. 1–22, 224–60, XIII. 245–79; art. "Bund," *PRE.*[3]; Giesebrecht, *Die Geschichtlichkeit d. Sinaibundes* (1900); H. C. Trumbull, *The Blood Covenant; Id., The Covenant of Salt; Id., The Threshold Covenant.*

11, 12. *Judgment upon Edom.* — After Syria and Philistia, and in connection with Tyre, the prophet, according to the present text, foretells the doom of Edom. This oracle, like those against Tyre and Judah, is evidently an interpolation from the exilic or post-exilic period. The specific arguments * are : (1) the similarity of structure with 1[9, 10] and 2[4, 5] and the difference of structure from that of the other fuller utterances ; (2) Petra, the most important city of Edom in the time of Amos, is not mentioned,[†] while the names Teman and Bozrah occur elsewhere chiefly in late writings [‡] ; (3) the vagueness of the description of Edom's offence ; (4) Edom in early times was subject to Israel, and suffered more from Israel than Israel from Edom. For two centuries before Amos Edom had been under Israel (1 K. 11[16] 2 K. 14[7]). The cruelty which furnished the basis for the ill feeling on the part of Israel came with the exile. It was not unnatural, therefore, that a later writer, devoid of historical perspective, and thinking that Edom deserved denunciation, should frame a section which in due time secured a place in the text of Amos. The clause "and his wrath, etc." (v.[11]) from the point of view of the interpolation, is a gloss, merely repeating the thought of the preceding phrase in synonymous words.

11. וישחת רחמיו] probably a gloss; 𝔊 ἐλυμήνατο μητέρα ἐπὶ γῆς; other versions follow 𝔐𝔗. Some codd. of 𝔊 read μήτραν for μητέρα. Hirscht accounts for the text of 𝔊 on the supposition that ארם crept in after רחמיו by mistake from the previous line and was then read with the preceding יו as בארם which then went over easily into בארמה. Gr., וְשָׁכַח or וְשָׁפַח for

* *V.* We. ; Che. *EB.* I. 151 f. ; Bu. *Jew. Enc.* I. 532 ; Now., Löhr, Baumann, Marti ; cf. GAS., Dr.

† The Sela, captured by Amaziah (2 K. 14[7]), is probably not to be identified with Petra, but with some unknown rocky fortress; so Kit. on 2 K. 14[7]; Che. *EB.* IV. 4344.   ‡ But cf. Gn. 36[33 f.] (J); and Che. *EB.* I. 602.

ושחת.—[ויטרף לעד אפו] 𝕲 καὶ ἥρπασεν εἰς μαρτύριον φρίκην αὐτοῦ. 'Α. καὶ
ἤγρευσεν εἰς τοὺς αἰῶνας ἐν ὀργῇ αὐτοῦ; similarly Σ., Θ. 𝔙 et tenuerit ultra
furorem suum. ܣ ܗ݂ܒ݂ ܠܥܠܡ ܘ݂ܪ ܘܐܡ݂ܘ. SS. retain 𝕸𝕿, but connect
אפו with following clause rendering עַד booty. Ols. (on Ps. 103⁹; so also
Gr., We., Gu., Dr., Elh., Oet., Oort Em., Hirscht), ויטֹר, which is apparently supported by ܣ and 𝔙 and favored by the parallelism.—[שמרה נצח]
𝕲 ἐφύλαξεν εἰς νῖκος; other versions follow 𝕸𝕿. Cf. ܣ ܢܛܪ ܠܥܠܡ. Marck
and Va., שֶׁמְרָה; so also J. A. Bewer (AJSL. XVII. 168), but with a different
meaning (v.i.). Ols., שמר לנצח (so We., Gu., Now., GAS., Oort Em., Elh.,
Oet., Hirscht) but this is unnecessary.—12. [תימן] 'Α., Σ., Θ., Arab., 𝕿,
south. 𝕲ܣ𝔙 follow 𝕸𝕿.—[ארמנות בצרה] 𝕲 θεμέλια τειχέων αὐτῆς; other
versions treat בצרה as a proper noun. 'Α., Σ., render ארמנות by βάρεις; Θ.,
οἰκήσεις; 𝔙 aedes.

11 a. *Edom*] The traditions recognize the Edomites as older,
so far as concerns national existence, than the Israelites.

Mt. Seir, extending from the southeast shore of the Dead Sea to the Gulf
of Aḳabah, a mountainous region, seems to have been their first home after
the migration from Mesopotamia. Some think it is the country mentioned in
Egyptian records as Adma or Atuma, near Egypt, the inhabitants of which
were called Shasu, nomads (Chabas, *Voyage*, 307; Brugsch, *Hist.* I. 146,
216; *DB.*² I. 855). This region, full of caves, gave them as freebooters
(Gn. 27⁴⁰) great protection, and was, likewise, favorable for caravan trade
between Egypt and Arabia, and Phoenicia and Philistia (cf. Ez. 27¹⁶, reading ארם for אדם; so 𝕲ܣ, and some Hebrew Mss.). From the table in
Gn. 36, it has been supposed (Ba.) that the Edomites conquered and incorporated the Horites (Dt. 2²²), also the Canaanites and Ishmaelites. Their
form of government was tribal (Gn. 36¹⁵⁻¹⁹. ²⁹ᶠ.); but for all the tribes there
was one king (Gn. 36³¹ᶠ.) probably elective (Buhl, *Gesch. d. Edomiter*, 47;
cf. Sayce, *DB.* I. 645). The cities, in order of importance, were Petra,
where two caravan routes crossed; Bozrah (Is. 34⁶ 63¹); the ports Elath
and Ezion-geber (1 K. 9²⁶). Some suppose them to have been sun-worship-
pers in view of the occurrence of the word הֲרַד (the name of the sun-god)
in their proper names (1 K. 11¹⁷ 1 Ch. 1⁵⁰ Gn. 36³⁹; Ba. 100; cf. Nö. *EB.*
II. 1187), but nothing really definite is known of their religion. Edom and
Israel were not always so bitter towards each other as in the later days (cf.
1 K. 11¹ᶠ.). While this hostility had some basis in Edom's treatment of Israel
at the Exodus (Nu. 20¹⁴⁻²¹ Dt. 2¹⁻⁸—the two accounts leave this matter quite
uncertain) and in events of the times of Saul and David (1 S. 14⁴⁷ 2 S. 8¹⁴),
the ground for complaint was rather on the side of Edom. Edom remained
subordinate to Israel under Solomon (1 K. 9²⁶), although Hadad sought to
throw off the yoke (1 K. 11¹⁴⁻²²), and to Judah under Jehoshaphat (1 K. 22⁴⁸ᶠ.
2 K. 3⁸ᶠᶠ.). Under Joram, Edom revolted and then followed a period of

independence, during which it had a king of its own (2 K. 8$^{20-22}$); but soon
Sela was captured by Amaziah (2 K. 14^7), and Elath was restored to Judah
by Uzziah (2 Ch. 26^2). For an interpretation of the Blessing of Esau
(Gn. 27$^{39f.}$, which had its origin about this time) as revealing the feeling of
Israel toward Edom, see Nö. *EB.* II. 1185.

11 b. *Because he pursued his brother with the sword*] Cf. Ob.^{10}.
If this contains a definite allusion, it must be understood, not of
Nu. 20$^{17 \text{ ff.}}$; * nor of Jehoram (2 Ch. 21$^{8-10}$ 2 K. 8$^{20-22}$); † but
rather of some incursion of Edom against Israel shortly before
the utterance. ‡ It is perhaps better taken of the general attitude
of Edom towards Israel, shown in the cases cited above and in
many others of which there is no record. § The title " brother"
was frequently thus applied, *e.g.*, Dt. 2^4 23^7 Ob.$^{10-12}$ cf. Gn. 27$^{40. 41}$.
Israel and Edom were more closely related than was Israel with
any other nation. — *And destroyed his compassion*] The rendering
of Cyril " did violence to the womb," referring to Esau's trading
his birthright, is fanciful; likewise that which makes רַחֲמָיו " his
brother." ‖ The choice must lie between " his compassions," *i.e.*,
the Edomites have destroyed their natural sense of compassion or
regard for a brother, ¶ or " his wombs," *i.e.*, pregnant women.**
Cf. Vater's opinion, which makes רַחֲמָיו *foetus.* This line seems to
be a comment in explanation of the preceding phrase, and its
omission greatly relieves the passage. — *And he cherished his
anger perpetually*] If 𝕸𝕿 is accepted, " anger " may be the subject = *And his anger did tear perpetually* (cf. Jb. 16^9); or an
accusative of manner = *And in his anger he did tear.* In either
case the meaning is the same, viz. that of a lasting hatred of
Edom for Israel (cf. Gn. 27^{41}).†† The emendation of Olshausen
(*v.s.*) here followed, which is based upon the parallelism and
implied in 𝔖 and 𝔙, *and retained his anger* (cf. Ps. 103^9 Lv. 19^{18}
Na. 1^2 Je. 3^5), makes a much easier rendering, but one which is
redundant, unless the following clause is treated as a gloss. — *And
he kept his anger forever*] (*v.i.*). — **12.** *Teman*] Used synony-
mously with Edom in Je. 49^7 Ob.^{9} Hb. 3^3 and in parallelism with

---

* Ra., Cyril.   ‡ Ew.   ‖ Cf. Ba.
† Schlier.   § Cal., Jus., Ros., Dr. ¶ Cal., Schrö., Ba., Pu., Ke., Dr.
** 𝕲, Doederlein, Dat., Jus.; but *v.* Marti.
†† So Cal., Jus., Ros., Ba., Pu., Ke., and in the second form 'A., Σ., Geb.

D

it in Je. 49²⁰. There being no mention of walls, we may, with
most commentators, understand that no "city" is intended. —
Bozrah] Probably the chief city of Edom. Referred to in Gn.
36³³ Je. 49¹³, and with Edom in Is. 34⁶ 63¹ Je. 49²² cf. Je. 49⁷ ᶠᶠ.
So called from its strength; Is. 34⁶. Note the rendering of 𝔊
(*v.s.*).

Teman was celebrated for its wisdom (cf. Je. 49⁷ ᶠᶠ.); Eliphaz, one of Job's
friends, came from it (Jb. 2¹¹ 4¹). It was probably named from Teman,
grandson of Esau; cf. Gn. 36¹¹· ¹⁵· ³⁴. Its location is not certain, but Ez. 25¹³
mentions "Teman even unto Dedan" as including the whole country, hence,
as Dedan was in the southeast, Teman was probably in the northwest or north
(Buhl, *Edomiter*, 30).

Bozrah is probably to be identified with the small modern village Buṣeire
or Buṣêra, meaning, little Bosra, although it has also been identified with the
later Petra (Wetzstein, in De. *Jesaja*,³ 704). Under Joram of Judah, Edom
probably gained its independence (2 K. 8²⁰ ᶠᶠ.). The text is doubtful, but cf.
Sta. *GVI.* I. 537; Buhl, *Edomiter*, 64; Kit. *in loc.* References of doubtful
date to Edom are found in Ps. 60⁸⁻¹¹ (= Ps. 108⁸⁻¹¹) Je. 49⁶⁻²² (cf. also Is. 11¹⁴
Je. 9²⁵ 25²¹), with which are to be contrasted the kindly references in Dt. 2⁵⁻⁸
23⁷ ᶠ. The kings of Edom before the time of Amos had paid tribute to
Adadnirari III. and soon after to Tiglathpileser III.

11. רדפו על] prep. with inf. expressing cause (*v.s.*). — ושחת] Pf. with ו cons.
fol. inf., to express freq. action; Dr. § 118; GK. 112 *i*, 114 *r*; H. 25, 1 *a*; Kö.
413 *d*. — רחמיו] abstr. pl.; GK. 124 *e*; Kö. 262 *e*. — ויטרף] the impf. with ו cons.
fol. a pf. with ו cons.; cf. Dr. § 118. — אפו] either subj. or obj. or adv. acc.
according to interpretation. — ועברתו שמרה נצח] This, for reasons given above,
is probably a gloss. The usual rendering has been "And his wrath he kept
forever," the הָ referring to עב׳, Mappîq dropped because of recession of
accent, GK. 58 *g*; or הָ paragogic (Ros.), cf. Zc. 5¹¹ Nu. 32⁴² Ru. 2¹⁴. Ew.'s
rendering of שָׁמְרָה "lieth in wait" (cf. Jb. 24¹⁵ Ps. 56⁷) is hardly tenable.
J. A. Bewer suggests a new rendering for this and the preceding clause, viz.
"His anger tore perpetually, while his fury raged forever;" cf. Je. 3⁵. This
involves a change of vocalization in one word (*v.s.*), and the giving to שמר of
the meaning *rage*, not elsewhere found in Hebrew, though quite common in
Assyrian (cf. Dl. *HWB. s.v.*) — ועברתו] casus pendens and chiasm for emphasis; GK. 142 *f*, n. 1.; Kö. 341 *d*. — נצח] adv. acc. of time; GK. 118 *k*;
H. 33, 3.

13–15. *Judgment upon Ammon.* — The list of Israel's enemies, the announcement of whose destruction would be gladly
received, included, besides Syria and Philistia (Phoenicia and
Tyre), also Ammon and Moab. These two are the next pair to

serve as the target of the prophet's indignant arrow. Ammon, because of her wickedness, shall, with the others, perish.

The arrangement of the strophes is 5, 3, and 3, and the general plan is that of the first two oracles. The clause בסער ביום סופה (v. 14) is but a weak repetition of the preceding clause and there is nothing to correspond to it in the parallel section on Moab (2¹⁻³), although in every other respect the parallelism is perfect. For these reasons we may regard it as a gloss. While the first two utterances (those concerning Syria and Philistia) are parallel, consisting each of three strophes with three lines in each, and the third and fourth utterances are parallel, consisting each of two strophes, one having four, the other two lines, the fifth and sixth utterances are also parallel, consisting each of three strophes, one of four, one of two, and one of three lines.

13. הרות] Val. בְּצָרוֹת(?).—[נבולם] 𝔘 = גבולי.—14. בחומת] 𝔊 pl. as in v.⁷; 𝔖 = בחוצת.—[בסער] 𝔊 καὶ σεισθήσεται (= וְסָעַר).—[ביום סופה] 𝔊 ἐν ἡμέραις συντελείας αὐτῆς (= בִּימֵי סוֹפָה). Gr. כיום.—15. מלכם] 𝔊 οἱ βασιλεῖς αὐτῆς. 'A., Σ., 𝔖𝔘 = מַלְכֹּם (so also Gr., Dr., Oort Em., Now.).—[הוא] read (with Gr. and Now.) כהניו, foll. 𝔊, οἱ ἱερεῖς αὐτῶν; so 'A., Σ., Θ.; cf. 𝔖 ܟܘܡܪ̈ܝܗܘܢ.

13 a. *The children of Ammon*] It was entirely proper to unite Ammon and Moab in treatment, because they were closely related to each other and to the Hebrews.

However untrustworthy the story of Lot's incest with his daughters may be, the fact which lies at the basis of the story may be credited, viz. that Ammon and Moab, as well as the Hebrews, belonged to the stock of the Terahites, who emigrated with Abraham (Kit. *Hist.* I. 24; Sta. *GVI.* I. 113). Just as tradition assigns to these nations a common origin, the law in later times (Dt. 23⁴ Ezr. 9¹ Ne. 13¹) refuses them admittance to the congregation of Israel. Moloch of Ammon, as well as Chemosh of Moab, was a man-eating fire-god, and to the worship of this god Israel frequently showed an inclination (Ju. 10⁶ 1 K. 11⁶ᶠ· 2 K. 23¹³). These nations, according to the traditions handed down, dwelt together, east of the Jordan, between the rivers Arnon and Jabbok, whence the original inhabitants, called Zamzummim by the Ammonites, and Emim by the Moabites (Dt. 2⁹ᶠ· ¹⁸⁻²¹), had been driven out. But they were subsequently separated by the Amorites, who, coming in between them, drove Moab south over the Arnon and Ammon to the east and north over the Jabbok, and established a kingdom in their original territory (Nu. 21²⁶ᶠᶠ·). At the time of the Exodus the Hebrews did not disturb Ammon, although they conquered the Amorites (Nu. 21²⁴ᶠ·). Ammon, now with Moab (Ju. 3¹³), and now alone (Ju. 10⁷ᶠ·), laid claim to the land taken from the Amorites by Israel (Ju. 11¹³; cf. Jos. 13²⁵). The contest was conducted on both sides of the Jordan. How much of all this is historically accurate we cannot affirm. Defeated by Jephthah (Ju. 11⁴ᶠ·), they appear next in Saul's time, under Nahash their king, at the siege of Jabesh-Gilead, where they were routed (1 S. 11; cf. 14⁴⁷). While at first on good terms with David (2 S. 10²; cf. 23³⁷), they later became hostile (2 S. 10³ᶠ·) and were defeated by him and treated with terrible cruelty (2 S. 8¹² 10. 12²⁶⁻³¹) at the capture of Rabbah. They do not occupy a very prominent place after this, but are mentioned as having been defeated by Jehoshaphat (2 Ch. 20) and as tributary to Uzziah (2 Ch. 26⁸) and Jotham (2 Ch. 27⁵). Allusion is made to them in Is. 11¹⁴. At the time of Amos they were probably independent.

13 b. *Because they have ripped up the women with child of Gilead*] This act of cruelty was not uncommon among the Hebrews (2 K. 8¹² Ho. 10¹⁴ 13¹⁶ 2 K. 15¹⁶ Is. 13¹⁶ Na. 3¹⁰ Ps. 137⁹; cf. *Iliad*, VI. 57 f., XXII. 163 f.).* The reference is in every way so specific as to suggest a particular event. This event may have been in connection with the attack of Nahash, the Ammonite, upon Jabesh Gilead (1 S. 11), or a league of the Ammonites with the Syrians under Hazael (2 K. 8¹² 10³²); cf. the league mentioned in 2 S. 10⁶ᶠᶠ·; *v.* also 2 K. 13³·⁷.† To this interpretation, in general, Jewish commentators have objected because of the cruelty involved, and have suggested that הָרוֹת be taken as = הָרִים *mountains*. This gives (1) *they broke through the mountains of Gilead, i.e.* violated the law of boundaries (Dt. 27¹⁷), or (2) the castles which were strong like mountains. ‡ For הָרוֹת it is also suggested to change the text (*v.s.*) and read *fortified places* as being more in harmony with the last clause of the verse. — *That they might enlarge their border*] This was the purpose of the war in which such cruelties were practised. The Ammonites had originally laid claim to this district (Ju. 11¹³) and were always presenting themselves as claimants for additional territory (Ju. 10⁸ 1 S. 11¹¹).—**14 a.** *But I will kindle*] Cf. *I will send*, v.¹⁰ and previously. This expression has been thought to mean that the fire is not only sent by Yahweh, but is also *directed* by him,§ or that it is a conflagration from *within.* ‖ — *Rabbah*] This is abbreviated for "Rabbah of the sons of Ammon" (Dt. 3¹¹ 2 S. 12²⁶ 17²⁷ Je. 49² Ez. 21²⁰). The town was

---

* Cf. Schultens, *Monumenta antiquissimae Historiae Arabum*, 135, cited in Michaelis, *Comm. on the Laws of Moses*, I. 327; Ba.; for Arabic usage We.¹ cites BAthir, IV. 256, 1; 258, 6; 260, 20; 262, 11 ff.; Kitâb al-'Agh. XIX. 129, 12 f.; XX. 128, 13; Tabard, II. 755, 19.

† Hi., Ba., Pu.   ‡ So Ki., Val.   § Geb.   ‖ Pu.

situated at the head of the Jabbok, about twenty-five miles N.E.
of the Dead Sea, and is to be distinguished from the post-biblical
Rabbah of Moab, the biblical Ar.

This is the only city of Ammon of any importance mentioned in the Bible,
though Jephthah is said to have captured twenty cities the names of which
are not mentioned, probably because they were small, all of which is a testimony to the essentially roving character of the people. Rabbah was besieged
and captured by David, but afterward regained its importance.

14 b. *With shouting in the day of battle*] The verb here rendered "shout," in Is. 15^4 Mi. 4^9 and Ho. 5^8 is used of the cry of those
in distress; cf. also Nu. 10^{1-10} Jo. 2^1. The substantive, contrary to
Marck, is used only of the joyful cry of victory or attack * (Jos. 6^5
Jb. 39^{25} Je. 4^{19} 49^2 Am. 2^2 Zp. 1^{16} Nu. $10^{5.6}$). — *With a storm in the
day of tempest*] This scarcely refers to an actual storm,† but
describes figuratively the assaulting of a city. ‡ Cf. Is. 27^8 28^2.§
— *And their king shall go into exile*] Upon the basis of $\mathfrak{S}$ and $\mathfrak{V}$,
some would read *Milchom*, the name of the Ammonitish idol, for
their king (*v.s.*). Upon the basis of Je. 49^3, where the same
phraseology is used, and Je. 48^7 (cf. also Zp. 1^5), where Chemosh
is spoken of in the same connection, others suggest *Molkam*, the
name of an idol. As opposed to these, and in favor of the ordinary
translation, *their king*, may be urged the use of "his princes";
the absence of any reference to idolatry in preceding passages, reference being made rather to cruelty; and the similarity of $1^{5.8}$ and
2^3 (cf. "judge," a substitute for "king" of this passage). ‖ — *His
princes*] The meaning will be determined by the interpretation
of the preceding מלכם, either royal princes, or the princes of
Milchom, *i.e.* the priests.

The fulfilment of this prophecy against the Ammonites is probably to be found in their subjugation by the Assyrians. Of this we
know simply that after the invasion of Tiglathpileser they always
appear as tributary to Assyria.¶ In the time of Nehemiah they

---

* Ba.   † Marck.   ‡ Ke., Dr., Marti.   § Hi.
‖ Hi., Gu., Val., Mit., GAS., Elh., Löhr, Hirscht, Oet., Hal.
¶ Sanipu, King of Ammon, is mentioned by Tiglathpileser III. in a list of tribu-
taries, including, among others, Salamanu of Moab, Metinti of Askelon, Ahaz of
Judah, Qaushmalaka of Edom, and Hanno of Gaza (*ABL.* 57; *KB.* II. 21).
Sennacherib (Taylor Cyl. II. 47–57) speaks of Buduilu of Ammon, along with

were still hostile to Israel. They are mentioned in the apocryphal books (Judith 5. 6. 7 1 Macc. 5[30–43]) as appearing in alliance with the Arabs (1 Macc. 5[39]), and manifesting the same characteristics and attitude toward Israel as in the earlier history. They are described as numerous by Justin Martyr,* but Origen † states that in his time they had become merged in the Arabs.

14. בתרועה] Note the rhythm in the two lines thus beginning, and the alliteration in the repetition of ב, and in סער. — סופה ... Cf. [הַעַר] שְׁעָרָה Na. 1[3]; it is to be compared with Assyrian šâru, *storm*, and sâru, *to be tempestuous*. The verbal root is used in Hebrew of any violent movement, *e.g.* Jo. 1[11. 13], of a raging sea. Hence comes for the noun the meaning, *storm.* — סופה] Cf. Ho. 8[7] Na. 1[3]; used of the storm-wind, especially of the hot wind from the south (Ba). Its derivation may be considered doubtful. It is ordinarily taken from סוף, to cease, bring to an end, which is not entirely satisfactory. — **15.** גולה] Another formation = גָּלוּת (v.[9]); Kö. 244*g.* — יחרו] Used to strengthen the ו; Kö. 375 *h.*

II. 1–3. *Judgment upon Moab.* — Ruin will come upon Moab for her sins; and the overthrow of the nation will be complete. Cf. Is. 15, 16, 25[10–12] Zp. 2[8–11] Je. 48 Ez. 25[8–11] Dn. 11[41].

In the text, as reconstructed, the line ומת בשאון מואב with the ו changed to ה, has been transferred to follow line 3 of strophe 1, and the last word of this line, לַשִׂיד (*to lime* (?)), restored to לשרד (cf. Je. 47[4]), is joined as first word to the line transferred. This reading, *in order to do indignity to the dead because of violence suffered by Moab,* or *in order to do indignity to the dead in Shaon of Moab* (*v.* Hoffm), makes the number of lines in this and the preceding oracle the same; the gloss in 1[14], בסער ביום סופה, having been omitted, allows the lines beginning ואכלה and בתרועה to stand together here just as in the previous oracle, provides a parallel line for the purpose-clause, למען וג׳; and removes the inexplicable לשיד from a line to which it does not belong, if the measure of the v. is to be considered. For a fuller discussion of the line, *v.i.* If this is accepted, the strophes have respectively 5, 3, and 3 lines.

1. שרפו] 𝕲 κατέκαυσαν; so 𝔖. 𝖁𝕿 3 sg. — לשיד] 𝕲 εἰς κονίαν. 𝖁 *usque ad cinerem.* 𝕿 וְסָדְנוּן בְּגִירָא בְּנֵיהֶ. Gr. לאפר. Hirscht, עצמות אָדָם לְמֹלֶךְ לַשִׂיד (cf. Ps. 106[37]; the reading אָדָם was proposed by Zenner, *Die Chorgesänge*

Menahem of Samaria, Ethobal of Sidon, Metinti of Ashdod, Kammusunadbi of Moab, Malikrammu of Edom, and others, as bringing him rich presents and kissing his feet (*ABL.* 71; *KB.* II. 91). The same king is included by Esarhaddon in his list of the twenty-two tributary kings of the Hittites (*ABL.* 86; *KB.* II. 149). Amminadbi, king of Ammon, is included in a similar list occurring in Ashurbanipal's Annals (*ABL.* 97; *KB.* II. 240 f.). * Dial. Tryph. † On Jb. 1.

im Buche der Psalmen 1896, I. 8). — **2.** הקריות] 𝕲 τῶν πόλεων αὐτῆς. 𝕿 כְּרְכָּא. 𝔙𝔖 proper name. — נשאון] 𝕲 ἐν ἀδυναμίᾳ. 𝔖 ܒܫܘܒܚܐ. 𝔙 *in sonitu*, for this and fol. word. — בקול] 𝕲𝔖, 3 codd. of Kenn. and 2 of de R. = ובקול (so Hirscht). — **3.** מקרבה] We. מקרבה, since Moab is masc.; so also שריו (so Now., Elh., Löhr, Oet.).

1 a. *Moab*] The account of the origin of Moab given in Genesis simply indicates * that the nation was closely related with Israel, and also with the weaker nation of the Ammonites. Their language was a dialect closely allied to the Hebrew. Their land (called הַמִּישׁוֹר, the level, or שרון, 1 Ch. 5¹⁶) was a plateau, fruitful and well adapted to agriculture (Is. 16⁸ᶠᶠ· Ru. 1¹ 2 K. 3⁴), which was their chief occupation. Its length was about fifty miles and its breadth thirty, and it was capable of supporting about 500,000 inhabitants. At the time of the Exodus, the Moabites had an organized kingdom (Nu. 22⁷·¹⁴·¹⁵).† Their religion was henotheistic, their only god mentioned in the Old Testament being Chemosh (Nu. 21²⁹ Je. 48⁴⁶). The form Ashtar-Chemosh also meets us on the Moabite stone, ‡ perhaps indicating the androgynous nature of the deity. § Their Baal-Peor, whom the Israelites were led to worship with unchaste rites (Nu. 25¹⁻⁵), was probably the same divinity, known as the Lord of Peor. ‖ It is improbable that there ever existed any ethical or spiritual movement in Moab similar to that found among the Hebrews.

Moab's boundaries to the west and south were constant, viz. the Dead Sea and the brook of the willows, Wady-el-Ḥasy (Is. 15⁷); but to the east and north they varied, although usually the boundary was near the river Arnon (Nu. 21¹³). The country seems to have had many cities. Whether Reuben and Gad occupied territory belonging to Moab (Nu. 32³⁴⁻³⁸) is doubtful (Sta. *GVI.* I. 116 ff.). No mention is made of Moab in the Amarna letters thus far published; but it was probably included as a part of the Egyptian province of Canaan. In a list of the conquests of Ramses II the name *Muab* occurs (Sayce, *Pat. Pal.* 21, 153). The aggressive character of the Moabites is alluded to in Is. 16⁶ Zp. 2¹⁰ Je. 48²⁹·⁴². The Baal-Peor and Balaam incidents are of special interest. There were wars with Israel in the time of the Judges, resulting finally in the defeat of Moab (cf. Nu. 21²¹⁻³¹ (E), Ju. 3¹²⁻³⁰ 11¹²⁻²⁸). There was little hostility, with the exception of a war in Saul's reign (1 S. 14⁴⁷), till late in the reign of David, when, for some un-

---

* Cf. Ba.; Sta. *GVI.* I. 27 ff.   † But *v.* Wkl. *GI.* I. 203 f.   ‡ Line 17.
§ Sta. *GVI.* I. 114.   ‖ Sta. *GVI.* I. 114 f.; Dr. *Dt.* 63 f.

known reason, he subdued them with cruel tortures (2 S. 8$^{2.\ 12}$ 1 Ch. 18$^{2.\ 11}$). They probably remained tributary till the division of the kingdom (1 K. 11^1). For a time they are not expressly mentioned. Then Omri of Israel subdued them (Mesha stone, ls. 4 ff.), and they continued tributary to the Northern kingdom (2 K. 3^4). After the death of Ahab or during his reign (2 K. 1^1 3^5), the Moabites under Mesha revolted and secured their independence (Mesha stone, cf. Sta. *GVI*. I. 532–6; English translations of this inscription may be found in Dr. *Sam*. pp. lxxxv–xciv; Bennett, art. "Moab," *DB*. III. 407 f.; Dr. art. "Mesha," *EB*. III.; Ball, *Light from the East*, 240), which, apparently, they never again lost to Israel. For the view that the Šalman mentioned in Ho. 10^{14} as having destroyed Beth-Arbel was a king of Moab, see the discussion *in loc*.

1 b. *Because they burned the bones of the King of Edom*] The nature of the act is uncertain. According to 𝕸𝕿 the words *to lime* follow *Edom*. This has been taken to mean the burning alive of the king mentioned,* or the burning of one who had been killed or buried.† The words *to lime* are supposed to describe the manner of the burning, as lime is burned; ‡ or the result, to dust, *i.e.* completely; § or, as many Rabbis, to make lime used as plastering. ‖ For the reading of Hirscht, *v.s.* Still more uncertain is the personal allusion which is intended. Is the reference to 2 K. 3^{27}, the son there being rather that of the King of Edom who is captured by the King of Moab before the battle begins?¶ But (*a*) a king, not a king's son, is mentioned; (*b*) no objection could be presented to the right of a conqueror to do as he pleased with a captive taken in war; (*c*) according to Josephus, the Moabite king offered his own son to Moloch.** Or is it to some incident in connection with 2 K. 3, *e.g.* the capture of the King of Edom himself immediately after the event related in 2 K. 3^{27}, of which the records do not speak?†† And did the crime consist chiefly in disturbing the peace of the dead in the grave (cf. 2 K. 23^{18}), by burning the body, perhaps, on the grave itself,†† and scattering the ashes upon water or in the air? Cf. Jos. 7^{25}. The Jews, like other nations of antiquity, considered offences against the dead as most impious acts. ‡‡ They identified,

---

* Os., Geb., Mau.   § Ki., and most modern comm.   ** Schrö.
† Jer., Cal., Hi., Ke.   ‖ So also Geb.   †† Hi.
‡ Ros.   ¶ Ki., Cyril, Abar., Geb., Mich.
‡‡ See *e.g.* Frey, *Tod, Seelenglaube und Seelenkult in alt. Israel*; Schwally, *Das*

to a certain extent, the grave with the world of spirits, so that only those buried together could associate with each other, while the unburied, as with the Greeks and Romans, were considered to wander as restless spirits with no fixed abode. Hence, cremation was condemned, while embalming was a common practice. These ideas may be gathered from various passages (Dt. 21[23] Jos. 10[27] 2 K. 23[16. 18] Ps. 79[2. 3] Is. 14[19] 66[24] Je. 36[30]).* Or was the crime connected with some incident of which no record is anywhere made, the date of which cannot therefore be fixed, though probably taking place shortly before this prophecy?† Or is this merely a different form of the tradition given in 2 K. 3[27], ‡ and was the King of Moab Mesha, whose character as presented in the Moabite stone seems to be entirely consistent with the representations here made? It has been noted § that the sin is against Edom, and not against Israel. The entire passage, although it is the key-note of the piece, is evidently obscure. It is therefore suggested that the text be modified as indicated above : *In order to desecrate the dead because of violence done to* (or *suffered by*) *Moab*] This purpose-clause now corresponds to a similar clause in 1[13]. In one case an act of vandalism was committed, viz. the ripping up of women with child, the purpose being, remotely, to increase their territory ; here is another act of vandalism, the burning of the bones of a royal personage, and the purpose is to take vengeance, by this desecration of the dead, for violence done to Moab. Not only is לשיד without significance, but also the clause, *And Moab shall die in a tumult,*] ordinarily interpreted as a description of the nation's death. — *The Palaces of Keryyoth*] Either a name for Kir-Moab, ‖ a city in the southern part of Judah captured by the Moabites (Jos. 15[25]) ; or (since where Ar is mentioned, Keryyoth is not found) another name for Ar-Moab,¶ mentioned Nu. 21[15] Is. 15[1], not appearing in

Leben nach dem Tode; Matthes, " De doodenvereering bij Israël," *ThT.* July, 1901 ; Sta. *Die Alttest. Vorstellungen vom Zustand nach dem Tode;* Jeremias, *Die Babyl.-Assyr. Vorstellungen vom Zustand nach dem Tode;* Now. *Arch.* I. 188 f., 329; Benz. *Arch.* 165 ff.; WRS. *Proph.* 398; Jos. *Ant.* XVI. 7; Grüneisen, *Der Ahnenkultus und die Urreligion Israels;* and the references to Arabic customs cited by We.[1], viz. *Kitâb-al-Aghâni* XII. 21, 11 ; *BAthir* V. 178, 12; 203, 23; *Maç.* V. 47, 1.

* Cf. Schrö., Hi., Or.; WRS. *Proph.* 397 ; Sta. *GVI.* I. 421 f.   † Ew.
‡ Ba.   § We.   ‖ Jus.   ¶ Ew., Mit.

Je. 48; or a place different from both of these,* of which mention is made in Je. 48$^{24.41}$.   Cf. ⅏, which treats it as a common
name.   The city probably stands for Moab, as Damascus represents Syria, from which it may be inferred that the city was an
important one.   The reference in the Moabite stone (l. 13) favors
Ewald's view that it is another name for Ar.† — *With shouting
and with the sound of the trumpet*] Cf. 1^{14} *with shouting in the
day of battle*; the trumpet is introduced as inciting them on to
conflict (cf. Je. 4^{19} Zp. 1^{16} Jb. 39^{25}). — **3**. *The Judge . . . her princes*]
In the narrowest sense the judge would be the head of the judicial
system ; ‡ but it is rather a word of general significance, applicable
to the king (cf. Mi. 5^{2}), one of whose functions was to judge §
(2 S. 8^{15} 15^{2} 1 K. 7^{7} Je. 21^{12}), and is thus used intentionally for
king ; ‖ perhaps, better still, a name for the highest officer (cf. the
Carthaginian *Sofetes*),¶ or regent ** (cf. 2 K. 15^{5}) ; or, in the
absence of a proper king, vassal, or prince appointed by the king
of Israel.††   The feminine pronoun must refer to the land, ‡‡
although Wellhausen would change it to the masculine as referring to *the judge*, to which word also *with him* refers.   The close
resemblance in thought between 2^{3} and 1^{15} should be noted.

Frequent mention of Moab is made in the Assyrian inscriptions,
e.g. that Salamanu paid tribute to Tiglathpileser III., §§ Chemoshnadab to Sennacherib, ‖‖ Muçuri to Esarhaddon and Ashurbanipal.¶¶   The policy of Moab seems for the most part to have been

---

* Ba.   † Ri. *HBA.*; Dr.   ‡ Ros.   § Jus., Dr.   ‖ Ba., Ke., Now.
¶ Pu.   ** We.   †† Ew., Hi., GAS.   ‡‡ Hi., Ba., GAS., Mit.

§§ Moab was subdued in the course of the western campaign which resulted in
the establishment of Assyrian supremacy over Ammon, Askelon, Judah, Edom,
Gaza, and some Syrian states.   See *ABL*. 57; *COT*. I. 249; *KB*. II. 21.

‖‖ The tribute of Chemoshnadab was received in connection with Sennacherib's
third campaign, which included the overthrow of Sidon and other Phoenician
cities; the subjection of Samaria, Arvad, Byblos, Ashdod, Ammon, Edom, Askelon,
and Ekron; the battle of Eltekeh, and the siege of Jerusalem. See *ABL*. 71 ff.;
COT. I. 284 ff.; *KB*. II. 91 ff.

¶¶ Muçuri of Moab is included among the "twenty-two kings of the land of
Ḥatti, of the sea-coast and the middle of the sea" named as tributary to Esarhaddon and to Ashurbanipal.   See *ABL*. 86, 96 f.; *COT*. II. 40 f.; *KB*. II. 149, 239 f.
A successor of Muçuri, whose name is quite uncertain, is mentioned by Ashurbanipal as having defeated Ammuladin, an Arabian chief: "Chemosh-Astarte (?),
King of Moab, a vassal submissive to me, brought about his defeat in the field of
battle."   See G. Smith, *History of Ashurbanipal*, 288; Wkl. *GI*. I. 209.

one of peaceful acceptance of the Assyrian lordship; at least no record of any struggle between Assyria and Moab is preserved other than one in the time of Sargon.*

1. שרפו] Inf. cstr. with suf. after על is a favorite construction in Amos; cf. על דושם (1⁸), על הגלותם (1⁶), על־הסגירם (1⁹), על־רדפו (1¹¹), על־בקעם (1¹³), על־מכרם (2⁶), על־מאסם (2⁴). The m. sg. pron. is used in two cases with collective force: GK. 135 p; Ew. 317, 1), 2). — לשׁדד] v.s. Inf. cstr. with ל expressing purpose, cf. להסגיר (1⁶) and למען הרחיב (1¹³); but of the other five instances where the similar construction might have been expected, one (1³) has nothing, while four (1⁹ 1¹¹ 2⁴ 2⁸) have synonymous clauses, all of which (except 2⁸) indicate the state of mind which led to the act of sin, e.g. forgetfulness of the brotherly covenant (1⁹), the stifling of compassion (1¹¹), non-observance of Yahweh's statutes (2⁴). The root שׁדד with its derivative שֹׁד, has the primary meaning of committing an act of violence, despoil, cf. Is. 16⁴ Je. 48¹·⁸ Ho. 10¹⁴. — **2.** On the art. in הקריות] cf. הגלגל and הירדן; H. 4, 3 e (4); GK. 126 e; Ew.⁸ 277 c. On identification with ער v. Dietrich in Merx, Archiv I. 320 ff.; also ZDPV. II. 10. — ומת] 𝕸𝕿 for המת, although ו might remain in the sense of even (cf. GK. 154, note 1 (b)). — בְּשָׁאוֹן] 𝕸𝕿 in a tumult (i.e. the nation is pictured as dying in the midst of the din of battle, cf. Ho. 10¹⁴ Ps. 74²³); so Pu., Dr., Mit., et al.; cf. emendation suggested above, בְּשָׁאוֹן in return for violence done to, with בְּ of price (cf. Gn. 29¹⁸ Dt. 19²¹), and a cstr. in objective relationship with a following genitive; H. 8, 1 b; GK. 128 h. The objective genitive is common with words of this class, denoting injury, etc.; cf. Ob.¹⁰ Hb. 2¹⁷. For שָׁאוֹן in the meaning, violence, destruction, cf. Ps. 40³ Je. 46¹⁷. Or. reads בִּגְאוֹן = in, or because of, Moab's pride, cf. Is. 16⁶, in which reference is made to the well-known pride of Moab. Some treat שאון as an old proper name, perhaps of the acropolis of ער מואב, corresponding to מואב as ציון to ירושלים; cf. Je. 48⁴⁵ Nu. 24¹⁷ (שׁת=שׁאת). So Hoffm. ZAW. III. 97; but v. Now. Perhaps שאון is for שרון, a word which, like מישור, seems to designate the land of Moab in 1 Ch. 5¹⁶. — בתרועה] Now modifies אכלה of preceding line, just as in 1¹⁴. — בקול] Note asyndeton as in ביום (1.¹⁴); the intended parallelism is evident. — שׁופר] This instrument was a horn; it is specifically called "ram's horn" in Jos. 6⁴ ff.; cf. Arab. سَوَافِر, ram's horns, and Assyr. šapparu, mountain goat. In early times, according to the Talmud, they were, naturally, crooked; but the modern shofar (used in the synagogue) is usually straightened and flattened by heat. It is the oldest form of wind instrument in the world still in use, having been employed in the Mosaic ritual from the beginning until the present day. The shofar was probably the earliest kind of trumpet, and was used in war (Ju. 3²⁷) and to raise the alarm at the approach of danger (Am. 3⁶). Later in Israel's history

---

* See KB. II. 64 f.; Wkl. Keilinschriftliches Textbuch zum A. T.² (1903), 41.

the trumpets were appropriated by the priests for use in worship, in some respects serving the purpose of the modern church bell.

4, 5. *Judgment upon Judah.* — As the text now stands, the climax of Amos's outburst against the neighboring nations, before Israel herself is denounced, appears in words uttered against Judah, whose punishment is predicted on the ground of abandonment of Yahweh's instruction.

The form of the piece, if the clause וַיַּתְעוּם כִּזְבֵיהֶם אֲשֶׁר־הָלְכוּ אֲבוֹתָם אַחֲרֵיהֶם is omitted as a gloss (*v.i.*), is identical with that of the oracles relating to Tyre and Edom, *i.e.* 5 + 2. Against the genuineness of the entire utterance it may be urged that the similarity in form just mentioned puts the section in the same category with 1⁹·¹⁰ and 1¹¹·¹², and any doubt which attaches to these oracles must attach also to this; furthermore, that the introduction of this oracle removes entirely the force of the surprise which the Israelites would have felt; that it is impossible to suppose that Amos would have treated Judah so cursorily, and in a manner so like that in which he treated the outside nations; that the terms of Judah's sin are of a Deuteronomic character and of later origin (cf. חֻקָּיו לֹא שָׁמָרוּ, Dt. 4⁶ 6²⁴ 16¹² 17¹⁹, as well as the frequently recurring phrases *to observe to do, to observe and do,* 4⁶ 5¹, etc.); that the style is tame, vague, and weak; that the term Israel in 2⁶⁻¹⁶ includes Judah (cf. 2¹⁰); that the concluding formula אָמַר יְ is lacking, and that the sin described, transgression of the "instruction" and the "statutes" of Yahweh, was too indefinite, not so flagrant as to call for its introduction in this place, in fact, unlike any charges made elsewhere by Amos, and out of harmony with the formula, *for their transgressions,* etc., since it could not be specified as one of the three or four. So Duhm, *Theol. der Proph.* 119; We.; Sta. *GVI.* I. 571; Val.; Che. in WRS., *Proph.* XVI. and *EB.* I. 153; Oort, *ThT.* XIV. (1880), 116; GAS.; Volz 19; Now., Löhr; Taylor, *DB.* I. 86; Baumann. But note the considerations offered on the other hand: that Judah is not included under Israel in 2⁶ᶠᶠ· and it is inconceivable that Amos should have omitted Judah in his written statement, even if, perhaps, he failed for certain reasons to mention it in his oral statement; that the phraseology termed Deuteronomic is to be found in Is. 5²⁴ Ex. 18¹⁶; that though the charges brought against Judah are general they are corroborated by Is. 2⁶⁻⁸·¹⁸·²⁰ 5⁷⁻²⁴; and Amos may have wished to reserve the more specific accusations for use against Israel. So WRS. *Proph.* 399 f.; Kue. *Einl.* II. 347; Gun., Mit., Dr. If the passage is genuine, its introduction by the prophet is due to his desire to prevent the charge of favoritism toward his own people (Cal.) The reasons for regarding the clause in v.⁴ beginning ויתעום וגו' as a gloss are : (1) the comparatively late date of the idea contained in it, cf. Ex. 32¹ Dt. 9¹²; (2) the use of כזבים to designate idols, a use which is parallel to that of הבלים which appeared after Jeremiah's time (Now.); (3) the

awkwardness of the syntax as it is here introduced (*v.i.*); (4) the fact that
the symmetry of the strophic arrangement is entirely destroyed.

4. יהודה‎] 𝔊 υἱῶν Ἰούδα.— שמרו‎ . . . מאסם‎] 𝔙 renders both by 3 p. sg.
— כזביהם‎] 𝔖 om. suff. 𝔊 adds ἃ ἐποίησαν. 𝔙 *idola sua.* — אחריהם‎ . . . אשר‎]
𝔊 fol. Heb. idiom, οἷς . . . ὀπίσω αὐτῶν. — ויתעום וגו'‎] a gloss (*v.s.*).

4. *Judah*] Outside of this oracle the only specific references to
Judah are found in 1² 6¹ 7¹² 9¹¹.* Judah represents the southern
kingdom, including Benjamin, in distinction from northern Israel
(1 K. 12²⁰ᵇ).† The relationship of the two nations was very close
in spite of the disruption, for however they may have differed
from each other in dialect, in religious ideas or in governmental
sympathy they were one nation in distinction from their Canaanitish neighbors. The impossibility of uniting all the interests of
the various tribes showed itself in the earliest times, and it was
only under David and Solomon that a union, even when effected,
could endure. The rivalry between the two kingdoms after the
division was intense and bitter (cf. 1 K. 12¹⁸· ²¹ f. ²⁶ ff· 15⁷· ¹⁶ ff. ³² 2 K.
14⁸ ff·). At this time there seems to have been no special cause for
bitter feeling between them. — *The law of Yahweh*] Four stages
in the history of this word may be traced : ‡ (1) direction or instruction from Yahweh, in general, without any technical meaning ;
cf. advice from elders, Pr. 1⁸, utterances of prophets, Is. 1¹⁰ 8¹⁶ ;
(2) technical direction given by the priest on specific matters of
ceremonial observance and conduct, Mi. 3¹¹ Je. 2⁸ 18¹⁸ Lv. 11⁴⁶
15³² ; (3) direction as to the general duty of an Israelite as found
in Dt. 1⁵ 1 K. 2³ 2 K. 10³¹ 14⁶ 17¹³ 21⁸ 22⁸ Je. 16¹¹ ; (4) the direction formulated and contained in the Pentateuch, Ne. 8¹ f· ¹³ f· 10³⁴· ³⁶.
The exact meaning intended here will depend upon the date
assigned to the passage. The use in the next member of the
parallelism of the word *statutes*] in a measure marks the idea as

---

* Cf. the query whether the story of the encounter of the prophet of Judah with
Jeroboam I (1 K. 13), may not have been worked up upon the basis of the encounter of Amos with Jeroboam II.; Kue. *Einl.* II. 342.

† Cf. especially Seesemann, *Israel und Juda bei Am. u. Ho.*

‡ Dr. *Dt.* 208, 209, 401 f.; WRS. *OTJC.*² 299 ff., 372 ff., 382 f., 425 f.; Kue.
Hex. § 10.4; Sm. *Rel.* (v. *Index*) ; We. *Prol.*, 394 ff.; McC. *HPM.*, §§ 457, 488, 610;
Benz. *Arch.*, 321, 324, 412; Now. *Arch.* II, 97 f.; Dr. 230 f.; Kent and Sanders,
"The Growth of Israelitish Law," in *Bibl. and Sem. Studies, critical and histor.
essays by the members of the Sem. and Bibl. Faculty of Yale Univ.* (1902), 41–90.

consistent with the third or Deuteronomic stage described above, 2 K. 17[19]. This word (sometimes with *judgments*, also with *testimonies* and *commandments*, prefixed), is especially frequent in Dt. and in books dependent on Dt. (cf. 4[5. 8. 14] 5[1. 31] 6[1. 20] etc.), and designates enactments or institutions whether moral, ceremonial, or civil (*e.g.* Dt. 7[1-3] 12. 14. 16. 17).* This "direction" of Yahweh and these "statutes," *they had rejected, had not observed*], a charge which accords well with the feeling of the prophets (Is. 5[24]), who narrated the stories of the kings of David's line (2 K. 17[15. 19]), although the charge is of sin against God, rather than against man. Cf. the frequent formulas, "evil in the sight of Yahweh," "provoked him to jealousy with their sins which they committed, above all that their fathers had done." Judah's rulers might be classified as (1) the *good* kings, Asa (1 K. 15[11] 2 Ch. 14[2]), Jehoshaphat (1 K. 22[43] 2 Ch. 17[3]), Joash (2 K. 12[2f.] 2 Ch. 24[2. 18]), Amaziah (2 K. 14[3] 2 Ch. 25[2]), who, nevertheless, fell far short of reaching the standard in the mind of the historian, a *standard* (fixed by Dt.) in accordance with which all worship on high-places was interdicted; (2) the *bad* kings, Abijah (1 K. 15[3], cf. 2 Ch. 13[10]), Joram (2 K. 8[18] 2 Ch. 21[6]), Ahaziah (2 K. 8[27] 2 Ch. 22[3]), who openly opposed the true Yahweh worship, while Athaliah (2 K. 11[3] 2 Ch. 22[12]) actually deserted the Yahweh religion.† If this representation of apostasy comes from Amos, allowance must be made for the fact that the general prohibition of worship on high-places was still a thing of the future (Josiah's reign); if from a later date, the charge may have been made from the point of view of Deuteronomy. That the accusation in general was true against the Judah of Amos's time cannot be doubted. The gloss, *And their lies have caused them to err*] (resembling Je. 23[13. 32]), is a still later interpolation in the original charge,‡ whenever made. These *lies*, in the mind of the interpolator, may have been the plausible but false excuses which they offered for their transgressions, § or the false prophets whose activity in later times was very great, ‖ or, better still, their idols, *i.e.* something which has no actual existence, and actually deceives;¶ for a similar

---

* Gun.; Lag. *BN.* 40; Barth. *NB.* 112, 119; Baentsch, *Das Bundesbuch,* 32; Dr. *Dt.* 62.   † See Mit., 81 f.   ‡ So Marti.   § Cal., Geb.   ‖ Ki., Abar.
    ¶ Jer., Drus., Dat., Schrö., Ros., Hi., Ba., Mit., Dr., Now., *et al.*

idea in connection with other Hebrew words *v.i.* — *After which their fathers walked*] An expression used of Yahweh worship (Dt. 13⁴), and also of idolatry (Dt. 4³ 8¹⁹ 11²⁸ 13²). The whole course of Judah's history was an illustration of this fact. Judgment, therefore, shall come upon Judah, and shall show itself particularly against *the palaces of Jerusalem*], a threat which would strike terror to the hearts of Israelites, for Jerusalem, even to the Northern Israelites, represented in a peculiar manner the Yahweh, in whose worship the two nations united.

According to tradition Jerusalem was in existence before Abraham (Gn. 14¹⁸ Ps. 76²). At the conquest of Canaan, Jerusalem (on the Amarna inscriptions, *cir.* 1400 B.C., Urusalim; hence the original name, Jebus being used to designate the non-Israelite population, Ju. 19¹¹, GFM. *Ju.* 20, 413) was not taken from the Jebusites (Jos. 15⁶³, cf. the substitution of "Benjamites" for "Judahites" in Ju. 1²¹, and note also the spurious character of 1⁸), but remained a Canaanitish city until captured by David (2 S. 5⁶⁻⁹), who fortified it and made it the capital of the kingdom. Under Solomon the city was magnificently adorned with buildings, most important of which was the temple. Between the time of Solomon and that of Amos, Jerusalem had been captured and plundered three times: (1) by Shishak in Rehoboam's reign (1 K. 14²⁵ f· 2 Ch. 12¹f·); (2) by Arabians and Philistines in Joram's reign (2 Ch. 21¹⁶f·); (3) by Israel under Jehoash in Amaziah's reign (2 K. 14¹³f· 2 Ch. 25²³f·). — **4.** מאס] used of rejection of people by Yahweh (Je. 6³⁰ 14¹⁹), as well as of rejection of Yahweh by his people, as here; cf. also 1 S. 15²³ 2 K. 17¹⁵; cf. in the same sense שׁלך, נטשׁ, עזב, נאץ, זנה. — תורה] from Hiph. of ירה = *direction*, used with חקים (חקות), משׁפטים, and מצות (Baentsch, *Das Bundesbuch*, 29–34; Dr. *Dt.* 62). Note the chiastic arrangement of תורה and חקיו. The change of subject from מאסם in the clause beginning ויתעם is very awkward and throws suspicion on the connection of the two clauses. — כזביהם] *their images*, cf. אָוֶן (Is. 66³), אלהים . . . לא (Je. 5⁷), הבל (Je. 8¹⁹), and אֱלִיל (Lv. 19⁴). — אשׁר] A good example of a full relative sentence H. 46, 1; GK. 138 *a*; Ew.⁸ 331, *c* (2). — **5.** ירושׁלם] Qᵉri for ירושׁלם; cf. Urusalim (Amarna), Ursalimma (Assyr.) (Dl. *Par.* 288; *COT.* I. 148 f.; *RP.²* V. 60 f.; *DB.²* I. 1582; BSZ. *s.v.;* BDB. *s.v.;* Grill, *ZAW.* IV. 134 ff.; Zimmern, *ZA.* 1891, pp. 252, 254, 263; Sayce, *HCM.* 176; Jastrow, *JBL.* XI. 105). 𝔊 Ἰερουσαλήμ, class. Grk. Ἱεροσόλυμα, Aram. ירושׁלם. Other proper names with the ending יַם _ are: רָמָתַיִם, קִבְצַיִם, קָרְיָתַיִם, דִּבְלָתַיִם, חֹרוֹנַיִם, מִצְרַיִם, עֶגְלַיִם.

§ **4. Judgment against the nation Israel.** 2⁶⁻¹⁶. If other nations are to be punished for their sins, surely Israel must suffer. (1) Her transgressions are many, and, above all, injustice and oppression prevail; (2) notwithstanding the divine purpose to do for her everything possible, every effort has been rendered futile; (3) therefore, now, a destruction shall come from which there shall be no escape. These three ideas are expressed in three distinct pieces, each of three strophes, and each strophe, originally, of four lines. The writer adjusts the form of his language to the character of the thought, and the logical movement is thus rendered wonderfully impressive.

6-8. *The injustice and oppression in Israel.* The nation is guilty of a treatment of the poor and needy so cruel as to be a profanation of God's holy name.

The three strophes of this piece have the trimeter movement. Each contains a single verse; but vs.⁷ ᵃⁿᵈ ⁸ have been transposed. V.⁷ is to be placed as the third strophe after v.⁸ because (1) the ptcp. השפים is less abrupt, connecting itself with the subject of the preceding imperfects; Torrey's statement concerning Amos's use of the ptcp. (*JBL.* XV. 152) is entirely in accord with this; (2) the order of thought thus becomes more regular; (3) the piece closes with the climax "profane my holy name"; and (4) the closing line, just quoted, sustains a striking relation to the first line of the succeeding piece "and yet I," etc. Cf. my presentation of this point in the *Biblical World*, September, 1898, p. 179, and Löhr (1901), who places v.⁸ between ⁷ᵃ and ⁷ᵇ, and then brings together ⁷' and ¹⁰ (v.⁹ following); on the other hand Oet. 66, regards the first of these changes as unnecessary, the second as pedantic.

6. [צדיק] Gr. דַּלִּים, cf. 8⁶. — [ואביון] 𝕿 connects with צדיק.—[בעבור נעלים] בְּדִיל דְיַחְסְנוּן 𝕿. Che. (*Crit. Bib.*), שָׁלוּם. — **7.** [השאפים] read הַשָּׁ[א]פִים, from שׁוּף (so Jer., Ba., We., Gr., Now., Torrey *JBL.* XV. 151, GAS., Löhr; cf. Hal.), supported by 𝕲, which connects השאפים with נעלים, rendering it τὰ πατοῦντα (some codd., τῶν πατούντων), by 𝕾, and 𝖅, *qui conterunt.* 𝕿 perhaps = שאטים (cf. Ez. 16⁵⁷; so Hal.). Oet. הַשָּׁמִים עָפַר ארץ על ראש. — [על] Elh. אֶל. (?) — [על עפר ארץ] Om. as a gloss, since it is unnecessary, in itself is very awkward, and altogether spoils the rhythm (so We., Now., Torrey *JBL.* XV. 151 ff., Löhr, Marti; cf. Dr., Elh., and Oet., who are unable to see how these words could have gotten in the text if they were not genuine; but *v.* Torrey's explanation of the origin of the gloss). Oort (*Em.*) om. the entire clause, beginning with השאפים. ἐπὶ τὸν χοῦν τῆς γῆς seems to be a later addition to 𝕲 (so We., Now.). — [בראש] 𝕾 om. 𝕲𝖅 pl. 𝖅 seems to om. ב (so also Löhr). Hirscht, בראש.—[וורך] Gr. ודרך. Oort (*Em.*), Marti, יִדְרְכוּ.—[ואיש] 𝕲 καὶ υἱὸς.—[הנערה] 𝕲 τὴν αὐτὴν παιδίσκην. Read with Hoffm. הַנַּעֲרָה (*v.i.*). Another reading suggested is הַנַּאֲרָה, *the accursed thing.* — **8.** [ועל] Oort, fol. 𝕲, om. עַל (so Now., Elh., Löhr); perhaps 𝔊 read וָאת.—[חֲבָלִים] 𝔊 δεσμεύοντες = חֹבְלִים (Vol.) or חֲבָלִים (Va., Seb., Gr.); so 𝔖. Gr., fol. 𝔊, adds יִרְעוּת.—[יטו] Ew. ידו. Sta. יצעו (cf. Je. 2²⁰). Hal. יטו.—[כל] 𝔊 om.—[עֲנוּשִׁים] 𝔊 ἐκ συκοφαντιῶν = according to Hirscht, עֲשׁוּקִים, a corrupt text. 𝔖 עֲתִיקָא, *old*, probably reading a form of ישׁן (Seb.). Gr. עִם נָשִׁים (?). 𝔊's rendering of ⁸ᵃ, καὶ τὰ ἱμάτια αὐτῶν δεσμεύοντες σχοινίοις παραπετάσματα ἐποίουν ἐχόμενα τοῦ θυσιαστηρίου, according to Ba. = וְאֵת בִּגְדֵיהֶם חֹבְלִים עָשׂוּ צְלָלִים לַמִּזְבֵּחַ; but according to Gr. בגדים קשרים בחבלים לירעות.

6. Though starting the indictment of Israel with the stereo-typed formula, *for three transgressions*, etc.] this is abandoned after the first sentence. — *Because they sell the righteous for money, and the needy for a pair of shoes*] The reference is not to the righteous and poor in spirit who, because of opposition to a royal edict, are seized and sold into slavery; * nor to the corrupt acts of judges in the oppression of the poor, at first for money, and later, as they become more corrupt, even for a pair of shoes; † but to the unjust and outrageous seizure (*sell* here being used figur-atively) of innocent men by the powerful for debt, and to the habit of selling the poor into slavery when the debt was only as much as a pair of shoes; ‡ cf. 2 K. 4¹ Mat. 18²⁵. The sin of Israel repeated in different forms is that of *injustice, oppression;* cf. the legislation which touches this, Ex. 23⁶⁻⁸ Dt. 16¹⁸⁻²⁰ Lv. 19¹⁵; and the attitude of the later prophets, Is. 1²³ 3¹⁴ᶠ· 5²³ 10¹ᶠ· Je. 5²⁸ 22³ Ez. 22²⁹ Mi. 3⁹⁻¹¹ 7³ Mal. 3⁵. The phrase *for a pair of shoes* (cf. Am. 8⁶ᵃ) seems to be a proverbial expression designating some-thing of the lowest value; § cf. Ez. 13¹⁹. A very plausible in-terpretation ‖ is based on the custom of using the shoe as a "conventional symbol in legal transactions" (cf. Ru. 4⁷ Ps. 60⁸). One of the commonest crimes of Amos's day was that of land grabbing (cf. Is. 5⁸) on the part of the rich, and it is this that Amos is here denouncing. The judges are charged with receiv-ing money for the betrayal of the innocent, and not only so, but also with cheating the needy out of his land. This interpre-tation is supported by 𝔊's reading of 1 S. 12³, viz. ἐκ χειρὸς τίνος εἴληφα ἐξίλασμα καὶ ὑπόδημα (from whose hand have I taken a

---

* Geb.
            ‡ Os., Va., Hi., Ew., Ba., Dr.
† AE., Theodoret, Crocius, Ros.
            § Dathe, Bauer, Jus., Schrö., Ros., Marti.
‖ G. H. Box, *Exp. Times*, XII. (1901), 377 f.; cf. Hoffm. *ZAW.* III. 97 ff.

bribe and a sandal?)* — **8.** *And because garments taken in pledge
they spread out*] These were especially the outer garments, or
mantle (Gn. 39^{12} 1 K. 22^{10}),† rather than bedclothing (1 S. 19^{13}),‡
held in pledge contrary to the command in Ex. 22^{26}, which provides for the return of the garment over night,§ or taken in payment for unjust fines.‖ Garments thus illegally and mercilessly
held, the upper classes spread out, in order to recline upon them, as
upon couches for sleeping,¶ or as at banquets in their feasting.**
Cf. Ewald's interpretation, *cast lots* (1 S. 14^{42}). — *Beside every
altar*] Referring to the sacrificial meals (cf. 1 S. 3^3 $9^{12. 13}$ Dt. $14^{26 f.}$,
also Ho. 8^{11} $10^{1. 2. 8}$ 12^{11}). — *And the wine of such as have been
fined they drink*] That is, wine purchased by money received
through unjust judgment.†† — *In the houses of their gods*] Not
in the house of their gods,‡‡ *i.e.* the calves worshipped as gods
in Bethel and Dan ; nor in the house of their God, *i.e.* Yahweh,§§
for this was at Jerusalem ; but in the *houses* of their gods ‖‖ (*v.i.*).
The whole is a protest of the simple ancient Jewish religion against
the metropolitan civilization,¶¶ carrying with it, as it does, corruption and greed. — **7.** *Who tread* [*to the dust of the earth*] *the
head of the poor*] Cf. 8^4 Gn. 3^{15}; that is, trample the poor into
the dust,*** or, omitting עַל עֲפַר אֶרֶץ, *who tread upon, or crush, the
head of the poor*, a reading based upon a slight change of 𝔐
(*v.s.*). Others have understood the phrase as meaning, "who
desire to destroy the heads of the poor who already are cast into
the dust,"††† or, "who long for the dust of the earth, *i.e.* earthly
things, gold, silver, which may be possessed only at the risk of the
heads of the poor," ‡‡‡ or, "who long for the person of the poor
in addition to his landed property," §§§ or, "who long to see dust
scattered upon the heads of the poor, *i.e.* to see their misery as
thus indicated," ‖‖‖ or, "who long for even the dust sprinkled by

---

* The correctness of 𝔊's reading is established by Ecclus. 46^{19} where the
original text (ed. of Cowley and Neubauer, p. 32) reads: כפר ונעלים מ[מי לקח]תי
= from whom have I taken a bribe or a pair of sandals ?

† Jus., Schrö., Ba.   ‡ Ros.   †† Cal., Os., Ros.   ¶¶ We.

§ Ra., Ki., Cal., Os., Jus., Va., Ros.   ‡‡ Or.   *** Ba., GAS.

‖ Geb.   ¶ Cal., Os., Jus., Va.   §§ Crocius.   ††† Cal., Jus.

** Ra., Ki., Luth., Geb., Ros.   ‖‖ Oort (*ThT.* XIV. 141), Mit.

‡‡‡ Geb., who cites for similar use of בְּ 2 S. 23^{17} בְּנַפְשׁוֹתָם; 1 Ch. 12^{19} בְרָאשֵׁי;
also Struensee, Mich.   §§§ Hoffm. *ZAW.* III. 99 f.

‖‖‖ Dat., and with slight variation, Ros., Ke., Or., Gun., Elh.

the mourner (cf. 2 S. 1[2] 15[32] La. 2[10]) upon his head, as indicative of his grief." * The general thought is the same in every case. — *And the way of the humble they turn aside*] Cf. 5[12] Is. 10[2] Ex. 23[6] Je. 5[4]. The word *way* is difficult to define, meaning "the judgment" † or "the cause, business"; ‡ better, however, is "the path in life, the walk by which they are characterized" (Ps. 1[6]). § The rich and powerful push the humble out of the path in which they would naturally walk, in other words, deprive them of the privileges to which they are entitled (Jb. 24[4] Mat. 18[6]). — *A man and his judge deal according to agreement*] So Hoffmann, changing ר to ד. ‖ This is in better harmony with the context, which is entirely occupied with the idea of corruption and oppression. The other reading, *a man and his father go unto the same maid*, makes the sin an exaggerated form of adultery, a father and son going to the same harlot,¶ or the same young wife,** or a girl (the article being generic), *i.e.* one of the temple prostitutes †† who were in the service of Baal and Astarte, and plied their business near the altars and temples (cf. Gn. 38[21. 22] Dt. 23[17] 1 K. 14[24]); or a servant taken as a concubine (Ex. 21[8. 9], cf. Ez. 22[11] Lv. 18[8. 15]); ‡‡ according to Reuss, it does not mean the same woman, but simply that the father sets an example to the son; while Hitzig explains that the expression נערה אחת is avoided, because it might have implied that intercourse with different maids would not be blameworthy. — *And so profane my holy name*] Any act inconsistent with God's character would be a profanation of his name — a phrase common in the Holiness Code (Lv. 17–26) and in Ezekiel. §§ This would apply equally well to (1) impurity of life, ‖‖ (2) idol worship involving impurity (cf. Lv. 18[21] 20[3]),¶¶ (3) corruption in the administration of justice.*** The thought is that this is the real result ††† of all such action. This phrase does not, as Nowack contends, settle beyond question that the preceding clause refers to the practices of the temple prostitutes.

---

* Va., Schrö., Hi., Pu., Hd., Duhm (*Theol.*), Dr.
† Ros., Ba., Gun.   § Mit.   ¶ Cal., Os., Hi., GAS.
‡ Jus.   ‖ *ZAW*. III. 99 f.   ** Rabbi Salomo, Geb.
†† Mich., Mau., Ew., Hd., Ba., St., Now., Dr., Elh.   ¶¶ St.   *** Hoffm.
‡‡ Ros.   §§ Cal., Os., Ros.   ‖‖ Most commentators.   ††† Ros.

6. מִכְרָם] with ĭ atten. from ă, instead of with ŏ, as if the Qal Impf. had ă; so also Ne. 13[15]; but מָכְרָה, Ex. 21[8]. Cf. נִפְלוּ, 2 S. 1[10] with נָפְלוּ, 1 S. 29[3]. V. Barth, NB. 77 c; GK. 61 b. — ב [בכסף] denotes price, cf. 8[6]; GK. 119 p; Kö. 332 o. — [צדיק] Cf. Barth, NB. 133 c; Lag. BN. 110; Ols. 185 a; Kautzsch, Ueber die Derivate des St. צדק in a.t. Sprachgebrauch (1881); WRS. Proph. 72; always used of persons except Dt. 4[8]. For the sense innocent (cf. נקי) v. Ex. 23[7] Pr. 18[17]. — [בעבור] May denote price, BSZ., s.v.; Ew.[8] 315 c, note 3; but for the sake of (1 S. 12[22]) here and in 8[6] gives better sense. Cf. Ba., who maintains the latter as the only meaning; Hoffm. (ZAW. III. 99) makes עבור here, 7[8] and 8[6] = עבור הארץ (Jos. 5[11]), i.e. produce, secured to the judge by the token of a pair of shoes; cf. Ru. 4[7]. — [נעלים] = something of the slightest value (cf. 8[6] Ez. 13[19]; so Dathe, Ba., Jus., Ros., Schrö., et al.), but cf. Ba., 264; ZA. VII. 296; Hoffm. ZAW. III. 98 f. —

8. על] not a prep. governing בגדים, but a continuation of על with מכרם = because, as in Gn. 31[20] Ps. 119[136]; cf. full form, Dt. 29[25]. Löhr shows clearly that ועל as a prep. is out of place, for Amos uses שכב and סרח for lie and recline; ᵹ om. it; and it is superfluous in the metre of the line. — יטו] by the transposition of vs.[7 and 8] now continues the inf. מכרם (H. 29, 5 b; GK. 114 r; Dr. § 118), having in itself and giving to the inf. the freq. force, H. 21, 2; GK. 107 g; Dr. § 33 a; Ew.'s use of יַטּוּ = הִפִּיל, cast lots, is unnecessary and without basis; cf. Is. 31[3] Je. 6[12], in which הִטָּה is used of stretching out the hand, a sense more easy to harmonize here with its use in v.[7] — ישתו] is coördinate with יטו. On the sacrificial meals of the Hebrews, see Di. on Lv. 3; WRS. OTJC.[2] 239, 448–51, and Proph. 98 f.; and other literature cited in my Constructive Studies in the Priestly Element in the O.T. (1902), 90 ff. — בית אלהיהם] = in the houses of their gods, the second noun pluralizing also the first, H. 3, 4; GK. 124 r; cf. בית עצביהם, 1 S. 31[9]. —

7. השפים] or, הַשָּׁאפִים (GK. 23 g); the article, as in Gn. 49[21] Ps. 49[7], adds a new statement, here in a tone of impatience and indignation; (GK. 126 b; Kö. 411 e; Mit.; Torrey, JBL. XV. 151 f.; cf. the frequent use of the ptcp. in this way, 3[10] 4[1] 5[7] 6[3. 4 ff. 13], etc.). Against the reading here adopted, Elh. (cf. Hirscht) urges (1) that in Gn. 3[15], where שוף occurs with ראש, the prep. ב is absent; (2) that in Gn. 3[15] שוף cannot possibly mean tread upon, when used of the serpent at least; (3) that it involves the rejection of על עפר ארץ, the presence of which words cannot be accounted for on the supposition that they are a gloss (but v.s.); (4) that ᴹᵀ makes satisfactory sense. — בראש] On use of ב after verbs of touching and taking hold of, GK. 119 k; Ew.[8] 217, 3, 2), a); but note that in 8[4] the ב is omitted after השפים. — [השאפים וגו' ᵹ τὰ πατοῦντα ἐπὶ τὸν χοῦν τῆς γῆς καὶ ἐκονδύλιζον εἰς κεφαλὰς πτωχῶν (cf. ᵴ = for the sake of sandals which tread upon the dust of the earth and who strike the poor with their fists) is explained as due to a double interpretation of השאפים, one rightly connecting it with the subject of the preceding inf., the other wrongly connecting it with נעלים; it is as an explanatory gloss to the latter that the על עפר הא' originated (so e.g. Torrey, JBL. XV. 152). The result is that the two interpretations appear side by side in ᵹ and ᵴ, השאפים being

represented in each, while 𝔐𝕋 presents a mixture of the two interpretations,
עַל עֲפַר הַאֹ' belonging to the secondary one. Hirscht objects to this that 𝔊
renders שָׁאַף in 8[4] by ἐκτρίβω ; cf. 2 K. 19[26] where 𝔊 confuses שׁרפה with שׁוף
and translates it πατήματα, and Is. 25[10] where דוש is rendered by πατεῖν.
Moreover, in Gn. 3[15], שׁוף is used of an action of the foot, not of the hand
(κονδυλίζω).   Hence only πατοῦντα can here be referred to שׁאפים, and
since this rendering of שׁאפים made the Hebrew unintelligible, καὶ ἐκονδύλιζον
was freely added by the translators after ἐπὶ τὸν χοῦν τῆς γῆς in order to
secure sense for the passage. Hirscht, therefore, would retain 𝔐𝕋 with one
change, viz., בְּרֹאשׁ instead of בְּרֹאשׁ, and, by considering בְּרֹאשׁ as the direct
object of הַשֹּׁאֲפִים and regarding עֲפַר הָאָרֶץ as an ironical expression for money
(cf. Assyr. " gold, the dust of his land " and "the dust of the earth of Susa
. . . I took to Assyria," KB. II. 14, 209), would secure the following interpretation : " the wicked already possess much, and yet it is nothing (dust),
and they ever covet more of this nothing from those who have nothing more."
This is scarcely an improvement upon 𝔐𝕋 and, to say the least, makes very
awkward syntax.— יַטּוּ] A more usual meaning of הטה than the above ; here
a continuation of the ptcp., as the other, of an inf.; H. 27, 5 b ; GK. 116 x ;
Kö. 413 l, 368 i ; Dr. § 117.— וְאִישׁ וְאָבִיו יֵלְכוּ אֶל הַנַּעֲרָה] In support of this
reading note (1) that 𝔐𝕋 is entirely outside of the scope of the author's
thought ; cf. Mi. 2[9] in which the casting out of the women is a part of the
picture of oppression ; (2) the parallel picture in Mi. 7[3] ; (3) the use of אב
= priestly judge, 2 K. 6[21] 13[14] Je. 17[10] (cf. Gn. 45[8] ; GFM. Ju. 385 f.), and a
similar usage in Egyptian (ZDMG. XXXI. 726) ; (4) the similar combination
of נער and הלך in 3[3].— לְמַעַן] H. 29, 3 a (a) ; GK. 107 q ; Kö. 407 f ; Ew.[8]
337, 2 ; expresses a necessary logical consequence but never simply result ;
" in rhetorical passages, the issue of a line of action, though really unde-
signed, is represented by it ironically as if it were designed " (BDB. 775),
e.g. Ho. 8[4] ; cf. Kö. 396 e. This is the only occurrence of לְמַעַן in Amos.

9–12. *The efforts made by Yahweh to build up Israel.* The present condition of Israel is not due to neglect on the part of Yahweh, for he (1) had taken Israel out of Egypt, led her through the wilderness and brought her to Canaan, (2) had driven out the Canaanites from before her, and (3) had raised up teachers through whom his will might be made known, — but all to no effect.

This piece stands in closest connection with the preceding (cf. the contrast
— they had profaned his holy name, when it had been *he*, who was, etc.), and
falls into three strophes each of three pentameters, or six alternating trimeters
and dimeters ; preferably the former, since the long drawn out lines picture
the historical details given, and form a contrast with the quick trimeter movement of vs.[13-15] which follow. It seems right to transfer v.[10] to precede v.[9]

and make it form the first strophe, because (1) this is a simple historical statement and the chronological order is self-evident, while (2) nothing is gained by the explanation that v.⁹, although later in time, is put before v.¹⁰ to emphasize the greatness of the victory over the tall and mighty aborigines, which was so remarkable in contrast with the weakness of Israel at the time of the prophet (Ew.), or to tell first what God did *for* the nation, and then what he did *to* the nation ; (3) the confusion grew out of the fact that both strophes began with ואנכי ; while (4) the whole of strophe 2 (v.⁹) grows out of the mention of האמרי in line 3 of strophe 1 (v.¹⁰). Cf. Löhr, Oet., Baumann, and Marti who makes both ¹⁰ and ¹² interpolations.

10. ואנכי העליתי] 𝔙 correctly renders, *ego sum qui ascendere . . . feci.* Before לרשת the insertion of ואביאכם found in 𝔖, *and I brought you to this place*, completes the rhythm and furnishes a basis for לרשת. — **9.** [השמדתי 𝔊 ἐξῆρα ; 𝔊ᴬ ἐξέγειρα. — מפניהם] Some codd. מפניכם. — ארזים . . . אלונים [ארזים 𝔊 sg. — ואשמיד] 𝔊 ἐξήρανα ; (some codd. ἐξῆρα) ; 'Α. καὶ συνέτριψα in second, but ΣΘ like 𝔊 ; cf. Ba.'s suggestion that ἐξήρανα is an early (because followed by Jer. and Arab.) modification of ἐξῆρα to fit the picture of a tree. — **11.** [ואקים 𝔊 καὶ ἔλαβον = ואקח (cf. Dt. 18¹⁸). — [לנזרים 𝔊 ἁγιασμόν = נֶזֶר. The line האף [אין זאת וגו׳ the concluding home-thrust of the piece — should stand at the end of v.¹², where it belongs logically and poetically (see *Biblical World*, September, 1898 ; so also Löhr, 6 ; on the contrary, Oet. 66). — [האף Gr. ־אֲפֹה. — [זאת Riedel, זֶה אות. — **12.** [נְזרים 𝔊 ἡγιασμένους ; other Greek versions τοὺς Ναζιραίους. — [לאמר לא תִנָּבֵא 𝔖 has the third person ; these words might well be omitted as a gloss and the line thus restored to its proper length.

10. *And yet it was I who*] Emphasizing, cf. 𝔙, the contrast between the ingratitude and wickedness of the people (v.⁸) and the readiness of Yahweh to pour out blessings upon them. For similar use of the conjunction, which is especially frequent with the personal pronouns, see Ju. 16¹⁵ Is. 53⁷ Gn. 26²⁷. — *Brought you up out of Egypt*] The usual form of expression, cf. Gn. 12¹⁰ 26² 44¹⁷ 45²⁵ 46³, not because Palestine was toward the north,* but rather because of the local elevation, the mountainous character of Palestine in contrast with Egypt.† The general thought here expressed is found elsewhere, Ex. 19⁴ Dt. 32¹⁰ Ps. 78⁵³ Je. 2². For the various explanations of the present order of vs.⁹·¹⁰, and for the reasons which suggest a reversal of the order, *v.s.* — *Forty years*] Cf. 5²⁵ Dt. 2⁷ 8² especially 29⁵ ; a reminder not only of the disobedience for which the wandering was a punishment, and in spite of which Yahweh was good enough to bring them into the land, but also of

---

* Ros.   † Hd. ; cf. GAS. *HG.* 45–59.

the power of Yahweh exhibited in his gracious act of feeding and
caring for them during all this time.*   On the duration of the wandering there is difference of opinion.†   For the use of the number
forty in Scripture,‡ see Gn. 7^4 25^{20} 50^3 Ex. 16^{35} 24^{18} Nu. 13^{25} Dt.
25^3 Ju. 3^{11} 5^{31} 8^{28} 13^1 1 K. 19^8 Ez. $29^{11ff.}$ Jon. 3^4. — *To possess the
land*] Cf. Dt. 6^{12} Ho. 13^4 (RV. *marg.*). This phrase has been
joined (1) to the preceding clause with the idea that this long
wandering was intended to prepare them for driving out their
opponents,§ (2) to the whole verse, explaining thus the purpose
of the Exodus as a whole ;‖ but it is better with $\mathfrak{S}$ (*v.s.*) to suppose
that the words *and brought you hither*] were a part of the original
text. — *The Amorite*] By whom Amos meant not a particular
people dwelling from the Jabbok to the Arnon on both sides of
the Jordan (cf. Nu. $21^{21.32}$), nor one (cf. Gn. $10^{15f.}$) of many Canaanitish peoples, used here to represent all¶ (cf. Gn. 15^{16} Jos. 24^{15}),
but the whole Canaanitish constituency, described by E (of the
Hexateuch) and by Amos as the Amorite (*v.i.*). — **9.** *And it was
I who destroyed from before them*] An emphatic expression as in
v.[10], and the usual word for the overthrow of the Canaanite race
(see in E, Jos. 24^8, the same phrase), especially frequent in Dt.
(cf. $2^{21f.}$) and in the later historical books. — *The Amorite . . .
whose height was like the cedars*] An hyperbolical description, based
upon the common opinion of the existence of giant nations, intended to magnify the goodness and the power of Yahweh, who
was able to overcome enemies of such stature.**   Specific mention
of the gigantic autochthones of the land is made elsewhere, viz.
of the sons of Anak (Nu. $13^{22ff.}$ Dt. 1^{28}); the Emim (Dt. 2^{10}); the
Zamzummim (Dt. 2^{20}); the Rephaim (Dt. 3^{11}); cf. also Nu. 13^{33}.
The cedar in the Hebrew mind was the ideal representation of gran-
deur, 2 K. 14^9 Is. 2^{13} Ps. 80^{10} 92^{13} Ez. $17^{22f.}$ 31^3 Je. 22^7. — *And he was
strong as the oaks*] Cf. Is. 2^{13} Zc. 11^2 Ez. 27^6. — *But I destroyed
his fruit . . . his roots*] That is, root and branch (cf. Ez. 17^9 Ho.
9^{16} Jb. 18^{16} Is. 5^{24}),†† a picture of complete destruction, ‡‡ and not a

---

* Cal., Ros., Ba., Pu.   † Cf. Sta. *GVI.* I. 132 f.; Dr. *Dt.* 32 f.   ‡ Cf. Kö. *Stil*, 54.
§ AE., Ki.   ‖ Ros.   ¶ Jus., Schrö., Ros., Ba., Hd., Pu., Or., *et al.*   ** Pu.
†† Cf. Eshmunazar Inscription (*Corp. Insc. Sem.* 1^1 p. 19, ls. 11, 12) : " May he
have no root underneath, or fruit above, or any beauty among the living under the
sun."   ‡‡ Cal., Jus., Ba.

reference to different classes, *e.g.* the fruit being the children, and the root the stock of the population as that which propagates the species.* The destruction, here poetically exaggerated, was not at first represented as so complete, cf. Ex. $23^{32\,f.}$ 34^{12}; but in later times, and especially in Dt. (cf. $7^{1\,f.}$ $20^{15\,f.}$ Jos. 11^{20}) it is treated as something practically finished even in the early days. Perhaps the gradual disappearance of the Canaanites furnished the occasion for this difference in representation. — **11.** Yahweh had shown his presence and his favor in the Exodus and in the Conquest; but when Moses, the great prophet, had died, who, in the divine plan, should serve as mediator between himself and Israel? *Moreover I raised up some of your sons for prophets*] (cf. Je. 6^{17}), and, through these, the connection of Yahweh with Israel had been maintained. All this was in strict accord with Dt. 18^{15}, the earliest announcement of which formed the constitution of the prophetic order. Up to this time Israel's prophets, not reckoning Moses, Samuel, and those sent also to Judah, included Ahijah (1 K. 14^2), Jehu (1 K. 16^1), Elijah (1 K. 17^1), Elisha (1 K. 19^{16}), Micaiah (1 K. 22^8), Jonah (2 K. 14^{25}), and the many prophets whose names are not given (1 S. 28^{15} Ho. 4^5 1 K. 13^1 20^{35}). Hitzig's interpretation, *aroused . . . so that they became*, is not so good as the ordinary *raised up*, or *ordained*. The phrase *your sons* limits the writer's thought to Israelites,† but "lays no stress upon the fact that youth is the time of inspiration and enthusiasm"; ‡ cf. Jo. 3^1. Nor does the blessing consist in the fact that their own sons have been taken as Yahweh's representatives, when angels might have been chosen. § The usual particle (מִן) is here used to express the partitive idea, *some of.* — *And some of your youths for nazirites*] Mitchell rightly distinguishes *Nazarite* from *nazirite*. The nazirite, as the word נזיר signifies, was *separated* (from men, ‖ or from wine ¶), *consecrated* to God; cf. the Rechabites, 2 K. 10^{15} Je. 35^6. Ordinarily the vow of the nazirite was made for a definite period, but in two cases, those, perhaps, in the mind of Amos, the obligation seems to have been assumed for life, viz. Samson (Ju. $13^{5.\,7.\,14}$ 16^{17}) and Samuel (1 S. 1^{11}). This has been thought to be the original form of the vow.** The custom had its origin in an

---

* Hi., Ke.   ‡ Cf. GAS. I. 11–30, 44–58.   ‖ Ba.   ¶ Jus.

† Ba.   § Cal.   ** WRS. *Proph.* 84; Gun. 45.

effort to counteract the self-indulgent habits introduced into Israel by the Canaanites. The law (Nu. 6^{2-21}) provided only for the temporary obligation, at the termination of which the hair, which meanwhile had been sacred, should be sacrificed (Nu. 6^{18}). It was also understood that the nazirite should abstain from pollution by contact with death, as well as from every product of the vine (cf. Ju. 13^{14} Nu. $6^{3f.}$). The nazirite (cf. also the cases of John the Baptist, Lu. 1^{15}, and, according to Eusebius,* James, the brother of Jesus) was introduced not as a reminder of Yahweh's goodness in establishing the institution as a set way for securing holiness,† nor because of the similarity of the nazirite's work to that of the prophet, the former teaching by example, the latter by precept ; ‡ but because it enabled the speaker to deal a severe blow against one of the great evils of his day. — **12.** *But*] Instead of observing the example and obeying the precepts of these divinely appointed agents, *ye made the nazirites drink wine*] and so debauched them, a fact which, in view of the nation's degeneracy, is easily credible, although no historical allusion to it is found. The influences used may have been either persuasion (Gn. $19^{32.34}$) § or compulsion (Nu. $5^{24.26f.}$) ‖. — *And the prophets ye commanded, "ye shall not prophesy"*] Cf. 7^{16}. The example of one class is made null and void, and the utterances of the other class are prevented, and so Yahweh himself, who had raised up these messengers, is insulted and rejected. Note the chiastic arrangement of the thought. Actual examples of the prohibition placed upon prophecy were not infrequent, *e.g.* Jeroboam I. (1 K. 13^4), Jezebel (1 K. 18^4 19^2), Ahab (1 K. $22^{8.26f.}$), Ahaziah (2 K. $1^{9ff.}$), Jehoram (2 K. 6^{31}) ; cf. later the case of Amos (7^{13}), also Is. $30^{10.11}$ and the persecution of Jeremiah. — *Is not this indeed so?*] Will any one deny these accusations ? Is Israel then not deserving of the punishment which is threatened? This question is in a better position here than at the end of v.^{11}, and concludes the entire accusation. — *It is the oracle of Yahweh*] The phrase used here and ordinarily translated *saith Yahweh* (also in 2^{16} $3^{10.13.15}$, etc.), is not the phrase used in 1^{15} 2^3 $5^{16.17.27}$, etc., but one of much stronger significance (*v.i.*).

---

* *Hist.* 11. 23.   † Cal.   ‡ Os., Geb., St.   § Ki.   ‖ Jus., Ba.

10. ‏ואנכי‏] Emphatic by position and expression, GK. 135 *a*; Kö. 362*g.* — ‏ואולד‏] Always without ‏י‏ in 1 p. sg. with ‏ו‏ cons.; GK. 69 *x.* — ‏במדבר‏] *V.* Baentsch, *Die Wüste in d. a. Schriften.* — ‏ארבעים שנה‏] Sg. of noun with pl. of numeral, H. 15, 4. — ‏לרשת‏] The inf. with ‏ל‏ expressing purpose, GK. 114 *f,* and notes. — ‏האמרי‏] According to We. (*Die Composition des Hexateuchs,* 341 f.), Steinthal (*Zeitschrift für Völkerpsychologie,* XII. 267), Meyer (*ZAW.* I. 121-7, 139 ff.), WRS. (*Proph.* 26, 379), Sta. (*GVI.* I. 110; cf. also Budde, *Bibl. Urgeschichte,* 344–8; De. on Gn. 48²²), Di. (*Gen.* I. 365), Kit. (*Hist.* I. 22), Dr. (*Dt.* p. 11), GAS., Buhl (art. "Amoriter," *PRE.*³), and Now., this is a name current as early as the sixteenth century B.C., and applied to the primitive population of Palestine in E and D of the Hexateuch (J using "Canaanite"), and in Amos, synonymous with Canaanite. Cf. Gn. 48²² Dt. 1⁷·¹⁹·²⁰, also Ju. 1³⁴ ⁱ· 6¹⁰ 2 S. 21². McC. (*HPM.* I. 406 ff.) maintains that "in the Old Testament the two names answer to two distinct peoples, though it is impossible as yet to say with certainty how far the one was removed from the other in point of origin, and date of settlement"; similarly Wkl. (*GI.* I. 52 ff.). The terms *land of Amar,* which occurs with *land of Kanāna* (Canaan) in the Egyptian inscriptions (Brugsch, *Hist. of Eg.*² II. 14 f., 154; Bu., *Bibl. Urgeschichte,* 346 f.; Dr., *Dt.* 12; GFM. *Ju.* 81 ff.), and *Amurri* of the Tel-el-Amarna tablets (Sayce, *Races of the O. T.* 55 f., 101 f., 110–17; Dr. *Dt.* 12; GFM. *Ju.* 83) are probably the same name. The word occurs frequently in the Assyrian inscriptions, if the name for Syria, *matu Aḥarri,* is to be read *matu Amurri;* so Delattre, *PSBA.* 1891, pp. 215–34; *ZA.* VII. 2; *RP.*² V. 95 rm. 4, 98 rm. 2; Muss-Arnolt, *Dict.* 30, 61; Sayce, art. "Amorites," *DB.*; W. M. Müller, art. "Amorites," *Jew. Enc.*; Paton, *Hist.* 16; Wkl., *KAT.*³ I. 178. — **9.** ‏השמדתי‏] The usual word for the destruction of the Canaanites, especially frequent in Dt. *e.g.* 1²⁷ 2¹²·²¹·²²·²³ etc. — ‏מפניהם‏] is a sudden change from the second person to the third, Kö., *Stil.* 241. — ‏וגבהו‏ . . . ‏אשר‏] *whose height,* the full form of the relative sentence (H. 13, 1; 46, 1; GK. 138 *a*; Ew.⁸ 331 *c,* 3). — ‏הלן הוא‏] The unusual order makes ‏הסן‏ (occurring only here and Is. 1³¹) very emphatic. — ‏כאלונים‏] On the generic art. in comparisons, H. 4, 3 *d* (2); GK. 126 *o.* On the Hebrew idea of giant nations much has been written (cf. especially *DB.*² I. 1173–6; Schwally, *Das Leben nach dem Tode,* 64 f.; *Id. ZAW.* XVIII. 135; Dr. *Dt.* 40; GFM. *Ju.* 39), but the subject is not yet entirely clear. The words ‏איל‏ (of which the sg. occurs only in proper names), ‏אילה‏, (noun of unity corresponding to ‏איל‏), ‏אילון‏, and the differently pronounced ‏אלה‏ and ‏אלון‏, though carefully distinguished in 𝕱𝕬𝕿, are hopelessly confused in the versions. In Aramaic this is one word ‏אילן‏, meaning *great tree.* The traditional idea (Celsus, *Hierobotanicon,* I. 34 ff.; J. D. Michaelis, *Supplementa,* p. 72 ff.; Ros. *Bibl. Alterthumsk.* IV. 229 ff.; Ges. *Thes.* 50 f.; but on the other side Lowth on Is. 1²⁹; GFM. *Ju.* 121 f.; *ZDPV.* XIII. 220 ff.; We. *Prol.* 248), that certain two or three of the words were used consistently for *terebinth,* and others for *oak,* is not borne out by the versions, and the distinction could not have been indicated in the unpointed text. The words signify "in Hebrew usually, if not exclusively, 'holy tree,' as the place, and, primitively, the object of wor-

ship, without regard to species " (GFM. *Ju.* 121). — ואשמיד] *Yea, I destroyed,*
a repetition of השמדתי, for the purpose of adding the phrase which would
characterize the destruction as *complete;* on 𝕲 ἐξῆρανα, *v.s.* Note î in Hiph.
after wāw cons., as frequently in 1 sg., GK. 53 *n.* — שרשיו] For the same
expression, Is. 5²⁴ 14³⁰ Mal. 3¹⁹. — **11.** מבניהם] The prep. used partitively,
GK. 119 *w*; Kö. 81; Ew.⁸ 217, 1, 1), *b*). — לנב׳] On the use of ל, GK. 119 *t*;
Kö. 327 *v β* 2). — **12.** ותשקו] With a double acc., H. 31, 1; GK. 117 *cc.* In
𝔐𝕿 the wāw cons. construction is continued, notwithstanding the break
caused by the insertion of האף וגו, Kö. 368 *b.* — ועל הנביאים] The chiastic order
again, for emphasis and variety; instead of צוה with acc. of person (*e.g.*
Gn. 26¹¹), the rarer construction of על (still more rare are אל and ל) is used
(cf. also Gn. 2¹⁶ 1 K. 2⁴³ Is. 5⁶ Na. 1¹⁴); the thing forbidden is here (according
to the present text) introduced by לאמר (sometimes with ל and the inf. *e.g.*
Je. 13⁶). — לא תנבאו] In the direct form of one of the "ten words," the negative
separated from the verb by the disjunctive accent, hence dag. lene in ת, GK.
21 *b*; not an entreaty, in which case אל would have been used, but an absolute
command, as if from heaven itself, H. 41, 1 *a, b*; GK. 107 *o.* — **11** *b.* האף]
The interrogative is for rhetorical effect, Kö. 371 *c*; אף (= really) giving
special stress to the following אין, cf. Gn. 18¹³. — נאם] This word occurs about
370 times in the O. T., being especially frequent in Je. (171 times), in Ez. (86
times), and in Am. (21 times). It is distinctively a prophetic word, appearing in all the prophets except Hb., Jon., and Dn., and occurring outside of
prophetic literature only three times, viz. Ps. 36² 110¹ Pr. 30¹. It is followed
by the divine name everywhere except in Nu. 24, where it is used of Balaam;
in 2 S. 23¹, of David; in Pr. 30¹, of Agur (a doubtful text); in Ps. 36², of
transgression personified; and in Je. 23³¹, where it is used as a cognate
accusative. נאם usually comes at the close of a prophetic statement or occurs
parenthetically in the midst of one; it introduces the utterance only in Nu. 24
2 S. 23¹ Is. 1²⁴ 56⁸ Zc. 12¹ Ps. 36² 110¹ Pr. 30¹. It is a noun of the form
qŭtâl like גבול, רכוש, etc. (so Barth *NB.* 82 *e*; Kö. II. 1 p. 501); rather than
a pass. ptcp. (Dr., and most of the older authorities). The root does not
occur in Hebrew in any other form (except Je. 23³¹, where it is a denominative vb.), but cf. Arab. *na'ama = groan, sigh, murmur, whisper,* etc. Hence
נאם probably denoted the divine communication as imparted secretly and mysteriously; cf. the phenomena indicated as accompanying the communication
of Yahweh's word to Balaam (Nu. 24³ᶠ· ¹⁵ᶠ·); the phrase " uncover the ear "
used of God speaking to man (1 S. 9¹⁵ Jb. 33¹⁶, etc.); and Eliphaz's description of the revelation given to him (Jb. 4¹²). נאם is the strongest word
denoting prophetic utterance and especially marks its divine character; it is
best rendered *oracle.* Cf. BDB., BSZ.

13–16. *The impending calamity.* The charge of wickedness
has been made (vs.⁸⁻¹⁰); the futile efforts of Yahweh to save the
nation have been narrated (vs.¹¹·¹²); the end has now come; Israel,

for her sins, must suffer : (1) Yahweh will bring a great calamity ; (2) the strongest will not be able to escape ; (3) the swiftest and most courageous will fall.

This piece, forming the last of the dreadful trilogy, goes back to the trimeter movement. The movement then becomes short and quick, as if by its very form to foretell the coming doom. In view of (1) the difficulties suggested by v.[13] (*v.i.*); (2) the serious interruption of thought between עמיר and ואבר (v.[14]); and (3) the irregularity of the first strophe as compared with the peculiar symmetry which elsewhere characterizes the form of these chapters, there seems to be good reason for assuming the loss of a part of the text, perhaps one or two lines, of the first strophe. On the other hand a complete strophe of four trimeters may be obtained by dividing as follows : —

[לכן] הנה אנכי
מעיק תחתיכם
כאשר תעיק העגלה
המלאה לה עמיר

This arrangement would be fatal to Gun.'s interpretation (*v.i.*).

13. הנה] 𝔊 logically reads לכן, διὰ τοῦτο, before this, לכן having dropped out, because of the frequency with which הנה is employed as an introductory particle, cf. ולכן הנה, Is. 8[7]. — מעיק] 𝔊 κυλίω; 𝔊[A] κωλύω; 'A. τριξήσω; 𝔙 *strideo; 𝔖 I will press* (same root as in Hebrew). Hi. מפיק (so also St., Or. (?), We., Gr., Val., Dr. (?), Now., BDB., Elh., Löhr, Oet.). — תעיק] 𝔊 κυλίεται; 'A. τρίξει; 𝔖 *presses;* 𝔙 *stridet.* Hi. הָפוּק (so St., We., Dr., Now., BDB., Oet., *et al.*). Gr. חפיק (so *e.g.* Elh., Löhr). — העגלה] Some suggest הָעֶגְלָה. — לה] Gun. om. as dittograph. — **15** *a.* יעמר . . . ותפש] Belongs with v.[14], in strophe 2; this arrangement is demanded by the meaning, as well as by the versification. — **14.** מקל] 𝔊 ἐκ δρομέως; 'A. and Θ. κουφοῦ; 𝔗 מְדִּקְלִיל. Gr. מְכֻלָּם. V.[15] is om. in some Mss. of Kenn. and deR., and in the Arabic, probably because of the similar endings of v.[14] and v.[15] as now separated. — **15** *b.* יְמַלֵּט] read יִמָּלֵט, as in 𝔊 διασωθῇ, 𝔖 ܢܬܦܨܐ, 𝔗 יִשְׁתֵּזֵי, 𝔙 *salvabitur* (so Hi., Gr., Seb., Now., Dr., Elh., Oort (*Em.*), Oet., Hirscht). Zeydner (*ThSt.*, IV. 201 ff.; so also Now.) regards the words from וקל (v.[15]) to בגבורים (v.[16]) as a later addition (*v.i.*), while Löhr om. v.[15] entirely as late; so Hirscht (with some hesitation); but cf. Je. 46[9]. Oet. is inclined to om. וקל נפשו . . . (v.[15]); *v.* Baumann, 31. — **16.** ואמיץ וגו׳] 𝔊 καὶ ὁ κραταιὸς οὐ μὴ εὑρήσει τὴν καρδίαν αὐτοῦ ἐν δυναστείαις, for which Wkl. (*Untersuch.* 184 f.), proposes this original text : ואמיץ לב ישכח לבו מִגְבוּרוֹת = "the stouthearted — his heart will forget heroic deeds." 𝔊, according to Wkl., read לב as לא and gave שכח its Aramaic sense, *find.* — בגבורים] 𝔖 כגבור. 𝔊[A] καὶ εὑρήσει τὴν καρδίαν (omitting ὁ κραταιὸς οὐ μὴ), similarly 𝔊[QT] and *Syr.-Hex.*, καὶ ηὑρέθη

ἡ καρδία σου; and 𝕲^{Bab} om. οὐ μή. In view of these facts Hirscht regards
the original text as being ומצא which was corrected to ואמיץ; 𝕲 transl. both
and since the result was in conflict with the preceding vs. added the negative
of his own accord. Similarly Vol., but v. Stek.

13. *I will make you groan in your places just as the threshing
wagon makes the (floor) filled with sheaves to groan*] This is Hoffmann's rendering,* and is the best of the many (v.i.) that have
been proposed. There is nothing in the words themselves, or in
the context, to suggest an earthquake.† The writer's mind is filled
with war, the coming of which (cf. 5^{27} $6^{7.14}$ $7^{9.17}$ $8^{9f.14}$) shall make
men *cry out* in their misery. The appropriate manifestation for
such grief would be uttering of groans, which not improperly might
be compared by the farmer-prophet to the creaking and groaning
of the threshing-floor under the weight of the threshing-sledge and
its full supply of sheaves. This does not differ essentially in thought
from the more common interpretation, *I will press your place, as
the wagon that is full of sheaves presses* ‡ *what is under it* § or *on
the earth;* ‖ or, *I will press that which is among you as a wagon
which is loaded (with stones) presses the sheaves;* ¶ or, *I will press
down upon you as a wagon presses that is full of sheaves;* ** or, *I
will make it totter* (מפיק) *beneath you as a cart tottereth that is
full of sheaves (v.s.).* The lack of clearness here is probably to be
explained by the loss of a part of the strophe. — **14, 15 a.** *Then
shall refuge fail the swift*] Cf. 9^{1b}. The strophe beginning with
these words presents, in four sharp utterances, the utter lack of hope
of any deliverance. Neither the swift (Je. 25^{35} 46^6 Jb. 11^{20}), nor the
strong (Pr. 24^5), nor the hero, experienced in war, nor the armed
man, skilled in handling the bow (Je. 46^9), shall find refuge, or be
able to assert his strength, or rescue himself, or stand (Ps. 102^{26}
Dn. $11^{6.8}$; also Je. 46^{21} Na. 2^8), when the great calamity shall come.
Everything in which men at such times trust shall fail, viz. swiftness,
strength, experience, and skill in the use of weapons of war. —
15, b, c, 16. *And the swift of foot shall not rescue himself*] Cf.
2 S. $1^{2.3}$ 2^{18} 1 Ch. 12^8. This strophe, omitted in some Mss. (v.s.),
repeats the same idea in largely the same words, though differently

---

* *ZAW.* III. 100 f.   ‡ Crocius, Schrö., Ges.   ‖ Schlier, Ke.   ** Ew., GAS.
† Cf. Mit. 96 f.   § So Hd.   ¶ Geb.

arranged. This is not a later insertion (*v.s.*) ; the poet would
picture again, with monotonous vividness, the impossibility of
escape.   Does the phrase *shall flee away naked*] (*i.e.* having abandoned his weapons, armor, or dress which might embarrass him)
contradict what has been said concerning the impracticability of
any effort to escape ?   No, for flight here means *rout*, not *escape*.
But upon the whole strophe and its correspondence to the preceding, *v.i.* — *In that day*] The day which was always uppermost
in the mind of the prophet, the day of Yahweh, described more
fully in 5¹⁸.

   13. הִנֵּה] For other cases of הִנֵּה used to introduce a solemn utterance,
cf. Gn. 6¹⁷ Is. 7¹⁴. — אָנֹכִי] Emphatic and in contrast with the suffix in תַּחְתֵּיכֶם;
otherwise the more common הִנְנִי would be used; cf. Gn. 24¹³ Ex. 4²³.
— מֵעִיק . . . תַעִיק] The ptcp. used here of the immediate future, H. 27, 2 *c*;
GK. 116 *d*; Dr. § 135, 3. This *a. λ.* has given rise to many and widely different interpretations, the chief of which may be classified : (1) Those in which
עוק is given the meaning of the Aramaic צוק *press*, cf. the derivative עקה
Ps. 55⁴, מועקה Ps. 66¹¹: (*a*) both verbs taken transitively : *I will press
you down* (for this use of תחת cf. Jb. 36¹⁶) *as a wagon* (or, *a cow*) *presses*,
etc. (Döderlein, Ew., GAS. *v.s.*); or, *I will make narrow the place for you*, etc.
(Rückert); or (= Arab. عَقّ), *I will cut in pieces, as a threshing roller*, etc.
(BSZ. *s.v.* עוק); (*b*) the first verb trans., the second intrans.: *I will press you
down as a wagon is pressed down*, *i.e.* gives way (Va., De Wette, Ros.,
Mau.); (*c*) both verbs intrans.: *I am pressed under you as a wagon is
pressed*, etc. (Cal., Ba., Pu.). (2) Those in which עוק is translated *creak,
groan* (cf. Arab. عمق), then *tremble, totter :* (*a*) *I groan under you as
the wagon groans* (Os., cf. 'A. and ₣, *v.s.*); (*b*) *I will make you cry out*,
etc. (Jus., Hoffm. *v.s.*). Against which Now. urges the unsuitableness of
the thought as preparatory to v.¹⁴; the uncertainty of the readings in Ps. 66¹¹
and 55⁴ cited in comparison; the difficulty of making המלאה an acc., and of
omitting הגרן. (3) Those involving change of text: (*a*) *I will make it
tremble under you as the wagon trembles* (*v.s.*), by changing עוק to פוק (cf.
1 S. 2²⁹, לפני for לעמי; 2 S. 24⁶, צפן for יען); (*b*) *I will make it tremble under
you as the full wagon makes the sheaves tremble*, with עמיר as object, and לה
omitted (Gun.). (4) עוק = Arab. عوج, *withdraw, flee away; I will cause
your place to yield as the wagon breaks down that is full*, etc. (Hi.'s later view),
the reference being to the earthquake of 1¹, though the words were probably not
spoken, but written afterward. The great majority of these interpretations are
based upon the conception of an earthquake (*v.s.*). (5) עוק = Arab. عوق,
hinder, I will cause a stoppage under you as the threshing sledge (Is. 28²⁷ ᶠ⁻) *stops
(i.e.* no longer turns) *which is choked with straw*; cf. 𝕲ᴬ (*v.s.*) (Wetzstein, *ZAW.*

III. 278).— Hal. renders תחת] as " body," citing Hb. 3¹⁶ Zc. 6¹². — כַּאֲשֶׁר] The
prep. governing the antecedent of the relative, not the relative; cf. H. 46, 3 *c*);
Kö. 63; GK. 138 *e*. — תָּעִיק] Impf. of indef. freq. action, H. 21, 3; Dr. § 33 *b*;
GK. 107 *g*. — הַמְלֵאָה] The art. with ptcp. equiv. to a rel. clause, H. 4, 3 *f*.; Dr.
§ 135, 7; on the Qal. ptcp. of stative verbs, GK. 50 *b*, *d*. — לָהּ] For another case
of ethical dative with ptcp. cf. בּוּדֵר לִי Ho. 8⁹; H. 11, 2 *c*; GK. 119 *s*; Kö. 36;
Ew.⁸ 217, 2, 2) *a*) 3); Dr. *Dt.* 10 *f*, 16.   Note Gun.'s suggestion that לָהּ is a
dittograph of the last syllable of the preceding word (cf. Kö. 402 *l*). — עָמִיר]
Either acc. after הַמְלֵאָה, *i.e.* acc. of spec. (cf. Kö. 327 *f*), or acc. after תָּעִיק
(Gun.).— **14.** מִן . . . וְאָבַד] The ו is consequential, following the ptcp. H. 25, 5;
Dr. § 113 (1); GK. 116 *x*. מֵן with אבר, cf. Je. 25³⁵ Jb. 11²⁰ Ps. 142⁵. — קָל]
Standing alone, even without the article, used as a superlative (so Va.;
GK. 133 *g*).— מָנוֹס] So far as form is concerned, either *flight* (so Ke., Val.),
the noun with מ having the force of the verb, or *place of flight, refuge* (Pu.,
Gun.), the מ denoting place; GK. 85 *e*; Barth, *NB*. 160 *c*. — **15** *a*. תֹּפֵשׂ הַקֶּשֶׁת
לֹא יַעֲמֹד] *i.e.* shall perish, or shall be put to flight. — **15,** *b*, *c*. A comparison
of the second and third strophes, ¹⁴· ¹⁵ᵃ· and ¹⁵ ᵇ· ᶜ·, shows a general purpose on
the part of the writer to repeat the thought with the same words arranged in
a somewhat striking manner.   If עָרוּם might be pointed עָרוּם (*skilled*) rather
than עָרוֹם, and two or three transpositions made, the similarities of the
strophes would become still more striking, the parallelism more perfect, and
a better sense gained.   The following is suggested as a plausible conjecture : —

וְאבד מנס מקל   וקל ברגליו לא יְמַלֵּט
וחזק לא יאמץ כחו   ואמיץ לבו בגבורים
וגבור לא ימלט נפשו   וערום לא ימלט נפשו
ורכב הסוס ינוס ביום ההוא ותפש הקשת לא יעמד

Note that after the first clause, those that remain are circumstantial, adding,
in a subordinate way, details to the main picture.   This may in part be reproduced by the use of the conjunction *while ;* H. 45, 1 *c* ; GK. 156 *d* ; Dr.
§ 162.

Zeydner (*ThSt.*, 1886, pp. 201 f.) supposes that 2¹⁴⁻¹⁶ contains several
glosses, and that, these being rejected, the original text was : —

וְאָבַד מָנוֹס מִקָּל
וְחָזָק לֹא יְאַמֵּץ כֹּחוֹ
וְגִבּוֹר לֹא יְמַלֵּט נַפְשׁוֹ
וְתֹפֵשׂ הַקֶּשֶׁת לֹא יַעֲמֹד
עָרוֹם יָנוּס בַּיּוֹם הַהוּא
נְאֻם יְהוָה

16. וְאַמִּיץ לִבּוֹ] *The stoutest of heart*, an epexegetical genitive, really superlative; GK. 128 *x*; cf. Kö. 336 *h*. — עָרוֹם] According to 𝔐𝕿 an acc. of state,
H. 33, 4; GK. 118 *n*; Kö. 332 *g*.

Summary. *A judgment on Israel:* (1) The nation has sinned grievously, treating the poor and needy unjustly, and oppressing them beyond all measure; until her behavior has become in the eyes of the world a profanation of Yahweh's holy name. (2) This moral condition is due to no lack of effort on Yahweh's part; since he had led Israel out of Egypt into Canaan, had driven out the Canaanites before her, and had given teachers who should declare righteousness to her; but all his care had been without result. (3) For her sins Israel must suffer, the nation shall perish; none, not even the swiftest and strongest, shall escape.

§ 5. The roar of the lion ; destruction is coming. 3^{1-8}. The prophet's first message concerning Israel's future has been delivered. The people, very naturally, refuse to credit his statements. Yahweh is not likely, in their opinion, to desert his own nation. Everything, politically considered, seems to be prosperous. Disaster of any kind is far removed from their thoughts. The leaders are blind to the actual situation. To meet this condition of things, the prophet delivers what may be regarded as the most striking of all his utterances, viz. 3^{1-8}. The ordinary view * which makes this passage an explanation of the prophet's mission, upon the ground that he was compelled by Yahweh's power to speak, although against his will, does not bear close examination.

The strophic arrangement of 3^{1-8} is 2, 4, 4, 4, and 2 lines, each line a pentameter, a movement better adapted to the thought than the trimeter. Strophe 2 seems to have lost one of its four lines, the restoration of which (something like, *But you have forsaken and rejected Yahweh your God*) greatly aids in securing an intelligible interpretation. The effort of D. H. Müller † to connect these vs. ($1-8$), as two strophes, with a third strophe (vs. $9-12$), in each of which there is an allusion to the "lion" in the last line but one, seems arbitrary when one measures the last line of the proposed third strophe, and observes that, in order to meet the exigencies of the theory, in other words, to get in "the lion," he makes it twice the length of any other line. Cf. the arrangement by Löhr which makes vs. $1-10$ consist of three strophes of 10, 6, and 6 lines respectively, involves the omission of vs. $1b.\ 4b.\ 5b$ and 7 and the transposition of $6a$ to follow $6b$, and disregards the irregularity of the length of the lines thereby secured. See also Baumann, 35 ff. Marti treats v.^{3} as a gloss.

---

* This is held by nearly all the commentators; *v.* the partial list of opinions given.   † *Die Propheten*, I. 70 f.

III. 1–3. *A message against the nation which Yahweh brought up out of Egypt : You were chosen for a special work ; but you have forsaken Yahweh, therefore you shall be punished for your iniquities, for there must be agreement between a nation and its God.*

1. Strophe 1 (v.[1]) is made up of two pentameters, and forms the introduction. — בני יש׳] is really superfluous after עליכם and before עַל כל־הם׳, and, since it lengthens the line unduly, may well be regarded as a gloss. — בני] Some Mss. have בית, so 𝕲 οἶκος, and Syr.-Hex. (so also Oet.); cf. 2^{11} 3^{12} 4^5 9^7 with $5^{1.2}$ 6^{14} 7^{10} 9^9. — עַל כל הם׳] 𝕲 connects with foregoing by καί. Löhr and Marti omit 1b as an interpolation due to a desire to make the following speech refer to Judah as well as to Israel. In favor of this might be urged (see Seesemann, Löhr; cf. Baumann): (1) that the sentence is complete with 1a; (2) 1b drags a little; (3) the change of person, from Yahweh to I, is a little awkward; (4) this expresses briefly Amos's theory of divine justice, but this theory in the vs. that follow is developed and applied only to Israel, not to Judah; (5) Amos never uses לאמר to introduce a divine oracle. But this conclusion is not necessary. Amos develops his thesis only against Ephraim, but it is not impossible that in the theme he has Judah in mind also; by means of an addition to an address to Ephraim he briefly indicates that what he is about to say in v.[2] applies to Judah as well as Israel. It is not his function, however, to apply it especially to Judah (so Seesemann). Since v.[3] is synonymous with v.[2b], this interpretation (*v.i.*) solving what has already become a difficult problem (Oort, *ThT.* XIV., 121 f., 138, failing to find any connection between v.[2] and v.[3], and considering the "particularism" of v.[2] inconsistent with the catholic spirit of Amos, regards vs.[1. 2] as an interpolation ; while Now. treats 3^{3-8} as having no logical relation to $3^{1.2}$), in order to secure a logical antecedent for v.[2b] and, at the same time, make the structure of strophe 2 complete, I would suggest that such a line as, *But you have forsaken Yahweh, your God*, once formed a part of the text. — **2.** רק] 𝕲 πλήν; Σ. μόνους. — ידעתי] Gr. יָעַרְתִּי. — מכל מש׳] 𝔖 precedes this with the phrase "from all the peoples," which is probably a marginal note, explaining משפחה, that has crept into the text (so Seb.). — עונותיכם] 𝕲 τὰς ἁμαρτίας (some codd. κακίας); 'A. ἀνομίας; Σ. ἀδικίας; Θ. ἀσεβείας; 𝔖 ܣܟ̈ܠܘܬܟܘܢ; 𝕿 חובֵיכוֹן; 𝖁 *iniquitates.* — **3.** יחדו] 𝕲 ἐπὶ τὸ αὐτὸ καθόλου. — אם נוערו] 𝕲 ἐὰν μὴ γνωρίσωσιν ἑαυτούς (= נורעו), so Marti; but 'A. συντάξωνται; Θ. συνέλθωσιν.

1. The form of statement is intended to arouse the attention of the people, cf. 3^{13} 4^1 5^1 8^4 ; the prophet, according to 𝕸𝕿, addresses himself to the *sons of Israel*] by whom he ordinarily means Northern Israel ;* but here he adds, as if by an afterthought, *the*

---

* So here Cal., Bauer, Schrö., Hi., Ew.

whole family that I brought up, etc.], thus giving to the common phrase a larger meaning.* A better sense is gained by treating בני יש׳ as a gloss, *v.s.* Cf. for this use of *family*, v.², Je. 8³ Mi. 2³. This phrase " reminded Israel proper that any preëminence among the nations of which they might boast was the inheritance of all the sons of Jacob, and it reminded Judah that any danger that threatened Israel threatened them also, so far as they had been guilty of similar transgressions." † The word uttered is *against*] not simply *in reference to* the nation Israel ; and here, as frequently among the prophets, there is the fond allusion to the time when Yahweh *brought her up out of the land of Egypt*] *i.e.* the time when Israel really became a nation. So intense has the thought of the prophet become that he identifies himself with Yahweh. — **2.** *You only have I known*] Not, *acknowledge* ‡ as of the elect, nor *take notice of = love* § (cf. Ho. 13⁵ Ps. 1⁶ Jb. 24¹⁶) ; with the following preposition *from*, the idea is *to distinguish from, to choose*, as in Gn. 18¹⁹ Je. 1⁵ Is. 58³. This thought is found also in Dt. 7⁶ 14² 28¹·⁸·¹³·¹⁴ Ps. 147¹⁹·²⁰. The doctrine that Israel has been chosen by Yahweh for a particular service to the world lies at the basis of every expression of Hebrew thought. Nor is it paralleled by a similar doctrine among other nations ; in any case, the teaching took a stronger hold of Israel. This thought, carried too far, furnished the basis for a superstition almost as deadly as any of those which the Israelitish religion was to displace. Against this superstition the prophets contend. The choice of Israel by Yahweh, they maintain, is not unconditional. Israel must cherish the right mind toward Yahweh, or punishment will come ; and when it comes, it will be all the more severe because of the special privileges which she has enjoyed. Was this idea true? or was it a fancy of the Hebrew people? To answer this question is to place an estimate upon the whole prophetic work. The thought of v.² ᵃ suggests the idea of failure on the part of Israel to fulfil the divine purpose (cf. Ho. 4¹⁰ Je. 5¹⁹ Dt. 31¹⁶ 1 S. 15²³ 2 K. 17¹⁵) because she has rejected Yahweh ; and now *I will visit upon you all your iniquities*] (cf. Ex. 20⁵ Je. 5⁹·²⁹ 11²² 23², etc.), because, Israel,

---

* Os., Geb., Ros., Ba., Hd., Pu., Ke., We.   ‡ Ke.
† Mit.   § Now., Dr., Elh.

you have rejected the unique privileges offered you; because,
although specially chosen, and given a knowledge of Yahweh's
will which others did not have, you have shown yourselves un-
worthy. Calamity is here, as everywhere, pictured as a visitation
of God. Too much stress must not be placed upon *all*, which
does not imply that, while all of Israel's sins shall be punished,
some of those of less favored nations might be overlooked.* Israel's
punishment, declares the prophet, will be the more severe because
her sins have been more heinous; the " all " refers to the sins of
the nation many times repeated. If, now, Yahweh and Israel
have no longer anything in common, can there be harmony and
coöperation as in the past? — **3.** *Can (they) two walk together, if
they be not agreed?*] If, on the one hand, Israel has left Yahweh,
and if, on the other, he is planning for Israel terrible punishment,
what will be the issue? The prophet sees, what other men of his
times do not see, viz. the dissolution of the covenant relationship
which has hitherto existed between Israel and Yahweh. In the
remaining strophes he proceeds to develop this thought. The
interpretations which connect v.[3] with what follows, and make it
to be the thought of the whole, that everything has a definite
cause and works out an ordained result (*e.g.* that two persons,
seen walking together in the wild moorlands of Tekoa, must have
arranged their meeting beforehand, *i.e.* have agreed to be together, cf. Jos. 11[5] Jb. 2[11]),† and that the presence of the prophet
against his will indicates a plan of action formed against them
by Yahweh himself, ‡ proceed from a wrong point of view. Notice should be taken of that other class of interpretations in
which a special allusion is found in נוֹעָדוּ to the agreement between Yahweh and the prophet, conveying authority to the latter, §
or the agreement between Joel and Amos, ‖ or the agreement
among all the prophets, an agreement which indicated the truth
of their message as coming from the Holy Spirit,¶ this assertion
of their authority being rendered necessary because the prophets had been forbidden (2[12]) to prophesy.** That the verse

---

* So Ke.
† Va., Schrö., Hi., Ew., Mit., Now., GAS., *et al.*
‡ St.
§ Cal., Dathe, Bauer, Ros., Mau., Ke., Or.

‖ Munster.
¶ Os.
** Ros., Pu.

refers to the relation between Yahweh and his people was rightly taught by Grotius, Gebhard, Marck, Harenberg, Justi, Schröder, Henderson, Pusey.

1. שִׁמְעוּ אֶת־הַדָּבָר הַזֶּה] does not mark a formal division of the matter (cf. 4¹ 5¹; *contra* Mit.); the prophet both at the beginning and in the middle of his utterances frequently uses this, or a similar phrase, to arouse attention. — דִּבֶּר] Pf. of indef. past, H. 17, 3; Dr. § 9. — עֲלֵיכֶם] The prep. is not used simply as a dat. (Va.; cf. Gn. 2¹⁶), nor does it mean *in reference to* (suggested by Va.); the common force *against* is more appropriate (Ros. and most comm.). — כָּל־הַמִּשְׁפָּחָה] On כל *totality of*, H. 5, 1 *a*, (1). On form of המש, Barth *NB.* 161 *a*; used in this strophe in both its narrower and wider sense, *family* and *nation;* on its derivation from שָׁפַח *pour out, v.* BSZ. 868. — הֶעֱלֵיתִי] On the sudden change of person, see Kö. *Stil.* 249. — אֶרֶץ מִצְרַיִם] Appos. annexion, H. 8, 3 *c*; GK. 128 *k.* — **2.** אֶתְכֶם] Emphatic, (1) in standing before its vb. rather than as a suffix in connection with it, thus furnishing one of the necessary usages of את, H. 11, 2 *b*, (1), GK. 117 *e*; (2) in being preceded by רק. — יָדַעְתִּי] Not a stat. pf. *do I know*, but a pres. pf. *have I chosen;* H. 17, 2; Dr. § 8; GK. 106 *g*, an act of the past the consequences of which, at least in part, continue down to and include the present. — עַל־כֵּן] Implying a statement of Israel's abandonment of Yahweh. — אֶפְקֹד] A future impf. H. 22, 1; GK. 107 *i*; Dr. § 29. — עֲוֹנוֹת] Strictly *error*, cf. the vb. in 2 S. 7¹⁴ 24¹⁷, etc., and Dr. on 1 S. 20³⁰. — **3.** יַחְדָּו] Fuller יַחְדָּיו (Je. 46¹². ²¹ 49³); lit., *in his unities*, acc. of manner (Barth, *ZDMG.* XLII. 356), GK. 118 *q*, Ols. 135 *c*; cf. Gn. 22⁶. ⁸. — בִּלְתִּי אִם From בָּלָה cstr. with archaic ending ‎וּ, H. 41 rm. *e*; GK. 90 *m*; Sta. § 343; found in Phoen. (Tabnith inscr. 5) as conj.; without אם, Is. 10⁴ Gn. 43³; cf. Kö. 392 *a.* — נוֹעָדוּ] lit. *they have made an appointment* (cf. מוֹעֵד *appointed time*).

4, 5. *The roar of the enemy may even now be heard; Israel, unconscious of the fact, is already within the toils.*

In a double figure, that of a lion and his prey, and that of a bird and its hunter, the situation of Israel, in the prophet's times, is portrayed. This situation is the result of the separation of Israel from Yahweh. The difficulty lies in the fact that Israel as a nation has long been deaf to the roaring of the lion, and blind to the hunter and his snare. Only the prophet hears and sees.

The structure of strophe 3 is clear.

4. בִּיעַר] 𝕲 ἐκ τοῦ δρυμοῦ αὐτοῦ. — מִמְּעֹנָתוֹ] Baumann om. — לֹכֵד] 𝕲 adds τί. Löhr om. ⁴ᵇ·⁵ᵇ as being superfluous both in form and thought. — **5.** עַל פַח על פח] 𝕲 ἐπὶ τὴν γῆν, which suggests either the omission of פח (so Oort

ThT. XIV. 134 and *Em.*, Gun, Mit., Val., Now., Elh., Hirscht, Löhr, Oet., Baumann), as having crept in by mistake from the last clause of v.⁵, or, better, the corruption into פח of an original פְגִי (Perles). — [מוקש 𝔊 ἰξευτοῦ (= מוקיש, or מוֹקֵשׁ Vol.); so 𝔖𝔗; Mit. יֻקַשׁ, but cf. Gun. — [יעלה 𝔊 σχασθήσεται, 𝔙 *auferetur* (= חֵיָעֶלה, so also Gr.). — [מן־הֵא' 𝔊 ἐπὶ τῆς γῆς. — [לֹא יִלְכוד 𝔊 adds τι. 𝔖 om. and renders ולכוד, ܠܐܝܣ, but this was not, as Seb., basing his idea upon a certain conception of the passage, suggests, the correct text; for it carries with it lack of rhythm and of good meaning.

4. The prophet is a countryman and deals with phenomena which are familiar to him. For a long time lions have not frequented Palestine, but the testimony is unquestioned that they were common down to the Christian era, and even later.* — *Does a lion roar in the forest when there is no prey for him*] *i.e.* Does he go hunting without securing something? or in declarative form, When a lion roars, his prey is near at hand ; let it beware. The second member is only a variation in form of the first : The young lion does not utter his voice unless he has caught something. In the prophet's mind the people, destined to suffer for their sins, are the prey, which is already, in vision, in the possession of the lion, whose roar, though uttered, the prey has not understood. The prophet's voice is one of warning ; and, now, with change of figure we hear it again ; and this time, likewise, it is a figure which appeals to a countryman. — **5.** *Does a bird fall upon the ground, if there is no hunter ? or does a snare fly up without catching anything ?*] Here, as Mitchell observes, " the order of thought is reversed." The prophet, with his keen insight, perceives that already the bird has fallen, the snare has sprung up. It follows, therefore, that there is a hunter near at hand, invisible perhaps, but none the less real. Cannot the people see that they are entrapped, that they are already within the toils ?

The first couplet (v.⁴) has been interpreted (1) as one of several illustrations of the principle of cause and effect ; nothing happens by chance ; there is always a cause (Reu., Val., Now., GAS., Dr., *et al.*); (2) as describing Yahweh under the figure of a lion (cf. v.⁸, also 1², Je. 25³⁰ Ho. 11¹⁰ ; and, on the roaring of the lion, cf. Ps. 104²¹ Is. 5²⁹ 31⁴ Je. 2¹⁵ Ez. 22²⁵), *i.e.* Yahweh's roar compels me to prophesy (Schrö., Hi.), or Yahweh's roar indi-

---

* Cf. Ju. 14⁵ 1 S. 17³⁴ 2 K. 17²⁵ ; Reland, *Palaestina*, I. 274 ; Van Lennep, *Bible Lands*, 247 ; G. E. Post, art. "Lion," *DB.*

cates imminent danger (Cal., Os., Pu.), or Yahweh's roar should lead to repentance (Geb.), or Yahweh does not threaten, and fail to send punishment (Dathe, Jus., Ros.). It is suggested by some (Ba., Hi.) that in the first clause the roaring precedes and is the cause of capture; while in the second, it is a different roar, viz. that which accompanies the eating and so follows as the result of the capture. According to Geb. the young lion is the prophet who joins with Yahweh in threatening punishment; Hd. suggests that the subject of לָכַד must be אַרְיֵה, not כְּפִיר, since the young lion in the den roars only when the old lion brings home the prey; but the second clause is generally understood to present the same thought as the first (Ros., Ke., *et al.*). Even greater difficulty has attended the interpretation of the second couplet : (1) a bird does not fall upon the ground, unless there be to it, *i.e.* the bird (Hi., Mau., Ba.), or the ground (Hes.), a snare (Cal., Os., Dat., Ros.), or a fowler (Luther, Ba.); in other words, people do not suffer except because of sin; or calamity never comes except by a net which God stretches (Cal., Os., Dat.), or calamity comes through the snare of Jeroboam's false worship (Geb.). The פַּח of v.⁵ ᵇ is " the large net of the bird-catcher which he has to draw up and which takes a number of birds at once" (Ew.). Hence, will the net go up, *i.e.* be taken away (Ew., Hes., Mau.), or treating יַעֲלֶה as Hiph., will the fowler remove the net before, etc. (Cal., Geb., Jus., Schrö.; cf. 𝔖); while many understand it as meaning, the net does not spring up unless a bird has entered it (Os., Hi., Hd., Ke., Now., GAS., Dr., *et al.*). From one or another of these renderings, the thought is inferred to be : Yahweh will surely not desist until his threatenings have been fulfilled (Cal., Os., Ros., *et al.*), or Israel is to be captured by the fowler Satan (Geb.). You cannot escape a punishment which God has announced through the prophets (Dat.). Just as none of these things happen without a cause, so the prophet's preaching is not without cause — Yahweh has revealed to him the coming calamity (so GAS., Now., Dr., Marti, *et al.*).

4. אַרְיֵה [כְּפִיר, אֲרִי)] and אֲרִי, which are but different forms of the same word (Ols. 216 *d*, Barth, *NB.* 237), are the usual words for lion. The original meaning is probably to be seen in the Ethiopic ኣርዌ, *wild beast*. The Arabic أُرْوَى, *wild goat*, is a different specialization of the same idea. Aram. אַרְיֵה, Syr. ‎أَرْيَا‎, Assyr. arû, all mean *lion*. It is the usual word in Hebrew; לָבִיא (Arab. لَبْأَة لَبُوَة, Assyr. labbu) is the poetic word and does not mean distinctly *lioness* (the old view, cf. Ges. *Thes.* 738) although in some cases it is feminine. כְּפִיר is the young lion, but old enough to seek prey, thus distinguished from גוּר *the cub*, usually of a lion. — [וְמֶרֶף אֵין לוֹ] Circ. clause, cf. v.⁵, וּמוֹקֵשׁ אֵין לָהּ, H. 45, 1 *d*; Dr. § 159; GK. 141 *e*. — [אֵין] Cstr. before לוֹ GK. 152 *o*; Ew.⁸ 321 *b*; Sta. § 371 *a*. — יִתֵּן קוֹלוֹ Cf. נְשָׂא קוֹל.— [בִּלְתִּי אִם] Cf. v.³; GK. 163 *c*. — **5.** צִפּוֹר] Here fem., but masc. in Ps. 102⁸ Pr. 7²³; cf. Kö. 252 *a*. — [הֻיעֲלֶה] On the various constructions, *v.s.* — [מוֹקֵשׁ] The whole bird-net or trap is probably expressed by פח (cf. Pr. 7²³ Ec. 9¹²), consisting of two frames covered with nets, which fly together, perhaps the lower one flying up, when the trap is sprung. מוקש is either the mechanism by striking which the bird springs the trap (cf. Wilkinson, *Manners and Customs of the Ancient Egyptians*, I. ser. iii. 37 f., 46; Hoffm. *ZAW*. iii. 101; BSZ.) or, better still, the bait (BDB., Dr.); in any case not a synonym of פח (*contra* Mit. and Hirscht). — לכוד] Inf. abs. prec. the finite vb., intensifying it; H. 28, 3 *a*; GK. 113 *n*, *q*. On the position of the negative, *v*. Kö. 352 *l*.

6, 7. *The calamity comes from Yahweh; but Yahweh always warns; why, then, do not the people tremble?*

Having announced that Yahweh and Israel must now separate and that the latter is to be punished (strophe 2), that a nation, even at this time, is ready to pounce down upon Israel as her prey (strophe 3), the prophet, in strophe 4, asks: Why, when the alarm has been given, do the people not tremble? This calamity, so soon to burst upon them, like every such calamity, is from Yahweh. Do they not understand that Yahweh sends no disaster without having previously made announcement through his prophets?

6. The structure of strophe 4 is chiastic, members 1 and 4 relating to the alarm, members 2 and 3, to the agency of Yahweh. Nothing can be more certain than the close relationship of these two couplets. The versions almost unanimously treat אם as a particle of condition. — רעה בעיר] Hoffm., רָעֶה בְּעֵר (*v.i.*). — עשה] Elh. שָׁנָה. Löhr and Baumann transpose v.⁶ᵃ and ⁶ᵇ. — **7.** Variations exist as to the tense rendering of גלה . . . יעשה, 𝔊 ποιήσῃ . . . ἀποκλύψῃ; 𝔙 *facit . . . revelaverit;* 𝔖 ܓܠܐ . . . ܢܥ . — סורו] 𝔊 παιδείαν (reading a formation from יסר, Vol.); the suffix αὐτοῦ is present in 𝔊ᴬᵠ; 'A. ἀπόρρητον; Σ. ὁμίλιον; Θ. τὴν βουλήν; 𝔖 ܪܙܗ. Oort's suggestion of כֹּה (*Th.T*. XIV. 135; adopted by Gun.) or כֵּן (*Em.;* so also Hal.) for כי (v.⁷) is superfluous. Oet. would place v.⁷ after v.⁸ on the ground that כי of v.⁷ finds no basis in v.⁶; while Löhr, Baumann, Marti, om. v.⁷ as a gloss.

6. *Shall a trumpet be sounded in a city*] as a summons to battle, or in order to give alarm against destructive animals (Jo. 2¹), or against an approaching enemy (Ho. 5⁸ Je. 6¹ Ez. 33³), *and the people not tremble?*] (cf. Ho. 11¹⁰·¹¹ 1 S. 16⁴). Why, then, should not the warnings of the prophet be heard and heeded? — *Can evil*] *i.e.* not moral evil, but misfortune, calamity, disaster (cf. 1 S. 6⁹ Je. 1¹⁴ 18⁸ Is. 45⁷ Gn. 19¹⁹ 44³⁴ Ex. 32¹⁴ Ez. 7⁵),

happen in a city and Yahweh not have caused it?] He is over
all and in all, the author of all fortune, good or ill. — **7.** *But*
(rather than *for*) *he does nothing*] in the way of sending calamity
upon men,* *except he reveal his* (*secret*) *purpose to his servants,*
the prophets] To the prophets, who are Yahweh's servants (cf.
the frequent use of this expression in Jeremiah's times, *e.g.*
2 K. 17¹³.²³ 21¹⁰ 24² Je. 7²⁵ 25⁴ 26⁵ 29¹⁹ 35¹⁵), and as such
represent him in his dealings with men (Gn. 18¹⁷ Dt. 18¹⁸), he
reveals the significance of the calamity, and the purpose which it
was intended to subserve. They are given the knowledge and
are expected to sound the alarm by forewarning and exhortation.
Since, then, every calamity comes from Yahweh to serve a purpose,
and since the prophets, who are the interpreters of the divine will,
have given the alarm, how strange that the people who are in such
danger do not hear and tremble !

6. אם] better understood as an interrogative (= *num*; so many, *e.g.*
Har., Jus., Ros., Ew., Hd., Pu., Reu., Or., We.) than as a conditional part.
(Schrö. apparently, Mit.); rarely (cf. Gn. 38¹⁷ 1 K. 1²⁷ Ju. 5⁸ Is. 29¹⁶) at the
beginning of an interrog. and still more rarely, as here, repeated (cf. Je. 48²⁷
Jb. 6¹²); cf. H. 42, 4 *a*, *b*; GK. 150 *h*; Ew.⁸ 324 *c*, (*c*)). — ועם לא יחררו] Circ.
clause ; note use of לא (not אין, see vs. ⁴·⁵; cf. ויהוה לא עשה), because the vb.
is finite; GK. 152 *a*, *b*; Dr. § 162. — רעה בעיר] Hoffm.'s reading, (1) רֶעָה
(fem. of רַע = תְּרוּעָה; cf. Ex. 32¹⁷), and (2) בְּעֵר, *through a watcher*, i.e. *a*
prophet, is, as Gun. (pp. 59–61) has said, open to the following objections :
1) The word רֶעָה cannot be shown to exist; in Ex. 32¹⁷ it is either to be read
רֵעוֹ with Qᵉrî, or רעה, with a fem. suffix, with Di. 2) רַע is not identical with
תְּרוּעָה, but means, in accordance with the original meaning of the root,
a *tumultuous noise* rather than a *warning cry* (Ex. 32¹⁷ Mi. 4⁹ Jb. 36³³).
3) The reading בְּעֵר for בְּעִיר is very questionable. No text is known in which
עֵר has the meaning proposed, synonymous with prophet. 4) The inference
which Hoffm. draws, that "false prophets do not warn," *i.e.* false prophets
sleep while the true are wakeful, is not warranted by the facts. 5) The
connection with ויהוה לא עשה would be difficult, and Hoffm. does not explain it. — עשה] The 3rd pers. is resumed here; cf. v.²ᵇ; Kö. *Stil.* 256. —
7. כִּי] Does not mean here *for* (to be joined with v.⁸; Schm., Or., Dr.),
nor *namely* (Hi.), nor *surely* (Geb., Hd., BDB., Now.; cf. GAS.), nor is
Oort's suggestion of a change to כה or כֵן necessary; the preceding sentence
is virtually a negative sentence, and כִּי = *but* (Mit.), H. 44 rm. (*d*); GK. 163 *b*;
Ew.⁸ 354 *a*. — וְיֵשֶׂה] Indef. freq., H. 21, 3; Dr. § 33 (*b*); GK. 107 *g*. — לֹא

---

* Cal., Geb., Ros.

דָּבָר . . .] A usual form of expressing *nothing* (cf. Ex. 9⁴ I K. 5⁷ 10⁸ Is. 39²);
cf. also לֹא . . . כל, *no one;* H. 14, 2 *d;* GK. 152 *b.* — כִּי אִם] *except =
unless previously,* H. 48, I *f;* GK. 163 *c;* Kö. 372 *h.* — נִגְלָה] Fut. pf., H. 19, 3;
Dr. § 17. — סֹודוֹ] The old derivation was from יסד, to establish, hence a decree, counsel (Jus.; Ges. *Thes.* 602; Hd.). It is now usually assigned to the
root סור of uncertain meaning (BDB.; Kö. II¹. p. 49; cf. Hom. *ZDMG.*
XLVI. 529). Similar is Syr. ܣ̈ܘܕ̈ܐ, *secret conversation.* סוֹד has the
meanings, (1) confidential discourse, (2) counsel, (3) secret, (4) assembly, here
probably secret, secret counsel, cf. Je. 23¹⁸·²². Löhr (*v.s.*, following Duhm,
and Che. *EB.* I. 154) urges against the authenticity of v.⁷ (1) the difficulty of
explaining כי; (2) the phrase עבדיו הנביאים belongs to Je., Dt., and later literature; (3) סודו occurs nowhere prior to Je.; (4) the poetic structure differs
from that of the context, hence it is to be regarded as an interpolated explanation of v.⁸ᵇ. But an argument from language is at best unconvincing; the
כי can be satisfactorily disposed of as above; and the v. fits well in the strophic
structure here presented.

8. *The enemy having manifested his presence, let every one fear;
Yahweh having spoken, let every one recognize the coming calamity.*

The utterance is the last of the rapidly rising climax, and sustains a close logical connection with what has been said; both
members are thus connected with strophe 2, the first, also, especially with strophe 3, and the second with strophe 4   In view of
the decision to punish Israel for his sins (strophe 2), a movement
has been inaugurated which makes Israel, though seemingly unconscious of the fact, the prey of a mighty nation (strophe 3);
the lion has roared, let every one fear (strophe 5 *a*); Yahweh is
the author of this situation, and has through his prophets announced it, though without effect (strophe 4); *the Lord God hath
spoken,* let every one hear and see beforehand the coming disaster
(strophe 5 *b*).

8. The parallelism is complete and synonymous, although "the lion" and
"the Lord God" do not have the same reference. — שָׁאָג] 𝕲 and 𝔜 render
by futures, ἐρεύξεται, *rugiet,* 𝕾 and 𝕿 by pfs., ܢܗܡ, נָהֵם. — For דִּבֶּר] all
have pfs. — מִי] 𝕲 καὶ τίς in both cases. — ינבא] We. יחרד (so also Now.); and
Che. (*EB.* I. 154) יְכָאֵב; but no change is necessary.

8. The prophet, as has been seen, recognizes in the tramp of
the Assyrian army, which his ear has been quick to catch, the fact
that *the lion has roared*], and, himself hearing it so distinctly, he

does not understand why others should be deaf to it. — *Who is there that does not fear ?*] The purpose of the roaring was to occasion fear ; why is it that every citizen of the kingdom is not terror-stricken and penitent before the approach of this terrible army from the north ? — *The Lord Yahweh hath spoken*] and the words have no uncertain sound. The message given, as always, through his servant, the prophet, and given for the purpose of carrying conviction to the hearts of those who would not see, has been uttered ; *who is it that cannot prophesy ? **] Who is there so blind as not to see this coming misfortune and proclaim beforehand its terrible significance ; in order that, if perchance Israel should hear and repent, Yahweh might order otherwise ? This was the purpose of all prophecy.

8. אַרְיֵה שָׁאָג] Circ. cl. with vb. in pf. (*the lions having roared*) preceding the principal sentence, H. 45, 3 *b*; Dr. § 165; GK. 156 *d*. — מִי לֹא יִירָא] *i.e. who should not fear ?* or *who is there that does not fear ?* or *let every one fear*. On the force of the tenses here and the conditional nature of the sentence *v.* GK. 159 *h*; Dr. § 154. — יְִנָּבֵא] It is not necessary to suppose (Schrö.) that there is here a reference to the event described in 7¹², and that consequently that event took place before the utterance of this passage. The substitution of יחרד for ינבא (*v.s.*) is too prosaic, but harmonizes with the general interpretation adopted above.

§ 6. The doom of Samaria. 3⁹–4³.

In still another form the prophet delivers the message given him to proclaim. (1) So great is the wickedness of the capital city, Samaria, that even Egypt and Philistia, called upon to look within Samaria's walls, are astonished at what they see. (2) But an enemy is coming who will quickly lay waste this beautiful and luxurious city. What remains will be as nothing. Even the altars of Bethel will be included in the dreadful destruction. (3) The women of Samaria, because of their debaucheries, must share the punishment. They shall be carried away captives through breaches in the wall.

This piece, which is entirely separate from the preceding and following, originally consisted of six strophes, each containing four pentameters. To restore this, certain minor changes in the text are necessary as well as the transfer of v.¹⁵ to follow v.¹¹ (see *BW.*, Sept. 1898, pp. 179–82; so

---

* Geb., Ros.; cf. GAS. "who can but prophesy?"

also Elh.; cf. Löhr who places v.[12] after vs.[13. 14. and 15]; and Baumann who places v.[13] between v.[10] and v.[11]). Here again Müller's arrangement of strophes (*Die Propheten*, I. 71) fails, because he has not observed that 4[1-3] belongs with 3[9-15] and, indeed, forms the climax of the piece (so We., GAS.) The first line of each strophe, as rearranged, contains a statement of proclamation or assertion on the part of Yahweh, thus giving great intensity to the whole passage. Still further, the six strophes logically divide them-selves into three groups, each of two, and in the first strophe of each group reference is made to Samaria. Strophes 1 and 2 (vs.[9. 10], vs.[11. 15]) present a judgment scene. Samaria is accused of tumult and oppression. Outside nations are summoned to witness her wickedness and to testify against her. The decision is rendered — punishment, viz. destruction by a foreign foe who will lay waste the whole city. Three clauses are probably interpola-tions: (1) וְאָמְרוּ (v.[9]) merely repeats the idea contained in הַשְׁמִיעוּ and, although in the form רָֽאֵמֹר it would be common, may be thrown out; (2) וַעֲשׁוּקִים בְּקִרְבָּהּ (v.[9]) is very awkward, meaning, not *oppression*, but *the op-pressed;* does not join well with מְהוּמֹת; is superfluous in view of שֹׁד (v.[10]); and entirely spoils the measure of the line (see *BW.*, Sept. 1898, p. 182; so Löhr). (3) נֶאֻם יהוה (v.[16]) does violence to the measure and is tautological after the same phrase in v.[11], which constitutes the first member of the strophe. The transfer of v.[15] to follow v.[11] is justified by the demands of the strophic arrangement, for otherwise all would be confusion; by the closeness of thought in vs.[11 and 15], everything having to do with houses (palaces, winter houses, summer houses); and by the fact that in its present position it makes an anti-climax, while by its removal v.[14] furnishes, in the destruction even of Bethel's altars, the highest point yet reached in the description.

9. ארמנות] Ⓖ χώραις (= ארמות; so also Elh.), or אֲרָצֹות (Vol.), so in vs.[10. 11]. — באשרור] Ⓖ ἐν' Ἀσσυρίοις (= באשור, so also Gr., Wkl. *Untersuch.* 185, Val., Oort *Em.*, Oet., Marti); Elh.: מאשור. — ועל] Elh., יער, omitting ב ארמנות. — ארץ מצרים] Ⓖ τῆς Αἰγύπτου, probably an error for γῆς Αἰγ', which appears in 22 Mss. (so Hirscht). — ואמרו] Baumann om. הרי] Read in sg. with ⒼⓈ and Syr.-Hex.; cf. 4[1] 6[1] (so Oort, *ThT.* XIV. 129; We., Now., GAS., Löhr, Elh., Oet., Baumann); Gr. הָרֵי. — מהומת] Ⓢ sg., Ⓖ θαυμαστά, reading incorrectly, תמוהות, pass. ptcp. of תמה (Drusius, Ba.), Σ. ἀχορτασίας. — בקרבה ... בתוכה] Oort (*ThT.* XIV. 129) בקרבה ... בתוכה — בקרבה ... בקרבה ועשׁוקים] om. as a gloss upon מהומת, which unduly lengthens the line (*v.s.*). — **10.** ידעו] Ⓖ sg. — עשות נכחה] Ⓖ ἃ ἔσται ἐναντίον αὐτῆς (= נכחה ... אֲשֶׁר, Va.). — נכחה] Ⓢ ܡܬܚܒܠܝ, (connecting with יכח, Seb.), Ⓣ אוריחא. — נאם י'] Löhr removes to the end of the v.; Baumann om. — **11.** צר וסביב הארץ] Ⓖ Τύρος κυκλόθεν ἡ γῆ σου ἐρημωθή-σεται, vocalizing צֹר, taking סου from fol. line, dropping י, and adding the vb. Ⓥ *tribulabitur et circuietur terra*. Read יסֹבֵב with Ⓢ (adopted by St., Gun., Seb., We., Gr., Val., Now., Dr., Löhr, Elh., Hirscht, Oet.); this is better than יַסֵּב (Ba.), or יְסָבֵב (Bauer); cf. Hoffm. and Gu., יְסָבִיב; Jus. צרו סביב (but v. Gun.); Oort (*Em.*) וסובב; Rahmer סביב (cited by Hirscht), a dialect form

for שביב = *flame;* Va. צלו סביב; Gr. מָצור, for צר, on basis of Θ; Hal. צר יְצוֹרֵר.
— [והורד] 𝔖 = ותירד, with fol. suffixes in 3 sg. fem. 𝔊 κατάξει. We., וְהֻרַד (so
also Gr., Now., Löhr, Elh., Oet., Hal.). — [ממך] Hal. מַמֶּה. — [ונבזו] Oet., וְנָבֹזּוּ.
— **15.** [והכיתי] 𝔊 συγχεῶ καὶ πατάξω, explained by Vol. as a double
rendering based on a reading, המחי or המותי; cf. 𝔊's rendering of יהֻּמֶם
in 1 S. 7^10. — [ויספו] 𝔊 προστεθήσονται = יספו or נוספו (Va., Oet.) or אספו (Vol.).
— [בתים רבים] 𝔊 ἕτεροι οἶκοι πολλοί; 𝔊^AQ οἶκοι ἕτεροι πολλοί. There is no need
to suppose, with Oort (*ThT.* XIV. 128), that 𝕸𝕿 is corrupt; cf. Baumann,
בתי השן. — [נאם יהוה] Löhr om. as a later addition (*v.s.*).

9–11. *Samaria's wickedness astonishes the neighboring nations.*

9. The opening words accord with the oriental usage of sum-
moning assemblies by proclamation. *Proclaim*] *i.e.* let it be
proclaimed, the word being used indefinitely,* and not addressed
specifically, either to the prophets † (for Amos seems everywhere
to be standing alone in his work), the hostile nations, ‡ or any
general messenger. § — *Over the palaces*] Because either the
upper classes are addressed, as corresponding to the upper
classes of Samaria, upon whom judgment was coming, ‖ or the
palace is the natural place from which proclamation is dissemi-
nated.¶ — *Ashdod . . . Egypt*] The prophets not infrequently
represent pagan peoples as morally superior to the rebellious
people of Yahweh, because the former sin in ignorance, but the
latter with full knowledge.** These two names are representative,
Ashdod standing for Philistia. In explanation of the selection of
these, it has been suggested that they, of all nations, rejoiced
most over Israel's humiliation; †† that these two in contrast with
Edom, Ammon, Moab, Syria, and Phoenicia, stood apart from
Israel; ‡ that they were the nations whose unrighteousness Israel
had experienced; ‡‡ that "even the chief cities of the Philistines
and Egyptians, who indeed are not weak and can tolerate much,
would be amazed, if they saw the mad extravagance and the
injustice in Samaria"; §§ that Ashdod especially was chosen because of its similarity to שד, the word used in v.^10 to denote the
violence of which Amos accuses the people. ‖‖ — *Gather ye upon
the mountain of Samaria*] If the plural is read, the reference

---

* Ros., Mau., Mit., Dr.	§ Hd.	** Cf. Hal.	§§ We.
† Hi., Ke.	‖ Hi., Mau., Ke., Mit.	†† Ew.	‖‖ GAS.
‡ Ba.	¶ Mercer, Ros., Ba.	‡‡ Ke.	

is to the mountains of Ebal and Gerizim, from which may be
seen the mountain or hill on which Samaria is built and on
which the witnesses might stand and look down into Samaria (cf.
1 K. 16²⁴) ; * but the better reading is הר, *i.e.* the mountain or
hill of Samaria (cf. 4¹ 6¹). — *Samaria*] is declared to have been
founded by Omri (1 K. 16²⁴). It is on a hill about three hundred feet high, surrounded on three sides by mountains, but
open toward the west. Later it was fortified, especially by
Ahab, so that it was strongly defended. It took a siege of three
years for Assyria to capture it. From that time on it was of
little importance. — *And see the manifold tumults therein*] In
other words, the turbulent and voluptuous life of the nobles
(Pr. 15¹⁶),† including oppression, ‡ confusion and overturning of
justice, § arbitrary deeds of might, ‖ strife of poor and rich,¶
terrores.** — **10.** *And* (*how*) *they know not to do good*] The ignorance carries with it indifference and hostility (cf. Je. 4²²). The
emphasis is on *know*, all ideas of right having been lost.†† The
reference is, of course, to the wealthy Samaritans. — *These who
treasure violence and oppression*] That is either (1) store up
money and goods which are the fruit of violence (cf. 2⁶·⁷), ‡‡ or
(2) heap up oppression as one heaps up treasure. §§ — **11.** *Therefore*] Because of the iniquities which have been mentioned, for
the existence of which there is ample evidence, *an adversary shall
surround the land*] An *enemy*, ‖‖ rather than *affliction,*¶¶ in view
of the following phrase ; in any case, the invasion is one which
shall include the whole country. — *And he shall strip from thee thy
strength*] The subject is the *adversary* of the preceding clause ;
this is better than to treat the verb as impersonal, *one shall strip,****
or to make it passive, *thy strength shall be stripped from thee,*††
or to understand the subject to be Yahweh. ††† — *And thy palaces
shall be plundered*] The beginning of the more detailed description
of the results of the invasion, the principal effect of which is seen
in the destruction of the more prominent and splendid buildings

---

* So Cal., Jus., Schrö., Ba., Mit., Dr.   † Hes.   ‡ Cal.
§ Jus., Schrö.   ‖ Va.   ¶ Ros.   ** Mich.   †† We.
‡‡ Dat., Va., Schrö., Ros., Ba., Hd., Gun., Now., Dr.   §§ Jus., Pu., We.
‖‖ Cal., Geb., Mich., Mau., Hd., Ke., Gun., We., Now., Elh.
¶¶ Jer., Hi., Hes., Ba., Dr.   *** Hi.   ††† Ba.

of the city. This is continued directly (according to the re-arrangement suggested above) in v.[15]. — *And I will smite the winter house together with the summer house*] The older opinion, that the winter and summer houses were distinct, being built and arranged differently, although close together,* seems to have little support. They were rather different parts of the same house,† the upper story, if there were two, or the exterior, if there was but one story, being used for summer. Cf. Ju. 3[20] Je. 36[22]. An inscription recently discovered at Zinjirli, dating but shortly after Amos's time, furnishes an interesting parallel to this expression. Barrekūb, King of Sham'al, a vassal of Tiglathpileser III., relates his activities in decorating his father's house in honor of his ancestors, the kings of Sham'al, and says, " and it is for them a summer house and a winter house." ‡ — *The houses of ivory*] That is, houses adorned with ivory (cf. Ps. 45[8] and Ahab's house, 1 K. 22[39]), an evidence of great luxury, for ivory was costly (cf. 1 K. 10[18]). All these were houses of nobles rather than of kings. § — *Many houses shall perish*] According to some רַבִּים may be translated *great*, cf. Is. 5[9]; ‖ but the more natural idea is that many houses (cf. 6[11] Is. 5[9] 2 K. 17[5. 6]), even those of the common people, shall be destroyed.¶ The writer sees a great catastrophe, the destruction of every structure in the city.

9. עַל] According to Massora Magna (cf. Mercer, Ba.), here and in twelve other cases, שמע with עַל instead of אל.— בְּאִשְׁדּוֹד] On prep. בְּ after noun in cstr. state to define more closely the force of annexion, H. 9, 2*b*; GK. 130*a*; Ew.[8] 289*b*; Kö. 336*u*; cf. also בארץ. Against 𝔐𝔗 and in support of his own reading (*v.s.*) Elh. urges (1) that the coupling of a Philistine town with the great land of Egypt is unlikely ; (2) that one would not expect only *two* people to be summoned to witness Samaria's corruption, but rather the whole world; (3) that the reference to "palaces" is strange; it is not uncommon to speak of the *land* when the inhabitants of it are really referred to, but "palaces" is never used for the people of the land ; (4) 𝔊's reading אדמות; consequently the reading, " Proclaim to the lands, from Assyria to the land of Egypt," etc., was

---

* Bauer, Ros., Dr.

† Van Lennep, *Bible Lands*, 115; Thomson, *LB.* I. 478; Ri. *HBA.* I. 574–80; Reu.; GFM. *Judges*, 96 ff; *DB.*[2] I. 1403–8; Benz. *Arch.* 111–24.

‡ Quoted by Dr. from an article by Sachau in *Sitzungsberichte d. Akademie d. Wissenschaft*, Berlin, Oct. 22, 1896, p. 1052.

§ Gun., We., Now. ‖ Ki., Cal., Geb., Bauer, Mau., Hd.

¶ Hi., Ros., Ba., Ke., Or., Gun., We., Gu., Mit., Dr., Now., GAS.

probably the original one. But (1) the plural אדמות occurs only once, Ps. 49[12], and there not in the sense of *lands, countries,* but as denoting the landed possessions of individuals; (2) Ashdod, a representative town of Philistia, and Egypt are summoned as two of the lands most closely concerned with Israel's affairs; (3) " palaces," a favorite word with Amos, are mentioned as representative of the ruling classes. — האספו] Niph., with its original reflexive meaning, GK. 51 *c.* — על־הרי] The difference between the sg. הר and the pl. הרי is important; if הר is read, the outside nations are invited into Samaria itself (cf. 4[1] 6[1], *v.s.*). — על] here and 2 S. 17[11] 2 K. 22[20], instead of אל after אסף, according to Massora Magna (cf. Mercer). — שמרון] The name of the city is in Aram. שָׁמְרָיִן, in Syr. سَامَرِين, Assyr. *Samerina.* It probably means watch-tower, from שָׁמַר. Cf. however, Sta. *ZAW.* V. 165–75 ; GAS. *HG.* 346–9. — מהומת] Cf. Pr. 7[11] 20[1]. The pl. may intensify the idea (GK. 124 *e*) or represent a condition finding frequent expression (GK. 124 *f*) ; according to Hi. made pl. by the proximity of the pl. עשוקים; elsewhere (1 S. 5[9. 11] 14[20] Zc. 14[13]) in sg. — עשוקים] Taken (1) as a pass. ptcp., *those oppressed, calumniam patientes* (Jer., Va., Ros.); (2) as connected with מהומת as a case of hendiadys = the great cry of the oppressed (Geb.); (3) as a ptcp. used as a noun (Jb. 35[9] Ec. 4[1]), cf. מלוכה, זבול (Hd., Ba.); (4) as a noun, *oppression* (Jus., Schrö., Mau., and most modern comm.), used collectively and then abstractly, GK. 124 *e*; Kö. 261 *d*; but evidently here it is a gloss (*v.s.*). — **10.** ולא ידעו] Grammatically dependent on ראו (v.[9]), *see . . . and how they do not know* (cf. Ho. 7[10] Je. 2[19] Ec. 6[10]). Cf. GK. 157; Ew.[8] 351 *b* ; Kö. 413 *h*, and *Stil.* 259. — עשות] The inf. as obj. of verb (cf. 1 K. 3[7]; Is. 1[14], etc.); cf. H. 29, 1 *d*; GK. 114 *c*; Kö. 399 *i.* — נכחה] Fem. for neut., cf. רעה, Gn. 50[20]; נקלה, Je. 6[14]; נכונה, Ps. 5[10] ; cf. H. 2, 2 *b* (2) ; GK. 122 *q.* — האצרים] Cf. construction of השאפים (2[7]); Kö. 411 *f*; GK. 126 *b.* — **11.** צר וסביב] Besides the textual changes above, the following constructions have been suggested: (1) the supplying of יבא (Ros.); (2) סביב = סביבות used as a prep., Ps. 50[8] (Hi.); (3) supply צר יהוה after ו (Ros.), the ו = *and indeed,* cf. Je. 15[13] Ez. 13[7. 22] (GK. 154 *b*); (4) בְּכָל־ = סביב; cf. 2 K. 17[5] (Hd.); (5) סביב לְ = סְביב; cf. Ex. 16[13] 40[33] Nu. 1[53], לְ here omitted on account of the sententious brevity of the message (Ba.,), cf. Kö. 319 *q*, 375 *d.* — וְהוֹרִד] î written defectively ; for subj. have been suggested, צר (Mau.), Yahweh (Ba.), הַמּוֹרִיד (Hi.), H. 37, 2 *c*; GK. 144 *d, e*; Ew.[8] 294 *b* (2); cf. v.[3] Is. 63[6]; We.'s reading וְהוּרַד is suggestive, but not really necessary. — חֻמֵּךְ עֻזֵּ] A change in the suffix from the 3d m. pl. to the 2d f. sg., *i.e.* to the city of Samaria or the Israelitish nation, GK. 122 *h* ; Ew.[8] 317 *b* ; עו = might, with the idea of glory (Ke.), not fortresses (Ew.), which would require a more specific word (Ba.); cf. כבוד, תפארת, Ps. 29[1] 96[6] 132[8]. — נָבֹזּוּ] On form, GK. 67 *t.* — **15.** וְהִכֵּיתִי] The use of the 1st p. is no more striking after נָבֹזּוּ (v.[11]) than, according to 𝕸𝕿, after . . . וְנִדְעֵעוּ וְנָפְלוּ (v.[14]); on יִ־, instead of יֵ־, GK. 75 *f.* — בֵּית הַחֹרֶף] On annexion as a substitute for the adjectival construction, H. 8, 3 *d* ; GK. 128 *q* ; here used collectively. — עַל] *together with* = *and,* cf. Gn. 32[12] 28[9] (Ros.,

Mau., Or., We., Mit., Now.), not *upon*, *i.e.* the stones of one falling upon those of the other (Ba., Ke., GAS.).—[בָּתֵּי הַשֵּׁן] On בָּתֵּי = bât-tê, GK. 96 ; Sta. § 187 *a* ; BSZ. and BDB. *s.v.* הַשֵּׁן (also 1 K. 10¹⁸; cf. Ez. 27¹⁵) is for the fuller שֶׁנְהַבִּים, *tooth of elephants* (cf. 1 K. 10²² 2 Ch. 9²¹). For further allusion to houses of this kind, see 1 K. 22³⁹ Ps. 45⁹.—[וְסָפוּ] Pf. 3 pl. of סוּף, cf. Is. 66¹⁷ (BDB.), or of ספה, cf. Je. 12⁴ (suggested by Ros., cf. BSZ. where it is assigned to both roots !).—[בָּתִּים רַבִּים] Singularly like the Assyr. *bîtu rabû*, the ideographic equivalent of the word *ekallu*, הֵיכָל, which has gone over into Heb., Aram., and Syr. The Assyr. *ekallu* is itself a loan-word, being the Assyrian form of the Sumerian *e-gal* = great house. The phrase here may then be equivalent to הֵיכָלִים = palaces.

12–14. *Nothing will be left to Samaria's luxurious nobles; and even the altars of Bethel will be destroyed.*

These strophes furnish pictures in detail of the coming destruction, the first, of its effect upon those who have been living lives of luxurious ease ; the second, of its effect upon the religious institutions of the period.

12. [כרל] Hoffm. (*ZAW.* III. 101 f.) לְכַד.—[וְנִגְלוּ] S ܢܰܦܫ = *shall be carried away*, which makes better sense, unless with We. we understand the last part of the line to have been lost, *e.g. from the invading enemy.*—[בשמרון] Oort (*ThT.* XIV. 128; so Baumann) om. as a later insertion.—[בפאת מטה] 𝕲 κατέναντι τῆς φυλῆς (explained by Hirscht as = לקראת מַטֶּה; by Oort, *loc. cit.* as = בפני מ'; cf. Stek. 102); cf. Θ. κατέναντι κλίματος; S ܣܬܘܢܐ ܕܥܠ ܣ̈ܦܣܝ (= בפתאם מַטֶּה, א and ת having been transposed, ס being a dittograph; Seb.); 𝕿 בתקוף שולטן = *in the strength of power.* Oort, בִּמְשִׁתֵּי מטה (so also Val.); Hal. בְּכָסַת מ'; Marti, צפית *cushion.*—[ערש] 𝕲 ἱερεῖς; against the explanation of Jer., adopted by most critics, that 𝕲 did not understand the meaning of the word and so merely transliterated it, ἐρες, and that it was afterward modified, Hirscht rightly urges the fact that in 6⁴ 𝕲 renders ערש correctly; 𝕲^{Q mg}, Σ., Θ., and Syr.-Hex. have κλίνη, and some codd. κλίνει, following Δαμασκῷ. S has ܟܡܐܠ (= ארץ), which may be a part of the translation of וּבְדֶמֶשֶׁק, as it was vocalized (Seb.), ערש being wholly omitted. 𝕿 רְחִיצִין = *trust*, which points to a different reading from 𝕸𝕿, since in 6⁴ ערש is rendered correctly. On the basis of 𝕲's rendering, and the supposition that 𝕲S𝕿 all point to a word ending with ם, while 𝕿 seems to have read a word beginning with כ, Hirscht proposes כִּסְלָם (= *their confidence*). 𝖁 has *Damasci*. Hoffm.'s proposal to read *Damascus*, and to connect ¹²ᵇ, beginning הישבים, with v.¹³, does not commend itself. We. suggests that דמשק is a corruption of some word corresponding to פאת. Löhr om. הישבים ונו' as a gloss combined from 3⁹ 4¹ 6⁴. Elh. proposes ובכר דַמֶשֶׁק ערש, the construction being like that of כלי חמדת בית יהוה in 2 Ch. 36¹⁰. Oet. וּבְמַרְבַּדֵּי ערש, cf. Pr. 7¹⁶. Gr. וּבְשָׂמִיכַה ערש, cf. Ju. 4¹⁸,

Margolis (*AJSL.* XVII., 1901, 170 f.), וּבְשִׁיק ערשׂ, translating: "So shall the children of Israel that dwell in Samaria rescue the corner of a couch and the leg of a bed," regarding ד as dittog. of ב, and מ as dittog. of שׂ, and treating ב as ב of accompaniment, נֵצֵל בְּ, meaning "escape with, rescue." Che. (*EB.* I. 149) substitutes משכב for דמשק; Duhm and Marti, דַּבֶּשֶׂת. — **13.** ארני יהוה אלהי הצבאות] 𝕲 κύριος ὁ θεὸς ὁ παντοκράτωρ, omitting ארני; so also 𝕻. 𝕾 "the Lord of Hosts, the Mighty One, the God of Israel," reading apparently ארני יהוה צבאות אלהי ישראל; probably the אלהי ישראל is a gloss explaining יהוה הצבאות (Seb.). Löhr om. the whole of v.[13b], נאם יה׳ וגו׳, as a later addition having no place in the original strophic structure. — **14.** מזבחות] Oort מַצֵּבֶת (*ThT.* XIV. 142; so also Val., Elh.; cf. Stade and Marti). We. om. v.[14b] as a later addition which is wholly foreign to the context (so also Now., Löhr; Che. *EB.* I. 154; Bu., art. "Amos," *Jew. Enc.*), but *v.i.*

12. *As the shepherd rescues from the mouth of the lion*]. The mind of the prophet reverts to his own experiences,[*] and not simply to a popular saying[†] (cf. 1 S. 17[34 ff.] Is. 31[4]). The shepherd (cf. Ex. 22[13]) was accustomed to produce the remains of a beast as evidence. Amos's references to lions are not infrequent; cf. 3[4. 8] 5[19]. The force of the comparison lies in the insignificant character of what is rescued, viz. *two legs or a piece of an ear*], the merest remnant, something, indeed, not worthy of mention. Some[‡] think of an allusion to a variety of goat with exceedingly large ears, which would be of sufficient value to account for the shepherd's rescuing them at such danger to himself; but this is unnecessary. — *So the children of Israel shall be rescued*] There is to be added, perhaps, *from the enemy* (*v.s.*) ; cf. the rendering *rescue themselves* ; [§] in other words, practically none of the Israelitish voluptuaries described shall be saved, there being no possible reference to the remnant referred to in 9[9], an idea so cherished by Isaiah (6[13]). [‖] — *They who sit in Samaria on the corner of a couch, on the damask of a divan*] One may put aside without much consideration most of the interpretations proposed for this passage, *e.g.* (1) the inhabitants dwelling in two particular streets in Samaria, viz. *Peath Mittah and Demesek Eres* ;[¶] (2) by hypallage, for in a bed of extremity,[**] *i.e.* brought from afar, and in a couch of Damascus,[††] *i.e.* covered with Damascene

---

[*] Ros., Schrö., Hd.   [†] Hi.   [‡] Jus., Hd.   [§] Ew., Ke.   [‖] *Contra* Ba.
[¶] Based upon the use of יֹשְׁבִים rather than שֹׁכְבִים (Drusius, cited by Geb.).
[**] בְּמִטַּת פאה.   [††] בערש רמשק.

G

stuff; * (3) those few should be saved who had crept into beds for safety, into couches covered with Damascene stuff; † (4) in Samaria, that is, in the corner of a bed, etc., the city being thus compared to a bed from its geographical position; ‡ (5) there shall be saved only the sick lying on couches; § (6) shall secure themselves with the corner of a couch, etc., connecting בפאת וגו׳ with יִנָּצְלוּ. ‖ We have a picture of Samaria's nobles lying free from care on soft couches (6¹).¶ Perhaps there is contained a thrust at the new court method of sitting on the corners of sofas instead of lying on them.** — **13.** *Hear ye*] Addressed, not to the Egyptian and Philistine nobles who are thus commissioned by Yahweh to make to his people the announcement of their doom,†† nor to Israel herself, ‡‡ nor to the few faithful, §§ nor to the prophets (*v.s.*); ‖‖ but for rhetorical purpose, to individuals among the people, or to any who might hear.¶¶ — *And testify against*] Meaning more than *declare unto*, cf. Gn. 43³ Dt. 4²⁶ 30¹⁹. — *The house of Jacob*] *i.e.* the house of Israel (cf. 9⁸ with 9⁹); but the writer means not all Israel (3¹), who would have an interest in and be witnesses of the sin and punishment; *** but rather the ten tribes (7¹⁰),††† as is indicated by the mention of Bethel. — *The declaration of the Lord Yahweh, the God of Hosts*] Cf. similar expressions in 5¹⁴ 6¹⁴ Ho. 12⁵ Is. 1⁹·²⁴, here either wholly or in part a gloss; *v.s.* for the great variations of the versions. — **14.** *That*] What follows is an object clause after *testify against* (v.¹³); cf. the renderings, *for,* ‡‡‡ *surely.* § — *In the day that I visit the transgressions of Israel upon him*] *i.e.* when the threatened disaster comes. — *I will inflict punishment upon the altars of Bethel*] Peculiar sacredness attached to the altars (cf. 2⁸) at Bethel, for here Abraham and Jacob had erected altars (Gn. 12⁸ 35⁷), and here sacrifice had been offered in all later times (1 S. 10³). Allusions to the worship at Bethel are found in 1 K. 12²⁸·³¹ 13¹·² Am. 9¹ Ho. 4¹⁵ 10¹·²·⁸. The destruction of these altars meant in reality the entire abolition of Israel's worship, and was the greatest blow which could be struck. Wellhausen argues that v.¹⁴ᵇ

is an interpolation, because (1) not the altars but Samaria's aristocracy are the sinners, (2) the sins of Samaria's aristocracy
could not be visited upon Bethel's altars, and (3) in the preceding
verses and in v.[15] Amos speaks of Samaria's excesses; but this is
not convincing, for (1) just as the punishment threatened, takes, in
one case, the form of destruction of dwelling houses, so it takes
here the form of destruction of religious structures; (2) Bethel is
described by Amaziah as a sanctuary of the king and a royal residence (7[13]), and its destruction would mark the humiliation of the
royal house, as well as the disappearance of the last refuge of the
people (1 K. 1[50] 2[28]);* (3) as has been shown above, v.[15] is to be
taken with vs.[11, 12], and this utterance is the highest yet reached in
the prophetic climax. — *Horns of the altar*] An important part of
the altar, since they were needed for the performance of a certain
part of the ceremony (Lv. 4[30]).†

12. ויציל] Impf. of def. freq., H. 21, 2; Dr. § 33 (*a*); GK. 107 *g*. — . . . הרעה
האריה] On the use of the article, GK. 126 *r*. — שׁתי] On form, GK. 97 *a*, note;
Sta. § 361 *b*. On use of the numeral with the dual to express a certain emphasis,
GK. 88 *f*; Kö. 257 *d*. — או] Used especially in legal expressions. — בדל] Only
here; cstr. of בְּדַל, *a piece*, from בָּדַל, in Hiph. *divide;* = תנוך, lobe of the ear,
Ex. 19[20]; but note the suggestion of לבד (*v.s.*); cf. Is. 26[13] (cf. Gun. *per contra*).
— הישׁבים] Hoffm.'s conjecture that with this word v.[18] begins, *O ye who dwell*,
etc., etc., hear, has nothing for its support; it goes better with what precedes.
The ptcp. with the art. = rel. clause, GK. 126 *b*. The usual objections to
the 𝔐 of this clause are: (1) on the basis of the rendering *Damascus*,
(*a*) that the presence of Israelites in D. is inexplicable, (*b*) that some word
corresponding to בפאת is necessary before ערשׂ; (*c*) that it requires a change
of pointing, viz. דַמֶּשֶׂק; (2) on the basis of the rendering *damask*, (*a*) that in
the time of Amos Damascus was not renowned for the manufacture of
the material now named after it, (*b*) the old versions are all against it,
(*c*) in Arabic the name of the material (dimaḳs) differs from that of the city
(Dimaksh), so that it is doubtful whether there really is any connection
between the two. Cf. Fränkel, *Aramäische Fremdwörter im Arabischen*, 40,
288; Kö. *Stil.* 26 f.; BDB. For the various attempts to emend the text *v.s.*
— **13.** ארני יהוה אלהי הצבאות] This is the only occurrence in the O. T. of this
full title. Other combinations with צבאות in Amos are יהוה אלהי הצבאות, 6[14];

---

* Mit.

† On an Aramaic inscription from Teima, to the S.E. of Edom, an altar is
represented with horns, curved like those of an ox, rising from the corner. Perrot
and Chipiez, *History of Art in Sardinia, Judaea*, etc., I. 304.

‫5¹⁶‬, ‫אלהי צבאות‬ ‫יהוה‬; ‫4¹³ 5¹⁴ f. 27 6⁸‬; ‫הצבאות‬ ‫יהוה‬ ‫אדני‬; ‫9⁵‬, ‫אדני‬ ‫צבאות‬ ‫אלהי‬ ‫יהוה‬. ⅌ has ‫צבאות‬ also in ‫9⁶, ¹⁵‬. Other divine titles used in Amos are: ‫יהוה‬, 54 times; ‫יהוה‬ ‫אדני‬, 19 times; ‫אדני‬, 3 times; and ‫אלהים‬, once, viz. ‫4¹¹‬. Löhr (p. 58) maintains (1) that of the titles in which ‫צבאות‬ appears, the oldest one is ‫צבאות‬ ‫יהוה‬, a form not appearing in Amos, but especially frequent in Is., Je., Hg., and Zc.; (2) that ‫צבאות‬ was not used at all by Amos, but is to be ascribed to later editors wherever it appears in the book; (3) that the earliest passage in which ‫צבאות‬ appears is 2 S. 5¹⁰, which belongs to the 9th century, and shows that the name has been long familiar to the people; (4) that the earliest use of ‫צבאות‬ that has come down to us was that which denoted Yahweh's warlike might, and (5) that later it came to denote Yahweh as the ruler of the powers of nature. The title is distinctly of a prophetic character, occurring only in the prophets, the prophetic histories, and in six Psalms of a prophetic tone. For other discussions of the meaning and use of the name see De. *ZLTh.*, 1874, pp. 217 ff.; Schra. *JPTh.*, 1875, pp. 316 ff.; Sm. *Rel.* 185; Kautzsch, *ZAW.* VI. 17 ff., 260; Dr.; BDB. — **14**. ‫בְּיוֹם‬] in cstr. relation with the following inf., which serves as protasis, H. 29, 1, *b*; GK. 114 *b*. — ‫וּפָקַרְתִּי‬] The ‫ו‬ marks the apodosis, H. 25, 2 *d*; GK. 112 *mm*; Kö. 367 *z*; acc. to Ew. the protasis includes all of v.¹⁴, the apodosis beginning with v.¹⁵. — ‫קַרְנוֹת‬ . . . ‫מִזְבְּחוֹת‬] Pl. fem., referring to inanimate objects, H. 2, 2 *b* (1); GK. 122 *m, n*.

IV. 1–3. *The women of Samaria who by their debaucheries have oppressed the poor will be carried away captive through breaches in the walls of the city.* The fifth and sixth strophes close the piece and present in form and thought an almost perfect climax.

At first sight the pentameter seems to have been abandoned; but a study of the double strophe, as a whole, shows a purpose in this on the part of the artist. One serious difficulty remains, however, upon any hypothesis of construction, viz. the evident shortness of strophe 5, line 2, ‫שֹׁמְרוֹן‬ ‫בְּהַר‬ ‫אֲשֶׁר‬ (4¹). It is probable that a word like ‫ישבו‬ has dropped out after ‫אֲשֶׁר‬. The tetrameter of lines 3 and 4 is explained by the evident desire for double phrases ending in ‫ות‬ and ‫ים‬‗, by the length and full sound of two of these phrases thus brought into juxtaposition, and by the preparation of the poet for the climactic effort which is to be made in strophe 6. This last point will perhaps also explain the shortness of strophe 6. Having now used every art at his disposal with which to prepare for the final scathing words of taunt and rebuke, line 3 is drawn out with words long and strong sounding, while line 4 is still longer and stronger, a fitting expression of the terrible thought which has been accumulating. Isaiah, in later times, adopted not only the idea of reaching a climax, in the description of a coming calamity, by charging the women with responsibility because of their debaucheries, but also the use of words ending in ‫ות‬ and ‫ים‬

for the effect of the sound. Cf. Is. 3$^{18-23}$, in which this method is developed at great length and most skilfully.

1. [הבשן] 𝔙 *pingues;* 𝕿 נְפְסַיָּא; Σ. αἱ βόες εὔτροφοι; other versions treat as proper name.— [לאדניהם] We. לאדניהן; so also עליכן and אתכן (v.²) (so Now., Elh., Oet., Löhr).— [הביאה] 𝔊𝔖 pl., and add *to us* (= לָנוּ); this, if original, would make five words in this line.—**2.** [אדני יהוה] 𝔊 om. one of these titles, having merely κύριος. Gr. בנפשו, 𝔊 κατὰ τῶν ἁγίων. Gr. בקדשו, [בקדשו] 𝔊 κατὰ τῶν ἁγίων. Gr. בנפשו, cf. 6⁸ Je. 51¹⁴.— [כי] Baumann om.— [ונשא] 𝔊 καὶ λήμψονται; similarly 𝔖𝔙. We. וְנִשָּׂאוּ (so Gr., Now., Elh., Oort *Em.*, Oet., Hirscht).— [בְּצִנּוֹת] 𝔊 ἐν ὅπλοις; 'A. ἐν θυρεοῖς; Θ. ἐν δόρασι; 𝔖 ܒܙ̈ܝ̣ܢܐ; 𝔙 *in contis;* 𝕿 עַל תריסיהון. — [ואחריתכן] 𝔊 καὶ τοὺς μεθ' ὑμῶν; 𝕿 ובנתכון.— [בסירות דוגה] 𝔊 εἰς λέβητας ὑποκαιομένους ἐμβαλοῦσιν ἔμπυροι λοιμοί, of which, according to Vol., εἰς λέβητας is the translation of בסירות, ὑποκαιομένους an explanatory addition, ἐμβαλοῦσιν a vb. supplied from the context, and ἔμπυροι λοιμοί (= *burning plagues*) an erroneous translation of דוגה. 𝔊^{AQ} om. ὑποκαιομένους ἐμβαλοῦσιν; 7 codd. om. ἔμπυροι λοιμοί; hence Hirscht regards 𝔊 as containing a double rendering of דוגה, which was either unknown to the translators or else illegible. — [סירות] 𝔖 ܣ̈ܝܪܐ.— [דוגה] Gr. דָגָה, on basis of 'A. ἰχθυδίων, and 𝔖 ܘ̈ܝ̈.— **3.** [ופרצים תצאנה אשה נגדה] 𝔊 καὶ ἐξενεχθήσεσθε (= ותוצאנה) γυμναὶ κατέναντι ἀλλήλων, of which γυμναὶ κατέναντι is probably a corruption of γυναῖκες ἔναντι (so Va., Ba., Hirscht), or perhaps γυμναὶ = פרוצות, cf. Lv. 13⁴⁵ Nu. 5⁸ (so Vol.). Gr. או פרצים. Hal. וְנֶגְדָּהּ.— ...וּפ' תְּצָאנָה א' [השלכתנה] 𝔊 ἀποριφή-σεσθε; so 𝔙, reading וְהָשְׁלַכְתְּנָה; cf. 𝔖 ܘܬܫܠܡ̈ܢ.— [ההרמונה] 𝔊 εἰς τὸ ὄρος τὸ Ῥομμάν (= הר הרמונה); Θ. εἰς τὸ ὑψηλὸν ὄρος; 𝔙 *in Armon;* 'A. Ἀρμονᾶ; Σ. εἰς Ἀρμενίαν; 𝕿 הרמני; 𝔖 ܘ̱ܝ̈ܡܢܐ. Many emendations have been suggested for these last two words, *e.g.:* Hi. וְהִשְׁלַכְתֶּן הַהַר מוּנָה (מוּנה being a contraction of מעונה) = and ye shall be cast out on the mountains as a refuge. Ew. ההר רמונה = and ye shall cast Rimmonah to the mountains. Ba. וְהָשְׁלַכְתֶּן הֲדַר רִמּוֹן. New. והשלכתינה החרמנה = and I will cast it forth utterly destroying it. Döderlein and Dahl, חֶרְמוֹן, the former translating "Schlachtbank," the latter "Verweisungsort." Meier (*SK.,* 1842, pp. 1028 f.) וְהִשְׁלַכְתֶּנָה הָהָר מוּנָהּ = and ye shall cast (each one of you) on the mountain her false god, מונה being derived from מון = divide, decide (cf. Arab. مَان, to lie), and meaning *an image, an idol;* cf. תְּמוּנָה (Jb. 4¹⁶ Dt. 4¹⁶ Ex. 20³). Gr. וְהִשְׁלַכְתְּנָה הָרָה ארמונה. Kö. (II. i. p. 459, N. 5), ההרה חרמונה. Hi. (1st ed.), וְהִשְׁלַכְתֶּן הֲדַר רִמּוֹן (so also St., Gun.). Elh. וְהֻלַּכְתֶּן הַהֲרֹמוֹנָה (so also Gun. *ThSt.* XVIII. 218). Oet. וְהִשְׁלַכְתֶּנָה אֶת הָרֲמוֹנָה (cf. Or. הָרֲמוֹנָה). Löhr. ההר רמון. Oort, ההרמונה. Mit. והשליך את ארמנות שמרון = toward the highlands of Ramman, *i.e.* Syria. Che. (*EB.* II. 1966), וְתִשְׁכַּלְנָה בַּקְּדֵשׁוֹת. Hal. הַכַּרְמֶנָה (cf. Is. 20¹⁰ Je. 22¹⁹). Marti, עֲרֻמּוֹת. The original text seems to be beyond recovery (so We., GAS., Now., Dr., *et al.*).

1. *Ye kine of Bashan*] The attention of the prophets is not infrequently turned to women (cf. Is. 3¹⁶ 4¹). The women of the times are here designated by a figure strikingly appropriate. Bashan * was the northernmost of the three great divisions of the mountainous range east of the Jordan, reaching to the Yarmuk, south of which were Mt. Gilead and Ha-Mîshôr, and was known for its *oaks* (Is. 2¹³ Ez. 27⁶ Zc. 11²), its *pastures* (Mi. 7¹⁴ Na. 1⁴ Je. 50¹⁹), and especially its *cattle* (Dt. 32¹⁴ Ps. 22¹² Ez. 39¹⁸), which are represented as being both fat and ferocious. The allusion is not to the men,† especially judges and counsellors, called *cows* by way of contempt, which supposition would explain the masculine form of שְׁמָעוּ ; but, in view of פרים, Je. 50²⁷ Ps. 22¹², where men are intended, and the feminine forms occurring so frequently in the passage, to the noble women and princesses ‡ who are now rebuked because of their sins.— *Who . . . in the mountain of Samaria*] Cf. above and on 3⁹.— *Injure the poor and crush the needy*] Not directly, to be sure, but through *their husbands*] (cf. 2⁷ 8⁶), not the rich, § of whom the rulers ask bribes, for oppressing the poor ; nor the kings and princes ‖ urged to intemperance by their counsellors ; nor the king, the plural being a plural of excellence (cf. Gn. 40¹ 2 S. 10⁸), but the lords, or husbands of the debauchees ¶ (cf. Gn. 18¹² 1 K. 1¹⁷ ff. Ps. 45¹¹), the masculine suffix being due to carelessness, to whom they say *bring that we may feast*], *i.e.* the husbands are induced to deal oppressively with the poor in order that they may procure the viands needed for their wives' debaucheries (cf. Is. 28¹ ff.), which, from the general character of the language, may be understood to have included drinking, feasting, and wanton luxury of every kind.— **2.** *The Lord Yahweh hath sworn*] Cf. similar expressions (6⁸ 8⁷).— *By his holiness*] Not by his sanctuary, § the temple at Jerusalem by which, as the symbol of his holiness, he may swear ; nor by his holy name ** (Je. 44²⁶) ; but rather by his majesty,†† " his sacred awe-

---

* Wetzstein, *Hauran*, 39–42, 83–6; Gu. *ZDPV.*, 1890, 230 ff. ; GAS. *HG.* 53, 549 ff. 575 f., and art. " Bashan," *DB.* ; Dr. art. " Bashan," *EB.*

† Jer. (fol. ℭ), Cal., Os., Mercer, Har., Dat., Hd.

‡ Geb., Jus., Va., Hi., Ba., Ke., Gun., We., Now., GAS., Dr. § Cal.

‖ Ros., Mau., Hd.

¶ Geb., Jus., Va., Ba., Hi., Ke., We., Dr. ** Va. †† Jus., Schrö., Ros., Now.

inspiring personality,"* with the implication that he will vindicate
his holiness by inflicting punishment for sin.† — *Days are coming
upon you*] The sad and serious forecast of gloom and wretched-
ness so common in prophecy (cf. 8¹¹ 9¹³ of the bright future, 1 S.
2³¹ 2 K. 20¹⁷ Is. 39⁶, and fifteen times in Je., *e.g.* 7³² 16¹⁴). —
And ye shall be taken with hooks] The translation *shields*‡ gives
no sense here ; the same is true of *thorns* ;§ the figure is that of
fish (no longer *cows*) caught by *hooks*.‖ This is better than to
understand the representation of animals led by rings in their
noses.¶ — *Even the last of you*] That Amos does not mean here
their *posterity* ** (cf. Je. 31¹⁷ Ps. 109¹³ Dn. 11⁴) is clear from 7¹⁷, in
which he looks forward to an immediate destruction.   In the
synonymous member, for the sake of emphasis, he adds that even
of those, if there are any, who may be left, the last without exception shall suffer in like manner, viz. be carried away *with fish-
hooks*] thus interpreting the expression already given.†† The
older interpretation *pots* was strange enough in connection with
the word הונה, fish.   Calvin's idea, that though they thought themselves so large they should be carried away by a very small instrument (fish-hooks), and Gebhard's, that the instruments were poles
sharp like thorns, which were to be used for rescuing the women
from fish-ponds into which they had fallen, are equally absurd ; cf.
the view of G. A. Smith that, the hooks ordinarily used for such
purposes having all been used on account of the great number of
captives, fish-hooks will be used for the last of them.   The correct
idea is the same as in Hb. 1¹⁴ᵇ, *i.e.* that of women as helpless as
the fish in the hands of the angler (Mitchell) ; cf. also the usage of
the Assyrians in leading captives by ropes fastened to rings in the
under lip. ‡‡ — **3.** *And through breaches*] Emphatic by its position; these could hardly have been prepared beforehand for secret
escape, §§ nor were they made by the people themselves in their
hurry to escape ; ‖‖ but were those made by the enemy, and,
according to the picture, are so many as to furnish the easiest
exit from the city ; cf. 2 K. 17⁵·⁶, also Gn. 38²⁹. — *Ye shall go forth*]

---

* Mit.   † Os., Hd., Ke.   ‡ 'A.; 𝕲𝕾 *weapons*.   § Döderlein.
‖ Cal., Ros., Schrö., Mau., Pu., Gun., Mit., Now., Dr.
¶ Jus., Hi., GAS.; cf. Duhm and Marti.   ** Geb., Hi., Ba., Gun., Elh.
†† Ros., Hi., Ke.   ‡‡ Rawlinson, *Anc. Mon.* I. 243.   §§ Hi.   ‖‖ So apparently Cal.

Direct address; not escaping as fugitives,* but carried away as captives.† — *Each woman straight before her*] *i.e.* not one after another; ‡ nor each caring *only* for herself § (cf. Jos. 6[5. 20] Is. 47[15]), nor each one alone, unaccompanied by a man, ‖ nor each one in a captive state, not permitted to turn to the right hand or the left; ¶ but each one straight forward " from the place where she is captured,"† *i.e.* through the breach which is directly before her ** (cf. here also Is. 47[15] Jos. 6[5. 20]). — *And ye shall be cast*] The passive is easier than the active with the object supplied, " ye shall cast yourselves." — *Toward Harmon*] In favor of understanding this word as the name of a place, however uncertain may be its exact significance (*v.i.*), may be urged (1) the general testimony of the versions, (2) the weight of interpretation, (3) the demands of the passage, and (4) that this piece, like other pieces of Amos, might be expected to close with a statement of the place to which Israel is to be sent captive; cf. 5[27] 6[14].††

1. שִׁמְעוּ] Masc., though women are addressed, because standing first (cf. Is. 32[11]) GK. 144 *a*, Kö. 205 *c.* — פָּרָה [פָּרוֹת הַבָּשָׁן for פָּרֶה, hence ־ָ unchangeable, even in cstr., GK. 25 *e*; the art. used in הַבָּשָׁן regularly in historical statements (*e.g.* Nu. 21[33] Dt. 1[4] Jos. 17[1] but not in 1 Ch. 5[23]), and frequently, though not in the majority of cases, in poetry; it is present, *e.g.*, in Is. 2[13] Je. 22[2)], but lacking in Ps. 22[13] 68[16. 23] Is. 33[9] Ez. 27[6] 39[19] Mi. 7[14] Na. 1[4] Zc. 11[2]; cf. Dr. *Dt.* 47; GAS. *HG.* 549; it is the distinctive art., as in הַיַּרְדֵּן, GK. 126 *e.* — הָעֹשְׁקוֹת] Art. with ptcp. = rel. clause; עשק is very general, including the doing of an injury whether open or secret; while רצץ refers rather to open attack and assault (Ho. 5[11] Ju. 10[8]); both words are found together, as here, in Dt. 28[33] 1 S. 12[3. 4]. שָׁבַר indicates a more entire destruction. — הָרֹצְצוֹת] Note asyndeton in case of the ptcps. with the art. — לַאֲדֹנֵיהֶם [הֵם is either an error in grammatical usage (Ba.), or the masc. because the cows (fem.) are used to represent men (Ros., Mau.), or a copyist's mistake (*v.s.*), or the masc. used, as including the fem. (Schrö.), cf. עֲלֵיכֶם אֶתְכֶם (v.[2]) with the use elsewhere of the fem.; see GK. 135 *o*; Kö. 14. — הָבִיאָה] Sg., although addressed to אֲדֹנֵיהֶם; to be urged perhaps in favor of interpreting אֲדֹנֵיהֶם king (Ros., Mau., Hd.); on Hē cohort., GK. 48 *i*; Sta. § 595 *b.* — וְנִשְׁתֶּה] The simplest expression for purpose, H. 26, 2 *a*, Dr. § 60, GK. 108 *d.* — 2. וְנִשְׁבַּע] Pf. of indef. past; H. 17, 3; Dr. § 9; GK. 106 *b.* — בְּקָ] This ב falls under the general head of *means* or *instrument*, cf. its use in בְּשֵׁם (Dt. 6[13], etc.); as here in Jos. 2[12] and fre-

---

* Hi., Or. † Mit. ‡ Jus. § Ew. ‖ Geb.

¶ Hd., Dr. ** Ros. †† Hoffm., *ZAW.* III. 102; but cf. Marti.

quently, Is. 62⁸; cf. Arab. بْ which must be used in swearing rather than بِ
or بْ, before a pron. suf., and when, as here, the vb. is expressed (Wright,
Arab. Gram. II. § 62). — כִּי] Either a part. of asseveration, *surely*, or equivalent to quotation marks (Hd.), GK. 157 *b.* — וְנִשָּׂא] Shall it be taken (1) as
a Niph. pf. used impers. (Hi.), cf. Gn. 11⁹ Ex. 13⁷ Is. 23¹, H. 25, 2 *d*,
or (2) as Qal. impf. 1 pl. (sugg. by Va.), or (3) as Pï'ēl pf. (GK. 75 *oo*)
with הָאוֹיֵב understood as subj. (Ke.), or used impersonally, cf. 1 K. 9¹¹
(Schrö., Ba., Ke.), or (4) with the text changed to נשאו (*v.s.*)? Preferable
is (3) or (4). On pf. with ו cons. here, GK. 112 *x* ; Kö. 361 *c.* — . . . בְּצִנּוֹת
בְּסִירוֹת]. This is the only case where סיר has the meaning *hook*, its usual
sense being *thorn*, and the only occurrence of the fem. form of the plural.
צִנָּה also is found only here, the usual form being צִנִּים, pl. of צֵן. The
primary force of both words, as also of חוֹחַ, is *brier*, *thorn* (cf. Pr. 22⁵ Jb. 5⁵
Is. 34¹³ Ho. 2⁸ 9⁶), and the meaning *hook* is of later origin ; cf. Assyr. ḥaḥin,
ḥiḥinu, *thorn*. Hal. urges that usage of the kind here described was
never accorded to women, but only to dangerous prisoners, and that תצאנה
of v.³ shows that women go forth voluntarily, hence that the statement
is made not of living women but of the carcasses of women that are
dragged out and cast upon the dung heap. — אַחֲרִיתְכֶן] Stronger than שְׁאֵרִית
(Ew). — **3.** וּפְרָצִים] Ancient interpreters (so Dat., Jus.) seem to have read with
בְּ = *through;* but it may be the acc. as obj. of יצא (Va., Schrö., Ba.); cf.
Gn. 44⁴ GK. 118 *d*; Kö. 211 *d*; on position, Ew.⁸ 309 *a*, 1. — אִשָּׁה] As distributive pron. GK. 139 *b.* — וְהִשְׁלַכְתֶּנָה] Read by 𝕲 and other versions (*v.s.*) as
a Hŏph. ; otherwise with an obj. supplied (Geb.), the ה‎ָ is either due
to the influence of the last syllable of הֵצֵאנָה (Ke., Mit.); or to be taken as
ה paragogic, though rare in pf. (Va., Ros.), cf. Is. 7² 2 S. 1²⁶; or, better,
as a case of dittography, GK. 44 *k* (*v.s.*). — הַהַרְמוֹנָה] In addition to the
explanations of this term involving emendation of the text (*v.s.*), the following renderings may also be cited : (1) הרמון has been regarded as a
stronger pronunciation of ארמון and interpreted (*a*) of the king's palace,
(*b*) of the fortresses or palaces of the enemy (so Jus., Schrö., *et al.*) ;
(2) it has been identified with Armenia (so 𝔖𝕿 Σ., Jer., *et al.*) ; (3) *highlands* which had to be crossed on the way to Assyria (so Hes., Mau.);
(4) the name of the mountain on which Samaria stood, or some portion of it
(AE.); (5) Mt. Amanus (Luther); (6) *pride* (Rashi); (7) it has been
connected with Arab. هَرَم and referred to the *harem* of a hostile king. It
is regarded as inexplicable by many (so We., Val., Dr., Now., GAS., *et al.*).
It is to be taken, in any case, as a place-name, and We.'s objection to this,
that such a name would be suitable if the people as a whole were spoken of,
while it does not suit where the women in particular are mentioned, does not
hold in view of the preceding ופרצים תצאנה. All efforts to discover such a
place as Harmon have thus far failed.

§ 7. Israel's failure to understand the divine judgments.   4⁴⁻¹³.

The occasion is perhaps a festival.* The prophet in an ironical
vein exhorts Israel to continue in the formal ceremonial worship
— the cultus at Bethel and Gilgal — but it is all an illusion, and
displeasing to the very God whose favor they thus seek to gain.
Again and again Yahweh has indicated his displeasure with their
conduct in drought, in famine, in blight of crops, in pestilence
and war, and in earthquake ; but alas ! they have not turned back.
It remains, therefore, to inflict upon them, — what ? In any
event, " Prepare, O Israel, to meet thy God ! " Who is he that
speaks thus ? The God of creation and history.

This piece, though very different in movement and structure from any that
has preceded, is none the less artistic. The arrangement presented here appeared
in *BW.*, October, 1898, pp. 251 f. In its original form the piece consisted of
nine strophes, each containing four trimeters. Of these, 1 and 2, which form
the introduction, are closely connected, likewise 8 and 9, which form the conclusion. Strophes 3–7, each of which is introduced by a vb. in the first person (7ᵇ and 8ᵃ are a gloss), and characterized by the refrain *But you did not
return to me, saith Yahweh*, make the body of the poem (cf. below on strophes
4, 5). Müller's arrangement (*Die Propheten*, I. 68 f.) of this section, including 4¹⁻³, is arbitrary and artificial. His attempt to secure strophes of
5 + 4 + 3 + 2 + 1, and refrain, *i.e.* 16 lines, with an introduction of 8 lines
and a closing strophe of 8 lines, is an utter failure. One need only examine the
lines to see that they have been arranged to meet the demands of the theory.
It is important to note the more serious changes of text involved in the
reconstruction here adopted. These will be discussed in detail in their
proper places : —

(1) the rejection in v.7ᵃ of the gloss בעור שלשה חרשים ; (2) the rejection
of v.7ᵇ and all of v.8, except the refrain, as a gloss ; (3) the rejection of
the gloss עם שבי סוסיכם ; (4) the treatment of v.13 as a later addition, although,
if the line יהוה אלהי צבאות שמו might be fitted into strophe 8, the place of a
lost line would be supplied in that strophe and an extra line avoided in
strophe 9.

The arrangement proposed by Löhr (in 1901) has much in common with
the present reconstruction, viz. (1) the rejection of vs.7. 8 as a later addition
(so also Baumann) ; 7ᵃ 8ᵇ, however, are regarded here as genuine ; (2) the
treatment of vs.12 ᵇ. 13 as an interpolation ; (3) Löhr finds in vs.4-6 and 9-11 six
strophes identical with strophes 1–3 and 5–7 of the present arrangement (except that he makes two lines out of the refrain instead of one, as here, and
retains עם שבי סוסיכם). But Löhr differs also in connecting 3¹⁴ᵇ 9¹ (as far

---

* We.

as הספים) and 9⁷ with the present piece, which he regards as only a fragment of the address against the sanctuaries at Bethel and Gilgal, the beginning and end of 4⁴⁻¹²ᵃ being lacking.

4, 5. *Continue, O Israel, your efforts by sacrifices to secure
Yahweh's favor,— but it is useless.*

The strophe consists of three couplets, each containing an ironical command
relating to the cultus, with a fourth couplet explaining Israel's strange conduct,
viz. their love for all this empty show. The structure is perfect, every line
being regular in length.

4. הגלגל] 𝔖 and 𝔗 precede by בְּ.—הרבו] Oort, והרבו (*ThT.* XIV. 143;
so also Gun., Elh., Oet.).—**5.** וקטר מחמץ תודה] 𝔊 καὶ ἀνέγνωσαν ἔξω νόμον=וְקָראו;
מְחוּץ תּוֹרָה; 𝔗 מחמס (so also Hirscht); Ew., וקטרו (so also Gun., Oort *Em.*,
Elh. and Oet., who omits conj.); cf. Margolis (*AJSL.* XVII. 171), who suggests
וִקְראו בַחוּץ תּוֹדָה, Call out in the streets, Thanksgiving!—וְקָראו נְדָבוֹת 𝔊 ἔτι
ἐκαλέσαντο = קָראו; 𝔖 ܠܰܦ ܣܘܰܣ = (=וְנִדְרי נ').—השמיעו] 𝔊 joins to fol. cl.,
while 𝔖 translates ܣܰܠܶܡ = וְשַׁלְמוּ.

4. *Go to Bethel and — transgress.*] It is only necessary to read
the whole phrase to see that the prophet is not serious; "going
to Bethel" carries with it transgression, the two are synonymous.
The tone of voice, doubtless, indicated the irony of the expression.
The transgression was not (1) the worshipping on high places,
a violation of the law of the central sanctuary at Jerusalem
(Dt. 12⁴⁻⁷),* for that law had not yet been promulgated; nor
(2) the changing of the details of the ceremonial by adapting
them to the heathen worship outside of Israel;† nor (3) the calf-
worship which was in vogue at Bethel (cf. Ho. 4¹⁵ 8⁵ ᶠ·);‡ nor
(4) the failure to give Yahweh a proper place in the worship;§
nor (5) the fact of engaging in worship though morally unfit,‖ —
but the fact of engaging in any kind of ceremonial worship for
the purpose of finding Yahweh, when, indeed, the more zealously
they observe the cultus, the farther do they remove themselves
from Yahweh.¶ — *In Gilgal*] For situation and description,** cf.
Jos. 4¹⁹ 15⁷; for the place which it had occupied in Israelitish his-

---

* Cal.   † Geb., Os.   ‡ Jus., Hd.   § So apparently Pu.   ‖ Dr.
¶ We.; WRS., *Proph.* 94–99; Now., Mit.
** Conder, *Tent Work,* II. 7 ff.; Rob. *BR².* I. 557; GAS. *HG.* 494; Bliss, art.
"Gilgal," *DB.;* GAS. art. "Gilgal," *EB.*; Marti.

tory, cf. Jos. 4[19. 20] 5[3-10] 1 S. 7[16] 10[8] 11[14] 15[10 ff.] 2 S. 19[15] Ho. 4[15] 9[15] 12[11]. The site has only recently (1865) been identified * as Jiljûl, 4½ miles from the Jordan, 1½ miles from Jericho. — *And bring every morning your sacrifices*] The ironical vein still continues; the sacrifices were those which were offered annually (1 S. 1[3. 7. 21]); the worshipper is invited to offer them daily instead of annually; † the exaggeration does not consist in offering instead of a usual morning offering an earlier one; ‡ nor is the sense satisfied by understanding the invitation to be merely the description of a custom, viz. that of making an offering *on the next morning* after arrival at the sanctuary. § — *Every third day your tithes*] The tithe ‖ was differently administered at different periods. According to the regulations of Dt. (14[28] 26[12]), which seem earlier than those of P (Nu. 18[21-28]), the third year was the tithing year κατ' ἐξοχήν,¶ because only in this year was the whole tithe given away, the offerer himself and his family eating it in the other years. In strict parallelism with the preceding line, the prophet urges the worshippers to offer their tithes every third day instead of every third year.** Note, however, should be made of the renderings, *every three years*, יָמִים = year †† (as in Lv. 25[29] Ju. 17[10] 2 Ch. 21[19]), *on three days* (= at the times of the three great feasts, which, it is claimed, lasted originally each a single day), ‡‡ *every three days, i.e.* frequently, §§ and especially, *on the third day* (after arrival), ‖‖ on the ground that Amos is exaggerating nothing, but as above, describing the custom of the visiting worshipper at Bethel, who offered his sacrifice on the morning after arrival and his tithe on the third day, a supposition for which no one offers a good reason. — **5.** *And burn of leavened bread a thank-offering*] The prophet exhorts the people still further to increase their zeal by burning

---

* By Zschokke; but Schlater (*Zur Topogr. u. Gesch. Palästinas*, 246 ff.); Buhl (*Geogr. des alt. Pal.*, 1896, pp. 202 f.) and BSZ. identify this Gilgal with Julêjîl, opposite Ebal and Gerizim, east of the plain.

† Mit.   ‡ Ba.   § Os., We., Now., Dr.

‖ Hermann, *Gottesdienstl. Alterth. d. Griechen*, § 20, 4; Ri. *HBA.* II. 1792-7; Di. on Lv. 27[33]; Ryssel, *PRE.*[2] XVII. 442 f.; We., *Die Composition des Hexateuchs;* WRS. *Sem.* 244-54; Sayce, *Patriarchal Palestine*, 175.

¶ Dr. *Dt.* 173.   ‡‡ Oort, *ThT.* XIV. 143 f.
** Ros., Ke.   §§ Schrö.
†† Cal., Va., Hd., Pu.   ‖‖ Os., We., Now., Dr., Marti.

(*i.e.* turning into sweet smoke) what ordinarily was not burned, viz. the leavened bread which formed a part of the thank-offering. Amos does not here refer to the transgression of any law in existence (*e.g.* Lv. 2^{11} 7^{12}); but to a new custom, just now being developed, the thought being that a thank-offering prepared with yeast or grape-honey (Ho. 3^1) would be more acceptable. This use of leaven (cf. the raisin-cakes of Ho. 3^1) was probably regarded as pleasing to the Canaanitish deities,* hence in later times it came to be forbidden (Lv. 7^{12} Ex. 23^{18}). The translation of 𝕿, *from violence* = that which is gained by violence (*v.s.*) seems to relieve a serious difficulty, but like the rendering *without leaven*† is quite far-fetched; cf. 𝕲 (*v.s.*). — *And proclaim free-will offerings, make them known*] The freewill-offering (cf. the later regulations Dt. $12^{6.\ 7}$ Ex. 35^{29} Lv. $22^{18.\ 21}$) was intended to be given as the freest possible expression of the heart's feeling. The irony, which still continues, lies in the prophet's urging the people, not the priests, ‡ to publish far and wide § their voluntary gifts, an action which was directly contrary to the spirit of such gifts. The language does not convey the idea, ordinarily assigned to it, of a command to the priests to make freewill offerings compulsory. ‖ — *For so ye love to do*] Cf. Je. 5^{31}. The prophet has described a tendency, indeed the fundamental error, of the Northern religion. This fault, which has now become an organic part of the national system, is not that the offerings, correct in themselves, were made at the wrong place,¶ but that Israel is laboring under a delusive idea; for outward forms of any kind, however zealously executed, will not take the place of the essentials of religion.

4. באו ביתאל וגו׳] The parallelism rules out the rendering, "Go to Bethel, and transgress at Gilgal," etc. (Hi.). — בית אל] Acc. of direction after באו, GK. 118 *d*. — הגלגל] This might be taken (1) with הרבו = place *in* which, GK. 118 *d*; cf. the ב of the versions (GAS., Dr.); (2) with באו of prec. member, or with a verb of motion supplied = acc. of direction (Jer., St., Or., Gun., We., Mit., Now., Elh.); (3) = acc. of specification, "as far as concerns Gilgal" (Ba.) GK. 118 *q*; (2) is preferable. The name is a reduplicated formation from גלל

* Cf. WRS. *OTJC.*[1] 434 and *Sem.* 220 f.   § Ba.
† Oort, *ThT.* XIV. 144; but cf. Gun.   ‖ Schrö., Hi., Pu., Ke.
‡ Os.   ¶ Cal., Os.

and means *the circle*, the reference being probably to a circle of sacred stones
(cf. Jos. 4⁵ 8²⁹ᶠᶠ·); for a similar formation, cf. כִּכָּר from כרר; the art., which
is always retained, except Jos. 5⁹ 12²³, is an indication that the appellative
force of the word was long felt; cf. Kö. 295 *b.*—[הרבו לפשע Lit., *multiply in
transgressing*, inf. with ל having the force of the gerund, H. 29, 3 *e*; GK. 114 *o*;
Kö. 399 *m.*— [לבקר Distributive, cf. Je. 21¹² (but here לבקר may = in the
morning, early), Ex. 29³⁸· ³⁹ 1 Ch. 16⁴⁰; Kö. 331 *f*; cf., however, Now., who
maintains that for the expression of the idea, *every morning, every third day*,
there would be used either the pl. (cf. Ps. 73¹⁴ Jb. 7¹⁸), or a repetition of
the word (cf. 1 Ch. 9²⁷); GK. 123 *d*. On the force of the art., *v*. Kö. 300 *b*.
Giesebrecht (*Die hebr. Praeposition Lamed*, p. 23) makes לבקר = *early* everywhere except Ps. 49¹⁵.— [ובחיכם, מעישרתיכם, קטר, חמץ, תודה, נדבות, This vocabulary
of religious worship is noteworthy for its size and scope, its definiteness, and
the peculiar connection in which it is introduced. If this passage is genuine,
and no one doubts this, it must be conceded (1) that a fully developed cultus
was in existence at this time; (2) that it was showing a pronounced tendency
towards a still fuller expansion; (3) that the priest-power was very considerable, and one with which the prophet was coming into antagonism; (4) that
the prophet, at all events, represented an idea in religion which did not have
much, if any, prevalence at this time.— **5.** [קטר Inf. abs. for imv., H. 28, 5 *c*;
GK. 113 *z*; Ew.⁸ 328 *c*; Ḳö. 218 *b*. The original meaning of the word is
to *give out vapor or smoke*, like Arab. قَتَرَ to *give forth vapor*, قُتَار *smoke*,
steam, Assyr. *ḳuṭru*, *smoke*. Pi'ēl and Hiph. are commonly used, meaning *to
burn on the altar*. It cannot be said that the Pi'ēl is the proper word to be
used for burning incense, and the Hiph. of sacrifices (Gun.). The Massorites
attempted to make the distinction that the Pi'ēl designates either irregular or
idolatrous sacrifice, the Hiph., lawful. But this is arbitrary (cf. 2 Ch. 34²⁵).
Rather, the Pi'ēl is the older expression, and the Hiph. the younger, used
chiefly in P; cf. Kö. 96 (We. *Prol.* 64; *ZAW.* VI. 298 f.; Kit. *Theol.
Studien aus Würtemberg*, II. 53; SS. 660; Now. *Arch.* II. 246 f.).— [מן Is
not partitive, *some leaven for a thank-offering*, but local, *a thank-offering
made up of leaven.*— [חמץ The usual term for leavened bread. In general,
all leavened bread was forbidden to be offered on the altar (Ex. 23¹⁸ Lv. 2¹¹).
Traces of greater freedom appear in Lv. 7¹³ 23¹⁷. This passage shows the custom
in Israel to have been different from that in Judah. Amos does not necessarily
regard it as unlawful (We.). Indeed, the custom may be regarded as in harmony with the original ideas of sacrifice (WRS. *Sem.* 220 f., 242; *OTJC.*² 345).
— [תודה The thank-offering is a particular kind of the שְׁלָמִים (Lv. 7¹²). It is
also called זֶבַח הַתּוֹדָה, Lv. 7¹² 22²⁹, and fully זֶבַח תּוֹדַח שְׁלָמִים Lv. 7¹³· ¹⁵ (Now.
Arch. II. 238; Benz. *Arch.* 446).— [נדבות The freewill-offering, a spon-
taneous offering, not one prescribed, often united with נדר *vow*, both being
extraordinary offerings (Now. *Arch.* II. 238 f.; Benz. *Arch.* 446, 451).
They might take the form of burnt-offerings (Dr. *Dt.* 143; Lv. 22¹⁸· ²¹),
but more usually of שלמים (Lv. 7¹⁶). The נדבות were often made the

occasion for free-handed hospitality, with perhaps a general invitation to
all to come and partake (We.; WRS. *Sem.* 254).—[אהבתם] Stative pf.,
H. 18, 1; Dr. § 11; GK. 106*g.*—[וזבחיכם] The root זבח means to slaughter
for sacrifice, as originally all slaughtering was connected with sacrifice.
זֶבַח is therefore the generic word for sacrifice, usually designating the sacrificial meal, for which in later times שלמים was commonly substituted as a
more specific term (WRS. *Sem.* 222, 237; Dr. *Dt.* 141 f., 145; BDB. *s.v.*;
Now. *Arch.* II. 210, 215; Benz. *Arch.* 435; We. *Prol.* 73).—[מעשרתיכם] The
tithe was a widespread institution in antiquity. On tithes in general, see
Spencer, *De Legibus Hebraeorum*, III. 10, § 1; Ew. *Antiquities*, p. 300;
Ryssel, *s.v.* "Zehnten," *PRE.*[2]; WRS. *Sem.*, Lecture VII., and *Proph.* 383 f.,
and art. "Tithes," *Enc. Br.;* We. *Prol.* 156 f.; Dr. *Dt.* 166–73; Now. *Arch.*
II. 257 f. Among non-Semites may be cited the Greeks, who tithed the
spoils of war, the annual crops, and other sources of revenue (Xenophon
and his followers, *e.g.*, reserved a tithe of the proceeds of the sale of captives
for a thank-offering to the gods, Xenophon himself using his own share to
erect a small temple in Scillus, near Olympia; *v. Anabasis*, V. 3; cf. Hermann, *Gottesdienstl. Alterth. d. Griechen* (2d ed.), § 20, 4); the Romans,
who paid tithes to Hercules (Diodorus, IV. 21; Plutarch, *Moralia*, II. 267 E),
and the Lydians, who tithed their cattle (Nic. Damasc. in Müller's *Fragm.
Hist. Gr.* III. 371). Among the Semites the custom was general; the Car-
thaginians sent an annual tithe of their increase to Tyre to the temple of Mel-
karth (Diodorus, XX. 14); there are many references to tithes and monthly
tributes in the records of the Babylonian temples (Jastrow, *Rel.* 668). A
common vow among the Arabs was, "If God gives me a hundred sheep, I will
sacrifice one in every ten" (Arnold, *Septem Moʿallakât*, p. 186). The only
pre-Deuteronomic references to the tithe in the O. T. are Gn. 28[22] and this
passage. It is to be noted that both connect the payment of tithes with
Bethel. It is probable that in early times the religious tithe of each district
was given for the support of the sanctuary of the district. This tithe was
probably not compulsory, but was spontaneously given; it is classed by Amos
with freewill-offerings, thank-offerings, and vows, and may have been used to
furnish a sacrificial banquet. The absence of any regulation concerning tithes
in the earliest legislation seems to point to the voluntary character of the gift.
It is not unlikely that in the earliest times the tithe and the "firstfruits" and
"firstborn" were identical.

6–8. *Famine and drought have failed to draw you unto me.*
These two strophes, with the later insertion, have never been made
entirely clear, either in structure or meaning.

6. נתתי] 𝔊 δώσω. —[נקיון] 𝔊 γομφιασμόν, *toothache*; 𝔖 ܫܶܢܳܐ; 𝔗 אקהיות,
all reading קהיון = bluntness, from קהה, to be dumb (Ba., Seb.; Lag. *BN.*
200 f.; BSZ., BDB.); cf. Je. 31[29] Ez. 18[2]; 𝔙 *stuporem;* 'Α., πληγήν; Σ., Θ.,

καθαρισμόν. — **7 a.** בעור שלשה חדשים לקציר] though in all the versions (cf. 𝕲 τρυγητοῦ but ᑫᵐᵍ θερισμοῦ), is a gloss, added as a meteorological calculation, and disturbing not only the strophic arrangement, but also the poetic generalization. — לא אמטיר] Closes the third member of the strophe, after which the refrain from v.⁸, ולא שבתם עדי נאם י, belongs. — **7 b.** חלקה] This word, with what follows in v.⁷ and v.⁸ as far as the refrain, is evidently an interpolation, repeating the idea of the famine already described. In favor of this are (1) the awkwardness of the two circumstantial clauses in their present position at the end of v.⁷, although necessarily dependent on ונע of v.⁸; (2) the redundancy in the repetition of עיר with the numerals; (3) the utter extravagance and lack of poetical force in the whole expression; (4) the impossibility of securing a symmetrical structure for the poem if this section is to be included; (5) the lack of reason for dwelling at such length on the drought, when other calamities are, in some cases, treated in a single line. — תמטיר] Gr. תִּמָּטֵר; Oort (*Em.*), fol. 𝕲, βρέξω, אמטיר (so Gun., Now., Elh.); but 𝕸𝕿, though unexpected, may be intended for the sake of alliteration (Oet.). — **8.** ונעו] Should, in any case, stand closely connected with what precedes; 𝕲 καὶ συνασθροισθήσονται, reading possibly ונערו; cf. Nu. 16¹¹ (Vol.), so 𝕾.

Löhr om. all of vs.⁷· ⁸ as a later insertion coming from two hands, the first of which contributed a strophe consisting of vs.⁷ ᵃ ᵃ· ⁷ ᵇ and ⁸ ᵇ (the refrain), while the second furnished a variation of this strophe, consisting of vs.⁷ ᵃ β· ⁸ (including the refrain), which crept into the text from the margin. These two strophes, according to Löhr, differ from the original strophes in having one more line each, and they interrupt the progress of the thought, while they also closely resemble 8¹¹ f· (endorsed by Now. *ThLZ.* XXVI. 164).

6. *I also it was who gave to you*] The pronoun is emphatic, and, with the particle גם, marks the contrast between Yahweh's attitude of punishment and their conduct described in vs.⁴· ⁵. — *Cleanness of teeth*] Nothing to eat, interpreted in the following member as "lack of bread," *i.e. famine;* on the frequency of famine in Palestine, cf. Gn. 12¹⁰ 26¹ 41⁵⁴ Ru. 1¹ 2 S. 21¹ 1 K. 17¹.* The meaning *stupidity,* favored by some of the versions (*v.s.*), does not accord with the etymology of the word, the parallelism, or the context. The idea of " innocency of eating what was forbidden,"† or that of " emptiness,"‡ is not to be found in the word. — *In all your cities*] The calamity referred to affected the whole country. Such famines are recorded as having taken place under Ahab (1 K. 17¹²), and under Jehoram (2 K. 4³⁸ 8¹), but the reference here is probably to a later famine of which no record has been

---

* See C. Warren, art. " Famine," *DB.*   † Geb.   ‡ Va.

preserved. — *But ye did not return to me*] Yahweh expected the
calamity to bring the people to their senses, but it failed to do so.*
This expression is common and important (cf. Ho. 6^1 $14^{1.\ 2}$ Is. 10^{21}
31^6 Je. $3^{1.\ 12.\ 22}$ 4^1 Dt. 4^{30} $30^{2.\ 8}$ Is. 44^{22} 55^7 1 S. 7^3 2 Ch. $6^{24.\ 38}$ Ps.
78^{34} Mal. 3^7), since it with the N. T. Greek ἐπιστρέφειν (*e.g.* Acts 3^{19}
9^{35} 11^{21} 1 Thes. 1^9) prepared the way for the later idea contained
in the word "conversion."† — **7.** *I also it was who withheld from
you the rain*] Lack of rain was, of course, the occasion of the
famine described in v.⁶. Perhaps this strophe originally preceded
that in v.⁶. In any case the famine and the drought are treated
distinctly. — *While yet there remained three months to the harvest*]
This clause, which is to be treated as a gloss, ‡ contains an explanation by some later hand as to the details of the withholding of
the rain. The interpolator may have had in mind either (1) the
so-called latter rains of the last of February or first of March, the
harvest beginning, in some sections of the country, April 1 and continuing into June ; this rain fell when the grain was beginning to
grow, and without it the crops would be ruined (but see Nowack,
135); § or (2) a drought for the entire three months preceding
harvest ; ‖ or (3) the rain which fell in the latter part of April, that
is, three months before the fruit harvest,¶ or within three months
of the last of the grain harvest in June ;** or (4) the heavy rain
due six months before harvest, *i.e.* in November and December,
which in this case Yahweh had withheld until three months
before the harvest time, that is, until sometime in January.†† —
Rain upon one city] Not at intervals, upon various occasions,‡‡
but in the particular case which the prophet has in mind, the
tense denoting vivid representation. §§ Yahweh is represented
as withholding rain, although he gave evidence of his power to
bestow it on certain cities, which stood in striking contrast with
those from which it was withheld. This phenomenon is not an
uncommon one in Palestine ; ‖‖ cf. Ju. $6^{36\ \mathrm{ff.}}$ — **7 *b*, 8.** *One field*

---

* On the ancient belief that natural calamities were an indication of displeasure
on the part of the deity, and consequently of sin on the part of the people, *v.* GAS.
I. 169f.; *HG.* 73–76.   † Dr.   ‡ So also Marti.
§ Jus., Va., Schrö., Hi., Ke., Or., Mit.   ‖ Ros.   ¶ Jer.   ** Ba.
†† We., Now., GAS., Dr.   ‡‡ Mit., Dr.   §§ Va., Ew.
‖‖ Thomson, *LB.* II. 66.

H

being rained upon and another field, which was not rained upon, drying up, two or three cities staggering unto one city to drink water without being satisfied] An insertion, which really adds nothing to the picture already presented, made by some one who felt perhaps that a description of a drought was imperfect if it did not include the country as well as the city; the interpolator, however, forgets himself and in a very tautological way goes back to the cities, two or three of which he represents as exhausted because of the drought, and as staggering in their weakened condition to a more favored city, where, after all, they are doomed to disappointment. How remarkably this picture resembles that given in 6[9. 10], which must also be treated as an interpolation ! * — *But ye did not return unto me*] The refrain, which contains, as Mitchell has said, "a world of pathetic tenderness."

6. גם] Correlation, expressing correspondence, here of a retributory character, not simply emphasizing אני (Pu.), nor נתתי (Mau.), but the whole thought (Ba., Reu., We.); cf. Gn. 20⁶ Jos. 24¹⁸ 2 S. 12¹³ Mi. 6¹³ (see BDB. *s.v.*, גם (4) p. 169; Kö. 394 *d*). — נקיון שנים] Versions (*v.s.*) seem to have read כֶּהְיוֹן, the root of which is used with שן in Je. 31²⁹⁻³⁰ Ez. 18²; this reading was favored without good reason in BSZ.¹²; cf. Lag. *BN.* 201; the phrase is peculiarly significant as a figurative designation of famine; cf. נקיון כפי Gn. 20⁵ Ps. 26⁶ 73¹³, *cleanness of my hands.* — עדי] Stronger than אֵלַי (cf. La. 3⁴⁰); אל represents only the *direction*, עד the *attainment* of the purpose (Fleischer, *Kl. Schriften*, I. 402 f.). — **7.** גשם] Really a *shower*, or *burst of rain*, used (1) of abundant rain (*e.g.* 1 K. 17¹⁴ 18⁴¹. ⁴⁴); (2) in poetry for מטר, the generic word for rain; but also (3) of heavy winter rains (*e.g.* Ct. 2¹¹; cf. Lv. 26⁴); cf. also יורה, Ho. 6³ Dt. 11¹⁴ Je. 5²⁴; מורה Jo. 2²³ Ps. 84⁷, *early rain;* מלקוש Je. 3³ Pr. 16¹⁵ Zc. 10¹, *latter rain.* On these words, see Rob., *BR.*² I. 429 f.; Chaplin, *PEF.* 1883, pp. 8 ff.; Klein, *ZDPV.* IV. 72 f. — בעור] Kö. 401 *x.* — שלשה] H. 15, 2 *b;* GK. 134 *b.* — והמטרתי] Not freq., Dr. § 114 (*a*), but equiv. to a vivid impf., GK. 112 *h*, note; so also אמטיר (v.⁸). — אחת . . . אחת] *one* . . . *another*, GK. 139 *e*, note 3. — חלקה] Introducing the first of the two circ. clauses, H. 45, 3 *b;* Dr. § 165. — תמטיר] Not 2d p. addressed to Yahweh, nor 2d p. addressed to the water (Va.), nor 3d p. used impersonally, nor with עב understood as subject (Ros., Schrö.), but 3d p. fem. (= neut.) impf. (Mau., Hi., Hd.), or to be read אמטיר with 𝕲 and 𝔙 (*v.s.*), GK. 144 *c*; Kö. 323 *k.* — **8.** וְנָעוּ] Freq.; lit. *to move with unsteady gait*, and so, of a drunkard

* On the method of water supply in Eastern cities, viz. by cisterns, cf. the Mesha inscription, ls. 9, 24 f.; Je. 2¹³ 2 K. 18⁸¹ Dt. 6¹¹ Is. 36¹⁶ Pr. 5¹⁵ Ec. 12⁶ 2 Ch. 26¹⁰ Ne. 9²⁵. See S. A. Cook, art. " Conduits and Reservoirs," *EB. ;* Benz. *Arch.* 51 ff., 230 f.; *ZDPV.* I. (1878) 132–76.

[שׁתים שׁלשׁ] (Is. 24²⁰), of a blind man (La. 4¹⁴), of one exhausted (Ps. 59¹⁶). —
Used to express an indefinite number, GK. 134 *s*; Kö., *Stil.* 163, 212. — [ולא] =
without.

9–11. *Blight of crops, pestilence and war, and earthquakes
have failed to draw you to me.* These three strophes conclude the
five which have the refrain.

9. [ובירקון] fol. in ﬡ by יֵרָקוֹן ‎ܣܘ̈ܩ‎ = ובנרב, an insertion from Hg. 2¹⁷; cf.
Dt. 28²² I K. 8³⁷ (Seb.). — [הרבות] ﬡ ἐπληθύνατε = הִרְבֵּיתֶם; so also Syr.-Hex.
(so also Oet.); but read הֶחֱרַבְתִּי, to which Oet. objects (1) that חרב elsewhere has only the sea and rivers as objects, ירב always being used of vegetation, and (2) that this emendation destroys the contrast intended by the
author, viz. "You increased your gardens and your vineyards, but your fig
trees and olive trees the locust devoured." But the contrast exists only after
the text has been emended by Oet. in order to produce it; the change to the
2d p. involved in Oet.'s reading is too abrupt; and חרב is used of other
things than rivers and seas, *e.g.* Je. 2¹² (the heavens); Ju. 16⁷ ᶠ· (green withes);
Ez. 19⁷ (palaces); Zp. 3⁶ (streets); 2 K. 19¹⁷ (land, though חרם should perhaps be read here). — [וגנותיכם] is joined by ﬡ with what precedes, while ﬧ
makes the division after וכרמיכם. — [לא] ﬡ οὐδ᾽ ὥς, so also in vs.¹⁰⁻¹¹. — **10.** [דבר
ﬡ θάνατον; ﬦ *mortem;* ﬡ ‎ܡܘܬܐ‎ ﬧ מוֹתָא. — [בחרב] Zeydner (*ThSt.* 1888,
pp. 249 f.; so also Val.) בָּחֳרֶב. — [שׁבי] There is no ground for the readings:
צְבִי (Gr., so also Elh., Oet.); שֶׁבִי (Hoffm. *ZAW.* III. 103); [בקרכם (= בחוריכם
(= צְבִי) עִם שׁבי (Hal.); or שֶׁרִי (Zeydner, *loc. cit.,* so also Val.). — [באשׁ ﬡ ἐν
πυρί, reading באשׁ; so also 6 Hebr. Mss. (so also Zeydner, *loc. cit.,* Val., Elh.). —
מחניכם] ﬡ in some Mss. om. suf. while ﬥ renders ‎ܣܝܢܟܘܢ‎ (*your stench*),
connecting it with ‎ܣܪܐ‎ (Seb.). — [ובאפכם] Omit ו with ﬡﬦﬧ, ᾽A., Σ. (so We.,
Gr., Now., Löhr, Hirscht, Oet., Hal., Baumann). Ethiopic = ואנגפכם; Zeydner,
וראפכם = ורפיכם (*loc. cit.,* so also Val.); Elh. באפי, following ﬡᴬᵠ. Marti om.

9. *I smote you*] Each of the five strophes begins with a verb in
the perfect 1st singular; cf. (1) *I it was who gave you* (*famine*),
(2) *I it was who withheld from you rain*, (3) *I smote you*, (4) *I
sent upon you pestilence*, (5) *I overturned you.* — *With blight and
decay*] Both words are used of human diseases in Dt. 28²². The
first is the scorching of the east wind, cf. 1 K. 8³⁷ 2 K. 19²⁶ 2 Ch.
6²⁸ Is. 27⁸ Ez. 17¹⁰; the second, mildew caused by dampness
and heat, having a yellow appearance, cf. Je. 30⁶. — *I laid waste
your gardens and vineyards*] This reading, on the basis of Wellhausen's emendation, satisfies every demand of the context. The
difficulties of the old text are seen in the efforts to translate it,

e.g. many of your gardens,* the multiplying of your gardens,†
your many gardens, ‡ or much mildew § (taking הרבות with what
precedes), or as an adverb, most, often. ‖ — *Your fig trees and olive
trees the locust devoured*] With this rendering it is no longer necessary to discuss whether of the four nouns, gardens, vineyards, fig
trees, olive trees, only the first depended on " I smote," ¶ or the
first two,** or none,†† all being taken as the object of " devoured."
The word for locust is a general word meaning the one that gnaws ;
cf. Jo. 1⁴ 2²⁵. This visitation was not infrequent, and was always
attended with the greatest possible destruction. ‡‡ — **10.** *The
pestilence after the manner of Egypt*] The many possibilities of
this ambiguous phrase have been seized upon ; the sending of
the pestilence was (1) *sudden* as was the destruction of Egypt's
firstborn ; §§ (2) a visitation upon the wicked, not the righteous,
as was the case of the Egyptians, as compared with the Hebrews ; ‖‖
(3) as if Israel were God's enemy as Egypt had been ; ¶¶ (4) sent
while they were on their way to Egypt ; ¶ (5) sent from Egypt,
lit. on the way on which one comes from or goes to Egypt ; ***
(6) in the same way as that in which it was sent against Egypt,
cf. Is. 10²⁶ ; ††† (7) just as in Egypt, the home of the pestilence, ‡‡‡
" a thoroughly Egyptian plague," §§§ " with the same severity and
malignity " with which it visits Egypt, ‖‖‖ after the manner of
Egypt.¶¶¶ Does the prophet have in mind a particular historical
event? No. For the estimation in which the Hebrews regarded
pestilence as a punishment for sin, cf. Lv. 26²⁵ 2 S. 24¹⁵. — *I slew with
the sword*] Reference is made not to any particular battle, *e.g.* the
slaughter by Hazael and Benhadad of Syria, when Jehoahaz was king
(2 K. 8¹² 13³⁻⁷),**** but rather to the long Syrian conflict, which
lasted many years.††††— *Together with the captivity of your horses*]
An interpolation, ‡‡‡‡ meaning that horses were captured and
slain, §§§§ or that, while the men were slain, the horses were captured. ‖‖‖‖ The word שבי is, however, here used in an uncommon

---

* GAS.   ‡ Ros., Mau., Mit., cf. Pu.   ‖ Ba., Ew., Or.   ** Ros., Schrö.
† Geb.   § Hd.   ¶ Jus.   †† Bauer.
‡‡ Thomson, *LB.* II. 102 ff.; Van Lennep, *Bible Lands,* 313.   §§ Os.
‖‖ Geb., Ros.   ¶¶ Cal.   *** Va.   ††† Hd., Pu.   ‡‡‡ Hi., Ke.
§§§ Ew., GAS.   ‖‖‖ Dr.   ¶¶¶ Ba., We. **** Ros., Schrö., Hi., Ba.
†††† We., Now.   ‡‡‡‡ So also Baumann.   §§§§ Va., Schrö., Hi., Hd., Ke.
‖‖‖‖ Os., Geb., Ros., Ba.

sense, viz., the act of taking captive (Ezra 9⁷ Dn. 11³³), but ordinarily it denotes either the condition of captivity or the sum of the
captives. In Ex. 22⁹, the verb is used as here of animals, though
elsewhere of men. The preposition עִם here = *besides* and is used
in a late or Arabic sense. The peculiar usage of the more important
words, the anti-climax, the fact that the line interferes with the strophe, and the evident afterthought implied in it show its character as
a later insertion. — *And I caused the stench of your camps to rise in
your nostrils*] The slaughter was so great, the unburied bodies and
carcasses so many (cf. Is. 34³), that pestilence arose, the result of
war. As above, drought followed famine, though the occasion of it,
so here war follows pestilence, though the occasion of it. Justi's
reading, "I caused your camps to burn in mine anger" (cf. 2 K.
5¹ 13³), although supported by 𝔊, cannot stand. — **11.** *I overthrew among you*] That is, some of your cities ; the overthrow was
evidently that of an earthquake, perhaps that mentioned in 1¹*
(which, it will be remembered, is from a later hand), or some
earthquake unspecified;† others understand an overthrow by a
hostile attack ; ‡ and still others, a general summing up of all the
preceding judgments. § The word הָפַכְתִּי is always used of the
destruction of Sodom and Gomorrah, cf. Gn. 19²⁵ Dt. 29²² Is. 1⁷ ‖
13¹⁹ Je. 49¹⁸ 50⁴⁰. The shortness of this line may be due to the
omission of some phrase.¶ — *As God overthrew Sodom and Gomorrah*] The point of comparison is not the manner of the overthrow, but its thoroughness.** The form of expression is so
similar to that in Gn. 19 as to lead some †† to suppose that Amos
had that text before him. The use of the word *Elohim*, in contrast with the subject of הָפַכְתִּי, strangely enough has been thought
to prove the existence of more than one person in the Godhead. ‡‡
The reading "the great overthrow," using *Elohim* as a superlative, §§ is grammatically possible, but out of harmony with the context. — *And ye were as a brand snatched from the blaze*] *i.e.* ye
were barely rescued, saved as by a miracle, cf. Zc. 3²,‖‖ not, the
destruction was only partial.¶¶ — *But ye did not turn unto me*]

---

* Schrö., Hi., We.   † Mau., Schlier, Pu., Mit.   ‡ Ke., St.   § Ba.
‖ Where סְרִם is probably to be read for זרים.
¶ See *BW.*, October 1898, p. 252; so also Löhr and Baumann.   ** Mit.
†† *E.g.*, Va.   ‡‡ Geb., Hes.   §§ New.   ‖‖ Jus., Va., Mit.   ¶¶ Hi.

Every effort was futile which Providence put forth to rescue Israel from total destruction.

9. [בשדפון] On the art., GK. 126 *n*; Kö. 297 *b.* — [החרבתי] Instead of הרבות, which is grammatically impossible (cf. Kö. 402 *g*); cf. We. (*v.s.*). — [תאניכם] On the masc. pl. ending, cf. Na. 3¹², Kö. 253 *f.* — [ויאכל] Impf. of vivid representation of past event, Dr. § 27 (1) (*a*); GK. 107 *d*; H. 20, 1 *a.* — [גזם] Cf. other names for locust, all of which are likewise descriptive terms: ארבה (Jo. 1⁴ 2²⁵), ילק (Na. 3¹⁶), חסיל (Jo. 1⁴ Is. 33⁴), חגב (2 Ch. 7¹³), צלצל (Dt. 28⁴²), גב (Is. 33⁴). — **10.** [בכם] ב = *against;* for other cases cf. Gn. 16¹² 2 S. 24¹⁷. — [עם] For other cases of עם in this sense, cf. Is. 25¹¹ 34⁷ Je. 6¹¹ Na. 3¹² Ps. 66¹⁵. — **11.** [בכם] ב partitive, *among* you, some of you; cf. Nu. 11¹⁷ Zc. 6¹⁵. — [כמהפכת] An old inf. form in the cstr. relation with 'א, GK. 115 *d*; Barth, *NB.* **171** *c, a*; Kö. 233 *c*; as an inf. it governs את־סדם as a direct object, GK. 115 *d.* We. regards this old inf. followed by the general title אלהים as an indication of an old and not distinctively Israelitish idiom. — [מֻצָּל] A Hoph. ptcp., ŭ appearing in the sharpened syllable.

12, 13. *Therefore you shall suffer. What? Prepare for the worst. It is Yahweh who speaks.*

The remaining strophes of the poem have suffered greatly in their text. It may be accepted, in general, that a part of v.¹² and all of v.¹³ are from the hand of a later writer (so Duhm, *Theol.* 109; Oort, *ThT.* XIV. 117 *f*; We., Sta. *GVI.* I. 571; Taylor, *DB.*; Löhr, Che. in WRS. *Proph.* XV. and *EB.* I. 153; Bu. *Jew. Enc.*; Now., Co. *Einl.* 176; Baud. *Einl.* 509; Marti; but on the contrary see WRS. *Proph.* 400; Kue. *Einl.* II. 347; Mit., Hoffm. *ZAW.* III. 103; cf. GAS. I. 201 ff.; Dr. 118 f.). It may be supposed that the original poem contained a conclusion, predicting a punishment more severe than any of those which had been described; that this prediction was in form consistent with the strophes which preceded, though, of course, without the refrain; that the later editor, for one or more of several reasons which might be given, substituted the present concluding lines, which are general in character, for the more specific statement in the original; that this later editor, here as everywhere, ignored, consciously or unconsciously, the poetic form of the production which he thus modified. It is not strange (*contra* We.) that the conclusion here, as perhaps in Is. 9, should thus be broken off. We may well understand that in a multitude of cases the closing words of earlier sermons, having lost in later times the direct and specific reference which they were intended to convey, have given place to utterances presenting more modern thought and form. In view of this we need not be surprised to find that while vs.¹². ¹³ as thus modified contain eight lines (the number for two strophes), they are so constructed that, except by a transposition which is more or less violent, the division is 3 + 5 instead of 4 + 4.

12. כה] 𝕍 *haec;* 𝕿 מה. Oort (*ThT.* XIV. 117) regards the phrase
כה ... ישראל as due to dittography.— [עקב כי 𝕲 πλὴν ὅτι; 𝕍 *postquam autem*
חֲלַף דְּלָא חַבְתְּ לְאוֹרְיָתָא דָא ;A. ὕστερον; Θ. ἔσχατον; 𝕿 ,كس,لا مذـــجلا ؟ �
אֶעֱבֶּד לָךְ; Elh. drops the clause עשה לך as a gloss on the preceding
clause. Oet. regards the first two clauses as doublets, but suggests also that
the original text may have read עקב כי זאת עָשִׂיתָ ישראל, with second clause לכן
כה אעשה לך. Oort (*Em.*) inserts ו before עקב.—[לקראת 𝕲 τοῦ ἐπικαλεῖσθαι =
לְקָרָא (Va.); � ܘܩܐ (= 𝕲, perhaps לקרא אֶת, Seb.); 𝕿 לְמְבְּלָא אוּלְפָן
אוֹרָיְתָא דֶאֱלָהָךְ; A. κατέναντι; Σ. = *ut adverseris;* Θ. εἰς ἀπάντησιν.—**13.** יוצר
הרים] 𝕲 στερεῶν βροντήν, reading חסר (Va.), or יוֹצֵב (cf. נצב, מציב; cf. Na.
2[8] La. 2[4], Vol.) and הרעם (Va. Vol.); � ܪ,ܡ for יוצר as well as ܒܪܐ.—
מה-שׂחו] 𝕲 τὸν χριστὸν αὐτοῦ = מְשִׁיחוֹ or מְשִׁיחוּ; so also Syr.-Hex. 'A. τίς ἡ
ὁμιλία αὐτοῦ; Σ. τὸ φώνημα αὐτοῦ; Θ. τὸν λόγον αὐτοῦ; 𝕍 *eloquium suum;*
� ܡܬܚܫܒ ܡܢ ܠܒܢܐ (= מה שבחו, Seb.); 𝕿 מָה עוֹבָדוֹהִי (= מעשׂהו). Oet.
regards מה' לא' סג' as a marginal gloss and reads מִשְׁפָּטוֹ for מה-שׂחו. Hoffm.,
ZAW. III. 103, שֵׂחוֹ (?) מֵי לְאָדְמָה וּמַגִּיר, seeking thereby to bring the clause
into harmony with the context. Hal. [שׂחר עיפה.—ומחולל ארץ משׂחו. 𝕲[A]
inserts καί; so some Hebrew MSS.; so also Oort, *ThT.* XIV. 117; 'A.
renders עיפה by χύμα, flood; Σ. ἐσπέραν, evening; 𝕍 *faciens matutinam*
nebulam; � ܘܥܒܕ ܨܦܪܐ ܘܚܫܘܟܐ.

12. *Therefore*] In view of the failure of Yahweh's previous
judgments to bring Israel to terms. — *Thus will I do to thee*] The
threat is addressed to each individual of the nation, and thus
becomes more vivid. But what is the threat implied in the word
thus ? It does not refer specifically to the punishments proposed
in the preceding statements, *e.g.* 4[2-3],* nor to punishments of such
a character in general,† nor to a complete destruction like that
just cited in the case of Sodom and Gomorrah. ‡ But as always
in the case of *thus* in Amos, § and as evident from the tense of the
following verb, ‖ the reference is to the future.¶ The prophet
thus theatrically ** predicts the *final* punishment, a punishment all
the more severe because it is left thus indeterminate. Whether of
purpose or not, the form is that of the Hebrew oath, *God do so to*
me and more also if, etc. (1 K. 2[23]), which is most terrible in its
significance because of its indefiniteness. — *Because I will do this*]
The words "this" and "thus" refer to the same thing; *i.e.*
because this punishment, so terrible in its nature, is to come upon

---

* *Contra* Ros., Schrö., Mau., Hd.　　　　† Os.　　　　‡ Geb.
§ Ba.　　　　‖ Ke.　　　　¶ So Now., Mit., GAS., Dr.　　　　** Ew.

you. — *Prepare to meet thy God*] This can scarcely refer to a rising
up in preparation like that of an accused person when the judge
approaches * or when sentence is about to be pronounced.† Nor
does the injunction have reference simply to the hard fate which
is before them, ‡ the inevitable doom (cf. Je. 46¹⁴ Ez. 22¹⁴) which
the nation could not escape, whatever might be true of the individual.§ It is not a challenge, ‖ calling upon Israel to endure
Yahweh's anger. It is, in accordance with the whole spirit and
purpose of prophecy, a call to repentance (cf. ⅌, to call upon thy
God), in other words the spiritual application of the threat; for
every prediction of disaster was in itself an exhortation to repentance, in order that, if possible, the disaster might be averted.
Whatever befell the nation, there was an opportunity for the
repentant individual to receive divine favor.¶ — **13.** The logical
connection between v.¹² and v.¹³ is somewhat uncertain. To make
v.¹²ᵇ a challenge and translate ¹³ᵃ, *But* (*remember*), — *who
formeth mountains*, etc., ‖ is un-Hebraic. The strophic arrangement would be satisfied, and a good thought obtained by combining ¹²ᶜ and ¹³ᵈ thus, (¹²ᶜ) *Prepare to meet thy God, O Israel,*
(¹³ᵈ) *Yahweh, God of Hosts is his name;* (¹³ᵃ) *for behold*, etc.]
In any case, an ellipsis in thought must be supplied, *e.g.*, Prepare
to meet thy God, O Israel! (and do not doubt his power to bring
the threatened punishment). *For, lo! he forms the mountains*]
"By his power the visible world, with all its grandeur, exists"
(Ps. 104⁸).** — *And he creates the wind*] The invisible world,††
not the spirit of man. ‡‡ — *And he tells man what is his thought*]
This seems out of place in the midst of an utterance, all the other
members of which refer to nature. Its uncertainty of meaning is
attested by the variety of interpretations accorded to it, *e.g.* ⅌ *his
Messiah;* ⅌ *how great is his glory;* ⅌ *what are his works;* ⅌ *his
declaration;* his (God's) thought to man, §§ his (man's) thought to
him; ‖‖ and the attempts to emend the text (*v.s.*). Hirscht proposes to take אדם as a proper name and interpret it in view of
Gn. 3¹¹. — *He makes dawn darkness*] Not dawn and darkness; ¶¶

---

* Ew.   † Reu.   ‡ Suggested by Jus.   § Hd.   ‖ Mit.
¶ So Cal., Os., Geb., Jus., Ros., Ba., Pu., Ke., Dr.   ** Bauer, Jus., Ros., Schrö.
†† Ros., Ew., Hd., Pu., and most comm.   ‡‡ Cal., Geb., Or.   §§ Geb., Ew.
‖‖ Cal., Jus., Schrö., Hd., Ke., Dr.   ¶¶ ⅌., fol. by Cal., Geb., Jus., Ke., *et al.*

nor spiritual light and darkness,* but either he changes dawn into darkness, *i.e.* the change from day to night,† or from night to day,‡ or better, the change of day at the approach of a storm (Ps. 18⁹). § — *He treads on the heights of the earth*] *i.e.* goes forth in storm and thunder (cf. Mi. 1³ Jb. 9⁸ Matt. 5³⁴).

12. לכן] Very similar in meaning to על כן. In usage, however, they vary, לכן being often used as in this case where the inference is important and of a threatening character, and also having sometimes the meaning, *nevertheless* (Je. 5²); cf. Ew.⁸ 353 *b* (2). — כה] Regularly refers to something that follows (BSZ., BDB., and SS., *s.v.*; Kö. 332 *b*, and *Stil.* 112); rarely of something present, Is. 20⁶. — עקב כי] Cf. the same expression in 2 S. 12¹⁰, and the similar עקב אשר in Gn. 22¹⁸ 26⁵ 2 S. 12⁶; cf. Kö. 389 *n*, and *Stil.* 171. — זאת] Neut., H. 2, 3 *a*; GK. 122 *q*. — הרים] Art. om., H. 5, 4; GK. 126 *h*; Kö. 277 *b*. — אדם] Here collective, H. 1, 2. — עשה] On the ptcp. in cstr. with the object and governing product in acc., see GK. 116 *g*, N. 2; Kö. 241 *f*. — שחר עיפה] Double obj. H. 31, 6, rm. *c*; Kö. 327 *w*. — בָּמֳתֵי] ֵ‑ is the archaic ending of fem. cstr.; cf. GK. 87 *s*; Ew.⁸ 211 *d*. The form is bâ-mᵒ-thê, perhaps a mistaken vocalization for bâ-mô-thê, the ô written defectively, Ols. 164 *b*; GK. 95 *o*.

§ 8. A dirge announcing Israel's coming destruction. 5¹⁻⁶, ⁸, ⁹.

A lamentation is pronounced : " Israel shall fall, her forces shall be reduced to a tenth ; for she has disobeyed Yahweh's direct command, ' Seek me ; not Bethel, nor Gilgal, nor Beersheba ! ' " and now again it is commanded, ' Seek Yahweh, lest ye perish.' [Who speaks? The creator of the luminaries, the controller of the seas, the destroyer of the strong.]

The original poem consisted of six strophes (vs.¹⁻⁶). The second and third strophes are elegiac in their movement, a short line (dimeter) following a longer line (trimeter). Bu., *ZAW*. II. 30, considers only the second strophe to be elegiac; so Mit., 125; Dr. 175. The קינה (dirge) was a formal composition, somewhat artistically constructed, the second or shorter line being intended to echo the first, " producing a plaintive, melancholy cadence." To the six original strophes were added, by a later hand, two strophes, each having four trimeters. V.⁷ belongs to the section which follows, and should precede v.¹⁰. The addition is after the analogy of the insertion already noticed in 4¹³. There is, notwithstanding the statements of Oort (*v.i.*) and Volz, entirely satisfactory connection between vs.⁴⁻⁶ and vs.¹⁻³.

---

* Grotius, Geb., Dathe.   † Gun.   ‡ Or.   § Mit., Dr.

V. 1–3. *Israel shall fall, never again to rise; only a tenth shall survive.*

1. בית — .(Va.) הזה for יהוה substituting perhaps ,κυρίου adds 𝕲 [הדבר הזה .
ישראל] 𝕲𝖄 join with following v. and make subj. of נפלה. — **2.** קום] 𝕿 adds שָׁתָּא
חדא = in one year. — בתולת ישראל] 𝕲𝖄 join with נטשה; 𝕿 *assembly.* — אדמתה]
𝕾 om. suf.; 𝕲 has *his.* — **3.** כי כה אמר אדני יהוה] To be transferred to v.[1] to
follow ישראל, thus relieving (1) a serious interruption in the thought of vs.[2. 3],
(2) the lack of a line in one strophe and superfluity of a line in another.
Baumann om. — העיר] 𝕲𝖄𝕾𝕿 add *from which*, thus making אלף subj. of היצאת.
— תשאיר] 𝕲𝖄 have passive (= תִּשָּׁאֵר) with מאה as subj. (Vol., so also Gr.);
𝕾𝕿 have Hithpa'ēl, while 𝕾𝖄𝕿 insert *in it;* so also in v.[3b]. — לבית ישראל]
To be transferred to fol. מאה, thus conforming to the קינה measure (so Now.;
Löhr places it after יהוה, v.[3]; Gun. and Oet. regard it as a repetition from v.[4]).

1. *Hear this word.*] The beginning of a new discourse, intended,
if possible, to strike terror to the hearts of the people and thus
lead them to repentance. Such a message, uttered in the prosperous days of Jeroboam II., would certainly seem to be in contrast with the time in which it was uttered. — *Which I take up
against you, even a dirge*] This rendering is to be preferred to
(1) *as I uplift a dirge,* making אשר = *as*; * or (2) *because I uplift,*
etc., † since it is the more simple and at the same time accords
better with the versification. The word "take up" (נשא) *i.e.*
on the lips, is found in the technical term מַשָּׂא, so often used by
the prophets; it means "to pronounce," "to denounce," and is
used regularly of a dirge (Je. 7[29] Ez. 19[1], etc.). Just as in the case
of an individual's death there was uttered a lamentation (cf.
2 S. 1[17] Ez. 28[12] 32[2] 2 Ch. 35[25]) so here, the death of the nation
being assumed, the mourner utters the dirge-song. This dirge is
not restricted to v.[2], ‡ nor does it include the entire chapter, § but
is contained in vs.[2 and 3]. — *O house of Israel*] The 𝕸𝕿 connects
these words with the preceding, as against 𝕲𝖄 (*v.s.*), thus greatly
increasing the pathos of the appeal. — *For thus says the Lord Yahweh*] Transferred from v.[3], introducing in the most solemn way the
sad and severe announcement which is to follow. — **2.** *Shall fall*]
The certainty of the event being indicated by the use of the perfect. Very unreasonable is the interpretation which renders the

---

* Ba., We.   † Os., Hi.
‡ Dahl, Ros., Hd., Hi., Ew., Bu., Ba., Pu., GAS., Dr.   § Ki., Schrö.

perfect literally, *and has fallen*, and upon this basis rejects vs.[1-3],*
because, as a matter of fact, Israel did not fall until after the reign
of Jeroboam II. The expression is used of violent death (*e.g.*
2 S. 1[19. 25. 27]), especially of death in battle, and of loss of honor or
possessions (*e.g.* 2 S. 1[10] Ps. 10[10] Pr. 11[28]). For its use of nations
cf. Is. 21[9] Je. 51[8]. — *Not to rise again*] *i.e.* as a people; the
prophet always held out hope of pardon and mercy to individuals. — *Virgin Israel*] In personifications the word "virgin"
is used alone with no other name besides Israel (Israel never
occurs with "daughter" in this sense); aside from this passage,
this expression is found only three times,† viz. Je. 18[13] 31[4. 21]. The
explanations of the phrase, used here for the first time, may be
classified according as the principal thought is found in (1) the
figure of chastity, whether political chastity, *i.e.* as being free,
unconquered, independent of other powers ‡ (cf. the use of
"daughter" in the same sense, and sometimes in combination
with "virgin," in connection with Idumea, La. 4[22]; Judah, La. 1[15]
2[1-5]; Egypt, Je. 46[11. 19-24]; Babylon, Is. 47[1. 5] Zc. 2[7]; Jerusalem,
Is. 37[22]; in La. 2[13] and Je. 18[13] the reference is to Jerusalem before
her capture), or religious chastity, *i.e.* freedom from contaminating
contact with other gods; § or (2) the idea of the delicacy and
self-indulgence of the people; ‖ or (3) the idea of collectivity,
the feminine being used to convey this thought, — in this sense it
has been taken (*a*) as a designation of the people in general; ¶
(*b*) as a poetic term for *state* (cf. Is. 37[22] Je. 14[17] 2 K. 19[21]); (*c*) as
the designation of a *city*, and usually the chief or capital city of
the kingdom, Samaria, or Jerusalem.** It here refers to northern
Israel †† (in Isaiah, Jerusalem), and is employed to mark the contrast between Israel's past and future condition. — *She shall be
hurled down upon her own soil*] A stronger figure than that contained in *fallen;* the description is expanded in Ez. 29[5] (leave thee
(thrown) into the wilderness), 32[4] (leave thee forsaken upon the
land); there is no thought of an uprooted and prostrate tree, ‡‡
nor of a depraved woman in difficult child-birth. §§ She will be
left to die where she has fallen. — *With none to raise her up*] An

---

* Oort, *Th.T.*, XIV. 118.   † Mit.   ¶ Va., Ros.   ‡‡ Geb.
‡ Geb., Har., Hi., Hd., Ke., Now., Dr.   ** Schrö., Ew.   §§ Har.
§ Os.   ‖ Cal., Pu.   †† Mit., Now., GAS.

advance upon what has preceded, for not only will she not be able to raise herself, but no one else will be able to render her assistance. The Jewish interpreters in general follow 𝕋, and regard the calamity as of temporary character. — **3.** *The city that goeth forth a thousand having (but) a hundred left*] The two circumstantial clauses of this verse add to the picture portrayed in v.² an additional feature, viz. the ninefold decimation of the forces sent out to war, a terrible slaughter. The statement is general, the *city* being any city in the kingdom. The thousand refers not simply to the levy or census,* but to the warriors who marched out for war.† While it is evident that in Amos's time the basis of military enrolment was the towns and villages, in earlier days it was tribes and families. ‡ For allusions to similar companies, cf. 1 S. 8¹² 2 S. 18¹·⁴ 2 K. 11⁴·¹⁹ Ex. 18²¹ etc. § — *Of the house of Israel*] Transferred (*v.s.*).

1. אשר] Depends for its construction upon קינה; if as a pronoun it refers to הדבר, קינה is either in apposition with it, or an acc. of purpose, GK. 131 *k*; Kö. 327 *v*, 384 *c* (Now.); but if אשר = "as" (Ew.⁸ 334 *a*, Ba., We.), קינה is the acc. after נשא; the former is preferable. — נשא] Ptcp. of immediate future, GK. 116 *p*; since the lifting up of a word, or of the voice, is but an Oriental phrase for *utterance* or *speech*, perhaps the word *speak* would fairly represent נשא; cf. נשא קול (= הרים קול, נתן קול), Ju. 9⁷; also נשא alone, Is. 3⁷ 42²·¹¹ (see, however, Paton, *JBL.* XXII. 201–7). — קינה] The verb קונן is doubtless a denominative from קינה. A plausible derivation (*Thes.*), for קינה is the Arabic root قَانَ, to forge, devise, hence a skilfully wrought production, so named either from its poetic form, or from its contents as glorifying the dead (Wetzstein, *Zeitsch. f. Ethnologie*, 1873, pp. 270 ff.). Bu. prefers the former reason (*ZAW.* II. 28). This derivation from the Arabic is doubted by some (*e.g.* Ba.). The closest parallel is found in the Syriac ܩܝܢܬܐ, which means both song and elegy. We may also compare Eth. ፈለየ: song, and ፈለየ: to sing. The קינה is an elegy, a poem of lamentation, thus distinguished from נהי, which means sometimes a song of lament, but sometimes simply the cry of mourning (Je. 31¹⁵); cf. the vb. in 1 S. 7². קינה is used commonly, as here, with נשא (Je. 7²⁹ 9⁹ Ez. 19¹ 26¹⁷ 27²·³² 28¹² 32²); with קונן (2 S. 1¹⁷ Ez. 32¹⁶), and with למר. With נשא, על generally precedes the person or thing which is the object of lamentation, but sometimes אל (Ez. 19¹ 27³²); על is sometimes used of the place (Je. 7²⁹). For the importance of elegies among Oriental nations, cf. Wetzstein (*v.s.*) and the Arabic work, *Hamasa*, 365–497. The principal rhythm of the קינה

---

* Ew.   † Hd., Ba., Schegg.   ‡ We., Now.   § Cf. Benz. *Arch.* 359.

is a long line followed by a shorter one, the favorite measures being 3 and 2 words, 4 and 2, and 4 and 3. However, a קינה may be written in another measure, and the Qînah measure may be used for other poems, as a later usage. On Qînah rhythm, see Bu. *ZAW.* II. 6 ff., 38–45; III. 299 f.; XI. 234 ff.; XII. 261 ff.; and in *Preuss. Jahrbücher*, 1893, pp. 460 ff.; Ley, *SK.*, 1896, p. 637; DHM. *Proph.* I. 209; Kö. *Stil.* 315 ff.; BDB. *s.v.* The principal examples of the קינה in the O.T. are the following: the Book of Lamentations; Is. 14[4-21] Ez. 19[1-14] 26[15-17] 27[2-36] 28[12-19] (doubtful) 32[2-16] Je. 9[9], and several separated vs. following, Is. 45[14-25] Ps. 137 2 S. 1[19-27] 3[33 f.] (the last two not in the technical measure) 2 K. 19[21-28] (= Is. 37[22 ff.]) Is. 1[21-23] Ho. 6[7 ff.] Am. 8[10]. — [בית ישראל] Vocative; not subj. of נפלה (v.[2]). — **2.** [נפלה] Proph. pf., H. 19, 2; GK. 106 *n*; Dr. § 14. — [לא תוסיף] Impf. in contrast with preceding pf., used to intensify the idea that the destruction will be permanent, H. 20, 2, rm. *b*; Dr. § 36; on the inf. with תוסיף, H. 36, 3 (2); GK. 120 *a*; Kö. 399 *b*. — [בתולת] On the cstr. state, GK. 128 *k*; Kö. 337 *g*. — [אין מקימה] Circ. cl., H. 45, 2 *e*; on force of אין, Kö. 361 *d*, 402 *m*. — **3.** [העיר] Stands first, not because emphatic, but in a circ. cl., H. 45, 3, rm. *d*. — [היצאת] On art. with ptcp., H. 4, 3 *f*; here joined poetically to העיר, the city being thus represented as going out to war. — [אלף] Acc. of limitation, or specification, H. 33, 3; GK. 117 *z*; Kö. 332 *k*; so also מֵאָה; for a similar construction, cf. 2 K. 5[2], גדורים, and 2 K. 9[25], צמדים. The same idea is expressed by ל with the numeral; cf. 1 S. 29[2]. — [לבית] Not a case of ל used when the preceding governing word is absent, but like לדוד in Je. 13[18] (Hi.); cf. Kö. 281 *n*.

4–6. *Israel shall fall* (vs.[1-3]) *because she has disobeyed the divine command given in the past to seek Yahweh alone.* [But even now the entreaty comes again] *Seek Yahweh, lest ye perish.*

These verses contain the second half of the dirge (strophes 4, 5) and the concluding strophe of the original poem, somewhat mutilated. The second half gives the explanation of the destruction announced in the first half; while in the concluding strophe, the prophet, as so many times before, turns in exhortation to the people to do the thing, the neglect of doing which in the past has cost them so dearly. The logical connection of vs.[4-6] becomes plain when אמר (v.[4]) is taken as historical pf., or plup. (*v.i.*); and, therefore, the proposal to throw out vs.[1-3] (Oort), or to treat v.[4] as introducing a new section (Now., Marti), may be rejected.

5. [ובאר שבע לא תעברו] To be transferred to the beginning of v.[5]; it is entirely rejected by Baumann, since (1) it spoils the strophic arrangement, (2) has nothing to correspond to it as in the case of Bethel and Gilgal; cf. 4[4], where only the two cities are mentioned; also 8[14]. — [ובאר שבע] 𝕲 has ἐπὶ τὸ φρέαρ τοῦ ὅρκου; cf. same in Gn. 26[31] 21[31], but in Am. 8[14] it has proper name. — [יהיה לאון] 𝕲 ἔσται ὡς οὐχ ὑπάρχουσα, similarly 𝕾 and 𝕿, all seeming to take לאון in the sense of לאין (Seb., so Hal.); 𝔙 *erit inutilis.* — **6**. It seems probable that an entire member has been lost, perhaps וְעָתָה בית ישראל. — יצלח] 𝔊 ἀναλάμψη with בית יוסף as subj. = צרב or דלק (Va.) or צמח, cf. Is. 4² (Voi.); 𝔙 *comburatur*, similarly 𝔖. Read י ישַׁלַח אֵש בבית (so We., Elh., Löhr, Gun. *Th. St.* XVIII. 221; cf. Baumann); cf. Gun. ישלח באש (in his comm., but abandoned later in favor of We.'s reading; so also Gr.). Now. 𝔖 יצית באש; Oet. יצַת כאש; Elh. ישליך אש(?); Hal. יֵעֶלֶה(?); Duhm (*EB.* 3799) and Marti, אש יצלח לַהַב אש. — אכלה] 𝔊 adds αὐτόν. Now. om. as gloss. — לבית אל] 𝔊 τῷ οἴκῳ Ἰσραήλ (cf. Ho. 10¹⁵); one cod. has τῷ Ἰσραήλ; so also one cod. of Kenn. לישראל, and one of de R. לבית ישראל (so also Dathe, Gr., Now., Elh., Hal., Löhr, Oort *Em.*). Ἀ. and Σ. τῷ Βαιθήλ; Θ. τῷ οἴκῳ Βαιθήλ. Hirscht explains the reading ישראל as due to a marginal note by a reader contrasting בית און and בית ישר, which resulted in the blending of בית ישר and בית אל into בית ישראל. We. and Now. om. לבית אל as a gloss; Marti transposes it to v.⁷. Oet. transposes thus: ואכלה בית ישראל ואין מ'. Löhr rejects v.⁶ᵇ as an interpolation based on 1⁴, and introducing a thought entirely foreign to Amos.

4. *For thus said Yahweh to the house of Israel*] The prophet has just described the coming desolation. This description suggests at once the question, Are we not zealously engaged in the worship of Yahweh? Why are we then to suffer? The answer is furnished: 'Yahweh in times past spoke thus and thus, — commands which ye have disobeyed.' The verb is not to be rendered *saith*, but *said*, referring to the injunctions of the past. The dirge may well describe the occasion of the impending calamity. The ordinary interpretation which makes this an exhortation uttered by the prophet, after announcing the calamity,* takes away the force of the most impressive portion of the piece, and compels the prophet to give two exhortations in practically the same language (see v.⁶). — *Seek me*] A common phrase for the expression of religious desire implying worship and obedience, and used alike of God and idols.† — *And live*] *i.e.* that you may live, implying that the danger ahead may not be averted otherwise; cf. Is. 1¹⁹ Am. 5¹⁵. The life of course includes national life and prosperity (Baur). For other examples of two imperatives used in this way, either conditionally, *if you seek me you will certainly live*, the conclusion being

---

* Nearly all comm.

† Besides דרש, the word here, בקש is also used in the same sense; cf. Ps. 24⁶ Is. 8¹⁹ 55⁶. The exact meaning here as gathered from the context is *to make effort to obey his will and to practise a righteous life.*

thus rendered more certain, or as an action with a purpose, *seek me in order that you may live*, the request being thus emphasized, cf. Gn. 42^{18} 1 K. 22^{12} 2 K. 5^{13} Je. 27^{17} Am. 5^{14}. There is no reference to the future life, nor, perhaps, even to spiritual life.* — **5**. *And to Beer-sheba do not (ye shall not) cross over*] (*v.s.*).   This line, probably corrupt, must be transferred to precede the line *and do not seek Beth-el*, which is required by the chiastic arrangement of the next strophe.   Several explanations have been given of the lack of a corresponding line, as in the case of Gilgal and Beth-el, *e.g.* a pun is evident in the very word באר שבע = באר שבי = fount of captivity ; † or, Beer-sheba is omitted because, being in Judah, it was not destroyed when Samaria fell ; ‡ or because Amos is prophesying only to the ten tribes ; § or because no suitable paronomasia could be found for Beer-sheba. ‖   If the present text is accepted, we must understand that the Israelites of Amos's day were not satisfied with visiting the sanctuaries of the North, but were so zealous in their worship as to cross over the border-land of their own territory ¶ and penetrate as far south as the ancient sanctuary of Beer-sheba, thirty miles southwest of Hebron on the road to Egypt.   Beer-sheba played an important part in the stories of the patriarchs, cf. Gn. 21$^{14. 31. 33}$ 26$^{23. 33}$ 28^{10} 46^{1} ; there is no authority for Driver's statement, " in Amos's time it was a popular resort for pilgrims from N. Israel," unless it is found in 8^{14} (a doubtful text).   After the captivity it was again occupied (Ne. 11^{27}). This worship was strikingly inconsistent with the assumption of Jeroboam I. that Jerusalem was too far away from the Northern tribes to be the place of central worship.   The most extreme form of corrupt worship, viz. that at Beer-sheba, is thus placed in contrast with the true attitude commended. — *Ye shall not seek Beth-el*] *i.e.* visit for the purpose of exercising rites and ceremonies. — *And Gilgal ye shall not enter*] Reference has already been made to these places as the seats of sanctuaries. — *For Gilgal shall surely go into exile*] The Gilgal, in which they now take such delight, will be laid waste.** — *And Beth-el shall become (Beth)aven*]

---

* *Contra* Pu., Ke.   ‡ Jer., Hi.   ‖ Ros.
† Har.   § Ba., Ke.   ¶ Jer., Har., Ros., Hi., Ba.
** The alliteration of the original הגלגל גלה יגלה cannot well be indicated in a translation. Cf. Ew., *Gilgal wird Galle weinen ;* Ba., *Gilgal giltig entgilt es ;* Or.,

The word אָוֶן has been variously taken as meaning *nought*,* *idol-atry*,† *iniquity* ‡ (cf. Ho. 4¹⁵ 5⁸ 10⁵) ; *trouble ;* § in a recent transla-tion it is rendered *des Teufels*. ‖   It is better to understand it as an abbreviation ¶ of בֵּית אָוֶן, the אָוֶן in either sense being the oppo-site of אֵל (Beth-el).   Cf. Hoffmann's suggestion ** that the wor-ship of the Northern kingdom had many Egyptian elements, such as the calf, that Yahweh was identified with Ra', and Beth-el with On, the sacred city.   Hence the use of אָוֶן by Hosea and Amos has a double sense; here " your On-Beth-el will become Aven, delu-sion."   It is of importance to note that not far from Beth-el, close to the edge of the desert, there was a village (the site of which is now uncertain) named Beth-aven (cf. Jos. 7² 18¹² 1 S. 13⁵ 14²³).†† — **6.** The dirge being now completed, it is the natural thing for the prophet to utter an exhortation.   This, found in v.⁶, completes the piece.   But, unfortunately, one line seems to have been lost ; perhaps it read, *And now, O house of Israel, seek Yahweh and live*] *i.e.* do as he long ago bade you. — *Lest he cast fire on Joseph's house*] ‡‡ The wrath of God is represented by fire (Dt. 32²² Ez. 22²¹).   Joseph, as well as Ephraim, is often used for Northern as distinguished from Southern Israel (cf. 2 S. 19²⁰ Ob.¹⁸ Zc. 10⁶ ; Joseph, without *house*, occurs in Am. 5¹⁵ 6⁶ Ez. 37¹⁶ Ps. 78⁶⁷). — *For Beth-el*] 𝔊, some Mss., and the demands of the parallelism incline some (*v.s.*) to read *for Israel ;* but the reading of 𝔐𝔗 is satisfactory, Beth-el being the centre of the religious cultus ; cf. 2 K. 22¹⁷ Is. 1³¹ Je. 4⁴. §

4. The Hebrew could not distinguish *has said* (indef.), *has just said* (pf. of immediate past), from the historical *said ;* the latter is intended here, H. 16, 1; Dr. § 7; GK. 106 *d.* — דְרָשׁוּנִי וַחֲיוּ] H. 48, 8 *b*; Dr. § 152, 1 ; GK.

Die Rollstadt rollt von dannen ; Mit., *Gilgal shall go into galling captivity ;* We., *Gilgal wird zum Galgen gehen ;* GAS., *Gilgal shall taste the gall of exile.* Cf. Ho. 12¹² for a similar alliteration of the same letters; and for other cases Is. 10²⁹ 15⁹ Je. 6¹ Mi. 1¹⁰. ¹¹. ¹⁴. ¹⁵ Zp. 2⁴.

* Mich., Jus., Ros., Ba., Or.	‡ Ew.	‖ We.; cf. GAS.
† Hd., GAS.	§ Dr.	¶ Hi., Mit.
** *ZAW.* III. 105 f.		†† GAS., art. " Beth-aven," *EB.*

‡‡ 𝔐𝔗 יַצְלַח has been translated *advance* (Cal.), *pass through consuming all* (Har., Jus., Hd.), *destroy* (Dahl), *kindle* (𝔊 and 𝔙, *v.s.*).   The translation adopted, which seems better, rests upon the suggestion that ה and כ are easily confused in sound, while the כ of כְּאֵשׁ is inserted after the analogy of dittography.

110 f.; Kö. 364 k.   דרש and בקשׁ are practically synonymous (cf. Ez. 34⁶); and are used alike of seeking Yahweh and of seeking idols (e.g. Lv. 19³¹ Is. 19³ Dt. 18¹¹ Je. 8² 21² Gn. 25²², etc.).   For original force of both see BSZ. and BDB. An early meaning, *resort to*, seems to appear in Am. 5⁵ Dt. 12⁵ 2 Ch. 1⁵. Both words were used commonly of consulting the deity, through an oracle or through a prophet, in reference to matters of all kinds, religious and secular (Ex. 18¹⁵ 1 S. 9⁹ 2 K. 3¹¹ 8⁸ Ez. 20¹·³, etc.).   From this usage came the broader meaning of seeking in prayer and worship and, in general, striving to act in accord with the divine will (Dt. 4²⁹ Ho. 5⁶ Zp. 2³ Ps. 40¹⁷ 69⁷ 105³, etc.).   In prophetic speech דרש is much the more common word of the two when used of religious affairs. — **5.** [אל תדרשׁו Deprecation, H. 41, 1 b; Dr. § 50 (a) Obs.; GK. 152 f; Kö. 352 g., but cf. לא (with תבאו) prohibition. — [ביתאל והגלגל marks the chiasm; perhaps לא after הגלגל is due to a desire not to repeat the sound al. — [גלה יגלה H. 28, 3 a; GK. 113 n; Kö. 329 r. — [כי הגלגל Note masc. form of the vb., though the feminine is more usual with names of towns; Kö. 248 c. The subj. first because emphatic, so [ביתאל; note the chiastic order of the proper names in ⁵ᵇ, as compared with that in ⁵ᵃ. — **6.** [ויצלח v.s. The difficulty is twofold (1) the use of צלח with acc. of the person, when it is regularly followed by על or אל (cf. Ju. 14¹⁹ 15¹⁴ 1 S. 10⁶), being used with the acc. in the sense of *to reach*, 2 S. 19¹⁸; and (2) the fem. vb. אכלה which points to אשׁ; hence the many emendations proposed (v.s.). Margolis (AJSL. XVII. 171), however, defends יצלח (but reads כאשׁ) on the basis of the usage of צלח in Ecclus. 8¹⁰, where it is followed by בנחלת (a mistake for בגחלת; cf. 𝔊) and rendered *kindle* by 𝔊. — [בית יוסף Subj., not obj. — [אכלה Fem. as ref. to אשׁ. — [לביתאל Correct, notwithstanding We. et al., v.s.; not acc. (ל = sign of acc.) after מכבה (cf. Hd.), nor to be connected with אכלה (Mau.); but dat. of adv. or disadv.; cf. Ez. 37¹¹; GK. 119 s.

8, 9. *Who is it that you are asked to seek?   Yahweh is his name, the creator of the luminaries, the controller of the seas, the destroyer of the strong.*

This addition from a later hand, "to relieve the gloom of the prophetic picture," falls into two strophes, each of four trimeters.   It bears the general character of the additions found in 4¹³ 9⁵·⁶, and resembles in style the Deutero-Isaiah (cf. Is. 40²² ᶠ·).   Note (1) the use of participles, and (2) the peculiar words; cf. Stickel, *Hiob* 276; Che. EB. I. 153 n. 3.   Vs.⁸ ᵃⁿᵈ ⁹ are placed by Elh. after 2⁷ ᶠ.   Their lack of connection with v.⁷ is generally acknowledged (so Ew., followed by GAS., who places them before v.⁷; Gr., who would place v.⁸ after 4¹³; Oet., who suggests the alternative of the end of the chap.; Che. EB. I. 153, who places them after 4¹³; Now., who regards them as a misplaced gloss on v.⁶; Dr., Marti, and others, who treat them as an interpolation; cf. Baumann).

I

8. יהוה שמו] To be transferred to the beginning of v.[8], some preceding word being lost ; or perhaps the line may be filled from 𝕋 = *Let there be fear in the presence of him who*, etc. Two codd. of Kenn. add צבאות and two codd. of 𝕲 read, *Yahweh, God of hosts*. — כימה וכסיל] 𝕲 πάντα καὶ μετασκευάζων = כל ומסב (Vol.) ; 'Α. Ἀρκτοῦρον καὶ Ὠρίωνα ; Σ. Πλειάδας καὶ ἄστρα ; 𝔙 *Arcturum et Orionem* ; Θ. Πλειάδα καὶ ἔσπερον ; 𝕋 כימה וכסילא ; 𝕾 ܟܣܝܠܐ ܘܟܝܡܐ. — צלמות] Read צַלְמוּת (cf. Ps. 23[4]) foll. 𝕲 σκιάν (Va.), not צלל (Vol.) ; 𝔙 *tenebras;* but 𝕾 ܡܘܬܐ ܘܛܠܠܝ (see BDB.). — לילה] Read ללילה, with ten codd. Kenn. and seven de R. (so Dathe, Mit., Oort *ThT*. XIV. 118, Elh.). — הקרא למי־הים 𝕋 = *who commands to gather great armies like the waters of the sea.* — **9.** המבליג] ὁ διαιρῶν = הַמַּפְלִיג (Now.) ; 𝕲ᴼ ὁ διορίζων ; 'Α. ὁ μειδιῶν ; Σ. τὸν ποιοῦντα καταγελάσαι ; 𝔙 *qui arridet* (*subridet*, cod. Am.) ; 𝕋 רמגבר ; 𝕾 ܡܚܝܠܐ. Gr. המלעיגים ; Oet. הַמְעַלְגֵל ; Oort מגבר ; Elh., המגדיל ; Oort (*Em.*) and Marti, המפליא. — שד] Read שבר, fol. 𝕲 συντριμμόν (so Ew., Hi., Oort, Gr., GAS., Now., Oet.). 𝕾 ܣܘܚܡܐ and 𝕋 חלשיו = רָשׁ (Seb.) ; 𝔙 *vastitatem;* Σ. ἀφανισμόν. Hoffm., שׁד here and in fol. clause. Elh., שׁח. — עז] 𝕲 ἰσχύν = עֹז (so also Oort) ; 𝔙 *robustum;* 𝕋 תקיפים ; 𝕾 ܚܣܝܢܐ ; Hoffm., עֵז (?). — ושד] 𝕲 καὶ ταλαιπωρίαν ; 𝔙 *depopulationem;* 𝕾 ܣܚܬܡܐ ; 𝕋 ובוזזין ; Hal. וּשֹׁדֵד. St. would read (so also Dr. and Oort *Em.*) ושבר on basis of 𝕲 and Is. 59[7] 60[18] Je. 48[3] ; but it is better to read שבר for the previous שד (*v.s.*) and retain 𝔐𝕋 here, since 𝕲 employs συντριμμός and σύντριμμα to represent שבר twenty-three times, but שד only four times, including this passage, while the vb. שבר is regularly rendered by συντρίβω. ταλαιπωρία, on the other hand, represents שד ten times and שבר only thrice, while שדד is regularly rendered by ταλαιπωρέω. However, the occurrence of the phrase שד ושבר in Is. and Je., where 𝕲 renders by συντρ. καὶ ταλ., makes the matter somewhat uncertain. — מבצר] Hoffm., מַבְצִיר (?). — יבוא] Read יָבִיא, with all the versions (so Va., Oort *ThT*. XIV. 118 and *Em.*, Hoffm., GAS., Now., Elh., Oet., Hal.) ; 𝕲 Σ. ἐπάγων ; 𝔙 *affert;* 𝕾 ܡܚܠܛ ; 𝕋 מַשְׁלִיט. — These vs. are evidently not genuine. V.[7] must be transferred to precede v.[10], see p. 105. So Bauer, Ew., Or., GAS.; cf. Mit., who strains himself in the effort to connect vs.[7 and 8] (p. 129) ; Gun., who rejects v.[7] ; WRS. *Proph.* (p. 400), who maintains that, though not closely connected with the immediate context, these vs. are in complete harmony with the general purport of the thought of Amos, and that the ejaculatory form is " not surprising under the general conditions of prophetic oratory, while the appeal comes in to relieve the strain of the intense feeling at a critical point in the argument." The suggestion has been made to transfer הניחו from v.[7], with 𝕾 (New. *v.i.* p. 118), or to supply דרשו (Mich., Jus.), or *seek Yahweh* (Geb.), or *He is the one who* (Ba.) ; but it seems best to supply part of a line which shall include the words taken from the end of the v., viz. יהוה שמו, since this phrase could not originally have stood in the midst of the description. In 4[13] it comes at the close of the sentence.

8. *Whose name is Yahweh*] The God who is Israel's national
God, and who desires Israel's strongest allegiance. — *The creator of
the Pleiades and Orion*] In two or three strokes the poet depicts
the omnipotence of the God for whom he pleads. He seizes upon
two of the heavenly constellations which are most conspicuous to
represent, by synecdoche, the universe that is visible. They are
referred to in Jb. 9^9 $38^{31f.}$ (cf. Is. 13^{10}) in the same way as a proof
of God's creative power. The Hebrew name for Orion, which
also = *fool*, may perhaps contain a trace of some old mythological
notion, which held this constellation to have been "originally
some foolhardy, heaven-daring rebel who was chained to the sky
for his impiety." * The thought is not different from that of the
Psalmist (8^3). This seems to be the meaning rather than (1) the
interpretation of כימה as "genial heat" and כסיל as "cold," † on
the ground that it harmonizes better with the context to speak
of present acts than of a far-distant creation (but cf. the custom
of the Deutero-Isaiah); or (2) that which finds the principal
force of the utterance in the star-worship, which was not uncom-
mon in Israel (cf. Je. 7^{18} $44^{17.18}$ 2 K. 17^{16} $21^{3.5}$, cf. 23^{11}), the
thought being "do not worship the stars, but the creator of the
stars"; ‡ or (3) that of כימה as "fortune," "destiny"; § or (4) that
which supposes the stars to have been mentioned because of their
influence upon the weather, and because the writer wished to show
the supremacy of Yahweh over all such forces.‖ — *Who turneth
deep gloom into morning*] The "darkness" thus turned is not
the darkness of death,¶ an interpretation based upon an incorrect
pointing of צלמות (*v.i.*), nor the original creation of light, ‡ but
the change from night to day, a most wonderful, although most
common, phenomenon. — *And day into night darkeneth*] This

---

* Dr.; so Di. (on Jb. 9^9), Che., BDB. For reference to these constellations in
early Greek literature, cf. Hom. *Il.* XVIII. 486–9 : —

> Πληϊάδας θ' Ὑάδας τε τό τε σθένος Ὠρίωνος
> Ἄρκτον θ' ἣν καὶ ἄμαξαν ἐπίκλησιν καλέουσιν,
> Ἥ τ' αὐτοῦ στρέφεται καί τ' Ὠρίωνα δοκεύει,
> Οἴη δ' ἄμμορός ἐστι λοετρῶν Ὠκεανοῖο.

Cf. also XXII. 26–31, and *Od.* V. 272–75.

† Parkhurst, cited by Owen in his translation of Cal.   ‡ Geb.   § Schlier.
‖ Hoffm. *ZAW.* III. 109.   ¶ Pu., Ke.

supplements and explains the preceding phrase; the idea is that of the regular order of nature, night succeeding day, under a great Director, not that of an extraordinary event like the darkness of the land of Egypt,* nor the shortening of the days in winter. — *Who calleth the waters of the sea and poureth them on the face of the earth*] Cf. Is. 48[13] Jb. 38[34]. Are these waters the rains drawn from the sea and descending upon the earth (cf. Jb. 36[27]) ; † or the fountains and streams by which the earth is watered ‡ (cf. Ec. 1[7] Jb. 12[15]) ; or an inundation, the Noachian deluge, the most terrible punishment in history? § In favor of the last are the use of the expressions *call* and *face of the earth*, the thought of the following, and the typical character of the illustrations of Yahweh's power, as thus interpreted, viz., "Jehovah, by whom the world was made, of whose will the order and harmony in nature are an expression, and at whose command the forces in nature may become as destructive as they have been beneficent." ‖ — **9.** *Causeth violence to burst upon the strong*] For the word המבליג (found elsewhere only in Jb. 9[27] 10[20] Ps. 39[14] and מבליגית in Je. 8[18]) there have been suggested the following : (1) *He that strengthens* (the spoiled against the strong, so that the spoiled, or a waster, shall ascend upon the very fortresses ;¶ or destruction (= the destroyed) against strength (= the strong) so that (through him) destruction comes upon the fortress) ; * (2) *He that manifests; ** (3) *He that causes to flash forth* (figure taken from the dawn),†† cf. Is. 47[11] Jo. 2[2]; also צמח in Is. 42[9] 58[8]; (4) *He that laughs at;* ‡‡ the third satisfies the context in all the passages in which the word occurs and accords with its derivation (*v.i.*). On Hoffmann's interpretation *v.i.* — *And causeth devastation to come upon the fortress*] This rendering is based upon the reading יביא (*v.s.*) instead of יבוא, although the Qäl of בוא (like שוב) sometimes has a transitive meaning.

8. עשה] has been treated as obj. of דרשו to be supplied (Mich., Jus.), as subject of יהוה שמו (Schegg), as predicate of a sentence of which הוא, to be supplied, is subject (Ba.). If regarded as an interpolation, its connection may be very loose, perhaps the answer to some implied question; cf. Kö. *Stil.*

* Geb.   § Pu., Ke., Reu., Mit.   ** Va.
† Jer., Cal., Os., Geb., Dahl, Ros., Or.   ‖ Mit.   †† Ros., Ba., Hi.
‡ Hi.   ¶ Cal.   ‡‡ 'A., Jer., Schegg, Pu.

214.—כימה] occurs elsewhere only in Jb. 9⁹ 38³¹; usually taken to mean the Pleiades (so 'A., Σ., Θ., and 𝕲 on Jb. 38³¹), from the idea that it is similar to Arab. كُومَة, a heap (Ba.; BDB.; Taylor, *DB*. III. 896). Other meanings given are Sirius (Stern, in *Jüd. Zeitschrift für Wissen. u. Leben*, III. 258 ff.; Nö. in *BL.;* Hoffm. *ZAW*. III. 107 ff.) and the Scorpion (*ZA*. I. 264).—כסיל] The derivation from כסל = *to be strong*, is very questionable. The word ordinarily means *a fool*. As used of a star it occurs only here and in Jb. 9⁹ 38³¹ Is. 13¹⁰. 'A. and 𝔙 and 𝕲 on Is. 13¹⁰ and Jb. 38³¹ translate by *Orion*, which is the usual meaning given; Saadia, Abulwalid, and others identify with Canopus. Cf., for further discussion, Wetzstein in De. *Job*,² 501 f.; Taylor, *DB*. III. 632; R. Brown, Jr., *Trans. of Ninth Congr. of Orientalists*, II. 457 f.—צלמות] The old derivation is as a compound of צֵל מָוֶת = shadow of death; so 𝕲,'A., Σ., Θ. (in places); 𝔖𝕿𝔙; Ges. *Thes.;* Schwally, *Das Leben nach dem Tode*, 194; Nö. *ZAW*. XVII. 183 ff.; BDB. The vocalization צַלְמוּת from צלם, *be dark* (cf. Assyr. *ṣalmu*) is also ancient, and has been accepted by many; Ew.[8] 270 c; De. and Hupfeld (on Ps. 23⁴); BSZ., Gun., Bu. (on Jb. 3⁵); Kö. *Lehrgebäude*, II. i. p. 415. Barth, *NB*. 259 c, would make the form צְלִמוּת (cf. Marti), while We.[3] proposes צְלָמוּת after analogy of Arab. *tzulamât*. The passages in which the word is found are, besides this, Jb. 3⁵ 10²¹ᶠ· 12²² 16¹⁶ 24¹⁷ 28³ 34²² 38¹⁷ Is. 9¹ Je. 2⁶ 13¹⁶ Ps. 23⁴ 44²⁰ 107¹⁰· ¹⁴.—לילה] For syntax according to 𝕸𝕿, cf. GK. 117 *ii*; Kö. 327 *v.*—החשיך] A pf. of experience fol. preceding ptcp., in chiastic order with יהפך, H. 18, 3; GK. 106 *k.*—הקורא] The art. here; in preceding ptcps. it has been omitted, the first being in cstr.; cf. GK. 126 *b*; Kö. 411 *h.*—וישפכם] Impf. with wāw cons. fol. a ptcp. H. 24, 5; GK. 111 *u.*—9. המבליג] Commonly derived from a Heb. root akin to Arab. بَلَجَ, *to be bright*, بَلِجَ, *to be bright, joyous*. In all the other passages in Heb. the meaning *be glad, cheerful*, is usually assigned; cf. Schultens, *Origines Hebrææ* (1761); Lane, *Arab. Lex.* 245; BDB., BSZ. It is here in chiastic order with יבא; here the impf. (indef. freq.) follows the ptcp. with the article, H. 21, 3; GK. 111 *u.*—שר] Hoffm., on the basis of an emended text, translates, *he causes Taurus to rise after Capella and causes Taurus to set after Vindemiator*. This is explained by the fact that Capella rises at the end of April before Taurus in May, and Taurus sets in November after the setting of Vindemiator in September. To this it is objected (We.) that this is too ordinary a matter to stand in so important a connection, and that if this had been the idea, the stars were so well known that so different a reading could not have grown up.

§ 9. Transgressors shall come to grief. 5⁷, ¹⁰⁻¹⁷. (1) A perverter of judgment and an oppressor of the poor, Israel shall not enjoy the gains which she has unjustly made (vs.⁷· ¹⁰ᶠ·). (2) Guilty of every sin, receiver of bribes, she must change her life, if she

would live and have Yahweh's presence; vs.[12-14]. (3) Only righteousness will furnish ground for mercy, in the great calamity which
is to bring lamentation to every heart (vs.[15-17]).

This poem consists of three double strophes, each double strophe including
one strophe of four and one of six lines. The first part of each double strophe
contains a characterization of the times; the second part, introduced by לָכֵן
describes the calamity which is coming upon Israel as punishment.

7, 10, 11. *Those who exercise injustice and shun him who
reproves them for it, shall forfeit all the privileges which otherwise
would accrue to them.* The reasons for placing v.[7] in this connection are : (1) its utter lack of connection with v.[6] and v.[8]; its
natural connection with v.[10]; and the fact that when joined to v.[10]
it permits a strophic arrangement of the whole section at once
simple and natural. This transposition has been adopted without
reference to the arrangement, upon the basis of the logical connection.* Unsatisfactory must be regarded the attempt to connect
it with the preceding verse as a contrast, *yet ye change*, etc. ; † or
with the following verse, supplying *consider* at the beginning of
v.[8]; ‡ or to supply, *Seek him, I say, ye who*, etc. ; § or to make it
a gloss belonging to 6[12], ‖ a suggestion growing out of the endeavor
to treat vs.[8. 9] as original with Amos (cf. Nowack *in loc.*).

7. ההפכים] 𝕲 ὁ ποιῶν = הפעל (Vol.), rendering by same word as for עשה
(v.[8]); cf. the different rendering of ההפך (v.[8]). Oort, on basis of 𝕲, ההפך
(*ThT.* XXV. 121 f.; so Val.).— ללענה] 𝕲 εἰς ὕψος = למעלה (Va.), or perhaps
לעולה, which Oort substituted in 1880, but later (*ThT.*, 1891) abandoned for
למעלה. 𝔙 *absinthium ;* cf. 𝕲 in 6[12], πικρίαν. — לארץ] New. לראש.— הניחו
𝕲 sg. (so Oort and Val.); 𝔖 ܡܨܡ, joined to fol. v.; Gr. הִגִּיעוּ.— **10.** [שנאו
Elh. שנאי.— בשער] 𝕲 pl. [מוכיח 𝔖 ܠܡܟܣܢ, corrected by Seb. to ܠܡܟܣܢ;
cf. Syr.-Hex. and Ez. 3[26]. — [דבר 𝕲, Θ., λόγον = דָּבָר; Σ. ῥῆμα.— תמים] 𝕲, Θ.,
ὅσιον; Σ. ἄμωμον. Hoffm. תְּמִים (but *v.* Gun.).— **11.** [בושסכם 𝕲 suf. 3 p. pl.;
𝔙 *diripiebatis ;* 𝔗 בְּמִבַּזְכִין; 𝔖 ܡܒܙܐ, perhaps = בוססכם (Seb.; so Hal.).
Read בוקכם (so Oet., Marti) or בוסכם (We., Now., Elh., Che. *EB.* I. 155, Löhr).
Gr. שׁוֹסֲסְכֶם מֵעַל; Oort, בוססכם. Some MSS. read שׁ for שׂ; others בושתכם,
בו ששכם, בושסכים (*v.* de R.).— [משאת בר 𝕲 δῶρα ἐκλεκτά, perhaps reading
some form of בחר for בר (Va.); so also 𝔖𝔙. Gr. וּמַשְׂאַת (cf. Dt. 24[10]). —

---

* Ew., Reu., Gu., GAS., Now.; Kö. 411 f.; Marti; Gun. would drop v. 7 as an
interpolation.   † Jus.   ‡ Schrö.   § Stru.   ‖ Kue.

בניתם [$\mathfrak{S}$ makes this and נטעתם rel. clauses, omitting in each case the following ו.— חמר] Some MSS. of Kenn. and de R. חמר; cf. Mi. 6¹³⁻¹⁵ Zp. 1¹³.

7. *They who turn judgment to wormwood*] The leaders are
especially meant, but the people are also not without guilt. The
arraignment begun thus with the participle, a favorite form of
expression with Amos, in impassioned speech, is continued by the
finite verb (cf. 2⁷ 4¹³). The figure is drawn from a bitter herb,
reckoned poisonous (cf. 6¹² Je. 9¹⁵ 23¹⁵ La. 3¹⁵· ¹⁹ Dt. 29¹⁸ Pr. 5⁴
Rev. 8¹¹) by the ancients. Instead of the sweetness of justice,
the bitterness of injustice is accorded. The very institutions
which were intended to secure justice produce injustice (cf. La. 3¹⁹
Am. 6¹²).— *And cast righteousness to the ground*] Righteousness,
here meaning civil justice, is personified, and represented as an
individual thrown down, and treated with violence and contempt,
"trampled under foot." This is stronger than the ordinary "turn
aside justice" (Baur) ; cf. 2 S. 8¹⁵ Is. 59¹⁴ Je. 22³.— **10.** *They
hate*] Referring, as before, to the upper classes, who have the
administration of justice.— *Him that reproveth in the gate*] *i.e.*
the gateway, the place where justice was administered (cf. Dt. 22¹⁵
Ru. 4¹ᶠᶠ· Ps. 127⁵ Pr. 31²³ 1 K. 22¹⁰ La. 5¹⁴) ; the phrase is dependent upon the word translated *the one who reproves, i.e.* the
prophet, or the judge, who rebuked injustice (cf. Jb. 13¹⁵ 19⁵
Is. 29²¹) — perhaps Amos himself.— *The one who speaks uprightly*]
Not one who advocates an unblamable manner of life,* nor one
who brings witnesses to prove his own integrity.† The word תמים
is not an object accusative = one who speaks the truth (cf. Is.
33¹· ⁵) ; ‡ but an adverbial accusative (cf. Ps. 15² Pr. 28¹⁸) and
means *sincerely, blamelessly*. § — *They abhor*] A synonym of *they
hate*, but stronger. ‖ — *Therefore*] The mark of the second part
of the strophe ; cf. vs.¹³· ¹⁶ (also 3¹¹ 4¹²).— *Because ye trample
upon the weak*] A more direct statement of the charge already
made in vs.⁷· ¹⁰.— *And take from him exactions of grain*] The
specific kind of oppression is here indicated ; the translations
load of grain, as much as a poor man could carry on his back ; ¶
great load; ** tax placed on every one over twenty years of age *

---

* Geb.	‡ Now.	‖ Hi., Ke.	** Lu.
† Har.	§ Ros., Hd., Dr.	¶ Cal.	

(cf. Ex. 30^{12-16}) ; *his share,** are far-fetched.   (Cf. Grätz's emendation ; *v.s.*).   The word has come to be a general designation
for gift ;† it was sometimes voluntary (cf. Gn. 43^{34} 2 S. 11^{8}
Je. 40^{5}), but also sometimes involuntary (cf. 2 Ch. 24^{6-9} Ez. 20^{40}).
In the latter case, as here, it was really a tax forced from the
poor by the rich ;‡ something more than a euphemism for inter-
est, and called such to evade the law § (Lv. 25^{37} Dt. 23^{19}).   Cf.
Hitzig's rendering which introduces the apodosis with this clause :
Ye shall have to take from him a present of corn, i.e. as alms. —
Houses of hewn stone] Cf. Zp. 1^{13} Mi. 6^{15} ; houses of exceptional
character, for the rich. — *But ye shall not dwell in them*] Cf.
Dt. 28^{30} Is. 65^{22} Am. 9^{14} ; there will be no opportunity to dwell in
them, because Israel is to go into exile. — *Vineyards of delight*]
Cf. Ez. 23^{6. 12. 23} ; Is. 32^{12} ; the poet pictures in the most tantalizing
manner the dire character of the doom which confronts them.

---

7. הרפכים] Cf. above; the art. is used almost as a vocative, but the fol. vb.
in the 3d pers. points rather to the relative usage, H. 4, 3 *f*; GK. 126 *b*; on
tense force cf. Kö. 237 *a*. — לענה] Commonly derived from לען = Arab. لعن,
to revile, abominate, hence *the detested* herb, cf. Ges. *Thes.* 758. The word
is used only figuratively in the O. T., *i.e.* either in comparisons (Pr. 5^{4},
where it is contrasted with honey), or as a figure of apostasy (Dt. 29^{17}), or
injustice (here and in Am. 6^{12}), or bitter grief (Je. 9^{15} 23^{15} La. 3^{15. 19}).
The plant belongs to the genus *Artemisium* and is common in Palestine,
many varieties of it existing there.   Cf. J. Löw, *Aramäische Pflanzennamen,*
80 f., 401, 421; Tristram, *Nat. Hist. of Bible,* 493. — הניחו] Pf. fol. ptcp., H. 27,
5 *b*; GK. 116 *x*; Dr. § 117; an Aramaicized pf., GK. 72 *ee.* — **10.** שנאו] Stat.
pf., H. 18. 2; cf. GK. 106 *g.* — בשער] According to the accent, the subj. of שנאו,
i.e. those who are in the gate hate him who reproves ; but it is better to connect
with מוכיח. — דבר] Cf. 𝕲 = דבר, and note the chiastic order. — תמים] Adv. acc.,
H. 33, 5; GK. 118 *n.* — יתעבו] Impf. of frequentative action. — **11.** בושסכם]
Has been taken from בוס, *oppress,* the ש being introduced to give the resemblance of בוש, *be ashamed* (Geb.); from בוס, the ש being a mistake of original
copy (Jus.), or a scribal error (Va.), or a dissimilation from בוס (Gun., Oort,
BDB. p. 143); from בוש = باس, *behave proudly, abuse* (Har., Hi.); from בוש
= be ashamed (Tuch, on Gen. p. 213, cited by Ba.); from בז, being read בוזזכם
(𝕿𝕰). It is ordinarily explained as a Po'ēl inf.; but it should be read בוסכם
(*v.s.*), Qāl. inf. cstr., the ש being a correction placed side by side with the
letter corrected; cf. עמשי, Ne. 11^{13}, and נפישסים, Ne. 7^{52}; cf. GK. 61 *e.* — דל]

דלל, from which this is derived, means *to be low, weak*. It is uncertain whether it is the same as the root דלל, *to hang*. It is probably the same as Arab. دَلَّ, *to be low, vile*, and perhaps Assyr. *dalâlu, to be humble, obedient*. Hence דל means (1) *weak*, (2) *lowly, humble, poor*. — משאת] Cf. Phœn. משאת = *tax, penalty;* BDB. 673. — בר] Means *grain*. Is perhaps similar to Arab. بُرّ, *wheat*. Usually derived from ברר = *to purify*. It is written בַּר here and in Am. 8⁶ Ps. 72¹⁶; elsewhere בָּר. — תקחו] Continuing the inf. בוסכם; cf. Kö. 413 *d*. — בָּתֵּי] GK. 96; Sta. 187 *a*. — גזית] An abstract noun = *hewing;* אבני is to be understood as preceding it; cf. Is. 9⁹ 1 K. 6³⁶; Kö. 243 *b*. — חמר] Cf. reading חמר; on the noun used as here for adj., GK. 128 *p*; for חמרה in same construction, Je. 3¹⁹ 12¹⁰ Ez. 26¹² Ps. 106²⁴.

12, 13, 14. *In view of Israel's many sins of persecution and bribery, prudence would suggest silence, in order that life and Yahweh may still be hers.* This double strophe has in the first part, as before, a description of Israel's wickedness, and in the second part a threat of punishment, viz. the death of the nation and abandonment by Yahweh. The first part has a reference to the "gate" as the forum of justice, and the second is introduced by "therefore."

The authenticity of vs.¹³· ¹⁴· and ¹⁵ has been questioned by Oort (*ThT.* XIV. 122, who suspects only v.¹⁵ and regards ¹³ and ¹⁴ as belonging to Amos, but as originally having followed v.²⁰), Val., Now., Volz, GAS., Löhr, Che. (*EB.* I. 154), *et al.* Oet. grants the late origin of v.¹³, but claims vs.¹⁴ f· for Amos, placing them, however, after v.²⁴. We. also regards v.¹³ as interrupting the connection between v.¹² and v.¹⁴, being only a parenthetic note. Elh. inserts v.¹² between 5¹¹ and 2¹³ ff·, and vs.¹³⁻¹⁵ between 2¹⁶ and 3¹ f·. Marti places vs.¹⁴ f· after v.⁶, and drops v.¹³ as late. The reasons for suspecting the passage are: (1) lack of relation to v.¹², since a threat (perhaps v.¹⁶) would be naturally expected to follow; (2) lack of connection with v.¹⁶, the לכן of ¹⁶ having no meaning after v.¹⁵; (3) lack of unity within these vs. themselves, ¹⁵ ᵃ being a repetition of ¹⁴ ᵃ, ¹⁴ and ¹⁵ being an imitation of 5⁴· ⁶; (4) the use of המשכיל in a technical sense as in Pr. 10¹⁹ Ecclus. 20⁷; (5) the lack of consistency between the thought of v.¹³ and the general spirit and teaching of Amos, whose tone was bold and fearless, rather than of the kind to encourage silence under difficult circumstances; (6) the nation, although treated as responsible, is only a remnant; but there is no time preceding 734 B.C. when this historical situation exists. It is to be conceded that the logical consecution of the passage is not as clear as might be expected from Amos; but it is possible (*v.i.*) to answer most, if not all, of these objections. If, however, these arguments are conclusive, the

original piece is one strophe shorter, the second part of strophe 2 and the
first part of strophe 3 being late, the original strophe 2 consisting of what is
now strophe 2 ^{a} and strophe 3 ^{b}.

12. חטאתיכם] Read חטאיכם, on account of the masc. עצמים (We., Now., Löhr,
Oet., Marti; cf. Elh., p. 148).— צררי צדיק לקחי כפר] 𝔖 seems to have read
מעיקין לֵה לְוַפֵּאָה כ׳ ררי צ׳ לקחו כ׳ (Seb.); 𝔙 *hostes justi accipientes munus;* 𝔗
𝔗 ירדם] —.ודין אב׳ ב׳ תטו Gr. ואביונים בשער הטו]—.בְּדִיל לְמַבְּלָא ממון דִשֻׁחַר
adds רעה]—.מן קרם רַשִׁיעַיָא 𝔊 πονηρῶν, perhaps = רעים (Vol., Hirscht), ה and
ס being similar in Aramaic script.—**14.** כאשר אמר] 𝔊 connects with v.[15].

12. *Surely I know*] A new strophe; Yahweh is now represented as speaking; however ignorant men may be, *he* knows (cf.
Ps. 73[11] Jb. 22[13]). — *Many are your transgressions*] *i.e.* in multitudes are they committed. — *And great are your sins*] The repetition is, of course, poetical, yet the two words mark different kinds
of iniquity, the first, deliberate rebellion; the second, habitual
variation from the right. The position of the adjective in each is
very emphatic. After making the general charges, the speaker
introduces more specific arraignment. — *Persecutors of the righteous*] Cf. 2[7] 3[9. 10]; all the more strong because of the singular, and
the lack of the article; the impassioned feeling is so marked that
the speaker passes in what follows from the second to the third
person. — *Takers of bribes*] Ordinarily כפר means *ransom*, the
price paid for life by wealthy criminals (Ex. 21[30] Nu. 35[31]); the
sin, if this be the meaning, consists in threatening the unprotected
with death in order to extort from them a new ransom; * but
here, as in 1 S. 12[3], the word means *bribe* given to the judge†
(cf. שחד). — *Yea the needy in the gate they thrust aside*] Cf. 2[7] Ex.
23[6] Dt. 16[19] 24[17]. In passing to the third person, there is not
simply a " relaxing of the tension of direct invective " (Mitchell);
the speaker, as if with gesture of the hand, indicates his contempt. ‡ The offence mentioned was not (1) making the feeble
fickle-minded by means of legal decisions,§ nor (2) giving unjust decision against the poor, and thus depriving them of their
just rights (cf. Is. 10[2] 29[21] Mal. 3[5] Pr. 18[5]),‖ but (3) the repell-
ing of those who wished to defend their cause (cf. Is. 10[2]).¶ —
13. *Therefore*] The mark of the second part of the double stro-

---

* So here, Ew.   ‡ Ke.   ‖ Ros.
† Ros., Hi., Ba., Or., Mit., Now., Dr.   § Geb.   ¶ Mit., Dr.

phe. — *Since the prudent man at such a time is keeping silence*]
This general meaning for משכיל is to be preferred* to (1) the
teacher, *i.e.* the prophet, whose function it was to rebuke evil at
any cost† (cf. 5¹ᶠᶠ· 7⁹ᶠᶠ· Dn. 12³ 1 K. 18¹³), perhaps Amos himself;‡ or (2) the official whose duty it was to restrain and punish
crime. § It includes all who might, under ordinary circumstances,
be expected to rebuke the public iniquity. The fact is stated,
that, *at such a time, i.e.* under the present circumstances, injustice so prevails that speech will accomplish nothing.‖ There
is no indication of reproach uttered against the prudent. The
translation, *therefore shall he who understands this time keep
silence, for it shall be an evil time,*¶ connecting " in that time "
with the preceding word, erroneously refers the utterance to a
future time rather than to the present. The whole clause is circumstantial, and as such subordinate, — a construction well expressed by the conjunction *since.* — *It is surely an evil time*] A time
which promises disaster. — **14.** *Seek good and not evil*] The advice has already been given to seek Yahweh (v.⁴; cf. v.¹⁵ Mi. 6⁸).
The force of the imperative is not really hortatory, but conditional,
and it implies a threat, that unless good rather than evil is sought,
national death awaits them. — *That ye may live*] In other words,
unless you seek good, a thing which you are not now doing, you
will die politically. — *That so*] *i.e.* in case ye do so; ‡ not, in like
manner as,** nor " so," corresponding to כאשר.†† — *Yahweh . . .
may be with you*] In the special sense of extending help and giving
prosperity. — *God of Hosts*] *i.e.* the God who rules heaven and
earth is able to render any and every kind of help. — *As ye have
said*] Israel, of course, always maintained that she was loyal to
Yahweh. She had always regarded herself as, in a peculiar sense,
the people of God (Je. 7¹⁰ Mi. 3¹¹). Has her life justified the
idea ? Unless her whole attitude changes, unless good and not
evil is made the end of her national life, that life shall cease, and
the much talked of fellowship of God will be lost.

12. כי] Not causal, but asseverative; cf. also v.¹⁸. — ירעתי] Stat. pf. H. 18, 2;
GK. 106 *g*; Dr. § 11. — רבים] Position and indeterminateness indicate a de-

---

* With Dat., Jus., Hd., Gun., Dr.   ‡ Ba.   ‖ Ke., We., Mit.   ** Hi.
† Dahl, Ros.   § Har.   ¶ Gun.   †† Ke.

pendent clause (Now., Kö. 384 *h*), or pred. acc., and by position emphatic, Kö. 334 *x*; so also צררי.—עצמים] With לקחי in appos. with subj. of הטו.—צדיק] Collective. — לקחי] Ptcp. in cstr., GK. 116 *g*. — כפר] The bribe given to a criminal officer, as distinguished from שחר, the bribe given to a civil officer in order to escape the punishment decreed (Hi., Now.). — ואני] Epexegetical ו = *even*. — הטו] Pf. of indef. past, H. 17, 3; Dr. § 9; continuing a ptcp., H. 27, 5 *b*; Dr. § 117; GK. 116 *x*. — **13.** המשכיל] Circ. cl., H. 45, 3 *b*; Dr. § 165. — כי] Asseverative. — היא] Copula. — **14.** אל] Deprecatory, H. 23, rm. *g*; GK. 152 *f*, *g*; with jussive understood, Kö. 355 *n*. — למען] On expression of purpose, Mit. *Final Constructions of Biblical Hebrew*; H. 47, 4 *b* (3); GK. 165 *b*, *c*; Kö. 396 *b*. — ויהי] On use of jussive here, cf. GK. 109 *k*; H. 44, 2 *b*; Dr. § 62; Kö. 355 *n*. — אמרתם] Pf. of indef. past, *as ye have all along said*.

15–17. *Only righteousness will avail against the calamity which is coming.* — The third and last of the double strophes does not at first sight seem so compact and logical as those which have preceded. Indeed, v.[15] (*v.s.*) is thought by most commentators to be the desired continuance of v.[14] and to have no connection with what follows.* In the preceding sub-sections, the prophet has pictured Israel's iniquity and ruin. In the first, all was dark; in the second, a slight suggestion of hope was given, provided her method of life was changed; in the third, the case is presented more strongly in the form of an exhortation, followed by the distinct assertion that *perhaps Yahweh will be gracious, etc.* There is seen, therefore, a gradually increasing representation of pardon, a thought which filled every prophet's heart, no matter how dark the picture which he painted. In this sub-section, as in the other, there occur the reference to the "gate," and the introduction of the conclusion by "therefore," although the logic of it here, it must be confessed, is not so clear as in the other case. (For another alternative, *v.s.*)

15. שנאו ... אהבו] 𝕲 1 p. pl. — טוב ... רע] 𝕲𝕾 pl.; 𝕿 infinitives = *to do evil* and *to do good*. — אולי] 𝕲 ὅπως. — **16.** לכן] Gr. אָכֵן. — אדני] Because of its anomalous position and on the authority of 𝕲𝕾 and seven Mss. is omitted by some (New., Löhr; Baumann omits the phrase לכן ... אדני); it is, however, probably a corruption of ארנין; cf. the suggestion of GAS. to read יהוה אדני, dropping אלהי צבאות as an intrusion; but the title אדני יהוה does not otherwise appear in Amos. — אבל] Baumann, אָבֵל. — ומספר אל יודעי נהי] 𝕲 con-

---

* Cf. Baumann, who drops 5[14. 15] as late.

nects ומספד with prec. and inserts καὶ after it, thus: καὶ κοπετὸν καὶ εἰς εἰδότας
θρῆνον.   Read with 𝔙 (so also Oort *Em.*, We., Now., Gr., Oet., Elh.), which
transposes אל before מספד thus: *et ad planctum eos qui sciunt plangere ;* cf. 𝔖,
which inserts אל before מספד and retains it also before יודעי. Σ. gives μέλος for
נהי.   Hal. וּמְעָפֵר(?) for ומספד (cf. 2¹³ עָמִיר). This whole clause is a gloss (cf.
Löhr, who omits אל אבל ומספד and is followed by Now. *TLZ.*, 1901, p. 164),
as is indicated by the awkwardness of the construction after the prec. clause,
and the impossibility of arranging it in harmony with the structure of the
strophe. — **17.** כרמים] 𝔊 ὁδοῖς = דרכים; cf. the reading כְּרָמִים (Hoffm. *ZAW.*
III. 112). — כי אעבר] 𝔗 = *I will reveal myself to perform vengeance of judgment.*   ¹⁷ᵇ is taken by Löhr as an addition; while Baumann rejects ¹⁷ᵃ.

15. *Hate evil and love good*] Already in the preceding strophe
a hint has been given of the possibility of pardon. The suggestion made, " Seek good and not evil," is now repeated in even
stronger form, as the condition on which pardon may be secured.
The abstract " evil " and " good " is better than the concrete " evil
man," " good man." *   The positive command is needed to sup-
plement the negative, for to hate evil is not sufficient unless one
seeks good.†   The speaker's purpose to impress his thought by
repetition is seen in comparing " hate " of v.¹⁴ with " hate " of v.¹⁰.
The standard of good and evil, in his mind, is conformity with
Yahweh's will. — *And establish justice in the gate*] In other words
reverse the present condition of things ; ‡ the reference is not to
the restoration of true worship instead of calf-worship, § nor to the
improvement of private morality, but to the execution of public
justice. ‖ — *Perhaps*] Cf. Gn. 16² Jo. 2¹⁴. Even if Israel should repent, the question of relief is not absolutely certain, for there are
many contingencies ; the suffering which has been predicted may
be necessary for the working out of great plans. — *A remnant of
Joseph*] Does the prophet here anticipate the doctrine of the
remnant, " the repentant and purified few," so strongly emphasized
by Isaiah (cf. 11¹¹) and Micah (cf. 4⁷),¶ or does he refer to the fact
that Israel is now only a remnant (cf. 7². ⁵) on account of the calamities (cf. 2 K. 10³² Am. 4⁶⁻¹¹) which she has already suffered ? **   The
objection †† to the latter view, that the kingdom had been restored

---

* AE.   † Ros.
‡ Cal., Ros., Mit. (cf. vs.⁵. ⁷. ¹⁰. ¹² with הציגו ; cf. the opposite הניחו, v.⁷).
§ Geb.   ‖ We.   ¶ Cal., Ew., Mau., Ba., Pu., Ke., Mit., Dr.
** Jus., Schrö., Ros., Hi., Hd., Or., We.   †† Ke.

by Joash and Jeroboam II. (2 K. 13$^{23\,ff.}$ 14$^{26-28}$), has little weight from the point of view of the prophet. This difference between the real fact and the appearance (for, after all, the prosperity under Jeroboam II. was only the last upward flash of the dying flame) makes it unnecessary to consider this verse as a gloss added after the fall of Samaria.* — **16.** *Therefore*] Refers not to a particular class, the hypocrites, of whom the prophet now speaks exclusively; † nor to the whole preceding paragraph, vs.$^{7.\ 10-12}$, in which their sins were enumerated; ‡ nor to v.^{13}.§ (The Massoretic space rests upon a misconception.) After a momentary pause, in which opportunity is given for an indication of assent, the poet, following the form of utterance already adopted in the preceding strophes, begins for the third time the announcement of doom. *Therefore, i.e.* "because they do not do what they have just been exhorted to do," ‖ because, indeed, they give no sign of doing it. — *I will cause shouting*] This is the translation of ארנין, suggested as an emendation of אדני (*v.i.*). — *In all squares*] The open places near the gates, the market-places (cf. Je. 48^{38} Is. 3^{26} 14^{31}) in which injustice had been substituted for justice; there is no restriction in the context to the squares of Samaria. — *For mourning*] The shout will not be for joy, but rather a lamentation for the dead, accompanied by beating on the breast. — *They shall say, Woe ! Woe !*] *i.e.* the mourners, who form the funeral procession, which marches through the streets, shall utter these words (cf. 1 K. 13^{30} Je. 22^{18} 34^5 Ez. 2^{10} 30^2). The mourning company would include also mourning-women and flute-players (cf. Je. 9$^{17\,f.}$ 48^{36} Mat. 9^{23}).¶ — *And the husbandmen shall summon to mourning*] Cf. Je. 9^{17}. This rendering ** is to be adopted, describing the effect of the judgment upon the country, as distinguished from the cities and towns. The ordinary interpretation, viz. *they* (people in general) *shall summon the husbandmen to mourning*, because their rustic voices would be loud enough,†† or because no inhabitants of the city would be left from the slaughter,‡‡ or because the occupation of the husbandmen would henceforth be useless,§§ does not so well accord with the context. The word "husbandmen" includes the

---

* So Oort (*ThT.* XIV. 122).   † Cal.   ‡ Ros., Hd.   § Stru., Ke.   ‖ We.
¶ Ba., Ke., Or., Thomson (*LB.* I. 145 f.) ; Van Lennep (*Bible Lands*, 586) ; Mit.
** Ew., Gun.   †† Hd.   ‡‡ Ros., Hd.   §§ Pu.

cultivators of the soil and, as well, those who had care of cattle.*
— *And unto wailing* (cf. עֵמֶק) *those skilled in lamentation*] This
has been added by a later hand to indicate, what the passage does
not elsewhere specifically express, the employment of professional
mourners ; † skilled and unskilled raise the mourning cry. ‡ These
were generally women (Je. 9$^{17\,f.}$); but cf. 2 Ch. 35^{25} Ec. 12^5, where
men are spoken of. § — **17.** *Yea in all vineyards*] Where, ordinarily, the joy is greatest (cf. Is. 16^{10} Jb. 24^{18}), there will be
mourning because of the failure of crops. The writer has now
described the mourning of the three great divisions of the nation,
people of the city, husbandmen, and vinedressers, the last two being distinguished from each other, and both from the first. ‖ The
transposition of this clause so as to follow *Woe ! Woe !* which G. A.
Smith proposes, is unnecessary. — *When I pass through the midst of
thee*] Laying waste the country ; an allusion to the passing through
Egypt (Ex. 11^4 12^{12}).¶ It is universally conceded that the idea
here is that of a punishment** which is to come upon Israel, either
pestilence or war (cf. v.^{27} 6^{14}).

15. וַהֲצִיגוּ . . . וְאָהֲבוּ . . . שָׂנֵא] Successive imperatives, H. 23, rm. (*i*);
GK. 110 *a* ; Dr. § 112. — בְּשַׁעַר] The adverbial modifier precedes the object,
GK. 142 *g*. — אוּלַי] = אוֹ and לִי (= לֹא) means *if not, whether not*, with מִי יוֹדֵעַ
supplied; cf. Assyr. *ûlai*, Jo. 2^{14}; Kö. 186. — יַחֲנֹן] GK. 67 *cc*; Kö. 210 *d*;
here trans. taking dir. obj. (cf. Ex. 33^{19}); cf. Ki. (*v.* Ros.) who makes it
intrans. and supplies עַל before שְׁאֵרִית. — שְׁאֵרִית יוֹסֵף] Indefinite = *a remnant*
(GK. 127 *e*); cf. Dt. 22^{19} 1 S. 4^{12}. — **16.** אַרְנִין] Emend. for אַדְנִי; רֹנֵן, cf.
رَنّ = to twang as of a bow, used of inarticulate sound, *e.g.* shout; while
generally expressing the shout of joy, it is used once (in Qăl) of mournful
cries, La. 2^{19}, the Hiph. *cause to shout* is seen in Ps. 65^9 Jb. 29^{13}, in both cases
with the idea of rejoicing. Here the verbal idea of shouting, intentionally
left indefinite for a moment, is later defined by the acc. מִסְפֵּד. — יֹאמְרוּ] Impers.,
GK. 144 *f*. — הוֹ־הוֹ] Only here in this form ; elsewhere הוֹי = *vae !* o!; cf. Is. 1^4
Je. 48^1, etc., in the sense of *threat;* Is. 18^1, of exhortation ; 1 K. 13^{30} Is. 17^{12}
Je. 22^{18}, in the sense of *affliction, grief*, as here. In the modern Syriac
dialect of Urmia the mourner's cry is *û hû, û hû ;* cf. Socin, *Die neuaramä-
ischen Dialecte am Urmia-See* (1882), p. 102. — קָרְאוּ] Not impers. as יֹאמְרוּ,

---

* So also in Aram., Syr., and Arab.; cf. Assyr. *ikkaru.*

† Cf. Wetzstein in *Zeitschrift f. Ethnologie*, 1873, pp. 295–301. Bu. in *ZAW.*
II. 26 f. and *ZDPV.*, 1883, pp. 184 ff.; Dr. 232 ff.

‡ We., GAS.   § *V.* Gun. and Marti *in loc.*   ‖ Ew.

¶ Cal., Ba., Ke., *et al.*   ** Va., Ros., Schrö., Hi., Ew., Ba., *et al.*

but with אכר taken collectively for subject; GK. 145 *b*; Kö. 346 *m*; with אל,
cf. Gn. 3⁹ Jon. 3². — [אָכָּר From אכר = اَكَّرَ, *dig*; on form, GK. 84, No. 22;
cf. Assyr. *ikkaru*, and اَكَّرَ; in Je. 31²⁴ נסעו בערך is joined to the word;
in 2 Ch. 26¹⁰ it is used with כרמים as here. — [אבל Cf. מספד, נהי, קול בכי.
יורעי נהי] On construction, GK. 116*g*; it is interesting to note that נהי outside
of this place, and Mi. 2⁴, occurs only in late literature, viz. Je. 9⁹·¹⁷·¹⁸·¹⁹ 31¹⁵;
cf. המקוננות and החכמות, Je. 9¹⁶. No sharp distinction can be made between
נהי and קינה; the former was perhaps a more general term than the latter
(Dr.). — [כי] = *when*, as in Ho. 11¹ Gn. 4¹² Dt. 4²⁵, etc.

§ 10. The doom of captivity. 5¹⁸–6¹⁴.

(1) A *woe* against
those who pray for Yahweh's day : it is a day of judgment; because of formal feasts and noisy songs, without justice and righteousness, the nation shall go into captivity, saith Yahweh (5¹⁸⁻²⁷).
(2) A *woe* upon those who are careless and indifferent : because
of the luxury, the licentiousness and the apathy of the people,
the nation shall go into captivity, saith Yahweh (6¹⁻⁷). (3) An
oath against the proud and self-confident Israel : because of
this pride and bold audacity, this self-dependence and disregard of justice, Israel shall be supplanted by a foreign nation,
saith Yahweh (6⁸⁻¹⁴).

This poem consists of three triple strophes, each strophe of the nine contains six lines. In each triple strophe, the first presents a woe (in the third,
this woe becomes an oath); the second presents a phase of the wickedness
of the situation (*e.g.* (1) the utter formality of worship, (2) the luxury of
life and apathy of feeling, (3) the pride and self-confidence); the third
pictures the coming captivity (*e.g.* (1) a captivity beyond Damascus, (2) a
captivity at the head of the captives, (3) the complete surrender of the
country to a foreign enemy). The symmetry of the three divisions is almost
perfect, — each beginning with a woe (or oath), each ending with *saith
Yahweh* in one form or another. The logic and symmetry of this section
are completely destroyed by Elh., who places 5¹⁸⁻²⁰ between 3⁸ and 3⁹; 5²¹⁻²⁵
between 3¹⁴ and 4¹; 5²⁶ f. between 4³ and 4⁴; 6¹⁻⁶ between 4¹¹ and 4¹²; 6⁷
between 4¹² and 4¹³; 6⁸ between 4¹³ and 5¹; 6⁹⁻¹¹ between 5³ and 5⁴; 6¹² f. between 5⁵ and 5⁶; 6¹⁴ between 5⁶ and 7¹. Löhr does not recognize the unity
and independence of this section, but treats it in connection with 5¹⁻¹⁷. He
arranges 5¹⁸–6¹⁴ in eight strophes, consisting of 4, 10, 4, 4, 10, 10, 4, and 4 lines
respectively. This involves the omission of 5¹⁹·²⁶ and 6²·⁹·¹⁰, the transposition
of 6⁵ to follow 6⁶ᵃ and the addition of an extra line after עלות in 5²² as well
as before והגלתי in 5²⁷, and disregards the logic of the passage at some
points. Baumann's reconstruction is still more radical.

18–27. *A woe upon ignorant zeal for a corrupt worship, in which no place is found for justice or righteousness! A captivity beyond Damascus awaits you.* — The unity of this section (consisting of three six-line strophes) appears in (1) the outer form, as compared with the other sections, and (2) the thought which centres about the cultus. This cultus includes the great doctrine of "Yahweh's day" as well as a regular set of feasts, and offerings; it is not wholly detached from images — all of which are wrongly understood, and wrongly practised, and for this reason lead to ruin.

It is best to regard as interpolations (1) למה־זה לכם יום־יהוה, v.[18]; (2) וישלם מריאיכם לא אביט, v.[22] (*v.i.*). It will be noted that in the third and fourth lines of each strophe the poet allows himself to prolong the measure, a pentameter being substituted for a trimeter evidently in order to lay emphasis upon the thought by increasing the details given. The fact that this occurs so uniformly in each strophe shows that it is intentional. It would be possible, of course, to make two trimeters in each case (or a trimeter and dimeter), the strophes having eight instead of six lines.

18. יום יהוה] 𝕿 twice in this v.: יומא דעתיד למיתי מן קדם יי .— למה זה].— 𝕲 and 𝖄 translate זה as a pron.: ἵνα τί αὕτη, *ad quid eam vobis.* — יום יהוה] 𝖄 connects with the following, *dies domini ista tenebrae, et non lux.* The entire clause beginning with למה bears the marks of an interpolation, for the sake of making clear the relation between the first and last clauses of the verse; cf. Löhr, who would treat הוא חשך ולא אור as a gloss derived from v.[20 a], having its origin in the later insertion of v.[19]. — הוא] 𝕲 adds before it ו = καὶ αὕτη. — **19.** ובא] 𝕲 εἰσπηδήσῃ suggests וברח (Oet.). — ידו] 𝕲 τὰς χεῖρας αὐτοῦ. Löhr makes the v. a proverb which has crept into the text from the margin; but for this there is no basis. — **20.** הלא] 𝕾 ܣܡ, making the sentence affirmative. — יום יהוה] Löhr om. — ואפל] Gr. ואֹפֶל (so Löhr, Elh.). — **21.** ולא אריח בעצרתיכם] 𝕲 inserts θυσίας. Gr. on basis of 𝕲 inserts מנחתיכם here and drops it from v.[22] as a dittograph. — **22.** כי אם] Elh. transposes כי to the beg. of v.[21]. — עולות] 𝕾 ܟܠܗܝܢ; omitted as a gloss to explain אָרִיחַ in BDB. p. 585. — ומנחתיכם] 𝕾 om. ו, connecting the word with ארצה. Baumann om. We. thinks that after עלות the apodosis to the preceding clause has fallen out (so Now., Löhr; but cf. Baumann; also Duhm and Marti, who treat כי . . . עולות as a gloss). — וישלם מריאיכם לא אביט] May be rejected as an interpolation added to give an apparently greater completeness to the catalogue of offerings; 𝕲 has καὶ σωτηρίου(ς) ἐπιφανείας ὑμῶν, reading מראיכם (Va., Vol.). Hirscht calls attention to the fact that in the nine other cases where 𝕲 renders שְׁלָמִים by the pl. it employs the *neuter* form, and suggests that 𝕲 read here שְׁלָמִים. 𝕾 has ܘܕܕܒܚܝܟܘܢ ܣܓܝܐܐ, instead of the more usual ren-

K

dering of שלמים, viz. ܘܩܪܒ ܡܚܬܐ. 𝔙 *et vota pinguium vestrorum*; 𝔗 וּנְכְסַת
קֻרְשֵׁיכוֹן. Gr., on basis of 𝔊, וְשַׁלְמֵי (so Hal.). Oet. suggests the transposition
of this clause to follow עלות.—23. [המון] Gr. הֵמְיַת (cf. Is. 14¹¹).—[נבליך] 𝔊
ὀργάνων σου; ᾽A. ναβλῶν σου; 𝔗 inaccurately, פִּנְּבָרֵךְ, so 𝔖; 𝔙 *lyrae tuae.*—
[לא אשמע] Probably a gloss.—24. [ויגל] 𝔖 ܘܢܬܓܠܐ, deriving the word from
גלה = to uncover; so 𝔙 *et revelabitur*, and 𝔗 וְיִתְגְּלֵי. Θ. ἀποικισθήσεται
= גלה, *to carry captive.*—25. [מנחה] 𝔊𝔖𝔗 pl. The order of words in v.²⁵
varies greatly in the Mss. of 𝔊, *e.g.* in 𝔊ᴬ בית ישראל follows במדבר; 𝔊ᴮ agrees
with 𝔐𝔗; Tischendorf's text places בית ישראל after לי, and במדבר after שנה
(so 𝔖). Cf. Acts 7⁴².—26. [סכות] Read סְכַּת (so Dozy, *Die Isr. zu Mekka*, p. 33;
Schmidt, *JBL.* XIII. 8), with 𝔊 and Σ. τὴν σκηνὴν; similarly 𝔖 ܡܛܠܬܐ
and 𝔙 *tabernaculum.* ᾽A. τοὺς συσκιασμούς; Θ. τὴν ὅρασιν, confusing with
שָׂכָה (Schmidt); 𝔗 סִיכּוּת (cf. Lag. *Proph. Chald.* 452). Cod. 196 of de R. סכּות
(so also Ba.). The reading סכּוּת is adopted by many (Schrader, *SK.* 1874,
pp. 324–35, and *COT.* II. 142; Oort, *ThT.* XIV. 142, 147 f.; Gun., Baethgen
Sem. Rel. 239; Mit., Now., Dr., Oet., BDB.), but *v.i.*—[מלככם] 𝔊 τοῦ Μολόχ =
מֹלֶךְ; ᾽A. Μολχόμ; 𝔖 ܡܠܟܟܘܢ; 𝔙 *Moloch deo vestro;* all taking it as name of
an idol; so also two codd. of de R. 𝔗 פתכומריכון. Σ. Θ. βασιλέως ὑμῶν.
Ba. מִלְכֹם; but see Düsterdieck, *SK.*, 1849, pp. 908–12.—[כיון] 𝔊 'Ραιφάν, a
copyist's error of ר for כ. Jus., Ba., and Schmidt cite: (1) J. D. Mich. *Supplementa*, pp. 1225 ff., who adopts Kircher's explanation (*Lingua Aegyptiaca resti-
tuta*, p. 49) of ΡΗΦΑΝ = Arab. רגל = נחל = *Saturn;* and (2) P. E. Jablonski,
Opuscula (1806), pp. 41 ff. (= *Remphah Aegyptiorum deus*, 1731), who reads
Ρομφα (cf. Complutensian, Origen), and explains it as *Ro-mphah* = king of
heaven = sun. 𝔗, ᾽A. Σ. read כִּיּוּן, taking it as a proper name. Θ. ἀμαύρωσιν,
and 𝔙 *imaginem*, both deriving from כון (*v.* Muss-Arnolt, *Exp.*⁶ II. 425).
𝔖 ܟܐܘܢ = כֵּאוּן (so also Jus., Ba., Dozy, *Die Isr. zu Mekka*, 33; Kue., *Rel. of
Isr.* I. p. 245; Schrader, *SK.* 1874, pp. 324 f.; Gun., Mit., We., Gu., Now.,
BDB., Oort, *Em.*; Dr., Elh., Oet.).—[צלמיכם] Dozy, צלמכם (so Muss-Arnolt,
*Exp.*⁶ II. 425). Gr. suggests that כוכב may be the name of a god and that
we should read צלמי ואת. Schrader transposes צ to follow אלהיכם (*COT.* II.
141 f.; Gun., Mit., Oort (*Em.*), Dr.(?), Elh., Oet.). We. om. as a gloss on
אלהיכם.—[כוכב] We. om. as a gloss on כיון (so independently G. F. Moore in
BDB., Gu., Schmidt, *JBL.* XIII. 10; Zeydner, *Stemmen voor Waarheid en
Vrede*, 1893, pp. 613 ff.; cf. Dr.). Cf. Now., who takes כוכב אלהיכם as a gloss
belonging before כיון.—[אלהיכם] 𝔗 טְעֲוַתְכוֹן. 𝔊 and 𝔖 have a different order
from 𝔐𝔗 in the latter part of this v., 𝔊 = and the star of your god, Raiphan
— their images which ye made for yourselves; 𝔖 = the star which you made
for yourselves a god (cf. 𝔙). We. takes v.²⁶ as a later addition which has
crowded out an original threat that connected closely with v.²⁷ (so also Now.,
Che. (*EB.*, but see *Crit. Bib.*), Löhr, Marti).—27. [שמו] We. om. (so Löhr).

18 a. *Alas!*] Not so strong as *woe*, implying "commiseration,
rather than denunciation" (Driver).—*For those who long for*]

Not the hypocritical Hithpôlēl = *pretend that they desire;* * nor
the simple Pĩʿel = *desire,* with the reflexive sense, *desire for themselves;* † but *earnestly desire and expect.* ‡ — *The day of Yahweh*]
Cf. Jo. 2² 3¹⁴ᶠ.   The prophet does not speak to (1) those who in
their misery and distress think that the coming of Yahweh, even
if it brought death, would be better than their present situation; §
nor to (2) the credulous and superstitious Israelites, who, trusting
in their Israelitish descent, and mindful of promises made to their
ancestors, but forgetful of the obedience on which the promises
were based, and of their own conduct which was the occasion
of the evil situation, blindly imagine that Yahweh's day can bring
only good; ∥ nor to (3) the bold and reckless sceptics who did
not believe that the day would ever come, and thus mocked the
suggestions by the prophet to this effect (cf. Is. 5¹⁹ Je. 17¹⁵ Ez.
12²²).¶   He has in mind, rather, (4) the great multitude, who
think that without reference to their conduct, or the attitude of
their mind, this "coming day" will be a "cure-all" for every
woe.**   It does not, however, follow from this, as Wellhausen
contends, that Amos would have "protested against the Messianic
belief, if he had known of it."

Amos found a well-established doctrine of the day of Yahweh cherished
among the people. They looked forward to it as a day when Yahweh would
give them triumphant victory over all their enemies and thereby establish
himself as supreme among the gods. This hope grew out of their monolatrous
conception of Yahweh and their belief in their own nation as destined to
become the great and powerful representative of Yahweh among the nations,
and was fostered by the long-continued hostilities between Israel and her
neighbors, in which Israel was not always victorious. The day must come,
therefore, in which Yahweh would gloriously vindicate himself and his people
by overthrowing all his foes and making Israel supreme. But the idea as
expressed by Amos was, in one essential point at least, directly contrary to
the prevailing thought ; instead of Israel triumphing over her enemies on that
day, she is herself to be humiliated, and that by Yahweh himself. This new
conception of the day was the direct outcome of Amos's new conception of
Yahweh as an ethical God, whose chief requirement of his people was righteousness. Amos felt that in view of the moral corruption of Israel it was
inevitable that Yahweh would punish her and thus vindicate his own righteous-

---

* Har., citing יִצְטַיָּרוּ, Jos. 9⁴; הִשְׁתַּנִית, 1 K. 14²; יִתְחַפֵּשׂ, 1 K. 20³⁸.
† Pu., Mit.   ‡ GAS.   § Os., cf. Cal.   ∥ Geb., Ba.
¶ Har., Dathe, Jus., Ros., New., Ew.   ** We.

ness in the sight of the world. Other nations, too, were to be punished, not, however, as enemies of Israel, but as transgressors of the moral law. The new way thus marked out by Amos was trodden by all his successors. The development of the idea kept pace with the growth of the conception of Yahweh, and further modifications through successive periods were caused by the ever changing historical and social environment. For a systematic historical treatment of this subject see J. M. P. Smith, "The Day of Yahweh," *AJTh.* V. (1901), 505–33. Other material will be found in R. H. Charles, *A Critical History of the Doctrine of a Future Life, etc.* (1899), 80–137; and the article, "Eschatology of the Apocryphal and Apocalyptic Literature," *DB.;* A. B. Davidson, art. "Eschatology of the O. T.," *DB.;* Marti, *Gesch. der Isr. Religion*, 180–6; WRS. *Proph.* 131 ff. 397 ff.

18 b. *What have ye to do with it ?*] This is plainly an interpolation, explaining the הוי of the preceding line, — *what concern is it of yours ? What good will it do you ?* (cf. Gn. 27⁴⁶). — *Yahweh's day is a day of darkness and not light*] It is better thus to connect יום ח with what follows.* The *darkness* is figurative, *i.e.* ruin, calamity, but it is also physical or literal, as appears from the following comparisons. It remained for Joel, in later days, to emphasize still more strongly the literal side (cf. Jo. 1¹⁵ 2¹ 3⁴·¹⁴), and represent nature itself as sharing in the gloom ; † cf. also Is. 5³⁰ 8²² 9² 58⁸ 59⁹ Je. 13¹⁶. — **19.** *As when one flees from a lion and a bear meets him*] The comparison is singularly appropriate in view of the occupation of Amos, for it was an everyday experience ; cf. Is. 24¹⁸. — *The lion*] Cf. 1 S. 17³⁴ La. 3¹⁰. — *The bear*] Once common and dangerous, although at present found only in the northern districts (cf. 1 S. 17³⁴ 2 K. 2²⁴ La. 3¹⁰). — *Or goes into the house . . . and a serpent bites him*] The *coming home* has no connection with the lion and bear episodes, as, for example, because of the terror and exhaustion which would follow such an encounter ; ‡ it is rather the sudden coming of misfortune when and where it would be least expected. § — *The serpent*] Probably an adder hidden in a crevice. Strange enough is the tendency of ancient commentators to refer the animals in these comparisons to particular individuals, *e.g.* the lion to Nebuchadnezzar,‖ Pul ; ¶ the bear to the Persians,** Tiglathpileser,¶ Ahasuerus ; ‖ the serpent to Shalmaneser,¶ Alexander the Great, or

---

* So Ros., Schrö.; on the contrary, Mit., GAS., Marti. † Schrö., Ba.
‡ Hi., Mit. § Ros., Dr., *et al.* ‖ Jer. ¶ Geb., Har. ** Abar.

Antiochus Epiphanes.* The thought is not climactic, a grada-
tion being intended,† but is general, and pictures a situation from
which there is no escape; cf. "incidit in Scyllam, qui vult vitare
Charybdim." ‡ — **20.** *Deep darkness without any brightness in it*]
After repeating the very words of v.[18], changed for greater forceful-
ness into the form of a question (perhaps Marti is right in treating
v.[20a] as a gloss on v.[18], and joining v.[20b] to [18]), the prophet employs
another phrase in which still stronger words are used for darkness
and light, viz. *deep darkness, gloom,* a darkness which grows greater
and greater, without even a ray of light (cf. Is. 50[10], and for the
opposite, Is. 9[1]). — **21.** *I hate, I despise*] Cf. Is. 1[14] Dt. 16[22] Ps. 11[5],
and likewise Je. 6[30] 7[29]. The prophet represents Yahweh as entirely
out of sympathy with the religious worship, and, indeed, hostile to
it. It is the cultus which seems to the prophet to be the occasion of all trouble, since to this may be charged "the illusion and
the obstinacy" of the people. — *Your feasts*] Such festal gather-
ings as the passover (1 K. 12[32]) and the feast of tents (1 K. 8[2]),
not sacrifices; religious, not profane. § Under this name were
included the three annual festivals (Ex. 23[14] 34[23]; cf. Dt. 16[16]).
The name has its origin not in the *dancing* (חגג) which was a
feature of the feasts, but in the *pilgrimage* which was involved. ‖
These festivals are hated by Yahweh (cf. Is. 1[10-15]), not because
they failed to comply with certain prescribed rules or regulations
as to place;¶ nor because of calf-worship;** nor because they
were external, not including worship of the heart,†† for, up to
this time, emphasis had not been placed on heart-worship; but
because they constituted a cultus which did not truly represent
Yahweh, and must be abandoned, if true ideas of Yahweh were to
prevail. ‡‡ — *I will not smell*] A relic of the old superstition that
the god actually smelled the savor of the offering (Gn. 8[21] Ex. 29[41]
30[38]). The term is used as one of several to express delight in,
or acceptance of, a sacrifice (Lv. 26[31] Is. 11[3]); cf. ארצה (5[22]).

---

* Jer.   † Mit.   ‡ Jus., Ros., Schrö.   § Hi.

‖ Nö. *ZDMG.* XLI. 719; We. *SV.* III. 106, 165; WRS. *Proph.* Lect. II.
note 6; Dr. *Sam.* 173; SS. 184-5; BDB. On Hebrew feasts in general see
the literature cited in my *Constructive Studies in the Priestly Element in the Old
Testament* (1902), pp. 104-6.

¶ Cal., Va.   ** Pu.   †† Jus., Ros., Schrö., Hd., Ke., Ba.   ‡‡ We.

While the old realistic idea has doubtless largely disappeared, the thought was originally like that which appears in the Babylonian story of the Deluge : * —

> " A peace-offering I made upon the height of the mountain;
> Each time I placed seven censers,
> Poured into them calmus, cedarwood and sweet-smelling . . .
> The gods inhaled the savor ;
> Yea, the gods inhaled the sweet savor ;
> The gods gathered like flies around the sacrificer."

Your festivals] Nowhere else does the plural of this word † occur. The singular means an *assembly*, especially of a religious character, is used as a synonym of חג, and designates especially the festival of the seventh day of the passover (Dt. 16[8]) and the eighth day of the Feast of Tabernacles (Lv. 23[36] Nu. 29[35] 2 Ch. 7[9]). ‡ — It contains the idea of *holiday*, § not that of *solemn assembly* ; ‖ cf. 2 K. 10[20] 1 S. 1[13] Jo. 1[14]. The usage here, as in Is. 1[13], is general. — **22.** *For, although ye offer*] This is better than *yea, if*, ¶ or simply *although ;* ** cf. the suggestion that the first line of v.[22] is to be taken as apodosis of אריח, v.[21].†† — *Your burnt-offerings and meal-offerings*] These words are not to be separated, ‡‡ but, taken together, are the object, not of ארצה, §§ but of תעלו. ‖‖ The use of the suffix with מנחות and not with עלות does not depend upon the fact that the former was offered regularly morning and evening, while the latter had no fixed rule ; ¶¶ nor is it an inconsistency in the use of the suffix ; *** the two words form *one* idea, and the suffix, attached to the second, modifies the whole expression (*v.i.*). The connective, *and*, is not *even*, ¶ on the ground that the מנחה was more important than the עולה. Cf. Wellhausen and Nowack, who understand that after עלות there originally stood an apodosis which has fallen out. Perhaps with BDB. (*s.v.* מנחה) עלות might be taken as a gloss explaining אריח. — *Meal-offerings*] Originally *a gift*, or offering of any kind (Gn. 32[13] 43[11] 1 S. 10[27]), but as other

---

* *V. KAT.*[3] p. 550; *BW.* III. 117.   † עצרות.

‡ Cf. its use in later times of the Feast of Weeks ; Jos. *Ant.* III. 10, 6 (= Ἀσάρθα), and in the Mishnah.

§ Mit.	¶ Ew.	†† Elh. p. 155.	§§ Hes.
‖ Cf. Ke.	** New., GAS.	‡‡ Ros.	‖‖ So most comm.
¶¶ So Hi.	*** We., Now.: Hal. om. the suffix with מנחות.		

sacrifices became more definitely indicated, in later usage, and especially in P, applied only to unbloody or vegetable offerings. — *The peace-offerings of your fatlings I will not regard*] This may be regarded as an interpolation, dating from the time when specific detail must be given regardless of monotony. It is distinctly superfluous and anti-climactic. The translation *peace-offerings** (only here in the singular) is preferable to *thank-offering*,† or *votive offering* ‡ or *meal-offering*.§ The fuller form is זבח שלמים (Lv. 3¹·⁶, etc.). — **23.** *Take away from me the noise of thy songs*] The verb is singular, showing the elevation and austerity of the language in keeping with the thought.‖ *Noise*, or *clashing*, is kindred to *tumult*,¶ and preferable ** to *multitude*. †† The objection is not to the musical drawl in worship, ‡‡ but to the entire worship, of which the music was a part. The parallelism shows that more was meant than merely the noise of the people's throng flowing like great waters (Is. 17¹²).§§ We know little or nothing of the music of Amos's period. — *And the melody of thy lyres*] Only here is זמרה used of instrumental rather than vocal music (Ps. 81² 98⁵ Is. 51³). The lyre or harp (also called psaltery) with as many as ten strings (Ps. 33²) was used in profane music (Is. 5¹² 14¹¹ Am. 6⁵; cf. Grätz, *Psalmen*, I. 66), but likewise in sacred music (2 S. 6⁵ Ps. 33² 144⁹).‖‖ This passage testifies to the early use of songs and music at the sacrifice ¶¶ (cf. 8¹⁰ Is. 30³²); but it is not so clear that this description evidences close connection of the ritual in Samaria with that in Jerusalem.*** — *I will not hear*] These words, taken separately by Calvin, are evidently an addition prompted by the desire to complete the parallelism.††† With these omitted the line would read, *Remove from me the noise of thy songs and the melody of thy lyres*, a strong pentameter. — **24.** *Let justice roll as waters*] Cf. Is. 1¹⁰⁻¹⁷. Yahweh wishes not the swelling sound of pilgrimages, nor that of liturgy, but rather that of judgment. We have here not a *threat*, ‡‡‡ that Yahweh in his wrath

---

* 𝔊; Ros., SS. (*s.v.*).   † Jos., Ew., Ke., GAS., *et al.*   ‡ Mich.
§ Di. on Lv. 3, Now. *Arch.* II. 211.   ‖ Ew.   ¶ Jer.   ** Geb., Ros., Mit.
†† Cal.   ‡‡ Or.   §§ Hoffm. *ZAW.* III. 112.
‖‖ Cf. the excellent essay, "Music of the Ancient Hebrews," in *The Book of Psalms (SBONT.)*, 217–34.   ¶¶ So We.   *** Ke.
††† On the other hand, Or., Gu.   ‡‡‡ Os., New., Hi., Ke.

will send judgment like a swiftly rolling, impetuous stream; nor a *prediction* * of the righteousness of the Messiah, nor an *answer* to certain hypocrites that Yahweh will give free course to (*i.e.* bless) their righteousness, if it be sincere; † nor an *assertion* that by their own efforts alone this ideal state can be secured; ‡ but *an exhortation* § to give up the old idea of religion, viz. a cultus, and adopt the new, viz. justice and righteous living.— *Justice . . . righteousness*] That is as practised among men in life; it is not the divine justice executed against men as in Is. 10²²; cf. Is. 51⁵ 59¹⁷ 63¹. ‖ — *As waters . . . as an ever-flowing stream*] The on-ward, unobstructed flow of a mighty mass of waters is, indeed, an admirable figure with which to describe the ideal progress of justice and righteousness. The " stream " was at the rainy season a tor-rent, at other times a small brook or even merely the dry bed of a stream. But the stream, to fit the figure, must be never-failing, ever-flowing.— **25.** *Was it (only) sacrifices and offerings that ye brought me in the wilderness during forty years*] Interpretations have greatly varied; according as they have represented Israel during this period, offering (1) idolatrous sacrifice to Yahweh; † (2) sacrifice acceptable in form, but not continuous because of lack of animals; ¶ (3) required sacrifices, but no freewill-offer-ings; ** (4) sacrifices to idols, but not to Yahweh; †† (5) sacrifice accompanied (v.²⁶) by idol-worship; ‡‡ (6) few sacrifices compared with their many rebellions; §§ (7) no sacrifices at all; ‖‖ (8) sacri-fices to be sure, but also something else, viz. " true worship of the heart and righteousness, public and private." ¶¶ This rendering places the emphasis in its proper place and does not compel Amos to say that there were no sacrifices or offerings in the wilderness. The ה of הזבחים has been taken as the article,*** as ה interrogative expecting an affirmative answer; ††† as ה interrogative expecting a negative answer. ‡‡‡ The real meaning is this: In the period of the wandering, " the golden age," ye brought me something more

---

* Schegg.   † Cal.   ‡ Ew.
§ Har., Mau., Hd., Pu., Or., Gun., We., Mit., GAS., Dr.   ‖ Ke.   ¶ Geb.
** Jus.   †† Jer., Os., Pu., Or.   ‡‡ Va., Ros., Mau.   §§ Schrö.
‖‖ Hi., Ew., Ba., We., Mit., GAS., Dr., Marti.   ††† Hd.
¶¶ Macdonald, *JBL.* XVIII. 214 f.   ‡‡‡ So most recent comm.
*** Dahl, Stru., Mau.

than sacrifices (cf. Je. 7²²) ; and the logical connection is with the following verse and not with the preceding, as appears from the strophic structure, and from the evident connection between הִגַּשְׁתֶּם (v.²⁵), and וּנְשָׂאתֶם (v.²⁶ ; *v.i.*). — *Forty years*] The same tradition concerning the sojourn in the wilderness as that furnished by the Hexateuch. — **26.** *But now ye lift up*] This has been taken as (1) a charge of idolatry against the time of the wandering in the wilderness * (= *and ye lifted up*) ; but what has the prophet's thought here to do with idolatry in the time of the wilderness ? (2) as a question coördinate with and parallel to the preceding, *Did ye carry about the tabernacle of your king, etc. ;* † (3) as a charge of idolatry for the entire period from the wandering to the days of Amos, ‡ and indeed such a charge would have been true ; cf. Jos. 24¹⁴ Ex. 32⁴⁻⁸. ¹⁹ Ju. 17⁴ᶠ. 1 S. 19¹³ 1 K. 12²⁵⁻³³ ; (4) as an accusation against the contemporaries of Amos (*and ye lift up*) ; § (5) as a prediction (*and ye shall lift up*) of a time when they shall carry their idols on their backs into captivity ; ‖ and (6) as a command (the wāw consecutive and perfect being treated as an imperative) to take up their idols and go into captivity ; ¶ cf. Is. chap. 2. The ו would be conjunctive in (1) and (2), adversative in (3) and (4), consecutive in (5) and (6). — *The shrine of your king and the image of your God which ye have made for yourselves*] This translation (1) is based upon a text which treats (*a*) כּוֹכַב as a gloss explaining כִּיּוּן, and having its origin at a time when the latter had come to be pronounced כֵּיָן and treated as the name of a deity (*v.s.*) ; (*b*) צַלְמֵיכֶם as a gloss explaining אֱלֹהֵיכֶם, occasioned by the phrase אֲשֶׁר עֲשִׂיתֶם לָכֶם (*v.s.*) ; and restores סִכּוּת to סַכַּת (*v.s.*) ; (2) accepts the proposition that according to the context Amos has in mind an *impure and corrupt worship,* in other words, a worship which included not only a wealth of sacrificial offerings in number and variety, together with extravagant and debauching sacrificial banquets, but also pretentious processions in which the sacred symbols of Yahweh were carried about with a view to gaining his favor ; (3) rejects the proposition that

---

* Os., Dathe, Jus., Hes., Ba., Hi., Ke., Pu., Bu. (*Rel. of Isr.*, 68).
† Schmidt, *JBL.* XIII. 1–15.   ‡ Geb., Har.
§ Tiele (*Gesch. d. Relig. im Altertum,* I. 336).
‖ Ew., Or., Val., GAS., Dr. ; Peters, *Hebr.* I. 242 f.   ¶ Mit.

idolatry was intended, whether this was the worship of Assyrian
gods,* viz. Sakkut (= Adar) and Kewan (= Saturn), including
the view which would make מלך and צלם proper names, viz.
Moloch (or Milcom) and Selem ; † or Phoenician gods, viz. *Koun
and Keiwan ;* ‡ (4) avoids the conjecture, occasioned by the
difficulty of ascribing the worship of Assyrian gods to Amos's time,
that the whole is either very late, *i.e.* after 722 B.C., or a late redaction of an earlier text which had become unintelligible (*v.s.*) ;
(5) involves the treatment of ונשאתם suggested in (4), p. 137.
The prophet has in mind the times of the wandering in the wilderness, times when Israel was treated with special favor by Yahweh,
a favor which was evidently secured in some other way than by
sacrifices and processions.   These were the times which antedated
the introduction of Canaanitish impurity into the Yahweh worship.
His face is set severely against recognizing this sort of thing as
pleasing to Yahweh.   This kind of worship will not merely fail to
turn away his anger; it is, in itself, an occasion of displeasure.
The condition of heart and mind which it represents is sufficient
evidence that only punishment of the severest character will meet
the exigencies of the situation. — **27.** *Beyond Damascus*] This
phrase in earlier days represented the climax of judgment, as did
Babylon in later days.   Cf. Acts 7[43] in which Stephen actually
substitutes Babylon for Damascus.

18. הוי] Used at times as a particle of denunciation and threatening; cf.
Is. 1[24] 5[8. 11. 18. 20. 21. 22], etc.; but also as expressing commiseration and grief;
cf. 1 K. 13[30] Is. 3[9. 11] 6[5] 24[16]. — המתאוים] Art. with ptcp. = rel. cl. with its
antecedent; H. 4, 3*f*; Kö. 411 *a*. Hithp. = an intensified Pi'ēl (cf. BDB.)
= to long after presumptuously; *v.* Je. 17[16]. — לָמָה זֶּה] On d. f. firm., cf. GK.
20 *k* and on d. f. conj., GK. 20 *c*; on force of זה, Kö. 42 *β* = adverb, giving
" directness and force " to the question (BDB.); *contra* Ros., who regards it
as either obj. of vb. *desire* understood, or as subj. of some phrase such as
come into your mind. — לא אור] לא with noun; cf. GK. 152 *d*; more emphatic
than אין; cf. Ex. 4[10] Am. 6[13] 7[14] Je. 2[11], etc. — **19.** ינוס] Freq.; fol. by
four pfs. with wāw cons., GK. 112 *m*, Kö. 367 *m*. — האִרי . . . הדוב . . . הנחש]
Art. denoting an individual not definitely known, GK. 126 *q, r*; Kö. 300 *b*.
— הבית] Art. = *his ;* Kö. 299 *e*. — **20.** לא נגה] לא, rather than אין, as in v.[18]. —

* So Schra. *COT.* II. 141 f.; We., Mit., Dr., Che., Now., Torrey, BDB., Muss-
Arnolt, Marti, *et al.*
† Baethgen (*Sem. Rel.* 239).   ‡ Tiele, *Rev. de l'Hist. d. Rel.* III. 211.

21. שְׂנֵאתִי] Stat. pf., GK. 106 g. Note asyndeton, GK. 154 a, N.; Kö. 370 g, h. — אריח ב] Cf. Ex. 30³⁸ Lv. 26³¹ Is. 11³, only other cases where this vb. is followed by ב of interest (cf. Kö. 212 c). — עַצְּרֹתֵיכֶם] D. f. dirimens, GK. 20 h. — **22.** כִּי אִם] = For even if (Kö. 372 h); Dr., § 143, treats it as an imaginary condition introduced by אִם taking imperf. in both protasis and apodosis. — כֶּם_] With the second of two nouns which, together, form one idea, cf. 2 S. 23⁵. Muss-Arnolt (Exp.⁶ II. 414, N. 3) calls attention to the frequency of this construction in Assyrian; e.g. Tig. Pil. I., Prism Inscr. col. I. 71, narkabâti u umma-nâ-te-ia (my chariots and my warriors), II. 6, III. 44, etc. For the opposite construction in which the suffix is used with the first of a series of nouns and omitted with succeeding ones, v. Ex. 15²; cf. Assurbanipal, Annals, V. 59 ff.; cf. GK. 135 m. — וְשַׁלֵם] On the nature of this offering, cf. Now., Arch. II. 211 f. Elsewhere שלם is always pl.; it is used sometimes with זבח preceding it (e.g. Ex. 24⁵ 1 S. 11¹⁵), and sometimes without זבח as here (e.g. Nu. 15⁸ 1 S. 13⁹). It is not unlikely that the pl. cstr. should be read here; the י might easily be lost sight of between two מ's. — מְרִיאֵיכֶם] Cf. Is. 1¹¹. Assyr. marû = fat; Ar. مَرِءَ = be digestible. The word is used generally, as here, of sacrificial animals, e.g. Ez. 39¹⁸. — **24.** וְיִגַּל] For advers. ו, cf. Kö. 360 c. Perles, Analekten, p. 75, following We., proposes to connect with גַּל = spring and to translate spring up, or bubble forth. — מִשְׁפָּט] Cf. Batten, JBL. XI. 206–10, on usage of this word; here evidently in the sense of justice. — **26.** וּנְשָׂאתֶם] GK. 112 x takes the pf. with wāw cons. as fut. (yea, ye shall take it up) and 112 rr as frequentative (cf. Ew., Oet., p. 71); Dr. § 119 a treats it as pf. with wāw cons. not attached to a preceding impf. but still retaining future force; Kö. 368 b, emphatic — copula going back to v.²⁴, and resuming the thought after the interruption of the parenthetical question in v.²⁶; cf. Am. 2¹² ª; Che. (EB.), the wāw is simply wāw-explic. so often prefixed to glosses; cf. Is. 45²⁰. — ... סִכֻּת] That this was the original pointing is supported by 𝕲 and Σ., although the next word Μωλόχ makes 𝕲, as a whole, interpret the passage of idolatry rather than impure worship; in its favor are also 𝔖𝔙 (v.s.). Under the influence of the anti-idolatrous feeling, and at an early time, although after the coming in of Assyrian ideas (Is. 2⁶⁻⁸), the striking resemblance of the Assyrian SAG-KUD, i.e. Ninib, the Assyrian god of war (cf. סֻכּוֹת בְּנוֹת, 2 K. 17³⁰, the name of a god; Dl. Pa. 215 f.), which name with the determinative kakkab = star (II. R. 32, 25; COT. II. 141 f.; Tiele, Bab.-Ass. Gesch. 528 f.; Sayce, Hib. Lectures, pp. 7, 151–154), as suggested by Jules Oppert, means the planet Saturn, led to a modification of the original סֶכֶת to סִכּוּת, the change from ă to ĭ being perhaps suggested by the form of שִׁקּוּץ, abomination (words denoting idolatry and idols frequently take the ground-form qiṭṭûl, e.g. קִבּוּצִים, גִּלּוּלִים; so Ba.; Baudissin, Sem. Rel. I. 95 f.; Nö. Gött. Gelehrt. Anzeigen (1884) II. 1022; Torrey, JBL. XIII. 61 f.; Che. Exp.⁵ V. 43; Muss-Arnolt, Exp.⁶ II. 421 f.), or due to a natural attenuation (v.i.). — כִּיּוּן] Especially interesting are 𝔙 which makes it a common noun, viz. imaginem (as adopted above), and 𝔖 כֵּיוָן, the pronunciation which expressed the later in-

terpretation involved in the reference to Assyrian gods.   For reference to the
use of this word in Babyl. texts, cf. Jensen, *Kosmologie*, 111 f.   For formation
as a common noun, cf. צִיּוּן (Ez. 39[15]); Sta. § 228.   In connection with this
interpretation may be noted (1) the suggestion of Muss-Arnolt (*Exp.*[6] II.
414–28), who transposes v.[25], placing it between vs.[23] and [24], omits v.[26] as
a marginal gloss, emending it as follows: יאלהיכם ואת־כיון כוכב צלמכם וגו׳,
translating: *And now ye worship Ninib as your decider* (or *king*), *and even
as your elohim ; and the star Saturn, as your idol which*, etc.   He takes נשא
here in the sense of the Assyr. *našû gâtâ* = lift up the hands = pray to, worship; and מלך as equivalent to the Assyr. *mal(i)ku* which is applied to
Ninib and other gods; and accounts for the selection of these names from
the many Assyrian gods by the fact that the star Kaimanu, the star of the god
Ninib, is spoken of as the star of justice and righteousness (kakkab kettu u
me-šar, II. R. 49, No. 3, 41), hence was chosen with reference to the thought
of v.[24].   (2) The opinion of Che. that the "proof of the Assyriological explanation is so nearly complete that we ought not to hesitate to accept it"
(*Exp.*[5] V. 42–44; abandoned, however, in *Crit. Bib.* in favor of a Jerahmeelite explanation); but the cultus here designated (that of *Sakkuth* and
Kaiwan) was not known in Israel until after 722 B.C. (cf. 2 K. 17[30]).   An
insertion of this kind is seen perhaps in Is. 10[4].   (3) The suggestion of
Baethgen (*Sem. Rel.* 239) that there are four proper names of deities, viz. *Sak-
kut, Kaiwan, Moloch, Selem.*   (4) The suggestion of G. A. Barton (*Oriental
Studies*, Philadelphia, 1894) that Amos refers to a cultus that was at least
probably present in his own day; since in one of the *El-Amarna* letters from
Jerusalem mention is made of a city *Beth-Ninib*, an evidence of the worship
of *Ninib*, or Saturn, in Palestine.   (5) The suggestion of Tiele (*Rev. d. l'hist.
d. rel.* III. 211), who makes these divinities purely Phoenician.   (6) The
objection to the interpretation which makes the prophet refer to the carrying
into exile, by Israel, of Assyrian gods, that, as a matter of fact, the victors
would carry off the idols of the vanquished nations (We.; cf. Hi.).   (7) The
reading of Haupt, *ZA.* II. 266, 281 f., כֵּאָמָן (for כְּאָמָן), the Hebrew form of the
Babyl. name Ka'âmânu.   (8) The opinion that *Sakkuth* and *Kaiwan* are perhaps two names for the same god; since *Sakkuth* is an ideographic writing
for the god *Ninib*, and *Ninib* seems to be the god of the planet Saturn
(= *Kaiwanu*), and *Sak-kut* and *Kaiwanu* are associated, as here, in the
Shurpu tablets; cf. IV. R. 52, col. 4, l. 9; and Zimmern, *Beitr. zur Kenntnis
der Bab. Rel.* (1896), p. 10, l. 179 (so R. W. Rogers, *EB.* I. 749; Muss-
Arnolt, *Exp.*[6] II. 414–28).   (9) The carrying of images in procession among
the Hebrews is not at all improbable in view of (*a*) the references to the
carrying of the ark in the wilderness, around Jericho (Jos. 6), and into battle
(as at Gilboa); (*b*) the same custom among the Assyrians, as at the New
Year's procession (cf. Jastrow, *Rel. of Bab. and Assyr.* 679; C. J. Ball, *Light
from the East*, 173); and (*c*) among the Egyptians (cf. Herodotus: "The
image being in a small temple of gilt wood, they carry out on the previous day
to another sacred habitation"; quoted by Hd. p. 159).   (10) The designa-

tion of Yahweh as מלך occurs also in Je. 48¹⁵ 51⁵⁷ Dt. 33⁵ Ps. 5³ 10¹⁶ 29¹⁰; and, as Elh. suggests, Israelites do not apply the term to the gods of foreigners. (11) The sugg. of Kö. II. i. 151, that the pointing כִּיּוּן is intended to suggest כּוּן, as something *established, firm*. (12) The explanation of Schmidt, who regards סִבָּה and כִּיּוּן as the original readings, but accounts for 𝔐𝕿 by supposing that at a later time מלככם came to be read מְלִכֹּם, that this suggested the reading כִּיּוּן, and that this in turn gave rise to the pointing סִכּוּת, the Palestinian equivalent for סְכּוּת, *ă* being attenuated as in *Rimmon* (= Rămmân) and *Tiglathpileser* (= Tukulti-apal-ê-šarra). (13) The suggestion of Hal. that three idols of Aramaean origin are mentioned, viz. סכות, the Aramaean name of Nabû, which was something like סְכָוָה, the Σεχὲς of Hesychius; כיון = Saturn; and כוכב = Venus (Aram. כּוכבתא); the translation being "And you shall carry Sakwé, your king, and Kaiwan and Kokab, your gods, the images which, etc." — 27. מהלאה ל] Is a circumlocution for the st. cstr.; Kö. 281 *p*; BDB.; cf. Je. 22¹⁹ Gn. 35²¹.

VI. 1-7. *A woe upon reckless and indifferent Samaria, who devotes herself to enervating luxury of every kind, — in food and drink, home-life and banquets, — but forgets the danger which threatens the country! She shall herself lead the captives who are soon to be dragged away.*

The unity of this section (the second section of three six-line strophes) is seen in (1) the outer form, and (2) the single thought which it presents, viz. the sinful luxury of the nation (v.², *pass over to Calneh*, etc., is a later insertion, *v.i.*). The structure of the section is characterized by the constant recurrence of the ptcp. with the article, followed by a finite vb. in cases in which it is desirous to prolong the thought. Each of the couplets (except the ninth) presents a single characteristic of the nation, viz. (1) recklessness, (2) conceit, (3) procrastination, (4) luxury, (5) gluttony, (6) enervation, (7) drunkenness, (8) hardness; therefore (9) captivity.

1. השאננים] 𝔊 τοῖς ἐξουθενοῦσιν = הַשָּׁאטִים, with Aramaic force (Bauer) or הַשְׁנָאִים; cf. Zc. 1¹⁵, where the same word was unknown to 𝔊 translators (Vol.); 𝔖 ﺤﺴﻨﻨﻴﺎ = הַשָּׁאטִים (Seb.); 𝔙 *qui opulenti estis;* 'Α. καταaσπαταλῶντες; Θ. εὐθηνοῦντες. Gr. שלאננים.—[בציון Che. בְּחֶרְזֶה (*JQR.* X. 573); Co. (*Einl.*) suspects genuineness (cf. Now., Volz, Löhr, Marti). — נקבי ראשית הגוים] 𝔊 ἀπετρύγησαν (= נקפו Vol.; Schleus. fol. Dru. corrects to ἀπετρύπησαν; cf. Arabic) ἀρχὰς ἐθνῶν. 𝔖 ﻓﺒﻴﻬ‍ = נִקְבֵי (Seb.) or וְקָבֵי (Hal.); 𝔙 *optimates; Σ.* οἱ ὠνομασμένοι ἐπὶ τοῖς ἀρχηγοῖς τῶν ἐθνῶν; Θ. οἳ ἐπεκλήθησαν ἀρχαῖοι τῶν ἐθνῶν; hence Gr. and Che. suggest הנקראים, but this is unnecessary since נקב in Ni. means practically the same thing; cf. Nu. 1¹⁷ 1 Ch. 16⁴¹ 2 Ch. 28¹⁵, etc.; in this case נקבי should be read הנקבים = *they who are desig-*

nated, or *designate themselves, as the first,* etc. This is supported by (1) Θ., Σ.;
(2) the grammatical consistency which it furnishes with the use of the ptcp.
fol. by a finite vb. throughout the entire passage; (3) the fact that, as Lagarde
has shown, the final ם of the pl. was not written in original Mss. Torrey's reading (*JBL.* XIII. 62 f.) נקפו (based on ᵬ, though ᵬ uses it in another sense),
an imv. (to be translated, "make the round of the foremost nations and come
to them, house of Israel! Pass over to Calneh, etc.") to be connected logically with v.², is suggestive but fails to relieve the difficulty, since it looks to
the preservation of v.² as a part of the original text.　Hal. נִקְבוּ = *Pronounce*
(the names of).— וּבָאוּ לָהֶם בֵּית יִשְׂרָאֵל] ᵬ καὶ εἰσῆλθον αὐτοί, connecting οἶκος
τοῦ Ἰσραήλ with the following v.; ܒ‍ܙ‍ܘ‍ = בְּזוּ (Seb.(?)); ᴟ *ingredientes
pompatice domum Israel;* ᵭ וְכָל דְּמָן דְּיִסְתַּמְכוּן.　Che., ברכו להם (*JQR.* X. 573),
but this means nothing.　The reading בְּזוּ (fol. ܣ) is in close sympathy with
the context, and is supported (1) on the side of the construction by Jos. 8². ²⁷
11¹⁴ Dt. 2³⁵ 3⁷; (2) as a charge against the rulers by Is. 3¹². ¹⁴. ¹⁵ 10²; cf.
Ez. 34¹⁰. ²² Am. 2⁶ ᶠᶠ. 4¹ 5¹² ᶠᶠ. (6³).　The reading בתולה מבית ישראל (Grimme,
ZDMG., 1897, p. 696), while ingenious, contributes nothing; much more
plausible is the reading וּבָאוּלֵהֶם (cf. 2 K. 24¹⁵) "und zu deren Vorderesten
das Haus Israel gehört" (Hirscht).　Oet. suggests either וּבָעֲלֵי בֵית ישראל, or
וְבַאלֹהִים (הֵמָּה) בְּבֵית יש׳; Gr. suggests וְכָנוּ.　Hal. וּבֹאוּ.— **2.** [כלנה ᵬ πάντες;
ܡ‍ܟ‍ܠ‍ܝ‍ܐ—[חמת רבה] ᵬ Ἐμαθ Ῥαββά.—[וורדו] ᵬ adds ἐκεῖθεν.—[גת] Hal. גם.—
[פלשתים] ᵬ ἀλλοφύλων, as usual.—[הטובים] ᵬ ܣᴟ have superlative, taking ה
as the article.　The whole v. is a later insertion (so Schra., Bickell in *COT.,*
We., Now., Löhr, Oet., Marti; cf. GAS., and Peters, *Hebr.* II. 175, who
suggests that Amos may have been still alive in 711 B.C.), as appears (1) from
the different form of the v. as compared with those which precede and
follow, *i.e.* the different rhythm (Bickell in *COT.* II. 144); (2) from the
marked interruption which it makes in the transition of thought from v.¹ to v.³
(the connection between ¹ and ³ being very close) and the grammatical dis-
turbance involved; (3) from the utter lack of meaning which it furnishes;
(4) from the historical fact (*v.i.*) that in the days of Amos these cities had not
yet been destroyed.　The text is to be emended (so Geiger, Oort, *Em.;* We.,
Val., Now., Oet., Marti, *et al.*) (*a*) by inserting the subj. of טובים, viz. אתם,
dropped perhaps because of similarity of sound, (*b*) by transferring the מן
connected with גבולכם to stand with גבולם.　Cf. Elh., אם רע גמולם מגמלכם, and
Gr., גם רב וגו׳.— **3.** [המנדים ᵬ οἱ ἐρχόμενοι, but ᵬᴬᵠ and Syr.-Hex. (in margin) οἱ εὐχόμενοι.—[המנדרים ܘܐ‍ܠ‍ܡ‍ܚ‍ܒ‍ ܣ the המחכים (Seb.), or המתאוים (Gr.);
ᴟ *qui separati estis;* ᵭ אנון מרחקין.　Baumann inserts הוי. Che.
המתחנדבים; Riedel, לאים.—[ותגשון] ᵬ οἱ ἐγγίζοντες καὶ ἐφαπτόμενοι, a double
rendering; Hoffm. וַתִּגְּשׁוּ; Riedel, וְתִגְשׁוּ.—[שֶׁבֶת] ᵬ σαββάτων = שַׁבָּת (so
also Hoffm., Hirscht); cf. ܣ ܠ‍ܫ‍ܡ‍ܒ‍ܐ. Che., זֶבַח; Gr. שבר; Riedel, לְשֶׁבֶת;
Marti, וְשֵׁר.

VI. 1. *Alas !*] Addressed to the ruling classes ; *they that are careless in Zion*] Judah as well as Israel is now rebuked, for (1) there is no good reason to omit בציון (*v.s.*) ; cf. Nowack, who would give a later date (the time of writing down the prophecy) to v.¹, if the reference to Judah is original ; and Cheyne, who would make v.¹ a late insertion or change ציון to תרצה (*v.s.*), the people being at ease because (2 K. 15¹⁶) the general resided there ; (2) the rendering of 𝕲 and 𝕾 *who despise Zion* * may not be sustained ; (3) there is no support for the translation " make a tumult in " ;† the usual interpretation, *at ease, secure, careless*, is supported by Is. 32⁹. — *Reckless in the mount of Samaria*] *i.e.* those in Samaria who are confident and therefore reckless,‡ not, those who trust in the strength of Samaria.§ — *Who specify themselves the chief of the nations*] According to 𝕳𝕿, נקבי, the rulers are here designated as *noted, marked by name* (cf. the later usage in Nu. 1¹⁷ 1 Ch. 16⁴¹ 2 Ch. 28¹⁵ 31¹⁹), there being no reference in these words to the cities of Jerusalem and Samaria. ‖ Justi's " *the princes of the first people of the earth* " (cf. Nu. 1¹⁶) well expresses the idea, a common one from the earliest times, that Israel was the most exalted nation of the entire world. It is better (*v.s.*) to make a slight change in the text and thus secure the rendering indicated. The expression is not ironical.¶ Cf. same phrase (without article) used of Amalek in Nu. 24²⁰, of spoil in 1 S. 15²¹, and of Ammon in Dn. 11⁴¹. — *Unto whom Israel's house comes*] Cf. Ex. 18¹⁶ 2 S. 15⁴. The pronoun *whom* does not refer to the nations whom Israel dispossessed,** nor to the mountains of Zion and Samaria, the land which Israel occupied,†† nor to these mountains as places where the Israelites assemble for worship and for judgment ;‡‡ but rather to the princes, to whom as leaders and judges Israel comes for justice (cf. 2 S. 15⁴), or to render service ;§§ cf. Gn. 19⁹ 1 K. 10¹⁴ Is. 49¹⁸. It is not necessary to omit ובאו להם, ‖‖ nor to understand ¶¶ that the phrase refers to the coming of the people to their leaders to learn foreign customs ; but it must be conceded (with

---

* Adopted by Dathe; Geb. so translates 𝕳𝕿.   § Os., Geb., Pu.   ** Ki.
† Har.   ‖ Cf. Cal.   †† Ros.
‡ Cal., Ros., Mau., Ba.   ¶ We., GAS., Dr.   ‡‡ Hes.
§§ Schrö., Mau., Umb., Hi., Hd., Ba., Schegg, Pu., Or., Dr.   ¶¶ With Hoffm.
‖‖ So We.

Nowack) that the phrase is an awkward one, and that some such
word as שְׁפַט might well have been expected.   Much may be said
for the reading of 𝕾 (*v.s.*), " and spoil for themselves the house
of Israel."   Cf. Marti, who reads " and in the gods of the house
of Israel," and calls it a gloss on " in the mount of Samaria."
— **2.** *Pass over to Calneh . . . Hamath and . . . Gath*] With this
verse must be compared Na. 3⁸ Ju. 11²⁵ 2 K. 19¹³. The determination of the localities depends somewhat upon the age of the
verse.   Is the verse as a whole *encouraging*, and intended (whether
by Amos or a later editor) to strengthen Israel's claim that she is
the first of the nations ?   In this case these cities are cited as examples of prosperity, and the argument is : " No city of your
acquaintance is more flourishing than yours ; yet ye treat Yahweh,
who has given you this prosperity, with neglect ; the punishment
for this conduct is exile." *   But (see Nowack) (1) contemporaries
of Amos needed no such encouragement in their faith ; (2) the
mention of Gath would have no meaning in such a comparison
while Assyria and Egypt were in existence ; (3) " these kingdoms " must mean Calneh, etc., not Israel and Judah.   Or, is the
verse *threatening*, and intended to warn Israel that she, however
" first " she may be, shall perish ?   In this case these cities are
cited as examples of "*fallen greatness*" (Driver), and the argument
is : " If cities that have been great are now in ruins, Israel, likewise, may perish." †   The latter view is to be accepted (*v.s.*). —
Calneh] (cf. כַּלְנֶה, Gn. 10¹⁰ ; כַּלְנוֹ, Is. 10⁹ ; כַּנֶּה, Ez. 27²³) is not
Ctesiphon, on the Tigris ; ‡ nor Niffer ; § nor Kullani, mentioned
in the Eponym Canon ‖ as conquered by Tiglathpileser III., B.C.
738 (= modern Kullanhou, six miles from Arpad ; cf. Calno and
Arpad, Is. 10⁹) ;¶ nor Kunulua (Kinalia), about seventy-five miles
north of Hamath, southeast of Antioch, capital of Patin ; ** but,
perhaps, the Kulunū †† conquered by Sargon, 711 B.C. — *Hamath
the great*] The modern Hamah (with 30,000 inhabitants), on the

---

* So Ew., Hi., Ke., Or., WRS. (*Proph.* 138), Dr.

† Ba., Pu., Schra., We., Now.   ‡ Ba., Or.   § G. Rawlinson (Smith's *DB.*¹).

‖ G. Smith, *The Assyr. Eponym Canon*, 50; Wkl. *Gesch. Bab. u. Ass.* 225;
Tiele, *Bab.-Ass. Gesch.* 230.   ¶ H. G. Tomkins, *PSBA.* V. 61.

** Gu. *Das Zukunftsbild des Jesaia*, 43; Di. on Is. 10⁹.

†† Dl. *Pa.* 225; *COT.* II. 143.

Orontes, 150 miles north of Damascus, the northernmost limit of
the territory promised to Israel (Nu. 34[8]). At times it was a part
of the Israelitish kingdom (as under David and Solomon, its king
being Toi, 2 S. 8[9], and perhaps under Jeroboam II., 2 K. 14[25. 28]
Am. 6[14]); at other times, it was independent and allied with neighboring nations against Assyria, as when it joined with Syria and
Israel against Shalmaneser II. and was defeated, 854 B.C. ; or with
Judah, against Tiglathpileser III., 741 ; or against Sargon, 720,
when at last its subjection was complete. After this date it is referred to as furnishing colonists for Samaria, 2 K. 17[24], and containing Israelitish exiles, Is. 11[11].* — *Gath of the Philistines*] That
one of Philistia's five cities nearest (cf. 1 S. 17[52]) Judah's border
(whether it is to be taken as *Tell es Safieh*,† or *Dikriu*, ‡ or to be
regarded as unknown §). It was destroyed by Uzziah (2 Ch. 26[6])
about 760 B.C. Here resided Rephaim (Jos. 11[22] 2 S. 21[18-22]). Cf.
Gimtu Asdudim, *COT*. II. 89, 91.|| — *Are they better than these
kingdoms ? Or is their border greater than your border ?*] With
this rendering the sense is, Are the cities just mentioned fairer
than the kingdoms of Israel and Judah ? No ; for God has so
punished them that they are reduced in size.¶ How ungrateful,
therefore, you are, in view of all that God has done for you above
your fellows.** The question is answered affirmatively by some †† :
Yes ; therefore how foolish it is of you to remain careless, having
seen the downfall of people more powerful than yourselves. Some
take the ה as article, instead of interrogative (cf. 𝔊 and 𝔖), and
translate as a clause in apposition with the names just given, "the
best of those kingdoms." ‡‡ The words have been put in the
mouth of the leaders, §§ saying : (*Go to*) *those which are better
than these kingdoms (just mentioned), and see if any is as great
as yours*, — this is the boasting of the leaders. The rendering, || ||
Are there fairer kingdoms than these (*i.e. Kalneh*, etc.) ? *And yet
they are not so large as the land of Israel*, does not add much
to a better understanding of the text ; but Pusey was approach-

---

* Cf. *COT*. II. 7 f., 143 ; GAS. 177 ; Buhl, *Pal*. 66, 110 ; Dl. *Pa*. 275-8.
† Porter in Smith's *DB*.[1] ; Che. *EB*.   ‡ Guerin, *Judée*, II. 108 f.
§ GAS. *HG*. 194 ff. ; Dr. || V. C. J. Ball, *Light from the East*, 93, 186.
¶ Va., Mau.   ** So Ros., Hi., Hd., Reuss, Mit.
†† Schrö., Kno.   ‡‡ Dathe, Mich.   §§ Schegg, Gun. || || Sugg. by Mit.
I.

ing the thought when he made it mean, " Are they, Israel and
Judah, better than these (*i.e. Calneh*, etc.)?" This leads us to
emend the text (*v.s.*) by supplying אַתֶּם and changing the position
of the pronominal suffixes : *Are ye better than these kingdoms ?
Is your border greater than was their border ?*] They have per-
ished, are you not afraid that you, too, will perish ? This interpretation is in strict accord with Na. 3⁸. With this interpretation
it becomes clear that the verse is an interpolation from the end of
the eighth century (*v.s.*). — **3.** *Who postpone the day of calamity*]
The connection of this with v.¹ is very close both logically and
grammatically. These leaders, like those described in Is. 5¹⁹, put
far away the day of disaster, *i.e.* declare that it is far off, or act
as if it were far away (cf. 9¹⁰ Is. 22¹³ 66⁵). — *And cause the seat of
violence to come near*] This may refer to tribunals or thrones in
which violence is in authority instead of justice, the word שבת
being a technical word for throne or judicial seat ; cf. Ps. 122⁵
74²⁰, or, perhaps better, to the sitting of injustice.* According to
some † the seat of violence has reference to Assyria, but the reference is rather to the encouragement of oppression in the midst
of Israel. ‡

<hr/>

1. הוי] *v.s.* on 5¹⁸. Followed by acc., Kö. 321 *b*; characteristic of Isaiah's
style, rarely met with elsewhere; Am. 5¹⁸ Mi. 2¹ Hb. 2⁶ ff.; cf. Ew.⁸ 327 *b*. —
השאננים] An intransitive adj. from vb. שאן = to be quiet, a root occurring
also in Syriac and Ethiopic with same meaning as in Hebrew. For formation,
cf. רענן; Barth, *NB.* 143 *a*; and Sta. § 230. — ראש] Equivalent to a superlative; cf. Kö. 309 *g*. — **2.** רבה] Article omitted before ר for sake of euphony,
GK. 126 *z*; cf. Kö. 334 *m* and 337 *u*. — גת־פלשתים] For proper names with
fol. gen., cf. GK. 125 *h*; Ew.⁸ 286 *c*. Article omitted as in Gn. 10¹⁴, etc.; cf.
Kö. 295 *f*. — הטובים] Subj. omitted in 𝕸𝕿; cf. Ew.⁸ 303 *b*, 1. — **3.** מנדים]
Cf. Is. 66⁵ for מְנַדִּים, Hiph. ptcp. of נדד, *v.* Oet. — ל]ליום introduces
acc., cf. Ho. 10¹², a common Aramaic construction; Ew.⁸ 282 *c*, Da. § 100,
rm. 5, Kö. 289 *h*. — ותגישון] Finite vb. cont. ptcp., cf. 2⁷ 5⁷. — שבת] Barth,
ZDMG. XLI, 619, connects this with the Arab. ثِبَ = to gather; cf.
Kö. 210 *f*.

<hr/>

* Cf. GAS. I. 174.   † Pu.

‡ So nearly all comm. There is neither occasion nor basis for the violent
emendation of Hoffm. (*v.s.*), furnishing the translation : *Ye who daily demand
unjust* [*tribute*], *and every Sabbath require unrighteous* [*gain*] ; cf. ⅁.

4. סרחים] ⑥ κατασπαταλῶντες = פֹּרְחִים, with Aramaic force (Vol.); so 𝔙 *lascivitis.* — מרבק] ⑥ adds γαλαθηνά = עוּלִים or עֲלָלִים, which resemble עֲגָלִים (Va.). — **5.** הפרטים] ⑥ ἐπικροτοῦντες; ⑥ᴮ ἐπικρατοῦντες; Gr. הֹפְּפִים, or הטפפים. — פי] Gr. פְּנֵי. — הנבל] ⑥ τῶν ὀργάνων; 𝔖 ‏عَبَل‎; 𝔙 *psalterii;* 𝔗 נִבְלָא. — כדויד] ⑥ ὡς ἑστηκότα, which Cappellus explained as due to confusion with דוּר, and Vol. as a reading of כְּרָם from דוּם, while Hirscht sugg. that there may have been a corruption of ΩΣΔΑΤΙΔ into ΕΣΤΩΤΑ. Gr. כַּדִּים. In any case the phrase is probably a gloss, since it has no place in the metrical structure of either the preceding or following line; cf. את־מלך וגו', Is. 8[7]; so Peters (*Hebr.* II. 175), Che. (*EB.*), Löhr, *et al.* — השבו להם] 𝔙 *putaverunt se habere;* ⑥ ἐλογίσαντο. BSZ., *s.v.* המה, sugg. that in להם lies a derivative from הָמָה, cf. הֶמְיָה. — כלי־שיר] ⑥ καὶ οὐχ ὡς φεύγοντα, according to Vol. = כְּלִי שָׁוֵּר, but according to Hirscht, due to a reading from שׁוּר = סוּר. Gr. כַּלֵּי שִׁיר. Now. כֹּל שִׁיר; so Oort (*Em.*). Elh. מְלֵי שִׁיר, since tradition does not ascribe to David the making of musical instruments. Che. (*Exp.T.*, 1898, p. 334), restores the entire v. thus: —

הַמְזַמְּרִים עַל־תֹּף וְנֵבֶל
וישמחו לקול שיר

Who play on timbrel and harp,
And rejoice at the sound of song.

(Cf. Jb. 21[12 b].) Marti reads v.[5b], כדויד נֶחְשְׁבוּ לְהַשְׂכִּיל בְּשִׁיר. — **6.** במזרקי יין] ⑥ τὸν διυλισμένον οἶνον = מְזֻקָּק יין; cf. Is. 25[6] Ps. 12[7] (Vol.); so 𝔖 ‏مُصَفًّى‎; 𝔙 *vinum in phialis;* 𝔗 adds כָּף = דִּכְסַף. Oort, במורקי יין (so Val.), or במורק יּ (cf. Je. 48[11]). Gr. במזרקים (so Elh., Hal.). — נחלו] Gr. חלו(?), from היל; cf. Je. 5[8]. Löhr places [6a] before [5], while Marti transposes [6b] to follow [13]. — **7.** גלים] ⑥ δυναστῶν = גְּדֹלִים (Va., Vol.). — מרזח סרוחים] ⑥ χρεμετισμὸς ἵππων ἐξ 'Εφράιμ, perhaps reading סוּסִים (so Oet.; but cf. Vol.). Σ. ἑταιρεία τρυφητῶν; 𝔖 ‏ܘܢܐܕ ܡܢ‎ 𝔖, perhaps reading סריהם = שָׁרֵיהֶם (Seb.). 𝔙 *factio lascivientium;* 𝔗 מְנָהוֹן מַרְזְחִין וּמְפַכִּין.

4. *Who lie on ivory couches*] Cf. 3[12]. These were couches inlaid with ivory, such as those which Sennacherib took from Hezekiah.* The use of such couches indicated the luxury and self-indulgence of the times. — *And stretch themselves out upon their divans*] Reference is intended to lying at the table; it does not include the specific idea of "romping," † nor that of abundant tapestry with which the divan was draped, ‡ nor the thought of

---

* *COT.* I. p. 286. † Schrö. ‡ Ki.

drunkenness,* but, in general, all of these, emphasis being placed on the wantonness and extravagance of their conduct ; cf. Is. 22[13] Ez. 23[15]. — *Lambs out of the flock*] i.e. those carefully selected from the flock on account of special fatness or daintiness, cf. Dt. 32[14] 1 S. 15[9],† rather than a general reference to the wealth of those persons who are rich enough to have flocks.‡ — *Calves from the midst of the stall*] i.e. calves reared artificially in a stall, a place in which they are shut up in order to be easily fattened. Cf. 1 S. 28[24] Je. 46[21] Mal. 4[2]. — **5.** *Who twitter*] Used sarcastically of the music rendered at feasts. The idea is not that of ordinary singing,§ nor dancing, ‖ nor cooing,¶ nor wanton silly talk or song,** nor parting the lips,†† nor bungling, doing something prematurely,‡‡ nor leading in the music without waiting for the professional musicians, §§ nor improvising idly ‖‖ ; but of derision, to indicate the prophet's contempt " for the perhaps really not unmusical songs with which feasts were enlivened " ¶¶ ; cf. Is. 5[12] 24[9]. — *To the sound of the harp*] Another rendering is, *in accordance with ;* cf. על פי in Gn. 43[7] Ex. 34[27] Lv. 27[18]. § — *Like David*] If this word is genuine, the leaders of Israel, whom the prophet would rebuke, are now brought into comparison with David. They are like him in that *they devise for themselves instruments of song*] It is not a *contrast,* viz. between their use of instruments for amusement, and that of David for worship.*** Nor is it correct to render ††† " they think, fondly imagine — make the mistake of supposing that the instruments are for them as for David." חשב = *devise, invent,* with reference to the popular idea that David was an inventor of instruments. No other passage of earlier times speaks of David as a poet or musician. ‡‡‡ But this reference does not imply that his reputation had only to do with secular music. §§§ The evidence is very strong, however, that the word is a gloss (*v.s.*). — *Instruments of song*] Musical instruments

---

* Ba. We. renders "ausgelassen sein," which is approved by Now., and cites its application in Arabic to animals pasturing freely, at liberty, and in Syriac to wild and rapacious beasts.

† Ba. *et al.*   ‖ Stru.   †† Schegg.   §§ Hd.
‡ Mau.   ¶ Schrö.   ‡‡ Ew.   ‖‖ Dr.
§ Ros.   ** Hi., Ke., Now.   ¶¶ Mit.; cf. Hoffm. *ZAW.* III. 114.
        *** Jer., Cal., Jus., Ros., Schrö.   ‡‡‡ Reuss.
        ††† So Ew., Mit.   §§§ We., Dr.

used to accompany the voice; but the context is not favorable to
the allusion to instruments, hence (*v.s.*) Cheyne's suggestion,
voice of song, Elhorst's *words of song*, Nowack's *all kinds of
song*, and Marti's *consider themselves like David in the understanding of song.* — **6.** *Who drink (from) bowls of wine*] Another
token of self-indulgence. Instead of the ordinary drinking-vessel,
the word is employed which is later used of the vessel from
which blood was poured or thrown (dashed) for sacrificial purposes (Ex. 38³ Nu. 4¹⁴ 7¹³ ff. Zc. 9¹⁵ 14²⁰), the large size thus being
emphasized. — *With the first of oils they anoint themselves*] Anointing in ancient times signified not only consecration, but joyousness
(cf. Ps. 23⁵ 92¹⁰ Is. 61³ Ec. 9⁸ with 10¹⁹). It was a hygienic custom, since the oil refreshed the skin and served as a protection
against heat. In this case the *first of oils, i.e.* the choicest
oils, are employed. To omit anointing was a sign of mourning
(2 S. 12²⁰ 14²). — *And do not grieve for the breach of Joseph*]
Their minds are so occupied with the mirth and joy that they
fail to see, and hence to appreciate, the terrible breach or wound
which, in the near future, will be inflicted upon Israel. Such
a sight as that which the prophet has gained would make them
sick in body and in mind (cf. 1 S. 22⁸); for a great affliction
or overthrow (cf. Je. 8¹¹·²¹) is near at hand. This word *breach*
does not refer to any specific political intrigue,* nor to the
present evil condition of Israel,† but to the future calamity
which even now threatens the nation. ‡ — **7.** *Therefore, now*]
The *now* is logical, rather than temporal, Ho. 2¹⁰ 5⁷. — *At the
head of the captives*] These, who were described as the ראשׁית
הגוים, נקבים, shall go forth at the head, in the very forefront; cf.
1 S. 9²² Mi. 2¹³. — *And the shout of the banqueters shall cease*]
The rendering, "the mourning of those who stretch themselves
out shall come," § is based upon an impossible meaning of סר.
Some use here the Aramaic meaning of מרזח, viz. feasting. ‖ The
rendering "shout" (either of joy or sorrow) is required here as
in Je. 16⁵ and is justified by the Arabic زَرِجَ.¶ The alliteration in the Hebrew words סר מרזח סרוחים is noticeable. —

---

* Mich.   † Schegg.   ‡ Hi., Mit.   § Cal.
‖ Har., Mich.   ¶ Jus., Va., Ros., Ba., Pu., Ke.

8 b. *Saith Yahweh God of Hosts*] This phrase, if retained at all, must follow this piece as a whole.

4. סרוחים] On force of pass. ptcp., cf. Kö. 235 d. — **5.** הפרטים] α.λ.; if text is correct, probably to be connected with فَرَطَ, *to precede*, fourth stem = *to hasten, exceed due bounds, be immoderate, talk excessively* (Lane, p. 2376); hence Dr., following Abul-Walid (Neubauer, *Abul-Walid's Lexicon*, col. 586), suggests "to extemporize poetry over-rapidly, without premeditation, in a hurried flow of unmeaning, unconsidered words" (*v.* Dr. p. 236 ; Now.). Observe, likewise, Hoffm.'s rendering, "those who strike the strings across the opening of the harp," which is based on the usage of פרט (Lv. 19[10]), *to tear* (cf. Buxtorf, *Lex.* 1811 f.; Payne Smith, *Thesaurus Syriacus*, p. 3311), and makes the על פי entirely superfluous. — נבל] The kinds of instruments denoted by the two names נבל and כנור are not certainly known. The two are the only stringed instruments mentioned in the O. T., and are frequently named together (Is. 5[12] 1 Ch. 15[16] 2 S. 6[5], etc.). Both seem to have been made of wood (1 K. 10[12]) and to have been portable (1 S. 10[5] 2 S. 6[5]). A full discussion of these and other instruments, with excellent illustrations of Assyrian, Babylonian, and Egyptian harps, etc., is given in *Bk. of Ps.* (*SBONT.*), 222 ff.; cf. Dr. 234 ff.; Benz. *Arch.* 273 ff.; Now. *Arch.* I. 273 ff. — **6.** שתה ב׳] = *to drink from*, cf. Gn. 44[5]; same force in Arabic and Aramaic (Dn. 5[2]). For the same phrase = *to drink of*, cf. Pr. 9[6]; GK. 119 m, N. — מזרקי] Used only here of *wine;* elsewhere, bowl or basin for *throwing or casting* a liquid, esp. blood ; *e.g.* at altar, Ex. 27[8] Nu. 4[14]; in temple, 1 K. 7[50] 2 K. 12[14]; in second temple, Neh. 7[70]. This meaning is borne out in the signification of the root, which in the cognates means *scatter, disperse;* cf. Aram. זְרַק, Assyr. zarâķu, Arab. زَرَقَ, *cast at.* — שמנים] On force of the pl., cf. Kö. 259 a. — ימשחו] For construction, etc., cf. Kö. 327 o and 319 m. On impf. continuing ptcp., cf. Dr. § 117 O. The original meaning seems to be shown by Arab. مَسَحَ = *stroke with the hand*. It is used of *painting* a house (Je. 22[14]) and *oiling* a shield (Is. 21[5] 2 S. 1[21]). Anointing as a part of the toilet is always expressed by another verb, סוך. משח, as used of persons, is limited to anointing *as a religious rite*, aside from this passage ; and this seems to be no exception, since the feast here was a *sacrificial* feast. The primitive significance of anointing was probably religious ; animal fat was the first unguent, and, being regarded as the special seat of life, was considered the best medium for the transmission of the vitality of the being from which it was taken ; hence "unction was primarily an application of sacrificial fat with its living virtues to the persons of the worshippers" (WRS. *Sem.* 383 f.). This accounts for the anointing of kings, priests, etc., and for the use of unguents in connection with religious rites. Olive oil was used later when agriculture was taken up (Ps. 92[11] Dt. 28[40]

Nu. 6[15]). — יוסף] This designation of N. Israel occurs twice elsewhere in Amos (5[6. 15]); other names are: *Jacob* (6[8] 7[2. 5] 8[7]); *house of Jacob* (9[8]); *house of Isaac* (7[16]); and regularly *Israel* (2[6. 11], etc.). Joseph is named as the ancestor of Ephraim, the largest tribe (cf. Ho. 6[4] 13[1]). The use of the title occurs each time in a connection implying a bond of sympathy between Israel and Yahweh, or at least a shade of tenderness in the feelings of Amos.

8–14. *Yahweh makes oath: I abhor Israel, and she shall be given over to her enemies for destruction; she has turned justice to poison, imagining herself strong; surely I will bring upon her a nation which shall overcome her entire territory.*

The striking difference between the grammatical expression in this piece (the third of three six-line strophes) and that in the preceding is evidence of distinctness; but when there is considered in connection with this (1) the opening oath (v.[8]), which is climactic to the woes introducing the other pieces, (2) the concluding words, which are parallel to those of the other pieces, we have sufficient basis for the assumption that this is one of three pieces making up a larger whole. Vs.[9. 10] are so peculiar in their thought and form as at once to raise suspicion of their genuineness; this suspicion becomes a certainty upon closer investigation (*v.i.*). The intensity of expression, as well as the definiteness of this section, is greater than in either of the two preceding. It thus furnishes a fitting climax for the entire piece, containing, in essence, the threefold thought of the whole, viz. (1) Yahweh's anger, because of (2) Israel's sin, and consequently, (3) Israel's destruction.

8. נאם יהוה אלהי צב׳] 𝕲 om. (so Now., Elh., Löhr, Baumann); it should follow עַתָּה, v.[7] (cf. We., Oet., Marti). — מתאב] Read מתעב (so Geiger, p. 349; We., Mit., Elh., Löhr, Oet., *et al.*). — את־גאון] 𝕲 inserts πᾶσαν; 𝕮 בֵּית מַקְדְּשָׁא דְּבֵיתֵהּ (so in London Polyglot, but in Paris Polyglot, רבותה).—ארמנתיו] 𝕲 τὰς χώρας αὐτοῦ; 𝖁 *domos ejus.* — והסגרתי] Gr. fol. 𝕲 καὶ ἐξαρῶ, —והכרתי.—ומלאה] 𝕲 σὺν πᾶσι τοῖς κατοικοῦσιν αὐτήν; 𝖁 *cum habitatoribus suis.* Hoffm. וּמְלֹאָהּ = *and her citadel;* so Matthes and Elh. — **9, 10.** These verses are a later insertion (so Now. and Löhr; We. and Che. consider them, at least, misplaced; but cf. GAS. and Marti), made in order to illustrate the last phrase of v.[8]. This is evident because of (1) the marked interruption of the continuity of thought between v.[8] and v.[11]; (2) the utterly strange and incongruous conception thus introduced; (3) the impossibility of arranging the material of these vs. (viz.[9. 10]) in any poetical form, much less the form which characterizes the remainder of the piece. The acceptance of GAS.'s suggestion to supply at the close of v.[8] the words *to the pestilence* only furnishes a still better basis for the addition of the gloss. Oet. sugg. the order [7. 11. 8. 9. 10]. — והיה אם] 𝖁 *Quod si;* 𝕾 ؋o. — ומתו] 𝕲 adds καὶ ὑπολειφθήσονται οἱ κατάλοιποι.—ונשאו דודו] 𝕲 καὶ λήμψονται οἱ οἰκεῖοι οἱ αὐτῶν. Hal. דודו. Riedel, וְנָשָׂאו דוד.—ונשאו—ומסרפו] Many Mss.

read יֵ. 𝕲 καὶ παραβιῶνται = ויפצרו (Va., Vol.), as in Gn. 19⁹ 2 K. 2¹⁷ 5¹⁶,
or ויפרצו (Vol.), as in 1 S. 28²³. 𝕾 ܡܫ ܦܩܒܬ ܟܠܗ = ומקרבו [Seb.];
𝕱 et comburet eum; 𝕿 מְיַקְּרָה. Now. ומספדו(?); Riedel, וּמַגְּרֵפָה = besom. —
After [עצמים 𝕲 adds αὐτῶν. — [לאשר 𝕲 pl. — [בירכתי 𝕲 and 𝕾 om. — [אפס
Riedel adds חי יהוה, to explain what follows. — [הם וגו' 𝕿 סָפוּ וַיִּמַּר סָלַק
reading ,ܟ̈ܐܦ̈ܐ ܚܡܫ̈ܐ ܒܒ̈ܬܐ = 𝕾, אֲרֵי כד הֲווֹ חַמְשִׁין לָא הֲווֹ מִצְלָן בְּשַׁמָּא דַיָי
[להזכיר — .(so Seb.; cf. Gr. Monatsschrift, 1886, p. 376) הם for אֶפֶס
𝕾 ܗܘܝܘ = ܡܬܕܟܪ = הַזְכִּיר (Seb.); 𝕱 recorderis. The following attempts at
reconstruction of the text may be noted : Oort, understanding that ואמר הס
is a dittog. of ואמר אפס (cf. Baumann, who om. ואמר אפס), that the material
has been largely transposed, and that the horrors of an earthquake are here
described, reads : (⁸ᵈ) והסגרתי עיר ומלאה (¹⁰ ᵈ) עד לא תזכר בשמה (¹¹) כי הנה י'
מצוה והכה הבית . . . בקעים (⁹) והיה אם עשרה אנשים בבית אחד מתו (¹⁰) ונשאו . . .
That is : (⁸ᵈ) And .מן־הבית ואמר לאשר בירכתי הבית העור עמך ואמר אפס
I will deliver up a city and its contents, (¹⁰ ᵈ) so that it shall no longer
be called by its name; (¹¹) for, behold, Yahweh commands and will smite,
etc., (⁹) and it shall come to pass that, whenever ten men shall have
died in one house, (¹⁰) their relatives will clear away the ruins in order
to carry the bones from the house, and they will say to whoever is in
the rear of the house, "Is there still another?" and he will answer,
"No!" Zeydner reads (ThSt. IV. 196 ff.; so Val.) : (¹⁰) ונשאר מְכָרָד להוציא
עצמים מן־הבית ואמר לאשר בירכתי הבית העור עמך ואמר אפס ואמר הסכילו אֶל
That is : (¹⁰) And an escaped one will remain to bring .הַזְכֵּר בשם יהוה
forth the bones from the house and he will say to whoever is within
the house, "Is there still any one with thee?" And he will say "No." And
he will say, "These have done foolishly. Remember the name of Yahweh."
(⁹) והיה אם יהיו עשרה אנשים בבית ואחד ימות וְיִוָּתְרוּ הָאֲחֵרִים (¹⁰) ונשאו : Ru. reads
ד' ומ' לה' עֲצָמָיו מן־הבית ואמר . . . העור עמָך אמֶר ואפס וגו'. That is : (⁹) And
it shall come to pass that if there be ten men in a house and one die
and the others be left, etc., . . . to bring forth his bones . . . "Is He
still with you who creates (= אֹמֵר) and annihilates?" . . . Gr. reads :
ונשאום עבריהם ושרפו (¹⁰), substitutes ואמרו for the sg., drops ואמר הס as dittog.
from ואמרו אפס, and adds אָבִו after לא. Hoffm. reads (¹⁰) ונשאו דורו מְסָרְפָיו
= and his burners erect a funeral pyre for him. Oet. sugg. (¹⁰) ונשא דוד אֹ
אֶלֶף, treats להוציא עצמים מבית as a gloss on the corrupt ומסרפו and declares the remainder of the v., beginning with the first ואמר, to be "un-
versehrt." Elh. reads ונשא דורו מספרו, and om. ואמר following עמך. Box and
Oesterley (Exp. T. XII. (1901) 235 f.) read ונשאו שאר ופרצו להוציא עצמים
as a ואמר הס (treating מן־הבית ואמר לאשר בירכתי הבית העור עמך ואמר אפס
dittog., and the last clause, ואמר הס, as a gloss on כי וו. Marti וְנִשְׁאַר דור מְסַפֵּר,
or וּשְׁאָר דורי מְסַפֵּר. — 11. [כי הנה יהוה מצוה Is an insertion (so also Baumann)
made to connect vss.⁹·¹⁰ with the interrupted thought in [והכה וגו' which is to
be read מַלְכּוּ 𝕿 .(so Oet.) וְהִכָּה or וְהִכּוּ. Gr. reads יוֹצֵא for מצוה. — [הבית Hi.
om. ה as due to homoioteleuton (so Gr.). — [הגדול 𝕾 ܦܠܓܐ. — [רסיסים ,בקעים

אם יחרוש‎ .12—. ‎וּבֵית‎ Gr. ‎ והבית‎] Gr. ‎רצוצים‎. —‎ .‎סלי‎ؤسم‎, سلنخكمسه‎ ‏ܠ‎
בבקרים‎] ⅏ εἰ παρασιωπήσονται ἐν θηλείαις = ‎נקבים‎ or ‎נקבית‎ (Va., Ba.), probably an error of vision. 𝔙 aut arari potest in bubalis; 'A. εἰ ἀροτριαθήσεται;
Σ. πέτρα διὰ βοῶν. Read ‎בבקר ים‎ (so Mich., Hi.; Oort, ThT. XIV. 120, and
Em.; Gr., We., Gu., Val., Mit., GAS., Now., Dr., Löhr, Elh., Oet., Marti);
cf. Hirscht, ‎בבקעים‎ (Jb. 39¹⁰); Hal. ‎כבקר רים‎.—‎ראש‎] ⅏ εἰς θυμόν, as in
Dt. 32³³ Jb. 20¹⁶; 𝔗 ‎לריש חמן בישין‎. —‎ 13. ‎ללא‎] Gr. ‎על לא‎. —‎ 14. ‎נאם י' וגו'‎]
Omitted in some Mss. of ⅏. Transpose to end of v. (so Löhr). ⅏ℵ
insert ‎גוי‎ before ‎נאם‎.—‎ מלבוא‎] ⅏ τοῦ μὴ εἰσελθεῖν.—‎ ער‎] ⅏ καὶ ὡς = ‎וער‎
(Hirscht); ⅏ᴬ and other codd., ἕως.—‎ הערבה‎] ⅏ τῶν δυσμῶν, a frequent
rendering of ‎מערב‎ and ‎ערבה‎; cf. Is. 15⁷. ‏ܠ‎ ‎ؤحـܠ‎. Oort sugg. the transposition of v.¹⁴ to precede 5²⁶.

8. *The Lord Yahweh hath sworn by himself*] Elsewhere
only in Je. 51¹⁴, in 4² the oath was *by his holiness.* For expressions similar to this, Gn. 22¹⁶ Nu. 14²⁸ Heb. 6¹³.—*I abhor*]*
Cf. Dt. 28⁶³ Ho. 5¹². ¹⁴ 13⁷ ᶠ·; also Am. 9⁴.—*The glory of Jacob*]
Not something that belonged to Israel as a special treasure, which
distinguished them from other nations, cf. Is. 2¹⁰· ¹⁹· ²¹ Ps. 47⁴,† in
other words, the true glory, which shall now be taken away; nor
the temple at Jerusalem, cf. 𝔗; ‡ but rather that of which Jacob
boasted as their glory, viz. palaces and cities (cf. Na. 2² Zc. 9⁶),§
the pride which has brought downfall (Is. 9⁹ Ho. 5⁵). ‖ —*I will
deliver the city and its contents*] *i.e.* men, cattle, goods, shall be
given to the enemy (1⁶· ⁹). Perhaps the thought refers more
specifically to the siege and capture of the city; ¶ cf. 2¹⁴⁻¹⁶ 3¹¹ ᶠ·
4². ³ 5¹⁶ 8³. The city is Samaria, the article being omitted in the
terse, poetical expression. — **9.** This verse and the following
introduce a new element into the description of the future punishment, and at the same time a new form and a new style.
After these verses (*i.e.* in vs.¹¹ ᵇ· ¹²⁻¹⁴) the old idea, style, and form
recur. The new element is the plague; the new form, an individual experience; the new style, conversational prose, the poetic

---

* The root ‎תאב‎ may better be read ‎תעב‎ (*v.s.*), whether the use of ‎א‎ in this text
is to be understood as an intentional change (Geiger, p. 349), a Samaritanism
(Eich, *Einl.* I. 185; Jus.), a provincialism (Ba.), or a copyist's error (Dahl., Now.).
The renderings "I find wanting" (cf. ‎תאבתי‎), Storr (see Va.), "I will paralyze,"
from ‎تَاب‎, *to be numb* (Va.), hardly deserve consideration.

† Cal., Hd.   ‡ Ki. and Jewish interpreters generally.
§ Ros., Ke., Mit.   ‖ Ba.   ¶ Hi., Ba., Pu.

form being abandoned. There is nothing in v.[8], or in vs.[12 ff.] which corresponds, or lends aid in interpretation. — *And it shall come to pass*] Cf. the series of pictures of devastation in Is. 8[15. 21. 22]. — *If there be left ten men in one house that they shall die*] The picture is that of a slaughter in war. If of the survivors there are as many as ten, all of them shall perish in a plague. According to some,[*] ten represents a large number, a numerous family, all of whom, however, shall die. According to others,[†] it means a very few, because the prophet has in mind especially the palaces which would contain hundreds. — **10.** *And one's uncle, even his burner, shall take him up to bring out the body from the house*] The relative,[‡] perhaps uncle,[§] father and brothers being dead, comes to care for the dead body. The relative is either himself *the burner*, or is accompanied by a *burner*. Inasmuch as burning of the dead was entirely exceptional among the Hebrews (cf. 2[1]; the cases of criminals, Lv. 20[14] 21[9] Jos. 7[15. 25] Gn. 38[24], and that of Saul and his sons), this has been taken as another exception, the prophet supposing it to be impossible to adopt the usual form of burial, and the burner represented as acting either within[||] or without[¶] the home, on account of the peculiar situation; or the burning, like the plague itself, has been considered a mark of divine anger.[**] The reference is not, however, to the burning of the body, but to the burning of spices in honor of the dead;[††] cf. Je. 34[5], and especially 2 Ch. 16[14] 21[19 b]. The suggestion has also been made[‡‡] that the lack of timber in Palestine would make cremation of any considerable number of bodies almost impossible. The pronoun *his* seems to suggest some *common* custom.[§§] — *And shall say*] It is the relative who speaks. — *To him who is in the innermost parts of the house*] *i.e.* to some one who is still alive,[||||] and, in his terror, has withdrawn to the inmost recesses of the house;[¶¶] not to a neighbor in an adjoining house,[***] nor to a servant,[†††] nor

---

[*] Os., Geb., Hi., Torrey, Marti.   [†] Jus., Ros., Schrö.

[‡] Jus., Ros., Schrö., Ba., Hd., Ke.   [§] A. V.

[||] Cal., Hi.   [¶] Ke.   [**] W. R. Smith, *Sem.* 372, N. 3.

[††] Har.; Thomson, *LB.* II. 493; Mit., Dr.   [‡‡] Mit.

[§§] Hi., Dr.   [||||] Jus., Va., Hi., Ba.

[¶¶] Cf. Ps. 128[8]; ירכתי is also used of a cave in 1 S. 24[4], of Sheol in Is. 14[15], of a ship in Jon. 1[5].   [***] Cal.   [†††] Schlier.

to a relative who remains weeping.* — *Is there yet any one with thee*] Are you altogether alone ? — *And he shall say*] Inserted to separate the two parts of the statement, cf. 2 K. 6²⁷ ᶠ⋅ Gn. 16⁸⁻¹¹ 21⁷. — *None*] The last survivor answers, and in his answer gives utterance to the deepest feelings of despair. — *And he shall say: Hush! one may not mention the name of Yahweh*] Cf. 8³ Hb. 2²⁰ Zp. 1⁷ Zc. 2¹³. This is not the utterance of the survivor, and thus to be taken as a word of repentance (being rendered, Ought we not to remember Yahweh's name?),† nor an explanatory statement by Amos of what was in the sick man's mind; ‡ but the utterance of the relative to the survivor, which partakes of the despair common to the situation: " No prayer will avail, all is lost," § or " recourse to Yahweh is of no use " ; ‖ " do not tempt Yahweh to farther outburst of anger " ; ¶ " do not mention his name and thus make him aware of your presence " ; ** cf. Is. 19¹⁷.††

— **11.** *For behold Yahweh will command*] A part of the gloss, intended to regain the connection which has been lost. What follows should, however, be joined directly to the last words of v⁸, viz. *I will give over the city and its contents, and one shall smite the great house and the small house*] Utter destruction is coming. *The great house* in connection with *the small house,* means either all houses, alike of rich and poor, ‡‡ for God is no respecter of persons ; cf. 3¹⁵ Is. 9¹⁷ ; or, as seems better, the nation Israel and the nation Judah,§§ the former of which suffered under Shalmaneser, the latter under Sennacherib. — *Into fragments . . . into fissures*] The distinction suggested that the destruction of the great house (whether taken of the rich, or of Israel) is to be more complete than that of the small house (*i.e.* the poor, or Judah), is not found in the text. The second word is as strong a word for destruction as the first. — **12.** *Do horses run upon crags ?*] It is just as unnatural and absurd for you to pervert justice, as for men

---

* Os.   ‡ Hi.   ‖ Jus., Schrö.   ** Ba., Reuss.

† Har.   § Dathe, Va., Ros.   ¶ Ew., Dr.

†† The collection of materials on conceptions of divine names among primitive peoples given by F. J. Coffin, in his dissertation on the Third Commandment, is of interest as illustrating the last clause of v.¹⁰; see *JBL.* XIX. 166 ff. Cf. also Baumann's sugg. that יהוה has displaced an original אלהים = *spirit* (1 S. 28¹⁸).

‡‡ Cal., Har., Ros., Schrö., Hi., Mit., Dr., Marti.

§§ 𝔗, Jer., Dahl, Dathe, Jus., Hd., Or., We.

to make horses run upon crags.* We are not to understand that
the rock represents the hard and stubborn people.† — *Does one
plough the sea with oxen ?*] This reading (*v.s.*) avoids the necessity
of supplying an important word in thought and, at the same time,
the very irregular plural form, בקרים. — *That*] כי can scarcely be
rendered *but,*‡ or *surely.* § — *Ye have turned justice into poison*]
Only a general word may be used, since the exact meaning of ראש
is uncertain (*v.i.*). "A moral order exists which it is as impossible
to break without disaster as it would be to break the natural order
by driving horses upon a precipice." ‖ — *The fruit of righteousness
into wormwood*] *i.e.* what would be good and helpful, into that
which is bitter and injurious. — **13.** *Who rejoice in that which is
not*] A strong effect is produced by using לא to negate a noun
(cf. לא עם, לא־אל, Dt. 32^{17. 21}; לא איש, Is. 31^8). The people, whom
the prophet rebukes, flatter themselves with self-deception, that
which is imaginary, not real¶; but *v.i.* — *Who say, Have we not
taken for ourselves horns by our own strength ?*] The nation is represented as boasting of the new power ** which they had acquired
under Jeroboam II. ; †† the horn represents power, Je. 48^{25} Dt. 33^{17}
Ps. 75^{5. 10} 89^{17}. An utterance of pride, similar to this, is placed in
Ephraim's mouth, Is. 9^{10}. Against Graetz's suggestion ‡‡ that לא
דבר is a city, viz. *Lo-debar,* 2 S. 9^{4 f.} 17^{27}, and קרנים another city
(1 Macc. 5^{26}; cf. *Ashteroth-Karnaim,* Gn. 14^5 ⑤), both on the
east of Jordan, and that the boast has to do with their recent
subjection by Jeroboam, the names of these towns being selected
because of their peculiar significance, §§ may be said : ‖‖ (1) the
Hebrew prophets are not accustomed to speak thus of victories,
(2) לקח is not the proper word for capturing a town, but rather
לכד, (3) לקח ל is a common idiom for the idea, *to provide oneself
with* (cf. Is. 8^1 Je. 36^{2. 28} Ez. 4^1 5^1 Zc. 11^{15}, etc.) ; (4) these towns
were not sufficiently strong to warrant such a reference to them,¶¶
(5) cf. 5^{15}; (6) the unanimous testimony of the versions. —
14. *Yea*] or *surely,* goes back again to v.^{11} after the digression

---

* Dathe, Schrö., Ba., Hd., Pu., Ke., Reuss, Mit., Dr.   † Cal., Os.
‡ Mit.   § Hes.   ‖ GAS.   ¶ Cal., Os., Geb., Ros.
** Geb., Har., Jus., Schrö., Dr.   †† Jus., Schrö., Ba., Ke., Dr.
‡‡ So We., GAS., Now., Elh., BDB., p. 520, Marti.   §§ GAS.   ‖‖ Dr.
¶¶ Cf. however GAS. I. 176 ff.

in vs.[12, 13] ; not *but* * nor *for* as "justifying the low estimate of their power, expressed in v.[13]," † nor " as a means of destroying you in spite of your imagined strength " ; ‡ nor *therefore,* because of your self-confidence. § — *Behold*] Here, as so often, in the announcement of the climax. — *I am raising up*] Cf. 7[8] Hb. 1[6] Is. 10[5] ; in the sense of giving to them a commission ; it is something which is even now in progress. — *Against you, O house of Israel, a nation*] By the removal of the clause beginning with נאם the object *nation* is brought nearer the verb. This nation was of course Assyria; cf. 5[27] Is. 5[26 ff.] — *And they shall crush you*] Cf. Ex. 3[9] Ju. 4[3] 6[9] Nu. 22[25]. — *From the entrance to Hamath*] Cf. 2 K. 14[25], which describes the restoration of Jeroboam II. in almost the same words ; also Nu. 34[8], which indicates this as the territory promised. This was the pass between the Lebanons, the northern limit of Israel's territory. Dan was at its mouth. — *Unto the stream of the Arabah*] This could not have been the Nile, ‖ nor the Dead Sea ¶ which in Nu. 34[3, 12] is the southern border, nor the river Arnon ; ** cf. 2 K. 14[25] ; nor the Kidron.†† We must decide between (1) the stream of Egypt, *i.e.* the *Wady-el-Arish,* Nu. 34[5] ; ‡‡ (2) the sea of the Arabah, *i.e. Wady-el-Ḥasy,* the old boundary between Moab and Edom, which flows into the southern end of the Dead Sea ; §§ or (3) a stream flowing into the north end of the Dead Sea ; ‖‖ in this case 2 K. 14[25] would mean that Jeroboam II. had extended his kingdom *as far as* the Dead Sea (cf. Dt. 3[16 f.]).¶¶

In many forms and under many figures the poet has thus pronounced the doom of captivity. With each new effort, he has become more clear and definite ; and with this direct statement the first part of the book closes.

---

* AV.   ‡ Mit.   ‖ Dathe.   ** Jus.; cf. Hoffm.
† Dr.   § Cf. Geb.   ¶ Dahl.   †† Ros., Schrö., Mau., Hd.

‡‡ Cf. We., who suggests that originally the reading was probably נחל מצרים, and that the present text is the work of a later writer who desired to exclude Judah from the threatened territory.

§§ Hi., Gun., Now., Dr.   ‖‖ Mit., GAS.

¶¶ The name נחל הערבה occurs only here ; as We. notes, the southern border is נחל מצרים when Judah is included and ים הערבה when it is excluded. A נחל הערבים is mentioned in Is. 15[7] as the boundary between Moab and Edom which is probably not referred to here.

8. ‏בנפשו‎] This is the ‏ב‎ of swearing; cf. Gn. 21²³ 22¹⁶ Am. 8¹⁴; Kö. 391 *a*; BDB. 89 f.; *his soul = himself;* cf. Ps. 25¹³ Gn. 49⁶, etc.; H. 8, 2 *c*, rm. (*d′*). — ‏מתעב‎] = ‏מחאב‎. Cf. the constant interchange of ‏על‎ and ‏אל‎; ‏געל‎ and ‏גאל‎; *v.* BSZ. 577. The weakening of ‏ע‎ to ‏א‎ is characteristic of the later development of the Semitic languages; it is especially frequent in Assyrian, Mandaic, Samaritan, Phoenician, and the later stages of Ethiopic and Aramaic; cf. Lindberg, *Vergleich. Gram. d. sem. Sprachen*, I. 21 f. — ‏גאון‎] *V.* note of Dr., pp. 238 f. — **9.** ‏ומתו‎] The ‏ו‎ marks apod., H. 44, 2 *c.* — **10.** ‏דודו‎] Most common force in Heb. as in other Semitic dialects (cf. Assyr. *dâdu*) is "loved one"; so Is. 5¹ and Ct. 1¹³ᶠ· *et passim;* but the meaning "uncle" is well attested; cf. Lv. 10⁴ 1 S. 14⁵⁰; so also in Syriac. A broader term, *e.g. kinsman*, would seem better here (Hi., Ba., Ke., Or., RV. m., BDB.). — ‏מסרפו‎] Cf. 1 K. 18²⁷, ‏שיג‎ for ‏סיג‎; La. 2⁶, ‏שך‎ for ‏סך‎; La. 4⁴, ‏פרש‎ for ‏פרס‎; 2 S. 1²², ‏נשוג‎ for ‏נסוג‎; for similar interchange in Aramaic, cf. Dalman, *Gram. d. jüd.-pal. Aram.*, p. 74. This use of the pron. suf. without reference to anything already mentioned is awkward, but not unknown; cf. Is. 17⁶ (where the text should probably be emended to read ‏קצֶר‎). For the use of sg. suffix referring to pl. antecedent, cf. Kö. 348 *a.* — ‏אפס‎] Used absolutely, GK. 152 *s*, cf. Ew.⁸ § 322 *b.* — ‏הם‎] Ordinarily as here (Ju. 3¹⁹ Am. 8³ Hb. 2²⁰ Zp. 1⁷ Zc. 2¹⁷) an interjection; cf. Ne. 8¹¹ Nu. 13³⁰ where it is treated as a vb. — ‏להזכיר‎] On construction, cf. Ew.⁸ § 295 *e*; Kö. 399 *β.* — ‏ב‎ ‏בשם‎] ‏ב‎ of interest, Kö. 212 *c.* — **11.** ‏רטיסים‎]

‏ا.λ.; cf. Ar. ‏رسّ‎ = "a fountain choked up by ruins"; and the related root in Assyr., *rêsu* (‏ראס‎) = *to shatter, kill*, etc.; cf. ‏רצץ‎ and ‏הרס‎, and ‏ירשש‎ (Je. 5¹⁷). In Ct. 5² the same word has the sense *drops* (of dew), but this must come from another ‏רסס‎ (cf. Ez. 46¹⁴). Cf. Hoffm. *ZAW.* III. 115. On use of acc., cf. Ew.⁸ § 284 *a*, (*c*); Kö. 327 *v.* — **12.** ‏בבקרים‎] It is urged against the reading ‏בבקר ים‎ (1) that the pl. ‏בקרים‎ appears in 2 Ch. 4³; cf. Ne. 10³⁷; (2) that the mention of oxen in connection with sea-ploughing is superfluous; (3) that the absence of the article with ‏ים‎ would be exceptional; and (4) that the figure would be too bold for a Semite; cf. Gun.; Kö. 254 *g.* — ‏ראש‎] Written ‏רוש‎, Dt. 32³². Ho. 10⁴ and Dt. 29¹⁷ show that the word denotes some plant, and its frequent association with ‏לענה‎ indicates that it was of a bitter (Ps. 69²²) and probably poisonous nature. Poison is clearly meant in Dt. 32³³ Je. 8¹⁴ Jb. 20¹⁶, etc. Some have thought that the poppy was the plant in question (*Thes.;* G. E. Post, *DB.* II. 104). — **13.** ‏ללא‎] GK. 152 *a*, N.; Ew.⁸ § 286 *g*; H. 8, 2 *d*, rm. (*f*); Kö. 380 *f* (‏אישר‎ being dropped from consciousness). — **14.** ‏הצבאות‎] The article in this title is exceptional. The full title ‏יהוה אלהי‎ ‏ה‎[‏צבאות‎ occurs 26 times in O. T., but the article appears with ‏צבאות‎ only four times, viz. Ho. 12⁶ Am. 3¹⁸ 6¹⁴ 9⁵. It occurs six times in Amos without the article (4¹³ 5¹⁴· ¹⁵· ¹⁶· ²⁷ 6⁸). Cf. Kö. 295 *i* and 285 *a.* — ‏גוי‎] "Indeterminate for the sake of amplification" (as in Arabic) = a terrible (?) nation; GK. 125 *c.* — ‏מלבוא‎] On construction, Kö. 406 *c.*

§ 11. Three visions of destruction. 7^{1-9}.

These three visions were probably announced at Bethel : * (1) a vision of devouring locusts, the destruction stayed by the interposition of Yahweh's hand (7^{1-3}) ; (2) a vision of devouring fire, the destruction stayed again by the interposition of Yahweh's hand (7^{4-6}) ; (3) a vision of a plumb-line, the destruction this time permitted to become complete (7^{7-9}).†

Contrary to the usual interpretation, this section, like those which have preceded, is a poem. I reached this conclusion in March, 1897 ; see *BW.* Nov. 1898, pp. 333 ff. ; cf. Elh. *De profetie van Amos* (1899); Löhr (1901); Baumann (1903). The form and style are in many respects similar to those found in the first pieces (chaps. I and 2). The poem consists of three stanzas of nine trimeters each. These stanzas present in common a remarkable symmetry, each falling logically into three subdivisions; the first and second are strictly parallel throughout : —

כה הראני אדני יהוה	כה הראני אדני יהוה
והנה [יהוה] יוצר גבי	והנה קרא לריב
בתחלת עלות הלקש	באש אדני יהוה
ויהי הא מכלה	ותאכל את־תהום רבה
לאכל את־עשב הארץ	ואכלה את החלק
ואמר אדני יהוה סלח־נא	ואמר אדני יהוה חדל־נא
מי יקום יעקב כי קטון הוא	מי יקום יעקב כי קטון הוא
נחם יהוה על־זאת	נחם יהוה על זאת
לא תהיה אמר יהוה	גם היא לא־תהיה אמר יהוה

Of the nine lines five in each are practically the same; in the remaining four there is a similarity of plan; cf. והנה, line 2, the forms of אכל in lines 4 and 5; and the same logical division comes at the end of each triplet. Concerning the corrections of the text, viz. (1) omission of והנה לקש אחר גזי המלך (v.¹) and (2) the reading of ויהי הא מכלה (v.²), *v.i.* The third stanza is from its nature essentially different, and yet the difference is one of thought rather than of form. With the omission of v.⁸ᵃ (*v.i.*) the arrangement is as follows : —

לא אוסיף עוד עבור לו	כה הראני
ונשמו במות ישחק	והנה אדני נצב
ומקדשי ישראל יחרבו	על־חומה ובידו אנך
וקמתי על בית ירבעם בחרב	ויאמר אדני הנני שם אנך
	בקרב עמי ישראל

---

* Note the suggestion of H. P. Smith, *Old Testament History* (1903), p. 211, that these visions belong to the opening of Amos's ministry.

† (1) On the relationship of chs. 7-9 to those which have preceded, see Introduction, p. cxxviii; (2) on the nature of the vision and its use in prophecy, see references on p. 388.

VII. 1–3. *A vision of destroying locusts, whose destructive work is stayed by Yahweh upon the prophet's urgent intervention.*

1. יוצר] 𝔊 ἐπιγονή = יֵצֶר (so also Ba., Hoffm., Gu., We.³, Marti); so 𝔖 and 𝔗 בְּרִית. Insert יהוה as subject of יוצר (so Oort, Now., Elh.). — תחלת] Baumann om. — והנה לקש אחר גזי המלך] Read יֶלֶק for לקש (so Hoffm., We., Löhr; Che., *Crit. Bib.;* Marti). 𝔊 βροῦχος εἷς Γὼγ ὁ βασιλεύς; ᾽Α. ὄψιμος ὀπίσω τῆς γάζης τοῦ βασιλέως; Σ. καὶ ὡς εἰπεῖν ὄψιμος μετὰ τὴν κουρὰν τοῦ βασιλέως; Θ. καὶ ἰδοὺ ὄψιμος μετὰ τὴν κουρὰν τοῦ βασιλέως. Gr. לְקֵשׁ אֵת גִּזֵּי. Oort, יֶלֶק for לקש (so Val.). Elh. והנה אחר גבי הילק. Volz (*ThLZ.* XXV. 1900, p. 292) וְהַלֶּקֶשׁ אַחַר עֵת הַמַּלְקוֹשׁ; cf. Marti. Schmidt (*EB.* 4332), מלך גוג or גוג המלך. Che. (*Crit. Bib.*) והנה ילק וְאַרְבֶּה וְגָזָם וְחָסִיל. This phrase is an explanatory insertion not belonging to the original text, as appears from the form, the thought, and the strophic structure (so Now., Baumann). — **2.** והיה אם כלה] Read וַיְהִי הָא מְכַלֶּה (so Torrey, *JBL.* XIII. 63; We.³, Dr., Oort, *Em.;* Löhr; cf. GK. 112 *uu;* but cf. Baumann). We.¹ ויהי טרם. Now. ויהי כאשר or ויהי כי or ויהי (so Elh.). Val. ויהי אם. Oet. הָנוּ = הֵנָּהוּ (cf. Je. 18³). Volz, לֶאֱכֹל[ל] ויאמר לה. Baumann and Marti om. אם כלה. — סלח־נא] 𝔊 ἵλεως γενοῦ; 𝔙 *propitius esto, obsecro;* 𝔖 ܚܘܣ. Gr. חדל־נא, as in v.⁵. — מי יקום] 𝔊𝔖𝔙 = Hiph'il (so also Os., Dathe, Gr., Seb., Oet.). Σ. τί ὢν ὑποστήσεται ᾽Ιακώβ. Cf. the frequently occurring phrase אין מקים (*e.g.* 5²). Oort, מַיְקוּם for מה יקום (so Val., Now. (?), Elh., Oet.); but the text may well stand. — **3.** נִחם] 𝔊 μετανόησον = וַחֵם (Vol.) or הִנָּחֵם (Va.); so 𝔖 ܐܬܪܚܡ. 𝔙 *misertus est;* ᾽Α. παρεκλήθη; Σ. παρακλήθητι.

1. *Thus the Lord Yahweh showed me*] This is the uniform introduction to all the visions except the fifth (9¹). There is no evidence to show whether the vision came in a dream, or in ecstasy. Indeed, it is not necessary to suppose that either of these methods was employed. They are, nevertheless, real visions, since the writer clearly distinguishes between them (together with the fourth vision in 8¹⁻⁴) and the historical episode in 7¹⁰⁻¹⁷. — *Yahweh was forming*] Cf. Gn. 2⁷. To supply Yahweh as the subject brings the form of expression into harmony with the corresponding line of the second stanza, and makes unnecessary the reading of יֵצֶר (*formation, breed*) instead of the participle, although this is favored by 𝔊𝔖𝔗 and many scholars (*v.s.*). The participle shows that the action was not yet finished. — *Locusts*] Perhaps, here, locusts in the larval stage.* Reference was made

---

* See Dr., pp. 82–91 (= Excursus on Locusts), and, in addition to the literature there cited, art. "Locusts," in *DB.* and *EB.*

in 4[9] to the sending of locusts for the purpose of bringing Israel
to see the error of her ways. This was, of course, an act of mercy
on the part of Yahweh. But here the mercy "appears not in
sending the locusts, but in withdrawing them before they had
utterly destroyed the vegetation of the country. It is the same
plague viewed from two slightly different standpoints, from the
first of which appears the active, from the second the passive side
of the divine mercy." * — *In the beginning of the coming up of the
aftergrowth*] The 'aftergrowth' was either (1) the second growth,
the first being cut off, as here, for taxes, or for royal use,† or
(2) a later grass which started up in March and April under the
influence of the late spring rains. ‡ Ordinarily grass was not
cut and made into hay, but was eaten, as it grew, by the
cattle. § Perhaps, however, in this case, it had been allowed to
grow for the king's levy for the support of the cavalry. ‖ —
*And behold there were full-grown locusts after the king's mow-
ings*] This is undoubtedly a gloss (*v.s.*) intended to fix more
definitely the exact time of the invasion of locusts. Does this
mean *the king's mowings*, which, as suggested above, were levied
for the army, the people making no use of the grass until
this levy had been taken away?¶ This seems satisfactory, yet
some take גֵּז in the sense of *shearings*, the time designated being
the time of the king's *sheepshearing*.** The translation *locusts*
involves a change of text based upon 𝔊 (*v.s.*). 𝔐𝔗 has *aftergrowth*. The appearance of the larvae of the locust in the
beginning of the coming up of the aftergrowth, and of fully
developed locusts after the king's mowings, is intended to represent a destruction of herbage which threatened to be complete,
since the latter appeared at a time when the rains were all past
and the summer heat was just beginning. — **2.** *And when they
were making an end of devouring*] Mitchell contends (1) that
והיה should be retained instead of the proposed ויהי; (2) that it

---

* Mit.   † Jus., New., Or., *et al.*   ‡ Mit., GAS., Now.

§ Burckhardt, *Travels in Syria*, 246; so Mit., Now., and others; but see
Gun. (*ThSt.* XVIII. 222 f.), who questions the statement that hay was unknown in
Palestine, and that לקש cannot mean aftergrowth, and cites Ps. 37[2] 72[6] 90[6] to show
that two growths of grass were customary.   ‖ WRS. *Sem.* 246.

¶ Ros., Ew., Ba., Now., Dr.   ** Hoffm., Mit.

M

has the inchoative force (cf. Is. 4⁴) ; (3) that to suppose that the locusts would first devour the herbage and then proceed to the grass is to make a distinction between עשב and לקש (viz. vegetables and grass)* which does not exist, and also to ignore the habits of locusts, who devour everything as they go. והיה = *and it was coming to pass*, *i.e.* an act not yet completed. This is better than the suggestion † to substitute טרם for אם ; but the reading וַיְהִי הָא מְכַלֶּה (*v.s.*) is adopted here as being still more plausible. — *Forgive*] *i.e.*, Israel has sinned ; the locusts have been sent to punish ; the punishment having been inflicted in part, forgive now the sins on account of which it was sent. — *How can Jacob stand*] The interrogative מִי is used here as in Is. 51¹⁹ = *as who*, i.e. *in what condition* is Jacob that he should stand? ‡ The reading יקים (*v.s.*) = who shall raise up Jacob? is not necessary ; nor is מִי used in apposition with the subject. § Cf. the reading מָקוֹם (*v.s.*). — *For he is small*] Notwithstanding his boasts he is insignificant in the sight, not only of God, but also of men. — 3. *Yahweh repented him concerning this*] The usual anthropomorphic expression ; cf. v.⁶ 1 S. 15³⁵ Jon. 3⁹ Gn. 6⁷ Jo. 2¹⁴. — *It shall not be*] The utter destruction proposed will not take place. Perhaps sufficient infliction has now been given to bring Israel to a realization of his sins. Cf. the similar description of Yahweh's method of work with Israel in chap. 4.

The first vision describes graphically a visitation of locusts sent upon Israel as a punishment, which, however, because of the intervention of the prophet was stayed before it had completely devoured the land. The prophet had in mind, according to some, an attack of locusts ; ‖ according to others, an Assyrian invasion, viz. that of Pul or Tiglathpileser III.,¶ or past punishment, of whatever kind, which had been only partial.**

1. וֹהנה וגו'] The equivalent of an obj. clause. Kö. 361 *g*. — נֹבֵי] From the root גבה (not found as such) meaning *gather ;* cf. جبا = נבא (whence גֵּבָא, Is. 30¹⁴, *pool*, *cistern*); Aram. גְּבָא. Three nominal forms occur : (1) גֵּב (in pl.), Is. 33⁴; also (2) גּוֹב, Na. 3¹⁷; (3) גובי orig. vowels *â*, *ă* ; cf. GK. 86 *i*; Ols. 216 *d*; Sta. 190 and 301 *a*. — גוי] Hoffm. and Mit. render *shearings*, main-

---

  * Hi., Ke.   ‡ Geb., Ros., Hd. ; Kö. 332 *i*.   ‖ Pu., Mit., Dr.   ** We.
  † We.   § Hi., Dr.   ¶ Har., Dathe, Ros., Hd.

taining (1) that mowing and haymaking are and always have been unknown in Palestine, (2) that גז = fleece in Dt. 18[4] Jb. 31[20], and in Ps. 72[6] *fleece* suits better than *meadow*. But as We. suggests, (1) the king's shearing would take place at the same time as that of other people, and the added genitive would be superfluous, (2) the rendering *mowing* is made probable by its occurrence in Arabic. However, Assyrian *gizzu* is always = *shearing*, *wool*. — **2.** והיה] If correct, freq. Dr. § 120; H. 25, 1 *a*; but better as above. — מכלה לאכל] On the use of the infinitive, GK. 114 *m*; Ew.[8] 285 *c*; H. 29, 4 *a*. — **3.** נחם] Niph. pf.; cf. Ar. ناكم = *to sigh deeply*, *groan;* with על as in v.[6] Je. 8[6] Ex. 32[12], etc., sometimes with אל Je. 26[3], and with a clause introduced by כי, Gn. 6[6f]. — זאת] *This thing;* fem. = neut. GK. 122 *q*.; H. 2, 3; not because it refers to a *plague*. — תהיה] Fem.; cf. זאת.

4–6. *A vision of destroying fire, whose destructive work is stayed by Yahweh upon the prophet's urgent intervention.*

4. והנה קרא לריב באש] 𝔊 for לריב has τὴν δίκην; 𝔖 حصني; 𝔗 לִמְדָן; Θ. καὶ ὁ καλῶν τὴν δίκην; 𝔙 *et ecce vocabat judicium ad ignem*. Ew. interprets (so Hi., We., Now.) קרא as = קֹרֶה (Is. 34[14]). Krenkel (*ZwTh*. IX. 271) לרביבי אש; cf. Dt. 32[2]; so Oort (*ThT*. XIV. 121, and *Em*.), Val.; but as Oet. says, רביב is not so used, the usage being as in Gn. 19[24], ממטיר אש. Gr. לְבָעֵר באש. Hoffm. לָרִב באש or לְרֹבֶב אש; cf. Ps. 18[14]. Elh. and Hal., להבת אש, flame of fire. Oet. קֶרֶב. Riedel, לִשְׁבִיב אש (Jb. 18[5]). — אדני] Gr. om. as dittog. — ותאכל] Elh. ויאמר תאכל. — החלק] 𝔊 adds κυρίου, cf. Dt. 32[9]. 𝔙 inserts *simul*. Krenkel, ואת חבל (*ZwTh*. IX. 271; so Oort, *Em*.; Val., Oet.). Hoffm. הַחֵלֶק. — **5.** חדל־נא] 𝔖𝔗 render in same way as סלח־נא v.[2]. — **6.** לא תהיה] 𝔊 in v.[3], οὐκ ἔσται, here οὐ μὴ γένηται. — אמר א' יה'] 𝔖 om. as in v.[3].

4. *The Lord Yahweh was calling to contend by fire*] Cf. Is. 66[16]. Yahweh is now in open controversy with his people. This representation is not infrequent; cf. Is. 3[13] Je. 2[9] Ho. 4[1] Mi. 6[2]. *Calling*, as in 5[8] 9[6], = giving command. Cf. also Is. 48[13] Jb. 38[34]. It is Yahweh who is calling, not an angel,[*] and the command is that punishment shall be inflicted by fire ; in other words, " fire is called into the quarrel." [†] Other suggestions are as follows : calling (Israel) to strife with fire ;[‡] one called that the Lord Yahweh would punish with fire.[§] The reference in any case is not to war,[||] but, as the context plainly shows, to summer heat[¶] which results in drought. If קרא is taken as = קֹרֶה (*v.s.*), the

---

[*] Ew.   [†] GAS.   [‡] Ba.   [§] Ew.   [||] Hd.   [¶] We., Mit.

meaning is (cf. Dt. 25[18] Is. 34[14]) *Yahweh meets* (*i.e. comes near*) *to strive;* but in favor of the ordinary interpretation is (1) the phrase in Am. 5[8], (2) the parallel in Is. 48[13]; cf. Jb. 38[34]; it is true, however, that these are all late passages. — *And it devoured the deep*] So intense is the drought that the great subterranean depths which supply the springs and streams with water are dried up.* Cf. Gn. 7[11] Dt. 33[13] Ps. 24[2]. For similar droughts, cf. Jo. 1[19. 20] Ps. 83[14] Is. 9[18].† There is no reference to large bodies of water like the Jordan. ‡ Elh. supplies "and he said," and then reads: "it shall devour the great deep and it shall devour the land." — *And had begun to devour the land*] This has been understood as meaning the land of Israel, *i.e.* the portion assigned by Yahweh to his people (cf. Mi. 2[4] and חלקה in Am. 4[7]) ; § by others, as the cultivated land (cf. Mi. 2[4] 2 K. 9[10. 36 f.]) ; ‖ but if we understand the framework of the land in distinction from sea, *i.e.* that which is apportioned to man for cultivation,¶ we obtain the climax which Wellhausen fails to see.**

The first and second visions are parallel with the list of inflictions in 4[6-11]; others might have been added, but these two were typical of all the efforts which had been made to turn Israel from her evil way. The fire may have been intended to represent a more severe punishment than that which the locusts represented.†† While there is no reference to an Assyrian invasion,‡‡ the two represent every past judgment which has befallen Israel. These visions are not premonitions of coming disaster, §§ but rather interpretations of actual afflictions. ‖ ‖

4. לריב] Davidson translates, *calling fire into the quarrel;* but see GAS., p. 110; H. 47, 3 *d;* Ew.[8] 338 *a.* — באש] On force of art., cf. Kö. 299 *c.* — ארני יהוה] On peculiar position, cf. Ew.[8] 306 *d.* — את תהום] On use of את and absence of art., Kö. 293 *c;* cf. Kö. 249 *i,* on feminine gender. — ואכלה] in contin. of ותאכל is peculiar; cf. GK. 112 *tt;* Dr. § 120 *n;* Kö. 370 *p* = it had just begun to eat, *i.e.* incipient impf. with pluperfect idea. Cf. Gun. (*ThSt.* XVIII. 223 f.), who regards this as indefensible (either a slip of the pen or an incorrect phrase) and would read ותאכל. — **6.** גם־היא] Emph.

---

* Hoffm., We., Mit., GAS., Now.
† Thomson, *The Land and the Book,* II. 228.
‡ Geb., Ba.
** Krenkel's suggestion of תֵּבֵל, *the world,* is unnecessary.
†† Cal., Dr.
‡‡ Geb., and many others.
§ Geb., Ros., Hi., GAS., Dr.
‖ Now.
¶ Cal., GAS.
§§ Or.
‖‖ GAS.

7-9. *A vision of the plumb-line, whose destruction is permitted to become complete.*

7. הראני] Add ארני with ⅏𝔊 (so Oort, *Em.;* Löhr, Oet.). — חומת אנך] Read חֹומָה, and om. אנך (so Oort, Gr., Now., Elh., Löhr, Oet.). Val. עֲנָכָה. Hal. אֶוֶן ח׳. Riedel sugg. that אנך is an abbreviation of אֲנָחָה, a pun being intended here as in 8¹. — אנך] 𝔊 ἀδαμαντίνου, ἀδάμας; so 𝔖; ᾿Α. γάνωσις; Θ. τηκόμενον; 𝔙 *litum*, and *trulla caementarii.* — ארני נצב] 𝔊 om. ארני (so Löhr); 𝔊ᴬQᵐᵍ and Syr.-Hex., ἀνὴρ ἐστηκώς. Hirscht explains 𝔊's treatment of ארני as due to the influence of the similar form in vs.¹·⁴ and 8¹, and perhaps also to a desire to avoid the anthropomorphism of 𝔐𝔗. — 8a. is a gloss. — ויאמר ארני] Oort (*Em.*) adds אלי. — עבור] Hal. sugg. כְּפֵר. — **9.** וישחק] 𝔊 τοῦ γέλωτος; so 𝔖. Σ. τοῦ ᾿Ιακώβ (cf. a similar change by 𝔊 in v.¹⁶). — מקרשי] 𝔊 αἱ τελεταί. Löhr adds נאם יהוה at close of v.

7. *The Lord stationed beside a wall*] 𝔐𝔗 reads *plumb-wall*, but this is very difficult.* According to this interpretation the picture represents the Lord as a builder, and describes his character. The wall beside which he stands is a token of his work, *i.e.* it is built by a plumb-line ; it is an ideal wall. It is only this kind of work which he will countenance. His work must be exact.† But all this is exactly contrary to facts, since the wall is condemned. The rendering of אנך by "adamant," ‡ referring to the unchangeableness of God's decrees, or by "sling" § as more striking and as representing (v.⁸) the beginning of war, or by "plaster" ‖ may not be accepted. The "wall" can hardly be taken allegorically as representing the people of Israel ; nor is the plumb-line intended to signify the law or revelation.¶ It is equally impossible to render the phrase "wall together with a plumb-line" or a "wall built to the plummet." ** We may therefore suppose that the word "plummet," which occurs legitimately in the next phrase, has crept in here by mistake. — *With a plumb-line in his hand*] *i.e.* the purpose of the builder is to test the character of the wall, in order to determine whether it has been built thoroughly and exactly (cf. Is. 28¹⁷). There is here an anticipation of the work of destruction which is to be spoken of later, for walls were destroyed by plumb-line, *i.e.* thoroughly †† (La. 2⁸ Is. 34¹¹ 2 K. 21¹³). It is not enough to understand that the plumb-

---

* Cf. We.   ‡ 𝔊𝔖, Stru.   ‖ Schegg.   ** Ke., GAS., Dr.
† Cf. Sm. *SK.*, 1876, pp. 622 f. *n.*   § Stäudlin.   ¶ Geb.   †† Hi., Pu.

line indicates the measurement of that part of the wall which is
to be destroyed.* — **8**. *I am setting a plumb-line in the midst of
my people Israel*] The builder will test the structure, and that
which does not stand the test shall be destroyed (cf. texts cited
above). — *And I will not again pass by them any more*] In the
former visions Yahweh had permitted the intercession of the
prophet, but now any request to this effect is anticipated and shut
off. *To pass by* or *over* is to pardon (Mi. 7¹⁸ Pr. 19¹¹). Hoffmann's
translation of עבור by " harvest " has nothing in its favor. — **9**. *The
high places*] Down to the days of Josiah the nation worshipped
Yahweh regularly and legitimately upon the so-called high places.†
These were natural or artificial eminences chosen as being nearer
the abode of the gods. Other nations had followed this same
custom (Dt. 12²; cf. also Is. 15² 16¹², and the Mesha-stone, l. 3).
On these high places, an altar was raised, which was attended by
priests (1 K. 12³¹ ff. 13³² f.). When, in and after Josiah's time, the
centralization of the worship had been effected, in connection with
the publication and acceptance of Deuteronomy, a ban was placed
upon worship at the high places. But in the days of Amos this
centralization had not taken place. When, therefore, he speaks
reprovingly of the worship conducted at these places, it is not
because of the many places as distinguished from one place, but
because of the unsatisfactory (*i.e.* unspiritual, perfunctory) character of the worship.— *Of Isaac*] A synonym used by Amos alone
for Israel. It may include Judah, but not Edom. ‡ Many suggestions have been made touching the use here of this word, *e.g.*
(1) because Isaac's example was often quoted in support of this
idolatrous practice ; § (2) with reference to the meaning of the
word " mockery " as descriptive of the worship here conducted ‖ (𝔊,
followed by Jerome and Theodoret, treats the word as an appellative, " mockery ") ; (3) for the altar at Beersheba, built by Isaac
(Gn. 26²⁵), greater antiquity and authority were claimed than for
the worship at Jerusalem ; ¶ (4) to contrast " their deeds with the
blameless, gentle piety of Isaac." ** The spelling ישׂחק for יצחק,

---

* Ew.

† See my *Constr. Studies in the Priestly Element in the O. T.*, pp. 74 ff., and
literature cited on pp. 78 ff. Now. *Heb. Arch.* II. 12-14.

‡ So We.   § Cal., Os.   ‖ Geb.   ¶ Har.   ** Pu.

found in v.[16] and in Ps. 105[9] Je. 33[26], has been thought to be pro-
vincial,* and to cast ridicule on the idol-worship.† — *And the
sanctuaries of Israel shall be laid waste*] The exactness of the
parallelism is to be noted ; ‡ but the order is chiastic. — *And
I will rise up against the house of Jeroboam with the sword*]
Cf. Ho. 1[4]. Drought was the punishment pictured in the first
vision, locusts in the second, and now the sword in the third ; cf.
the parallel in 4[6–11]. The prediction is plainly one against Jeroboam's dynasty ; the great destruction is coming in Jeroboam's
time ; and, in the prophet's mind, the destruction of the dynasty
and that of Israel are synonymous. The ruin of Jeroboam's house
is not an incident in the general destruction, but the climax. The
sword stands for the Assyrian army ; cf. 6[14]. The application in
the third vision is made directly to Israel. One application serves
for all three visions.

7. נצב] Indicates something more formal and fixed than עמד (Dr.). —
וביריו אנך] Characteristic Hebrew idiom, cf. Is. 6[6 a] 2 S. 16[1] Zc. 2[5] 2 Ch. 26[19].
For order of words in circ. cl. cf. H. 45 rm. (*d*); Kö. 362 *c*; GK. 156 *b*. On
meaning of אנך, cf. Lag. *BN.*, p. 175, l. 5 ; Jensen, *Hittiter u. Armenier*,
p. 209 ; Dl. *HWB.* p. 101 ; Riedel, p. 31. — **8.** רנני שם] Ptcp. refers to
present, not to future time. — לא אוסיף עור] Usual idiom to express the idea
of doing (or not doing) a thing once more, *e.g.* 5[2] 7[18] Dt. 5[19] Gn. 8[12] Is. 23[12],
etc. — עבר ל] *Pass by, forgive*, cf. עבר בקרב (5[17]), *pass through, destroy*. —
9. נשמו] Other words expressing the idea of *waste, desolation* are ראב, חרב,
שאה.שדד — ב [בחרב] of instrument.

§ 12. An Accusation and a Reply. 7[10–17].

(1) The priest of Bethel, to whose ears have come the words
of Amos's utterances, charges him to the king as a conspirator ;
and, acting doubtless for the king, orders him to leave Bethel,
the king's headquarters, and return to Judah.

(2) The prophet Amos, in reply to the charges of the priest,
asserts that he is not one of the prophetic guild, but a herdsman
sent by Yahweh directly to speak to Israel ; and, acting as
Yahweh's spokesman, declares the fate of the priest, his family,
and his country.

---

* Va., Schrö.   † Ros.
‡ יחרבו = ונשמו ; ישחק = ישראל ; כמות = מקדשים.

This passage has always until recently (see my strophic arrangement in *BW.*, Nov. 1898, pp. 333–8) been taken as a piece of historical prose thrown in between the first and second groups of visions. It is clear that it is an episode growing out of former utterances of Amos (cf. Riedel's suggestion that 7^{10-17} was placed after 7^9 because the name Jeroboam occurs nowhere else in the book). At first sight it would seem to be prose; and yet mere prose would scarcely be expected even in an episode if we remember (1) the very early date of the work of Amos, and the tendency, at this early date, to describe all events in poetry; cf. Ju. chap. 5, Ex. 15^{1-18}; (2) the fact that Amos in his introductory address, which was prosaic enough from one point of view, and very monotonous, nevertheless adopted the poetic form and worked out the various statements in so careful a manner as to make them seem almost artificial. If, now, we note still further (3) the many parallelisms which the passage contains; (4) the logical division into two parts (vs.$^{10-13}$ and vs.$^{14-17}$); (5) the triple division of the first part, viz. v.^{10} six lines, v.^{11} three lines, vs.$^{12. 13}$ six lines; (6) the similar triple division of the second part, viz. vs.$^{14. 15}$ six lines, v.^{16} three lines, v.^{17} six lines; and (7) the measure of the first part, regular trimeter, and that of the second, regular tetrameter, we have sufficient data for supposing that this was originally intended to be poetry. The artistic skill which put the accusation in a trimeter movement, and the strong and terrible reply in the heavier and statelier tetrameter is characteristic of Amos. The symmetry is throughout extraordinary. Löhr (1901) also maintains the poetical character of this narrative and arranges it in five strophes of four lines each, the introductory statements in vs.$^{10.12. 14. 17}$ being regarded as prose: str. 1 = vs.$^{10. 11}$; str. 2 = vs.$^{12. 13}$; str. 3 = vs.$^{14. 15}$; str. 4 = v.^{16}; str. 5 = v.^{17}. But this arrangement involves (1) the omission of ויאמר אלי יהוה from v.^{15}; (2) the omission of יגלה מעל אדמתו ישראל גלה from v.^{17}; (3) considerable irregularity in the length of lines; (4) the treatment of אתה אמר as a line, although the corresponding line, לכן כה אמר יהוה, in v.^{17} is not counted. Elhorst (1900) treats the passage as poetry and arranges it in three strophes: (1) vs.$^{10-15}$ = 18 lines; (2) vs.$^{16. 17 a}$ = 6 lines; (3) v.$^{17 b}$ = 3 lines. This arrangement exhibits neither symmetry nor logic. See also Baumann's strophic arrangement. For a discussion of the authenticity and date of this portion of the book of Amos *v.* pp. cxxiv, cxxix.

---

10. כהן] 𝔗 רַבָּא as usual. — קשר] Σ. ἀνέπισεν ἀναταρασσό, a corruption of ἐποίησεν ἄνταρσιν (*v.* Field, *Hex.*). — **11.** ימות] Gr. adds בֵּית. — **12.** חֹזֶה] 𝔊 ὁ ὁρῶν; 𝔙 *qui vides.* — אכל . . . לחם] 𝔊 καταβίον. — **13.** הוא] Löhr and Baumann om. the second time. — **14.** אנכי] 𝔊𝔖 om. the second (so also Löhr and Baumann). — בוקר] Lit. *cow-herd*, is inconsistent with צאן in v.^{15}, and must therefore either be changed to נוקר, cf. 1^1 (so Hi., Gr., We., Gun., Mit., Dr., Now., Oort, *Em.*; Elh., Löhr, Oet., Baumann), or be taken in a general sense, the larger including the lesser. — ובולס שקמים] Σ. ἔχων συκομόρους. 𝔗 וְשָׁקְמִין לִי בִשְׁפֶלְתָּא, and adds "because of the sins of the people Israel, I afflict my soul." — **15.** מאחרי] 𝔊 ἐκ; 𝔙 *cum sequerer.*

—אל‎] ‎𝔖 = על‎ (so also Elh., Oort, *Em.*; Oet.).—**16.** לא תטיף‎] ‎𝔊 οὐ μὴ
ὀχλαγωγήσεις, perhaps = תָּאֱלֶף‎ (Vol.), cf. ‎𝔖𝔗, חליף‎ (*v.* Seb. *in loc.*). ‎𝔙 *non
stillabis;* Σ. οὐκ ἐπιτιμήσεις; 'Α. οὐ σταλάξεις = ‎𝔐𝔗.— ישחק‎] ‎𝔊 'Ιακώβ;
‎𝔙𝔗 = v.⁹.—**17 a.** בעיר חונה‎] Hoffm.'s reading, בָּעֵר תְּזֶנֶה‎, is unnecessary, and
is rightly objected to by Gun. because: (1) ער = צר‎ only in Aramaic (Dn. 4¹⁶);
(2) זנה‎ with ב‎ is not used to express such an action; (3) other words, *e.g.*
שגל‎, are regularly used to denote violation of this sort; (4) ‎𝔐𝔗 is perfectly clear. Hal. תְּעֶנֶה‎.—**17 b.** Löhr and Baumann om. last clause. ‎𝔊 adds,
from beginning of chap. 8, the words: οὕτως ἔδειξέ μοι Κύριος.

10. *And Amaziah the priest of Bethel*] This outbreak led by
the priest, perhaps a high priest (certainly not the only priest),
was provoked by the scathing words which now for some time
Amos had been preaching. It is not impossible to suppose that
the interruption was due immediately to the utterance of v.⁹.*
But from the beginning the prophet had antagonized the priestly
order. The interests of the priest were identical with those
of the king. — *Amos has conspired against thee*] The prophet is
not charged with having entered into actual conspiracy; but
rather with conduct of a deceitful and seditious character which
would produce conspiracy. — *The land is not able to contain all
his words*] Either the land is too small,† the prophet's words
being too many and too atrocious; or, the people cannot endure
the prophet's work, because it is so hostile, the priest thus pro-
claiming in hyperbolical fashion his own thought as that of the
people. — **11.** *Jeroboam shall die by the sword*] The words of
Amos here quoted by the priest contain only the subject of his
preaching, and this, indeed, is given in a form which would be
most likely to incite the king, for it will be noted that (1) the
actual statement of Amos was not personal; he said the house
of Jeroboam (7⁹), ‡ although, while Jeroboam was still alive he was
the principal member of the house; § (2) the reasons for Amos's
words are not given, viz. Israel's sins and the prophet's intercession. Perhaps, on the other hand, no concise statement of
this kind could be more accurate, and it may therefore be an
injustice to charge the priest with distorting or perverting the
prophet's words. ‖ — *Israel shall surely go away into captivity*]

---

* Ke., We. † Va., Ros., Hd., Dr. § Hi., Ke., We.
‡ Os., Geb., Har., Jus., Schrö., Pu. ‖ So Now.; per contra GAS., Dr.

These words had been uttered by the prophet many times;
cf. 5⁵·²⁷ 6⁷.—**12.** *And Amaziah spoke unto Amos*] This message
was sent by the priest to Amos, either (1) because his words
to the king produced no effect, and he was compelled therefore to act upon his own authority;* or (2) after the message
had been sent to the king and before the answer had been
returned; in this case they were prompted by a friendly desire
to have the prophet avoid the king's wrath,† or, as seems most
plausible, (3) on the authority of the king, the statement to that
effect being omitted;‡ such ellipses in conversation are very
common; cf. Is. 7¹⁰⁻¹³. There is no evidence (4) that an unsatisfactory answer had been received from the king, and is
left unmentioned because it was unsatisfactory.§ — *O thou Seer!*]
Cf. the rendering, *visionary.* ‖ The history of חֹזֶה is brief: ¶ in
pre-exilic literature it is used only of Gad (2 S. 24¹¹, cf. 1 Ch. 21⁹);
in later literature it occurs 2 Ch. 29²⁵ (Gad), 1 Ch. 25⁵ (Heman),
2 Ch. 9²⁹ 12¹⁵ (Iddo), 19² (Jehu, son of Hanani), 29³⁰ (Asaph),
35¹⁵ (Jeduthun), and (in the plural) Is. 29¹⁰ 30¹⁰ Mi. 3⁷ 2 Ch. 33¹⁸·¹⁹.
The other word translated *seer*, רֹאֶה, is said (1 S. 9⁹) to be the
oldest designation for prophet, and is used as a title only of
Samuel (1 S. 9⁹·¹¹·¹⁸·¹⁹ 1 Ch. 9²² 26²⁸ 29²⁹), of Hanani (2 Ch. 16⁷·¹⁰),
and in plural, Is. 30¹⁰. Amos had just announced three visions;
it was appropriate to apply to him this title;** but it is also
probable that mockery was intended, much as if we should say,
"O thou gazer!" †† — *Go, flee thee to the land of Judah*] This
is not the advice of a friend; but the command of one in authority. In Judah, the prophet's own land, he might say concerning Israel what he pleased. — *Eat bread there and prophesy
there*] To understand this it must be noted (1) that in the earlier days there were soothsayers, rather than prophets, ‡‡ whom
the people consulted about the affairs of life, making a gift for
the privilege of the consultation (cf. 1 S. 9⁷·⁸); (2) that these
soothsayers constituted local guilds (*i.e.* the schools of the prophets), and, for the most part, restricted their work to a particular
locality, securing their livelihood by means of the gifts received,

---

* Dr.   † Ros.   ‡ Ew.   § Cal.   ‖ GAS.   ¶ See Dr., p. 206.
** Dahl, Mit., Dr., Da. (*DB.* IV. 109).   †† Merc., Jus., Ros., Hd., Dr.
‡‡ Cf. Da., art. " Prophecy and Prophets," *DB.*

i.e. from charity; (3) that in later times the great mass of the so-called prophets were only soothsayers of this character, receiving rewards from the people for speaking according to their wishes (cf. Is. 30^{10} Mi. 3^5 Ez. 13^{19} 1 K. 22^{13} Je. $23^{16.17}$ 28^{1-4} $29^{8f.}$); (4) that, in every case, those whom time has shown to be true prophets were, like Amos, bold in their utterance, and regardless of public opinion. The priest is anxious to dismiss Amos, for he supposes him to be a soothsayer, and therefore one who is in sympathetic touch with the masses of the people, and these, as always, are ready to rise against those who are in authority. He orders him to go to Judah, where he will have no difficulty in making a livelihood by uttering invectives against Israel, for the people of Judah will be pleased to hear of any calamity which threatens Jeroboam II. — **13.** *But at Bethel thou shalt no longer prophesy*] Cf. 2^{12}. Then follow two reasons for this banishment: (1) Bethel is the place of the king's sanctuary, *i.e.* the principal headquarters in the kingdom for the national religion; and (2) it is the royal residence; these, of course, were the very reasons why Amos desired to preach in this place. — **14.** *And Amos answered and said*] With these words the movement leaves the lighter trimeter, and becomes a heavier, more sonorous tetrameter. The opening words are strong: *I am no prophet, nor a prophet's son, etc.*] "Amos was the founder and the purest type of a new phase of prophecy."* The use of the past tense, *I was no prophet, etc.* (*i.e.* when I was called), to avoid a contradiction † with v.[15], is based upon a misconception of the meaning of the prophet's words, which is, " I am not a prophet by profession, nor am I a member of a prophetic guild." ‡ The literal use of the phrase, *prophet's son*, has been defended § on the ground that among false prophets the office was transmitted from father to son; but for this no evidence exists. The other interpretation depends upon (1) the general use of the word " son " in Semitic in the sense of *belonging to*, (2) the name applied to the companies of prophets at Bethel, Gilgal, etc. (cf. 1 K. 20^{35} 2 K. $2^{3.5.7.15}$, etc.). — *A shepherd am I*] See on 1^1.

---

* We. *Prol.* 472. † So 𝔊𝔖, Ros., Schrö., AV., RV., Dr.
‡ 𝔙𝔗, Cal., Mau., Hd., Ke., We., Mit., Dr., GAS. § Har.

—And a dresser of sycamores] This occupation was of the lowest in rank, and, joined with that of herdsman, it indicates the humble origin of the prophet. בולם has been thought * to refer to the "piercing" of the fruit in order that it might ripen; but the verb is better understood as signifying "to tend or dress the fruit of the sycamores" (*v.i.*). This fruit resembles a small fig, although it is very insipid in taste. The tree "grew abundantly in the mild climate of the Shephēlāh, or Maritime Plain (1 K. 10²⁷ 1 Ch. 27²⁸), as it does still in that of the deep Jordan valley; in Egypt, where it also grew (Ps. 78⁴⁷), and where it is found still, its wood was used for doors, boxes, coffins, and articles of furniture (Wilkinson-Birch, *Anc. Eg.* II. 416). It attains the size of a walnut tree, has wide-spreading branches, and, on account of its shade, is often planted by the wayside (Lk. 19⁴). The fruit grows, not on the branches, but on little sprigs rising directly out of the stem, and in clusters like the grape — it is something like a small fig in shape and size, but insipid and woody in taste" (Driver, p. 207).† — **15.** *Go, prophesy against my people, Israel*] It was while he was following his occupation that the message of Yahweh came to him, a message which he could not refuse to obey, a command, indeed, to go north to Israel, and to preach against her. The prep. אֶל is euphemistic for עַל (cf. v.¹⁶). This usage in a bad sense (cf. Je. 26¹¹ ᶠᶠ· 28⁸ Ez. 6²) is clearly indicated by the context.‡ "There is a note of yearning" in the suffix ִ of עַמִּי (cf. "thy" in 9¹⁵). § — **16.** *Now, therefore*] All that has been said thus far is preliminary, the real word is yet to be spoken. — *Thou sayest*] A marked antithesis is made between the *thou sayest* of Amaziah and the *Yahweh hath said* (v.¹⁷). — *Thou shalt not preach*] נטף in Hiph. is here first used of prophecy (cf. Mi. 2⁶· ¹¹ Ez. 21²· ⁷ Jb. 29²² also Ct. 4¹⁶ Dt. 32²). The transfer of *drop* to *preach* may rest upon the idea that the word of prophecy drops refreshingly like dew upon the obedient, wearisomely upon the disobedient; ‖ or, better, may have been suggested by the flow of prophetic speech when in the ecstasy.¶ The verb is here essentially synonymous with נבא of the parallel clause,

---

* 𝔊ᴮ, Ba.; cf. Lagarde, *Mit.* I. 68 f.; Che. in WRS. *Proph.* 396 ; Mit., Dr.

† Cf. G. E. Post, art. "Sycamore," *DB.*   ‖ Pu.

‡ Mau., We.   § Mit.   ¶ Dr.

and does not carry with it any contemptuous idea.— **17.** *Thy wife shall be a harlot in the city*] This does not imply that she is already one of the קדשות of Baal;* or that she shall enter voluntarily into whoredom, in order to obtain her accustomed luxuries;† or that she will be seduced by the conquerors;‡ but that she shall be forcibly ravished,§ and that *in the city, i.e.* in public (cf. 1¹³ Is. 13¹⁶ La. 5¹¹ Zc. 14²), the disgrace being all the greater. ‖ — *Thy sons and thy daughters shall fall by the sword*] *i.e.* thy children. The daughters were generally taken as wives for the soldiers, but the punishment is here extraordinary.— *Thy land shall be divided by line*] This distribution of land to colonists was in accordance with the Assyrian policy after the time of Tiglath-pileser III. (cf. 2 K. 17²⁴ Mi. 2⁴ Je. 6¹²). The line was, of course, the measuring-line. — *Thou shalt die in an unclean soil*] This is characteristic of the early Israelitish thought. Any land in which Yahweh was not present was unclean (1 S. 26¹⁹). More-over, Yahweh could not be present, unless he could be properly worshipped (cf. Ho. 9³·⁴ Ez. 4¹³).¶ The reference is probably to Assyria. It was for this reason, in part, that no place of wor-ship was established in Babylon during the exile.— *Israel shall surely go into captivity away from his land*] The very words (v.¹¹) with which Amaziah had charged him are now repeated. This shows his daring. These words were, after all, the sum and substance of his preaching. Perhaps he expected the captivity immediately. In any case, about twenty-five years passes before Tiglathpileser III. attacks Israel, and thirty-five before Samaria is destroyed by Sargon.

10. תּוּכַל] From וכל; cf. Arabic كَلَّ. The י of the preformative has arisen through a depression of the vowel from יוכל (ground-form *yaukhal* = *yawkhal*); GK. 69 *r*; so Kö. I. i, 36, 2; Böttcher, § 475 f., Bickell, § 33, Stade, § 486. On the basis of the proper name יְהוּכַל (Je. 37⁸; cf. 38¹), Ew.⁸ § 127 *b*, explains it as a Hoph. always used instead of the Qal. — לְהָכִיל] From another root, but similar in sound to תּוּכַל. — **11.** בחרב] Emph. position; chiastic order; and the emph. inf. הָרֹג; cf. 5⁵ 7¹⁷; GK. 113 *n*; Ew.⁸ § 312 *a*. — **12.** ברח] Imv. fol. by another imv., and this by an impf., — a rare combi-

* Jus.; cf. Har.   † Ew.   ‡ Geb.
§ Cal., Ros., Mau., Hi., Hd., Pu., We., GAS., Now., Dr.   ‖ See *RP*. III. 51.
¶ Now. *Arch.* II. 275 f.; WRS. *OTJC.* 249 f.

nation.— חנבא] GK. 110*f*; H. 23, rm.(i).—לך] Eth. dat.; H. 39, 7; Ew.⁸, § 315 *a*; Kö. 35.—**13.** בית־אל] Emph. pos.; acc. of place.—הוא] Showing that בית־אל is masc., as are all names of towns in which בית appears; Kö. 248 *c*.—לא תוסיף עוד] Cf. 5² 7⁸ 8². —מקדש מלך] Note omission of art. with מלך in this common phrase, cf. Da. § 22, rm. 3.—**14.** ויען] Here used in the technical sense of *retort*, or *reply to an accusation*; cf. Jb. 9³·¹⁴·¹⁵·³² 16³ etc.—בולס] The vb. seems to be a loan-word, being a denominative from the Arabic بَلَس, *a fig*, or Ethiopic *balasa = fig*, or *sycamore* (Di. *Lex. Aeth.* col. 487; Lag. *BN.* 108), and evidently = *to care for*, or *dress, figs*, or *sycamores*. 𝔊 renders κνίζων = *scraping;* Θ. similarly (χαράσσων); this, perhaps, points to some process of nipping the fruit to aid it in maturing. (Cf. Lag. *Mit.* I. 68 f.; Tristram, *Nat. Hist. Bib.* 399.)—**15.** ויקחני] The wāw cons. = *but.* — אתה אמר] In contrast with כה אמר יהוה.

§ 13. A fourth vision of destruction, with an explanatory discourse. 8¹⁻¹⁴.

(1) A vision of summer fruit, the ripeness of which indicates that its end has come; 8¹·². (2) *An address:* O ye who are corrupt, who practise every manner of wrong-doing, against whom the earth quaked, but in vain—the day is coming when the sun shall be darkened, when slaughter shall prevail, when mourning shall be universal, when a famine for the presence of Yahweh shall fill the land, for he may not be found; when the strongest shall faint, when men shall swear by their gods, and when they shall fall, never to rise. 8⁴⁻⁶· ⁷ f· ⁹ and ³· ¹⁰· ¹¹ f· ¹³ f·.

This section is a logical unit. It is composed of seven strophes of trimeter movement, each of six lines. Each strophe represents a step in the progress of the thought: str. 1 (vs.¹· ²), the vision that the end has come; str. 2 (vs.⁴⁻⁶), a pointed arraignment of those who stand accused; str. 3 (vs.⁷· ⁸), the threat of earthquake; str. 4 (vs.⁹· ³), the darkening of the sun, the slaughter of multitudes; str. 5 (v.¹⁰), deep and universal mourning; str. 6 (vs.¹¹· ¹²), the abandonment of his people by Yahweh; str. 7 (vs.¹³· ¹⁴), despair, confusion, destruction.

The most important modifications of the text are the following: (1) The omission of v.²ᵃ, — the question and answer, a gloss, after the style of Zechariah, which has crept in and supplanted the original third line of the strophe. This third line contained, perhaps, a further description of the כלוב קיץ, cf. a similar expanded form in 4⁷ 7¹; (2) the transposition of v.³, describing the wailing because of slaughter, to follow v.⁹, thus making with v.⁹ a complete strophe. In its present place v.³ has no meaning, while, after v.⁹, it not only continues the thought of terrible punishment, but prepares the way for the following strophe, which is wholly given up to the thought of mourning; (3) the omission of v.⁶, which consists of the repetition, with slight changes, of 2⁶ᵇ, and the gloss ומפל בר נשביר; (4) the omission of the stereotyped phrases in v.¹¹ᵃ: הנה ... יהוה. Hal.'s transposition of vs.¹¹ ᵃⁿᵈ ¹² to precede 9¹¹ is at least unnecessary.

VIII. 1, 2. *The fourth vision of destruction — the basket of summer fruit.*

1. [כלוב קיץ] 𝔊 ἄγγος ἰξευτοῦ, perhaps = כְּלִי יוֹקֵשׁ (Schrö.); 'A., κάλαθος ὀπώρας (= 𝔐𝔗); Σ., κάλαμος ὀπώρας; Θ., ἄγγος ὀπώρας θερινῆς; 𝔖 ܢܣ݂ܚ; סוף קֵץ=ܬܘܡ, or כָּלָה קֵץ (Seb.); 𝔗 מָאן מְלֵי סִיּוּפֵי קַיְטָא; 𝔙 *uncinus pomorum.* — **2.** [ויאמר] 𝔖 adds אלי יהוה.— [הקץ] Hoffm. הַקֵּיץ (so Gu.).

1. *Thus the Lord Yahweh showed me*] Each of the first four visions begins with the same words. — *A basket of summer fruit*] The word כלוב occurs only once outside of this passage, viz. in Je. 5²⁷, where it is "cage" (cf. Assyr. *kilubi*, bird-net). The word was doubtless a general term for receptacle (cf. كَلَب, *stitch, braid*), used alike for cage or basket. The use of קָיִץ, *summer fruit* (cf. Je. 24¹ ᶠᶠ·) is to be connected with the קֵץ (end) of v.². The picture in the vision is suggested by the thought concerning Israel. — **2.** *The end has come unto my people Israel*] The advance in thought between this and the former visions will be noted. The end is now close. Paronomasia, or punning, is not infrequent among the prophets.* It is not to be supposed that the words קֵץ and קָיִץ are at all connected etymologically.† — *I will not again pass them by*] Cf. 7⁸. For v.³, *v.i.*, p. 181.

This vision is really a reassertion of the thought contained in the third vision, which had been interrupted. Three interpretations are suggested : (1) As summer fruit, when ripe, may not last long, so Israel, ripe in her sins, shall now come to an end. ‡ (2) As summer fruit is plucked when ripe, so that it may not rot, so shall Israel be removed from home and carried into captivity. § But it is better to adopt another, viz. (3) the summer fruit is late

---

* See Je. 1¹¹ ᶠ· 50²⁰· ³⁴ 51²⁰ Ez. 25¹⁶ Mi. 1¹⁴ ᶠ· Ho. 1⁵; cf. Casanowicz, *Paronomasia in the O. T.*

† Cf. Hoffm., who substitutes קָיִץ for קֵץ, and treats עבור as in 7⁸.

‡ So Cal., Mau., Now., Elh.   § Merc., Ros., Hes., Schlier.

and poor, the best being gathered earlier ; a receptacle containing summer fruit shows the last of the crop, the end of the year, and, by analogy, the approaching end of Israel's kingdom.*

4–6, 7 f., 9 and 3, 10, 11 f., 13 f. An address, growing out of the vision, directed to the corrupt and wicked Israelites, announcing the certain and immediate destruction of the nation. V.⁴ has no connection with v.³, which for this and other reasons is transferred to follow v.⁹.

4. [השאפים] Read הַשֹּׁאֲפִים = who tread upon (so We., Now., Oet.). 𝔊 οἱ ἐκτρίβοντες εἰς τὸ πρωΐ, the last three words being, perhaps, a dittog. of ἐκτρίβοντες (so Hirscht). 𝔖 ܘܕܕ̈ܝܫܝܢ = הַשֹּׁאֲפִים (Seb.), cf. 𝔗 דִּישְׁטִין.— [אביון] 𝔖 om.; [ולשבית] 𝔖 om.; 𝔊 καταδυναστεύοντες; Θ. λύοντες; 𝔙 deficere facitis. Gr. לעשק את. Hoffm. וְלַשְׁבָּת. Now. וְהִעְשִׁקִים (so Oort, Em.; Marti). Oet. לַשְׁבִית, omitting ו (so Bewer, AJSL. XIX. 116 f., who considers it an adverbial expression meaning altogether). Elh. לישחית, which he transposes between השאפים and אביון.— [ארץ] 𝔊 ἀπὸ τῆς γῆς. Bewer adds יִרְצוּ.— **5.** [החרש] Gr. הֶחָרָשׁ.— [שבר] 𝔙 merces; 𝔊 om. (so Marti).— [והישבת] 𝔖 adds a predicate, viz. ܘܡܟܝܠ. Gr. הישו.— [בר] 𝔊 θησαυρὸν = אוצר; so 𝔖 (so also Oort, ThT. XIV. 155, and Em.; Gr., Elh.). 𝔙 frumentum.— [להקטין] 𝔖𝔗, 1 p. pl., as also for the remaining infinitives.— [לעית] Oort (Em.) לְעַשּׂוֹת. We. וּלְעַוֵּת (so Marti, Now.²).— **6.** [מפל] 𝔊 ἀπὸ παντὸς (= מִכֹּל); 𝔖 ܚܠ.— [בר] 𝔊 γενήματος; 𝔊^Qᵐ, πράσεως; perhaps = ברא (Va., Stek.), or שֶׁבֶר (Vol.). Gr. בֵּבַר or בַּבַר.— [נשביר] Hoffm. נִשָּׁבֵר. Oort rejects the last three words of v.⁶; while Löhr and Oet. consider the first six a repetition from 2⁶, and doubt whether the last three words should be connected with v.⁵, or be looked upon as the conclusion of a missing sentence. We., Now., Baumann, and Marti reject the entire verse.— **7.** [בגאון יעקב] 𝔖 om. ב and renders as an appos. to יהוה. Gr. לְגָאוֹן.— [אשכח] 𝔊 ἐπιλησθήσεται; so 𝔗. [לנצח] 𝔊, misunderstanding, renders εἰς νῖκος (cf. 1¹¹).— [מעשיהם] 𝔊 = מעשיכם (so Marti).— **8.** [תרגז] Hal. adds וְתָמוֹג (cf. 9⁵).— [עלתה] 'A., Σ. σκεπασθήσεται = עֻטְפָה (Hirscht).— [כאר] Read כיאור (so Oort, We., Gr., Gu., Now., Oet., Marti). All versions render river. Riedel, בְּאֵר (cf. Baumann).— [כלה] 𝔊 συντέλεια = כָּלָה (Vol., Seb.; adopted by Hirscht); so 𝔖 ܣ̈ܦ; 𝔙 universus; other Greek versions πᾶσα.— [ונגרשה ונשקה] 𝔊 uses one vb., καταβήσεται, the first being probably a gloss (so Now., Elh., Oort, Em., Oet.; Gr. regards it as a dittog.; but cf. Hirscht). Hoffm. ונגרשה, for ונגרשה (so We.³). Read with Qᵉrî and several codd. נשקעה (cf. 9⁵) (so Gr., Hoffm., Gu., Now., Oet., et al.).— Elh. om. 8ᵇ as a repetition from 9⁵. We. om. entire v. (so Now., Löhr, Marti).

---

* Ba., Pu., Dr.

4. *Hear this*] The beginning of a new strophe; the actual threat will be given later in v.[7]; cf. 3^1 4^1. — *Oh ye that tread upon*] This rendering, based upon the text הַשֹּׁאֲפִים (*v.s.*), is preferable; cf. 2^7. — *And are for making the poor to cease*] The idiom is a peculiar one but well established.* To translate " even to make," etc.,† or, connecting it with השאפים, " panting after the needy and to destroy," ‡ is unsatisfactory. Nor is it advisable to read " and on the Sabbath after the poor of the land " (*v.s.*), which spoils the parallelism, and fails to furnish a consistent thought; or, " ye who oppress the poor " (*v.s.*), on the basis of 4^1 and ᴳ. — *The poor of the earth*] Kᵉthîbh עֲנָוֵי; in Qᵉrî, עֲנָיֵי; the latter = *poor, wretched* (of the physical state), § the former = *humble, meek* (of the spiritual). ‖ The emphasis here is on the low and miserable social state of the poor (cf. 2^7 Jb. 24^4 Is. $3^{14f.}$), for which either form would be a correct expression.¶ — **5.** *When will the new moon pass*] The day of the new moon was celebrated as a religious festival (cf. 1 S. $20^{5.\ 18.\ 24.\ 27.\ 34}$; also 2 K. 4^{23} Is. 1^{13} 66^{23} Ez. $46^{1.\ 6}$ 1 Ch. 23^{31}, with מוֹעֵד; Ho. 2^{11} Nu. 28^{11-15} Ne. $10^{32f.}$). On this observance cf. Di. *Lev.* 578 f.; Benz. *Arch.* 464 f.; also Muss-Arnolt, *JBL.* XI. 72 ff., 160 ff. The reference here is to such observance; it is to be inferred that, like the Sabbath, it included suspension of trade.** The view that החדש means *month*, the desire being that some disaster would come which would increase the price of grain,†† or that the month is the harvest month during which the poor might gather what they needed,‡‡ scarcely deserves mention. Note also the suggestion of Graetz (*v.s.*) to read " how long till the new (corn) will pass away . . . and the old (corn) " etc. — *That we may sell grain*] The eager desire to resume a business in which profit might be gained, with utter disregard of all conventional and legal restraints, is rebuked. One can see no occasion for the suggestion of Wellhausen that this reproach is strange, because ordinarily the corn-merchant is no loser by delay in disposing of his wares. — *And the Sabbath that we may offer corn*] This is better §§ than " open (our) storehouses," " grain " by metonymy for " storehouse " ‖‖ (cf.

---

* Dr. *Tenses*, § 206; Da. *Syn.* § 96, rm. 4; GK. 114*p*. ‖ Geb., Har., Mit.
† AV.   ‡ Mit.   § Ros.   ¶ Hi.
** Va., Schrö., Ros., Hi., Mau., Ke., Mit.   ‡‡ Ki.
†† Merc.   §§ So generally.   ‖‖ Ros.

N

Gn. 41[56]). This is the earliest allusion to the Sabbath in prophetic literature. — *Diminishing the ephah and enlarging the shekel*] The size of the ephah is not definitely known, being estimated at from 21.26 quarts (Thenius) to 40.62 quarts (Josephus).* The shekel given in gold or silver has been variously estimated, perhaps in gold 16.37 grains (= $10.80); in silver 14.55 grains (= $.60).† — *Perverting balances of deceit*] *i.e.* providing false balances. A third kind of deceit is here mentioned. The attitude of the right-minded toward these practices is seen in Ho. 12[7] Jb. 22[6] Pr. 11[1] 20[23]. The legal attitude is given in Lv. 19[35, 36] Dt. 25[13-15]; cf. also Ez. 45[9, 10]. — **6.** This verse consists of two elements, both of which are glosses or interpolations : (1) *To buy the poor for silver and the needy for a pair of shoes*] A double phrase, of which the first part is a modification and the second a repetition of 2[6]. ‡ These lines stand in no close relationship with those which precede (vs.[4 and 5] refer to dealers in grain ; [6a] has nothing to do with this) ; are entirely out of grammatical harmony with those which follow ; are a mere repetition (but in a different context) of 2[6]; and may not be adjusted to any satisfactory construction of the strophic system. — (2) *And we sell the refuse of the corn*] This phrase is interpreted, " and buy (the needy) for a share by lot in the wheat for sale " ; § is declared unintelligible by one, ‖ and at least out of place by another.¶ It is impossible to connect it grammatically or logically with what precedes, although it is sometimes called the climax** of the indictment, or the final proof of their avarice.†† The whole is therefore to be taken as two later explanatory glosses, coming from different hands. Nowack suggests that perhaps in [6b] we have a fragment of an old saying by Amos, which, with the addition of the material in 2[6] (suggested by השאפים in 8[4] and

---

* Benz. *Arch.* 183 f.; cf. Now. *Arch.* I. 203; and art. "Weights and Measures," *DB*.

† Benz. *Arch.* 194; cf. Dr. p. 211; WRS. *PEF.*, 1894, p. 229; A. R. S. Kennedy, art. "Money," *DB*; Madden, *Coins of the Jews*.

‡ קנה is used for מכר, and דלים for צדיק, without any serious modification of the sense. The infinitive לקנות has been taken as indicating the purpose of the fraud described in v.[5], the inf. there indicating the method (Geb.) ; as indicating result rather than purpose (Hi.), and as (like לעות) parallel with להקטין and להגדיל. § Hoffm., changing text, *v.s.* ‖ Oort.

¶ We. (who calls the entire v. suspicious). ** Mit. †† Dr.

2⁷), makes up the verse.* — **7.** Here begins a new strophe (vs.⁷·⁸), marked by the solemn introduction : *Yahweh hath sworn by the glory of Jacob*] The oath is an evidence of indignation, and here, as in 4² 6⁸, "is provoked by the spectacle of some crying moral wrong." † 𝕲 has ‡ *against the pride of Jacob*, but בְּ after נשבע = *by*. The glory of Jacob is not Palestine, the possession of Jacob (although citation may be made of Je. 13⁹ Ne. 2³ Ps. 47⁴ Dn. 8⁹) ; nor, the greatness which he has given Israel ; § nor = *by myself* (cf. 6⁸), ‖ for although Yahweh himself is Israel's glory (1 S. 15²⁹), the author of 6⁸ could hardly have described Yahweh as "the glory of Jacob" : it is rather the vainglorious boasting of Israel (cf. 6⁸ Ho. 5⁵ 7¹⁰), by which, as an unchangeable fact, Yahweh swears scornfully.¶ — *I will never forget all their deeds*] *i.e.* the multitude of their wicked deeds. The elliptical form of the oath is here employed ; for the full form see 2 S. 3⁹ 19¹³, etc. — **8.** Contrary to the arrangement usually adopted,** v.⁸ is to be closely connected with v.⁷, forming with it a strophe. The indignant feeling of Yahweh is shared by nature, and in proof of this the earth will quake. — *On this account shall not the earth tremble?*] Not on account of the oath just sworn,†† but on account of the wickedness and corruption of Israel, Yahweh (cf. 9⁵) will bring a convulsion of the land itself. רגז describes the movement up and down, the restlessness which characterizes the earthquake. Some ‡‡ have thought this refers to the earthquake in Uzziah's time (Am. 1¹ Zc. 14⁵). — *And every inhabitant in her shall mourn*] Its universality and its grievous character are thus vividly depicted. — *And shall not the whole of it rise like the Nile?*] כאר has been read *like light*, §§ but is almost universally taken for כיאר, like the Nile (cf. 9⁵).

---

* Elh. rearranges the text of vs.⁴·⁶ᵃ·⁵· and ⁶ᵇ, and translates as follows : —

(4)   Hear this, ye who long to plunge the poor and the miserable in ruin,
(6 a)   To buy the poor for money and the miserable for a pair of shoes,
(5 6 b) Who say, when will the new moon be over that we may sell grain
        And the Sabbath, that we may open the granary, and sell the chaff of the grain?
        Who diminish the measure
        And advance the price
        And falsify the deceitful balance.

† Dr.   ‡ So also Jer., Os., Jus., Schrö.   § Bauer.   ‖ Hes., Ke., Marti.
¶ We., Now., Dr.   ** Dr.   †† Schegg, Ke.   ‡‡ Or.   §§ Rashi.

The reference is to the annual inundation. The rendering, " the whole land shall be inundated as by the Nile," * makes the subject of עלה not the thing which goes up, but that unto which something goes (cf. Is. 34¹³ Pr. 24³¹). The interrogation continues as indicated in the translation given. — *And heave*] A gloss ; omitted by 𝔊, lacking in 9⁵ and superfluous ; probably due to inability to understand ונשקה.† Cf. Hoffmann's suggestion (*v.s.*). ‡ — *And sink like the Nile of Egypt*] Cf. Is. 24¹⁹·²⁰. This phenomenon was known throughout the world. The usual translation makes כיאר = as by the Nile.

9. Löhr and Marti reject the first six words as a later addition. — הבאתי] 𝔊 3 p. with שמש as subj., δύσεται. Similarly Σ., Θ.; 𝔙 *occidet ;* 𝕮 אכסי. — החשכתי] 𝔊 3 p.; but 𝔙 *tenebrescere faciam.* — ביום אור] Gr. ביום ; Che. (*Crit. Bib.*) בעור יום. — **3.** — והילילו] 𝔖 ܬܐܠ.ܣ. — שירות] Read שָׁרוֹת, *singing-women*, since שירים would be expected for *songs*, and the present text yields no sense (so Hoffm., Oort, We., Gu., Now., Elh., Löhr, Oet., Baumann, Marti). 𝔊 τὰ φατνώματα, variously explained, *e.g.* as = שורות (Dahl), שירות (Va.), ספונים (Vol.), קורות (Riedel). 'Α. στρόφιγγες; Θ. τὰ ἐπάνωθεν; Σ. ᾠδαί; 𝔙 *cardines* = צירות (Dahl). — היכל] 𝔊𝔖 have article (so Gr.). — ביום ההוא] Superfluous (so Löhr, Marti); cf. 8⁹. 𝔖 has this phrase twice, connecting it the first time with the preceding, and the second time with the following context. The presence of ܣܒ between the two occurrences renders dittog. improbable (Seb.). — נאם אדני יהוה] Löhr transposes to the end of the v. Baumann, Marti, and Now.² om. — רב הפגר] 𝔊 πολὺς ὁ πεπτωκώς; 𝔙 *multi morientur;* 𝔖 ܬܐܠ. — השליך הס] Read הָשְׁלַךְ, and om. הס as a dittog. (so Oort, Gun.). 𝔊 ἐπιρρίψω σιωπήν = אשליך הס; 𝔙 *projicietur silentium;* 𝔖 ܠܐ̇ܡ.ܣ ܐ̇ܣ.ܣ. Zeydner (= יכבש) הַשִּׁיר יִכְבַּךְ (*ThSt.*, 1886, pp. 205 ff.; so Val.). Elh. כעם הָשְׁלִיךְ. Oet. and Hal. הָס. הַשְׁלֵךְ. Löhr suggests that ה of הס was originally the article, while ס, or מ, is the initial letter of a lost word, perhaps מזבחות. — **10.** יהיד] 𝔊 ἀγαπητοῦ. 𝔊 τοὺς μετ' αὐτοῦ; Σ., Θ. τὸ ἔσχατον τῆς γῆς. Gr. והעכרתיה. — **11.** The first six words are a gloss (so also Baumann). — רעב בארץ] Gr. inserts יצמא. — Before לשמע] 𝔊 inserts λιμὸν = רעב. — דברי] Read sg. with 𝔊𝔖𝔙𝕮 and many Mss. (so Dr., Marti). — **12.** ונעו] 𝔖 ܣ.ܠܡ̇ܠ.ܣ. — מים] 𝔊 ὕδατα τῆς θαλάσσης, a double rendering. — תתעלפנה] Gr. מזרח ישוטטו] Gr. תימן יחרדו וישוטטו (?). — **13.** — 𝔊 ἐκλείψουσιν. — בצמא] Om. as superfluous to sense and metre (so Löhr). — **14.** Löhr om. 14 *a* as a later addition. — באשמת] 𝔊 κατὰ τοῦ ἱλασμοῦ, with אשם in

---

* Dathe, Jus., Ros.   † Now.
‡ There is no good reason for treating (with We.) the whole v. as a gloss.

mind; ‎ܠ‎ ‎ܒܚܫܒܬ‎. Oort ‎באשרת‎ (so Gr., Elh.).—‎אלהיך‎] Baumann ‎אלהי‎.—
‎דרך‎] ⅏ ὁ θεός σου. Oort, ‎בְּרֶךְ = בְּאֶרֶךְ‎ (so We., Elh.). Hoffm. ‎דְּרָךְ‎ (so von
Gall, *Altisr. Kultstätten*, 49; Oet.; Marti; Now.[2]; cf. Wkl. *AOF.* II. 194 f.).
Dozy, ‎אֱלֶךְ‎ (*Isr. zu Mekka*, 31 f.; so Now.). Gr. ‎אלהיך‎ (so Gu.). Gun. ‎אֲרְגֵיךְ‎.
Houtsma, ‎פחרך‎ (*ThT.* X. 91). Hal. ‎אַדְרֶךָ‎.

9. The next strophe is made up of vs.[9 and 3].— *I will cause the
sun to set at noon*] The writer has in mind the day of Yahweh,
which is characterized by great natural changes. These are suggested by those with which the prophet is familiar. An eclipse
had occurred June 15, B.C. 763,* the centre of which passed
through Asia Minor at about 38–39° N. At Jerusalem (31°
46′ N.) it would be visible "as a fairly large partial eclipse." †
Reference to an eclipse of the sun has been found by some,
also, in Mi. 3[6] Zc. 14[6] Jo. 2[10.31] 3[15] Je. 15[9] 2 K. 20[11] Is. 38[8]
(689 B.C.) ; ‡ Ez. 30[18] 32[7.8] (556 B.C.) ; but it is to be noted that
nowhere in the Old Testament is there direct mention of an
eclipse, and that in all the cases cited greater or less doubt
exists whether there was really any thought of an eclipse. This
leaves our passage as the only clear case of an indirect character.— **3.** The result of such an eclipse is the terror and dismay
which first appear in connection with the palace life : *the singing
women of the palace shall wail*] For text *v.s.* The word ‎היכל‎,
Assyrian *ekallu*, means *large house*, used ordinarily of temple in
Hebrew, although just as regularly of palace in Assyrian. § Another rendering is "walls" (‎שׁוּרוֹת‎). ‖ Some urge against the translation *palace* the representation in 6[4-9], and the use by Amos of
‎ארמנות‎ to express the idea of *palace* (6[8] 1[4.7.10.12] etc.) ¶ ; but this
is not conclusive. Wailing was the ordinary sign of grief for the
dead (Is. 15[2.3] 16[7] etc.).— *A multitude of carcasses*] The eclipse
foretells and accompanies the direst of all disasters — an indis-
criminate slaughter. — *In every place they are cast*] The impersonal *one casts* is used for the passive,** or better (*v.s.*) vocalize as

---

* According to Michaelis, Feb. 9, 784 B.C.; but cf. Dr. who cites von Oppolzer,
Canon der Finsternisse = vol. 52 (1887) of the *Denkschriften* of the Vienna Academy; G. Smith, *Eponym Canon*, 46 f., 83.   † Dr.

‡ *V.* Bosanquet, *TSBA.* III. 31 ff., V. 261; Pinches, *DB.* I. 193.

§ Cf. Boutflower, *AJSL.* XVII. 244-9.   ‖ ⅏, Dahl.   ¶ Schrö.

** Geb., Va., Mau., Ba.

passive. So great is the slaughter that the burial is thus promis-
cuous. Some prefer to take the verb as imperative, "throw them
anywhere." *   If the text is allowed to stand, הס is translated
Hush!] So deep is the despair, and so great the danger, that
silence is enjoined by those who are removing their dead (cf.
the gloss in 6[9. 10]). But this is quite doubtful. The principal
treatments of הס have been: (1) as an adverb, *in silence;* †
(2) as an imperative, *be silent;* ‡ (3) as an interjection; §
(4) as connected with the following sentence; ‖ (5) as a marginal note added to express the feeling of some reader; ¶
(6) omitted as unintelligible; ** (7) rendered, with a change of
text (*v.s.*), "casts bitterness"; †† (8) it is, most probably, a corruption of הֵשַׁ, an abbreviation for הַשְׁלֵךְ (*v.s.*). The strophe is the
most picturesque of this series. It is strictly logical — the eclipse
— the slaughter — the confusion and despair of the burial. The
dramatic effect is probably not so definite nor so strong as is suggested by G. A. Smith. — **10.** *And I will turn your pilgrimages
into mourning*] The pilgrimages or festivals were the types of
rejoicing (Is. 30[29] Ho. 2[11] La. 5[15]). — *And all your songs into
dirges*] Cf. v.[3] and 5[1]. — *Sackcloth*] *i.e.* a coarse cloth made of
goats' hair or camels' hair. It was the garb of prophets (Is. 20[2]
Zc. 13[4] 2 K. 1[8] Mk. 1[6]) and mourners (Is. 15[3] 22[12]), and was worn
next to the skin (1 K. 21[27] 2 K. 6[30] Jb. 16[15] Is. 32[11]), being bound
about the loins (Ez. 7[18]), sometimes as the only garment (1 K. 20[31]
21[27]), and sometimes under an outer cloak (2 K. 6[30]). It is probable that a loin cloth of sackcloth was the earliest dress of the
Hebrews (cf. Erman, *Life in Ancient Egypt,* 200 ff.), and the use of
it in mourning is an illustration of the general custom of retaining
ancient forms and usages in religious ceremonies. ‡‡ — *Baldness*]
This was another sign of mourning; it was artificially produced,
the hair on the forehead being shaved off (Dt. 14[1]). It was a
custom common to Hebrews, Moabites (Is. 15[2]), Phoenicians
(Ez. 27[31]), Philistines (Je. 47[5]), Arabs (Agh. xv. 12), and many
others. It seems to be a relic of ancestor-worship, the object of

---

* 𝔗, Merc., Hd.   ‡ Merc., Har.   ‖ SS.   ** We.
† Cal., Os., Va., Schrö., Mau., Ba., St.   § Drusius.   ¶ Gun.   †† Elh.
‡‡ Cf. Schwally, *Das Leben nach dem Tode,* 12 ff.; Kennedy, art. "Sackcloth,"
DB.; Now. *Arch.* I. 193.

it being to establish an inviolable covenant between the living and
the dead, whereby the aid and protection of the latter are assured
to the former. In Arabia the hair was deposited on the tomb.
Hair, on account of its rapid growth, was thought to be a special
seat of life and strength (cf. the story of Samson) ; hence, like
blood, it was considered especially efficacious as a bond of union.
For the later Hebrew use of the custom, cf. Is. 3^{24} 22^{12} Mi. 1^{16}
Ez. 7^{18} etc.* — *And I will make it*] Not the land and its people,†
but the lamentation and sorrow of Israel on this terrible day. ‡ —
Like the mourning for an only son] An expression of the most
intense sorrow, cf. Je. 6^{26} Zc. 12^{10}. There is no reference to Tammuz, the Assyrian Adonis. — *And the end of it*] That is, of the
mourning ; § not of the Messianic times, ‖ nor of the land.¶ — *As
a bitter day*] Theirs will be a hopeless sorrow, the end of which is
worse than the beginning.** — **11.** *And I will send a famine*] In
such misery the people will naturally turn to Yahweh, but there
will be a famine and thirst, not for bread nor for water, but *for
hearing the word of Yahweh*] The singular, as in versions (*v.s.*). —
12. *And they shall wander from sea to sea*] *i.e.* from the Dead
Sea to the Mediterranean †† (cf. Ps. 72^8 107^3 Zc. 9^{10} Jo. 2^{20}) ; or,
perhaps, the term is a more general one, meaning the ends of
the earth. ‡‡ — *And from the North even to the rising of the sun
they shall run to and fro*] A brief expression designating the earth
with reference to its quarters. — *They shall not find it*] Cf. 1 S. 28^6
Ez. 7^{26} Je. 37^{17}. This is the climax of distress.

The arguments for treating this strophe (vs.[11, 12]) as an interpolation
(Oort, We., Kö. (*Einl.* 304 *d*), Now., Che. in *EB.*, Löhr, *et al.*) have little
force. It is urged: (1) that literal and figurative thirst cannot properly
be so closely joined; (2) that the formula in v.[13] points back to v.[9], and not
to "Lo, the days are coming" (v.[11]). But in answer it is to be said that
(1) the word בצמא (v.[13]) is a gloss; (2) likewise the words, "Behold, the
days are coming; it is the oracle of the Lord Yahweh" (v.[11]); (3) these
verses make a complete strophe, the essential thought of which, abandonment

---

* Cf. WRS. *Sem.* 323 ff.; arts. on "Baldness," by Macalister, *DB.*, and W. Max
Müller, *Jew. Enc.*; art. "Cuttings" (§ 3), by C. J. Ball, *EB.*

† Cal., Merc., Ros., Hd., Or., Mit.   § We., Dr., Elh.   ¶ Or.

‡ Geb., Hi., Ke., We., Dr., Elh.   ‖ Schegg.

** Oort and Gun. are unwarranted in pronouncing v.[10 b] unintelligible.

†† Va., Jus., Ros., Or., Mit., Marti.   ‡‡ Ke., Now.

of the people by Yahweh, is most appropriate after the description of the bitter mourning (in the preceding strophe). Marti om. [11b. 12b] as glosses.

13. A new strophe now begins, — the last, which describes the pitiable plight of the nation. *The fairest maidens and the youths*] The flower of the people, and its strength, *shall faint*] This is no anticlimax; nor is there real force in the argument for omitting this verse instead of vs.[11. 12].* The moment one recognizes the division into strophes, it is perfectly clear that no difficulty arises in going from v.[12] to v.[13]. — **14.** The flower of the people have been they *who swear by Samaria's guilt*] The calf at Bethel; cf. חטאת יש׳, Ho. 10[8]; but since Amos nowhere else attacks any special feature of the cult, and since Samaria is not used elsewhere by him for Israel, Wellhausen supposes that originally there stood here the name of the god of Bethel.† Notice should be taken of the emendation adopted by W. R. Smith, Oort, Graetz, and Elhorst of אשרת, Asherah, for אשמת; but cf. Stade, *ZAW*. III. 13, and Hoffmann, *ibid.* 123. — *And say: as liveth thy God, O Dan*] The calf at Dan, in northern Israel, near the base of Mt. Hermon (1 K. 12[29]).‡ Swearing was a part of the routine of worship, cf. Dt. 6[13] 10[20] Is. 48[1] Je. 12[16]. Under the Canaanitish influence, there had come to be different Yahwehs at different places, with different names; cf. Gn. 16[13] 21[33] 33[20] 35[7]. § — *And by the way of Beersheba*] On account of the difficulty of דֶּרֶךְ, there have been suggested (*v.s.*): (1) thy darling, (2) thy well, (3) thy lord, (4) thy god. It is possible to understand "way" of the method of worship at Beersheba (cf. Ju. 2[22] Je. 10[2]); but, on the whole, it seems preferable to take it of the pilgrimages to Beersheba, with which may be compared those to Mecca. || — *And they shall fall and not rise again*] The conception of God is so far from the true one, and the worship based upon it is so far from that which Yahweh desires, that utter ruin awaits the people.¶

1. כְּלוּב] A noun of the same form as גְּבוּל, לְבוּשׁ, from the ground-form כְּלוּב (*i -û*) as is shown by the Assyrian equivalent *kilûbi, bird-net* (cf. Winckler, *ZA.* VI. 145; Zimmern, *ibid.,* 157), which occurs as a Canaanitish gloss in the

---

* GAS. 185.   † So Now., Che. (*EB.*). Marti.   ‡ Stanley, *Sin. and Pal.* 461.
§ Now. *Arch.* II. 8 f. || GAS., Dr.   ¶ Paton, *JBL.* XIII. 88 ff.

Tell-el Amarna letters. Cf. GK. 84 *a*, *p*. — **2.** ל עֲבוּר] Cf. 7⁸; these are the only two cases of this phrase; the more common expression for *forgive* is עבר על (Mi. 7¹⁸). — **4.** לְשַׁבִּית] With syncopation of ה, GK. 53 *q*. Inf. cstr. continuing a ptcp., H. 29, 5 *a*; Kö. 413 *v*; Dr. § 206. — עֲנוּי] For which Qr. עניי. עֲנוּי in Kt. and Qr. is found in one Ms. which is followed by the second and the third editions of the Hebrew Bible (Naples, about 1491–1493, and Brescia, 1494); while another Ms., followed by the fourth edition of the Bible (Pesaro, 1511–1517) and by the Complutensian Polyglot, has עֲנִי in both Kt. and Qr. (see Ginsburg). For explanations of forms cf. Barth, *NB.* § 113; Lag. *BN.* pp. 48, 188, 190, and *Mit.* I. 81; BDB. עָנוּ and עֲנִי differ in meaning (*v.s.*, and cf. Lag. *Mit.* I. 81), but the line between them cannot be very strictly drawn, for they are frequently interchanged, — a confusion no doubt partly due to the Massoretes. — **5.** וּנְשַׁבִּירָה שֶׁבֶר] Impf. with וְ to denote purpose; cogn. acc. — לְהַקְטִין] This infinitive and the following are parallel with לֶאמֹר at the beginning of the verse, the construction being that of concomitant circumstance, equivalent to the gerundive; cf. Dr. § 206; GK. 114 *o*; H. 29, 3 *e.* — מֹאזְנֵי] Cf. Pr. 11¹ 20²³ Ho. 12⁸ Mi. 6¹¹ (מֹאזְ רֶשַׁע); and the opposite (צֶדֶק מֹאזְ) Lv. 19³⁶ Ez. 45¹⁰ Pr. 16¹¹ Jb. 31⁶. Other words are פֶּלֶס and הָגָה (Is. 46⁶). — **7.** אִם אָשְׁכַּח] Ellipt. form of oath; Ew.⁸ 356 *a*; GK. 149 *b*; H. 48, 9 *a*; Kö. 391 *k.* — לָנֶצַח] Other phrases denoting the same idea are לְדוֹר וָדוֹר; עַד עוֹלָם; עַד דֹּר וָדֹר (Je. 7⁷ Ps. 103¹⁷); לְעוֹלָם (Gn. 3²²); לָעַד (Am. 1¹¹ Ps. 19¹⁰); עֲדֵי עַד (Ps. 83¹⁸). — **8.** לֹא . . . הֲ] The two particles separated. — וְנִשְׁקְעָה] Kt. וְנִשְׁקָה. In some Mss. וְנִשְׁקְעָה is found in Kt. and Qr., and so also in the Complutensian Polyglot. Cf. נָבַח = נָבַע. — **9.** צְהָרִים] According to Lag. *BN.* 129, 16, this is connected with Arab. ظَهَرَ (= *to step forth*), and, like the Arab. ظَهْر, literally = *back* (cf. Assyr. ṣēru), and denotes the midday as the highest point in the sun's course. Kö. II. i. p. 93 derives it from צהר = זהר (*to shine*). It occurs (צהרים) in Mesha-Stone, l. 15. It appears to be a dual form; cf. ערבים (Ex. 16¹²). — לָאָרֶץ ל introducing the obj., a common Aramaic usage; Kö. 289 *d.* — **3.** הֵיכָל] Probably a loan-word from Sumerian *é-gal* (= *great house*), which has passed over, directly or indirectly, into Assyr., Arab., Aram., Syr., Ethiop., and Heb. (Oppert; Schra. *Höllenfahrt der Istar*, p. 148; *COT.* II. 39; Haupt, *E-vowel*, 11 f.; Lehmann, *Šamaššumukîn*, 126). Aram. and Syr. היכלא, and Assyr. *ekallu* = *palace* or *temple*, but the latter meaning is rare in Assyr. (Dl. *HWB.*), while in Ethiop. and Heb. it is the prevailing one. It is used of *palaces*, as here, in 1 K. 21¹ 2 K. 20¹⁸ Is. 13²² 39⁷ 2 Ch. 36⁷ Na. 2⁷ Ps. 45⁹·¹⁶ Ho. 8¹⁴ Jo. 4⁵ Pr. 30²⁸. The word is much more frequent in post-exilic literature than in early writings, which may be due to Assyrian influence or to the greater prominence of the temple in Hebrew thought, or to the combined influence of both causes (cf. BDB. **228**). — הֵילִילוּ] Other words used in mourning are : אֵבֶל, נוּד, סָפַר, קִין, נָשָׂא קִינָה; **10.** קִינָה] Cf. 5¹. — נָחָה, הָמָה, שִׂיחַ, אָנָה, קָדַר. The elegiac measure appears in this verse with the introduction of the word קִינָה; the evenly balanced members of the preceding verses are dropped, and their place is taken by members consisting of long and short lines, with the long line each time containing the predicate of the short line. It is limited to this verse (cf. Bu. *ZAW*. II. 30 f.). — הָ-] Neut., GK. 135 *p*; H. 2, 3. — יחיד] Obj. gen.; GK. 128 *h*; Kö. 336 *d*. — **11.** כי אם] Here adversative; not, as frequently, exceptive; cf. GK. 163 *c*. Note Kö. 372 *h*. — והשלכתי] Pf. with Wāw cons. in apodosis following a ptcp., H. 25, 2 *d*; Kö. 361 *c*. — לשמע] On use of ל cf. Kö. 281 *p*. — **12.** צפון, מזרח] In Heb. the points of the compass are denoted in three ways: (1) with reference to one's position facing the east they are קדם or קדים (*east*), ימין or תימן (*south*), אחרית (*west*), שמאל (*north*); (2) with reference to the sun they are מזרח or מזרח שמש (*east*), דרום (*south*), מבוא שמש or מערב (*west*), צפון (*north*); (3) geographically, נגב (*south*), ים (*west*). — ישוטטו] Denotes an uncertain roaming up and down in order to find something (2 Ch. 16⁹ Je. 5¹ Zc. 4¹⁰ Dn. 12⁴ = to search through a writing). — **13.** תתעלפנה] On form cf. GK. 54 *k*, 146 *g*. — **14.** נשבע] The custom of attesting the truth of a matter by oath was exceedingly common among the Hebrews. Most commonplace affairs were ratified by oath (Gn. 21²⁵ ᶠᶠ·); in certain cases a man's oath was sufficient to establish his own innocence (Ex. 22⁶ᶠ· ⁹ᶠ· ¹²); treaties were made binding by oath (Gn. 21²³ᶠ·), likewise promises (Gn. 24³⁷ 50⁵ᶠ·). This frequent usage caused it to become little more than an emphatic form of statement, as is seen by the fact that Yahweh himself is spoken of as swearing to do or not do certain things (*e.g.* 6⁸ Je. 49¹³). Since oath was usually taken in the name of the god worshipped by the one swearing, it came about that swearing by a god was considered synonymous with worshipping a god (Dt. 6¹³ 10²⁰ Je. 12¹⁶ Is. 48¹). — חֵי] Not the st. cstr. of the substantive חַי (Ew.⁸ 329; Kö. II. i. p. 42), but a contracted form of the adj. חי (whose st. cstr. appears only in Dn. 12⁷), the two forms of the adj. having been differentiated by the Massoretes who reserved חֵי for oaths sworn by Yahweh, and used חַי in oaths sworn by false gods and other non-enduring persons and things (Hoffm. *ZAW*. III. 124; GK. 93, *aa*, note; BSZ., BDB.).

§ 14. A fifth vision of destruction, with a passionate description of the ruin. 9¹⁻⁸ ᵇ.

(1) A vision of the downfall of the altar at Bethel, the chief seat of the Northern religion, and of the utter ruin of the votaries; 9¹. (2) A vivid expression of the thought that *escape is impossible*, whether they flee to the underworld, or to the heavens, to the top of Carmel or to the bottom of the sea; or even if they are captives in a foreign land; 9²⁻⁴. (3) An assurance that, after all, Israel, because of sin, will be treated like other nations, whose migrations, as well as that of Israel, Yahweh has conducted; and that complete destruction awaits the nation, in spite of her feeling of false security; 9⁷⁻⁸ ᵇ.

This section is clearly composed of four strophes of six lines each. The movement is for the most part tetrameter, although occasionally for the sake of more vivid description it falls into the trimeter. Strophe 1 (v.[1]) presents the vision of the catastrophe; strophes 2, 3 (vs.[2-4]) describe the utter impossibility of escape; strophe 4 (vs.[7-8 b]) silences the objection, which, of course, an Israelite would urge, that Yahweh, as Israel's God, could not thus humiliate her.

The more important modifications of the text are: (1) the treatment of vs.[5. 6] as a later interpolation, on the same grounds as assigned for 4^{13} $5^{8.9}$; (2) the omission of v.[8 c], "except that I will not utterly destroy the house of Jacob; it is the oracle of Yahweh," as a gloss inserted by a later hand to modify the absolute assertion of destruction made by Amos, and as a connecting link to the section of promise which was added, perhaps by the same hand.

1. חָזִיתִי יַת יְקָרָא דַיְיָ אִסְתַּלַּק מִכְּרוּבָא וּשְׁרָא עַל־מַדְבְּחָא 𝕿 [רָאִיתִי . . . עַל־הַמִּזְבֵּחַ.
[הַךְ] Gr. ἀφὲ(?); Volz (*ThLZ.* 1900, p. 291) and Marti, וַיַּךְ. [הַכַּפְתּוֹר] 𝕲 ἐπὶ τὸ ἱλαστήριον (= הַכַּפֹּרֶת); 𝔜 *cardinem;* Ἀ. (τὸ) οἰκοδόμημα; Σ., Θ. ἐπὶ τὸ κιβώριον; 𐊖 ‎ܠܟܦܘܪܐ‎. Gr. הַכַּרֻכֹב(?). Löhr calls attention to the possibility of dittog. in הַך הכפתור.—[הַסִּפִּים] 𝕲 τὰ πρόπυλα; 𝔜 *superliminaria;* 𐊖 ‎ܐܣܟܘܦܬܐ‎.—[בְּצַע] Imv., so 𝕲 διάκοψον; 𝔜 *avaritia;* 𐊖 ‎ܩܛܘܠ‎. Seb. וּבְצָעֵם. Lag. (*Anmerk. z. gr. Uebers. der Prov.* V. *f.*) בִּצְעָם = בְּוָעָם, *in wrath*, cf. Hb. 3^{12}. Oort, אֲזוֹב or אֲבָצְעֵם. Elh. ובצעי בצע מבר אישכלם. Gr. ואבצעם = וָאֶבְצָעֵם(?). Oet. וּנְפַצְתֵּם. Volz (*op. cit.*) and Marti, וַיֹּאמֶר אֲבָצֵעַם בְּרַעַשׁ.—[כֻּלָּם] 𝕲 πάντων; so 𝔜.—**2.** [יַחְתְּרוּ] 𝕲 κατακρυβῶσιν. Oort, יָחְתְּרוּ (so Gr.). Gun. יֶרְדוּ, with fol. ב omitted. Löhr and Baumann om. v.[2] as late and as out of harmony with the strophic arrangement.—**3.** [וְאִם] 𝕲 ἐὰν.—[מִנֶּגֶד עֵינַי] Baumann and Now.[2] om. as gloss.—[קִרְקַע] 𝕲𝕾 pl. שָׁמֵּם—Oort om. מ.—**4.** [עֵינִי] 𝕲 pl. Löhr and Now.[2] om. [4 b] as Jeremianic.—**5.** 𐊖 inserts אמר at beginning (so Gr.). Before הַצְּבָאוֹת 𝕲 inserts ὁ θεὸς = אלהי (so Elh., Oet.); cf. the remark of We., "Am. does not say יהוה הצבאות, but י' אלהי הצ'."—[וַתָּמוֹג] 𝕲 καὶ σαλεύων αὐτήν; 𐊖 ‎ܘܡܬܬܙܝܥܐ‎.—[כֻּלָּה] 𝕲 συντέλεια αὐτῆς (= כָּלָה), the pron. being absent in 8^8; so 𐊖; 𝔜 *omnis*, but in 8^8 *universus.*—[וְשָׁקְעָה] Gr. וְנִשְׁקְעָה.—[וְאָבְלוּ כֹל יֹשְׁבֵי בָהּ] Elh. om. as repetition from 8^8.—Oet. om. [5 b] as repetition from 8^8.—[כַּיְאֹר] Riedel, בְּאֵר.—**6.** [מַעֲלוֹתָו] מ is a dittog.; read עֲלִיֹּתָיו or עֲלִיָּתוֹ; cf. Ps. 104^3 (so Oort, Gun., Gr., We., Mit., Now., Elh., Oet., Marti). 𝕲 sg.—[וַאֲגֻדָּתוֹ] 𝕲 καὶ τὴν ἐπαγγελίαν αὐτοῦ; 𐊖 ‎ܘܡܠܟܘܬܗ‎; both possibly deriving it from נגד; cf. Jb. 21^{31} Is. 44^7 (Va., Seb., Vol., *et al.*). Other Greek versions, δέσμην. Gr. ואגדתו.—[יהוה] 𝕲𝕾 add צבאות (so Gr.). Vs.[5. 6] are to be associated with 4^{13} $5^{8.9}$, and treated as an insertion; for the argument in full *v.i.*—**7.** [הֲלֹא] 𐊖 = הִנֵּה.—[כַּפְתּוֹר] 𝕲 Σ. Καππαδοκίας; so 𝕿𝕾𝔜.—[קִיר] 𐊖 βόθρου, deriving it from קוּר; Θ. τοίχου; Ἀ., Ε'. Κεἰρ; 𐊖 ‎ܩܝܪ‎; Σ. Κυρήνης; 𝔜 *Cyrene;* 𝕿 קִירֵנֵי.—**8.** [הַחַטָּאָה] 𝕲 τῶν ἁμαρτωλῶν.—[עֵינֵי אֲדֹנָי] Oort, עֵינֵי נָאֻם.—[אֶפֶס כִּי וגו'] A gloss.

IX. 1–4. *The vision of destruction; the impossibility of escape.*

1. *I saw*] This vision has an entirely different introduction from those of the preceding visions. Here Yahweh himself appears, the symbol being no longer used.* — *By the altar*] The translation *on* † is too specific (but cf. 7⁷) ; the idea is that of leaning, or hovering, *over;* cf. Nu. 23³·⁶ 1 K. 13¹ 1 S. 25²⁴ Is. 6². ‡ The altar in the prophet's vision was not the altar in general as a place of refuge, § nor the altar at Jerusalem, including the temple and all that the temple represented, ‖ nor in particular the altar of burnt offering at Jerusalem ; ¶ but, rather, the altar at Bethel,** reference being made to the form of religion practised at the northern sanctuaries (cf. 8¹⁴), concerning which already much has been said. The chief temple of Northern Israel was located in Bethel. — *And he said*] The person commissioned to do the work of destruction is not mentioned. It was not the prophet,†† but rather one of the angels ‡‡ in Yahweh's court (cf. 2 S. 24¹⁶ 1 Ch. 21¹⁵). — *Smite the capitals*] Originally כַּפְתּוֹר was, perhaps, the ornament or knop (cf. Ex. 25³¹·³³ ᶠᶠ·) at the top of the column (Zp. 2¹⁴) ; later, the capital itself, here used collectively. These capitals at the top of the columns, on which rests the roof of the altar-building, shall be smitten with a violent blow. — *That the thresholds may shake*] The posts, §§ or thresholds, ‖‖ or sills which really formed the foundation. Some of the old interpreters ¶¶ understood these phrases to be intended figuratively of the kings, princes, and high priests. According to Ewald both terms apply to the altar ; כפתור to the knop, *i.e.* the horns ; ספים to the bottom of the altar ; so that the whole altar is shivered, and the pieces fly upon the assembled people. — *Yea break them off (?)*] וּבְצַעַם is so difficult that Wellhausen and Nowack give it up. It is perhaps an imperative.*** The suffix evidently refers to the parts of the temple, *i.e.* the capitals, or the sills, or both.

---

* Cf. Hi., Ba. ‡ Ew., Ba., Dr. ‖ 𝔗, Cal., Ros., Ke.
† Düsterdieck, *SK.*, 1849, p. 914. § Dahl., Mit. ¶ Os., Merc.
** Har., Mi., Ew., Hi., Ba., Schlier, Pu., Or., Gun., We., Now., GAS., Dr., Elh., Marti. †† Jus., Ba.
‡‡ Jer., Theod., Os., Merc. = Ros., Hi., Ew., Ke., Pu., Now., Dr. §§ Cal., Geb.
‖‖ Jus., Hd., We., Mit., GAS., Now., Dr., Marti. ¶¶ *E.g.* Merc., Geb.
*** So 𝔊, Merc., Va., Ros., Schrö., Ew., Hd., Or., Gun., Mit., BDB., GAS., Dr.

Elhorst by emendation of this and the two following words (*v.s.*)
gets this sense : "Those who seek unjust gain from corn, I will
deprive of children." — *And the residue of them*] Cf. 1⁸ 4². This
is not the beginning of a new verse, but a continuation of the
vision,* for the picture includes the falling altar, those crushed
beneath it, and also those who escape and flee to meet a death
even more terrible, death by the sword. There is no reference
to the common people.† The phrase means *the last one* of
them,‡ *i.e.* the one left from the destruction of the temple. —
There shall not escape a fugitive] There can be no escape from
Yahweh. It is this thought which is expanded in the strophe
that follows. — **2.** *Dig through to Sheol*] The under-world, the
abode of the dead (Is. 14⁹·¹¹ Jb. 11⁸ 26⁵ᶠ·), located in the very
centre of the earth (Eph. 4⁹), and therefore a most appropriate
and significant, though hyperbolical, example of inaccessibility.
— *Climb up to heaven*] The utmost height (Je. 51⁵³). The two
terms שְׁאוֹל and שָׁמַיִם are often thus employed as points of
extreme opposition ; cf. Jb. 11⁸ Ps. 139⁷·⁸ Is. 7¹¹ Mat. 11²³. § —
3. *At the top of Carmel*] Carmel was another example of inaccessibility, not only for its height (1800 ft. above the sea),
but more especially for its limestone caves (said to exceed 2000
in number, and to be so close together and so serpentine as to
make the discovery of a fugitive entirely impossible), and its
forests, which in the days of Strabo, ‖ were the retreat of robbers.
Cf. Ju. 6² 1 S. 13⁶ 1 K. 18⁴².¶ — *Bottom of the sea*] The only
place remaining for a fugitive compelled to leave the land, of
which Carmel, projecting into the sea, was the last portion.**
The sea was of course the Mediterranean, and hence *the serpent*] could not have been the crocodile,†† nor the venomous
marine serpents found in tropical regions ; ‡‡ the reference must
be to the imaginary sea-monster supposed by the ancients to
have its abode in the depths of the sea ; Gn. 1²¹ Is. 27¹. §§

---

* On the contrary We., Now.   ‡ Ew., We., Mit., GAS., Now., Dr.

† Cal., Os., Geb., Ros.

§ Cf. Stärk, *SK.* LXXVI. 157 ff., who uses this clause to prove that Yahweh
was thought of as dwelling, not in the heavens, but in the temple at Jerusalem.

‖ XVI. 2, 28.   ** Dr.   †† Ki.   ‡‡ Pu.

¶ Cf. Pu., Ke., Dr.   §§ Or., Mit., Now., Dr., Marti.

—**4.** *If they go (about) in captivity*] Cf. 5²⁷. The prophet has no definite place in mind — either in Egypt or Assyria. It is perhaps an allusion to another Israelitish conception, viz. that outside of Palestine Yahweh had no power over them; since in a strange and foreign land they would be under the power of the god or gods of that land; cf. Jon. 1¹. From this point of view, the remark, " Elsewhere exile is the worst threat; here that is surpassed," * has no place. — *The sword and it will slay them*] The serpent, upon Yahweh's command, would bite them; the sword, spoken of as a thing of life (cf. Ez. 32¹¹ Ho. 11⁶ Is. 34⁵⁻⁶), at the same command, will slay them. — *I will put my eye on them for evil*] This phrase, used elsewhere, "to keep watch over" (Gn. 44²¹ Je. 24⁶ 39¹²), *i.e.* in a good sense, is here defined in the bad sense. With it may be compared "set the face against" (Je. 21¹⁰ Ps. 34¹⁶ Lv. 20⁵ Ez. 15⁷). The purpose which was ordinarily good is now hostile. — **5.** *The Lord Yahweh Sabaoth*] The proposed logical connection of this verse with the preceding, " God is able to bring such punishments, because he is the almighty one " † is unnatural and far-fetched. We have here a dignified and heartfelt utterance introduced by one who has been reading the words of Amos in the light of the history of the centuries which have followed. It is better to treat the phrase as practically independent, ‡ rather than to make it the subject of what follows § or an oath, " by the Lord," etc. ‖ Elsewhere, as has been noted,¶ Amos always says " God of Hosts." ** With these verses may be compared 4¹³ 5⁸ᶠ. — *He that touches the earth and it melts*] Cf. Ps. 46⁶ 97⁵ 104³² 144⁵ Na. 1⁵. The manifestation of Yahweh's power in lightning, storm, or earthquake brings terror. Cf. also Mi. 1⁴ Ju. 5⁴ Ps. 75³. — *And it rises up, etc.*] A repetition, almost *verbatim*, of 8⁸ᵇ. — **6.** *He that builds his chambers in the heaven*] This is the Hebrew picture of Yahweh's dwelling-place. " The Hebrews pictured the sky as a solid vault (*firmamentum*), resting at its extremities on the earth (Jb. 26¹¹); in this vault the heavenly bodies were imag-

---

* We.   † Merc., Ros., Jus., Mit., Dr.   ‡ Hi., Ke., Or., GAS., Now.
§ Mit., Dr.   ‖ Ew.   ¶ We., Mit., Now.
** See GAS., p. 205 f., for statement on Amos's use of divine names. Cf. Löhr, pp. 38–67.

ined to revolve : ' in front of it' (*i.e.* in the open air below its
lower surface) the birds flew (Gn. 1²⁰) : above it were reservoirs
in which rain was stored (as also snow and hail) ; and above
these 'waters above the firmament' Jehovah sat enthroned."*
The slight change of text (cf. Je. 22¹⁴ Ps. 104³) here adopted
(*v.s.*) does away with the interpretations, (1) *ascents, i.e.* air,
fire, and spheres which successively approach nearer to heaven ; †
(2) *heaven of heavens*, or third heaven (cf. Dt. 10¹⁴ 1 K. 8²⁷
Ps. 148⁴) ; ‡ (3) *clouds*, as formed by the ascent of moisture ; §
(4) *heavenly orbs*, supposed to be in steps one above another
leading to Yahweh's throne. ‖ — *His vault upon the earth he has
established*] אֲגֻדָּה, used in Ex. 12²² Is. 58⁶ 2 S. 2²⁵ of something
held firmly together, *e.g. a bundle*, has been explained as (1) *promise* (from נגד) ; ¶ (2) *arch* = רָקִיעַ, firmament, something beaten
out, the vault which overhangs the earth.** — *He that calleth
for the waters*, etc.] Repeated from 5⁸ᵇ. The arguments which
have been urged against the genuineness of these two verses
are : †† (1) the abruptness of their connection with the context ;
(2) the fact that they repeat much from 8⁸ and 5⁸ ; (3) their
similarity to 4¹³ and 5⁸˙⁹, which are interpolated passages ; (4) the
use of the title אֲדֹנָי יהוה צב' as compared with Amos's use of
יהוה אֱלֹהֵי צְבָאוֹת ; (5) the style resembles that of Deutero-Isaiah
and other late writers ; (6) their metre and strophic form differ
from the structure of the original material. — **7.** *Are ye not
as the sons of the Cushites unto me ?*] The Cushites or Ethiopians, ‡‡ in Amos's times, occupied Nubia, with Napata as capital. About this time upper Egypt with Thebes became a part
of the Ethiopian territory. The king of Ethiopia, Piankhi, after
overcoming most resolute resistance and capturing Memphis, established his authority over the petty princes of Egypt, receiving
homage and tribute from them and preventing all attempts on their

---

* Dr., p. 218.   ‡ Pu.   ‖ Merc., Ros.; cf. Hes.
† Cal.   § Geb.   ¶ So 𝔊𝔖 and Stru.
** Mich., Ros., Jus., Hi., Ba., Hd., Mit., Now.

†† So *e.g.* Duhm (*Theol.* 119), Oort (*ThT.* XIV.), Sta. (*GVI.* I. 571), Gieseb.
(*Beiträge*, 190 f.), Co. (*Einl.*), Che. (in WRS. *Proph.* xv f. and *EB.*), Taylor (*DB.*),
We., Now., Löhr, Marti ; but cf. WRS. (*Proph.* 400), Kue. (*Einl.* § 71, 6), Kö.
(*Einl.* 303 f.).

‡‡ Brugsch, *Egypt under the Pharaohs*, 387 ff.

part to unite in opposition to him. However, Shabako, probably
the grandson of Piankhi, was the first Ethiopian ruler to seat himself upon the throne of Egypt and actually administer its affairs.
Israel, says the prophet, is no more to me than the far-distant,
uncivilized, and despised black race of the Ethiopians; cf. Je. 13²³.
No reference is made to their Hamitic origin,* or their black
skin;† and yet their color and the fact that slaves were so often
drawn from them added to the grounds for despising them.‡ —
Did I not bring up Israel out of the land of Egypt?] This is
not to be read separately from what follows. The sense and
syntax will be seen either by treating this clause as a protasis,
viz. "If I brought Israel up from the land of Egypt (as you
assert), did I not also bring the Philistines from Caphtor?"
etc.; or, more literally, by reading the three clauses in close
connection. — *Did I not bring up Israel out of the land of Egypt,
and the Philistines from Caphtor and Aram from Kir?*] Yahweh
from his point of view was equally concerned in many, or indeed
all, historical movements, of which three are cited as examples
and placed side by side with that of the Israelites. This thought
was probably not new with Amos; it was involved in the general
idea of the day of Yahweh, and must therefore have existed before Amos's day. § All this is in answer to the objection made
by certain narrow Israelites that Yahweh could not, if he would,
desert Israel at this stage of his connection with them. — *Caphtor*]
Not a part of the Nile Delta,‖ but Crete;¶ cf. Dt. 2²³ Je. 47⁴
Gn. 10¹⁴ (in which, "from whom the Philistines came forth"
should be transposed to follow "the Caphtorim"). Cf. also
Cherethites, Ez. 25¹⁶ Zp. 2⁵ 1 S. 30¹⁴. — *Syrians from Kir*] See
under 1⁵. Some groundless inferences have been drawn from this
verse, *e.g.* that the Philistines and Arameans had also been deliv-

---

* Ba.   † Ke.

‡ Cush (Gn. 10⁶·⁷ Is. 11¹¹ 18¹ 20³⁻⁵ 37⁹ 43³), often mentioned = *Soudan* (Arabic,
aswâd = black). In Egyptian inscriptions, *Kêsh* (cf. Dr.). Che. (*EB.* 968) interprets Cush here as designating the N. Arabian district of that name, which adjoined
the land of Muṣri. See Wkl. *Muṣri*, 2 (1898), and *Hibbert Journal*, II. (1904),
571–590.   § Sellin, *Beiträge*, I. 95 f.

‖ Ebers, *Ægypten u. d. Bücher Mose's*, 130 f.; Brugsch, *Egypt under the Pharaohs;*
see, however, Sayce, *Academy*, April 14, 1894, p. 314.

¶ De Goeje, *ThT.* IV. 257 f.

ered from slavery; * that according to Amos the Philistines and
Syrians were Cushites.† — **8.** *The eyes of the Lord Yahweh are
upon*] Cf. 9⁴. The use of ב marks the unfavorable look; cf.
Ps. 34¹⁵·¹⁶. In v.⁴ it was declared that Yahweh would look with
disfavor upon Israel; v.⁷ asserts that, in reality, no greater reason
exists for the exercise of favor toward Israel than for its exercise
toward other nations; v.⁸ goes back again and reasserts the unfavorable attitude of Yahweh to Israel and its consequent ruin.
This is a clear logical sequence. — *The sinful kingdom*] This is not
every sinful kingdom, ‡ nor Judah, § nor both Israel and Judah, ‖
but Israel alone.¶ With the article it might well be rendered *this*
sinful kingdom.** — *I will destroy it from off the face of the earth*]
This is the statement of absolute destruction which has been
made so frequently and which, made now for the last time, is
expanded, vs.⁹·¹⁰. — *Save that I will not utterly destroy the house
of Jacob*] A later Jew, who saw that the words of Amos had
not been literally fulfilled, adds this saving clause. The line is
an extra one from the point of view of the strophic arrangement; it is flatly contradictory to the thought which precedes
and follows; it has the tone of the later environment. The
entire verse is late in the opinion of some.†† The efforts made
to explain the clause as a part of the text show at a glance the
futility of the effort, *e.g.* "the favor here granted to Israel is a
special one because of the covenant with their fathers." ‡‡ It is
true that in later days (cf. Je. 5, 30, Ez. 14) this argument was
urged by prophets and others; but at this time the prophet had
just announced an exactly opposite position. — *The house of Jacob*]
is, of course, the northern kingdom (5¹·⁴·⁶ 6⁸·¹⁴ 7²·⁵·¹⁰·¹⁶ 8⁷), for the
prophet has had nothing else in mind from 7¹. The context
directly opposes the view which would refer these words to
Judah; §§ nor is there any reason to suppose that Israel in
general is meant. ‖‖

1. וירעשו] ו of purpose; H. 26, 2 *a.* — וכצעם] For form of suffix, cf. GK.
61 *g*; but see Margolis, *AJSL.* XIX. 45-48, for a better explanation. — להם]

---

* Geb.	‡ Cal., Merc., Pu.	‖ Ke.	** Va.
† Cf. Hi.	§ Jus.	¶ Dahl, Ros., *et al.*	

†† *E.g.* We., Che. in WRS. *Proph.* p. xv, and in *Exp.* 5th ser. V. 46; Volz,
Jahweproph. 23 f.; Now., Marti.   ‡‡ Merc.   §§ We.   ‖‖ Ew., Ke.

= dat., Kö. 286 *d.* — נס ... ינום] A somewhat uncommon expression for the impers. idea; cf. Is. 16¹⁰ Nu. 6⁹ Dt. 17⁶; GK. 144 *e*; Kö. 324 *l.* — פלט... ימלט] Same as prec. except that the cognate root פלט is used as subj., with פ instead of מ on account of preceding מ of להם. — **2.** אם] Here with impf. in a cond. sent. assuming an imaginary case = "*though* they were to dig ... my hand *would* fetch them"; GK. 159 *l*; H. 48, 4; Kö. 390 *u*; Dr. § 143. — **3.** חבא, סתר [חבא = *to withdraw, hide* (BDB.). סתר, as Arabic سَتَرَ shows, means *to cover, veil, protect,* etc. They are practically synonymous in Hebrew, and neither of them is used in the Qal. חבא, however, is, with one exception where it is used figuratively (Jb. 38³⁰), always used with reference to man; while סתר is used indiscriminately of men and things (cf. Ps. 19⁷ Ho. 13¹⁴ Gn. 31⁴⁹). Hence סתר is of more frequent occurrence than חבא. — הכרמל] On art., cf. H. 5, 1. — קרקע] Root perhaps קור, "to dig out" (so Kö. II. i. p. 91); cognates, Assyr. *qaqqaru* and Arabic قَرْف = ground. On form (*pilpel*) GK. 84 *o*; Sta. 243, 1); change of ר to ע is for sake of euphony; cf., for other cases of dissimilation in reduplicated stems, כבכב = נרכב ; כרכם = כמכם (Kö. II. i. p. 465). The word occurs in five other passages (Nu. 5¹⁷ 1 K. 6¹⁵·¹⁶·³⁰ 7⁷), each time denoting the floor of a building. Here it is the floor of the sea. — **4.** והרגתם] On suf., GK. 59 *g*; on ending ־ת, GK. 59 *a*; on vowel-change, GK. 59 *c, g.* — **5.** ואדני] There is much force in Ew.'s treatment of this ו as the ו of the oath; other possible examples of this usage are Ho. 12⁶ Jo. 4²⁰ Je. 29²³ Is. 51¹⁵ Dt. 32³¹ Ps. 71¹⁹ 89³⁸; cf. Ew.⁸ 340 *c*; H. 44, 1 *d*, rm. (*e*). — הנוגע] The ptcp. here is followed by ותמוג, *i.e.* impf. with ו cons., and this by ואבלו (also ועלתה and ושקעה). GK. 112 *tt* regards this case (*i.e.* the pf. with ו cons. following an impf. with ו cons.) as one of a few instances due to error in the text, or to incorrect modes of expression; cf. Kö. 366 *i* who treats the ptcp. as referring to past time; Ew.⁸ 343 *a*. In Am. 7⁴ what seems to be a similar case proves on examination to be different, since ואכלה is equivalent to an incipient impf. (*v.s.*). The proper explanation is this: the ptcp. together with ותמוג expresses not a descriptive action, but a fact of general experience, a construction ordinarily denoted by the pf.; GK. 106 *k*; Dr. § 12; H. 18, 3. The whole expression = "he causes the earth to melt." This was the principal statement, which is followed by three clauses each giving a detail of the concurrent phenomena. These clauses are not subordinated as circumstantial clauses would be by placing the subject before the predicate; they are concurrent and coördinate, yet descriptive, and hence the pf. with ו consec. (= impf.) is employed. It is possible that this peculiar const. points to a late and unclassical date for vs.⁵·⁶. — **6.** אגדתו] *His vault;* from the root idea of *binding* (Talm. and Aram. אגד) come four different ideas, each of which occurs but once, viz. *bunch* (of hyssop), Ex. 12²², *company* (of men), 2 S. 2²⁵, *bands* (of ox-bow), Is. 58⁶, and here the heavens, *as bound or fitted together into a vault.* Cf. Ar. إِجَّاس. — **7.** כשיום] On ־יים, GK. 87 *a.* — הלא] Given concessive force in

GK. 150 *e.* — אֶת־יִשְׂרָאֵל] The force of the position may be expressed by placing emphasis on the word *Israel.* — **8.** — אֶפֶס כִּי] An adv. of limitation, = *save that;* the other cases of this are Nu. 13[28] Dt. 15[4] Ju. 4[9]; also (according to We., Sta. *GVI.* I. 199, Dr., Kit., and BDB.), 1 S. 1[5]. — לֹא] For unusual position (elsewhere only in Gn. 3[4] Ps. 49[8]) cf. GK. 113 *v;* H. 28, 3 rm. f; Kö. 352 *l.* — הַשְׁמִיד] Intens. inf. abs., here written fully; cf. Dt. 15[14] Is. 59[4] Je. 3[15]; etc. (GK. 53 *k*).

§ 15. A later voice of promise. 9[8c–15]. (1) A modification of the prophetic utterance concerning the exile, which shall not be doom, but a source of discipline, destruction coming upon the wicked only; 9[8c. 9. 10]. (2) There will be a lifting up and repairing of David's hut, now fallen, and the acquisition of all the territory originally intended for Israel; 9[11. 12]. (3) There will be a return of numerous and plenteous harvests, a rebuilding of cities, and a replanting of vineyards; and Israel shall be permanently reëstablished; 9[13–15].

This section is composed of three strophes of six lines each. Strophe 1, introduced by the transition clause, *save that I will not utterly destroy, etc.,* furnishes the ground for what follows, viz. only the wicked of Israel shall perish; strophe 2 describes the political reëstablishment of Israel, including Judah; strophe 3 pictures the prosperity and permanency of restored Israel.

The chief reasons for denying this section to Amos are: (1) the many linguistic affinities between it and the works of exilic and post-exilic times (see especially Che. *Exp.* 5th ser. VIII. 44 f.; Volz, 23; Dr. 119; Day and Chapin, *AJSL.* XVIII. 81; Grimm, *Liturgical Appendices,* 91); *e.g.* הַשְׁמִיר (v.8[b]), יִפּוֹל (v.9), דָּוִיד (v.11), חוֹרֵשׁ and קוֹצֵר (v.13) *scriptio plena;* the late formula הִנֵּה יָמִים בָּאִים (v.13); the phrase כִּימֵי עוֹלָם; cf. Mal. 3[4] Mi. 7[14] Is. 51[9] Je. 46[26], which are late passages; the phrase שׁוּב שְׁבוּת, which is post-exilic; אֱלֹהֶיךָ, cf. Is. 41[10] 52[7] 54[6] 66[9] Ps. 147[12] Jo. 4[17]; עָסִיס is later than תִּירוֹשׁ, occurring only in Jo. 1[5] 4[18] Is. 49[26] Ct. 8[2]; חֲרִיסַת, cf. חֲרִיסָה, Is. 49[19]; מוּג in Hithpa. only in Na. 1[5] Ps. 107[26]; (2) the fact that this picture of restoration is inconsistent with Amos's repeated announcements of entire destruction (cf. 5[1. 2] 9[1–4. 7]); (3) a favorable attitude towards Judah, as distinct from Israel, is not characteristic of Amos; (4) the emphasis laid upon material blessings, extension of territory, etc., to the exclusion of every moral characteristic, is inconsistent with the attitude of Amos, whose whole message is ethical; (5) the fact that the passage contains echoes of later writings, *e.g.* cf. v.11 and Is. 11[1], v.13 *a* and Lv. 26[5], v.13[b] and Jo. 4[18], v.14 and 2 K. 19[29] Je. 14[9] 29[5. 28] Is. 54[3] 65[21] Dt. 28[30 f. 39] Zp. 1[13]; (6) the abruptness of transition from the announcement of destruction to the promise of restoration in v.8[b]; (7) the use of the title אֱלֹהֶיךָ is in opposition to the usage and thought of Amos (4[12] being a

questionable passage); (8) Amos always represents the whole people as the
object of punishment, but here a distinction is made between the righteous
and the sinner which is characteristic of later thought; (9) the passage
seems to look back upon a ruined nation (vs.[11. 14f.]); (10) Amos always contemplates an exile in Assyria, not a scattering among the nations as here.
(So *e.g.* Sta., We., Oort, Marti (*Gesch.* 191 and *Dodekapropheton*), Sm. (*Rel.*
183); Houtsma (*ThT.* XXXIV. 433), Co. (*Einl.* ed. 3, p. 184), Che. (WRS.
Proph. XV. and *Exp.* Jan. 1897, pp. 44–47, and *EB.*), Preuschen (*ZAW.*
XV. 24–27), Now., GAS., Volz, Löhr, Taylor (*DB.*), Bu. (*Jew. Enc.*), Baudissin (*Einl.*), Grimm (*Liturgical Appendices*, 88 ff.); but cf. Val., Dr., Mit.,
Oet. (pp. 24 f.), Co. (*Einl.* 1st ed.).)

Some interpreters make the interpolation begin with v.[11]; so *e.g.* Torrey
(*JBL.* XV. 153 f.; cf. Schwally, *ZAW.* X. 227; Seesemann, p. 15), who
saves vs.[8-10] for Amos by pruning them of later additions, viz. v.[8b], and the
last clause of v.[9], which were added in order to prepare the way for vs.[11 ff.].

9. [צרור] 𝔊 σύντριμμα = שֶׁבֶר (so also Elh.), 𝔖 ܚܣܡܬܐ. Oet. נְרֻנַּר (?),
cf. Is. 17[6].—**10.** [ימותו] 𝔊 τελευτήσουσι; 𝔙 *morientur;* 𝔖 ܢܡܘܬ.—[הרעה]
𝔊 τὰ κακά.—[תגיש] Read תַּגֵּשׁ (so We., GAS., Now., Torrey, Dr., Oort
Em., Elh., Oet., Marti). Cf. Hi. who reads תשיג as in 1 Ch. 21[12] Jb. 41[18],
and cites the substitution of מגיש for משיג in 1 S. 14[26].—[תקדים] Read תְּקַדֵּם,
since Hiph. occurs only in Jb. 41[3] (so We., Torrey, GAS., Now., Oort *Em.,*
Elh., Oet., Marti).—[בעדינו] 𝔊 ἐφ᾽ ἡμᾶς. Read עָרֵינוּ (so Hoffm., We., Gr.,
Oort *Em.,* Torrey, Now., Elh., Oet., Marti). Riedel, בְּעָרֵינוּ.—**11.** [סכת]
𝔗 מַלְכּוּתְהָא רבית Hoffm. סִכּוּת and הַנֹּפֶלֶת (so Preuschen, *ZAW.* XV. 25;
Schwally, *ibid.* X. 226; Gu.). At end of v.[11] 𝔖 adds, ודור דור כשנות; cf.
Dt. 32[7].—[פרציהן והרסתיו] 𝔖 3 m. pl. suffixes; 𝔙, for פר, *aperturas murorum
ejus.* We. פְּרָצֶיהָ וַהֲרִסֹתֶיהָ (so Gr., Val., Now., Elh., Oet., Marti).—**12.** [יירשו]
𝔊 ἐκζητήσωσιν = ידרשו.—[את־שארית אדום] 𝔊, omitting את, οἱ κατάλοιποι τῶν
ἀνθρώπων (= אָדָם), and inserting as obj. of יירשו in some Mss. με, in others,
e.g. 𝔊[A], τὸν κύριον; cf. Acts 15[17].—[אשר] ... עליהם Gr. כאשר. 𝔊 ἐφ᾽ οὓς ...
ἐπ᾽ αὐτούς; 𝔙 *eo quod . . . super eos.*—[ואת] 𝔊𝔙𝔖 pl.—**13.** [וגיש 𝔖 ܠܦܘ
= הָשִׂיג (Seb.).—[חורש בקוצר] 𝔊 ὁ ἀμητὸς τὸν τρυγητόν. Vol. sug. as basis
of 𝔊 חריש בקציר, but חריש = *seedtime,* while ἀμητὸς = *harvest.* 𝔗 רדיא בחצודא;
𝔖 ܐܝܟ ܚܨܕܐ. Oet. הֶחָרִישׁ. Gun. קוצר בחורֵשׁ.—[הדרך ענבים בם׳ הי׳ 𝔊 καὶ
περκάσει ἡ σταφυλὴ ἐν τῷ σπόρῳ, perhaps reading בְּבֶר for דרך; cf. Ez. 47[12]
(Vol.). 𝔖 ܟܠܗܘܢ ܟܠܢ ; cf. 𝔗 זַרְעָא בַר בְּמַפֵּק עִנְבִין וְיֶעֱצַר—[עסיס
𝔗, freely, חֲמַר מְרִית.—[תתמוגגנה] 𝔊 σύμφυτοι ἔσονται, perhaps reading התמוגגנה,
cf. Ho. 11[8] (Vol.); 𝔙 *culti erunt;* 𝔗 וְיִתְפַּלְחָן 𝔖 ܢܬܚܣܡܢ—**14.** [נשמות
𝔊, freely, ἠφανισμένας.—**15.** [ינתש] 𝔙 *evellam eos.*—[ארמתם] 𝔊[NB] om. suff.
—[אלהיך] 𝔊 ὁ θεὸς ὁ παντοκράτωρ; hence Gr. אלהי צבאות.

9. *For behold I command*] The later writer preserves the
continuity of expression, by placing the words in the mouth of

Yahweh. The importance of the utterance is indicated by the use of *Behold*. The participle represents the action as on the point of occurrence. — *I will shake the house of Israel among all the nations*] Every Israelite, good or bad, shall be subjected to the discipline (no longer doom) which is coming. Instead of a particular people, among whom Israel is to go captive, as else-where, the phrase " all the nations " occurs, as in later prophets ; cf. Je. 43⁵ Ez. 36²¹. — *Just as one shakes with a sieve*] The sieve is ordinarily constructed in such a way as that the good grain is retained, while the light grain, the dust, and chaff fall through to the ground when the sieve is shaken. So the captivity is to be a means of sifting out of Israel all the wicked and worthless who are a disgrace and offence to the true people of Yahweh. — *And not a kernel shall fall*] The good shall remain in the sieve, *i.e.* in exile, but the bad shall fall, *i.e.* perish. צרור = kernel or pebble ; cf. the following views : (1) that the nation is entirely chaff ; * (2) that צרור = small stones which remain with the wheat, not one of them shall fall ; † (3) that it means firm and solid grain, *i.e.* something pressed together ; ‡ (4) that *pebble* = wicked, who shall remain in the sieve, *i.e.* captivity, while the righteous fall out or escape ; § (5) that צרור = pious, who are bound in a *bundle* that they may not be lost. ‖ In favor of the interpretation of צרור as grain are : (1) the fact that what remains in the sieve is the good element according to the description here, while the bad falls through ; (2) the idea of destruction could not be expressed by the figure of preservation in the sieve, nor deliverance by falling through the sieve.¶ — **10**. *All the sinners of my people*] This is the point of differentiation. It cannot mean, " all my sinful people," ** a thought more naturally ex-pressed through an adjective. These sinners must be removed through the process of sifting ; a violent death awaits them. — *Disaster shall not touch or befall us*] For change of text, *v.s.*

---

* Cal.   † Merc., Ros.   ‡ Ba.

§ Hoffm., Preuschen (*ZAW*. XV. 24). This interpretation supposes the sieve referred to here to be the *Kirbal* described by Wetzstein, *ZDPV*. XIV. 1 ff., as a sieve with large meshes into which the grain was first thrown in order to screen out of it small stones, clods, straws, and imperfectly threshed ears, which could not be blown out by throwing the grain against the wind. Cf. Ecclus. 27⁴.

‖ Hes.   ¶ So Now.   ** Torrey, *JBL*. XV. 154 f.

For a similar attitude of mind on the part of the wicked, cf.
Am. 6³. Looking forward to Yahweh's day as a time of joy and
blessing (cf. 5¹⁸), they scornfully refuse to heed the prophet's
warnings of calamity. With this picture of Yahweh's day as a
time of discipline and purification resulting in the preservation
and strengthening of the righteous, that of Amos is in striking
contrast; cf. 5¹⁸⁻²⁰ 8⁹. ¹⁰. ¹². ¹³. — **11.** *In that day*] Cf. the introductory phrase in v.¹³, and the occurrence of both together in 8¹¹. — *I
will raise up the hut of David*] This expression presupposes the
exile, for the Davidic house is here reduced to a hut; cf. Hoffmann (*v.s.*) who reads *huts*, and interprets the phrase, not as
having reference to the union of the two kingdoms, but as a
picture of the coming restoration of the simplicity of Davidic
days which Amos loved, the *huts* of David being contrasted with
the palaces and forts of the age of Jeroboam. — *Build it as in
the days of old*] This would hardly be appropriate in Amos's
days, but entirely so in later times. — **12.** *That they may possess
the remnant of Edom and all the nations*] Cf. Ps. 60. This
hostility towards Edom in particular seems to reflect the feelings
of the exilic age; cf. Ob., Is. 63¹⁻⁶, etc. This political exaltation
of Israel at the expense of the nations in general is strangely
discordant with the teachings of Amos; cf. v.⁷. — *Which are called
by my name*] This does not mean "those to whom he shall have
revealed his divine nature, and manifested himself as a God and
Saviour"; * nor "those who have been solemnly proclaimed by
him as his property or subject-lands, which was done in his
promises to Israel and David's house"; † but refers rather to the
thought (cf. Je. 7¹⁰ Dt. 28¹⁰ 2 S. 12²⁸) that an owner's name will
adhere to what he owns, and to the fact that David had actually
subdued extensive territory and made it submissive to Yahweh. ‡ —
13. *The ploughman shall overtake the reaper*, etc.] Cf. Lv. 26⁵.
Ploughing and reaping will press close upon one another, the time
of ripening will be so short; before the farmer has his crops all
sown, it will be time for him to begin reaping those first sown. —
And the treader of grapes him who soweth seed] *i.e.* the vintage
will be so abundant that seedtime will arrive before the vintage is

---

* Ke.   † Or.   ‡ Now.

finished. Vintage begins in September, while seedtime begins as soon as the October rains have made ploughing possible. — *And the mountains shall drop sweet wine*] Cf. Jo. 3¹⁸. The vineyards were commonly planted on the mountain slopes. — *And all the hills shall melt*] It will appear as though the hills themselves were being dissolved in the copious streams of wine flowing from the vineyards on their sides. — **14.** *I will lead back the captivity of my people*] In Ho. 6¹¹, and everywhere in later writings (*i.e.* eleven times in Je., three times in Ez., Dt. 30³ Ps. 126¹·⁴ La. 2¹⁴ Ps. 14⁷ 53⁶ Zp. 2⁷ 3²⁰), except in Jb. 42¹⁰, the phrase שוב שבות may be given this meaning (*v.i.*). The other interpretation *turn the fortune* (*turning*) *of my people*, based on the derivation of שבות from שוב rather than שבה, is favored by some scholars (*v.i.*). The latter meaning is more general. In either case, the post-exilic origin of this utterance is clear in view of the detailed description which follows, and seems to have been written in the light of experience. — *They shall rebuild waste cities and inhabit them*] Cf. Je. 33¹⁰ Is. 54³ 65²¹. The opposite is seen in Zp. 1¹³ Dt. 28³⁰. — *And they shall plant vineyards and drink their wine, and they shall make gardens* (*i.e.* orchards), *and eat their fruit*] For similar ideals of the future see Is. 65²¹ Ez. 28²⁶; and note the contrast between this and Amos's outlook, 4⁹ 5¹¹; cf. Dt. 28³⁰·³⁹ Zp. 1¹³. — **15.** *I will plant them upon their land*] Cf. Ho. 2²³ Je. 24⁶ 32⁴¹ 42¹⁰ 45⁴ 2 S. 7¹⁰ Is. 60²¹ Jo. 3²⁰. The nation is here represented as a tree (cf. Ps. 1³). — *And they shall not again be plucked up from their land which I have given them*] A promise of permanent possession, qualified by no conditions ; but the nation is thought of here as righteous, and therefore enjoying the favor of Yahweh. — *Saith Yahweh thy God*] Cf. 4¹² Is. 41¹⁰ 52⁷ 54⁶ 66⁹. This is a phrase expressive of the close relationship now existing. It is not used by Amos.

9. וינוע] Indef. freq.; literally, *is shaken*, the subj. 'grain' being understood. — כברה] *α.λ.* Apparently from כבר = intertwine, weave. There seems to be no sufficient reason on either lexicographical or exegetical grounds to connect it with the modern غِرْبَال, described by Wetzstein, *ZDPV.* XIV. 1-7. — צרור] Etymol. uncertain; perhaps from צרר = *to press together*. The meaning *pebble* is assured for 2 S. 17¹³, the only other occurrence. *Grain of corn* suits the present context better. — **10.** חטאי עמי] Partitive genitive, GK. 128 *i*;

not "my sinful people" (so Torrey), cf. Da. § 24 *a*. — חגיש] Hiph. never occurs elsewhere meaning "draw near," but rather with causative force, "bring near." Hence the original consonants חגש should probably be pointed as Qal. Likewise תקריס] must be pointed as Pi.; Hi. occurs only in Jb. 41[8], where also Pi. was probably original (so Duhm). — בעריגו] If 𝕳𝕿 be retained, י is to be explained as *scriptio plena*, since בער is regularly used in sg. before suff. But (1) this unusual pointing, (2) the inappropriateness of this prep. after the vbs. used here, and (3) the rendering of 𝕲 (*v.s.*) support the change to עָרֵינו adopted here. The objection of Gun. that עד does not elsewhere occur with suffix of 1 p. pl. is of little force. — **11.** סכת] Used here fig. of the fallen Davidic dynasty; cf. its use in 2 S. 22[12] of the clouds as the dwelling-place of Yahweh. This is preferable to pointing it as pl., with Hoffm. (*v.s.*), and requires less change in the following suffixes, involving merely the reading of masc. sg. suff. instead of f. pl. in פרציהן, whereas the reading סְכּוֹת necessitates reading חרסתיהן, and בניתין, and גְּפָלֹת. Perhaps, however, it is better to read all three suff. as fem. sg., with We., and refer them to סכת. — דויד] The *scriptio plena* is a distinctively late characteristic, not becoming customary until the close of the fourth century B.C. In 6[5] it occurs again, but there it is certainly a later addition. See Eckardt, *ZAW.* XIII. 89 f.; cf. BDB. *s.v.*; for the statistics of the two forms of writing the name, see Bonk, *ZAW.* XI. 127 ff. — הרסתיו] α.λ.; a passive ptcp. formation (Barth, *NB.* 126 *c*), from הרס = "to tear down." If the masc. suffix be retained it must be explained as influenced by, or referring to, דויד. — כימי] For this use of כ cf. Ho. 2[5]. — **12.** אשר נקרא שמי עליהם] This phraseology regularly denotes the fact of possession; cf. Is. 4[1] 63[19] Dt. 28[10] Je. 7[10] 15[16] 2 S. 12[28]. — עשה זאת] This use of the ptcp. to express an attribute of Yahweh is found also in 4[13] 5[8f.] 9[5f.], and is common in late literature. — **13.** עסיס] Pass. ptcp. formation (Barth, *NB.* 126 *c*), from עסס = crush by treading; cf. Mal. 3[21]; Syr. ܟܣܣ = to explore; Arab. عَسَّ = to prowl about. This was probably a sweet wine made by not allowing fermentation to continue the usual length of time; cf. Dr., and Pliny, *Hist. Nat.* XIV. 9. In Ct. 8[2] this word is used of wine made from pomegranates, a kind of wine still made in Persia. — תתמוגגנה] Cf. the use of this same vb. with reference to the land in v.[5], and of the hills, as here, in Na. 1[5]. In Jo. 4[18], where this statement is repeated, the more ordinary phrase הלך חלב is substituted for this striking expression. — **14.** שבות] Best explained as derived from שבה, not from שוב. Cf. the effort of Barth (*ZDMG.* XLI. 618) to connect it with שבה = to gather (Arab. ثبا), translating, "I will gather a gathering."

A COMMENTARY ON THE BOOK OF HOSEA.

———◆———

§ 1. The superscription. I[1].* This superscription states the authority, the parentage, and the period of Hosea, the prophet whose writings make up the collection. The superscriptions of the prophetic books, like those of the psalms, had their origin in many cases in an age later than that of the prophecies themselves. This fact explains the inconsistencies so frequently found between the contents of the superscriptions and the contents of the books. The data for determining the value of the statement must be gathered from the book itself. In the case before us, aside from the formal utterance concerning the prophet's inspiration and the name of his father, the questions of special interest are : (1) Why should Jeroboam alone be mentioned of the Northern kings, when, if the other part of the date is correct, the prophet must have worked also during the reigns of several of the Israelitish kings, viz. Zechariah, Shallum, Menahem, Pekahiah, Pekah, Hoshea? (2) If Hosea was a Northern prophet, why is the work dated by Southern kings? (3) Did Hosea really prophesy during the period designated? (4) Consideration must also be given to the question of his home and nationality. These points, already referred to in the Introduction, will be taken up in the order suggested by the text.

I. 1. *The word of Yahweh*] While " law " or " instruction " (תורה = decision by oracle) was the technical word for the divine communication through the priest, and " counsel " (עצה = " the faculty of self-determination or devising of measures " †), cf. Je. 18[18], for

---

* Cf. Che. 9–15 ; Sayce, *JQR.* I. 162–172 ; Kirk. *Proph.* 107–110 ; Riehm, *Einl.* II. 46–50; Now. 2–6; GAS. I. 211–226; WRS. *Proph.* 144 ff.; Marti, 13 f.

† Cf. Siegfried in art. "Wisdom," *DB.*

that of the sage, "word" (דבר) is the term employed in connection with the work of the prophet (cf. Am. 1^1 Is. 2^1 Je. 1^2 $2^{1.4}$ 7^1 Ez. 6^1 7^1 12^1 13^1 Jo. 1^1 Jon. 1^1 Mi. 1^1 Zp. 1^1 Hg. 1^1 Zc. 1^1 Mal. 1^1). — *To Hosea, the son of Beeri*] The word *Hosea* (הוֹשֵׁעַ) means deliverance (cf. p. 205); with it may be compared the form Joshua (יְהוֹשׁוּעַ). The same name was borne by the last of the Israelitish kings (733–722 B.C.), but the effort to identify this king with the prophet is without success. The name Beeri occurs only here; cf., however, Beerah, 1 Ch. 5^6. Among various traditions concerning Hosea may be mentioned (1) that which locates his birth and death in Belemoth * or Belamon † or Bethshemesh ‡ of the tribe of Issachar; (2) that which represents his death as having taken place in Babylon and his burial in Tsepath in upper Galilee; § (3) that which makes his burial place in Almenia, in Northern Africa. Leaving these stories, we turn to the book which bears his name for the information not elsewhere given. *He was of Northern Israel;* this appears from (1) the language of the book, which contains Aramaisms; ‖ (2) the phrases ¶ "our king," 7^5, "in the house of Israel I saw a horrible thing," 6^{10}; "the land" applied to Northern Israel, 1^2; (3) the special interest shown in Israel; ** (4) the peculiar information displayed in reference to their religious †† and political conditions, their past history, ‡‡ and the topography of the country; §§ (5) his familiarity with the Northern love-poem, *Song of Songs,* ‖‖ but this point can scarcely be substantiated; (6) "the tone of Hosea's religion, which is, on the whole, both warmer and more joyous (cf. chaps. 2 and 14) than that which prevails in the great Judahite prophets." ¶¶ It has been suggested that Hosea, like Amos, went up from Judah to Israel; *** because (1) frequent references are made to Judah ($1^{7.11}$ 4^{15} $5^{5.10-14}$ $6^{4.11}$ 8^{14} 11^{12} 12^2), but these passages are doubtful,

---

* See Wü. pp. iii, iv; Now. *Hosea,* p. ix; Kno. *Proph.* II. 154; Pseudepiphanius, *de vitis prophet.* chap. 11.　　　† Pseudodorotheus, *de prophetis,* chap. 1.
‡ Jer. on 1^1.　　　§ שלשלת הקבלה, fol. 19.
‖ Sim. 38; Ke., Giesebrecht, *ZAW.* I. 258; Che., Kö. *Einl.* 311 f.; Now.
¶ Cf. Hi. and Ew.; *v.,* however, Che. p. 10.
** Wü. p. v.　　　†† Dr. *LOT.* 304.　　　‡‡ Now., *Hosea,* pp. viii f.
§§ Ew. I. 210 f.; Wü. p. vii.; Now. 3.　　　‖‖ Hi. 5; Che. 34.
¶¶ Che. p. 10; cf. Wü. p. viii.
*** Jahn, *Einl.* II. i. § 94; Mau. *Observat. in Hoseam,* cited by Ros.

and in any case do not involve such an implication ; (2) the superscription dates the life of the prophet principally according to
the kings of the Southern Kingdom, the name of Jeroboam being
given to indicate the period of his prophetic activity in Israel;
but, as will be shown, the superscription is from a late hand, and
consequently cannot be trusted for evidence of a character so
subtle ; (3) the prophet's attitude toward the people of Judah as
compared with that manifested toward Israel ; but under Uzziah,
the people of Judah were comparatively upright, while idolatry
with all its evils, and oppression with all its accompaniments, were
rampant in Israel.*   Nor does the use of the names of kings of
both kingdoms indicate birth in one and work in another.†   Moreover, the failure to give the birthplace of a prophet does not indicate that he was a native of Jerusalem.‡ — *In the days of Uzziah,
Jotham, Ahaz, Hezekiah, kings of Judah, and in the days of
Jeroboam, son of Joash, king of Israel*] This translated into
dates reads : Between *ca. 785* and *ca. 715*, reckoned by Southern
kings ; between *ca. 780* and *ca. 745*, reckoned by Northern kings.
If genuine, this would mean that Hosea's work began, at least
before *745* B.C., and continued probably through *722* B.C.

As favoring this, and in explanation of the difficulties which have arisen,
it has been suggested : (1) That the names of the Southern kings are inserted
(*a*) because the line held a more permanent and dignified position, and its
chronology was more trustworthy (Ma. 4); (*b*) because, as the prophet
knew, they were the true kings (Häv. *Einl.* II. ii. 278; Ke. I. 11 f.; Hng. I.
166 f.; Pu.); (*c*) because they were the righteous kings, Jeroboam's name
being added for the reason that he too was righteous in not heeding the
calumny against Amos (7¹⁰); or (*d*) because it was customary to date one's
prophecies by the kings of one's native land (Hosea being from Judah)
(Mau.). (2) That the name of Jeroboam is added (*a*) in order that the
prophet may give evidence of his knowledge to foretell future events, since
he first threatens the evil in the prosperous time of Jeroboam (Cal. 38 f.;
Os. 509; Hng. 167; Ke. I. 12 f.); or (*b*) because the prophet's work
was done in Israel (so most comm.); but the fanciful character of such
suggestions is obvious. (3) That the names of the remaining kings of
Israel are omitted because they were not regarded as real kings (Cocceius
in Marck, 6; Hng. 168). In favor of the genuineness of the super-

---

* Kit. *Hist.* II. 310 f.; Kno. *Proph.* II. 155, Anm. 5; Wü. p. vi.; H. P. Smith,
O. T. Hist. 221 ff.   † Ros. p. 5.   ‡ Wü. p. vii.   Cf. Ew. I. 210–214.

scription it has been urged (1) that "Shalman" (10^{14}) refers to Shalmaneser (Hng. I. 169 f.; Pu.); (2) that Jareb (5^{13} 10^6) is the natal name of Sargon (Sayce, *HCM.* 417); (3) that the predictions of Assyrian invasion in $10^{5.6}$ 13^{16} seem to refer to the immediate future (Huxtable); (4) that the allusions to the Egyptian relations (7^{11} 11^{11}) are satisfied by the events of Hoshea's reign (Ma. 341; Ke. I. 15 f.; Hng. I. 170 f.); (5) that 8^{10} refers to tribute paid by Menahem to Tiglathpileser (Schm. p. 73); (6) that the whole description is one that accords literally with the period of the last days of Israel (Hng. I. 171 f.; Ke. I. 16). Against the genuineness of the superscription may be urged (Ew., Sim., Wü.; WRS. *Proph.* 406 f.; Che.; Dr. *LOT.* 301 f.; We., Or., Bach., Val., Now.; Da. *DB.* II. 420; Marti, *EB.* II. 2121, *et al.*; Oet.) : (1) the inconsistency of placing the later date (Uzziah, etc.), *ca. 780* to *715*, before the earlier (Jeroboam) *ca. 780* to *ca. 745*, when chaps. 1–3 seem to belong to the reign of Jeroboam (cf. the description of prosperity in chap. 2, which is applicable only to Jeroboam's time; and the announcement of a yet future destruction awaiting the dynasty of Jehu, 1^4), and chaps. 4–14, to the times which immediately followed; (2) the improbability that a Northern prophet would use for his dates the reigns of Southern kings; (3) the fact that in the prophet's time Gilead was still Israelitish, 6^8 12^{11}; cf. 5^1; although in 734 B.C. its inhabitants were carried away by Tiglathpileser; (4) the absence of any reference to the attack of Pekah upon Judah in 735 B.C. (cf. Is. 7); (5) the probability that Hezekiah did not come to the throne until after the fall of Samaria, to which event Hosea looks forward (13^{16} 14^1) (We. *Jahrbb. f. deutsche Theol.* XX. 630; Wkl. *Untersuch.* 77 ff.; McCurdy, *HPM.* II. 250; Marti, *EB.* 796; Che. *EB.* 2058; Gu. *Gesch.* 200; *et al.*)

The evidence points to the conclusion suggested above, that at least a portion of the superscription comes from the hand of a post-exilic scribe, who thus inexactly represents Hosea as a contemporary of Isaiah (cf. Is. 1^1) and of Micah (cf. 1^1), the name of Uzziah being omitted from the date of the latter to show that he was younger.*

---

* Various opinions regarding the origin of the superscription are : Hi. reads as original, " In the days of Jeroboam, son of Joash, king of Israel; then spake Yahweh to Hosea," thus including a part of v.². Sim. and Wü. treat the whole as late. Ew. takes the specification of the kings of Judah as a later addition from the hand to which we owe Is. 1^7, and considers the rest of the heading as original but belonging only to chaps. 1 and 2. Che. says, " The first part, ' the word,' etc., may have been originally prefixed to a roll containing chaps. 1–3; the latter part was intended for the complete book; both parts were joined thoughtlessly at a late date." Sayce declares the title to be older than the age of ⅏, and to be the work of a native of Judah. It is inexact and imperfect and comes from a later

1. הושע] From ישע = *to be wide* ; this earlier form was changed to יהושׁע
(Nu. 13⁸·¹⁶ 32¹²·²⁸).   𝔊 'Ωσῆε; 𝔙 *Osee* ; Jerome (on 1¹) notes the writing
Αὐσή, Ause; Rom. 9²⁵ 'Ωσής; 𝔖 ܐܘܫܥ; Arabic غُوزَيَّ. On the original
pronunciation of הושע, cf. Haupt. *ZA.* II. 261, Anm. 2; Jäger, *BAS.* I. 468.
The form is not (1) an imv. (Hiph.) = *Save thou* (Ma. 2; Ros. 10.), for this
would require הושׁע; nor (2) pf. 3 m. sg., which would require הושׁיע; nor
(3) a compound of הו = יהו, a form of יהוה and שׁע = ישׁע, (Jer.; cf. Sim. 7, and
Wü. pp. 1 f.), for this is the explanation of יהושׁע; but (4) an inf. abs., (Sim. 6;
Wü. p. 1; Or. 4 ; BDB.); cf. Je. 11¹² 1 S. 25²⁶·³³.

§§ 2–5. Hosea's call to the prophetic work, in connection with the unfaithfulness of his wife, a picture of Israel's relationship to God.

1²–3⁵. A family experience leads Hosea to understand in some measure the love of Yahweh for Israel. This experience was, in a word, the adultery of his own wife, and the birth of children in this adultery. Some time after the events themselves have occurred, he tells the story, mingling with its details the new and precious truth which he has gained from the experience concerning Yahweh and Yahweh's bride, the nation Israel. His narrative, like that of Isaiah's vision (Is. 6) and Jeremiah's later feeling in reference to the message concerning the purchase of the field (Je. 32⁸), reads into the events the significance which the later history suggests. The present text as rearranged includes : § 2. The harlotry of Gomer, the prophet's wife, 1²⁻⁹ (v.⁷, a later addition). § 3. The purchase of Gomer as a slave and her retention " many days," 3¹⁻⁵ (v.⁵, a later addition). § 4. The harlotry of Israel and her punishment therefor, 2⁴⁻⁷·¹⁰⁻¹⁴·¹⁹ (vs.⁴ᵇ·⁶·¹² being glosses or later additions). § 5. Later voices

---

hand. Dr. supposes the original title to have had simply, " In the days of Jeroboam," and to have referred only to chaps. 1–3 ; and the names of the Judean kings, contemporaneous with and subsequent to Jeroboam, to have been added in order to indicate that the book as a whole referred to a later period. We. and Now.² say that only the beginning of the superscription, " The word of Yahweh which came to Hosea, son of Beeri," is old. Now. thinks that if any part of the superscription is genuine, it must be " The word of Yahweh which came to Hosea, son of Beeri, in the days of Jeroboam, king of Israel." This belongs only to chaps. 1–3. Marti (*EB.* II. 2121), suggests " words of Hosea, the son of Beeri " as the original form. Da. (*DB.* II. 420) grants the possibility of an early date for " the words of Yahweh which came to Hosea, the son of Beeri." Oet. rejects the entire chronological statement as coming from a later hand.

describing Israel's return to Yahweh and his acceptance of her,
2$^{8-9.\ 16-18.\ 20-25.\ 1-3}$.* With slight exceptions the material is poetical.†

§ 2. The harlotry of Hosea's wife. 1$^{2-9}$.

A man of sensitive temperament marries a young woman who later proves unfaithful to her marriage vows. The children born in infidelity are named *Jezreel, Un-loved, "No kin of mine"* (lit. *not-my-people*). These names, like those of Isaiah's children, were significant. The woman, after some years, goes from bad to worse. The prophet (1) is led to see in this a parallel with Israel's treatment of Yahweh; and (2) through this domestic affliction is called to preach to his sinful countrymen.

2. דבר] 𝕲𝖄𝕾𝕿 read as a substantive (דְּבַר) or inf. cst. (דַּבֵּר); but 'A. ἀρχὴ ἦν ἐλάλησε. — בהושע] 𝕾 = על־הו. 𝕸𝕿 places pisqa after this, thus indicating it as an independent sentence; so 𝕲, but 𝕾𝖄 connect with what follows. Hi. regards the clause בהו . . . תחלת as a gloss (so Bach., Now. (?)). Oet. om. יהוה אל הושע.—ילדי זנונים] 𝖄 (*Cod. Amiat.*) inserts *fac* before these words. Bach. (*Pr.*) om. as a gloss on זנה.—אשת זנונים 𝕲 ἐκπορνεύουσα = זֹנָה; so 𝖄. — **3.** לו] Omitted in some Mss. of Heb. and 𝕲, and in Arabic, but present in Ethiopic *Franckfurter Bibel-Cod.* (Bach. *Pr.*). — **4.** יהוא] 𝕲 Ἰούδα; Σ., Θ. Ἰνοῦ.—ממלכות] Oet. and Now.² sugg. that this is a confusion of מלכות and מֶמְלָכָה, and would read מַמְלֶכֶת. — **6.** ויאמר לו] 𝕾 inserts יהוה as subj. and reads לי for לו; so also in v.⁹. — לא רחמה] 𝕲 οὐκ ἠλεημένη; 𝖄 *absque misericordia*, both pointing toward a ptcp. as orig. form; but 𝕾 has finite vb. Loft. sugg. לא רחמיה.—כי נשא אשא להם] 𝕾 treats ל as sign of acc., and renders נשא, *carry away;* 𝖄 *sed oblivione obliviscar eorum* (reading נשה); 𝕲 ἀλλ' ἢ ἀντιτασσόμενος ἀντιτάξομαι αὐτοῖς; 𝕿 takes נשא as = *forgive*. Gr. would place this clause in v.⁷ after ארחם. Bach. would insert אל (= not that I should forgive) before כי, its loss being occasioned by preceding ישראל. Hal. inserts לא = I will not pardon. — **7.** Omit as a Judaistic insertion (*v.i.*). Oet. would transpose to chap. 14. — **9.** לא אהיה לכם] Read לא אלהיכם (cf. 2²⁵ Zc. 8⁸) (so 𝕲 codd. 42, 44; Orig. IV. 618; We., Gr., Loft., Now., Oet., Hal., Marti).

2 a. *In the beginning when Yahweh spoke*] is the proper rendering of 𝕸𝕿, and is favored by 𝕲𝕾𝖄; *v.s.* It refers to the

---

beginning of the prophet's work, which is, therefore, made syn-
chronous with his marriage. It is unquestionably awkward, and
many suggestions have been made to relieve this difficulty; *v.i.*
— *With Hosea*] Yahweh is here represented as speaking *with* the
prophet, *i.e.* as entering into communication with him, the person
who speaks being a superior being* (Nu. 12[2, 6] Zc. 1[9 ff.]) ; rather
than *through* or *by* (1 K. 22[28]). — *Yahweh said unto Hosea*] The
marriage which is commanded is a means of educating the prophet
to an understanding of Yahweh's will. That Yahweh was actually
speaking to him when his heart was led to take the step, later
events testify. — *Take to thee*] Used by zeugma with a double
object, viz. Gomer and the children, and denoting here, as elsewhere, marriage (cf. Gn. 4[19] 6[2] 19[14] 1 S. 25[43] Ex. 21[10] 34[16]), and not
concubinage.† — *A wife of whoredoms*] Not (1) one who was unchaste, *i.e.* a harlot, at the time of marriage, ‡ because (*a*) Hosea
would scarcely have attributed such a command to Yahweh;
(*b*) this would be inconsistent with the symbolical representation
which makes Israel (and, therefore, the woman) at first faithful
(Je. 2[2]) ; (*c*) the ordinary word זָנָה would better have been used.
Nor (2) one who, like all Israelites of the day, was spiritually
unclean, *i.e.* addicted to idolatry. § But (3) one who, although
chaste at the time of marriage, had in her a tendency to impurity
which later manifested itself. ‖ For a fuller summary of the different interpretations *v.i.* — *And children of whoredoms*] Not
(1) children already born in adultery to the mother before
marriage with the prophet; ¶ because (*a*) as Gomer is the wife
of whoredoms, the children to be named (vs.[4, 6, 9]) must be the
children of whoredoms ; (*b*) the symbolical interpretation points
to children born in sin after the marriage ; ** nor (2) children
who, like all Israelites, were guilty of idolatry ; †† nor (3) children,
born to the prophet by his wife, who inherited from the mother
this tendency toward lewdness ; ‡‡ but (4) children born to her
after marriage and begotten by another than the prophet.**

---

* Ew.   † Thomas Aquinas, Schmidt.
    ‡ So most older commentaries, and recently, Volz, " Die Ehegeschichte Hosea's,"
ZwTh. XLI. 321–335.   § New., Preiswerk, Sharpe, Riedel.
    ‖ So Geb., Mau., Ros., Hd., Che., We., WRS., Kue., GAS., Now., Da., Marti, *et al.*
    ¶ So Abarb., Grotius, Kurtz, Ke.   ** So most recent comm.   †† Hal.
    ‡‡ Sanctius, Or.

A summary of the more important interpretations of the marriage of
Hosea is here given.

I. A vision, a transaction in a dream or trance, and never carried out in
real life (so Maimonides, AE., Ki., Hng., Ke., Wü., Tött., *et al.*). II. Closely
allied to I., and, like it, based upon objection to a literal interpretation, is the
view which makes it a parable, or allegory, or figurative mode of speech (so
Rashi, Cal., Pareus, Crocius, De Wette, Schrö., Hes., Hi., Sim., Bleek, Schm.,
Reuss, Kö., *et al.*). In defence of both the above as against a literal interpretation it is urged (*a*) that to take it literally is a reflection upon the holiness
of God, and imputes to Hosea conduct out of harmony with the character
of a prophet; (*b*) that the woman in 3^1 is not the same as the wife in
chap. I, and that Hosea should have made two such marriages is improbable;
(*c*) that too much time was consumed by these events for Hosea ever to
have used them as the basis of a striking appeal to the nation; (*d*) that
prophets often represent themselves as being under command to do things
which could not have been done (*e.g.* Ez. $4^{2\,ff.}$); (*e*) that the chief emphasis
in the whole narrative is on the symbolical names; (*f*) that the interpretation
of the act is attached immediately to the command to perform the act, altogether after the fashion of vision and symbol rather than as in actual life;
(*g*) that it would have been psychologically impossible for a man of Hosea's
character to have received such a command from Yahweh.

Against the preceding views, and in favor of a literal understanding of the
narrative, it is urged (*a*) that what is morally and religiously objectionable
in actual practice becomes no more defensible by being presented as vision or
parable; (*b*) that no indication is given by the prophet that this is vision or
parable and not fact (but cf. Je. $25^{15\,ff.}$ Zc. 11); (*c*) that the name Gomer
bath Diblaim yields no symbolical significance; (*d*) that no symbolical
meaning can be attached to the fact that the second child (v.^{6}) is a girl
rather than a boy; (*e*) that the literal view suits the realism of early prophecy better than the supposition that it is a product of literary imagination;
(*f*) that prophets were accustomed to give symbolical names to real children
(cf. Is. 7^3 8^3); and (*g*) that a real experience such as this furnishes the best
explanation of Hosea's message, — it was the outcome of the sufferings of his
own heart.

III. Those who have maintained that a real marriage took place have
differed widely among themselves. It has been held: (1) That Gomer was
an acknowledged harlot (*a*) who had already borne children (so Abarb.,
Grotius, Kurtz); or (*b*) who bore children to Hosea in lawful wedlock (so
Böckel and Mau., interpreting לו as showing that the children were Hosea's
own); or (*c*) who bore, after her marriage, children whose parentage was
uncertain (so Jer., Theodoret, Merc., Sanctius, Burkius, Dathe, Bauer, Ew.,
Hofmann (*Weissagung u. Erfüllung*, 205 ff.), Pu., Val., *et al.*). The chief
arguments in support of this view are (*a*) that the marriage thereby becomes
a direct, obvious sermon against Israel; (*b*) the extraordinary character of
the act was for the express purpose of attracting attention (cf. Ez. $12^{9\,ff.}$)

and leading the people to question the prophet, and thus furnish him an opportunity to teach the lesson he desired; (*c*) if the act of 3[1] was a public one, as is generally maintained, why not also that of 1[2], since the form of the divine command is practically the same? (*d*) the divine purpose of the marriage becomes clear — viz. to open the eyes of the people to its sins against Yahweh. The interpretation of Umbreit is worthy of mention in this connection, viz. that Hosea, thinking of Yahweh as the husband of Israel, and of himself as Yahweh's representative to Israel, feels that he himself has contracted marriage with a harlot, since he by virtue of his prophetic calling sustains the same relation to Israel as Yahweh does. Against the view that Gomer was a public harlot are urged two objections which seem decisive : (*a*) that if this had been intended זֹנָה would have been used instead of אשת זנונים; (*b*) that it is contrary to the regular custom of Hosea and the prophets in general, who always represented Israel as pure at the time of her union with Yahweh.

(2) Another phase of this view is that spiritual fornication is meant here, Gomer being a worshipper of idols, like all the Israelites of Hosea's time (so New., Preiswerk, Sharpe, Riedel, Hal.). But if such were the case, Hosea's preaching and his use of his wife for illustrative purposes would have had little force with people who were all sinners like his wife and saw no evil in their conduct.

(3) Some have held that Hosea took Gomer, the harlot, not as a full wife, but only as a concubine (so Thomas Aquinas, Schmidt). But this is even less acceptable than (1).

(4) Another attempt to escape difficulty is the view that makes the wife and children virtuous and honorable, but says that Hosea *called* them adulterous for parabolic purposes (so Luther, Os.). However, this is out of keeping with his character, and might have brought upon him open ridicule abroad and misunderstanding at home.

(5) Finally, it is held that the disposition toward adultery in Gomer did not manifest itself until after her marriage (so Geb., Ma., Ros., Eich., Stuck, Theiner, Hd., Schegg, Schlier, Che., We., WRS., Kue., GAS., Da., Marti, *et al.*). The advantages of this view are (*a*) that it accepts the narrative as being the simple recital of historical facts which it apparently is, while, at the same time, it does away with the moral difficulties involved in other views that do the same; (*b*) that it furnishes a reasonable basis for Hosea's evident love for his wife; (*c*) that it most easily explains the processes through which Hosea came to a realization of the mutual relationship of Yahweh and Israel; (*d*) that it is strongly supported by chap. 3, which describes Hosea as taking back his wife who had been dismissed on account of her adultery, which dismissal would not have been justifiable if Hosea had married her with full knowledge of her having been previously immoral. The objections that have been made to it (cf. Volz, *ZwTh*. XLI. 321–35 ; Da. *DB*. II. 422) are (*a*) the fact that it necessitates the supposition that Hosea, after an experience running through many years, looked back upon it all, and in-

P

terpreted as a direct call of Yahweh what was in a large measure due to his own natural impulses; (*b*) the fact that to take out of Hosea's life the number of years necessary for the occurrence of the events narrated here leaves comparatively little of his life to be spent in prophetic activity; (*c*) if we accept the view of We. (so WRS., Kue., GAS., Now.) that Hosea did not discover his wife's infidelity until after the birth of their first-born, it follows that his domestic experience had little to do with his conception of his mission, for he foretells the doom of Israel in the name of his first child, Jezreel; (*d*) however, whether he learned of his wife's faithlessness before the birth of Jezreel (so Che. in WRS. *Proph.* p. 112), or after that event, and before the birth of the other two, it is scarcely probable that he would have kept Gomer in his house and permitted her to go on in adultery; (*e*) the fact that the wife's infidelity did not develop until after the marriage would have been too important an item to have been completely ignored in the text (cf. Marti's view that Gomer's infidelity was not discovered till after the birth of all three children); (*f*) it is no easier to think of Yahweh as commanding Hosea to marry a woman whom Yahweh knows to be about to break her marriage vows than it is to think of him as commanding Hosea to marry a recognized harlot; (*g*) the purpose of the marriage does not appear on this supposition; it was not necessary to teach Hosea the idea of Yahweh as Israel's husband, for this was a common Semitic conception; nor could he have passed immediately from the thought of his own love for his wicked wife to that of Yahweh's love for Israel, — he must have had a special revelation of this thought, — hence the marriage was unnecessary; nor was it necessary in order to arouse the prophetic spirit in Hosea, for he could not have seen in his own experience an analogy to Yahweh's experience with Israel had he not previously had a prophet's realization of Israel's wickedness; nor is it sufficient to say that the marriage was to teach Hosea how deep was Yahweh's love and anguish and how base was Israel's ingratitude, — such sympathy could come only through clear insight into Israel's complete revolt from Yahweh in cultus and life; (*h*) while it is *per se* possible that the revelation contained in the marriage was limited to Hosea himself, the brevity of the representation and its close intermingling with the remaining utterances speak against it, as well as the fact that in such cases the mediating position of the prophet between Yahweh and Israel always appears.

2 *b*. *For the land goes a-whoring from after Yahweh*] The land represents the individual inhabitants and is used in the narrower sense of Israel, excluding Judah.* The sense of the symbol is plain : (1) the prophet represents Yahweh ; (2) Gomer who is married to the prophet, is Israel who is

---

* Wü., Che., Now., *et al.*

married to Yahweh; (3) as Gomer after marriage goes astray, so Israel, after a period, goes a-whoring after other gods.—**3**. *And took Gomer, the daughter of Diblaim*] Much fruitless effort has been spent in seeking a symbolical meaning for Gomer. This has been due to the fact that the prophet so interprets the names of the children, and because " Gomer " is not an ordinary name ; *e.g.* (*a*) "consumption," and this with Diblaim = " corrupt mass of figs " ;* (*b*) "completeness " (cf. Jer. τετελεσ-μένη), with Diblaim = " cakes of figs, sensual pleasure " ;† (*c*) destruction, ruin,‡ referring to the punishment coming ; (*d*) coals ;§ (*e*) marriageable maiden, daughter of wantonness. ‖ Besides the interpretations of Bath Diblaim given above may be mentioned *doppelgattige*,¶ 𝕿 which reads : " Go prophesy against the inhabitants of the city of idolatry, etc.," and " Gomer, daughter of raisin-cakes," *i.e.* ardent worshipper of Baal.** Kimchi suggests that Gomer was a well-known harlot of the prophet's time. But no symbolical meaning attaches to the word, since the prophet gives none, although to the others he gives it, and since the emphasis rests upon the children rather than upon the mother. In this case Gomer is a historical person,†† and Diblaim may refer to her father, or to her home, *bath* having both usages ; cf. Diblathaim, a city of Moab, Nu. 33⁴⁶ Je. 48²².—*And bore him a son*] Some Mss. (*v.s.*) omit " him " ; in any case, the context demands that the son be one born in sin, though recognized for the mother's sake. Any son born while Gomer is recognized as his wife will be his son.—**4**. *Call his name Jezreel*] Four points may be noted : (1) The name is symbolical and refers to the great battle-ground (cf. Ju. 4¹³ ff. 6³³ ff. 7¹ ff. 1 S. 29¹ ff.) on which Jehu had massacred the family of Ahab (2 K. 9, 10). In giving this name to the bastard son, he plainly characterizes Jehu's act as wicked and ruinous. This opinion, differing from that of 2 K. 10³⁰, represents the opinion of Hosea and the moral reformers of his time, a century after the event. A century had given the prophets a better point of view. The cult of Jehu and his descendants was not one which the prophet of the period could endorse. (2) Per-

---

* Cal.	§ Ges., Mau.	** Riedel.
† Crocius.	‖ Hi.	†† Geb., Ew., Sim., *et al.*
‡ 𝕿, Marck, Schlier.	¶ Meier, cited by Sim.	

haps, as Nowack suggests, the prophet had before him Elijah's prediction of the downfall of Ahab's home on account of Naboth's blood (1 K. 21²⁰ ᶠᶠ·). (3) The prophet does not yet know, if we may judge from the name of the son as compared with the name of the daughter (v.⁶), that his wife is faithless to him.* (4) From the words that follow : *I will avenge the blood of Jezreel upon the house of Jehu, and will cause the kingdom of Israel to cease*] it appears that Hosea expected the end of Jehu's dynasty and the end of the kingdom to come at the same time. As a matter of fact about twenty-one years (743–722 B.C.) passed before the kingdom ceased to exist, and during this period six kings sat upon the throne. This is all the more interesting in view of the fact that the prophet himself lived for some time after the death of Zechariah, and might easily have changed this definite expression which was not fulfilled to one more nearly in accord with the facts ; which goes to show that neither the prophet nor his contemporaries were accustomed to place emphasis upon the letter of prophetic speech. While, on the other hand, it is clear from history that with the fall of Jehu's dynasty the end in the larger sense had begun to show itself. — **5.** *The bow of Israel*] *i.e.* power (cf. Gn. 49²⁴ Je. 49³⁵ Jb. 29²⁰). — *In the valley of Jezreel*] Jezreel was the scene of the slaughter of Ahab's family by Jehu ; hence the valley of Jezreel is selected as the most fitting place for the infliction of vengeance for this deed. † — **6.** *And she bare a daughter*] Now the prophet has discovered the unfaithfulness of his wife, for he is instructed : *Call her name No-pity*] Literally, *She is not pitied* or *loved*, an independent sentence used as a proper name ; the explanation follows : *I will no longer have pity* (or *love*) *for the house of Israel, that I should at all forgive them*] Other renderings of the last clause are : (1) but will utterly take them away ; ‡ (2) but I will take away from them (everything) ; § (3) but I will completely forget them ; ‖ (4) but I will lift up my hand (in solemn oath) against them.¶ Marti omits this clause. — **7.** *But I will have pity upon the house*

---

* So We., WRS., Kue., Now. ;. but cf. Che. (*v.s.*).

† Meinhold, p. 64, treats v.⁵ as a later addition.

‡ Hd., AV., *et al.*   § Hng., Pu., *et al.*   ‖ 𝔙, Scholz, *et al.*   ¶ Abarb.

of Judah] This verse is from a later hand * because (1) it occasions an interruption in the description of the prophet's domestic history, and its connection with Yahweh and Israel; (2) the phrase "Yahweh their God" does not occur in pre-Deuteronomic literature; (3) other verses relating to Judah are suspicious; (4) it reflects the deliverance of Judah in Sennacherib's time (701 B.C.). — *And will deliver them by Yahweh their God*] The interpolator apparently forgets that he is representing Yahweh himself as speaking, and thus drops into the use of the third person. — *And not . . . by bow, nor by sword, nor by equipment, nor by horses, nor by horsemen*] This repudiation of all human help and this absolute confidence in Yahweh's ability and willingness to deliver his people in miraculous ways represent a characteristically late conception (cf. Ez. 39$^{1-10}$ Jo. 2^{32} 3$^{14-17}$ Zc. 14$^{3\,ff.}$). —
8. *And she weaned . . . and bare a son*] The period of time between the birth of the first child and that of the third would cover from six to eight years, since children were not weaned until they were two or three years old.† — *Call his name Not-my-people, for ye are not my people and I am not your God*] This expresses the complete estrangement existing between Israel and Yahweh, and Yahweh's purpose to leave Israel to its fate. This translation involves a slight change of text (*v.s.*) which seems to be demanded by the context. 𝕳𝕲𝕿 "I will not be to you" furnishes essentially the same thought.

2. תחלת דבר] Cstr. foll. by relative clause with relative omitted; two possible constructions: (1) the beginning of that which Yahweh spoke, cf. Ps. 81^6 Jb. 18^{21} (Ma., Mau., Sharpe); or (2) in the beginning when Yahweh spoke, cf. Gn. 1^1 = In the beginning when God created, etc., Ps. 4^8 90^{16}; GK. 130*d*; H. 8, 2*e*; Kö. 385*h* (Ew., Ke., Now.). Other constructions have been suggested: (1) to regard ד׳ חי as in apposition with בימי (v.^{1}) = "In the days of Jeroboam, etc., in the beginning when Yahweh spoke, etc."; but in this case we should expect a repetition of the prep. ב with חי and the omission of ו before בימי; (2) to take the phrase as the subject of the preceding verse, "In the days of Jeroboam, etc. (was) the beginning of

---

* So We.; Sta. *Gesch.* I. 577; Co. *ZAW.* VII. 285; Kue. *Einl.;* Gieseb. *Beiträge*, 213; Schwally, *ZAW.* X. 227; Che. in WRS. *Proph.* p. xx.; Oort, *ThT.* XXIV. 345 f.; Now., GAS., Gu., Seesemann, Meinhold, Marti; but cf. Kö. *Einl.* 309; Böhmer, *ZwTh.* XLV. 5.

† Cf. *ZDPV.* IV. 65; Now. *Arch.* I. 171.

that, etc."; (3) to make תחלת the subj. of what follows, "the beginning
which Yahweh spoke with Hosea was that Yahweh said to Hosea"; (4) to
treat the clause תחלת . . . בהו׳ as a gloss, and, connecting vs.[1 and 2], to read
(omitting ו), "In the days of Jeroboam, etc., Yahweh said to Hosea" (Hi.).
Other readings have been suggested for דבר, viz. דַּבֵּר (𝔅), inf. const.; דְּבָר
(𝔊𝔖𝔗); and also דָּבָר as a noun, cf. שֶׁלֶם and Je. 5¹³ (Merc., Hd.). — [בהושע]
On the following pisqa, or space, cf. Baer's note, p. 59; GK. 17 e; and Weir,
Hebr. Text, 94.   This is one of the twenty-eight verses in which pisqa is
inserted immediately after athnah. — [קח לך] For other cases of zeugma see
2²⁰ ᵇ Gn. 1¹¹ 1 S. 1²¹ ᵇ Je. 19¹ Ez. 6⁹ (cf. Kö. *Stil.* 122 f.). — [אשת זנונים] On
pl. in abstr. to express intensity, GK. 124 f.; H. 3, 2 *b*; Kö. 261 *d*; Ew.⁸ 179;
on the use of annexion to express characteristic qualities, GK. 128 *p*; Kö. 335 *a*.
— [זנה תזנה] Intens. inf. abs.; the impf. (a fut. in 𝔊 and 𝔅) is a freq. of the
pres.; H. 21, 2; GK. 107 *g*. This word זנה as distinguished from נאף means
to commit fornication, and is used almost wholly of the woman, either married
or unmarried (used of man only in Nu. 25¹, with הָעָם as subj.); while נאף means
to commit adultery, and is used usually of the man, always with another man's
wife; sometimes of the woman (Lv. 20¹⁰ Ho. 4¹³ f., etc.). — [מאחרי] Lit. *from
after*, cf. Dt. 7⁴ 2 S. 7⁸ 20² Is. 59¹³; frequent constr. for *from going after*,
used of those who abandon a person or party whom they have before followed; Kö. 213 *d*. — **3.** [בת דבלים] On cstr. cf. Kö. 306 *m*. — **4.** [יזרעאל] *God
sows;* cf. similar formations in ישמעאל, ירפאל, ישראל; Lag. *BN.* 131. — [ופקרתי]
ו marks apod. after prec. protasis, עוד מעט (cf. ושברתי, v.⁵); GK. 112 *oo*
and 143 *d*; Kö. 367 *p*. — [דמי] On force of pl., Kö. 259 *c*. — **5.** [והיה] The
familiar formula, GK. 112 *y*; Dr. § 121, *Obs.* 1; H. 25, 4. — [עמק יזרעאל] The
prop. name is used in this paragraph of the city, the plain, and the son of
Hosea; for other examples of the plain, Jos. 17¹⁶ Ju. 6³³; cf. also Ho. 2². ²⁴. —
6. [ויאמר] Either impers. or with the subj. (Yahweh) to be supplied. — [לא רחמה]
This has been taken as a Pu. ptcp. with מ dropped, but the regular negative
with the ptcp. is אין; it is probably a pausal form of the pf. 3 sg. f. (cf. Is. 54¹¹
Pr. 28¹³).   On this use of the neg. in proper names, GK. 152, note 1;
Kö. 352 *p*. — [לא עוד] = Lat. *non jam*. — [אוסיף ארחם] Verbal appos.; H. 36,
2; GK. 120 *g*.   On the transl. *pity* or *love*, the Grk. transl. (*v.s.*) vary, 𝔊 using
for ארחם, ἐλεῆσαι; Complut. ἀγαπῆσαι (cf. Paul, in Rom. 9²⁵).   The word is
used of the love of a father for his son (Ps. 103¹³), and of God for man
(Is. 30¹⁸). — [כי נשא ונו׳] כי indicates result (Mau., Hi., Ew., Sim., Ke., Che.,
Now., GAS.; Kö., 395 *b*), and is not adversative (𝔊𝔗𝔅, New., Hd.), while נשא
here = עון נשא = *take away guilt* = *forgive* (Kö. 209 *b*).   Cf. this usage with
acc. in Ex. 32³² Ho. 14³ Mi. 7¹⁸, etc.; but also as here with עון omitted and
ל of person, Gn. 18²⁶ Nu. 14¹⁹ Is. 2⁹ Ps. 99⁸. — **7.** [ואת־בית יה׳] Emph. being
suggested in contrast with בית יש׳ (v.⁶).   It is easy to see the origin of this
gloss. — [ביהוה אלהיכם] Cf. 12⁷ Zc. 10¹² Is. 26¹³ 45¹⁷ Ps. 18³⁰ 44⁶. — [בקשת ונו׳]
Note the arrangement of the five nouns: (1) *by bow and by sword*, (2) *and
by battle*, (3) *by horse and by horsemen;* war includes all the others and
is altogether superfluous in the list, especially in the middle of it.   Now.

and Marti om. it ; Che. translates "equipment of war." Perhaps the thought
is to be divided thus : "and I will not deliver them by bow nor by sword;
nor in battle by horse nor by horsemen." In any case the rhythm demands
that וכמלחמה go with the two following instead of, as according to the
accents, with the two preceding nouns.

§ 3. The purchase of Gomer as a slave, and her retention "many days." 3[1-5].

The prophet was compelled by his love for
Gomer, faithless as she was, to purchase her, out of the depths of
infamy into which she had fallen, at the price of a slave. He does
not, however, at once reëstablish the old relationship ; she is to
be disciplined, to lead a life shut off from men, even from her
husband. This period of seclusion will last "many days." The
prophet is led to see in this also (1) a parallel of Yahweh's
treatment of Israel ; and (2) this together with the first act of the
domestic tragedy constitutes his call to preach, and furnishes him
the fundamental factor in his preaching.

The literary form of this section is distinctly poetic. In no portion of the
book is the parallelism more marked, or more perfect. The first person is
employed instead of the third, as in chap. 1. There are three strophes of 6,
6, and 5 lines, in which the trimeter movement prevails. The first (v.[1])
describes the faithlessness of both Gomer and Israel; the second (vs.[2, 3]) is
devoted to Gomer, picturing her degradation and seclusion; the third (v.[4])
is devoted to Israel, picturing her degradation and seclusion. V.[5] is a
later addition (v.i.) In this piece, which stands closely related with the
contents of chap. 1, both in form and thought, the artistic element is
seen in (1) the distribution of the contents into the three strophes (v.s.);
(2) the regularity of the rhythm (falling to a dimeter only once, in ואמר
אליה); (3) the parallelism; (4) the use of poetical phrases like אהבת רע
מנאפת; (5) the use of rare and poetical words, like אשישי (v.[1]) and לתך
(v.[2]); (6) the use of the first person throughout; (7) the assonance prevailing in the closing lines of each strophe, viz. the recurrence of ים֖ in lines
5 and 6 of strophe 1; of י֖ in lines 4–6 of strophe 2; and of אין in lines 3–5
of strophe 3.

1. אהבת רע] Ⓖ ἀγαπῶσαν πονηρά (= אֹהֶבֶת רַע); so Ṡ (so also Hermann,
SK. 1879, p. 515; the reading אֲהֻבַת is adopted by Mich., Oort; Patterson, *Hebr.* VII. 194; Gu.; Volz, *ZwTh.* XLI. 331; Oet., Marti); but 'A.
ἠγαπημένην τῷ πλησίον; Σ. ὑφ᾽ ἑτέρου (= אַחֵרֶת). Gr. רֵעָה. Hal. אֹהֲבַת רֵעִים.
Bach. (foll. Benary) points אֲהֲבַת = *with the love of a friend*, and om. ומנאפת
as a gloss on זנוּי, suggesting that the whole expression is a later correction
made to offset the narrative of the prophet's relation to Gomer in chap. 1.

—'שי בני] Bab. Cod. בית ש'.—**2.** ואכרה] 𝔊 καὶ ἐμισθωσάμην (= וָאֶשְׂכְּרֶהָ);
so 𝔖 (so also Hal.).— לחך שערים] 𝔊 νέβελ οἴνου (= נֵבֶל שֵׁכָר); so Syr.-Hex.
𝔖 om. the first שערים. Gr., foll. 𝔊, יין נבל (so We. (?), Oort, *Em.*).—אשישי
ענבים] Gr. אשרים וחמנים.(?).—**3.** לי חשבי] 𝔙 *expectabis me;* so Σ. προσδο-
κήσεις με.— לאיש] 𝔊ᴬᴼ, ἀνδρὶ ἑτέρῳ.—אליך וגס־אני] 𝔙 *sed et ego expectabo
te;* 𝔊𝔖 om. גם. We. inserts אבוא לא before אליך (so Gr., Now., Oort, *Em.*;
cf. AE. and Ki., who supplied it in thought). Linder (*SK.* 1860, pp. 739 f.;
cf. Riedel, אלך לא) substitutes אֵלֵךְ for אליך. St. adds איננו after אני. Bach.
inserts אֵל with some such voluntative as אבואה implied. Oet. לָךְ אֲנִי וגם, or
אֵלָי אֲנִי וגם, taking אני as imv. of אנה, *to sigh.* Read אליך אֵינֶנִי וגם (cf. Marti);
for the idiom אל אין, cf. Gn. 31⁵.—**4.** שר ואין מלך אין] Co. and Now. om.
as gloss.—מצבה] 𝔊 θυσιαστηρίου (= מזבח); so 𝔖𝔙. Other Greek versions,
στήλης.—ותרפים אפור ואין] 𝔊 οὐδὲ ἱερατίας οὐδὲ δήλων, which latter word
represents הָאֵפֹים elsewhere, *e.g.* Dt. 33⁸ 1 S. 14⁴¹ (Gr.; cf. Che. *Crit. Bib.*).
'A. καὶ ἀκούοντος δι' ἐνδύματος καὶ διὰ μορφωμάτων; 𝔖 ܣܡܠ ܟܣܐ ܐܒܢ̈ܝ;
ܣܡܐܠ ܣ(ܣ); 𝔙 Σ., Θ. simply transliterate the Hebr.—**5.** פחדו] 𝔊 ἐκστή-
σονται; Σ. ἐπαινέσωσι; 𝔖 ܣ.ܢܠܝ.—הימים באחרית] 𝔙 *in novissimo dierum.*
V.⁵ as a whole comes from a later period (so Stärk, *ZAW.* XI. 249; Co.
ZAW. VII. 285, and *Einl.* 172; Oort, Volz, Now.; Marti, *EB.* 2122; but
cf. Seesemann, 42 and Now.²); this appears from (1) the lack of anything
in the narrative of Hosea and his wife to which the statement here might
correspond. Hosea, clearly, did *not* take back his wife; he went only so far
as to place her in seclusion. Not a word in the narrative points to her re-
instatement in the family. (2) The tone and contents of this verse accord
completely with those of 2¹⁻³·⁹·¹⁶ᶠ·, which for many reasons must be treated
as of later origin (*v.i.*). (3) The language of the verse points to a later
time: (*a*) פחד occurs only in Dt., Je., Ps., Pr., Jb., late parts of Is., and
Mi. 7¹⁷ (a late passage), where the usage here is exactly paralleled;
(*b*) הימים אחרית occurs besides in Dt., Je., Ez., Dn., Is. 2² (Mi. 4¹) Gn. 49¹
Nu. 24¹⁴—the last two passages having been edited late (cf. Stärk, *ZAW.*
XI. 247 ff.); (*c*) מל' דויד,—the expectation of a Messianic king is of later
origin, having its beginning with Isaiah; and the name David is not applied
to him until the days of Jeremiah and Ezekiel. Moreover, the full writing
דויד is late (this phrase is taken as an interpolation by We., Sta. *GVI.* I. 577;
Gu., Val., Seesemann, Now.², Meinhold); (*d*) טוב, as applied to Yahweh, is
found only in later writings, *e.g.* Je., Ne., Ps., Is. 40–66.

III. 1. *Once more go, love (this) woman*] The עוד is thus to be
taken with לך,* and not with ויאמר in contrast with "in the beginning" (1²).† The "woman" is unquestionably the same woman,

---

* So the accents, 𝔊𝔖𝔙, Cal., Merc., Ma., Hi., Sim., Wü., Or., Che., Bach., Gu.,
We., Now., GAS., Marti.

† Ew.(?) Umb.; Oort, *ThT.* XXIV. 355 (who shows that in the majority of cases
עוד follows its verb); Gr.

Gomer, described in chap. 1,* because (1) she is later defined as an adulteress; (2) she plays the part, in parallelism with Israel, represented by Gomer; (3) *her*, of *and I bought her* (v.^{2}), refers to a particular woman, viz. the one described in v.^{1}; (4) if this is another woman, why is not some reference made to the fact? (5) the introduction of two women would entirely spoil the essential thought. The only considerations for supposing this a different woman† are (1) the lack of an article with אשה; but *v.i.*; (2) the lack of historical data concerning the treatment of the first wife, but, on any hypothesis, the account must be reckoned meagre and defective; (3) the money of v.^{2} is the dowry, but this is, in itself, a wrong assumption; *v.i.* In order to avoid the force of the evidence which chap. 3 furnishes for the prevailing interpretation, it has been argued that the chapter is from a later date, ‡ because (1) in 1^2 and in chap. 2 the marriage relation is between Yahweh and the land, but in 3^1 between Yahweh and the *sons of Israel;* Hosea might have learned to substitute *Israel* for *land*, but not *sons of Israel;* the latter involves such a weakening of the figure as is scarcely possible in the imagination of one man; (2) in 3^1 the Israelites are said to have turned to "other gods," while elsewhere Hosea speaks only of images of Yahweh set up at local shrines which he never accredits with real existence as gods; (3) chap. 3 represents Hosea as arriving at the thought of Yahweh's love for wicked Israel; if he had done so, this thought must have ruled his later utterances; but, on the contrary, no such thought appears; the opposite feeling is rather dominant (cf. 9$^{15, 17}$ 13^{14}); (4) chap. 3 is in reality an allegorical narrative which was added to the literal account of facts in chap. 1 at a later date. It is evident that, either intentionally or otherwise, something has been omitted, viz. how Gomer came into the situation in which chap. 3 finds her. Did she abandon her husband? or, did

---

* Geb., Burkius, Stuck, Ew., Hd., Kurtz, Pu., Che., Paton (*JBL.* XV. 15), We., Gu., Now., GAS., Hal.

† Schmidt, Bauer, Ma., Eich., New., Ke., Or., Seesemann, Marti.

‡ So Volz, *ZwTh.* XLI. 321–5; cf. also Marti, *EB.* 2123, note 2, and in his *Dodekapropheton,* who makes it a later addition intended as an allegory concerning Israel, chap. 1 having been taken as relating to Judah; in which case Hosea had two wives, one literal, viz. Gomer (= Judah), one allegorical (chap. 3)= Israel; cf. Ez. 23.

he drive her from his house? — *Beloved of a paramour and an adulteress*] The first words are read *loving evil* (*v.s.*), a general term followed by one more specific (but see Nowack) ; *loving a lover, i.e.* one not her husband (*v.s.*), (cf. the use of אהבי in this verse) ; *loved by her husband,** thus making her sin all the greater (cf. רֵעַ Ct. 5[16], and the parallelism in the next member in which Yahweh's love for Israel is indicated) ; *with the love of a friend, like,* etc. (*v.s.*). The 𝔐 is, however, to be preferred,† and, if adopted, greatly intensifies the degradation into which the woman had fallen. The thought is, go love this woman, disgraced and fallen as she is. רֵעַ means *paramour* also in Je. 3[1] La. 1[2]. ‡ — *As Yahweh loves the sons of Israel*] This modifies the principal verb of the command : Love her, and in so doing you will only be doing what Yahweh does for Israel under similar circumstances. — *Although they turn to other gods*] Cf. 2[7. 12 f. 16 f.] ; these gods were the Canaanitish Baalim who were looked upon as the givers of the products of the soil. — *And are lovers of cakes of grapes*] A clause parallel with the preceding, and describing, not the gods § (who were foreign and lovers of, etc.), but the Israelites, ‖ who, in becoming lovers of *raisin-cakes*, are adopting the customs of the Canaanitish cult in their worship of Yahweh. While elsewhere (1 S. 25[18] 2 S. 6[19]) this phrase refers to an ordinary article of food, although in the latter case, doubtless, associated with a sacrificial feast, it is here used with some sarcasm, as one of " the Dionysiac features " of the worship of the gods ¶ who were supposed to be the givers of the grapes. For the rendering *flagons of wine,* and the interpretation of it as a reference to ordinary debauchery,** there is no support. — **2.** *And so I bought her to me*] This is the inexplicable point in the entire transaction. We may only guess why the purchase was necessary. There are three possibilities : (1) she had been divorced, and was now the wife of another ; but if this were the case, according to Je. 3[1 ff.] she could not have returned to her former husband even if the second had died (cf.

---

* Rashi, Cal., Schmidt, Bauer, Ma., Stuck, Ros., Ke.

† AE., Os., Merc., Geb., Eich., Mau., Ew., Hd., Sim., St., We., Now.

‡ Che.   § Hi.

‖ Ew., Hd., Sim., Pu., Ke., Schm., St., Or., Val., Gu., Now., GAS., Marti.

¶ WRS. *OTJC.*[1] 434.   ** AE., Ki., Cal.

Dt. 24$^{1-4}$) ; perhaps, however, this law was not yet in existence in Hosea's times ; * or (2) she had actually become the slave-concubine of some one, and the price paid is the price of a slave ; or (3) the whole proceeding is exceptional, and a price is paid merely to prevent altercation with the man with whom she has been living.† In any case, to regard the money as the price paid for a slave ‡ is easier than to understand that the prophet here describes : (1) the provision which he makes for a decent support until she shall be fully reinstated, § or (2) the dowry which always goes with a marriage. ‖ — *For fifteen pieces of silver, and a homer of barley, and a lethek of barley*] Five difficulties present themselves here : (1) the unknown word "lethek" (*v.i.*) ; (2) the absence of the preposition ב (= price) from the words "homer" and "lethek" ; (3) the apparent uselessness of the repetition of the word "barley" ; (4) the lack of any explanation for the payment of this price partly in money and partly in grain ; (5) the uncertainty as to the value of barley. The text is clearly suspicious. The piece of silver is, as usual, the shekel (= 75 cents(?)). A homer = 10 ephahs (cf. Ez. 45^{11}) = 30 seahs = 8 bushels. A seah of barley, according to 2 K. 7^{18}, was worth one-half a shekel ; but this was at the close of a siege. The "lethek" (*v.i.*) by tradition = one-half of a homer. Accepting this traditional valuation of the "lethek," and rating the seah at one-third of a shekel, the price of the grain would be a second 15 shekels. The value of a slave (Ex. 21^{32}) is 30 shekels, the sum here named. There is no good basis for ⅏'s *bottle of wine* (*v.s.*).¶ — **3.** *Many days shalt thou sit still for me*] *Sitting still* is intended to be the opposite kind of life to that which she has been pursuing (cf. Is. 30^7 Je. 8^{14}). The designation is emphatic, but indefinite. The purpose of this quiet and secluded life is a moral discipline, which in the end will prepare her "*for me*," *i.e.* to resume her former position as wife. The

---

* Now.   † Che.   ‡ Hes., Ew., Hd., Or., We.

§ Os., Geb., Po., Pu., Hux., Patterson (*Hebr.* VII. 220) ; cf. Cal., who makes the money a purchase price, and the grain provision for the wife.

‖ Ma. (the woman being another than Gomer), Ros., Stuck, Theiner, Mau.

¶ As a curiosity of interpretation may be cited the view of AE. that the 15 pieces of silver = the 15 kings, beginning with Rehoboam, and counting the sons of Josiah as one, the חמר and לתך being the chief priests of the kingdom of Judah who were in Jerusalem.

prophet adds three specifications to this general statement, which throw light upon this purpose : *thou shalt not play the harlot; thou shalt not have a husband; nor will I be to thee*] This is climactic. The first specification goes without saying ; but two others follow : she may not have another husband, a thing in itself entirely proper ; and, stronger yet, her own husband will grant her no intercourse, she is restrained " from even the legitimate gratification of her natural instincts " (Cheyne) ; she must give up her licentious life ; the proper conjugal life is denied her " many days." Literally, *thou shalt not be to a man* (cf. Ru. 1¹² Lv. 22¹² Nu. 30⁷ Dt. 24², etc.), an ordinary expression for marriage. The third clause reads literally according to the present text, *and also I unto you;* according to the text as amended, *nor will I be unto thee* (*i.e.* as a husband). This has been treated in many ways (*v.s.*) : (1) " And also I shall be so unto you," *i.e.* he, the prophet, will have no connection with any other woman ; * (2) " And yet I am kind unto thee " ; † (3) " And also I, even I, shall not be unto you " (*v.s.*), but the repetition of the pronoun is not probable ; (4) " And also I will go away from thee " (*v.s.*) ; (5) " And also I . . . not unto thee " (inserting אֵל, *v.s.*) ; (6) " And also I will be against you " ; ‡ (7) " And also I will not be unto thee," the force of לֹא being carried over from preceding clause ; § (8) " And also I will not come in unto you " (*v.s.*). —**4.** *For it is many days that the sons of Israel shall sit still*] In other words, like Gomer, — like Israel ; *i.e.* Israel shall be put in seclusion, retention, until she shall have acquired a new spirit. As in the preceding case the time is indefinite ; the discipline consists in certain deprivations ; and as before, these deprivations are distinctly designated in climactic order : — (1) *Without king and without prince*] The king and prince represent the rulers of the state (cf. Ex. 3¹⁶ 2 S. 19¹¹ 1 K. 8¹ 20⁷ Je. 26¹⁷, also Ho. 7³ 8¹⁰ 13¹⁰, where king and prince occur together). If they are here viewed as " lovers " with whom Israel has been faithlessly dallying, the demands of the context will be satisfied ; ‖ and Hosea seems to regard them in 1⁴ as guilty of injury to Israel. Others think this is too forced and prefer

---

* Che., GAS.   † Ew.   ‡ Wü.   § Mau., Reuss.   ‖ We., Che.

to regard the words as a gloss (*v.s.*). (2) *Without sacrifice and without pillar*] For *sacrifice* 𝔊𝔖𝔙 read " altar." The conse-crated pillar * was a stone erected as an abode or sanctuary for the Deity at any place where Deity had clearly manifested its presence and power. There were ' pillars ' at Shechem (Jos. 24²⁶), Bethel (Gn. 28¹⁸ ᶠᶠ·), Gilead (Gn. 31⁴⁵ ᶠᶠ·), Gilgal (Jos. 4⁵), Mizpah (1 S. 7¹²), Gibeon (2 S. 20⁸), En-rogel (1 K. 1⁹). They were a common feature of Canaanitish, Phoenician, and Arabic worship, and in early times were in good repute among the Hebrews, being a regular accompaniment of every sanctuary ; but the later legislation prohibited them as idolatrous (Dt. 12³ 16²² Ex. 23²⁴ 34¹³). A part of Jehu's work as the champion of Yahweh was the destruction of the " pillars " of Baal (2 K. 10²⁶ᶠ·). Two of these sacred stones were discovered in 1900 by Professor George L. Robinson near the road up to the high place at Petra.† " Sacri-fice " and " pillar " make a pair representing worship, or the work of the priest. (3) *Without ephod and teraphim*] These represented means of discovery of the divine will and were used in worship. The ephod ‡ was an image of the deity. This appears most plainly (1) from the account of the making of an ephod by Gideon (Ju. 8²⁶ ᶠ·), for which 1700 shekels of gold were used, which was ' set up ' (יַצֵּג) in Ophra and became an object of worship : (2) from the statement that the sword of Goliath was hung behind the ephod at Nob (1 S. 21⁹), showing that the ephod stood out from the wall and was not a garment hung on the wall ; (3) from its connection with teraphim and with graven and molten images (Ju. 17¹⁻⁵ 18¹⁴· ¹⁷· ¹⁸· ²⁰). § The ephod was probably

---

* Whitehouse in *DB.*, art. " Pillar "; We. *Reste arab. Heidenthums* ², 101, 171 ; Now. *Arch.* I. 91, 192, 261 f.; II. 15, 18 f.; Benz. *Arch.* (Index) ; WRS. *Sem.* 203 ff., 457 ; G. F. Moore, art. " Massebah," *EB.* III.; Dozy, *Die Israeliten zu Mekka ;* Kue. *Rel. of Isr.* I. 390–5 ; Von Gall, *Altisraelitische Kultstätten ;* Evans, *Mycenaean Tree and Pillar Cult.*

† See *BW.* XVII. 6-16 ; S. I. Curtiss, *PEFQSt.* 1900, pp. 350–5.

‡ Sellin, *Beiträge*, II. 115 ff.; Baudissin, *Gesch. des alttest. Priestertums*, 205 ff.; Dr. *DB.* art. " Ephod "; Now. *Arch.* II. 21 f., 92 f., 118 ff.; Sm. *Rel.* (Index) ; Lotz, *PRE.*³ V. 402–6 ; Benz. *Arch.* (Index) ; Sta. *GVI.* I. 466, 471 ; We. *Pro.* 130 ; Foote, *Johns Hopkins Univ. Circulars*, XIX. No. 145, p. 40 ; G. F. Moore, *Judges*, 232, 380 ff., and art. " Ephod," *EB.* II.; Kö. *Hauptprobleme*, 59–63 ; Lag. *Mit.* IV. 17 ; Marti, *Rel.* 29, 101 ; Reuss, *Gesch. d. heilig. Schrift.* §§ 102, 139.

§ The phrase " to carry an ephod before me " in 1 S. 2²⁸ seems opposed to the an image of wood or stone, covered with gold or other precious metal, — hence its name אֵפוֹד (cf. אֲפֻדָּה, Is. 30²²) ; cf. the use of the same word for the garment, or covering, of the priest (Ex. 25⁷ I S. 2¹⁸). On the basis of this connection with the priestly ephod and of its relation to the sacred lot (1 S. 23⁹ ᶠᶠ· 30⁷ ᶠᶠ·) it is argued with much force that the primitive ephod was not an image, but a loin-cloth, or apron, containing pockets from which the lot was drawn.* The sanctuaries at Dan (Ju. 17 and 18) and at Nob (1 S. 21⁹ 23⁶) are mentioned as having ephods. The *teraphim* were penates, images of ancestors † (cf. 1 S. 19¹³· ¹⁶ Gn. 31¹⁹· ³⁴ ᶠ·). That they had human form appears plainly from the story of Michal's ruse in substituting the teraphim for David her husband. This, added to the fact that they were consulted for oracles (Ez. 21²¹ Zc. 10²), are mentioned alongside of האבות and הידענים (2 K. 23²⁴), and were common to both Aramaeans and Hebrews (Gn. 31¹⁹· ³⁴ ᶠ·), makes it probable that they were relics of ancestor worship. ‡ If Schwally's proposal to connect the word with רפאים (= *shades*) be accepted, no doubt remains as to their original significance. They came to have a place at the sanctuaries along with the ephod. Are these things regarded as ungodly and unauthorized ; has the use of them been idolatry, parallel with Gomer's adultery ; and are these the occasion of the captivity which is now predicted? Or, as marriage and conjugal intercourse (something under ordinary circumstances proper enough) were denied to Gomer for a certain period as a punishment for her sins, are these something which under ordinary circumstances are proper enough, but which in this case are taken away from Israel in order to punish her? Or does the prophet's thought include both Yahweh-worship and idol-worship? That is: in the same manner as Hosea's wife is to be restrained from all intercourse, both lawful and unlawful, so Israel is to be cut off from all worship, both true

idea of the ephod as an image of God; but the word לפני does not appear in 𝔊ᴮ and 𝔖.

* So T. C. Foote, " The Ephod," *JBL.* XXI. 1-47.

† Benz. *Arch.* 257, 382; Now. *Arch.* I. 260; II. 23; Sm. *Rel.* (Index) ; Reuss, *Gesch. u. s. w.* § 139.

‡ So Sta. *G VI.* I. 467; Schwally, *Leben nach dem Tode,* 35 ff.; Che.

and false.* Much turns on the answer given to these questions.
If the first is true, Hosea, looking at the case from the point of
view of Judah, regards the Northern kings as usurpers, and the
sacrifice and pillars as alien to the orthodox cult and as
the source of Israel's difficulties.† If the second is true, he
regards these things as legitimate and natural; he enters no
protest against them, just as he enters no protest against marriage; but for this very reason, the deprivation is all the more
severe, since it is to be a deprivation of what was legitimate
and not of what was illegitimate. ‡ In this case, as Wellhausen
says, "It is not without a touch of scorn that Hosea here with
an air of innocence enumerates maççeba, ephod, and teraphim
as something which will be sorrowfully dispensed with in exile."
— 5. *Afterward the sons of Israel shall return and seek* (or, *again
seek*) *Yahweh, their God.*] V.⁵ is an addition (*v.s.*, p. 216), and
must be so interpreted; cf. 2⁹·¹⁷. A reader, living at a time when
the period of seclusion is concluded, and realizing that Israel's
return was the next step in the manifestation of the divine grace,
adds the thought which makes more complete the wonderful statement in vs.¹⁻⁴. It is a picture of the very "last times." — *And
David their king*] This, interpreted from the point of view of
the Judaistic period, is not (1) merely a king of the Davidic
dynasty, *i.e.* the dynasty itself (cf. Am. 9¹¹); § but (2) the Messianic king, ‖ the second David, an idea which had its roots in
Isaiah's time, and thenceforward developed (cf. Ez. 34²³ 37²⁴ᶠ·
45⁸·⁹ Je. 30⁹). — *And they shall tremble before Yahweh and his
goodness*] The punishment inflicted will have been so terrible
that ever afterward, Yahweh will be approached with awe and

---

* So Stuck, Mau., Ew., Hd., Sim., Pu., Ke., Wü., St., *et al.* Cf. W. R. W. Gardner
(*AJSL.* XVIII. 178), who takes the three double expressions as a series of contrasts, viz. the *king*, God's representative; the *prince*, Baal's representative; *sacrifice*, God's offering; *pillars*, signs of Baal-worship; *ephod*, means by which God
revealed himself; *teraphim*, means by which Baalim were consulted. In short the
people were to be without God and his worship, but also without Baal and his
worship. But the use of the ephod was as truly an act of superstition as was that
of the teraphim.

† So Ros., Reuss, Or., Sharpe, Now.   ‡ So We., Che.

§ Ma., Ros., Mau., Hi., Sim.; Duhm, *Theol.* 63; Che.; Di. *Alttest. Theol.* 165;
WRS. art. "Hosea," in *Encyc. Brit.;* Or., Wü.

‖ ₵, AE., Os., Geb., Lu., Stuck, Hd., Ke., Marti.

trembling (cf. Ps. 119[161]) ; and not only Yahweh, but his goodness
(טוב), *i.e.* his blessing. — *In the end of the days*] Here, as in
Is. 2[2] (Mi. 4[1]) Dt. 4[30], and perhaps Je. 23[20], characteristic of a
post-exilic interpolation.* This great time, perhaps first suggested in Ezekiel's day, becomes in later prophetic thought the
date when all that is wrong will be set right.

1. [עור] Cf. עור קח לך, Zc. 11[15]; for other cases of עור prec. a finite vb., cf.
Ps. 84[5] Jb. 24[20] Ec. 3[16] 12[9] Je. 2[9] (Oort, *ThT.* XXIV. 355). Cf. GK. 142 *g*.—
[אשה] The article is lacking acc. to a usage common in Arabic of which several
cases are found in Hebr., called 'indeterminateness for the sake of amplification'; here expressed by *such a woman;* cf. בער, Is. 28[2]; גוי, Am. 6[14];
GK. 125 *c*; Reckendorf, *Die syntaktischen Verhältnisse des Arabischen,* 163 f.;
but cf. Kö. 293 *d.* — [אהבת רע] For construction, cf. Kö. 336 *o.* — י כאהבת
[את־בני] Inf. fem. with י for subj. and את־בני obj., GK. 115 f.; H. 29, 2 *c*; Kö.
229 *c* and 232 *a*. Barth (*NB.* I. 174 ff.), followed by BDB., retains pointing
of 𝔐, and regards it as a ptcp. act., citing several similar cases in Hebrew.
It cannot be denied that the renderings ordinarily adopted for אֲהָבַת do not
harmonize in paral. with this phrase; but cf. Bach.'s reading above. — [והם פנים
Circ. clause = *while they are,* etc., or *although they are ;* GK. 141 *e*; Dr. § 160;
H. 45, 1 *b*; Kö. 362 *p* ; הם is also subj. of אהבי. — [אלהים אחרים Cf. Ex. 20[8]
23[13] Dt. 5[7] 6[14] Jos. 23[16] 24[2] Ju. 2[12] 1 S. 8[8] Je. 1[16] 2 Ch. 7[19]. — [אשישי] The root is
אשש, *to found* (cf. أسس and Assyr. *ashâshu,* with same force). Thus it seems
to mean "cakes of *pressed* grapes." Here only is ענבים expressed; and here it
is evidently an offering to the gods (cf. Je. 7[18]). In 2 S. 6[19] (= 1 Ch. 16[3]) it is
spoken of as an article of food; so also in Ct. 2[5] where it seems to be regarded
as stimulating nourishment (cf. BDB., BSZ.; Ritter, *Erdkunde,* XV. 719, cited
by Benz. *Arch.* 92; Now. *Arch.* I. 237; WRS. *OTJC.* Lect. XI. note 7; Che.;
Riedel, pp. 15 f.). This meaning is questionable in Is. 16[7], where *Thes.* takes it
as = *foundations* (so 𝔖, Ki., Jarchi; but cf. De. on Is. 16[7] and Riedel, p. 15).
Cf. Che. *CB.* — **2.** [וָאֶכְּרֶהָ] Cf. 𝔊 (*v.s.*); if from כרה dag. forte
dirimens, GK. 20 *h*; Ew.[8] 28 *b*. — עָשִׂתׂר עֲרָכִים. [בסף] For use of sg., cf. H. 15, 3, rm. (*d*). For
omission of שקל, cf. Kö. 314 *h*, and *v.* Ex. 21[32] Nu. 7[18] Lv. 27[3 f.]. — [לתך] *a.λ.*
The Mishnah tradition that this measure = ½ כֹּר = ½ חֹמֶר is the only source of
information concerning it (cf. Levy, *NHWB.* II. 531). The corresponding
Syriac root seems to have no connection with this word (cf. Lag. *Or.* II. 32 f.;
Benz. *Arch.* 183; Now. *Arch.* I. 203). — [אליך] Cf. Kö. 319 *r* and 352 *u* for
explanation of construction here on the basis of 𝔐. — **4.** [אין] Circ. cl., cf.
𝔊, gen. abs. in this case; the repetition is intended to emphasize the monotonous emptiness which the sound of אין itself represents. — [תרפים] On significance of pl. form, cf. Kö. 263 *o.* — **5.** [את־דויד] The full writing is found regu-

---

* So Stärk, *ZAW.* XI. 252; Seesemann, 42; Now.[2]; cf. Meinhold.

larly in Zc., Ch., Ezr., Ne.; also in Am. 6⁵ 9¹¹ (both late passages), Ez. 34²³ Ct. 4⁴ 1 K. 3¹⁴ 11⁴· ³⁶ (these three verses are from R^d); cf. GK. 2, *v.* note 2, where the full writing in the Minor Prophets is called a caprice of the Massoretes. — ‏פחדו אל‎] Cf. Kö. 213 *a*.

§ 4. Israel's harlotry and her punishment therefor. 2⁴⁻⁷· 10-14. 15 (18). 19 [English, 2²⁻⁵· 8-12. 13 (16), 17].

Let Israel put away her harlotry, lest I destroy her; for she has sinned shamefully in entering into union with those whom she supposed to be the authors of her prosperity; and she has forgotten that it was I who gave her all these things. But I will take away my corn and wine and wool and flax; I will destroy her vines and fruit trees; yea, I will cause all her gladness to cease; I will punish her for her indulgence in unholy things. I will even cause these things to be forgotten.

This is (1) independent of chaps. 1 and 3, which go together; and (2) independent of the insertions from later times in vs.⁸· ⁹· ¹⁶· ¹⁷· ²⁰⁻²². ²³⁻²⁵· ¹⁻³. There is no very close connection between this and chaps. 1 and 3.

This piece may be treated as a literary unit (vs.⁴ᵇ· ⁶· ¹² being regarded as glosses; *v.i.*). Its thought is the simplest possible: *Israel has played the harlot; she shall be punished.* For the passages which have been inserted by later writers (four such insertions may be distinguished), *v.i.* It is made up of four strophes, 8, 9, 8, 9; and its movement is trimeter. This is almost perfect throughout. Strophe 1 (vs.⁴· ⁵) : Plead with your mother to put away her sin, lest I destroy her. Strophe 2 (vs.⁷· ¹⁰) : She has sinned in seeking the Baalim from whom she imagined she received benefit, not knowing that it was I who bestowed upon her all her comforts. Strophe 3 (vs.¹¹· ¹⁴) : Therefore I will take back these things which I have given her, the evidences of her prosperity, her corn and wine, her vines and fig trees. Strophĕ 4 (vs.¹³· ¹⁸· ¹⁹) : I will cause all joy to cease and will punish her for these indulgences, and their very names shall be expunged and forgotten. In this treatment the following modifications of the present text have been made: (1) 2⁸· ⁹· ¹⁶· ¹⁷, ²⁰⁻²², ²³⁻²⁵, ¹⁻³ are taken as four distinct and independent utterances and treated separately (see pp. 236–248); (2) 2⁴ᵇ (‏כי . . . אישה‎), v.⁶, v.¹⁰ (‏עשו לבעל‎), v.¹², v.¹⁴ (‏אשר נתנו לי מאהבי‎) are glosses; (3) v.¹⁸ is treated as a gloss; (4) v.¹⁴ is placed after v.¹¹, leaving v.¹³ and vs.¹⁵ ᵃⁿᵈ ¹⁹ in close connection. These passages will be considered in their proper places.

4. ‏ריבו‎] 𝕲 κρίθητε; 'A., Σ., δικάσασθε; 𝔙 *judicate;* in all, *judge,* rather than *plead;* cf. 𝔖. — ‏ותסר‎] 𝕲 καὶ ἐξαρῶ; so Ethiopic; 'A. ἀφελέτω. —

מפניה] 𝕲 ἐκ προσώπου μου; so Ethiopic; = מפני (so also Vol. and Loft., regarding 𝕸𝕿's change to 3 p. as made on theological grounds). — 5. פן] 𝕲 ὅπως ἂν, the opposite of 𝕸𝕿; but 'Α., Σ., Θ. μήποτε. — כמדבר... כארץ] Gr. and Hal. ב for כ. — ושתיה] 𝔖 om. — ציה] 𝖅 inviam. — 7. שקוי] 𝕲 πάντα ὅσα μοι καθήκει; similarly 𝔖; 𝕿 וכל פרנוסי. — 10. וכסף וגו] 𝕲 And silver I have multiplied for her. This one, however, made (things) of silver and gold for the Baal; 𝔖 and silver and gold I multiplied to her, and from it they made Baal; similarly 𝕿. Bach. עָשׂרוּ for עָשׂו. Oet., on basis of 𝕲 and Syr.-Hex., עָשְׂתָה. — 11. צמרי] 𝕲 τὰ ἱμάτιά μου. — לכסות] 𝕲 τοῦ μὴ καλύπτειν; cf. Sievers, Now.²; 𝖅 quae operiebant; 𝔖 ܠܡܟܣܝܘ ; Gr. מכפסות. — 12. מורי] 'Α. ἐκ χειρὸς αὐτῆς. — 14. האנתה] 𝕲 συκᾶς. — אתנה] We. אֶתְנָן (so Bach., Now., Oet., Marti). — ויער] 𝕲 μαρτύριον = לעד (Vol., Treitel). — 13. והשבתי] 𝕲 ἀποστρέψω (= הֲשִׁיבֹתִי). 𝕲 pluralizes all nouns of this verse and inserts καί between each pair except the first. — 15. להם ... אשר] 𝕲 ἐν αἷς ... αὐτοῖς; 𝖅 quibus; 𝔖 refers להם to ימי. — תקטיר] Now. and Marti, תְּקַטֵּר. — חליתה ... נומה] 𝕲 pl. — 18. תקראי] 𝕲 adds לי after the first vb. and renders both verbs καλέσει; so 𝖅, vocabit. Oort (Em.), תקרא. — בעלי] 𝕲 βααλείμ; 𝖅 Baali, both treating it as a proper name; 'Α. ἔχων με. Marti, foll. 𝕲 and Duhm. — 19. תקרא לאישה ולא תקרא עוד לבעלים. יזכרו] Gr. יזכירו (so Loft.). — שמות] 𝔖 sg. — בשמם] 𝔖 has sg. suff. Hal. om. this phrase. — מפיה] Gr. מפיהם.

II. 4. *Strive with your mother, strive*] Yahweh is represented as addressing the individual Israelites * (this is better than to understand merely the faithful Israelites†). The mother with whom they are to strive is the nation Israel as a whole. The repetition of the imperative gives intensity; cf. נחמו נחמו, Is. 40¹. It is with the mother, viz. Israel herself, that complaint must be made, not with Yahweh. — *For she is not my wife, and I am not her husband.*] This is not (1) the word of judgment pronounced, כִּי being = ὅτι ; ‡ nor (2) is it merely a parenthetical phrase inserted by the original writer by way of explanation ; § but rather (3) a gloss ; ‖ because it interrupts the connection between ריבו and ותסר, and because, as a matter of fact, Hosea does not dissolve all relation to his wife nor represent Yahweh as wholly abandoning Israel. — *That she put away her whoredoms from her face*] A clause depending closely upon

* So Cal., Grotius, Schmidt, Dathe, Bauer, Böckel, Mau., Hes., Ros., Hi., Sim., Ke., We.　　　　† Hux., Sharpe.　　　　‡ Geb., Ma., Ros.

§ Bauer, Böckel, Ew., Hd., Sim., Wü., Che.

‖ Volz, Now.; Marti om. only the latter half ; Now.² retains both clauses.

ריבו; this is the message which the children are asked to convey to the mother, because it is the mother's "whoredoms" that have brought shame and disgrace upon the children.   Noteworthy is 𝕲 *and I will take away her*, etc., *i.e.* by carrying her into captivity.* *From her face*,† rather than *from before her*, ‡ the former contrasting better with *breasts* of the following clause (cf. Hor. *Odes*, I. 19, ls. 7, 8).— *And her adulteries from between her breasts*] A strong parallel for the preceding, breasts here standing for shamelessness, while face there indicated obstinacy. § Cf. also Kimchi, who makes the breasts = the law, written and oral; Crocius, who makes face and breasts mean open and secret sins, *i.e.* the life and the heart; Hitzig, who, following Kimchi and Abarbanel, understands *whoredoms* as the paint upon the face, and *adulteries* as the ornaments which hung down upon the breasts (cf. v.¹⁵).— **5.** *Lest I strip her naked*] Cf. Ez. 16³⁹. In five successive and climactic phrases there is pictured the punishment which awaits the adulteress, Israel. It is still Yahweh who speaks. The representation is at first true to the figure, and speaks of Israel as a woman; but almost imperceptibly it passes over in the latter part to the thought of the land. Stripping naked the adulteress was the custom of other nations (*e.g.* among the Germans ‖). According to Lv. 20¹⁰ and Dt. 22²² as interpreted by the Talmud, she was to die by strangling; but Ez. 16³⁹. ⁴⁰ (cf. John 8⁵) refers to death by stoning.— *And set her as in the day of her birth*] When Israel's history as a nation began, whether we date it from the time of the Egyptian bondage,¶ or from the time of her becoming independent (cf. Ex. 9¹⁸. ²⁴),** or from the time of the exodus,†† she was a nomadic people without house, or possession of any kind. This former low and hard condition will be hers again.— *And make her as the wilderness*] But now the writer identifies the nation and the land. Israel, *i.e.* her land, is to become a wilderness. ‡‡ This is better

---

* Theophylactus; see Wahrendorf, *In Theophylacti* ἀνεκδότους, *etc., super initium cap. II. Hoseae, etc.* (1702), p. 11.

† Schmidt, Böckel, Ros., Theiner, Mau., Hng., Hes., Hd., Ke., Or., Che., Now.

‡ Dathe, New.   § Che.   ‖ Tac. *Germ.* §§ 18, 19.

¶ Ki., Ke., Wü.   ** Sim., Now.   †† Cal., Hi.

‡‡ So Eich., Theiner, Hes., Hi., Sim., Che., We., Now.; Seesemann, p. 37.

than to read it *as in the wilderness*,* or to interpret the suffix
directly of the nation, thus made desolate.† — *And set her as
dry land*] A poetic parallel of the former clause, but stronger,
since the wilderness was not always a desert. — *And slay her
with thirst*] He still speaks of the land (cf. Ez. 19[13] Koran
30 : 18).   One finds important material for consideration in
this verse with its splendid climactic arrangement, with its
beautiful and natural blending of two ideas, land and people,
which were really one, with its representation of Israel's future,
so distinctly different from that of v.[16] in this same chapter. —
6. *And upon her children I will have no mercy, because they are
the children of whoredom*] This (1) is merely a repetition of
1[6] and 1[2]; (2) interrupts the very close connection between
vs.[5 and 7] (*v.i.*) ; (3) may not itself be treated as preceding v.[7] ;
(4) is inconsistent with the strophic structure. It is a gloss. ‡
A reader, seeing (v.[5]) that the land had been laid waste, added,
for the sake of completeness and in language already at hand,
a statement concerning the people of the land, the Israelites.
— **7.** *For their mother has become a harlot*] The change of
person from באמכם (v.[4]) is not unusual. This is the reason for
the dire punishment threatened in v.[5]. Of what now has Israel
really been guilty ? Not of worshipping the Baalim as gods
who existed in opposition to, or alongside of, Yahweh, as the
givers of the blessings of field and flock ; § but rather of having
put Yahweh in the place of the Baalim and having retained as
an essential element of the worship of Yahweh the rites formerly
carried on as a part of the cultus of the Baalim. They do worship Yahweh as the source of these material blessings, but they
have corrupted his worship with so much that pertains in reality
to the cultus of the Baalim, that they might as well be worshipping
the latter. ‖ — *She that conceived them has behaved shamefully*]
For this idea of acting shamefully, cf. Pr. 12[4] 17[2]. — *For she said,*

---

* So Jarchi, Böckel, Stuck.

† So *e.g.* Cal., Os., Merc., Schmidt, Geb., Dathe, Bauer, Ma., Ros., Schrö.,
New., Hng., Ew., Hd., Pu., Ke., Wü.

‡ So Volz, Now.; but cf. Marti, who om. only 6[b], and Now.[2], where the entire
verse is retained.

§ Böckel, Or., Che., Val., Gu., Seesemann.   ‖ We., Now.

I will go after my lovers] Israel's paramours were not the peoples round about,* nor the gods of these people ;† but the Baalim ‡ whose cult had completely corrupted the more pure Sinai-cult which had been Israel's in the early days. — *Who give me my bread and my water, my wool and my flax, my oil and my drink*] Three couplets, of which the first, *bread and water*, describes nourishment ; the second, *wool and flax*, clothing ; the third, *oil and drink*, satisfaction and happiness. It is the gods of the land that give these, hence they must be followed after. The word for *my drink* does not mean " strong drinks," § or artificial drinks in general ; ‖ but, although rare, has the meaning of drink in general, as in Ps. 102⁹ ; cf. its figurative meaning in Pr. 3⁸, the only other occurrence of the word. In view of the reference to *water* in connection with *bread*, and the frequent use elsewhere of the phrase *oil and wine*, drink may be taken here as = wine. — **10**. *For she has not understood that it was I who gave her the corn, etc.*] This verse fits so closely to v.⁷ that one can scarcely see how a separation ever arose. It is not to be taken as an interrogative sentence,¶ but as a declarative sentence, continuing the thought of v.⁷.** Corn, wine, and oil represented the wealth of Palestine (Dt. 7¹³ 11¹⁴, etc.). — *And multiplied her silver and gold*] Did Israel's silver and gold form part of the country's mineral resources ? Or did they come from the sale of the country's products, such as those just mentioned? The knowledge we have of ancient mining points to the latter, since in Syria proper there were no mines for gold. The gold came from Spain, India, Arabia, and perhaps South Africa. Silver was mined in Spain and in Upper Egypt. The single passage in the O. T. which refers to mining of any kind (Jb. 28) must have been written by one who had seen mines operated in other lands.†† However, gold and silver were used as media of trade in Palestine in the earliest times, as appears from references to them in the Tel-el-Amarna letters ; ‡‡

---

* 𝔗, Jer., Rashi, Ki., Ma., Grotius, Ros.   † Bauer.

‡ Böckel, We., Che., Or., Val., Gu., Now., Marti.

§ Ki., Schmidt, Ros., Stuck, New., Ke., Wü., Che., *et al.*   ‖ Mau., Hi., Hd.

¶ Ew., We.   ** Volz, Now., Marti.

†† See Hull, " Mines, Mining," in *DB.* ; cf. art. " Mines," *EB.* III.

‡‡ Letter 191, l. 10 ; 192, Reverse, l. 7 ; 239, l. 50 f. ; 265, l. 12 ; 280, l. 8.

and it was probably in exchange for the products of the land that gold and siver came to Palestine in Hosea's time. That there was much gold in Palestine is seen from the Black Obelisk of Shalmaneser, "The tribute of Jehu, son of Omri, silver, gold, basins of gold, bowls of gold, cups of gold, buckets of gold, lead, etc." Sennacherib also (Taylor Cylinder, col. III. 34 ff.) says of Hezekiah, "Along with thirteen talents of gold and eight hundred talents of silver I made him bring after me precious stones, etc." — *Which they have used for the Baal*] This has been taken to mean the overlaying of images with silver and gold (cf. Is. 30²²) ; * (2) the golden calves established by Jero-boam I., the clause in this case limiting only the preceding word "gold" ;† (3) molten images of the calf, found in the various high places; (4) gold offered to Baal. ‡ But in any case these words are a gloss as is shown by their loose connection (cf. the absence of the relative pronoun) ; by the use of the article with the singular of בעל ; by the 3d plural of the verb instead of the 3d feminine singular as in the preceding clause; and by their departure from the thought of the context which is con-cerned with Yahweh's actions rather than with those of Israel. §
— **11.** *Therefore I will take back again*] Cf. Gn. 26¹⁸ 2 K. 21³ 24¹ Je. 18⁴, in which as here שוב denotes ‖ "not merely the repetition of the same action, but also repeated occupation with the same object, though along a different line." — *My corn in its time, and my wine in its season*] The harvest season was not uniform throughout Palestine on account of the varying climatic conditions of the land ; but in general it began with the barley-harvest (2 S. 21⁹) early in April, and lasted about seven weeks (Dt. 16⁹). The beginning was marked by the Feast of Maṣṣoth and the close by the Feast of Ingathering. The gathering of grapes for eating began as early as June in some regions, but the vintage proper began in September and continued on into October. The vintage festival was the Feast of Booths.¶ — *And I will rescue my wool and my flax*] These

---

* Hd.   † Hi., Or., Che.   ‡ New., Hng.
§ So We., Now.; Marti om. also *and gold;* but, *per contra v.* GAS.   ‖ Sim.
¶ Now. *Arch.* I. 231, 236; Benz. *Arch.* 209, 212; Paterson, *DB.* I. 49 f.; Hogg, *EB.* I. 76.

gifts had hitherto been put to wrong uses and ascribed to wrong sources. By withdrawing them Yahweh would not only chastise Israel, but also teach her to recognize him as the bestower of these blessings. — *Given to cover her nakedness*] Cf. Ez. 16⁸. — **12.** *And now I will uncover her shame*] *i.e.*, and consequently, cf. 5⁷ 10³ Am. 6⁷ ; but this is only another form of expressing the thought of v.¹¹ᵇ, and interrupts seriously the consecution of vs.¹¹ᵇ ᵃⁿᵈ ¹³. The entire verse is to be taken as a gloss. — *In the presence of her lovers*] These must be the Baalim, whose actual existence seems to be taken for granted by the interpolator ; cf. Ps. 96⁴.*
— *And none shall deliver her out of my hand*] Israel's lovers, the false gods, must stand by and look upon her reproach without being able to render help of any kind. — **14.** *And I will lay waste her vines and her fig trees*] Cf. Jo. 1⁷. Here, as frequently, the vine and fig tree stand for the greatest blessings of God (Jo. 2²² 1 K. 4²⁵ Zc. 3¹⁰). Wool, flax, vine, and fig tree are representative of all the products of the earth and their removal signifies general destitution. — *Of which she has said, these are my rewards, which my lovers have given me*] *i.e.* the hire of the prostitute (cf. 9¹ Gn. 38¹⁷). — *And I will make them a thicket*] Another representation of desola- tion (cf. Is. 5⁶ 7²³ 32¹³ Mi. 3¹²), יער being here, however, not the dig- nified and stately forest (as in Is. 7² 10¹⁸ Dt. 19⁵ Je. 46²³ Ps. 96¹²), but the inaccessible brushwood (so also in 1 S. 14²⁵· ²⁶ Is. 21¹³ Je. 26¹⁸). — *And the beasts of the field shall eat them*] *i.e.* the wild beasts of the open country. — **13.** *And I will also cause to cease all her mirth, her feasts*] This verse should follow † v.¹⁴ instead of preceding it, as in 𝕸𝕿. The cessation of mirth and feasting is the climax, and not only logically but chrono- logically follows the desolation of the vine and the fig tree. Lit. *make to rest;* used in Ps. 46⁹ of war, Pr. 18¹⁸ of strife, Is. 16¹⁰ of shouting. In the earlier times joy and mirth were the most marked characteristics of sacrifice and feasts (Ex. 32⁵ ᶠ· Ju. 21¹⁹ ᶠᶠ· 1 S. 1³· ⁷· ¹³ ᶠᶠ·). — *Her mirth, her feasts*] *i.e.* the mirth of her feasts. The *feasts* were either the three annual feasts mentioned in Ex. 23¹⁴⁻¹⁷ (cf. Is. 9³ 29¹), ‡ or the great harvest festival of

---

* Cf. Marti, who retains the verse as a whole, but treats this clause as an inter- polation.   † So Volz, Now., Hal.   ‡ Wü., Che., *et al.*

which mirth was so conspicuous a feature (cf. Ju. 21[19] 1 K. 8[2]
12[32]).* This is the only one of the three great feasts which
is named in the historical books. For a similar threat see
Am. 8[10]. — *Her new moon, and her sabbaths and her festal assemblies*] The festival in connection with the first appearance
of the new moon probably dates back to a very early period
in Israel's history,† as appears from the fact that it and the
passover are the only feasts having no connection in origin and
significance with agriculture, and that it seems to have been an
occasion for clan reunions and sacrifices (1 S. 20[4 ff.]). It was
also regarded as a fitting occasion for visiting the prophets
(2 K. 4[23]). The ordinary occupations of life were suspended
on this day as also on the Sabbaths (Am. 8[5]). There seems
to have been connected with its celebration a large amount
of superstition and corruption which was objectionable to the
prophets, for Isaiah also threatens Israel with its removal (2[13 f.]),
while JE and Deuteronomy completely ignore it. However,
later legislation incorporated it in the regular sacrificial system
(Ez. 46[1-7] Nu. 28[11 ff.] 29[6] 1 Ch. 23[31] 2 Ch. 2[4], etc.). ‡ The *Sabbath* § is often mentioned alongside of the new moon (Am. 8[5]
Is. 1[13] 2 K. 4[23] Ez. 46[3]), and seems to have been closely connected with it originally, the new moon being observed on the
first day of the month, and the Sabbath probably on every
seventh day after. In course of time, however, the Sabbath
came to have more importance than the new moon, and its
recurrence on every seventh day became independent of any
relation to the new moon. The Sabbath was originally a day
of sacrifice and of propitiation of the deity, as appears from

---

* Now.; cf. We. *Prol.* 94 f.; Now. *Arch.* II. 150 f.; Benz. *Arch.* 468.

† This early origin is made certain if הלולים (Ju. 9[27]) be derived from הלל, *to
shine*, and thus connected with the Arabic *hilâl* = new moon. Thus the general
word for feast would originally have been used only of the new moon feast. So
Sprenger, *Leben u. Lehre d. Mohammads*, III. 527; Lag. *Orientalia*, II. 19 f.;
Now. *Arch.* II. 138 f.

‡ Now. *Arch.* II. 138 ff.; Benz. *Arch.* 464 f.; and art. "New Moon," *EB.* III.;
Abrahams, "New Moon," *DB.* III.

§ See especially Jastrow, "The Original Character of the Hebrew Sabbath,"
AJT. II. 312–352; cf. also We. *Prol.* 112–116; Now. *Arch.* II. 140–144; Benz.
Arch. 202, 465 f.; Harding, *DB.* I. 859; and other literature cited in my *Const.
Studies in the Priestly Element in the O. T.* (1902), 114 ff.

the regulations controlling corresponding days in Babylonia, and
from O. T. references to it in earlier days as a day of religious
observances (1 K. 4²³ Is. 1¹³ Ez. 46¹ᶠᶠ·), a day when trade ceased
(Am. 8⁵), and when the manna was withheld (Ex. 16²⁵), and the
day upon which the showbread was renewed (1 Ch. 9³²). The
rest from ordinary labors which was a consequence of this effort
to propitiate deity came to be in later days the most conspicuous feature of Sabbath observance. Two traditions exist in the
O. T. concerning the origin of the day : Ex. 20¹¹ traces it back
to God's resting after his creative work (cf. Gn. 2²), while Dt. 5¹⁵
makes it a memorial of the Exodus. *Festal assemblies* * is a
term used to designate a sacred season or feast ; literally it is
an appointed time or *place*. It is a broader term than חג, which
is properly applied only to feasts involving pilgrimages. It is
thus used of the Sabbath (Lv. 23²ᶠ·), the Passover (Lv. 23⁴ᶠ·),
the New Moon (Ps. 104¹⁹), the Year of Release (Dt. 31¹⁰), the
Day of Atonement (Lv. 23²⁷), the Feast of Unleavened Bread
(Lv. 23⁶), and the Feast of Booths (Dt. 31¹⁰ Ho. 12⁹). In Gn. 1¹⁴
this word is used probably of the sacred seasons as determined
by the moon's changes, rather than of the seasons of the year.
In Ho. 9⁵ it is used in a general sense in parallelism with *feast of
Yahweh*. Thus in the terms " feasts," " new moons," " Sabbaths,"
and " festal assemblies," the prophet has included every variety of
sacred feasts ; they are all to be brought to an end. — **15.** *And I
will visit upon her the days of the Baalim*] *i.e.* I will punish her
on account of the days, etc. *The days of the Baalim* is an
expression referring especially to the festivals just enumerated
and in general to the whole period during which corrupt Yahweh-
worship had prevailed, since the festivals and even the entire
cultus, though nominally carried on in honor of Yahweh, were
in reality, from the prophet's point of view, corrupt rites and
sensual orgies devoted to the Baalim.† — *In which she made
offering to them*] For this interpretation of קטר *v.i.* (p. 235).
— *And decked herself with her earrings and her jewels*] It was
a common Semitic custom to don special attire for all festive

---

* See *EB*. I. 346 ; BDB. 417 ; We. on Ho. 12¹⁰; Now, *Arch*. II. 155. Marti
om. this word as a gloss.

† Cf. We., Che., Marti.

and sacred occasions. The clothes worn in the performance of everyday duties must be either laid aside or thoroughly washed, lest they should defile the sanctuary; while clothes made holy by contact with holy things could not be worn afterwards in ordinary life, unless they were previously washed, since they would render holy, *i.e.* taboo, everything touched by them. Jewels, too, seem to have been a usual feature of the sacred dress; the Syriac word for "earring" means "the holy thing," and the word for "pearls" in the dialect of South Arabia seems to denote the same idea. Moreover, jewels were common as amulets.* — *And went after her lovers, and forgot me*] The nature of their Yahweh-worship was such as to give them an entirely false idea of the character of Yahweh; under his name they were virtually doing homage to the Baalim. — **18.** *And it shall be at that day*] A very common form for introducing a gloss. The reasons for regarding this as a gloss † to v.[19] are (1) the use of the terms *Ishi* and *Baali*, (2) the fact that it is in part a repetition of the thought of v.[19], (3) its metre differs from that of both preceding and following context, (4) it is superfluous in the strophic structure. — *Thou shalt call me Ishi*] *i.e.* my husband; this implies Israel's return to a proper understanding of her relation to Yahweh and of the kind of service acceptable to him, — a thought which lies beyond Hosea's outlook for his people. It gives the positive aspect of Israel's future conduct, which is represented only negatively in the next clause and in v.[19]. — *And shalt call me no more Baali*] *i.e.* my Baal; Hosea regularly uses the plural form *Baalim* when speaking of Canaanitish elements in the Yahweh-worship; the singular occurs only here and in the gloss to v.[10]. The two words *Ishi* and *Baali* express practically the same idea, but the use of the latter is condemned on account of its connection with the Baalim. — **19.** *And I will remove the names of the Baalim from her mouth*] Cf. Zc. 13[2]. This verse connects closely with v.[15]. Whereas in the past Israel has devoted herself assiduously to the cultus of the Baalim, thus neglecting the proper worship of Yahweh, in the coming days Yahweh will utterly destroy all

---

* WRS. *Sem.* 452 f.; Now.　　　　　† So We., Volz, Now.

trace and memory of Baal worship. — *And they shall no more
be mentioned by their names*] Their names even shall be forgotten.

4. ריבו ... ריבו] For other cases of epizeuxis, *v.* Is. 21⁹ 26⁸ 40¹ Je. 4¹⁹; cf.
Kö. *Stil.* 155 f. רִיב בְּ occurs in Gn. 31³⁶ Ju. 6³²; רִיב אֶל in Ju. 21²² Jb. 33¹³,
etc.; more common are רִיב עִם (Gn. 26²⁰ Jb. 9³) and רִיב אֵת (Ju. 8¹ Je. 2⁹).
— לֹא] Instead of אֵין in a noun clause with pronominal subject; cf. GK.
152 *d*; Kö. 352 *m.* — וַתָּסַר] Impf. with ו of purpose. — זְנוּנֶיהָ] Now.'s rendering "nose-ring" is without philological or exegetical support, as is also his
transl. of נַאֲפוּפֶיהָ] by "necklace." These renderings imply an evil significance
for nose-rings and necklaces, such as does not seem to have belonged to them.
נאפופים is a syn. of נאפים (Je. 13²⁷ Ez. 23⁴³). For force of the pl., cf. Kö.
261 *d, f.* — **5.** פֶּן] Controlling five verbs. — אַפְשִׁיטֶנָּה] On form *v.* GK. 58 *i.* —
כַיּוֹם] On the force of כ *v.* GK. 118 *u*; Kö. 319 *d.* — כְאֶרֶץ] Without article;
cf. Kö. 299 *l.* — וַהֲמִתִּיהָ] On form *v.* GK. 72 *w.* — **6.** אֲרַחֵם] Seghol in pause,
a Massoretic peculiarity; cf. יְרַחֵף, Dt. 32¹¹; cf. GK. 52 *n.* — בְּנֵי זְנוּנִים] On
use of בֵּן *v.* BDB., *s.v.* (8); GK. 128 *s.* — **7.** הֲבִישָׁה] A pres. pf., GK. 106 *g*;
on formation from יבש rather than בוש *v.* GK. 78 *b*; BDB. p. 102. — **10.** הִיא
אָנֹכִי ...] Strong contrast. — וְזָהָב ... וְכֶסֶף] Without article, though preceding
nouns have it. — עָשׂוּ לַבָּעַל] Rel. clause with rel. particle omitted. On force of
ל cf. 8⁴ Is. 44¹⁷. Hosea uses pl. בְּעָלִים except here and in 13¹. — **11.** אָשׁוּב
וְלָקַחְתִּי] Cf. GK. 120 *e*; Kö. 369 *q, r.* — לִכְסוֹת] A purpose clause depending
upon the preceding nouns; cf. Gn. 24²⁸ Mi. 5¹; Kö. 385 *c.* — **12.** נַבְלֻתָהּ á.λ.,
meaning *shamelessness, lewdness;* stronger than the more common נבלה,
disgraceful folly. — לְעֵינֵי] A less frequent idiom than בְּעֵינֵי. — **13.** חָגָּה] This
and foll. nouns are all collective singulars. — שַׁבַּתָּהּ] On dag. f. in ת cf.
Assyr. *Šabattu; v.* Barth, *NB.* § 15; Kö. II. i. pp. 180 f. — **14.** אֶתְקָלֵם] On
form cf. GK. 59 *g.* — **15.** הַבְּעָלִים] On signif. of pl., cf. Kö. 264 *f.* Special
names of Baalim are: בַּעַל בְּרִית (Ju. 8³³ 9⁴), בְּ זְבוּב (2 K. 1² f. 6. 16), בְּ פְּעוֹר
(Nu. 25³·⁵), בְּ גָּד (Jos. 11¹⁷ 12⁷ 13⁵), בְּ חֶרְמוֹן (Ju. 3⁸ 1 Ch. 5²³), בְּ חָמוֹן (Ct. 8¹¹),
בְּ צְפוֹן (Ex. 14²·⁹ Nu. 33⁷), בְּ חָצוֹר (2 S. 13²³), בְּ מְעוֹן (Nu. 32³⁸ 1 Ch. 5⁸ Ez. 25⁹),
בְּ פְּרָצִים (2 S. 5²⁰ 1 Ch. 14¹¹), בְּ שָׁלִשָׁה (2 K. 4⁴²), בְּ תָּמָר (Ju. 20³³); cf.
בַּעֲלַת בְּאֵר (Jos. 19⁸). — הִקְטִיר] Impf. denoting customary action. קטר, in pre-
exilic literature, is used of the offering up of sacrifices in general; not until
the times of Jeremiah and later is it applied to offerings of incense; these
latter were probably among the foreign customs brought in by Manasseh
(cf. Sta. *ZAW.* VI. 298 f.; Moore, art. "Incense," *EB.*; Now. *Arch.;* Benz.
Arch.; BSZ., *s.v.*). The vb. is used chiefly in Pi. and Hiph. and means "to
cause smoke, or odor, to ascend"; cf. Assyr. *ḳutru* = smoke. Now.'s change
to the Pi'ēl form is unnecessary, since the Hiph. occurs in preëxilic passages,
e.g. 1 S. 2¹⁶ 1 K. 9²⁵ 2 K. 16¹⁵. — וְתַעַד] Impf. cons. foll. an impf. of past
time; but cf. Kö. 366 *g.* — הֶלְיָתָהּ] á.λ. from חלה, *to adorn;* חֲלִי (Pr. 25¹² Ct. 7²)
means a *necklace,* and this fem. form coupled with נֶזֶם probably denotes some

specific neck or breast ornament, rather than *jewellery* in general. — [אתי
Emph., and in chiastic order with מאהביה. — **18.** [תקראי לי קרא לְ is the
regular idiom for naming; cf. Gn. 1⁵. — **19.** [יזכרו ב׳ For a similar use of
זכר ב, implying "longing after," cf. Je. 3¹⁶.

§ 5. Later voices describing Israel's return to Yahweh.
2⁸· ⁹ 2¹⁶· ¹⁷ 2²⁰⁻²² 2²³⁻²⁵ 2¹⁻³.   [English, 2⁶· ⁷ 2¹⁴· ¹⁵ 2¹⁸⁻²⁰ 2²¹⁻²³ 1¹⁰⁻2¹.]

*A. Israel, compelled to separate herself from her lovers, returns
to Yahweh; 2⁸· ⁹.* Israel finds herself cut off from her lovers by
impassable barriers; she searches for them, but they have disappeared, together with the prosperity which she had associated
with them; she returns therefore to her former husband.

This is a single strophe of six tetrameters, or two strophes, each of three
tetrameters. The measure is rough and irregular. These verses do not come
from Hosea himself (so Now., Volz; Oort, *ThT.* XXIV., 345 ff., regards
vs.⁸⁻¹⁰ as misplaced, and inserts them between 2¹⁵ and 2¹⁶; Marti om. only ⁹ᵇ)
because: (1) they break the otherwise close connection between vs.⁷ ᵃⁿᵈ ¹⁰;
(2) they do not harmonize with 3³, since here a voluntary return of the
woman is described while there she is held in forcible restraint; (3) they
are rendered superfluous by 3³; (4) they prematurely introduce the element
of chastisement which comes in naturally in v.¹¹; (5) the rhythm and
strophic structure differ from those found in the context.

8. [דרכך Read דְּרָכֶּהָ with 𝕲 (so Oort, *ThT.* and *Em.*; Gr., We., Loft., Gu.,
GAS., Oet., Marti, *et al.;* Bach., *Alttest. Untersuch.* I. 11, reads דרכיה; so also
Now.; this is favored by 𝔖𝕿, Syr.-Hex., and the following נתיבותיה). —
[ואת גְּדֵרָהּ (Seb.). — וגזרתי = ואפסוק 𝕿 וגדרתי This pointing is supported
by Θ., Cod. Babyl., and Complut. (so Baer, Ginsburg, Loft., Now., GAS., Marti,
et al.). 𝕲 τὰς ὁδοὺς; 𝕲ᴬ𝕼 add αὐτῆς; hence Oort, דרכיה. 𝔙 *eam maceria;*
hence Gr. אׁתָהּ גְּדֵרָה. — [בסירים 𝕲 ἐν σκόλοψιν. — **9.** [תמצא 𝕲𝔖 and Syr.-
Hex. = תְּמָצֶאם (so also Oet., Marti).

8. *Therefore*] The later writer builds this insertion upon the
thought of v.⁷: Because now Israel has expected her food and
clothing from her lovers, *therefore, — Behold, I am going to hedge
up her way with thorns*] As if Israel were a traveller and, as
such, finds in the course of her journey a thorn-hedge directly in
front of her, which proves to be impassable; cf. Jb. 3²³. "It is
very common in the East to put thorns and the branches of thorn
trees along the sides of fields by which sheep are driven to pas-

ture, so that they may not wander in." * — *And build her a wall that she may not find her paths*] If the path comes suddenly up to a wall, and she cannot proceed further, it is evident that the path beyond the wall cannot be found. This wall, as well as the thorn-hedge, represents circumstances and events which render continued action of any kind impracticable, " some dark calamity utterly paralyzing the vital powers." † — **9.** *And she will pursue her lovers and not overtake them*] *i.e.* the blessings upon which she confidently counted as coming from the Baalim will fail her, and as a consequence she will no longer feel their " mystic presence." רדפה is intensive, and represents the pursuit as earnest and eager. — . . . *Seek and not find them*] For a similar use of בקש, cf. 5⁶ 2 Ch. 11¹⁶. — *Let me go and return unto my former husband*] This implies a feeling that in an earlier period there was something, at all events, different. This earlier religion stood out distinctly in contrast with the later religion which now included contaminating elements from the Canaanitish cults. It was this primitive, severe, and unimaginative religion which Elijah represented, and which was still observed by such as Jonadab the Rechabite (Je. 35⁵⁻¹⁰) and his comrades. — *For it was better with me then than now*] An expression of opinion on the part of one who has seen in Israel's later history the facts which seem to him to prove this statement. It was not an idea that could have been clearly comprehended in Hosea's times. The reference is to Israel's earliest times, before she had become tangled up with Canaanitish civilization. ‡ This is no genuine repentance (cf. 6¹⁻³), but only a desire for change, because change is expected to bring relief (cf. Je. 44¹⁷).

8. הנני] הנה presents a new thought and with pron. suf. and a ptcp. expresses the immediate future (Kö. 237 *g*; GK. 116 *p*); the pron. with the ptcp. = an object clause; Kö. 410 *b*. — שך] Only here and 1¹⁰; allied with שכך from which שך, *thorn;* cf. شَكّة, Assyr. *sikkatu;* also סוך, נסך, סכך, שכך (Fränkel, 90; Dl. *Prol.* 195 f.); literally *to twine*, here the twisting of thorns into a hedge. — סירים] Cf. Na. 1¹⁰ Is. 34¹³ Ec. 7⁶; and with meaning of *hooks*, Am. 4². — גדרתי גדרה] *Her wall, i.e.* a wall (for, *i.e.*) against her. This is a

---

* W. R. W. Gardner, *AJSL.* XVIII. 177.   † Che. *in loc.*
‡ Cf. Now. *Arch.* I. 104, 223; II. 2.

late word (Am. 9¹¹ also being an interpol.); cf. use of גדר with ארח (Jb. 19⁸), דרך (La. 3⁹). The suggestion of Gardner (*AJSL*. XVIII. 177) to retain 𝔐𝕿, translating "and build a sheepfold" (cf. Nu. 32¹⁶ 34³⁶), is not in harmony with the context which describes methods of discipline rather than means of protection. Note the cogn. acc. (again in Ez. 22³⁰) and the chiastic arrangement of the last two clauses of v.⁸. — On גְּרֵרָה֫ *v*. Baer, p. 60. —
9. ואלכה ואשובה] Cohortative = strong resolution, — *I will go and I will return*, *i.e.* I will go back to; or better, *Let me go back to.* On the verbal appos., H. 36; GK. 120 *d*. — אז מעתה] The comp. מן after טוב foll. by *adv. of time* which represents a temporal clause, so that the prep. becomes in reality a conj.; cf. Kö. 308 *b*.

B. Israel, after a season of separation from her lovers, will be restored to former favor; 2¹⁶· ¹⁷.   Israel is kindly and gently separated from her lovers, and, as in the coming out of Egypt, is guided to the wilderness for discipline ; after this her possessions will be given back to her, and she will again be strong and fresh as in the days of her youth.

This, like the former addition, consists of one strophe of six tetrameters. It differs from 2⁸· ⁹ (1) in the different usage of הנה, cf. הִנְנִי (2⁸) with הנה אנכי (2¹⁶); (2) especially in the entirely different point of view, 2⁸· ⁹ representing Israel as forced away from her lovers, 2¹⁶· ¹⁷ as enticed away; 2⁸· ⁹ representing the discipline as coming in one way, 2¹⁶· ¹⁷ as coming in another. This piece is clearly late (so Volz, Now., Marti; cf. Now.'s later views, (1) in *Die Zukunftshoffnungen Israels in der Assyr. Zeit* (1902), p. 43, that these verses belong to a late utterance of Hosea; (2) in Now.² (1903) that they are *not* from Hosea, and in any case belong in another connection) because of : (1) the different point of view taken from that in vs.¹¹ ᶠᶠ·; there the thought is that of *punishment* pure and simple, here it is tender-hearted *chastisement* with a view to repentance and reformation; there punishment only is in mind, here promises of blessing prevail; (2) the different representation here from that in v.⁵; there the land where Israel dwells is to become a barren waste; here Israel is to be driven from its land into the desert by Yahweh; (3) the thought of Israel's obedience to Yahweh in her youth (v.¹⁷), which does not agree with the representations of 11¹ᶠ· and 12⁴; (4) the order of thought in v.¹⁷, which is characteristic of later days; Israel's return to Yahweh is here represented as due to Yahweh's generous bestowal of blessings which awaken gratitude, but if Hosea ever contemplated a return it must have been as a result of punitive discipline at the hands of Yahweh, blessings coming only after repentance; (5) late expressions; *e.g.* "the valley of Achor" is mentioned in Is. 65¹⁰; the figure of allurement in the wilderness has parallels in Ez.; (6) the different rhythm and strophic structure from those employed in the genuine verses of the context.

16. לכן] Gr. אכן.—מפתיה] ⅊ πλανῶ αὐτήν. St. מְתַעְיֶהָ. Buhl (*ZAW.* V. 179 ff.)—מְפַתֶּחָה.—המרבר] ⅊ ὡς ἔρημον. Gr. המרברה.—17. כרמיה] ⅊ τὰ κτήματα αὐτῆς; ⅊ *vinitores ejus* (= כְּרְמֶיהָ); so ⅏] משם ואת] Oet. and Marti, וְשַׂמְתִּי אֶת. Hal. וְאִשִׁים אֶת.—לפתח תקוה] ⅊ διανοῖξαι σύνεσιν αὐτῆς = לִפְתֹחַ תְּבוּנָה (Oet.); ⅊ *ad aperiendam spem;* ܣܟܐ̈ܒ ܠܡܦܬܚ, vocalizing לְפַתַּח (Seb.) and following ⅊ in the rendering of תקוה.—ענתה] ⅊ ταπεινωθήσεται; so ܣ; ⅊ *canet.* Buhl and Marti, עֲלְתָה.

16. *Therefore*] Not *nevertheless,* nor *but;* * but as in v.[8] consequently, *i.e.* because she has gone away after her lovers,† v.[15] being thus fitted in by the later writer. Cf. Keil's attempt to coordinate the "therefore" of vs.[8, 11 and 16].—*Behold I am going to allure her*] From the first word, there is seen here in contrast with 2[8, 9], as also with 2[11], the purpose to use kind words and gentle means by which to bring back erring Israel. She will be *allured* or *wooed back.* This meaning is assured by the parallel furnished in the following line, *speak to her heart.* The word פתה does not necessarily have a bad meaning (cf. ⅊, πλανῶ). Other explanations suggested are (1) I will loose her bonds (Je. 40[4]); ‡ (2) I will put it into her head to return while she is yet in exile; § (3) I will cause her to err. ∥ — *And bring her into the wilderness*] The wilderness recalls the events which followed the exodus from Egypt. It has been taken (1) as a place of hope as well as of affliction; ¶ (2) as a place for deliverance, not for punishment.** It means the captivity which included the idea of the desert between Palestine and Babylon, and also the idea of sojourn in a foreign land, for this was in itself like living in a desert (Is. 41[17]). Cf. Wellhausen, who seems to favor the idea suggested in 2[5], that the writer does not have in mind a wilderness, but the waste condition of Palestine, a condition which will be changed. — *And I will speak to her heart*] *i.e.* speak kindly and encouragingly to her. —17. *And I will give to her from there her vineyards*] This means that out of the wilderness, when the purposes of discipline sought to be gained thereby have been secured, the vineyards which have been taken from her will be restored,†† a reference to the time when she leaves the desert. ‡‡ With the present text the

---

* Dathe, Ros., New., Hd.
† Ew., Ke., Pu., Wü., Or., We., Now., GAS.
†† Wü., Now., Che., *et al.*

‡ So Buhl (*v.s.*).
§ Ki. ∥ St.
‡‡ Ma., Ke.

¶ Sim.
** Ke.

interpretations (1) And there I will give to her, etc.,* (2) that the words are spoken ironically, because there are no vineyards in a wilderness,† (3) and I will make thereof her vineyards for her, ‡ (4) vinekeepers (Ϋ), are impossible ; (5) the suggestion § that " I will give to her " = the fuller expression " I will bring to her mind " has no parallel in usage ; (6) the interpretation ‖ of כרמיה as " her nourishment," on the basis of Ϭ and the Assyr. *kurmu, kurmatu* = nourishment, finds no support in Hebrew usage. — *And the valley of Achor for a door of hope*] In contrast with the *troubling* of Israel which took place when Israel was first entering into the land ; Jos. 7²⁵·²⁶. This valley is situated on the northern boundary of Judah (Jos. 15⁷) and probably ran back from Jericho into the hills of Judah (Jos. 7²⁴).¶ It is praised as a valley of great fertility (Is. 65¹⁰). Its use here like that of *wilderness* (v.¹⁶) is large and free, designating by this historical reminiscence the second entrance of Israel into her own land. This entrance will be one through *a door of hope*, a promise of success.** Some understand that the valley of Achor is here mentioned because of its fertility ; †† and others that this was a prediction of the exact way by which Israel was to return. There is no need for the emendations of Oettli and Halévy (*v.s.*), though they furnish a smoother connection, viz. " And I will make the valley of Achor, etc." — *And there she shall respond as in the days of her youth*] Israel, once more, will now yield herself to Yahweh's will, make response to his advances, conform herself to his wishes ; ‡‡ cf. 2¹⁹·²². This is better than (1) *she will sing*, §§ the reference being to antiphonal singing like that of Miriam (Ex. 15⁶·²¹), for such singing here and in vs.²¹⁻²³ would be out of place, (2) *she will humble herself*, ‖‖ or (3) *she will go up thither*,¶¶ which certainly goes well with the ה of שמה, but is not consistent with the identification of שמה with משם, and anticipates the עלותה of the following line. — *And as in the day when she came up from the land of Egypt*] The memory

---

* We.   † Hi., We.   ‡ Sim.   § Bach.   ‖ Hal.

¶ *EB.* I. 36; cf. Conder, "Achor," in *DB.*   ** So most comm.

†† Cal., Ma., *et al.*

‡‡ 'A., Θ., ᵂ, Stuck, Hes., Hi., Ew., Ke., Che., We., GAS., Now.

§§ Ϋ, AE., Ki., Cal., Grot., Ros., Mau., Umb., AV., Wü.

‖‖ Ϭ. Σ.   ¶¶ Buhl (*v.s.*).

of the exodus is one firmly fixed in the minds of the Hebrew nation; cf. 12⁹·¹³ 13⁴ Am. 2¹⁰ 3¹ 9⁷ Mi. 6⁴ 7¹⁵ Je. 2⁶ 7²²·²⁵ 11⁴·⁷ 16¹⁴ 23⁷, etc.

16. מפתיה] On the form, *v.* GK. 93 *ss.* פתה is used chiefly of persuasion to evil, *e.g.* Dt. 11¹⁶ Ex. 22¹⁵ Jb. 31⁹ Pr. 1¹⁰; it is employed to express Yahweh's influence upon prophets in Je. 20⁷ Ez. 14⁹. There is no need to change the text with St. and Buhl (*v.s.*); 𝕸𝕿 is supported by the parallelism of the last clause of the verse. — המדבר] Adv. acc. denoting the end of motion. — על לבה] The regular Hebr. idiom for *cheeringly, comfortingly;* cf. Gn. 34³ 50²¹ Ju. 19³ 2 S. 19⁸ Ru. 2¹³ Is. 40². — **17.** משם] Though literally local, *i.e.* from that place, it is in effect temporal, *i.e.* when she has reached that place I will give, etc. The proposal of Oet. and Hal. to read ושמתי or ואשים (*v.s.*) relieves the difficulty of this phrase, but leaves the clause preceding too indefinite, and spoils the tetrameter of both clauses. — עכור] i.e. *trouble;* for an early etymological explanation of the name, *v.* Jos. 7²⁴ ᶠᶠ. — שמה] The long form may have been used for the sake of euphony; note the three ā-endings of this line. The force of the word is purely local. — כימי] Lit. *according to that which happened in the days of,* i.e. *as in the days of;* on omission of ב after כ, *v.* GK. 118 *u*; BDB. 455. — נעוריה] Abstr. pl.; by formations of this kind are regularly denoted stages of life, *e.g.* זקונים, *old age,* בתולים *maidenhood;* cf. Barth, *NB.* 55 *e.*

C. Israel rescued from all harm, and remarried to Yahweh; **2²⁰⁻²².** A new ordinance is established that beasts and men shall do Israel no harm ; and again shall Israel be betrothed to Yahweh, this time in loving kindness, mercy, and faithfulness ; and at last Israel shall really know Yahweh.

We have here two somewhat ragged pentameter strophes of four lines each. This, like *A* and *B*, is independent of the chapter as a whole, as well as of the other divisions. It is peculiar in: (1) its rhythmic structure, (2) its repetitiousness and prolixity, (3) its point of view. It is to be regarded as distinct from the chapter as a whole (so Volz, Now.; Marti, *EB.* 2122) because: (1) this idyllic picture of a state of universal peace represents later ideals (cf. Is. 4⁶ ᶠ· 65²⁵); (2) the thought of vs.²¹ ᶠ· has no parallel in the story of Hosea's marriage, which is the basis of chaps. 1-3; (3) the vocabulary and phraseology of v.²⁰ are characteristic of a later age; cf. Gn. 9² Lv. 26³ ᶠᶠ· Ez. 34²⁵ ᶠᶠ· Is. 11⁶ ᶠᶠ· 35⁹ 2⁴ Zc. 9¹⁰; (4) a new metre and strophic structure appear. Now., in his *Zukunftshoffnungen Israels in der Assyr. Zeit,* p. 43, withdraws his earlier view that vs.²⁰⁻²⁵ are from another hand, and suggests that they come from a late utterance of Hosea; in Now.², however, the Hoseanic authorship of v.²⁰ is once more abandoned.

R

20. [אשבור] 𝕋 איבטיל; so 𝔖, both = אשבית (Seb.).—[השכבתים] 𝔊 κατοι-
κιῶ σε; similarly Σ., Θ., reading הוֹשַׁבְתִּים (Oet.); 'Α. κοιμήσω αὐτούς.—
21. [ארשתיך] Σ. λήψομαί σε; 𝕋 וַאֲקַיְמִנָּכִין.—[בצרק ובמשפט] A gloss (so Now.),
incongruous in view of context.—**22.** [וידעת את־י׳] 𝔙 et scies quia ego
Dominus; Babyl. Cod., כי אני י׳, now corrected to agree with 𝕸𝕋. Gr. וְרָעַת.
Marti, וּבְרָעַת.

20. *And I will make for them a covenant with the beasts, etc.*]
The pronoun refers to Israel; and, now, between Israel and the
lower world of animals a covenant will be established, the essence
of which will be peace between man and animals. Just such a
covenant restraining the beasts from harming Israelites, Zc. 11[10]
represents Yahweh as breaking; cf. also Ez. 34[25]. Such a covenant was rather an "ordinance" than a "treaty" (Cheyne). Is
there here and in prophetic references to close relationship of
animals and men (cf. Nu. 22[21-30] Is. 11[6-9] 65[25] Jb. 5[22 f.] Gn. 3[1 ff.]
Ez. 34[25]) a survival of the totemistic conception involving a belief
in a real blood connection? * — *And the bow and the sword and
war I will break out of the land*] There will be peace likewise
between Israel and other nations (Ps. 46[9] 76[3] Je. 49[35] Is. 9[4]). *War*
(cf. 1[7]), including everything that relates to battle, is here joined
with *break* by zeugma.† This late expression finds analogies
in Is. 2[4] Mi. 4[4] Je. 23[6] 33[16]. — *And I will make them lie down
in safety.*—**21.** *Yea, I will betroth thee to me forever*] Security and
confidence are the great ends sought in the administration of the
affairs of a nation. *To lie down in safety* (cf. Jb. 11[18] Is. 14[30]
Lv. 26[6]) is the naïve and childlike designation of complete assurance. But, in order to strengthen the thought and to bring it
into harmony with the context, the writer goes back to the figure
of betrothal and marriage, a relationship which, now, shall last
throughout all time (cf. Je. 31[35-37] Is. 54[8-10]). — *In kindness and in
mercy*] The preceding words, *in righteousness and in judgment*,
are to be omitted as a gloss (*v.s.*), since they are superfluous by
the side of v.[22]; are inapplicable in the strictest sense to the
figure of betrothal; present, as they stand, a bizarre arrangement
of thought; interfere with a smooth strophic structure; and ex-

---

* Cf. Gunkel's defence of the genuineness of this verse on the ground of the
antiquity of this conception, *Genesis*, p. 112.   † Cf. Kö. *Stil.* 122 f.

press the thought of a later period.   For the manifestation of *kindness* and *mercy* on the part of God to Israel, cf. Is. 14^1 30^{18} 49^{10} 54$^{8.\ 10}$ Je. 31^{20} Ez. 39^{25}. — **22.** *I will betroth thee to me in faithfulness, and thou shalt know Yahweh*] The thrice-repeated statement of betrothal makes it both emphatic and solemn. *Faithfulness* from the time of Isaiah (cf. Is. 11^5) had been one of the characteristics of Yahweh most frequently dwelt upon in his relation to man.   Three gifts will thus be brought to Israel as bridal gifts, viz. love, mercy, and faithfulness, and as a result Israel *will know Yahweh* (cf. 4^1).   The custom originally was to pay the dowry to the bride's family (cf. Gn. 34^{12}) as a compensation for the loss of her labor ; later this dowry came to be regarded as the possession of the wife (cf. Gn. 31^{15}) which provided for her needs in case of her husband's death, or her divorce without due cause.* The fact that the gifts of Yahweh here are all such as would tend to the happiness of Israel makes it evident that the later marriage custom is alluded to.†   Everything is given by Yahweh, and nothing is asked of Israel in return.

---

20. כרתי] The ordinary word for the making of a covenant ; the original significance of the expression may be seen from Gn. 15^{10} Je. 34^{18}.   Other phrases used of making a cov. are באו בברית, Je. 34^{10} ; הגביר ברית ל, Dn. 9^{27} ; הקים ברית את, Ez. 16^{62} ; שם ברית, 2 S. 23^5.   The breaking of a cov. is expressed by עבר ב', Jos. 7^{15} ; הפרו בר', Is. 24^5 ; חלל ב', Mal. 2^{10} ; מאס ב', 2 K. 17^{15}. — עם] This prep. often foll. כרת ברית, but ל is more frequent ; other preps. used are את and בין. עם is used with the first two nouns here, and understood with the third. — חית השדה] The phrase used by J in the creation account, Gn. 2^{19} ; cf. P's חית הארץ, Gn. 1^{25}. — **21.** וארשתיך] With the change of figure it becomes necessary to change from the 3d pl. m. pron. of v.^{20} to the 2d fem. sg. ; abrupt changes of this kind are not infrequent, *e.g.* 2$^{3.\ 18}$ 4^6 Gn. 49$^{25\ a.\ 26\ a}$ Dt. 32$^{14\ d.\ 15\ b}$; cf. Kö. *Stil.* 238 ff. The threefold occurrence of the vb. not only adds emphasis, but also affords opportunity to add several adverbial modifiers without cumbering the sentence ; cf. Kö. *Stil.* 298. — בצדק] The prep. with this and foll. nouns is ב of price, which usually follows ארש with the gift of the bride. The original force of ארש ב is seen in Ar. اِرْش, *a fine, price.* — **22.** אמונה] A common formation for abst. nouns ; cf. גבורה, *might ;* קבורה, *burial ;* מלוכה, *rule ;* רפואה, *healing ;* Barth, *NB.* § 82 *e.*

D. Yahweh's response in faithful love; 2²³⁻²⁵. — "Jezreel (Israel) asks the plants to germinate ; they call upon the earth for
its juices ; the earth beseeches heaven for rain ; heaven suppli-
cates for the divine word which opens its stores, and Yahweh
responds in faithful love." (Cheyne).

This addition consists of three strophes of trimeter movement, of 4, 3, and
4 lines. Its characteristics as a piece are clear and beautiful thought, and
perfect, artistic form, the metre being regular, the parallelism progressive,
and the strophic structure symmetrical; cf. in the last line of each strophe
the pronoun followed by a vb. of saying. Both thought and form are highly
poetic. It is from later times than those of Hosea (so Volz; Marti omits
2¹⁵ᵇ⁻²⁵), as is seen from: (1) the fact that it contemplates the full restoration
of Israel to Yahweh's favor; (2) the eschatological phrase והיה ביום ההוא,
which belongs to later times; (3) the use of ענה, which is found in this sense
only in late passages, *e.g.* 14⁹ Ps. 65⁶ Ec. 10¹⁹; (4) the materialistic blessings
spoken of here which are not in keeping with the spirit of the teachings
of Amos and Hosea; (5) the new metre and strophic structure; (6) the
presupposition of the exile contained in v.²⁵ ᵃ.

23. אענה] 𝔊𝔖, and Syr.-Hex. om. the first (so also Seb., Oort, Marti). —
25. וזרעתיה] We. וזרעתיהו (so Bach., Now., Oet.), the suff. referring to יזרעאל.
— עמי־אתה] 𝔖 om. אתה.— אלהי] 𝔊 κύριος ὁ θεός μου εἶ σύ, adding אתה (so
also Hal.); so 𝔙, Syr.-Hex.

23. *I will respond to the heavens*] The petition from Israel for
prosperity comes last of all through the heavens to Yahweh, who
is the fountain head of authority. The representation is not
merely poetical ; for it was the popular belief that rain and dew
came as the direct gifts of Yahweh. It was at his command that
the clouds were opened or remained closed ; cf. Am. 9¹³ Jo. 3¹⁸
Ez. 34²⁵· ²⁸ 47¹⁻⁸, also Dt. 28²³ Lv. 26¹⁹. — **24.** *And they shall respond to Jezreel*] The corn, wine, and oil will respond to Israel,
here called Jezreel with reference to the meaning of the word,
God sows; cf. the use made of it in v.²⁶. — **25.** *And I will sow
her unto me in the land*] Cf. Je. 31²⁷· ²⁸. Jezreel = Israel restored,
is to be sown again in the land, this time unto, *i.e.* for, Yahweh.
All Israel, wherever scattered, will return to the land of their
ancestors. The purpose of the sowing is, of course, that they may
bring forth fruit. — *I will have pity upon the un-pitied one*] The
name of 1⁶ is here reversed. — *And to not-my-people I will say,*

thou art my people] The name of 1⁹ is likewise reversed. — *And they will say, thou art my God*] Israel's confession; cf. Zc. 13⁹ Rom. 9²⁵ 1 Pet. 2¹⁰.

23. וְהָיָה בַיּוֹם הַהוּא] For the use of this phrase in other late passages, cf. v.¹⁸ Jo. 4¹⁸ Mi. 5⁹ Zc. 13². Other phrases of similar import are: בַיּוֹם הַהוּא וְהָיָה (Zc. 13¹); וְהָיָה בְּעֵת הַהִיא (Am. 9¹³); וְהָיָה אַחֲרֵי־כֵן (Am. 5¹³); הִנֵּה יָמִים בָּאִים (Jo. 3¹); וְהָיָה בְּאַחֲרִית הַיָּמִים (3⁵ Mi. 4¹). — אֶעֱנֶה] Repeated for the sake of rhetorical effect; to omit it once, as some do, spoils the rhythm of the passage, and robs it of its dignity in some measure. — וְהֵם] From this point on through v.²⁴ the clauses are all circumstantial, depending upon v.²³ᵃ.

E. Israel's vast numbers, united as one family under Yahweh, and victorious against all enemies; 2¹⁻³. — In the future time, Israel's numbers will be beyond calculation; instead of estrangement from Yahweh, her people will be recognized as the sons of the living God; and instead of schism between north and south, there will be united action resulting in victory over all opposers.

We have here two strophes of four lines each, in the pentameter movement. Each strophe contains an important idea, and both together form a splendid unity. Strophe 1: Israel's numbers will be great, and she will again become Yahweh's people. Strophe 2: She will be reunited, and thus enabled to meet all enemies. This piece has been recognized as occupying an impossible place, and has been transferred to the end of chap. 2 (so Heilprin, *The Historical Poetry of the Ancient Hebrews*, II. 125 f.; St., Kue. *Einl.* II. 319; Che., Kö. *Einl.*; Gu., GAS., Oet.). The grounds urged for this are the fact that it avoids the abrupt transition from threat to promise involved in passing from 1⁹ to 2¹; the better connection secured in placing 2¹⁻³ after the promises of 2²⁰⁻²⁵; and the very similar arrangement found in Rom. 9²⁵ ᶠ· where these verses are quoted. But it is superfluous after 2²⁵, being little more than a repetition of vs.²³⁻²⁵; it uses הָאָרֶץ (v.³) in an altogether different sense from that in vs.²⁰ and 25; לֹא־עַמִּי is given a different interpretation from that in v.²⁵; and it forms a very poor ending for chap. 2. It is better to treat it as an entirely later piece (We.; Sta. *G VI.* I. 577; Co. *ZA W.* VII. 285, and *Einl.* 172; Giesebrecht, *Beiträge zur Jesaiakritik*, 213 ff.; Oort, *ThT.* XXIV. 358 ff.; Loft.; Che. in WRS. *Proph.* p. xviii; Volz, Now.; Seesemann, 33; Da. *DB.* II. 425; Marti, *EB.* 2122; Grimm, *Liturg. Append.*, 61 ff.); because, in its present position, it breaks the connection, nor can it be satisfactorily placed elsewhere; the reference to Judah is suspicious, the rest of the chapter speaking only of Israel; it presupposes the exile (v.²); its vision of Israel's future passes beyond Hosea's horizon; the tremendous increase of Israel is a later eschatological conception (Gn. 22¹⁷ 32¹² Is. 48¹⁹); and it differs in poetic form from every other section of this chapter. Skipwith (*JQR*. VI. (1893) 298) joins 2¹·² to end of chap. 3, but rules out 3⁵, 2¹, and 2², with the exception of the last clause, כי גדול וגו׳, as an exilic interpolation. 𝔊 and 𝔖 give vs.¹⁻² to chap. 1, and v.³ to chap. 2.

1. והיה] 𝔊 and 𝔏 use past tense, changing to fut. in the second והיה. 𝔖, by mistake, inserts negative. Gr. suggests the insertion here of Is. 2²⁻⁴ (Mi. 4¹⁻³). —במקום] Transl. literally in all versions, viz. *in the place where;* 𝔖 introduces the apodosis with *there.* — **2.** ראש] 𝔊 ἀρχήν; so 𝔏. —אחד] Gr. would add here: ...ויגברו על איביהם בעמק יזרעאל — **3.** אחיכם]... אחותיכם. Read both nouns in sg. with 𝔊 and 𝔏 (so We., Now., GK. 96, Marti). Oet. retains pl., but vocalizes the second noun, לַאֲחִיֹתֵכֶם.—ועלו וגו׳] Bach. reads וְעָלוּ, and would transfer the whole clause to the conclusion of 1⁶.

1. *And it shall come to pass that the number of the children of Israel shall be*] It is of Northern Israel that he speaks,* for in v.² Judah is distinguished; cf. also 1⁶·⁷. — *As the sand of the sea*] Cf. Gn. 13¹⁶ 22¹⁷ 32¹² Jos. 11⁴ Is. 10²². Prosperity always includes numbers; cf. Mi. 2¹² Is. 48¹⁹. — *Instead of its being said*] Better † than *in the place where it was said*, which has many supporters. ‡ — *Ye are "not my people"*] The name designating their estrangement from Yahweh (1⁹) will no longer be used. In its place will be given to them a title denoting the closest fellowship with him, viz. *the sons of the living God*], not sons of idol-gods. This phrase (cf. 1 S. 17²⁶ Dt. 5²⁶) includes two important elements, viz. (1) *sons* (cf. Nu. 21²⁹ Mal. 2¹¹) of God, in accordance with the common Semitic conception that the nation is the offspring of the deity; § (2) the expression *living God, i.e.* a god who is the fountain or source of life (cf. Ps. 42² 84²) ; here used for the first time (except perhaps the use by J in Jos. 3¹⁰) ; cf. its later usage in oaths, Ju. 8¹⁹ 1 S. 14³⁹·⁴⁵, placed even in the mouth of the deity, Dt. 32⁴⁰ Nu. 14²¹·²⁸, etc.; *v.* especially Am. 8¹⁴. This verse is not entirely consistent with 2²⁵, *v.s.* — **2.** *And the children of Judah and the children of Israel shall be gathered together*] The separation of north and south at the death of Solomon, although brought about by prophetic influence (cf. 1 K. 11²⁹ ff. 12²²⁻²⁴), is regarded by Hosea (3³ f. 8⁴ 13¹⁰·¹¹) and by the writer of this passage as lacking

---

* Merc., Hd., Sim., Ke., Che., Now., Marti, *et al.;* on the contr., Hi.

† Ki., Grot., Hi., Ew., AV., Che., We., Now., Marti, *et al.*

‡ 𝔊𝔖𝔙, Dathe, Ros., Umb., Ke., Wü. § See WRS. *Sem.* 40 ff.

divine approval. This schism, therefore, will be healed (cf. Is. 11[13]
Ez. 37[22]). — *And they shall appoint for themselves one head*] This
head is a king, probably of the Davidic family. — *And they shall
go up out of the land*] *i.e.* the land of exile (cf. Ezr. 2[1] 7[6] Ne.
12[1]), the whole reference being to the time and circumstances of
the scattering.* Some prefer to understand *go up* of marching
to battle (cf. Na. 2[2] Jo. 1[6]), the land in this case is Palestine, now
too small for the inhabitants, who therefore seek to enlarge their
territory (Am. 9[12] Is. 11[14] Mi. 2[12, 13]).† Besides, it is urged, the
going up from the land of captivity could not have preceded the
appointment of a common king. Still others ‡ understand Egypt
to be referred to (cf. Ex. 1[10]) and used symbolically of all captivity.
Notice also may be taken of the translation, *they shall grow up
from the ground, i.e.* like grain after it is sowed. § — *For great
shall be the day of Jezreel*] Does this mean the day of scattering, ‖
referring to the dispersion? Or does it mean the day of *sowing?* ¶
Clearly the latter, for the name Jezreel has been given a new
meaning. In the former case, *great* means *terrible;* in the latter,
glorious. By this name the writer evidently described the day of
Yahweh, the time when punishment was to be meted out to Israel's
foes and blessings showered upon Israel herself. — **3.** *Say ye to
your brother, " my people," and to your sister, " compassionated"*]
This is only a repetition of 2[25]. The words have been taken as
addressed (1) to the people of Judah bidding them greet the returning Israelites and welcome them back to the land; ** (2) to
the disciples of the prophet bidding them announce to the whole
nation the news of its restoration to Yahweh's favor; †† (3) to the
members of the united kingdom bidding them greet each other as
Yahweh's people; ‡‡ (4) to those who had been allowed to remain
in the land, bidding them welcome the returning exiles; §§ and
(5) as a fragment of some lost statement. ‖‖

1. יִמֹּר] Potential impf. denoting possibility; H. 22, 2 *a*; cf. Je. 31[37] 33[22], the
only other occurrences of the Niph. used of impossible acts as here. — בְּמָקוֹם
[אֲשֶׁר = תַּחַת אֲשֶׁר]; for another instance of this use, cf. Is. 33[21]. The regular

---

* Ki., Cal., Ros., Mau., Hd., Wü., We., Now., Marti, *et al.*
† Hi., Ew., Umb., St., Che.   ¶ Hi., Ew., Umb., Marti.   §§ Marti.
‡ *E.g.* Ke.   § Reuss.   ** So Hi.   †† Che.   ‖‖ Meinhold.
‖ Theod., AE., Cal.   ‡‡ Hng., Ke., Wü., Or.

significance of the phrase is local, *in the place where* (Lv. 4²⁴ 2 S. 15²¹ 1 K. 21¹⁹ Je. 22¹² Ez. 21³⁵ Ne. 4¹⁴); cf. GK. 130*c*; Kö. 337*x*, and 393. — [ויאמר] Customary impf. in the first instance; simply future in the second. — **2.** [יחדו] Really a noun in adverb. acc. = in his unitedness; always having the force of an adv. = together, in union. — [ראש] Used of the head of the state; cf. 1 S. 15¹⁷ Nu. 14⁴. The phrase שים ראש is found only here; cf. Nu. 14⁴, נתן ראש; Is. 3⁴, נתן with acc. of person and שׂר in apposition; Ps. 18⁴⁴, שים with acc. of person, followed by לראש. — **3.** [אחותיכם] = אֲחִיוֹתֵיכֶם, the final radical has disappeared here as in Jos. 2¹³ Ez. 16⁵¹·⁵⁵·⁶¹; cf. GK. 96. The context, however, requires the reading אֲחוֹתְכֶם; but cf. Kö. 258 f.

§ 6. Yahweh's contention with Israel, on account of sins encouraged by the priests. 4¹⁻¹⁹.

Yahweh has a contention with Israel; for on every side is wickedness. In this wickedness the religious guides, the priests, take the lead; and for their failure to perform their duty they shall be rejected, degraded, and put to confusion. Because of their example the people of Israel indulge in idolatry and adultery. May Judah not join in iniquity with Israel, who is committed to vice, and will continue until the enemy utterly confounds and destroys her.

This piece contains five strophes of twelve lines each; the measure is trimeter, occasionally falling into dimeter. Strophe 1 (vs.¹·²·³) describes the situation; Strophe 2 (vs.⁴·¹⁴ᵈ·⁵·⁶) places the responsibility upon the priests; strophe 3 (vs.⁷·⁸·⁹·¹⁰·¹²ᵃ) describes further the priest's responsibility; strophe 4 (vs.¹¹·¹²ᶜᵈ·¹³·¹⁴ᵃᵇᶜ) pictures the madness of the people in their sensual indulgence; while strophe 5 (vs.¹⁵·¹⁶·¹⁷·¹⁸·¹⁹) depicts Israel's sins and her consequent destruction. Cf. Ew., who makes four strophes, ¹⁻⁵·⁶⁻¹⁰·¹¹⁻¹⁵·¹⁶⁻¹⁹; also Wü., who divides, ¹⁻³·⁴⁻¹⁰·¹¹⁻¹⁴·¹⁵⁻¹⁶; and Marti, who secures thirteen strophes of four lines each, omits vs.³·⁵·⁶ᵃ·¹⁰ᵇ·¹⁵·¹⁶ᵇ, and transposes v.¹¹ to follow v.¹⁴. In the present arrangement the following transpositions have been made, viz. (1) of v.¹²ᵃ to precede v.¹¹; this leaves (*a*) a better connection with v.¹⁰, than v.¹¹ afforded; (*b*) a better connection with v.¹²ᵇ, than v.¹²ᵃ afforded; (*c*) a much easier connection for the circ. clause in ¹²ᵃ; and (*d*) no good ground for calling v.¹¹ an interpolation (Ru., Now.), although it is proverbial in form and contents; (2) of v.¹⁴ᵈ to precede בֹהֵן, the last word in v.⁴ as the text now stands. These words (וְעַם לֹא־יָבִין יִלָּבֵט) (*a*) are evidently out of place where they are, the context contrasting הם (the priests) with the young women of the nation; (*b*) fit in perfectly with the last clause of v.⁴ as amended (*v.i.*), adding still another circumstantial detail of the picture, *Yea, a people*, etc.; (*c*) perfect the symmetry of strophe 2, while they completely destroy that of strophe 4, in which they are now found; and (*d*) on this supposition need no longer be regarded (Ru., Now.) as a gloss.

IV. 1–3. *The announcement of Yahweh's contention and its occasion.* Listen, Israel, to Yahweh: The land lacks everything good; it abounds in everything bad: consequently it, with all its life, is now suffering.

In this strophe the parallelism is less regular than in the remaining strophes; but the irregularities greatly heighten the artistic effect. These consist of (1) the elegiac measure (3, 2) with which it opens; (2) the gradual abandonment of shorter for longer lines, until in lines 7 and 8, the climax is reached in the long series of infinitives, making tetrameters, in which the very vowels (â and ô) add to the strength of the passage (cf. the repetition of אין in the preceding line, the sound of which is well adapted to the thought); (3) the gradual falling away again of the sound in lines 9–12. The whole strophe is a magnificent example of the musical swell (crescendo and diminuendo) expressed in measure and sound.

1. ריב] 𝕲 κρίσις.— **2.** פרצו] 𝕲 κέχυται; 𝓥 *inundaverunt;* 𝕊 ܤ. All disregard the pausal accent. 𝕲 and 𝓛 add ἐπὶ τῆς γῆς, perhaps = ברץ (= בארץ), a wrong reading of פרצו, which was later corrected, the old reading being allowed to remain (Vol.). — רמים] 𝓛𝓥𝕊 sg. — נגעו] 𝕊 ܣܠܟܬ. — **3.** ואמלל וגו׳] 𝕲 καὶ μικρυνθήσεται σὺν πᾶσιν τοῖς, κ.τ.λ.; 𝕲ᴬᑫ, Θ. καὶ σμικρυνθήσεται, κ.τ.λ.; 𝕊 ܣܠܟܦܘ.— השרה] 𝕲 adds καὶ σὺν τοῖς ἑρπετοῖς τῆς γῆς; so 𝓛.— גם] 𝕲 om.— יאספו] 𝓥 *congregabuntur;* 𝕲 ἐκλείψουσιν.

1. *Hear the word of Yahweh*] This word was spoken after the death of Jeroboam II. (743 B.C.), and during the anarchical period which immediately followed (Zechariah, Shallum, and Menahem all coming to the throne within a year),[*] or a little later, perhaps in the reign of Pekah (736 B.C.).[†] It is with these words that Hosea's public ministry really begins, the preceding chapters (1–3) being intended rather to picture the internal and domestic struggle which led him to enter upon the ministry. Hosea's experience, as described in chaps. 1–3, sustained a relation to his prophetic work similar to that which Isaiah's vision (chap. 6) sustained toward his ministry.[‡] While nothing is said, the sense is evident that these words are spoken through Hosea and to Northern Israel, for in v.[15] Judah is distinguished from Israel.— *Yahweh has a contention with*] This was not merely "a just cause," nor a reproof, accusation,[§] but

---

[*] So Ma., Ros., Schrö.   [‡] Cf. WRS. *Proph.* 183.
[†] Riehm, *Einl.* 48.   [§] Schmidt, Now.

contention, quarrel (cf. Mi. 6² Je. 2⁹).* A relationship has
existed between Yahweh and Israel, the terms of which Israel
has not observed. The time has come when Yahweh will enter
into contention with the nation. — *For there is no truth* . . .
love . . . *knowledge of God*] This is a negative statement of
Hosea's ideal. By *truth* he means fidelity, honesty, constancy,
trustworthiness in thought, word, and deed (cf. Je. 9³·⁴) ; by *love*
he means not love of man for God, nor love of God for man ;
but love for fellow-men (cf. Gn. 21²³ ; cf. for the use of these
two words together, Gn. 32¹⁰ (of God) ; Gn. 24⁴⁹ 47²⁹ Ps. 85¹⁰ (of
man)). The opposite of fidelity and love are indicated in the
following verse. These elements of character and of conduct
are lacking, because there is lacking also *the knowledge of God*
in which they take root. By this he means not knowledge of
Yahweh (cf. 2²⁰ 4⁶ 5⁴ 6⁶), which would be from the standpoint
of those times something less broad, more *national;* but "the
general, legal, divine duty of humanity."† — **2.** *Swearing and
lying*] *i.e.* perjury (cf. אלות שוא, 10⁴). אלה alone means simply
swearing, of which in itself there was no prohibition, unless,
perhaps, the reference is to *cursing,* which is so common in the
East (cf. Mat. 5³⁴ ᶠᶠ·). ‡ The two together stand in opposition
to "truth." § — *And killing and stealing and committing adultery*]
Violation of the 6th, 8th, and 7th commandments. The infinitives absolute are used instead of the finite form of the verb
for vividness and emphasis ; cf. 𝕲 above. These are in opposition to "love." The fancied "security in Samaria" (Am. 6¹)
no longer exists. There is every reason to suppose that the
decalogue in its original form was at this time in existence. ‖
— *They break into*] *sc.* the houses of their neighbors (Jb. 24¹⁶), or,
acts of violence.¶ Cf. also the word פרצים = *robber* (Ez. 18¹⁰) ;
and the interpretation which makes the act a breaking into the
law.** Cf. 𝕲 above. — *Blood striking blood*] The plural = blood-

---

* Wü., GAS.

† Carl Abel, *Ueber den Begriff der Liebe in einigen alten und neuen Sprachen*
(Berlin, 1872), p. 63.   ‡ So Cal.   § Now.

‖ See WRS. art. "Decalogue," *Enc. Brit.;* Paterson, art. "Decalogue," *DB.;*
Ew. *Gesch. Isr.*³ II. 231 ; Kue., *Rel. Isr.* I. 285 ; but cf. W. E. Addis, art. "Decalogue," *EB.;* We. *Comp. Hex.* 331 f.; Sta. *GVI.* I. 457 ff., and Marti.

¶ Che.   ** Rashi, Ki.

shed ; *i.e.* murder follows immediately upon murder. The phrase
is a striking one, but this fact and the change of subject need not
excite suspicion.* — 3. *Therefore the land mourns*] The prophet
evidently speaks not of some future † or past ‡ calamity, but of
one present, a severe drought existing at the time. § It is doubtful whether he has in mind, at this point, the anarchy which followed Jeroboam's death. ‖ — *And every denizen in it languishes*]
This refers not merely to animals, ¶ but as well to men. — *Even
to the beasts of the field, etc.*] *Even to* ** or *including* (cf. Gn. 7²¹)
is preferable to (*a*) *through*,†† making the beasts the agents, as also
to (*b*) *together with* (cf. Gn. 9²), ‡‡ (*c*) *among*, putting birds and
beasts on a level with men, §§ and (*d*) *for the lack of.* ‖‖ — *While
even the fish of the sea are taken away*] This is the climax of
the presentation, the drought being so great that the streams are
dried up, the phrase דְגֵי הִים not being restricted to fish actually
in the sea.¶¶ The association of the animal world and even the
inanimate world with man in his suffering is an idea widely held
among the prophets (Am. 8⁸ Is. 16⁸ 24³⁻⁶ Zp. 1². ³ Je. 12⁴ Jo. 1¹⁰. ¹⁸ ;
cf. Rom. 8²²), and is based upon the early belief that land and
man and animal were in some way closely connected.*** Cf. the
totemistic conception referred to on 2²⁰.

---

1. כִּי] Used demonstratively, as in Ps. 118¹⁰ f. (cf. BDB. p. 472), as a particle
of asseveration = "surely, etc"; or better, to introduce direct discourse, as
in Gn. 21³⁰ Ju. 6¹⁶ (cf. BDB. p. 471; H. 47, 3 *a*); not causal (Wü.), nor
explanatory and introducing a parenthetic clause (Sim.). — רִיב] Cf. the
forensic terms מִשְׁפָּט, *lawsuit* or *case*, as in Dt. 10¹⁸ Jb. 13¹⁸ 23⁴ 1 K. 8⁴⁹, and
Mi. 7⁹, where the two words are used as parallels; and דִּין used in similar
sense in Dt. 17⁸ Ps. 140¹³ Jb. 35¹⁴. — אֵין] Its repetition is significant. Cf.
also Ho. 3⁴ Nu. 21⁵ Jos. 6¹ 1 K. 18²⁹ Jb. 34²² Is. 41²⁶ 1 S. 26¹²; for cases of
אֵין joined with two or more words, cf. Ne. 4¹⁷ Gn. 41³⁹ 45⁶ Dt. 12¹² Je. 22¹⁷.
— **2.** אלה וגו׳] These five infinitives furnish one of the best examples of the
use of the inf. abs. for a finite vb.; H. 28, 5 *a*; GK. 113*ff*; Kö. 217 *a*, *b*;
cf. also Is. 21⁵ Je. 8¹⁵ Ec. 4². — פָּרְצוּ, נָגָעוּ] Pfs. denoting an action begun in
the past and still continuing. Cf. Dr. § 8; cf. also Am. 5¹⁴ Ps. 2¹ Is. 21³.
— וְרֹמִים וגו׳] Is clearly a circ. clause, H. 45, 1; GK. 142 *a*, *c*; Dr. § 156 f. —

---

* We., Now.; cf. Hal.	¶ Marti.	§§ Schmidt.
† Ros., Wü.	** So Ew., GAS.	‖‖ Geb.
‡ Ke.	†† Abar.	¶¶ Now.
§ Sim., Now. ‖ Che.	‡‡ Stuck, Wü.	*** WRS. *Rel. Sem.* 126.

3. [האבל] Descriptive, H. 21, 1. — [אמלל] Pŭ'lăl; cf. also Jo. 1¹⁰ Is. 33⁹ Je. 14². — [כל] Distributive; GK. 127 *b*; BDB. p. 481 *a*. — [בעוף ... בחית] On force of ב, cf. Gn. 7²¹ 8¹⁷ 9¹⁰·¹⁶ Ex. 12¹⁹ Nu. 31¹¹. — [וגם דני וגו'] Another circ. clause, adding a new feature in the details of the description.

4–6. *The Priest responsible for Israel's wickedness.* The people need not blame each other for the wretched condition of things on every side. It is thou, O priest, who dost cause this mischief, and for this reason thou shalt fall. Thy whole stock shall perish. As thou hast rejected knowledge, so I will reject thee; as thou hast forgotten me, so will I forget thee.

The poetic form is a regular trimeter movement in twelve lines. Three important modifications of the text require to be made. These are: (1) A change in the reading of עמך כמריבי כהן, which will place כהן in the following verse (*v.i.*). (2) The connection of לילה (v.⁵) with what follows, and the omission of ו in ודמיתי; this secures a better division of the words, as well as better thought. (3) The transfer of ועם לא יבין ילבט from v.¹⁴ to follow v.⁴. This clause is plainly out of place where it now stands. In the new position it fits well and completes the strophe.

4. [אך] ⅏ ὅπως; 𝔙 *veruntamen;* ⅏ = because no one is, etc. — Bach. אך איש יוכח ואל בו ירב אל איש = only let no one strive with him (*i.e.* Yahweh) and let no one reprove for my people, etc. Ru. כי כמוכח כמוכח = for the blamer is as the blamed one and my people, etc. — [ועמך כמריבי כהן] ⅏ ὁ δὲ λαός μου ὡς ἀντιλεγόμενος ἱερεύς = עמי כמרד כהן (Vol.); ⅏ ܘܥܡܝ ܐܝܟ ܟܗܢܐ = ועמך מריב ככהן (Seb.); 'A. ὡς ὁ ἀντιδικῶν ἱερεῖ; Σ. ὡς ἀντίρρησις ἢ πρὸς ἱερέα. Read ועמי (with Beck, Böckel, Bach., Ru., GAS., Now., Oet., *et al.*) and ככמריו (with Beck, Böckel; Mosapp, *ZAW*. V. 185; GAS.), and transfer כהן to beginning of v.⁵ as a vocative (GAS.). Beck reads הכהן as voc. at end of v.⁴. Mosapp (*ZAW*. V. 185), ועם ככמריו יכהן = and the people worship like their priestlings. Hermann (*SK.*, 1879, p. 516; so Kö. 360 *c*), וְעִמְּךָ מְרִיבִי כהן = and with thee is my strife, O priest. Mich. וְעִמְּךָ מריבי כהן = and thy people act like those who strive with me, O priest. WRS. (*Proph.* 408; so Che.), וַעַמְּךָ מרו בי כהן = and thy people have rebelled against me, O priest. Oort (*ThT.* and *Em.*; so Val., Gu.), עִמְּךָ רִיבִי הכהן, the כמ being due to dittog. Bewer (*JBL*. XXI. 110 f.), וַעַמְּךָ מֶרִיב כֵּן = "and thy people is striving thus," the phrase being a gloss explanatory of 4*a*. Gr. וַעַמְּךָ מְרִיבָה כהן, and Hal. וַעַמך מְרִיבֶיךָ כהן = and thy people it is that blames thee, O priest. New. וכעם כמריבת כהן = and as is the people, so is the provocation of the priest. Heil-prin, ועמך כמריביו כהן. Ru. (so We.³, Now.), ועמי כמוך הכהן = and my people are like thee, O priest. Marti, fol. Duhm, וְעַם כַּמֶּר וְנָבִיא כַּכֹּהֵן. — **14 *d*.** ועם לא [יבין ילבט] ⅏ καὶ ὁ λαὸς ὁ συνίων (some codd. οὐ συνίων) συνεπλέκετο μετὰ πόρνης, connecting the first two words of v.¹⁵ with v.¹⁴; so ⅏. Gr. יָלְבַד.

Gardner (*AJSL*. XVIII. 179), ועם מנאפים ילבטו = and with adulterers they lie down. — **5.** [כשלת 𝕲 ἀσθενήσει (= וכשל); 𝕾 ܟܘܠܗ܀ܡ (= יִשְׁקֻלְּתָּ (?)). Read כָּשֶׁלְתָּה יוֹמָם (so We., Now., Oet., Marti). Cf. Bach's sugg. that [היום may represent an original vocative, *e.g.* הָעָם or הַכֹּהֵן. — [עמך Some Mss. of 𝕲 μετ' αὐτοῦ (so also Ru.). — [לילה 𝕲 reads ללילה, and joins to following clause; 𝕾 makes it a separate clause. Ru. — [ודמיתי אמך 𝕲 ὡμοίωσα (= דְּמִיתִי); 'A., Θ. νυκτὸς ἐσιώπησα; 𝔙 *nocte tacere feci matrem tuam ;* 𝕾 ܐܦ ܟܘܠܗ. Gr. וְהַדְמֹית עַמָּך. Bach. וְדָמֶיךָ אֲמָחֶה (in *Praeparationen* (1892); but later in *Untersuch.* (1894), כָּל־יְלָדָיו דָּמִיתִי עַמָּך, for (לילה וגי). Ru. וְדַמּוּ תְרָפֶיךָ. Wkl. ללילה דָּמִיתִי יוֹמָךְ = I will turn thy day into night (*Untersuch.* 181; so Val.). For אמך, Now. בָּנֶיךָ, and Hal. עַמֶּךָ. Gardner (*AJSL*. XVIII. 178) om. ודמיתי אמך as a dittog. Marti, בֵּן וְדָמִתִי אִם. — **6.** [נדמו 𝕲 renders like דמיתי (*v.s.*), but in pass.; so 𝕾; 𝔙 *conticuit.* Gardner, נדמה. — [אתה הרעת מאסת Marti, אֶת־הַדַּעַת מָאַסוּ. — [אמאסאך Read with many Mss. אמאסך. Bach. (*Pr.*) — [בניך Wkl. בָּךְ (?); Bach. (*Pr.*) בְּרִיתָךְ. וְאֶמְאַס אֹתְךָ מַקַּהֵלִי. Marti changes all 2 pers. forms to 3 pers. in vs.5. 6.

4. *Still let none find fault, and let none reprove*] Who speaks? The prophet, and of his own words uttered in vs.1-3. This reproof of Israel, he concedes, is really out of place ; it is at all events useless. — *Since my people are but like their priestlings*] This meaning (*a*) is supported in part (*my people*) by 𝕲 (*v.s.*) ; (*b*) furnishes clearly the thought demanded by the context (cf. the reading "since my people are like thee, O priest" ; but this makes it necessary to keep "priest" where it stands, thus maintaining two difficulties) ; (*c*) is in accord with the use of "priestlings" elsewhere, this word always having a bad sense (cf. 10⁵ 2 K. 23⁵ Zp. 1⁴). This circumstantial clause, giving a reason why the people should not be upbraided, is strengthened by another, transferred from v.¹⁴. — **14** *d. Yea, a people stupid (and) falling to ruin*] A more appropriate juxtaposition could scarcely have been effected. — **5.** *O priest! thou shalt fall by day*] For text, *v.s.* According to another interpretation this should read *thou dost stumble,* and refers to the actual sin* in which the priest is engaged, rather than to the punishment which is to fall upon him.† The rendering *by day* is given, though incorrectly, to היום by 𝕲𝕾 and others. ‡ — *And the prophets also shall fall with thee*] These are the prophets, the word being collective, who prostituted their calling for the

---

* So Marck, Sim.   † So Ki., Ros., Ew., Now.   ‡ *e.g.* Hal.

sake of support ; they were in great numbers at many times, cf. Je. 5³¹ 6¹³ 14¹³·¹⁴ 1 K. 22⁶ᶠ·, and made prophecy a means of livelihood (Mi. 3¹¹ Am. 7¹²). They would perform their functions even while in a drunken condition, Is. 28⁷.* — *And by night I will destroy thy mother*] Cf. 𝕲𝕴. Confusion has arisen between the two meanings of the verb, "to be silent," and "to destroy" (*v.i.*). *Thy mother* hardly means the nation (cf. 2²),† for the pronoun evidently refers to the priest, and it is the priest of whom the prophet now speaks ; but rather, *thy stock,* ‡ *i.e.* a portion of the nation, the caste or clan of priests ; cf. *city* used in this sense (2 S. 20¹⁹ Ps. 149²), with which may be contrasted "I will also forget thy children" (v.⁶). Indeed, Nowack so renders the phrase here, changing the text (*v.s.*). — **6.** *My people will be destroyed by reason of their lack of knowledge*] This sentence determines the meaning to be attached to the verb of v.⁵ᵇ, and also seems to favor the conclusion there reached on "thy mother," — since now the people are dealt with as a whole. The knowledge lacking is knowledge of God (cf. v.²). The ordinary rendering *without knowledge* utterly fails to express the sense. The reference is not to the present situation, but to the future destruction of the people because of the sins into which the priest has led them. Nowack and Wellhausen, without good reason (viz. because it is unnecessary to the connection, and because it has no corresponding parallel member), treat this line as a gloss. — *Because thou hast rejected knowledge*] It is evidently the priest who is addressed § (both on account of the preceding context, and on account of the phrase following), and not the nation ; ‖ and besides, the idea of the nation as a priest-nation is probably late. " Knowledge, viz. of God's revealed will, was theoretically a deposit in the priestly order (Dt. 33¹⁰ Ez. 44²³ Mal. 2⁷)." ¶ — *I reject thee from being priest to me*] Clearly Hosea had at one time recognized the

---

* *V.* Da. *Exp.* 5th ser. II. 1–17; and art. "Prophets and Prophecy," *DB.*; Maybaum, *Proph.* 85–130; Sm. *Rel.* 248–255; WRS. *OTJC.* 278 ff.

† Jer., Ki., Ma., Ros., Hi., Sim., Ke., Wü., GAS.; cf. Or.

‡ Schmidt, WRS. *Proph.* 407; Che.

§ So AE., Ki., Cal., Bauer, Eich., Ros., Mau., Ew., Che., We., GAS., Now.

‖ Stuck, Schrö., Hi., Umb., Sim., Ke., Wü.

¶ Che. On the importance attached to knowledge of God by Hosea, see especially GAS. chap. XXI.

Northern priesthood as legitimate. This is a rejection of the
entire priest-clan ; and not of the priest-nation (Ex. 19⁶ is early
preëxilic ; Dt. 7⁶, barely preëxilic ; Is. 61⁶, exilic). מאס is the
opposite of בחר. — *And (because) thou hast forgotten the law of
thy God*] The *torah*, instruction, was supposed to be a deposit
with the priests, and God was supposed to be particularly near to
them. This instruction was in considerable part oral ; but even
at this date there must have been a written code (the Covenant
code, Ex. 20²³–23³³).* — *I will forget thy children, even I*] i.e.
the members of the clan, Winckler's suggestion of "thee" for
"thy children" being unnecessary in view of Dt. 33⁸ ᶠᶠ.

4. אך] Here in its limitative sense, *however* (Wü.), cf. Gn. 9⁴ Ps. 49¹⁶
Jb. 13¹⁵, rather than asseverative (Ki.), of which examples occur in Gn. 44²⁸
Ps. 73¹. — איש . . . איש] Note chiasm ; cf. the view which would make the
second איש the object of the vb. (Hi.). 𝕿 paraphrases the first איש by ספר,
the second by נביא. — עמי וגו׳] A circ. clause, H. 45, 1 *d* ; GK. 141 *e* ; cf. Kö.
360 *c*. — 14 *d*. ועם לא יבין ילבט] The impf.'s are coördinate and are adjectival ;
H. 21, 4 ; GK. 155 f. — 5. וכשלת] If כהן is placed in v.⁵, either (*a*) ו is used
to mark apodosis (cf. Is. 6⁷ Ho. 8¹⁴ Am. 1⁴), GK. 112 *x* ; Kö. 415 *s* ; or (*b*)
the ו may be omitted and the vb. treated as a proph. pf. In any case it is
future in idea, not frequentative. — היום] It is difficult to treat יום with the
article, when the corresponding לילה has none ; the natural rendering *to-day*
is inappropriate ; hence the suggestion of We. (*v.s.*). — דמיתי] Cf. confusion
in versions. To be distinguished are : דמה I., to be like ; and דמה II., to
be silent, to cease, to cause to cease, to destroy (= מחה ; cf. דמם, to be dumb,
silent, Wü., p. 146), which occurs four times in Hosea, viz. here and in 4⁶
10⁷·¹⁵, elsewhere in sense of destroy, Is. 6⁵ 15¹ Zp. 1¹¹ Je. 6² 47⁵ Ob.⁵ Ez. 32²
Ps. 49¹³·²¹. — 6. נדמו] Pl. the subj. being collective, H. 40, 4 *b* ; GK. 145 *b* ;
not to be taken as future (so Kö. 129) but as present pf. ; the change of time
is marked by the dropping of the ו cons. which appears in previous verse. —
מן [מבלי דעת] is causative ; *from lack of knowledge ;* cf. the use of מבלי in
which מן is neg., the בלי being a second neg. (as in מאין) = *without knowing*
= suddenly, Is. 5¹³ ; cf. Kö. 403 *e*. — ואמאסאך] א (after ס), a mistake retained
on account of the superstition entertained concerning the letter ; it is designated (note the º over it) by the Massoretes as יתיר *i.e.* superfluous, and is
lacking in nearly a hundred Mss. (cf. Kenn. and De Rossi *in loc.* ; cf. cod.
Babyl. 1010 A.D.) ; so BSZ. and BDB. ; Ew. § 247 *e*, treats the word as an
Aramaic form. The ו with Šᵉwā (De. *Complutensische Varianten*, 18 f. ; Baer,
Duodecim Prophetarum, 61) marks the apodosis ; GK. 112 *x* ; Kö. 415 *z*. —
מכהן] Reg. use of מן = that thou no more shalt be priest ; H. 41, 4 *d* ; GK.

---

* See Kit. I. 94 ; Di., We., Kue., Co. *Einl.*, Bu. *ZAW.* XI.

119 *x.* —וַתִּשְׁכַּח] Paral. with מָאַסְתָּ and dependent on כִּי, presenting an additional point, *and further, because thou hast forgotten;* cf. GK. 111 *x.* — תּוֹרַת
אֱלֹהֶיךָ] Hosea uses תּוֹרָה three times, viz. here and in 8¹· ¹². In all three cases there is evident reference to a body of priestly instruction; on the original meaning of the word, see We. *Prol.* 394; Sm. *Rel.* 36; Benz. *Arch.* 408, and art. "Law and Justice," *EB.;* Now. *Arch.* II. 97; Dr., art. "Law," *DB.;* but cf. Kö. *Offenbarung,* II. 347; Baudissin, *Priesterthum,* 207. — גַּם אָנִי] Triple emphasis; (*a*) as expressed by גם, (*b*) as expressed by the use of the pronoun; (*c*) as indicated in the position of the pronoun.

7–10, 12 a, b. *The priests' wickedness, their contagious example, and their abandonment of Yahweh.* The wickedness of the priests is great in proportion to their number. They live on the vices of the people. Their punishment shall come upon them as a reward for their deeds. They shall perish, because, filled with sensuality, they have abandoned Yahweh their God, and gone to consulting with that which is wood.

This strophe presents no irregularities; v.¹¹ being made to follow v.¹²ᵇ, the logical difficulty involved in going from v.¹⁰ to v.¹¹, and from v.¹¹ to v.¹² is avoided. Every line is a good trimeter.

7. כְּרֻבָּם] 𝕲 = פְּרֻבּוֹתָם. — כֵּן] Bach. כֹּהֲנִים, without necessity, yet with force. — כְּבוֹדָם Geiger (*Urschrift,* p. 316; so Gr.), foll. Jew. Sopherim, כְּבוֹדִי. — אָמִיר] Om. with 𝔖. — הֵמִירוּ] Read הֵמִירוּ with 𝔖𝕿 (so Geiger; Houtsma, *ThT.* IX. 60; Oort, *ThT.* and *Em.;* Val., Ru., GAS., Marti; cf. Buhl, *ZKW.* 1881, pp. 227 f.). Gr. יָמִירוּ. — **8.** חַטֹּאת] 𝕲𝕿 pl. (so Oort, *Em.*); Θ. ἀμαρτίας ὁ λαός μου ἐσθίει. Köhler (*Bibl. Gesch.* II. Pt. ii. 33 ff.), חַטַּאת. — יֹאכֵלוּ] Bach. יֹאכְלוּ (?); Gardner, יֹאבוּ לֹה = they consent to it. Bewer (*JBL.* XXI. 111 f.), יֹאכְלוּ. — עֲוֹנָם] 𝕲 pl. Oet., Marti, and Now.² עֲוֹנוֹ. — יִשְׂאוּ] Bewer would either read יִשָּׂא and om. previous אֶל, rendering, "My people's sin shall devour it and their guilt shall take away its life," or change אֶל to עַל = "and because of their guilt shall they take, etc." נַפְשׁוֹ] In some Mss. נַפְשָׁם; so in all versions (so also Hi., Oort, Gr., Bach., Ru., Now., Oet.). Wü. and Marti, וְנֶפֶשׁ; cf. GK. 145 *m.* — **9.** כַּכֹּהֵן] Ru., on basis of 𝕿's וְאִישִׁי דִיקִיר לְרַבְסִיר inserts כְּבוֹדוּ. — עָלָיו] 𝔖 pl. suff. as also in לוֹ and מֵעֲלָלָיו. — **10.** יְפֹרְצוּ] Read יְחָרֵצוּ, foll. 𝕲, κατευθύνωσιν (so also We., Oort, Val., Bach., Now.). Σ., Θ. πληθυνθήσονται; 𝖵 *cessaverunt;* 𝔖 ‏ܬ‏. Ru., וּפִרְצוּ. Gr. יִצָּרֵרוּ. — הִזְנוּ] Perhaps to be read יָזְנוּ (We., Oort, Now., Oet., Marti). — לִשְׁמֹר] 𝕲 transl. as inf. expressing purpose and connects זְנוּת of v.¹¹ with it as object; 𝔖 joins to v.¹¹ and renders, ‏ܢܡܝܘ‏. Oort (*ThT.* and *Em.*) om. as gloss. Bach., foll. Saadia, supposes a זְנוּת to have been lost from end of v.¹⁰. Now. and We., לֹא שָׁמָר (?). Gardner connects with it as obj. the first word of v.¹¹, pointing זְנוּת. Oort and Marti suspect the last five words of v.¹⁰ to be an editorial addition. — **12** *a, b.* בעוצ] ⅏ ἐν συμβόλοις, perhaps originally συμβουλαῖς = בעצות (so Stru., Seb.); cf. ⅏ ܣܘܠܟܠܐ = בעצתו (Seb.). — ישאל, יגיד [⅏ pl. Gr. שאל. — מקלו] ⅏ ἐν ῥάβδοις αὐτοῦ = במקלות (Vol.).

7. *According to their number, so they sin against me*] Cf. the rendering, "As many as they be, so many have sinned against me." * This is spoken of the priests,† not of the people,‡ as is shown by the meaning of v.⁸. The priestly numbers and influence have prospered and grown with the progress of the kingdom under Jeroboam II. — *They have exchanged their glory for shame*] Thus following the Syriac (*v.s.*), and a reading current among Jewish writers. The substitution of *my* (*i.e.* God's) *glory* (*v.s.*) is forbidden by the context, which is dealing with the priest's degradation. For similar expressions, cf. Je. 2¹¹ Ps. 106²⁰. *Their glory* = their position. — **8.** *They feed on the sin of my people*] This describes more distinctly the manner of the priests' sin. Sin (חמאת) does not here mean *sin-offering* § (the thought being that the priests encouraged the people to sin in order that they, the priests, might have the larger number of sin-offerings, *i.e.* greater perquisites), for four reasons: (1) the parallel word is עון, iniquity; this seems to demand for חמאת the meaning *sin;* (2) in Hosea's times, while compensation was given to the priests (cf. 2 K. 12¹⁶), it was not counted as an offering to Yahweh; (3) to eat the sin-offering was no sin (Lv. 6²⁵·²⁶); (4) the sin-offering was unknown prior to Ezekiel. ‖ Nor does it mean *money* paid as an expiation for sin,¶ since "eat" can hardly be used with such an object. Nor may it be interpreted of the whole cultus as described in vs.¹¹⁻¹⁸.** Nor can the rendering (*v.s.*) "My people shall eat sin, etc.," be justified in view of the context, which is concerned primarily with the priest. The word is to be explained therefore as *sin*, or with the versions *sins*, and is interpreted (1) by עון of the next line, (2) by 8¹¹ (cf. Am. 4⁴), in which Israel's sin is defined as belief in the efficacy of offerings to satisfy Yahweh, viz. "for Ephraim has made many altars to sin." The sin of the priests

---

* GAS.   † Ki., Che., Now.   ‡ Sim., Ke., Wü., Or.
§ Sim., Ke., Wü., Che., Or.; Sellin, *Beiträge z. isr. u. jüd. Rel.* I. 160 f.; II. 303 f.
‖ We. *Prol.* 73; Now.   ¶ Marti, *Rel.* 113 f.   ** Baudissin, *Priesterthum*, 236.

consists in encouraging the people in a false conception of
Yahweh, in order that they may increase their gain. — *And unto
their iniquity they lift their souls*] They direct their greed, their
longing, their appetite, to the guilt of the people; "they live
upon the vice of the day";* cf. Je. 22²⁷ Ps. 86⁴ 143⁸ Pr. 19¹⁸.
The singular suffix is either to be changed to the plural (with
versions), or read distributively. — **9.** *And so it becomes like
people, like priest*] The priest has become like, no better than,
the people, his special privileges and his nearness to Yahweh
now serving him no good.† It does not mean that the people
have become like the priest, *i.e.* "they have fallen under ritual,
doing from lust what the priests do from greed." ‡ In the latter
case v.⁹ would mark the transition from the priests to the people,
who, contaminated by the priests' example, are corrupt and
sensual; the thought here and in v.¹⁰ is of the people, and
not of the priests. In the former case, v.⁹ continues the description of the priests' wickedness and approaching punishment.
— *But I will visit punishment upon his ways, and his deeds I
will requite to him*] The priest shall suffer for his failure to
perform aright his functions, for the conduct which has brought
reproach upon his religion, and for his deeds which have been
in violation of his vows. — **10.** *And they shall eat and shall not
find satisfaction*] Mi. 6¹⁴ Lv. 26²⁶. This is still spoken of the
priests, as even those agree who would assign the following clause
to the people. § The reference is to the sacrificial meal, in which
the priest would take part with the worshipper. — *They shall
commit adultery and shall not find satisfaction*] The sin referred
to here is a part of the Baal cult which the Israelitish priests
have introduced into the Yahweh-service. According to this,
every woman was required to prostitute herself once in the
temple with a priest.‖ Against the ordinary interpretation of
the second clause, *they shall not increase, i.e.* the punishment
of childlessness, is to be urged (*a*) the fact that increase of offspring was not expected or desired from this immorality, (*b*) the
𝕲 reading (*v.s.*), which (cf. 1 S. 29⁴) means *to find satisfaction.*

---

* GAS. *in loc.*   ‡ GAS.   § Wü.
† Che.   ‖ Herodotus, I. 199; Strabo, XI. p. 532.

If the sin is that of the people, the ordinary interpretation is more appropriate. Cf. *non dirigentur;* * es soll ihnen nicht gelingen.† — *For they have left off heeding Yahweh*] The priests by their conduct have actually abandoned Yahweh, and now there follows what would naturally be expected and what furnishes the transition to the next strophe. — **12** *a, b. (Yea) My people ask counsel at their wood*] This is the climax. The priests have turned the people away and will no longer themselves have occupation, for the wooden teraphim are sought for advice; cf. 8⁶ 2 S. 2¹ 16²³. — *Their staff declares to them the oracle*] This may be (1) a staff with a wooden image carved on the top; ‡ (2) the diviner's wand (cf. Ez. 21²¹, where the king of Babylon combines divination by arrows with consultation of the teraphim); (3) a miniature *asherah,* or sacred tree, the foregoing "wood" being applied to the ordinary *asherah;* thus the entire charge would be directed against surviving elements of tree-worship.§

7. כֵן . . . . כ] Correlation, cf. 1 S. 9¹³ Ps. 127⁴ Jo. 2⁴; Kö. 371 *o.* — [כבודם Position emph. — [בקלון ב = price; cf. Ps. 106²⁰ Je. 2¹¹; and GK. 119 *p;* Kö. 332 *o.* — [אמיר] This is not impossible; but המירו seems much better. — [המירו, חטאו Pres. pfs. — **8.** חטאת] Emph. pos.; cf. Kö. 339 *m.* — [ישאו, יאכלו Freq. impfs. — [נפשו] = appetite, desire; cf. Sellin, *Beiträge,* II. 303 f.; Briggs, *JBL.* XVI. 25 f. On force of suff. cf. Kö. 348 *v.;* GK. 145 *m.* — **9.** [והיה] = and it shall be, not, "thus it comes to be" (GAS). — [כעם ככהן The כ is really a subst., lit., the similitude of the people, etc.; cf. Kö. 371 *g.* — [דרכיו ומעלליו Chiasm; sg. suff. used collectively. — **10.** [עוב לשמר] This expression is awkward, and might be improved by omitting לשמר, which stands in a peculiar place, and furnishes a construction of which no other example appears (*i.e.* ל with inf. after עוב). For other suggestions *v.s.* — **12** *a, b.* [עמי] Pathetic: — My people, consulting their wood, while their staff declares to them the divine will!

11, 12 *c*–**14** *c. The madness of the people in their sensual indulgence.* Indulgence in wine and harlotry has driven the people mad; everywhere is sensuality to be seen; but the young women who engage in lewdness do not deserve punishment; it is rather their fathers, whose example they follow, who shall suffer.

* Jer.   ‡ Pococke.
† Lu.; cf. Stuck.   § So WRS. *Sem.* 196; cf. Foote, *JBL.* XXI. 36.

The poetic form of this strophe is simple and regular. Two points only
deserve notice : (1) v.$^{14\,d}$ has already been transferred to follow v.^{4}; (2) כי
טוב צלה (v.^{13}) is probably a gloss (cf. Now.), added for explanation when
the usage had died out. Such an explanation would not have been needed
in Hosea's time.

11. זנות] 𝔊 connects with v.^{10} (*v.s.*). 𝔖 (*v.s.*) renders, *And they loved
fornication;* Arabic seems to use לשמר from preceding verse, *that they may
serve fornication and drunkenness.* — יין] Versions prefix וְ. — לב] 𝔊 makes
subj., joining with it עַמִּי of following verse. 𝔖 adds suff. = לבם. Ru. regards
vs.$^{11\,\text{and}\,14\,d}$ as a proverb originally placed on the margin by some reader (so
Now.). — **12** *c, d.* התעה] Read with 𝔖𝔙, התעם (so Gr., Bach., Ru., We., Now.,
Oort (*Em.*), Oet., Hal.). Marti, הִתְעָהוּ. — **13.** ואלה] — אֲהֵלֵיהֶם Bach. אֱלֹהֵיהֶם. — אליהכם] Bach.
Now. sugg. that a vb. has dropped out after this word, which expressed the
licentious practices of the men, or that it stood in place of כי טוב צלה, which
may well be a gloss. We. would supply the missing vb. after כי טוב צלה.
In view of these suggestions Gardner proposes to read לבנות יעלו = they go
up to the harlots, or לבמות יעלו for לבנה ואלה. — צלה] 𝔊 om. suff. Gr. צֶלֶם. —
14. לא אפקוד] 𝔊 joins to v.^{13} by καί; so 𝔏. Bach. (*Pr.*) הֲלֹא אִם. — בנותיכב
כלותיכם . . .] Gr. changes suff. to 3d pl. הֶם. — תנאפנה] Bach. (*Pr.*) adds
after this, וְעַל בְּנֵיהֶם. — הם] 𝔖 fem. = הֵנָּה. — יפרדו] Gr. יֻפְרָדוּ (so Oet., Marti).
Hal. יַקְרִיבוּ, they sacrifice.

11. *Harlotry, wine, and new wine take away the brain*] The
prophet introduces the new strophe with one of the many " wise
sayings " which were familiar to him, moral sayings which constituted the stock in trade of the wise men who sat in the gate.
Other examples of the use of wisdom sayings may be found in
4$^{1\,b.\,14\,d}$ 6$^{4\,b}$ 8$^{7\,a}$ 10$^{12\,f.}$ 14^9. This saying formed a most appropriate
introduction to a strophe which pictures the wildest possible in-
dulgence of passion. — **12** *c, d. For the spirit of harlotry has led
them astray*] They are actuated by an impulse which leads to
harlotry ; cf. the use of " spirit " in this same sense with " jealousy " (Nu. 5^{14}), " perverseness " (Is. 19^{14}), " uncleanness " (Zc.
13^2).* — *And they have played the harlot from under their God*]
Cf. 1^2. — **13.** *Upon the tops of the mountains they sacrifice*] Cf.
1 K. 14^{23} 2 K. 17^{10} Je. 2^{20} 3^6. This was the Canaanitish practice,
and, as such, is condemned. Mountains and hilltops were sacred
because regarded as nearest the abode of the deity ; cf. the " bare
places " of Je. 3^2. — *And upon the hills they make offerings*] Cf.

* Che.

Am. 4⁵; also *v.s.*, pp. 133 f. — *Under oaks, etc.*] Something seems
to be wrong here. Gardner's suggestion (*v.s.*) is not without merit.
Besides the difficulty already mentioned is the logical connection
with what follows : — *Therefore your daughters, etc.*] This is a
natural element in the situation ; it could hardly be otherwise,
for the religion thus cultivated demands licentiousness. — **14.** *I
will not punish your daughters . . . nor your spouses*] The parallelism corresponds exactly to that of v.¹³. Guilty as they may be,
these women do not deserve punishment. — *For they themselves
with harlots go aside*] *i.e.* the elders, the priests ; to the leaders
belongs the blame for the situation. Observe the change from
2d pers. *ye* to the 3d pers. *they ;* cf. Gn. 49²⁵ ᵃ· ²⁶ ᵃ Jos. 7¹² ᵇ Is. 1⁵
1 K. 1²ᵇ.* — *And with consecrated harlots they sacrifice*] *i.e.* professional prostitutes connected with the ceremonial of worship
(*v.i.*).

11. ויין ותירוש] Fermented and unfermented wine. Omission of ו with יין
favors the reading of 𝕲 which takes זנות with v.¹⁰. — יקח] Frequentative
impf.; H. 21, 3; Dr. § 33 (*b*). The vb. is in sg., because the compound subject expresses one idea, debauchery; Kö. 349 *r.* — **12 c, d.** Note the chiastic
arrangement of these two clauses. — **13.** אלון] Oak, a tree closely related to
the אלה, *terebinth*, as the two words evidently go back to the same root.
— לבנה] If the text is accepted, is of uncertain meaning; its only other occurrence is in Gn. 30³⁷. Its Arabic cognate لُبْنَى favors the meaning *storax*,
and so 𝕲 translates in Gn. 30³⁷. But here 𝕲 and 𝔖 render λευκή (poplar)
which seems to be the only suitable sense (Löw, *Aramäische Pflanzennamen*).
These three nouns, standing in the sg., and without the article, are used in a
generic sense, each representing its class. — **13.** Note chiasm in last two
clauses. — **14.** יפרדו] *They go apart, i.e.* from the sanctuary. It is clear that
the קדשות and their companions withdrew from the sanctuary itself; cf.
Herod. I. 199, ἔξω τοῦ ἱεροῦ, and other evidence cited by WRS. *Sem.* 455.
There seems to be no occasion to follow Ru. in supposing that פרד designated
any special ceremonial action.— הקדשות] Literally, *consecrated ones, i.e.* women
who had sacrificed their virtue in honor of Astarte; cf. Assyr. *kadištu.* Such
sacred prostitutes were common in ancient sanctuaries; cf. Strabo, XI. 532;
Gil-ga-meš Epic; WRS. *Sem.* 455; Jeremias, *Izdubar*, 59 f.; Benz. *Arch.* 428 f.;
Now. *Arch.* II. 132, 307; Jastrow, *Rel.* 485; Che., art. "Harlot," *EB.*; W. P.
Paterson, art. "Harlot," *DB.*; and the many references to the devotee, or
sacred prostitute, in the Hammurabi Code, *e.g.* §§ 110, 127, 178, 182; see

---

* See Kö. *Stil.* 238 f. Marti unnecessarily changes all the suffixes in vs.¹³· ¹⁴ to
the 3d pers.

R. F. Harper, *Code of Hammurabi* (1904); Cook, *The Laws of Moses and the Code of Hammurabi*, 149 f. Religious prostitution of this sort was distinctly prohibited by the Deut. Code (Dt. 23^17f.).

15-19. Though Israel is committed to idolatry may Judah not follow her example, nor resort to the places of idolatrous worship. Israel is given over to idols; she goes from bad to worse; her rulers are enamoured of infamy. An enemy will suddenly and violently carry her away.

If v.^15 is authentic, this strophe, like the preceding one, consists of twelve lines. Here, strangely enough, as in strophe 1, the 7th and 8th lines are lengthened, as if to indicate by their very length the sadness and seriousness of the situation. The authenticity of v.^15, or at least of 15 *a*, is denied by many (so *e.g.* We.; Sta. *GVI.* I. 577; Co. *Einl.* 172; Che. in WRS. *Proph.;* Gu., GAS., Now.; Seesemann, 20 f.; Marti, *EB.* 2122; but cf. Hal.) on the following grounds: the reference to Judah is forced and unnatural, lying aside from the prophet's thought in the preceding and following context; the sentiment concerning Judah is radically different from that expressed elsewhere in Hosea *e.g.* 5^5. 10. 13. 14 6^4; and the awkwardness of the address to Israel when the thought is directly concerned with Judah; but it may perhaps be said that Judah's affairs were always closely connected with those of Israel, and this mention would serve only to make more pointed the rebuke of Israel.

15. אם־זונה] 𝕲𝕾𝕷 join with v.^14. — אל יאשם [אל 𝕲 μὴ ἀγνόει = אל תאשם; 𝕾 = אל תאשם (so also Ru.), with ישראל subj. and יהודה obj. — יהודה] 𝕲 inserts καὶ before it, and joins with foll. vb, so 𝕷; 𝒴 supplies *saltem.* — בית און] 𝕲 εἰς τὸν οἶκον Ὤν; 'A., Σ., Θ. εἰς οἶκον ἀνωφελοῦς; 𝕮 וביתאל; 𝕷 *in domum Og.* One cod. of 𝕲 adds here the end of Am. 5^5. — תשבעו] Insert here, with We. and Now., שבע בבא (*v.i.*). Ru. supposes some such word as בְּאַשְׁמוֹתָם to have fallen out. — **16.** סררה] 𝒴 *lasciviens.* — יִרעם] Oort (*Em.*), הירעם. Hal. לא ירעם. — **17.** חבור] We. חבר (so Ru., Now.). Bach. (*Pr.*), בַּעֲבוּר. הנח לו 𝕲 ἔθηκεν ἑαυτῷ σκάνδαλα, (so 𝕷); perhaps 𝕲 represents some word that has been lost; 'A., Θ. ἀνέπαυσεν ἑαυτῷ; 𝒴 *dimitte eum.* Gr., foll. 𝕲, הניח לו מכשול. Bach. (*Pr.*), יְנַחֲלוּ. Ru. הניח לו מוסרים, using סר of v.^18; cf. 𝕲. Oort (*Em.*), הנחילו. Müller (*SK.* 1904, p. 124), הנח לו (cf. 2 K. 17^29). Marti om. as gloss. — **18.** סר סבאם] 𝕲 ᾑρέτισεν Χαναναίους (= בָּחַר בִּכְנַעֲנִים), so 𝕷; 𝒴 *separatum est convivium eorum;* 𝕾 om.; 'A. ἄρχων συμποσίου αὐτῶν; Σ. ἐπέκλινεν τὸ συμπόσιον αὐτῶν. 𝕮 evidently read שר for סר. Jer. renders 𝕲 by *provocavit Canan,* which represents ᾑρέθισε; hence, Vol. proposes מרה for סר. Read סר סבאים (so Houtsma, *ThT.* IX. 60; We., Oet., Marti). Ru. בָּאוּ בְּכִנְעֲנִים. Hd. אם סר סבאם = when their carousal is over (so Che., GAS.). Gr. שָׂרֵיהֶם סְבוּאִים. Oort (*Em.*), למו סבאָם כלם הזנה. Bach. (*Pr.*), סָרָבִים וְסַלּוֹנִים,

to be joined with v.[17].   Gardner, סָךְ סִכָּאִים .—[אהבו הבו] 𝕲 ἠγάπησαν;
𝔜 *dilexerunt;* 𝔖 ٥سحبو; Σ. ἠγάπησαν ἀγάπην. With 𝕲𝔖𝔜 and some
Heb. Mss., omit הבו (so, *e.g.*, Dathe, New., Hi., Oort (*ThT.* and *Em.*), Val.,
Gu., Gr., Ru., GAS., Now., Hal.).   Wü. אֲהֵב אָהֲבוּ.   Sim. אָהֹב אָהֲבוּ (Houtsma,
Wkl. *Untersuch.*).   Bach. הֵבֵל הֵבֵל .—אהבו מגניה [קלון מגניה] 𝕲 ἀτιμίαν ἐκ φρυάγματος
αὐτῆς; 𝔜 *afferre ignominiam protectores ejus;* Σ. οὗ ἡ βοήθεια ἀτιμία;
𝔖 ٥سكٰٰن مَجۡ.   Many, foll. 𝕲, מִגְאוֹנָהּ ק or ק׳ מִגְּאוֹנָם or מִגְּאוֹנָהּ (Houtsma, Gr.; Oort,
ThT. and *Em.*; Vol., Val., Gu., GAS.).   Cappellus, ק׳ מִגְּנֶיהָ.   Ru. ק׳ בְּנֶיהָ.
Bach. מָצֹר (or *Pr.* מֵאֹנְיֵהֶם) קֵלוּ מַקְלֵיהֶם, connecting first word of v.[19] with v.[18].
Wkl. (*Untersuch.*), קָלוֹנָם גְּאוֹנָם, the last word being joined with v.[19].   Böttcher,
ק׳ מִגְּנֶיהָ.—19. [צרר] 𝕲 συστροφή; ᾽Α. ἐνδεσμῶν; Σ. ὡσπερεί τις δήσειε;
𝔖 يُحۡز = will howl; 𝔏 *haec conversio.* Gr. תְּצָּר Ru. צרור. Oort (*Em.*),
צררה. Oet. צְרָתַם(?).—[רוח] Bach. (*Pr.*) would insert some such vb. as
לָקְחָה, or נָשָׂאה, or נָטְלָה; cf. Oet., who sugg. נְשָׂאתַם.—[אותה] 𝕲 σὺ εἶ (= אַתָּה);
᾽Α. (πνεῦμα) αὐτῆς; 𝔖𝔗Σ. om.; 𝔜 *eum.* Wkl. אוֹתָהּ or אֹתִי. Oort, אֹתָם (so
Gr., Val., Now., Hal.).—[מזבחותם] Read מִמִּזְבְּחוֹתָם with 𝕲 ἐκ τῶν θυσιαστη-
ρίων αὐτῶν; so 𝔖𝔗𝔏 and Arabic (so also We., Wkl. *Untersuch.*, Bach.,
Oort, *Em.*; Val., Ru., Gu., Now., Da. *DB.* II. 425, Oet., Marti).   Gr. מזנותם(?).

---

15. *Although thou, Israel, play the harlot*] For the reasons
urged against regarding v.[15a] as genuine, *v.s.* Noteworthy is the use
of the participle to express the continuance of the action.—*Let
not Judah become guilty*] *i.e.* let Judah keep herself free from
contact with that by which Israel has been contaminated. The
admonition to Judah closes with this brief exhortation.*—*Come
not to Gilgal*] cf. Am. 4⁵ 5⁵ also Ho. 12¹¹; addressed to Israel,†
not Judah, ‡ although Judah may have been prone to go to Gilgal
(cf. 2 K. 8¹⁸ 16³ Ez. 23¹³). The northern Gilgal is of course intended (*v.s.*, pp. 91 f.).—*Nor go up to Beth-aven*] Cf. Am. 4⁵ 5⁵ 1 K.
12²⁹⁻³³; copied from Amos, § and as before an intentional pun on
the name of Bethel. On "go up" with Bethel, cf. Ju. 1²² 1 S. 10³.
—*And swear not in Beersheba, " By the life of Yahweh"*] Cf.
Am. 8¹⁴: "As thy way, O Beersheba, lives." The insertion of
"in Beersheba" ‖ is justified by the parallelism of the context,
which demands in this line the name of a town, and by the
analogy of Am. 5⁵ 8¹⁴. Swearing by Yahweh was not regarded as
sinful (Je. 38¹⁶), but was permitted (Je. 4²) and, indeed, later

---

* Cf. Hi., who would extend it to v.[17] or v.[19].   † Abar., Cal., *et al.*
‡ Ki., Os., Schmidt, Geb., *et al.*   § Ew.   ‖ We., Now., GAS.

commanded (Dt. 6¹³ 10²⁰).   In Am. 5⁵ the prohibition is against coming to Beersheba for worship.   It is quite certain therefore that a word designating the place has fallen out.   Without this word the passage has been taken to prohibit (1) the blending of the name of the true God with those of idols (cf. Zp. 1⁵ Ez. 20, 2 Cor. 6¹⁵) ; * (2) swearing by Yahweh as a *local* god, cf. Am. 8¹⁴, ᛞ.† — **16.** *Yea, like a stubborn heifer, Israel acts stubbornly*] Cf. 11⁴ Je. 31¹⁸ Dt. 32¹⁵. This stubborn rebelliousness is seen in Israel's unwillingness to follow the leadings of her master Yahweh ; there is no reference, however, to the yoke of the law. ‡ — *Can Yahweh now feed them like a lamb in a broad place ?*] Not a declarative sentence indicating that Israel will be like a lamb in a great pasture-field, open to attack on every side and without proper protection, § but, although no interrogative particle is found, a question implying surprise. The connection with the preceding clause is close ; Israel being a stubborn heifer, how can she expect to be shepherded like a lamb? The " broad place " = plenty and prosperity ; cf. Ps. 18¹⁹ 31⁸ 118⁵ Is. 30²³. כִּי here means *yea*, not *but;* and the connection with v.¹⁵, while not close, is assured. ‖ — **17.** *Ephraim is wedded to idols ; leave him alone*] The figure is that of husband and wife (cf. Mal. 2¹⁴) ; ¶ of such a character was the " mystic relationship " of the idolater and his God (Is. 44¹¹ ; cf. 1 Cor. 10²⁰).** The accusation here is not that of following strange gods, but of using idols to represent Yahweh, as, *e.g.* in the case of the calves and the Baalim. The latter half of the verse is a rhetorical imperative addressed to the audience ; the thought being that it is useless to try to reform Israel ; he must be left to meet his well-deserved fate. — **18.** *A band of topers ! they devote themselves to harlotry*] The text of vs.¹⁸· ¹⁹ is very difficult, perhaps hopelessly corrupt (so Nowack). This rendering is based upon a slight change of text (*v.s.*). The A.V. " their drink is sour "†† is impossible ; likewise " their drinking is degenerated " (cf. Je. 2²¹) ; ‡‡ and " he is gone after

---

* Ki., Abar., Cal., Ros., Hd., Pu., Ke., Wü.   † Hi., Or., We.
‡ Ki., Abar., Geb., Bauer, *et al.*   § Cal., Os., Ros., Hd., Ke., Wü.
‖ So Abar., Ew., Hi., St., Che., We., Now., GAS.   ¶ Ros., Sim.   ** We.
†† Lit. *departs* (cf. Is. 1²²) ; so Ros., Pu.; cf. rend. *putrid, of offensive smell;* so Ki., Cal.   ‡‡ Ew., Ke.

their wine." *   On the basis of 𝕸𝕿 it will be "their drunkenness over (*i.e.* when their carousal is over) they indulge in harlotry." † Following the example of the versions (*v.s.*) many have attempted to find an interpretation by changing the text (*v.s.*), *e.g.* Ruben, "he provoked the Sabaeans"; Graetz, "their princes are drunken"; Gardner, "they have turned aside (they have become) drunkards"; Bachmann, "briers and thorns" (to be taken with v.[17]). Neither the causative idea, viz. "they strive to lead others to idolatry" (cf. 4^{10} 5^{3} 2 Ch. 21^{13}) ; ‡ nor the idea of threat, "they shall commit whoredom enough," *i.e.* will exhaust themselves in it (cf. inf. abs. in Am. 9^{8}) § seems to have been intended ; but rather the thought that when weary of drunkenness, they plunge into licentiousness ; they go from bad to worse. — *Her rulers have fallen in love with shame*] Here again the text is uncertain ; the rendering adopted involves a slight change of text (cf. Ps. 88^{17}). ∥   "Shield," the literal rendering, is used figuratively of *rulers* (cf. Ps. 89^{18} 47^{9}). With 𝕸𝕿 as basis, the sin mentioned was that of : (1) bribery, "the princes love (to say) give ye (a bribe for the perversion of justice), and this is a shame"; ¶ or, (2) loving shame, "her princes love, they give shame," *i.e.* so love shame as to give it to others.** Of special interest are the following interpretations (*v.s.*) : (1) 𝕲, "they love shame rather than her pride," *i.e.* Yahweh ; (2) "their sceptres, or scales, are lighter than a grain of corn" (the first word of v.[19] being joined with v.[18]) ; †† (3) "in their gardens they love shame"; ‡‡ (4) "they loved their shame; their pride the wind carries, etc." (the last word of v.[18] being read with v.[19]) ; §§ "on account of their gardens their faces shall blush." ∥∥ — **19.** *A wind has enveloped (i.e. will sweep) her in its wings*] Israel shall be carried away with the suddenness and violence of a wind-storm (cf. Is. 57^{13}).¶¶   It is not the disappointment which comes from finding oneself wholly dependent upon what proves to be wind, *i.e.* nothing.*** With this idea may be compared the expression "wings of the wind" (Ps. 18^{10} 104^{3}), and in 13^{15} "the east wind." ††† — *And*

---

* New.   † Abar., Hd., GAS., *et al.*; cf. RV.   ‡ Ros.   § Hi.
∥ So many, including Hi., Che., Gr., Ru., Val., Oort, Gu., Now., GAS., Hal.
¶ AE., Ki., Grot.   ** Abar.   †† Bach.   ‡‡ Ru.   §§ Wkl.   ∥∥ Marti.
¶¶ Ki., Ros., Hi., Che., *et al.*
*** So AE., Ki., Abar., Cal.; cf. Schmidt, pp. 186 f.   ††† Wü., Now.ᴴ

they shall be ashamed of their altars] Cf. 8[11]. This requires the adoption of 𝔊 and 𝔖 (*v.s.*).

15. אם] With concessive force, *though;* and so representing Israel's case as irremediable (Wü.); cf. GK. 160 *a*; Kö. 394 *a*. — זנה] Used figuratively, in emphatic position. — ויאשם] The use of the 2d pers. by 𝔊 and 𝔖 makes the construction much more natural; however, sudden transitions from one person to another are not so uncommon as to necessitate adoption of the reading of 𝔊 (cf. 1 K. 1[2] Is. 1[5] Ez. 20[40] 29[6 f.], and *v.* Kö. *Stil.* 238 ff.). — יהודה] Is construed here as masc., the thought of the people being dominant; cf. Kö. 249 *b*. — בכאר שבע] An additional argument for this insertion is the pun that it furnishes; cf. בית און and common prophetic usage, *e.g.* Mi. 1[14 f.]. — חי יהוה] Lit. *living is Yahweh;* cf. our *as true as I live;* Ew.[8] 329 *a*. — **16.** Note the alliterative recurrence of ר in [16 a]. — כפרה] Cf. Am. 4[1] for use of same figure. — **17.** חבור] On the use of the cstr., cf. Kö. 336 *o*. — הנח-לו] For similar use of this vb., *v.* 2 K. 23[18]; cf. Kö. 289 *d*. — **18.** סר סבאים] (*v.s.*) *A band of topers!* This reading satisfies the context and involves but slight change in the consonants of the text. The phrase may be taken as exclamatory or as a *casus pendens*. — אהבו הבו] הבו seems to have arisen through dittography, not being found in the chief versions. Bach.'s conjecture (*v.s.*) is unnecessary. Other treatments of הבו are: (*a*) denom. from هَيَبَ, *to fear, i.e.* love and fear shame (Mich.); (*b*) from הוב, *consecrate*, used as adv., "they bring with zeal their shameful gifts" (Bauer, transl. מגן as *gift*); (*c*) = יהבו in pf. and in verbal appos. with אהבו = *they love to give shame* (𝔗, Jer., Ros.); (*d*) the two words to be read as one: אהבוהבו (cf. מתחתני, Ps. 88[17]), (Fürst, *Lex.;* Mau., Hi., Hd., Pu., Ke., Or.). — **19.** צרר] The versions, with the exception of 𝔖, support the existing text. It is unnecessary (1) to supply לקחה or נשאה (Bach.; cf. Oet.); (2) to make the verb צרר fem. pf. (Oort), or impf. (Gr.), or verbal noun (Ru.). A proph. perf. Note the use of רוח as masc. with this vb., but as fem. with suff. אותה. — כנפיה] The use of the fem. sg. suff. here is difficult to account for, being preceded and followed by masc. pl. forms referring to Israel. Moreover, Hosea rarely uses the sign of the definite object (Now.). Bach.'s conjecture that this is a corruption of אתם, which was a remnant of an original נשאתם, is attractive, but involves the connection of צרר with the preceding verse, for which there is no sufficient ground. — ויבשו] An impf. with ו conjunctive following a proph. perf. and denoting a coördinate circumstance; cf., however, Kö. 147 *a*. — ממזבחותם] This reading is supported by 8[11] and by the fact that זבח does not form a plural with fem. ending.

§ 7. The Guilt of Priests and Princes, and their Punishment.

5[1-14]. Israel has become defiled under the leadership of the priests and princes, who do not know Yahweh, and, therefore, have

been faithless to him.   Punishment will be inflicted ; this will
be twofold, viz. from without, an invading army which will lay
waste the land ; also, from within, corruption and anarchy with
civil war ; *the moth, and the lion.*

This piece, consisting of four twelve-line strophes, trimeter movement, has
suffered little or no change.   Strophe 1 (vs.^[1-3]) indicates the responsible persons ; strophe 2 (vs.^[4-7]) describes the relation of these persons to Yahweh.
Strophe 3 (vs.^[8-11]) pictures the destruction as coming from without, viz. an
invading army ; strophe 4 (vs.^[12-14]) pictures the destruction as coming from
within, viz. corruption and anarchy.   The four strophes divide themselves
very naturally into two groups of two each (cf. the Massoretic Perasheth, ס).
Each double strophe is introduced with a phrase inviting attention, viz.
Hear this (v.^1) and *Blow the trumpet* (v.^8).

V. 1-7. *The priests and princes, a snare to Israel* (^[1-3]) *; their
ignorance of Yahweh and consequent faithlessness to him* (^[4-7]).
(1) The priests and princes have proven to be a snare in which
Israel has been entrapped ; for Israel has been led by them into
harlotry, and has become unclean.   (2) They are filled with the
spirit of harlotry and do not understand Yahweh.   They will fail
to find ' him when they seek him ; for he will have withdrawn.
Alas, they have dealt treacherously with Yahweh ; for they have
abandoned him for another.

1. בית ישראל] Oet. and Meinhold treat these words as a gloss. — [למצפה
𝔊 τῇ σκοπιᾷ, not treating it as a name; so 'A. τῇ σκοπεύσει; Σ. τῇ πλατείᾳ;
𝔙 *speculationi;* 𝕿 וְלְמַלְפָּיכון; 𝔖 ܠܡܣܟܪ; 𝔏 *speluncae in visitatione.* — [תבור
𝔊 τὸ 'Ιταβύριον; 'A. Θαβώρ; Σ. τὸ ὅριον; Θ. τὸν δρυμόν; 𝕿 תבור רם; 𝔏 *in
statum in se.* — **2.** ושחטה שטים העמיקו] 𝔊 ὃ οἱ ἀγρεύοντες τὴν θήραν κατέπηξαν
= שָׁטוּ שְׁטִים (so also Bauer); Σ. and E', καὶ θυσίαν . . .; 𝔙 *et victimas
declinastis in profundum.* 𝔖 ܘܡܨܝܕܬܐ ܠܨܝܕܐ ܥܡܩܘ; 𝔏 *quam qui
venantur confixerunt bestiam.*   The following readings for this clause deserve
consideration : Vol. וְשְׁחֵטִי שֶׁטָחִים הע׳.   Seb. וְצֵידִים הַשִּׁטִים הע׳ = and hunters
going round about lay snares.   Umb. וְשַׁחַת הַשִּׁטִים הע׳ = and the pit of Shittim
they have made deep (so We., Che., Ru., GAS. Now., Oort (*Em.*), Marti).
Val. foll. a sugg. of We. ושחת בשטים עמוקה.   Gr. וְשְׁחֵטָה מַשְׁטֵמָה הע׳.   Houtsma,
וּשַׁחַת הַשֹּׁטְמִים הע׳.   Bach. (*Pr.*) וְשָׁם שָׁחֲטָה שֹׁחֲטִים הָעַמִּים.   Linder (*SK.* XXXIII.
741), שַׁחַת שֵׁטִים הע׳.   Oet. וְשַׁחַת הַשֵּׁטִים הע׳.   Bach. וְשַׁפְטֵי הָעַמִּים.   Ew.
וּשַׁחֲתָה שֵׁטִים הע׳ (so Sim.).   Oort, וְשַׁחַת הע׳.   Hal. בשחטה or בשחטם הע׳.   Che. (*CB.*),
ושחת חרטמים הע׳.   Müller (*SK.* 1904, p. 124), וְשְׁטְחָה. — [ואני Read ואין (so Che.,

Marti).—[מוסר] 𝔊 παιδευτής = מְיַסֵּר (so also Oort (*Em.*)); 𐤔 רֹןֹיֹ; 𝔙 *eruditor*. Umb. מוּסָר, fetter (so Linder, *SK*. XXXIII. 742). Gr. אֱיסָר. Oort, מוֹסִיר. Hal. מוּסָר.—[לכלם] 𝔊 ὑμῶν (= לכם).—3. עתה] Read אַתָּה (so We., Now., Oet.).—[הזניתה] 𝔊 ἐξεπόρνευσεν = הזנה; so 𐤔𐤏 (so also Ru., Oort (*Em.*)). Some Heb. Mss. הזנתה. Oet. and Marti, זָנִיתָ. We. and Now. treat 3 *b* as an explanatory gloss.—4. יתנו] We. suspects the text and suggests some vb. meaning "forsake." Oet. foll. 𐤔 יתנו (so Hal., Now.², Marti). Bach. יַתְכְּנוּ.—[מעלליהם] 𝔊 τὰ διαβούλια αὐτῶν. 'Α. ἐπιτηδεύματα; Σ. βουλάς; Θ. γνώμην. Oort, עֲלֵיהֶם.—5. ועָנה] 𝔊 καὶ ταπεινωθήσεται; cf. 𐤔 כלאמֹצֹא = וְעָנה (Seb.; so also Oort). Marti, וְעָנה.—[וישראל ואפרים] Om. one of the words (so Oet., Marti). We. om. both.—[יכשלו] 𝔊 ἀσθενήσουσιν.—[כשל] 𝔊𐤔 = וכשל (so also Oort, *ThT*. and *Em.*; Ru., Oet.), or יכשל (so also We., Gr.).—6. בצאנם ובבקרם] 𝔊 om. suff.—[ימצאו] 𝔊 adds αὐτόν.—[חלץ] 𝔊 precedes by ὅτι (= כי); so also 𐤔. Oort (*ThT*. and *Em.*), חלף. Oet. חֵלֵץ or יֵחָלֵץ.—7. ביהוה וגו'] 𝔊 ὅτι τὸν κύριον, κ.τ.λ. Marti, כי הם בי בגרו וכי חלץ (so Now.²).—[ילדו] 𝔊 ἐγεννήθησαν αὐτοῖς (= ילדו). 𐤔 ܐܟܣܐ.—[עתה] 𐤔 om. the entire clause.—[חרש] 𝔊 ἡ ἐρυσίβη, mildew (= חֵרֶש = חֵרֶם); We. sugg. that 𝔊 may be a corruption of ερυς, which was a transliteration of חרש.

Arabic, القَمْل. Grotius and Che. (*CB*.), חָסִיל. Ru. מְחָרֵש. Bach. חֹרֵב or (*Pr*.), חֵרֶב (so Hal.; cf. Oet.). We. יחריב(?). New. העש. Oort, משחית (*ThT*. and *Em*.; so Val., and Marti, who supposes a verb, וְיַחְרִיב or וְיֶחֶרְבוּ, to have fallen out from after it). Gr. יָרֵש ואת. Oet. חֵרֶם or חֵרֶב.—[חלקיהם] תֹּאכְלֵם חֵרֶב. Oet. חמוריהם.

1. *O priests . . . house of Israel, and house of the king. . . .*] The address is threefold, viz. to *the priests*, who have especially received rebuke in former statements ; to *the people* (viz. the entire Northern Israel, not the elders *), who likewise have been entangled by and with the priests; and then, a step forward being taken as if by an afterthought (the chiasm is noticeable), there is added, *the house of the king* (cf. Isaiah's address to the house of David, Is. 7¹³), *i.e.* the court, including the royal family. In this addition, the thought of the prophet begins to concern itself, as it has not before done, with the political side. A little later, this thought becomes predominant ; for it is true that, after all, the king and court could control the priests. The prophet, however, does not direct the sermon especially to the court.† With this arraignment, cf. Is. 1² Mi. 1² Jo. 1².—*Hear . . . hearken . . . give ear*] These three verbs present a climax, the second being

---

* AE. † So We.

more specific than the first, and the third than the second. — *For
for you is the judgment*] Very different from Mi. 3¹, " Is it not for
you to know judgment?" but all the more true because Micah's
statement holds good. The "you" does not refer exclusively to
the court ("Yea, O house of the king, give ear, because to you
belongs the administration of judgment"), although this would
(*a*) explain the בִּי which is otherwise difficult, (*b*) suit the parallelism, and (*c*) be favored by Mi. 3¹ Dt. 1¹⁷.* It refers rather
to all the persons addressed. *Judgment*, here, is not the act of
judging as in Mi. 3¹, but the sentence of the judge, 1 K. 3²⁸ Ps. 17²,
here unfavorable, as in Is. 53⁸ Je. 1¹⁶ 4¹² 39⁵. This *sentence* (cf.
also v.¹³) points to the position occupied by Israel in relation to
Assyria, perhaps in the reign of Menahem (cf. 2 K. 15¹⁹·²⁰), and
to the ultimate destruction of the Northern kingdom which was
soon to follow. — *A snare . . . a net. . . .* (v.²) *a pit*] This is the
triple figure, borrowed from the hunter, employed to designate the
entanglement into which Israel has fallen. For similar usage, cf.
Am. 3⁵ 1 S. 26²⁰ Ps. 10⁹ 11². The rendering *pit* rests upon a
restored text (*v.s.*). — *On Mizpah . . . on Tabor . . . of Shittim*]
Mizpah = Mizpah of Gilead, Ju. 10¹⁷ 11¹¹·²⁹; also = Ramoth
Gilead, Jos. 20⁸ 21³⁸ 2 K. 9¹·⁴·¹⁴; also = Ramath-Mizpeh, Jos.
13²⁶. This was the place consecrated by Jacob (Gn. 31⁴⁵⁻⁵⁴);
perhaps es-Salṭ in Belk'a.† *Tabor* (= Jehebet Tor) was in the
territory of Issachar and Zebulon (cf. Ju. 4⁶). — **2.** *Shittim* (cf.
text above), also called אָבֵל הַשִּׁטִּים, was a camping-place of Moses
and Joshua (Nu. 25¹ Jos. 2¹ 3¹). It was here that the affair of
Baal-Peor took place. These three places were celebrated, perhaps, for the peculiarly seductive character of the worship which
they represented. For other renderings of the first clause of v.²,
v.i. — *And there is no correction for any of them*] This ‡ is more
consistent with the context than, "And I am a rebuke to all of
them," § although the latter is the more commonly accepted
meaning, and, according to Wellhausen, furnishes the transition
from the priests to the people, from the seducer to the seduced.
— **3.** *I know Ephraim, and Israel is not hid from me*] *i.e.* "It is

---

* Cf. Rashi.   ‡ Che.
† But cf. GAS. *HG.* 587 f.   § Ew., Hi., Sim., Now., GAS.

I who know, etc.," in striking contrast with the oft-repeated statement that Israel does not know Yahweh. — *Yea thou, O Ephraim,
hast committed harlotry, and Israel is defiled*] For text (*v.s.*).
The כִּי cannot mean *for* unless it goes back to v.^{2b}. — **4.** *Their
doings do not suffer them to return to their God*] This rendering,*
making "doings" the subject, is preferable to the other rendering,
"They do not frame their doings to return, etc.," † which makes
it the object. For one use of נתן, 1 Ch. 22^{19}; for the other, Ju. 3^{28}
15^1 1 S. 18^2 24^7 Gn. 20^6. — *For the spirit of harlotry is within
them*] *i.e.* in their constitution. — *And Yahweh they do not know*]
See 2$^{8.\ 20}$ 4^6 6^6 8^2. This is the burden of Hosea's preaching ; lack
of a proper appreciation of the character of Yahweh has led Israel
into all sorts of corruption. ‡ — **5.** *But the pride of Israel shall testify to his face*] This rendering of ענה § (= עני, cf. عني), (1) goes
better with the following preposition בְ ; (2) suits better the context in 7^{10} than the rendering *is humbled* (which takes ענו = ענה
= عنو ‖). *The pride of Israel* has been taken as a title of Yahweh
(cf. Am. 8^7),¶ in which case it would mean that Yahweh has delivered a judgment (cf. Ru. 1^{21}) against Israel which signifies destruction ; but the context ** is dealing with Israel's "material
grandeur" (cf. Zc. 10^{11} Ez. 32^{12}), *i.e.* arrogance ; in this case it
would mean : Israel's arrogance is a testimony against Israel himself. This arrogance (*v.* Wellhausen) is the trust in the ritual, and
the feeling that there is no need to turn from that and to repent
(cf. 7^{10}). — *And Ephraim shall stumble in his guilt*] The word
stumble is of frequent use among the prophets to designate dis-
aster and ruin ; cf. 4^5 14$^{1.\ 9}$ Is. 31^3 59^{10} Je. 50^{32} Na. 2^5 3^3. — *Judah
also shall stumble with them*] These words are suspected as a
gloss by some †† without sufficient reason. An occasional side
glance at Judah, a people so intimately connected with his own,
must not be denied to the prophet. — **6.** *With their flocks and
their cattle*] Ready to be offered as sacrifices. — *They will go to*

---

* So 𝕿, Eich., Mau., Ke., Wü., Che., GAS.   † Umb., Hi., Ew.

‡ Marti om. v.^{4b} as a gloss based on 4^{12}.

§ Ki., Eich., Dathe, Umb., Ew., Hi., Ke., Che., We., GAS.

‖ 𝕲𝕿𝕾, Rashi, AE., Ros., Schrö., Mau., Huxtable.   ¶ Che.

** So We.; GAS. I. 262.

†† So Oort (*ThT.* XXIV. 485), Now., Marti (*Rel.* 119, *EB.* 2122, and *Dodeka-
proph.*).

seek Yahweh] It is Northern Israel, not Judah,* of whom the
prophet speaks. — *He has withdrawn from them*] Yahweh's patience has an end (cf. Mi. 3⁴) ; their superstitious ritualism and
self-sufficiency can no longer be tolerated.† — **7**. *They have dealt
faithlessly*] Used of adultery, Je. 3²⁰ ; cf. Mal. 2¹⁴. Hosea is here
keeping up the figure of the nation's marriage to Yahweh, and
characterizes the syncretism in worship as a breach of the marriage contract. — *For they have begotten strange children*] The
figure is continued ; these words are not to be taken literally as
a charge brought against the Israelites for marriage with heathen
women, from which unions " strange " children were born ; ‡ but
rather, the parents having departed from the true worship of
Yahweh, their children have naturally followed, and are consequently strangers to Yahweh, having no place among his children. §
— *The (next) new moon may destroy them with their portions*]
i.e. within a month ruin may overtake them. ‖   The ordinary
interpretation, which makes the new moon represent the prevailing cult with all its corruption and superstition,¶ is untenable,
because, at this time, the new moon did not occupy an important
place in the cult.   Other attempts (*v.s.*), based on change of text,
have not been successful, *e.g.* the locust shall devour, etc.** ; mildew shall devour, etc. ; †† the sword shall devour, etc. ; ‡‡ he will
hinder them from ploughing. §§

1. זאת] Neut., H. 2, 3 *a*; GK. 122 *q.* — האזינו] . . . הקשיבו] Both words
are poetical synonyms of שמע, the ordinary prose word. האזינו seems to
mean more precisely *turn the ear* and so give close attention, while הקשיבו
is *drink in eagerly.* — כי] Must be either asseverative = *surely* (cf. μέν) or
(cf. ὅτι) equivalent to quotation marks. — שחת] . . . רשת . . . פח] On פח
cf. Am. 3⁵. The רשת was a net laid upon the ground to catch birds; while
the פח was a pit dug in the track of large game and concealed by a covering;
cf. Ps. 94¹³ Pr. 26²⁷. — **2.** וישחטה שטים העמיקו] The reading of Che. and We.
is the most satisfactory (*v.s.*). The chief interpretations of 𝔐𝔗 have been:

---

* So AE., Ki.

† Marti om. this phrase because (1) חלק is not elsewhere used intransitively,
and (2) the thought that Yahweh could be found at the altars is not in harmony
with Hosea's conceptions.

‡ Theodoret, Rashi; for still other views, cf. Jer., Eich.

§ Ki., Cal., Ew., Hi., Sim., Ke.   ‖ Cf. Now., GAS.   ¶ Ke., Wü.
** Grotius, Che. (*CB.*).   †† Ru.   ‡‡ Bach., Hal., Oet.   §§ We.(?)

(1) and they slaughter numerous victims for idols (𝕿); (2) and slaughter have they heaped up (Rückert, cited by Wü.); (3) through sacrificial slaughter have they sunk deep into error (Hes.); (4) through slaughter have they become absorbed in their course (Lu.); (5) and excesses have they spread out deeply (Ke.); (6) and revolters are sunk deep in corrupt ways (Or.); (7) and backsliding they sinned deeply (Ew.). Cf. the many emendations proposed (*v.s.*). — **3.** אני] Used for rhythmic reasons; GK. 135 *a*. — [אפרים וישראל Chiastic. — [כי] Asseverative. — עתה] = אַתָּה; the same confusion of these two words occurs in 1 K. 1¹⁸, 𝕲, and 2⁹, 𝕲 and *Luc.* The ordinary usage of עתה in Hosea is to introduce the punishment or consequence (4¹⁶ 5⁷ 7² 8⁸· ¹⁰· ¹³ 10²); cf., however, 10³. — **4.** . . . יתנו ל] This is the only case where the accusative of the obj. is omitted in this kind of construction (*v.s.*), but the obj. is here easily supplied. — **5.** ועּנה] On the roots ענו and ענו cf. p. 185 and Rahlfs, *עני und ענו in d. Psalmen* (1892). — [וישראל] Omit; Ephraim and Israel are wholly synonymous terms, used interchangeably by Hosea (cf. 4¹⁶ f. 5³· ¹¹ ff. 7¹ 11⁸), hence one of them is superfluous here. — **6.** The parallelism in vs.⁶ and ⁷ is quite irregular, and thus in contrast with the prec. verses of the double strophe. — חלי] Intrans. only here (We.). — **7.** חדש] Means *within a month* (Jer., Ros., Mau., Hi., Umb., GAS.); and although this seems indefinite (cf. Zc. 11⁸), the usage is confirmed by the fuller expression חדש ימים (cf. Gn. 29¹⁴ Nu. 11²⁰· ²¹).

8–14. *Destruction is coming from without and from within.*
(3) An invading army will bring devastation; (4) corruption and anarchy, like moth and rottenness, produce a fatal disease.

8. בגבעה] 𝕲 ἐπὶ τοὺς βουνούς (= בגבעות); 𝔖 ܣܘܰܓܺܝ. — 𝕲 ἠχήσατε = חצרו.—[ברמה 𝕲 ἐπὶ τῶν ὑψηλῶν = ברמות; 𝔖 same as for בגבעה. — בית און] בּית אָוֶן 𝕲 ἐν τῷ οἴκῳ "Ων; 'A. εἰς οἶκον ἀνωφελοῦς; Σ. ἐν Βὴθ "Ων; 𝔖 ܘܶܐ ܣܘܳܐ. Sayce (*Babyl. and Or. Record*, II. 20), בית און. Read with We. and Now. — אחריך] בבית אל 𝕲 ἐξέστη = חרד or הֶחֱרד (Vol.), or יחרד (Sim.); 'A., Σ., Θ. ὀπίσω σου; E´, κατὰ νώτου σου; 𝖵 *post tergum tuum;* 𝖑 *et expavit.* We., foll. 𝕲, sugg. החרידו (imv.) (so Gr., Ru., Now., Oort (*Em.*), Marti). Bach. אחרים or אחריך אחרים. Meier (*SK.* XV. 1028 f.), אחרית. Sayce (*Babyl. and Or. Record*, II. 20), חֲרד בן-אוֹני. — **9.** נאמנה] 𝕲 πιστά; 𝔖 ܣܰܡܟ̈ܠܳܐ = אמונה (Seb.). — **10.** יהודה] Read ישראל here and in vs.¹² ff. (Marti, *Rel.* 119, and *EB.* 2122; so Now.). — [גבול] Gr. adds גם. — **11.** עשוק] 𝕲 κατεδυνάστευσεν τὸν ἀντίδικον αὐτοῦ = עשק (Vol.). — רצוץ] 𝕲 κατεπάτησεν = רָצַץ (Vol.). Read both ptcps. as active (so Oort, *ThT.* and *Em.*; Val., We., Now., Oet., Marti). Gr. would join ¹¹ ᵃ to v.⁹ and connect v.¹⁰ with vs.¹² f. — משפט] Che. (*ExpT.* X. 375; *OLZ.* 1899, p. 137), מְשׁפָּטָי. — [הואיל 𝕲 ἤρξατο = הֵחֵל. — צו 𝕲 τῶν ματαίων and 𝔖 ܣܘܰܬܣܰ = שָׁוְא (so Dathe, Bauer, Vol., Seb., Che.); so 𝕿 (cf. Geiger, *Urschrift*, 411); 𝖵 *sordes* = צי = צוא. Read שוא, written שׁ; cf. Jb. 15³¹ (so Dathe, Bauer, St., Sim., Che.; Oort, *ThT.* and *Em.;*

Gr., Ru., Loft., Gu., GAS., Now., Oet., Marti). Bach. יֵצֶר. Che. (*loc. cit.*) אַשּׁוּר. Brüll (*Jahrb. f. jüd. Gesch.* 1883, pp. 1–62), בְּצַע (cf. Ez. 33³¹). Fürst (*Lex.*) = צִיּוּן, a pillar, finger-post. — **12.** כעש] ⅗ ὡς ταραχή = כבעס (Vol.) or כרעש (Seb.); 'A. ὡς βρωστήρ; Σ. ὡς εὑρώς; 𝕴 *quasi tinea;* جمثـا أبـر. — כרקב] ⅗ ὡς κέντρον = כרקר; 'A., Σ. σῆψις; 𝕴 *quasi putredo;* أنـل = leprosy, elephantiasis. — **13.** מזורו] ⅗ τὴν ὀδύνην = צור (Vol.); 'A. ἐπίδεσιν; 𝕴 *vinculum.* — וישלח] ⅗ adds πρέσβεις. Some insert יהורה (Sayce, *Babyl. and Or. Record,* II. 21; We., Oet., Hal.); but ישראל is better (Bach. (*Pr.*), Now., Che. (*EB.* 2331); cf. Marti). — ירב] ⅗ Ἰαρείμ; جمـت; 'A. δικασόμενον; Σ. φονέα; Θ. κρίσεως; 𝕴 *ultorem.* Bach. יְרֵפָא or יָרֵפָא, in view of foll. לרפא. W. M. Müller (*ZAW.* XVII. 334 ff.) and Riedel (cf. McCurdy, *HPM.* I. 415 f.), מַלְכִּי רָב, the old nominal ending being retained because the whole expression was thought of as a proper name (so Now.², Marti). Che. (*Exp.*, Nov. 1897, p. 364), מֶלֶךְ רָב or מֶלֶךְ רָם; but in *EB.* 2331, מֶלֶךְ עֲרָבִי (cf. Weber, *Arabien vor dem Islam,* 1901, p. 24), also changing אשור to מצור. Wkl. (*Muṣri* (1898), 32; cf. *KAT.*³ 150 f.), יתרב, a district on southern border of Muṣri. Hal. מלך רחב = king of Egypt. — ויגהה] Read יִגְהֶה (so We., Now., Bach. (*Pr.*), Oet., Marti). Gr. יהנה. — **14.** שחל] ⅗ πανθήρ. — כפיר] ⅗ λέων. אני אני] ⅗Ⳙ and ℭ om. one אני (so also Loft.).

8. *Blow the trumpet . . . the cornet*] Cf. Am. 3⁶. The announcement of approaching attack; cf. 8¹ Je. 4⁵ 6¹. The prophet sees in vision the coming of destruction. Here, as in many cases (cf. Is. 6⁹·¹⁰), the imperative serves as the most vivid expression for prediction, the real meaning being: the time is near at hand when the trumpet *will blow* in token of the enemy's approach. On the form and character of the musical instruments here mentioned, *v.s.*, p. 43 f., 150. — *In Gibeah . . . in Ramah*] Gibeah means *hill,* Ramah (cf. ⅗) *height,* both being located on eminences. It is improbable that these names are chosen solely with reference to their meaning and the practice of idolatry on high places; * but they represent all hill-towns from which alarm could easily be sounded. Gibeah (cf. 9⁹ 10⁹) was the same as Gibeah of Benjamin (1 S. 13².¹⁵ 14¹⁶ 2 S. 23²⁹), and as well, Gibeah of Saul (1 S. 11⁴ 15³⁴). It was situated near the road leading from Jerusalem to Nablûs, and has been identified with Tell-el-Fûl.† Ramah is the village where Samuel lived (1 S. 15³⁴; cf. Ju. 4⁵ 19¹³), and is the modern Er-Râm, some two hours north of Jerusalem, on

---

* Sim.

† *ZDMG.* XII. 161 ff.; Rob. *Pal.* I. 577–9; and art. "Gibeah" in *DB.* and *EB.*

T

the road to Bethel.   From 1 K. 15²¹ Is. 10²⁹ we may suppose that
these towns were in the territory of Judah. — *Cry aloud in Bethel*]
The 𝕸𝕿 Beth-aven (cf. 4¹⁵) seems to have arisen as a term of
reproach for Bethel,* whether *aven* be interpreted as *nothingness*,
or as denoting the city of On (𝕲 *Ωv), or Heliopolis, whence
idolatry was imported.   Bethel, situated on the border between
Ephraim and Benjamin, about ten miles north of Jerusalem (modern name, Beitin), was selected as a place which, equally well
with those already mentioned, would serve as a source of signal to
the surrounding people.† — *Make Benjamin to tremble*] Based on
Wellhausen's emendation (*v.s.*); cf. 𝕲 and Am. 3⁶. The 𝕸𝕿,
After thee, O Benjamin, has been, (1) taken as the ancient war-
cry of the tribe; cf. Ju. 5¹⁴, where, however, it is used in a different sense; ‡ (2) interpreted *the enemy is after thee, O Benjamin,* §
now that Ephraim has been captured; cf. Je. 48² Ez. 5¹² Ho. 11⁶
Ju. 16²⁰; (3) also, Benjamin is after thee, *i.e.* attacking thee; ‖
(4) understood to be the proclamation which is to be announced from Bethel (or Aven); ¶ (5) treated as a description
of Bethel from the standpoint of the writer in Judah.** For various emendations of text, *v.s.*; note especially that of Sayce, " tremble, O Benoni." On Hosea's failure to mention Jerusalem, and
the suggestion that his reference to Benjamin is really a hint in this
direction, *v.* Cheyne, p. 74. — **9.** *Ephraim shall become a desolation in the day of punishment*] This is the announcement toward
which v.⁸ pointed.   It includes the fate of the people at large
(v.⁹), and likewise, that of the leaders in particular (v.¹⁰).   The
word rendered " desolation" has been wrongly interpreted " astonished," †† " speechless "; ‡‡ it means rather final and utter destruction with no apparent opportunity for repentance. §§   The threat
was fulfilled by Shalmaneser (2 K. 17). The "day of punishment," lit. judicial decision, wrongly connected by some with
the following phrase ‖‖; cf. Ps. 149⁷. — *Concerning* (or *against*)
Israel's tribes do I make known that which is sure] So the prepo-

---

* *V.s.*, pp. 263, 272; so Hi., We., Now., Marti.   † Ew., Che., *et al.*
‡ GAS.; cf. on this Hävernick (*Einl.* II. 283, 4), Ke., Bach., Or., and Now.
§ Ki., Dathe, Bauer, Ros., Hi., Mau., Pu., Ke., Wü., Or.
‖ Sim.   ¶ Hi., Che., GAS.   ** Grot., Ew.
†† Rashi.   ‡‡ R. Abhu, cited by Ki.   §§ Cal., Pu., Ke., *et al.*   ‖‖ Ki.

sition is to be taken,* and not = among.† In parallelism with Ephraim, *tribes of Israel* = the Northern tribes,‡ and not all Israel, including Judah.§ The judgment announced is one of sure fulfilment (cf. Hb. 2^3), something of absolute endurance (cf. Dt. 28^{59}). — **10.** *The princes of Israel*] The priests have been rebuked; it is now the turn of the princes. These had already been included in the exordium. Upon the whole it is well to substitute *Israel* for *Judah* of the 𝕳𝕰𝕿 here and in the following verses. With this slight change, all difficulty in the logical connection of v.[10] with the preceding verses disappears. This change is supported by the frequent interchange and coupling of the terms "Ephraim" and "Israel" in Hosea; *e.g.* $5^{3.5.9}$ 6^{10} 7^1. — *Are like landmark removers*] The commonest sort of thieves. This is not a reference (following 𝕳𝕰𝕿) to Judah's seizure of Northern territory in the times of anarchy; ‖ nor to the efforts of Ahaz to introduce idolatry into Judah (2 K. 16^{10-18}) ; ¶ nor is it a specific rebuke of the policy of the rulers (as in Is. 5^8 Mi. 2^2) to acquire all the land and thus disturb the boundaries fixed by their fathers (cf. Dt. 19^{14}) ; ** but is, perhaps, a proverbial phrase for the lowest wickedness, a type of the most degraded practices.†† Cf. the idea that "landmarks were under the protection of religion (Pr. 22^{28} 23^{10} ; cf. Jb. 24^2), and to remove them laid the offender under a curse (Dt. 19^{14} 27^{17})." ‡‡ — *Upon them will I pour out my wrath like water*] Cf. Is. 8^7 Je. 14^{16}. The poetic description of Yahweh's wrath is at one time the fire which devours, at another the flood which drowns, the object of its attack. — **11.** *Ephraim practises oppression! he breaks down right*] The 𝕳𝕰𝕿 presents two difficulties, viz. the use of the participle passive in a consecution of imperfects relating to Ephraim's future; and the use of "justice" with the passive participle interpreted, (1) *broken* or *crushed in judgment, i.e.* God's judgment, the idea being so familiar that no more distinct designation was necessary §§; (2) *one whose right is broken,* ‖‖ *i.e.* the right of national independence; (3) *is rightly*

---

* Hi., Ke., Now., Marti.   ‡ Now.   ‖ Hi., Sim., Pu., Or.   ** We.
† Wü.   § Che.   ¶ Grot., Hd.
†† Bauer, Ros., Wü., Now., Che., GAS.; cf. Hull, art. "Landmark," *DB.*
‡‡ Che.   ‖‖ BSZ., *s.v.*, רוצץ.
§§ Ros., Hng., Ke., Che.

crushed; * (4) *crushed by judgment.*† The 𝕸𝕿 is supported
by the occurrence of the same two participles in Dt. 28³³. But it
seems better to follow 𝕲, and read the participles as active (*v.s.*),
thus furnishing another charge in the indictment against Ephraim,
for which punishment is coming. That משפט = *right* appears
from its usage in 2¹⁹ Am. 5⁷·¹⁵·²⁴ 6¹². — *Because he has determined
to go after vanity*] The explanation of the national deterioration.
But was it *vanity* (= שוא) that Hosea really used? It cannot
have been צו, meaning the commands of Baal-prophets ; ‡ or the
commands of men ; § or the commands of Jeroboam I., ‖ which
were of so destructive a character, an ironical turn being imparted
by the use of צו, as in Is. 28¹⁰·¹³ ; or commands in a bad sense ; ¶
or God's commands, *i.e.* he went after evil, even after God's commands against it had been given ; ** or a log of wood = a wooden
god ; †† or pillar = finger-post ; ‡‡ for no one of these meanings
makes adequate sense. In the same category belong the following suggestions, viz. : (1) (the god) *Zaw,* §§ a deity whose name
is found in the Palmyrene proper names (*e.g.* אמתצא, *handmaid of
Zaw;* תימצא, *gift of Zaw;* עברצו, *servant of Zaw* ‖ ‖), who represented the rays of the moon,¶¶ whose worship prevailed in ancient
times from South Arabia to the Syro-Arabian deserts ; but (*a*) the
context speaks of Assyria, and there was no such God among the
Assyrians ; *** (*b*) the phrase *walk after* does not require after it
the name of a god ; ††† (*c*) Palmyrene inscriptions are comparatively late, viz. first century A.D. ; (*d*) Hosea would hardly charge
all of Israel's sin to the worship of a moon-god nowhere else mentioned in the O. T. (2) צו = צוא, *filthiness,* צו: ואני, arising from
haplography of א ; ‡‡‡ (3) *imagination;* §§§ (4) *Assyria,* or *Asshur.* ‖ ‖ ‖ We come back to the rendering *vanity* (based on שוא,
v.s. ; suggested by 𝕲 and 𝕾 ; ¶¶¶ nor is it an objection (cf. König)
that the emendation is so easy), *i.e.* idols ; cf. Je. 18¹⁵ Ps. 31⁶. —
12. *And it is I who am like a moth . . . like rottenness*] Cf. Jb.

---

* Marck.　　† Schm.　　‡ Rashi.　　§ AE., Schrö., Ke., Wü., Or.
‖ Ki., Mau., Hd., Pu.; Kö. *Exp T.* X. 376 ff.　　¶ Ki.　　** Ros.　　†† Ew.
‡‡ Fürst (*Lex.*).　　§§ Hommel, *Exp T.* X. 329 f.　　‖ ‖ Cf. *ZDMG.* LIII. 98–101.
¶¶ Cf. *PSBA.* XXI. 75.　　*** Che. *Exp T.* X. 375.
††† Kö. *Exp T.* X. 376–378 ; cf. also *Stil.* 264 ff.　　‡‡‡ Cf. Geiger, *Urschrift,* 411.
§§§ Bach.　　‖ ‖ ‖ Che. *Exp T.* X. 375.　　¶¶¶ So Bauer, *et al.; v.s.,* p. 272.

13[28]. Internal dissolution, for destruction was coming from within, viz. through anarchy and civil war; cf. 13[1]. The figure denotes slow but certain progress. The pronoun is emphatic, designating Yahweh himself as the author of this approaching calamity. — *To Ephraim . . . to the house of Israel*] It is better, as above, to read "Israel" for "Judah." — **13.** *And so Ephraim saw his sickness, and Israel his sore*] Here again we read "Israel" rather than "Judah." Similar figures are used to describe political decay in Is. 1[5. 6] 3[7]; cf. also Ho. 6[1] 7[1]. Ephraim comes at last to recognize the serious character of the situation. The sickness and the sore were not only political, viz. anarchy and civil war (*v.s.*), but also religious and moral deterioration. — *And Ephraim went to Asshur, and Israel sent to king Jareb*] To preserve the parallelism which, up to this point, has been so regular, we insert "Israel" (*v.s.*). But who is king Jareb (cf. 10[6]), and to what circumstances is reference made? The opinions offered have greatly varied: (1) the name of a place in Assyria,* or a symbolical name for Assyria itself, like Rahab for Egypt;† (2) the name of a king of Egypt;‡ (3) = Aribi, a district in Northern Arabia, the oldest form being probably Jarîb (cf. proper names Jerîb and Jerîbai), and a reminiscence of it appears in the later Sabaean word *Marjab*;§ (4) an appellative (= "king combatant") describing some king of Assyria, *e.g.* Ašur-dân-ilu (771–754),‖ or Tiglath-pileser;¶ (5) an appellative to be connected with Syriac ܡܰܪܒ (be great), and equivalent to הַמֶּלֶךְ הַגָּדוֹל, which is used of an Assyrian king;** (6) an appellative = one who pleads, *i.e.* a patron, used of the Assyrian king;†† (7) the original name of Sargon, king of Assyria, which was dropped when he ascended the throne, in the same way that Pul became Tiglath-pileser, and Ululâ became Shalmaneser IV. when they began to reign;‡‡ (8) to be read with a different division of consonants

---

* AE., Ki., Geb.   † Sim.; W. T. Lynn, *Babyl. and Or. Record*, II. 127 f.

‡ Theod., Eph. Syr.; Wkl. *GVI.* 63; but see W. M. Müller, *ZAW.* XVII. 334 f.

§ Hommel, *Aufsätze u. Abhandlungen*, II. 231; but see Kö. *Fünf neue Arab. Landschaften im A.T.*   ‖ Schra. *COT.* II. 136 ff.

¶ Now. *Hosea, in loc.;* so also Whitehouse in *COT.* II. 137, note.

** See Wü.; so McC. *HPM.* I. 415 f.   †† Reuss.

‡‡ Sayce, *JQR.* I. 162 ff., and *Babyl. and Or. Record*, II. 18–22, 145 f.; cf. *HCM.*

(*v.s.*), "the great king" = Assyr. *šarru rabû*; * (9) a corrupt text (*v.s.*), the original having read "king of Arabia," † or "king of Jathrib"; ‡ (10) = Assyr. *irbu*, tribute, the rendering being "and sent tribute to the king" § (but, according to Winckler, *irbu* always denotes internal taxes; tribute from foreign nations is *biltu, madattu,* or *tamartu*); (11) = "king who should bring healing," the text being changed (*v.s.*). ‖ — *But he cannot heal you, nor will he relieve you of your wound*] This is an illustration of the characteristic attitude of the prophets toward alliance with other nations. It is not only wrong, but useless, to seek for outside help (cf. Is., chaps. 7, 8, 31^{1ff.}). — **14.** *For I, myself, will be like a lion to Ephraim, and like a young lion to the house of Israel*] Cf. Is. 31^4. The strongest possible metaphor of destruction. This verse states the reason for the uselessness of Israel's efforts spoken of in v.^{13}. The affliction of Israel is divinely ordained, hence appeal to human aid is of no avail. — *I, even I, will rend and go my way*] The repetition of the pronoun lays emphasis on the fact that Yahweh is the agent of the coming destruction. — *I will carry off, and none shall rescue*] Cf. Is. 5^{29}. The figure is that of the lion dragging away the prey, and none daring to interfere.

8. הריעו . . . [תקעו] Imv. = an emphatic prediction; cf. GK. 110 *c*. — שפר . . . [הצרה] Art. omitted; indef. — בְּרָמָה . . . [בַגִּבְעָה] Art. is indicative of original appellative force; cf. Kö. 295 *b*. — [אחריך] Cf. Ju. 5^{14}, where 𝕲 offers אחיך and the text is regarded as corrupt by all recent commentators (so *e.g.* Moore, Bu., Now.), some, indeed, considering it a gloss having its origin in this verse of Hosea (so Bickell, *Carmina*, 196; Marquardt, *Fundamente;* Wkl. *GI.* I. 158). The impossibility of making sense of 𝕸 here renders some emend. necessary; that of We. offers the least objection and has the support of 𝕲. On construction according to 𝕸 cf. GK. 147 *c.* Two artistic elements may be noted in this verse: (1) the collocation of *ā* sounds in 8^*a*; (2) the elegiac rhythm. — **9.** ישראל . . . [אפרים] Note chiastic arrangement. The elegiac movement continues through this verse, but the line בשבטי יש' is short; has a word dropped out after בשבטי? — [נאמנה] Fem. expressing neut. — **10.** [כמסיגי] Aram. form; GK. 72 *ee*. — **11.** [רצון מ'] If

---

417; so also Neubauer, *ZA.* III. 103; Hommel, *GBA.* 680; but see McC. *HPM.* I. 416; and Selbie, *DB.* II. 550.

* W. M. Müller, *ZAW.* XVII. 334 ff.; cf. the almost identical view of Che. (*v.s.*).
† Che. *EB.* 2331.   ‡ Wkl. *Muṣri* (1898), 32; cf. *KAT.*^3 150 f.
§ Paul Rost, quoted by Wkl. *KAT.*^3 151.   ‖ Bach. *Untersuch., in loc.*

MT be retained, the pass. ptcp. is followed by a genitive having the force of an acc. of limitation; cf. Kö. 336 *h.*—[הואיל הלך] Verbal appos.; cf. הואיל בּער, Dt. 1⁵; cf. Kö. 361 *h.*—[אחרי צו] צו in Is. 28¹⁰· ¹³ is probably not a genuine word, but merely a sound coined by the prophet in mockery of the drunken and unintelligible babblings of his opponents. In any case the use of the word there throws no light upon its meaning here. The indefiniteness of the charge speaks against taking צו as a synon. of מצוה, as does also the fact that none of the versions so take it. Nor does the pointing צו = *excrement, filth* (for which צאה is the regular form) mend matters; this word is never used of idols, and the idea of human iniquity (cf. Is. 4⁴ Pr. 30¹²) is scarcely strong enough here. For the use of the phrase הלך אחרי = *worship, serve*, with abstract terms, cf. Is. 65² Je. 18¹² (thoughts); Je. 3¹⁷ 9¹⁴ 16¹² (stubbornness); and with names of gods, Dt. 4³ 1 K. 14⁸; cf. Je. 2⁸. The Assyr. *alâku arki* is used in the same sense. With the confusion of ש and צ presupposed here by the adoption of the reading of 𝔊 cf. interchange of צ and ש in יצחק and ישחק.—13. [מלך] On absence of art., cf. Kö. 333 *x.*—[ורוא] Emphat. pos. in contrast with אנכי (v.¹⁴).—[יוכל] Best explained as *Qal* with ו depressed to ו; *v.* GK. 69 *r*; Kö. I. 407; Wright, *Comp. Sem. Gram.* 237; others explain as a *Hŏph*, which was always used instead of the *Qal.*—[לכם] On use of prep., cf. Kö. 289 *a.*—[יגהה] ἁ.λ.; cf. the subst. גּהָה, Pr. 17²², and Syr. ‏ܓܗ‎ = be freed. Since (1) the subj. of יגהה is naturally the same as that of יוכל, and (2) גהה is intrans. in Syr., it is better to point יָגְהֶה, with Now. (*v.s.*).—14. שחל . . . כפיר [שחל] is a poetic word for *lion*, occurring, aside from this passage and 13⁷, only in Job, Psalms, and Proverbs. כפיר denotes the young lion, but one old enough to hunt prey.—[ואלך] Impf. with ו conj. coördinate with prec. impf.; cf. Dr. § 134.—[ואין מציל] Circ. clause; cf. Kö. 362 *i.*

§ 8. Israel's blind and fitful repentance does not remove the guilt which will one day be manifest to all; which, indeed, is seen to-day in the affairs of the king. 5¹⁵–7⁷. (1) Israel may put on the form of repentance, but she is so blind to the situation and to the true nature of God that such repentance is only on the surface. (2) This is true in spite of the fact that the most earnest teaching and the most definite warnings have been given concerning Yahweh's will. (3) Israel is faithless, and her chief towns are headquarters of every kind of vice, and all this is encouraged by the priests. (4) But now when the time comes, *i.e.* the day when " the great turning-point in her fortunes arrives, the day of mingled punishment and mercy," * this iniquity

* Che.

will be recognized and appreciated. (5) Nay, even to-day it is apparent in the situation as it stands connected with the kings — enthroned and assassinated, "surrounded by loose and unscrupulous nobles: adultery, drunkenness, conspiracies, assassinations; every man striking for himself; none appealing to God." *

This piece contains five strophes of 12, 10, 10, 10, and 12 lines. The movement is the trimeter, but occasionally it falls into the elegiac style; cf. Bu. *ZAW*. II. 32 f. This arrangement secures a complete unity of thought and shows close consecution of strophic arrangement. Strophe 1 (5^{15}–6^3) presents in dramatic form two soliloquies: the first, of Yahweh, who now turns himself away with the feeling that in distress Israel will seek him out; the second, of Israel, who in shallowness of heart assures himself complacently that Yahweh has wounded him, simply that he might heal him; that as soon as he seeks Yahweh, he will find him. Strophe 2 (6^{4-6}) describes the incredulity and impatience with which Yahweh receives this fitful repentance. Had he not given him warning? Had he not expressly declared that it was love which he desired, and not sacrifice? Strophe 3 (6^{7-10}) portrays the terrible wickedness of Israel's chief places, the robbery and murder, the corruption and adultery which Israel, encouraged by the priests, has committed in transgression of the covenant. Strophe 4 (6^{11}–7^2) pathetically suggests that in the future a time will come, the day of Israel's turning, when the iniquity of Ephraim will be laid bare, although perhaps at present their consciences do not prick them, so entangled are they in the meshes of sin. For, in fact, strophe 5 (7^{3-7}), the immorality of the nation, from king down, is so apparent, the hopelessness of the situation is so great, that repentance is really impossible, the very capacity for it being absent. In this arrangement the following points deserve consideration: In strophe 1, line 8 seems exceedingly long, especially in contrast with line 7, which is unusually short. It is possible that ונחיה לפניו is a gloss explaining יקמנו. With this exception the parallelism is close and regular. In strophe 2 a line seems to be missing after 6^4, the על־כן of 6^5 failing to connect properly with what precedes. This fact, pointed out by Now., accords with the need of a line to complete the otherwise almost perfect parallelism of the strophe. It is worth while to suggest that perhaps the line ומשפטי כאור יצא (as reconstructed) was originally joined with the line now lost. It is surely not closely connected with the two preceding lines. In this case the strophe would be ideally symmetrical. In strophe 3 (6^{7-10}), (1) the form of the elegy appears quite distinctly; (2) lines 1 and 2, and 3 and 4 are satisfactory; line 5 might be read *assassins in troops, a gang of priests*, but cf. p. 287; (3) דרך of line 7 is probably wrong, for it is impossible to separate it thus from שכמה; (4) perhaps line 8 might be transferred to follow what is now line 9, thus

* GAS.

improving the sense and as well the measure; (5) $6^{11\,a}$ is, of course, a gloss. In strophe 4 (6^{11}-7^2), (1) v.$^{11\,b}$ is suspected, but *v.i.;* (2) v.$^{11\,c}$ is clearly to be connected with what follows in spite of the chapter division. In strophe 5 (7^{3-7}), (1) v.^{4} from כמו חנור is a gloss explaining v.^{6}; (2) the remainder of the strophe is regular and symmetrical.

V. 15-VI. 3. *Israel feigns repentance.*

In a wonderfully conceived pair of soliloquies, the poet represents Yahweh as waiting for Israel to come back, and Israel as, in fact, coming back, but with a conception of Yahweh so false and an idea of repentance so inadequate as to make the whole action a farce.

The genuineness of $5^{15\,b}$-6^3 is denied by some (Che. in WRS. *Proph.* xx ff.; Marti, Volz, *Jahweprophetie,* 33; Grimm, *Lit. App.* 69 ff.; Che. includes also $^{15\,a}$ and 6^4 in the insertion, and Marti $^{15\,a}$ and $6^{5\,b}$) on the ground that: (1) it breaks the close connection existing between 5^{14} and 6^4; (2) its phraseology is an echo, in part, of the following verses; (3) the interpretation of 6^{1-3} as an expression of superficial repentance, which interpretation is necessary to the retention of these verses in the text, is forced; (4) it bears close resemblance in spirit to other late insertions, *e.g.* 14^{1-9} and 6^{11}-7^1; (5) the exile seems to be presupposed by the strong expressions יחינו and יקמנו, 6^2; (6) the language supports the argument for a late date (Volz cites the following terms: בצר להם; שחר; טרף = tear; רדף with ל in fig. sense only here; מלקוש; יורה).

15. ויאשמו] ⑤ ἀφανισθῶσιν, ᵴ *deficiatis,* and ℒ *exterminentur,* deriving it from שמם (cf. Ho. 2^{14} Jo. 1^{17} Am. 7^9 Zp. 3^6 Zc. 7^{14} 11^5 (⑤), Ez. 6^6). Read יִשָּׁמוּ = startled, puzzled (We., Now., Oet., Marti); cf. Gr. יָשָׁמוּ. — בקשו] ᵴ *quaeratis.* — בצר להם ישחרנני ⑤ᵴℒ and some Heb. Mss. join to the following verse and chapter. ⑤ᵴℒ add לאמר (so also, *e.g.,* Gr., We., GAS., Oet.). — **VI. 1.** לכו] ⑤ πορευθῶμεν (= נלך); so ᵴ (so also Oort). — יהוה] ⑤ adds τὸν θεὸν ἡμῶν. — טרף] ᵴ *cepit.* — יך] ℒ om. this and following word. Read with ᵴ, וַיַּךְ (so We., Bach. (*Pr.*), GAS., Now., Oet., Marti). Oort, הכה. — **2.** מִיֹּמָיִם] ᵴ om. מן and renders by pl. Gr. בַּיֹּמָיִם. Bach. (*Pr.*) מְיָמִים(?). — ביום השלישי] Join with preceding context, and perhaps ו should be inserted as in ᵴ. Bach. (*Pr.*) בְּיוֹם הַשָּׁלוּם(?). — יקמנו] ⑤ ἀναστησόμεθα (= נקום). — **3.** ונדעה] Ru. וְנִרְאֶה, deriving from דעה = غَلَا, come early. Gr. sugg. that it may be dittog. from נרדפה. Bach. (*Pr.*) transfers this and foll. three words to the end of this verse. — כשחר נכון] Read כְּשַׁחֲרֵנוּ כֵן (Giesebrecht, *Beiträge,* 208; We.; Sm. *Rel.* 210; Val., GAS., Now., Oort (*Em.*), Marti); cf. Ru. כְּשַׁחֲרֵנוּ כֵן. — מצאו] ⑤ εὑρήσομεν αὐτόν (so ℒ); E', ἡ ἐπιφάνεια αὐτοῦ. Read, foll. ⑤, נִמְצָאֵהוּ (Giesebrecht, *Beiträge,* 208; We., Val., GAS., Now., Oort (*Em.*), Marti); cf. Sm. *Rel.* 210; Oet. נִמְצָאֶנּוּ. — יורה]

𝕲 precedes by καί. Read יְרְוֶה with 𝕾 ﺭﯜﻯ? (so also Seb., Perles (p. 90), Now., Oort (*Em.*), Oet., Marti). Oort (*ThT.*) foll. 𝕲, ויורה לארץ.

15. *I will return again to my place*] Yahweh is soliloquizing. This is not the figure of the lion returning to his den;* but (cf. Mi. 1³) is a survival of the older form of expression in accordance with which interest in human affairs is expressed by the phrase "coming down." The *place* is the heavenly temple; to this he will return, and, as it were, from a distance observe the conduct of Israel (Is. 18⁴ Ps. 14²).† The expression, as a whole, indicates Yahweh's non-activity in Israel's fate ‡ (cf. 9¹² Je. 14⁸·⁹ Ps. 80¹⁴), and is parallel with the common expressions, "hide the face" (cf. Ps. 10¹¹ 30⁷ 104²⁹), § and "stand afar off" (cf. Ps. 10¹ 38¹¹). — *Until they are confounded*] This rendering, involving a slight textual change, is easier ‖ (cf. Ez. 6⁶ Zc. 11⁵ 𝕲, Jo. 1¹⁷) than the usual one, based upon 𝕸𝕿, which is rendered : (1) acknowledge their offence,¶ or feel their guilt ** (cf. Lv. 5⁴·⁵ Zc. 11⁵) ; (2) suffer the consequences of their guilt †† (cf. Ps. 34²¹·²² Is. 24⁶ Pr. 30¹⁰ Ho. 13¹⁶). — *In their distress*] Cf. Ps. 18⁶ ‡‡ Dt. 4³⁰ Ps. 66¹⁴ 106⁴⁴ Is. 25⁴ 26¹⁶ 2 Ch. 15⁴. — *They will seek me*] This does not mean "seek in the morning," emphasis being placed on careful and earnest seeking §§ ; but simply *seek*, being synonymous with בקש, but used only in poetry ‖‖ (cf. Jb. 7²¹ 8⁵ 24⁵ Pr. 1²⁸ 7¹⁵ 8¹⁷ 11²⁷ 13²⁴ Ps. 63¹ 78³⁴ Is. 26⁹). — **VI. 1.** *Saying, Come and let us turn unto Yahweh*] Israel is represented as soliloquizing. Note the "saying" which precedes, according to 𝕲 and 𝕾. These words (vs.¹⁻³) are not: (1) an example of the confession of penitence with which Israel will approach Yahweh in the future, employed by Hosea as an occasion for warning Israel that Yahweh's favor will not manifest itself, as they expect, immediately upon their turning to him;¶¶ nor (2) the words of Hosea himself expressing his desire to lead his people back to the right way, which will bring them divine favor again;*** nor (3) the language of the prophet

---

* Theod., Ros., Ke.
† Rashi, Ki., Cal., Ew., Ke., Wü., Schm., Che.
‡ Sim.   § Wü.   ‖ We.
¶ Cal., Ros., AV., Pu.
** Ras., Ki., Che., GAS.   †† Hd., Wü., Schm.

‡‡ Cf. Hupfeld-Now. *in loc.*
§§ Ros., Pu., Ke.
‖‖ Rashi, Cal., Hd., Now.
¶¶ Now.
*** Giesebrecht, *Beiträge*, 207 f.

addressed to the people ; * but with 5[15] and 6[4ff.] are (4) a dramatic representation, in the form of soliloquy and dialogue, of the attitude of the people to Yahweh and of Yahweh to the people. It is, therefore, an expression of *assumed* repentance.† — *For he has torn that he may heal us*] Cf. Dt. 32[39]. The same action is ascribed to Yahweh in 5[14]. — *And he has smitten that he may bind us up*] For the slight textual change *v.s.* — **2.** *He will revive us after two or three days*] Lit. "after a couple of days, or on the third day." This "collocation of a numeral with the next above it is a rhetorical device employed in numerical sayings to express a number which need not or cannot be more exactly specified." ‡ "Three days" is to be connected directly with "after two days" without the conjunction, as in 2 K. 9[32] Am. 4[8]; cf. Is. 17[6]; this is syntactically correct, and gives a better parallelism. The thought is, he will deliver us in a short time. For this use of "revive," in the sense of healing the sick, cf. Jos. 5[8] 2 K. 8[9] 20[7]. This passage is really the basis of Ez. 37[1-10]. § Cf. Ho. 13[1]. — *He will establish us that we may live before him* ‖] "To live before him" is to live acceptably or under his protection ¶ (cf. Gn. 17[18] Is. 53[2] Je. 30[20]). — **3.** *Yea, let us know, let us be zealous to know Yahweh*] This appeal is coördinate with that contained in v.[1],** and is not to be coördinated with "that we may live." †† The second phrase explains the first, and, at the same time, intensifies it ; cf. Dt. 16[20] Is. 51[1] Ps. 34[14]. Thus the verb means more than "endeavor," ‡‡ "grow continually," §§ "hunt after." ‖‖ — *When we seek him, then we shall find him*] For text, *v.s.* The people are not disturbed, for they are confident of success just as soon as they make the effort.¶¶ If the אור be retained, the rendering will be, *his going forth is certain as the gray of morning.* On "going forth," cf. Ps. 19[6]; שחר means not morning-red,*** but morning-gray.††† — *He will come as the winter-rain, and as the spring rain which waters the earth*] The word rendered winter rain (גשם) denotes a heavy, pouring rain ; it is used of the winter rains, as here, also in Ezra 10[9. 13]. The heavy winter rains last

---

* Ke., Or.   ‡ GK. 134 *s*.   ** Ke., Schm., Now., Che.
† Ew., Che., GAS.   § Che.   †† Reuss.   ‡‡ Ew.   §§ Pu.   ‖‖ Ke.
‖ On הקים as a syn. of היה, cf. Ps. 41[9].   ¶¶ Cf. We.; Giesebrecht, *Beiträge*, 208 f.
¶ Ke., Wü., Schm., Che., Now.   *** Hi., Sim.   ††† Wü.

from the beginning of December to the end of February; this is the rainy season *par excellence* (cf. Ct. 2[11]). The spring rain (מלקוש) falls during March and April, coming just before harvest, and is of the greatest importance for the proper ripening of the crops.*

15. ואלך אשובה] Vb. appos., H. 36, 2; GK. 120 *g*.— ויאשמו] Is impossible because neither of its three meanings (cf. BDB.) suits the context. — להם] On force of ל, cf. Kö. 281 *oβ*. — ישחרנני] The defective *û* and the nun epenth., uncontracted; cf. Pr. 1[28] 8[17]; GK. 8 *l*, 58 *k*, 60 *e.* — **VI. 1.** לכו ונשובה] Corresponding to the first words of 5[15].— וירפאנו] ו of purpose; so also in ויחבשנו and ונחיה; H. 26, 2 *a*; GK. 165 *a.*— יד] Cf. GK. 109 *k*; Kö. 194 *e.* — **2.** מימים] (1) on מן = *in the course of*, GK. 119 *y*, note 2; cf. Kö. 401 *g* (= after), and BDB. p. 581 *b*; (2) on similar use of the dual, cf. Is. 17[6] 7[21]; (3) the ־ should stand with השלישי; (4) on the use of two numerals, *v.s.*, and cf. Am. 1[3 ff.] 4[8].— **3.** נרעה] The ה־ is hortatory, H. 23, 2 *b*; GK. 48 *e*; not indicative of determination, H. 23, 2 *a*.— יורה] Adjectival impf.; this reading is better than ṀṪ יורה from ירה = throw: יורה in the sense of *rain* occurs again only in Ho. 10[12], and there also the text is questionable.

4–6. *Yahweh's incredulity and impatience.*

4. מה] After אפרים, $ precedes with ן. We. supposes that something has been lost from the end of v.[4] and the beginning of v.[5]. — **5.** הצבתי בנביאים] ⅏ ἀπεθέρισα τοὺς προφήτας ὑμῶν = חצדתי, an Aramaicism, with ב omitted (Vol.). Σ. οὐκ ἐφεισάμην; E'. ἐξέκοψα; 'Α., Θ. ἐλατόμησα; $ ܢܨܒ ܐܨܡܝ (omitting ב); 𝔙 dolavi in prophetis; Oet. and Hal. הצבתים ב׳ Oet. sugg. also מְחָצְתִּיח or לחצתים. — הרגתים] ⅏ and $ refer suf. to נביאים. Oort (*Em.*) drops the suffix, while Marti changes it and preceding to ר — ומשפטיך אור] Read ומשפטי כָאוֹר, with ⅏ καὶ τὸ κρίμα μου ὡς φῶς; so also ᚦ (so Dathe, Bauer, Ros., Hi., Ew., Sim., Ke., Wü., Now.; WRS. *Proph.* 389; Or., Che.; Oort, *ThT.* XXIV. 486, and *Em.*; Bach., We., Gr., Val., Ru., Gu., GAS., Oet., Hal., *et al.*). E'. καὶ ἡ δικαιοκρισία. Marti, מִשְׁפָּטֵנוּ כָאוֹר. Ru. omits this phrase as interrupting sequence of thought.— ויצא] Hi., foll. $ and ᚦ, וַיֵּצֵא or יָצָא. — **6.** ולא] ⅏ ἤ (= rather than); cf. ᚦ מְפָרְבַח.

4. *What can I make of you, O Ephraim*] Yahweh now speaks. The tone is not so much that of rebuke as of despair. Every effort thus far made has failed. What hope is there that any of the plans of Yahweh for Israel will be realized? The inter-

---

* Cf. GAS. *Hist. Geog.* 63 ff.

rogative is really a negative : *I can make nothing of you.** There
is no allusion to a method for bringing about the good mentioned in the preceding verse,† nor to punishment in addition
to that which they have already received. ‡ — *Since your love is
like the morning cloud*] Not (1) the love of God for you will
be quickening, etc. ; § nor (2) the love of God for you which
will be transient ‖ like yours for him ; but (3) your love for God,
your goodness, your piety, is fleeting, transient.¶ The morning
clouds disappear very early during the hot season in Palestine,
the sky being usually perfectly clear by 9 A.M.** — *Yea, like the
dew which early goes away*] The dew of Palestine is very heavy
in the summer time and resembles a fine rain or Scotch mist
rather than the phenomenon so familiar to us.†† It is thus of
the greatest importance for vegetation during the long dry
season, and is a favorite illustration with O. T. writers. Here,
however, the reference is to its transitory character, with no
thought of its beneficial effects. — **5.** *Wherefore I have hewn
them by the prophets*] The connection between vs.[4 and 5] is not so
broken as is represented by some commentators. ‡‡ V.[4] describes
Israel as a people whose fitful and irresponsible conduct has
occasioned anxiety and despair to their God. This situation
explains why in the past he has hewn them by the prophets,
i.e. punished them. There is no reason why these words should
not stand in the text, ‡‡ for their specific meaning is clear and
strong. The verbs here refer to the past, §§ not to the present or
future. ‖‖ Israel is compared with stone or wood, which is being
shaped ; the hewing is the punishment intended for discipline ; ¶¶
the work of the prophets is elsewhere spoken of as destruction,
e.g. Is. 11[4] 49[2] Je. 1[10] 5[14] 1 K. 19[17]. — *I have slain them by the
words of my mouth*] This simply repeats and explains the preceding line, the pronoun referring to the people.*** The prophets
in the past had not hesitated to threaten the people with death

* Ras., Ros., Hi., Hd., Pu., Wü., Or., Che., Now.

† Lu.   ‡ Schm.   § Cyril.   ‖ Jer.

¶ Š, Ras., Ki., Cal., Hi., Wü., Che., Now.   ** Cf. *ZDPV.* XIV. (1891), 110 ff.

†† See Neil, *Palestine Explored* (1882), pp. 129-151; GAS. *Hist. Geog.* 65; Che.,
art. " Dew," *EB. ;* Hull, art. " Dew," *DB.*   ‡‡ We., Now.

§§ Ros., Hi., Sim., Che., Or., Now., GAS.   ‖‖ Umb., Mau.

¶¶ Jer., Geb., Pu., Ke., Wü., Schm.   *** Cal., Hd., Pu., Ke., Wü., Now.

for disobedience; and every kind of calamity was interpreted as from God for failure to comply with his wishes. The words of Yahweh, because of their power, are compared with arrows, Ps. 45⁵, and with a sword, Ps. 45³ Heb. 4¹² Rev. 1¹⁶; cf. also Is. 11⁴ Je. 23²⁹. — *And my judgment is like the light which goes forth*] This is based on a slight change of 𝕳𝕿 (*v.s.*). The judgment is that of which the execution now hangs over Israel. This judgment is like the light which all may see and fear, the rise of the sun being a symbol of gracious visitation.* The older rendering, "thy judgments are like a light that goeth forth," was interpreted in various ways, *e.g.* thy way of living religiously was plain as the light; † the judgments belonging to thee went forth like the lightning; ‡ the judgment upon thee when it comes will be just, clear. § Notice should be taken of the rendering, "my law (or judgment) shall go forth as the light." ‖ It is better, however, to regard the clause as circumstantial and dependent upon the preceding perfects (*v.i.*). — **6.** *For it is love that I delight in, and not sacrifice*] The mistake of the people consisted in their notion that sacrifices were sufficient to gain Yahweh's favor. What Yahweh delights in, *i.e.* that which will gain his favor, is love; cf. 1 S. 15²², in which obedience is emphasized. This love is not love for God as distinguished from love for one's fellow-men, but both. — *Knowledge of God and not burnt-offerings*] Here, as in many places in this piece, we have an example of Hosea's ability to make a perfect parallelism. Knowledge of God and love of God go together. On the attitude of the prophets to the priests and that for which they stood,¶ *v.* Is. 1¹¹⁻²⁰ Mi. 6⁶⁻⁸ Je. 7²². ²³ Ps. 40⁶ 50⁸ ᶠᶠ. 51¹⁷; cf. Mat. 9¹³ 12⁷.

4. מה] In interrogation is capable of varying meanings: (1) *how?* in rhetorical questions, implying negative answer; (2) *why?* in sense of "do not"; (3) *what?* simple interrogative; (4) *what?* implying answer *nothing;* cf. BDB. — ישראל [יהורה, and note the parallelism which is (almost)

---

* Che. † Cal. ‡ Hd. § Pu. ‖ Ew., Che., Or.

¶ Cf. this saying, attributed to Buddha: "If a man live a hundred years, and engage the whole of his time and attention in religious offerings to the gods, sacrificing elephants and horses, and other life, all this is not equal to one act of pure love in saving life." (Beal's *Texts from the Buddhist Canon;* quoted by Che.)

artificially regular.—[וחסדכם Introduces a circ. clause; Kö. 362 p.—[בקר]
On absence of article cf. Kö. 294 e, 299 m.—[וכטל] ו epexeg., *Yea, like
the dew.*—[משכים הלך] Verbal apposition with second vb. containing the
principal idea (GK. 120 g). The absence of the art. is exceptional in view
of its presence in כטל.—**5.** [על־כן] This phrase is very flexible = (1) on
account of this, *e.g.* Gn. 10⁹ Is. 13⁷; (2) with adversative force, Ps. 42⁷;
(3) to introduce an inference, Ps. 45⁸.—[הרגתים, חצבתי, יצא] The pfs. are
pfs. of indef. past, H. 17, 3; GK. 106 d. The impf. is adjectival.—[ומשפטי]
As thus reconstructed, introduces a circ. clause.—**6.** [חסד] Emphatic.—
[מעלות] The parallel ולא shows that מן is not comparative, but neg.; so GK.
119 w; cf. Kö. 308 b.

7–10. *Israel's wickedness.*

7. [כאדם] 𝔙 *sicut Adam;* 𝕿 כדריא קדמאי. Mich. כְּאָדָם. We. באדם (so cod.
554 of De Rossi, and Che. *EB*, col. 58). Oort (*ThT.* and *Em.*), בָּאֲדָמָה.
Oet. מֵחֶרֶם. Gr. בְּאוֹן. Sellin (*Beiträge*, I. 168 f.), כַּאֲדָם. Preuschen (*ZAW.*
XV. 28; so Gardner), בִּשְׁכֶם. Pfeiffer (cited by Sim.), בָּאֲדָמָה. Che. (*CB.*)
בריתי.—[בָּאָדָם G παραβαίνων = עָבַר, agreeing with אדם.—[עברו] (so Ru., Gardner).—[בגדו] G κατεφρόνησεν, with גלעד of foll. verse as subj.
—**8.** [גלעד Oort, גִּלְעָל.—[פעלי] G ἐργαζομένη, sg. to agree with קריה.—עקבה
אדם] G ταράσσουσα (= עכר (Cappellus), or עכרה (St.), or קבעת (Vol.)) ὕδωρ
(= מים); 'Α. περικαμπὴς ἀπὸ αἵματος; Σ. διώκεται ἀπὸ αἵματος; Θ. ἡ πτέρνα
αὐτῆς ἀφ' αἵματος; Ε', ὑποσκελίζουσα καὶ δολοφονοῦσα; 𝔙 *supplantata sangu-
ine;* 𝔖 ܥܩܒ̈ܬܗܘܢ. Bach. עקביהם דם, their footsteps are blood. Oet.
עֲקֻבָּת דָּמִים. Ru. עֹקֶבֶת אָדָם. Val. עֲקֻדָה (so Hal.).—**9.** [וכחכי איש גדודים] 𝔊 καὶ
ἡ ἰσχύς σου ἀνδρὸς πειρατοῦ; 'Α. καὶ ὡς θυρεὸς ἀνδρὸς εὐξώνου; Σ. καὶ ὡς
φρύαγμα ἀνδρὸς ἐνεδρευτοῦ; Θ. . . . πειρατοῦ; Ε', ὡς λόχος πολυχειρίας
λῃστρικῆς; 𝔙 *et quasi fauces virorum latronum;* 𝔖 ܘܐܝܟ ܐ̈ܢܫܝ ܓܝܣܐ
ܘܚܒܪܐ = וּכְחֶדֶר כָאִישׁ גְדוּדִים (Seb., *et al.*). 𝔊 and 𝔖 join to preceding verse.
Ru. חפכו איש. GAS. ומחבת איש. Oet. מְחַכֵּי גד'. Gardner, וּכְחַבֵּל אַנְשֵׁי גד'.
or כֶּחָבָא אַנְשֵׁי גְדוּדִים. Marti, וַחֲכִיָּא גְדוּדִים חִבְּאוּ כֹּהֲנִים דַּרְכֵי רֹצְחִים שֶׁכְמָה. Bach.

[חֶבֶר.—[גְּדוּדִים מַכֵּי אִישׁ Read חִבְּאוּ with 𝔊 ἔκρυψαν (Cap., Vol.). 𝔖 ܐܚܒܐܘ
= חברו (Seb.; so also Oet.). Ru. חִבְּאוּ. Gardner, יחבאו. Marti, וַחֲכִיאוּ.—
[דרך Ru. בְּדַרְכֵּה.—[דרך] 𝔊 joins with preceding; so 𝔖 ܐ̈ܘܪܚܬܐ; 𝔊^AQ ὁδὸν
Κυρίου. Ru. יְרָחוֹ. Hal. and Marti transpose to foll. ירצחו.—[ירצחו] Oet.
וירצחו, (so Marti), which should foll. שכמה.—[שכמה] 𝔊 Σίκιμα, as obj. of
ירצחו; so 𝔖 and Σ.; 𝔙 *pergentes de Sichem.* Ru. הִשְׁכִּימוּ, for שכמה כי. We.
considers חכי, דרך, and ירצחו corrupt.—**10.** [בבית יש' 𝔊 joins to v.⁹. Read
with We. בנביתאל; cf. 10¹⁵ Am. 5⁶ (so Oort. *ThT.* and *Em.*; Preuschen,
ZAW. XV. 30; Ru., Now., Oet., Marti).—[שם] 𝔊 joins to preceding.—
[זנות לאפרים 𝔖 ܐܦܪܝܡ ܘܢܝ זנה א'. We. זָנִית א' (so Preuschen, *ZAW.*
XV. 30; Now., Oet.). Oort, זָנָה א'. Gardner, זְנוּת. Marti, זָנָה א'.

7. *But they like men have transgressed the covenant*] Israel
as a whole is spoken of,* not merely the priests,† nor the
prophets. ‡ Upon the whole "like men," § *i.e.* after the manner
of men, human-like, is to be preferred to "like Adam" (for
which are urged 𝕿 and 𝕵; the fondness of Hosea for early
allusions, cf. 2^3 9^{10} 11^8 12^4; the other occurrences of this phrase,
Jb. 31^{33} Ps. 82^7, and the parallel in Rom. 5^{14}), ‖ because of (1) 𝕲
(*v.s.*); (2) the absence of any account of a covenant with Adam
in Genesis; (3) the fact, that not until P is אדם used as a
proper name; ¶ (4) this is satisfactory in sense,** viz. ordinary
men, who have not had the privileges accorded to Israel. Cf.
the reading "in Admah" (*v.s.;* cf. 11^8). — *Have transgressed the
covenant*] This does not refer to the unknown covenant between
Yahweh and Israel,†† cf. 8^1; but to an ordinance (cf. 2 K. 11^4
Je. 11^6 $34^{13.18}$ Jb. 31^1 Ps. 105^{10}). Cf. the synonymous phrase
הפר ברית (Gn. 17^{14} Dt. 31^{16} Ju. 2^1), and the phrase "the book
of the covenant," Ex. 24^7. Notice is to be taken of the following renderings: (1) like Edom, they broke their covenant
with Israel; ‡‡ (2) they are as men who transgressed the covenant, §§ or who break a covenant; ‖‖ (3) they in Adam (a place)
did . . .¶¶ — *There they have betrayed me*] *There* is not an
adverb of time as in Ps. 36^{12} 53^5; *** nor an allusion to the land
which had received so many benefits; ††† nor a reference to the
ceremonial worship; ‡‡‡ but it refers to certain localities, either
unknown, §§§ or those cited in the following verses, ‖‖‖ which were
the scenes of the sin designated. The utterance carried with
it "a gesture of indignation." ¶¶¶ — **8.** *Gilead is a city of evil-
doers*] Much difficulty attaches to this proper name. It has been
taken as the district or land of Gilead; **** or the cities of
Gilead in general; †††† or Jabesh-Gilead; ‡‡‡‡ or Mizpah, the
capital of Gilead; §§§§ probably Mizpah, or in any case a seat of

---

* Cal., Hd., Ke., Now.ᴴ, *et al.*   † Sim.   ‡ AE., Hi., *et al.*
§ So Ki., Cal., Sim., Hi., Hd., Mau., Ew., Che., GAS.
‖ So Jer., Rashi, Umb., Ke., Pu., Or., Wü., Hal.
¶ Budde, *Urgeschichte*, 161 ff.   ** But *v.* Now.
†† Cf. Krätzschmar, *Die Bundesvorstellung*, 106.   ‡‡ Mich.   §§ Ew.   ‖‖ Hd.
¶¶ We.; Che. *EB.* art. *Adam.*   *** Hi.   ††† Ras., Ki., Bauer.
‡‡‡ Cal.   §§§ Ke., Now.   ‖‖‖ Wü., Or.   ¶¶¶ Che.   **** Pu., Ke., Or.
†††† Dathe.   ‡‡‡‡ Hi.   §§§§ Ew., Mau., Sim.

worship ; * or Ramoth Gilead (cf. Jos. 21³⁸ 1 K. 4¹³).† We may
understand it to be a city called Gilead mentioned in Ju. 10¹⁷,
but not identified. ‡ On the ground of some codexes of 𝕲 of
the Lucian revision which have Γαλγαλα, Gilgal has been suggested (v.s.; cf. 4¹⁵ 9¹⁵ 12¹¹). — *Tracked with bloody footprints*]
The versions (v.s.) except 𝕾 are far wide of the mark and give
no aid. None of the proposed changes of text seems to be necessary ; cf. 1 K. 2⁵. Other renderings are " spotted," " smeared," §
" hilly." ‖ There is no reference to historical events with which
we are familiar ; although Hitzig refers it to the murder of
Zechariah. — **9.** Although the text of this verse is hopelessly
corrupt, its general meaning seems clear, viz. that the priests are
really bandits occupying the highways and murdering travellers.
Of the four lines all present serious difficulties except the last.
The words of the first line (v.s.) have been taken (a) *thy
strength is that of bandits,*¶ but no good analogy for this expression can be found (yet cf. Pr. 20²⁹ Ne. 8¹⁰) ; (b) *assassins in
bands* (מחבי), *i.e.* those who lie in wait for men, in companies **
= companies of assassins ; but this is harsh and unnatural ; (c) *in
. . .* (the name of some city having originally stood where we
now have חבי) *is a band of robbers,* thus corresponding to Gilead
of v.⁵ ;†† (d) *the priest is a robber* ‡‡ (כהן), but this will make the
כהנים of the next line tautological ; (e) *as one hides robbers, the
priests hide themselves,* §§ but this gives no satisfactory meaning.
For still other suggestions v.s. ; upon the whole the rendering
And as bandits lie in wait for a man ‖‖ (cf. the slight variation
secured by treating איש as construct with גדודים, *and as bandits
lie in wait* ¶¶) seems best, the reference being to the wicked
work of Israelitish bandits (cf. 7¹), or to that of outside nations
like Moab, Aram, etc. (cf. 2 K. 5² 13²⁰). For other cases of
גדוד in this sense cf. 7¹ 1 S. 30⁸·¹⁵·²³ 2 K. 5². — *The priests hide
themselves on the road*] For text, v.s. 𝕳𝕿 reads (*so does*) *the
gang* (or *company*) *of priests, i.e.* an organized company (cf. in
later times, the Pharisees ***) of bad priests, but דרך must be taken

---

* We.   ‖ Hi.   ¶ 𝕲𝕾.   §§ Bach. (v.s.).
† Ros., Hd., Wü.   ** GAS.   ‖‖ So AV., RV.
‡ Oort, Now.   †† Preuschen (v.s.).   ¶¶ Hi., Ew., Che.; cf. Now.
§ Ros., Or.   ‡‡ Gardner.   *** Che.
  U

with what precedes.* — *They murder those going to Shechem*]
Some have regarded שכמה as = שכם אחד, *with one consent* (cf.
Zp. 3⁹);† but it is now understood to be the proper name,
Shechem,‡ which was at the same time a city of priests and a
city of refuge (Jos. 20⁷ 21²¹). The reference is to the abuse of
the right of asylum without allusion to any special event, cf.
Ju. 19²⁵·⁴⁵ 1 K. 2³¹ ᶠᶠ. § If דרך is taken with what precedes (*v.s.*),
we may suppose that some word (*e.g.* ההלכים) has dropped out.
Such a word seems necessary to secure the proper length of the
line. — *Yea, villainy they commit*] כי is asseverative, ‖ not causative.¶ The word זמה is not used here of some unnatural crime
(cf. Lv. 18¹⁷ 19²⁹),** nor of *lewdness ;* †† but of general wickedness
which was deliberate, thought out, *i.e.* villany ; cf. Pr. 10²³ 21²⁷.
— **10.** *In Bethel I have seen a horrible thing*] *In Bethel* (*v.s.*)
is better than 𝕸𝕿, *in the house of Israel,* because of 10¹⁵ Am. 5⁶,
and the use of "there" in v.¹⁰ ᵇ. 𝕲's connection of this word
with the preceding phrase is interesting and perhaps right. In
any case *Bethel* is intended. ‡‡ The thing seen is something to
cause terror (the word is an intensive form (*v.i.*), cf. Je. 18¹³), and
is explained by what follows. — *There, Ephraim, thou hast played
the harlot*] For text, *v.s.;* the harlotry is both literal and spiritual,
since the latter carried with it the former. Israel's calf-worship
in Bethel and Dan seems to be the occasion of these accusations. — *Israel is defiled*] The poetic parallel of the preceding.

7. והמה] ו is advers.; the pron. inserted not only for emphasis, but also to
give prominence to בגדו ב.—באדם] Cf. Ho. 5⁷; used of faithlessness and
deceit in various human relationships, and in general conduct; ב occurs
usually, but sometimes מן, cf. Je. 3²⁰.—שם] Kö. 373 *k.*— **8.** גלער] Emph.
by pos. and accentuation.—פעלי און] Cf. Is. 31² Ps. 5⁶; also similar use of
רע, Mi. 2¹; cf. עולה, Ps. 119³; cf. שֶׁקֶר, Ho. 7¹.—מדם] מן = cause; here דם
sg., frequently pl. in this sense; for the idea of the land polluted by blood,
Nu. 35³³ Ps. 106³⁸.— **9.** חכי] Here inf. cstr., GK. 23 *l,* 75 *aa;* not inf. abs.,
Kö. 225 *b.*—איש] May be: (*a*) the abs. after כחכי, גדודים being acc. of

* So 𝕲𝕾; cf. Hal.'s transpos. (*v.s.*). † AE., Ki., Cal., AV.
‡ Jer., Geb., Bauer, Dathe, Ros., Hi., Ew., Hd., Sim., Pu., Ke., Wü., Schm.,
Or., Che., Reu., We., Now.
§ Dathe, Ros., Hi., Ew., Sim., Wü., Or., Now.
‖ Hi., Ew., Wü., Ke., Now., Reu.
¶ Pu., Or. ** Ke. †† Sim.
‡‡ So Geb.

manner; or, (*b*) a cstr. with גר (*v.s.*); cf. Kö. 232 *a*. — [וּרְצַחוּ־שֶׁכְמָה An unusual case of the use of Măqqēph, cf. Gn. 6⁹ 7¹¹. — [שֶׁכְמָה Cf. שְׁכֶמָה, Gn. 37¹⁴ Jos. 24¹ GK. 93 *s*. — **10.** [שְׁעַרוּרִיָה Of the form qătlûl, GK. 84 *b*, *m* (cf. שְׁפרוּר Jer. 43¹⁰ [Kᵉth.]), with the addition of ־יָ (and the fem. end. ־ה); cf. שַׁעֲרוּרָה, Je. 5³⁰ 23¹⁴; also שַׁעֲרֻרִת, Je. 18¹³.

VI. 11-VII. 2. *Ephraim, to-day hardened in sin, will in the future discover his iniquity.*

11. [גַּם יהודה 𝔊 καὶ Ἰούδα, joining with v.¹⁰. Gr. (*Monatsschrift f. Gesch. u. Wiss. d. Judenthums*, 1887, p. 528) גם יהוה — .[שת קציר לך 𝔊 ἄρχου (= שָׁרַי, Aramaicizing (Vol.)) τρυγᾶν σεαυτῷ; E´, παρεσκεύαζε σαυτὸν εἰς τὸ ἐκθερισθῆναι; 𝔙 *pone*; 𝔖 ܚܨܒ. Gr. עֵת קֵץ לך (?). Read with Che., שִׁית (so Now., Oet., Marti). Ru. שָׂם שְׁקֵצִיךָ, supposing that something like לכן לא תשוב לבטח has dropped out from after שם. Bauer, שָׁתָ, addressed to Judah. Oort would read שת as imv. We. takes this and ¹¹ᵇ as a gloss on כרפאי לישראל (7¹) (so Now., who also rejects ¹¹ᵃ as a later addition; similarly Marti, *Rel.* 119, and *Dodekapropheton;* Preuschen, *ZAW.* XV. 31; cf. Oort and Oet.). — **VII. 1.** [כרפאי ליש' 𝔊 joins to 6¹¹ (so also We. and Che. (*CB.*)) and seems to read ב (*ἐν*) for כ (so also Ew., Oort, Marti). Bach. (*Pr.*) כְּרָאתִי לישראל. We. and Now. consider these words "ganz verloren." — [וְנִגְלָה We. om. ו (so Now., Oort (*Em.*), Che. (*CB.*), Marti; but cf. Oet.). — [רָעוֹת 𝔊𝔖𝔙𝔗 sg. (so Marti). Meinhold (p. 84), וַיִּרְעָתִי ר'. Marti, רָעָה ש' ר' — .[שקר 𝔖 adds ܫ̈ܥܟܒ. — [וְגָנֵב יבוֹא Add בֵּיתָה with 𝔊, whose πρὸς αὐτόν is probably an error for πρὸς οἶκον (so Oet., Marti, Now.²); cf. the parallel בחוץ. Bach. (*Pr.*) וגנבים בו (Gr. also reads בו for יבוא, but retains גנ' in sg.). Ru. inserts עָלֶיךָ before יבוא and transposes these words with the remainder of the verse to precede בשובי וג' and form the close of 6¹¹. — [פשט גדוד 𝔊 ἐκδιδύσκων (= פָּשַׁט) λῃστής, perhaps to be corrected to πειρατής, cf. 6⁹ (Vol.); Σ. ἐκδύον δὲ λῃστήριον; E´, λωποδύτης δὲ λῃστεύει; 𝔙 *spolians latrunculus;* 𝔖 ܚܣܟܕ. — **2.** ܘܟܠܗܘܢ ܚܛܝܗܘܢ 𝔖 [וּבַל יֹאמְרוּ לִלְבָ' Read בל יעמדו בלב' 𝔊 joins with v.¹ and renders ὅπως συνᾴδωσιν ὡς ᾄδοντες τῇ καρδίᾳ αὐτῶν, which Vol. explains as a double rendering, ὅπως συν' being a later correction of ὡς ᾄδοντες, which represents an original כַּמְּזַמְּרִים. Bach. (*Pr.*) proposes לחבר כאמרים בל' as the original text of 𝔊. Gr. בל' ואל יאמרו. We. and Now. suspect the text. — [סבבום Bach. (*Pr.*) הֲסַבּוּ. Hal. סְבָבוּנִי.

11. *Judah, for thee also is set a harvest*] An evident gloss suggested to the later writer by the sins of Judah which so resembled those here charged to Israel. Taking the 𝕳𝕿, שת, much variety of opinion has existed as to the subject; was it Judah preparing a harvest for Israel * (but in this case גם is difficult); or Israel,† or

---

* AE., Cal.   † Bauer.

Yahweh,* doing the same for Judah ; or is the verb to be treated
as impersonal— *one has set for thee*, etc. ? †   It is better to read
שִׁית (*v.s.* ; cf. Ps. 104[20]), the passive participle.   Judah, adds the
reader, will also suffer disaster ‡ (cf. 8[7] 10[13]; also Is. 17[11] 28[24-29]
Je. 51[33]) just as Ephraim, for has she not committed the same
sins?   Unsatisfactory is the meaning *branch* (cf. Jb. 4[9] 18[16] 29[19])
= *it has grafted a branch* (*i.e.* of the impurity mentioned in v.[10]) ; §
and entirely aside is the idea that the harvest is to be taken in a
good sense, viz. blessing, deliverance. ‖ — *When I would turn the
captivity* (or *fortune*) *of my people*] See Am. 9[14].   The grounds for
treating this phrase as a gloss are by no means so clear (*v.s.*) in
this passage as in some others ; and while, in general, the clause
may be taken as post-exilic, something may be said for its pre-
exilic authorship here, especially if the more general of the two
interpretations is adopted.   The reference is not to an actual
return from captivity,¶ nor merely to the bringing of the people
back to God,** but rather to the coming of a time of blessing or
good fortune.††   It is therefore in any case parallel with the first
clause in 7[1] and to be taken with it. ‡‡— **VII. 1.** *When I would
heal Israel*] *i.e.* when in mercy I would visit Israel, when my heart
would prompt me to forgive her ; cf. 5[13] 11[3] Je. 17[14].   בְּ is better
than כְּ (*v.s.*).   Perhaps with Nowack we should understand that
the apodosis has been dropped out of the text, since it is difficult
so to regard וְנִגְלָה (*v.i.*) ; or with Bachmann we should change the
text (viz. בִּרְאֹתִי, *when I look at*) to adapt it to the apodosis ; the
former suggestion is the more satisfactory.   Perhaps this line read
like this, " my hope and desire is frustrated." — *For the guilt of
Ephraim discovers itself*] Something (*v.s.*) has been lost with
which the ו of וְנִגְלָה was connected.   The verb is to be taken of
the past or present, §§ and not of the future. ‖‖   It is Israel's past
and present sin which makes it impossible now to relieve her of
the threatening calamity.   On Wellhausen's suggestion for omission of ו, *v.s.* — *And the evils of Samaria . . .*] Here a word is
needed to complete the parallelism as well as the metre, — per-

---

* Geb., Pu.   † Ros., Hd., Schm., Ke., Or.

‡ Bauer, Dathe, Ros., Hi., Wü., Now., Che., Reu.   § Ew.   ‖ Pu., Or.

¶ Pu., Wü., Schm.   ** Ke., McC.   †† Now.   ‡‡ So 𝔊, Ew.

§§ Ras., AE., Cal., Ros., Hd., Pu., Ke., We., Now.   ‖‖ 𝔊, Theod., Ew., Che.

haps *appear* (נראו). — *How they practise fraud*] כי here might
also mean *for*. שקר = corruption of every kind* (Je. 6¹³ 8¹⁰)
rather than idolatry ;† cf. דברו שקר, Mi. 6¹² Is. 59³. — *And the thief
comes into the house*] Two illustrations of the character of the
times are given, one the prevalence of ordinary thieving, the other
(*v.i.*) that of highway robbery. For the words, *into the house, v.s.*
The imperfect represents the frequency of this act. — *And bandits
roam abroad without*] Cf. 6⁹. — **2.** *They are not steadfast in their
heart*] For text, *v.s.* Another doubtful clause, the use of the
preposition ל being uncommon, 𝕲 having evidently something
different ; ‡ and although connection with the following clause is
demanded, it is difficult to find. Something is gained by substituting ב for ל, but 𝔐 *they say not* = *they think not* is hopeless.
On this use of עמד, cf. Dt. 25⁸, and for the general characteristic
here affirmed, viz. lack of loyalty, fickleness, cf. 4¹ᶠ· 6⁷ 7¹³ 10⁴·¹³
11¹² 12¹. — *All their evil I will record*] *i.e.* remember and punish ;
cf. 8¹³ 9⁹ Je. 14¹⁰ 44²¹. — *Now their deeds have encompassed them*]
i.e. as witnesses of their crimes, § or have beset them about so that
they are entangled. The situation is that of the past and present,
and not, as some maintain, ‖ the future (cf. 2⁸ 4¹⁹ Am. 3¹¹ Is. 13³).
The result is strongly introduced by *now*. — *They have come to be
before me*] A restatement of the fact already given in 7¹.

11. שבות] Cf. Am. 9¹⁴; also Kö. 329 *i*. — **VII. 1.** כְּרֹ] On the difference
between כ and ב, cf. BDB. 90 f. and 454 *b* ; the two are frequently interchanged by copyists. — ונגלה] If the apod. after prec. clause, ו has its common use, Kö. 415 *y*; otherwise something has been omitted with which ו had
originally a connection (*v.s.*). — רעות] Fem. pl. with neut. idea frequent ;
masc. pl. only in Ps. 78⁴⁹; Kö. 245 *a*. — יבוא פשט] Chiasm, with change of
tense, Kö. 155. — **2.** כל] Only used in more formal speech. — ללבבם] Ordinarily
the shorter form לב occurs in earliest poetry, Amos and Hosea ; *v.* Briggs's
"Study of the Use of לב and לבב in the O. T.," in *Semitic Studies in Memory
of Dr. Kohut*, Berlin, 1897, and BDB. — היו] Cf. Kö. 389 *c*, who suggests
יהיו, a י being dropped after פני.

3–7. *Repentance is impossible ; the situation is hopeless.*

3. ברעתם] 𝕲 has noun in pl. Ru. בְּרִיקֵיהֶם on basis of 𝕿. — בסריקתהון. — ישמחו]
Read with We. ימשחו (so Oort, *Em.;* Val., Now., Marti); but cf. Oet. —

---

* Cal., Ros., Now.ᴴ, *et al.*   † Jer., Theod.   ‡ We., Now.
§ Mau., Ew., Hd., Pu., Or., Reuss.   ‖ Ros., Hi.

[מלך] 𝔊𝔖, Θ., pl., but still construe it as obj. of ישמחו (so Ru.). — [ובכחשיהם
𝔖 connects with preceding. — [שרים] 𝔖 joins to foll. verse and reads שריהם. —
4. We., Now., and Marti treat this verse as a gloss on v.⁶, while Oet. would
place it after v.⁵. GAS. suggests that if there be a gloss, it begins with
ישבת. — [כלם מנאפים] These words, foll. 𝔖, are to be connected with שרים of
v.³ (so Houtsma (*ThT.* IX. 62), We., Now.). Oort (*ThT.* and *Em.*) reads
כלם מְנָפְחִים on basis of E´, εἰς τὸ μοιχεύειν ἐκπυρούμενοι. — [בערה מאפה] 𝔊
καιόμενος εἰς πέψιν = לַאֲפוֹת (Vol.); 𝔙 *succensus a coquente.* Read with Oort
(*ThT.* and *Em.*) בֹּעֵר הֵם אֹפֵהוּ (so We., Val., Now., Oet.). New. הַמְאֵפָה(?).
Hal. מַאֲפֶה ב´. — [ישבת] 𝔊 κατακαύματος; 𝔏 *conbustio.* Vol., foll. Grabe, corrects to καταπαύματος. GAS. suggests לחבת אש as original text of 𝔊. —
[מעיר] 𝔊 ἀπὸ τῆς φλογός = מִבָּעֵר (so also Oort (*ThT.* and *Em.*), Val., Now.,
Oet.). 𝔏 *flammae.* 𝔖 ܡܥܡܪܠ; 𝔙 *paululum civitas.* E´, πρὸς ὀλίγον
ἡ πόλις. Gr. מֵהַבְעִיר(?). Hal. מִבָּעֵר. — [מלוש בצק עד חמצתו] 𝔊 ἀπὸ φυρά-
σεως στέατος ἕως τοῦ ζυμωθῆναι αὐτό; 𝔖 ܠܐܡܬ ܚܡܠ ܟܡܐ ܢܣܟܐ;
𝔗 מעין מלש לישא עד לא חמע; 𝔙 *a commixtione fermenti donec fermentaretur
totum.* Ru., by comparison with v.⁷ ᵃ 𝔊, which he considers a repetition of this
verse, secures the foll. text: כֻּלָּם מְנָאֲפִים יֵחַמּוּ כְתַנּוּר בֹּעֵרָה אֵשׁ אֹפֶחָם לָהֶם אֶפְחָם וְיִשְׁבּוֹת מְעַט.
Marti transposes and reads: כְּמוֹ תַנּוּר בֹּעֵר הֵם כֻּלָּם מִן אֹפִים אֹפֶה יֵשׁ וגו´. —
5. [יום מלכנו] 𝔊 both nouns pl.; 𝔖 2d noun pl.; so many Heb. Mss. Oort
(*ThT.*) sugg. יומם (but in *Em.* ביום) מלכם. Ru. reads מַלְכֵיהֶם and takes
יום as a corruption of some such vb. as "they have stupefied." Gardner
om. יום as a dittog., ו arising from preceding ו and ם from foll. מ. Marti,
הֵם and וְשָׂרֵינוּ for שָׂרִים. — [החלו] 𝔊 ἤρξαντο; so 𝔖𝔙 = הֵחֵלּוּ (so also Dathe,
New., Hi., Houtsma). Gr. הִתְהֹלֲלוּ(?). Hal. הֵחֵלָה (so, independently, Gardner). Oet. נֶחֱלוּ. — [חמת] 𝔊 θυμοῦσθαι; 𝔖𝔙 also have infin. (so also Dathe,
New.). Gr. מֵחֲמַת יִין (so Oet., Hal.). Gardner, חמו. Müller (*SK.* 1904,
p. 125), הֵמִיתָם יָיִן. — [משך ידו] 𝔖 both words pl. Gr. מָסַךְ יֵינוֹ(?). We. and Now.
consider these and foll. words corrupt. Oet. אִמְצוּ יְדֵי הַלֵּצִים. Oort connects
משך with preceding context. Ru. מֵשֹׁכְרֵי אַף רְצִיחֶם(?). Gardner sugg. רצצים
for the last word. Redslob om. vs.⁵⁻⁷ as a marginal gloss on vs.³·⁴. — **6.** [קרבו]
𝔊 ἀνεκαύθησαν; 𝔖 ܩܪܒ = קרה (Seb.); 𝔙 *applicaverunt;* ´A., Σ., Θ. ἤγγισαν.
Read, with 𝔊, בערו (Vol.). Cappellus explained 𝔊 as = חרבו; Gr. = קרהו;
Bauer = זרבו. Michaelis reads קרבי (so Böckel, New., WRS.). Schorr (cited
by We.), קֹרְבָּם (so Che., Perles (*Analekten*, 32), We., Oet., Now.²). Marti,
קָרְחָה. Ru. considers it a corrupted correction of the foll. ארבם. Oort and Val.
connect first two words of v.⁶ with v.⁵. — [לבם] 𝔊 transl. by pl. and makes it
subj. of קרבו. — [כארבם] 𝔊 ἐν τῷ καταράσσειν αὐτούς, joining with the following (Vol., foll. Bahrdt, corrects to καταρᾶσθαι, which represents an
original ארב); 𝔖 ܟܡܐܢܗܘܢ; 𝔙 *cum insidiaretur eis;* ´A., Σ., Θ. ἐνεδρεύειν;
𝔗 בְּאִתְכְּמוֹנֻתְהוֹן. Schorr, בער בם (so Che., Gr., Perles (*Analekten*, 37), We.,
Now.²). Ru. בְּקָרְבָּם. Oet. כְּאָרְבָה. Marti om. as gloss. — [ישן] 𝔊 freely, ὕπνου
. . . ἐνεπλήσθη. Houbigant, עָשַׁן (so Böttcher, Wü.). WRS. (*Proph.* 413)
treats it as = יעשן. — [אפהם] Read אַפֵּהֶם with 𝔖 ܐ̈ܦܝܗܘܢ; so 𝔗 and many

Heb. Mss. (so Dathe, Wü., Houtsma (*ThT.* IX.), Schm., Che., WRS. (*Proph.* 413), We., Val., Ru., Gu., Now., GAS., Oet., Marti). ᴳ Ἐφράιμ (so New., Gr.); 𝔙 *coquens eos;* ʾΑ. ὁ πέσσων; Θ. ὁ πεσών; Σ. *pistor αὐτῶν.* Oort (*ThT.* and *Em.*), אָפָם.—בער הוא בקר] ᴳ πρωὶ ἐνεγενήθη, ἀνεκαύθη. Now. בְעָר.—7. Ru. om. first three words as a repetition from v.⁴.—ואכלו את ש'] ᴳᴬ κατέφαγεν πύρ; Ru. וְאָכְלָה אֵשׁ.—נפלו] Gr. יִפֹּלוּ.

3. *In their wickedness they anoint kings*] According to 𝔐 the charge made is that the highest authorities, the royal personages, indulge in the most sensual pleasures;* or that the king is rejoiced by the violence practised and boasted of (cf. Is. 3⁹ Pr. 20⁸·²⁶) by his subjects.† It is better, however, to read (cf. 8⁴·¹⁰) *anoint* (*v.s.*); the thought then is that one king after another comes to the throne through acts of wickedness and crime.—*And in their treacheries, princes*] Secret intrigue, involving faithlessness to both fellow-man and God.—**4.** *Since they are all adulterers*] viz. king, princes, and people. These words belong with the preceding verse as a circumstantial clause. ‡ For Oort's reading, *v.s.*—*They are like a burning oven whose baker*] These words, with the remainder of v.⁴, are a gloss to v.⁶. § This is the beginning of a new sentence, and this distribution of letters (*v.s.*) avoids the serious difficulty of treating תנור as feminine.—*Ceased to stir up the flame*] Using מִבְעָר for מעיר. ‖—*From the kneading of the dough until its leavening*] *i.e.* during the period in which fermentation was taking place.

Much variation has arisen in the interpretation of details: *e.g.* Ew., as the baker rests from heating only a short time, *i.e.* while he is compelled so to do (viz. during the few hours which intervene between the kneading of the dough and its fermentation), so the rulers rest from inflaming their passions only while they recuperate their strength for new pleasures (so Ras., Hd., Pu.). Others understand that the greatest heat of the oven is from the kneading of the dough to its leavening, because refuse, not wood, is used for fuel, and some hours are needed to secure the greatest heat, and that to the heat of this period is compared their passion (Ki., Cal., Dathe, Bauer, Ros., Wü., Schm.). Some desire to allegorize the statement by making Israel the dough, the king the baker (cf. Geb., Hi.); others think that actual persons and events are

---

* Che., GAS.   † Bauer, Ros., Pu., Or.

‡ 𝔖, Houtsma, We., Oort (*v.s.*), Val., Now.

§ This appears from (*a*) the repetitions involved; (*b*) the relation to v.⁶; (*c*) the use of כמו (*v.i.*).   ‖ So ᴳ, GAS., *et al.*

referred to, but that these are now unknown to us (Reuss). Some make the fire represent lust, while the oven is the heart; thus: "The baker ceases from kindling when the oven has reached a certain heat, and then he leaves the fire to smoulder, till the fermentation of the dough is complete, and a fresh heating is necessary. So after passion has once been gratified, it smoulders for a time, but is afterward kindled to a greater heat than before, when some attractive object comes within its range" (Che.; so Now.).

5. *On the day of our king they are become sick*] יום, = *on the day*, has been omitted as a case of dittography (*v.s.*) ; read in the plural ; * translated *by day ;* † interpreted as the day on which the king was chosen, ‡ the annual coronation day, § the birthday ‖ (Gn. 40²⁰ ; cf. Mat. 14⁶), any festival day appointed by the king,¶ — in any case a day of carousal. מלכנו, our king, has been read in plural.** החלו, *they are become sick,* or *have made themselves sick* is to be taken with *princes* as the subject ; †† others treat it as a causative = they made him (*i.e.* the king) sick ; ‡‡ or derive it from חלל, *to profane,* §§ or *begin.* ‖‖ — *The princes, with fever from wine*] The result of drunken carousal. Many render *from the heat of wine ;* ¶¶ but it is perhaps stronger; cf. Mi. 1⁹ 2¹⁰.*** Of no value is the suggestion, חמת (cf. Gn. 21¹⁵) = bottles full of wine.††† — *He stretched forth his hand with loose fellows*] Very difficult, perhaps impossible, to understand. ‡‡‡ *V.s.* for suggested readings, none of which is satisfactory, except perhaps that of Gardner, who reads רצצים for לצצים. Some kind of association or familiarity has been generally understood, either with drinking

---

* 𝕲.

† So Oort (*v.s.*) whose translation of the verse is : "By day the princes make their king sick; he is inflamed in long succession with wine, and holds forth with scorners whenever they are near him." This joins משך with *preceding* clause, and connects כי קרבו of v.⁶ with v.⁵. Against this rendering Now. urges the meaningless יומם which calls for a contrasted לילה; the difficulty of understanding החלו; the unusual position of חמת מיין as obj. of משך; the use of משך in such a connection; the meaningless כי קרבו; and the very doubtful use of the phrase יד וג׳ to denote the idea of good fellowship.

‡ Rashi, AE., Ki.　　§ Cal., Geb., Che.　　‖ Bauer, Wü., Schm., Ew., Che.
¶ Marck, Ros., Hi., Sim.　　　　　　** 𝕲𝕾, and many Heb. Mss.
†† Rashi, Bauer, Ros., Ew., We., Now.　　‡‡ AE., Ki., Pu.
§§ Geb.　　　　　‖‖ 𝕾𝔙, Hi., Wü., *et al.* (*v.s.*).
¶¶ Rashi, Geb., Ros., Hi., Hd., Wü., Or., Che., We.　　*** Ew., GAS.
††† AE., Ki., Cal.　　　　　‡‡‡ Marti om. ⁵ᵇ as a corrupt gloss.

companions (cf. 1 S. 22[17] Ex. 23[1]),* or with conspirators in a law-less project.† Wellhausen considers this a reference to the con-spiracy which resulted in the death of the last king (or perhaps the last *legitimate* king). The occasion for the murder was a ban-quet given by the king to his princes, and the conspirators were, not these same princes, but some unmentioned individuals. —

6. *For like an oven their hearts burn with their intriguing*] This translation (reading בערו on basis of 𝕲 for קרבו) furnishes an ex-cellent sense ; something which cannot be said of 𝔐𝕿, for which there have been proposed several interpretations (*e.g.* they prepare beforehand, ‡ bring near their heart to evil works, § turn, ‖ make nearly like,¶ have made ready ; ** they draw near, like an oven is their heart, etc. ; †† they draw near together, *i.e.* king and scoff-ers ; ‡‡ they have brought their heart into their ambush as into the oven, cf. Ju. 19[13] Ps. 91[10] ; §§ they have laid their cursing to their heart as to an oven ; ‖‖ they have made their hearts like an oven with their intriguing¶¶), nor of most of the emendations suggested ; *e.g. their inward part is like an oven, their heart burns in them;* *** *for like an oven is their heart within them;* ††† *for their inward part is like an oven, their heart like a smoke-hole.* ‡‡‡ The כי does not carry the thought back to v.[4], §§§ nor does it connect v.[6] with לצצים, ‖‖‖ but serves as an asseverative particle.¶ The thought, in general, is that of conspiracy, which is kept secret while it is maturing, but which after a period breaks out. The night is the time for development ; in the morning it becomes public. There seems to be no basis for the attempts of many commentators to connect this language with specific classes or events ; ¶¶¶ the reference is rather to the many conspiracies and murders following Jeroboam II.**** — *All night their anger sleeps*] With אפהם, or אפם, instead of אֹפֶהם (*v.s.*). There seems no neces-sity for changing the text to read *smokes* †††† (*v.s.*) instead of *sleeps.* The anger is that of the conspirators against those who are to be their victims ; this sleeps only in the night. — *In the morning it*

---

* Dathe, Cal., Ros., Ke., Wü., Or.   † Che., We.   ‡ Rashi, Cal.   § Ki.

‖ Geb.   ¶ Ew.   ** Pu.   †† Sim.   ‡‡ Böttcher, Schm.   §§ Ke.   ‖‖ Or.

¶¶ GAS.   *** Schorr, (cited by We.), *et al.* (*v.s.*).   ††† Ru.   ‡‡‡ Oet.

§§§ Sim., Ke.   ‖‖‖ Hi., Wü., *et al.*   ¶¶¶ Hi., Ew., Or.

**** Ros., Hd., Che., We., Marti, *et al.*   †††† Sug. by WRS., adopted by Che.

blazes like a flame of fire. — **7.** *All of them glowing like an oven*]
This is either an unnecessary repetition from v.⁴, or if v.⁴ (beginning
with כמו) * is a gloss (*v.s.*), it resumes in a single line the thought
expressed figuratively in v.⁶, preparatory to the presentation of the
same thought in literal form. The order of words shows that this
clause is subordinate ; it expresses the occasion of the actions next
described. The entire people are represented as filled with the
passion of conspiracy, and consequently — *they devour their rulers*]
It will be remembered that the reigns of Zechariah, Shallum, Menahem, Pekahiah were respectively six months, one month, six
years, one year. These were followed by Pekah (six years) and
Hoshea (eight years). In the period of about twenty years six kings
sat on the throne ; cf. 2 K. 15.† The term שפטים, commonly rendered *judges*, here means *rulers, i.e.* the nobles, including kings
and princes. It is frequently applied to kings, cf. Is. 40²³ Ps. 2¹⁰.
— *All their kings have fallen*] A poetic parallel for the preceding
line. Some fell by assassination, others by the hand of a foreign
enemy. This statement could not have been written earlier than
Menahem's time. — *No one among them calling for me*] A circumstantial clause added to give a prophetic touch to the historical
statement which preceded. Notwithstanding the serious situation
("four regicides within forty years") none among the people ‡
(cf. vs.⁹·¹⁰·¹⁴·¹⁶), rather than the princes, § call on Yahweh for help.

4. כלם] Subj. of circ. cl. joined with prec. — כמו] Poet. for כְּ; cf. 8¹² 13⁷;
מו is another form of מָה, *what;* the usage is a pleonastic one; cf. Arab. مَا
in بِمَا. — חנור] No art., according to Kö. 299 *l*, because the accompanying
attribute does not denote a permanent characteristic. — בּוֹעֵרָה מאפה] On basis
of 𝔐𝔗, the fem. ה‑ without accent is discussed, GK. 80 *k*; and מ as denoting agent, Kö. 107. — חמצתו] י is subj. — **5.** מיון] On prep. after cstr. H. 9,
2 *b*; Kö. 336 *w*, and note the om. of מן from חמת, where it is syntactically
required; Kö. 330 *n*. — לצצים] Not Qăl ptcp., but Pôlel, with מ omitted.
— **6.** כל־הל׳ . . . בקר] Emph. pos.; acc. of time. — לֵהָבָה] _, instead of ă or ā
before הָ, in the second syl. before the tone; cf. הֶהָרִים; GK. 27 *q*. — **7.** כלם]
Subj. introd. circ. cl. — ואכלו] = Impf. frequent., describing the repeated conspiracies; Dr. § 113 (4), *a.* — כל־מלכיהם] Chiastic order. — אֵין־קרא] The

---

* So Ru. (*v.s.*).

† For an account of the seditions and conspiracies which filled this period,
v. WRS. *Proph.* 151 ff.; Sta. *G VI.* I. 575–602.

‡ Pu., Ke., Wü., Che., We., *et al.*   § Geb., Ros., Ew.

verse closes as it began with a circ. cl., the two intervening lines being
arranged chiastically.

§ 9. The confusion of the nation. 7^8–8^3. Israel is losing
herself among the nations, and yet she is blind to the fact.
In her arrogance she is turning away from her God, thus chal-
lenging his punishment. Israel is a silly dove turning hither and
thither, only to be caught in the net; 7^{8-12}. Destruction awaits
her; for against me, though ready to redeem her, she has lied.
Instead of sincere worship, her people merely howl for corn and
wine, and cut themselves and rebel. They desire evil; they are
a deceitful bow; their princes shall perish; 7^{13-16}. Assyria is
about to attack them; they may cry unto me, but it will not avail,
for they have spurned the good; 8^{1-3}.

In this piece we may note: (1) a change of measure, the lines containing,
for the most part, four words instead of three; (2) a remarkable use of
parallelism, the entire piece falling into couplets; (3) an apparent grouping
of these couplets in pairs; (4) a division into three strophes, the first having
three such pairs of couplets, *i.e.* twelve lines; the second the same; while the
third, which forms the climax to the whole piece, contains one such pair, or
four lines; (5) a more conspicuous effort than has heretofore been noted to
introduce those points which conduce to symmetry. In the arrangement here
proposed the following modifications of the text are adopted: (1) the clause
איסירם כשמע לעדתם in ^{12c} is transferred to follow immediately upon v.^{10}. (2) It
is understood that the line now consisting of ואנכי אפדם (v.^{13c}) is incomplete,
two words being lost. (3) The words זו לעגם (7^{16}) are treated as a gloss.
(4) The two clauses forming the second half of 8^1, beginning יען, are treated
as a later interpolation.

8. בעמים] ⅏ ἐν τοῖς λαοῖς αὐτοῦ = בעמיו. — הוא יתבולל] ⅏ συνεμίγνυτο;
Syr.-Hex. מתחלט הוא. Oet. הוא יבול (so Marti, Now.²); Gardner, היה בליל. —
אפרים] Gr. om. as dittog. — עגה] ⅏ ἐγκρυφίας; so 𝔙 subcinericius panis;
E', ὡς ἐν σποδιᾷ πεσσόμενος ἄρτος. — בלי הפוכה] ⅏ adds ܠ; so ℭ.
Hence Ru. בלא הפוכה תאכל. — **9.** ⅏ supplies ܣ at beginning. — ידע]
⅏ ἔγνω; hence Ru. ידע. — גם] 𝔙 sed et. — זרקה בו] ⅏ ἐξήνθησαν αὐτῷ;
E', ἤδη τυγχάνων; ⅏ ܠܒܫ; ℭ מטחנון; 𝔙 effusi sunt in eo. Ru.
הרב רקתו; Gr. זרחה בו (so BDB.(?)); Oet. זרקה בו (so Marti, Now.²). —
10. וענה] ⅏ καὶ ταπεινωθήσεται; so ⅏ and 𝔙; cf. 5⁵. — ולא] Oet. om. ו. —
בכל זאת] ⅏ ἐν πᾶσι τούτοις; so 𝔙 in omnibus his; ⅏ om. — **12** c. איסירם]
Ru. אאסיר; Oet. אאסרם(?); Gr. איסרם (so Now., Oet., Hal., et al.). Marti,
אאסרם = אסרם. — כשמע לעדתם] ⅏ ἐν τῇ ἀκοῇ τῆς θλίψεως αὐτῶν, reading לרעתם

(Cap., Vol., Now.), or לצרחם (Cap.); 𝔖 ܘܢܣܒܘܢ ܡܬܩܠܐ = אסו; לעדותם‎
(Seb.); Σ. μαρτυρίας [αὐτῶν]; 𝔗 בְּשֵׁם לעצתם = על רשמעו לעצחתוין‎ (Sim.,
Seb.); 𝔙 and 'A. = 𝔐𝔗. Ru. שמע לעזרתם or בְּמֵכְל צַעֲרַיהֶם. Gr. לעזריהם‎ or
Hal. כְּשֶׁמְעַ לעַר or וּכְנִשׁׁמָע. Oet. שָׁכֵם עַל רָעָתָם (cf. Marti); Gardner, בשבע
לצרחם. Müller (SK. 1904, p. 125) כש לַחֲצָם — 11. [קראו 𝔖 ܢܣܒܘ = קרבו‎
(Seb.). — [אשור] Gr. אַשׁׁוּרָה. — 12. [כאשר 𝔖 ܥܠܝܗ; 𝔗 באתר = כאשר‎
[עליהם — .באשר = באשר] Gr. אַשׁׁוּרָה. — 12.
E', κοινῇ· ὅτι καὶ κοινῇ πάντες ἐξημαρτήκασιν. — 13. [שר להם 𝔊 δείλαιοί εἰσιν;
𝔖 ܣܚܝܦܝܢ܂ ܐܝܟ ܡܦܠܬܐ 'A. προνομὴ αὐτοῖς; E', ἐκπορθήσονται; Θ. ταλαι-
πωρία. Gr. להם אִיד. — [ואנכי Ru. om. ו. — 14. [בלבם 𝔊 αἱ καρδίαι αὐτῶν, as
subj. of יעקו, omitting ב; 𝔖 ܟܣܝܐ ܡܢ — .[משכבוחם 𝔖 sg. noun;
'A., Σ. ἀσελγῶς; Sm. (Rel.[1] 125), מִשְׁאֲרִוחָם; Oet. מִשְׁפָּחֵיהֶם. Read, with Gardner, מִזְבְחוֹתָם. — [יחגוררו] Read, with 𝔊, κατετέμνοντο, יחגודדו (so also Houtsma,
Seb., Vol., Che., Gr., We., Gu., Ru., RV. m., Now., GAS., BDB., Oet., Marti,
et al.). 𝔙 ruminabant; 𝔖 ܡܬܓܘܣܝܢ; 'A. περιεσπῶντο; Σ. ἐμηρυκῶντο;
E' om. Hal. יְחְנוֹדְדוּ. — [יסורו 𝔖 ܢܣܛܘܢ; 𝔊 joins with foll. verse, ἐπαιδ-
εύθησαν = יְסְרוּ (Cap., Vol.), or ימרו (Gr.), or יִסְרוּ (Wü.); Σ. ἐξέκλιναν; E',
ἀπέστησαν. Ru. סָרְרוּ; Gr. יָמְרוּ (so Hal.) Read, with Houtsma, יָסֹרוּ (so
Now., Oet.). Marti, סָרוֹר יָסֹרוּ, using יסרתי of v.[15]. — 15. [ואני יסרתי חזקתי
𝔊 κἀγὼ κατίσχυσα, omitting יסרחי (so also Ru. and Oet., who also om. ו
from before אני); Σ. ἐγὼ δὲ ἐπαίδευον αὐτούς. Perles (Analekten, 60), וַיִּסְרֵהוּ;
Gr. יִסֵּרְתִּים. Hal. אֲסָרְתִּי. — [זרועתם] Gardner, זְרֹועַ אתם. Ru. om. v.[15] as breaking the connection and repeating v.[18] in form and thought. — 16. [וישובו Ru.
וַיָּשׁׁוּבוּ; Oet. יָבֹשׁׁוּ. — [לא על 𝔊 εἰς οὐδέν = על לא (Vol.); 𝔖 ܠܐ ܬܩܠܐ;
𝔙 ut essent absque jugo; Σ. εἰς τὸ μὴ ἔχειν ζυγόν; E', ἵνα διάγωσιν ἄνευ ζυγοῦ.
New. [לא יועיל; Oort לא יועילו (so Val., Oet.), or לא להועיל; Marti לבעל
(Rel. 147; Ru., Now.; but cf. Sellin, Beiträge, II. 306); Gr. יועיל ללא
— [קשת Sellin (Beiträge, II. 306) רֶשֶׁת. — [רמיה 𝔊 ἐντεταμένον; Σ. ἀνεστραμ-
μένον; E', διάστροφον. [זעם 𝔊 and Θ. ἀπαιδευσίαν = מֶרַעַם (Gr.); 'A. ἀπὸ
ἐμβριμήσεως; E', διὰ μανίαν; 𝔗 מעקמות. Ru. מֵעֲמֶק. Marti, מִזַּעֲמִי. — [לשונם
Oet. לְשׁׁוֹנִי. Marti, שְׁפָּחֵיהֶם. — [לֹעְגָם] 𝔊 φαυλισμὸς αὐτῶν = עֲלֵיהֶם (Gr.);
𝔖 ܡܓܘܕܦܘܬܗܘܢ = עזלם (Ru.); 'A. μυχθισμός; Σ. ὅ ἐφθέγξαντο; E', αὐτὴν
ἐβλασφήμησαν; 𝔗 מעשׂיהם = עברייהון (Ru.). Gr. עֲלֵיהֶם; Oet. כְּפֻלָם. Oort om.
זו לעגם as a dittog. — VIII. 1. [אל חכך שפר 𝔊 εἰς
κόλπον αὐτῶν ὡς γῆ = כעפר [ם]חיק אל (Vol.), or כשפר (Gr.); 𝔖 ܐܣܘ ܡܪܝ =
חכך כשפר = חֲרֶשׁ (Seb.). Ru. אֱחֹול, omitting כשפר as dittog.
of כנשר; Oort עפר ילחכו, to be joined with the last two words of 7[16];
Houtsma, כשפר. Gr. קֹול for אל. — [כנשר] Gr. sugg. it may be dittog.
from כשפר; Hal. כַּצִפָּה; Gardner, מְבַשֵּׂר. Read שֶׁר כִּי (so We., GAS.). —
בית יהוה Ru. ביתי. Gr. בית יהודה. — [ועל] Gr. וְגֻמַל; Now. om. 1[b] as a later
addition. Marti, foll. a suggestion of Che. (Exp. 1897, p. 364), reads 1[a]:
ישראל]‎ 𝔊𝔏 — 2. [יזעקו 𝔖 adds ܣܓܝ. — אֶל־תִּתְחַשׁ כַּשׁׁוֹפָר הָרֵם קֹולְךָ עַל־כ' י'
and 𝔖 om. (so Dathe, Gr., Now., Oet., Marti). — [אלהי 𝔊 ὁ θεός; 𝔖 1st

p. pl. suff.; hence Oet. and Marti אלהים or אלהינו.—Ru. om. v.² as in part
a repetition of 7¹⁴ and in part a dittog.; Marti om. vs.¹·² as glosses.—**3.** זנח]
𝔊 ὅτι, κ.τ.λ.; hence Gr. כי זנח (so Ru., Now.).—ואיב ירדפו] 𝔊 ἐχθρὸν κατε-
δίωξαν (= ירדפו or רדפו). Ru. און רדפו להם, joining first word of v.⁴ with
v.³; Hal. אֲוֶן יִרְדְּפוּ.

8. *Ephraim—among the nations he lets himself be mixed*]
On יתבולל, *v.i.;* although somewhat uncertain,* it may be accepted as a fairly satisfactory reading. The meaning is not
is kneaded,† referring to the loss of independent existence in
exile; nor does it refer to the seeking for help from the outside
nations;‡ but rather to the acceptance of the foreign fashions
and ideas which came in upon Israel in connection with the
opening up of commercial relations with the outer world.§ This
is the third or fourth time in Israel's history when the nation
is brought into intimate relations with the outside world. From
the association with Assyria, much good will come; for a new
and larger horizon will be secured and important steps forward
will be taken toward higher conceptions of God and of the
world: but with this good, there is coming also much that is
bad, much that can "dissipate and confuse" the weaker of the
nation. "The tides of a lavish commerce scattered abroad the
faculties of the people, and swept back upon their life alien
fashions and tempers, to subdue which there was neither native
strength nor definiteness of national purpose." ‖ — *Ephraim —
he has become a cake not turned*] As a result of mingling with
the foreign nations and accepting their ideas, Israel has become
an unturned cake — the round, flat cake, baked on hot stones ¶
(cf. 1 K. 19⁶) — a striking figure, which describes the condition
of things at home as growing out of that abroad. The point of
emphasis does not rest on the fate of the unturned cake, which,
of course, is destroyed; nor on the fact that, such a cake being
half-ruined, Israel, likewise, is half-ruined; ** nor on any specific
reference to their opinions concerning the worship of idols; ††
but rather upon that weakness of the national character which

---

* We.   † Ras., Bauer, Or.   ‖ GAS. I. 271.
‡ AE., Eich., Mau., Che., Reuss.   ¶ Now. *Arch.* I. 111.
§ Ki., Cal., Ros., Hd., Wü., *et al.*   ** Che.   †† AE., Ki.

was exhibited, in the inconsistencies of which they were guilty, the lack of thoroughness with which their plans were executed, the wrong direction pursued by those in charge of the national policy, and the lack of proportion in national effort. "How better describe a half-fed people, a half-cultured society, a half-lived religion, a half-hearted policy, than by a half-baked scone?"*
— **9.** *Strangers have devoured his strength and he knows it not*] The strangers are the foreign nations already mentioned. The reference is a general one, taking in all with whom Israel had come in contact in these times, viz. the kings of Syria, Hazael, and Benhadad in the times of Jehoahaz (2 K. 8^{12} 10^{32} 13^7); Tiglath-pileser, the king of Assyria, called Pul (2 K. $15^{19.\ 20}$), who exacted tribute from Menahem, and took away territory from Pekah (2 K. 15^{29}); and likewise the Philistines (Is. 9^{11}), and Egypt, with whom Israel was always warring. For other cases of כֹּחַ, *strength*, used in the sense of *property*, cf. Pr. 5^{10} Jb. 6^{22}. לֹא יָדַע (cf. Is. 1^3) = he does not understand the meaning of the punishment (2^7 5^{15}); rather than, he does not understand anything,† *i.e.* has not come to discretion, or does not know Yahweh. ‡ —
Yea, gray hairs are sprinkled upon him and he knows it not] Cf. 7^{11} Is. 46^4 Ps. 71^9. The nation is represented as passing through the various stages of human life. Israel has lost his strength; but that is not all, he has reached such an old age, as is seen from the appearance here and there of gray hairs, that there is no hope of regaining the strength which has been lost. The inevitable accompaniment of old age is weakness. This representation of the state as an individual, called personification, is one of the most interesting features of Hebrew style; cf. the suffering servant of Is. 42^{1-9} $44^{1\ f.}$ 52^{13}–53^{12}, and the collective "I" of the Psalter. — **10.** *The pride* (or *arrogance*) *of Israel has witnessed against him*] See on 5^5; cf. Am. $4^{6.\ 11}$. Yahweh is not the witness, § but their own pride of heart which blinds them to the sure fate that is rapidly overwhelming them. The evidence of arrogance has been very clear in the historical events of the period, especially in their attempt now to secure

---

* GAS. I. 273; so We., Now., *et al.* ‡ 𝕋, Theod., Abarb.
† Hi., Pu., Wü., Or. § Hi., Ke., Che.

Assyria's favor, and again, that of Egypt.* — *Yet they do not return to Yahweh their God and seek him for all this*] Cf. Is. 9[12. 17. 21]. The logical relationship of the verbs in this verse is somewhat obscure on account of the use of the tenses.† Some treat the three clauses as coördinate;‡ others § make עִנָה the predicate not only of אֵין ‎" but also of the two following clauses, translating: *Then testifies against him the pride of Israel and that they do not return to Yahweh, etc.;* but this construction is cumbersome and unnecessary; for this use of וְעָנָה, *v.i.* — **12 c.** *I will chastise them by the abundance of their afflictions*] This translation (reading בְּשֵׁבַע לְצָרָתָם (*v.s.*)) is one of several attempts (*v.s.*) to get a tolerable meaning out of the clause. 𝔐𝕿 *as their congregation has heard,* if accepted, would mean in a general sense, *as has been publicly proclaimed,* either through the prophets (cf. Am. 2[11 f.] 2 K. 17[13]), ‖ or if the passage is late, through the reading of the law (Dt. 27 and 28).¶ Of considerable interest is the interpretation of Rashi, who without noticing the anachronism understands this of Jeremiah (37[3] 42[3] 30[8]) ; that of Hitzig, who reads : *according to what is heard of* (= *concerning*) *their congregation, i.e.* the Assyrian party which (note יֵלְכוּ) relied especially on the foreign power; and that of Ewald, who interprets : like a prophetic oracle prophesying this very thing announced to their congregation by a former prophet. But with 𝔊𝔖𝕿 most commentators have found this peculiarly difficult, only 𝖄 and 'A. supporting it. For the reading proposed, Ps. 16[11] Jb. 14[1] 10[15] furnish analogies. This clause is detached from v.[12 b] and placed here because (1) it is superfluous in v.[12], the thought of punishment being there already fully expressed; moreover, this prosaic statement is not in keeping with the figurative language of vs.[11. 12] ; (2) it furnishes just the required conclusion for the thought of v.[10]. — **11.** *And so Ephraim has become like a foolish dove without understanding*] The dove, celebrated in proverbs ** for its simplicity and unsuspicious nature, flies thoughtlessly from one danger, that of the pursuing hawk, to another,

---

* Cf. especially GAS. I. 337.   ‡ GAS., *et al.*   ‖ Dathe, Or., Wü.

† Marti om. [10] as a gloss.   § Ew., We., Now.   ¶ Bauer, Pu., Ke., *et al.*

** Cf. the Arabic proverb, "There is nothing more simple than the dove"; a similar proverb was current among the Greeks and Romans,

HOSEA

the fowler's net; * or having in search of food lost its home,
flutters hither and thither without purpose or plan.† Such has
Israel become (cf. Je. 5²¹). The words "foolish" and "without
understanding" are here connected with the dove, ‡ not Ephraim. §
Cf. the parallel phrase חֲסַר לֵב (Pr. 6³², 7⁷ 10¹³·²¹), and the phrase
of opposite meaning חכם לב (Pr. 11²⁹). — *To Egypt they cry; to
Assyria they go*] By some these statements are supposed to be
specific allusions to certain historical events, *e.g.* the former to
2 K. 17³, the latter to 2 K. 15¹⁹ (cf. 5¹³ 8⁹·¹³ 12¹). ‖ But it is
better to take it in a more general sense as referring to the
foreign policy, controlled now by the Assyrian party, now by
the Egyptian, — a policy of hesitation and indecision which
marked the entire period of the monarchical supremacy.¶ —
12. *As they go, I will spread over them my net*] Cf. Ez. 12¹³
17²⁰ 19⁸ 32³ Jb. 19⁶. כאשר = not *wherever* ** nor *the more*,†† but
as soon as, ‡‡ *i.e.* as soon as they seek the help of other nations,
whether Egypt §§ or Assyria. ‖‖ The spreading over them of the
net signifies the calamity which is about to fall upon them, viz.
the captivity. — *Like birds of the air I will bring them down*]
A poetic parallel for the preceding phrase, expressing destruction. Yahweh will bring them down, just as birds of the air
are brought down, *i.e.* by a bait which allures them,¶¶ or by
missile weapons.*** — **13.** *Alas for them that they have strayed
from me*] This wandering away from Yahweh does not refer to
their acceptance of the calves,††† nor generally to their lack of
obedience (cf. Ps. 21¹¹ᶠ·) ; ‖ but, while the language may have
been drawn from the figure of the foolish dove wandering away
from its nest ‡‡‡ (cf. Is. 16² Pr. 27⁸), the special sin rebuked is that
of seeking the help of Assyria and Egypt. For other cases of
אוֹי cf. 9¹² Is. 6⁵ Nu. 21²⁹ Je. 13²⁷. — *Destruction to them, that they
have rebelled against me !*] Here a stronger expression is employed, viz. that of rebellion, apostasy, which means (*a*) the

---

* So Hi., Hd., Che., Reuss.   † Ew., Or.   ‡ Ros., Now.   § Ke.   ‖ Ros.
¶ Cf. McC. *HPM.* §§ 631-633, 650, 652 ff., 677 ff., etc.; Gu. *Gesch.* pp. 188, 206 f.,
210, 216, 222, 224, and art. "Israel," *EB.* §§ 30, 34, 36; Barnes, art. "Israel, History
of," *DB.* II. 512 f.
** Pu.   ‡‡ Wü., Che., GAS., Now.   ‖‖ Jer., Ros.   *** Hd.
†† Ew.   §§ Ras., AE.   ¶¶ Wü., Che.   ††† Ki.
‡‡‡ Hd., Ke., Wü., Che., Or., Now.

breaking of bonds that have existed, and (b) the claiming of release from former responsibility. On שׁד, *v.s.* — *And shall I redeem them . . .*] Cf. 13[14]. The imperfect אפדם has been treated (1) as expressing desire,* *I have desired to redeem them, but, etc.;* (2) as a frequentative of past time,† *I have often redeemed them, but, etc.;* (3) as conditional,‡ *if I should, etc., they would only, etc.;* but it is simpler to understand the clause as interrogative, although no interrogative particle is prefixed § (*v.i.*); or as exclamatory, ‖ *I redeem them when they, etc.!* This explains the presence of אנכי in the principal clause, although it is not especially emphatic. There had been frequent instances of redemption in the past, but these do not bear upon the present situation. — *When they have spoken lies about me*] *i.e.* represent me wrongly, misunderstand me, and think evil of me; meaning by this not simply that they were acting as hypocrites in their worship,¶ nor that they thought Yahweh unable to help them (Je. 14[9] 44[8]),** but rather that their entire conception of him was wrong, — in other words, they did not know Yahweh. **—14.** *And they have never cried unto me with their heart*] Cf. Ps. 119[10]; the cry which has gone forth has not been honest and sincere, *i.e.* from the heart, or with 𝕲, *their hearts have not cried unto me.* Cf. 1 S. 12[8. 10] Is. 29[13] Ps. 84[2]. — *But they keep howling beside their altars for corn and new wine*] *i.e.* for material blessings, — the beastlike cry of the animal for food, etc., and not the true cry of a soul for God. 𝕸𝕿 *on their beds* cannot stand, for it must mean that they eat the meal of the sacrifice, offered to secure these material blessings, while reclining upon divans, or couches; and this is hardly supposable. The emendation adopted (*v.s.*) is quite simple and natural, and better than others proposed, *e.g.* משארת, kneading-trough (*v.s.*), which Nowack rightly characterizes as affording no adequate sense; but Nowack is wrong in supposing that על with מש must have the same meaning as על with the other words. For an example of a preposition used in two senses in the same verse cf. ב in 4[3] 5[5]. — *They cut themselves, they rebel against me*] This ren-

---

* Ras., AE., Ki., Hi., Ke., Wü., Or., Che.   § Geb., Reuss, Now.
† Theod., Cal., Ros., Hd., Pu.   ‡ Eich.   ‖ We.   ¶ Bauer, Ros.
** Hi., Ke., Che., *et al.*

x

dering of an emended text (יתגדדו, *v.s.*) represents the people as engaged in the well-known mourning custom, forbidden in Dt. 14¹ Lv. 19²⁸ 21⁵, but kept up even in the latest times (cf. 1 K. 18²⁸ Je. 16⁶ 41⁵ 47⁵ 48³⁷).* 𝕸𝕿 (יתגררו), in which ר occurs instead of the suggested ד, has been translated : (1) *they collect themselves*, *i.e.* to rebel † or to eat and drink, ‡ or to buy wheat and wine offered for sale, § or to make solemn processions to their idols (cf. Jo. 1¹³ ff. 2¹⁶ ff.) ; ‖ (2) *are in distress ;* ¶ (3) *excite themselves ;* ** (4) *howl, roar* (cf. Je. 30²³).†† The second word (יסורו) also needs emendation, for סור is invariably followed by מן ; סרר (*v.s.*), cf. 4¹⁶ 9¹⁵ Is. 1²³, gives the right idea. ‡‡ — **15.** *Although it was I who trained and strengthened their arms*] To be taken with the following clause. The pronoun is emphatic, and the circum-stantial clause expresses the idea of concession. The usual mean-ing of יסר, *chasten, punish,* §§ *i.e.* strengthened by chastisement, gives no sense. If 𝕸𝕿 is retained it must mean *trained*, or *dis-ciplined,* ‖‖ and be taken with *their arms* (cf. Ps. 18³⁴ 144¹), unless we read יסרתים, *I trained them* (*v.s.*). For the phrase *strengthen their arms*, cf. Ez. 30²⁴· ²⁵, also Ps. 10¹⁵ 71¹⁷ 1 S. 2³¹ 2 Ch. 32⁸ Is. 48¹⁴ Zc. 11¹⁷.— *Yet concerning me they keep thinking (only) evil*] The base ingratitude is pictured with which they treat the very one who gave them strength to secure their victories. This puts more strongly the thought already expressed in v.¹³. That they do think evil of him is evident from the abandonment of him involved in going after Egypt and Assyria, for there could be no association with these nations without some recognition of their deities. Such recognition was of course inconsistent with a right conception of Yahweh. There is probably no reference to the calf-worship.¶¶ — **16.** *They turn, (but) not upwards*] Cf. 11⁷. This is the accepted rendering of 𝕸𝕿, but is unsatisfactory. For discussion

---

* So 𝕲. On this custom cf. WRS. *Sem.* 321 f.; We. *Reste*², 181; C. J. Ball, art. "Cuttings of the Flesh," *EB.* §§ 1, 2; Schwally, *Das Leben nach dem Tode*, 16 ff.; Frey, *Tod, Seelenglaube und Seelenkult im alt. Isr.*, 134 ff.; Grüneisen, *Der Ahnenkultus u. die Urreligion Isr.*, 73; Zapletal, *Der Totemismus u. d. Rel. Isr.*, 106–112.

† Ras. § Ki. ¶ 𝔖, Bauer, Schm. †† Hi.
‡ AE., Ke. ‖ Ros., Hd., Or. ** Ew. ‡‡ Now.
§§ So Ras., AE., Geb., Pu.
‖‖ Bauer, Ros., Hi., Ke., Now., Or., Che., Reuss, *et al.* ¶¶ Ros.

of על as a substantive, *v.i.* Some understand על as used for
עלה = height, here the highest;[*] others, as = עליון, *the high,
exalted one* = God;[†] others, simply as an adverbial accusative
= *upwards;*[‡] others with 𝕲 and 𝕾 turn the words around and
read על לא = על שׁוא, *to that which is nothing* = *idols.*[§] The
suggestion of לַבַּעַל, *to Baal,* seems to relieve the difficulty and
is probably to be accepted; *v.s.* for other suggestions. — *They
have become like a bow which swerves*] Ps. 120[2 f.]. The comparison (cf. Ps. 78[57]) is not to a bow (1) whose string has lost
its elasticity, and consequently the arrow fails to reach its mark,[‖]
nor (2) one which cannot be used because it is relaxed,[¶] nor
(3) one whose string breaks without shooting the arrow,[**] nor
(4) one which strikes and wounds the bowman,[††] but rather (5) to
a bow which is expected to shoot in one direction but actually
shoots in another, thus failing to accomplish its end.[‡‡] It is
thus with Israel. Cf. the vineyard which was expected to yield
good grapes, but actually yielded wild grapes, Is. 5[1-7]. — *Their
princes shall fall by the sword because of the insolence of their
tongues*] For are not the princes (*i.e.* the leaders) everywhere
represented as being primarily responsible? Upon them especially will fall the doom which the sword of Assyria[§§] will execute.
It is because the Egyptian party has secured the supremacy that
this evil fate is announced. The leaders who have persuaded
their followers to adopt a policy hostile to Yahweh's teachings
and threatenings will now suffer the misery which must surely
follow. But what was the character of their tongue or language,
which has led to this result? Was it its roughness,[‖‖] its deceptive tone,[¶¶] its haughty boasting,[***] its pride, depending upon
Egypt as protection,[†††] its mockery and scepticism, its insolence as displayed toward Yahweh,[‡‡‡] its bitterness?[§§§] Why
should we have expected "falseness"? Only here and Je. 15[17]
is זעם used of men; elsewhere (*e.g.* Is. 10[5. 25] 13[5], etc., *v.i.*)

---

[*] Mau., Hes.   [†] Ki., Cal., Hd., Pu.

[‡] Hi., Ew., Sim., Ke., Wü., Or., Che., Reuss.   [§] Bauer.

[‖] Ke., Reuss, We.   [¶] Ew.   [**] Σ. (*v.s.*), Ros.   [††] Jer., Or.

[‡‡] Rashi, Ki., Cal., Geb., Hi., Hd., Sim., Pu., Wü., Now., Che., GAS.

[§§] Cf. Meinhold's view that Syria is alluded to, not Assyria.   [‖‖] Rashi.

[¶¶] Ki., Ros., Pu.   [***] Cal.   [†††] Hd.   [‡‡‡] Wü., Now., Or., Che.   [§§§] GAS.

only of Yahweh; hence the suggestion of *my tongue* (*i.e.* Yahweh's); but upon the whole the rendering *insolence* satisfies the context. This *insolence of tongues* has been exhibited especially — *in the land of Egypt*] Cf. Isaiah's sermons at this same time against the representatives of the Egyptian party. The words *this their scorn* are a gloss* explaining the ‎לֹ ‎זעם (*v.s.*). While they are depending upon Egypt, boasting of their strength, only scorn and derision will Egypt accord them.† For other treatments of ‎לענם, *v.s.;* but cf. Ewald — *that is their scorn with the land of Egypt.* Nothing now may interpose to stay the doom of a people whose apostasy and treachery are so evident. Destruction is certain. — **VIII. 1.** *To thy mouth with the trumpet!*] The text is difficult and perhaps corrupt, both 𝔊 and 𝔖 grouping the consonants so as to make words different from those in 𝔐𝔗 (*v.s.*). Nothing is to be said for the emendations proposed (*v.s.*); nor is the case quite so bad as is thought by Nowack, who leaves the clause untranslated. ‎חֵךְ = *mouth* (Pr. 5[3] 8[7] Jb. 31[30]; cf. also Ct. 5[16] 7[9]). ‡ It is the sounding of the alarm uttered to the prophets by Yahweh, for the enemy is now approaching (cf. 5[7 ff.] Am. 5[1 ff.] Is. 5[25 ff.] 7[17]). — *For an eagle (comes down) upon the house of Yahweh*] For text, *v.s.* The Assyrian, cf. Dt. 28[49] (not including Nebuchadnezzar and the Roman armies§), will come with the swiftness of the eagle (cf. the description of his march in Is. 5[26–30]). This is the explanation of the alarm; ‖ and not a further command to the prophet to fly like an eagle to Yahweh's house.¶ The attack will be made upon Yahweh's house, *i.e.* not the temple in Jerusalem,** nor the temple in Samaria,†† nor the people of Israel ‡‡ (Nu. 12[7]), but rather the *land of Israel,* as also in 9[15] (cf. 9[3]). §§ Here is to be compared the Assyrian name for Palestine, *bît Ḥumri,* ‖‖ and for a kingdom in North Syria, *bît Adini.* — *Because they have transgressed my covenant* (= *ordinance*) *and trespassed against my law*] Clearly a later addition.¶¶ For this use of ‎ברית, cf. 2 K. 11[4]

---

* Oort (*v.s.*); Marti om. 16*b* as a gloss.

† Cal., Ros., Hd., Sim., Pu., Ke., Wü., Now., Or.   ‡ Ki., Hd., GAS., BDB.

§ Jer., Pu.   ‖ Ros., Hd., Ew., *et al.*   ¶ AE.; cf. Hi.   ** Jer., Theod.

†† Ew.   ‡‡ Cal., Bauer, Hd., Ke., Wü., Or.   §§ Hi., Now., Che.

‖‖ Cf. *KAT.*[3] 247.   ¶¶ Cf. Now., Oort (*v.s.*).

Je. 11⁶ 34¹³·¹⁸ Ps. 105¹⁰; * but these ordinances (consider the Book of the Covenant or Ordinances) are based upon the constitutional agreement which was understood to have been entered into between Israel and Yahweh at Sinai (*v.i.*). תורתי here (cf. also 4⁶) refers to a written law which was "more ethical and religious than ceremonial." † — **2.** *To me they will (then) cry, My God, we know thee, we Israel*] *To me* is in strong contrast with those to whom they have turned in the past. This will take place when the disaster is upon them, cf. 5¹⁵ 6¹ ᶠᶠ. The cry will be one claiming relationship with and intimate knowledge of Yahweh, which is urged as a ground for deliverance. Just so Yahweh is represented as recognizing Israel in Is. 43¹. The utterance is intentionally broken and rough. The singular *my God*, used of each individual ‡ (cf. Is. 5³⁸ 1 S. 5¹⁰), passes abruptly into the plural, the nation as a whole. It is interesting that 𝕲 and 𝕾 omit *Israel* (*v.s.*), which is in apposition with the *we* of the preceding verb. § This is simply a prediction of the coming time when Israel will view the situation in a different manner from that employed at present. It is not a question of astonishment, ‖ nor is the language ironical, ¶ or potential.** Cf. Wellhausen's suggested translation : "to me, they cry : ' My God ' ; but I know thee, O Israel." — **3.** *For Israel hath spurned the good*] Yahweh's thought — hardly an answer, as most commentators take it. "The good" thus rejected with loathing (*v.i.*) includes everything for which Yahweh has stood — as opposed to the turning to Assyria and Egypt — as well as Yahweh himself; †† cf. Am. 5⁴·⁶·¹⁴. Seek me = seek the good. טוב without the article is especially strong. כי found in 𝕲 is to be restored. The whole case has been stated ; again goes forth the proclamation : *let the foe pursue him*] On the form, *v.i.*

8. אפרים] Emph. pos.; to drop the second one (*v.s.*) leaves the construction with היה awkward. — יתבוללו] Cf. Ar. بَلَّ, *moisten;* Assyr. balâlu = *pour out;* Syr. ܚܒܠ (in derivatives) *mix.* This is only occurrence of Hithpo.; Qal. = *mix*, is used of confusion of speech in Gn. 11⁷·⁹ (J), but

---

* See Che.   † Now.; cf. Or. on 8¹².   ‡ Hi., Hd., Ke., Wü., McC., Now., Che.
§ Geb., Ros., Hi., Ew., Hd., Pu., Ke., Che., Now., *et al.*   ‖ Ew.   ¶ Hi.
** Hd.   †† So Jer., AE., Ki.

chiefly of the mixing of flour with oil in sacrifices, *e.g.* Nu. 7¹³ Lv. 2⁵; it is distinctly characteristic of P. This verb is used intentionally in view of the figure of the cake in the next clause. The derivation from בלל = בלה *waste away* (so Ew., BSZ.) is unnecessary and without support, and renders the significance of בעמים obscure, while no sufficient reason for the use of Hithpo. appears (Now.). — בלי] Here with a ptcp., more frequently with nouns; cf. 2 S. 1²¹ Ps. 19⁴. Note the perfect symmetry of the two lines and the recurrence of ָ in ⁸ᵇ (four times). — **9.** והוא] Introducing a circ. cl. with vb. in pf. — זרקה] This is the only case where this vb. is used intransitively (Ki., Hi., Sim., Ke., Wü., Now.); cf. Ex. 24⁶ 29¹⁶· ²⁰. Its regular meaning is *to throw, scatter copiously* (cf. Assyr. zarâḳu), and it is most commonly used of the dashing of the sacrificial blood against the altar, *e.g.* Lv. 7². Perhaps here used in a middle sense; cf. חלץ, 5⁶ (Or.). — **10.** בכל זאת] On concessive force of ב, cf. Kö. 394 *i*; BDB. 90 *b*. — **11.** אין לב] Circ. cl. — מצרים... אשור] Emph. pos.; קרא = *call for help* is more often construed with a prep. than with acc. as here. אשור = acc. of end of motion; on omission of ָה directive, cf. Kö. 330 *c*. — קראו] Recession of tone and retention of vowel are due apparently to a desire to secure the same rhythm in ק מצ as in אש הל. This artistic effort reminds us of some of Isaiah's uses of paronomasia; cf. Is. 3¹⁸ᶠ· ²²ᶠ·. — **12.** איסירם] For other examples of retention of the initial י in Hiph. of פ״י verbs, cf. מימינים (= מיסינים) 1 Ch. 12²; וישרו, Pr. 4²⁵; הישר, Ps. 5⁹; but the unusual form and the fact that this is the only instance of the Hiph. of this vb. make it probable that this is an error for אֱיַסְּרֵם; cf. Bö. 437 *f*; GK. 24 *f*, 70 *b*; Kö. II. i., p. 356 *d*); Ew.⁸ 131 *c*. — שמע לעדתם] שֵׁמַע is regularly followed by a gen., which may be either attributive (Ex. 23¹), subjective or objective; in the latter case it = *report concerning*. The construction here with a following prep. is duplicated only in Is. 23⁵ = כאשר שמע למצרים, where the translation *when the report reaches Egypt* is required by the context (Gr. and Marti, however, declare the construction in Isaiah ungrammatical and emend to יִשָּׁמַע). But *according to a report to their congregation* furnishes no sense here; and it seems necessary to regard the text as corrupt. — **13.** אוי ... שד] אוי expresses denunciation here rather than grief, as appears from the parallel שד. This is the only instance of שד used as a denunciatory particle; a closely related usage appears in Je. 20⁸. — ואנכי] Emph. = *and will I*, the contrast being both with the previous and the following clauses; for the interrog. without particle, cf. GK. 150 *a*; on use of impf., cf. GK. 107 *n*. — והמה] Introd. circ. clause with concessive force = *though they*, or *while they*. — **14.** ייליל] Other cases of this formation in this same vb. are Is. 15²ᶠ· 16⁷ Je. 48³¹ and Is. 65¹⁴ (= תילילו); cf. ייטיב, Jb. 24²¹. For explanation, cf. GK. 70 *d*; Kö. I. i., p. 421. — על משכבותם] The various emendations proposed (*v.s.*) are due to a feeling: (1) that על should have same force here as with דגן and תירוש; (2) that ייללו and יתג both refer to sacrificial customs; cf. 1 K. 18²⁸. — יתגוררו] Has been connected with: (1) גור = *to sojourn* and rendered *they assemble themselves* (so AE., Ki., *Thes.*, Wü., AV., RV.); (2) גור = *to quarrel*, and rendered, *they excite themselves* (so Ew.), but, (1) is inappropriate here and (2) always implies a stirring up of strife or war; moreover, Hithpo. of גור is otherwise not found. 𝔊's reading, which involves the slight change from ר to ד, is entirely satisfactory to the context. — יסורו] סור, *turn aside, depart,* is never construed with ב; hence it seems necessary to point יְסוֹרוּ from סרר = *rebel,* though impf. of סרר does not elsewhere occur. Note the parallel phrase in v.¹³. — 15. ואני] כי פשעו בי Emph.; note exactly parallel const. Am. 2⁹; cf. v.¹³ of this chap. — ואלי] For other instances of חשב, followed by אל = על, cf. Je. 49²⁰ 50⁴⁵. — 16. לא על] Cf. אל על, 11⁷; הֵקֵם עַל, 2 S. 23¹; and the reverse idea, פנה למעלה, Is. 8²¹. If 𝔐𝔗 be correct, על is here a subst. used adverbially, and an adversative particle = *but* must be supplied; at best the construction is exceedingly irregular. In both cases על has ָ because of strong accent. — זו] Only here and Ps. 132¹², where it has relative force; but in Mishnah it is the regular fem. of זֶה; cf. זֹה, 2 K. 6¹⁹, etc., and זוֹ, Ps. 62¹², etc.; cf. GK. 34 b, Kö. 44. According to Ki., Ros., and Now., זו = זאת; while Ew. (fol. by Ke.) makes it = זֶה by a dialectical difference in the method of pronunciation; cf. Ew.⁸ 183 a. — לעגם] Suffix in view of יפלו בח must be taken as an objective gen. = *scorn over them.* — VIII. 1. אל חכך] For similar abrupt utterances see 5⁸ Ju. 5¹⁴ Is. 8²⁰ Ex. 27¹⁹ Pr. 20²⁵; cf. Kö. 355 l, m. חך is derived from חנך (of unknown meaning) as appears from Syriac ܚܶܢܟܳܐ Arab. حَنَكٌ. It regularly denotes *palate, gums,* etc., always referring to the interior of the mouth, never to the lips. — כנשר] The נשר is probably to be identified with the griffon-vulture, eagles being rare in Palestine; cf. Now. *Arch.* I. 84; Tristram, *NHB.* 172 ff.; Dr. on Dt. 14¹². This vulture was an eater of carrion (Jb. 39³⁰ Pr. 30¹⁷) and was often mentioned in Assyrian inscriptions (našru). For other references to its swiftness, 2 S. 1²³ Je. 49²². — 2. אלהי וגו] The sg. suff. is strange in view of foll. pl. vb.; אלהי occurs also in 2²⁵ (a late passage), 9⁸·¹⁷. Other suff. with אלהים are הֵ-, 4⁶ 9¹ 12⁷·¹⁰ 13⁴ 14²; יו-, 9⁸; הָ-, 14¹; הֵם-, 1⁷ 3⁵ 4¹² 5⁴ 7¹⁰. The use of suff. with the divine name is much more frequent than in Amos, where it occurs only in 2⁸ (הֶם-); 4¹² 8¹⁴ and 9¹⁵ (הֵ-); 5²⁶ (כֶם-), at least two of these passages being late. — 3. ירדפו] On unusual form of suff. cf. GK. 60 d. It is jussive, not indic., and this is thought to account for the ו (Now.). — בית יהוה] Cf. οἶκος θεοῦ, 1 Tim. 3¹⁵ Heb. 3⁶ (cf. 3²) Zc. 9⁵.

§ 10. Israel's kings and idols displeasing and destructive.

8⁴⁻¹⁴. — Israel's kings are of no divine appointment; and the calf set up at Samaria will be utterly destroyed, 8⁴⁻⁶. The storm of destruction will overwhelm the entire nation; the fact is, Israel is already being swallowed up among the nations, 8⁷⁻¹⁰. Israel's zeal in worship is only zeal in sinning, no regard being paid to the divine admonitions. Yahweh, instead of granting acceptance of his sacrifices, will bring visitation and exile, 8¹¹⁻¹³.

This piece has been greatly modified by insertions. These are as follows:
1) ‏ככלי אין חפץ בו‎ (v.⁸); 2) ‏למען יכרת‎ (v.⁴); 3) ‏עד מתי לא יוכלו נקיון‎ (v.⁵);
4) the whole of v.¹⁰ (v.i.); 5) the whole of v.¹⁴ (v.i.). The following transposition is necessary: ‏חרה אפי בם‎ (v.⁶) to follow ‏עצבים‎ (v.⁴), ‏צמה‎ (v.⁷) being
treated as going with what precedes. With these modifications of the text,
the piece falls simply and naturally into three strophes of eight lines each,
each strophe in turn including two halves of four lines each. The measure is
a mixture of tetrameter and trimeter.

4. ‏השירו‎] Hal. ‏הֲשִׁרוּ‎.— ‏ידעתי‎] 𝕲 ἐγνώρισάν μοι.— ‏עשו‎] Read ‏עֲשׂוּ‎.—
‏יכרת‎] Read pl. with 𝕲𝔖𝔙𝔗𝕷, viz. ‏יִכָּרְתוּ‎. Ru. ‏הָמְרֹתִי‎.— 5. ‏זנח עגלך‎] 𝕲 ἀπό-
τριψαι τὸν μόσχον σου = ‏זְנֵחוּ‎ (Vol.; so also Hal.), or ‏זָנַח‎ (Stek., Gr.), or ‏זָנַח‎
(Kö. Stil. 241). Complut. and codd. 22, 36, 42 = ἀπόρριψον; cod. 86,
ἀπόρριψε; 𝔖 ‏ܚܘܡ‎ = ‏זְנֵחוּ‎ (Seb.); 'A., ἀπώθησαν μόσχους σου; Σ., ἀπεβλήθη
...; Θ., ἀπόρριψαι; E', ἀποβλητός σου ἐστὶν ὁ μόσχος; 𝔙 projectus est vitulus
tuus; 𝔗 ‏טְעִי בְּתַר עֶגְלָא‎; 𝕷 coniri, etc. Read, with Oort, ‏אֲנַח‎ (ThT. and
Em.; so We., Val., Now.). Wkl. (Untersuch. 182), ‏זָנַחְתִּי‎ (so Marti).
BSZ. ‏זָנַח‎.— ‏אפי‎] Umb. ‏אַפּוֹ‎ (so Wü.).— ‏בם‎] Oort (ThT. and Em.), ‏בי‎.—
‏יוכלו‎] Hal. ‏תּוּכְלוּ‎. One cod. of de R. ‏יוּכַל‎ (so also Oort, ThT. and Em.).
— ‏נקיון‎] 𝕲 καθαρισθῆναι; 'A., ἀθῳωθῆναι; Σ., καθαρθῆναι; 𝔙 emundari;
𝔖 ‏ܠܡܬܕܟܝܘ‎. Wkl. (Untersuch. 182), ‏נקיונכֶם‎, using ‏מ‎ כי from beginning of v.⁶.
Gardner, ‏בִן‎, the ‏נ‎ of ‏נק‎ being a dittog. of prec. ‏ו‎, and the ‏ק‎ an error for ‏ב‎.
Oort, ‏נְקֹיא‎ or ‏הֵקָּוֹת‎, inf. Niph. of ‏קוא‎.— 6. ‏כי מישראל‎] 𝕲 ἐν τῷ Ἰσραήλ,
joining with v.⁵; 𝕷 in Istrahel. Gr. ‏מוסר אוילי‎. Oort om. ‏כי‎ and joins ‏מיש‎
to v.⁵. Meinhold, ‏כי מיד איש‎. Hal. ‏בית יש‎, joining to v.⁵. Ru. reconstructs
‏כִּי מֵעֲלֻוחַךְ הֲרֵשִׁי עֲשֵׂהוּ‎, to follow ‏שמרון‎ (v.⁵), the words ‏הרה וגו׳‎ being misplaced.
— ‏והוא‎] Om. ‏ו‎ with 𝔖 (so also Scholz, We., Gr., Gu., Now., Oet., Gardner,
Marti).— ‏כי שבבים‎] Another reading, ‏ואלהים לא אלהים הוא‎.—‏ואלהים הוא‎
𝕲 διότι πλανῶν = ‏שׁוֹבֵב‎ or ‏שׁוֹבֵב‎ (Vol.); Σ., ἀκατάστατος; E', ρεμβεύων;
𝔙 in aranearum telas; 𝔖 ‏ܓܘܓܝ‎ = ‏שֹׁבָבִים‎ (Seb.); cod. 86, παραπλησίως
τῷ τῆς ἀράχνης ἱστῷ. Read, with Oort and Now., ‏כשבבים‎. Gr. ‏כשממית‎,
spider-webs. Ru. ‏קוֹרֵי עַכָּבִישׁ‎, or ‏עַכָּבִים‎ (cf. Ju. 12⁶). St. ‏כי שברים‎.—
‏עגל שמרון‎] 𝕲 and 𝔖 = ‏עגלך‎, as in v.⁵. Wkl. om. as gloss; Ru. om. as
repetition.— 7. ‏יזרעו‎] Ru. ‏זָרְעוּ‎.— ‏וסופתה‎] 𝕲 καὶ ἡ καταστροφὴ αὐτῶν =
‏וסופתם‎, Aramaicism (Vol.); Σ., καὶ συσσεισμόν; Θ., καὶ καταιγίδα. Gardner,
‏וסופתָה‎ = and its end.— ‏יקצרו‎] 𝕲 ἐκδέξεται αὐτά = ‏יַקְצְבוּ‎ (Vol.).—. . . . ‏קמה‎
‏יעשה קמח‎ 𝕲 δράγμα οὐκ ἔχον ἰσχὺν τοῦ ποιῆσαι ἄλευρον; Σ., στάχυες
ἄκαρποι, μὴ ποιοῦντες ἄλευρον.— ‏לי‎] Read, with We., ‏לה‎ (so Marti). Oort
(ThT. and Em.), ‏להם‎. Gr. ‏לָמוֹ‎.—‏יעשה‎ ‏ב׳‎] Marti, ‏עָשָׂה‎.—‏ב׳‎. — 8. ‏היו‎] Oet.
and Marti, ‏הָיָה‎. Ru. ‏הוֹרוּ‎ (cf. Je. 22²⁸).—‏אין חפץ בו‎] 𝕲 ἄχρηστον; 𝔙 im-
mundum.— 9. ‏המה עלו‎] Ru. ‏הֵנָּה הֶעֱלוּ‎.—‏אשור‎] Oort (Em.), ‏אשורה‎.—‏פרא‎
‏בורר לו‎] 𝕲 ἀνέθαλεν καθ᾽ ἑαυτόν; Σ., καὶ οὐκ ἀνέθαλεν ἐν ἐμοί; cod. 86, ὡς
ὄναγρος μονάζων καθ᾽ ἑαυτὸν διαιτώμενος. Gr. ‏פ׳ נורד‎ (cf. Is. 14³¹). Marti
transfers this phrase to follow ‏נבלע יש‎ (v.⁸), and reads ‏אפרים וגו׳‎—‏אפרים‎

𝔊, 'Α., Σ., and Θ. join with preceding context. We. מצרים (so Val., Oet., Now.², Marti). Oort (*Em.*), וּלְמִצְרָיִם, for לו א' — [החנו אהבים] 𝔊 δῶρα ἠγάπησαν = אתננים אהבו (Vol.); 𝔙 *munera dederunt amatoribus suis;* 𝔖 ܐܬܢ ܐܗܒ = אתן אהבם אתנו (Seb.). Gr. אתנו אהבו (cf. 9¹). We. יְתְּנוּ (so Val., Oet., Marti). Ru. נחתנו בגוים. Oort (*Em.*), נתנו אהבים. — 10. גם כי] 𝔊 διὰ τοῦτο; cod. 86, ἀλλὰ καὶ ὅταν. — יתנו] 𝔊 παραδοθήσονται, and 𝔖 ܢܬܟܢܫܘܢ (= יְתְּנוּ). — עתה] 𝔖 om. — אקבצם] Oet. אֲפִיצֵם (so Meinhold) or אֲנַפְּצֵם. Ru. יְקַבְּצֵם, with the subject עתה, which is to be taken as the name of some Assyr. people. — ויחלו] Read, with 𝔊, καὶ κοπάσουσιν, וְחָדְלוּ (so also We., Or., Ru., Now., Oort (*Em.*); cf. GAS.). 'Α., καὶ λιτανεύσουσιν; Σ., καὶ μενοῦσιν; Θ., καὶ διαλείψουσι; 𝔙 *et quiescent;* 𝔖 ܘܢܬܬܢܝܚܘܢ = וינוחו (Seb.); 𝔗 יחכמון. Gr. וילאו or וילאו (so Val., Oet., Marti). Oet. וְיָנוחוּ or וְיָחֵדְלוּ. Hal. וְיֵחֵלּוּ. Ru. וְנָחוּ(?). Gu. וְיָחֵלּוּ. — מעט] Ru. בְעַט, עַט being the name of some Assyrian province. — ממשא] Read, with 𝔊 and Θ., τοῦ χρίειν, מִמְּשַׁח (so Oort (*ThT.* and *Em.*), Kue. (*Einl.*), Che., Gr., Val., Ru., Loft., GAS., Hal., Marti). 'Α., ἀπὸ ἄρματος; Σ., ἀπὸ φόβου. — מלך] 𝔖𝔗 and Σ., pl.; 𝔊𝔖𝔙𝔗, 'Α., Arab., and many codd. of Kennicott and de R. join to following word by ו (so also Oort (*ThT.* and *Em.*), We., Gr., Ru., GAS., Now., Hal.). — שרים] Linder (*SK.* XXXIII. (1860), 746), שָׂרִים. — 11. לחטא] 𝔊 joins with foll. clause, εἰς ἁμαρτίας. Omit with We. (so Now., Oet., Marti). Or. לַחֲטֹא (so Oet.; cf. Gu., Now.); Oort (*ThT.* and *Em.*), לַחֲטֹאות. Hal. מַצֵּבות. לחטא] 𝔊 om. (so also Gu.), and adds ἠγαπημένα from v.¹³ (Vol.); Σ., εἰς ἁμαρτίαν; 𝔙 *in delictum;* 𝔖 ܕܚܛܐ ܣܓܝ = גדול לחטא, or לְ רב (Seb.). Oort and Ru. om. last two words of this verse as a repetition. — 12. אכתוב־לו] 𝔖 adds "and" (so also Gr.). Zeydner (*ThSt.* VI. 249), אֶכְתֹּב. — רבי תרתי] 𝔊 πλῆθος καὶ τὰ νόμιμά μου (= רב ותורתי); 'Α., πληθυνομένους νόμους; Σ., πλήθη νόμων μου; 𝔙 *multiplices leges meas;* 𝔖 ܘܟܬܒܬ ܠܗ ܣܘܓܐܐ. Gr. (*Gesch.* II. i. 469; so Oort, *ThT.* and *Em.*), דִּבְרֵי תורתי. Hi. רב תולֹתִי (so We., Val., Sm. (*Rel.* 283 f.), Gu., Loft., Marti). Zeydner (*ThSt.* VI. 249), רב וְתּולֹתִי. Oet. תּולֹתָי. — כמו] Ru. רַבּות־תּולֹתִי = חשב with obj. (Seb.). — 13. זבחי נחשבו] 𝔖 ܣܡ ܐܠܒ ܐܠܐ ܣܡ, וַאֲמָרֵי — הכרבי.

זבחי]𝔊 θυσιαστήρια τὰ ἠγαπημένα = זבחים אהובים (Vol.), joined to v.¹²; Σ., θυσίας ἐπαλλήλους; Θ., θυσίας μεταφορῶν; 'Α., θυσίας φέρε φέρε; 𝔙 *hostias offerent;* 𝔖 ܕܒܚܐ ܕܪܚܡ. Oort and Ru. om. Marti, זֶבַח אֲהָבַי; Sim. זִבְחֵי ה'. — יזבחו] 𝔖, 'Α., and Θ. join to prec. context; 𝔊 διότι ἐὰν θύσωσιν θυσίαν. Oort (*Em.*). — בשר ויאכלו] 𝔊 καὶ φάγωσιν κρέα. Oort (*Em.*), וַיִּזְבָּחוּ. Oort and Ru. זבח ויאכלו ב'. Oet. וּבָשָׂר יאכלוּ — [ויפקר. We. om. ו. Oort ופקר (cf. 𝔊). מצרים ישובו] 𝔊 adds (so also Gu.) καὶ ἐν 'Ασσυρίοις ἀκάθαρτα φάγονται. Hal. transposes יש מ' המה to end of v.⁹. — 14. היכלות] 𝔊 τεμένη. Besredka (*Rev. études Juives*, 1893), הליכות. — ארמנתיד] 𝔊 τὰ θεμέλια αὐτῶν (so 𝔏). Ru. אַרְמְנֹתָיו (so Oort (*Em.*), Marti). Gr. ארמנתיהן. Oort treats v.¹⁴ as inserted later from Amos (so Scholz, We., Ru., GAS., Now., Marti; cf. Seesemann).

4. *Since they have made kings, but not from me*] This is not a
reference to (1) a contemporary king, *e.g.* Menahem (cf. 7^{16}) ; *
nor to (2) the godless way of choosing kings referred to in $7^{3.\,5.\,7}$; †
nor to (3) the fact of frequent choosing and deposition of kings
in the time of the prophet (cf. $7^{3.\,7}$ 8^{10} 2 K. 15). ‡ The prophet
has in mind rather the circumstances under which the kingdom
was divided, the establishment of Jeroboam I., and the history
in detail, which followed these events. §   He clearly condemns
the schism, although this had come about in part as the result
of prophetic work (1 K. $11^{29.\,31}$ $12^{15.\,24}$).   This contradiction is
one which is to be expected as between prophets of a higher
and lower rank, and between those of an earlier and later period.
"A prophet could only declare the will of God with regard to
the particular case laid before him." ‖   The contradiction is
not reconciled by the statement that while Jeroboam was God's
choice the people did not consult him (God) at the time, or
that Jeroboam, after being told God's purpose, took wrong means
to accomplish it.¶   The two accounts proceed from different
points of view.   In one, the schism is a punishment upon Rehoboam and his followers ; in the other, it is the source of the evils
in existence in the prophetic times. — (*And*) *since they have made
princes, but I knew* (*them*) *not*] This is only the poetical repetition
of the idea contained in the former line, referring perhaps to the
subordinate officers of the royal administration ; ** cf. 3^4 7^3 8^{10} 13^{10}.
To know is to recognize, *i.e.* to approve, regard as one's own, cf.
Jb. 9^{21} 34^4 Ps. 1^6.   Others, without sufficient ground, treat השׁירו
as = הסירו, *and they remove them* †† (*v.i.*). — *With their silver and
gold made by them into idols*] Here for the first time a prophet
speaks against making images of Yahweh, and while the calves of
Jeroboam are included (some limit the reference to these ‡‡), the
wider reference is to Israel's religious history. §§   The prophet
desires to place together two facts in Israel's history, and to show
that they are correlated.   These are the kings established by men,
and the gods manufactured by men ; as with one, so with the

---

* Hi.   † Ros.   ‡ Bauer, Wü., We., Marti.
§ AE., Ki., Ew., Hd., Sim., Pu., Ke., Che., Reu., Now.   ‖ Che.; cf. Reu., Now.
¶ Ki., Cal., Pu.   †† Ras., AE.   §§ Sim., We.
** Hi., Sim.   ‡‡ Now.

other.* — *That they may be cut off*] For text *v.s.* The subject is either the *silver and gold*, or *the idols*,† but not *the people.* ‡ If 𝕸𝕿 is retained, the verb is collective. Destruction was, to be sure, the *result* of their idolatry ; but since Israel " knew or could have known " the result, to engage in idolatry was to purpose destruction. Purpose and result are not always clearly to be distinguished. § This clause breaks the continuity of thought, anticipates the idea that is to follow, makes an incomplete line, and spoils the symmetry of the strophic division ; it is better to regard it as a gloss. — *Mine anger is kindled against them*] This clause, transferred from [5b], fits better in this place, furnishes the principal idea, and prepares the way for the more specific statement with which v.[5] begins. Its removal from between [5a] and [5b] assists greatly in improving the thought of vs.[5 and 6] ‖ (*v.i.*) ; cf. Nu. 11[33] 2 K. 23[26] Is. 5[25]. — **5.** *I loathe thy calf, O Samaria*] This rendering (based upon the emendation of אנח for זנח) accords with the clause which precedes (*mine anger*, etc.), and comes appropriately into close connection with the first part of v.[6] (cf. 10[15]). Other renderings based on slight modifications of text (*v.s.*) are : (1) he loathes thy calf, etc. ; ¶ (2) he has rejected thy calf ; ** (3) thy calf has rejected thee ; †† (4) thy calf is loathsome ; ‡‡ (5) my anger has rejected thy calf. §§ " Calf " is diminutive and sarcastic for bull ; these representations of Yahweh were placed in Dan and Bethel, perhaps also in Samaria and Gilgal ; but it is possible that Samaria is here a district ; cf. 7[1] 8[6] 10[5.7] 13[16]. On [5b] *v.s.* — *How long will they be incapable of punishment ?*] This gloss is an expression of the feeling of some later reader, ‖‖ being entirely parenthetical in its tone ; cf. Je. 13[27]. The thought is not clear. Is it interrogation ¶¶ or exclamation? *** Is it incapacity for innocency, *i.e.* inability to clear themselves of guilt,††† or freedom from punishment ‡‡‡ which is despaired of ? Although the former mean-

---

* *V.* GAS. I. 277.

† Ki., Hi., Ew., Ke., Wü., Che., Reu., Now., Marti.

‡ Ros., Sim., Pu., Or.   ‖ Cf. Dathe, Bauer, Ru.   ** Hi., Umb., RV.

§ Ros., Hd., Sim., Pu., Or., Now.   ¶ GAS. ; cf. Ew.   †† AV., Stuck.

‡‡ Ma., Dathe, Hd., Wü., Sim., Ke., Or., Che.; Kö. *Stil.* 241.   §§ Mau.

‖‖ So Marti, who om. also [6a]; but *v.* Now.[2].

¶¶ Ros., Hd., Or., Che., GAS., *et al.*   *** Sim., We., Now.

††† Ros., Sim., Or., Che., GAS., *et al.*   ‡‡‡ Hi., We., Now., BSZ., BDB.

ing for נקי is found in Gn. 20⁵ Ps. 26⁶ 73¹³, the context which describes the anger and loathing of Yahweh favors the latter, and this is supported by Je. 25²⁹ (cf. Ex. 21²⁸). The presence of כפי in so many cases favors the former view. It is unnecessary to read *ye* for *they* (*v.s.*). For other unapproved suggestions, *v.s.* — **6.** *For out of Israel is it*] This clause states the ground for Yahweh's loathing of the calf, and, with ⁵ᵇ transferred and ⁵ᶜ treated as a gloss, joins itself directly to the principal clause. The images of Yahweh have never been sanctioned by him. The fact that these images are of entirely human origin furnishes the basis for Yahweh's scorn (cf. 13² Is. 37¹⁹ 40¹⁹. ²⁰ 41⁷). The ו of והוא seems to be superfluous. If retained, it would be read *is this also*, referring to the kings, who, like the idols, were without divine approval. This calf is something which has its origin in Israel. The phrase in contrast with Israel is not " other nations," as if the prophet was meeting the plea that this custom was of foreign origin.* The next clause finishes and amplifies the thought. — *A smith made it and it is not God*] Cf. 13²; it has no real existence. The people addressed have evidently come to believe that the image and God are identical. The prophet assures them that it is from Israel and is not God.† — *Like splinters Samaria's calf shall become*] Utter destruction awaits this emblem of and substitute for deity. This reads כ for כי (*v.s.*), and makes the clause a part of the general sentence beginning with this verse. On שבבים *v.i.*

4. הם] Not emph., but introducing the circ. cl., GK. 142 *a, b*. It is possible to omit it as a dittograph, in which case the first two vbs. would be coördinate with עשׁו; but *v.i.* — השׁירו] Cf. הסירו, Dn. 11³¹; so here one cod. of Kenn. and two of de R.; cf. also Dn. 9¹¹. For the form, cf. GK. 67 *v*; cf. Ru.'s reading (*v.s.*).— כספם וגו׳] The subj. of the pass. עשׁוי, which in the act. would take double obj., Kö. 327 *w*. This makes a third consec. circ. cl. — עשׁו] To be read עשׁוי pass. ptcp., followed by the ל of agent (GK. 121 *f*) although ל might also mean here *for*. — למען] Here points to an end inevitably involved in the action described by the principal vb., but none the less deplorable; cf. Kö. 396 *e*. — **5.** אזנח] Cf. 𝕲 imv. It is not to be connected with זנח = *to stink* (cf. Is. 19⁶), but with זנח = *to loathe, reject* (cf. v.³ Ps. 43²); cf. Assyr. zinû = *to be angry* (BDB.) — יוכלו] Not Hoph., but an old Qäl pass.; cf. Kö. I. i. p. 407; GK. 69 *r*.— **6.** והוא] If ו is retained, it is strengthening and = *also*, Kö. 375*g*.— חרשׁ] Emph. pos. — שבבים] This has been: (1) connected

---

* So Jer., Cal., Hd.   † Sim.

with the Arab. شَبَّ, to *kindle, burn* (cf. Schultens on Jb. 18⁵), *i.e.* the splinter with which one kindles a fire; also with Arab. *Sebtbah = slice, little piece* (Ew.); (2) corrected to שְׁבָרִים (cf. Is. 1²⁸ 30¹⁴) (St.); (3) derived from the Aram. שׁבב = *break;* cf. שבא *fragment* (*Thes.;* Kö. II. i. p. 71; Now.), and سَبَّ, to *cut. V.* Nö. *Mand. Gram.* 140; Hoffm. *ZAW.* III. 121; We. *in loc.* — עֶגֶל שׁ''] Cf. Kö. *Hauptprobleme*, 53 ff.

7. *For they sow wind and they reap whirlwind*] A further statement and explanation of the coming destruction. *Wind* represents the nothingness, the utter failure, of their present policy; but the outcome is still more serious, viz. *whirlwind*, that which is itself destructive; cf. 10¹³. — *A seed which has no stalk*] לוֹ is difficult (*v.s.*). According to 𝔐, *it has no stalk*, the pronoun refers to Israel, but in that case לָמוֹ would be expected. If taken as suggested,* לה would be expected instead of לוֹ, for קמה is feminine. The fact of the symmetry gained by this reading is, however, convincing. — *Which yields no grain*] *i.e.* is utterly worthless. — *If perchance it were to yield, strangers would devour it*] All that Israel might hope to gain will pass over into the hands of the enemy.† The figure continues through to the end, ‡ and does not go over in the latter half to a description of actual events. § — **8.** *Israel is swallowed up*] The nation is, as a matter of fact, practically ruined. The prophet is speaking of the present, not the future, ‖ as appears from the tense (cf. יבלעהו v.⁷), and from the following parallel phrase עתה היו.¶ It does not mean that the nation as well as the fruit shall be swallowed, for נבלע is not a prophetic perfect.** — *Already are they among the nations*] This is the simple prose interpretation of the figures which have been used (cf. 7⁸). The process of scattering, *i.e.* the loss of independence, has begun, though they do not appreciate it. With this clause there has been associated the gloss, *like a vessel in which is no pleasure*] This, however, is entirely foreign to the thought of the context. It is a not uncommon simile, denoting something unserviceable and worthless; cf. Je. 22²⁸ 48³⁸.— **9.** *For they have gone up to Assyria*] This fact is cited, not as a punishment to

---

* We.   † Marti, without good reason, om. this sentence as a gloss.
‡ Ros., Mau., Ew., Sim., Che., We., Now.   § Marck, Hi., Umb.
‖ So Hi.   ¶ Now.   ** Marck.

be inflicted upon them, viz. the exile, but as an act of faithlessness and guilt. This statement presents still more literally and specifically the exact situation. Note (1) Israel is swallowed up; (2) (the more prosaic form of the same thought) they are already among the nations; and now (3) (the very specific expression) they have gone up to Assyria. The going up to Assyria was for assistance and marked dependence upon a foreign power. — *A wild ass taking his way by himself*] This is not Assyria,* but Israel; † for (1) it is to Israel that the application of the figure is appropriate, viz. wilfulness; (2) there is a pun on the words פרא and אפרים. The wild ass usually moves in droves, ‡ but this representation of solitariness marks Israel's case as all the more peculiar. Perhaps this clause should go with the following, § but it is more natural ‖ to take פרא as figurative of wilfulness than as denoting love of independence (cf. Gn. 16¹² Jb. 39⁵ ᶠᶠ·), as the connection with the following would involve. — *Ephraim gives love-gifts*] These are the gifts by means of which Israel sought connection with Egypt and Assyria. Wellhausen's suggestion to substitute " Egypt " for " Ephraim," rendering, *to Egypt they give love-gifts*, is strongly supported by the parallelism; cf. 𝔊. — **10.** *Also if they give themselves among the nations, I must now gather them in*] This verse is a later addition.¶ This is at once apparent if אקבצם is taken as a promise to gather them after they have been scattered among the nations in exile; but it is clear also upon the other interpretation. As Simson has pointed out, no single word of this entire verse is of certain meaning. In ¹⁰ᵃ the thought turns on the interpretation of אקבצם ; the suffix refers to Israel,** not to the nations.†† The verbal idea is not a promise, ‡‡ but a threat. §§ If the nations were to have been gathered against Israel, something indicating this would have been inserted. It is Israel that is to be gathered in, *i.e.* brought back home, put under restraint, imprisoned, deprived of judgment, taken into exile; cf.

---

* Dathe, Bauer, Eich., Schrö.

† Ma., Ros., Hi., Sim., Or.

‡ See art. "Ass," *EB.*

** AE., Cal., Ew., Wü., Che., We., Now., *et al.*

†† Ki., Os., Mau., Hi., Or., *et al.*

§§ Stuck, Wü., Che., We., Now., *et al.*

§ Sim., *et al.*

‖ So Now.

¶ Marti om. ¹⁰ᵃ as a gloss.

‡‡ Umb., Hd., *et al.*

2¹⁴ᶠ· 3³ᶠ· 8¹³ 9³. This entering into relationship with outside nations must cease. "The time has come for me to check their misplaced activity." גם כי means therefore *even if* (cf. 9¹⁶ Is. 1¹⁵ Ps. 23⁴) rather than *yea though*.* יתנו is treated, of course, like the התנו of the preceding verse. — *And they must cease for a while from the anointing of kings and princes*] Here the uncertainty turns first upon the treatment of ויחלו. Three principal suggestions may be considered according as the word is taken from : (1) חלל, *to begin, i.e.* they begin to be diminished † (מעט = inf.), or to become less (מעט = adv.) ‡ on account of the burden, etc. ; (2) חול, *to be in pain, to grieve,* and pointed without the Daghesh וַיָּחֵלוּ (so 10 Mss. and 44 Editions §), *i.e.* and they shall suffer, or grieve a little on account of, etc. ; ‖ (3) חדל, the text being changed to וְחָדְלוּ (*v.s.*), *i.e. And they will cease for a little* (or *soon*), etc. Adopting the third, it is better also to adopt the 𝕲 text, מִמְשֹׁחַ, *from anointing,* instead of ממשא (*v.s.*). The latter has been thought to refer to the tribute imposed by the king of Assyria, מלך שרים being taken in annexion, *king of princes.*¶ With the second suggestion made above, this would fulfil the demands of the context in yielding a statement having the force of a threat. The 𝕲 text, however, furnishes an easier solution, and one especially appropriate. There will be a ceasing, says the prophet, from this continual anointing of kings and princes (a case of asyndeton). In this interpretation, מעט may be taken in the sense of *soon* (cf. Ps. 2¹² 81¹⁴) or *for a little while.* The latter is of course the more usual and, here, the more caustic.

7. כי] Cf. vs.⁶· ⁹· ¹⁰. — סוּפָתָה] On the final הָ cf. עוּלָתה, 10¹³ Ez. 28¹⁵; also עזרתה, Ps. 44²⁷; רִכְלָתְךְ, Ez. 28¹⁶; an acc. cf. Kö. 287 *b*; GK. 90 *f*; Dr. § 182 *Obs.* Note the assonance in קמה, צמח, and קמח. — בלי] Cf. Kö. 352 *c*; GK. 152 *t.* — אולי] Cf. Kö. 390 *s*; BSZ. 18. — 8. כבלי וגר] An elliptical rel. cl., GK. 155 *i*; Kö. 380 *c.* — 9. פרא] On gender, Kö. 247 *f*; Albrecht, *ZAW.* XVI. (1896) 68; on deriv. Jensen, *Kosmologie,* 110; cf. Assyr. parû, which, however, means *mule,* wild ass being purîmu; for other figures, cf. Je. 2²⁴ Jb. 24⁵. — התנו] Pl. with coll. noun, cf. Ju. 5¹⁴ᵃ. — אהבים] Pl. of psycholog. experience; cf. also דרים, Ct. 1²· ⁴; עגבים, Ez. 33³²; cf. Kö. 262 *b.* — 10. גם כי] Kö. 339 *t.* — ויחלו] Cf. GK. 111 *w,* N. Impf. continuing a historical present, Kö. 366 *g.* — מִמְּשׁ]

---

* But cf. BDB. 169, Dr. 143.   † Ma., Ros., Ke.   ‡ Hi.   § de Rossi.
‖ Cal., Stuck, New., Hd., Sim., Wü.; cf. Gu.   ¶ Eich., Hi., Ke., *et al.*

On dag. cf. GK. 20*g*; Kö. I. p. 54 *b*. On relation to vb., Kö. 412 *a*.— מלך
שרים] With superlative force, according to Kö. 309 *k*.

11. *For Ephraim has made many altars*] It was the common
notion (Is. 1[11]) that the more sacrifices offered (or altars built)
the more pleasing was it to the national deity. The לחטא, if
retained, indicates that the opposite of this is true, viz. that this
multiplication of altars results merely *in sinning*.* If retained
with the pointing לַחֲטֹא † (the inf. *absolute* being used for the sake
of the rhythm), the meaning would be that Ephraim's purpose
in all this was *to make atonement, i.e.* to secure expiation of sin ; a
purpose which the second member shows to have been futile ; but
this idea is scarcely consistent with this period. It seems better,
therefore, to omit the word in this line (*v.s.*). — *They are to him
altars — for sinning*] What was thought to be action deserving
commendation is condemned. The more altars, the greater and
deeper is Israel's guilt. לחטא is not used in a double sense, ‡ viz.
the sin of the act and the calamity resulting from the act, since
the latter idea is not possible in this connection. § To retain the
לחטא of the first line involves a repetition amounting to tautology,
and greatly weakens, instead of strengthening, the sense. ‖ It is
not enough to use the word in one sense in the first line, and in
another in the second. — **12.** *Were I to write for him by myriads
my laws*] Each word of this much-disputed sentence presents
difficulties. Is (*a*) the Q*e*rî רֻבֵּי to be accepted with the rendering *the multitudes of my law(s)*, or *my many laws*,¶ or *the excellencies of my law*,** or *the great things of, etc.;* †† or (*b*) the
K*e*thîbh רִבּוֹ, *by myriads,* ‡‡ or *the ten thousand things of, etc.;* §§ or
(*c*) רֹב ‖‖ or רִבּוֹת,¶¶ *multitudes;* or (*d*) דִּבְרֵי,*** *the words of my
law(s)* ? Is (*a*) the sg. תּוֹרָתִי, *my law,* ††† or (*b*) the pl. תּוֹרֹתִי ‡‡‡
to be preferred? Cf. also (*c*) the combination רֹב וְתוֹרֹתִי. §§§ Is
אכתוב (*a*) to be taken as Qăl, or (*b*) changed to Hiph. = *cause
to write;* ‖‖‖ and, in the former case, is it (*c*) an historical present

---

* Che.	‡ Ma., Hi.	§§ RV.	¶¶ Oet.
† Or.	§ Hd.	‖‖ We. *et al.*(*v.s.*).	
‖ So Now. against Ew., Hd.		*** Gr., Oort (*v.s.*).	††† Sim.
¶ Bauer, Dathe.	†† AV.	‡‡‡ 𝔊𝔙 and most modern comm.	
** Ma.	‡‡ Hi., Ew., Hd., Sim., Ke.	§§§ 𝔊.	‖‖‖ Zeydner (*v.s.*).

indicating that what had occurred was continuing still; * or (*d*) a future, *I will write;* † or (*e*) a present perfect, *I have written;* ‡ or (*f*) a past, *I wrote;* § or (*g*) an imperfect of customary action, *I am wont to write;* ‖ or (*h*) hypothetical, *were I to write, etc.,* *though I wrote, etc.*¶ The importance of this utterance lies in the testimony which it furnishes to the existence of laws or a code of laws in Hosea's time. We decide first in favor of רִבּוֹ, *myriad* (although this occurs elsewhere only among late writers, *v.i.*), because: (*a*) רִבֵּי as a plural occurs nowhere else; (*b*) nothing is gained by substituting רב or any of its cognate forms, all conveying the same idea, that of *multitude,* an idea which itself is identical with that of רבו, *ten thousand;* (*c*) while דברי is easy and plausible, it is impossible to imagine how, if once it had a position in the text, anything could have been allowed to take its place. It follows, almost without argument, that *my laws* (pl.) (for which no consonantal change is required) combines more easily with *myriad* or *ten thousand* than does *my law* (sg.); for the thought plainly in Hosea's mind was the multiplicity, and not the unity, of the laws. Little can be said for the Hiph., *I cause to write;* it only remains to settle the tense force of אכתוב. If the writer had intended past or present perfect, *i.e.* if he had wished to mark it as a definite fact, he would naturally have used the perfect tense. The present, whether historical or voluntative, fails to meet the demands of the context, although both would emphasize the idea that the laws were still in process of being written or collected, or, in other words, that the collection was not yet finished. The future makes no sense whatever. Upon the whole the hypothetical force seems to be preferable, *Were I to write my laws by myriads, i.e.* if I were to write laws so many that they could not be numbered; or, if the laws that have been written should be increased indefinitely (to ten thousand), — a statement which presupposes: (*a*) that in Hosea's time the custom was established of reducing instruction to writing; ** (*b*) the possibility of increasing the number, *i.e.* a conception that the list was incomplete; †† (*c*) that the laws in existence were not being ob-

---

* Ke.   † 𝔊𝔙.   ‡ 𝔖𝔗, AV.   § RV.   ‖ Che.
¶ Hi., Hd., Ew., Or.   ** Cf. Holzinger, *Einl.* 8.
†† Cf. Kue. *The Hexateuch,* 178: "With the prophets then the torah of Yahweh

Y

served, although the prophets were defending them (cf. 4[6-8]) ; and consequently (*d*) that they were not the *ceremonial* laws regulating the work of the priests, for this work the prophet condemns because he does not regard it as a part of Yahweh's instruction (cf. Is. 1[11.12]),[*] but rather prophetic instructions, laws relating to "civil justice and the applications of a plain but religiously sanctioned morality (cf. the so-called Book of the Covenant, Ex. 20[23]–23[33])." [†] Among the prophets *tôrah* = instruction, and refers to the admonition of the prophets (cf. Is. 1[10] 2[3] 8[16] Je. 18[18] 26[4.5] Ez. 7[26] Is. 42[4] Hg. 2[11] Zc. 7[12]. In Deuteronomy *statutes and judgments* is the phrase which expresses the idea of law ; while *tôrah* is still used of oral instruction. [‡] It is urged [§] against this interpretation : (1) that the analogy of other Semitic religions, in which, from the first, the ceremonial and ethical appear together, is against the position that the instruction referred to was ethical rather than ceremonial ; (2) that this proposition does not explain the fundamental significance of the symbolism of ceremony in ancient religions ; and (3) the existence of such ceremonial elements in the Decalogue and Book of the Covenant ; while (4) there stands against it the presupposition of an extensive priestly law in Deuteronomy. It is maintained, still further [‖] : (1) that even granting the hypothetical translation, the passage proves "the existence of a detailed and copious law embracing the subject of sacrifice, which the prophet held to be from God, and charged both priests and people with neglecting" ; (2) that, however, the tense (pf.) of נחשבו renders the hypothetical construction impossible, and favors the treatment of אכתוב as historical (cf. Ps. 103[7]) ; and (3) that the hypothetical explanation involves certain incongruities which are fatal, *e.g.* would ten thousand requirements be more likely to secure obedience than a smaller number? [¶] — *As those of a stranger they would be accounted*] and therefore of no

---

is by no means a closed and completed whole, handed down from antiquity, but the continuous and ever renewed indication to Israel of Yahweh's will."

[*] We. *Prol.* 57.

[†] Che; cf. Briggs, *The Hexateuch*, 14; Carpenter and Harford-Battersby, *The Hexateuch*, I. 19.

[‡] Cf. Addis, *The Documents of the Hexateuch*, II. 34, N. 1.   [§] Or.

[‖] Green, *Moses and the Prophets*, 114.

[¶] Cf. Sm. *Moses apud Prophetas*, 13; Now.[H].

binding force ; for how could the laws of one nation be regarded as authoritative by another? Cf. Gn. 19⁹. The matter may be summed up : Hosea condemns those of his time, priests and people, who are observing in great detail a sacrificial cult (v.¹¹) and accuses them, although they are very busy in the observance of this cult, of having forgotten Yahweh (4⁶⁻⁸). These people, he says, would count even a myriad of Yahweh's laws, if they were written for them, as the prophecy of a stranger and therefore as not binding. They have in mind nothing but offerings ; they forget the divine instructions delivered by the prophets. — **13.** *My offerings of . . . they sacrifice flesh, and they eat it*] The easiest disposition of the words זבחי הבהבי, and the one most common, is to render *my sacrificial gifts* (*v.i.*) *they sacrifice*, etc., which is interpreted to mean that sacrifice, with them, is merely formal, the important thing being the " luxury of a dinner of flesh-meat " ; * but this is almost meaningless in this connection. The same thing may be said of the slightly varying translations, *sacrifices of my own gifts,*† *as a sacrifice of my gifts,* ‡ etc. Essentially different are the interpretations which understand הבהבי to mean *raw flesh* (*v.i.*), § or roast sacrifices (*v.i.*). ‖ 𝕲 (*v.s.*) connects the first two words with the preceding, viz. " and my laws were reckoned as those of a stranger, the beloved sacrifices " ; while some treat them as a gloss and thus secure the simple reading, *they sacrifice flesh and they eat it.*¶ There is not very great choice in the midst of so many difficulties. — *Yahweh having no delight in them*] On רצה, *v.i.* This is the important point.** Whatever the preceding words mean, they were intended to describe a cultus, a worship, in which Yahweh took no pleasure, and consequently *Now must he remember their guilt*] Now ≐ *at last ;* the consummation has been reached. Patience is exhausted ; *he must remember, i.e.* he feels himself obliged to remember and to take notice of their guilt (cf. 7² 9⁹ Je. 14¹⁰ ; in all of which, as here, the verb in the parallel member is פקד, *visit, punish.*) — *And visit their sin*] The usual and frequent technical term for punishment. — *Since they to Egypt shall return*] Cf. 9³.⁶ 11⁵. This is either a

---

* Ki., Hd., Ke., St., Che., BDB.   ‡ Sim.   ‖ Or.

† Stuck, Hes.; cf. Bauer.   § Ew.   ¶ Oort, Ru.

** But Marti om. this phrase as a gloss.

poetical expression for captivity in general; or a prediction of captivity in Egypt, parallel with the more frequent prediction of an
Assyrian captivity. In favor of the second supposition may be
cited (1) the repetition of the threat (*v.s.*), (2) the threat in
Is. 7[18] of a double invasion from Egypt and Assyria, (3) the constant vacillation between the two political parties, one of which
advocated alliance with Egypt, the other with Assyria; but above
all (4) the predictions of restoration from Egypt in Is. 11[11]
Mi. 7[12]. It would be interesting if in this connection it could be
shown that 𝔊's addition to this verse (*v.s.*), *and in Assyria they
shall eat the unclean thing*, were anything but a gloss borrowed
from 9[3].* — 14. *And so Israel forgot his maker and built palaces*]
This verse is a later addition,† for (1) the reference to Judah is
uncalled for; (2) the style resembles that of Amos rather than
Hosea; (3) the natural conclusion of the discourse is in v.[13];
v.[14] only weakens the climax; (4) the thought of Yahweh as
Israel's creator is unexpected in Hosea's time; (5) the verse is
superfluous in the strophic system. The abandonment of Yahweh
in the opinion of the prophet is contemporaneous with and in
proportion to the steps taken to exhibit self-dependence. *Palaces*
(rather than the more common rendering of היכלות *temples*) must
be understood (*v.i.*), since we may ascribe neither to Hosea
nor to a later author the opinion that the building of the
temple was a wicked thing. — *And Judah multiplied fenced
cities*] The poetic parallel for the preceding statement. — *And
so I will send fire upon his cities, and it shall devour his palaces*]
Cf. Am. 1[4]–2[5].

11. מִי לחטא] If 𝔐𝔗 stands, an interesting case of repetition of a series
of words, H. 39, 5 *a*, rm. (*e*). — 12. אכתוב] Q[e]rî shortens the longer form of
K[e]thîbh. — רבו] Q[e]rî changes ו of K[e]thîbh to י, thus securing a pl. cstr. —
נֶחְשָׁבוּ] For pass. used with acc., *v.* Pr. 17[28]; also frequently, as here, with כ,
cf. Is. 5[28] 29[16] Jb. 18[3]; Kö. 338 *v, y,* є. On d. f. in שׁ, cf. GK. 13 *c*. —
13. יוכר . . . ויפקד] Parallel acts, hence ו rather than ויפ. Kö. 370 *f*. —
14. וישלחתי] Wāw consec. with pf. = impf. of threat, as seen from the context, although no determining word precedes; cf. also 4[5 a] 10[14]; Kö. 367 *y*.

---

* Cf., however, Gu. Marti treats *since they to Egypt*, etc., also as a gloss.

† So Sta. *G VI.* I. 577; Scholz, Oort, We.; Che. in WRS. *Proph.* XVII. ff.; GAS.,
Now.; Marti, *EB.* 2122; *et al.;* but cf. Kue. *Einl.* § 67, 8–10; Co. *Einl.* § 27, 3.

§ 11. Israel's exile — a breaking up of social and religious habits. 9[1-9].

Israel should not rejoice too loudly in her harvest and vintage feasts, since, on account of her adultery, the time is at hand when there will be no threshing-floors nor winevats, no libations nor offerings; for all food will be unclean, and all who eat unclean (vs.[1. 2. 4]). Israel is to be carried into exile in Assyria or Egypt, where it will be impossible to celebrate feasts and festivals, and her own land will be thorns and thistles (vs.[3. 5. 6]). Israel's days of visitation are coming, — days of bitter experience, when prophets and spiritual guides will have been driven mad because of Israel's faithlessness, and because of the opposition which they encounter, — days of dire punishment (vs.[7. 8]).

This piece is marked by a peculiar definiteness and clearness. Perhaps v.[8] forms an exception to this statement. It consists of three strophes, each of which is introduced by a three-membered clause, after which come perfectly regular couplets: strophe 1, 3 + 2 + 2 + 2 + 2; strophe 2, 3 + 2 + 2 + 2; strophe 3, 3 + 2 + 2 + 2. Strophe 1 warns against the heathenish joy of their celebrations, for soon there will be no libations nor sacrifices. Strophe 2 announces the exile, during which the celebration of feast-days and festivals will be impossible. Strophe 3 describes days of visitation. The following modifications are to be adopted: (1) the transfer of v.[3] to precede v.[5]; (2) the treatment of v.[9] as a gloss.

1. אל־גיל] ⅏ μηδὲ εὐφραίνου; so ⅏𝔙𝔗, all reading אל. Om. as a gloss repeating אל תשמח. Marti, אל תגל.—כעמים] Some codd. of Kenn. and de R. בעמים (so also Abarb., Ros., Gr.). 𝔏 adds *terrae.* — על־כל] ⅏ מֶ֫ה. — גרן] Om. with ⅏ as a dittog. of גרן (v.[2]); this yields a trimeter line and permits גרן (v.[2]) to follow closely upon גרנות, a construction demanded by the context. — **2.** ירעם] Read, with ⅏, ἔγνω αὐτούς = ידעם (so Houtsma, We., Oort (*ThT.* and *Em.*), Gu., Ru., GAS., Now., Oet., Marti). ⅏ نصحبّ = יֵרַעֵם (Seb.). — בה] Read, with ⅏⅏𝔙𝔗, בם; so Bab. cod. (so also Dathe, Ew., Bauer, We., Gr., Oort, Loft., Ru., Gu., GAS., Now., Oet., Marti). — **3.** וישבו] ⅏ κατῴκησαν = יָשְׁבוּ.—וישב] ⅏ κατῴκησεν = יָשַׁב; 𝔙 om. ו.—**4.** יערבו] Read יֶעֶרְכוּ (so Kue. *Hibb. Lect.* 1882, pp. 312 f.; Oort, *ThT.* and *Em.;* Val., We., Gu., Loft., Ru., GAS., Now., Marti). Gr. יערב. Gardner, יערבו (cf. Ex. 13[12] Lv. 18[21]). — זבחיהם] Join, contrary to accents, with what precedes; so ⅏; but ⅏𝔙 join with following. — כלחם] Gardner, כי לחם.—אונים] ⅏ اَكْلُهُمْ.—לחם] 𝔏 *ejus.* Read לַחְמָם (so Kue. *Hibb. Lect.* 1882, pp. 312 f.; Oort, *ThT.* and *Em.;* We., Val., Gu., Ru., Loft., GAS., Now., Oet., Marti).—יבוא] GAS. יָבִיאוּ. — **5.** ליום]

𝔊 pl. (so also GAS.). — **6.** [הנה הלכו] Gr. הן הלכו = *if*, etc.; Marti, הלכים ה'. Read, with We., Val., and Now., וילכו. — [משר] 𝔖 כמשׂר = בשר. Read, with We., אשׁור (so Val., Now., Oet., Marti). Ru. om. as a double of [מצר]ים, and supplies the town-name התפּנחס before תקבצם. — [מחמד] 𝔊 Μαχμάς (= מחמש), due to confusion of ר with foll. ל and consequent resemblance to familiar מכמש (Vol.). Σ. τὰ ἐπιθυμήματα. Gr. מטמון. Marti, מחמדיהם. Read, with Hi., מחמדי for ל מח (so We.; Oort, *Em.;* Val., Oet., Hal.). — [לכספם] Gardner, לכרמם. Hal. בתיהם. Some codd. of Kenn. and de R. לנפשם (so Ru.). Marti om. as gloss. — [קמוש] 𝔊 ὄλεθρος = מוקש (Vol.). 𝔖 בבמין. — [יירשם] 𝔊 κληρονομήσει αὐτό = יירשׁו (so also Ru.). — **7.** [ירעו] 𝔊 κακωθήσεται = ירע. Now. and We.[3] ידע. — [ישראל] Ru. adds אפי and transfers here from v.[8], אפרים זעם אלהיו, the text being changed. — [על רב עונך ורבה משטמה] על רב עונך זעם אלהיו רבה = 𝔊 ὑπὸ τοῦ πλήθους τῶν ἀδικιῶν σου ἐπληθύνθη μανία σου = משטיכה (Vol.); 𝔖 om. conj. with 𝔊, and derives משטמה from שטה = *forsake* (Seb.); 𝒱 renders last clause *et multitudinem amentiae.* Read ורב החטאה (so Ru., Now.; *v.i.*), and, with Now., transfer משטמה to beginning of v.[8]. Gr. ורב המשטמה (so We., Oort (*Em.*)). Oort, רבה משטמה, omitting ו with 𝔊. Hal. ירבה מש". Ru. om. משטמה צפה as a correction of the foll. משטמה. **8.** [צפה] Gr. צדה. Che. and Hal. צופה. Oet. צפה פה. — [עם] Grotius, עם (so Mich., Gr.). Che. מעם. Oet. על. Ru. and Hal. זעם. Oort om. — [אלהי] 𝔊 om. suff. Some codd. אלהיו (so also Oort, *ThT.* and *Em.;* Ru., Hal.). Oet. om. as dittograph of last word in verse. — עם אלהי is to be omitted, with Now., as a gloss. — [יקוש] Oort, יקש. — [משטמה] Om. as dittog. of מ in v.[7] — **9.** [העמיקו] 𝔊 joins with v.[8] (so also Oort, Gr., We., GAS.). Oort, העמיק. — [שחתו] 𝔊 ἐφθάρησαν = שׁחתו (Vol.). Read, with We. and Now. שׁחתו. — [כימי] Hal. מימי. — [הגבעה] 𝔊 τοῦ βουνοῦ; so 𝔖. — [יזכור] 𝔖 inserts עתה before יו (so also Ru.). 𝕷 adds *dabitur* after יו.

IX. 1. *Do not rejoice, Israel, like the peoples*] The words are addressed to Israel at a time when the nation is engaged in the midst of the wild and exuberant celebration of a harvest feast. It is, perhaps, also a time when Assyria's hand, for a moment, seems to have been lifted, and Israel permitted to breathe more freely (cf. 2 K. 15[19]). Instead of (1) retaining אל־גיל = unto exultation = *too loudly*, cf. Jb. 3[22]; * or (2) reading אל־גיל (*v.s.*), which is irregular in that an imperfect would have been expected; it is better (3) to omit the phrase as a gloss on אל תשמח.† This harvest-rejoicing places Israel on a plane

---

* So Hd., RV., *et al.*

† Cf. Hal.'s sug. that גיל here = produce of the soil, being allied to Aram. גילא (stalk), Arab. جيل (tribe), and Ethiop. *ĕgyâl* (child) ; cf. Dn. 1[10] Ps. 65[13].

with other nations, *i.e.* makes her *like the peoples*, the heathen.
What, in the prophet's mind, constituted the difference ? The
people in their celebration acknowledge the harvest to be a
gift of the god of the land in return for their sedulous worship,
thus making material gain the goal and the reward of worship ;
while it is the prophet's contention that divine blessings are
bestowed for real worth and character (Dt. 28¹⁻⁶). Here is
opposition between the folk-religion and the true Yahweh-religion
as preached by the prophet. It is here that עמים is first used
in the sense of *heathen.** — *That thou hast played the harlot
from thy God*] Is this the ground of the command not to
rejoice,† or is that ground to be found later in the statement
that *threshing-floor aud wine-vat will not know them* (v.²).‡ In
the latter case, כי = *that, in that,* and the following clauses
furnish the substance of the rejoicing, not the reason or occasion.§
— *Thou hast loved a harlot's hire upon all threshing-floors*]
Accepting the harvest-fruits as from the Baalim commits Israel
to the service of the Baalim. Every celebration of a local
festival is, therefore, an act of harlotry, in which the harlot
acknowledges her paramour and accepts his gift, *i.e.* the harlot's
hire. The sin here is not worshipping on the high places, but observing a cult in which debasing tendencies are at work, instead
of those which would elevate and ennoble. It is, in other words,
a case of the material *vs.* the spiritual (cf. Zc. 14¹⁶⁻¹⁹). דנן is
unnecessary and may be omitted. — **2.** *Threshing-floor and wine-
vat shall not know them*] *Feed them* ‖ (cf. 4¹⁶) is not an easy
expression with the subject here indicated. The reading יֵדָעֵם
is very natural and is supported by the parallel phrase יְכַחֵשׁ. The
floor and the vat (the place within the press into which oil or
wine flowed, cf. Jo. 2²⁴) stand, concretely, for the grain and oil
and wine, these henceforth will not know, *i.e.* be known to,
Israel, not because a failure of crops is to be expected,¶ but
because they are to be carried into exile.** — *And the new wine
shall play them false*] Cf. Hb. 3¹⁷. The reading *her*, if correct,
is due to Israel's representation as a harlot ; but (1) the versions

* We.

† Ke., Or., *et al.*

‡ Hi., Ew., Now.

§ Now., Marti.

‖ So 𝔊𝔗.

¶ Dathe, Mau., Hi., Ew., *et al.*

** Marck, Stuck, Umb.

(*v.s.*) read *them;* (2) everywhere else in chaps. 4–14, Israel is spoken of as *he* (thou) or *they* (ye) (even in 4[16] 10[11], in comparison with feminine animals).* — **4.** *They shall not pour libations to Yahweh*]† In eating and drinking at sacrificial meals a portion of the wine was devoted to the deity and poured out as a libation, the rest was drunk in connection with the offering (cf. Am. 2[8] 1 S. 1[24] 10[3]). If this custom be interfered with in the exile, the whole of the wine in general will become unclean, and therefore unpleasing to Yahweh. — *Nor prepare for him their sacrifices*] This is the simplest treatment, although it requires the change of יערבו to יערכו (*v.s.*) and the connection of זבחיהם with this verb as object contrary to the accents.‡ To represent the sacrifices as *unpleasing* to Yahweh § (cf. Je. 6[20] Mal. 3[4]) is inconsistent with v.4[a] and with chap. 3, which say that there shall be no sacrifice at all. The word ערך, used of laying in order the parts of the sacrifice, is common (Lv. 1[7 f. 12] 6[5] Ex. 40[4. 23]; cf. Ps. 23[5]). It must be remembered that sacrifice and feasting upon animal food were inseparable. || — *Their bread shall be like the bread of mourning*] *i.e.* לחמם for להם. Just as the wine they drink and the flesh they eat will be taken without giving thereof a due portion to Yahweh, and consequently will be unconsecrated and unclean, and without " the joy of the sense of the divine favor," so the bread which they eat will be unclean; it will be, in fact, like *the bread of mourning, i.e.* the bread eaten during the days of mourning for the dead (Nu. 19[14]), or, better, the bread used at the funeral feasts and broken for the dead (cf. Je. 16[7] Dt. 26[14]).¶ No stronger impression for impurity could have been found; and yet all bread eaten in exile will be thus impure. — *All who*

---

* Ew.

† Cf. Oort, *ThT.* XXIV. 491 f., who rejects vs.4 and 5 as a later addition for the following reasons: (1) the difficulty of explaining בית יהוה (v.4) as coming from Hosea, since it cannot denote the temple at Jerusalem, and there was more than one temple in North Israel; (2) these verses break the connection; (3) they do not reflect the sentiment of Hosea's time, but that of the Deuteronomic period; (4) they are inconsistent with vs.1–3. Marti makes 4[b. 5] late.

‡ Cf. RV., which takes this word with what follows.   § So 𝕲𝕾𝕿.

|| WRS. *Sem.* 222 f.; Sm. *Rel.* 140 f.

¶ Ros., Hi., Ew., Hd., Sim., Ke., Now., Marti.

eat shall defile themselves] The idea of cleanness and uncleanness is very old; it is to be connected closely with the ideas
of ancestor worship and totemism, and is, in fact, only another
name for taboo;* and there is, therefore, nothing in this to
prove the observance at this time of the Levitical cult. — *For
their bread shall be only for their hunger*] Instead of the double
purpose involved in eating as heretofore, viz. worship of, or
communion with, the deity, and satisfaction of desire for food,
only the latter shall now exist. All that was holy and sacred,
all that was spiritual, will have disappeared. This is the idea
whether we render לְנַפְשָׁם *for themselves,*† or *for their belly,*‡ or
for their desire or *hunger* § (cf. also Is. 29[8] 32[6] Ps. 63[5] 107[9]). —
It shall not come into Yahweh's house] *i.e.* any place consecrated
to Yahweh, *e.g.* the temple, or a high place. — **3.** *They shall not
dwell in the land of Yahweh*] This is the explanation of the
dire threat contained in vs.[1. 2. 4]; they will be compelled to
abandon their home land, *the land of Yahweh.* This expression
furnishes the key to an understanding of the O. T. religion down
to the exile. The old Arabic tribal conception of God, involving on the one hand a belief in the personality of God which
opposes a tendency toward pantheism, and on the other, a belief
in the deity as an abstract representation of irresistible power
and force, which was opposed to polytheism, developed into
henotheism or monolatry, according to which each nation had
its own god (Chemosh, the god of Moab; Milcom, the god of
Ammon). In this way Yahweh was the god of Israel (Ju. 11[24]).
This was a worship of one god, but also an acknowledgment
of the existence of other gods for other lands and peoples.‖
As clear cases of this belief, cf. Naaman the Syrian, who takes
home earth from Palestine on which to worship Yahweh, who
had cured him (2 K. 5[17]); the flight of Jonah, who thought he
could thus escape the presence of Yahweh (Jon. 1[1]); and the
feeling of David that in being driven out of Israel into another

---

* Cf. Sta. *GVI.* I. 481–487; WRS. *Sem.* 446 ff.; Now. *Arch.* II. 275 f.; Benz.
Arch. 478–484; G. A. Simcox, *EB.* I. 842 f.; Matthes, *ThT.* XXXIII. 293–318;
and other literature cited in my *Priestly Element, etc.*, 126 ff.

† Ma., Umb., Hd., Ke., *et al.*   ‡ Ew.   § Hi., Che., Now.

‖ WRS. *Proph.* 54 f.; Sm. *Rel.* 113 f.; Schultz, *Theol.* I. 176 ff.

land he was being forced to transfer his worship to other gods
(1 S. 26¹⁹). — *But Ephraim shall return to Egypt*] Cf. on 8¹³.
This reference is not simply a " type of the land of captivity,"
Assyria being intended and designated thus as a new Egypt.*
The fact is, that at this time Israel was between two great
threatening powers. It is not yet certain in the prophet's mind
whether Egypt or Assyria, or both, shall be the agent of Israel's
exile. Both are tyrannizing over her. Toward both Israel leans
(cf. 5¹³ 7¹¹). Time will determine the issue more definitely. —
And in Assyria they shall eat what is unclean] Cf. Ez. 4¹³.
Living in a foreign land and eating that which is unclean are
synonymous terms. The situation is now squarely before them.
Perhaps they will consider (cf. 𝕲's addition to 8¹³). — **5**. *What
will ye do on the day of a festival?*] How will the Sabbath and
the day of the new moon be properly celebrated ? How, indeed,
will they be celebrated at all in a foreign land, where Yahweh's
sanctuaries do not exist ? These days were the great days of
rejoicing, recurring weekly and monthly.† — *Or on the day of
feasting to Yahweh*] The חג was the great harvest feast ‡ (cf.
1 K. 8² 12³² Ju. 21¹⁹ Ez. 45²⁵ 2 Ch. 5³), and not a general term
for all feasts and synonymous with מועד. § — **6**. *For behold they
will go to Assyria*] This reading ‖ (*v.s.*) relieves two difficulties :
(1) the absence of a reference to Assyria in connection with
the mention of Egypt; (2) the confusion involved in the
rendering of the present text, *they will go from the devastation*,
i.e. they will leave their wasted land ; ¶ or *they will die of hunger;* **
or *yea, if they are gone from the ruins,* †† a protasis, — all of which
describe a departure on account of devastation, rather than a
deportation. ‡‡ — *Egypt gathering them, Memphis burying them*]
Rapid strokes in a picture, intentionally left somewhat indefinite. §§
In this description reference is made to the numerous and vast
burial grounds of Egypt, one of the largest being at Memphis.
Memphis occupied an important position on the Nile, a short
distance south of Cairo, whence it commanded the whole of
Egypt, of which it was the most important city during the

---

* Ke.   † See my *Priestly Element in the O. T.*, p. 96.   ‡ Sim., Now.

§ Ke.   ‖ We., Now.   ¶ Cal., Bauer.   ** Ki., Dathe.   †† Ew., § 357 *b*.

‡‡ Or.   §§ Marti om. מצ׳ תק׳ as a doublet of מף תק׳.

greater part of its existence.* — *Nettles inheriting their precious things of silver*] Another side of the picture ; cf. 9[16]. The plural מַחְמַדֵּי is probably to be read.† This has been taken : (1) as a reference to idols of silver;‡ (2) as meaning treasure-houses or palaces;§ (3) as a proper name;‖ (4) as connected with תְּכַבְּרֵם, and meaning "on account of longing for their silver."¶ — *Thorns coming up in their tents*] Cf. Is. 34[13]. Their dwellings, not tabernacles, or places of worship (cf. Ez. 16[16]).—**7.** *The days of visitation will come*] The perfect is prophetic. This and the following line tell what it is that Israel shall know, or experience. — *The days of recompense will come*] שִׁלֻּם (cf. similar formation in פִּגּוּל, חִתּוּל) is an abstract noun, parallel in thought to *visitation* (פְּקֻדָּה),** and is hardly a play on the proper name Shallum.††— *Israel shall know*] It is better thus to connect this clause with the preceding,‡‡ than to make it a parenthetical clause and connect it with what follows, כִּי being understood. §§ — *A fool, the prophet ; mad, the man of spirit*] Two uncertainties exist here : (1) Is this phrase (a) the direct object of יֵדְעוּ, *i.e.* Israel shall know (that) the prophet is a fool, etc., this entire clause, יֵדְעוּ . . . הָרוּחַ, being parenthetical, and the following עַל־רֹב וְגוֹ׳ depending upon בָּאוּ ; ‖ or (b) is the phrase independent of what precedes and to be taken only with what follows ?¶¶ (2) The other question concerns the sense in which נָבִיא and אִישׁ הָרוּחַ are taken, whether (a) of the false prophets, who have deluded the people by their prediction of prosperity and are now convicted of folly and made insane by the divine judgment;*** or (b) of true prophets ?††† Against the interpretation of *false* prophets it may be urged that the terms "fool," "madman," are not likely to have been used by the people of false prophets who had led them astray (Orelli), that אִישׁ הָרוּחַ must be used of a truly inspired prophet, notwithstanding Mi. 2[11], and that v.[8] sup-

---

* See arts. "Memphis," *DB.*, and "Noph," *EB.*, by W. M. Müller.
† Hi., We., Now.   ‖ 𝔊.   †† We., Marti.
‡ Hess., Hi., We.   ¶ Marck, Ros.   ‡‡ We., Or., GAS., Now., *et al.*
§ 𝔗, Jer., Ra., Ki., Wü., *et al.*   ** Ki., Wü.   §§ 𝔗, Marck, Hi.
‖ 𝔗, Jer., Ki., Ra., Marck, Mau., Hi., Bauer, Ros., Wü.
¶¶ Umb., Sim., Che., Or., Now.
*** Ki., Abarb., Marck, Dathe, Ros., Mau., Hi., Hd., Ke.
††† Ew., Umb., Sim., Che., We., Now., Marti,

ports strongly this interpretation as a whole. The sentence is
to be taken with Nowack as a quotation from the mouth of the
people (cf. 6[1] Is. 28[9, 10]).* The prophet seems to say: You,
the people, maintain, do you, that the prophet has become a
fool, and the man of spirit a madman? It is true, just as you
say, but learn that this great calamity has come upon them
*because of the greatness of thine iniquity and the greatness of thy
sin*] It is Israel's iniquity and sin (adopting Ruben's suggestion
to substitute חטאה, *sin*, for משטמה) that have driven mad the
inspired messengers of Yahweh. This same thought is ampli-
fied in the following verses. — **8.** This verse is almost hopelessly confused. The more important solutions proposed are
the following: (1) *Ephraim's watchman, appointed by my God,
even the prophet — a fowler's snare is in all his ways;* † this
interpretation involves the reading of מעם for עם, a מ having
dropped out after אפרים; and uses the word "watchman" as in
Je. 6[17]. The result is a sentence giving an appropriate thought,
but so involved in expression as to make it very doubtful.
(2) *Ephraim acts the spy with my God; the prophet is a
fowler's snare upon all his (Israel's) ways.* ‡ Variations of
this interpretation are three: (*a*) Ephraim lays ambush against
the people (עַם instead of עִם) of my God; § (*b*) Ephraim looks
round about outside of (away from) my God (for foreign help); ‖
(*c*) Ephraim looks after prophecies in addition to those from
my God.¶ (3) *Ephraim expects help from my God,* ** treating
צפה as in Ps. 5[3] Mi. 7[7] La. 4[17], and עם as for מֵעָם (cf. Jb. 27[13]).
(4) *There is hostility to the watchman in the house of his God;
the prophet (finds) the snares of the fowler on all his ways.* ††
This interpretation involves considerable change in the text, viz.
(*a*) the transfer of משטמה from the end of v.[7] to the beginning of
v.[8]; (*b*) the omission of אפרים עם אלהי (cf. Ruben's suggestion
that these words stood originally in connection with ירעו ישראל
(v.[7]) in this form: ירעו ישראל אפי אפרים זעם אלהיו, the אפי having
dropped out, זעם being for עם); (*c*) the omission of משטמה in [8b]
as useless repetition; (*d*) the transfer of א' בבית to follow צפה,

---

* Cf. Ew., Oort, We., Che. § Mich. ** Hd.
† Che. ‖ Struensee, Sim. †† Now.
‡ GAS.; cf. Ew., Umb., Ke., Or. ¶ Dathe, Hi.

— all this disorder being due to efforts to restore the meaning, when by mistake משטמה was placed at the end of v.[7], instead of the beginning of v.[8]. The parallelism is perfect, and the sense excellent.* I desire, however, to suggest the following arrangement, which renders unnecessary certain omissions and changes involved in Nowack's interpretation : *Enmity exists towards Ephraim's watchman; the prophet (finds) the snares of the fowler in all his ways; in the (very) house of his God they dig for him a deep pit*] This interpretation follows Nowack only in transferring משטמה from the end of v.[7] to the beginning of v.[8], and in the omission of עם אלהי. A preposition, ל or על, must be inserted. It adopts Wellhausen's suggestion to place the first two words of v.[9], העמיקו שחתו, at the end of v.[8], giving them another pointing. With this interpretation v.[8] supplements v.[7], adding three expressions, of which the first is the simple statement, the second and third poetical pictures and illustrations. The watchman (cf. Ez. 3[17 ff.]) of Ephraim meets persecution on every side; fowler's snares compass about the prophet; a deep pit is digged for him even in the house of his God. House here, as in v.[15], means Canaan. — **9.** *As in the days of Gibeah*] A gloss from 10[9];† here inconsistent because the thought has to do only with Ephraim's persecution of Yahweh's prophets; cf. Ju. 19[22-30] 20[46-48]. — *He will remember their iniquity, he will visit their sin*] An insertion from 8[13].‡

1. ואל־גיל] If retained = inf. abs. or cogn. acc. with תשמח, although of different stem; Kö. 329 *h*. For similar cases of combination of different stems, *v.*, *e.g.*, Jb. 3[22] 2 S. 19[5] Zc. 8[2] — אתנן] Deriv. from תנה (BDB; cf. 8[9. 10]; but cf. We. who regards these forms as corrupt and from נתן) with א prosthetic and affix ‍ַ‍ן; or from נתן (BSZ.) for אנתנן; cf. Kö. II. i. p. 96. — **2.** גרן] Position of words chiastic with prec. verse and emphatic. — **4.** וזבחיהם] The objection of Oet. and Hal. to the reading ד ערך on the ground that it is

---

* Marti reconstructs vs.[7. 8] as follows : —

(7*a*) באו ימי הפקרה	(7*b*) אויל הנביא
באו ימי השלם	משגע איש הרוח
יֵרַע ישראל קצפי (אַפִּי or)	על רב עונך
(8*a*) יֵרַע אֶפְרַיִם עַמִּי	ורבח חַטַּאתָם
	(8*b*) פח יקוש על כל דֶּרֶךְ
	וּמַשְׂטֵמָה בבית אֱלֹהִים

† So Now.   ‡ So Now., Marti.

not good Hebrew, cannot be maintained in view of the occurrence of ערך עורה Lv. 6⁵. In any case the poetic and prophetic use of ערך must not be measured by the later strict and ceremonial usage.— אונים] The phrase לחם אונים occurs only here according to 𝔐; but cf. Ez. 24¹⁷·²², where אונים is probably to be read for אנשים. On this and similar practices see Sta. *GVI.* I. 387 ff.; Schwally, *Leben nach d. Tode;* Frey, *Tod Seelenglaube u. Seelenkult.* — ויטמאו] On assim. of ר, cf. GK. 54 *c*, and cf. the Hothp. Dt. 24⁴; the Hithp. is not pass. but reflex.— לנפשם] If rendered *for themselves,* it is emphatic in contrast with *their gods;* Kö. 40.— **3.** ושב . . . וישבו] Intentional similarity of sound.—
5. ל [ליום is rarely used of *time* to express concurrence (*at* or *on*) rather than duration *in;* cf. Is. 10³ Je. 5³¹; *v.* BDB. 517; Kö. 331 *f.* — **6.** הלכו] Acc. to 𝔐, proph. pf.; cf. also באו, v.⁷.— מצרים] . . . תקברם The rhythm and picturesqueness of these circ. clauses is to be noted; the nouns beginning with מ, the first and second radicals of both vbs. being קב; each word closing with ם‍ֵ; cf. similar change in one consonant of a word in Is. 5⁷. — מף] Is elsewhere (Is. 19¹³ Je. 2¹⁶ 44¹ 46¹⁴·¹⁹ Ez. 30¹³·¹⁶) מ נף; here is perhaps due to influence of preceding מ. The ancient Egyptian name was Men-nofer (= the good abode) which was shortened into *Mennefe* and *Menfe,* which forms were transferred to other languages, *e.g.* Assyrian *Mimpi.* — מחמר] On the cstr. fol. by prep. H. 9, 2 *b*; GK. 130 *a*; Kö. 336 *w*; cf. also Kö. 280 *n*, on the expression of indeterminateness by cstr. with ל.—קמוש] On form cf. Kö. II. i. pp. 147, 461; Barth, *NB.* 45; Lag. *BN.* 117 f., 181 f.; Baer, *in loc.* In some Mss., קימוש.יירשם] On pl. suf. used as collective, *v.* Kö. 346 *q.*—חוח] cf. Assyr. *haḥin,* "a thorny growth" (Dl. *HWB.*). Used as here parallel to קמוש, Is. 34¹³. Later with meaning *hook,* 2 Ch. 33¹¹; cf. סיר which also has both meanings. Che. (*EB.*) emends this verse freely and finds here the names of four North Arabian districts.— **7.** הפקדה] On d. f. in 3rd radical, cf. A. Müller, *ZDMG.* 1891, p. 234; Kö. II. i. pp. 199, 461.—השלם] On art. with nouns of this form, Kö. 241 *l*; cf. 261 *e.* — **7.** משטמה] ἁ.λ. from שטם, a by-form of שטן, *to oppose, be hostile;* cf. Gn. 27⁴¹ Jb. 16⁹. Cf. the sugg. of BSZ. to connect it with the Syr. ܣܰܟ, *Pa.* = bind with cords, the word being omitted from v.⁷ — **8.** פח יקוש] יקוש only here; cf. יָקוֹשׁ with same meaning, Ps. 91³ Pr. 6⁵ Je. 5²⁶. For the phrase *snare of the fowler,* cf. Ps. 91³ 124⁷. On פח, *v.* Am. 3⁵. — **9.** העמיקו] Vb. appos.; H. 36, 2; GK. 120 *g*; a case of asyndetic appos.— כימי] כ = *as in,* used pregnantly; cf. Is. 5¹⁷ 9³ Jb. 29²; cf. BDB. p. 453, on original force of כ as subst.; Kö. 319 *d* on the adv. force of preposition.— הגבעה] Art. with this proper noun sometimes used, at others omitted; cf. Jos. 15⁵⁷ 18²⁸; Kö. 295 *b.*

§ 12. Israel is corrupt ; the life of old as well as young licentious. 9¹⁰⁻¹⁷.

Israel started out with freshness and purity of youth ; but contamination came at Baal-peor, and the abominable thing took hold of them (9¹⁰). Ephraim's glory is gone ; no children, no mothers ; no fruit (vs.¹¹·¹⁶*ᵃ·ᵇ*). Even when children are born they are slain before maturity; they are destined only for slaughter (¹⁶ᶜ·¹²ᵃ·ᵇ·¹³). Give them, O Yahweh, barrenness; in Gilgal they have shown their wickedness, and for it I will drive them forth (¹⁴·¹⁵ᵃ·ᵇ·). I will cease to love them, because of their rebellion; woe upon them. My God will make them vagabonds for their disobedience (¹⁵ᶜ·¹²ᶜ·¹⁷).

This piece is commonly recognized as complete in itself; so Mich., Dathe, Stuck, Mau., Hi., Ew., Ke., Che., Or., Val., Now., GAS., *et al.;* cf. however Hd., Sim. It consists of five four-line strophes, in a movement essentially tetrameter. Strophes 1 and 2 might be united; so also strophes 3 and 4; with this combination the order would be $8 + 8 + 4$. Strophes 1 and 2 describe the immoral life of the people and their consequent decay — no fruit. Strophes 3 and 4 assert that even those born are destined to captivity and slaughter before they are grown, for they will be cast off — because of wickedness in Gilgal. Strophe 5 declares that Yahweh, instead of loving them, will make them wanderers in the earth — on account of their rebellion. This arrangement involves the following transpositions: (1) v.¹⁶ to follow v.¹¹ (*v.i.*); (2) v.¹²ᶜ, כי־גם־אוי להם בשורי מהם, to follow v.¹⁵ (*v.i.*). Gr. arranges as follows: 10. 11 *a.* 14. 11 *b.* 12. 13. 15. 16.

10. ענבים] 𝕲 sg. — כבכורה] 𝕲 ὡς σκοπόν. — בראשיתה] Om., with 𝔖, as a gloss; 𝕲 πρόιμον; 𝒴 *in cacumine ejus.* — אבותיכם] 𝕲𝔖𝒴 3 pl. suff. (so also Ru.). — המה] 𝕿𝔖 = והמה (so Ru.). — לבשת] Read, with We., Now., and Marti, לבעל. — שקוצים] 𝕲, Σ. οἱ ἐβδελυγμένοι = שקוצים (Vol.); so 𝒴; 'Α. βδελύγματα. — כאהבם] 𝕲 ὡς οἱ ἠγαπημένοι = כאהבים (Vol.); 'Α. ὡς ἠγάπησαν; Σ. ὅσῳ ἠγαπήθησαν; 𝒴 *sicut ea quae dilexerunt;* 𝔖 ܐ̈ܝܟ ܕܪ̈ܚܡܝܢ. Gr. כמאהביהם. Gardner, באהליהם or באהלם. — 11. כבורם] 𝕲 and 𝒴 join with foll. clause. 𝕲 renders this and three foll. nouns as plurals. — מבטן] BSZ. and Marti, מבטן. — 16. הכה] 𝕲 ἐπόνεσεν = חלה (Stek.). Gr. ממכת. — שרשם] 𝕲 τὰς ῥίζας αὐτοῦ; 'Α., Σ. ἡ ῥίζα αὐτοῦ; 𝔖 connects with הכה as acc. of specification. — יבש] Gr. יבש. — בלי] Read, with Qᵉrî, בל; so 40 codd. of Kenn. (so also Gr., Ru., Oet.). — 12. ושכלתים] 𝕲 ἀτεκνωθήσονται; Ru. ושכרתים. Gr. ושכלתם. — מאדם] 𝕲 ἐξ ἀνθρώπων; 𝒴 *in hominibus.* Gr. אדמתם. Oort, מאדמה. — בשורי מהם] 𝕲, Θ. σάρξ μου (= בשרי) אוי להם Ru. and Hal. — עויליהם. — 𝔖 ܡ̈ܢܗܘܢ which Seb. corrects to ܡ̈ܢܗܘܢ (from סור), or αὐτῶν; 𝔖 ܡ̈ܢܗܘܢ. Read, with Hi., בשורי (so Ew., Sim., Gu.). Ru. בהם. Gr. יבאשו. — מבשר בניהם] Hal. פשעים הם. Bauer, בסורי (so Oort (*Em.*)). — 13. אפרים כאשר ראיתי] 𝕲 'Εφ. ὃν τρόπον; 𝕲ᴬᵩ· add εἶδον. Omit כ'ר' (*v.i.*). Gr. om. אפ' as dittog. from ¹³ᵇ. Ew. כאשר for כאשׁר. Hal. (or ואיה ואית ופרה). — לצור] Read, with 𝕲, εἰς θήραν, לציד or לצור (so also Houtsma, We., Ru., GAS., Oort (*Em.*), Oet., Marti); 'Α., Σ. ὡς ἀκρότομον; Θ. εἰς πέτραν; 𝒴 om. ל and treats צור as the subj. of שתולה. 𝔖 takes ר' as 2 p. sg. with לצור, treated as proper name, as its obj. Hal. בצור. — שתולה] 𝕲 παρέστησαν = שתלו (so also Hal.),

or שתו את (Houtsma). Read שְׁתוּ. Gr. שְׁכוּלָה. Oet. שָׁתוּ לה. Scholz, לְ שַׁח.
Ru. לְרָשִׁית.— [בנוה Read, with 𝔊, τὰ τέκνα αὐτῶν, בְּנֵיהֶם (so also Scholz, Ru.,
Hal.), or better בניו (so also Houtsma, We., Now., GAS., Oort (Em.), Oet.,
Marti); similarly Θ. Gr. בְּנֶיהָ. 𝔖 ܟܣܠܠܠܠ, reading בְּנֶיהָ, as pl. (Seb.).
— [ואפרים Oort suggests that this represents some vb. — [אל הרג Read, with
𝔊, εἰς ἀποκέντησιν, אל הֶרֶג (Vol.), or better להרגה (so also We., Now., GAS.,
Oort (Em.), Marti); similarly 𝔖. Ru. לְהֶרֶג.— 14. Om., with 𝔊, the second
תֵן לָהֶם (so also Bauer).— [צמקים Another reading צִמֻקוֹת.— 15. כָּל] Gardner,
עַל or עַל כָּל.— [רעתם 𝔊 κακίαι αὐτῶν.— [רַע 𝔊 τὰς κακίας.— [אוֹסֵף Oet. אִיסֵף.
— 17. אֱלֹהֵי] 𝔊 ὁ θεός; so Arabic and one cod. of Kenn.

10. *Like grapes in the wilderness I found Israel*] *i.e.* with the
same satisfaction and pleasure with which one finds grapes in
a wilderness, I found Israel; this connects במדבר closely with
כענבים,* and not with מצאתי † (= I found Israel in the wilderness
like wild grapes belonging to no one, and under no one's protection, *i.e.* poor and helpless), nor with both במדבר and כענבים ‡
(= like grapes which have no place in the wilderness, and are
not expected to be found there, so was Israel; and the discovery
of Israel in this unexpected place brought with it surprise and
joy). This interpretation is supported by the position of the
words, and by the parallel thought of the next line; cf. Je. 2²,
also Ho. 2¹⁵ 13¹. This expression is an allusion to the dwelling
of Israel in the wilderness. — *Like the first-fruit on a fig tree I saw
your fathers*] The first ripe fig, on account of the lateness of the
fig harvest in Palestine, § was always a great delicacy (cf. Is. 28⁴
Mi. 7¹). In Je. 24². ⁵ the better class of people are compared to
the first ripe figs. *In its first time, i.e.* when it begins to ripen,
is evidently a gloss, intended to make the statement still more
explicit. It is shown to be superfluous by the rhythm and the parallelism. 𝔖 omits it. — *(But) they came to Baal-peor*] The whole
of ¹⁰ᵇ is clearly in contrast with ¹⁰ᵃ, although no conjunction expresses this contrast. Although Israel was so favorably regarded
and so tenderly treated by Yahweh, yet in the very beginning of
her history she showed her ingratitude and her faithlessness by
the episode of Beth-peor ‖ (cf. Nu. 25³·⁵ 23²⁸ 31¹⁶ Dt. 3²⁹ 4⁴⁶) for

---

＊ Theod., Rashi, Mich., Stuck, Hd., Sim., Wü., Or., Che., Sharpe, Now., Marti.
† Hi., Ew.   § Cf. G. E. Post, art. " Figs," *DB.*
‡ AE., Ki., Umb., Ke., Schm.   ‖ Creuzer, *Symbolik und Mythologie*, II. 411.

which Baal-peor (perhaps an abbreviation of Beth Baal-peor *) here stands. Peor was situated somewhere in the vicinity of the hill of Pisgah † (Nu. 23¹⁴· ²⁸ Jos. 13²⁰) ; cf. Wellhausen's suggestion ‡ that it was identical with Pisgah. — *And separated themselves to Baal*] בֹּשֶׁת = shame, is of later origin than Hosea, and by a later copyist has here been substituted for the original " Baal." § Yahweh is called Baal in 2¹⁸. ‖ נזר in the Niph'al refers to that formal separation of oneself which may be called *consecration.* — *And they became abominations like the object of their love*] It may be questioned, with Wellhausen, whether שִׁקּוּצִים is not also an insertion, used perhaps instead of the word which stood here originally. כְּאׇהֳבָם may be taken as here, *i.e.* an infinitive construct ; ¶ or as active participle or noun, *like their lover,*** or *loved object,*†† *i.e.* the thing loved at Baal-peor. — **11.** *Ephraim — his glory flies away like a bird*] With the swiftness of the bird's flight will Ephraim's glory depart. The construction places special emphasis upon Ephraim, to bring the former fruitfulness (the idea contained in the name) into contrast with the coming calamity, which shall consist in lack of everything which made up Ephraim's glory, *i.e.* prosperity, honor among the nations, and, as a prominent element, children. — *There shall be no more birth, no more motherhood, no more conception*] This, the greatest possible curse, was the ⸝punishment threatened for their lack of chastity. The construction is singularly terse and strong. The order is climactic : women will not conceive ; if they do, the child will die in the womb ; if it should survive the embryonic period, it will die at birth. Cf. 4¹⁰. Does not their sin against chastity deserve this? Cf. Halévy's interpretation of these words, in which he reverses the order of the climax. — **16.** *Ephraim is smitten, their root withered*] This verse interrupts the thought in its present position, but fits in perfectly between vs.¹¹ ᵃⁿᵈ ¹² ; it is, therefore, to be transferred.‡‡ This change

---

* *EB.* 406.   ‡ *J. d. Th.* XXI. 580; cf. Di. on Nu. 23²⁸.
† Cf. Dr., art. " Beth-peor," *EB.*   § We., Che., Gu., Now.
‖ On the use of בֹּשֶׁת as a substitute or nickname for בַּעַל, cf. Dr. on 2 S. 4⁴; Di. in *Monatsberichte der Kön.-Preuss. Academie der Wissenschaften zu Berlin,* 1881, June 16 ; Morris Jastrow, Jr., in *JBL.* XIII. 19-30.
¶ Kö. I. p. 395.   ** BSZ., Ke., Or., Now.   †† Hi., BDB.
‡‡ So We., Now., GAS., Oet. ; Marti transfers only ¹⁶ᵇ.

z

also relieves an important difficulty in the strophic structure. The
figure of the tree is adopted; Ephraim is like a tree smitten by
worms (Jon. 4[7]) or by heat (Je. 17[8]); and, worst of all, the very
root is destroyed, thus leaving no hope of further growth (cf.
Am. 2[9] Mal. 4[1], and for the opposite idea, Is. 11[1] Ps. 1[3]). — *Fruit
they cannot produce*] This is the sum and substance of the whole
thing. — *Yea, though they beget children, I will slay the darlings of
their womb*] This means practically that they will bear no fruit. —
12. *Yea, though they bring up their sons, I will bereave them that
there be not a man*] Cf. 1 S. 15[33]. This statement follows naturally upon [16b], and is in strict accord with the Hebrew method of
statement, viz. to make a general and absolute statement, and
then to add the exception or modification (cf. Jb. 31[23] Pr. 7[4f.]).
V.[12c] should follow v.[15] (*v.i.*). — **13.** *Ephraim — for a prey are
his sons destined*] This rendering * is based upon ⅏ (*v.s.*); in
addition, it involves the omission of כאשר ראיתי as unnecessary,
and inconsistent with the rhythm. The old rendering, *Ephraim,
as I saw Tyrus, is planted in a pleasant place,*† means nothing,
(1) for Tyre (צר, not as here צור) is entirely out of place;
(2) שתולה = *planted*, does not fit as predicate to Ephraim; (3) כ
would have been used with Tyre, not ל. Other renderings of צור
are: *the palm;* ‡ *like pleasure groves of Tyrians,* reading אשר as
a noun (*v.s.*); § *Ephraim as I selected it for a Tyre,* etc.; ‖ *a
rock;* ¶ *as I saw is like a tree planted in Tyre;* ** *if I look as far
as Tyre,*†† or *toward Tyre.* ‡‡ — *Ephraim must lead forth his
sons to slaughter*] Hosea still continues his description of the
coming judgment. ⅏'s להרגה (*v.s.*), the abstract, *slaughter,* is
to be preferred to the 𝕸𝕿 אל הרג = *unto the slayer.* §§ —
14. *Give them, O Yahweh — what wilt thou give?*] This is
imprecation, ‖‖ not deprecation. ¶¶ The entire context pictures

---

* Cf. Houtsma, We., Now., GAS. Marti reads [13] as follows: —

אפרים כְּאִישׁ ראיתי לַצַּיִד שָׁת לֹה בָּנָיו
והוא ישראל הוציא לַהֲרֵנָה בָּנָיו

† AV.; cf. RV.   ‖ Ke.   †† De Wette.
‡ Cf. Arab. صون, *palm;* Hi.   ¶ ⅏., Bauer, Böckel.   ‡‡ Mau.
§ Ew.   ** Cal.   §§ Ew., AV., Or., Gu., *et al.*
‖‖ Mau., Hd., Sim., Ke.   ¶¶ Cal., Ros., Hi., Ew., Umb., Or., Che., Now., Marti.

Ephraim's ruin; and this is an appeal for that absolute ruin which is involved in the failure of a tribe or nation to propagate itself. To understand that this ejaculation is born of a sympathy which asks for the prevention of births that those born may not be compelled to suffer is far-fetched. The imperative, *give*, implies the opposite. The question is rhetorical, indicating excitement, and is intended not merely to furnish a basis for the repetition of v.[11], nor to ascertain the divine mind,[*] but = *what would I have thee give?* i.e. the prophet's own wish and prayer. — *A miscarrying womb and dry breasts*] The *give them* found in 𐤌𐤕 is superfluous and spoils the line. It is omitted in 𐤂. Unfruitfulness was regarded as a special and definite punishment from the deity; cf. Gn. 25^{21} $30^{1.2}$. This punishment stands related as a climax to that which has before been uttered; it also bears upon one of the chief sins of Jeroboam's time, the pride taken by the people in their numbers and prosperity; cf. Am. $6^{1.4-6}$ Ho. 2^8 10^1 12^8.[†] — **15.** *All their evil being in Gilgal*] A circumstantial clause = *since the consummation of their mischief* (or *calamity* [‡]) *is in Gilgal;* this use of כל (cf. Ec. 12^{13}) [§] is strained in order to secure paronomasia in connection with גלגל. Gilgal was the seat of Baalistic practices (cf. 4^{15} 12^{11} Am. 4^4 5^5); but there is no evidence of its being the headquarters of human sacrifice;[||] cf. 13^2. — *Yea, there I conceived hatred for them*] כי is resumptive, *yea* or *therefore;* the verb is inchoative, = not *I hated,* nor *I learned to hate,*[||] but *I formed* or *conceived hatred.* — *For the evil of their doings I will drive them out of my house*] The house here is not the temple, but Palestine, the land of Israel; cf. 8^1. On the use of גרש cf. Gn. 3^{24} 21^{10} (but there is no reference here to the Abraham episode).[¶] The figure of the husband and wife is again the basis of the expression (Nowack); cf. Lv. $21^{7.14}$ 22^{13}. — *I will no more love them, all their nobles being rebels*] A strong anthropomorphic expression for the decision to withdraw all favor and mercy from Israel. The reason assigned, one of the most important in the whole list of causes of the coming destruction, is the apostasy of the leaders. The same phrase with its

---

* Umb.   ‡ Oort. || Hi.
† Marti om. 14. 16 a β. 17 as glosses.   § Ma.   ¶ On the contrary, Ke.

paronomasia is cited in Is. 1²³. The court power is plainly in large measure responsible; cf. 7⁵ ᶠᶠ. — **12** *c.* *Yea, even woe upon them, when I look away from them*] For text, *v.s.* This clause is out of place in 𝕳𝕿, in which it not only has no logical connection with what precedes, but actually interrupts a closely connected passage.* Here it forms a fitting climax to a series of strong assertions, the idea of all of which is the abandonment of Israel by Yahweh. כי, here asseverative, is tautological if joined with ¹² ᵇ, which also is introduced by an asseverative כי. The גם, here indicating the climax, is impossible after ¹² ᵇ, as is seen by the effort of interpreters to make it refer to להם rather than to† אוי. The strophic structure is disturbed by its position in v.¹², but entirely satisfied by the order here proposed. — **17.** *My God will cast them away, for they have not hearkened to him*] The prophet now speaks, summing up the thought of Yahweh as it has been given in vs.¹⁵· ¹²ᵉ. Yahweh had said, "I will drive them out of my house; I will no more love them; yea, even woe upon them!" The prophet says, *My God* (for since they will no longer listen to him he may no longer be called Israel's God) *will cast them away.* They had been chosen (בחר) from among all the nations; cf. Dt. 32⁸ Ez. 5⁵ Am. 6¹ Mal. 3¹². — *And they shall become wanderers among the nations*] They will *become* (not be) wanderers, or fugitives, Je. 4¹; cf. use of נוד, of birds who have been cast out of their nest and fly hither and thither (Is. 16² Pr. 27⁸); cf. the use of Cain, Gn. 4¹². In 7¹³ it is used figuratively of wandering away from Yahweh.

10. ענבים] Hebrew is particularly rich in different words for the *grape* (cf. Che. *EB.* 1916 f.). Among these ענב (the usual term, being found also in Aram., Arab., and Assyr.) is the true word for the berry, אשכל being used for the cluster (Gn. 40¹⁰ Nu. 13²³).— הנמה באו] On circ. cl. with pf., H. 45, 1 *a*; GK. 142 *b*; Dr. § 163. — בעל פעור] For ב׳ פ׳ בית; for discussions on site, cf. also (*v.s.*) Conder, *Heth and Moab,* 142 f.; *PEF.* 1882, pp. 85 f.; Buhl, *Geogr. d. alt. Pal.* 123. — בשת] Cf. Je. 3²⁴ 11¹³; the substitution of בשת for בעל is especially frequent in proper names, *e.g.* ירבשת, 2 S. 11²¹ = ירבעל, Ju. 6³². — שקוצים] On form, Barth, *NB.* 102 *d*; GK. 84 *b, i.* Its use is always late, Je. 4¹ being apparently the earliest passage aside from this. As used for idols,

---

* Marti therefore makes it a gloss.

† Mau., Hi., We., Or., Gu., GAS., Now., *et al.*

cf. also 2 K. 23²⁴ Je. 7³⁰ Ez. 20⁷·⁸ Dn. 9²⁷; *v.* Gunkel, *Schöpfung u. Chaos,*
141.—[כאהבכם] On form, BSZ. and BDB.; only here and Pr. 7¹⁸.—**11.** [יתעופף
Hithpôlēl, only here; cf. Pôlēl, Gn. 1²⁰ Is. 6² 14²⁹ 30⁶.—[מן] Three times
with the force of negative, H. 41, 4 *d*; GK. 119 *x*; Kö. 406 *p.*—[לרה] Rare
formation = [לֶרֶת], GK. 69 *m.*—**16.** [אפרים שרשם] Chiastic order.—[גם] On force,
Kö. 394 *c.*—[בלי] Kᵉthîbh, but י is prob. dittog.; so בל (Qᵉrî) is better; בלי
is rarely used with finite vb., Kö. 352 *c, d.*—[יעשון] On ן, GK. 47 *m.*—
12 c. [בשורי] For various readings *v.s.* In favor of בְּשׂוּרִי is the appropriateness
of the meaning thus obtained, the slightness of the change involved, and the
fact that גם is thus given its proper force. Against the interpretation of
בְּשׂוּרִי = בסורי (so 'A., 𝔙𝔗, Ros., Mau., Ke., We., Or., Now., *et al.*) is the fact
that Hosea regularly writes ס; so 2⁴·¹⁹ 7¹⁴.—**16.** [והמתי] ו marks apodosis;
H. 48, 2 *b*; GK. 159 *f*; on form of עו vb. without inserted ô, GK. 72 *k.*—
[מחמרי] Cf. 9⁶; also La. 2⁴ Jo. 4⁵; on form, Barth, *NB.* 174.—**12.** [אם] = לי,
GK. 159 *m*; cf. Kö. 372 *h.*—**13.** [להוציא] On ל, H. 29, 3 *b*; Kö. 399 *z.*—
14. [מה־תחן] On optative force, GK. 151 *b*; Kö. 354 *h.*—**15.** [איפף] One of
the few jussives of 1st pers. used for cohort.; GK. 109 *d*; cf. Kö. 191 *c, g*;
also 197.

§ 13. Israel is wicked in proportion to her prosperity: but an end is coming of all that she has falsely trusted. 10¹⁻⁸.

Israel was
a luxuriant vine, but in proportion to her prosperity she multiplied
altars and pillars; however, she will now be declared guilty, and
her altars and pillars will be destroyed (10¹·²). On account of the
idol-calf, people and priest shall mourn; for it shall be carried to
Assyria, a token of Ephraim's shame (10⁵·⁶). The high places
shall be destroyed, thorns and thistles growing over them; the
king of Samaria shall be cut off; and the people shall even pray
to the mountains and hills to fall upon them (10⁸ᵃ·⁷·⁸ᵇ).

This piece consists of six four-line, or perhaps better, of three eight-line
strophes. Removing the glosses in vs.⁶·⁸ᵃ (*v.i.*), the arrangement becomes
8 + 7 + 7. The movement is trimeter, although dimeters are occasionally
employed, and in the last strophe the elegiac movement is used. Strophe 1
(vs.¹·²) pictures Israel as a fruitful vine, and with the increase of fruitfulness,
has come also an increase of idol-serving; but now that she has been found
guilty these emblems of idolatry shall be destroyed. Strophe 2 (vs.⁵·⁶)
describes the carrying away to Assyria of the idol-calf in which she has taken
such pleasure, which, therefore, has been her shame. Strophe 3 (vs.⁸ᵃ·⁷·⁸ᵇ)
declares that the high places shall be destroyed, the altars grown over with
thorns and thistles, while even the king shall be cut off, and men in the confusion of the judgment will call upon the mountains and the hills to fall
upon and cover them up.

This arrangement involves the following modifications: (1) vs.[3. 4] are to be taken as a later insertion (*v.i.*); (2) v.[7] is to be transferred to stand between [8a. and 8b] (*v.i.*).

1. בקק] 𝕲 εὐκληματοῦσα; 𝔙 *frondosa*; 'A. ἔνυδρος; Σ. ὑλομανοῦσα; 𝔖 ܘܡܫܒܚ = שׁוֹרֵק (Seb.; so also Gr.); 𝕿 בזיזא. Oet. בֹּהֶקֶת. ישׂראל] Ru. ישׁוה.—אֶפְרָיִם. 𝕲 (ὁ καρπὸς) εὐθηνῶν = ישׁלה or שׁלו (Vol.); 'A., Σ. ἐξισώθη; 𝔙 *adaequatus*. Oort and Gu. פֶּרְיוֹ שָׁוֶה לוֹ, or merely שׁלו פריו. Gr. לוֹ ישׁוה פריו. Marti, נָאֶה. Gardner, שָׁוָה. Read, with Oet., וישׁגיא (cf. Jb. 12[23] 36[24]), an Aramaicism.—לפריו] We. om. ל (so Now., Oet.).—הרבה למ'] Gr. מ' לו ה'.—היטיבו] 𝕲 ᾠκοδόμησεν; 'A. ἐσπούδασε (περὶ στηλῶν).—2. חלק לבם] 𝕲 ἐμέρισαν καρδίας αὐτῶν = הִלְקוּ לֵ' (Vol.); 'A., Σ., ἐμερίσθη καρδία. Read חָלָק (so Oort, Val., Now.). Oet. חָלָק. Ru. יַכֵּלֶּם, ח', חלק being the name of some hostile tribe. Brüll ("Beiträge zur Erkl. d. Buches Ho.," *Jahrb. f. Jüd. Gesch. u. Lit.*, v.-vi. (1883) 1-62; so Gr.), החליפו מלכם.—עתה] Ru. takes it here and in 8[10] as the name of some hostile tribe.—יאשמו] 𝕲 ἀφανισθήσονται (cf. 5[15]); A., Σ., Θ. πλημμελήσουσι; 𝔙 *interibunt*. Gr. ישׁמו. Ru. יְשַׁמֵּם.—יערף] 𝕲 κατασκάψει = יערה or יערער (Vol.).—ישׁדד] 𝕲 ταλαιπωρήσουσιν = ישׁדר (Vol.).— 3. כי לא] 𝔖 om. כי.—4. דברו] 𝕲 λαλῶν, = דַּבֵּר, agreeing with מלך of v.[3]; 𝔙 *loquimini*. Oort, מְדַבֵּר or דֻּבַּר (so Val.). Read, with We., דַבֵּר (so Gu., Ru., GAS., Now., Oort (*Em.*), Oet.).—דברים] Gr. כזבים (cf. 7[13]). Ru. דִּבְרֵי.—אלות] 𝕲 προφάσεις = עלות, an Aramaicism (Vol.); 𝔙 *visionis*. Ru. מֵעַל.—שׁוא] Ru. הַשָּׁיא.—כרת] 𝕲 διαθήσεται. Oort and Val. כָּרַת. Gr. בִּכְרֹת. Hal. בָּזֹה.—וכרת] Ru. רָאשׁ] 𝕲 ἄγρωστις = דֶּשֶׁא (Vol.); Σ. and Θ. λάχανον (sc. χλωρόν); 𝔖 ܪܝܫ. Loft. רוֹשׁ.—משׁפט] Ru. עַל תלמי שׂדי] Oet. מִשְׁפָּה or מִשְׁבָּה (cf. 11[7] 14[5]). Hal. מַשְׂחַת.

ܠܥܓܠܬ ܘܐܟܠ ܟܡܪܐ 𝔖; 𝕲 ἐπὶ χέρσον ἀγροῦ.—5. לעגלות] Read, with 𝕲, Θ., and 𝔖, לְעֵגֶל (so New., Oort, *ThT*. and *Em*.; We., Gu., Loft., Ru., GAS., Now., BDB., Oet., Marti). Dathe, Val. and Che. (*CB*.) לְעֶגְלַת. Gr. עַל עֵגֶל.—בית און] 𝕲 τοῦ οἴκου Ὢν; 'A. τοῦ οἴκου ἄς; Θ. τοῦ οἴκου ὄν. Oort and Marti, בית אל.—יגורו] 𝕲𝔖, Σ. render *dwell;* 𝔙 and 𝕿 *worship;* 'A., Θ. *fear*. Gr. יגודו or יתגרדו. Ru. יְתְגּוֹדָד. Che. ינודו.—שׁכן] Read, with 𝕲, κατοικοῦντες, שֹׁכְנֵי (so New., Oort, *ThT*. and *Em*.; We., Val., Loft., Gu., Now., GAS., Oet., Marti).—כי] Ru. כַּחִיר or כָּאֵב.—אבל] We. יֶאֱבַל (so Gr., Val., Now., Oet., Marti).—כמריו] 𝕲 καθὼς παρεπίκραναν αὐτόν (Vol.); 𝔖 joins with preceding.—עליו] 𝔖 = ועליו; 𝕲 om.—יגילו] Read יחילו (so Oort, Gr.). We. יְלִילוּ (so Val., Now., Oort (*Em*.), Oet., Hal., Marti). Ru. יְיֵלִילוּ.—עַל־כ'] Gr. וְעַל־כ'.—6. אותו] 𝕲 takes as obj. of an inserted δήσαντες, which GAS. accepts as belonging to original text.—יובל] 𝕲 ἀπήνεγκαν = יוּבִילוּ (so 𝔖𝕿 and Arabic; so also We., Loft., Now., Oet., Marti).—מנחה] 𝕲𝔖 pl. מלך ירב] 𝕲 τῷ βασιλεῖ Ἰαρείμ; 𝔙 *regi ultori;* 'A., Θ. δικάζοντι; Σ. ὑπερμαχοῦντι. For other readings see on 5[13].—בשׁנה] 𝕲 ἐν δόματι = במנה (Vol.); 𝔙 construes as subj. Gr. מַתְּנַת. Gu. and Marti, בֹּשֶׁת. Hal. כְּלִמָּה. Mich. בֻּשָׁנָה.—מעצתו] We. מֵעֲצֹבוֹ (so Val., Now., Marti). Oort (*Em*.), מעצמו.—7. נדמה]

𝕲 ἀπέρριψεν = רמה (Vol.); 𝔙 *transire fecit;* 𝔖 ܠܡܚ̈ = רמה (Seb.); some codd. of de R. נִרְמָה (so Oet.). Cornelius à Lapide, ירפה. Cappellus, נרמה.— שמרון] Hal. מִשׁ׳. Che. (*EB.* II. 2125, note), מִקְרָשׁ.— בקצף] 𝕲 ὡς φρύγανον; so 𝔖. Gr. בַּחֶמֶף. We. כקצב. Che. (*loc. cit.*), om. as corrupt dittog. of preceding מקרש (*v.s.*).— על פני מים] Che. (*loc. cit.*), גאון אפרים.— 8. [חטאת 𝕲𝔗 = pl.; so some codd. of de R. We. om. ח און as gloss (so Ru., Now., Marti), while Che. (*CB.*) om. חטאת ישראל. Gr. suggests that בית has been lost from before און, because of likeness to מות.— עלינו] 𝔖𝔗 have suff. in 3d p.

X. 1. *A luxuriant vine is Israel*] *i.e.* a vine running luxuri- antly, sending out shoots, a fruitful vine, prosperous.* With this may be compared the view † that makes Israel a pillaged vine, *i.e.* stripped of its fruit, which, however, after the robbing will lay up fruit for itself; and the very common view ‡ which renders בקק *empty*, *i.e.* one which pours out into leaves, but has no fruit. This statement is an extension of 9[10. 16]; cf. the vine סרחת, Ez. 17[6]. Halévy makes בקק predicate with the meaning *lay waste, destroy* (cf. Is. 24[1] Na. 2[2]) = *Israel lays waste the vine which has fur- nished him its fruit;* but this is not supported by the history of interpretation, nor by analogy (*v.s.*).—*He multiplies fruit for him- self*] The thought here is obscure. The following have been suggested : (1) *Which yields fruit for itself*, referring to the vine ; § (2) *Who yields fruit for himself*, referring to Israel; ‖ (3) *He putteth forth his fruit*; ¶ (4) *And the fruit is like him*; ** (5) *Her (the vine's) fruit flourishing* (so 𝕲 using perhaps שלו or ישלה; cf. Zc. 7[7] Jb. 21[23] Ps. 73[12] 122[6] Ez. 16[49].) But none of these gives an adequate sense. Perhaps the rendering given above †† (reading ישניא), which furnishes an idea corresponding to בקק of the preceding line, may be adopted. G. A. Smith (using שוה or שיה) renders, " he lavishes his fruit," while Gardner's read- ing gives just the opposite, " an evil fruit is his."—*In proportion to the increase of his fruit he multiplied altars ; in proportion to the prosperity of his land, he made beautiful the pillars*] *i.e.* the more fruit, the more altars did he build ; the more prosperous the land, the more beautiful were the pillars (or statues) which he

---

* 𝕲𝔙, Theod., Bauer, Ma., Hi., Ew., Sim., Ke., Schm., Or., Che., GAS., BDB., Now.   † Cal.   ‡ 𝔗, AE., Schmidt, Os., Ros., Pu., Sharpe.
§ Ma., Hi., Ke., Or., RV.   ¶ Hd.   †† Oet.
‖ Ew., Pu.   ** 𝔙, Mich.

erected.[*] This points to a recognition by the prophet of the
influence exerted on Israel by the agricultural life which Israel
had come to adopt, for with this life there came the influence of
the Baal-cult. On the pillars, or maṣṣebahs, *v.* on 3^4.— **2.** *Their
heart is false*] Was their heart " divided," resting now on Baal,
and now on Yahweh?[†] Or was it not rather " slippery, false,
deceitful "[‡] (*v.s.* for text), since Hosea particularly inveighed
against a certain kind of Yahweh-worship? Cf. the use of the
word with reference to tongue, lip, mouth, throat, and speech
(Ps. 5^9 12^3 55^{21} Pr. 5^3 and in Ez. 12^{24}, where in parallelism
stands (חזון שוא . . . מקסם חלק).—*Now must they bear punishment
for it*[§]] Other renderings are : be guilty, [||] deserve punish-
ment,[¶] suffer,[**] be punished.[††] Ruben's hostile tribes (*v.s.*)
seem to be the offspring of a fertile imagination. *Now* is logical
= *consequently.* — (*But*) *he will break the neck of their altars ; he
will ruin their pillars*] " Breaking the neck " is a strong figure in
this connection. It is unnecessary to suppose there is any reference to the striking off of horns (Am. 3^{14}) ; [‡‡] the word used
elsewhere only of animals is here used metaphorically. The parallelism of order between these lines and the first of the strophe
is to be noted. This representation of punishment is in contrast
with the picture of prosperity just presented. — **3.** *For soon
they will say : we have no king*] This confession is clearly inconsistent with the context and dates from a later period, probably
the exile. The inconsistencies of vs.[3 and 4], as pointed out by
Nowack and Marti, [§§] are : (1) they furnish an entirely different
explanation for the coming judgment, as compared with vs.[5 to 8] ;
(2) the lack of fear of Yahweh is not a true charge against the
Israel of Hosea's time ; (3) עתה in v.[2] refers to the present or
immediate future, but in v.[3] to a more remote future ; (4) they
break the connection of thought between vs.[2 and 5], which are both
concerned with the destruction of Israel's high places. If from
the exile, the phrase *we have no king* means what it says ; if from

---

* So Ew., Ke., Or., *et al.*   ¶ Bauer.
† Mich., Bauer, Hi., Hd., Pu., Or., RV.   ** Ew.
‡ We., Val., Now., GAS., Marti.   †† Hd.
§ Hi., Sim., Ke., We., Gu., GAS., Now.   ‡‡ We., Che., Marti.
|| Cal.   §§ *Rel.* 168 and *Dodekapropheton ;* so also Ru.; but cf. Now.[2]

an earlier period, it means, we have no king worthy of the name
or from whom help can come, *i.e.* an expression of despair.* Cf.
(1) the view which places the sermon in the interregnum following the death of Jeroboam II.; † (2) the view that makes the
basis of this statement, the fact that all of Israel's kings were
established in opposition to Yahweh; ‡ and (3) the view that
makes the statement interrogative, *Have we not a king? i.e.* the
king of Egypt. § — *For Yahweh we have not feared*] This is the
evident point of inconsistency with the context. No Israelite of
Hosea's time could have acknowledged that he did not fear
Yahweh; as a matter of fact he was engaged most assiduously in
a worship every part of which pointed in this direction. The
expression is not one of Hosea's time, but comes from that later
age when rightly it might have been uttered. — *And the king,
what could he do for us?*] For עשה, cf. Ec. 2². If [3a] means, *we
have no king*, this means, *if we had a king, what could he do;* if [3a]
means, we have no king worthy of the name, [3b] means, what can
the king we have do for us? In either case the answer is nothing.
— **4.** *Speaking words, swearing false oaths, making bargains*]
With דַּבֵּר the infinitive absolute (*v.s.;* cf. 4²; $\mathfrak{G}$ = דֹּבֵר) we have
speaking words, i.e. mere words, words from the lips (Is. 36⁵ 58¹³)
in which there is no truth, — falsehoods (Is. 29²¹). On *swearing
false oaths,*‖ cf. 4²; on *making bargains, i.e.* making covenants,
cf. 5¹³ 7¹¹; not in the ordinary affairs of life; ¶ nor with the
sanction of idols;** but rather with the great powers, Assyria
(or Babylon) and Egypt; †† cf. 10⁶ 12¹. — *And law springs
forth like weeds in the furrows of the field*] We expect here
the punishment which is to be inflicted for the conduct described in the preceding clause; but, as Nowack has pointed
out,‡‡ (1) משפט does not mean judgment in the sense of infliction, execution, but *right* (cf. 5¹¹, also Am. 5⁷·¹⁵·²⁴ 6¹²), an
indefinite term without special application; (2) the comparison
כראש is hardly clear or satisfactory; (3) while *on the furrows
of the field* fits in well in 12¹², it is here awkward, being sep-

---

* Mau., Ew., Hd., Sim., Or.

† Mich., *et al.*

‡ Hi., Pu., Ke., Che., *et al.*

** Ros.

§ Dathe; cf. Schmidt.

‖ See Coffin, *JBL.*, 1900, p. 107.

¶ Pu.

†† Mau., Hd., Ke., Che., Or., Schm.; Val. *ZAW.* XIII. 247.   ‡‡ Cf. Ke.

arated from ראש, to which it belongs. Perhaps this is a continuation of the preceding picture of wickedness, and in this case (1) *law* may be used in the sense of *lawsuit*;* or (2) *law* may be used ironically in the sense of *legal injustice*,† cf. Am. 6[12]; or (3), after all, *punishment*, which shall be as bitter (cf. Dt. 29[18] La. 3[19] Je. 9[15]), and as plenteous as ראש.‡ Cf. ⅁'s interpretation = *grass*. It has been suggested by Nowack that either another word be substituted for משפט, which shall mean "evil," or that הפכו לראש be read after Am. 6[12] (cf. Ho. 4[2]), *i.e. and judgment they turn to poppy;* but (3) above seems satisfactory. Cheyne suggests that this judgment began with the man who was foremost in those illegitimate covenants — the prophet's royal namesake, Hoshea (2 K. 17[4]). ראש has been rendered *bitterness*,§ *poppy*,‖ *weeds*,¶ *poison*, or *wormwood*,** *hemlock;* †† and משפט has been emended (*v.s.*) to *murder* or *backsliding*,‡‡ *falsehood, like thistles*,§§ *destruction*.‖‖ — **5.** *For the calf of Beth-aven the inhabitants of Samaria shall tremble*] We come back now to the original utterance, and to the beginning of the second 8-line strophe. The occasion of the approaching punishment is here stated to be the worship of the calf (cf. the different representation in v.[4a]). The connection with v.[2b] is very close. While now Israel identifies the calf-image with Yahweh, the prophet sees no relationship between them. There are no words too scornful for him to use of the calf. *Calf* (cf. ⅁) is to be preferred to *calves*, because of the singular suffix in עמיו and כמריו and because probably only one image was set up in each place. For explanations of this feminine plural, see p. 348. Beth-aven is probably ironical and contemptuous for בית אל, cf. 4[15] Am. 7[14].¶¶ On שכן, *v.i.* Cheyne's *bemoan* instead of *tremble for* is interesting in view of the parallelism. For other readings, *v.s.* — *Yea, his people shall mourn for him*] The perfect, if retained, is prophetic; perhaps the imperfect should be read (*v.s.*). — *And his priestlings shall writhe for him*] יחילו for יגילו, *v.s.* The word כמר is used only of idol-priests; cf. 2 K. 23[5] Zp. 1[4]. In Syriac and Aramaic

---

* GAS.	‖ *Thes.*, Hd., Che.	‡‡ Oet.
† Ke.	¶ Ew., Or., GAS.	§§ Ru.
‡ Ew., Hd., Che.	** Ki.	‖‖ Hal.
§ ⅁.	†† AV.	¶¶ Kö. *Stil.* 297 f.

it is used of priests in general without discrimination between those of the true God and those serving idols. It is perhaps to be connected with the Assyr. *kamâru, to lay prostrate*, the priest being *one who prostrated himself.** It is evidently used here as a term of contempt. The interpretation *rejoice* is impossible. — *On account of his glory, that it is banished from him*] Cf. 1 S. 4²². This is an insertion from a later hand, as is evident from the fact that the suffix cannot possibly go back to עגל, although this is intended, and the connection with what follows is impossible.†
— **6.** *Yea, this they will carry to Assyria*] The emphatic word *this* (אותו) refers to the image. — *As a present to king Jareb*] Probably a gloss based on 5¹³, *v.s.* It was not uncommon to carry presents of gold and silver from the temple to a foreign king; cf. 2 K. 12¹⁸ 16⁸ 18¹⁵ᶠ. — *Ephraim shall take disgrace, and Israel shall be ashamed because of his counsel*] The reading מֵעֲצָבּוֹ = *because of his idol* (*v.s.*) is good, but not necessary. Shame and reproach will rest upon Israel for the counsel which has been adopted as the basis of the national policy. — **8a.** *The high places of Aven shall be destroyed, the sin of Israel*] This arrangement of the verses prevents the interruption of the thought, and preserves the climax. Perhaps the reading, *the high places of Israel shall be destroyed*, both און and חטאת being taken as glosses (*v.s.*), is better. — *Thorn and thistle shall come up on their altars*] Cf. 9⁶. — **7.** *As for Samaria, her king is cut off*] This is better than to put *king* with the following clauses. ‡ The perfect is prophetic; cf. 8⁸. No particular king is intended; nor is the reference to an idol-god. § — *Like a chip on the face of the waters*] *i.e.* tossed about, without ability to move in a definite path. קצף means *chip*, ‖ rather than *foam.*¶ — **8 b.** *And they shall say to the mountains cover us; and to the hills, fall on us*] This petition goes up in order that they may not fall into the power of their enemies (cf. Lk. 23³⁰ Rev. 6¹⁶ 9¹⁶).

1. בקק] But for the context and the general usage in this figure (*v.s.*), it would be unjustifiable to adopt here a meaning found nowhere else; and

---

* Cf. BDB.; Dl. *Hebr. Lang.*, 40 ff.; Che.   ‡ Wü., We., Gu., Now., GAS.
† We., Now., Oet.   § Hess.
‖ 𝔊𝔖, Ki., Theod., Ma., Hi., Ew., Hd., Pu., Ke., Or., Che., Now., Marti.
¶ 𝔙𝔗, Σ., Rashi, Marck, Umb.

yet the Arabic بَقّ = to be abundant (v. Lane), furnishes good ground for this interpretation. BSZ. treats this case as an intrans. of the same בקק (found in Is. 24¹ and elsewhere, to empty) = to pour oneself out, to spread out. From this root Jabbok, the river, is probably named. — ישוה] Cf. GAS. I. 286, note; Barth, ES. p. 66. — כ] On the more . . . the more, Kö. 371 o. — רב] Is inf. cstr. fol. by ל, indicating dative of advantage (cf. Dt. 1⁶ 2³ 3²⁶, etc.); Kö. 286 d, 402 t, 407 c; and not subst. in cstr. before a gen. with ל, cf. Ew.⁸ 295 a. — שוב] Inf. cstr. like רב (v.s.). — הושיבו] Pl., while הרבה is sg.; Kö. 346 d. — 2. חלק] This is not the Pu'al (ב⤬𝔗, Hi.) of חלק = خَلَقَ, measure off; cf. Assyr. eklu, field, cf. Is. 33²³ Zc. 14¹ (Jäger, BAS. II. 296); nor Qäl of חלק = خَلَقَ, make smooth, lie (Ke., Wü., We., RVm.); but probably an adj. from latter, viz. חָלָק; cf. Pr. 5³. — עתה] Lit., at the time, an acc. of עת; cf. اَلآنَ, at the time, now. Here without ו, used of present or immediate future, a favorite construction of Hosea; cf. 4¹⁶ 5⁷ 8⁸·¹³. — יאשמו] On ☰, GK. 63 e. On the dagh. in ש, GK. 13 c. On impf. of obligation, H. 22, 3 b; Dr. § 39. אשם = to do a wrong (Ez. 25¹²); then to be guilty (cf. 4¹⁵ 13¹); then to be treated as guilty, to receive punishment (cf. 5¹⁵ 14¹). Here in this third sense. The word seems to be a favorite with Hosea. — יערף] A denom. vb. from ערף, neck; on the privative force of denom. vbs. (cf. Pi'ēl) GK. 52 h. The other cases, Ex. 13¹³ 34²⁰ Dt. 21⁴·⁶ Is. 66³, all refer to the breaking of the neck of an animal, e.g. calf, dog. — הוא] Emph. — 3. כי עתה] The ordinary meaning, for then, does not fit here; it refers to an action in the future and = at that time = soon (v.s.). — 4. דברים] Cogn. acc. = emph. — אלות] For אָלֹה, the usual form of inf. abs.; here with ה under influence of כרת, cf. Is. 22¹³; GK. 75 n; Kö. 402 e. On this use of inf. abs., H. 28, 5 a; GK. 113 ff. — ופרח] Pf. with wāw cons., continuing inf. abs., Kö. 367 o. — משפט] Cf. Sellin, Beiträge, II. 252; Sm. Rel. 389 f.; Duhm, Theol. 114 f. — ראש] See on Am. 6¹². — שדי] Art. omitted, Kö. 293 a; cf. this form with שדה. — עגלות] Read עגל (v.s.); the only case of the fem. used of the calf-idols in North Israel. The fem. pl. of ⤬𝔗 (cf. the masc. suff. of the vs.) has been explained (1) as heifers for calves used contemptuously (Jer., Cal., Bauer, Pu.); (2) because the images were those of young animals in which sex was not prominent (Sim.); (3) because they were lifeless, man-made things, cf. GK. 122 u (Ki.); (4) as an expression of indefinite generality, the fem. being the proper form for the abstract (Ke.). — שכן] Sg. with preceding predicate pl., Kö. 349 f. — כמריו] Suf. collective, Kö. 348 v. — 6. אותו] On acc. with pass. according to ⤬𝔗 (cf. Zc. 13⁶), GK. 121 b; Kö. 110; as obj. of יובל (𝕲), its position is emphatic. — בשנה] From בוש with affix ן shortened from an; Ew.⁸ 163 f; cf. Barth, NB. 210 c; Kö. II. i. p. 185. Perhaps בּשֵׁת should be read (v.s.). — 7. נרמה] Ptcp., perhaps to be read, ונרמה; Kö. 349 p. This same word occurs also in 4⁶ 10¹⁵. — שמרון מלכה] The order of words is difficult unless with Kö. 349 p (cf. 330 p) we suppose ו to have dropped out before the labial מ and read (v.s.) Samaria and her king;

cf. Ex. 8²⁰ᵇ Dt. 32⁸ᵇ, etc.—נפלו] Masc. for fem., the obj. added being fem.,
Kö. 205 c.

§ 14. Israel's history consists of sin, guilt; the fruit of such seed is a sad harvest, desolation, destruction, and death,— even of the king. 10⁹⁻¹⁵.

From the days of Gibeah, Israel has
sinned : Ephraim is a heifer desiring to tread the corn, but I will
spoil her beauty with a yoke upon her neck, and she shall be made
to draw, to plough, and to harrow (⁹·¹¹). Sow in righteousness
and reap in love ; break off evil habits ; there is still time to seek
Yahweh and obtain his favor ; (I exhort you thus) for hitherto you
have sowed wickedness and reaped punishment ; you have made
it your policy to lie, and to trust in chariots and warriors (¹²·¹³ᵃ).
But for this reason ruin is coming, tumult, the destruction of
fortune ; and in a morning your king shall be cut off (¹³ᵇ·¹⁴·¹⁵).

This piece consists of three strophes, each having seven lines of the trimeter movement. The strophic structure and measure prove conclusively that
the piece is entirely distinct from 10¹⁻⁸, although treating of the same subject.
For that matter, all of the chapters now treat of the same subject. Strophe 1
brings up out of the past "days of Gibeah," when Israel sinned; however
beautiful and prosperous she may be, hard burdens are before her — burdens
which will prove very heavy (vs.⁹·¹¹ᵃ). Strophe 2 recites the fact that it is
not too late to secure Yahweh's favor, if the right methods are followed, if
old habits are broken off; but to this end an entire change of policy will be
demanded in comparison with that of the past, in which deceit and faithlessness to Yahweh have been the principal elements (vs.¹²·¹³ᵃ). Strophe 3
pictures the ruin which for this reason is coming quickly and surely — a ruin
that will involve land, city, and king (vs.¹³ᵇ·¹⁴ᵃ·¹⁵). In this arrangement,
vs.¹⁰·¹⁴ᵇ are regarded as later additions (v.i.).

9. מימי] Gr. כימי (so Marti, *Rel.* 168).— הגבעה] 𝔊 οἱ βουνοὶ = הגבעות;
⅏ ܘ.ܒ݂ܐܓܠ.— חטאת] 𝔖𝔗 take as 2d p. of vb; 𝔊𝔙 = 3d p. Gr. חטָא (so Oort
(*Em.*)). Ru. חטאתָ. Read חטאת (We., Now.).—עמדו] We. בגדו. Gr. מערו.
Hal. אמרו. Oet. מרדו. Gardner, יברו.—לא] Oort (*Em.*), ולא. תשינג] Linder
(*SK.* XXXIII. 747), תסינג. Gr. and Hal. תשיגנו. Gardner, השיגה.—בגבעה]
Gr. כגבעה. Oort (*Em.*) om. Marti om. בגבעה ... חטאת as a gloss.— על] Read,
with Gr., Ru., Now., עלי. Gardner, אל.—על בני עלוה] Transfer to follow עמדו
(so Ru., Now.). Ru. inserts after this phrase, וישימו עגל בבית אל (cf. 1 K. 12²⁹).
Dathe joins to v.¹⁰ (so Oort, Oet.).—10. באותי ואסרם] 𝔊 παιδεῦσαι αὐτούς,
omitting בא and joining וא = יסרם (Vol.) to v.⁹. 𝔊ᴺ and some codd. render
בא by ἦλθε = באתי; ⅏ ܘ ܠ݂ ܐ ܘܒ ; probably ⅏ should
be corrected to ܘܒ݂ܐ݂ ܣ = בעברתי (Seb.; so also Gr., Ru., Now.). Oort

(*Em.*), בָּאתִי וַאֲסֻרֵם וְאֶאֱסֹף (so Marti; Dathe and Oet. also read וְבָאתִי). Hal.
ב'. אֶאֱסְרֵם Read בְּעָבְרָתִי אֲיַסְּרֵם (so Gr., Now.). — [בַּאסרם 𝕲 ἐν τῷ παιδεύεσθαι
αὐτοὺς = ביסרם; cf. Ps. 132¹, עֻנּוֹתוֹ (Vol.); 𝕾 مَدْرُوَمَا = מכֹ = בחוסרם (Seb.;
so also Oet.). Oort om. as dittog. We. לְיַסְּרָם (so Oort (*Em.*)). Hal. בְּאָסְרָם
(= בְּהֵאָסְרָם). — [לְשָׁתֵּי עִינֹתָם Qᵉrᵉ לְ עֵינֹתָם (so also Scholz, Gr., Gu., Now., Oet.,
et al.); so 𝕲. Hal. ע' יִשָּׂאוּ. Oort, וּלְעֵנִיתָם BSZ. לְ עֵינֹתָם (cf. 𝔗). Marti
om. בַּאס' לַע'. — 11. [וְאֶפְרַיִם 𝕲 om. ו (so also Now.). — [מַלְמֹדָה Om. as a gloss
(so We., Now.). Hal. לֹא מל'. — [לָדוּשׁ 𝕲 νεῖκος = דִין (Vol.). — [עָבַרְתִּי Hal.
עֲבַרְתִּי (cf. 1 K. 6²¹). Ru. om. as dittog. from v.¹⁰ (𝕾). Marti, הֶעֱבַרְתִּי עֹל עַל.
— [טוּב 𝕾 om. — [אַרְכִּיב Insert וְעַתָּה before אר'. Oort (*ThT.*) and Val.
וָאֶרְכִּיבָה; but, in *Em.*, אֶרְכַּב. Ru. substitutes אר' for preceding עב', and inserts
עֹל as its obj. — [אֶפְרַיִם Ru. om. — [יַחֲרוֹשׁ 𝕲 παρασιωπήσομαι = אחריש; 'A.,
Θ. ἀλοήσει; 𝕾 سُلَامَا = ידוש (?) (Seb.). — [יְהוּדָה Read, with Now., ישראל.
— [יְשַׂדֶּד 𝕲 ἐνισχύσει = ישׂרר (Vol.); 𝕾 نَصَبَ = לֹו — 𝕾 om. Gr. לֹי. — לפרי
12. [לִצְדָקָה 𝕾 renders as an accusative. — [לְפִי חֶסֶד 𝕲 εἰς καρπὸν ζωῆς = לפרי
חיים. Read לפרי חסד — [נִירוּ לָכֶם נִיר 𝕲 φωτίσατε ἑαυτοῖς φῶς; so 𝕾; 𝕽 *in-
novate vobis novale.* — [וְעֵת 𝕲 γνώσεως = דַעַת (so also Oort, *ThT.* and *Em.*,
Val., Oet.). Ru. וְעֵת (cf. Dt. 9²¹). — [לִדְרוֹשׁ 𝕲 ἐκζητήσατε. Ru. דִּרְשׁוּ. — [עַד
Gr. עֵד. — [וְיוֹרֶה Read, with 𝕲, γενήματα, פְּרִי (so also Oort, We., Val., Now.).
𝕽 *qui docebit;* similarly, 𝕾𝔗. Ru. וְיוֹרֶר (cf. Jo. 2²⁸). — [צֶדֶק 𝕾 = צִדְקוֹ (so
also Ru.). — [לָכֶם 𝕲 ἡμῖν. Oort, לָמֶה (cf. 𝕲), joining it to v.¹⁸. — 13. [חֲרַשְׁתֶּם
𝕲 ἵνα τί παρεσιωπήσατε = לָמֶה וגו', perhaps dittog. from לָכֶם. 𝕾 con-
nects with preceding. — [אֲכַלְתֶּם Ru. וַאֲכַלְתֶּם. — [בְּדַרְכְּךָ 𝕲 ἐν τοῖς ἁμαρτήμα-
σίν σου, a corruption of ἅρμασι = בְּרִכְבְּךָ, which occurs in 𝕲ᴬ𝕼; so read with
Ma., Dathe, Eich., Ew., Duhm (*Theol.* 130), Houtsma, We., Or., Che., Gr., Ru.,
Loft., Gu., GAS., Volz, Now., Oort (*Em.*), Oet., Hal. — [גִּבּוֹרֶיךָ 𝕲 δυνάμεώς
σου = גבורתך (Vol.); so 𝕾. — 14. [עֲמִיךָ 𝕲𝕾𝔼, sg. We. בְּעַמֶּיךָ (so Gr., Ru.,
Oet., Che. (*CB.*), Hal.; cf. Marti). Oort (*Em.*), בְּעַמֶּךָ. — [יוּשַּׁד 𝕲 οἰχήσε-
ται = ישׁר (Vol.). We. יֻשְׁדוּ (so Oet., Marti). — [כִּשֹׁד 𝕲 ὡς ἄρχων = כְּשַׂר;
'A. ὡς προνομή; Σ. καθὼς ἠφανίσθη. — [שַׁלְמַן 𝕲 Σαλαμάν; 'A. ἀπηρτισμένη;
𝕽 *Salmana;* 𝕾 حَلْمَا ; Syr.-Hex. = צלמנע. Che. (*Exp.,* Nov., '97, p. 364,
and art. "Beth Arbel," *EB.*), שַׁלּוּם. N. Herz (*AJSL.* XIV. 207 f.), צֶלֶם. —
[בֵּית אַרְבֵאל 𝕲 ἐκ τοῦ οἴκου Ἱεροβοάμ = בֵּית יָרָבְעָם (so also Che. *loc. cit.;* cf.
Gr. מִבּ' יר'); 𝕾 كَمَا كَمَا مَنْ ; 𝕽 *a domo ejus qui vindicavit Baal;*
𝕲ᴬ Ἱεροβαάλ; 'A. τοῦ οἴκου τοῦ δικάζοντος; Σ. ἐν τῷ οἴκῳ τοῦ Ἀρβεήλ; Θ. ἐνέ-
δρου; 𝔗 בְּכִמְנָא. N. Herz, מבית אַרְבָּעֵאל, reference being made to Ju., chaps. 17,
18. — [יוֹם 𝕲 pl. — [רֻטָּשָׁה 𝕲 ἠδάφισαν = רֻטְּשׁוּ (Vol.); so 𝕾. — 15. [עָשָׂה Read,
with 𝕲, ποιήσω, אֶעֱשֶׂה (so also We., Gr., Ru., Now., Oort (*Em.*), Oet., Marti);
𝕾 = עָשׂוּ. Hal. יֵעָשֶׂה. — [בֵּיתְאֵל Read, with 𝕲, οἶκος τοῦ Ἰσραήλ, בֵּית ישראל (so
also Oort (*ThT.* and *Em.*), We., Gr., Gu., Ru., GAS., Now., Oet., Marti). —
[רָעַת Oort (*ThT.* and *Em.*) and Gr. om. as dittog.; so 𝕲ᴬ𝕼. — [רָעֲתְכֶם
𝕲𝔼𝔗 pl. Hal. מַעֲשֵׂיכֶם or עֲצָתְכֶם. — [בַּשַּׁחַר Some codd. of Kenn. and de R.
כ"שׁ (so also Oort, Gr.); so some codd. of 𝕲, ὡς ὄρθρος. Oort (*Em.*), בשׂערה
(cf. We., Now.², Marti). Ru. כְּעַנַן שַׁחַר. — [נִדְמֹה נ' 𝕲 ἀπερίφησαν ἀπερίφη

‎נדמו נרמה‎ =; cf. 10⁷ (Vol.); 𝔊𝔖𝔙 connect last clause of v.¹⁵ with 11¹.
'A. κατεσιωπήθη. Ru. ‎אֲנָֽנֵם וְנִרְמֶה‎.

9. *From the days of Gibeah is Israel's sin*] *i.e.* the sin (‎חַטַּאת‎
for ‎חָטָֽאת‎ because the address is not continued *) of Israel is
something which goes back to earliest times.   But what is meant
by the days of Gibeah, *from* which (not *more than in which,*† nor
as in which = ‎כ,ימי‎,‡ Israel now sins) this sin dates?   Three
answers have been given : (1) The episode of the Benjamites at
Gibeah (Ju. 19²²) ; § but since there Israel (the eleven tribes)
was taking vengeance on one tribe (Benjamin) for an infamous
act, and here Israel is represented as committing sin, the allusion
is inappropriate ‖ (cf., however, Cheyne's statement : " True, Israel as a people took summary vengeance on the Benjamites for
the outrage of Gibeah ; but the seed of wickedness remained,
and developed into evil practices worthy only of the Gibeah of
old "). (2) The beginning of the kingdom under Saul which
occurred in Gibeah ¶ (cf. 13¹⁰·¹¹), which (according to Wellhausen) Hosea seems to regard as a sin perhaps second only to the
cult ; but does Hosea as a matter of fact oppose the kingdom as
such?   Is it not rather the schism?   (3) The idolatry of Micah
(Ju. 17³ ff.), which marked the beginning, according to tradition,
of that which has now spread so far and wide.** — *At that time
there stood against me the sons of unrighteousness*] This rendering
involves the reading of ‎עלי‎ for ‎על‎, and the transfer of ‎עלי בני עולה‎
from the end of the verse to follow ‎עמדו‎,†† a change which permits
the passage to give a sensible meaning, and relieves two lines, one
of which is too short, the other too long.   ‎שם‎ is here temporal ‡‡
rather than local ; cf. 2 K. 15²⁰ Ps. 14⁵.   The sons of unrighteousness are either the Benjamites (*v.s.*), the Israelites as a whole in
the case of the selection of Saul, or those associated with Micah.
Wellhausen's suggestion, ‎בגרו‎, is unnecessary.   Other interpretations of ‎עמדו‎ are : " stood still," as if Ephraim had acted traitor-
ously (cf. the great defeat of the eleven tribes, Ju. 20¹⁹⁻²⁵) ; §§ " have

---

* We., Now.   ‡ Ma., Gr., Meier (*SK.* XV. 1030).
† AE., Bauer, Ros., Sim.   § Mich., Mau., Hd., Pu., Ke., Or., GAS., *et al.*
‖ Now.   ¶ 𝔗, Sharpe, We., Now.; Sm. *Rel.* 219.
** Jer.   †† Ru., Now.   ‡‡ Hi., Sim.   §§ Mich.

remained (*i.e.* sinful), should there not overtake them in Gibeah a war against the sons of wrong?"* "stood firm against the sons of wrong," in contrast with present attitude; † "there they stand (now) defiant like the old Benjamites." ‡ For interpretations involving textual change, *v.s.* — *Shall not war overtake them even in Gibeah?*] Interpreters (*e.g.* Ruben) have been greatly perplexed to find any meaning for this line. The removal to the preceding line of עלי בני עולה seems to relieve somewhat the difficulty. § This difficulty is seen, *e.g.*, in G. A. Smith's rendering, "there have they remained, and this without war overtaking them in Gibeah against the dastards;" also Cheyne's, "there they stood that the war against the sons of unrighteousness might not overtake them at Gibeah," — both utterly unintelligible, even with the authors' additional remarks. The sense of the rendering adopted above is easy and natural. Inasmuch as they have sinned, beginning at Gibeah, war shall overtake them, reaching down even to Gibeah; *i.e.* a war which, coming from the north, shall cover the whole land, and reach even to the southernmost limit, Gibeah; ‖ for Gibeah was most probably situated about four miles north of Jerusalem, where the *Tell-el-Fūl* now stands.¶ —
10. *In my wrath I will chastise them*] A reading based on 𝔖 (*v.s.*). Other interpretations are : **(1)** 𝔊𝔄 "against the children of unrighteousness I have come (= בָּאתִי) to chastise them;" ** **(2)** most common, "in my desire," "at my will," "when I desire," cf. Is. 1²⁴ Ez. 5¹³ 16⁴².†† — *And peoples shall be gathered against them*] It is this sentence, together with the strophic structure, that makes the authenticity of the verse suspicious. The indefinite "peoples" marks a later date, it being the invariable custom of the prophets down to Ezekiel to name distinctly the hostile country intended. Hosea always indicates Egypt or Assyria. ‡‡ Giesebrecht (*Beiträge zur Jesaia-Kritik*), in support

---

* Marck, Ew., Umb., Hd., GAS. † Sim., Pu. ‡ Or.

§ Perhaps Hal. has come still nearer to the true solution in his rendering: "there they said (אמרו) : the war against the sons of iniquity shall not reach us (נו_) as (it has reached) Gibeah (כגבעה)." Worthy of note also is Oort's suggestion (based on 𝔊) : "Against the sons of iniquity (connecting these words with v.¹⁰), I come (באתי) and I will chastise them." ‖ Ru., We., Now.

¶ Cf. Robinson, *Bib. Res.* I. 577 ff.; Stenning in *DB.*; Now. ** Cf. Oort.

†† 𝔙, Ki., Rashi, Cal., Bauer, Or., Che., Reuss, GAS., RV. ‡‡ Cf. Now. *in loc.*

of Hosea's authorship, cites Is. 8^9 29^7 Mi. $4^{11\,ff.}$ Je. $3^{17\,f.}$. But Mi. $4^{11\,ff.}$ is late (v. in loc.), and Je. $3^{17\,f.}$ is suspicious (v. Duhm in loc.), while in Is. 8^9 29^7 עמים probably refers to the various peoples constituting Assyria's armies (cf. Stade, ZAW. IV. 260). Some read (v.s.), And I will gather, etc.— To chastise them for their double sin] Reading לְיַסְּרָם לשתי עֲוֹנתָם (v.s.), following 𝔊 and 𝔖.* Both words of 𝔐𝔗 have been in doubt, and interpretations have varied according to the reading of the text; e.g. (1) "When they have bound themselves (אסר) in two furrows" (עונה ; cf. מענה, 1 S. 14^{14} Ps. 129^3),† a reference to ploughing; i.e. however Israel might join together and thus strengthen themselves, Yahweh could easily gather people and destroy them; (2) when I give them over to captivity (אסר) because of their two sins; ‡ (3) when I chastise them, etc.; § (4) when I chastise them before both their eyes (using the kᵉthîbh), i.e. openly, in the sight of the heathen, ‖ but עֵינוֹת means "fountains," not "eyes" (cf. Ewald, who assumes a Syriac plural, עֵינוֹת, and Schultens, Animadversiones phil. (v. Wünsche), who reads ad potationes (שתי) fontium eorum); (5) when they are bound to their two transgressions.¶ What now are the two sins? The idolatry of Micah and Jeroboam?** The calves of Dan and Bethel?†† Apostasy from Yahweh and acceptance of idols? ‡‡ Rather, the cult and, not the desertion of David's house (3^5), §§ but (with Nowack) the establishment of the kingdom.—
11. Ephraim, indeed, is a heifer loving to thresh] מלמדה, well trained, is a gloss, for it is inappropriate beside אהבתי ‖‖ (cf. Halévy, who inserts לא = untrained, cf. Je. 31^{18}). Israel, in her past history, is compared to a young heifer to whom is assigned the easy task of walking round and round the threshing-floor, an occupation that carries with it the privilege of eating freely, for no muzzle was allowed (Dt. 25^4). This pleasing and delightful work she is still doing; cf. again Halévy, who (following the hint given in 𝔊, νεῖκος) interprets דּוּשׁ as in Hb. 3^{12}, strike with the foot, i.e.

---

* Cf. Ew.

† 𝔗, AE., Ki., Cal., Sim., Pu., AV., BSZ.; cf. Mich. ("ploughshares").

‡ Dathe, Bauer, Hi., Umb., Hd.   § Che.

‖ Here again Hal. interestingly suggests (v.s.), "in their being chastised they will expiate their sins."

¶ Or., RV.   †† Dathe, Hi., Marti.   §§ Hes., Ke., Wü., Che.

** Jer.   ‡‡ Theod.   ‖‖ We., Now.

to hurt or injure. — *And even I myself have spared the beauty of her neck*] Upon the rendering of עבר turns the decision between this translation and a second having almost the opposite meaning, viz. " but I have come on her fair neck," * or " but I will come," etc.,† or "I will pass on beside her fair neck," ‡ as a driver beside his ox. § The rendering given ‖ is to be preferred because (1) it continues the thought of the preceding member, and thus divides the strophe more satisfactorily as between the description of Israel's past and her future ; (2) the real transition is marked by the ועתה, to be supplied (for various reasons) in the following line ; (3) this usage of עבר *to pass by* is fully justified by its occurrence in Mi. 7¹⁸ Pr. 19¹¹, cf. Am. 7⁸ 8², although commonly in this sense ל follows with the person ; (4) " it adds a beautiful distinctness to the figure, for the heavy yokes used in the East not only gall the necks of the animals, but often produce deep wounds " (Cheyne) ; (5) the rendering "come over on," or "pass over" ¶ (cf. 1 S. 14⁴ (על) 14¹ Ju. 11³² 12³ (אל)) utterly fails to fit the connection ; while (6) ואני, although possibly adversative, is more appropriately emphatic = *and even I myself. — But now I will make Ephraim draw*] This is to be the fate of Israel, viz. captivity, in which heavy labor will take the place of the easy life hitherto enjoyed. רכב in Hiph. = " cause to ride," or " give a rider to," ** but from the context (*i.e.* יחרוש, ישדד), the secondary meaning " draw " or " yoke to " (a plough or cart) is required ; †† no analogy for this occurs ; cf., on the other hand, Halévy, " J'ai placé haut " = "J'ai fait monter sur mes bras " (cf. 11³). — *Israel must plough, Jacob must harrow for himself*] Another kind of work, that which precedes threshing, is now assigned to Israel, viz. the rougher work of ploughing and reaping. Israel (not Judah as in 𝕸) must be intended, ‡‡ for there is nowhere in

---

* GAS. ; and, essentially, Cal., Ma., Ew., Umb., Pu., Wü.

† We., Now.   ‡ Hd.

§ Hal., citing 1 K. 6²¹, renders, " J'ai pourtant bien doucement mis la chaîne à son cou," and contrasts, with this loving and lenient treatment of Israel, Yahweh's more severe attitude towards Judah, whose citizens as slaves will be compelled to hard labor.   ‖ BSZ., Che.   ¶ So Now.

** Ew., Umb., Pu.   †† Mich., Ma., Sim., Ke., Or., Che., GAS., Now., BSZ.

‡‡ Now. ; Seesemann, 20 f. ; cf. Oort and Val., who regard יהודה as originally a marginal note.

the passage even the most remote reference to Judah. This line, with "Israel" instead of "Judah," is original (cf. Marti,* who suggests that יהודה and ארכיב should be omitted as a gloss), since (1) its thought is necessary to complete the picture of Israel's change of occupation, and (2) the line is needed to complete the strophe. No good reason exists for reading לי † instead of לו.

— **12.** *Sow for yourselves righteousness; reap the fruit of love; break up your fallow ground*] Here are given three successive commands, each independent of the others, and all three making up the total of the activity which in the prophet's thought is demanded of Israel. ‡ The second is not to be taken as the consequence of the first; the three are necessary, as the preparatory steps toward *seeking Yahweh*. The figure thus employed to express the desired kind of life is taken from the field of husbandry (cf. 8[7]), with which Israel for so long a time had been familiar : (1) *Sow for yourselves righteousness*, a rendering which makes ל = the accusative, § instead of *according to* or *in*,‖ *i.e.* act righteously, let your deeds be righteous, direct your lives in such manner as that the result will be a proper sense of justice towards your fellows. (2) *Reap the fruit of love*, a rendering which reads לפרי (with ⑤) ¶ for לפי in proportion to,** *i.e.* let your lives be filled with the spirit of love, let the outcome of your activity be characterized by love ; חסד here = not love of God for man, but love of man for fellow-man,†† and with it, love of man for God ; perhaps piety expresses the idea as well as any other English word ; cf. Ho. 4[1] 6[4. 6]. With this interpretation compare that which binds together the two imperatives, זרעו and קצרו, giving them the conditional force *if you will sow . . . you shall reap*,‡‡ a construction in itself entirely legitimate, but not adapted to the context §§ because of the absence of ן and the presence of the third imperative, נירו. (3) *Break up your fallow ground*] Cf. Je. 4[3] Vergil, *Georg.* 1. 71. The third and most significant of the

---

* *Rel.* 119.   † Gr.

‡ Volz, 33 f., questions authenticity of vs.[12. 13 a]; Marti om. v.[12] as a gloss based on Je. 4[3], and also [13 b. 14 a β].

§ ⑤, We., Now., GAS.   †† Hi., Ke. ; cf. Wü., p. 463.

‖ AV., RV., Che., and many others.   ‡‡ Ros., Mau., GAS., *et al.*

¶ Gr., GAS.   ** Che.   §§ Wü.

prophet's injunctions; before sowing the seed prepare the ground which has hitherto been neglected, and in consequence has become full of weeds and thorns, *i.e.* plough virgin soil; in other words, no result may be expected unless the old habits are changed and new character formed.—*Since there is time to seek Yahweh*] *i.e.* there remains sufficient time; * not it is high time to seek.† — *To the end that the fruit of righteousness may come to you*] In favor of this rendering ‡ and the text which underlies it are : (1) 𝔊 (*v.s.*); (2) the recurring phrases " fruit of righteousness " (v.[12]), " fruit of lies " (v.[13]) ; (3) the usage of עד to express purpose (cf. Jb. 14[6] Is. 22[14]); (4) the impropriety of the idea of teaching (יורה הֵ) in this connection. The two most common renderings (upon basis of יורה) are *till he come and rain righteousness*, § for which Is. 45[8] and Ps. 85[11] are cited as analogies; and *till he come and teach you righteousness.*‖ Righteousness here = *salvation, deliverance*, as frequently in Is. 40–66 (cf. Is. 46[12] 54[17] 32[16] 33[5] Dn. 9[24]). " Righteousness is the divine principle *of* action, salvation the divine principle *in* action " (Cheyne).—**13.** *Ye have ploughed wickedness; injustice ye have reaped*] Here, as before, the terms used are not intended to designate consequence; *sow, reap*, and *plough, reap*, represent the ordinary activities, and these are, in effect, wickedness and injustice or disaster. This is in direct contrast with the demands set forth in v.[12].— *Ye have eaten the fruit of lies*] The end of your present policy is already in sight, utter disappointment.— *Because thou dost trust in thy chariots, in the multitude of thy mighty ones*] Here begins a new strophe, as is seen from (1) the change of thought, for כי בטחת must go with the following rather than with the preceding lines, since (*a*) the reason for the disappointment expressed in אכלתם וגו׳ has already been cited in *Ye have ploughed*, etc.; (*b*) the ו in וקאם is resumptive, pointing to an occasion or reason already given; (2) the change of form from second plural to second singular. Nowack's first objection (that the ground of the judgment in v.[14] is by this assigned to something which is not elsewhere emphasized in Hosea) is insufficient, for this is (*a*) only another way of saying

---

that they no longer trust in Yahweh, and (*b*) exactly what Isaiah
in his early sermons (2⁵ ᶠᶠ·) emphasizes so strongly; while his
second objection (that the idea of arrogant self-trust is inconsistent with the actual weakness and hesitation of the time implied
in their throwing themselves into the arms, now of Assyria, now
of Egypt) is contradicted by Isaiah's representation concerning
Judah for the same period (cf. Is. 2⁷). Cf. Wellhausen, who likewise regards the lines as unauthentic. (3) The strophic structure,
which with these lines makes a strophe of seven lines corresponding with the two preceding strophes. Volz * regards vs.¹². ¹³ᵃ as a
later insertion and v.¹¹ as misplaced because (1) they interrupt the
connection, breaking into the middle of a threat of punishment
with a warning accompanied by a promise of deliverance to which
no reference is made in the context; (2) the figure changes, —
in v.¹¹ Judah-Jacob is the animal engaged in agriculture, in v.¹²
it is the sower; (3) there are linguistic difficulties, *e.g.* צדקה, which
occurs only here in Hosea, and צדק denote a right state of heart,
the common meaning in late literature, while in Amos and Isaiah
they refer to external, forensic righteousness; this usage of לפי is
paralleled in Pr. 12⁸ 27²¹; נירו ניר seems more original in Je. 4³
than here; רשע (v.¹³) is a late word; (4) there are echoes of 6³ in
יבוא and יורה and in לדרש את־דעת יהוה (following ⅏). In reply to
these objections, Nowack urges (1) that the original significance
of vs.⁹· ¹⁰ is too uncertain to make the connection of v.¹⁴ with them
certain, and (2) that the deeper significance of צדיק was doubtless
known in early times. The reading, *in thy chariots* (*v.s.*) ברכבך
for בדרכך) rather than *in thy way* † (= in thy policy) is based
upon (1) ⅏ (*v.s.*), Jerome, Syro-Hexaplar text; (2) the parallelism
thy heroes; (3) Ho. 14³ Is. 2⁷; (4) the demands of the entire context. — **14.** *Therefore the tumult* (*of war*) *shall arise among thy
peoples*] The ב with קם may mean *against* (Ps. 27¹² Jb. 16⁸ Mi. 7⁶) ‡
or *in, among.* § The tribes are understood as peoples (cf. Dt. 33³
Lv. 21⁴· ¹⁴ Jo. 2⁶) ; but cf. the suggested emendation (*v.s.*) *in thy*

---

* Pp. 33 f.; cf. also Ru. who regards v.¹² as having "no connection with its surroundings," and as being made up of two fragments, the first of which may, perhaps,
be restored by adding וַאֲכַלְתֶּם פְּרִי אֱמֶת after לפי חסר. Ru. and Grimm, *Lit. App.*
72 f., also reject v.¹².   † Ke., Wü., AV., RV., *et al.*

‡ So Ke., Wü., *et al.*   § Umb., Sim., We., Now., GAS., *et al.*

cities, which is hardly necessary. On *tumult*, cf. Am. 2² Is. 17¹²
Je. 48⁴⁵ (sons of tumult = warriors). — *And all thy fortresses shall
be ruined*] We cannot fail to note here another idea which Isaiah
later develops (cf. 2⁹). The heroes and the fortified cities in
which Israel had put her trust shall be laid waste. — *As Shalman
ruined Beth-arbel in the day of war*] Both proper names have
been the subject of many conjectures. *Beth-arbel* has been identified (1) with the Assyrian Arbela on the Tigris,* but this was
too far away to have produced so strong an impression on the
Israelites; (2) with Arbela near Pella;† (3) with Arbela on the
west of the Sea of Tiberias (cf. 1 Macc. 9²; Jos. *Ant.* XII. 11, 1;
XIII. 15, 4);‡ cf. the corresponding words in the versions
(*v.s.*); 𝔊ᴬ, rendering *Jerubbaal*, interprets the passage of Zalmunna (Ju. chaps. 7 and 8).§ *Shalman* has been identified
with (1) Shalmaneser IV., the name being abbreviated (cf.
Coniah for Jehoiachin, Je. 22²⁴·²⁸ 37¹) for the sake of rhythm,
who became king 727 B.C. and besieged Samaria 724–722;‖
(2) Shalmaneser III., who made an expedition to Lebanon (the
cedar-country) in 775 B. C. and to Damascus in 773–772, when he
may have invaded the country across the Jordan;¶ (3) Salamanu,
a Moabitish king, contemporaneous with Hosea, mentioned ** by
Tiglathpileser as paying tribute;†† (4) Zalmunna (*v.s.*); (5) the
name of a North Arabian tribe who invaded the Negeb.‡‡ To be
noted further are the following points: (*a*) the name occurs in
Arabian poetry and on a Palmyrene inscription; (*b*) the reference is evidently to some great city and well-known king; this
would throw out the Moabitish Shalman and the Palestinian
Arbela; (*c*) the entire clause is a later insertion because the
most reasonable supposition is that the reference is to an Assyrian
king; but Hosea elsewhere speaks of the Assyrian king as מלך
ירב, and the king here spoken of would seem to be Shalmaneser IV.,
who lived after Hosea's time; cf. Am. 6². Steiner takes שלמן בית
ארבאל as a compound place-name, after the analogy of Abel beth-

---

* Eich., Ew.   † Hi., Or., Che.

‡ Hd., Pu., Schr., Ke., Now.; cf. Robinson, *Bib. Res.* II. 399.

§ Also Syr.-Hex., Old Latin, 𝔙, Horsley, Geiger, New.

‖ Ros., Umb., Pu., Hd., Ke., We.   †† *COT.*, Hal.; cf. Ru.

¶ Or.   ** II. R. 67, l, 60.   ‡‡ Che. (*CB.*).

Maacah (2 S. 20[14f.]) and Almon-beth-Diblathaim (Nu. 33[46f.]).—
The mother being broken with the children] Cf. Gn. 32[11] 2 K. 8[12]
Ps. 137[8.9].—**15.** *Thus shall I do to you, O house of Israel*]
This rendering adopts 𝕲's אעשה for עשה, it being impossible to
find for עשה an appropriate subject;* also 𝕲's בית ישראל for
ביתאל (cf. 6[10] 8[5]).† Various subjects for עשה have been given, *e.g.*
Bethel, ‡ Yahweh, § Shalmaneser; ‖ but none of these is satisfactory. The reading of 𝕲, βηθ 'Ισραηλ instead of βηθηλ, has arisen
according to some from the shortened Iηλ; ¶ according to others
from the fact that the two are synonymous.**—*Because of the
evil of your evil*] *i.e. your great wickedness*, the doubled form expressing intensity.—*In the dawn utterly undone shall be the king
of Israel*] The king is to be cut off either (1) in the morning of
his work, *i.e.* at the very beginning; †† or (2) in the morning
dawn, when prosperity is once more to present itself; ‡‡ or
(3) as suddenly as comes the dawn after a night of slumber (cf.
Ps. 90[5]); §§ or (4) like the dawn (כשחר), Is. 58[8]; ‖‖ or (5) in
the storm (בשער).¶¶ The probability lies between (3) and (5).

---

9. הגבעה] With art., cf. בג'; Kö. 295 *b*.—עלוה] = עולה; for other cases of
metathesis cf. כבש for כבש; זועה for זועה; שמלה for שלמה.—**10.** ואאסרם] If 𝔐
is retained, on ו cf. Kö. 415 *s*; on assimilation of ו, GK. 71; on ֵ in pause,
GK. 60 *a*.—אפרים] Circ. cl. *Ephraim being a heifer*, etc.—**11.** אהבתי] For
other examples of the old case-ending in ptcp., *v.* GK. 90 *l*; on ־ֹ before
prep. ל, Kö. 272 *b*; cf. 336 *w*.—וישדד] Very doubtful; only here and Is. 28[24]
Jb. 39[10]; cf. H. W. Hogg, *EB.* 77; Vogelstein, *Landwirtsch. in Pal.* 36.—
12. לצ'] On ל here and in לפרי, GK. 117 *n*; Kö. 289.—נירו . . . ניר] Here
and Je. 4[3] with cogn. acc.; the only other occurrence Pr. 13[23].—לדרוש] = genitive; cf. 2 K. 5[26] Ps. 102[14] Ec. 3[2-5]; Kö. 281 *p*, 400 *b*.—**13.** עולתה] Chiastic,
Kö. 339 *f*; on ה־, Kö. 287 *b*; GK. 90 *g*.—**14.** ויקאם] On the full (and rare)
writing of â, GK. 9 *b*, 72 *a*, 23 *g*.—וישר] Cf. Massoretic note; really a Qal
pass. (GK. 53 *u*; Böttcher, 906; Barth, *Festschrift z. Jubiläum Hildesheimer*,
(1890) pp. 145 ff.), though commonly called Höph.; only here and Is. 33[1].—
כשר] Inf. with subj. and obj.—אם על בנים] Circ. cl., GK. 156 *c*; cf. Kö. 402 *k*.
על = *together with*, GK. 119 *aa*, note 3; cf. Gn. 32[12].—רעת רעתכם] After
analogy of *Holy of Holies, Song of Songs;* GK. 133 *i*; Kö. 309 *i*; but cf. sugg.
of dittog. (*v.s.*); on ֵ retained after removal of tone, GK. 25 *e*.—נדמה] Niph.
inf. abs. intensive.

---

* We., Gr., Now.	‖ Hes.	‡‡ Ke. §§ Che.
† Oort, We., Gr., Now.	¶ Cf. Baudissin, *Rel.* I. 39.	‖‖ Oort, Gr.
‡ AV., Rashi, Wü. § Ew.	** Marck. †† Bauer, Hi.	¶¶ We.

§ 15. Israel a child ; Yahweh his father, with all the love of a father, even in the face of ingratitude and desertion.

11$^{1-11}$. I called Israel out of Egypt, but he wandered away from me, rendering worship to other gods ($^{1. 2}$). And yet it was I who brought him up, teaching him to walk, carrying him in my arms ; leading him kindly, treating him mercifully, gently feeding him ($^{3. 4}$). He must go back to Egypt, or take Assyria as his king, for he has cast me off (and the sword shall consume him for his bad policy) ; he . . . ($^{5-7}$). But how can I give him up to destruction like Admah or Zeboim ! For I am God and not man. My voice, like that of a lion in the distance, will call them to return (?) ($^{8a. 9b. 10a}$).

This piece is made up of four strophes, each of six or seven lines, having the trimeter movement. The first strophe ($^{1. 2}$) describes Israel's rebellious attitude toward his father, Yahweh. The second ($^{3. 4}$) pictures, in contrast, the loving and fatherly attitude of Yahweh toward Israel. The third ($^{5-7}$) declares that he must go into a foreign land, his cities be destroyed, etc. The fourth ($^{8a. 9b. 10a.}$) depicts the agony of the father, who, indeed, is unable to give up the son thus condemned to destruction and to exile, and consequently sends forth the summons which calls him back. The following parts are from a later hand : (1) וכלחה ברזו (v.^{6}) ; (2) the closing section (vs.$^{8b. 9a. 10b. 11}$).

XI. 1–4. *Israel has wandered away from Yahweh, although he cared for him most tenderly.*

1. לבני] Ⴌ τὰ τέκνα αὐτοῦ = לבניו; so Ⴒ (so also Val., Gu., Marti). Σ. υἱός μου (so Ⴑ); Θ. (ἐκάλεσα) αὐτὸν υἱόν μου. Wkl. לי בְּנִי (*Untersuch.* 182; so Ru., Che. *Exp.* Nov. '97, p. 365; Hal.). Gr. לִי בְּנִי. Oort, לִבְנַי. Read, with We., לִי כְּדִי, כֹּי belonging to v.^{2} (so Now.^{2}). — **2.** קראו] Ⴌ καθὼς μετεκάλεσα = כקראו (so also Oort, Wkl., Val., Gu., Ru., Loft., GAS., Oet., Hal., Che. (*CB.*), Marti); Ⴑ also inserts כְּ. Read, with We., קְרָאִי, with כרי from v.^{1}. Gr. כַּאֲשֶׁר קראו. Oort (*Em.*) קראתי. — מפניהם] Read מִפְּנֵי הֵם, with Ⴌ, ἐκ προσώπου μου (so Ⴑ, Mich., Dathe, Bauer, Oort, We., Val., Gr., Gu., GAS., Now., Oet., Hal., Che. *CB.*; Marti). Wkl. מִפְּנֵי, omitting הם as dittog. of לחם (*Untersuch.* 182; so Ru., Loft., Oort (*Em.*)). — **3.** חרגלתי לאפרים] Ⴌ συνεπόδισα; Σ. ἐπαιδαγώγουν; Θ. κατὰ πόδας; Ⴑ ܪܓ̈ܠܝ. Gr. א 'נֲחַלְתִּי לִי. Oort and Hal. הרגלתי. — קחם] Read, with Ⴌ, ἀνέλαβον αὐτόν, אֶחֱםֶם (so also Ew., Umb., Olsh. (§ 232 a), St., Or., Che., Oort (*ThT.* and *Em.*), We., Ru., Gu., Loft., Now., Oet., Marti). Hal. לקחתים or לקחתיו. Gr. יַחֲחֵם. — על זרועתיו] Ⴌ ⰔⰈ have suff. of 1st p. (so also Dathe, Or., Oort (*ThT.* and *Em.*), We., Gr., Ru., Gu., Loft.,

GAS., Now., Oet., Hal., Che. *CB*., Marti); 𝔊 also makes noun sg. — [רפאתים
Now. sugg. וְדַלְתִּים or רוֹמֲמְתִּים (cf. We. and Is. 1²). Gr. פריתים. — **4.** [חבלי
𝔊 διαφθορᾷ = חבל, with Aramaic force (Vol.). — [אדם] Gr. (*Psalmen*, 144), חֶסֶד,
cf. We. (so Ru.; Che. *Exp*. Nov. '97, p. 365; Now.², cf. Marti). Gr. (*Em*.) sugg.
רחמים or נחומים (so Ru.; cf. Che. *Exp*.). — [אהבה] 𝔊 ἀγαπήσεώς μου = אהבתי.
Ru. adds here, וַיֹּאמְרוּ בִי, on the basis of Σ. ἐνομίσθην. — [ואהיה] Ru. גם אני אהיה,
foll. 𝔊ᴬ καὶ ἐγὼ ἔσομαι. — [להם] Oort, לוֹ. — [כמרימי] 𝔊 ὡς ῥαπίζων ἄνθρωπος
= כְּמֹרֵט (so also Houtsma, Ru.) or כְּמַכֵּה אָדָם (Vol.; so Marti); Arab. = *as a
man smiting*. Read, with 𝔖, sg. כמרים (so also Oort (*ThT*. and *Em*.), Gr.,
Val., Gu., Now., Hal.); 'Α. ὡς αἴρων; Σ. ὡς ὁ ἐπιθείς. — [עֹל] 𝔊𝔗 om. (so
Ru.). — [על] Read, with 𝔖, מֵעַל (so also Oort (*ThT*. and *Em*.), Val., Now.,
Oet., Hal.). Ru. om. — [לחיהם] 𝔊 τὰς σιαγόνας αὐτοῦ. Houtsma, לחיו (so
Oort, Val., Gu.). Oet. לְחָיֵהֶם or לְחָיֵיהֶם. Hal. כְּחֵתֶם. — [ואט אליו] 𝔊 καὶ ἐπι-
βλέψομαι (= וְאַבֵּט, so also Houtsma, Oort, Val.) πρὸς αὐτόν; 'Α. καὶ ἔκλινα
πρὸς αὐτόν; similarly Σ., Θ.; 𝔖 ܣ؎ܟ̣ ܐܠܘܕ؎ = ואם אליהם. Ru. וַיַּבֵּט אֵלַי.
Read, with Hi., וְאַט (so Sim., We., Gu., Now., Hal.). Scholz, וְאֵט (so Oet.,
Now.², Marti). — [אוכיל] 𝔊 δυνήσομαι; 'Α. βρώματα; Σ. τροφήν; Θ. βρῶσιν;
𝔖 ܐܘܟܠ؎ = ואכלו. Oort (*ThT*. and *Em*.), ואאכיל. Gr. סֶבֶל. Ru. אוּכַל.
Val. וָאֹכִיל. Hal. אֹהֲלֵי. Marti, וָאֹכַל לוֹ. — **5.** [לא] Read לוֹ, with 𝔊 αὐτῷ, and
join to v.⁴ (so Dathe, Ma., Böckel, Eich., Houtsma, Scholz, We., Val., Gu.,
Ru., GAS., Now., Oet.). Gr. sugg. הֲלֹא (cf. Or.). Oort (*Em*.) om. — [ישוב
𝔊 κατῴκησεν = ישב; 𝔖𝔗 = pl.; so one cod. of Kenn.; three codd. have
ישוב. — [אל ארץ] 𝔊 Ἐφράιμ ἐν = אפרים ב. [הוא—] Ru. וְנָחָה; cf. Now.'s sugg.
that it is the remnant of a vb. of which מלכו was obj. Gr. יהיה. — [מלכו
𝔖 pl. suff. Between אשור and הוא מלכו, Hal. inserts לא ילך כי יהוה, and transfers כי מאנו לשוב to the end of v.⁶.

---

1. *When Israel was young, then I came to love him*] As
before (cf. 9¹⁰ 10⁹), the prophet goes back to Israel's earliest days
— this time (cf. 2³ in which the national existence dates from the
wandering in the wilderness) to the sojourn in Egypt. In 2¹⁵
this same period is designated as the days of his youth. It was
at this period that Yahweh fell to liking him. The verb אהב is
inchoative; * cf. שנא, 9¹⁵. כִּי is temporal, not causal. נער is very
indefinite, including any age from youngest childhood (cf. הנער
נער, 1 S. 1²⁴) to some degree of maturity (Gn. 34¹⁹ 1 K. 20¹⁵
1 S. 30¹⁷); but in its use here of the nation, it is evidently intended of the child age. This representation of Israel as a man
— at one time young (as here), at another with gray hairs (7⁹) —
is very striking. — *And out of Egypt I called him*] The 𝔐𝔗 here

---

* Hi., We., GAS., Hal.; but, on contrary, Wü.

presents serious difficulties of text and interpretation ; viz. (1) לבני,
my son, implies a call out of Egypt to become Yahweh's son ; but
in Ex. 4²² Dt. 14¹ Je. 3¹⁹ 31⁹·²⁰, the standard passages for this
idea, no such statement occurs, he is already represented as
Yahweh's son ; * (2) Hosea everywhere represents Israel and
Yahweh as husband and wife, not as father and son † (but cf.
vs.³ᶠᶠ·) ; (3) 𝔊 and 𝔗 read "*his sons* " ; (4) difficulties in connection with v.² (*v.i.*). In view of these difficulties, the following
renderings have been made : (1) *and called my son out of
Egypt*, ‡ but this does not do justice to the preposition ; (2) *and
. . . I called him to be my son*, § but *v.s.* ; (3) *and out of Egypt
I called his sons*, ‖ following 𝔊 and 𝔗, but this is inconsistent with
נער as used of ישראל ; (4) *and out of Egypt I called him* ¶ (reading לו כרי instead of לבני and taking כרי with following verse) ;
this is to be preferred. The use of this phrase in Matthew 2¹⁵
has been understood (1) to determine the meaning of Hosea's
words as predictive of the Messiah ; ** (2) to represent Israel as
a type of Christ ; †† (3) to furnish an illustration of the historical
event which the evangelist was describing. ‡‡ This, however, is
but one of many instances in which the N. T. interpretation
has proceeded upon lines other than those which may be called
historical. — **2.** *The more I called them, the farther they went
away from me*] This reading rests upon a text, in which, (1) כרי
(*v.s.*) has been substituted for בני and קראי for קראו (cf. 𝔊),
= *according to my calling ;* (2) according to 𝔊, מפנידם has been
separated into מפני הם (cf. 𝔖). The ordinary text, *they called
them, so they went from them*, (1) has nothing to which כן may
correspond, although in AV. and most translations this is supplied ;
(2) leaves the subject (prophets, §§ or idols, ‖‖ all agencies ¶¶)
unexpressed, thus giving rise to unnecessary confusion ; (3) requires the הם of מפנידם to be the prophets (subject of קראו) though
the הם of להם is Israel, — all of which is inconceivable. This,
then, is Yahweh's ground of complaint, that with every new effort
made by him through the prophets of succeeding centuries, Israel
became more and more hardened (Is. 6¹⁰ Je. 7²⁵·²⁶). If this were

---

* We., Now. § GAS. ** Hux. §§ Cal., Ew.
† Now. ‖ Now. †† Meyer, Broadus, Weiss. ‖‖ Eich.
‡ AV., RV. ¶ We. ‡‡ Kübel. ¶¶ Pu.

true, why should the work of the prophets have been continued? "It kept up a church within the nation, and it developed ideas which bore fruit in due time" (Cheyne). But was it true? No; for, as a matter of fact, Israel was making progress all the time. Every century was raising Israel farther and farther away from the heathenism on every side, and preparing the nation for the time when the great doctrine of monotheism could and would be accepted. The prophet's statement, thus placed in Yahweh's mouth, must be judged from the prophet's own point of view at the time of utterance, and not from the larger point of view gained in the comparative study of centuries of history. — *They kept sacrificing to the Baalim, making offerings to images*] Cf. 2⁸⁻¹³. These are details of the departure. The Baalim and the images (wood, metal, stone) of 2 K. 17⁴¹ Dt. 7⁵·²⁵ are the same, viz. the calves at Dan and Bethel. The imperfects are frequentative, expressing customary action. — **3.** *Yet it was I who taught Ephraim to walk, taking them up in my arms*] The "I" is in contrast with the Baalim, and introduces another description of Yahweh's exhibition of paternal love. Here again 𝔊, reading אֶקְחֵם (*v.s.*) and *my arms*, furnishes a better text. Only Ephraim is in the mind of the prophet, although he is speaking of a time when Ephraim and Judah were together. *Teaching them to walk* = keeping them on their feet; *i.e.* directing in a providential way their footsteps. To this is added *taking them up in my arms*, another term expressing paternal fondness and care, exercised when the child is weary (cf. Is. 63⁹ Dt. 1³¹ 32¹¹). The rendering of 𝕸𝕿 *he took them up* has been interpreted of Moses.* — *But they did not know that I healed (?) them*] Another reproachful touch; for, notwithstanding all that Yahweh did, they failed to recognize his presence and participation. The figure of "healing" is common in Hosea (5¹³ 6¹ 7¹; cf. Ex. 15²⁶), but it does not seem in place here, unless, perhaps, we supply the thought,† when they fell and hurt themselves in their learning to walk. Wellhausen regards רפאתים as a disturbing element; Nowack suggests that "I reared them" (Is. 1²) might have been expected; the suggestion of Graetz, "I redeemed them," is not bad. — **4.** *With the cords of a*

---

* Rashi, Ki., Sim.   † GAS.

man I would (or *used to*) *draw them*] The figure, as Hebrew usage permits, now changes, and it goes back to that of the "team of bullocks, in charge of a kind driver. Israel are no longer the wanton young cattle of the previous chapter (10¹¹) which need the yoke firmly fastened on the neck, but a team of toiling oxen mounting some steep road." * The driver, Yahweh, uses *cords of a man* not *cords of a heifer; i.e.* cords adapted to men, such as men could bear. — *With bands of love*] A parallel member interpreting אדם; the first time the word "human" is made synonymous with "love." † It is a tempting opportunity to suggest a gloss ‡ inserted to make clear the difficult phrase חבלי אדם, but the thought may well be attributed to the prophet himself, and not to a later reader. — *And I was to them as one who lifts up the yoke from upon their jaws*] This continues אמשכם. The particular action here described is somewhat obscure, because of our lack of knowledge of the form of ancient yokes; but the general sense is clear. The driver so disposes the yoke as to afford relief to the animal, perhaps while eating, perhaps while resting. The singular, מרים (= *lift up*, not *take away* § nor *lay upon* ‖), is to be adopted with 𝕲 and 𝕾 (*v.s.*) instead of the plural, 𝕸𝕿. על is better read מעל with 𝕾. Strangely enough, 𝕲 omits על, *yoke*. For *jaws*, cf. Ju. 15¹⁵. ¹⁶ Dt. 18³ Jb. 41² Is. 30²⁸; cf. also the proper name רמת לחי, Ju. 15¹⁷. Halévy's "shoulders" for "jaws" is unnecessary. — *And I inclined unto him and would give him to eat*] For ואט, read ואט; the object *my ear* being implied.¶ Others have taken this to be the adverb אט = *gently;* cf. 1 K. 21²⁷ 2 S. 18⁵ Is. 8⁶ Gn. 33¹⁴ Jb. 15¹¹; ** but the construction thus obtained is harsh beyond measure. 𝕲 reads ואבט, and makes אוכיל Hiph. of יכל, "to be able." In either case the figure is that of one approaching his people with food in a most indulgent and compassionate manner. The לא of v.⁵ is to be read לו and joined to the end of v.⁴ with 𝕲.

1. נער] Predic., though noun precedes. — ואהבהו] ו = *and so;* on form of אהב, GK. 68 *f.* — כדי] For בני, literally *according to the sufficiency*, or *abundance of;* cf. Dt. 25² Ne. 5⁸; the more usual correlative of כן is כאשר. —

---

* GAS.   † Ew.   ‡ Now.   § Or.   ‖ Bauer, Böckel.
¶ Hi., Sim., We., Now.   ** Ma., Hes., Ew., Umb., Ke., Che., GAS.

2. ל קראו] *Call to* a person, cf. 1 K. 1[32] Lv. 9[1]; also with אל, Gn. 3[9] Ps. 50[4];
even without a preposition, Gn. 27[1]. — כן] = *so* = in the same proportion; here,
either without the preceding כאשר (cf. other cases of omission, Is. 55[9] Je. 3[20]
Ps. 48[6]; Kö. 371 *l o*), or with כרי instead of כאשר (*v.s.*). Cf. the use of other particles for כן, viz. כה, בכה, כזאת. — יקטרון] On pl. end. ־ון, GK. 47 *m.* — **3.** תרגלתי]
A Tāph'ēl; *i.e.* a causative with ת preformative, denominative from רגל, *foot;*
other cases are יתחרה, Je. 12[5] 22[15]; מתרגם, Ezra 4[7]; GK. 55 *h;* Kö. II. i. p. 380;
but against the existence of such a stem, Barth, *NB*. p. 279. — ל לאפרים]
here probably sign of acc., but this usage is very rare indeed in so early an
author; Kö. 289 *a.* — קחם] Corrupt for אקחם; but cf. GK. 19 *i*, 66 *g.* —
4. אוכיל] Hiph. of אכל; *δ = â*, GK. 68 *i*; Kö. II. i. p. 544. — אמשכם] *I would,*
or *sought to, draw them;* Kö. 181. — אהבה] Elsewhere of God's love for Israel,
Je. 31[3] Is. 63[9] Zp. 3[17]. — ואט] So, rather than ואט; apocopation of אטה; cf.
Jb. 23[11] Je. 15[6]. Cf. Che.'s emendations on vs.[1-4] in *EB*. col. 2826, and his
additional ones in *CB*., which involve Jerahmeel here as everywhere.

5–11. *Israel must be punished by going into exile, and yet how can I, Yahweh, execute the punishment?*

5. מאנו] ⅏ sg. (so also Oort (*Em.*)). — לשוב] Σ. μετανοῆσαι. — **6.** וחלה]
⅏ καὶ ἠσθένησεν, and ܐ ܣܘܡ܏ܠܒ, both derive from חלה = *be sick;*
Σ. καὶ τραυματίσει; 𝔙 *coepit.* Gr. וגלה or וגללה (cf. Je. 23[19] 30[23]). Marti
om. as corruption of וכלתה. — וכלתה] ⅏ καὶ κατέπαυσεν = וכלה (Vol.); Σ. καὶ
συντελέσει. Om. as corrupt dittog. of וחלה. — בריו] ⅏ ἐν ταῖς χερσὶν αὐτοῦ
= בידיו; cf. ܐ; Σ. τοὺς βραχίονας αὐτοῦ; 𝔙 *electos ejus;* 𝕿 גברוהי. Read,
with We., בעריו (so Marti). Gr. sugg. בחריו (so Oet.) or בריחיו. Scholz, בער.
Gardner, בניו. — ואכלה] ⅏ καὶ φάγονται; so ܐ; Σ. καταναλώσει. Oet. ואכלתה.
Gardner, ואכלום, taking first מ of ממע' as vb. suff. — ממעצותיהם] Ru. בעצמותיהם.
Oort (*ThT.* and *Em.*), מצדותיהם (so Val., Gu.). Gr. עצמותיהם (La. 1[13]).
Read, with We. and Now., במבצריהם (cf. Marti). — **7.** ועמי] ⅏ καὶ ὁ λαὸς
αὐτοῦ = ועמו. — תלואים] ⅏ Σ. ἐπικρεμάμενος = תלוא; 𝔙 *pendebit.* Oet. נלאה
or הלאני, which is to be adopted (cf. Now.[2]). Marti, נלוים. — למשובתי] ⅏ ἐκ
τῆς κατοικίας αὐτοῦ = למושבו (Vol.) or ממשבתו (Now.). 'A. τῇ ἐπιστροφῇ
μου; Θ. εἰς ἐπιστροφὴν αὐτοῦ; Σ. εἰς τὸ ἐπιστρέφειν πρός με; ܐ ܠܡܗܦܟ.
Gr. למושבתיו. Oort (*Em.*), למשובתו. Oet. משובבתו or במשו, which is to be
adopted. Marti, אל־עצבים. — ואל על] ⅏ καὶ ὁ θεὸς ἐπὶ = ואל על. 'A. καὶ πρὸς
ζυγόν; Θ. εἰς ζυγόν; Σ. ζυγὸς δέ; 𝔙 *jugum autem* — all reading על (so also
Oort, Oet.). ܐ ܠܒܐ = ואל אל (Seb.; so also Gr.). Read, with Oet., אל על.
Ru. ואל הבעל (so Marti, *Rel.* 147). Hal. יעל על. Müller (*SK*. 1904, p. 126),
ואל על. — יקראהו] ⅏ τὰ τίμια αὐτοῦ = יקריו; 'A., Θ. καλέσει αὐτόν; Σ. συναντή-
σει αὐτῷ; 𝔙 *imponetur eis;* ܐ 3 pl. without suff. or with suff. taken as subj.
of foll. vb. Read יקראהו. Gr. יקראו והוא. Ru. יקרא הוא. Marti (*Rel.* 147),
יקרו. Oet. יאצרהו. — יחד לא ירומם] ⅏ θυμωθήσεται, καὶ οὐ μὴ ὑψώσῃ αὐτόν
= יחרה ולא ירוממהו (Vol.); Σ. ὁμοῦ, ὃς οὐκ ἀρθήσεται; 𝔙 *simul, quod non*

auferetur, reading יר׳ as a passive; 𐤔 ܢܓ݂ܠܐ ܘܢ ܐܣܢ݂ ܢ ܠ ܘ, taking יחר as adv. and joining with preceding. Read הוא חָדַל לְרַחֲמוֹ. Gr. יַחַר ולא יְרַחֲמֵם; cf. Ru. יְרַחֲמוֹ. Oort and Hal. ירוֹם. Oet. אַחַר לא ירומם.— 8. 𐤔 [איך אתנך]ܐܬܠ݂. ܐܣܡܟ—[אמגנך] 𐤂 ὑπερασπιῶ σου; ᾿Α. ὅπλῳ κυκλώσω σε; Θ. ἀφοπλίσω σε; Σ. ἐκδώσω σε; ℭ אשיצנך; 𐤔 ܐܚܕܟ. Hal. אֲמַגְּרֵךְ or אֲשִׁימֵךְ.—[כאדמה] 𐤂 joins with foll. vb.— 𐤔 om.— [יחד] 𐤂 ἐν τῷ αὐτῷ (cf. 2²); Σ. ἐν τούτῳ; ℣ *pariter.*— Gr. [נכמרו]— [נחומו] Read רַחֲמַי, with Θ. τὰ σπλάγχνα τοῦ ἐλέους μου, and 𐤔 ܐܬܚܡܬ (so also We., Gr., Ru., Now., Oet., Marti); cf. Gn. 43³⁰ 1 K. 3²⁶ Lk. 24³². — 9. [חרון] 𐤂 κατὰ τὴν ὀργήν. Read, with Gr., חֲרוֹן. — [אשוב] 𐤂 ἐγκαταλίπω = עזב (Schleusner), or אשאיר (Vol.).— [בקרבך] 𐤔 joins with איש ולא. Hal. בְּקִרְבּוֹ. — [ולא אבוא בעיר] Read, with Volz (p. 34) and Now., ולא אדם יִנְעַר, the last word being joined to v.¹⁰. One cod. of de R. בָעִיר. Houbigant, לְעִיר. St. לְבָעֵר (so Oort (*ThT.* and *Em.*), Val., Oet.). Marti (*Rel.* 133), ולא אַבְעִיר. We. and GAS. ולא אוֹכָה לבַער. Ru. and We.³ ולא אֶבְעָר (so Marti). — 10. [אחרי] Oort (*ThT.* and *Em.*), אחריך, joined with v.⁹ (so Val., Ru., We.³). Volz and Now. כַּאֲרִי. — [ילכו] 𐤂 πορεύσομαι = אלך (so also Ru.). Oort, יֵלֵךְ (so Val., We.³). Om., with Volz and Now., as gloss. — [כי הוא ישאג.—אֶשְׁאָג 𐤔 = adjectival impf. Ru. אֶשְׁאָג.— 𐤀. pl.; ܝܫܐܓ ᾿Α. pl.; Omitted in Lucian's text, in three codd. of Kenn., and in three of de R. (so also Ru., Oet.). — [בנים מים] 𐤂 τέκνα ὑδάτων; בני מים = 𐤔; בנים מִיָּם Ru. בָּנֵי מְשַׁבְּיָם. Gr. ב׳ מעמים Che. (*EB. s.v.* "Javan"), בנים מֵאָרֶץ. Now. בנים מאי ים (cf. Is. 11¹¹). Oort (*Em.*), בניך מים. Oet. om. ב׳ מ׳ as a corrupt repetition of the first three words of v.¹¹. Hal. adds וּמִצָּפוֹן after מים in view of the parallel "Egypt" and "Assyria" in v.¹¹. Müller (*loc. cit.*), בָּנֵי מִיָּם. Marti, בָּנֵי מִיָּם. — 11. [יחרדו] ℣ *avolabunt*, but in v.¹⁰ *formidabunt.* Oet. וַיֶּחֱ׳. — [והשבתים] 𐤂 ἀποκαταστήσω = והשיבותי. 𐤔 ܐܢ݂ܒ = ܣ݂ܘܐܦ݂ = וְהֵשַׁבְתִּים (Seb.). Read, with Gr., וַהֲשִׁיבֹתִים (so Now., Oort (*Em.*), Oet., Marti).— [על בתיהם] 𐤔 ܟ݂ܣܡ݂ܬ݂ܣ݂ܘ, probably corrupted from ܟ݂ܣܡ݂ܬ݂ܣ݂ (Seb.). Now. אֶל־בַת׳ (so Oort (*Em.*), Oet.).

5. *He must return to the land of Egypt*] Cf. 8¹³ 9³⁻⁶ 11¹¹. The prophets had both Egypt and Assyria in mind as places of exile; both powers are constantly threatening invasion; cf. Is. 7¹⁸. Predictions are made of restoration from both countries (cf. Is. 11¹¹ Mi. 7¹²). The sense here is perfectly clear, whether it is obtained (1) by transferring לֹא = לֹו to the preceding verse (*v.s.*), or (2) by using לֹא interrogatively, *Shall he not return?** but the latter is hardly consistent with the following clause. The prophet does not intend here to say that the people's desire to be free from Assyria's influence, and to go back to Egypt (to be in alliance with Egypt †) is not to be realized, for this was never true

---

* Mau., Schrö., Ew., Or.   † Jer., Ros., Hes.

of the entire people, as this statement would indicate. Nor may we take this reference to Egypt literally, and the others, cited above, merely as types of a place of exile.* — *Or Assyria will be his king*] The use of הוא in this connection is difficult. Nowack suggests that it is the survival of a verbal form ; perhaps יהיה (*v.s.*) is to be accepted. Halévy's insertion is far wide of the mark. — *For they have refused to return* (*to me*)] The poet plays with שוב ; Israel must *turn* back to Egypt, because they have refused to *turn* (*i.e.* to me). This refusal has been shown in the nation's attitude, on the one hand towards the prophets, and on the other towards Baalism. — **6.** *And so the sword will whirl in their cities*] The ו is consecutive ; the reference is to the coming devastation, in which the sword, the chief instrument of destruction, is represented as twisting or whirling about in their cities as a *person* (cf. Ez. 14[17] Gn. 3[24]). — *And will destroy their branches*] These words have probably crept into the text in explanation of the words in the preceding line. The word בדי has been taken of (1) *branches*, the suffix referring to Ephraim, the whole being the figure of a tree (cf. 9[10.16]),† but this is hardly appropriate in this connection ; (2) *great ones*, *princes* of the land, ‡ or *his chosen ones*, § or *his sons ;* ‖ (3) *hands*, 𝔊𝔖 ; (4) his *bars* (Je. 51[30]), *i.e.* the fortresses (cf. Na. 3[13] Mi. 5[6]) which protect the land ; ¶ (5) *Magi, i.e.* false prophets.** But in view of the uncalled-for change of figure, it is better to understand בדיו as a modification of בעריו, and כלתה of חלה, and to drop out the entire clause.†† This is in harmony with the strophic structure. — *And will devour them in their fortresses*] This clause furnishes the parallel for *and the sword will whirl in their cities*. In this rendering במבצריהם is substituted for ממעצותיהם, because the latter gives no satisfactory sense, or the first מ may be attached to the preceding verb (*v.s.*). — **7.** *And my people having wearied me with their rebellions, unto the yoke* (i.e. *captivity*) *Yahweh will appoint them, since he has ceased to love them*] For text, *v.s.* This verse is declared wholly corrupt by modern commentators. ‡‡ Of the verse as given in

---

* Ke., Wü.   ‡ יצע, Rashi, Böckel, *Thes.*   ¶ Hes., Ew., Wü., Che., BDB.
† AE., Ki., Hi.   § Gr.   ‖ Gardner.   ** Hal.
†† We., Now.; cf. GAS., who suggests that v.[6] may be an insertion, in view of corrupt text, and the fact that it weakens the climax of v.[5].   ‡‡ We., Now.

מִת, Nowack says in substance : While a representation of Israel's sin must be expected, תלואים למשׁ׳ makes no sense ; the expression " call upward " is extraordinary in the sense of calling to repentance, and the lack of an object after ירומם is unusual. With the thought of this line, cf. Is. 7[13]. On the reading יַקְרָאֵהוּ instead of יִקְרָאֻהוּ, *i.e.* Hiph. of קְרָה = קרא, cf. the exact equivalent in Je. 32[23], " and thou causest this evil to fall upon them " ; also Nu. 35[11]. The י of יחד is the remnant of הוא lost because of the preceding suffix, חד with the ל of לא = חֲדַל ; for ירומם read לְרַחֲמוֹ *to love him.** For parallel expressions, cf. 4[6] 9[15].

V.[7a] has been rendered by others as follows : (1) My people are fastened to defection (Cal.); (2) Since my people inclineth in order to fall away from me (Ew.); (3) My people is bent upon apostasy from me (Ke.; cf. AV., RV., Or.); (4) And my people is in doubt whether to turn to my law (ℭ); (5) And his people is suspended from its dwelling (ℭ; cf. 𝔜); (6) My people is hung up; *i.e.* is crucified, by the revolt from me (Oort); (7) My people is weary because of its revoltings (Oet.); (8) My people have a bias to turn from me (GAS.); (9) My people persists in its rebellion against me (Hal.); (10) And my people has joined itself to idols (Marti). V.[7bc] has been rendered by others as follows : (1) Upwards it is called; nevertheless it striveth not upwards (Ew.); (2) One calls it to the yoke (of the law) but no one takes the yoke upon himself (Mich.); (3) They call them to him on high; no one raises up himself (Cal.); (4) And unto the Baal (cf. Sellin, *Beiträge* II. 306, who thinks בעל impossible in view of לא ירומם) he calls; he does not pity him at all (Ru.); (5) And unto God they call; he is angry; he pities them not (Gr.); (6) And though they (the prophets) call them upwards, none of them can lift them (GAS.); (7) To a yoke will one call (or bind) him, which no one afterwards shall take away (Oet.); (8) Unanimously they call the most high God, Lo-Yeromam, *i.e.* he who should not be exalted (Hal.); (9) And they all meet the Baalim (Marti, *Dodekapropheton;* cf. *Rel.* 147, note); (10) And even if they should all together, even to the suckling, call upon him, he would not lift them up (Müller). The case is certainly a desperate one. Perhaps the suggestion given above is as satisfactory as any that has been offered.

8. *How can I give thee up, O Ephraim !*] Here begins the struggle in the prophet's mind between what seems to be the demand of justice and the claim of love. The *How* is exclamatory† and not interrogative;‡ it carries with it the negative

---

* Çf. Gr., Ru.   † Wü., Or.   ‡ Umb.

force : there is no way in which I can give thee up ; it is impossible (cf. Gn. 39⁹ 44⁸ Is. 20⁶ Ps. 137⁴). — *How can I surrender thee, O Israel !*] A poetic repetition of the former line in which מגן, further defining נתן, expresses the idea of "deliver into the hands of an enemy" (cf. Gn. 14²⁰), a surrender (as in Σ.), not a deliverance (as in 𝕲 and 'A.). — *How can I make thee as Admah ! How can I place thee as Zeboiim !*] These cities were associated with Sodom and Gomorrah (cf. Gn. 14².⁸, but the statement in that passage is probably based upon this *) ; cf. Dt. 29²³ Je. 49¹⁸ Mt. 10¹⁵ Lk. 10¹² ; but Hosea, like the author of Dt. 29²³, has ·sources of his own on which he draws for information concerning this catastrophe, *i.e.* sources other than Gn. 19 (*v.i.*). Amos and Isaiah use Sodom and Gomorrah in this same way (cf. Am. 4¹¹ Is. 1⁹ᶠ· 3⁹ 13¹⁹). It is better, in accord with the parallelism, to take כאדמה with what precedes than (cf. 𝕲) with what follows.† The איך is expressed only twice, viz. in the .first and third lines, being omitted in the second and fourth, thus giving us a beautiful example of the elegiac measure, 3 + 2, 3 + 2. — *My heart is turned upon me*] This and the three lines following (vs.⁸ᵇ·⁹ᵃ) are evidently late (*v.s.*). The thought of surrendering Ephraim produces paroxysms of sympathetic feeling in the divine breast. George Adam Smith (p. 297) says, "There follows the greatest passage in Hosea, — deepest, if not highest, of his book — the breaking forth of that exhaustless mercy of the Most High which no sin of man can bar back nor wear out." On the phrase *upon me* (עלי), *within me*, cf. 1 S. 25³⁶ Je. 8¹⁸. On נהפך, of the heart turned in sorrow, La. 1²⁰. — *My compassions grow hot together*] נחום occurs elsewhere (Is. 57¹⁸ and Zc. 1¹³) only in the sense of *comfort;* consequently רחמי, *my compassions* (cf. 2¹⁹ Am. 1¹¹) is suggested ‡ as a better reading here. כמר in Niph'al occurs elsewhere only with רחמים (Gn. 43³⁰ 1 K. 3²⁶; cf. also Lk. 24³²), and once with עור, *skin* (La. 5¹⁰). Light upon the meaning of the root is obtained from the modern Syriac, *kemr, fermentation.*§ יחד = כלם, begins the clause with emphasis (cf. v.⁷; also Dt. 33⁵ Ps. 41⁸). — **9.** *I will not act according to the*

---

* Cf. Kue., We., Sta., Co., Bu., Bacon, Wkl., Ball, Che., and Gunkel, who make Gn. 14 later than P.   † We.
‡ We., Ru., Now.   § Wetzstein, *ZDPV.* XIV. (1891), 6.
2 B

fierceness of my anger] Cf. 1 S. 28[18]. This follows the strong expression of sympathy (v.[8b]), and is only another way of saying what has been said in [8a]. So close is the connection between [8b] and [9a] (the expression of compassion, and the determination, in consequence, not to carry out his purpose of destruction), and so complete a parallel does this furnish for [8a] and [9b] (*I cannot give thee up, because I am God and not man*) that [8b] and [9a] are best treated as an insertion of a later writer.* — *I will not turn to destroy Ephraim*] Cf. 2[11]. This has been thought to mean : (1) I will not turn from pity to destroy Ephraim ; † (2) I will not again destroy Ephraim ; ‡ (3) I will not bring back Ephraim to noth- ing. § In any case, the expression is a confession of inability to do the thing it has been asserted he would do. — *For God am I, and not man*] *i.e.* divine and not human (cf. Nu. 23[19]). God may have sympathy and compassion ; he may have still other human attributes, *e.g.* anger ; but this anger may not divert Yahweh, as it might divert a man, from the execution of a well- considered purpose. — *Holy in the midst of thee*] *i.e.* holy in a truly ethical sense. — *And not human*] 𝕸 reads, *and I will not enter into the city;* ‖ but this means nothing (cf. Ex. 20[24]); it has been interpreted (1) any other city ; ¶ (2) I am not one of those who live in a city, *i.e.* a man (cf. 2 Ch. 6[18]) ; ** (3) of the omnipresence of Yahweh, occupying no space ; †† (4) of the thought that Yahweh's presence in a town must bring punish- ment. ‡‡ None of these being satisfactory, it has been suggested (1) to read עִיר = *hate, terror*, from עוּר *to boil* (cf. Je. 15[8]; cf. Rashi on 1 S. 28[16]) ; §§ (2) to read לִבְעֵר, *yet I come not to con- sume;* ‖‖ (3) to read לֹא אוֹבֶה לִבְעֵר, *I am not willing to consume;* ¶¶ (4) to read לִבְעֵר אַחֲרִיךְ, joining first word of v.[10], with a slight change, to v.[9] (cf. 1 K. 14[10] 16[3] 21[21]) ; *** (5) to read אָדָם *man*, for אָבִיא, and close the verse with this, thus securing a perfect parallelism (cf. Is. 31[8]). ††† This last suggestion seems, perhaps,

---

* Now. ; cf. We.[3].   † ᵞ.   ¶ Rashi.
‡ AV., RV., Or., We., Now., Hal.   ** Jer. ; Lowth, *De sacra poesie*, 242.
§ Che.   †† Stuck.
‖ Marck, Stuck, Ros., Hi., Pu., *et al.*   ‡‡ Hi.
§§ Schrö., Dathe, Eich., Mau., Ew., Umb., Sim., Ke., Wü., Or.
‖‖ St., Che., GAS.   ¶¶ We.   *** Oort, Val.   ††† Volz, Now.

the most plausible, and may be adopted. — **10.** *Yahweh will cry like a lion*] This is based on Volz's emendation,* which takes בעיר, last word of v.⁹, and אחרי, first word of v.¹⁰, with יהוה, reading ינער כארי ᵓ. The ילכו following יהוה is a gloss from the hand of some one attempting to improve the passage in order to make sense of it. This roar, like that of the lion calling together its young, is the summons of Yahweh to the scattered people to return (Am. 1² 3⁸ Je. 25³⁰). In Is. 27¹³ the summons is conveyed by means of a great trumpet. A different figure is employed in Ho. 5¹⁴ and 13⁷. The remainder of v.¹⁰, together with ¹¹, is from a later hand, explaining and amplifying the force and significance of the summons to return. The *return* is one of the most common and significant elements in the prophets' descriptions of the glorious future (cf. Is. 11¹¹·¹² 27¹³ 43⁶ Je. 3¹⁸ Am. 9¹⁴ Mi. 7¹² Zc. 10¹⁰). As a matter of fact, נער, *to growl, roar*, occurs only in Je. 51³⁸, where, as here (if this emendation is adopted), שאג is the corresponding word in the parallel line. Other treatments of these words (*v.s.*) are : (1) *I will go, like a lion I will roar,*† joining אחרי with v.⁹, and omitting יהוה ; (2) *Yahweh will go, like a lion he will roar ;* ‡ also joining אחרי to v.⁹. — *As a lion he will roar, yea, he himself will roar, and there shall come hurriedly . . .*] Once more, with greater emphasis than before, the thought of the summons and the return is repeated. Here emphasis is placed on the fact that Yahweh himself will send the summons, § and there will *come hurriedly* (*i.e.* eagerly, tremblingly ; cf. 3⁵ (פחד), Ps. 18⁴⁶ (חרג)) ; — who? whence? According to 𝕸, *sons from the sea, i.e.* faithful Israelites ‖ (or also the heathen ¶) from the west (𝕲 *children of water, v.s.*) ; the west being (perhaps מים = ים מאיי, Is. 11¹¹) "the same as 'the islands (or coastlands) of the sea' in the latter part of Isaiah, except that Hosea's knowledge of the coasts and islands of the western sea would be much vaguer than that of his fellow-prophet" (Cheyne). But how can the Israelites be called בנים in this connection, and how can they come from the west when they have been represented as living in Egypt and Assyria? The reading משבים, *from*

---

* Adopted by Now. † Ru. ‡ Oort.
§ In six Mss. of Kenn. and de R. כי הוא ישאג is lacking.
‖ Wü., Che. ¶ Hes.

*their captivity,** would make good sense, but has no real basis. Perhaps it is necessary here, as in some other cases, to acknowledge our inability to meet the difficulties, and to leave the subject of יחרד untranslated.† These words have been emended variously (*v.s.*); *e.g.* (1) *my children from their captivity;* ‡ (2) *sons from Aram;* § (3) *sons from the nations;* ‖ (4) *sons from the west and from the north;* ¶ (5) *my sons from the west;* ** (6) *builders from the west.* †† — **11.** *They shall come hurriedly, like sparrows, from Egypt, and like doves from the land of Assyria*] The birds represent the speed ‡‡ (cf. Ps. 55⁶ Is. 60⁸) with which they come, not the timidity and faint-heartedness; §§ cf. 7¹¹, in which the stupidity or foolishness of the dove is made a point of comparison. ‖‖‖ — *And I will bring them back to their houses*] Cf. Je. 32³⁷. This rendering ¶¶ really represents הֲשִׁיבוֹתִים instead of 𝕸𝕿, הושבתים, which means *I will cause them to dwell.**** — It is the declaration of Yahweh*] These words are questioned by Nowack, since they occur elsewhere in Hosea only in verses that are unauthentic or suspicious (2¹³·¹⁶·²¹). The closing verses of this chapter (vs.⁸ᵇ·⁹ᵃ·¹⁰ᵇ·¹¹) are probably late,††† because (1) they introduce an element of promise in the middle of a series of threats, there being no preparation for this word of promise and no reference to it in the following context; cf. also chap. 14, where a promise appears, although introduced in a wholly different way; (2) the expression, "I will not again destroy Ephraim," is explicable only at a time after Ephraim has experienced some severe chastisement; (3) there is no connection between vs.⁹ᵇ ᵃⁿᵈ ¹⁰.

5. ישוב] *He must not,* etc.; cf. Dr. § 39; Kö. 180; GK. 107 *r.* — ואש]] = *or,* here connecting alternative propositions; cf. Ex. 20¹⁰·¹⁷ 21¹⁶ Jb.

---

* Ru.   § Che. (*v.s.*).   ** Müller (*v.s.*).
† So Oort, We., Gu., Now.   ‖ Gr.   †† Marti.
‡ Ru.   ¶ Hal.   ‡‡ Che., Now.   §§ Wü.

‖‖‖ On doves and sparrows cf. Now. *Arch.* I. 82 f.; G. E. Post, "Dove," in *DB.;* A. E. Shipley and S. A. Cook, "Dove," in *EB.;* Tristram, *The Natural History of the Bible,* 201 f., 211-220.

¶¶ We., Now., GAS.   *** Ew., Reuss, Or., Che., Gu., BDB.

††† So Sm. *Rel.* 215 (¹⁰·¹¹ certainly late); Volz (⁹ᵇ genuine); Now. (⁹ᵇ·¹⁰ᵃ genuine; but Now.² makes 8ᵇ-11 all late); Marti, *Rel.* (¹⁰·¹¹ late); Grimm, *Lit. App.* 73. But cf. Seesemann, 28 f.; Giesebrecht, *Beiträge sur Jesaia-Kritik,* 211 f.

31¹³·¹⁶·²⁶.— 6. וחלה] Accent on ultima, although following syllable (חֶרֶב) has
tone.—מִמְּעַצּוֹתֵיהֶם] With two accents.— 7. וְעַמִּי] Introd. circ. cl.—תְּלוּאִם]
Treated as ל״א not ל״ה; cf. Dt. 28⁶⁶; GK. 75 *rr.* —עַל] If 𝕳𝕿 is correct,
a noun; cf. 7⁶ 2 S. 23¹. On going over of the local idea into the temporal,
then into *ideal* (as in Arabic), cf. Kö. 318 *a.* — 8. אֲתֶנְךָ] *Can*, impf. of possibility; Dr. § 37; GK. 107 *r.*—צְבָאִים] Q⁽ᵉ⁾rî, צְבוֹיִם; but regularly צְבֹיִם, Gn. 14²·⁸
Dt. 29²². 𝕲 Σεβωειμ. The city was one of "the five cities of the plain,"
but its exact site is unknown.— 9. לֹא־אִישׁ] Kö. 352 *m.*— 11. בָּתֵּיהֶם] On
form, GK. 96; Kö. II. i. p. 56; Sta. § 187 *a*; Wright, *Comp. Gram.* p. 88;
Philippi, *ZDMG*, XLIX. 206; Rahlfs, *ThLZ.* 1896, p. 587.

§ 16. Israel's falsity and faithlessness from the first, in spite of efforts through prophets, must bring retribution and ruin. 12¹⁻¹⁵.

[English, 11¹²–12¹⁴.] Israel is false and faithless,
always doing that which ends in nothing; turning now to Assyria,
now to Egypt; he must be punished; even before his birth he
was a supplanter (¹ᵃ·²⁻⁴ᵃ). Israel is a trader using false balances;
rich and self-satisfied; but his riches will count him nothing, for I
will cause him to dwell again in tents (⁸⁻¹⁰). Israel has been given
prophets, but with no effect; lies and demon-worship prevail;
bitter enmity has been aroused; sudden retribution will come
upon him; his altars shall be like stone-heaps in the furrows of
the field (¹¹·¹⁵·¹²).

The patriarchal episodes in vs.¹³·⁴ᵇ⁻⁷ (this is the correct order) and the
historical allusions in v.¹⁴ are from a later hand, and from a different and
conflicting point of view (*v.i.*), as compared with that of the original material.
The original piece (omitting vs.¹ᵇ·⁴ᵇ⁻⁷·¹³·¹⁴) consists of three very symmetrical
strophes of ten lines each, in trimeter movement. The first strophe describes
Israel as he is and has been from the earliest times, viz. a faithless one, a
vacillating one, never knowing his mind, surely deserving punishment, since
all this has been so from the life of the patriarch in his mother's womb. The
second strophe (adopting the elegiac movement 3 + 2) characterizes Israel
as Canaan, a trader cheating all with whom he trades, becoming rich thereby,
but destined, in spite of present riches, to dwell again in tents as in days past.
The third strophe narrates the efforts put forth by prophets sent from Yahweh
to teach him the right way, the lack of any results, the prevailing falseness
and idolatry, the bitter enmity thus aroused, and the sudden punishment
which is its consequence. Three exceedingly interesting additions have been
made from the post-exilic period (1) v.¹ᵇ, which includes Judah; (2) vs.⁴ᵇ⁻⁷,
which recalls certain traditions of Jacob, putting him in a most favorable light;
viz. as having had intimate relationship and great influence with God; (3) on

vs.^{13. 14} *v.i.* The order according to this arrangement is 1 *a.* 2-4 *a.* 8-10. 11. 15. 12 (v.¹⁵ preceding v.¹² logically), with the additions 1 *b.* 13. 4 *b*-7. 14. Cf. the arrangement of Oet., viz. 1-5. 13 f. 7. 6. 8-12. 15; that of Hal., viz. 1-10. 13. 11. 12. 14. 15; and that of Gr., viz. 1-11. 13. 15. 12. 14.

1. 𝕲 and 𝖄 connect with chap. xi. — ויהורה] 𝕲𝕾 connect with preceding. Bewer (*JBL.* XXI. 109 f.) om. as later addition. — [ער רד עם אל 𝕲 νῦν ἔγνω αὐτοὺς ὁ Θεός = עת[ה]ירדש אל (so also Scholz; cf. Loft. who follows 𝕲, but reads אלהים for ועם אל); 'A. ἐπικρατῶν . . . ; 𝖄 (*Judas*) *autem testis descendit cum Deo*; 𝕾 ܟܡܥܢ ܘܢܣܐ ܚܣܐ ܘܐܣܐ = ער ירד עם אל (Seb.). Brüll and Gr. ער רב וגו׳. Read, with Marti (*Rel.* 119; so Now.), ער ירע וגו׳. Che. (*Exp.* Nov. '97, p. 365) חרד עם אל. Oet. מרד עם אל. Hal. סורר וגו׳. Bewer, וער ירדעם אל. Müller (*SK.* 1904, p. 126), עוד דעת-אל. — [ועם קרושים נאמן 𝕲 καὶ λαὸς ἅγιος κεκλήσεται θεοῦ = ועם קרוש נאמר לאל (Vol.); 𝕾 . . . ܐܣܐ ועם ק׳ (Seb.); so 𝕿. Gr. ועם קרשים יאמר Co. ועם קרשים נצמר (*ZAW.* VII. 286 ff.; so We., Gu., Oort (*Em.*)). Hal. ועם קרוש לא נאמן Che. (*loc. cit.*) ועם קרשו נאמן Kö. § 348 *d*, ועם קרוש ימ[א][ז] אמן Oet. ועם קרשים נטמא. Böckel, ועם קרשים נאמר. — **2.** [רעה רוח 𝕲 πονερὸν πνεῦμα = רעה רוח Oort (*ThT.* and *Em.*), רע הרוח. Marti, רצה ר׳. — [כל היום 𝕲𝕾 join with preceding clause. — ושר] Read, with 𝕲, καὶ μάταια, ושו[א] (so also Oort (*ThT.* and *Em.*), We., Val., GAS., Now., Hal., Marti). — [ירבה Read, with 𝕾, ירבו (so also We., Now., Oet., Marti). — [וברית With We. and Now., om. ו. — [ויכרתו 𝕲𝖄 = sg. (so also Hal.). — [יובל 𝕲 ἐνεπορεύετο = יובל (so Hal.); 𝖄 *ferebat*. Read, with 𝕾, ܐܠܟܡܣܐ, יובלו, taking ו from beg. of v.³ (so also We., Now., Oort (*Em.*), Oet., Marti). — **3.** [ורוב 𝕲𝕬𝕷 om. ו (so also Now., Oort (*Em.*)). — [יהורה Read, with Oort, ישראל (so Now., GAS., Oet.). — [ולפקר Om. ו, with 𝕲 (so We., Gr., Now.). Marti, ואפקר. — [כרכיו 𝖄 joins with foll. vb. — **4.** [כבטן Gr. inserts אביו before כב. — [ובאונו 𝕲 καὶ ἐν κόποις αὐτοῦ. Om. ו as dittog. from prec. — [שרה] 𝖄 *directus est;* 'A. κατώρθωσε. — [אלהים Gr. איש א׳ (cf. Gn. 32²⁵). — **5.** [וישר 'A., Θ. καὶ κατώρθωσε; 𝖄 *et invaluit;* 𝕾 om. — [אל-כ׳ם] Read, with We., Now., Oet., Marti, את-כ׳ם. — [בכה וית׳ 𝕲 ἔκλαυσαν καὶ ἐδεήθησάν μου (Vol.); 𝕾 om. בכה. — [לו] Gr. adds לא. — [ביתאל 𝕲 ἐν τῷ οἴκῳ "Ων = בבית און (so also Gr.); 𝕷 *in templo meo.* — [ימצאנו 𝕲 Arab., and one cod. of Kenn. have 1 p. sg. suff.; 𝕿, 'A., Σ., Θ. suff. 3 p. sg. (so also Gr.). — [וישם Oort (*Em.*) and Marti om. ו. — [עמנו 𝕲 πρὸς αὐτούς = עמהם (Vol.). Read, with 𝕾, ܚܡܣܐ, עמו; so 'A., Σ., Θ., 𝕲𝔁, and also Dathe, Oort (*ThT.* and *Em.*), We., Beer (*ZAW.* XIII. 285), Val., Gu., Loft., GAS., Now., Oet., Marti. — **6.** [ויהוה Oort (*ThT.* and *Em.*) om. ו (so Val., Oet., Marti). — [יהוה זכרו 𝕲 ἔσται μν' = ד יהיה׳; 𝕾, Θ. take ז as 3 p. sg. of vb. with suff. Gr. ד הוא(?). Hal. זכרו. — **7.** [באלהיך 𝕾𝖄 = אל-א׳ (so also Oet.), or לא׳ (so also Gr.). Marti, באלהיך. — [תשוב We. תשוב. — [שמר Gr. תשמר. — [קוה 𝕲 ἐγγίζε = קרב. — **8.** [כנען Seb. ככנען (so Gr. (or (ככנעני)). — [לעשק 𝖄 *calumniam.* Read, with We., Now., and Marti, לעקב. Gr. לעשר or לעשיר. — **9.** [ויאמר Gr. om. ו. — [און לי 𝕲 ἀναψυχὴν ἐμαυτῷ; 'A. ἀνωφελὲς αὐτῷ; 𝖄 *idolum mihi;* 𝕾 ܚܣ ܐ܀ܐ Gr. הון לי. —

[יגיעו] Read, with 𝔊, οἱ πόνοι αὐτοῦ, יגיעיו (so We., Gr., Beer (*ZAW.* XIII. 288), Val., Now., Oet., Marti). — [ימצאו] 𝔊 εὑρηθήσονται = יִמָּצְאוּ (so also Gr., Oort); 𝔖 ܡܚܣܢ. — [לי עון] 𝔊 αὐτῷ δι᾽ ἀδικίας = לו בעונים; 𝔖 ܟܠ ܟܣܝܐ|ܐ = לי לעון. Read, with Gr. and Now., לו לעון. We. לעון (so Beer, Oet., Marti). Oort, לי מֵעָין. Oet. sugg. לַעֲוֹנִי. — [אשר חטא] Read, with 𝔊, ὡς ἥμαρτεν, אשר חָטָא (so also We., Gr., Beer, Val., Now., Oet.). Oet. וְלָאֲשֶׁר חטא(?). — 10. [מארץ] 𝔊 inserts ἀνήγαγόν σε = הֶעֱלִיתִיךָ, before מא׳ (so Oort (*Em.*)); 𝔖 inserts ܘ|ܐܣܩܬܟ = אשר הוצאתיך (Seb.); so ℭ. — [באהלים] Gardner, באלהיך. — [כימי מועד ℭ כיומי קדם = כיומי חרם = כִּימֵי חֶרֶם (so Marti). Perles (*Analekten*, 44), כימי עד. Gardner, במועד. Gr. and Now., כימי עולם (cf. Mi. 7[14f.]). Bu. (*New World*, Dec. '95) and We.[3] כימי נעוריך. — 11. [על] We. and Now., אל. — [חזון] 𝔊𝔖 pl. — [ביד] 𝔊 pl. Gr. — ובידי. — [ארמה] 𝔊 ὡμοιώθην = אֲדַמֶּה as in Is. 14[14] (Vol.); 𝔙 *assimilatus sum;* 𝔖 ܐ|ܬܕܡܝܬ. Gr. ומראה(?). Hal. אֲמַשֵּׁל. Oet. אֲדָמֶה אֲמֵר, taking first word of v.[12] with v.[11] (cf. 4[5]). Cf. We. Marti, אֲמָרָה. — 12. [אם גלעד עון 𝔊 εἰ μὴ Γαλαὰδ ἐστιν = אם ג׳ אין; so Θ. Read, with 𝔖, ܒܓܠܥܕ, 'ג בגל (so We., Now., Marti). Oort (*ThT.*), אם גלגל א׳, foll. Complutensian, Γαλγαλα; Oort (*Em.*) om. אם. Gr. — אך. — אם ג׳ ובית און [שוא היו] 𝔊𝔖𝔙ℭ, 'A., and Σ. join with foll. clause. 𝔖 reads לשוא and with Σ. om. היו. Gr. אך ש׳ הם. We. אך ש׳ עָשׂוּ, of which עשו is to be adopted (*v.i.*; so Marti). Now. sugg. יהיו for היו and would transp. it to 12[b]. — בגלגל שורים [זבחו] 𝔊 ἐν Γαλαὰδ ἄρχοντες θυσιάζοντες = בג׳ שָׂרִים זֹבְחִים (Vol.); several codd. of 𝔊, with Complutensian and Syr.-Hex., Γαλγαλοις; 'A. θυσιάζοντες; 𝔙 *in Galgal bobus immolantes;* 𝔖 ܟܝ ܠ|ܬܘܪܐ ܕܒܚܝܢ; ℭ לִמֵעָוָן (for שורים). Read, with Hi., לַשֵּׁדִים (so We., Now., Oort (*Em.*), Oet., Marti). Gr. — לִשְׁעִירִים. — [מזבחותם] 𝔖 2 pl. suff. — [גלים] 𝔊 χελῶναι; cf. Θ. on Ec. 12[8] and Nestle (*Exp. Times*, XIV. 189). — 13. [שמר] Gr. adds צאן, foll. ℭ. — 14. [כנביא 𝔖 pl. — [נשמר] Gr. יִשָּׁמֵר. — 15. [הכעיס] Oet. הִכְעִיס. — [תמרורים] 𝔊 καὶ παρώργισεν; 𝔖 ܣܟܣ. Oet. וַיְמָרְרֵהוּ. — [ודמיו] 𝔊𝔙 sg. Oet. om. ו. — [עליו] Oet. עָלָיו. Oet. — [ראשו. — [יטוש] 𝔊 ἐκχυθήσεται; 𝔙 *veniet;* 𝔖 ܢܫܒܘܩ. Gr. יִטּוֹר. Oet. עָל. — [אדניו] 𝔊 om. suff. Oort (*ThT.* and *Em.*) transp. to foll. אפרים. Marti reads v. 14, הִכְעִיסַנִי א׳ וּמְרֹרְנִי ישראל ודמיו עליו אֶשְׁפֹּךְ וחרפתו אָשִׁיב לוֹ.

XII. 1.

The past is here, as in other discourses, uppermost in the prophet's mind. *Ephraim has compassed me with lies, and the house of Israel with deceit*] Yahweh is the speaker, and he speaks out of an environment made up of Ephraim's lies, for these lies are so many as wholly to compass him about. Not infrequently has the charge been made, and with these same words, כחש and מרמה (cf. 4[2] 6[7] 7[1. 3. 13] 10[4. 13]). The lies and deceit have to do with Yahweh, for in another strophe their cheating of each other is taken up. Israel is false to Yahweh whenever she turns to Egypt or Assyria, just as a wife is false to her husband in joining with another man. With כחש may be compared בגד, Je. 5¹¹; and פשע, Is. 59¹³; while the opposite of all these words is אֱמֶת. "Ephraim" and "the house of Israel" are synonymous. — *And Judah is still known with God*] The question is, have the words of ¹ᵇ a *good* sense, and are they then from a later hand (for no motive can be conceived for Hosea's inserting here a eulogy of Judah); or have they a *bad* sense, and are they then really from Hosea's own hand? עֹד רָד עִם אֵל is difficult. The verb רוד occurs only here and in Je. 2³¹ Gn. 27⁴⁰ Ps. 55³. It has been taken (1) as = רדה = משל, *rule; i.e.* only Judah rules with God (= only Judah's kings have power with God);* (2) *Judah still serves his God;* (3) with עֵד instead of עֹד and רד = ירד, come down, *Judas autem testis descendit cum deo;†* (4) as = Arab. *râda* = rove about, stagger, waver, hesitate, be wayward with God;‡ (5) as = ידע, so 𝔊 (*v.s.*) = *and as for Judah, God knows them now;* but as Nowack says, neither is עֵת intelligible, nor do we expect a statement of this sort after v.¹ᵃ; (6) as = יְדָע, *but Judah is still known* (= betrothed, affianced) *with God,* which accords well with the following line;§ (7) as = rebellious;‖ (8) as = רָב, *great;¶* (9) *but Judah walks tremblingly with God;** (10) and still God knows them,* Judah being a later addition.†† — *And with the holy one faithful*] This seems upon the whole the most satisfactory interpretation of another difficult clause. נאמן followed by עִם is unknown; but cf. Ps. 78⁸ (אֶת ׳ע). The plural in קדשים is like that of אלהים; cf. Pr. 9¹⁰ 30³. The absence of the article indicates that it is used as a proper noun. This construction is preferable to (1) that which makes נאמן an adjective modifying קדשים‡‡ (although this is possible if קדשים is regarded as an intensive plural; cf. Ps. 7¹⁰ Is. 19⁴), because the parallelism is preserved; or (2) that which makes קדשים plural, and refers it to angels, saints, patriarchs, prophets, etc.; §§ or (3) 𝔊, which seems to have read ועם קדשים [לל]אל נאמר (*v.s.*); or (4) the reading ‖‖

---

* Rashi, Ki., Cal., Pu., AV.   † ע.

‡ Bauer, Schrö., Ew., Hi., Hd., Ke., Wü., Or., Che., BSZ.; Co. *ZAW.* VII. 287.

§ Marti, *Rel.* 119; Now.   ¶ Brüll, Gr.   †† Bewer.   §§ Jer.

‖ Hal.   ** Che. (*Exp.*) *v.s.*   ‡‡ Wü.   ‖‖ Böckel.

נאם יהוה, *i.e.* oracle of Yahweh, for נאמן, or, perhaps, worst of all, (5) the reading עִם קְדֵשִׁים נִצְמָד, "and with temple-prostitutes joined himself," * referring to the custom of having such attendants at the temples (cf. Nu. 25³⁻⁵ Dt. 23¹⁷⁻¹⁸ Gn. 38¹⁵· ²¹· ²² Ho. 4¹⁴). The chief grounds urged for this reading are (1) the parallelism thus secured between ¹ᶜ and ¹ᵈ; (2) the נאמר of 𝕲, which is considered an intermediate form between the original נצמד and נאמן; (3) the fact that נצמד in the only other places it occurs is used of a licentious cult (Nu. 25³· ⁵ Ps. 106²⁸); (4) in the only other passages where קְדֵשִׁים are mentioned (1 K. 14²⁴ 15¹² 22⁴⁶ 2 K. 23⁷), they are connected with Judah as here. In favor of regarding ¹ᵇ as late † may be urged, therefore, (1) the favorable estimate given of Judah, which Hosea could have had no occasion to utter; (2) the evident interruption made by ¹ᵇ in the prophet's statement concerning Israel, which is continued in v.²; (3) the peculiar, late usage seen in קדשים (as plural and proper name). Other renderings based on emendations (*v.s.*) are : (1) and with the Holy One is not faithful; ‡ (2) and the people of the Holy One it is called; § (3) and with temple-prostitutes is defiled. ‖

— **2.** *Ephraim herds the wind, and hunts the sirocco*] Ephraim is a shepherd, a hunter; but is the outcome of his occupation profitable ? His time is spent in herding — not flocks, but the wind, in hunting — not game, but the sirocco, the deadly southeast wind, ¶ which in its course destroys everything that it touches (cf. Ez. 17¹⁰ Jon. 4⁸ Ho. 13¹⁵ Is. 27⁸). The outcome of Ephraim's activity is, according to the figure, something absolutely void and empty; still more, something which is, in itself, not only useless, but fatally injurious. This use of רֹעֶה is bold and strong, but not too much so for Hosea; so that (1) Wellhausen's comparison of רָצָה (cf. Jb. 20¹⁰), *seek the favor of*, is unnecessary, although it is supported by the parallelism; (2) we are reminded of the רעות רוח of Ecclesiastes; (3) the

---

* Co. *ZAW.* VII. 286–289; adopted by We., but opposed by Oort, *ThT.* XXIV. 498 f.

† So We. *Prol.* 417; Oort, *ThT.*; Gu., GAS., Now.; Marti, *Rel.* 119, *EB.* II. 2122, and *Dodekapropheton.*　　‡ Hal.　　§ Gr., Bewer; cf. 𝕲.　　‖ Oet.

¶ Cf. Wetzstein in De. *Job,* on 27²¹; GAS. *Hist. Geog.* 67–69; Robinson, *Phys. Geog.* 305 f.

Jewish interpretation, *idolatry*,* is too specific; (4) "friend of the wind" † is forced; (5) there is here a touch of "Wisdom," but Hosea is full of wisdom-thought (*v.* on 14⁹). — *All day long they multiply falsehood and fraud*] This line explains the preceding; without cessation the activity goes on, but the result is that they increase (ירבו for ו ירבה ‡) falsehood (*i.e.* a false attitude toward Yahweh, § not simply toward one another ‖) and fraud (שָׁוְא being substituted for שֹׁד חמם, cf. Ⓖ שָׁו; since "violence" is not appropriate here, and the combination of falsehood and violence does not elsewhere occur).¶ — *They strike bargains with Assyria, and carry oil to Egypt*] Here the thought of the prophet becomes still more clear and explicit. Ephraim's activity was fruitless and injurious; it was false and deceptive; but how so? Because it involved relationship with and dependence upon other nations, and consequently acknowledgment of those nations' gods. Of the four expressions for entering into covenant, or alliance with, הקים ברית, or נתן, or שום, or כרת, the latter is chosen (cf. 5¹³ 7¹¹ Is. 2⁶). Oil, one of the most important products of Palestine (Dt. 8⁸ 1 K. 5¹¹ Ez. 16¹⁹ 27¹⁷), was carried to Egypt, which had no oil, as a present (Is. 57⁹) and as an article of commerce.** Here the former is intended. Read ריב : יֹבְלוּ ††

instead of וריב : יוּבָל. It would be difficult to find a more interesting parallel than is furnished for this verse in almost every particular by Is. 30⁶. The great sin is against Yahweh, and consists in alliance with foreign powers, which involves distrust of and faithlessness toward Yahweh. This is seeking for wind and multiplying of falsehood. And for this reason, — **3.** *Yahweh has a quarrel with Israel, to punish Jacob according to his ways*] It is impossible to suppose that Judah is here spoken of, because (1) Judah is not in the thought of the prophet here, nor often elsewhere, but *v.* p. clix; (2) if the text is correct, Judah is given the place of prominence, even before Jacob

---

* Rashi, Ki.
† Rashi, Oort (*v.s.*).
‡ Now., We.
§ Hd., Ke., Now., *et al.* ‖ Hi., Sim.
¶ Che., We., Now., GAS. On the use of שוא cf. Coffin, *JBL.* XIX. 168–171.
** See Macalister, art. " Oil," *DB.;* Kennedy, art. " Oil," *EB.*
†† We., Loft., Now., GAS.; on basis of Ⓖ, and to secure uniformity of verbal form in יובלו, יכרתו, ירבו.

(Cheyne's suggestion that Jacob is here used for Judah, as in
Ps. 77[15], is plainly incorrect) ; (3) to accept the text is to accept
the impossible combination, viz. Yahweh has a strife with Judah
(even) *in order to* punish Jacob (for (*a*) 𝕲 thus omits ו with
ולפקד, and (*b*) if retained, it must be rendered as above unless
the verse is assigned to a later period of the language, in which
the construction with ל is used to continue the ordinary imperfect*). We must, therefore, understand that some one changed
the original text, substituting Judah for Israel, perhaps when [1b],
which refers to Judah, was inserted.† With the phraseology
here, cf. 4[1] Mi. 6[2]. The omission of ו before לפקד (cf. 𝕲 and
statement above) makes the second member dependent on the
first ; *i.e.* the purpose of the contention is to punish Israel, and
this is to be measured *according to his ways ; i.e.* in return for
and in proportion to his faithless conduct toward Yahweh. The
prophet desires to place special emphasis on the basis of judgment which Yahweh will adopt, and to that end adopts a double
and striking rhetorical method of expression, repeating substantially what he has just said, and then illustrating the statement by a significant example. This he proceeds to do in the
next two members of the parallelism. ‡ — *According to his deeds he
will requite him* (— **4 a**) ; *in the womb he supplanted his brother*]
The two clauses expressing the same thought are arranged
chiastically, and are followed suddenly and strikingly by a statement concerning Israel's ancestor, Jacob, handed down by
tradition, which in a single stroke both announces and explains
the whole case. Jacob's supplanting of his brother in the womb
before birth indicates that fatal characteristic of the nation
which, as exhibited again and again in its history, has now
reached the point at which punishment must be administered.
This reference to traditional lore clearly carries with it reproach
(cf. the unfavorable sense in which the same verb is used,
Gn. 27[36]), and stigmatizes the nation as deceitful and untrust-

---

* GK. 114*p* ; H. 29, 5 *a*. † We., Now., GAS.

‡ In view of the peculiarly symmetrical and artistic expression found in this
section, and of its highly poetic character, one wonders whether Che. was not
sleeping when he wrote (p. 113) in connection with chap. 12, " Again poetry is
dispelled by prose."

worthy. In evident contrast with this single line, the long addition in vs.[4b-7] is occupied in the praise of Israel. עקב is rendered (1) "took by the heel," on the basis of וידו אחזת עקב (Gn. 25[26]), "and his hand was having hold of Esau's heel"; (2) "supplanted," on basis of Gn. 27[36], *i.e.* Jacob's supplanting (עקב) Esau twice, in the matter of the birthright and the blessing. But two things are clear: (1) there is no basis for the rendering "took by the heel"; (2) the word בבטן used with עקב indicates a source of authority distinct from the two Genesis sources.* The statement, therefore, is to be taken as an additional reproach upon Israel, and as indicating that his deceptive character is inborn and ineradicable;* in distinction from the view which makes this clause a statement of praise uttered of the ancestor Jacob (in contrast with the degraded condition of his descendants), since, even before birth he showed his preëminence, how he was destined to anticipate his brother;† for in this case the prophet would surely have designated as subject of [4a] the patriarch Jacob in distinction from the people Jacob; or (3) the view that this "catching hold of Esau's heel" was presented to Israel in order to encourage and stimulate them, and to show that not merit but the mercy of God was the source of the preëminence.‡ Of the three views, the first interprets the statement concerning Jacob as bad and in accord with what has been said of Israel; the second and third, as good, but as in contrast with what has been said.—
13. *And Jacob fled to the field of Aram*] This verse seems unquestionably to stand with [4b-7].§ Like these verses it is historical, and like them it is commendatory in its tone. The abruptness of v.[13] was observed as far back as Rashi. Cf. Gn. 27[43] 28[2], for the fuller account. The phrase "field of Aram" is a translation of the word Padan- (or Paddan-) Aram.— *And Israel served for a wife, and for a wife he herded (sheep)*] Cf. Gn. 29[18-20] 30[31] 31[38-41]. Nowack's suggestion of a contrast between "wife" and "prophet" (cf. v.[14]) is imaginary, and disappears with the separation of the two verses.—**4b.** *In his man's strength he*

---

* Now.   † Ew., Wü., Che.   ‡ Cal., Ros.; Beer, *ZAW.* XIII. 281-293.
§ Cf. Now., Oet.; Grimm, *Lit. App.* 74-77.

contended with God] שרה is also rendered "wrestled," * "had power with." † As the writer puts together יעקב and עקב, "supplant," so also ישראל and שרה, "contend." The pun is evident (cf. Mi. 1¹⁰·¹⁴). Note that (1) the ו of ובאונו is a dittograph of the ו of the preceding אחיו, dating, of course, from a time subsequent to the disarrangement of the original order ; (2) this line is parallel with that which follows, not with that which precedes ; (3) it is the first of four lines in close connection with each other ; (4) the contest with God (or the angel), occurring on the return from being with Laban (Gn. 32²⁵), is here placed first in order, whereas in Genesis, the Bethel story, occurring on his outward trip (*v.i.*) precedes ; (5) whatever specific interpretation is adopted of these four lines, it is understood to be praise of the patriarch Jacob. On באונו *v.i.* אלהים designates any form of superhuman character : (1) as here, angel ; (2) disembodied spirits (1 S. 28¹³) ; (3) judges, as representing God (Ex. 22⁸·⁹). This line praises Jacob, and is therefore inconsistent with ⁴ᵃ ; yet some make ⁴ᵇ synonymous with ⁴ᵃ, ‡ and understand the change to have taken place at the beginning of v.⁵. — **5.** *Yea, he contended with the angel and prevailed*] The poetical repetition of the preceding line, with one modification (angel for God) and one addition (the fact that he prevailed). For אל read את. § מלאך = אלהים ; cf. Gn. 16¹⁰ and 17¹⁸⁻²⁰ Ex. 13²¹ and 14¹⁹ ; and so in pre-exilic literature in general. ‖ It is E who in the Hexateuch makes large use of angels (cf. Gn. 21¹⁷ 22¹¹ 28¹² 31¹¹ 32¹·² Ex. 23³⁰). ¶ Of course it was Jacob who prevailed (ויכל) and not the angel.** Here the thought is that of praise, *i.e.* the persistency and energy with which the patriarch sought the divine blessing (cf. Gn. 32²⁹). — *He wept and besought mercy of him*] *i.e.* Jacob wept. While 𝕲 makes both Jacob and the angel weep, and 𝔐 only Jacob, J (Gn. 32²⁴⁻³²) says nothing about weeping. Jacob's attitude is exactly that which the writer would have Israel adopt, viz. anxiety, sorrow, and repentance, not victory. But is this consistent with the thought of ⁴ᵃ? Is it, moreover, the point of view maintained in Gn. 32²⁵ ? — *At Bethel*

---

* Ew.   † AV., RV.   ‡ Or.   § Now.   ‖ G. B. Gray, art. "Angel," *EB.*
¶ My statement, *Hebraica*, V. 261 ; cf. Carpenter and Battersby, *The Hexateuch*, I. 112 f.   ** Hi.

he met him (*Yahweh*) *and there he* (*Yahweh*) *spoke with him*] Cf.
Gn. 28[11 ff.] 35[9 ff.]. $\mathfrak{S}$ *him*, is better than *us* (*v.s.*), (cf. Ewald, who
on the other hand (1) treats נו of ימצאנו as 1st pl., not 3rd sg.,
(2) makes Yahweh subject* and not object, and (3) makes the
imperfects futures (in prediction) and not vivid pictures from past
history). Here is an allusion to Jacob's dream, but the point
of view is different from that of Gn. 28. That vs.[4b-5] present
a different and conflicting point of view as compared with vs.[2-4a] is
apparent. The unfavorable עקב of [4a] is changed into a favorable
term, שרה, in [4b], and this favorable point of view is maintained
through v.[5] in striking contrast with the condemnation expressed
in vs.[2-4a]. — **6.** *And Yahweh is God of Hosts; Yahweh is his
name*] This is an interjectional gloss or addition from the hand
of some pious reader of very late days † (the ו being confirmatory
of what precedes, and practically = *as truly as* ‡) rather than
the subject (ו being omitted) of the preceding ידבר, § for this
gives a cumbersome set of clauses for subject, and the ו of ואתה
does not fit in. *His memorial;* i.e. *his name*, cf. Ex. 3[15]. —
7. *So thou by the help of thy God shouldst turn back*] The
address is to Jacob ‖ (these being the words spoken at Bethel,
the clause being the object of ידבר (v.[5])), rather than to Israel; ¶
it has the tone and the coloring of the later times. *By thy
God, i.e.* by his help,** rather than *to thy God,* †† or *in thy God,
i.e.* "such being the character of God, who lets himself be won
by wrestling prayer, return thou to thy God and rest in him" ; ‡‡
but none of these explanations is wholly satisfactory. Cf. Wellhausen's suggestion (*v.s.*), *thou shalt swear* (Gn. 21[23] Dt. 6[13] 10[20]).
Halévy urges in defence of v.[6] that Hosea, after sharply contrasting
Israel's present dispirited and feeble state with the energy and
courage of their early days (vs.[4 and 5]), continues in v.[6] by assuring
them that Yahweh is the God of armies and is able to defend
the weakest against the strongest; therefore they should call
on him (reading זכרו, imv.) instead of appealing to outside
nations. — *Keep kindness and justice*] In relation to men, cf.

---

* So Sim.   ‖ Hi., We., Now.
† So We., Volz, GAS., Now.   ¶ Ma., Hd., Sim., Ke., Schm., GAS., *et al.*
‡ BDB. 253; cf. Am. 9[5-6] Is. 5[5].   ** Hi., GAS.
§ Oort, Val.   †† AV., RV., Sim., *et al.*   ‡‡ Che.

Ho. 4[1f.] 6[6] Am. 5[7. 10-12. 15].—*And wait on thy God without ceasing*]
i.e. cultivate absolute faithfulness, cf. 11[12] 9[1] 11[7] 7[11]. Nowack
calls attention to the difficulty of taking v.[7] as an address to
Israel, and suggests that were such the case, the verse must be
regarded as from another writer than the author of [4b-6]. In
favor of regarding vs.[4b-7] as a later addition * he urges (1) the
poor connection between [4a] and [4b]; (2) the extraordinary reversal of the historical order of events in the narrative of Jacob's
life; (3) the bad connection of v.[6] with v.[5]; (4) the fact that
v.[8] continues the thought of v.[4a]. This addition was occasioned
by the fact that one of the patriarchs was represented in the
original narrative in an unfavorable light, altogether at variance
with the ordinary view of the patriarchs. Effort has been made
to interpret vs.[1-7] as a unit,† thus: Ephraim on account of his
persistent sins is threatened with punishment from Yahweh.
His ancestor Jacob should be his example. Jacob sinned once
(viz. בבטן); but afterwards in sorrow and anguish he returned to
God (באונו שרה), who received him graciously and promised him
aid on certain conditions. But this interpretation implies an
unnatural contrast between בבטן and באונו.

1. סכבני] On extended (or uncontracted) form cf. GK. 67 *a*.— רד] The
possibilities of this word are very great in view of the several roots from
which these consonants might be taken; *e.g.* רדד (cf. Ps. 144[2] Is. 45[1]), רדה
(*v.s.*), ירד (*v.s.*), רוד (*v.s.*), but the corruption of the text seems certain.—
קרשים] The intensive plural *Most Holy One*, H. 3, 2 *c*; GK. 124 *h*; see
especially Kö. 348 *d*; cf. 263 *d*. Chiastic with עם־אל.—נאמן] Foll. קרשים as
predicate of יהורה.—**2.** יובל] Or יובילו, with ל of pers.; cf. Ps. 68[30] 76[12]; for
other cases of final ו connected wrongly with following word, *v.* Je. 22[14], ו חלוני
= חלוניו; 1 S. 14[21], סכבו גם = סביב וגם; Je. 17[11], עשרו ולא = עשר לא; cf. Dr.
Sm. xxx f.—**3.** ולפקר] Cf. GK. 114 *p*; also 114 *r*; Kö. 413 *v*; but *v.s.*—
4. שרה] Only here and Gn. 32[29]; in one case עם is the preposition, in the
other את. On the connection of שראל with this root, cf. BDB., BSZ.; Nestle,

---

* Cf. We.[8] (suspects [5-7]), Sm. *Rel.* 215 (rejects [7]), Volz (who considers [4b-7] an
archaeological note from a learned reader), Grimm (who rejects [4-7] as a "liturgical
appendix"), Wkl. *GI.* I. 59 (makes [4-6] late), Stärk, *Studien z. Religions- u.
Sprachgeschichte d. A. T.* II. 8 ff. (rejects [4b-7]), and Luther, *ZAW.* XXI. 67
(makes [5-7] late). Marti om. 3 *a.* [5-7] as later additions.

† Beer, *ZAW* XV. 281 ff.; Procksch, *Geschichtsbetrachtung u. geschichtlicher
Überlieferung bei den vorexil. Proph.* (1902), 19-23.

Isr. Eigennamen, 60 ff.; Gray, *Hebr. Prop. Names*, 218; Che. *EB.* 2311; Dr. *DB.* II. 530. — **5.** וישר] Generally treated as Qal. impf. of שׂוּר, a cognate of שׂרה (*v.s.*); GK. 72 *t.* The prep. אל is hardly appropriate, and in view of Gn. 32²⁹ את is preferable (*v.s.*, We.). — וַיִּכַל] With ַ for ׀, and ַ because of Zaqēph qātôn; on form, GK. 69 *r*; cf. 53 *u.* — בּיתאל] Acc. of place; Kö. 330 *k.* — יִמְצָאֶנּוּ] For either הו or נו (*v.s.*); on impf., Kö. 157 *b.* — **6.** ויהוה] This ו is almost the Arab. wāw of the oath (*v.s.*); cf. BDB., also H. 44, 1 *d*, rm.; Ew.⁸ § 340, 3. — אל־ש׳] The full form of the divine title; cf. Löhr, *Untersuch. z. B. Amos*, 39 ff.; Kö. 295 *i.* — **7.** קוה] For the use of this word in Psalms, cf. Ps. 27¹⁴ 37³⁴.

8. *Canaan !*] Strophe 2 begins in a startling fashion, with the derogatory epithet — *Canaan.** The thought is a direct continuation of strophe 1 (¹⁻⁴ᵃ). This strophe shows no recognition of the personal story of Jacob in vs.¹³· ⁴ᵇ⁻⁷. There is no reason for supposing, as does Nowack, that after ⁴ᵃ there originally existed a line or sentence which explained ⁴ᵃ, for ⁴ᵃ needs no explanation; it is on account of its perspicuity and suggestiveness that the later writer is led to give in contrast with it the interesting traditions which point to another conception of Jacob's character. V.⁸ follows ⁴ᵃ most fitly. *Canaan* is not (1) an address, direct or indirect, to the Canaanites or Phoenicians, whose reputation for dishonesty was widely known; † nor (2) a common noun, *merchant;* ‡ but (3) a proper noun used as a figurative epithet for degenerate Israel, and equivalent to *merchant*, for the work of merchandising in the cities had been in the hands of Canaanites so long that "Canaanite" had become a synonym for "merchant" (Pr. 31²⁴ Jb. 41⁶, also Zp. 1¹¹ Ez. 17⁴; cf. כנעה = *wares*, Je. 10¹⁷). In the same way "Chaldean" and "astrologer" became synonymous. To be rejected are (1) the making of כנען an appositive of Ephraim (v.⁹); § (2) its treatment as a vocative; ‖ in favor of (3) the construction as an independent nominative or accusative. — *In his hand are false balances, he loves to defraud*] Cf. Am. 2⁶ 8⁵ᶠ. לעקב (cf. ⁴ᵃ), *to defraud*, should be read ¶ instead of לעשק, *to oppress*, since the latter idea is not under consideration.

---

* On the etymological meaning, see Moore, *PAOS.*, 1890, pp. lxvii–lxx; GAS. *HG*, 4 f.; Buhl, *Pal.* § 42; M. Jastrow, Jr., art. "Canaan," § 6, *EB.*

† Cf. *Odys.* XIV. 290, 291, and the Latin *fides Punica.*   ‖ Cal.

‡ ⳦, Rashi, Marck, Ros., AV.   § Böckel.   ¶ We., Now.

The second line (two words) seems lacking in proportion, the preceding line having four words; but as suggested above, this strophe seems to have the elegiac movement $(3 + 2)$; it is surely an elegy in its tone. — **9.** *And does Ephraim say, Yes, but I have become rich; I have secured for myself wealth*] This verse contains (1) Israel's supposed reply to the charge of deceit and dishonesty; together with which comes (2) Yahweh's reply concerning the gains thus unrighteously acquired; * and not a continued statement by Israel that his wealth will not be reckoned as sin.† Israel's reply is of the self-congratulatory order, and furnishes his defence for this apparent dishonesty toward God and man (cf. Zc. 11[5]). ויאמר = *and has Ephraim said?* i.e. a condition (cf. Ps. 104[28 ff.]). אך is not asseverative = *surely, indeed;* ‡ but restrictive, and in contrast with what precedes = *howbeit, still, yes, but,* with something of astonishment on the part of the speaker that such charges should be made.§ Israel's defence is twofold: (*a*) I am prosperous, that's enough; (*b*) I have obtained my wealth by my own efforts, and neither by the help of God ‖ nor as a Canaanite (trafficker), cf. Zc. 14[21]. און (= *strength* v.[4]) must here be taken (cf. חיל) in sense of "*wealth*" (cf. Jb. 20[10]); cf. also the reading אָוֶן, *idol*, of 𝔙. — (*Let him know*) *that all his gains are insufficient for the guilt which he has incurred*] This rendering rests on 𝔊 and differs from 𝔐𝔗 in (*a*) substituting ו (3d pers.) for י (1st pers.); (*b*) in prefixing the preposition ל to עֹון; (*c*) in reading חָטָא,¶ pf. 3 m. sg., for חֵטְא. ימצאו, here without the רי (*sufficiency*), which is the fuller construction; cf. Lv. 12[8] 25[26. 28] (with רי) and Ju. 21[14] ** Nu. 11[22].†† Cf. also the interesting play on מצא between [9a] and [9b]. 𝔐𝔗 has been rendered (1) *all my profits shall bring me no iniquity which is sin;* ‡‡ (2) *as for all my profits, etc.;* §§ (3) *they will not find in all my profits, etc.;* ‖‖ but whatever the specific rendering, two fatal objections present themselves: (*a*) these words furnish the basis of v.[10], and must be a part of the divine rejoinder, not the continuation of Israel's defence, and must have the tone (as these do) of punishment; (*b*) there is implied an "unnatural distinction between iniquity

---

* Cf. Che., We., Now., Oet.	¶ We., Che., Now.	‡‡ So Wü.
† Cal., Hi., Ew., Pu., Or., *et al.*	** So BDB., and GFM. *in loc.*	§§ Mau.
‡ Che. § Wü. ‖ AE.	†† Also Now.	‖‖ AE.

2 C

and sin." * — **10.** *For I, Yahweh*] אנכי יהוה is not an independent sentence,† but the subject of אושיבך. ‡ — *Thy God from the land of Egypt*] Cf. 13⁴; the God who brought you up out of Egypt, who has since that day remained the same, and, therefore, has given no just cause for your unfaithfulness. — *Will again make thee to dwell in tents*] Is it a promise or a threat? (1) A promise § that they will *yet* be delivered out of the degraded and dishonest national life of the present into the pure, simple, and beautiful life of primitive times, before the curse of civilization had produced its dire results; *i.e.* "although it is true that Israel has incurred condemnation, I, being the same that I have been from the beginning of their history, will deliver them, and cause them to renew their joy before me." This view is supported (*a*) by that interpretation of כימי מועד (*v.i.*) which makes it represent an occasion of joy; (*b*) by the absence of any definite reference in this verse to the wilderness; (*c*) by the actual case of the Rechabites, whose ideal it was thus to live apart from civilization (Je. 35⁶ᶠᶠ·); (*d*) by the fact that 11¹¹ may be interpreted consistently with this; (*e*) by the combination in 2 K. 13⁵ of the same ideas; viz. deliverance and dwelling in tents. ‖ (2) A threat¶ that they will *again* be driven away from home and compelled as in the days of the wilderness to live in tents; *i.e.* a wandering, nomadic life. Being the same God as of old, he will now punish as he punished in the past (Nu. 14²⁶⁻³⁰). This view is supported (*a*) by the demands of the context, for what but a threat could be uttered after the heartless and defiant words of Israel as expressed in ⁹ᵃ? (*b*) by the analogy of 2¹⁴, which is unquestionably a threat; and (*c*) by a correct understanding of כימי מועד (*v.i.*). The evidence clearly favors taking the statement thus, nor is it, as has been suggested, a threat with an indirect promise in the far distant future, an idea growing out of the analogy of the wilderness followed by deliverance; ** or a suggestion that Yahweh "*could* destroy all this commercial civilization"; †† it is rather the plain and definite prediction, in language borrowed from past history and used figuratively, of certain destruction. — *As in the*

---

* Che. † Wü. ‡ Che. § Jer., Ki., Cal., Marck, Hd., Pu., Marti.
‖ The late origin of 2 K. 13⁵ is to be taken into consideration; cf. Benz., Kit. *in loc.*
¶ Grotius, Dathe, Ew., Umb., Or., We., Now. ** Ke. †† GAS.

days of the festal assembly] This phrase, in 𝕸𝕿 כִּימֵי מוֹעֵד, has received widely differing interpretations: (1) *According to the appointed days*, using מוֹעֵד as an appellative = an adjective.* (2) = Feast of booths (Lv. 23³⁹⁻⁴³; cf. 1 K. 12³² Dt. 31¹⁰), the time of "ingathering" (cf. Ex. 23¹⁶). The significance of this feast lay in the fact that it was an occasion of joy and thanksgiving, celebrating the completion of the harvest, and as such it was an expression of the characteristically Canaanitish idea that the deity was the lord, the *ba'al* of the land and the dispenser of its fruits. The dwelling in booths is explained by W. R. Smith as occasioned by the fear that the house and its contents should become *taboo* and unfit for ordinary use, through contact with the consecrated person of the worshipper during the progress of the feast; while Wellhausen attributes it to "the custom of the whole household, old and young, going out to the vineyard in time of harvest, and there camping out in the open air under the improvised shelter of booths made with branches." † That the feast was a reminder of the tent life of early days is, of course, a late idea (P). Wellhausen's objection that a feast characterized by unlimited expressions of joy would not be appropriate to the wilderness is met by Cheyne's statement that life in tents in the feast-time was a matter of amusement, out-of-door sport; but in contrast, Israel will be *compelled* so to live, and this would be another matter. ‡ (3) A national feast, § *i.e.* a day of national assembling. (4) *Days of appointed season*, i.e. *festivals* (cf. 9⁵ La. 2⁷·²²). (5) Although the real wilderness-feast was the Passover (Ex. 4²³), it is to be remembered that there is no reference to dwelling in tents in connection with the Passover, ‖ and nothing is known concerning the rites of this feast. In view of the difficulties involved in the interpretation of 𝕸𝕿, textual changes (*v.s.*) have been proposed, *e.g.*, (1) Yet shall I bring thee back to thy God in the appointed time; ¶ (2) as in the days of thy youth; ** (3) as

---

* Ma.

† On the feast of booths *v.* Now. *Arch.* II. 150 ff.; Benz. art. "Feasts," *EB.*; WRS. *Sem.* note K; We. *Prol.* 85, and my *Constructive Studies in the Priestly Element*, §§ 96–106.

‡ Mich., Bauer; also Grotius, Dathe (although regarding it as a threat (*shall I longer cause them to dwell in booths?*)).

§ Hi.   ‖ Cf. We., Now.   ¶ Gardner.   ** We.⁸; cf. Perles.

in the days of old,* cf. כימי נעוריה וכיום עלותה, 2[17], used of the times of the wilderness, and note the full significance which עד now receives. Wellhausen says that vs.[11. 12] belong in another context and that there is no connection between them. The latter part of his statement is correct, the first part wrong. G. A. Smith says of vs.[11-15], "I cannot trace the argument here." Marti treats vs.[9b-11. 13. 14] as later additions. If v.[11] is taken as introducing a new strophe, to be followed by v.[15] and then by [12] (v.[13] being placed before [4b] and v.[14] being regarded as a later addition from the same hand as vs.[13. 4b-7]), there is symmetry of artistic form, together with regular and close consecution of thought. — **11.** *And I spake by the prophets*] As so frequently (cf. Am. 2[9 ff.] Is. chap. 5) the prophet, before saying the last word, recalls the fact that earnest effort has been put forth to teach Israel the right things. This is a new thought in this piece, and quite appropriately introduces a new strophe; close connection with either [10a] or [10b. c] is not to be expected (cf. on the contrary Nowack). ודברתי, perfect with wāw consecutive, expresses frequently repeated action, *and I used to speak.* על means *by, by the hand of, through;* † no good reason exists for substituting אל; ‡ cf., however, ⅏ עם and Ⅎ πρός. — *For it was I who multiplied vision and by the hand of the prophets gave parables*] Special emphasis rests on "I." § *Parables, i.e.* similitudes, sometimes implied, as in 9[10], at others, definite, 7[4-7] Is. 5[1-7]. The suggestion to read ‖ אֲדַמֶּה אֲדָמֶה אִמֵּך (taking אם from v.[12], 𝕸𝕿) is favored (*a*) by the parallel in 4[5]; (*b*) by the non-occurrence of the absolute meaning *use parables* elsewhere for דמה, (*c*) by the failure of אם to make sense at the beginning of v.[12]; (*d*) by the meaning of [12b] which requires [12a] to be absolute and not conditional (cf. 6[8]); (*e*) by the easier interpretation of היו as well as זבחו as historical perfects; and (*f*) by the fact that the idea of destruction through a prophet is quite a common one (6[5]); but

---

* Gr., Now.   † Cf. Kno. *Prophetismus*, I. 201; Ke. *in loc.*   ‡ Now.ᴴ

§ On *visions*, cf. Giesebrecht, *Die Berufsbegabung der Alttest. Propheten*, 38–72; Duhm, *Theol.* 86 ff.; Maybaum, *Die Entwickelung d. isr. Proph.*, 1–6; Briggs, *Mess. Proph.* 17 f.; Sm. *Rel.* 82 ff.; Kö. *Der Offenbarungsbegriff d. A. T.* II. 9–60; Borchert, *SK.* 1895, pp. 217 ff.; Kue. *Prophets and Prophecy in Isr.*, 78–89; Schultz, *O. T. Theol.* I. 275–9, 281 ff.   ‖ Oet.

this is just the opposite idea from that which the prophet is trying to express (cf. [11a, 11b]), and is consequently impossible. — **14.** *And by a prophet Yahweh brought Israel up from Egypt; and by a prophet he was shepherded*] With v.[12] following v.[15], and v.[13] transferred to precede [4b], we have next v.[14], which is a later insertion intended to state, still more fully and definitely than Hosea had done, how Yahweh had made use of prophets in Israel's instruction. This explains why in v.[11] the 1st person is used, but in v.[14] the 3d, of Yahweh. In this verse, naturally, the idea of warning (so prominent in the original utterance) is absent. Although נביא is indefinite, only one prophet is in mind, Moses (cf. Dt. 18[18]). Nowack's remarks (p. 76, foot) are no longer in place, because v.[13] has nothing to do with v.[14]. It is possible that נשמר had a subject (*e.g.* Jacob), which has been lost; the shortness of the line is noteworthy. For this use of שמר, cf. Is. 21[11] 62[6]. — **15.** *Ephraim has given bitter provocation*] I gave Israel instruction and warning in every possible way (v.[11]), and what is the result? Ephraim has, by his conduct, given me bitter provocation; literally, *he has provoked bitterly*, no object being expressed; cf. 1 K. 21[22] 2 K. 21[6]. — *And his bloodshed he will leave upon him*] Nowack * is in error in demanding for נטש the meaning *to sling, to cast down;* its original use is *to leave, let alone* (cf. Ex. 23[11] = *let the field lie fallow;* Nu. 11[31], *and left* (*the quails*) *by the camp*) ; so here Yahweh will leave † upon him (Ephraim) his bloodshed, *i.e.* his guilt for the acts of bloodshed, of whatever form (not, however, in connection with children offered to Moloch ‡) which he has committed (cf. 1[4] 4[2]). § — *And his reproach his Lord will return to him*] *i.e.* Yahweh will repay Israel (cf. Is. 65[7]) for all reproach brought upon him (Yahweh), ו in הרפתו being the objective genitive ; ‖ or for the reproach of which Israel is guilty, ו being a subjective genitive ¶ (just as ו in the parallel phrase דמיו). — **12.** *In Gilead is iniquity, only vanity they have wrought*] The text is again corrupt. With אם no sense can be made ; perhaps we may read בְּ.** After the analogy of פעל in 6[8] we may change היו to עָשׂוּ.†† *Only, nought but* (cf. similar force in Nu. 12[2] Jb. 19[13])

---

* Also Ew., Che., BSZ.

† Ke., Or. (thrust upon him) ; GAS., p. 303, seems to have overlooked this word.

‡ Hi.   § BDB.   ‖ Che.   ¶ Wü., Now.   ** ﬡ, Now.   †† We.

is satisfactory, and the proposed change of אך to אָף * is unnecessary. Gilead is singled out, as in 6⁸, as a place in which Israel's
wickedness has especially manifested itself. אם of 𝕳𝕿 has been
taken (1) as introducing an ironical, or rhetorical, question, *Is
there iniquity in Gilgal?* † (2) as a particle of asseveration = *surely
there is wickedness in Gilgal;* ‡ (3) as a conditional particle,=
if there is iniquity in Gilgal. § — *In Gilgal they sacrifice to demons*]
Cf. Dt. 32¹⁷ Ps. 106³⁷. לשדים for שורים (*v.s.*), the ל having been
dropped after the final ל of גלגל. The difficulty with 𝕳𝕿 is ‖
(1) that the plural of שור appears only here ; (2) that the sacrificing of oxen was nothing in itself reprehensible ; (3) if the
meaning is "sacrifice to oxen," we should expect לשורים or, more
in accordance with prophetic usage, לעגלים ; and, in any case, the
worship of the calves is nowhere else mentioned as being conducted at Gilgal. 𝕲's שרים is clearly a misreading of ר for ד. ¶
The ordinary translations have been either (1) *they sacrifice
bullocks in Gilgal;* ** *i.e.* they insult Yahweh by sacrificing in
connection with idolatrous places (cf. 4¹⁵) ; or (2) they sacrifice
to the bullocks in Gilgal,†† but nowhere else is שור used of the calf-
worship. — *So their altars shall be as stone-heaps among the furrows of the field*] This is the consequence of it all (cf. Mi. 1⁶)
— a scene of desolation. The fulfilment is seen in 2 K. 15²⁹,
concerning which event Tiglathpileser himself says in a badly
broken passage, "The town of Gilead, . . . Abel [beth Maachah?]
. . . which is a part of the land of bit-Ḥumri [*i.e.* Samaria] . . .
the broad, throughout its extent I added to the territory of
Assyria ; and established my officer as governor over them." ‡‡

8. כנען] On *casus pendens* as a genitive attribute of the following clause,
cf. Kö. 341 *h*. — לעשק] On use of ל, H. 29, 4 *c*. — **11.** ואנכי] Peculiar position,
Kö. 339 *n*. — **12.** אם] Retaining 𝕳𝕿, Kö. (389 *p*) makes this conditional in
form, but causal in force. — והיו] Dr. (§ 136 γ) and Kö. (415 *c*) treat this as an

---

* We.   § Hi., Ew., Sim., Ke., Or.
† Cal., Pu.   ‡ Stuck, Hd.   ‖ Cf. Now.
¶ On demon-worship, cf. Di. and Dr. on Dt. 32¹⁷; Gray, art. "Demons," *EB.*;
Che. on Ps. 106³⁷; WRS. *Sem., v.* Index; Baudissin, *Studien zur sem. Rel.* I. 130–36.
** 𝕿, Ke., Wü., *et al.*   †† 𝕐, Marck, *et al.*
‡‡ Annals, *v.* III. R, 10, 2, ls. 17 ff.; cf. *KB.* II. 30 ff.; *KAT.*² 264 f.; Dr. in
Hogarth's *Authority and Archaeology*, 98 f.

apodosis expressing certain future. — שׂדי] On absence of art., Kö. 293 a. —
13. באשה] A good example of the בּ of price, or substitution, Kö. 332 o. —
15. תמרורים] Adv. acc., Kö. 332 e; on pl., Kö. 262 f.

§ 17. The utter destruction of Israel. 13¹⁻¹¹. Israel in the

days of old stood high; but they sinned and died; and now grow
worse and worse in their devotion to idols, treating them as gods
(¹·²ᵃ·ᵇ); therefore, idolatrous through and through, they shall van-
ish like cloud or dew, like chaff or smoke (²ᶜ·³). It was I who rescued them from Egypt; they have had no other god or saviour.
It was I who cared for them in the wilderness, but the more
prosperous they became, the farther they departed from me
(⁴·⁵·⁶). Therefore I will destroy them as if I were a wild beast
— jackal, or leopard, or bear, or lion (⁷·⁸). In this impending
calamity, O Israel, who will help you? There will be no king to
save you; for your kings, given in my anger, will be taken away
in my wrath (⁹⁻¹¹).

The unity of this passage is evident; its symmetrical structure is more
than usually marked. In five strophes (8 + 6 + 8 + 6 + 8) announcement
is made of absolute destruction. The movement is trimeter, with occasional
dimeters and tetrameters. Strophe 1 contrasts the honored Israel of the past
with the fallen Israel of the present, all on account of faithlessness to Yahweh
(vs.¹·²ᵃ·ᵇ). Strophe 2 presents a picture of destruction, — an utter vanishing
away, consequent on Israel's apostasy (vs.²ᶜ·³). Strophe 3 contrasts Yahweh's
love and care, as manifested in their past history, with their ungrateful attitude of neglect and forgetfulness in degree proportionate to the blessings
granted them (vs.⁴·⁵·⁶). Strophe 4 presents a second picture of destruction —
a horrible devouring, as of wild beasts (vs.⁷·⁸). Strophe 5 announces sternly
that no deliverance will be possible, since no leaders will remain to guide
them (vs.⁹⁻¹¹). No important modifications of the text are involved in this
arrangement.

1. כרבר] ⑮ κατὰ τὸν λόγον = כְּדָבָּר; similarly 'A. — רתח] ⑮ δικαιώματα
= חֻקֹּת, or, better, דח (Aramaic) in pl. (Vol.); Σ., Θ. τρόμον; 'A. φρίκην;
ﺱ |ܘܣ ܪ܆ = רָתַח with 'אפ as subj. (Seb.). Gr. אֱמֶת(?). Oort (ThT. and
Em.) and Val. רֵעַת. Hal. חֲתָת. — נישׂא] ﺱ ܠܘܪ |ܘܣܣ = [הוא[היה = נשׂיא הוא (Seb.);
similarly ⓣ. Read, with ﺱ and Oort, נָשִׂיא (so We., Gr., Val., GAS., Now.,
Oet.). Oort (Em.) and Marti, נָשָׂא — [הוא] Gr. היה(?). — ויאשׁם] ⑮ καὶ ἔθετο
αὐτά = וַיְשִׂימֵם (Vol.). — ויטם] Gr. וימוט. — 2. עתה] ⑮ om. — כחבונם] ⑮ κατ'
εἰκόνα; ﬗ quasi similitudinem; ﺱ ܣܟܡ̣ܟܣ = כתבניתם (Seb.); cf. ⓣ. One
cod. of de R. כתבונתם. Oort (ThT. and Em.), foll. ⑮, כִּתְמוּנַת (so Gu., Loft.) or

כתבנית. Ew. פְּתַבְנְתָם (so Gr., GAS., Oet., Now.[2]). Hal. בִּתְבוּנָה. Read, with
We., Val., Now.[1], פִּתְמוּנָתָם.—כלה] 𝕲 συντετελεσμένα = כָּלָה; 𝔖 om. Several
codd. of Kenn. and de R. כֻלְי, and 6 codd. of Kenn. כֻלָּם (so Loft., Hal.).—
להם] 𝕲 joins with preceding. Read, with Sta. (ZAW. III. 12; so Brüll,
Jahrb. f. jüd. Gesch. u. Lit. (1883); Gr.), אלהים, or, with Now. and We.[3],
insert אלהים before להם.—זבחו] 𝕲 θύσατε = זִבְחוּ; Σ. θυσιάσατε; 𝔙 immolate.
ד is perhaps a fragment of an original line, עַם זבחים לַשֵׁדִים (v.i.). Gr. וְנֵחִי(?).
Ru. זְבָחִי, to be taken with אמרים, which is to be rendered, they assign.—אדם]
Duhm (Theol. 132), דם(?).—וישקון] 𝕲 ἐκλελοίπασιν, with עג as subj.; probably derived from שפק (Vol.); 𝔙 adorantes; Θ. προσκυνήσετε; 𝔖 ܡܣܬܚܒ.
—3. ויסער] Oort, וִסֵער (so Gr., Now., Oet., Marti).—מארבה] 𝕲 ἀπὸ δακρύων
= מִאַרְבֶה (Vol.); 'A. ἀπὸ καταράκτου; 𝔖 ܟܣܝܐ.—4. ואלהיך] Foll. this
𝕲 inserts: "the one establishing the heavens and creating the earth, whose
hands created all the host of the heavens, and I did not show them to thee in
order that thou mightest follow after them; and I led thee," etc. On basis of
𝕲 and 𝔖 insert אשר הוצאתיך; cf. Oort (Em.), who inserts העליתיך (cf. 12[10]).—
5. ידעתיך] Read, with 𝕲, ἐποίμαινόν σε, רעיתיך (so 𝔖, Seb., We., Gr., Gu., Loft.,
GAS., Marti); cf. 𝕿.—בארץ] Now. and Oet. insert רעיתיך before בא.—
תלאבות] 𝕲 ἀοικήτῳ; 𝔙 solitudinis; 𝔖 ܥܒܐ ܘܥܠ ܣܡܟܐ, "a double rendering,
the latter being a gloss from the Alexandrine transl." (Seb.). Gr. תְּלָאֹות.—
6. כמרעיתם] 𝕲 κατὰ τὰς νομὰς (Σ. sg.) αὐτῶν; 𝔖 ܐܠܗܐ ܕܒܣܠ. Oort (ThT.
and Em.), כמרעיתם, joining it with v.[5]. We., Now., and Marti, כרעותם. Gr.
במרעיתם. Hal. כמו רעיתם 𝔖 om.; 𝕲 εἰς πλεσμονήν. Read, with Oort,
שָׁבֵעַ (cf. 𝕲); Oort offers an alternative, לִשְׂבַּע.—לבם] 𝕲 pl.—7. ואהי] 𝕲 καὶ
ἔσομαι = וְאֶהְיֶה (so also We., Now., Oet., Marti). Gr. and GAS. וָאֶהִי.—אשור]
Read, with 𝕲, Ἀσσυρίων, אַשּׁוּר (so 𝔖𝔙, We., Val., Now., Oet.). Brüll, Gr.,
Meinhold, Now.[2], and Marti, אשקר (cf. Je. 5[6]). Hal. אֲשׁוּרֵם.—8. שכול] Oort,
foll. 𝕲 and 𝔙, שכולה.—ואכלם] 𝕲 καὶ καταφάγονται αὐτούς = וַאֲכָלָם (so also
Oort, ThT. and Em.; Gu., Now., Marti). 𝔖 ܣܠܐܒܐ = וְיֹאכְלֵם or וְיֹאכְלָם (Seb.),
with לביא as subj.—שם] Meinhold, Now.[2], and Marti om.—כלביא] 𝕲 σκύμνοι
δρυμοῦ = כַּלְבִיא (Aramaicizing, Cappellus), or לביא (Schleusner), or כפירים (so
also Oort, ThT. and Em.; Gu., Now.), or כְּפִירֵי יַעֵר (Oet., Marti); 𝔖 om. כ.—
9. One cod. of de R. om. v.[9].—שחתך] Read, with 𝕲, τῇ διαφθορᾷ σου, שַׁחְתְּךָ
(so GAS.); 𝔙 perditio tua; 𝔖 ܡܚܒܠܟ. Val. שְׁחַתִּיךָ (so Gu., Now., Oet.,
Hal., Marti). Gr. בְּשַׁחְתְּךָ.—כי בי בעזרך] One cod. of Kenn. om. בי. 𝕲 τίς
βοηθήσει = [ד]מי יעזר (so also Oort, ThT. and Em.; Gr., Val., Gu., GAS.,
Now.). Read, with 𝔖, ܡܢ ܢܚܠܦܝ, מֵי בְעֶזְרֶךָ, cf. Ps. 118[7] (so also Seb.,
Scholz, Dr. Exp. 3d ser. V. 260 f.; Hal.). כי may be taken as a remnant of
אנכי (cf. Now.). Oet. מי בְעֶזְרֶיךָ (cf. Marti, כי בי בעזרך).—10. אהי] Read, with
𝕲𝔖, איה (so most comm.).—אפוא] 𝕲 οὗτος.—בכל] 𝔖 = וכל (so also Houtsma,
We.; Oort, ThT. and Em.; Val., Gu., GAS., Now., Oet., Marti). 𝔏 et in
omnibus. Gr. מכל.—עריך] Gr. צריך. Houtsma, שָׂרֶיךָ (so Oort, ThT. and
Em.; We., Val., Gu., GAS., Now., Oet., Marti).—וישפטוני] 𝕲 κρινάτω σε
= ישפטך (Vol.); 𝔖 sg.; so Arab. and some codd. of de R. Read, with

Houtsma, וִישְׁפָּטוֹף (so Oort, *ThT.* and *Em.*; We., Gu., GAS., Now., Marti). Val. and Oet. וּשְׁפָטוֹף. Gr. וִישָׁפְטֵף. Hal. transposes to precede בכל עריך. [וישרים — .(Seb.) שאלת ממני ואמרת = וֹمارُکֹامب هוلاعُ ⳨ [אשר אמרת — ⳨⳨ = sg. — **11.** [אתן ⳨ καὶ ἔδωκα (= ואתן); so ⳨. — [ואקח ⳨ = ואקחֵהוּ; ⳃ *et habuisti.* — [בעברתי ⳃ *in impetu tuo.*

XIII. 1. *When Ephraim used to speak, men trembled*] The many interpretations of this line may be classified in three lists: (1) Those which make רתת an apodosis, following the temporal clause expressed by an infinitive with a preposition, "When Ephraim spoke (or used to speak, referring to the time of Ephraim's prosperity, *e.g.* in the time of the judges*), there was trembling," † *i.e.* respect for him, reverence in his presence; cf. Is. 52[15]. (2) Those in which רתת as an infinitive or participle (רֹתֵת) is made to modify the infinitive דבר as an object or adverbial accusative, the next line serving as apodosis. Here belong the renderings: "When Ephraim spake stammeringly," ‡ or "spake confusion, ambiguously, etc." § (*i.e.* when Jeroboam introduced the calf-worship); "when Ephraim spake trembling" ‖ (*i.e.* humbly); "when Ephraim spake of revolt" ¶ (*i.e.* alarm, uproar, the opposite of שלום). (3) Those in which change of text has been suggested for רתת (*v.s.*), *e.g.* "judgment," or "decree," ** "truth," †† "knowledge," ‡‡ "terror." §§ Nowack's statement that (1) is grammatically impossible, and is devoid of good meaning, is too strong. It furnishes a fair meaning, and, although unusual, is permissible; cf. Gn. 4[7] (if שאת be correct; cf. Gunkel). — *He was a prince in Israel*] Reading נשיא for נשא of 𝕸. By some this is made (*v.s.*) the apodosis of the preceding line, *e.g.* "when he exalted himself in Israel" (*i.e.* made effort to get the ascendancy; ‖‖ or, "they rose to the exalted position which their prophet-ancestors foreshadowed," cf. Gn. 49[22-26] ¶¶); by others, as a parallel line, whether used in the good *** or bad ††† sense. Upon the whole, it seems clear that these lines, in contrast with the following (cf. עתה, v.[2]), describe Ephraim

---

* Hi.   † Cal., Bauer, Hi., Sim., Or., GAS., Marti.   ‡ Mich.   § Ma.
‖ Pococke, Pu.; cf. Che. "when the Ephraimites in trembling accents responded to the divine call (2[15]), etc."
¶ Ew.   †† Gr.   §§ Hal.   ¶¶ Che.   ††† Ma., Ew.
** ⳨.   ‡‡ Oort.   ‖‖ Hi.   *** Or.

in the glory of his past, before his fall, — a time when he needed
only to speak to produce awe among his fellow-tribes, — when he
stood highest in the nation, the prince. This, in the prophet's
mind, was either in the days of the judges (Ju. 8[1f.] 12[1]), or in
those of Jeroboam I. when the people took a retrograde step in
religion; or he refers more indefinitely to the general position
always occupied in the past by Ephraim, as shown in its furnishing
leaders like Joshua and in its acknowledged supremacy throughout its history. — *Then he became guilty through Baal, and died*]
On אשם, cf. 10[2]. Ephraim became guilty through accepting Baal-
ideas, and thus contaminating the purer form of his earlier religion. This corruption came about when, giving no heed to the
spiritual conceptions of the prophets, they devoted themselves to
the realistic worship of Yahweh in accordance with rites borrowed
from their Canaanitish neighbors (2[13. 16]). He died, to all intents
and purposes, in so far as it concerned his place in the progress
of religious thought (cf. Pr. 9[18] 1 Tim. 5[6]). Each step in this
direction was a step nearer death as a nation. Ephraim, in
Hosea's time, had been dying for a long time. The moment of
actual death was now not far distant. Such was early Israel and
later Israel. — **2.** *And now they continue to sin*] The Israel of the
prophet's time is no better; they, too, sin; in fact, they continue
to sin; they keep up the national retrogression. And then the
prophet gives in detail the several actions which constitute this
sin. Two quite distinct cults are here treated as one, the Baal-
cult and the image-cult. — *And they make for themselves molten
gods from their silver*] As early as in the smaller book of the
Covenant (Ex. 34[17]) there had been prohibition of the " molten
gods." In Isaiah's time (2[8]) the land came to be full of idols,
and, in the later days of Isaiah, Hezekiah (2 K. 18[4]) undertook to
root them out. The history of the relation of the prophets and
sages to the image worship is a most interesting one. This passage is one of the earliest in the long list of such utterances.* It
is always to be remembered that the stage of image worship in

---

* Cf. George F. Moore, arts. on " Idol " and " Idolatry and Primitive Religion,"
EB. 2146-58; P. Scholz, *Götzendienst und Zauberwesen bei den alten Hebräern und
den benachbarten Völkern* (1877); Baudissin, *Studien zur Sem. Rel.* I. 84; WRS.
Sem. 204.

the development of religion is a late one. With the attitude
of the Hebrew prophets towards image worship, and the actual
historical results of that attitude, may be compared the similar
attitude of the earliest Greek philosophers, together with the lack
of any such results.* — *Idols according to their own model*] Reading כתמונתם. 𝔐 " understanding," if retained, must be understood as used sarcastically. 𝔖, " according to their figure," and
𝔊𝔙𝔗 favor the rendering adopted above. Other readings (*v.s.*)
vary but slightly. — *Smiths' work, all of it*] This is the point of
real importance; there is nothing divine about it; the whole
affair is human.† — *To such they say: O God*] אלהים is to be
read either as a substitute ‡ for להם, or directly before להם.§
This seems necessary to meet the requirements of אמר, and is
justified by the similarity of the letters in להם and אלהים.
Others reach the same result by allowing אמרים to stand without an object (cf. Ps. 4⁵) ; *e.g.* " to such they speak ! " ‖ while
ordinarily these words have been closely connected with the following clause : *e.g.* " to even these speak men who sacrifice,
etc.," ¶ or " they say to one another while they sacrifice, etc." **
This statement concerning the ascription of deity to human handi-
work is the climax in the prophet's representation of Ephraim's
sin. What, indeed, could be more heinous? With this the strophe closes. Those interpretations which join with this line those
that follow fail to show a correct understanding of the logical
structure of the piece. — *With a people sacrificing to demons*]
𝔐 is impossible. Since אדם עגלים ישקן furnishes an admirable
meaning, and complies with the demands of the measure, it is to
be accepted.†† This leaves זבחי as the only fragment of a complete line requiring three words. The meaning of this last line
must have been synonymous with that of the line beginning with
אדם. In view of the parallelism thus required, and of 12¹¹, I venture to suggest עם זבחים לשדים. It was easy for עם to have dropped
out when note is made of the several preceding words, ending in
ים_ and הם_ ; furthermore, לשדים precedes a word not dissimilar
in form, אדם. Perhaps little can be said for this conjecture, but

---

* Welcker, *Griechische Götterlehre*, II. 114 f.
† Marti om. the phrase מכספם . . . כלה as a later substitute for the original text.
‡ Sta., Brüll, Gr.   § We., Now.   ‖ Che., GAS.   ¶ Ew.   ** Cal.   †† So Ru.

certainly as much as for the many efforts hitherto made to meet the difficulties in this passage. Some of these are: (1) "they say to one another, sacrificers of men, let them kiss, etc.; " * *i.e.* the absurdity of sacrificing men and worshipping calves is derided. (2) "Those among men who sacrifice, let them kiss the calves," † this construction being similar to that found in Is. 29¹⁹ Jb. 31²⁷ Mi. 5⁵ I K. 19¹⁸. In the latter case, the emphasis rests upon the absurdity involved in human beings paying homage to calves. Ewald's connection of these words with those preceding is interesting; viz. *to even these speak men who,* etc.; cf. also Keil's discussion. Concerning the first of these general interpretations, it is to be said that (*a*) calf-worship and human sacrifice were never combined; (*b*) human sacrifice did not exist in Israel until much later than Hosea's time, ‡ viz. that of Ahaz; (*c*) this erroneous interpretation originated with ᴳ, and has influenced commentators up to modern times; (*d*) the prophet would hardly have treated human sacrifice in such a fashion. Concerning the second interpretation, it is to be said that (*a*) the passages cited are not satisfactory analogies, and (*b*) the awkwardness of the expression, thus interpreted, is very great. § Concerning both interpretations, it may be said that (*a*) no adequate sense is conveyed; (*b*) the parallelism, elsewhere scrupulously observed, is ignored; (*c*) the demands of the strophic structure are not met (cf. Ruben and Duhm; *v.s.*). ‖ — *With men kissing calves*] A second circumstantial clause strictly parallel with the preceding one. For various interpretations, *v.s.* The *kiss* was a token of homage or adoration, and is referred to in the case of kings (Ps. 2¹²), and, as here, idols (I K. 19¹⁸ Jb. 31²⁷).¶ From the last passage, we learn that it was customary to kiss the hand towards the idol. — *3. Therefore they shall be like the morning cloud, and like the dew that early passes away*] A repetition, word for word, of 6⁴ᵇ (*v.s.*), but

---

* ᵍ, Rashi, Theod., Jer., Cal., Mich., Stuck, Schrö., Umb., Hi., Wü., BDB.

† ᔆ, AV., RV., Ki., Marck, Ma., Ros., Mau., Eich., Ew., Sim., Pu., Ke., Che., GAS., We., Now.

‡ On human sacrifice, *v.* Kamphausen, *Das Verhältnis d. Menschenopfers z. isr. Rel.;* on Molech-worship, *v.* arts. "Molech" in *DB.* and *EB.*   § Cf. Or.

‖ Cf. Marti's suggestion to (1) om. אלהים להם אמ׳ as a gloss, thus leaving הם וזבחי אדם, *they are sacrificers of men,* as the original text; or (2) point אֲמֹרִים, i.e. *they are Amorites, sacrificers of men.*   ¶ Cf. We. *SK.* III. 105.

this is no ground for omitting it here, as is done by Nowack.
The quadruple figure (cf. the following) is very striking. These
lines, moreover, are demanded to complete the structure of the
strophe. — *Like the chaff which whirleth up from the threshing-
floor*] Cf. Is. 17¹³ 41¹⁵ ᶠ· Ps. 1⁴. The threshing-floor was usually
situated on an eminence which the wind would easily strike (cf.
1 S. 19²² (𝕲) 2 S. 24¹⁸ 2 Ch. 3¹).* The active form, יְסֹעֵר 𝕸𝕿,
is satisfactory, and need not be changed to the passive (*v.s.*).
— *And like smoke from the window*] אֲרֻבָּה, used of the win-
dows of heaven, whence comes rain (Gn. 7¹¹ 2 K. 7²· ¹⁹ Mal. 3¹⁰),
occurs also of the openings of a dove-cote (Is. 60⁸), of the eyes
(Ec. 12³) ; and here, of the *latticed opening* or *window* through
which smoke escapes. The comparison is not found elsewhere.
The strophe, as a whole, is very strong. This people, sacrificing
to demons and kissing calves, shall become nothing, just like the
cloud, the dew, the chaff, and the smoke. — **4.** *And it was I, the
Lord thy God, who brought thee up from the land of Egypt*] *i.e.* I
do not forget, in thus threatening total extinction, that it was I
who brought them into existence as a nation. For other references among the prophets to the Egyptian residence, cf. 2¹⁵ 9³
11¹ Am. 2¹⁰ 3¹ 9⁷ Mi. 6⁴ Is. 10²⁶ 11¹⁶, etc. *Who brought thee up* is
from 𝕾 and 𝕲. 𝕲 inserts much additional material after *thy God*
(*v.s.*). — *And a god besides me thou knowest not*] Cf. Dt. 32¹².
The meaning becomes clearer from the parallel line ; it is God
as saviour, deliverer, that is meant ; *i.e.* Israel has received
no favors from any other god. It may not be assumed that
Hosea believed in the existence of only one God. At all events,
this expression does not show this. He says, however, that no
other god has exerted his power on behalf of Israel. — *Nor has
there been a saviour except me*] A poetic parallel of the preceding
line. — **5.** *It was I who shepherded thee in the wilderness*] This
reading follows 𝕲 and 𝕾 (*v.s.*). *It was I who knew thee* (cf. Am. 3²
Is. 58³ Na. 1⁷ Ps. 73¹¹ 144³) is a common expression = show favor,
cf. Ps. 1⁶ ; but its use of Israel in the preceding line seems to
justify this slight change of text. This, too, seems to be presupposed in v.⁶. Nowack allows *I knew thee* to remain in this line,

---

* Cf. Now. *Arch.* I. 232; Benz. *Arch.* 209; *DB.* I. 50; *EB.* 82 f.

and supplies, for the sake of the parallel, *I shepherded thee*, at the
beginning of the next line. — *In the land of drought*] Cf. Dt. 8¹⁵.
תלאבות, *drought*, occurs only here (*v.i.*). — **6**. (*But) when they fed,
they filled themselves full*] This reading connects שבוע (for שבעו)
with the preceding verb, as a strengthening infinitive absolute. So
bounteous was the supply furnished that Israel, although filling
himself to the full, failed to recognize the source of the supply
(2⁸ 4⁷ 10¹; cf. Dt. 8¹¹ ᶠ· 31²⁰ 32¹⁵· ¹⁸). This is expressed most
pathetically in the next line : *And their heart was lifted up ; consequently they forgot me*] The history is thus epitomized of the
evil results which often flow from prosperity ; * cf. 8¹⁴ Is. 17¹⁰.
— **7**. *And so I will be to them like a lion*] Because they have
forgotten me in the pride of their heart, I will treat them as
a lion treats his prey ; cf., for a similar expression, 5¹⁴. Some
prefer to render *I have become*, with reference to the fact that
the punishment has already been inflicted (7⁸⁻¹⁰), but ⅏ has the
future ; the imperfect with wāw consecutive may = prophetic
perfect, or the word may be pointed (*v.s.*) וָאֱהִיֶ. — *Like a leopard on the way to Assyria*] If אשור is pointed as in ⅏⅏, Yahweh
is represented as concealed upon the way, ready to jump or leap
upon † (cf. Je. 5²⁶, but this is doubtful ‡) the passing traveller. §
According to ⅏⅏ and ⅄, some Mss. and certain editions of the
Hebrew Bible (*v.i.*), the word should be pointed אַשּׁוּר, and be
rendered "to Assyria." ‖ Cheyne's objection to this translation,
that "the prophet has now to deal with the disease itself, not with
a mere symptom," seems hardly to meet the case. With "on the
way to Assyria" may be compared the more common treatment
of דרך שכמה (6⁹). The strongest argument for treating אשור as a
verb is the parallelism ; but (*v.s.*) the meaning required here is
hardly to be derived from שור, and besides, שם (v.⁸) seems to
require something more definite than על דרך. — **8**. *I will fall
upon them like a bear robbed of its young*] Cf. La. 3¹⁰ 2 S. 17⁸. —
And will tear the enclosure of their hearts] *i.e.* the breast. — *And
there I will devour them like a lion*] *v.s.* for the various suggestions for ⅏. Evidently the line was treated by ⅏ like the following

---

* Marti om. 6ᵇ as a gloss.   ‡ Cf. Giesebrecht and Duhm *in loc.*
† So GAS. I. p. 305, note 4.   § So Ew., Hd., Sim., Pu., Ke., Or., GAS.
‖ So Stuck, Hi., We., Val., Now., Oet. ; cf. de Rossi's Mss. (16).

line, " and lions shall devour them," the personal " I " being abandoned. — *While wild beasts tear them*] A circumstantial clause. —
9. *I am thy destruction, O Israel. Yea, who is thy help ?*] This
reading is gained by two slight changes in the text (*v.s.*). שִׁחֶתְךָ
may be pointed so as to be read as perfect 3d masc. " he has
destroyed thee "; * or perfect 1st sg. " I have destroyed thee," or
" I destroy thee." † It has also been taken as a noun with 2d
person suffix " thy destruction = thou hast destroyed thyself," ‡ or
with the following כי as a remnant of אנכי (cf. Nowack), " I am
thy destruction." Still another group of interpreters have made
the following clause the subject ; § viz. " it has destroyed thee, that
(thou art) against me, etc." (*v.i.*). According to Kimchi it is
the calf which has wrought the destruction. Upon the whole, the
1st person is to be preferred as continuing the person already in
use. The perfect is prophetic. The logical relationship of this
clause is thus clear : when I destroy thee, as I am now about to
do, who then is to be thy help? (מי for בי ; *v.s.*). כי may be
taken (*v.s.*) for אנכי, or as the particle of asseveration, *yea, then ;*
𝔊 and 𝔖 are so clear on this reading that we may not doubt it.‖
Oettli's pointing עֹזְרֶךָ, " thy helper," does not affect the sense.
בְ = " in the capacity of " or " in the character of," the so-called בְ
essentiae. ¶ Ewald's translation, " that (thou) to me, (*i.e.* to thy
help !) becomest unfaithful " (these last words to be supplied, the
abruptness being attributed to the " laboring voice, interrupted by
sobs "), is an interesting but ineffectual effort toward the reconstruction of this sentence. The verse, as read above, is strictly
in accord with the context. Who is to help thee ? (cf. Ex. 18⁴ :
for the God of my father was my help, lit. was *in* or *as* my help).
No one. — **10.** *Where is thy king now ?*] Reading איה for אהי
(*v.s.*).** The renderings, " I will be thy king," †† " Woe to thy
king," ‡‡ do not accord with what follows. The question calls for
a negative answer ; this, however, does not mean that Israel's

---

* Cal., Che., GAS.   † 𝔖, Bauer, Now., Oet., Hal.   ‡ Hd.
§ Hi., Ew., Sim., Ke., Or., RV.
‖ Dr. (*Exp.* 3d ser. V. 260 f.) points out in detail the difficulties of this passage,
and translates : " Thou art destroyed, O Israel, for who is there as thy help ? "
¶ Cf. De. on Ps. 35².   ** 𝔊𝔖𝔙𝔗, Pococke, Ew., Hi., Hd., Pu., Ke., Or., *et al.*
†† Cal.   ‡‡ Ma.

kings have passed away, that kings no longer sit upon the throne ; but rather that they are powerless to help. On אפוא, *v.i.* — *That he may save thee*] This is to be closely connected with the preceding, and closes the first line. The accentuation in 𝕸𝕿 is wrong. — *Or all thy princes that they may rule thee?*] This line, following Houtsma (*v.s.*), is the poetic equivalent of the preceding, matching it in every particular. — *Those of whom thou hast said*] At different times in the history of the northern kingdom when new dynasties were established.* — *Give me kings and princes*] Other passages in which Hosea refers to the kings are 7³ ᶠᶠ· 8⁴·¹⁰ 10⁷·¹⁵.† — **11.** *I give thee kings in my anger*] The imperfect here is frequentative in so far as it relates to the past ; but the history is still in progress. — *And I take them away in my wrath*] The history of the northern dynasties has been one the only interpretation of which must mean divine displeasure. Israel's experiment had proven to be a failure. "Indulged self-will brought with it its own punishment, — hardening of the heart in apostasy. Thus our passage seems to mediate between the two different views of Jeroboam's act presented in 1¹¹ and 1 K. 11²⁹⁻³⁹. In one sense Yahweh ' gave ' ; in another he ' gave not.' " ‡

1. כְ] = *quum*, ב = *quando*, in expressions of time; GK. 164 *g*; Kö. 401 *k–n*. The inf. here refers to the past; Kö. 216. — רחת] For form, cf. חתת, Jb. 6²¹; Lag. *BN.* 173; Kö. II. i. p. 68; Sta. § 199 *b*; Barth, *NB.* 7 *b*; Ew.⁸ p. 384; Nö. *Mand. Gramm.* p. 116. Cognate words are : Aram. רְתִיתָא = *trembling;* Arab. اَلرِّجْيَب = *trembling;* רֶמֶט = *terror*, Je. 49²⁴. — **2.** ויספו] Although separated from ו by עתה, the force of ו really continues; H. 24, 3 *b*; Kö. 368 *h*. — להם] With reflex. force, Kö. 28; GK. 135 *i*. — מסכה] From נסך = *pour out;* hence מ' = *molten metal, molten image.* — כחבונם] So 𝕸𝕿; on form, GK. 91 *e*; Ew.⁸ p. 645. For similar interchanges of ב and מ, Kö. 330 *o*. — עצבים] On d. f. in ב, GK. 93 *ee.* — כלה] Qᵉrî, כֻּלֹּו; perhaps כְּלֵה, referring to מסכה, or כֻּלָּם, referring to עצבים, should be adopted (*v.s.*). — להם] Refers logically to מסכה, but grammatically to עצ'; Kö. 349 *i*. — אמרים] For cases in which אמר is used absolutely, *i.e.* without an obj., cf. Gn. 4⁸ Ex. 19²⁵. — זבחי] Explained by GK. 128 *l* as a gen. of *genus;* by Kö. 337 *d* as an appositional gen.; but *v.s.* — **3.** משכים] On subordination of ptcp., GK. 120 *g*; treated as ptcp. circ. cl. by Kö. 412 *c*. — **4.** זולתי] Lit. = with the removal of ; cf. 2 S. 7²² Ps. 18³²

---

* Marti om. this and foll. clause as a gloss.
† On the relation of 1 S. 8⁵ ᶠ· as the basis of this, cf. Sellin, *Beiträge*, II. 185.
‡ Che. *in loc.*

Is. 45⁵·²¹ 64³. On the obsolete ending ‑ִי (cf. בְּלִתִי), cf. GK. 90 *m.* —
5. תלאבות] Only here; pl. intens.; GK. 124 *e*; Kö. 348 *a.* — **6.** מרעית] Verbal noun = inf.; Kö. 233 *d.* — וישבעו] ו cons. marks apodosis, in continuation of an inf. cstr.; Kö. 366 *h.* — שכחוני] On ‑ in stative vb., GK. 43 *a.* — **7.** כמו]
On poetical form, GK. 103 *k.* — **8.** דב] On gender, cf. GK. 122 *e*; Kö. 247 *h,*
and 253 *a*; *contra*, Ew.⁸ § 175 *a.* — לביא] Cf. Assyr. *labbu;* Arab. لَبُؤَة;
Lag. *BN.* 93; Erman, *ZDMG.* XLVI. 113; Hommel, *Säugethiere*, 288 f. —
9. כי] On its function as connecting protasis and apod., cf. Kö. 415 *l.* — נִי]
= מִי; on confusion of ב and מ, Kö. 330 *m.* — **10.** אפוא] Renders question more vivid; GK. 150 *l*; Kö. 353 *s.* — **11.** מלך] On frequency of collective usage, GK. 123; Kö. 254. — ואקח] The impf. with simple ו to express the frequentative idea.

§ 18. Ephraim condemned to Sheol. 13¹²⁻¹⁶.

Ephraim's sin is complete; judgment approaches, but he is unprepared; he cannot escape from the calamity which is bearing down upon him. Shall I, now, rescue him from this certain death? No! it is too late; let Sheol's plagues attack him. I will no more show compassion. To Ephraim, although heretofore fruitful, an east wind will bring drought and death; all precious things shall be carried away by the foreign invader. Samaria must suffer the consequences of rebellion against Yahweh, viz., sword and horrible destruction.

This section bears all the marks of unity, and is taken as a separate address by many modern commentators (*e.g.* We., Now., Marti). Some, on the other hand, connect it closely with 13¹⁻¹¹ (Ew., Or., Che., GAS.). It is true the general subject is the same, but, after all, this is the subject of the greater portion of the book. There are four strophes of trimeter movement, with 6 + 5 + 6 + 5 lines. The elegiac measure is strongly marked; while in strophe 4 the dimeter is adopted for the purpose of adaptation to the terrible content of the poem. Strophe 1 announces the end, the judgment, and the collapse of Israel. Strophe 2 pictures a momentary reconsideration, which results in a reannouncement more direful than before. Strophe 3 puts the matter in a more exact form, destruction by drought, by foreign invasion. Strophe 4 explains that it is on account of Israel's sin, viz. rebellion, that the sword and war will blot them out of existence.

12. צרור] Ⓖ συστροφὴν (taken as obj. of אקח, v.¹¹). — **13.** הוא] Now. והוא (so Marti). — בן לא חכם] Ⓖ υἱός σου ὁ φρόνιμος; ὁ must be corrected to οὐ (so Cappellus, Schleusner, Vol.; cf. Oet., who also om. σου); Ⓢ interprets the clause as causal. — כי עת] Ⓖ om. עת; 𝕷𝕾𝕰𝕿 = כי עתה (so also Scholz, Seb., Gu.(?)).

Oort (*ThT.* and *Em.*), כְּעֵת (so Gr., Now., Marti). Oet. כִּי כָעֵת. Hal. מֵעֵת.
— יעמר] Gr. יעברו.—במשבר] ᵹ ἐν συντριβῇ = 𝔙 *in contritione,* both literal or
etymological renderings. Gr. and Now. בְּמִשְׁבָּר. Hal. בְּמִשְׁפָּט.—בניס] 𝔏 *filio-*
rum tuorum. Gr. transposes to precede לא (cf. 2 K. 19⁸). Now. om.—
14. אפרס] ᵹ ῥύσομαι καί, "perhaps ᵹ read מ as ו" (Vol.).—אהי] Read,
with ᵹ𝔖, איה (so Gr.); ʼΑ., Σ. ἔσομαι; Θ. καὶ ἔσται; so 𝔗. 𝔙 *ero.*—דבריך]
Many codd. of de R. have sg.; cf. ᵹ, Θ. ἡ δίκη σου = ריבך (Vol., Loft.);
𝔖 اصلك; 𝔙 *mors tua.* Oet. דְּבָרֶךָ. Hal. דְּבָרְךָ.—קטבך] ᵹ τὸ κέντρον σου;
ʼΑ. δηγμοί σου; Σ. ἀκηδία σου; Θ. πληγή σου; 𝔙 *morsus tuus;* 𝔖 حمهمته.—
נחס] Hi. נָחַם. Gr. רחמים (cf. 11⁸). Hal. רַחֵם.—**15.** בין] Gardner, עין (fountain). Gr. בנים (?). Read, with We. כְּבֵין (so Val., Now., Oet.).—אחים] Oort
(*ThT.* and *Em.*), אָחוּ (so We., Val., Now., Oet., Marti). Gr. ואחים (?). BDB.
אָחִים. Gardner, חיים. Read, with We., מים אחו.—יפריא] ᵹ διαστελεῖ =
יפריד (Schleusner, Vol.; so also Seb., Gr.); so 𝔙 *dividet;* and 𝔖 جفلة.—
יבוא] ᵹ ἐπάξει = יביא (Vol.; so also Gr.), with ר as subj.; so 𝔙; similarly
𝔗.—עלה] ᵹ ἐπʼ αὐτόν = עליו; so Arab.; 𝔖 محمة.—יבוש] ᵹ ἀναξηρανεῖ
= יובש (so 𝔙𝔖, We., Gr., Now., Oet., Marti). Read יבֵשׁ.—מקורו] ᵹ𝔙𝔖 pl.
—יחרב] ᵹ ἐξερημώσει = יַחֲריב; so 𝔙 *desolabit* (so also We., Gr., Now., Marti).
—מעינו] ᵹ𝔖 pl. ישסה] ᵹ καταξηρανεῖ, probably a misreading for καταξανεῖ,
due to previous αναξ. (Vol., fol. Bahrdt). Gr. יובֵיש.—אוצר] ᵹ = אוצָר (so also
Oort, Gu.). Gr. ארץ. Read אוצַר; cf. GAS.—כל] Gr. וכל.—כלי] ᵹ𝔖𝔗 pl.
Hal. פְּרִי.—**XIV. 1.** תאשס] ᵹ ἀφανισθήσεται, deriving from שמס; cf. 5¹⁵ 10²
(Vol.). Gr. תְּשׁם. Marti, תֵּשַׁם.—יפלו] ᵹ πεσοῦνται αὐτοί; hence Oort (*Em.*)
inserts המה after יפ׳, and Gr. הם.—עלליהם] ᵹ𝔖𝔗 and Arab. = ועל (so also
Gr.).—והריותיו] Gr. והריות. Marti, הָרוֹתֵיהֶם.—יבקעו] Oet. יְבַקֵּעַן or יְבַקְּעָנָה (so
Marti).

12. *The iniquity of Ephraim is gathered up; his sin is laid by*
in store] This is no word of promise = shall be forgotten;* the
context and the language itself indicate the opposite. The figure
(cf. Jb. 14¹⁷) is taken from the custom of tying up money in bags
and hiding it in some secret place for preservation. Ephraim's
guilt is collected, carefully bound up; it will be well guarded and
preserved, and no part of it will be lost sight of in the day of
judgment. In other words, the case is closed. No longer is
there opportunity to atone for their misdeeds. Cf. the noteworthy
parallel in Is. 8¹⁶, where, however, it is the teaching of Yahweh,
the testimony of the prophets, that is gathered up. On v.¹²ᵇ cf.
Jb. 21¹⁹.—**13.** *The pangs of childbirth come upon him*] This
figure for anguish and distress is not uncommon (cf. Is. 13⁸ 21³

---

* Umb.

Mi. 4⁹ Je. 4³¹ 13²¹); the pain and suffering of a woman in travail is a most striking representation of an inevitable period of affliction, since it is something which no power can turn aside. In this instance the figure represents the woman as unable to perform the act; *i.e.* Israel is unable to extricate himself from the troubles which have come upon him. But with the privilege of a Hebrew poet, the figure suddenly shifts from the mother to the child that is to be born. — *He is an unwise son*] This child is represented as failing to do the part assigned him by nature; and in this failure he shows himself unwise and foolish. The result will be that, instead of an occasion for rejoicing, viz. a new birth, there will rather be an occasion for grief, for the parturition will be fatal to both mother and son. Not only is there no new being in the world; that one which did exist is taken away. Israel, in order to continue life, must be born again; without such new birth, old Israel must perish. The very failure to produce the new destroys the old. This is explained in the following line. — *For at this time he should not stand in the mouth of the womb*, or more freely, *this is no time to stand in the mouth of the womb* *] Whether עֵתָה be read,† or כָּעֵת = "at this time," the meaning is not affected. Graetz's "do not break through (the womb)" affords no real help in the interpretation of the passage. The exact meaning rests upon the modal usage of יעמד. If it is indicative, it signifies that the child at the (right) time (cf. Ez. 27³⁴) does not stand, ‡ *i.e.* has not come forward to that place in the womb whence egress at the proper moment is possible; if it is optative, that the child should not (at this time, or now) remain stationary in the womb, thus failing to make the progress necessary to a normal birth. § What is Israel doing? By his lack of will-power or inclination to do the necessary thing, viz. make timely repentance, he prolongs the agony and endangers even the possibility of the new régime which the prophets have pictured and promised. The figure has been interpreted of (1) premature birth; *i.e.* a child who is impatient and waits not for the proper time, thus remaining in the womb an insufficient period; and this is coupled with the interpretation of the passage as one of comfort; ‖ (2) retarded

---

* GAS. † 𝔖𝔙𝔗. ‡ Ew., Ke., Or., Che., Now. § Cal., Hd. ‖ Stuck, Hes., Umb.

birth; * but also (3) to a state of vacillation on the part of the
child at the critical moment. † — **14**. *Shall I deliver them from the
hand of Sheol?*] It seems necessary, first of all, to determine what
is required by the context, — a promise ‡ or a threat ? Vs.[12. 13]
seem (*v.s.*) to announce punishment; vs.[15 and 16] certainly have this
meaning; v.[14] itself contains (*v.i.*) the statement *repentance* (not
resentment) *is hid from my eyes.* How now can [14a] be taken in
any other way than as a threat ? But it has been suggested
(1) that the simple translation is "From the hand of Sheol,
I will redeem them," there being no interrogative particle; and
(2) that this translation is strictly in accord with the feeling of
a father who is thus represented as unable to contemplate the
thought of his son's final ruin; (3) that it is also consonant with
Hosea's expression of ultimate redemption elsewhere, cf. 1[10 f.] 2[15 f.]
3[5] 14[4-8]; (4) still further, that the language has been so taken by
𝕲𝖘𝖚𝕿, by Paul in 1 Cor. 15[55]; AV. and RV. In this case,
"repentance" (*v.i.*) must be changed to "resentment," and the
words treated parenthetically, *i.e.* "as an ejaculation of promise
in the midst of a context that only threatens." The argument is
almost if not entirely conclusive on the side of those who treat
the entire verse as a threat. But from this point of view, different
treatments have been accorded the passage : (1) (making the
imperfect a frequentative) "I have in past times repeatedly
delivered them, but, etc."; § (2) (making the imperfect conditional) "I would have delivered them, etc. (if they had been
wise, but — being foolish —) I will bring on them the plagues of
death, etc."; ‖ (3) (treating the sentence as interrogative, as
above) "shall I, or should I deliver them, etc.,"¶ a negative answer
being implied. The "hand of Sheol" (cf. the "mouth," Is. 5[14],
the "belly," Jon. 2[2]) is here used poetically for "power," and
perhaps to give the line a third word. *Sheol* = underworld. —
Shall I redeem them from death?] The poetic equivalent of the
preceding line; on the synonyms נאל and פדה, *v.i.*; on the
synonymous use of "Sheol" and "death," cf. Is. 28[15] Ps. 6[5] 49[14].
— *Where are thy plagues, O death ? Where, thy destruction* (or

* So most comm.   † Sim., Pu.
‡ Cf. Cal., Dathe, Ros., Umb., Mau., Ew., Hi., Ke.   § Rashi.
‖ Ki., Eich., Sharpe.   ¶ Sim., Wü., Schm., We., Gu., GAS., Now.

pestilence), *O Sheol ?*] אֵיָה = אֱהִי, *where ?* * So rendered by many, who treat it in entirely opposite ways; *e.g.* (1) as an expression of triumph over Sheol and death, their plagues and pestilence being powerless to do harm, inasmuch as Yahweh has determined to deliver Israel; † and (2) as a command to Sheol and death to do their worst, *i.e.* to bring on plagues and the pestilence which shall destroy Israel = " come on, death, with thy plagues, and thou, O Sheol, with, etc." ‡ Others (reading אֱהִי as 1st singular imperfect apocopated of הָיָה) render *I will be*, § or *I would be;* ‖ but (1) the 1st person singular is rarely apocopated ; (2) if Yahweh asserts positively that he will deliver them from Sheol, this clause must mean, *I would be thy plagues, if it were necessary*, but the context seems to require a positive declaration.¶ Whether we read *pestilence* as singular or plural is unessential (*v.s.*). Everything that points toward death (*mille viae leti*) is to be reckoned a pestilence ; while קָטָבְךָ (*v.i.*) = *destruction* in general (Is. 28²) ; in particular, *epidemic, disease, plague* (cf. Dt. 32²⁴ Ps. 91⁶).— *Repentance is hid from my eyes*] For this reason, Yahweh, having determined not to deliver, calls upon Sheol to do its fatal work. נֹחַם, occurring only here, has been emended to a form of רחם = compassion. Ewald, on the basis of Gn. 27⁴² (" thy brother resents thee unto death "), translates *resentment, i.e.* a secret, treasured, ancient grudge, which will result in the death of an enemy ; and this is something which God himself will not permit. But the word means neither *resentment* nor *compassion*.** It is the technical word for *repentance*. It refers therefore, either (1) to the threat of v.¹², †† of which Cheyne suggests it may once have been the third member, but surely in its present position it could not go so far back ; or (2) to ¹⁴ᵃ taken as a promise, ‡‡ *i.e.* a promise which should never be repented of = irrevocable ; but the promise is regarded, even by those who so accept it, as of so transient a tone as to make this doubtful ; or (3) to ¹⁴ᵃ taken as a threat, §§

---

* *V.s.* 𝕲𝕾𝕰𝖁𝕿 on Ho. 13¹⁰ and 𝕲, 'A., 𝕾, here ; so New., Hi., Ew., Hd., Umb., Sim., Ke.

† Ew., Umb., Hd., Ke., Che.

‡ We., GAS., Now.

§ עַם, AV., Cal., Dathe, Ros., Mau., Pu.

‖ Mich., Bauer. ¶ So Pu., Che.

** We.; cf. *Thes., s.v.*

†† Che.

‡‡ Mau., Hd., Ke.

§§ Or., GAS. Now., *et al.*

in view of what has already been said, and of the fact that there is evidently needed here a statement of threat, in preparation for what follows in v.¹⁵. — **15.** *Although he, as does the reed-grass in the midst of water, show fruitfulness*] A pun on the word אפרים, cf. also 14⁸ Gn. 49²², and Ewald's rendering, "though he be among brothers a fruit-child." His name (for name = nature or character) would have given ground for the expectation of fruit-fulness; *i.e.* prosperity. The reading adopted (*v.s.*) is favored by the continuation of the same figure in v.¹⁵. It would have seemed impossible that there could have been disaster with every-thing so prosperously situated (for the reed-plant in the midst of the water,* cf. Gn. 41². ¹⁸ Is. 19⁶). As fatal to 𝕸 † is the fact that Ephraim cannot be taken as one tribe among its brethren the other tribes, because clearly it is used here, as elsewhere, of all the northern tribes. ‡ — *There shall come an east wind,* — *Yahweh's wind*] This wind, coming over the desert, is both violent and scorching (cf. Arab. Sirocco = Eastern); cf. (with רוּחַ) Ex. 10¹³ Jon. 4⁸ Ps. 48⁷; as here, standing alone, Ho. 12¹ Is. 27⁸, etc. The figure represents Assyria, who comes from this direction, cf. Is. 21¹. It is Yahweh's wind, because it is Yahweh himself who executes the judgment pronounced, Assyria being the instrument (cf. Is. 10⁵. ¹⁵) § ; or because it is a mighty wind, in-tensity being expressed by the use of the divine name (cf. Gn. 23⁶ Is. 14¹³ Ps. 36⁶).‖ רוח ק is thus to be taken as in apposition with קדם, and so as closely connected with it, and not as subject of עלה. — *Coming up from the wilderness*] *v.s.* — *And his fountain shall dry up, and his spring shall be parched*] A continuation of the figure in ¹⁵ᵃ, the source of fruitfulness will be destroyed. For יֵבוֹשׁ read יִבַשׁ (*v.s.*), as is clear from the parallel word : יחרב; cf. 𝕲's treatment of the nouns as objects. — *While he will strip the treasure of all precious vessels*] The *he* is not emphatic, but used as expressing the subject of the circumstantial clause. It does not refer to Ephraim,¶ who is thereby represented as himself

---

* So Rashi, Or., We., Val., Now., Oort, Oet., *et al.*

† Retained by Ki., Cal., Marck, Bauer, Hi., Ew., Ke., Wü., Che., *et al.*

‡ So Now.   § Hd., Sim., Pu., Or.

‖ So Bauer, Ew.,; cf. Da. *Heb. Syntax*, p. 49; Kö. 309 *l*; Kelso, *AJSL.* XIX. 152–8; on the contrary, Green, *Heb. Gram.* p. 298; *Revue biblique*, Oct., 1901.

¶ Sharpe, GAS.

despoiling the treasury and turning over its precious things to
the enemy; but rather to the enemy itself * — Assyria (*i.e.* the
east wind; for here the figure changes) which carries off the
treasure consisting of all, etc. The change is confessedly abrupt,
but no greater than often occurs; nor is it so great as to justify
Nowack's suggestion that this line is the survival of a stanza or
sentence in which the antecedent of הוא appeared as Assyria.
The *precious vessels* (also rendered *pleasant vessels,†* *precious
jewels* ‡) include all articles of value. — **16.** *Samaria shall* (or
must) *bear the guilt*] This now is the final summing up. Some
make אשם = *be laid waste,* § but the rendering adopted is in
accord with 10² 13¹. The measure now falls to two words in each
line. — *For she has rebelled against her God*] Cf. Is., chap. 1.
— *They shall fall by the sword; their children shall be dashed in
pieces; and their women with child shall be ripped up*] The
gender and number of the verb change from feminine singular
to masculine plural. For parallel expressions, cf. 10¹⁴ Ps. 137⁹
2 K. 15¹⁶ Am. 1¹³. The change back to masculine singular and
the *hapax legomenon* הריות are not sufficient to raise suspicion
concerning the last clause. The customs of ancient warfare were
indeed horrible; ‖ cf. Jos. 10²⁴ 2 Ch. 25¹² Ju. 1⁶ᶠ· 2 K. 8¹².

12. On order of words, *v.* H. 39, 1; GK. 141 *l, m.* — **13.** חבלי] Subj. here
emphatic. — הוא] GK. 141 *a.* — לא חכם] A shortened attributive clause; Kö.
385 *d.* — עֵת] If = עֵתָּה, cf. Kö. 331 *b*; Ez. 16⁵⁷ 27⁸⁴ Hg. 1² Ps. 69¹⁴ Ec. 8⁹.
If = כְּעֵת, note demonstrative use of art., GK. 126 *b.* — **14.** מיד] Cf. ביד לשון,
Pr. 18²¹; מיד להבה, Is. 47¹⁴, etc. On the interrog. sense without particle,
GK. 150 *a.* — שאול] On Hebrew conception of ש, *v.* Charles, *Crit. Hist. of
the Doctr. of a Future Life* (*v.* Index, *s.v. Sheol*); Grüneisen, *Ahnenkultus u.
Urrelig. Isr.* (Index); Frey, *Tod, Seelenglaube, u. Seelenkult,* 188–228; Da.
DB. I. 739 f.; Schwally, *Leben nach dem Tode.* — אפדם . . . אגאל] גאל = *act
the part of a kinsman;* hence always implies a more personal and intimate
relation between the redeemer and the redeemed than does פדה, which is a
more general term denoting *ransom.* — קטבך] On the form before the suff.,
GK. 93 *q.* The masc. suff. (referring to שאול) is used under the influence of
the preceding ך_; Kö. 249 *f.* — **15.** יפריא] On intentional confusion of ל"א

and לה forms for the sake of the pun, GK. 75 *rr*. The Hiph. may be treated as intensive, GK. 53 *d*. — יבוש] For other cases of confusion between בוש and יבש, *v.* Ew.[8] § 122 *e*; GK. 78 *b*.

§ 19. Later words of hope. 14[1-8].

Israel will return from her apostasy with words of true repentance ([1. 2a]), saying to Yahweh, "Forgive the past, and we will render praise and thanksgiving, for in thee the fatherless finds pity ([2b. 3c]). We will henceforth enter into no alliance with Assyria or Egypt; nor will we treat as God dumb idols" ([3a. b]). (Yahweh will reply) "I will forgive the past, and love them; instead of being angry with them, I will show mercy ([4. 5a]). As a result they shall flourish; their prosperity shall be like the olive, like Lebanon" ([5b. 6]). "Ephraim will no longer serve idols; it is I who will care for him eternally and sustainingly" ([8]).

This piece, a picture of the final triumph of Yahweh's love, is added in accordance with the prophetic thought of a much later period. Cf. § 5, pp. 236–248, and also Introduction, pp. clix ff. Six short strophes of the trimeter movement (exceedingly regular) are evenly divided between Israel and Yahweh in their loving discourse with each other. Strophe 1 announces the return, in the form of command, and prescribes the gift which they are to carry (vs.[2. 3a]). Strophe 2 presents the petition for forgiveness and the ground for the same (vs.[3b. 4c]). Strophe 3 contains the pledge given, never again to desert Yahweh for dependence on outside powers or on graven images (v.[4a. b]). Strophe 4 announces in reply Yahweh's readiness to forgive, to forget, and to be merciful (vs.[5. 6a]). Strophe 5 pictures their great prosperity now that they are loyal to Yahweh (vs.[6b. 7]). Strophe 6 asserts that henceforth Yahweh, not idols, shall be their everlasting support (v.[9]). If it were not so clear that each of these four-line strophes contained a separate and distinct thought, it might be well to arrange the piece in two strophes of twelve lines each. In this arrangement, the following general modifications of the text have been assumed: (1) the transfer of v.[4c] to follow v.[3] (*v.i.*); (2) the omission of v.[7 aa] as a gloss (*v.i.*); (3) the treatment of v.[8] as a later addition. There has been a growing tendency on the part of the most recent writers to deal with this passage (vs.[2-9]) as with Am. 9[8b-15], *i.e.* assign it to a later age than that of Hosea (so We.; Che. in WRS. *Proph.* XIX. and in *Exp.* Nov. '97, p. 363; Marti, *Rel.* 119, *EB.* 2122, and *Dodekapropheton;* Volz(?); Grimm, *Lit. App.* 91 ff.; on contrary, *v.* GAS. I. 309 ff.; Now.). In behalf of this position it may be urged (1) that there is total lack of connection between vs.[1 and 2]; (2) that "to have added anything to the stern warning of 14[1] would have robbed it of half its force" (Che.); (3) that 2[b], in contrast with 5[b], looks back upon the punishment as completed; (4) that the allusion to a covenant with Egypt (v.[4]) is incomprehensible in Hosea's time; (5) that Hosea certainly could not have spoken of Yahweh's wrath as having departed from Israel; (6) that the spiritual tone of vs.[2-4] is in striking contrast with the picture in 5[6]; (7) that the emphasis laid upon physical blessings (vs.[6 ff.]) is strange on the lips of Hosea, who constantly rebuked the Israelites for their longing after material blessings rather than ethical and spiritual; (8) that the "whole description is wanting in unity; entirely different features are simply combined one with another" (Grimm); (9) that the language and phraseology are very similar to those found in writings from the time of Jeremiah and later (on language, v. especially Volz and Grimm); (10) that the emphasis here laid upon *words* is in striking contrast with Hosea's demand for *deeds*. On the other hand, it is claimed (see especially GAS.), (1) that Hosea must have given utterance to such a hope as is here set forth, his point of view being different from that of Amos, in that he was of an affectionate disposition, and utterly unable to believe repentance impossible, and had indeed already predicted restoration on the basis of repentance (chap. 2); but cf. pp. 236, 238; (2) that the epilogue introduces no idea which was not already contained in the previous promises of the book; "there is, in short, no phrase or allusion of which we can say that it is alien to the prophet's style or environment, while the very key-notes of his book — *return, backsliding, idols — the work of our hands, such pity as a father hath*, and perhaps even the *answer* or *converse* of v.[9] — are all struck once more" (GAS.); (3) the similarity between the epilogue and such passages as Je. 31[10-20] is to be explained as due to the influence of Hosea on later writers; (4) while it is unlikely that Hosea's ministry closed with this word of promise at a time so close to the downfall of Northern Israel, it is probable that it comes from some earlier portion of his career, when the moral failure of Israel was not so clear, and the outlook still furnished occasion for hope. The present position in the book, it is suggested, is due to Hosea or some editor who thought it unfitting that the prophet's message should go down through the ages closing with a threat of punishment. But the weakness of the old position is seen in the unreadiness of those who hold it to permit this chapter to stand at the end of the book.

2. [כשלח] 𝕲 ἠσθένησας. — 3. [דברים] 𝕃 *multos*. Gr. דברי (cf. Pr. 4[10]). With 𝕲 and 𝔖 insert "your God" after "Yahweh." — [אמרו] 𝔙 and many codd. of de R. = ואמרו. — [כל חשא] 𝕲 ὅπως μὴ λάβητε = בַּל־תִּשָּׂאוּ (Vol.); 𝔖 ܘܠܐܚܒܡ = כי חשא (?) (Seb.); 'Α. πᾶσαν ἄρατε; Θ. ἱλασθῆναι. Some codd. of 𝕲, δύνασαι πᾶσαν ἀφαιρεῖν (ἁμαρτίαν); hence Oort (*ThT.* and *Em.*) and Val. יִכְלַת שְׂאֵת. Gr. הֲבַל־תִּשָׂא. Scholz, אל־ת׳. Gardner, בל־חשע (= *regard not*). — [וקח] 𝕲𝔖 pl. Oort (*ThT.* and *Em.*), וְנִקְחָה (so Val., Oet. (or וְנִקָּח), Now.[2], Marti). Gr. וחטאא for וקח טוב קח being dittog. of prec. קחו. — [ונשלמה] 𝔖 3 p. sg. = וישלם. Gardner, ונשל, connecting מה_ with following. — [פרים] Read פְּרִי with 𝕲 καρπόν; so 𝔖 (so also Duhm, *Theol.* 132; Oort, *ThT.* and *Em.*; We., Val., Loft., Now., Marti); 𝔙 *vitulos* = פָּרִי (so also Oet.). Hi. פָּרְיוֹן. Gr.

נְדְרֵי. Gardner, מרמה.—שפתינו] S = שפתיכם. L adds *et aepulabitur in bonis
cor vestrum.* Duhm, משפתינו. Gardner, משפותינו.—4. S begins with ויאמרו.
—מעשה] GꞀꞀ pl.—אשר בך] G ὁ ἐν σοί; Ꞁ *quia ejus, qui in te est;* Θ. ὅτι
ἐν σοί; S ܘܒܟ· Oort and Gr. אשרי בך. Hal. precedes by כי אתה.
ירחם]—יתום] G ἐλεήσει = יְרַחֵם (Vol.); Ꞁ *misereberis;* S ܒܟ ܡܬܪܚܡ.—
Oort and Gr. om. as dittog. of ירחם.—5. ארפא] Gr. ארפאם.—משובתם]
G κατοικίας αὐτῶν = מושביהם (Vol.); SꞀꞀ take in sense of *penitence, conversion.* Gr. ממשובתם. We. ממנו(?).—נדבה] S ܒܢܕܒܬܐ. Hal. מִנְדְּבָה.—
שב] G ἀπέστρεψεν.—ממנו] Hal. מהם.—6. לישראל]—ויך] Ꞁ *erumpet,* with
שר' as subj. Houbigant, ויט. Oort, יכה. Read, with We. and Now., וילכו.
Oet. ויסבכו—כלבנון] L *sicut thus.* Oort (*ThT.* and *Em.*), כַּלְּבֶנֶה (so Val.).
We., Now., and Marti om. as dittog. from v.8.—7. וילכו] S ܘܢܬܒܣܡܘ. Gr.
יצלחו—כלבנון] LꞀ = כלבונה (so also New., Gr.).—8. וישבו] S ܢܬܒܘܢ,
probably an error for ܢܬܒܣܡܘ (Seb.). Val. וַיְשֻׁבוּ.—וישבי] G καὶ καθιοῦνται
= וְיֵשְׁבוּ (Vol.); so S; similarly Ꞇ. Read, with Oort (*ThT.* XVI. 298 f.,
and XXIV. 503), וְיָשֻׁבוּ (so We., Val., Loft., GAS., Now., Oet., Hal., Marti).
Oort (*Em.*), יֵשְׁבוּ, omitting preceding יָשֻׁבוּ—בצלו] We., Now., Oet., and Marti,
בְּצִלִּי—יחיו] G ζήσονται = יְחִיוּ (Vol.); so SꞀ; cf. Ꞇ. G inserts here καὶ
μεθυσθήσονται = ירויו (Vol.); some codd., στηριχθήσονται. Oort (*ThT.* and
Em.), יִחְיוּ. Perles, Now., and Marti, וְרִוְיוּ, foll. G, and considering ζήσονται
a later correction based on ꟿꞀꞀ. Oet. וְיִחְיוּ. Read, with GAS., foll. G, ויחיו
ורויו.—דגן] Oort (*ThT.* XVI. 299, XXIV. 503, and *Em.*), ברגן, and adds
ושכרו ביין (in *Em.* יִשְׁכּוּ). Marti, רֶשֶׁן or מִדְשֶׁן or עֲדָנוֹ. Read, with GAS. and
Oet., כַּנָּן.—יפרחו] G sg. Oort, ופרח, with אפרים, from beginning of v.9., inserted after גפן as subj.—זכרו] S = זכרם. Oort (*ThT.* and *Em.*) and Oet.
om. last three words of v.8 as a marginal note. Ew. זָכְרוּ. Gr. יִשְׁכְּרוּ. Marti,
וְיִזְכְּרוּ. Read, with GAS., זָכְרוּ (cf. Is. 66³).—לבנון] Some codd. of de R. כָּל.
Gr. and Hal. חלבון (cf. Ez. 27¹⁸). Che. (*Exp.* Nov. '97, p. 365), לְבָנֶה.
—9. S begins v. with ܢܘܥܒܪ, and treats אפ' as its subj.; so Ꞇ.—לי] Read,
with G, αὐτῷ, לו (so also New., Ew., Or., We., Gr., Loft., GAS., Now., Oort
(*Em.*), Oet., Marti).—לעצבים] G = ולע' (so also Gu.).—עניתי] G ἐταπείνωσα
αὐτόν = עֲנִיתִיו (so also Dathe, Oort, *ThT.* and *Em.*; Volz, Oet., Now.²); so S.
One cod. of Kenn. אענהו. We. עֲנָתוֹ. Gr. and Marti, עֲנִיתָיו. Hal. עֲנִיתִיךָ.—
אשורנו] G κατισχύσω αὐτόν = אֲשֻׁרֶנוּ (Vol.); S ܐܚܡܣܢܝܘܗܝ = אֲאַשְׁרֶנּוּ (Seb.);
Ꞁ *dirigam eum.* Oort, ואזרנו. Gr. וַאֲאַשְׁרֶנּוּ. We. וַאֲשֻׁרָתוֹ. Val. וַאֲשׁוּרָה. Oet.
וַאֲשַׁבְּבֶנּוּ (so Now.²). Gardner, וַאֲשֻׁרֶבֶנּוּ. Marti, וְאַשְׁרִבֶנּוּ. Volz, תִּירוֹשׁ וְדָגָן. Che.
(*Exp. T.* IX. (1898) 331), כברוש—רֶנָּי וְתִירוֹשִׁי. Hal. כזית or כְּאֹרַח.—פריך
Gr. פריו(?) (so Volz, Oort (*Em.*), Marti).—נמצא] Volz, יִצְמָח.

1. *Return, Israel, to Yahweh thy God*] The introductory words
of the utterance. The imperative is predictive (cf. Is. 23¹ 47¹)
= the time will come when thou shalt return. For the consistency of this prediction with the announcement to the effect that

there was absolutely no hope, reference is made to (1) other similar passages, viz. $1^{10}-2^1$ 2^{14-23} 3^{1-4} 11^{8-11}, but these are mostly late; (2) the suggestion that while the passages without hope applied to the nation as such, such expressions as these were addressed to the faithful few; (3) the proposition that in all predictions of disaster there is a conditional element (cf. Je. $18^{8\,ff.}$); but these are not sufficient to overcome the difficulties suggested above.   Israel's apostasy was the cause of the whole trouble (cf. Je. 2^{19}); his return is the first step to be taken toward reconciliation. — *For thou hast stumbled by thine iniquity*] Cf. 4^3 5^5. Israel's iniquity (crookedness) occasioned the fall; for the calamity has already come (cf. $5^{13\,f.}$ $7^{8\,f.}$). — **2**. *Take with you words and return unto Yahweh your God*] The last two words are found in ⅊ and ⅏, and are required by the measure. *Words* (not *my words (v.s.)*, nor Yahweh's words,* for (*a*) in this case something more definite would be required, and (*b*) this would not be consistent with the following lines; nor words which are to be taken to heart †) are to be the gift carried to Yahweh, for (Ex. 23^{15} 34^{20}) none shall appear before Yahweh empty; *words*, rather than sacrifice and burnt offering (cf. 5^6). These words must express repentance, not fitful, but true and strong.‡ — *Say unto him: Do thou wholly remove* (i.e. *forgive*) *iniquity*] The prayer begins with petition for pardon.   The emphatic כל used adverbially (cf. 2 S. 1^9 Jb. 27^3) describes the pardon called for as one *entirely complete; v.i.* Oort's emendation (*v.s.*), "thou art able to forgive," is very ingenious, but *v.* Nowack; cf. also Graetz, "Wilt thou not forgive?" — *And do thou take good*] *i.e.* take it well § that we pay, etc.; or accept what is good, viz. that we pay, etc.; ‖ or graciously receive (us); ¶ or let thyself be gracious; ** or take good things †† (cf. Ps. 107^9 Pr. 13^2 Is. 55^2). Graetz's suggestion (*v.s.*) means nothing; but Oort's, "and let us receive good," furnishes a good meaning. ⅊ and ⅏ have the imperative 2d person plural "take ye," but this is inconsistent with what follows. — *And we will pay the fruit of our lips*] *i.e.* if thou wilt forgive, etc., we will pay, etc.; or do thou forgive, etc.,

---

* Hi.　　　　‡ Umb., Sim., Now., and most comm.　　** We., Now.
† Bauer.　　§ Dathe, Sim.　　‖ Ke.　　¶ Hd., AV.　　†† Pu., BDB.

that we may pay, etc. 𝕸𝕿 "We will pay the calves of our lips " * is ungrammatical and senseless; it is hardly any improvement to render "we will pay (as if with) bullocks, (with) our lips." † Cf. Hitzig's rendering (*v.i.*), " thoughtless utterances " (Je. 5¹²). It is impossible to find any satisfactory treatment of פרים; nor is it necessary when 𝕲's suggestion of פרי is so close; ‡ cf. Is. 57¹⁹. The fruit of the lips is, of course, the words spoken in praise and thanksgiving (Ps. 51¹⁶ ᶠ· 69³⁰ ᶠ·). On שלם, cf. Ps. 50¹⁴. — **3 c.** *For in thee the orphan finds mercy* (or *pity*)] This line stands better here, because (1) בך has nothing in v.³ to which it may refer, while here it connects closely with the 2d person of the verbs תשא and קח; (2) it explains here the ground of their praise and thanksgiving, viz. for mercy shown, while with v.³ᵃ·ᵇ it makes no logical connection; (3) in its position in 𝕸𝕿 it has nothing with which it stands in parallelism, and it interferes with the strophic structure, while in the position here suggested it not only relieves strophe 3, but completes strophe 2, which otherwise would be incomplete. *The orphan* is " das von Menschen verlassene, rein auf Yahweh angewiesene Israel " (Wellhausen) ; cf. Jn. 14¹⁸. — **3 a. b.** *Assyria shall not save us*] A pledge to give up looking for help toward Assyria (cf. 5¹³ 7¹¹ 8⁹). — *We will not ride upon horses (from Egypt)*] A second pledge to leave off trusting in Egypt, for alliance with Egypt included the provision of cavalry by Egypt (cf. 1⁷ 10¹³ with Is. 30¹⁶ 31¹). From the times of Solomon horses were brought into Palestine from Egypt (1 K. 10²⁸ Ez. 17¹⁵). See the prohibition in Dt. 17¹⁶. — *And we will no more say: " Our God," to the work of our hands*] Cf. 13². This is the third pledge, viz. not to treat as God images which were made by themselves. This is the climax of the pledge. With these three points covered, Israel will be at one with Yahweh. The chief planks in the platforms of both political parties of earlier times are here rejected. In the phrase, "work of our hands," is seen an example " of the splendid morsels of irony in which " later prophecy " lashes idolatry " (cf. Is. 42¹⁷ 44⁹⁻²⁰). § — **4.** *I will heal their backsliding*] Although no words are used to

---

introduce a different speaker, the context leaves us in no doubt. Yahweh in his turn replies not directly to them, but in an indirect way, as if speaking to the prophet concerning them; cf. 11⁷. Their apostasy, or backsliding, is regarded as a disease, which will be healed. — *I will love them freely*] *i.e.* of my own free will; because of that which is in me, not because of anything in them. This is added as a poetic parallel to the preceding, and is grammatically independent. — *Since* (= *now that*) *my anger is turned away from them*] The pronoun is 3d singular, *i.e.* collective. The Babylonian Codex has *from me*, a mistake growing out of Je. 2³⁵. כִּי furnishes the ground for what follows in ⁵ᵃ, not what precedes. This connection of ⁴ᶜ with ⁵ᵃ is clearly shown by the parallelism. It is only in ⁵ᵇ and following that the subject changes from Yahweh to Israel. For other cases in which כִּ (= ὅτι), with its explicative clause, precedes the clause explained, cf. Gn. 3¹⁴·¹⁷ 18²⁰ 27²⁰ Ex. 1¹⁹ 18¹⁵ 2 S. 19⁴³ Is. 28¹⁵. — **5.** *I will be as the dew unto Israel*] The dew is here a figure of beneficence, kindness; cf. its very different force in 6⁴. טַל = night-mist or vapor, which comes in the summer with the west wind. This counteracts much of the evil effect wrought by the sirocco or east wind; cf. 13¹⁵. — *He shall blossom as the lily*] Cf. Ecclus. 39¹⁴. This figure suggests beauty and fruitfulness. On שׁוּשַׁן, *v.i.* — *And his root shall spread (like Lebanon)*] Cf. Is. 11¹⁰ 53². Whether the cedars of Lebanon * are intended, or the mountains,† is secondary, in view of the doubt which attaches to the word כַּלְּבָנוֹן, partly because of the abruptness of the change and the obscurity of the sense gained, and partly because of the frequent occurrence of the word in these last verses; cf. v.⁷. On וַיֵּלְכוּ for יֵלְכוּ, *v.s.* — **6.** *And his saplings shall spread*] This seems to be a gloss intended to explain ⁵ᶜ; cf. Is. 53², where יוֹנֶקֶת occurs as here, in the sense of *sucker*, the superfluous shoots about the roots, which ordinarily are cut out in order to strengthen the main stock. — *And his beauty shall be like the olive-tree*] Cf. Je. 11¹⁶ Ps. 52⁸. This figure suggests beauty, but also something of the greatest value. — *And his smell like Lebanon*] *i.e.* like the smell of the cedars and

---

* ⬦, Jer., AE., Ki., Geb., Mau., Sim., Pu., Wü., *et al.*
† New., Hes., Ke., Schm., Or., GAS., *et al.*

aromatic trees (cf. Ct. 4[11]). *Smell* = name; cf. Ct. 1[3]. — **7.** *They shall return and dwell in his shadow*] Cf. Ez. 31[6]. This cannot be a continuation of Yahweh's words, because it reads *his shadow;* but whose shadow could it be if not Yahweh's (cf. v.[8])? The shadow of Lebanon,* or Israel himself?† (cf. Je. 31[5. 12]). V.[7] contains only a repetition of what has been said. It is therefore best to regard it as an interpolation by a still later hand,‡ and to suppose that it was intended to be the utterance of the prophetic writer, not of Yahweh. The text is difficult. Reading וישבו for ישבי (*v.s.*), the sense becomes clear: *Once more they will dwell* § *under his shadow*. This is better than (1) to connect ישובו with יחיו = *once more shall they that dwell, etc., bring corn to life* (*i.e.* cultivate corn),‖ or (2) 𝕸 = *shall turn those who dwell in his shadow (and) they shall revive.*¶ — *And they shall live well watered like a garden*] = ויחיו כן ורויו (*v.s.*); cf. Ps. 36[8]. With this translation may be compared (1) *they shall revive (as) the corn;* ** (2) *bring corn to life* †† (cf. the statement in 7[14]), neither of which seems satisfactory. — *And they will sprout like the vine*] The vine is frequently mentioned in figurative speech; *e.g.* 10[1] Ps. 80[8. 14] 128[3] Ct. 7[8] Is. 34[4] Je. 2[21] 6[9] Ez. 17. — *And their renown will be like the wine of Lebanon*] Ct. 1[3]; cf. also ריח of preceding verse, and Ho. 12[5]. Contrary to Nowack's *a priori* suggestion that good wine could not be produced so far north, cf. the testimony of von Troil (cited by Henderson), "On this mountain are very valuable vineyards, in which the most excellent wine is produced, such as I have never drunk in any country, though in the course of fourteen years I have travelled through many, and tasted many good wines." ‡‡ Perhaps זכרו should be read with G. A. Smith, זְכְרוּ, and in the sense given this word in Is. 66[3], *they shall be fragrant;* cf. 𝕲. — **8.** *Ephraim, what more has he to do with idols*] Yahweh speaks here. V.[8] is in close connection with v.[6]. לי should be read לו (*v.s.*). If 𝕸 is retained, the translation is, *Ephraim (shall say)*: *What have I to do any more with idols?* §§ On the form of utterance, cf. Ju. 11[12] 2 S. 16[10], etc. — *I respond (to him) and look after him*] *i.e.* it is I who, etc.;

---

* Rashi.　　　　　† AE., Wü., Che.　　　　　‡ So Now.
§ So Oort, We., Val., Loft., GAS., Now., Oet., Hal.　　‖ Hi., Ew., Sim., Ke., Che.
¶ Wü., AV.　** Hd.　†† Che.　‡‡ Cf. Pliny, *Nat. Hist.* XIV. 7.　§§ 𝕾𝕿, AV.

cf. 2¹⁴· ²⁰· ²¹. Yahweh now replies or gives response to Israel in the same temper as that with which Israel met Yahweh, and besides, he looks upon him for the purpose of rendering assistance (Ps. 84⁹ 119¹³² Jb. 33¹⁴), *i.e.* he looks after his needs. Cf. the opposite, "to hide his face," Dt. 31¹⁷. Wellhausen's "his Anath and Asherah" is a freak of the imagination. Volz's "I answered him with wine and corn" is better, but not strong.— *I am like an evergreen cypress*] It is difficult to read this of Yahweh, but it is still more difficult to place it in Israel's mouth. In favor of the former * is the fact that it is demanded by the following clause of which Yahweh is certainly the subject. Yahweh's shelter and protection of his people are likened to the refreshing shade of the cypress. If the words be referred to Israel, there is the difficulty that Israel is likened in two successive clauses to two different kinds of tree, for the cypress is not a fruit tree. As opposed to this, and in favor of the latter,† is the fact that Yahweh is nowhere else likened to a tree. If the figure is used of Israel, the punctuation of 𝕸 must be disregarded, and this clause be taken with ואשורנו = *and I look after him like an evergreen cypress*. With all its difficulty, the former is to be preferred.— *From me is thy fruit found*] This is clearly in Yahweh's mouth, and announces, as the last word of the dialogue, that from Yahweh comes all of Israel's prosperity.

2. עד] For אל; for other cases, *v.* Dt. 4³⁰ 30² Jo. 2¹² Am. 4⁶· ⁸· ⁹⁻¹¹ La. 3⁴⁰. 3. קחו ... ושבו] Two consec. imvs.; H. 23, rm. *i.* On the change to pl. from sg. of v.², cf. Kö. *Stil.* 237.— כל] With adverbial force; GK. 128 *e*; but cf. Kö. 277 *m*, 339 *r*.— פרים] Other cases of stat. abs. in place of stat. cstr., Ju. 5¹³ Pr. 22²¹ Dt. 33¹¹.—4. אשר בך] On causal force of אשר, Kö. 389 *a*, 344 *c*; *contra* Ew.⁸ § 331 *d.* On ב marking agent, Kö. 106. בך = *through thee alone,* Kö. *Stil.* 196.—5. אהבם] With δ only in 1 p. sg.; elsewhere ‗‗, GK. 68 *f.*— נרבה] = כנ׳, Kö. 332 *r*, cf. Dt. 23²⁴.—6. שושנה] A noun of unity, Kö. 255 *b.* For literature on form and origin, cf. BSZ. The reference is, perhaps, to the fragrant white lily with six bell-like leaves, which grows wild in Palestine and "is unsurpassed in its fecundity, often producing fifty bulbs from a single root" (Pliny, *Hist. Nat.* XXI. 5). Possibly ܡܠܟܬܐ ܫܘܫܢ, the royal lily, is meant. This is three or four feet high, with a stem of the thickness of a

---

* Rashi, Ki., Hd., Wü., Or., Now., *et al.*

† So 𝔙𝕿, Sim.; Ma. treats v.⁹ as a dialogue between Israel and Yahweh, this clause belonging to Ephraim.

finger and flowers of great beauty. — **7.** ‏וילכו‎] Masc. with fem. subj., Kö. 205 *e*.
— **8.** ‏לבנן‎] Without art. (cf. vs.6 and 7), Kö. 295 c. — ‏ישבי ב׳‎] If retained, stat.
cstr. before prep., Kö. 336 *w*. — **9.** ‏מה־ל׳ . . . ל׳‎] More usual ‏מה־ל׳ . . . ו‎ (but
cf. Je. 2¹⁸); Kö. 376 *f*.

§ 20. The lesson to be learned. 14⁹.

A man who desires
wisdom will study such things as these that are found in Hosea's
prophecy. It will be seen from these chapters that Yahweh's
ways are straight, and that by them men stand or fall.

In a five-line stanza (trimeter movement), a reader from a late period adds
his own understanding or interpretation of Hosea's writings as a whole. Two
elements in the verse betoken the lateness of the conception, viz. the strong
coloring of the wisdom-speech, and the division of humanity into two classes,
viz. the righteous and transgressors; cf. Pr. 11⁵ 15¹⁹; also Ecclus. 39²⁴.

10. ‏ויכשלו‎] 𝔊 ἀσθενήσουσιν, cf. 5⁵. — ‏בם‎] Hal. ‏בעונם‎.

9. *Whoso is wise, let him discern these things*] Here ‏מי‎ is used
indefinitely, in the sense of *whoever*, or *if any one*. The words
wise (‏חכם‎) and *discern* (‏בין‎) are technical terms of the wisdom-
vocabulary; *these things* means, of course, the preceding discourses of the prophet Hosea. The reader's advice is this:
Notice how things work out in history, *as in the case of Israel*, and
acquiesce therein; for to do this is a mark of "wisdom." — *Prudent, then let him know them*] A parallel statement, reënforcing
what has just been said, expressed likewise in wisdom-language
(cf. ‏נבון‎, from ‏בין‎ (*v.s.*), and ‏ידע‎, which might mean here either
acknowledge, *confess* (as in Je. 3¹³ Is. 59¹² Ps. 51³) or *observe, perceive*, *i.e.* secure the lessons of wisdom they were intended to
teach; cf. the absolute use of ‏ידע‎ *be wise*, in Is. 1³, and its use
with ‏חכמה‎ in Pr. 24¹⁴). — *For Yahweh's ways are straight*] ‏כי‎
= *for*, not *that*. The word *Providence* would, perhaps, suitably
represent the frequently recurring phrase, *Yahweh's ways*, which
includes the ways in which he acts, as well as those in which men,
under his guidance, move. The reference is to Hosea's interpretation of these ways. Yahweh's dealings put men on *straight* (*i.e.*
not crooked, but lying in an unbroken level; cf. Is. 26⁴) or *right*
(*i.e.* righteous) ways; cf. Dt. 32⁴ Ps. 19⁹. — *The righteous walking*

in them] This word *righteous* (צדיקים) is not used elsewhere in Hosea. This is not explained by the fact that there were none such in his days,* but is due to the fact that this technical phrase had not yet come into use. The clause is subordinate to the preceding, not coördinate † with it. To walk in Yahweh's ways is to adopt a course of conduct in harmony with Yahweh's will, and consequently one which permits them to *go forward prosperously.* — *But sinners stumbling by them*] That is, they fall and suffer utter ruin. The same *ways* lead in one case to life, but in the other to death; cf. Dt. 30[19. 20] 1 Cor. 1[18].

10. מִי] Although apparently an indefinite pronoun here, it is really interrogative, *who is wise? let him, etc.* (cf. similar cases after מִי, Je. 9[11] Ps. 107[43]). — וַיֵּרַע . . . וַיֵּלֶך] On וַ with jussive marking what is really the apodosis of a conditional sentence, GK. 166 *a*. — צדיקים] In the sense of *just, i.e.*, right in one's cause, this word occurs in E (Ex. 23[7. 8]), Am. 2[6] 5[12], but in the general ethical sense it does not occur earlier than Jeremiah (cf. 20[12], Is. 3[10] being late). The two clauses at the end of the verse are closely parallel, and should be taken together, both being subordinate to the preceding; *v.s.*

---

* Hd.   † As We., Now., and most others make it.

INDEX.

I. SUBJECTS.

Adam, 288.
Adultery, punishment of, 227.
Alliteration, clxxii, 111.
Amorite, 55, 58.
Amos, occupation of, civ f., 2 f.
——, literary skill of, 12.
——, personal life of, c ff.
——, home of, ci.
——, date of, cii ff.
——, preparation of, cvi ff.
——, vision of, cviii.
——, antecedents of, cviii.
——, character of, cviii f.
——, message of, cx ff.
——, popular conceptions opposed by, cxi ff.
——, convictions of, cxiii ff.
——, anthropomorphisms in, cxv f.
——, monotheism of, cxvi ff.
——, ministry of, cxxiv ff.
——, political activity of, cxxvii.
——, literary form of, cxxx ff.
——, analysis of, cxxxii.
——, insertions in, cxxxi ff.
——, general structure of, cxxxiv ff.
——, history of Book of, cxxxvi f.
——, style of, cxxxviii ff.
——, discussions of poetical form of, clxv f.
——, syntax of, clxx f.
——, rare words in, clxxi.
——, favorite words in, clxxi.

Amos and Hosea, poetical form of, clxiv ff.
——, language and style of, clxx ff.
——, text and versions of, clxxiii ff.
——, literature on, clxxvii ff.
Ancestor-worship, 182 f., 329.
Angels, 381.
Anointing, 149, 150.
Assyria, relation to Israel, 20 f.

Baalim, names of, 235.
Baalism, nature of, xc.
Baldness, 182 f.
Bear, 132.
Book of the Covenant, lxiv ff.
——, reconstruction of, lxv f.
——, relation to E, lxvi f.
——, prophetic element in, lxviii f.
Bribe, 122, 124.

Canaan, 384.
Civilization, opposition of prophets to, xxxiii, xxxvi, lxxvi f.
Clean and unclean, 173, 329, 330.
Commandment, date of second, lxii.
Compass, points of, 186.
Covenant, 30 f.
Covenant Code, 255.
Cultus, 136.

David, 148, 198, 223.
Day of Yahweh, 62, 131 f., 181, 247.

419

II. GEOGRAPHICAL.

III. HEBREW.

The Geography of
Amos and Hosea

The following places cannot at present be
identified:

HARMON   BETH-ARBEL
BETH-EDEN   SODOM
KIR   GOMORRAH
ACHOR   ADMAH
SHITTIM   ZEBOIIM
BAAL-PEOR

"A decided advance on all other commentaries." — THE OUTLOOK.

DEUTERONOMY.

By the Rev. S. R. DRIVER, D.D., D.Litt.,

Regius Professor of Hebrew, and Canon of Christ Church, Oxford.

Crown 8vo.   Net, $3.00.

"No one could be better qualified than Professor Driver to write a critical and exegetical commentary on Deuteronomy. His previous works are authorities in all the departments involved; the grammar and lexicon of the Hebrew language, the lower and higher criticism, as well as exegesis and Biblical theology; . . . the interpretation in this commentary is careful and sober in the main. A wealth of historical, geographical, and philological information illustrates and elucidates both the narrative and the discourses. Valuable, though concise, excursuses are often given." — *The Congregationalist.*

"It is a pleasure to see at last a really critical Old Testament commentary in English upon a portion of the Pentateuch, and especially one of such merit. This I find superior to any other Commentary in any language upon Deuteronomy." — Professor E. L. CURTIS, of Yale University.

"This volume of Professor Driver's is marked by his well-known care and accuracy, and it will be a great boon to every one who wishes to acquire a thorough knowledge, either of the Hebrew language, or of the contents of the Book of Deuteronomy, and their significance for the development of Old Testament thought. The author finds scope for displaying his well-known wide and accurate knowledge, and delicate appreciation of the genius of the Hebrew language, and his readers are supplied with many carefully constructed lists of words and expressions. He is at his best in the detailed examination of the text." — *London Athenæum.*

"It must be said that this work is bound to take rank among the best commentaries in any language on the important book with which it deals. On every page there is abundant evidence of a scholarly knowledge of the literature, and of the most painstaking care to make the book useful to thorough students." — *The Lutheran Churchman.*

"The deep and difficult questions raised by Deuteronomy are, in every instance, considered with care, insight, and critical acumen. The student who wishes for solid information, or a knowledge of method and temper of the new criticism, will find advantage in consulting the pages of Dr. Driver." — *Zion's Herald.*

The International Critical Commentary.

"We believe this series to be of epoch-making importance."
— The N. Y. EVANGELIST.

JUDGES.

By Dr. GEORGE FOOT MOORE, D.D.,
Professor of Theology, Harvard University.

Crown 8vo. Net, $3.00.

"The typographical execution of this handsome volume is worthy of the scholarly character of the contents, and higher praise could not be given it." — Professor C. H. TOY, *of Harvard University*.

"This work represents the latest results of 'Scientific Biblical Scholarship,' and as such has the greatest value for the purely critical student, especially on the side of textual and literary criticism." — *The Church Standard*.

"Professor Moore has more than sustained his scholarly reputation in this work, which gives us for the first time in English a commentary on Judges not excelled, if indeed equalled, in any language of the world." — Professor L. W. BATTEN, *of P. E. Divinity School, Philadelphia*.

"Although a critical commentary, this work has its practical uses, and by its divisions, headlines, etc., it is admirably adapted to the wants of all thoughtful students of the Scriptures. Indeed, with the other books of the series, it is sure to find its way into the hands of pastors and scholarly lay-men." — *Portland Zion's Herald*.

"Like its predecessors, this volume will be warmly welcomed — whilst to those whose means of securing up-to-date information on the subject of which it treats are limited, it is simply invaluable." — *Edinburgh Scotsman*.

"The work is done in an atmosphere of scholarly interest and indifference to dogmatism and controversy, which is at least refreshing. . . . It is a noble introduction to the moral forces, ideas, and influences that controlled the period of the Judges, and a model of what a historical commentary, with a practical end in view should be." — *The Independent*.

"The work is marked by a clear and forcible style, by scholarly research, by critical acumen, by extensive reading, and by evident familiarity with the Hebrew. Many of the comments and suggestions are valuable, while the index at the close is serviceable and satisfactory." — *Philadelphia Presbyterian*.

"This volume sustains the reputation of the series for accurate and wide scholarship given in clear and strong English, . . . the scholarly reader will find delight in the perusal of this ~~admirable~~ commentary." — *Zion's Herald*.

The International Critical Commentary.

The Books of Samuel

BY

REV. HENRY PRESERVED SMITH, D.D.,

Professor of Biblical History and Interpretation in Amherst College.

Crown 8vo, Net $3.00.

"Professor Smith's Commentary will for some time be the standard work on Samuel, and we heartily congratulate him on scholarly work so faithfully accomplished."—*The Athenæum.*

"It is both critical and exegetical, and deals with original Hebrew and Greek. It shows painstaking diligence and considerable research."—*The Presbyterian.*

"The style is clear and forcible and sustains the well-won reputation of the distinguished author for scholarship and candor. All thoughtful students of the Scriptures will find the work helpful, not only on account of its specific treatment of the Books of Samuel, on which it is based, but because of the light it throws on and the aid it gives in the general interpretation of the Scriptures as modified by present-day criticism."—*The Philadelphia Press.*

"The literary quality of the book deserves mention. We do not usually go to commentaries for models of English style. But this book has a distinct, though unobtrusive, literary flavor. It is delightful reading. The translation is always felicitous, and often renders further comment needless."—*The Evangelist.*

"The treatment is critical, and at the same time expository. Conservative students may find much in this volume with which they cannot agree, but no one wishing to know the most recent conclusions concerning this part of sacred history can afford to be without it."—*Philadelphia Presbyterian Journal.*

"The author exhibits precisely that scholarly attitude which will commend his work to the widest audience."—*The Churchman.*

"The commentary is the most complete and minute hitherto published by an English-speaking scholar."—*Literature.*

"The volumes of Driver and Moore set a high standard for the Old Testament writers; but I think Professor Smith's work has reached the same high level. It is scholarly and critical, and yet it is written in a spirit of reverent devotion, a worthy treatment of the sacred text."—PROF. L. W. BATTEN, of P. E. Divinity School, Philadelphia.

The International Critical Commentary.

PROVERBS

By the Rev. CRAWFORD H. TOY, D.D., LL.D.

Professor of Hebrew in Harvard University.

Crown 8vo. Net, $3.00.

"In careful scholarship this volume leaves nothing to be desired. Its interpretation is free from theological prejudice. It will be indispensable to the careful student, whether lay or clerical."—*The Outlook.*

"Professor Toy's 'Commentary' will for many years to come remain a handbook for both teachers and learners, and its details will be studied with critical care and general appreciation."—*The Athenæum.*

"The commentary itself is a most thorough treatment of each verse in detail, in which the light of the fullest scholarship is thrown upon the meaning. The learning displayed throughout the work is enormous. Here is a commentary at last that does not skip the hard places, but grapples with every problem and point, and says the best that can be said."—*Presbyterian Banner.*

"Professor Toy's commentary on Proverbs maintains the highest standard of the International Critical Commentaries. We can give no higher praise. Proverbs presents comparatively few problems in criticism, but offers large opportunities to the expositor and exegete. Professor Toy's work is thorough and complete."—*The Congregationalist.*

"This addition to 'The International Critical Commentary' has the same characteristics of thoroughness and painstaking scholarship as the preceding issues of the series. In the critical treatment of the text, in noting the various readings and the force of the words in the original Hebrew, it leaves nothing to be desired."—*The Christian Intelligencer.*

"A first-class, up-to-date, critical and exegetical commentary on the Book of Proverbs in the English language was one of the crying needs of Biblical scholarship. Accordingly, we may not be yielding to the latest addition to the International Critical Series the tribute it deserves, when we say that it at once takes the first place in its class. That place it undoubtedly deserves, however, and would have secured even against much more formidable competitors than it happens to have. It is altogether a well-arranged, lucid exposition of this unique book in the Bible, based on a careful study of the text and the linguistic and historical background of every part of it."—*The Interior.*

"While this commentary is called 'critical' and is such, it is not one in which the apparatus is spread out in detail; it is one which any intelligent English reader can readily use and thoroughly understand "—*The Evangelist.*

The International Critical Commentary.

" We deem it as needful for the studious pastor to possess himself of these volumes as to obtain the best dictionary and encyclopedia."
— The Congregationalist,

ST. MARK.

By the Rev. E. P. GOULD, D.D.,

Late Professor of New Testament Exegesis, P. E. Divinity School, Philadelphia.

Crown 8vo.   Net, $2.50.

" In point of scholarship, of accuracy, of originality, this last addition to the series is worthy of its predecessors, while for terseness and keenness of exegesis, we should put it first of them all." — *The Congregationalist.*

" The whole make-up is that of a thoroughly helpful, instructive critical study of the Word, surpassing anything of the kind ever attempted in the English language, and to students and clergymen knowing the proper use of a commentary it will prove an invaluable aid." — *The Lutheran Quarterly.*

" Professor Gould has done his work well and thoroughly. . . . The commentary is an admirable example of the critical method at its best. . . . The Word study . . . shows not only familiarity with all the literature of the subject, but patient, faithful, and independent investigation. . . . It will rank among the best, as it is the latest commentary on this basal Gospel." — *The Christian Intelligencer.*

" It will give the student the vigorously expressed thought of a very thoughtful scholar." — *The Church Standard.*

" Dr. Gould's commentary on Mark is a large success, . . . and a credit to American scholarship. . . . He has undoubtedly given us a commentary on Mark which surpasses all others, a thing we have reason to expect will be true in the case of every volume of the series to which it belongs." — *The Biblical World.*

" The volume is characterized by extensive learning, patient attention to details and a fair degree of caution." — *Bibliotheca Sacra.*

" The exegetical portion of the book is simple in arrangement, admirable in form and condensed in statement. . . . Dr. Gould does not slavishly follow any authority, but expresses his own opinions in language both concise and clear." — *The Chicago Standard.*

" In clear, forcible and elegant language the author furnishes the results of the best investigations on the second Gospel, both early and late. He treats these various subjects with the hand of a master." — *Boston Zion's Herald.*

" The author gives abundant evidence of thorough acquaintance with the facts and history in the case. . . . His treatment of them is always fresh and scholarly, and oftentimes helpful." — *The New York Observer.*

The International Critical Commentary.

" It is hardly necessary to say that this series will stand first among all English serial commentaries on the Bible."

— The Biblical World.

ST. LUKE.

By the Rev. ALFRED PLUMMER, D.D.,

Master of University College, Durham.   Formerly Fellow and Senior Tutor of Trinity College, Oxford.

Crown 8vo.   Net, $3.00.

In the author's Critical Introduction to the Commentary is contained a full treatment of a large number of important topics connected with the study of the Gospel, among which are the following: The Author of the Book — The Sources of the Gospel — Object and Plan of the Gospel — Characteristics, Style and Language — The Integrity of the Gospel — The Text — Literary History.

FROM THE AUTHOR'S PREFACE.

If this Commentary has any special features, they will perhaps be found in the illustrations from Jewish writings, in the abundance of references to the Septuagint, and to the Acts and other books of the New Testament, in the frequent quotations of renderings in the Latin versions, and in the attention which has been paid, both in the Introduction and throughout the Notes, to the marks of St. Luke's style.

" It is distinguished throughout by learning, sobriety of judgment, and sound exegesis. It is a weighty contribution to the interpretation of the Third Gospel, and will take an honorable place in the series of which it forms a part." — Prof. D. D. SALMOND, in the *Critical Review.*

" We are pleased with the thoroughness and scientific accuracy of the interpretations. . . . It seems to us that the prevailing characteristic of the book is common sense, fortified by learning and piety." — *The Herald and Presbyter.*

" An important work, which no student of the Word of God can safely neglect." — *The Church Standard.*

" The author has both the scholar's knowledge and the scholar's spirit necessary for the preparation of such a commentary. . . . We know of nothing on the Third Gospel which more thoroughly meets the wants of the Biblical scholar." — *The Outlook.*

" The author is not only a profound scholar, but a chastened and reverent Christian, who undertakes to interpret a Gospel of Christ, so as to show Christ in his grandeur and loveliness of character." — *The Southern Churchman.*

" It is a valuable and welcome addition to our somewhat scanty stock of first-class commentaries on the Third Gospel. By its scholarly thoroughness it well sustains the reputation which the INTERNATIONAL SERIES has already won." — Prof. J. H. THAYER, of Harvard University.

This volume having been so recently published, further notices are not yet available.

" For the student this new commentary promises to be indispen-sable." — The METHODIST RECORDER.

ROMANS.

By the Rev. WILLIAM SANDAY, D.D., LL.D.,

Lady Margaret Professor of Divinity, and Canon of Christ Church, Oxford,

AND THE

Rev. A. C. HEADLAM, M.A., D.D.,

Principal of King's College, London.

Crown 8vo. Net, $3.00.

"From my knowledge of Dr. Sanday, and from a brief examination of the book, I am led to believe that it is our best critical handbook to the Epistle. It combines great learning with practical and suggestive interpretation." — Professor GEORGE B. STEVENS, *of Yale University.*

" Professor Sanday is excellent in scholarship, and of unsurpassed candor. The introduction and detached notes are highly interesting and instructive. This commentary cannot fail to render the most valuable assistance to all earnest students. The volume augurs well for the series of which it is a member." — Professor GEORGE P. FISHER, *of Yale University.*

"The scholarship and spirit of Dr. Sanday give assurance of an interpretation of the Epistle to the Romans which will be both scholarly and spiritual." — Dr. LYMAN ABBOTT.

" The work of the authors has been carefully done, and will prove an acceptable addition to the literature of the great Epistle. The exegesis is acute and learned . . . The authors show much familiarity with the work of their predecessors, and write with calmness and lucidity." — *New York Observer.*

" We are confident that this commentary will find a place in every thoughtful minister's library. One may not be able to agree with the authors at some points, — and this is true of all commentaries, — but they have given us a work which cannot but prove valuable to the critical study of Paul's masterly epistle." — *Zion's Advocate.*

"We do not hesitate to commend this as the best commentary on Romans yet written in English. It will do much to popularize this admirable and much needed series, by showing that it is possible to be critical and scholarly and at the same time devout and spiritual, and intelligible to plain Bible readers." — *The Church Standard.*

" A commentary with a very distinct character and purpose of its own, which brings to students and ministers an aid which they cannot obtain elsewhere. . . . There is probably no other commentary in which criticism has been employed so successfully and impartially to bring out the author's thought." — *N. Y. Independent.*

" We have nothing but heartiest praise for the weightier matters of the commentary. It is not only critical, but exegetical, expository, doctrinal, practical, and eminently spiritual. The positive conclusions of the books are very numerous and are stoutly, gloriously evangelical. . . . The commentary does not fail to speak with the utmost reverence of the whole word of God." *The Congregationalist*

The International Critical Commentary.

EPHESIANS AND COLOSSIANS.

By the Rev. T. K. ABBOTT, B.D., D. Litt.

Formerly Professor of Biblical Greek, now of Hebrew, Trinity College, Dublin.

Crown 8vo. Net, $2.50.

" The latest volume of this admirable series is informed with the very best spirit in which such work can be carried out—a spirit of absolute fidelity to the demonstrable truths of critical science. . . . This summary of the results of modern criticism applied to these two Pauline letters is, for the use of scholarly students, not likely to be superseded."—*The London Academy.*

" An able and independent piece of exegesis, and one that none of us can afford to be without. It is the work of a man who has made himself master of his theme. His linguistic ability is manifest. His style is usually clear. His exegetical perceptions are keen, and we are especially grateful for his strong defence of the integrity and apostolicity of these two great monuments of Pauline teaching."—*The Expositor.*

"It displays every mark of conscientious judgment, wide reading, and grammatical insight."—*Literature.*

" In discrimination, learning, and candor, it is the peer of the other volumes of the series. The elaborate introductions are of special value."— Professor GEORGE B. STEVENS, of Yale University.

"It is rich in philological material, clearly arranged, and judiciously handled. The studies of words are uncommonly good. . . . In the balancing of opinions, in the distinguishing between fine shades of meaning, it is both acute and sound."—*The Church.*

" The exegesis based so solidly on the rock foundation of philology is argumentatively and convincingly strong. A spiritual and evangelical tenor pervades the interpretation from first to last. . . . These elements, together with the author's full-orbed vision of the truth, with his discriminative judgment and his felicity of expression, make this the peer of any commentary on these important letters."—*The Standard.*

" An exceedingly careful and painstaking piece of work. The introductory discussions of questions bearing on the authenticity and integrity (of the epistles) are clear and candid, and the exposition of the text displays a fine scholarship and insight."—*Northwestern Christian Advocate.*

"The book is from first to last exegetical and critical. Every phrase in the two Epistles is searched as with lighted candles. The authorities for variant readings are canvassed but weighed, rather than counted. The multiform ancient and modern interpretations are investigated with the exhaustiveness of a German lecture-room, and the judicial spirit of an English court-room. Special discussions are numerous and thorough."—*The Congregationalist.*

" I have already expressed my conviction that the International Critical Commentary is the best critical commentary, on the whole Bible, in existence."—DR. LYMAN ABBOTT.

Philippians and Philemon

BY

REV. MARVIN R. VINCENT, D.D.

Professor of Biblical Literature in Union Theological Seminary, New York.

Crown 8vo, Net $2.00.

"It is, in short, in every way worthy of the series."—*The Scotsman.*

"Professor Vincent's Commentary on Philippians and Philemon appears to me not less admirable for its literary merit than for its scholarship and its clear and discriminating discussions of the contents of these Epistles."—DR. GEORGE P. FISHER.

"The book contains many examples of independent and judicial weighing of evidence. We have been delighted with the portion devoted to Philemon. Unlike most commentaries, this may wisely be read as a whole."—*The Congregationalist*

"Of the merits of the work it is enough to say that it is worthy of its place in the noble undertaking to which it belongs. It is full of just such information as the Bible student, lay or clerical, needs; and while giving an abundance of the truths of erudition to aid the critical student of the text, it abounds also in that more popular information which enables the attentive reader almost to put himself in St. Paul's place, to see with the eyes and feel with the heart of the Apostle to the Gentiles."—*Boston Advertiser.*

"If it is possible in these days to produce a commentary which will be free from polemical and ecclesiastical bias, the feat will be accomplished in the International Critical Commentary. . . . It is evident that the writer has given an immense amount of scholarly research and original thought to the subject. . . . The author's introduction to the Epistle to Philemon is an admirable piece of literature, calculated to arouse in the student's mind an intense interest in the circumstances which produced this short letter from the inspired Apostle."—*Commercial Advertiser.*

"His discussion of Philemon is marked by sympathy and appreciation, and his full discussion of the relations of Pauline Christianity to slavery are interesting, both historically and sociologically."—*The Dial.*

"Throughout the work scholarly research is evident. It commends itself by its clear elucidation, its keen exegesis which marks the word study on every page, its compactness of statement and its simplicity of arrangement."—*Lutheran World.*

"The scholarship of the author seems to be fully equal to his undertaking, and he has given to us a fine piece of work. One cannot but see that if the entire series shall be executed upon a par with this portion, there can be little left to be desired."—*Philadelphia Presbyterian Journal.*

" The best commentary and the one most useful to the Bible student is The International Critical."

—THE REFORMED CHURCH REVIEW.

ST. PETER AND ST. JUDE

By the Rev. CHARLES BIGG, D.D.

Regius Professor of Ecclesiastical History in the University of Oxford.

Crown 8vo. Net, $2.50.

" His commentary is very satisfactory indeed. His notes are particularly valuable. We know of no work on these Epistles which is so full and satisfactory."—*The Living Church.*

"It shows an immense amount of research and acquaintanceship with the views of the critical school."—*Herald and Presbyter.*

"This volume well sustains the reputation achieved by its predecessors. The notes to the text, as well as the introductions, are marked by erudition at once affluent and discriminating."—*The Outlook.*

"Canon Bigg's work is pre-eminently characterized by judicial open-mindedness and sympathetic insight into historical conditions. His realistic interpretation of the relations of the apostles and the circumstances of the early church renders the volume invaluable to students of these themes. The exegetical work in the volume rests on the broad basis of careful linguistic study, acquaintance with apocalyptic literature and the writings of the Fathers, a sane judgment, and good sense."—*American Journal of Theology.*

NUMBERS

By the Rev. G. BUCHANAN GRAY, D.D.

Professor of Hebrew, Mansfield College, Oxford.

Crown 8vo. Net, $3.00.

" Most Bible readers have the impression that 'Numbers' is a dull book only relieved by the brilliancy of the Balaam chapters and some snatches of old Hebrew songs, but, as Prof. Gray shows with admirable skill and insight, its historical and religious value is not that which lies on the surface. Prof. Gray's Commentary is distinguished by fine scholarship and sanity of judgment; it is impossible to commend it too warmly."—*Saturday Review (London).*

The International Theological Library.

EDITORS' PREFACE.

THEOLOGY has made great and rapid advances in recent
years. New lines of investigation have been opened up,
fresh light has been cast upon many subjects of the deepest
interest, and the historical method has been applied with
important results. This has prepared the way for a Library
of Theological Science, and has created the demand for it.
It has also made it at once opportune and practicable now
to secure the services of specialists in the different departments of Theology, and to associate them in an enterprise
which will furnish a record of Theological inquiry up to
date.

This Library is designed to cover the whole field of Christian Theology. Each volume is to be complete in itself,
while, at the same time, it will form part of a carefully
planned whole. One of the Editors is to prepare a volume
of Theological Encyclopædia which will give the history
and literature of each department, as well as of Theology
as a whole.

The Library is intended to form a series of Text-Books
for Students of Theology.

The Authors, therefore, aim at conciseness and compactness of statement. At the same time, they have in view

that large and increasing class of students, in other departments of inquiry, who desire to have a systematic and thorough exposition of Theological Science. Technical matters will therefore be thrown into the form of notes, and the text will be made as readable and attractive as possible.

The Library is international and interconfessional. It will be conducted in a catholic spirit, and in the interests of Theology as a science.

Its aim will be to give full and impartial statements both of the results of Theological Science and of the questions which are still at issue in the different departments.

The Authors will be scholars of recognized reputation in the several branches of study assigned to them. They will be associated with each other and with the Editors in the effort to provide a series of volumes which may adequately represent the present condition of investigation, and indicate the way for further progress.

CHARLES A. BRIGGS.
STEWART D. F. SALMOND.

Theological Encyclopædia.	By CHARLES A. BRIGGS, D.D., D.Litt., Prof. of Theological Encyclopedia and Symbolics, Union Theol. Seminary, N. Y.
An Introduction to the Literature of the Old Testament.	By S. R. DRIVER, D.D., D.Litt., Regius Professor of Hebrew, and Canon of Christ Church, Oxford. (*Revised and enlarged edition*).
The Study of the Old Testament.	By the Right Rev. HERBERT EDWARD RYLE, D.D., Lord Bishop of Winchester.
Old Testament History.	By HENRY PRESERVED SMITH, D.D., Professor of Biblical History, Amherst College, Mass. (*Now ready.*)
Contemporary History of the Old Testament.	By FRANCIS BROWN, D.D., LL.D., D.Litt., Professor of Hebrew, Union Theological Seminary, New York.
Theology of the Old Testament.	By the late A. B. DAVIDSON, D.D., LL.D., Professor of Hebrew, New College, Edinburgh. (*Now ready.*)

AN INTRODUCTION TO

The Literature of the Old Testament

By Prof. S. R. DRIVER, D.D., D.Litt.

Canon of Christ Church, Oxford

New Edition Revised

Crown 8vo, 558 pages, $2.50 net

"It is the most scholarly and critical work in the English language on the literature of the Old Testament, and fully up to the present state of research in Germany."—Prof. PHILIP SCHAFF, D.D.

"Canon Driver has arranged his material excellently, is succinct without being hurried or unclear, and treats the various critical problems involved with admirable fairness and good judgment."
—Prof. C. H. TOY.

"His judgment is singularly fair, calm, unbiassed, and independent. It is also thoroughly reverential. . . . The service, which his book will render in the present confusion of mind on this great subject, can scarcely be overestimated."—*The London Times.*

"As a whole, there is probably no book in the English language equal to this 'Introduction to the Literature of the Old Testament' for the student who desires to understand what the modern criticism *thinks* about the Bible."—Dr. LYMAN ABBOTT, *in the Outlook.*

"The book is one worthy of its subject, thorough in its treatment, reverent in its tone, sympathetic in its estimate, frank in its recognition of difficulties, conservative (in the best sense of the word) in its statement of results."
—Prof. HENRY P. SMITH, *in the Magazine of Christian Literature.*

"In working out his method our author takes up each book in order and goes through it with marvelous and microscopic care. Every verse, every clause, word by word, is sifted and weighed, and its place in the literary organism decided upon."
—*The Presbyterian Quarterly.*

"It contains just that presentation of the results of Old Testament criticism for which English readers in this department have been waiting. . . . The whole book is excellent; it will be found helpful, characterized as it is all through by that scholarly poise of mind, which, when it does not know, is not ashamed to present degrees of probability."—*New World.*

". . . Canon Driver's book is characterized throughout by thorough Christian scholarship, faithful research, caution in the expression of mere opinions, candor in the statement of facts and of the necessary inferences from them, and the devout recognition of the divine inworking in the religious life of the Hebrews, and of the tokens of divine inspiration in the literature which records and embodies it."—Dr. A. P. PEABODY, *in the Cambridge Tribune.*

The International Theological Library.

An Introduction to the Literature of the New Testament.	By S. D. F. SALMOND, D.D., Principal of the Free Church College, Aberdeen. (*In press.*)
Canon and Text of the New Testament.	By CASPAR RENÉ GREGORY, D.D., LL.D., Professor of New Testament Exegesis in the University of Leipzig.
The Life of Christ.	By WILLIAM SANDAY, D.D., LL.D., Lady Margaret Professor of Divinity, and Canon of Christ Church, Oxford.
A History of Christianity in the Apostolic Age.	By ARTHUR C. MCGIFFERT, D.D., Professor of Church History, Union Theological Seminary, New York. (*Now ready.*)
Contemporary History of the New Testament.	By FRANK C. PORTER, D.D., Professor of Biblical Theology, Yale University, New Haven, Conn.
Theology of the New Testament.	By GEORGE B. STEVENS, D.D., Professor of Systematic Theology, Yale University, New Haven, Conn. (*Now ready.*)
Biblical Archæology.	By G. BUCHANAN GRAY, D.D., Professor of Hebrew, Mansfield College, Oxford.
The Ancient Catholic Church.	By ROBERT RAINY, D.D., LL.D., Principal of the New College, Edinburgh. (*Now ready.*)
The Later Catholic Church.	By ROBERT RAINY, D.D. LL.D., Principal of the New College, Edinburgh.
The Latin Church.	By the Right Rev. ARCHIBALD ROBERTSON, D.D., Lord Bishop of Exeter.
The Greek and Oriental Churches.	By W. F. ADENEY, D.D., Professor of Church History, New College, London.
The Reformation.	By T. M. LINDSAY, D.D., Principal of the United Free College, Glasgow.
Symbolics.	By CHARLES A. BRIGGS, D.D., D.Litt., Prof. of Theological Encyclopedia and Symbolics, Union Theol. Seminary, N. Y.
History of Christian Doctrine.	By G. P. FISHER, D.D., LL.D., Professor of Ecclesiastical History, Yale University, New Haven, Conn. (*Revised and enlarged edition.*)
Christian Institutions.	By A. V. G. ALLEN, D.D., Professor of Ecclesiastical History, P. E. Divinity School, Cambridge, Mass. (*Now ready.*)
Philosophy of Religion.	By ROBERT FLINT, D.D., LL.D., sometime Professor of Divinity in the University of Edinburgh.
The History of Religions.	By GEORGE F. MOORE, D.D., LL.D., Professor in Harvard University.
Apologetics.	By the late A. B. BRUCE, D.D., sometime Professor of New Testament Exegesis, Free Church College, Glasgow. (*Revised and enlarged edition.*)
The Doctrine of God.	By WILLIAM N. CLARKE, D.D., Professor of Systematic Theology, Hamilton Theological Seminary.
The Doctrine of Man.	By WILLIAM P. PATERSON, D.D., Professor of Divinity, University of Edinburg.
The Doctrine of Christ.	(Author will be announced later.)
The Doctrine of Salvation.	By GEORGE B. STEVENS, D.D., Professor of Systematic Theology, Yale University. (*In press.*)
The Doctrine of the Future Life.	By S. D. F. SALMOND, D.D., Principal of the United Free College, Aberdeen.
Christian Ethics.	By NEWMAN SMYTH, D.D., Pastor of Congregational Church, New Haven. (*Revised and enlarged edition.*)
The Christian Pastor and the Working Church.	By WASHINGTON GLADDEN, D.D., Pastor of Congregational Church, Columbus, Ohio. (*Now ready.*)
The Christian Preacher.	(Author will be announced later.)
Rabbinical Literature.	By S. SCHECHTER, M.A., President of the Jewish Theological Seminary, New York City.

OLD TESTAMENT HISTORY

By HENRY PRESERVED SMITH, D.D.

PROFESSOR OF BIBLICAL HISTORY AND INTERPRETATION, AMHERST COLLEGE

Crown 8vo, 538 pages, $2.50 net

This book gives a history of Old Testament times. This it does by a narrative based upon those Biblical books which are historical in form. The nature of these books is carefully considered, their data are used according to historical methods, and the conclusions of recent criticism are set forth. The other books of the Old Testament with the more important of the Apocrypha are given their proper place so far as they throw light on the development of the Old Testament people.

" Professor Smith has, by his comprehensive and vitalized history, laid all who care for the Old Testament under great obligations."
— *The Independent.*

" The volume is characterized by extraordinary clearness of conception and representation, thorough scholarly ability, and charm of style."— *The Interior.*

" Dr. Smith's volume is critical without being polemical, interesting though not imaginative, scholarly without pedantry, and radical but not destructive. The author is himself an authority, and his volume is the best single presentation with which we are familiar of the modern view of Old Testament history."— *The Outlook.*

"This volume is the result of thorough study, is free from the controversial spirit and from any evidence of desire to challenge older theories of the Bible, is written in straightforward, clear style, does not linger unduly in discussion of doubtful matters, is reverent and at the same time fearless. If one has accepted the main positions of the Higher Criticism, while he may still differ with Professor Smith's conclusions here and there, he will find himself in accord with the spirit of the author, whose scholarship and achievement he will gladly honor."— *The Congregationalist.*

" We have a clear, interesting, instructive account of the growth of Israel, embodying a series of careful judgments on the countless problems that face the man who tries to understand the life of that remarkable people. The 'History' takes its place worthily by the side of Driver's Introduction. The student of to-day is to be congratulated on having so valuable an addition made to his stock of tools."
— *The Expository Times.*

The International Theological Library.

The Theology of the Old Testament.

BY THE LATE

A. B. DAVIDSON, D.D., LL.D., Litt.D.

Professor of Hebrew and Old Testament Exegesis, New College, Edinburgh.

EDITED FROM THE AUTHOR'S MANUSCRIPTS

BY

S. D. F. SALMOND, D.D., F.E.I.S.

Principal of the United Free Church College, Aberdeen.

Crown 8vo. 568 pages. $2.50 net.

"It is one of those monumental works whose publication the scholar hails with gratitude. Principal Salmond has edited Professor Davidson's manuscripts with care and fidelity. It would require much more space than we can give this volume in our crowded columns even to indicate the many points in which this, one of the greatest of Hebrew scholars, shows himself a lineal descendant and successor of the ancient prophets whom he loved so well; but it is enough to say that the work is fitted by its scholarship and its tone to become a standard in every theological seminary. Great pains have been taken with the Hebrew text, so frequently quoted, and its use is distinctly illuminative. His learning is never introduced to dazzle, but always to enlighten the reader." — *The Interior.*

"We hope every clergyman will not rest content till he has procured and studied this most admirable and useful book. Every really useful question relating to man — his nature, his fall, and his redemption, his present life of grace, his life after death, his future life — is treated of. We may add that the most conservatively inclined believer in the Old Testament will find nothing in this book to startle him, while, at the same time, the book is fully cognizant of the altered views regarding the ancient Scriptures. The tone is reverent throughout, and no one who reads attentively can fail to derive fresh light and benefit from the exposition here given." — *The Canadian Churchman.*

"Dr. Davidson was so keen a student, and yet so reverent as to his Bible, that anything from his pen must be of profit. The book gives evidence that his eyes were wide open to all modern research, but yet he was not led astray by any of the vagaries of the schools. Through all the treatment of the theme he remains conservative, while seeking to know the truth." — *Examiner.*

"No one can fail to gain immense profit from its careful study. We rejoice that such a work is added to the store of helpful literature on the Old Testament, and we express the hope that it may find wide reading among ministers and teachers of the Bible." — *The Standard.*

"In its treatment of Old Testament theology, there is nothing to equal it in the English language, and nothing to surpass it in any language. While it is prepared for scholars it will prove an education in the Old Testament to the intelligent laymen or Sunday-school teachers who will give it a faithful reading. The style is so clear that it cannot help but prove interesting. We commend this book with a special prayer, believing that it will make the Old Testament a richer book; and make the foundation upon which the teachings of the New Testament stand more secure to every one who reads it."
— *The Heidelberg Teacher.*

A HISTORY OF

CHRISTIANITY IN THE APOSTOLIC AGE

BY

ARTHUR CUSHMAN McGIFFERT, Ph.D., D.D.

Washburn Professor of Church History in the Union Theological Seminary, New York.

Crown 8vo, 681 Pages, $2.50 Net.

"The author's work is ably done. . . . This volume is worthy of its place in the series."—*The Congregationalist.*

"Invaluable as a résumé of the latest critical work upon the great formative period of the Christian Church."—*The Christian World* (London).

"There can be no doubt that this is a remarkable work, both on account of the thoroughness of its criticism and the boldness of its views."
—*The Scotsman.*

"The ability and learning of Professor McGiffert's work on the Apostolic Age, and, whatever dissent there may be from its critical opinion, its manifest sincerity, candid scholars will not fail to appreciate."
—DR. GEORGE P. FISHER, of Yale University.

"Pre-eminently a clergyman's book; but there are many reasons why it should be in the library of every thoughtful Christian person. The style is vivid and at times picturesque. The results rather than the processes of learning are exhibited. It is full of local color, of striking narrative, and of keen, often brilliant, character analysis. It is an admirable book for the Sunday-school teacher."—*Boston Advertiser.*

"For a work of such wide learning and critical accuracy, and which deals with so many difficult and abstruse problems of Christian history, this is remarkably readable."—*The Independent.*

"It is certain that Professor McGiffert's work has set the mark for future effort in the obscure fields of research into Christian origin."
—*New York Tribune.*

"Dr. McGiffert has produced an able, scholarly, suggestive, and constructive work. He is in thorough and easy possession of his sources and materials, so that his positive construction is seldom interrupted by citations, the demolition of opposing views, or the irrelevant discussion of subordinate questions."—*The Methodist Review.*

"The clearness, self-consistency, and force of the whole impression of Apostolic Christianity with which we leave this book, goes far to guarantee its permanent value and success."—*The Expositor.*

THEOLOGY OF THE NEW TESTAMENT.

By GEORGE B. STEVENS, D.D.

Professor of Systematic Theology, Yale University.

Crown 8vo, 480 pages, $2.50 net.

"In style it is rarely clear, simple, and strong, adapted alike to the general reader and the theological student. The former class will find it readable and interesting to an unusual degree, while the student will value its thorough scholarship and completeness of treatment. His work has a simplicity, beauty, and freshness that add greatly to its scholarly excellence and worth."—*Christian Advocate.*

"Professor Stevens is a profound student and interpreter of the Bible, as far as possible divested of any prepossessions concerning its message. In his study of it his object has been not to find texts that might seem to bolster up some system of theological speculation, but to find out what the writers of the various books meant to say and teach."—*N. Y. Tribune.*

"It is a fine example of painstaking, discriminating, impartial research and statement."—*The Congregationalist.*

"Professor Stevens has given us a very good book. A liberal conservative, he takes cautious and moderate positions in the field of New Testament criticism, yet is admirably fair-minded. His method is patient and thorough. He states the opinions of those who differ from him with care and clearness. The proportion of quotation and reference is well adjusted and the reader is kept well informed concerning the course of opinion without being drawn away from the text of the author's own thought. His judgments on difficult questions are always put with self-restraint and sobriety."—*The Churchman.*

"It will certainly take its place, after careful reading, as a valuable synopsis, neither bare nor over-elaborate, to which recourse will be had by the student or teacher who requires within moderate compass the gist of modern research."—*The Literary World.*

International Theological Library.

THE ANCIENT CATHOLIC CHURCH

From the Accession of Trajan to the Fourth General Council (A.D. 98=451)

By ROBERT RAINY, D.D.
Principal of the New College, Edinburgh.

Crown 8vo. 554 Pages. Net, \$2.50.

"This is verily and indeed a book to thank God for; and if anybody has been despairing of a restoration of true catholic unity in God's good time, it is a book to fill him with hope and confidence."— *The Church Standard.*

"Principal Rainy has written a fascinating book. He has the gifts of an historian and an expositor. His fresh presentation of so intricate and time-worn a subject as Gnosticism grips and holds the attention from first to last. Familiarity with most of the subjects which fall to be treated within these limits of Christian history had bred a fancy that we might safely and profitably skip some of the chapters, but we found ourselves returning to close up the gaps; we should advise those who are led to read the book through this notice not to repeat our experiment. It is a dish of well-cooked and well-seasoned meat, savory and rich, with abundance of gravy; and, while no one wishes to be a glutton, he will miss something nutritious if he does not take time to consume it all."—*Methodist Review.*

"It covers the period from 98–451 A.D., with a well-marked order, and is written in a downright style, simple and unpretentious. Simplicity, indeed, and perspicuity are the keynotes, and too great burden of detail is avoided. A very fresh and able book."—*The Nation.*

"The International Theological Library is certainly a very valuable collection of books on the science of Theology. And among the set of good books, Dr. Rainy's volume on The Ancient Catholic Church is entitled to a high place. We know of no one volume which contains so much matter which is necessary to a student of theology."—*The Living Church.*

"Of course, a history so condensed is not to be read satisfactorily in a day or even a week. The reader often will find ample food for thought for a day or more in what he may have read in two hours. But the man who will master the whole book will be amply rewarded, and will be convinced that he has been consorting with a company of the world's greatest men, and has attained an accurate knowledge of one of the world's greatest and most important periods."—*Christian Intelligencer.*

"As a compend of church history for the first five centuries, this volume will be found most useful, for ready reference, both to those who possess the more elaborate church histories, and for the general information desired by a wider reading public; while the temperate presentations of the author's own theories upon disputed points are in themselves of great value."— *Bibliotheca Sacra.*

"Principal Rainy of the New College, Edinburgh, is one of the foremost scholars of Great Britain, and in Scotland, his home, he is regarded by his countrymen as the chief figure in their ecclesiastical life. There can be little doubt that this recent volume will enhance his reputation and serve to introduce him to a wider circle of friends."—*Congregationalist, Boston.*

History of Christian Doctrine.

BY

GEORGE P. FISHER, D.D., LL.D.,

Titus Street Professor of Ecclesiastical History in Yale University.

Crown 8vo, 583 pages, $2.50 net.

" He gives ample proof of rare scholarship. Many of the old doctrines are restated with a freshness, lucidity and elegance of style which make it a very readable book."—*The New York Observer.*

"Intrinsically this volume is worthy of a foremost place in our modern literature . . . We have no work on the subject in English equal to it, for variety and range, clearness of statement, judicious guidance, and catholicity of tone."—*London Nonconformist and Independent.*

" It is only just to say that Dr. Fisher has produced the best History of Doctrine that we have in English."—*The New York Evangelist.*

" It is to me quite a marvel how a book of this kind (Fisher's 'History of Christian Doctrine') can be written so accurately to scale. It could only be done by one who had a very complete command of all the periods."—PROF. WILLIAM SANDAY, *Oxford.*

"It presents so many new and fresh points and is so thoroughly treated, and brings into view contemporaneous thought, especially the American, that it is a pleasure to read it, and will be an equal pleasure to go back to it again and again."—BISHOP JOHN F. HURST.

" Throughout there is manifest wide reading, careful preparation, spirit and good judgment."—*Philadelphia Presbyterian.*

" The language and style are alike delightfully fresh and easy . . . A book which will be found both stimulating and instructive to the student of theology."—*The Churchman.*

"Professor Fisher has trained the public to expect the excellencies of scholarship, candor, judicial equipoise and admirable lucidity and elegance of style in whatever comes from his pen. But in the present work he has surpassed himself."—PROF. J. H. THAYER, *of Harvard Divinity School.*

" It meets the severest standard; there is fullness of knowledge, thorough research, keenly analytic thought, and rarest enrichment for a positive, profound and learned critic. There is interpretative and revealing sympathy. It is of the class of works that mark epochs in their several departments."—*The Outlook.*

" As a first study of the History of Doctrine, Professor Fisher's volume has the merit of being full, accurate and interesting."
—Prof. MARCUS DODS

" . . . He gathers up, reorganizes and presents the results of investigation in a style rarely full of literary charm."
—*The Interior.*

CHRISTIAN INSTITUTIONS.

By ALEXANDER V. G. ALLEN, D.D.

Professor of Ecclesiastical History in the Episcopal Theological School
in Cambridge.

Crown 8vo, 577 pages, $2.50 net.

" Professor Allen's Christian Institutions may be regarded as the mos important permanent contribution which the Protestant Episcopal Church of the United States has yet made to general theological thought. In a few particulars it will not command the universal, or even the general assent of discriminating readers ; but it will receive, as it deserves, the respect and appreciation of those who rightly estimate the varied, learned, and independent spirit of the author."—*The American Journal of Theology.*

" As to his method there can be no two opinions, nor as to the broad, critical, and appreciative character of his study. It is an immensely suggestive, stimulating, and encouraging piece of work. It shows that modern scholarship is not all at sea as to results, and it presents a worthy view of a great and noble subject, the greatest and noblest of all subjects."—*The Independent.*

" This will at once take its place among the most valuable volumes in the ' International Theological Library,' constituting in itself a very complete epitome both of general church history and of the history of doctrines. . . . A single quotation well illustrates the brilliant style and the profound thought of the book."—*The Bibliotheca Sacra.*

" The wealth of learning, the historical spirit, the philosophic grasp, the loyalty to the continuity of life, which everywhere characterize this thorough study of the organization, creeds, and cultus constituting Christian Institution. . . . However the reader may differ with the conclusions of the author, few will question his painstaking scholarship, judicial temperament, and catholicity of Christian spirit."—*The Advance.*

" It is an honor to American scholarship, and will be read by all who wish to be abreast of the age."—*The Lutheran Church Review.*

" With all its defects and limitations, this is a most illuminating and suggestive book on a subject of abiding interest."—*The Christian Intelligencer.*"

" It is a treasury of expert knowledge, arranged in an orderly and lucid manner, and more than ordinarily readable. . . . It is controlled by the candid and critical spirit of the careful historian who, of course, has his convictions and preferences, but who makes no claims in their behalf which the facts do not seem to warrant."—*The Congregationalist.*

" He writes in a charming style, and has collected a vast amount of important material pertaining to his subject which can be found in no other work in so compact a form."—*The New York Observer*

Apologetics;

Or, Christianity Defensively Stated.

By the late ALEXANDER BALMAIN BRUCE, D.D.,

Professor of Apologetics and New Testament Exegesis, Free Church College, Glasgow; Author of " The Training of the Twelve," "The Humiliation of Christ," " The Kingdom of God," etc.

Crown 8vo, 528 pages, $2.50 net.

Professor Bruce's work is not an abstract treatise on apologetics, but an apologetic presentation of the Christian faith, with reference to whatever in our intellectual environment makes faith difficult at the present time.

It addresses itself to men whose sympathies are with Christianity, and discusses the topics of pressing concern—the burning questions of the hour. It is offered as an aid to faith rather than a buttress of received belief and an armory of weapons for the orthodox believer.

" The book throughout exhibits the methods and the results of conscientious, independent, expert and devout Biblical scholarship, and it is of permanent value."—*The Congregationalist.*

"The practical value of this book entitles it to a place in the first rank."—*The Independent.*

"A patient and scholarly presentation of Christianity under aspects best fitted to commend it to 'ingenuous and truth-loving minds.'"—*The Nation.*

"The book is well-nigh indispensable to those who propose to keep abreast of the times."—*Western Christian Advocate.*

"Professor Bruce does not consciously evade any difficulty, and he constantly aims to be completely fair-minded. For this reason he wins from the start the strong confidence of the reader."—*Advance.*

" Its admirable spirit, no less than the strength of its arguments, will go far to remove many of the prejudices or doubts of those who are outside of Christianity, but who are, nevertheless, not infidels."—*New York Tribune.*

" In a word, he tells precisely what all intelligent persons wish to know, and tells it in a clear, fresh and convincing manner. Scarcely anyone has so successfully rendered the service of showing what the result of the higher criticism is for the proper understanding of the history and religion of Israel."—*Andover Review.*

" We have not for a long time taken a book in hand that is more stimulating to faith. . . . Without commenting further, we repeat that this volume is the ablest, most scholarly, most advanced, and sharpest defence of Christianity that has ever been written. No theological library should be without it."—*Zion's Herald.*

Christian Ethics,

By NEWMAN SMYTH, D.D., New Haven.

Crown 8vo, 508 pages, $2.50 net.

" As this book is the latest, so it is the fullest and most attractive treatment of the subject that we are familiar with. Patient and exhaustive in its method of inquiry, and stimulating and suggestive in the topic it handles, we are confident that it will be a help to the task of the moral understanding and interpretation of human life."
—*The Living Church.*

" This book of Dr. Newman Smyth is of extraordinary interest and value. It is an honor to American scholarship and American Christian thinking. It is a work which has been wrought out with remarkable grasp of conception, and power of just analysis, fullness of information, richness of thought, and affluence of apt and luminous illustration. Its style is singularly clear, simple, facile, and strong. Too much gratification can hardly be expressed at the way the author lifts the whole subject of ethics up out of the slough of mere naturalism into its own place, where it is seen to be illumined by the Christian revelation and vision."—*The Advance.*

" The subjects treated cover the whole field of moral and spiritual relations, theoretical and practical, natural and revealed, individual and social, civil and ecclesiastical. To enthrone the personal Christ as the true content of the ethical ideal, to show how this ideal is realized in Christian consciousness and how applied in the varied departments of practical life—these are the main objects of the book and no objects could be loftier."
— *The Congregationalist.*

" The author has written with competent knowledge, with great spiritual insight, and in a tone of devoutness and reverence worthy of his theme."
—*The London Independent.*

" It is methodical, comprehensive, and readable; few subdivisions, direct or indirect, are omitted in the treatment of the broad theme, and though it aims to be an exhaustive treatise, and not a popular handbook, it may be perused at random with a good deal of suggestiveness and profit."
— *The Sunday School Times.*

" It reflects great credit on the author, presenting an exemplary temper and manner throughout, being a model of clearness in thought and term, and containing passages of exquisite finish."—*Hartford Seminary Record.*

" We commend this book to all reading, intelligent men, and especially to ministers, who will find in it many fresh suggestions."
—Professor A. B. Bruce.

THE CHRISTIAN PASTOR AND THE WORKING CHURCH

By WASHINGTON GLADDEN, D.D., LL.D.

Author of "Applied Christianity," "Who Wrote the Bible?" "Ruling Ideas of the Present Age," etc.

Crown 8vo, 485 pages, $2.5o net.

"Dr. Gladden may be regarded as an expert and an authority on practical theology. . . . Upon the whole we judge that it will be of great service to the ministry of all the Protestant churches."—*The Interior*.

"Packed with wisdom and instruction and a profound piety. . . . It is pithy, pertinent, and judicious from cover to cover. . . . An exceedingly comprehensive, sagacious, and suggestive study and application of its theme."—*The Congregationalist*.

"We have here, for the pastor, the most modern practical treatise yet published—sagacious, balanced, devout, inspiring."—*The Dial*.

"His long experience, his eminent success, his rare literary ability, and his diligence as a student combine to make of this a model book for its purpose. . . . We know not where the subjects are more wisely discussed than here."—*The Bibliotheca Sacra*.

"This book should be the *vade mecum* of every working pastor. It abounds in wise counsels and suggestions, the result of large experience and observation. No sphere of church life or church work is left untreated."—*The* (Canadian) *Methodist Magazine and Review*.

"A happier combination of author and subject, it will be acknowledged, can hardly be found. . . . It is comprehensive, practical, deeply spiritual, and fertile in wise and suggestive thought upon ways and means of bringing the Gospel to bear on the lives of men."—*The Christian Advocate*.

"Dr. Gladden writes with pith and point, but with wise moderation, a genial tone and great good sense. . . . The book is written in an excellent, business-like and vital English style, which carries the author's point and purpose and has an attractive vitality of its own."—*The Independent*.

"A comprehensive, inspiring, and helpful guide to a busy pastor. One finds in it a multitude of practical suggestions for the development of the spiritual and working life of the Church, and the answer to many problems that are a constant perplexity to the faithful minister."

The Christian Intelligencer